Strategic Management of Health Care Organizations

Second Edition

Strategic Management of Health Care Organizations

Second Edition

W. JACK DUNCAN
University of Alabama at Birmingham

PETER M. GINTER
University of Alabama at Birmingham

LINDA E. SWAYNE
University of North Carolina at Charlotte

First published 1995
Reprinted 1995, 1996

Blackwell Publishers Inc.
238 Main Street
Cambridge, Massachusetts 02142
USA

Blackwell Publishers Ltd.
108 Cowley Road
Oxford OX4 1JF
UK

Library of Congress Cataloging-in-Publication Data
Duncan, W. Jack (Walter Jack)
    Strategic management of health care organizations (W. Jack Duncan. Peter M. Ginter.
      Linda E. Swayne.—2e.
        p.   cm.
    Includes bibliographical references and index.
    ISBN 1-55786-534-5
    1. Health facilities—Administration.   2. Strategic planning.
I. Ginter, Peter M.   II. Swayne, Linda E.   III. Title.
RA971.D78   1995
362.1′1′068—dc20
                                                       94-27573
                                                            CIP

British Library Cataloguing in Publication Data

A CIP catalogue record for this book is available from the British Library.

Typeset in Times Roman on 10/12 pt
by Modern Graphics, Inc.
Printed in the USA by Quebecor Printing Inc./Book Press

This book is printed on acid-free paper

Preface

"Tactics is knowing what to do when there is something to do.
Strategy is knowing what to do when there is nothing to do."
— *Savielly Tartakover*
Polish Chess Grand Master

A thaw in the Cold War and better U.S./Soviet relations was the major favorable trend in the world as ranked in a recent edition of the *Future Survey Annual*. The second trend cited by futurists was "the growth of strategic planning and organizational renewal, creating a better structure for problem solving." In this text, we have chosen to refer to this process as *strategic management*. The editor of the *Annual* noted that strategic management in the past few years, "has taken on a new and promising form that is more holistic, qualitative, visionary, and action-oriented toward shaping the future."

At the same time that strategic management is showing positive results for business enterprise, study after study cites a lack of strategic thinking and generally poor management as the most important problems facing the health care industry. Clearly, health care has had difficulty in dealing with a dynamic environment, holding down costs, providing universal access, diversifying wisely, defining quality, and balancing capacity and demand. Not coincidentally, the health care sector has been slow to adopt modern management methods, particularly strategic management.

The widespread call for the adoption of strategic management in health care is to a great extent the result of the phenomenal growth of the industry over the past thirty-five years. Since 1960, the percentage of the U.S. gross national product (GNP) attributed to health care has more than doubled. During that period, health care went from $11.5 billion and the tenth largest portion of the economy to nearly $1 trillion and the second largest portion (real estate is the first). Further, some analysts predict that health care may account for as much as 18 percent of the GNP by the year 2000.

Compounding the problems associated with rapid growth, the health care industry has experienced significant environmental change. Political and regulatory "health care reform" changes have initiated a complete restructuring of the industry. Technological advances have continually and rapidly evolved the "state of the art." The economy and competition have forever altered the vision and mission of many of the industry's institutions. In some areas health care professionals are in short supply, and many of those who remain in the industry have become disenchanted.

Today, no decision-making environment is more difficult or complex than that of health care. The industry presents a truly unfamiliar, unexpected, ambiguous, and uncertain environment. Dramatic change will continue to take place within the technological, social, political, regulatory, competitive, and economic context of health care delivery. For this reason, strategic management is gaining a prominent role in the administration of modern health care. Today, health care organizations that do not have a clear strategy are doomed to mediocrity at best – and failure at worst – resulting in a poor quality of life for the community.

Health care managers will have to understand the changing environment, develop clear, feasible strategies that will posture their organizations for long-term success, and consistently and logically implement the adopted strategy. Managers will have to make strategic decisions today that will influence their organizations for many years.

For these reasons, students of health care administration need to develop a strategic management perspective – a clear understanding of the dynamics of the health care environment and the methods and constructs to position their organizations for success. At the same time, today's professional health care managers need further experience in assessing strategic health care situations, proposing strategies, and discussing the advantages of their proposals.

The objective of this text is to provide readers with a strategic perspective and an understanding of its logic and structure. The book draws upon the literature and experience of the business and health care communities as well as research and practice in both the public and private sectors. This approach provides thought processes and analysis methods from business and health care that have proven effective in dealing with complex tasks in dynamic environments. In combining business and health care methods, we have not lost sight of the fact that health care management has its own unique setting, managerial parameters, and strategic considerations.

The book provides a strategic management perspective through fourteen chapters and twenty cases dealing with strategic issues that allow vicarious experiences in developing pragmatic strategies. In addition, the book contains five appendices that aid in the analysis, research, and presentation of health care strategy. The book is divided into seven parts including An Introduction to Strategic Management of Health Care Organizations, Situational Analysis, Strategy Formulation, Strategic Implementation: Operational Strategies, Controlling and Creating the Strategy, Appendices, and Cases in the Health Care Sector. The first five parts introduce the theory and practice of strategic management for health care organizations. The appendices provide important information and develop skills necessary for effective strategic analysis and presentation. The cases provide further insight and understanding of the complexity of the issues that organizations face, practice in discerning critical issues, application of theory, understanding of the interrelatedness of administrative functions, and a format for discussion of the issues facing the industry.

The text contains features that will help the reader understand the nature and application of strategic management. First, each chapter contains Learning Objectives that direct attention to the important points or skills introduced in the chapter. An Introductory Incident is placed before the beginning of the text material as a practical example of concepts introduced and discussed within the chapter. In addition to these features appearing at the beginning of the chapter, the text contains a generous number of examples and exhibits. To provide further insight, each chapter contains several "Perspectives" drawn from actual health care organizations' experiences. These sidebars allow the student "to relate to a concept" presented in the text. Finally, each chapter concludes with Summary and Conclusions, Key Terms and Concepts in Strategic Management, Questions for Class Discussion, Notes, and Additional Readings. We believe that these features provide an informative, interesting, and pedagogically sound survey of strategic management of health care organizations.

The second edition contains some new features and changes. A new classification of strategic decisions is included to provide a clearer logic for strategy development. Strategies are classified as directional, adaptive, market entry, positioning, or operational. In addition, the chapters have been rewritten and revised to provide better linkage among strategies, from directional (mission, vision, values, and objectives) to adaptive (expansion, contraction, and stabilization) to market entry (purchase, cooperation, and development) to positioning (market-wide and segmentation) to operational (functional and organization-wide) strategies. Expanded coverage includes environmental analysis and strategy evaluation methods, culture and organizational excellence. In addition, there is an expanded bibliography and a more comprehensive index. New topics include strategic alliances, strategic information systems in health care, facilities management, total quality management (TQM/CQI), ethical and social responsibility, plus an entire chapter that applies the actual strategic management process and methods presented in this text to a state public health department. Finally, rather than sixteen cases, there are now twenty cases; of the twenty cases eleven are new, three are revised, and six are favorites that reviewers indicated should be retained. Of the cases 70 percent are new or updated.

The book has applications for both students and professional health care managers. Students will find the book provides an integrative experience that helps pull together their knowledge, skills, and experiences into a unified understanding of health care management. Many highly skilled professionals in health care are seeking to expand their expertise in strategic management. Hospital administrators, long-term-care facility managers, medical practice managers, home health care managers, and state and federal public health administrators will find the text a useful guide for developing and implementing strategy.

Acknowledgments

We are indebted to many individuals for their assistance and encouragement in the preparation of this book. First, we would like to thank the appendix contributors – Mahmud Hassen (Appendix B), and Gary F. Kohut and Carol M. Baxter (Appendix C). Their work provides additional fundamental skills important in strategic management. Also Kay Webb and Marian S. Lambert made an invaluable contribution typing manuscripts, proofing, and generally supporting all of our activities.

A special note of thanks is due to Dean M. Gene Newport of the Graduate School of Management/School of Business at the University of Alabama at Birmingham, Dean Edward M. Mazze of the Belk College of Business Administration at the University of North Carolina at Charlotte, Dean Dale O. Williams of the School of Public Health at the University of Alabama at Birmingham, and Dean Charles L. Joiner of the School of Health Related Professions at the University of Alabama at Birmingham, who have continued to be supportive of all our projects. We appreciate the support and encouragement of Charles J. Austin, chairperson of the Department of Health Care Organization and Policy and Department of Health Services Administration at the University of Alabama at Birmingham and Eli I. Capilouto, acting vice chair of the Department of Health Care Organization and Policy.

In addition, we have benefited greatly from the stimulation and encouragement of other faculty including Stuart A. Capper, Janet M. Bronstein, Myron D. Fottler, Cynthia C. Haddock, Robert S. Hernandez, Tee H. Hiett, Howard W. Houser, R. L. Jordan, Joyce A. Lanning, Stephen T. Mennemeyer, Gail W. McGee, Robert A. McLean, Robert L. Ohsfeldt, John E. Sheridan, and Richard M. Shewchuk. Rarely are individuals fortunate enough to have such a large number of supportive colleagues who are so willing to give of their time to facilitate the work of others. Michael A. Morrisey, director of the Lister Hill Center for Health Policy has generously provided use of office space, logistical support, and unfailing encouragement.

We also thank Barbara A. Mark of the Medical College of Virginia, Arnold Kaluzny of the University of North Carolina at Chapel Hill, Judith W. Alexander of the University of South Carolina, Stephen M. Shortell of Northwestern University, and Howard L. Smith of the University of New Mexico for their initial insights and contribution to the first edition and their encouragement to write it. An additional thanks to all the fine people at Blackwell Publishers and Blackwell Scientific Publication, Inc., for their constant help and guidance, especially Rolf A. Janke who always believed in us and in this book and whose enthusiasm motivated us all the more. We would also like to thank the reviewers – John A. Baker, University of Arkansas at Little Rock; John D. Blair, Texas Tech University; James O. Hacker Jr., Winthrop University; Roice D. Luke, Medical College of Virginia; and Woodrow D. Richardson, University of Alabama at Birmingham. These colleagues provided valuable guidance in blending concepts from the business and health care fields. They have given a great deal of time and effort to contribute to the education of tomorrow's health care leaders.

A very special note of thanks is extended to a number of people in health care organizations who have opened their organizations to us and allowed us to use them as laboratories to test and refine our ideas and approaches. Chapter 14, Creating the Strategic Plan: An Example, could not have been developed without the support and encouragement of several people at the Indiana State Department of Health (ISDH). John C. Bailey, M.D., state health commissioner, provided us the opportunity to interrelate theory and practice and use the ISDH as the integrative example in this text. Joe D. Hunt, director of policy coordination, kept the project alive and served as the catalyst at every stage. Nancy C. Blough, J.D., deputy commissioner, supported the process, insisted that it stay on schedule, and stepped in to make things happen when the process slowed. Keith Main, director of public health research, believed in the process and in us, and made the experience enjoyable and a genuine learning experience. Finally, we express our appreciation to all of the employees of the ISDH who participated in the project.

A special thanks to Carole W. Samuelson, M.D., health officer of the Jefferson County Department of Health, who has allowed us valuable access to the health department. Dr. Samuelson's enthusiasm for medicine and her commitment to leadership keeps us motivated and encouraged. Clyde A. Sellers, assistant health officer for management, has also provided support and has "run interference" for us in a series of management development and strategic planning projects at Jefferson County.

Other health care professionals who have been instrumental in helping us formulate and refine ideas and concepts are Donald E. Williamson, state health officer, Alabama Department of Public Health, Clyde Bargainer, director at the Alabama Department of Public Health, and Pat Cleavland, director of the New Mexico Division of Pubic Health.

The book would not have been possible without the case writers. Case writing is a difficult art, requiring many hours of library research, personal interviews, and detailed analysis. The case contributors listed in this text represent some of the finest case researchers anywhere. We think you will appreciate and enjoy their craft.

Finally, strategic management is about organizational survival. We live in a competitive world, and health care organizations are no longer protected from the challenges of competition. Health care institutions must compete for patients, markets, revenues, appropriations, employees, and more. Only through a sound, logical process of strategic management can a health care organization understand the changing health care environment and meet the competition now emerging from all sectors. As Avinash Dixit and Barry Nalebuff suggest: "Good strategic thinking . . . remains an art. But its foundations consist of some simple basic principles – an emerging science of strategy."

W. Jack Duncan
Peter M. Ginter
Linda E. Swayne

Contents

An Introduction to Strategic Management of Health Care Organizations

Part 1 provides an introduction to strategic management of health care organizations through two chapters. Chapter 1 discusses the need and rationale for strategic management in today's turbulent health care environment. The chapter defines *strategic management,* traces its foundations, and presents a broad conceptual paradigm for thinking strategically.

Chapter 2 introduces a structured process for conducting strategic management in a health care organization. The process is presented as a model; discussion includes a description of the external environment and processes for conducting situational analysis, strategy formulation, strategic implementation, and strategic control. In addition, the chapter discusses strategic change and the benefits of strategic management models.

CHAPTER 1

The Nature of Strategic Management

> "To be in hell is to drift, to be in heaven is to steer."
> – *George Bernard Shaw*

LEARNING OBJECTIVES

After completing this chapter you should:

1. Be able to provide a rationale for the importance of strategic management for all types of health care organizations.
2. Understand the benefits of strategic management for health care organizations.
3. Be able to trace the evolution of strategic management and discuss its conceptual foundations.
4. Be able to define and differentiate between strategic management, strategy, and strategic planning.
5. Understand the characteristics of strategic decisions and be able to discuss different types of strategic decisions.
6. Be able to discuss the four major stages of strategic management.
7. Be able to define the different organizational levels where strategy may be developed and discuss how strategies at these levels are interrelated.
8. Understand that strategic management is a creative process that fosters innovation and change within the organization.

It was the best of times because the United States created the most advanced health care system in the world. In the early 1990s, hospitals in America's largest cities spent enormous sums on sprawling megaplexes and high-tech medical equipment. They were constantly pushing the limits of modern medicine producing one breakthrough after another. People who could afford it traveled from all parts of the world to America to receive the finest medical treatment available.

It was the worst of times because double digit increases in health care costs were bankrupting the system. Insurers and the public alike were in a furor over the escalating costs. In addition, approximately 37 million Americans were without health insurance. The industry was awash with uncertainty as the nation debated health care reform. The mid-1990s were a period of turbulence and "white water change."

Stark, but not unusual, examples of the problems in health care across the nation can be found in a tale of two cities.

Boston

In an environment of increasing costs, calls for reform, an aging population, an overabundance of duplicated services, declining birth rates, declining admissions and lengths of stay, and insurers cutting payments, Boston's largest and most prestigious hospitals were expanding and vying for dominance in a costly market niche. Beth Israel Hospital, a leading medical facility and the site of many major medical advances, is one of the teaching hospitals affiliated with Harvard Medical School. In 1993, it proudly opened a $5 million facility devoted to saving the lives of critically ill babies. With twenty new neonatal beds of its own, Beth Israel no longer had to transport its babies who needed intensive care across the street to the world famous Children's Hospital or three blocks away to Brigham and Woman's Hospital, both Harvard teaching hospitals with international reputations. Tufts University's New England Medical Center opened a multimillion-dollar maternity unit in downtown Boston and St. Elizabeth's Medical Center, another Tufts affiliate in nearby Brighton, opened a new wing dedicated to women's and infant's care. At the same time, Massachusetts General Hospital, perhaps the best known of the Boston hospitals, opened a new obstetrics facility.

Nashville

Although buffeted by market forces for years, many of the nineteen hospitals in the Nashville area were not fully aware of the magnitude of the looming environmental changes in their health care market. The city of Nashville, with a population of about 500,000, had ten general hospitals with revenues of approximately $1.2 billion. In the seven counties surrounding the city were nine additional hospitals, each with about 100 beds. In the past, these county hospitals sent 40 to 60 percent of their patients to Nashville for treatment – a situation likely to change.

Nashville's ten hospitals – three for-profit and seven not-for-profit – had an average occupancy rate of approximately 66 percent. Here, the for-profits may not ultimately squeeze out the not-for-profits as in some other of the nation's cities. The strongest hospitals are Nashville Baptist and St. Thomas, not-for-profit hospitals competing to take a larger share of the market by offering a full continuum of care and building statewide networks. Vanderbilt Teaching Hospital may survive under the wing of the university. Nashville Memorial Hospital and Tennessee Christian are insulated by politics and religion, respectively, but are in remote parts of the city and struggling financially. Meharry-Hubbard, a not-for-profit, teaching hospital in a predominantly black area, has allied with the city's public hospital, Metro-General. Metro-General, where about half the doctors who run the 500 community-health centers in the poor rural and inner-city areas in the United States were trained, needs more paying patients, and its management fears that poor people, given a choice of hospitals, will choose to go elsewhere.

A New Paradigm of Health Care

Can all these hospitals survive? During the 1990s, a new paradigm of health care delivery will be created in the United States. But what will it look like? How do organizations know where to compete and where not to compete? How can individual health care organizations chart their way through the changes occurring in the industry? What strategies will help health care organizations cope with all the changes and position them to survive?

Source: Terrie Reeves, Ph.D. Candidate, Health Services Administration, University of Alabama at Birmingham. Adapted from Laura Walbert, "Reality Is at the Bedside," *CFO* (December 1993), pp 22–25.

MANAGING IN A DYNAMIC ENVIRONMENT

The dramatic changes currently occurring in the health care industry will continue in the last half of the 1990s. At no previous time have both public and private health care institutions faced a more turbulent, confusing, and threatening environment. Impetus for significant change will come from many sources, including federal, state, and local health care reform efforts; international as well as domestic economic and market forces; demographic shifts and lifestyle changes; and technological advances within the health care industry. Certainly, the hospitals in Boston and Nashville, described in the Introductory Incident, as well as health care institutions across the nation, will look very different by the year 2000. Which health care institutions will survive these changes and prosper?

The greatest challenge for health care organizations is identifying and planning for these changes. As a result, the remainder of the decade promises to be challenging and exciting for health care managers. Interviews with health care professionals and a review of the health care literature suggest that health care organizations will have to cope with some or all of the following by the year 2000:

- Additional legislative health care reform efforts to provide health care access to the 37 million Americans who are without health insurance.
- A more restrictive reimbursement environment as a result of intensified efforts by the federal government and the health care industry to curb burgeoning medical costs.
- Payment of a larger portion of total health spending by third-party payers such as government, insurance companies, and corporate employers.
- Demographic shifts that will place capacity burdens on some health care organizations as a lessening of demand threatens the survival of others.
- Population mobility that will test the flexibility of medical coverage programs and make facility planning more difficult.
- An aging population that will increasingly strain the capacity of health care institutions.
- The high costs of purchasing new, sophisticated, largely computer-based technologies to meet the demand for high-quality health care.
- Further consolidation within the health care industry because of cost pressures and intensified competition.
- The development of integrated networks of care (the combining of the financing and delivery of care).
- The continuing expansion by health care corporations into segments that have less regulation and their entry into businesses outside of the traditional health care industry.
- The increasing importance of market niche strategies and services marketing.
- Growth in outpatient care and the development of innovative alternative health care delivery systems.
- The rapid growth of home health care influenced by limitations in reimbursement (prospective payment) and the high costs of hospital care.

- The decreasing viability of many of the nation's small, rural, and public hospitals and a reconfiguration of the rural health delivery system.
- An increase in the popularity of health maintenance organizations (HMOs) and preferred provider organizations (PPOs) to the point where managed-care plans will cover nearly one-third of the United States population by the year 2000.
- Critical shortages of nonphysician health care professionals and a surplus of physicians within some specialties and in some geographic regions.
- More emphasis on preventive care through wellness programs and healthy behavior.
- A changing role for public health moving back to "core public health" activities (prevention, surveillance, disease control, assurance) and away from the delivery of primary care.
- Increased pressure to reduce the cost of administration of health care.[1]

How can health care managers deal with these important, complex, and sometimes conflicting issues? Which ones are most important or most pressing? Furthermore, what new issues will emerge in the last half of the 1990s? It is likely that there will be new opportunities and threats to health care organizations in the remainder of this decade that have yet to be identified or fully assessed. It seems certain that there will be more change in the health care industry in the next ten years than there was in the past ten.

We need only look at some of the changes that took place during the past several years to appreciate the number and magnitude of the changes that may occur as we approach the year 2000. For instance, because of health care cost escalation during the previous twenty years, Medicare's prospective payment system (PPS) was implemented in 1983. PPS initiated reform of the nation's health care delivery system, and yet because of the extensive reform efforts of the 1990s, its tenth anniversary passed virtually unnoticed.[2] As a result of PPS, health care delivery today is quite different than it was in the mid-1980s. PPS shifted national priorities from insisting on high-quality care regardless of cost to holding health care delivery costs in check. These changes greatly affected the basic structure of the health care industry in a very short period of time.

Another significant change that occurred during the 1980s and early 1990s was the dramatic increase in managed-care systems such as preferred provider organizations and health maintenance organizations. Although often referred to as health care providers, these organizations are actually interposed between providers and payers and attempt to "manage the care" on behalf of the health service consumer and the payer. Growth of these organizations is fueled by the prospect of health care reform. In the 1990s, managed care has fostered the growth of integrated health systems. Employers embraced these organizations as a way to control their health care costs. Now more than 60 percent of major employers offer managed-care plans and over 70 percent of inpatient care is covered by some fixed-price, managed-care payment system. In an effort to control rising health care costs and improve quality, managed-care organizations and integrated networks became major forces shaping the health care industry.

Perspective 1–1 describes the evolution of managed care and its impact on the industry.

In a similar fashion, the health care industry has been greatly affected by the dramatic rise in the number of acquired immune deficiency syndrome (AIDS) cases. Yet, the long-term impact of HIV, the AIDS virus, on medical procedures, as well as on institutional operations, policy, and strategy, is only beginning to be acknowledged.

The health care industry will be very different in the future. Indeed, a restructuring of the health care industry is already underway.[3] The large number of failures of health care organizations, on the one hand, and the large numbers of mergers, acquisitions, alliances, and cooperatives, on the other, indicate the magnitude of the restructuring taking place (see Perspective 1–2).

Coping with the Environment

Health care managers may assume with confidence that in the last half of the 1990s they will have to guide their organizations through more change than at

---

PERSPECTIVE 1 – 1
The Evolution of Managed Care

The idea of managed care has had a profound and lasting influence on the nature and delivery of the nation's health care. Managed health care systems attempt to manage the cost and quality of health care. The methods of managing care have evolved over the past twenty-five years through three distinct phases or generations. First-generation managed care was directed toward limiting benefits and providing utilization reviews, including second opinions for surgery. First-generation managed-care efforts were typically employer-based health insurance plans. Second-generation managed care provided benefit differentials, provider networks, and utilization management. These second-generation systems were managed by health maintenance organizations and preferred provider organizations. Third-generation managed-care systems include quantitative quality measures, patient-care management teams, and advanced physician selection and monitoring. Third-generation managed care increasingly involves integrated networks of care. Integrated networks are beyond HMOs in both structure and function. Consumers receive vertically integrated health services from family-oriented medical care to tertiary hospital care, nursing homes, home and mental health services, and perhaps long-term care. One umbrella institution organizes and manages this continuum of care. In some cases, the institution owns all or most of the diverse components of the system although in other cases webs of contractual relationships form the continuum of care.

Source: Steven Findlay, "Networks of Care May Serve as a Model for Health Reform," *Business & Health* 11, no. 2 (1993), pp. 27–31.

PERSPECTIVE 1-2

Structural Change Within the Health Care Industry

The 1990s promise significant structural change within the health care industry. Evidence that structural change is already underway is provided by the large number of hospital and other health care delivery failures in the early 1990s. Typical of health care industry problems experienced in larger cities is the situation in Philadelphia, the nation's fifth most populated metropolitan area.

In Philadelphia, most hospitals are sick or dying. Recently, more than 60 percent of the city's forty-six hospitals lost money. In the early 1990s, six of the hospitals were under Chapter 11 bankruptcy protection from creditors. Two other hospitals laid off a total of 270 employees, and at least one hospital is spending its endowment fund to survive. Temple University Hospital, the 504-bed teaching facility, lost $19 million in fiscal 1989. Added to Philadelphia's problems, more than 50 percent of the region's hospitals had negative profit margins as compared with only 22 percent in 1985.

The CEO of Mount Sinai Hospital, which only recently reopened as a psychiatric and rehabilitation facility, indicated that "the whole system is in a state of crisis." The present system may have allowed too many hospitals, too many beds, duplication of high-tech services, heavy concentration of hospitals in certain areas, and low concentration in others. In addition, inadequate Medicaid and Medicare payments have contributed to losses. Henry Nicholas of the National Union of Hospital and Health Care Employees stated, "There is no strategy, no plan, no leadership at the state level – no strategy, no plan, no leadership at the local level."

Source: Dean Mayer, "The Philadelphia Story: Hospitals in State of Crisis," *HealthWeek* 4, no. 5 (March 12, 1991), pp. 1, 56.

---

any previous time. Both the amount and speed of change have increased, indeed, change itself has changed. Change has become so rapid, so complex, so turbulent, and so unpredictable that it is sometimes called simply *chaos* or *white water change.*[4] Health care managers will have to cope with this type of change and position their organizations to take advantage of emerging opportunities while avoiding external threats. Strategic management can help health care managers cope with both the anticipated and the white water change that is occurring in health care.

Strategic management has become a major thrust guiding the management of all types of contemporary organizations. In the United States, more than 97 percent of the top 100 industrial companies and more than 92 percent of the top 1,000 industrial companies report corporate strategic planning efforts.[5] Business has embraced strategic management as a way to anticipate and cope with a variety of external forces beyond its operating control. The environmental uncertainties and competitive pressures that have moved business organizations to adopt strategic management now beset health care organizations. Indeed, health care has become a complex business using many of the same processes and much of the same language as our most sophisticated business corporations.

As more and more health care organizations adopt strategic management and incorporate strategic processes into their operations, it is important that health care managers understand the concept, language, and process. Strategic management provides a basic understanding of how and why an organization survives and grows.

The Benefits of Strategic Management

The adoption and further development of strategic management will provide many benefits to health care organizations. Although a number of empirical studies indicate that organizations that successfully adopt a strategic management approach may reasonably expect improved financial performance[6] strategic management is not simply a technique for improving long-term financial results.

Strategic management is a philosophy or way of managing an organization; therefore, the benefits of strategic management are not always quantifiable. Strategic management ties the organization together with a common sense of purpose and shared values. It enables the organization to develop a clear self-concept, specific goals, and consistency in decision making. Strategic management asks managers to understand the present and think about the future.

The process of strategic management requires that managers communicate both vertically and horizontally within the organization. Because all levels of managers are asked to think strategically, overall coordination is often improved dramatically. Finally, strategic management encourages innovation and reduces resistance to change within the organization in order to meet the needs of dynamic situations. In fact, strategic managers realize that change, which often "flies in the face of tradition," is the key to success. The benefits of strategic management are summarized in Exhibit 1–1.

When Strategic Management Fails

Strategic management has been studied carefully, and there is general agreement that there are no fatal flaws in the concept. However, the full range of potential benefits will *not* be realized if there is:

- less than full commitment from top management,
- too little emphasis on building the data base needed for decision making,
- misconceptions that, once set, objectives will take care of themselves,
- failure to integrate planning and budgeting, or
- lack of attention to implementation strategies.[7]

When top management does not fully embrace strategic management or sees it as only a technique, it will most assuredly fail. The passion for managing strategically should run from the top of the organization to the bottom. Moreover,

---

EXHIBIT 1–1
The Benefits of Strategic Management

1. It is likely that strategic management will improve long-term financial performance.
2. Strategic management provides the organization with a self-concept, specific goals, guidance, and consistency in decision making.
3. In organizations practicing strategic management, managers understand the present, think about the future, and recognize the signals that suggest change.
4. Strategic management requires managers to communicate both vertically and horizontally.
5. Overall coordination within the organization is often improved in strategically managed organizations.
6. Strategic management encourages innovation and change within the organization to meet the needs of changing situations.

---

managers who lack adequate external and internal information will find it difficult to develop realistic strategies. Another common problem is that managers may spend a great deal of time developing objectives but fail to assure the necessary implementation support or to integrate planning with operations.

The Strategic Management Perspective

As suggested in the preceding discussion, strategic management is a method of thinking about and managing organizations. It is a unique perspective that requires managers to cease thinking solely in terms of internal operations and adopt what may be a fundamentally new attitude, an *external* orientation. It is basically optimistic in that it integrates "what is" with "what can be." Strategic management is the exciting future of effective health care management.

THE FOUNDATIONS OF STRATEGIC MANAGEMENT

Before discussing the nature of strategic management, it is important to explore its origins, evolution, and contemporary use. In addition, it is important to adopt a broad conceptual paradigm for understanding and integrating the many complex variables involved in strategic management.

The Evolution of Strategic Management

The concept of strategy in a political and military context has a long history. For instance, the underlying principles of strategy were discussed by Sun-tzu, Homer,

Euripides, and many other early strategists and writers. The English word *strategy* comes from the Greek *strategos,* "a general," which in turn comes from roots meaning "army" and "lead."[8] The Greek verb *stratego* means "to plan the destruction of one's enemies through effective use of resources."[9] As a result, many of the terms commonly used in relation to strategy – *objectives, mission, strengths, weaknesses* – were developed by the military.

Over the past fifty years, strategic management has been developed primarily in the business sector. The first modern writers to relate the concept of strategy to business were Von Neumann and Morgenstern in their theory of games in the late 1940s.[10] Another early formulation of strategic management was planning, programming, and budgeting systems (PPBS), which was introduced in the late 1940s and early 1950s and practiced on a limited basis in business and government.[11] Planning was central to these early strategic management approaches.

The 1960s and 1970s were a time of major growth for strategic planning in business organizations. Leading companies such as General Electric were not only practicing strategic planning but also actively promoting its merits in the business press. Strategic planning provided these firms with a more systematic approach to managing business units and extended the planning and budgeting horizon beyond the traditional twelve-month operating period. In addition, business managers learned that financial planning alone was not an adequate management framework.[12]

In the 1980s, the concept of *strategic planning* was broadened to *strategic management.* This evolution acknowledged the importance of strategy implementation and control as well as strategy formulation and established strategic management as an approach to managing complex enterprises. Many types of nonbusiness organizations, including organizations in education, government, and health care, embraced strategic management during the 1980s as a way to deal with the competitive environment.

Strategic management concepts have been employed within health care organizations only in the past twenty to twenty-five years. Prior to 1970, individual organizations had few incentives to employ strategic management because most health care organizations were independent, freestanding, not-for-profit institutions, and health services reimbursement was on a cost-plus basis. Efforts at health planning were initiated by either state or local governments and implemented through legislation or private or nongovernmental agencies. For the most part, these planning efforts were disease oriented; that is, they were categorical approaches directed toward specific health problems (for example, the work of the National Tuberculosis Association, which stimulated the development of state and local government tuberculosis prevention and treatment programs).[13] More recently, a variety of state and federal health planning or policy initiatives have been designed to (1) enhance quality of care – studies on outcome measures; (2) provide or control access to care – Hospital Survey and Construction Act (better known as the Hill-Burton Act), Medicaid, Medicare, state certificate of need laws; and (3) contain costs – National Health Planning and Resource Development Act, implementation of DRGs. Exhibit 1–2 presents the evolution of health planning since 1900.

As suggested in Exhibit 1–2, there has been substantial health planning in the

EXHIBIT 1-2
Stages of Health Planning

Stage	Time Period	Major Concern	Control
Private Sector	1900 to late 1950s	Quality of care	Professional
Public Sector, Initial Stage	Late 1950s to early 1970s	Access to care	Administrative, grounded in volunteerism
Public Sector, Advanced Stage	Early 1970s to end of 1970s	Cost containment	Administrative, combined with regulation
Regionalization of Health Planning	1980 to 1994	Managerial efficiency	Market
Health Reform	1994 –	Access and cost containment	Market, combined with regulation

Source: Adapted from G. Budrys, *Planning for the Nation's Health: A Study of 20th Century Developments in the U.S.* (Greenwood Press, 1986), p. 4a. Reprinted by permission.

United States, however, strategic management is organization specific. Strategic management helps an individual organization respond to state and federal policy and planning efforts, as well as to a variety of other external forces. The major differences between strategic planning and other forms of health planning are that strategic planning:

- is a market-driven and market-based approach,
- puts more emphasis on qualitative rather than quantitative analysis,
- places the development of strategic plans under the direct control of the chief executive officer without delegation,
- requires that the strategy must be clearly stated and persuasively communicated throughout the institution,
- creates final planning goals, objectives, and programs that must be vigorously implemented,
- requires that middle management be carefully educated and prepared to engage in strategic planning,
- emphasizes data collection and analysis for the "nuts and bolts" of the health institution's business,
- requires that strategic planning be integrated with other management functions, and
- places a strong focus on gaining and sustaining a competitive advantage.[14]

In recent years the expansion of health care systems, the fragmentation of markets, the growth of investor-owned hospital companies, and an emphasis on cost containment have induced individual health care organizations to investigate strategic management. Today, increased emphasis is placed on strategic management in health care organizations as well as in the health care management literature. The following statement released by Barnes Hospital in St. Louis illustrates this new emphasis: "With the formulation of a strategic plan based on differentiated quality provided in a continuum of care, built by resource management, a service focus, and superior talent, Barnes has laid the groundwork for growth from a single hospital into a complete health care system."[15]

The Systems Approach as a Broad Conceptual Paradigm

The problems facing health care organizations are so complex that they defy simple solutions. Understanding the nature of the health care environment, the relationship of the organization to that environment, and the often conflicting interests of internal functional departments requires a broad conceptual paradigm, but it is difficult to comprehend so many complex and important interrelationships.

Systems Thinking Managers have found *general systems theory* (GST) or "systems thinking" to be a useful framework for organizing and understanding the variables of strategic management. A systems framework provides a basis for understanding and integrating knowledge from a wide variety of highly specialized areas so important to today's health care manager.

A *system* may be defined literally as "an organized or complex whole; an assemblage or combination of things or parts forming a complex or unitary whole."[16] The use of the systems approach requires managers to define the organization in broad terms and attempt to identify the important variables and interrelationships that will affect a decision. A systems approach in management may be defined as a logically consistent method of reducing a complex problem to simple components that can be used by decision makers in conjunction with other considerations to arrive at a best solution. It permits managers to concentrate on those aspects of the problem that most deserve attention and allows a more focused attempt at a resolution. In simple terms, systems thinking enables managers to see the "big picture" in proper perspective and helps them to avoid devoting excessive attention to relatively minor aspects of the total system.[17]

Thinking Like a Manager Today, health care organizations are placing increased emphasis on the scientific analysis of managerial decisions. Systems approaches can provide a logical and consistent conceptual framework for analyzing these decisions. Exhibit 1–3 illustrates the value of the systems concept to the management of a hospital in terms of three aspects of the strategic manager's job. First, rapid environmental change from diverse sources requires the manager to identify and monitor the systems likely to affect the organization. Second, the health care manager strives to achieve overall organizational effectiveness and avoid allowing the parochial interests of one organizational element to distort overall performance. Third, the strategic manager must do this in an organizational environment that

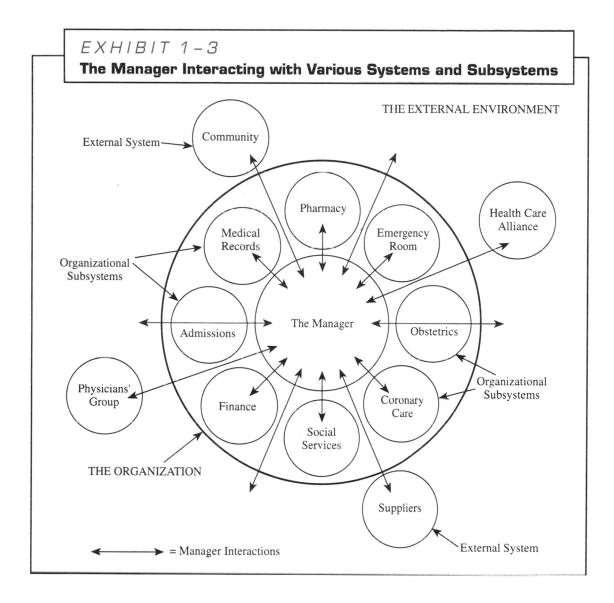

EXHIBIT 1-3
The Manager Interacting with Various Systems and Subsystems

THE EXTERNAL ENVIRONMENT

Community

External System

Pharmacy

Medical Records

Emergency Room

Health Care Alliance

Organizational Subsystems

The Manager

Admissions

Obstetrics

Organizational Subsystems

Physicians' Group

Finance

Coronary Care

Social Services

THE ORGANIZATION

Suppliers

External System

◄──────► = Manager Interactions

invariably involves conflicting organizational objectives.[18] As suggested in Perspective 1–3, in a strategic context this process is sometimes called *strategic thinking.*

Recognizing the importance of systems thinking, health care managers commonly refer to the *health care system* or the *health care delivery system* and strive to develop logical internal *organizational systems* to deal with the environment. Typical of organizations that understand the need to think in terms of systems is Memorial Health Systems (MHS) of York, Pennsylvania. MHS management reorganized the company into logical groups of related health care organizations

PERSPECTIVE 1–3

Strategic Thinking: Are You a Strategic Thinker? A Planner? Or Both?

Strategic thinkers built and continue to build the health care systems that will serve major metropolitan and rural areas during the next fifty years. Strategic thinkers are visionaries. They know what they want to become and what they want their organization to be. Strategic thinkers look at assumptions, understand system interrelationships, create scenarios, and calculate the odds. Strategic thinkers forecast external technological and demographic changes, as well as critical changes in the political and regulatory arenas. Planners, on the other hand, figure out how to get where the strategic thinkers want to go. A planner gathers and evaluates data and tells the strategic thinker what it will take to achieve an objective.

In large organizations such as hospitals and health care systems, successful strategic thinkers are good politicians and leaders. They know how to articulate the vision and sell it to their boards, medical staffs, employees, and communities. The health care strategic thinker not only has a vision, but also determines the mileposts that must be passed on the road to achieving that vision.

Strategists are thinkers about the future, playing what-if games and plotting several steps ahead. They pay their dues, working in several organizations and in many capacities. Most important, however, strategic thinkers are never satisfied. They are always asking questions; talking with customers, friends, and competitors; and reading everything they can. Strategic thinkers use their own experiences and the experiences of others to shape their vision and develop strategies.

Source: Johnson, Donald E. L., "Strategic Thinking About Collaboration and Integration," *Health Care Strategic Management* 11, no. 3 (1993), pp. 2–3.

(subsystems) to better deal with the "medical, economic, and social changes that may further challenge . . . traditional health care."[19] Memorial Health Systems thus moved from a functional organizational structure to one composed of semi-autonomous subsystems: Memorial Health Systems Corporation, the parent holding company; Memorial Hospital, a 165-bed community hospital; Memorial Enterprises, a company engaged in various diversified activities such as diagnostic centers, outpatient surgical facilities, and a retirement community; MHS Title Holding Company, a real estate acquisition firm; and MHS Management Corporation, which provides professional services to other companies. The management of Memorial Health Systems reported that organizing around systems resulted in profound improvements in Memorial Hospital's fiscal stability and allowed the organization to expand services significantly.[20]

In a similar manner, health care managers must use systems thinking to understand and relate to the external environment. The community and region may be thought of as an integrated health care system with each part of the

---

EXHIBIT 1–6

Strategic Planning, Strategy, and Strategic Management Definitions

Strategic planning is the set of processes used in an organization to understand the situation and develop decision-making guidelines (the strategy) for the organization.

A *strategy* is a pattern in a stream of decisions positioning an organization within its environment and resulting in the "behavior" of the organization. Additionally, a strategy is a future-oriented plan that provides decision-making guidelines for managers.

Strategic management is a philosophy of managing the organization that is externally oriented and links strategic planning to operational decision making. Strategic management attempts to achieve a productive and creative fit between the organization's external environment and its internal situation.

Many academic medical centers have had to develop these abilities and commitments in the past several years. Some academic medical centers have been less responsive to change because they felt their unique mission and diverse, specialized services such as educating medical students, conducting research, providing expensive tertiary services, and serving a growing uninsured patient caseload insulated them from the problems encountered by other community providers. However, as illustrated in Perspective 1–5, some academic medical centers understand the requirements of strategic management and are committed to change.

What Strategic Management Is Not

Strategic management is a philosophy of management. As such, it provides no guarantees nor does it promise specific results. Adopting strategic management will not assure success or even survival for an organization. Rather, strategic management provides a logical way to think about the organization, the environment, and the competition.

Strategic management should not be regarded as a *technique* that will provide a "quick fix" for an organization that has fundamental problems. Quick fixes for organizations are rare; successful strategic management often takes years to become a part of the values and culture of an organization. If strategic management is regarded as a technique or gimmick, it is doomed to failure.

Strategic management is not a process of completing paperwork. If managers have reached a point where strategic management has become a process of filling in endless forms, meeting deadlines, or changing the dates of last year's objectives and plans, the process is not strategic management. Effective strategic management requires little paperwork. It is an attitude, not a series of documents.

PERSPECTIVE 1-5

Academic Medical Centers Develop the Required Strategic Abilities and Commitments

Greg Hart, general director at the University of Minnesota Hospital and Clinic in Minneapolis, says that academic medical centers in the past have not had to respond as proactively as other providers to the demands of their local markets. But this situation has changed. He stated, "Academic medical centers have to reposition their organizations to be more valued patient care partners by being more cost-competitive, emphasizing quality, and becoming leaders in outcomes research and measurement."

This understanding of the system of competitive behavior has resulted in the University of Minnesota Hospital and Clinic becoming much more aggressive in its marketplace. It has obtained 75 to 80 percent managed-care penetration and has developed new relationships with local HMOs. For example, the hospital signed a participating provider contract with Minnesota's largest managed care organization, Medica, which has 450,000 members. In addition, U of M Hospital and Clinic is studying strategic alliances with three other local hospitals, partly in response to the passage of Minnesota's health care reform bill, which encourages more integrated service networks.

In a similar manner, the University of Pennsylvania Health System in Philadelphia has committed to strategic thinking. The university adopted a new governance, corporate, and management structure, that joined the former medical center with many primary physician practices in its tristate region. The new university system is developing satellite facilities to offer more local care and is seeking affiliations and relationships with existing community hospitals and other continuum-of-care providers. In addition, the university plans a management services organization to support the system's community-based physicians and its own managed-care entity.

The University of Minnesota Hospital and Clinic and the University of Pennsylvania Health System understand the interaction of competitors, customers, money, people, and resources. In addition, these institutions have an understanding of how they will fit in the competitive equilibrium and are committing resources to be a part of the changing future.

Source: Jim Montague, "Academic Medical Centers Begin Retooling for the Future," *Hospitals & Health Networks* 67, no. 8 (1993), pp. 36–41.

Strategic management is not a process of simply extending the organization's current activities into the future. It is not based solely on a forecast of present trends. Strategic management attempts to identify the issues that will be important in the future. The questions facing strategic managers are not just "*How* will we provide this service in the future?" but rather, "*Should* we provide this service in the future?" "What *new* services will be needed?" and "What services are we providing now that are no longer needed?"

THE CHARACTERISTICS OF STRATEGIC DECISIONS

Strategic management is, in large part, a decision-making activity. The strategy of an organization is the result of a series of managerial decisions. Although these decisions are often supported by a great deal of quantifiable data, strategic decisions are fundamentally judgmental. Because strategic decisions cannot always be quantified, managers must rely on "informed judgment" in making this type of decision. Generally, the more important the decision, the less quantifiable it is and the more we will have to rely on the opinions of others and our own best judgment.

The Attributes of Strategic Decisions

To differentiate from other types of organizational decisions (tactical, policy, procedural, and so on), it is useful to discuss the characteristics of strategic decisions. Just because a decision is important to the success of an organization does not mean that it is necessarily a strategic decision. What, then, is a strategic decision? For a decision to be strategic it must meet all of the following characteristics. The decision must:

- be directed toward defining the organization's relationship to its environment;
- take the organization as a whole as the unit of analysis;
- be multifunctional in character, that is, it must depend on inputs from a variety of functional areas;
- provide direction for, and constraints on, administrative and operational activities throughout the enterprise; and
- be important to the success of the enterprise.[24]

Decisions that exhibit all of these characteristics are strategic decisions. For example, a decision by a multiunit hospital system to gain an edge over competitors by its entry into a new geographic market through the purchase of a community hospital is strategic in nature. Such a decision relates the organization to its environment (the new market and the organization's relationship with competitors), determines the strategic direction of the entire organization, involves the resources of all the organization's functional areas, provides decision-making guidance for all of the hospital's managers, and will surely affect the ultimate success of the hospital.

Decisions that reflect only one of these characteristics are generally not strategic in nature. For example, decisions to change operational procedures or the development of hospital advertising copy are not normally considered strategic in nature.

Types of Strategic Decisions

Considering the characteristics of strategic decisions, Robert C. Shirley has identified seven decisions that are strategic in nature and accomplish the overall function of formulating the strategy:

- *Mission:* the fundamental purpose and broad aims of the organization;
- *Customer mix:* the specific target market(s) to be served by the organization;
- *Product mix:* the specific products or services to be offered by the organization to serve the needs of the target market;
- *Service area:* the geographic service area determined by the physical boundaries established for the organization's activities;
- *Goals and objectives:* the specific results that the organization is seeking to accomplish;
- *Competitive advantage:* the means by which the organization seeks to differentiate itself from other organizations in the same industry or across industries;
- *Outside relationships:* relationships with government, suppliers, financing sources, and other major constituencies and interest groups.[25]

Once an organization has made decisions in these seven areas, it has defined the scope of its operations, mapped its future direction, and stated its overall relationships to its environment in terms of product/market scope, geographic boundaries, competition, and goals and objectives to be achieved. In short, the organization has developed its strategy. Exhibit 1–7 illustrates these decision areas for a rehabilitation hospital. It is clear from these decision areas that executives at Rancho Los Amigos Medical Center have a clear picture of their strategy.

The Responsibility for Strategic Decisions

Strategic decision making for health care organizations is the responsibility of top management. The chief executive officer (CEO) is a strategic manager with the ultimate responsibility for positioning the organization for the future. If the CEO does not fully understand or support strategic management, it will not happen.

In the past, formulation of the strategy was primarily a staff activity. The planning staff would formulate the strategy and submit it for approval to top management. This process resulted in plans that were often unrealistic or did not fully consider the realities and resources of the divisions or functional departments.

Over the past decade, many large formal planning staffs have been dissolved as organizations learned that strategy development cannot take place in relative isolation. Today, the *coordination and facilitation* of strategic planning typically is designated as the responsibility of a key manager (often the CEO), and *development* of the strategy has become a line job with each manager responsible for the strategic implications of his or her decisions. The rationale underlying this approach is that no one is more in touch with the external environment (regulations, technology, competition, social change, and so on) than the line manager who must deal with it every day; however, someone must coordinate the organization's overall strategy and facilitate strategic thinking throughout the organization. As a result, the strategic planner acts as an extension of the chief executive officer to ensure that an organized and used planning process ensues.[26] Perspective 1–6 illustrates the changing role of the strategic planner over the past three decades.

EXHIBIT 1-7

**Seven Strategic Decision Areas
of Rancho Los Amigos Medical Center**

Mission

To maximize the performance, function, and mobility of each of our patients and to afford them the greatest possible opportunity for achieving independence in the activities of daily living.

Customer Mix

Those with congenital and acquired disabilities from Los Angeles County, Southern California, the nation, and foreign countries.

Product Mix

Surgical services, rehabilitation nursing, children's services, patient progress conferences, physical therapy, occupational therapy, pathokinesiology, communication disorders therapy, spinal injury service, recreation therapy, rehabilitation engineering, and other related services.

Service Area

Primarily Los Angeles County and Southern California, but also drawing nationally and internationally.

Goals and Objectives

- Maintain and improve traditionally high level of patient care
- Reduce dependence on financial support from public funds
- Foster innovation
- Upgrade and replace facilities

Competitive Advantage

- Image
- High-quality services
- Excellent, widely recognized staff
- County support
- Emphasis on management and financial management

Outside Relationships

- Excellent relationship with the County of Los Angeles
- Established board of directors from large locally based organizations
- Medical school affiliation
- Received high commendations from both the Joint Commission on Accreditation of Hospitals (JCAH) and the Commission on Accreditation of Rehabilitation Facilities (CARF)

Source: Rancho Los Amigos Medical Center publications.

PERSPECTIVE 1–6
Position Advertisements for Strategic Planners

1970s

An expert at strategic planning, knowledgeable in all strategic planning functions. Will be required to develop a strategic planning process for corporate and divisional units. An ability to build and manage a staff of planning specialists as they perform strategic analysis and complete the strategy formulation and selection process.

1980s

A strategic planning specialist who can guide the CEO and direct reports to explore and identify the strategic alternatives available and evaluate and select the most beneficial for the organization. Will be responsible for conducting strategic analysis and providing input to the CEO and the direct reports.

1990s

Knowledge of strategic planning models and responsible for establishing and monitoring the strategic planning schedule, handling the logistics of planning group meetings, providing strategic analysis and assessments to the strategic planning group, and documenting and distributing strategic planning group meeting results. To function as an extension of the CEO to make strategic management effective in fulfilling the vision for the organization. Assist the CEO to establish, articulate, communicate, and educate those responsible for putting into practice strategies that pay off. Major efforts will be in establishing the criteria for effective strategy and ensuring that they are applied.

Source: Donald L. Bates and John E. Dillard, Jr., "Wanted: A Strategic Planner for the 1990s," *Journal of General Management* 18, no. 1 (1992), pp. 51–62.

In organizations that have seriously adopted strategic management, all managers are strategic managers. As part of the job, every manager must be concerned with change and innovation. Each must ask critical questions: "Should we be doing this in the future?" "How should we be doing this?" "What new things should we be doing?"

Long-Range and Short-Range Planning

In the general management and health care literature, you will see references from time to time to "long-range" planning or plans and "short-range" planning or plans. In such references, long-range planning typically pertains to a period of time that extends three to five years into the future, whereas short-range planning refers to plans that are expected to be accomplished in one to three years.

These time references are purposely missing from our definitions of strategic management, strategy, and strategic planning. The terms *long-range* and *short-range planning* lack the richness implied in the terms *strategic management, strategy,* and *strategic planning.* Long-range and short-range planning have the connotation of simply extending present operations to some point in the future. Strategic management, on the other hand, constantly questions the environment/organization relationship and the basis for competition.

Although strategies typically take considerable time to implement, and thus are generally long-range in nature, the time span is not the principal focus of strategic management. In fact, strategic management compresses time. Competitive shifts that might take generations to evolve instead occur in a few short years.[27] Therefore, it is better to use long range and short range to describe the time it will take to accomplish a strategy rather than to indicate a type of planning.

MODES OF STRATEGY MAKING

Obviously, some organizations grow and prosper with relatively rudimentary strategic management systems. Are these organizations successful because of pure luck or have their leaders managed to develop successful strategies without going through the formal process? An organization may have a strategy even though it lacks a formal planning system as long as its decisions are consistent over time. Thus, strategic management may be viewed as taking place in several different ways or modes. The process of strategic management may range from a formal process to an intuitive one.

As illustrated in Exhibit 1–8, the development of strategy may be the result of strategic thinking, formal strategic planning, or opportunistic decision making.[28] Henry Mintzberg referred to these strategic management modes as the entrepreneurial mode, the planning mode, and the adaptive mode.[29]

Strategic Management Modes

In the *strategic thinking* or *entrepreneurial mode,* an implicit strategy is worked out by a dominant or powerful leader without the support of a formal process. In this mode, the entrepreneur has a "good feel" for the market and competition – a kind of sixth sense that enables him or her to judge what to do next.[30] Decision consistency is derived from the strong vision for the future of the organization by the entrepreneur or leader. An example of successful strategic thinking can be seen in the careers of two early leaders of the South Carolina Baptist Hospitals, Reverend W. M. Whiteside and William Arthur Boyce. Rev. Whiteside was the first full-time administrator of the hospital and served in this capacity for forty years, guiding the facility as it struggled through its early years. Rev. Whiteside managed through a strong, dominant personality; without his leadership South Carolina Baptist Hospitals would not have survived. William Arthur Boyce was his successor. Boyce was intent on building the facility's reputation for progress and eagerly began pursuing opportunities for expansion. As with Rev. Whiteside, he dedicated forty years of his life to the healing ministry. Boyce's vision, without

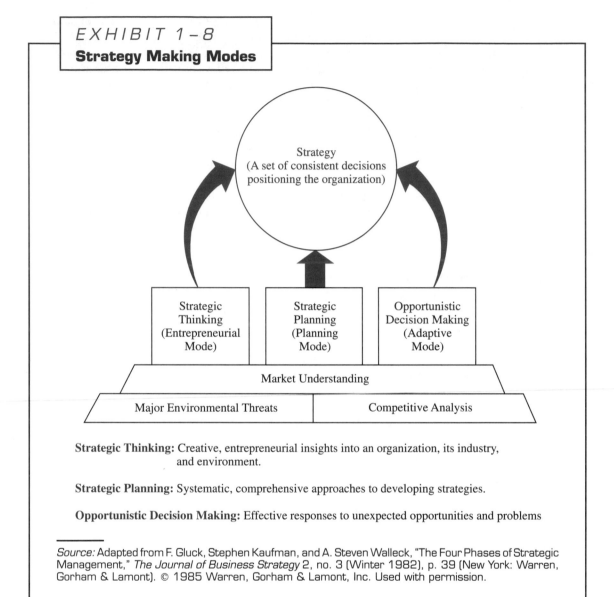

EXHIBIT 1–8
Strategy Making Modes

Strategy
(A set of consistent decisions positioning the organization)

| Strategic Thinking (Entrepreneurial Mode) | Strategic Planning (Planning Mode) | Opportunistic Decision Making (Adaptive Mode) |

Market Understanding

| Major Environmental Threats | Competitive Analysis |

Strategic Thinking: Creative, entrepreneurial insights into an organization, its industry, and environment.

Strategic Planning: Systematic, comprehensive approaches to developing strategies.

Opportunistic Decision Making: Effective responses to unexpected opportunities and problems

Source: Adapted from F. Gluck, Stephen Kaufman, and A. Steven Walleck, "The Four Phases of Strategic Management," *The Journal of Business Strategy* 2, no. 3 (Winter 1982), p. 39 (New York: Warren, Gorham & Lamont). © 1985 Warren, Gorham & Lamont, Inc. Used with permission.

the aid of a formal planning process, led South Carolina Baptist through an era of phenomenal expansion. Boyce intuitively understood the factors for success in his environment.[31] The strategic thinking mode is common in the founding and early development of organizations. This was certainly the case of Richard Scrushy in the founding of HealthSouth Corporation. Scrushy provides a classic example of the entrepreneurial mode as illustrated in Perspective 1–7.

The *formal planning* mode, on the other hand, may be described as a highly

---

PERSPECTIVE 1-7
Entrepreneurial Response to Opportunity

Third-party payers limit reimbursement to hospitals and physicians by reimbursing them according to diagnostic-related groupings (DRGs). Therefore, hospitals cannot afford to consistently keep patients beyond what the preset fee schedule allows. However, rehabilitation facilities (facilities that teach victims of strokes, accidents, and injuries how to function again) are not subject to the DRG system because it is very difficult to predict how long it will take to rehabilitate a patient; each person responds differently to treatment.

Richard Scrushy saw the squeezing of reimbursements in the health care system and saw a way to take advantage of that change. Scrushy indicated, "My idea was to provide high-quality hospital-type rehab services in a low-cost setting." As a result, Scrushy started HealthSouth Rehabilitation Corporation in 1984. As of

1994, HealthSouth is one of the largest comprehensive rehabilitation companies in the country, operating 265 facilities specializing in orthopedics, rehabilitation services, and sports medicine in thirty-two states, Canada, and the District of Columbia. HealthSouth revenues have surpassed $1 billion with a profit margin of approximately 20 percent.

The rehabilitation industry is growing at a dramatic pace. Rehabilitation revenues are over $10 billion and expected to grow 20 percent annually. In addition to being outside the DRG system, another factor contributing to the growth of the rehabilitation industry is the belief by third-party payers that rehab can save more money than it costs. For example, one study showed that for every dollar spent on rehabilitation, $30 is saved in disability benefits.

---

ordered process resulting in strategies developed by a purposeful organization. The assumption underlying the planning mode is that strategic management can be a logical process through which managers can understand the forces in their environment and thus make better decisions concerning the positioning of the organization. The theory and practical implementation of the formal planning mode is the central concern of this text.

As the name implies, in *opportunistic decision making* or the adaptive strategic mode, managers react to changes rather than anticipate and plan for change. Mintzberg describes this mode as one in which decision makers with conflicting goals bargain among themselves to produce a stream of incremental, often disjointed, decisions.[32] Again, a consistent plan may emerge from such a process, but it is much more likely that the strategy of the organization will become vague or "lost" over time. For organizations in dynamic environments, such as health care organizations, the opportunistic mode appears somewhat dangerous.

Which of the strategic management modes is appropriate for health care organizations? What factors are important in making the decision?

The Case for the Planning Mode

Whether an organization should adopt a formal planning mode depends on three structural factors: (1) the demographic features of the organization, (2) the nature of the organization, and (3) the nature of the market and environment.[33] These factors are presented in Exhibit 1–9.

Demographic Features Three demographic features of the organization will affect the need for formal strategic planning: the size of the organization, the diversity of its operations, and its profitability (the cost-revenue relationship). Generally, the larger the organization, the greater is the need for a formal strategic management system to achieve internal coordination and communication. Similarly, the greater the diversity of the organization (multiple markets, divisions, and so on), the greater is the need for a formal approach to strategic management. Moreover the need for formal strategic management grows as the gap between revenues and costs narrows, as there is less room for error.

Nature of the Organization Several internal aspects of the organization affect its need to adopt the planning mode. These factors include the number of important

---

EXHIBIT 1–9
Health Care Structural Factors Suggesting the Planning Mode

Structural Factors	Conditions Requiring More Formal Planning
Demographic Features	
Size of the Organization	Large
Diversity of the Organization	Great
Profitability	Low
Nature of the Organization	
Number of Important Functions	Many
Shared Markets	High
Complexity of Markets	High
Fixed Assets	High
Nature of Market and Environment	
Market Growth Rate	Low
Competitive Threats	High
Rate of Environmental Change	High

Source: Adapted from G. S. Yip, "Who Needs Strategic Planning?" *The Journal of Business Strategy* 6, no. 2 (Fall 1985), p. 39. (New York: Warren, Gorham & Lamont). © 1985 Warren, Gorham, & Lamont, Inc. Used with permission.

functions in the organization, the number of shared markets, the complexity of the markets, and the nature of strategic investments (fixed assets).

Many organizations tend to be dominated by one function. Traditionally, in hospitals the dominant function has been medical services. However, should more than one function play a strategic role, the need for a formal process that involves all functions increases. Similarly, achieving synergy via strategic coordination depends on the capability to share customers, programs, and costs among products or services within a division or among divisions. A formal strategic management process can actively search for sharing opportunities.

The more complex the market, the greater is the need for a formal approach to ensure that as many aspects of the market as possible are considered. This is especially true when there is extensive use of all the elements of the marketing mix, when there are regional variations with which to contend, and when there are legal or regulatory burdens. Finally, an elaborate strategic management process is more critical for organizations that deal with large fixed-asset investments such as a hospital's physical plant than for those that deal with expense investments such as advertising.

Nature of the Market and Environment External concerns affect the need for formal strategic management. These include such factors as rate of market growth, level of competition, and environmental change. A formal planning mode becomes increasingly important to organizations when their markets stop growing and when there is an increase in the level of competition. In addition, when the rate of change in such environmental factors as legal, regulatory, economic, demographic, social, and so on increases, the need for a formal, systematic method of coping with change is needed.

An organization may be evaluated as to its need for a formal strategic management process. Such an evaluation has been completed for Barnes/Jewish/Christian Health System, a large metropolitan, nonprofit, voluntary hospital in St. Louis (see Exhibit 1–10). As illustrated with Barnes, most contemporary health care organizations should use a formal process. These organizations are often quite large and growing, are very diverse and offer a wide variety of patient services, and are subject to constant pressure by various groups to reduce costs and increase revenue. In addition, they must integrate diverse organizational functions and deal with the growing emphasis on entering related complex markets that require extensive capital investment. Finally, for most health care organizations there is increased competition within the various markets, which are themselves experiencing a great deal of environmental change. A formal planning system is required to deal with all of the variables involved in managing a modern health care facility.

STAGES OF STRATEGIC MANAGEMENT

Strategic management has four stages or groups of processes: situational analysis, strategy formulation, strategic implementation, and strategic control. To strategically manage an organization, we must understand the forces in our current

EXHIBIT 1 – 10

Barnes/Jewish/Christian Health System

Structural Factors	B/J/C Health System	Need for Formal Planning
Demographic Features		
Size of Organization	Share of Metro St. Louis health care market: 29.5% System Beds: 3,136	High
Diversity of Organization	Barnes Hospital (1,053 beds), 12 hospitals, 7 nursing facilities, 2 retirement centers, affiliations and alliances with 20 additional hospitals within 150-mile radius of St. Louis; affiliated with Washington University School of Medicine; coordinated programs for women's and children's health	High
Profitability	Medium on $1.4 billion annual revenues	Medium
Nature of the Organization		
Number of Important Functions	Many interrelated functions, e.g., research, education, patient care, marketing, staffing, a complete continuum of services	High
Shared Markets	Regional and local, linkage of services, teaching and community hospitals, home care markets	High
Complexity of Markets	High technology: in the top ten of U.S. hospitals in pioneering research, e.g., islets cells, lung transplants, kidney nephrectomy through lapriascopic technology	High
Fixed Assets	More than 3,100 system-wide beds; latest technology as required for research, teaching, and patient care	High
Nature of Market and Environment		
Market Growth Rate	Growth in the Midwest and in St. Louis is stable	Medium
Competitive Threats	Fifty hospitals in the St. Louis market	High
Environmental Change	Constant technological change/frequent regulatory change	High

Source: 1988 Annual Report, Barnes Hospital, St. Louis, Missouri; Modern Health Care 24, no. 24 (June 13, 1994), p. 6.

situation, develop from that understanding a plan or strategy that will move the organization toward our vision for the future, develop the operational-level programs that will accomplish the strategy, and periodically evaluate the success of the strategy and make necessary changes.

In reality, these stages are highly interrelated and may be initiated at any point. For instance, an organization may find that action has to be taken before the strategy has been formalized or before the situational analysis has been completed or fully understood. Similarly, the process of controlling may create a whole new understanding of the competition and thus a new strategy. These stages are illustrated in Exhibit 1–11.

Situational Analysis

Situational analysis consists of investigating the external environment to determine key external forces; analyzing the internal strengths and weaknesses of the organization; and evaluating the organization's mission, vision, values, and objectives. An organization's strategy must take advantage of opportunities in the environment, avoid external threats, capitalize on internal strengths, and reduce the organization's weaknesses. Therefore, before a strategy can be developed, managers must have a clear sense of what the organization *should* do, what it *can* do, and what it *wants* to do.

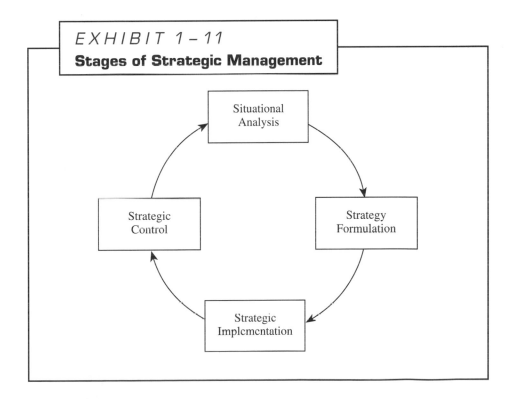

EXHIBIT 1–11
Stages of Strategic Management

Strategy Formulation

Based on the results of the situational analysis, organizational goals must be established, strategic alternatives generated and evaluated, and a strategy determined. This process is referred to as *strategy formulation*. Based on the organizational setting, the formulation stage determines the course of action for the organization. As previously discussed, strategic planning is made up of the situational analysis and strategy formulation stages of strategic management.

Strategic Implementation

Strategic implementation is the process of translating the strategy into specific programs. Therefore, in the implementation stage, employees and managers are mobilized to translate formulated strategies into action. Operational (functional and organization-wide strategies) are developed that will accomplish the broader organizational strategies. It is in the implementation stage that managing human, financial, informational, and physical resources becomes most important. During this stage, the strategy is accomplished.

Strategic Control

The final stage of strategic management is strategic control. The basic objective is to assess whether the strategy and supporting implementation are still appropriate, which is accomplished by periodically evaluating the effectiveness of the strategy and its implementation and making any necessary modifications. The fundamental activities of the control stage of strategic management include (1) reviewing the goals of the organization, (2) measuring the performance of the organization, (3) comparing the goals with the performance, (4) assessing the strategy, and (5) taking corrective action if necessary.

LEVELS OF STRATEGY

The strategic management process may be applied at different levels in the organization. The resulting strategies will differ in scope as well as in purpose as we move from one organizational level to another. As illustrated in Exhibit 1–12, strategic management creates a hierarchy of strategies. Each level provides the "means" for accomplishing the "ends" of the next higher level. Thus, the operational level provides the means for accomplishing the ends of the divisional level. The divisional level, in turn, is the means for the ends established at the corporate level.

Corporate-Level Strategy

The corporate level is the broadest level of strategic management. At the corporate level, the strategic management process defines the general markets or businesses in which the organization will operate and addresses the question, "What business(es) should we be in?" It focuses on integrating semi-autonomous organizational units into an effective portfolio.[34] (These organizational units are often

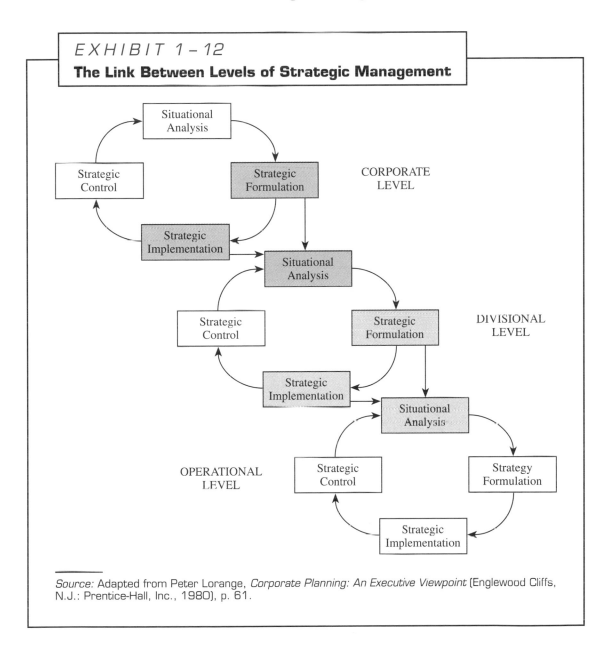

EXHIBIT 1–12
The Link Between Levels of Strategic Management

CORPORATE LEVEL

DIVISIONAL LEVEL

OPERATIONAL LEVEL

Source: Adapted from Peter Lorange, *Corporate Planning: An Executive Viewpoint* (Englewood Cliffs, N.J.: Prentice-Hall, Inc., 1980), p. 61.

called *strategic business units* or SBUs. Because health care organizations provide services, these units are sometimes referred to as *strategic service units* or SSUs.)

Corporate-level strategy must consider multiple markets and the diverse products and technologies unique to each market. At the corporate level, strategic managers determine in which separate businesses the corporation will select to compete. Therefore, at this level there is a wide range of strategic alternatives (diversification, vertical integration, divestiture, and so on).

The organizational structure of InterMountain Health Care, Inc. (IHC), a regional system serving the intermountain area of Utah, Idaho, and Wyoming, is illustrated in Exhibit 1–13. At the corporate level is a parent holding company, InterMountain Health Care, Inc., which owns various semi-autonomous "businesses" or SSUs operating in several different markets, each headed by a central board member.

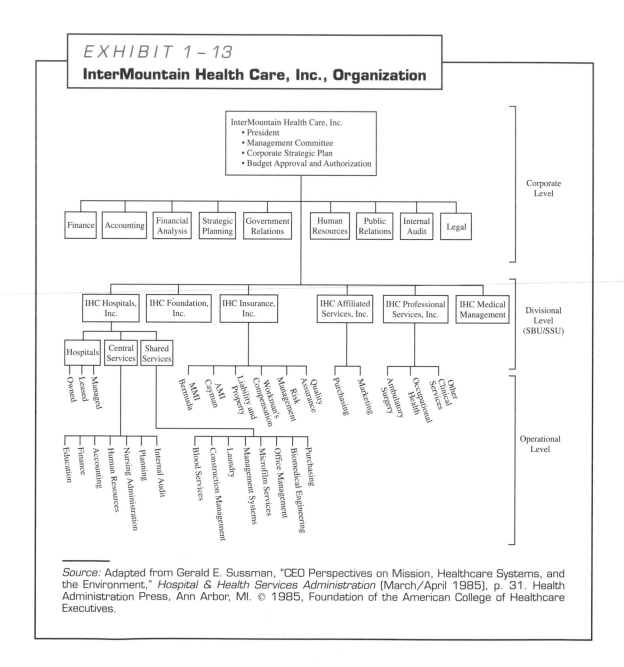

EXHIBIT 1–13

InterMountain Health Care, Inc., Organization

Division-Level Strategy

Division-level strategy deals with the question of how an organization should compete in a given market; that is, how it should position itself among its rivals to reach its goals and allocate its resources to achieve a competitive advantage over its rivals.[35] Division-level strategic management is concerned with competition in a single market, with a single product line, using technology appropriate for that market. These semi-autonomous units are often referred to as SBUs or SSUs. Therefore strategic managers are most concerned with a specified set of competitors within a well-defined market. Strategies at this level are usually limited to the organization's current area of operations (market development, product development, and so on).

In Exhibit 1–13, InterMountain has several subsidiaries carrying the IHC brand name, including IHC Hospitals, Inc., which manages the system's twenty-three hospitals; a foundation, which does fund development; an insurance company; IHC Affiliated Services, which provides shared services; IHC Professional Services, which develops and supports alternative modes of health care delivery including ambulatory surgery centers; and a medical management company, which provides professional services to other companies. These SBUs or SSUs are allowed a great deal of operating independence, and yet there is strong central leadership and control of finances.

Operational-Level Strategy

Operational strategies may be developed within the functional departments of an organization such as marketing, finance, information systems, human resources, and so on. Similarly, organization-wide operational strategies that affect all of the functional departments may be developed by SBU managers. Functional strategies address two issues. First, they are intended to integrate the various subfunctional activities. Second, they are designed to relate the various functional area policies with any changes in the functional area environment.[36] Organization-wide strategies are directed toward integrating the functions themselves and creating internal changes across functions (for example, quality programs or changing the organization's culture). At InterMountain Health Care in Exhibit 1–13, each division has the appropriate supporting functional units to carry out the mission of the division.

Development of strategy at this level still involves situational analysis, strategy formulation, strategic implementation, and strategic control. Strategies at the operational level are developed to support higher level strategies.

Exhibit 1–14 summarizes some of the important characteristics of corporate, divisional, and operational strategies and demonstrates the scale of each. Corporate strategies are concerned with the entire organization and its relationship to the entire industry. Such strategies consider multiple, sometimes unrelated, markets and typically are based on return on investment and market share or potential market share. Divisional strategies are much more focused and provide direction for a single division or SSU within a specific product area or market. Divisional

---

EXHIBIT 1 – 14

**Characteristics of Corporate,
Divisional, and Operational Strategies**

Attribute of Strategy	Corporate	Divisional SBU/SSU	Operational	
			Functional	Organization-wide
Scope	The entire organization	A single SBU/SSU	A single functional area	Across all functional areas
Type of Decision	Industries	Products/ markets	Market approach	Internal/ organization-wide
Market	Multiple	Single	Segment	Internal
Performance Criteria	Return on investment/ market share	Market share	Contribution to strategy	Contribution to strategy

---

strategies are most often concerned with maintaining or increasing market share. Operational strategies are concerned with individual functional areas such as marketing, finance, human resources, and staffing, or are directed toward organization-wide internal change. Operational strategies support divisional strategies in addressing market segments.

ORGANIZATION OF THE BOOK

In our view, health care managers require a comprehensive strategic management approach for guiding organizations through the environmental and industry changes that will occur in the last half of the 1990s. We believe that the strategic management concepts, processes, and methods presented in this text will prove to be valuable in coping with the 1990s and beyond. In addition, the internal, nonquantifiable benefits of strategic management discussed in these chapters will aid health care organizations to better integrate functional areas to strategically utilize limited resources to satisfy the various publics served.

The processes of strategic management for health care organizations are described in fourteen chapters organized around a comprehensive model. This chapter provided an overview of the nature of strategic management in health care organizations. The remaining chapters present a specific model of health care strategic management and examine the strategic processes included within the model.

Following the chapters are five appendices designed to aid in the analysis, discussion, and presentation of health care case studies. Appendix A presents a suggested method for case analysis, and Appendix B provides additional information concerning the specifics of financial analysis for health care organizations.

Appendix C provides insights into making presentations to health care professionals (or future health care professionals). Appendix D presents sources for obtaining additional health care and business information. Finally, Appendix E is an extensive bibliography of strategic management references helpful to the health care researcher or strategist. In addition to the chapters and appendices, twenty comprehensive health care case studies are included to provide actual and timely strategic management situations for analysis by the student.

SUMMARY AND CONCLUSIONS

This chapter discussed the nature of strategic management. Many changes are taking place in the environment that will profoundly affect the success of health care organizations. Strategic management provides a philosophy of health care management that considers these changes in relation to the capabilities of the organization and provides a framework for positioning the organization within the environment.

The concept of strategic management has been successfully used in politics, by the military, and by business organizations. Health care managers are finding it essential for their organizations. Strategic management is useful because it involves systems thinking, allowing managers to consider and integrate the many important external and internal variables that health care organizations now face.

This chapter has provided some important definitions of strategic management that will be used throughout the book. In the process of defining strategic management, strategy, and strategic planning, we have illustrated that strategic management is not a panacea for success or an end in itself. Both the product and the process of strategic management are important.

In exploring the nature of strategic management, it is important to note that strategic management decisions are largely judgmental, yet are crucial to the success of the organization. More specifically, these decisions relate the entire organization to its environment, consider all of the organization's functions, and provide guidelines for all management decisions regarding the organization's mission, customer mix, product mix, service area, goals and objectives, competitive advantage, and outside relationships.

The process of strategic management may be either formal or informal. The decision to adopt a formal system may be based on the demographic features of the organization, the nature of the organization, or the nature of the market and environment. A great deal of evidence suggests that modern health care organizations should adopt a more formal method of strategic management.

The stages of strategic management were examined. Strategic management may be thought of as having a sequence of interdependent stages, including situational analysis, strategy formulation, strategic implementation, and strategic control. Further, these stages may be applied at various levels within the organization. Thus, the strategic management process often involves developing strategies at the operational level to achieve strategies at the divisional level. Division-level strategies, in turn, are the means to achieving corporate-level ends.

In the next chapter, we will develop and discuss a comprehensive model for strategic management.

KEY TERMS AND CONCEPTS IN STRATEGIC MANAGEMENT

competitive advantage
corporate level
customer mix
divisional level
entrepreneurial mode
formal planning
functional strategies
general systems theory
goals and objectives

mission
opportunistic decision-
    making
operational level
organization-wide strategies
outside relationships
product mix
service area
situational analysis

strategic business unit (SBU)
strategic control
strategic implementation
strategic management
strategic planning
strategic service unit (SSU)
strategy
strategy formulation
system

QUESTIONS FOR CLASS DISCUSSION

1. Why is strategic management an important management perspective for health care organizations in the 1990s?
2. Explain and illustrate the possible benefits of strategic management. What types of health care institutions may benefit most from strategic management?
3. Is strategic management more of a philosophy of managing organizations or a management technique? Explain your answer.
4. Why is "systems thinking" helpful to strategic managers?
5. Trace the evolution of strategic management. Have the objectives of strategic management changed dramatically over its development?
6. What is a strategy? How is a strategy different from strategic planning? From strategic management?
7. What is meant by the statement, "Strategic managers should try to create the future"?
8. Strategic management results in important decisions concerning the organization. What are the characteristics of such decisions?

9. In a for-profit hospital or long-term care facility, suggest some types of managers that would be concerned with making strategic decisions.
10. How has the role of the strategic planner changed over the past several decades? What new skills will be essential for the strategic planner in the 1990s?
11. How does the entrepreneurial strategy mode differ from the planning mode?
12. Under what circumstances is the adaptive mode most appropriate in health care management?
13. For a health care organization with which you are familiar, apply the three sets of structural factors presented in Exhibit 1–9 to determine if formal strategic management is required.
14. What are the stages of strategic management? What types of processes occur within each stage?
15. At what organizational level(s) may a strategy be developed? If more than one level, how are these levels linked by the planning process?

NOTES

1. This partial list of issues in the health care industry is the result of numerous interviews with both public and private health care professionals conducted by the authors and is substantiated by such publica-

tions as R. Amara, J. I. Morrison, and G. Schmid, *Looking Ahead at American Healthcare* (Washington, D.C.: McGraw-Hill Publishing Co., Health Care Information Center, 1988); Arthur Andersen &

Co., *The Future of Healthcare: Changes and Choices,* (Chicago: American College of Healthcare Executives, 1987); Committee for the Study of the Future of Public Health, *The Future of Public Health,* Division of Health Care Services, Institute of Medicine (Washington, D.C.: National Academy Press, 1988); John T. Foster, "Hospitals in the Year 2000: A Scenario," *Frontiers of Health Services Management* 6, no. 2 (Winter 1989); and various surveys and forums in such publications as *Modern Healthcare, Federation of American Health Systems Review, Hospitals, Journal of Allied Health, Journal of the American Medical Association,* and so on.

2. David Burda, "What We've Learned from DRGs," *Modern Healthcare* 23, no. 40 (October 4, 1993), pp. 42–44.

3. Pam Autrey and Dennis Thomas, "Competitive Strategy in the Hospital Industry," *Health Care Management Review* 11 (1989), p. 7.

4. H. B. Gelatt, "Future Sense: Creating the Future," *The Futurist* 27, no. 5 (September–October 1993), pp. 9–13.

5. Harold E. Klein and R.E. Linneman, "Environmental Assessment: An International Study of Corporate Practice," *The Journal of Business Strategy* 5 (1984), pp. 66–75.

6. See Stanley S. Thune and Robert J. House, "Where Long-Range Planning Pays Off," *Business Horizons* (August 1970), pp. 81–87; H. I. Ansoff, J. Avener, R. G. Brandenberg, F. E. Portner, and R. Radosevish, "Does Planning Pay? The Effect of Planning on Success of Acquisition in American Firms," *Long Range Planning* (December 1970), p. 207; David M. Herold, "Long-Range Planning and Organizational Performance: A Cross Validation Study," *Academy of Management Journal* (March 1972), pp. 91–102; Delman Karger and F. A. Malik, "Long Range Planning and Organizational Performance," *Long Range Planning* (December 1975), pp. 60–64; P. H. Grinder and D. Norburn, "Planning for Existing Markets: Perceptions of Chief Executives and Financial Performance," *The Journal of the Royal Statistical Society* 138, Series A (1975), pp. 70–97; J. S. Ang and J. H. Chua, "Long-Range Planning in Large U.S. Corporations," *Long Range Planning* (April 29, 1979), pp. 99–102; D. Robley Wood, Jr., and R. Lawrence Laforge, "The Impact of Comprehensive Planning on Financial Performance," *Academy of Management Journal* (September 1979), pp. 516–526; Ronald J. Kudla, "The Effects of Strategic Planning on Common Stock Returns," *Academy of Management Journal* (March 1980), pp. 5–20; Richard B. Robinson, Jr., "The Importance of Outsiders in Small Firm Strategic Planning," *Academy of Management Journal* (March 1982), pp. 80–93; Jonathan B. Welch, "Strategic Planning Could Improve Your Share Price," *Long Range Planning* (April 1984), pp. 144–147; J. S. Bracker and J. N. Pearson, "Planning and Financial Performance of Small, Mature Firms," *Strategic Management Journal* (November–December 1986), pp. 503–522. For an extensive survey of the strategic planning/financial performance literature, see Lawrence C. Rhyne, "The Relationship of Strategic Planning to Financial Performance," *Strategic Management Journal* 7, no. 5 (September–October 1986), pp. 423–436.

7. James L. Webster, William E. Reif, and Jeffrey S. Bracker, "The Manager's Guide to Strategic Planning Tools and Techniques," *Planning Review* 17, no. 6 (1989), p. 5.

8. Jeffrey Bracker, "The Historical Development of the Strategic Management Concept," *Academy of Management Review* 5, no. 2 (1980), pp. 219–224.

9. Ibid.

10. Ibid.

11. Webster, Reif, and Bracker, "The Manager's Guide," p. 5.

12. Ibid.

13. Ernest L. Stebbins and Kathleen N. Williams, "History and Background of Health Planning in the United States," in William A. Reinke, *Health Planning: Qualitative Aspects and Quantitative Techniques* (Bal-

timore: Johns Hopkins University, School of Hygiene and Public Health, Department of International Health, 1972), p. 3.

14. C. Clemenhagen and F. Champagne, "Medical Staff Involvement in Strategic Planning," *Hospital & Health Services Administration* 29, no. 4 (1984), pp. 79–94.

15. Barnes Hospital, St. Louis, Missouri, 1988 *Annual Report,* p. 15.

16. David I. Cleland and William R. King, *Systems Analysis and Project Management* (New York: McGraw-Hill Book Company, 1983), pp. 19–20.

17. Ibid.

18. Ibid., p. 17.

19. Company Documents, *We're with You for Life,* Memorial Health Systems Corporation, p. 1.

20. Ibid.

21. Henry Mintzberg, "Patterns in Strategy Formulation," *Management Science* 24, no. 9 (1978), p. 935.

22. David P. Smith, "One More Time: What Do We Mean by Strategic Management?" *Hospital & Health Services Administration* 32 (1987), pp. 219–233.

23. Bruce D. Henderson, "The Origin of Strategy," *Harvard Business Review* (November–December 1989), p. 142.

24. Robert C. Shirley, "Limiting the Scope of Strategy: A Decision Based Approach," *Academy of Management Review* 7, no. 2 (1982), pp. 264–265.

25. Ibid., pp. 265–266.

26. Henderson, "The Origin of Strategy," p. 142.

27. Donald L. Bates and John E. Dillard, Jr., "Wanted: A Strategic Planner for the 1990s," *Journal of General Management* 18, no. 1 (1992), pp. 51–62.

28. Frederic Gluck, Stephen Kaufman, and A. Steven Walleck, "The Four Phases of Strategic Management," *The Journal of Business Strategy* 2, no. 3 (1982), pp. 9–21.

29. Mintzberg, "Patterns in Strategy Formulation," p. 934.

30. Gluck, Kaufman, and Walleck, "Four Phases," pp. 11–12.

31. South Carolina Baptist Hospitals, *Horizon* 32, no. 4 (Winter 1989), pp. 2–5, and an interview with Lewillar Kelley, director of medical records, South Carolina Baptist Hospitals, an employee since 1947.

32. Mintzberg, "Patterns in Strategy Formulation," p. 934.

33. George S. Yip, "Who Needs Strategic Planning?" *The Journal of Business Strategy* 6, no. 2 (Fall 1985), pp. 30–42.

34. Dan E. Schendel and Charles W. Hofer, "Introduction," in *Strategic Management: A New View of Business Policy and Planning,* ed. D. E. Schendel and C. W. Hofer (Boston: Little, Brown and Company, 1979), p. 12.

35. Ibid., p. 13.

36. Ibid.

ADDITIONAL READINGS

Bigelow, Barbara, and John F. Mahon, "Strategic Behavior of Hospitals: A Framework for Analysis," *Medical Care Review* 46, no. 3 (1989), pp. 295–311. The authors apply theoretical models that provide insight into the interaction between the environment and a hospital's choice of strategy. Further, the article explains how strategic behavior differs both on the basis of environmental characteristics and with respect to the resources available.

Enthoven, Alain C., "The History and Principles of Managed Competition," *Health Affairs,* Supplement (1993), pp. 24–48. Managed competition relies on a sponsor (employer, government, or cooperative) to structure and adjust the market for competing health plans, to establish equitable rules, create price-elastic demand, and avoid uncompensated risk selection. More specifically, Enthoven defines *managed competition* as a purchasing strategy to obtain maximum value for consumers and employers, using rules for competition derived from microeconomic principles. The author's definition of managed competition is a blend of the competitive and regulatory strategies that have coexisted for years in the U.S. health care system. Enthoven examines the development of managed competition and articulates its principles.

Nutt, Paul C., and Robert W. Backoff, *Strategic Management of Public and Third Sector Organizations: A Handbook for Leaders* (San Francisco: Jossey-Bass Publishers, 1992). The authors consider the unique needs of public and third-sector organizations and provide strategic approaches designed especially for these institutions. The book offers a framework for understanding strategic issues, explains strategic management concepts, describes their step-by-step process, examines planning techniques, discusses specific examples, and includes forms and worksheets for carrying out the process.

Smith, Howard L., and Neill F. Piland, "Does Planning Pay Off? A Look at the Experience of New Mexico's Rural Hospitals," *Hospital Topics* 71, no. 1 (1993), pp. 27–35. The authors asked the question, "Do hospitals respond to significant changes in their environment or to external pressures through increased emphasis on strategic planning?" Further, "Does strategic planning pay off in terms of performance?" In addressing these key questions the article examined the extent to which rural hospitals modified strategic planning in response to external forces, explored the relationship between planning and hospital performance, and discussed the practical implications for hospital admin-

istrators. The authors found that, when faced with a turbulent environment, rural hospitals adjusted their strategic planning over time to have a more external focus and that strategic planning was associated with better performance.

Spiegel, Allen D., and Herbert H. Hyman, *Strategic Health Planning: Methods and Techniques Applied to Marketing and Management* (Norwood, NJ: Ablex Publishing Corporation, 1991). Using a six-step strategic planning process framework, the authors provide an extensive and comprehensive compilation of methods and techniques for each aspect of health care planning. They provide insight into identifying and resolving problems existing in the delivery of health care services. The book is particularly helpful in pinpointing needs in geographic service areas; garnering material, financial, and staff resources; creating, selecting, and ranking strategic options; implementation; and evaluating outcomes.

Stanfield, Peggy S., *Introduction to the Health Professions* (Boston: Jones and Bartlett Publishers, 1990). The author provides an excellent and up-to-date overview of health care professions. In the process, she explores the health care system and details numerous careers that involve patient care as well as twenty health-related careers that do not directly involve patient care. The book is designed to help interested students zero in on professions that will match their aptitudes and desired level of responsibility, training, and remuneration.

CHAPTER 2

The Strategic Management Process

"Natural competition . . . is inherently conservative in the way it changes a species' characteristic behavior. By contrast, strategic commitment is deliberate, carefully considered, and tightly reasoned. But the consequences may well be radical change in a relatively short period of time."

– Bruce D. Henderson

LEARNING OBJECTIVES

After completing this chapter you should:

1. Understand the need for and limitations of a comprehensive model of the strategic management process for health care organizations.
2. Be able to cite examples of how the external environment influences the actions and success of health care organizations.
3. Understand that the internal strategic processes developed by health care managers can significantly aid in understanding and coping with environmental change.
4. Be able to describe the strategic management process and its interrelationships, and understand its purpose.
5. Be able to apply the strategic management process to an actual health care organization.
6. Understand strategic change, the frequency of such change, and the forces that put pressure on organizations to engage in strategic change.
7. Be able to describe and discuss *muddling through* and *logical incrementalism.*
8. Be able to describe how an organization may realize a strategy that it never intended.

45

Daughters of Charity National Health System Strategic Management Components

Daughters of Charity is the world's largest religious community of women, with almost 33,000 members. It is one of the largest not-for-profit health systems in the United States. The Daughters of Charity coordinate their national systems from the headquarters in St. Louis, although each region develops its own strategic plan following systemwide guidelines.

The Daughters of Charity National Health System (DCNHS) guidelines for the development of strategy suggest that strategic plans should be clear, concise, flexible, and communicated. Listed here are the seven minimum elements expected in the strategic plan for each region.

1. *Planning Process Description.* The strategic plan should include a written narrative and a diagram that describe how the local planning process relates to the values and objectives of the DCNHS and the external environment.
2. *Role Statement.* The organization's role statement should be reviewed before, during, and after the planning process to ensure consistency with the environmental analysis.
3. *Environmental Analysis.* As a part of the annual strategic planning process, a thorough environmental analysis should be conducted. The environmental analysis should include both marketplace analyses (e.g., patient origin, market share, competitor assessment, physician supply and distribution, market research, and so on) and internal analyses (e.g., organizational strengths and weaknesses, medical staff, clinical service lines, financial condition, payer mix, and so on).
4. *List of Selected Goals and Strategies.* The listing of the goals and strategies should in some way clearly indicate which part of the organization is responsible for meeting each goal and implementing each strategy.
5. *Mission, Business, and Finance Considerations.* For each goal, the strategic plan should document the major analyses and considerations that led to the adoption of that goal (e.g., to support the mission, results of local needs assessment, market demand, financial analysis, and so on).
6. *Identification of Current and Proposed Strategic Service Units.* Local health ministries should specifically identify and define their major service lines.
7. *Impact on Organization Structures.* The strategic plan should at a minimum include a copy of current management organization charts and indicate that the plan's impact on the organization has been considered.

Source: Daughters of Charity National Health System publications.

THE NEED FOR A MODEL OF STRATEGIC MANAGEMENT

Strategic management has been described as a management process that has the objective of making the organization compatible with and successful in its external environment. In managing to achieve that compatibility, many constantly changing external and internal factors must be considered. Without some type of organizing framework, strategic management becomes an overwhelming task. As illustrated by this chapter's Introductory Incident, logical guidelines and well-thought-out procedures facilitate the strategic management process and assure consistency in its application.

Strategic management is most easily understood, studied, and applied by using a *conceptual model* of the process. Models are abstractions that attempt to identify, simplify, and explain processes, patterns, and relationships inherent to a phenomenon. As a result, models are quite useful because they circumvent the need to store masses of data and allow us to recognize the logic underlying a series of interdependent processes.

An understanding of the rationale and logic of strategic management is essential for future-oriented managers. The use of a descriptive model, based on systems thinking as discussed in Chapter 1, provides an overview of the rationale, logic, context, and processes of strategic management. In addition, managers can gain an appreciation of the required inputs to strategic management, the processes involved, and the outputs of the process. Finally, a better understanding of the interrelationships inherent in the process can be gained.

A MODEL OF THE STRATEGIC MANAGEMENT PROCESS

A model of the strategic management process that illustrates and organizes the major components for health care organizations is presented in Exhibit 2–1. This comprehensive model serves as the basis for much of the discussion in this chapter. The model represents a clear and practical approach to understanding the setting (the external environment) for health care as well as the organization itself. In the practice of strategic management, as portrayed in the model, managers engage in several strategic management processes: situational analysis, strategy formulation, strategic implementation, and strategic control. In addition to the organization's setting, each of these elements of the strategic management process will be discussed.

The Organizational Setting

The external environment exerts a powerful influence on the organization and may be referred to as the *organization setting*. Conceptually, the setting may be viewed as being made up of the broader general environment and the more specific health care environment or health care industry. As indicated in the model, these environments affect each other as well as directly affecting the organization.

The General Environment The *general environment* comprises all organizations and individuals outside of the health care industry. Such organizations may include government institutions, business organizations, educational institutions, religious

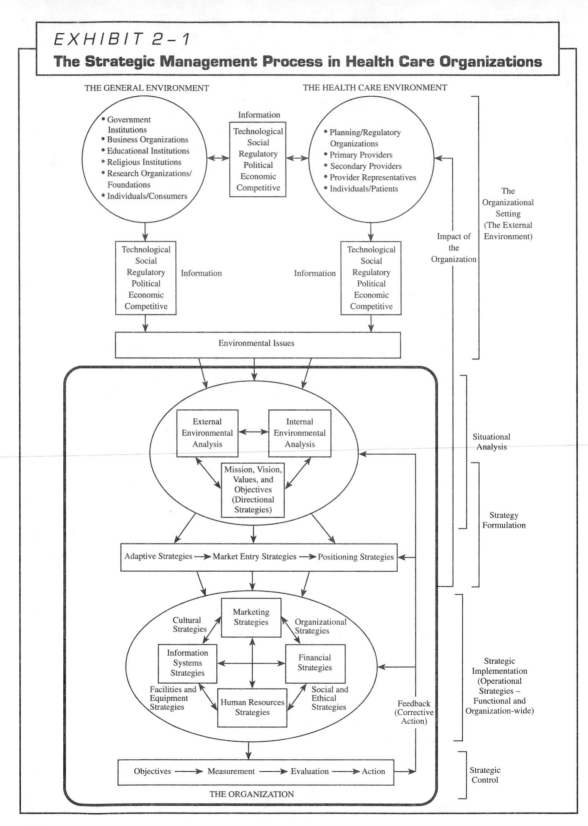

EXHIBIT 2-1

The Strategic Management Process in Health Care Organizations

THE GENERAL ENVIRONMENT   THE HEALTH CARE ENVIRONMENT

Information

• Government Institutions
• Business Organizations
• Educational Institutions
• Religious Institutions
• Research Organizations/Foundations
• Individuals/Consumers

Technological
Social
Regulatory
Political
Economic
Competitive

• Planning/Regulatory Organizations
• Primary Providers
• Secondary Providers
• Provider Representatives
• Individuals/Patients

The Organizational Setting (The External Environment)

Technological
Social
Regulatory
Political
Economic
Competitive

Information

Information

Technological
Social
Regulatory
Political
Economic
Competitive

Impact of the Organization

Environmental Issues

External Environmental Analysis

Internal Environmental Analysis

Mission, Vision, Values, and Objectives (Directional Strategies)

Situational Analysis

Adaptive Strategies → Market Entry Strategies → Positioning Strategies

Strategy Formulation

Cultural Strategies

Marketing Strategies

Organizational Strategies

Information Systems Strategies

Financial Strategies

Facilities and Equipment Strategies

Human Resources Strategies

Social and Ethical Strategies

Feedback (Corrective Action)

Strategic Implementation (Operational Strategies – Functional and Organization-wide)

Objectives → Measurement → Evaluation → Action

THE ORGANIZATION

Strategic Control

institutions, research organizations and foundations, and individuals and consumers.

Organizations and individuals in the general environment, acting alone or in concert with others, initiate and foster the macroenvironmental changes within society. These organizations and individuals generate technological, social, regulatory, political, economic, and competitive *information* that will, in the long run, affect many different industries (including health care). Therefore, external organizations, engaged in their own processes and pursuing their own missions, are developing new information that will affect other industries, organizations, and individuals. Perspective 2–1 provides an excellent example of activities by business organizations in the general environment that affect both the health care environment and specific health care organizations.

Information flows in the general environment usually affect a number of different sectors of the economy (industry environments). For example, the shift in the general regulatory environment toward less government oversight and more deregulation that occurred during the Reagan and Bush administrations affected not only the health care industry but also many others, including transportation, banking, and telecommunications. Similarly, health care reform initiatives of the Clinton administration affected virtually all institutions in the general environment, not just health care organizations.

PERSPECTIVE 2–1

Business Institutions in the General Environment Affect Health Care Organizations

In the past, multihospital systems and nursing home chains dominated the development and operation of retirement centers. The 1990s may see a fundamental change in this business, a change that is coming not from within the health care industry, but rather from business institutions in the general environment. Health care systems are facing new competition from hotel chains such as Marriott Corporation and Hyatt Corporation. For instance, through 1995, Marriott plans to invest more than $1 billion in 150 retirement communities nationwide (some will be joint ventures with hospitals). As competition increases from the business sector, social activities, meals, and housekeeping may become more important competitive factors.

Multihospital systems (such as National Medical Enterprises, Convenant Benevolent Institutions, and Adventist Health System) and nursing home chains (such as Good Samaritan Society, National Benevolent Association, and Forum Group) will have to be aware of activities outside the health care environment. Competitive information concerning the strategies of the business organizations will prove to be important for health care organizations as they develop their own retirement center strategies.

Source: Karen Pallarito, "Slowdown Signals Transition for Retirement Centers Run by Nursing Homes, Hospitals," *Modern Healthcare* (May 21, 1990), pp. 77–80.

A business that develops a breakthrough in computer technology (new information) or a government organization that fosters changes in the general regulatory climate (new information) contributes to macroenvironmental changes that, although perhaps not specifically related to health care, may have a significant and long-lasting impact on the delivery of health care. Although initially developed in the business sector, innovations in computer systems and information processing technologies have significantly affected the delivery of health care.

As illustrated in Exhibit 2–1, the organization itself may be affected *directly* by the technological, social, regulatory, political, economic, and competitive information initiated and fostered by organizations in the general environment. In aggregate, these information flows represent the general direction of societal change, which may affect the success or failure of any organization. Therefore, an organization engaging in strategic management must try to sort out the general information being generated in the external environment and detect the major shifts taking place. This process is often referred to as *macroenvironmental analysis.* A shift in health care consumer attitudes and expectations is an example of a societal change that may affect the success or failure of health care organizations. Perspective 2–2 illustrates baby boomer health care attitudes that will have a direct impact on health care organizations in the late 1990s.

Typically, as information is accumulated and evaluated by the organization, information flows will be summarized as *environmental issues* affecting the industry or organization. The identification and evaluation of the issues in the general environment are important because the issues will accelerate or retard changes taking place within the industry and may affect the organization directly as well.

The Health Care Environment The *health care environment,* on the other hand, concerns information generated within the health care industry. Obviously, this information more directly and immediately affects other health care organizations. For example, the development of new genetic splicing techniques, new Medicare regulations, and the proliferation of freestanding emergency clinics directly affect most health care organizations.

Rapid expansion of the health care system throughout the past decade and increasing specialization have resulted in many different types of health care organizations. Therefore, there are a number of ways to group or classify health care providers and services. For example, providers have been classified as inpatient, outpatient, community based, voluntary, institutional, governmental, hospice, comprehensive health maintenance, centers, cooperatives, ambulatory care, and physicians' offices.[1]

In addition to the wide range of provider types, health care organizations have greatly expanded their roles and services. One of the most significant trends in the evolution of the health care industry is that health care services are moving toward the consumer. After the nation built the world's most elaborate and costly centralized hospital system to bring patients *to* the health care system, today many health care organizations have reversed this attitude and are taking their services to the consumer. For instance, many hospitals have started outpatient surgical centers, free-

---

PERSPECTIVE 2-2

Baby Boomer Consumers Will Have a Major Influence in the 1990s and Beyond

Broad changes are in store when a generation of health care consumers as large as the baby boomers increasingly gain access to the health care system. Seventy-six million strong, the baby boom generation and its buying habits have helped drive the cost-and-quality revolution in industries ranging from automobile manufacturing to retailing. Health care has had to follow the trend, leading to widespread release of outcomes data through quality report cards and similar mechanisms.

The baby boom generation has different expectations and a far different background for those expectations than older generations. This group generally does not see their doctors as gods and will routinely:

- Ask questions about treatment options and costs, then take charge of the decision;

- Demand more products and services that promote youthful and healthy aging, because they are uncomfortable with physical decline;
- Pore over self-help books, videos, and data bases and use hot lines, workshops, survivor groups, and more;
- Refuse to accept advice – and advice givers – at face value;
- Demand convenience and excellent service;
- Ask for evidence of quality and expertise;
- Expect continuity of care; and
- Explore alternative therapies.

Source: Kevin Lumsdon, "Baby Boomers Grow Up," *Hospitals and Health Networks* 67, no. 18 (1993), pp. 24–34.

---

standing diagnostic units, alcoholism clinics, community-outreach programs, mobile units complete with a physician to make house calls, and health-fair stores in shopping malls. An additional example of health care organizations moving toward the consumer can be seen in the phenomenal growth of home health care (70 percent of the nation's hospitals are involved). The search for new sources of revenues to finance modernization, "free care," and educational programs may lead some institutions to open unrelated for-profit businesses such as restaurants, parking lots, office buildings, and fitness centers.[2] Perspective 2–3 illustrates yet another emerging organization form – the group practice without walls.

The variety of these organizations defies easy categorization. However, the health care system may be generally grouped into the five segments as shown in Exhibit 2–1. These groups include organizations that plan and regulate primary and secondary providers, organizations that provide health services (primary providers), organizations that provide resources for the health care system (secondary providers), organizations that represent the primary and secondary providers, and individuals and patients.[3]

PERSPECTIVE 2–3

The Group Practice Without Walls – An Emerging Organizational Form?

A *medical group practice* is a group of three or more physicians formally organized to provide medical care, consultation, diagnosis, or treatment through the joint use of equipment, records and personnel, with practice income distributed according to a prearranged plan. During the past two decades, this practice model has become the health care delivery system of choice for physicians in the United States. In the mid-1990s, a variation of this model – the group practice "without walls" – emerged as an important alternative form of health care delivery. The group practice without walls builds on the group practice concept, except that the group's physicians practice medicine in offices dispersed throughout a particular geographic area rather than physically located in one facility.

Until the mid-1990s, the group practice without walls was praised as the health care delivery system of the future but a concept that had yet to be fully implemented. The benefits of the group practice without walls are:

- maintenance of physician autonomy and practice style,
- centralized administration (professional managers) but a decentralized system of health care delivery,
- economies of scale provided by a larger organization (purchasing power),

- new marketing opportunities,
- additional legal protection afforded by the group model, and
- greater ability to respond to the changing health care marketplace.

The Premier Medical Group in Denver is one of the early organizations of this kind. The Denver-based practice has approximately 45 physician employees, and it is expected that the group will eventually include over 100 physicians and their practices. The majority of its owners are primary-care physicians – internists, pediatricians, and family practitioners. Specialists will likely become involved as owners at some point in the future. Each outpatient facility is organized as a separate unincorporated operating division. Ultimate decision making for the group is vested in the corporation's nine-member board of directors – a group elected by, and from the physician owners.

Will this form of practice be *the* model for the future? Which practices will be the first to join groups of innovators? Where will such practices develop? What will be the long-term impact of group practices without walls?

Source: Darrell L. Schryver, Gerald A. Niederman, and Bruce A. Johnson, "Establishing a Group Practice 'Without Walls'," *Health Care Strategic Management* 11, no. 1 (1993), pp. 18–21.

As indicated in the model of the strategic management process and analogous to the general environment, health care organizations as well as individuals engage in their own processes that create technological, social, regulatory, political, economic, and competitive information flows into the environment. This information affects other organizations both within and outside of the health care industry. For example, the increased costs of health care have become a major negotiating point in management/labor disputes. Companies such as American Telephone & Telegraph Company (AT&T), Allied-Signal Inc., Sears, Marriott Corporation, and others have experimented with preferred provider organizations (PPOs) to curb rising health care costs. AT&T was the first major company to negotiate managed care as a part of a union contract with the Communications Workers of America and the International Brotherhood of Electrical Workers.[4]

In addition to the general environment and health care environment information flows, the health care organization must be aware of the competitive changes taking place within the industry. Therefore, the health care organization will be affected by competitive information flowing within the industry as well.

Organizations and individuals within the health care environment develop and employ new technologies, deal with changing social issues, address political change, develop and comply with regulations, compete with other health care organizations, and participate in the health care economy. Therefore, strategic managers should view the health care environment with the intent of understanding the nature of changes taking place in technology, social issues, regulation, political attitudes, economic realities, and competition. Focusing attention on these major change areas (information flows) facilitates the early identification and analysis of industry-specific environmental issues that will affect the organization. This process is often referred to as *industry analysis*. Industry analysis has been extremely important to hospital managers as they chart the growth of hospital systems and the changing nature of competition as examined in Perspective 2–4.

The Organization

Although the organization and its members are influenced by the external environment, internal processes exist to help the organization understand, interpret, and cope with its external environment. These processes are situational analysis, strategy formulation, strategic implementation, and strategic control. As suggested in Chapter 1, these processes aid the organization in understanding competitive behavior and the impact of a strategy. The organization can then decide to commit resources to a new strategy, predict risk and return, and encourage a willingness to act in light of the strategy.

The internal processes of situational analysis, strategy formulation, strategic implementation, and strategic control lead the organization through a structured process designed to best position the organization within the external environment and to implement a strategy that will help assure success. As stated in the quote at the beginning of this chapter, "strategic commitment is deliberate, carefully considered, and tightly reasoned."

Situational Analysis

Analyzing and understanding the situation is accomplished by three separate processes: (1) external environmental analysis; (2) internal environmental analysis; and (3) the development of the organization's mission, vision, values, and

PERSPECTIVE 2-4
The Growth of Hospital Systems

The development of hospital systems in the United States was driven by the horizontal integration of facilities and resulted in the creation of multihospital systems that provided similar acute care services across multiple locations. The transition to multihospital systems began with investor-owned acquisitions in the late 1960s. Improved access to capital markets and federal reimbursement programs that encouraged growth made it extremely profitable for investor-owned facilities to expand by acquiring hospitals. By the mid-1970s not-for-profit hospitals began to form multihospital systems in response to competition from investor-owned chains and state regulatory and certificate of need (CON) planning constraints. Until the mid-1980s, both investor-owned and not-for-profit systems pursued acquisition strategies, but these strategies differed in terms of magnitude and intensity. Investor-owned systems adopted aggressive growth strategies and concentrated on service delivery in large national markets whereas not-for-profit systems tended to expand more slowly and in local markets.

More recently, expansion of system capability has occurred by way of vertical integration and related and unrelated diversification activities. This expansion represents the evolution of hospital systems from providers of acute care to providers that are capable of addressing a continuum of health care needs. The result is that multihospital systems have been redefined as multihospital health care systems and have incorporated structural changes in organizational arrangements to reflect the provision of a wide range of services beyond acute care in the hospital. Thus, multihospital health care systems can be expected to provide a variety of services across multiple locations.

The transformation of multihospital systems to multihospital health care systems was precipitated in large part by changes in government policy that involved a shift to risk-based payment programs and dramatic increases in health care costs that sensitized consumers, employers, and insurers to health care prices. With the implementation of PPS and DRGs, the government stopped subsidizing hospital acquisitions and horizontal growth of systems. Without government support for acquisitions, the health care industry recognized that there was no national market for health care. The delivery of health services occurs locally, and systems must compete in local markets.

Written by Donna Malvey, Ph.D. Candidate, Health Services Administration, University of Alabama at Birmingham.

objectives. The interaction and results of these processes form the basis for the development of strategy. These three interrelated processes drive the strategy.

As indicated in the model in Exhibit 2–1, issues in the external environment directly and simultaneously affect all three situational analysis processes. Issues in the external environment will affect the process of environmental analysis, provide the context for internal analysis, and influence the mission, vision, values, and objectives of the organization. For example, a regulatory change may very well affect independently the analysis of the external environment, what is determined to be a strength or weakness of the organization, and how managers view the mission, vision, values, and objectives. Moreover, the three situational analysis processes affect one another. They are not completely distinct and separate; they overlap, interact with, and influence one another.

External Environmental Analysis To operate in today's changing environment, managers of health care organizations need a method for scanning external information that will affect the organization. This process is referred to as *external environmental analysis*. As information is accumulated and classified, managers must determine the *environmental issues* that are significant to the organization. They must also monitor these issues, collect additional information, evaluate their impact, and incorporate them into a strategy.

External environmental analysis is the process by which an organization crosses the boundary between itself and the external environment in order to identify and understand changes (issues) that are taking place outside the organization. These changes will represent both *opportunities* and *threats* to the organization and may emanate from either the general environment or the health care environment. It is important that health care managers understand the nature of these opportunities and threats well before they affect the organization. Managers must understand and respond to external opportunities and threats because they represent the fundamental issues that will spell success or failure for the organization. Opportunities and threats should influence the strategy adopted by the organization, that is, what the organization *should* do. Chapter 3 examines more closely the general and health care environments and the process of external environmental analysis.

Internal Environmental Analysis The organization itself has an internal environment that represents the capabilities of the organization (what the organization *can* do). An understanding of the organization's capabilities requires an extensive, in-depth analysis of the internal functions, operations, structure, resources, and skills.

An internal environmental analysis should reveal the *strengths* and *weaknesses* of the organization. An understanding of the strengths and weaknesses provides a foundation for strategy formulation and is essential if a strategy is to be developed that optimizes strengths and deemphasizes and overcomes weaknesses. Chapter 4 examines the processes of internal environmental analysis.

Mission, Vision, Values, and Objectives The mission, vision, values, and objectives of an organization greatly affect the strategy it ultimately adopts. The organization's *mission* represents the consensus and articulation of the organization's understanding of the external opportunities and threats and the internal strengths and weaknesses. It is a general statement of what distinguishes the organization from all others of its type and answers the questions "Who are we?" and "What do we do?" *Vision,* on the other hand, is that *view of the future* which management believes is optimum for the organization (ideally, based on an understanding of the external opportunities and threats and internal strengths and weaknesses) and is communicated throughout the organization. Vision profiles the future and constitutes what the organization *wants* to do.

The *values* of an organization are the fundamental beliefs or "truths" that the organization holds dear. Values are the best indicator of the philosophy of the organization and specify what is important (honesty, integrity, customers, and so on) in the organization. Values are sometimes referred to as guiding principles. The *objectives* of the organization broadly specify the major direction of the organization and link the mission to organizational action. Unlike the mission statement, objectives are specific and measurable.

Mission, vision, values, and objectives may be considered part of the situational analysis because they rely on and influence external environmental analysis and internal environmental analysis. Taken together, an organization's mission, vision, values, and objectives express an understanding of the situation, what the organization is now and what it wants to be. However, mission, vision, values, and objectives are also a part of strategy formulation, because they provide the broadest direction for the organization and are referred to as *directional strategies*. The development of mission, vision, values, and organizational objectives are explored in more detail in Chapter 5.

Strategy Formulation

Situational analysis involves a great deal of gathering, classifying, and understanding information. Strategy formulation involves making decisions concerning that information. These decisions will result in a strategy for the organization. As previously mentioned, the first set of decisions concern the mission, vision, values, and organizational objectives. These decisions provide the general direction for the organization and are, therefore, called directional strategies. Next, more specific strategic decisions must be made. These decisions include determination of the adaptive strategies, market entry strategies, and the positioning strategies. When these decisions have been made the general strategy for the organization will have been developed. As illustrated in Exhibit 2–1, the three processes in the situational analysis component of the model (external environmental analysis, internal environmental analysis, and mission, vision, values, and objectives) simultaneously affect the formulation of strategy and provide input to the strategy.

Directional Strategies As suggested in the preceding section, mission, vision, values, and objectives – the *directional strategies* – are a part of both situational analysis and strategy formulation. They are included in the strategy formulation process as well as in situational analysis because they are decision-making activities that set the broadest direction for the organization. Directional strategies provide the basic philosophy of the organization.

Adaptive, Market Entry, and Positioning Strategies After the mission, vision, values, and broad objectives have been established, strategy formulation involves the evaluation and selection of (1) adaptive strategies, (2) market entry strategies, and (3) positioning strategies. The *adaptive strategies* are more specific than the directional strategies and indicate the method for carrying out the directional strategies. The adaptive strategies specify how the organization will expand (diversification, vertical integration, market development, product development, or penetration), contract (divestiture, liquidation, harvesting, or retrenchment), or stabilize (enhancement or status quo) operations.

The *market entry strategies* indicate whether the adaptive strategy will be accomplished by buying into the market (through acquisitions, licensing, or venture capital investments), cooperating with other organizations in the market (through mergers, alliances, or joint ventures), or internal development. *Positioning strategies* delineate how the organization's products and services will be positioned vis-à-vis other organizations' products and services in a given market and might include strategies such as cost leadership or product differentiation.

Decisions concerning these strategies are sequential. That is, directional strategies are developed first, then adaptive strategies are formulated. Next, market entry strategies are selected. Finally, positioning strategies are formulated. These strategic decisions explicitly answer the questions: What business(es) are we in? What business(es) should we be in? How are we going to compete? At this point, the broad organizational strategies have been selected. In addition, the strategic decisions outlined in Chapter 1 – mission, customer mix, product/service mix, service areas, goals and objectives, competitive advantage, and outside relationships – will have been made. The strategy formulation process is further explored in Chapters 6 and 7.

Strategic Implementation

Once the strategy for the organization (directional, adaptive, market entry, and positioning strategies) has been formulated, *operational strategies* that support (accomplish) the organizational strategy are developed. Operational strategies are made up of strategies developed within the functional areas of the organization and organization-wide operational strategies. *Functional strategies* and supporting programs and budgets must be developed for the key functions in the organization, such as the marketing, information systems, finance, and human resources functions. These functional areas are directly and independently affected by the strategy formulation process, yet functional strategies must be integrated to move the organization toward realizing its mission. In addition to the functional strategies, organizations often develop *organization-wide strategies*. These operational strategies include initiatives such as changing the organization's culture, reorganization, upgrade of facilities and equipment, and social and ethical strategies. These strategies generally affect the entire organization and cut across all functional areas.

Operational strategies are developed in a manner similar to the development of the organization's general strategies. For instance, a functional-level manager must understand the situation (the functional environment, the functional strengths and weaknesses, the mission, vision, values, and objectives of the organization, and the organization's strategic plan), develop a functional mission, set functional objectives, and develop a functional strategy that is supported by specific functional programs and budgets. Similarly, organization-wide strategies draw upon situational analysis (particularly internal analysis), have specific objectives, and must support the strategy of the organization. Implementation strategies are discussed further in Chapters 8 through 12.

Strategic Control

The final stage of strategic management is strategic control. This process includes (1) the establishment of standards (objectives), (2) the measurement of performance, (3) the evaluation of organizational performance against the standards, and (4) the taking of corrective action if necessary.

The strategic control process will, in turn, affect the operational strategies, the organization's general strategy, and situational analysis processes. As managers monitor these various organizational processes, they learn what is effective and take corrective action as necessary. The strategic control processes are discussed in Chapter 13.

Impact of the Organization

The final element of the strategic management model presented in Exhibit 2–1 is the impact of the organization on the external environment. Actions taken by the organization will affect the other organizations and individuals in the health care industry as well as organizations and individuals in the general environment. Thus, implementation of a strategy may cause other organizations that are monitoring their environment (collecting competitive information) to react. For instance, introducing a new medical procedure, engaging in an innovative health care delivery joint venture, or merging two corporations will not go unnoticed in the industry and may very well permanently and substantially affect the nature of the environment. Health care organizations are not only affected by the environment but, through their behavior, they affect the environment as well.

The model of strategic management provides a useful framework for conceptualizing and developing strategies for an organization. The model may be applied to a variety of types of health care organizations operating in dramatically different environments. The model is useful for both large and small organizations and facilitates strategic thinking at corporate, divisional, and operational levels.

STRATEGIC CHANGE

The adoption of a new directional or adaptive strategy suggests a major strategic change for an organization. Such change, although relatively infrequent, is often very difficult for an organization and is implemented over an extended period of time. For example, a decision by a multihospital corporation to expand by diversifying into nursing homes would be relatively dramatic and change the nature of the corporation. Such major shifts in strategic direction are not made frequently or arbitrarily.

As illustrated in Exhibit 2–2, changes in directional or adaptive strategies essentially are a reorientation of the organization and have been called "revolutionary" or "frame breaking."[5] Thus, in *revolutionary change* the pattern of decision making is dramatically altered. Changes in the market entry, positioning, or operational strategies, on the other hand, may be viewed as refinements (strategic adjustments or "frame bending") and represent periods of incremental or *evolutionary change;* that is, change that takes place within the confines (guidelines) of the established and accepted broader strategies. Changes in market entry, positioning, and operational strategies typically do not represent a major strategic reorientation but may require internal (operational, structural, human resource, and so on) alterations. These changes, though sometimes dramatic, are still viewed as evolutionary in nature.

Frequency of Change

For most organizations, changes in strategy occur only at *strategic pressure points.* Thus, there are relatively short periods of strategic change between longer periods of relative stability during which few changes occur. These periods have been described as "waves of change and continuity" and "spurts and pauses" – bold, risky leaps into the future followed by a time of catching up or consolidation.[6] Spurts may be viewed as a way of focusing resources and energy to take advantage of strategic windows of opportunity, while pauses provide time for maintenance and stability.[7] The concept of strategic change is illustrated in Exhibit 2–3.

Change occurs at strategic pressure points. Pressure for change builds to the point where management feels change is more important than the "costs" associated with the change. Generally, pressure for revolutionary change (shifts in

---

EXHIBIT 2-2
The Strategies and Revolutionary and Evolutionary Change

	Type of Change					
	Revolutionary Change		**Evolutionary Change**			**No Change**
Strategies	Changes in directional strategies	Changes in adaptive strategies	Changes in market entry strategies	Changes in positioning strategies	Changes in operational strategies	No change, same strategies
Nature of Change	Reorientation (frame breaking)	Reorientation (frame breaking)	Adjustment (frame bending)	Adjustment (frame bending)	Adjustment (frame bending)	Same frame
Example	Change the mission	Diversify into new business	Move from merger strategy to alliances	Move from one market segment to another	Change marketing strategy	Continuity

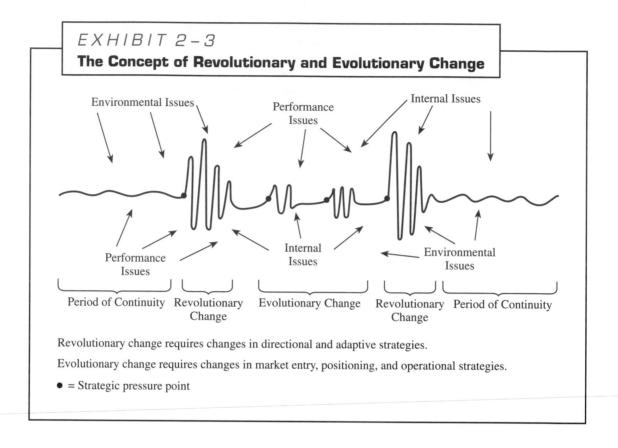

EXHIBIT 2-3

The Concept of Revolutionary and Evolutionary Change

Revolutionary change requires changes in directional and adaptive strategies.

Evolutionary change requires changes in market entry, positioning, and operational strategies.

● = Strategic pressure point

directional and adaptive strategies) do not occur frequently; changes in market entry, positioning, and operational strategies occur more often and are followed by periods of continuity.

Forces for Change

A vast number of forces are pressuring for changes in the strategies of health care organizations. These forces may be categorized as external issues, internal issues, and performance issues.[8] External issues that may influence strategies could be technological, regulatory, political, social, economic, or competitive. Such issues are explored more fully in Chapter 3. As a result of analysis of the external environment, management may conclude that a revolutionary or frame-breaking change is required or, perhaps, that the basic strategy is sound and only a change in the operational-level strategy is needed. Perhaps the most significant change facing health care in the 1990s is the growth of managed care. As illustrated in Perspective 2–5, the phenomenal growth of managed-care plans have forced many physicians and physician groups to adopt frame-breaking (backward vertical integration) and frame-bending (entering into alliances) strategies.

PERSPECTIVE 2-5

Physicians and Physician Groups Adopt Frame-Breaking/ Frame Bending Strategies

Until the early 1990s, most physicians and physician groups had neither the desire nor the incentive to become a part of the growth in managed-care plans. Being a part of a managed-care plan would mean being a part of the payer group (vertical integration) and represented a fundamental change (frame breaking) in strategy for most physicians. Managed care was perceived as a much-maligned novelty that severely limited traditional physician autonomy. Despite the growth of managed-care plans, many doctors predicted that their patients would never leave them. However, HMOs have significantly eroded patient loyalty. Harsh economic realities are forcing many physicians nationwide to reevaluate some traditional beliefs about their patients and practices. Concerning the growth of managed care, Don Shubert of the National Institute for Medical Management, observed that "events like these are giving some physicians a real wake-up call. They're realizing they've got to get involved in managed care if they want to survive."

Managed care involves a whole new way of "doing business" for physicians. Many doctors perceive managed care to be discount medicine and overregulation. They do not understand operating in an environment of resource-based relative value scale (RBRVS), capitation, and health reform. Therefore, to be successful, physicians and physician groups will have to adopt new evolutionary (frame bending) strategies by entering into alliances, repositioning as cost leaders, and changing clinic operations. Such strategies will involve greater dependence on and interaction with other types of health care professionals and organizations. In addition, physicians will have to take a broader look at their patients' health (under capitation the incentive is to keep patients healthy) than was required by the traditional fee-for-service approach.

Source: Jim Montague, "Wake-Up Call," *Hospitals & Health Networks* 67, no. 16 (1993), pp. 40–43.

In addition to external issues, internal issues may suggest a need for a strategic change. The internal assessment process (examined in Chapter 4) may indicate strengths or weaknesses that call for change in strategies. For instance, the results of new drug research by the organization may suggest a new strategy in a certain market or new functional-level promotional strategies to inform the public.

Organizational performance, especially financial performance, may alert management that strategic change is required. Typically, low financial performance mounts pressure on management to engage in evolutionary (market entry, positioning, or operational) strategies in the short term and revolutionary strategies (directional or adaptive) in the long term. Chapters 8 through 12 examine strategic implementation as it is affected by revolutionary and evolutionary change.

External, internal, and performance issues may, of course, work together to create pressure for strategic change. As management becomes aware of these issues (separately or in concert), pressure builds until the "strategic pressure point" is reached and management makes a decision and takes action.

THE MODEL OF STRATEGIC MANAGEMENT AND REALITY

There are many ways to think about the strategic management process in organizations. In fact, Henry Mintzberg identified ten distinct schools of thought concerning organizational strategy.[9] As described in Exhibit 2–4, three of these approaches were prescriptive: the design (conceptual) school, the planning (formal) school, and the positioning (analytical) school. Six schools of thought were described as descriptive and dealt with approaches to the strategic management process: the entrepreneurial school (a visionary process), the cognitive school (a mental process), the learning school (an emergent process), the political school (a power

---

EXHIBIT 2–4
Strategy Formation Schools of Thought

School of Thought	Basic Process	Brief Description
Design School	A conceptual process, simple, judgmental, deliberate (prescriptive)	Strategy formation as a process of informal design, essentially one of conception, process of fitting the organization to its environment
Planning School	A formal process, staged, deliberate (prescriptive)	Formalized the design approach, describing strategy as a more detached, sequential, and systematic process of formal planning
Positioning School	An analytical, systematic process, deliberate (prescriptive)	Focuses on the selection of strategic positions considered generically, emphasizes the content of strategy, selection of the optimal strategy
Entrepreneurial School	A visionary process, intuitive, largely deliberate (descriptive)	Strategy is associated with the vision of a single leader, focuses on personal intuition, judgment, wisdom, experience, insight

EXHIBIT 2-4   *cont'd*

School of Thought	Basic Process	Brief Description
Cognitive School	A mental process, overwhelming (descriptive)	Strategy is viewed as a cognitive process of concept attainment, an understanding of the strategist mind, how individuals handle information to develop strategies
Learning School	An emergent process, informal, messy (descriptive)	The world is too complex to develop clear plans or visions, hence strategies must emerge in small steps or stages, strategy is a process of doing and learning
Political School	A power process, conflictive, aggressive, messy, emergent (descriptive)	Strategy is a process of exploiting power within organizations and by organizations with regard to their external environment
Cultural School	An ideological process, constrained, collective, deliberate (descriptive)	Strategy is rooted in the culture of the organization and thereby depicts it as collective, cooperative, and based on the beliefs shared by the members of the organization
Environmental School	A passive process, emergent (descriptive)	Strategy formation is a passive process and power over it rests not in the organization but the force in the environment
Configurational School	An episodic process, integrative, sequenced (descriptive)	Strategy is composed of behavioral typologies, stages, episodes, or cycles

Source: Developed from Henry Mintzberg, "Strategy Formation Schools of Thought" in *Perspectives on Strategic Management,* ed. James W. Fredrickson (New York: Harper Business, 1990), pp. 105–197.

process), the cultural school (an ideological process), and the environmental school (a passive process). The final school of thought, the configurational school, specifies the stages and sequence of the process and attempts to place the findings of the other schools in context.[10]

Given the carefully contemplated reasoning of the proponents of these various approaches, it is safe to assume that there is no one best way to think or learn about strategy making in complex organizations. The model of strategic management discussed in this chapter is based *first* on the design school and is meant to provide a framework (concept) for understanding strategy making in organizations. The design school provides an excellent starting point for understanding the *concept* of strategy and a foundation for comparing and contrasting strategy approaches. It does not, however, perfectly represent reality. As suggested in the other schools of thought, strategic management is not always a structured, well-thought-out exercise. In reality, thought does not always precede action, perfect information concerning the environment and organization never exists, and rationality and logic are not always superior to intuition and luck. Sometimes organizations "do" before they "know." However, the model does provide a framework for understanding strategy and it serves as a pedagogical starting point for an introductory course in strategic management. Upon this framework, throughout the remaining chapters, contributions of the other schools (optimal strategies, the power of entrepreneurial vision, emergent strategies, political power, culture, environmental forces, and strategy cycles) will be integrated into the design framework.

OTHER DIMENSIONS OF STRATEGIC MANAGEMENT

Several additional dimensions of strategic management should be acknowledged and discussed. For instance, intended strategies are often not the realized strategies. Sometimes managers are able to just "muddle through," or managers may have a broad master plan or logic underlying strategic decisions but, because of the complexity of the external and internal environments, incremental adjustments are the best they can do.

Intended vs. Realized Strategy

Defining strategies as patterns that emerge in a stream of decisions suggests that strategies may be viewed as the ex post facto results of decision-making behavior as well as a priori guidelines to decision making. Of course, a strategy does not always work out as planned (an *unrealized strategy*). In other cases, an organization may end up with a strategy that was quite unexpected as a result of having been "swept away by events" (an *emergent strategy*).

Exhibit 2–5 presents three outcomes for an organization. These outcomes may be summarized as follows:

1. Intended strategies that are realized *(deliberate strategies);*
2. Intended strategies that are not realized, perhaps because of unrealistic expectations, misjudgments about the environment, or changes during implementation *(unrealized strategies);* or

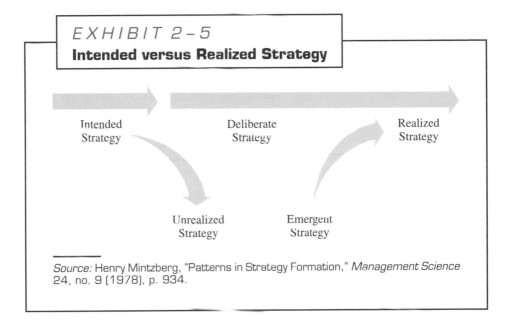

EXHIBIT 2-5
Intended versus Realized Strategy

Intended
Strategy

Deliberate
Strategy

Realized
Strategy

Unrealized
Strategy

Emergent
Strategy

Source: Henry Mintzberg, "Patterns in Strategy Formation," *Management Science* 24, no. 9 (1978), p. 934.

3. Realized strategies that were never intended, perhaps because no strategy was developed at the outset or perhaps because the strategies somehow were displaced along the way *(emergent strategies).*[11]

Obviously, health care organizations formulate strategies and realize them to varying degrees. For instance, as a part of a deliberate strategy to broaden their market, improve service to the community, and retain referral patients, many community hospitals began offering cardiac services such as catheterization and open-heart surgery.[12] As a result, many of these hospitals have built market share and increased profitability. However, some community hospitals have not fared so well. Their managers had unrealistic expectations concerning the profitability of cardiac services and the volume required. A large volume is crucial to cardiac services because it allows the hospital to order supplies in bulk and provides physician experience that produces better outcomes and shorter lengths of stay. In addition, some community hospital managers misjudged the level of reimbursements from Medicare, thereby further squeezing profitability margins. The strategies of those community hospitals that left the market were not realized.

Still other community hospitals seemed to move into a full range of cardiac services without an explicit strategy to do so. In an effort to retain patients and enhance their images, these hospitals began by offering limited cardiac services but shortly found that they were not performing enough procedures to be "world class." They added services, equipment, and facilities to help create the required volume and, without really intending to at the outset, ended up with emergent strategies to build significant market share in cardiac services.

Mintzberg added several possible outcomes to those presented in Exhibit 2–5. For example, he discussed strategies that, as they were realized, changed form and became, in part at least, emergent; emergent strategies that were formalized as deliberate ones; and intended strategies that were overrealized.[13]

It is quite possible that a strategy may be developed and subsequently realized. However, we must be realistic enough to understand that when we engage in strategic management the theoretical ideal (strategy developed, then realized) may not and in all probability will not be the case. A great deal may go wrong. The possibilities include the following:

1. There is a reformulation of the strategy during implementation as the organization gains new information and feeds that information back to the formulation process, thus modifying intentions en route (a function of strategic control).
2. The external environment is in a period of flux and strategists are unable to accurately predict conditions; the organization may therefore find itself unable to respond appropriately to a powerful external momentum.[14]
3. Organizations in the external environment, implementing their own strategies, may block a strategic initiative forcing the activation of a contingency strategy or a period of "groping."

Muddling Through

As the term implies, *muddling through* is an approach in which the organization moves step-by-step in small degrees. A muddling-through approach to strategic management suggests that there is often difficulty in gaining a consensus concerning organizational objectives and values and the appropriate strategy. Additionally, in social and organizational settings, we cannot assume that preferences are stable over time; a highly valued strategy in one circumstance may not be prized at all in another.

The result is that managers choose among values and strategies at the same time and make adjustments at the margin concerning which satisfactions will be willingly sacrificed to achieve another strategic alternative. More specifically, strategy makers simultaneously choose a strategy designed to obtain certain objectives and the objectives themselves. In doing so, managers focus on marginal or incremental values. Because marginal values are the only relevant ones, the manager has little incentive to attempt to clarify the objectives in advance of the choice.

Strategy formulation when muddling through is dynamic and ongoing. It is a process of successive approximations toward a desired objective in which "what is desired itself continues to change under reconsideration."[15] This provides the important advantage of avoiding serious long-term mistakes in strategic analysis. This is the case because (1) past sequences of strategy formulation provide experience and knowledge to be applied to future steps; (2) giant leaps toward outcomes beyond cognitive limits are not required as any given alternative or outcome is not expected to be a final solution; (3) previous predictions can be tested as we move toward each successive step; and (4) minor errors are more easily corrected than when decision making takes place through distinct steps widely separated by time.[16]

Logical Incrementalism

Some authors argue that managers rarely employ normative, sequential strategic management processes. Instead, strategic analysis is an artificial blend of formal analysis, behavioral techniques, and power politics.[17] The objective is to bring about cohesive, step-by-step movement toward ends that are broadly conceived initially and constantly refined and reshaped as new information appears.

Logical incrementalism proceeds by steps, although the steps are not necessarily linear. Strategic issues often emerge as anomalies, paradoxes, or inconsistencies in an organization's current operation. They may even amount to crises, but rarely are they discovered in the process of formal environmental scanning. Instead, strategic managers develop networks (usually informal ones) to acquire objectives and other information. This type of networking is accomplished with people and groups outside as well as inside the organization. Studies have shown this type of skill to be so important that it is a major determinant of managerial success.[18]

This information, however, is not always accepted as final. Successful strategic managers tend to develop or consciously generate broad arrays of alternatives. Politically, these managers "systematically alert wide audiences" to the fact that they are shopping for ideas among trusted colleagues. A few special studies may even be commissioned. Only when a sufficient number of people are alerted, enough support is built to ensure acceptance, and data have become persuasive are commitments finally made.[19]

In this process, an appreciation of organizational culture is a key to successful strategic change. Decision makers skillfully "change the symbols" to build credibility and prepare the organization for change.[20] Initial moves in strategic change are partial, tentative, and experimental. They may appear as little more than tactical adjustments. Political support is built by key appointments to task forces, committees, chair positions, and other critical positions during implementation. Frontal attacks on old strategies are not employed. Instead, organizational politics are used to coopt, neutralize, or at least find "zones of indifference" where opposition will not be overwhelming.

As progress is made, the gains have to be solidified. This is accomplished in a variety of ways, all of which require the skillful use of organizational politics. Executives support actions that facilitate acceptance of the new policy. Usually prime movers avoid direct involvement with projects at this stage, when success is less than certain. Although they keep a low profile, they may provide visibility, support the change with added resources, and so on. Eventually, as champions emerge and are identified, the desired changes will be recognized in the formal planning system.

In logical incrementalism, strategy formulation is seen as a continually evolving analytical-political process. It is a "groping, cyclical process" that circles back on itself with frequent interruptions and delays. It is more like "fermentation in biochemistry, rather than an industrial assembly line."[21]

The process, although incremental, is not piecemeal. It requires constant assessment and reassessment of the organization's capacities and needs. Formal planning processes are used to interrelate and evaluate the resources required, benefits sought, and risks taken. Bargaining does much to ensure balance and breadth. In fact, much of strategic change is little more than consensus building. A comparison of muddling through and logical incrementalism is presented in Exhibit 2–6.

Lessons for Health Care Managers

Strategic management is a complex and difficult task. The 1990s will place a higher premium on effective management and leadership than ever before (see Perspective 2–6). Yet, no single approach may be adequate to understand social and organizational processes. The model presented in this text is designed to provide the essential logic of the process involved in strategic management. However, the model must not be applied blindly or with the belief that "life always works that way." We must realize that, once introduced, our strategies are subject to a variety of forces both within and outside the organization. Sometimes we learn by doing.

EXHIBIT 2–6
Comparison of Muddling Through and Logical Incrementalism

Management Activity	Muddling Through	Logical Incrementalism
Goal Setting	Goals are rarely specific or explicit enough to provide direction or offset uncertainty but the recognition of only a few compromising values simplifies goal setting.	Goals and issues evolve from inconsistencies, anomalies, and paradoxes. Goal statements are rare in that they evolve and develop. Considerable uncertainty and little direction.
Organization Design	Requires a base or organizational infrastructure to pursue the few well-defined values and organization slack to respond to new opportunities. Structure is typically outdated because of reliance on experience and incremental thinking.	Demands more extensive use of temporary (project) groups that can be rapidly formed and dismantled as needs change. Potential for excessive confusion since some aspects of strategies are being implemented before the strategy is finalized.
Implementation Motivation	Motivation is to pursue core goals. Little incentive for pursuit of emerging goals. Likely confusion between ends and means.	Significant confusion over real and transitional goals. Difficult to build adequate reward systems. Creation of uncertainty with frequent change in symbols and culture.

EXHIBIT 2-6   cont'd

Management Activity	Muddling Through	Logical Incrementalism
Leadership and Power	Leadership retains a more formal connotation. Leader must keep morale and enthusiasm high through many interactions required in the refinement of goals.	Power relationships are more informal and the politics of implementation operate at many stages as the decision maker attempts to build support and consensus. Power also operates in the changing of symbols. Politicking becomes a valuable management tool.
Communication	Communication is less directive, and more attention is given to ensuring that all people have opportunity for upward communication. Considerable emphasis is placed on mechanisms to sense happenings in the external environment.	Networking is a key to managerial success. Communication is centered within the organization but networks also move outside into the external environment.
Control	Difficult to define good and bad performance levels because the standards (goals) are frequently changing. Most logical basis for evaluating behavior is the goodness of the policy itself rather than what it is designed to accomplish.	Behavior is evaluated in terms of the changing and vague aspirations that arise in response to anomalies between the present state of affairs and the demands of the environment.

SUMMARY AND CONCLUSIONS

Models of complex phenomena are useful in understanding the various processes involved and their interrelationships. Models provide an abstract overview and conceptual anchors for managers to consider as they struggle to deal with complexity. Without some conceptual framework, it would be difficult to begin the process of strategic management. This chapter has presented a model that delineates the major processes and illustrates the interrelationships.

The model of strategic management may be thought of as having two major segments: the setting and the organization itself. The setting consists of the broad general environment and the more specific health care environment. These

---

PERSPECTIVE 2-6
Chief Executives View the Health Care Industry

A survey of 291 health care chief executive officers of top hospitals and health care systems showed that the CEOs believe that management and leadership will be the key to success in the last half of the 1990s. The survey suggested that an effective strategy will be more important than ever. The survey found:

- Approximately 67 percent of the CEOs believed that many hospitals faltered in the 1980s because health care leaders were inflexible or unable to anticipate and meet the need for alternative health services and products.
- About 96 percent of the CEOs said ambulatory care would be a key feature of hospitals as they redesign.
- Approximately 70 percent said their hospitals either would begin or continue a salaried relationship with one or more hospital-based physician groups.

- Revenue from managed-care plans would rise to 30 percent of total revenue by 1995.
- Virtually all respondents – 90.9 percent – said rising health care costs were likely to result in rationing services.
- Some 60 percent said self-perpetuating hospital boards would not evolve fast enough to keep pace with the external changes in health care.
- More than 81 percent believed that CEO turnover rates likely would rise during the 1990s to reach the double-digit rates of the late 1980s.
- About 55 percent believed that hospitals and systems have insufficient management depth or "bench strength."

Source: Jay Green, "Management to Blame for 80's Woes – CEOs," *Modern Healthcare* 23, no. 16 (1993), p. 3.

---

environments affect one another as well as the organization itself. The general and health care environments are composed of organizations and individuals that, in pursuit of their own missions and objectives, create information. The strategic manager must consider this information and determine if there are any emerging issues to which the organization could, should, or must respond.

The organization component of the model was investigated by describing the internal processes (situational analysis, strategy formulation, strategic implementation, and strategic control) that are designed to help managers understand and respond to the external environment. The subprocesses within each (as well as the processes themselves) are not inherently discrete but rather overlap and affect one another. The processes within situational analysis combine to influence the process of strategy formulation. The strategy formulation process in turn affects strategic implementation at the operational level. Finally, the strategic management process must be evaluated and controlled.

The development and adoption of a new strategy for an organization represents a major change. However, major changes in the organization's strategy (directional or adaptive strategies) are relatively infrequent and represent revolutionary change for the organization. Changes in market entry, positioning, and operational strategies occur more frequently and may be viewed as evolutionary change or strategic adjustments. Typically, change occurs when pressure from external issues, internal issues, and performance issues reaches the point that management believes that it must act. The point at which a change is made is referred to as a *strategic pressure point.*

We must understand that the normative model of strategic management is not itself reality but rather a framework for dealing with reality. The behavior of an organization probably cannot be accurately modeled. In reality, the stages of strategic management may be blended together as the strategy is formed and reformed through organizational learning and incrementalism. Organizational values may never be clear, nor will the organization always reach consensus as to what the values should be. The mission and organizational objectives may surface as a strategy emerges. The process of implementing the strategy may actually create an entirely new, unintended strategy.

Health care managers must understand that, although the normative model provides a framework for thinking about the organization and its future, they must deal with powerful internal and external forces, which in many cases are beyond their control. As Mintzberg has said, "practice is always more complicated – and more interesting – than theory . . ."

KEY TERMS AND CONCEPTS IN STRATEGIC MANAGEMENT

adaptive strategies	**intended strategies**	**organizational setting**
deliberate strategies	**internal organizational**	**organization-wide strategies**
directional strategies	**analysis**	**positioning strategies**
emergent strategies	**logical incrementalism**	**realized strategies**
environmental issues	**macroenvironmental**	**revolutionary change**
evolutionary change	**analysis**	**strategic change**
external environmental	**market entry strategies**	**strategic choice**
analysis	**mission**	**strategic pressure point**
functional strategies	**muddling through**	**unrealized strategies**
general environment	**objectives**	**values**
health care environment	**operational strategies**	**vision**

QUESTIONS FOR CLASS DISCUSSION

1. Why are conceptual models of management processes useful for practicing managers?
2. How is *systems thinking* used as a foundation for model development?
3. Describe the "setting" for health care management. Is the setting too complex or changing too rapidly to accurately predict future conditions?

4. How are the general environment and the health care environment related? How does one affect the other? How do they affect the health care organization?
5. What are some of the major subsystems of the general and health care environments? Why is it important that we focus on the subsystems rather than on the environment as a whole?

6. How will the attributes of the baby boomers, as described in Perspective 2–2, affect the nature and delivery of health care in the last half of the 1990s?

7. In general, what are the organizational processes that managers develop to understand their situation and formulate strategies?

8. How are situational analysis, strategy formulation, strategic implementation, and strategic control linked together?

9. Do health care organizations change directional and adaptive strategies often? Why are these changes called *revolutionary?*

10. What is *evolutionary* strategic change?

11. What events can create pressure on an organization and lead to a *strategic pressure point?*

12. What is meant by *realized strategies?* How can strategies be realized if they were never intended?

13. What can go wrong with well-thought-out strategies that were developed using all the steps of our model of strategic management?

14. What is *muddling through?* Is muddling through an appropriate approach to strategic management?

15. What is *logical incrementalism?* Does the concept of logical incrementalism seem realistic? Can health care managers operate in an environment of incrementalism?

16. Select a health care organization you are familiar with and discuss the demands of strategic management for the organization.

NOTES

1. Peggy S. Stanfield, *Introduction to the Health Professions* (Boston: Jones and Bartlett Publishers, 1990), p. 16.

2. Ibid.

3. Beaufort B. Longest, Jr., *Management Practices for the Health Professional,* 4th ed. (Norwalk, Connecticut: Appleton & Lange, 1990), pp. 12–18.

4. Ron Winslow, "AT&T's Plan on Health Costs May Set Pattern," *Wall Street Journal* (July 19, 1990), pp. B-1, B-3.

5. M. L. Tushman, W. H. Newman, and E. Romanelli, "Convergence and Upheaval: Managing the Unsteady Pace of Organizational Evolution," *California Management Review* 29, no. 1 (1986), pp. 29–44.

6. Sharon Topping, "Strategic Change in Multi-Hospital Systems: A Longitudinal Study of the Nature of Change," dissertation, The University of Alabama at Birmingham, 1991.

7. Ibid.

8. Ibid.

9. Henry Mintzberg, "The Design School: Reconsidering the Basis Premises of Strategic Management," *Strategic Management Journal* 11, no. 3 (1990), pp. 171–195.

10. Ibid.

11. Henry Mintzberg, "Patterns in Strategy Formation," *Management Science* 24, no. 9 (1978), p. 945.

12. Mary Wagner, "Cardiac Services Find a New Home in Community Hospitals," *Modern Healthcare* (October 29, 1990), pp. 23–31.

13. Mintzberg, "Patterns in Strategy Formation," p. 946.

14. Ibid.

15. C. E. Lindbloom, "The Science of Muddling Through," *Public Administration Review* 19, no. 2 (1959), p. 85.

16. Ibid.

17. J. B. Quinn, "Managing Strategic Change," *Sloan Management Review* 21, no. 4 (1980), pp. 3–20.

18. J. P. Kotter, *The General Managers* (New York: The Free Press, 1982); and Fred Luthans, S. A. Rosenkrantz, and H. W. Hennessey, "What Do Successful Managers Really Do?" *Journal of Applied Behavioral Science* 21, no. 3 (1985), pp. 255–270.

19. J. B. Quinn, "Strategic Change: Logical Incrementalism," *Sloan Management Review* 19, no. 1 (1978), pp. 7–22.

20. T. E. Deal and A. A. Kennedy, "Culture: A New Look Through Old Lenses," *Journal of Applied Behavioral Science* 19 (1983), pp. 498–505; and V. Sathe, "Implications of Corporate Culture: A Manager's Guide to Action," *Organizational Dynamics* (Autumn 1983), pp. 5–23.

21. J. M. Pfiffner, "Administrative Rationality," *Public Administration Review* 20, no. 4 (1960), pp. 125–132.

ADDITIONAL READINGS

Hax, Arnold C., "Redefining the Concept of Strategy and the Strategy Formulation Process," *Planning Review* 18, no. 3 (May/June 1990), pp. 34–40.

An MIT professor, Arnold Hax provides a fresh look at the concept of strategy and the strategy-formation process. Hax reviews the critical dimensions of strategy and examines different processes contributing to its formation. In addition, the article explores explicit versus implicit strategy, formal analytical processes versus behavioral approaches, strategy as a pattern of past actions versus the forward-looking plan, and deliberate versus emergent strategy.

Hofer, Charles W., and Dan Schendel, *Strategy Formulation: Analytical Concepts* (St. Paul: West Publishing Company, 1978). This book defines the concept of strategy and explains the reasons for its central role in the management of organizations. Distinctions of strategy formulation and content are drawn at the corporate, divisional, and functional levels of the organization. Many of the concepts, models, and techniques useful for the formulation of strategy are discussed.

Pettigrew, Andrew, *The Management of Strategic Change* (Oxford: Basil Blackwell, 1987). This book is a collection of thoughts by leading strategic thinkers concerning the understanding and management of dynamic environmental and organizational change. The book covers a wide range of strategic issues associated with managing change, including the process of change, the impact of technology, organizational methods to deal with change, and errors in managing strategic change.

Pettigrew, Andrew, Ewan Ferlie, and Lorna McKee, *Shaping Strategic Change* (London: Sage Publications, 1992). This book examines the processes of the management of strategic service change within a health care setting – the National Health Service (NHS) of England. In exploring the nature of change, the book reviews the literature that has been used to study organizational change processes and explains why an approach based on the study of organizational transitions and adaptations is preferred. In studying strategic change, the authors examine the introduction of general management within the NHS, explore the influences of and barriers to strategic change, and examine the skills associated with change management. In addition, the book provides a generic model for understanding strategic service change.

Spender, J. C., *Industry Recipes: An Enquiry into the Nature and Sources of Managerial Judgment* (Oxford: Basil Blackwell, 1989). J. C. Spender indicates that new management models are necessary to deal with uncertainty and change. In this book organizations are considered bodies of knowledge, and management is the process of creating, manipulating, and communicating this knowledge. The key to successful management is creativity and judgment in thinking about and dealing with the organization and its relationship with the external environment.

Stacey, Ralph, "Strategy as Order Emerging from Chaos," *Long Range Planning* 26, no. 1 (1993), pp. 10–17. The author provides some excellent examples of Mintzberg's concept of unintended strategy and organizational learning. In doing so, Stacey introduces the strategic frame of reference of *chaos* and *self-organization*. Stacey suggests that it is impossible for managers to plan or envision the long-term future of an organization in a dynamic environment. Managers must create and discover an unfolding future, using their ability to learn together in groups and interact politically in a spontaneous, self-organizing manner. When there are pro-

vocative atmospheres conducive to complex learning, organizations change and develop new strategic direction. In such atmospheres the destination as well as the route may turn out to be unexpected and unintended. As a result, strategy emerges spontaneously from the chaos of challenge and contradiction, through a process of real-time learning and politics.

Situational Analysis

The starting point in the process of strategic management is to determine precisely where the organization is today and where it wants to be in the future. Situational analysis, covered in Part 2, is the process that determines precisely where the organization is today.

Chapter 3 contains a comprehensive investigation of the external environment. Because the external environment provides strategic managers with clues as to what they *should* be doing, this is a critically important aspect of situational analysis.

Assessment of the internal environment is accomplished through an analysis of the organization's subsystems as examined in Chapter 4. Once these subsystems are understood, strategic managers have a better appreciation for *strategic capabilities* or what the organization *can* do.

Finally, mission, vision, and values are examined in Chapter 5. The process of developing a mission forces members of an organization to think about their distinctiveness today; the vision forces them to think about their hopes for the future; and the values makes them aware of the things that should be cherished and not compromised as the mission and vision are pursued.

3

Understanding and Analyzing the External Environment

"You can observe an awful lot just by watching."
– *Yogi Berra*

LEARNING OBJECTIVES

After completing this chapter you should:

1. Appreciate the significance of the general external environment's impact on health care organizations.
2. Understand and be able to discuss the specific goals of environmental analysis.
3. Be able to point out some limitations to the process of environmental analysis.
4. Be able to describe the various types of organizations in the external environment and how they produce information flows that may be important to other organizations.
5. Be able to identify major environmental trends affecting health care organizations.
6. Be able to identify key sources of environmental information.
7. Discuss important techniques used in environmental analysis.
8. Be able to conduct an external environmental analysis for a health care organization.

The design, services, name, and location of hospitals will undergo a major transformation by the first decade of the twenty-first century. Most health care procedures will be dispersed to alternative sites and, therefore, the hospital will not be a place. The health care system of the twenty-first century will be spread over a wide geographic area and into sites such as homes, churches, and workplaces rather than being bundled together in a very congested and intimidating hospital environment. *Hospital* will no longer mean one monolithic building but a distributed campus. The health care system will be linked together, not by bricks and mortar, but by a common management structure and a uniform computer system.

Hospitals will take on a totally new role and become data centers. Patients will be treated at home through interactive television, while specialists and "super specialists" back at the hospital work with and manipulate the systems to treat them. The hospital will not be a place you go, but something that comes to you.

Something resembling a hospital will continue to be needed for emergency services, intensive care, and some diagnostic work. Other services can be mobile or housed in satellite locations, such as traveling MRIs and radiology clinics located in shopping malls. There will be a blurring between the definition of hospital and ambulatory care centers. Horizontal development may be more important than vertical development for the hospital of the future.

Hospital designers will abandon the institutional features of today's hospitals and create environments more conducive to healing and comfort. Architecture will have more fluid organic shapes becoming more therapeutic and will break the institutional grid of 90 degree angles that has become so characteristic of hospitals. Hospital rooms of the twenty-first century will be larger and resemble a comfortable bedroom. Additional space will accommodate family visits, because hospitalized patients in the future will be there principally for critical care.

Source: Rhonda L. Bergman, "2013: The Hospital Is Not a Place," *Hospitals & Health Networks* 67, no 19 (1993), p. 29.

THE IMPORTANCE OF ENVIRONMENTAL INFLUENCES

Fifty years ago the delivery of health care was usually an uncomplicated relationship of facilities, physicians, and patients working together. Government and business stood weakly on the fringes, having little significant influence. As medical expertise expanded, so did the institutions affecting health care. Today, a multitude of interests are directly or indirectly involved in the delivery of health care. For instance, private-sector businesses are largely responsible for the development and delivery of drugs and medical supplies; and government agencies regulate much of the actual delivery of health care services. The external environment increasingly has become a factor in the success of health care organizations.

To be successful, health care organizations must have an understanding of the external environment in which they operate and anticipate and respond to the significant shifts taking place within that environment. As indicated in the Introductory Incident, the nature of health care institutions will change dramatically in the next two decades as a result of external technological, social, regulatory, political, economic, and competitive forces. Because of this change, it is unlikely that today's concept of a hospital could be successful in the twenty-first century. Those institutions that recognize the significant external forces and modify their strategies and operations accordingly will prosper. Those organizations that ignore the external forces or resist change will find themselves out of touch with the needs of the market, especially because of antiquated technologies, ineffective delivery systems, and outmoded management systems.

The introduction of an early recognition system to identify external opportunities and threats is a major task for health care management. This task has evolved because of the growing impact of economic factors, new technologies, increasing government influence on the industry, new centers of power, demographic shifts, changes in motivation for work, and changes in values and lifestyles, as well as changes in the kind and extent of competition. An excellent example of an organization identifying opportunity and taking advantage of demographic shifts was M. D. Anderson Comprehensive Cancer Center at the University of Texas in Houston. After research, Anderson selected central Florida as an area for expansion because the state was projected to have 80,000 new cancer cases annually by the year 2000. In their research, Anderson found little competition in place in the central part of Florida and approximately 2,000 patients were leaving the area for care.[1]

Health care organizations must understand the impact of external factors and be flexible and open enough to consider new methods and approaches. An additional example of organizations "reading" shifts in the external environment and being open to change is the development and growth of outpatient clinics specializing in alternative medicine as illustrated in Perspective 3–1.

Because the success or failure of a health care organization depends for the most part on influences from outside of the organization, the key to strategic management and, indeed, to the organization's success is to "do the right thing" (effectiveness) and not just "do things right" (efficiency). Organizational effectiveness has an external orientation and suggests that the organization is well

PERSPECTIVE 3-1
Market Opening up to the Nontraditional

Several shifts in the external environment have created new market opportunities in alternative or nontraditional medicine. These opportunities are the result of a growing acceptance of some unconventional forms of medicine, such as chiropractic therapy, massage therapy, alternative wound care, nonsurgical cardiac care, and mind/body medicine (mind/body medicine utilizes nutrition, massage therapy, meditation, and other natural stimuli to treat an array of illnesses, from arthritis to cancer).

Environmental shifts that have opened up this growing market include changes in the health care delivery system, institutional support, and changes in the public's attitudes. The phenomenal growth of outpatient clinics away from the influence of traditional medicine practiced in a hospital has provided a setting conducive to the growth of unconventional forms of medicine. The serious consideration of including alternative medicine and technologies in overall health care reform has fostered the growth of nontraditional approaches. The National Institutes of Health's Office

of Alternative Medicine has been given a $2 million budget to explore previously unaccepted and unconventional medical treatments. In addition, consumers appear to be giving wider support to alternative medicine. A *New England Journal of Medicine* survey indicated that one-third of 1,500 respondents to a survey were treated with unconventional therapy. Americans spend over $15 billion a year on alternative medicine.

Despite the controversy surrounding alternative medicine, it appears that there will be many opportunities (and threats) for organizations in this growing market. No doubt, traditional health care organizations will carefully monitor these trends. In addition, it may be an opportune time for providers of alternative health care to form new relationships with hospitals, nursing facilities, insurers, and managed-care groups.

Source: John Burns, "Market Opening up to the Non-Traditional," *Modern Healthcare* 23, no. 32 (August 9, 1993), pp. 96–98.

positioned to accomplish its mission. Efficiency, on the other hand, has an internal orientation and suggests that economies will be realized in the use of capital, personnel, or physical plant. However, if an organization is doing the wrong thing, no amount of efficiency or good management will save it from decline. Health care organizations, of course, should strive to be both effective and efficient. But, given the choice, an organization should always choose effectiveness.

Strategic management should be directed toward positioning the organization most effectively within its changing environment. Environmental analysis is an integral part of the situational analysis section of the strategic management model presented in Chapter 2 and highlighted in Exhibit 3–1. This model shows the role of the environmental analysis process and its relationship with mission, vision,

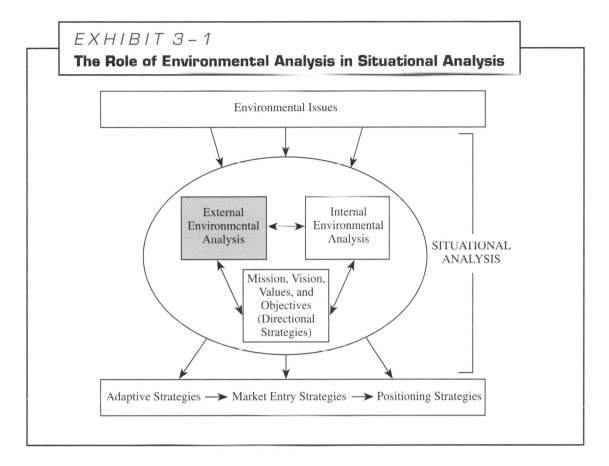

EXHIBIT 3–1
The Role of Environmental Analysis in Situational Analysis

values, objectives (the directional strategies), and internal analysis. Environmental analysis includes the process of understanding the issues of the external environment and determining their implications for the organization. As illustrated by the arrows, the results of the environmental analysis process directly influence the development of the organization's mission, vision, values, objectives, and internal analysis. In combination, external environmental analysis, internal environmental analysis, and the formulation of mission, vision, values, and objectives affect the strategy of the organization.

The *external environmental analysis* process attempts to identify, aggregate, and interpret environmental issues; provides information for the formulation of organizational mission, vision, values, and objectives; and provides the context for internal analysis. As suggested from the double-headed arrows in Exhibit 3–1, each of the other situational analysis processes simultaneously influences the environmental analysis process. For instance, the mission, vision, values, and objectives of the organization will influence which environmental issues are most important (or even perceived) and the internal analysis process determines the relevancy of the external issues. These processes in aggregate influence the strategy formulation process.

The Need for Environmental Analysis

Do all health care organizations need environmental analysis? Based on extensive experience in business, A. H. Mesch developed a series of questions to determine if an organization needs environmental analysis. The questions include:

1. Does the external environment influence the capital allocation and decision-making processes?
2. Have previous strategic plans been scrapped because of unexpected changes in the environment?
3. Has there been an unpleasant surprise in the external environment?
4. Is competition growing in the industry?
5. Is the organization or industry becoming more marketing oriented?
6. Do more and different kinds of external forces seem to be influencing decisions, and does there seem to be more interplay between them?
7. Is management unhappy with past forecasting and planning efforts?[2]

Answering "yes" to any of the questions suggests that management should consider some form of environmental analysis. Answering "yes" to five or more indicates that environmental analysis is imperative. In today's dynamic environment, most health care managers would answer "yes" to more than one of these questions and should be performing environmental analysis. This is certainly the case for public hospital managers, as illustrated in Perspective 3–2.

Because capital expenditures such as investing in new technology or expanding facilities take many years to "pay for themselves," environmental analysis is essential when allocating capital. An understanding of the emerging trends within the environment would aid in determining the long-term viability of such capital expenditures. Similarly, strategies of the organization are more likely to be sound and will have greater longevity if the dynamics of the external environment are considered.

Environmental analysis seeks to eliminate many of the surprises in the external environment. Organizations cannot afford to be surprised. As one writer has pointed out, "to the blind all things are sudden." Often managers who practice environmental analysis are so "close" to the environment that by the time change becomes apparent to others, they have already detected the signals of change and explored the significance of the changes. Rarely are such managers completely surprised by external events.

When competition is increasing, environmental change will be accelerated and managers must be particularly concerned with meeting consumers' needs. For example, if a hospital does not consider the latest technology, emerging social trends, or new regulatory realities, patients and physicians may choose to go to another hospital where the latest technology has been adopted, the staff is sensitive to emerging social issues, or the administration has adapted to regulatory change. Under these conditions organizations generally become more marketing oriented, which calls for an effective environmental analysis function.

In many health care organizations, forecasting and planning have not been successful. Often, the lack of success is due to forecasting and planning processes

---

PERSPECTIVE 3-2

Public Hospitals Need Environmental Analysis

Health care reform and the increase in managed competition have caused the nation's 1,400 public hospitals to scrap previous strategic plans or initiate serious strategic planning efforts. This new environment may require them to compete with other health care providers. Historically, public hospital and competition were rarely used in the same sentence. Government-sponsored hospitals were created to serve the people that other providers did not want. Now, the rules are changing and public hospitals are scrambling to compete.

Many public hospitals have been financially strapped, and their physical plants are outdated and deteriorating. Yet, competition will require capital investments in additional primary-care sites, health maintenance organizations, improved links between providers in their health care systems, and the formation of partnerships with private health care providers. It has been estimated that capital needs of the nation's largest urban providers will exceed $15 billion this decade. The challenge for public hospitals is to develop networks that meet the needs of the traditionally underserved and at the same time attract new markets.

Clearly, for public hospitals, there has been a strategic surprise (health care reform initiatives) and the rules for success are rapidly changing. Previous plans have little relevance and the new environment will dramatically affect capital allocations. Competition is growing and forces in the external environment will continue to influence public hospitals' decisions.

Source: Karen Pallarito, "Going Public: Government-Sponsored Hospitals Court Patients by Expanding Primary Care," *Modern Healthcare* 23, no. 42 (1993), pp. 30–36.

---

directed internally toward efficiency rather than externally toward effectiveness. Such planning systems have not considered the growing number and diversity of environmental influences. Early identification of external changes through environmental analysis will greatly enhance the planning efforts in health care organizations. For example, as it became clear that health care reform would move toward some form of managed care or managed competition, many physicians group practices and solo practitioners were joining together to create large physician-driven health care organizations that could compete for prepaid health care contracts. These physicians viewed such organizations as a way to evolve competitively to ensure their survival.[3]

The Goals of Environmental Analysis

Although the overall intent of environmental analysis is to position the organization within its environment, more specific goals may be identified. The specific goals of environmental analysis include:

1. to classify and order information flows generated by outside organizations;
2. to identify and analyze *current* important issues that will affect the organization;
3. to detect and analyze the weak signals of *emerging* issues that will affect the organization;
4. to speculate on the *likely* future issues that will have significant impact on the organization;
5. to provide organized information for the development of the organization's mission, vision, values, objectives, internal analysis, and strategy; and
6. to foster strategic thinking throughout the organization.

There is an abundance of information in the external environment. For it to be meaningful to the organization, managers must identify the sources as well as aggregate and classify the information. Once classified, important issues that will affect the organization may be identified and evaluated. This process encourages managers to view change as external issues that may affect the organization.

In addition to the identification of current issues, environmental analysis attempts to detect weak signals within the external environment that may portend a future issue. Sometimes based on little hard data, managers attempt to identify patterns that suggest emerging issues that will be significant for the organization. Such issues, if they continue or actually do occur, may represent significant challenges to the organization. Early identification aids in developing strategy.

Strategic managers must go beyond what is known and speculate on the nature of the industry, as well as the organization, in the future. This process often stimulates creative thinking concerning the organization's present and future products and services. Such speculation is valuable in the formulation of a guiding vision and the development of mission and strategy. For example, the Introductory Incident, describing the nature of a twenty-first century hospital, was developed through a process of extending and analyzing emerging external issues and speculating on future likely issues and their impact upon the hospital. Perspective 3–3 provides some of the emerging and speculative trends and issues that led to the conclusions reached in the Introductory Incident.

When top managers, middle managers, and front-line supervisors throughout the organization are considering the relationship of the organization to its environment, innovation and a high level of service are likely. Strategic thinking within an organization fosters adaptability, and those organizations that "adapt best will ultimately displace the rest."

The Limitations of Environmental Analysis

Environmental analysis is an important process for understanding the external environment, but it provides no guarantees for success. The process has some practical limitations that the organization must recognize. These limitations include:

1. environmental analysis cannot foretell the future;
2. managers cannot see everything;

PERSPECTIVE 3-3

Trends and Issues Influencing Health Care Delivery Systems of the Twenty-first Century

Looking beyond the basic structural changes of health care reform can be helpful in planning for the future. These are some of the forces influencing the vision of the hospital of the twenty-first century described in the Introductory Incident of this chapter. Although some of the following changes are twenty years or more in the future, early signs are apparent now:

- Health care moves from its current "diagnose-and-treat" to "predict-and-manage" approach allowing for intervention well before problems become acute.
- Many acute care services become broadly decentralized.
- A decline in surgical rates.
- Surges in ambulatory and home care.
- Greater focus on trauma and serious infection in hospitals.
- Cures for diseases such as cancer, AIDS, and Alzheimer's disease.
- Extension of life and a need for more geriatric-health professionals.

- Widespread use of alternative therapies and providers.
- More use of advanced practice nurses (APNs).
- Advances in telemedicine and information management bring specialized services and expertise to remote locations.
- "Wearable" personal computers.
- "Biosensor" self-care devices.
- Health risks analyzed using a data base of a patient's genetic information.
- Reversal of genetic damage by replacing damaged or defective genes.
- Artificial intelligence or expert systems used routinely in clinical diagnoses.
- Increase in endoscopic techniques and the movement from inpatient to outpatient surgery.

Source: Rhonda L. Bergman, "Quantum Leaps," *Hospitals & Health Networks* 67, no. 19 (1993), pp. 28-35.

3. sometimes pertinent and timely information is difficult or impossible to obtain;
4. there may be delays between the occurrence of external events and management's ability to interpret them;
5. sometimes there is a general inability on the part of the organization to respond quickly enough to take advantage of the issue detected; and
6. managers' strongly held beliefs sometimes inhibit them from detecting issues or interpreting them rationally.[4]

Environmental analysis was never envisioned to foretell the future but rather to read the signals that indicate what the requirements for competition will be in the near future. Even the most comprehensive and well-organized environmental analysis process will not detect all of the changes taking place. Sometimes events occur that are significant to the organization but that were preceded by few, if any, signals of the event. However, for most major environmental shifts there are adequate precursors if managers are paying attention.

Uncovering information is the key to environmental analysis. However, in some cases, timely and pertinent information may be difficult to obtain. This difficulty is particularly apparent when there is an important proprietary development by a competitor. Even when information is available, it may be difficult to interpret its real significance, the organization may be slow in mobilizing to take advantage of the information because decisions require too many levels of approval, or the strategy formulation process may be viewed as a yearly cycle.

Perhaps the greatest limiting factor in external environmental analysis is the preconceived beliefs of management. In many cases, what managers already believe about the industry, important competitive factors, or social issues inhibits their ability to perceive or accept signals for change. Because of each manager's beliefs, signals are ignored that do not conform with what he or she believes. Despite long and loud signals for change, in some cases organizations do not change until "the gun is at their head," and then it is often too late.

A DESCRIPTION OF THE EXTERNAL ENVIRONMENT

Organizations and individuals create change. Therefore, if health care managers are to be aware of changes taking place outside of their own organization, they must have a good understanding of the types of organizations that are creating change and the nature of the change. Exhibit 3–2 illustrates the concept of the external environment for health care organizations.

The Creation of Information

As suggested in Exhibit 3–2, the external environment is made up of a variety of organizations and individuals. Some of the organizations and individuals have little direct involvement with the health care industry and may be classified as making up the *general environment.* Other organizations are directly involved with health care and are considered part of the *health care environment.* However, the distinction between the general and health care environments is not always clear, as information in the general environment is continually "breaking through" to the health care environment. For instance, laser technology was developed outside of the health care industry but has been quickly adopted within health care in a variety of surgical applications. Today, further development of laser technology is continuing both within the health care environment and the general environment. This phenomenon sometimes is referred to as *environmental slip.*[5]

Organizations within both the general environment and the health care environment create information flows through their normal operations that may affect a variety of other organizations. Some organizations create more significant information than others. A medical equipment company may develop a new diagnostic technology that will offer the health care providers that purchase it a

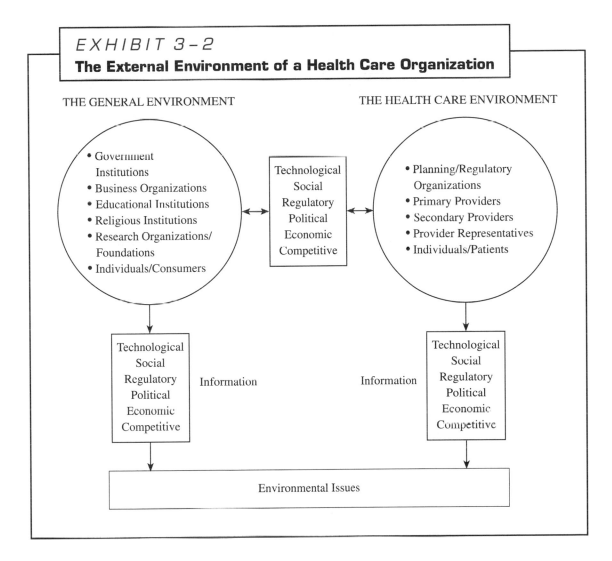

EXHIBIT 3-2
The External Environment of a Health Care Organization

THE GENERAL ENVIRONMENT

- Government Institutions
- Business Organizations
- Educational Institutions
- Religious Institutions
- Research Organizations/ Foundations
- Individuals/Consumers

Technological
Social
Regulatory
Political
Economic
Competitive

THE HEALTH CARE ENVIRONMENT

- Planning/Regulatory Organizations
- Primary Providers
- Secondary Providers
- Provider Representatives
- Individuals/Patients

Technological
Social
Regulatory
Political
Economic
Competitive

Information

Information

Technological
Social
Regulatory
Political
Economic
Competitive

Environmental Issues

competitive advantage. For example, magnetic resonance imaging (MRI) gave freestanding diagnostic clinics a significant competitive advantage over some hospitals. Similarly, new Medicaid or Medicare regulations may change the advantages or disadvantages of certain types of health care delivery strategies. It is important that the organization understand this new "information" and be in a position to respond. Management must decide whether to adopt the new technology or whether to react to Medicaid or Medicare regulation changes, and if so, how.

In most instances, the information flows that are generated in the general environment have less immediate impact on a health care organization than information flows created within the health care environment. However, information occurring within the general environment subsequently will affect the health care industry as organizations within the industry adopt the information for their own use. In addition, these general environment information flows may have a direct impact on any one health care organization if it is the member of the health care industry that most immediately sees an application for the information. Therefore, it is important that health care organizations not only identify and monitor information generated within the health care environment but also have a "window" on the general environment.

Classification of Information Flows

Information generated by organizations may be quite varied. However, to understand and analyze the information, it is often convenient to classify it by type. Many organizations classify environmental information as being technological, social, political, regulatory, economic, or competitive.[6] Information, of course, is not inherently technological, social, and so on. However, using this "systems approach" helps us to understand the nature of the information and to evaluate its impact. Such a classification also helps aggregate information and organize it for the identification of important issues that may affect the organization. Through the aggregation and organization process, patterns may be identified and evidence accumulated to support an issue.

As illustrated in Exhibit 3–2, once it is conceptually categorized by management, information may be seen as technological, social, political, regulatory, economic, and competitive information streams. These information flows may then be evaluated as to their significance to the organization.

Components of the General Environment

All types of organizations and independent individuals generate important information within the general environment. For example, a research firm that is developing imaging technology may provide "information" that could be used by a variety of other organizations in very diverse industries such as hospitals (magnetic resonance imaging) and manufacturing (robotics).

The members of the general environment may be broadly classified in a variety of ways depending on the strategic management needs of the organization analyzing the environment. These groups of organizations and individuals make up the broad context for the health care industry:

1. government institutions,
2. business organizations,
3. educational institutions,
4. religious institutions,
5. research organizations and foundations, and
6. individuals and consumers.

Further, these organizations and individuals generate information (technological, social, regulatory, and so on) that may directly affect the entire health care industry or a specific health care organization.

Components of the Health Care Environment

The variety of health care organizations make categorization difficult. However, the health care system may be generally grouped into the five segments shown in Exhibit 3–2:

1. organizations that plan and regulate primary and secondary providers;
2. organizations that provide health services (primary providers);
3. organizations that provide resources for the health care system (secondary providers);
4. organizations that represent the primary and secondary providers; and
5. individuals involved in health care and patients (consumers of health care services).[7]

Exhibit 3–3 lists the types of organizations and individuals within each segment and provides examples. The categories of health care organizations listed

---

EXHIBIT 3–3
Organizations in the Health Care Environment

Organizations that Plan for and/or Regulate Primary and Secondary Providers

- Federal Regulating Agencies
    Department of Health and Human Services (DHHS)
    Health Care Financing Administration (HCFA)

- State Regulating Agencies
    Public Health Department
    State Health Planning Agency (e.g., Certificate of Need (CON))

- Voluntary Regulating Groups
    Joint Commission on Accreditation of Healthcare Organizations (JCAHO)

- Other Accrediting Agencies

Primary Providers (Organizations that Provide Health Services)

- Hospitals
    Voluntary (e.g., Barnes/Jewish/Christian Health System)
    Governmental (e.g., Veteran's Administration hospitals)
    Investor-Owned (e.g., Columbia/HCA, American Medical International, National Medical Enterprises)

- State Public Health Departments
- Long-Term-Care Facilities
    Skilled Nursing Facilities (e.g., Beverly Enterprises, Upjohn Healthcare Services, Mediplex)
- Intermediate-Care Facilities

EXHIBIT 3-3   *cont'd*

- HMOs and IPAs (e.g., Care America, Complete Health, PruCare)
- Ambulatory-Care Institutions (e.g., Wellesley Medical Management, National Rehabilitation Centers)
- Hospices (e.g., Hospice Care, Inc., Melinda House, Connecticut Hospice, Inc.)
- Physicians' Offices
- Home Health Care Institutions (e.g., Care Givers Home Health, Olsen Healthcare, Visiting Nurses Association (VNA), Kimberly Quality)

Secondary Providers (Organizations that Provide Resources)

- Educational Institutions
  Medical Schools (e.g., Johns Hopkins, University of Alabama at Birmingham (UAB))
  Schools of Public Health
  Schools of Nursing
  Health Administration Programs

- Organizations that Pay for Care (Third-Party Payers)
  Government (e.g., Medicaid, Medicare)
  Insurance Companies (e.g., Prudential, Metropolitan)
  Businesses (e.g., AT&T, IBM)
  Social Organizations (e.g., Shriners, Rotary Clubs)

- Pharmaceutical and Medical Supply
  Drug Distributors (e.g., Bergen Brunswig, Walgreen, McKesson)
  Drug and Research Companies (e.g., Bristol Myers Squibb, Merck, Pfizer, American Home Products, Eli Lilly, Upjohn, Warner Lambert)
  Medical Products Companies (e.g., Johnson & Johnson, Baxter International, Abbott Labs, Bausch & Lomb)

Organizations that Represent Primary and Secondary Providers

- American Medical Association (AMA)
- American Hospital Association (AHA)
- State Medical Associations (e.g., Illinois Hospital Association, Kentucky Medical Association)
- Professional Associations (e.g., Pharmaceutical Manufacturers Association (PMA), American College of Healthcare Executives)

Individuals and Patients (Consumers)

- Independent Physicians
- Nurses
- Nonphysician Professionals
- Nonprofessionals
- Patients and Consumer Groups

Source: Adapted from Beaufort B. Longest, Jr., *Management Practices for the Health Professional,* 4th ed. (Norwalk, Connecticut: Appleton & Lange, 1990).

under each of the health care segments is not meant to be all-inclusive, but rather to provide a starting point for understanding the wide diversity and complexity of the industry.

Organizations that Plan and Regulate A number of organizations plan for or regulate primary and secondary health care providers. These organizations may be generally categorized into four groups: federal regulating agencies, state regulating agencies, voluntary regulating groups, and accrediting groups.

Federal involvement in the regulation of the health care industry has increased in the past thirty years. The passage of the Medicare and Medicaid programs in the mid-1960s and the 1974 enactment of the National Health Planning and Resources Development Act dramatically increased the federal government's participation in the regulation of health care.[8] Important federal health care regulating organizations include the Department of Health and Human Services (DHHS) and the Health Care Financing Administration (HCFA). In a similar manner, state governments have become concerned about the provision of health care and have created a variety of organizations and agencies to regulate health care within the states.

In addition to federal and state government regulating agencies, there are a number of voluntary regulatory groups and accrediting agencies. These groups include the Joint Commission on Accreditation of Healthcare Organizations (JCAHO) as well as a number of separate discipline accrediting agencies such as the American Dietetic Association, the National League of Nursing, and the Commission on Accreditation of the American Dental Association. With a growing emphasis on quality, it is likely that these types of organizations will expand their role within the industry.

Primary Providers The most visible component of the health care system, there are a number of ways to classify the wide and diverse range of primary providers. (Primary and secondary providers should not be confused with primary, secondary, and tertiary levels of hospital care.) Exhibit 3–3 suggests one approach that has eight, sometimes overlapping, groups: hospitals; state public health departments; long-term-care facilities; HMOs, PPOs, and IPAs; ambulatory-care institutions; hospices; physicians' offices; and home health care institutions.

These types of organizations make up the delivery portion of the health care industry. In the past, hospitals have been the dominant segment, but as the industry becomes more specialized and fragments further, other primary providers will grow in importance. Institutions that are likely to be more dominant in the future are long-term-care facilities, hospices, and home-care institutions.

Secondary Providers Essentially composed of support organizations for primary providers, the secondary provider component includes educational institutions, organizations that pay for health care, and pharmaceutical and medical supply companies. Educational institutions, through their medical, nursing, schools of public health, and allied health care programs, educate health care personnel. Organizations that pay for care (third-party payers) include the government (prin cipally through Medicare and Medicaid), commercial insurance companies, and employers.

Another segment of the secondary provider category includes pharmaceutical and medical supply organizations. This is a particularly important segment supporting the research and material needs of primary providers. Major pharmaceutical and medical supply organizations include drug distributors, drug and research companies, and medical products companies.

Representation of the Primary and Secondary Providers The various providers of health care are typically represented by associations whose main purpose is to foster the disciplines and represent the interests of their constituencies. Examples include national associations such as the American Medical Association, the American Hospital Association, the Pharmaceutical Manufacturers Association, and so on. In addition, there are a variety of state and local health care associations.

Individuals and Patients The final segment of the health care industry includes individuals working within the industry (either independently or in health care organizations), patients, and consumer groups. Individuals working within the industry create the culture of the industry and are the source of many issues. Patients are the reason that health care organizations exist. In the past, this group was treated as a mere component of the health care system, but in today's competitive environment the needs and wants of the users of health services are driving the system. Patients create important issues for health care managers. In addition, groups of consumers such as the American Association of Retired Persons (AARP) and the American Cancer Society make their voices heard about health care issues.

Analysis of the Service Area

Health care organizations generally focus their environmental analyses primarily on their service areas. The service area is considered to be the geographic area surrounding the health care provider. It is usually limited by fairly well-defined geographic borders. Beyond these borders services may be difficult to render due to distance, cost, time, and so on and are probably not competitive. Therefore, a health care organization must not only define its service area but also analyze in detail all relevant and important aspects of the service area.[9]

In most cases, the service area is product specific as well as geographically oriented. Health care organizations must define the service areas for each of their products or services. For instance, the service area for inpatient services is not necessarily the same as the service area for emergency room services or open-heart surgery. The opportunities and threats for each of these multiple service areas may be quite different; therefore, considerable analysis may be directed toward understanding the nature of the service areas.

Service areas will be different for different organizations. For instance, a national for-profit chain may define its service area quite broadly, whereas an individual hospital, home health care organization, or HMO may define its service area much more narrowly. Most health services are provided and received within a well-defined service area, where the competition is clearly identified and critical forces for the survival of the organization originate. For example, hospitals in rural areas have well-defined service areas for their particular services. These hospitals must be familiar with the needs of the population and with other organizations providing competing services. Similarly, the service areas for public health departments vary within a state, depending on whether they are metropolitan or rural, and may suggest quite different opportunities and threats.[10]

THE PROCESS OF ENVIRONMENTAL ANALYSIS

There are a variety of approaches to conducting an environmental analysis. For instance, some management authors suggest identifying the major groups that have a stake in the success of the organization. An analysis of the needs of these "stakeholders" will provide the organization with an understanding of its immediate environment. Other authors view the external environment as being made up of several environmental subsystems such as the technological environment, social environment, political environment, and suggest an analysis of these subsystems.

Regardless of the approach, it appears that four fundamental processes are common to all environmental analysis efforts: (1) scanning to identify signals of environmental change, (2) monitoring identified issues, (3) forecasting the future direction of the issues, and (4) assessing the organizational implications of the issues.[11]

Environmental analysis may be carried out by a special staff whose primary duty is to understand the issues in the external environment, or it may be part of the line manager's job. However, these four processes are required in any environmental analysis effort and should be assigned to individuals responsible for the environmental analysis process. Exhibit 3–4 illustrates the four processes and their interrelationships.

Scanning the External Environment

As suggested earlier in this chapter, the external environment is composed of a number of organizations and individuals in the general and health care environments. These organizations and individuals, through their normal operations and activities, are generating information that may be important to the future of other organizations. The environmental *scanning* process acts as a "window" to these organizations. Through this window, managers engaged in environmental scanning carry out three functions:

1. view external environmental information,
2. organize external information into several desired categories, and
3. identify issues within each category.

Strategic issues are trends, developments, dilemmas, and possible events that affect an organization as a whole and its position within its environment. Strategic

EXHIBIT 3-4
The Environmental Analysis Process

SCANNING

- View external environmental information
- Organize information into desired categories
- Identify issues within each category

MONITORING

- Specify the sources of data (organizations, individuals, or publications)
- Add to the environmental data base
- Confirm or disprove issues (trends, developments, dilemmas, and possibility of events)
- Determine the rate of change within issues

FORECASTING

- Extend the trends, developments, dilemmas, or occurrence of an event
- Identify the interrelationships between issues and between environmental categories
- Develop alternative projections

ASSESSING

- Evaluate the significance of the extended (forecasted) issues to the organization
- Identify the forces that must be considered in the formulation of the vision, mission, internal analysis, and strategic plan

issues are often ill-structured and ambiguous and require an interpretation effort (forecasting and assessment).[12]

The scanning function, conceptualized in Exhibit 3–5, serves as the organization's "window" or "lens" on the external world. The scanning function is a process of moving the lens across the array of external organizations in search

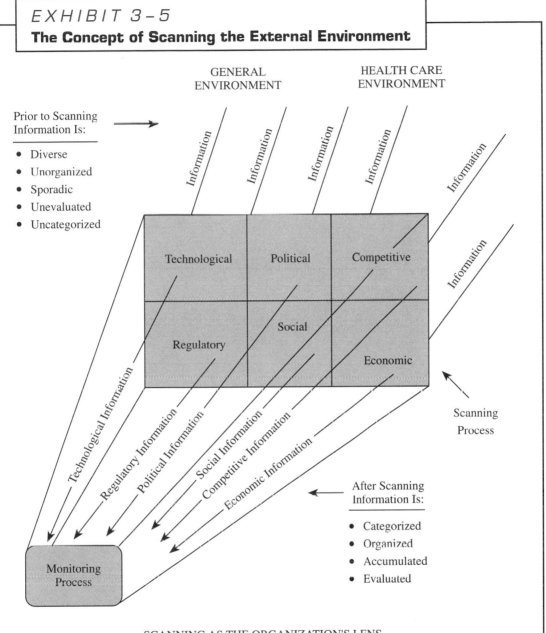

EXHIBIT 3-5
The Concept of Scanning the External Environment

GENERAL ENVIRONMENT   HEALTH CARE ENVIRONMENT

Prior to Scanning Information Is:

- Diverse
- Unorganized
- Sporadic
- Unevaluated
- Uncategorized

Information

Technological   Political   Competitive

Regulatory   Social   Economic

Technological Information

Regulatory Information

Political Information

Social Information

Competitive Information

Economic Information

Scanning Process

After Scanning Information Is:

- Categorized
- Organized
- Accumulated
- Evaluated

Monitoring Process

SCANNING AS THE ORGANIZATION'S LENS

The scanning process allows the organization to focus on technological, political, competitive, regulatory, social and economic issues, trends, dilemmas, and events important to the organization. The "viewing process" must sort diverse, unorganized information. This process also filters out information not relevant to the mission of the organization.

of current and emerging patterns of information. Using the lens, the viewer can focus on diverse and unorganized information generated by external organizations and individuals, and compile and organize it into meaningful categories. Thus, information generated in the external environment is organized in the scanning process. Prior to this interpretation process, information is diverse, unorganized, sporadic, and mixed and has not been assessed. The scanning process categorizes, organizes, accumulates, and, to some extent, evaluates this information. This organized information is then used in the monitoring function.

Information Categories To monitor and further analyze the information, it must be lumped together in some logical categories. Categories not only aid in tracking but also facilitate the later assessment of the impact of the information on the organization. As suggested earlier, the categories most used to classify information are:

- technological,
- social,
- political,
- regulatory,
- economic, and
- competitive.

These streams of information are assessed and their impact incorporated into the strategy of the organization.

Information Sources There are a variety of sources for environmental information. Although organizations create change, they themselves are often difficult to monitor directly. However, a variety of secondary sources (published information) are readily available to most investigators to monitor other organizations. Essentially, people and publications both outside and inside the organization serve as the lens to the external world. These sources are outlined in Exhibit 3–6.

For most organizations, personal sources are far more important than impersonal sources. Within the organization, there is typically a variety of experts who may be familiar with information created outside the organization and who may be the greatest single source of such information. Outside the health care organization, nonmembers and patients may be considered important personal sources. Impersonal sources are largely accounted for by publications such as newspapers and journals, television, libraries, and public and private data bases. (Appendix D of this text provides a comprehensive list of impersonal sources of health care and business information.)

Scanning Importance Environmental scanning is perhaps the most important part of environmental analysis because it forms the basis for the other processes. In the scanning activity, information flows are specified and sources identified. It is from this beginning that a data base for decision making will be built. In light of the importance of this process the following scanning guidelines have been suggested:

1. The purpose of the scanning process is to plot the issues likely to have an impact on the organization and prepare to cope with those issues should they arise.

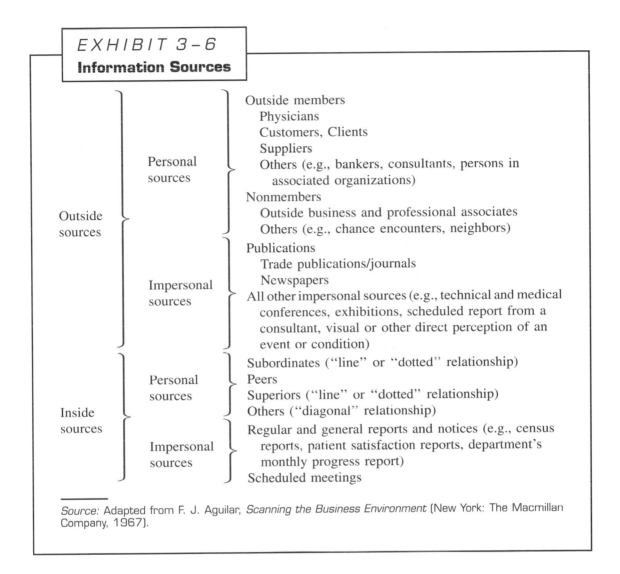

EXHIBIT 3-6
Information Sources

Outside sources

Personal sources

Outside members
  Physicians
  Customers, Clients
  Suppliers
  Others (e.g., bankers, consultants, persons in
    associated organizations)
Nonmembers
  Outside business and professional associates
  Others (e.g., chance encounters, neighbors)

Impersonal sources

Publications
  Trade publications/journals
  Newspapers
All other impersonal sources (e.g., technical and medical
  conferences, exhibitions, scheduled report from a
  consultant, visual or other direct perception of an
  event or condition)

Inside sources

Personal sources

Subordinates ("line" or "dotted" relationship)
Peers
Superiors ("line" or "dotted" relationship)
Others ("diagonal" relationship)

Impersonal sources

Regular and general reports and notices (e.g., census
  reports, patient satisfaction reports, department's
  monthly progress report)
Scheduled meetings

Source: Adapted from F. J. Aguilar, *Scanning the Business Environment* (New York: The Macmillan Company, 1967).

2. Scanning must take into consideration all the possible influences on an organization. Only after all issues have been considered should the refining process and the setting of priorities take place.
3. The results of environmental scanning should be a proactive rather than a reactive stance by the organization toward its environment.
4. It is not sufficient for managers to accept the plan that results from the environmental scan; it is crucial that they understand the thinking that led to the development and selection of strategic and tactical issues from among those identified in the scanning process. It is therefore advantageous if as many managers as possible take part at some level in the scanning process.

5. An important aspect of environmental scanning is that it focuses managers' attention on what lies outside the organization and allows them to create an organization that can adapt to and learn from that environment.[13]

Monitoring the External Environment

The monitoring function is the tracking of trends, issues, and possible events identified in the scanning process. Monitoring accomplishes four important functions:

1. it researches and identifies additional sources of information for specific issues delineated in the scanning process;
2. it adds to the environmental data base;
3. it attempts to confirm or disprove issues (trends, developments, dilemmas, and the possibility of events); and
4. it attempts to determine the rate of change within issues.

The monitoring process investigates the sources of the information obtained in the scanning process and attempts to identify the organization or organizations creating change and the sources reporting change. Once the organizations creating change and the publications or other information sources reporting change have been identified for a given health care organization, special attention should be given to these sources.

The monitoring function has a much narrower focus than scanning; the objective is to accumulate a data base around the identified issue. The data base will be used to confirm or disconfirm the trend, development, dilemma, or possibility of an event and to determine the rate of change taking place within the environment.

The intensity of monitoring is reflected in management's understanding of the issue. When managers believe they understand the issue well, less monitoring will be done. However, when environmental issues appear ill-structured, vague, or complex, issues will require a large amount of data to arrive at an interpretation.[14]

Forecasting Environmental Change

Forecasting environmental change is a process of extending the trends, developments, dilemmas, and events that the organization is monitoring. The forecasting function attempts to answer the question: "If these trends continue, or if issues accelerate beyond their present rate, or if this event occurs, what will the issues and trends 'look like' in the future?"

Three processes are involved in the forecasting function:

1. extending the trends, developments, dilemmas, or occurrences of an event;
2. identifying the interrelationships between the issues and environmental categories; and
3. developing alternative projections.

Assessing Environmental Change

Assessing environmental change is a process that is largely nonquantifiable and therefore judgmental. The complexity of what we find and the grossness of most of the data that we collect are not consistent with traditional decision-making methods.[15] There are few procedures for incorporating "fuzzy" issues into the planning process.[16] In addition, even when exposed to identical issues, managers may interpret their meaning quite differently. Different interpretations are a result of a variety of factors such as beliefs, perceptions, and past actions.[17]

The assessment process contains the following general steps:

1. evaluation of the significance of the extended (forecasted) issue upon the organization; and
2. identification of the issues that must be considered in the formulation of the vision, mission, internal analysis, and strategic plan.

An excellent example of organizations attempting to assess the significance of an issue upon the organization occurred in late 1993 and throughout 1994 as many organizations tried to anticipate health care reform efforts. One of the lessons learned from experience with DRGs was that organizations should not wait for the first set of reform implementation regulations to position themselves but rather they must adapt *before* the change.[18] Perspective 3–4 presents the results of the North Carolina Public Health Department's effort to forecast and assess the effects of health care reform initiatives and to redefine the role of public health in the state.

The assessment or interpretation of a strategic issue is often represented by general labels such as *opportunity* or *threat*. These labels capture management's belief about the potential effects of environmental events and trends. Other dimensions may be used, such as positive/negative, gain/loss, and controllable/noncontrollable.[19]

Unfortunately no comprehensive conceptual scheme or computer model can be developed to provide complete assessment of environmental issues. The assessment process is not an exact science, and sound human judgment and creativity may be bottom-line techniques for a process without much structure. Fahey and Narayanan conclude that the fundamental challenge

> is to make sense out of vague, ambiguous, and unconnected data. Analysts have to infuse meaning into data; they have to make the connections among discordant data such that signals of future events are created. This involves acts of perception and intuition on the analysts' part. It requires the capacity to suspend beliefs, preconceptions, and judgments that may inhibit connections being made among ambiguous and disconnected data.[20]

ENVIRONMENTAL ANALYSIS TOOLS AND TECHNIQUES

External environmental analysis (scanning, monitoring, forecasting, and assessing) is the process for understanding the external environment. This understanding is an essential part of strategy formulation. However, in performing

PERSPECTIVE 3-4

The Role of Public Health Under Health Care Reform

I. *The Unique Functions and Responsibilities of Public Health in North Carolina.* Public health is unique in its emphasis on prevention and its regard for the community as the "patient." The functions of public health in North Carolina that need to be preserved under health care reform include:

- Monitoring community health status,
- Coordinating and convening of planning and evaluation activities,
- Assurance of health care system accountability,
- Public information on community health status,
- Assurance of services to special populations,
- Assessment of environmental risks to health and assurance of protection from these risks, and
- Assurance of preventive services.

II. *The Role of Public Health in the Delivery of High-Quality Clinical Services.* Increased access to health care services will strain the existing health care system. Funds that support the unique functions of public health should not be diverted to provide primary care. A "trade-off" between clinical services and core public health functions can be inefficient, costly, and detrimental to the health status of North Carolina's communities. With regard to the provision of clinical services:

- All people must be served under health care reform, including those who have traditionally been disenfranchised.

- Some personal health services may always need to be provided in local health departments (e.g., communicable disease treatment).
- The extent and nature of public health clinical services should be determined by community consensus of local needs, balanced against the availability of service resources in the community.
- In the transition to full implementation of health care reform, the extent to which any local health department provides direct care will vary widely by community.
- For the immediate future, the public health system may need to provide direct health care for special populations when they lack access to other providers.

III. *The Financing of Population-Based Services.* Population-based services are underrecognized and underfunded despite their critical contribution to the health of North Carolina's citizens. Full funding of population-based services is necessary even if the primary care and clinical services currently provided by health departments are subsumed in the private sector.

- Public Health in North Carolina should be financed as a proportion of the state's aggregate health care expenditures.
- Formal education for public health practitioners needs to be supported by an additional *set aside.*
- Creative training approaches will be necessary to ensure that public health personnel remain adequately trained.

- The *cost containment objectives* of health care reform can be achieved only through a strengthened public health system.
- The *cost effectiveness objectives* of health care reform can be achieved only through healthy lifestyles, behavioral change, and primary prevention.

IV. *Local Health Department Preparation for Health Care Reform.* The changes in North Carolina's health care delivery system will be felt acutely at the local level, where health departments/districts will be responsible for ensuring the continuity of quality health care services to an expanded service population.

- Local public health officials and personnel must understand and embrace the inherently political nature of health care reform.
- There will be a continued need to emphasize the role of prevention as basic to health.
- There is a continued and expanding need to project a positive public health image.
- Local public health officials should make every effort to become well informed about all aspects of health care reform.

- Local public health officials need to assess the current capacity of their communities to deliver needed services.
- Local public health officials need to participate actively in the identification of human resources within their local communities that can be brought to bear on existing and anticipated health care needs.
- State and local public health officials need to actively assess training and professional development needs as health care reform is implemented.
- Local public health departments should take a leadership role in working with their local communities to facilitate consensus on issues related to health care.
- Local public health officials should increase their focus on *health outcomes* as service and program assessment indicators.
- Local public health officials should focus on developing and maintaining organizational flexibility for an uncertain and exciting future.

Source: Conference on "The Role of Public Health Under Health Care Reform," University of North Carolina, School of Public Health, Chapel Hill, July 1993, pp. 1–2.

the scanning, monitoring, forecasting, and assessing processes, several different analysis tools and techniques may be utilized. These techniques, which are informal and generally not overly sophisticated, have been variously described as "judgmental," "speculative," or "conjectural."[21] Indeed, environmental analysis is largely an individual effort and is directed to person-specific interests. Environmental analysis techniques usually are not limited to just one of the environmental analysis processes, but rather encompass scanning, monitoring, forecasting, and assessing.

To address the problem of determining the importance of environmental issues, the literature recommends simple trend extension, solicitation of expert opinion, stakeholder analysis, critical success factor analysis, scenario writing, competitive analysis, and diffusion studies. An investigation of U.S. industrial and nonindustrial firms and foreign industrial firms found that trend extrapolation was the most widely practiced analysis method, perhaps because of its relative simplicity.[22]

Simple Trend Identification and Extrapolation

Trend identification and extrapolation is a matter of plotting environmental data and then, from the existing data, anticipating the next occurrence. Obviously, such a method works best with financial or statistical data. However, environmental issues are rarely presented as a neat set of quantifiable data. Rather, environmental issues are ill-structured and conjectural. Thus, in many cases, trend identification and extrapolation in environmental analysis is a matter of reaching consensus on the existence of an issue and speculating on its likelihood of continuance.

An example of trend identification and extrapolation concerns the Children's Memorial Hospital (CMH) in Chicago, which was opening a satellite clinic and surgical center in a Chicago suburb. Decision makers at Children's noted that many pediatric hospitals such as La Bonheur Hospital in Memphis, Children's Hospital and Medical Center in Seattle, and Cincinnati Children's Hospital succeeded in establishing similar clinics. In addition, the decision to build the clinic was influenced by careful analysis of CMH's patient population, a substantial portion of which came from the suburban regions where the clinic was to be located. Projected population growth in the service area indicated sufficient demand for the satellite clinic.[23]

In the case of Lake Villa Nursing Home, demographic trends as well as others are of interest. As illustrated in Exhibit 3–7, the trend identification and extrapolation process includes the identification of issues by environmental category, the designation of an issue as an opportunity or threat, and the determination of its probable impact on the organization. Additionally, managers may assess the likelihood that the trend, development, or dilemma will continue or that the event will occur and identify the sources for additional information.

These issues may then be plotted on the chart shown in Exhibit 3–8. The assumption is that the issues to the right of the curved line in the exhibit have a significant impact (high impact) on the organization and are likely to continue or occur (high probability) and should be addressed in the strategic plan.

The formats illustrated in Exhibits 3–7 and 3–8 are useful for organizing environmental data and providing a starting point for speculating on the direction and rate of change for identified trends. However, as with Children's Memorial Hospital, trend extrapolation of environmental issues requires extensive familiarity with the external environment (the issues) and a great deal of sound judgment.

EXHIBIT 3-7

Trend/Issue Identification and Evaluation Lake Villa Nursing Home

Trend/Issue	Opportunity/ Threat	Evidence	Impact on Our Organization (1–10)	Probability of Trend Continuing (1–10)
Aging Population	Opportunity	1 in 5 Americans will	9	9
		be at least 65 by 2030		
Wealthier Elderly	Opportunity	Income of those 60+	7	6
		has increased 10%		
		faster than any other		
		group		
Local Competition	Threat	Over past 5 years,	7	9
		number of nursing		
		homes in the service area		
		has increased from 5		
		to 7		

10 = High probability of occurring
 1 = Low probability of occurring

Solicitation of Expert Opinion

Expert opinion is often used to identify, monitor, forecast, and assess environmental trends. Experts play a key role in shaping and extending the thinking of managers. For example, Perspective 3–5 presents expert opinions of the new managerial skills that will be required in health care organizations throughout the remainder of the decade. Health care managers can use these opinions to stimulate their strategic thinking and begin developing human resources strategies.

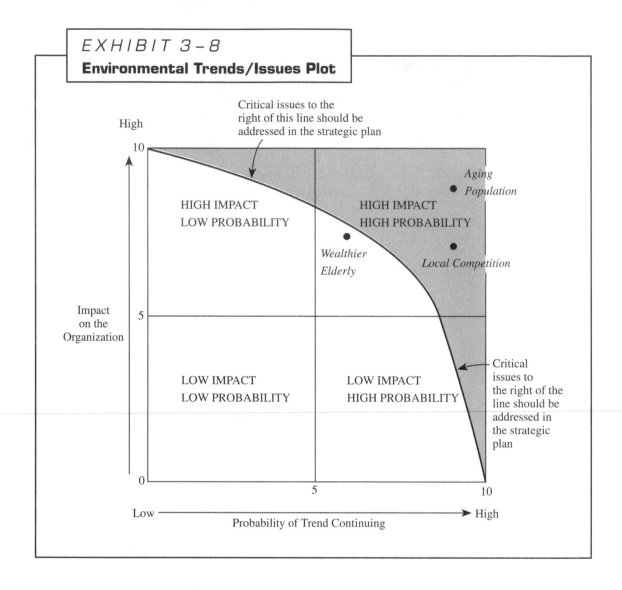

EXHIBIT 3–8
Environmental Trends/Issues Plot

Critical issues to the right of this line should be addressed in the strategic plan

High

Impact on the Organization

HIGH IMPACT
LOW PROBABILITY

HIGH IMPACT
HIGH PROBABILITY

Aging Population

Wealthier Elderly

Local Competition

LOW IMPACT
LOW PROBABILITY

LOW IMPACT
HIGH PROBABILITY

Critical issues to the right of the line should be addressed in the strategic plan

Low — Probability of Trend Continuing — High

To further focus managers' thinking and generate additional perspectives concerning the issues in the external environment, there are a number of more formal expert-based environmental analysis techniques. These techniques help solicit and synthesize the opinions and best judgments of experts within various fields. These techniques include the delphi technique, the nominal group technique, brainstorming, focus groups, and dialectic inquiry.

Delphi Technique   The delphi technique is a popular, practical, and useful analysis technique for considering environmental data. The delphi method may be used to identify and study current and emerging trends within each environmental

PERSPECTIVE 3-5
Experts Agree on Need for New Management Skills for the Future

According to Gary L. Filerman, associate director of the Pew Health Professions Commission, the convergence of the forces of reform, technology, and changing organizations is about to uncap the most turbulent managerial environment in health care we have ever faced. A major part of that turbulence is going to be the upheaval and restructuring of the work force. A changing health care environment will call for different skills for managing organizations and systems in that environment. Managers of the future will have the responsibility to see that quality services are delivered at a reasonable cost, and the competence of the managers will be judged on the health status of the community or population served.

Stephen J. Kratz, principal at the health care consulting firm Tyler & Co., observed that managers of the future will have to have new skills and be strong negotiators and entrepreneurs with the ability to gain the respect of the business and medical communities, as well as an under-

standing of integrated and managed care-issues. Consultant Robin Orr added that health care managers will no longer direct workers but empower them, as hierarchies flatten and traditional boss/subordinate relationships gradually fall by the wayside. Joseph C. Rost, professor of leadership and administration at the University of San Diego, indicated that health care managers will have to work with a variety of stakeholders to find ways to meet the needs of patients, reduce expenses, and take care of community health needs. Ellen Morrison, associate director for the Institute for the Future, concludes that leadership and managerial performance will be based on outcomes (not patient volume) and satisfaction. To be effective, health care managers will have to break old patterns and traditions.

Source: Jill L. Sherer, "Future Leaders Show Workers the Way," *Hospitals & Health Networks* 67, no. 19 (1993), p. 35.

category (technological, social, economic, and so on). More specifically, the delphi technique is the development, evaluation, and synthesis of individual points of view through the systematic solicitation and collation of individual judgments on a particular topic. In the first round, individuals are asked their opinions on the selected topic. Opinions are summarized and then sent back to the participating individuals for the development of new judgments concerning the topic. After several rounds of solicitation and summary, a synthesis of opinion is formulated.[24]

S. C. Jain found that the traditional delphi method has undergone a great deal of change in the context of environmental analysis. Jain suggests that the salient features of the revised delphi method are to:

1. identify recognized experts in the field of interest;
2. seek their cooperation and send them a summary paper (based on a literature search); and
3. conduct personal interviews with each expert based on a structured questionnaire.[25]

In contrast to traditional delphi methods, there is no further feedback or repeated rounds of questioning. The major advantage is being able to recruit recognized experts because less of their time must be committed.

The delphi technique is particularly helpful when health care managers want to understand the opportunities and threats of a specific environmental issue. For instance, there are indications that, because of the aging population, home health care is becoming more popular. However, the home-care industry has seen profits decline due to Medicare reimbursement changes and cuts in home medical equipment funding. In addition, HCFA regulations requiring a physician to demonstrate the medical necessity for home health care has, along with increased competition, dampened enthusiasm. A delphi panel can help health care managers better understand the opportunities and threats in the home health care market.[26]

Nominal Group Technique, Brainstorming, and Focus Groups   The nominal group technique, brainstorming, and focus groups are interactive group problem identification and solving techniques. In the nominal group technique (NGT), a group is convened to address an issue, such as the impact of consolidation within the health care industry or the impact of an aging population on hospital facilities. Each individual independently generates a written list of ideas surrounding the issue. Following the idea-generation period, group members take turns reporting one idea at a time to the group. Typically, each new idea is recorded on a large flip chart for everyone to consider. Members are encouraged to build on the ideas of others in the group. After all the ideas have been listed, the group discusses the ideas. After the discussion, members privately vote or rank the ideas. After voting, discussion continues and the group generation of ideas continues. Typically, additional votes are held until a reasonable consensus is reached.[27]

In brainstorming, a group is convened for the purpose of understanding an issue or assessing the impact of an issue on the organization or generating organizational strategic alternatives. In this process, members present ideas and are allowed to clarify them with brief explanations. Each idea is recorded but, generally, evaluation is not allowed. The intent of brainstorming is to generate fresh ideas or new ways of thinking. Members are encouraged to present any ideas that occur to them, even apparently risky or impossible ideas. Such a process often stimulates creativity and sparks new approaches that are not as risky, crazy, or impossible as first thought.[28] As illustrated in Perspective 3–6 computer technology can enhance and facilitate brainstorming sessions.

NGT and brainstorming could be used to understand and respond to the trend of women's increasing preference for midwives rather than OB/GYN physicians. Women are increasingly fed up with high-tech, highly impersonal prenatal care and delivery. This trend is due, in part, to the high risks and high insurance costs for obstetricians. For example, one in eight OB/GYN doctors has stopped

PERSPECTIVE 3-6
GDSS Facilitates Brainstorming

Group decision support systems (GDSS) are configurations (local area networks) of computer hardware and software that enhance the decision-making process by merging computer and communication technologies. Accordingly, GDSS are interactive, electronic meeting support systems with the goal of enriching meetings, thereby improving the quality and quantity of alternatives and decisions. One powerful use of GDSS is for electronic brainstorming. A typical brainstorming session occurs in a conference room where members have their own private microcomputers. Arranged in this central "room of the future," group members generate messages that display on a central "public" projection screen. A skilled facilitator provides guidance throughout each session. Increased creativity occurs by providing group members the ability to generate and share comments simultaneously while remaining anonymous. Possible gains include increased information, synergy, ob-

jectivity, stimulation, and learning. Anonymity can prove useful when there are differences in power and status within the group and helps prevent domination and intimidation. Further, simultaneous or parallel communication helps prevent rationing or blocking of speaking time.

Most GDSS field research suggests that larger groups obtain greater benefits. Second, improved meeting outcomes result in improved performance, efficiency, and satisfaction. Third, GDSS are most appropriate for complex tasks. Finally, repeated use increases performance and reactions. Other GDSS tools include a meeting manager, idea organizer, vote compiler, alternatives evaluator, and a policy formulation application.

Source: Written by John Frank Patton, Ph.D. Candidate, Health Services Administration, University of Alabama at Birmingham. Adapted from L. M. Jessup and J. S. Valacich, *Group Support Systems* [New York: Macmillan Publishing Company, 1993].

delivering babies, one in four will not handle a high-risk pregnancy, and more than one-third do not accept Medicaid patients. In addition, nearly 26 percent of all counties nationwide lack prenatal care clinics. European countries, where infant mortality rates are significantly lower than those in the United States, use midwives for approximately 70 percent of all births. NGT and brainstorming provide a forum to explore the strength of the midwife trend and clarify the forces underlying the trend.[29]

Similar to brainstorming, focus groups bring together ten to fifteen "experts" to develop, evaluate, and reach conclusions regarding environmental issues. Focus groups provide an opportunity for management to discuss particularly important organizational issues with qualified individuals. For example, a hospital considering the establishment of a satellite clinic might develop a focus group of physicians. On the other hand, if a hospital wanted to understand the patient's viewpoint on the use of a midwife, different perspectives could be explored by convening a focus group of women who used a midwife and another group composed of women who would not use a midwife. The individuals involved can provide new insights for understanding the issues and suggest fresh alternatives for their resolution. Hospitals and large group practices have used focus groups of patients to better understand the perceived strengths and weaknesses of the organization from the patient's view.

Dialectic Inquiry Dialectic inquiry is a "point and counterpoint" process of argumentation. The nineteenth century German philosopher Hegel suggested that the surest path to truth was the use of dialectic, an intellectual exchange in which a thesis is pitted against an antithesis. According to this principle, truth emerges from the search for synthesis of apparently contradictory views.[30]

More specifically, in environmental analysis dialectic inquiry is the development, evaluation, and synthesis of conflicting points of view (environmental issues) through separate formulation and refinement of each point of view.[31] For instance, one group may argue that health care costs will be declining by the year 2000 (thesis) because of the prospective payment system, pressure by businesses and labor, health care reform, physician reimbursement reform, and so on. Another group may present a case that the trend toward rising health care costs will continue (antithesis) because of hospital failures, the high cost of new technology, failure of health care reform initiatives, and so on. Debating this issue will unearth the major factors influencing health care costs and implications for the future.

Any health care provider can utilize this technique by assigning groups to debate specific external issues. The groups make presentations and debate conflicting points of view concerning the environment. After the debate, the groups attempt to form a synthesis position concerning the likely future.[32]

Stakeholder Analysis

Stakeholder analysis is based on the belief that there is a reciprocal relationship between an organization and certain other organizations, groups, and individuals. They are referred to as *stakeholders,* that is, organizations, groups, and individuals that have an interest or "stake" in the success of the organization. Examples of possible health care stakeholders, shown as a "stakeholder map," are presented in Exhibit 3–9.

Stakeholders may be categorized as internal, interface, and external. Internal stakeholders are those who operate primarily within the bounds of the organization, such as managers and other employees. Interface stakeholders are those who function both internally and externally, such as the medical staff and the corporate officers of the parent company. External stakeholders operate outside the organization and include such entities as suppliers, third-party payers, competitors, regulatory agencies, the media, the local community, and so on.[33]

Some of these stakeholders are almost always powerful or influential, others are influential regarding only certain issues, still others have little influence and power. If the stakeholders can be identified and evaluated, then the "forces" affecting the organization may be specified. The needs and wants of these constituencies may dramatically affect the strategy of an organization.[34]

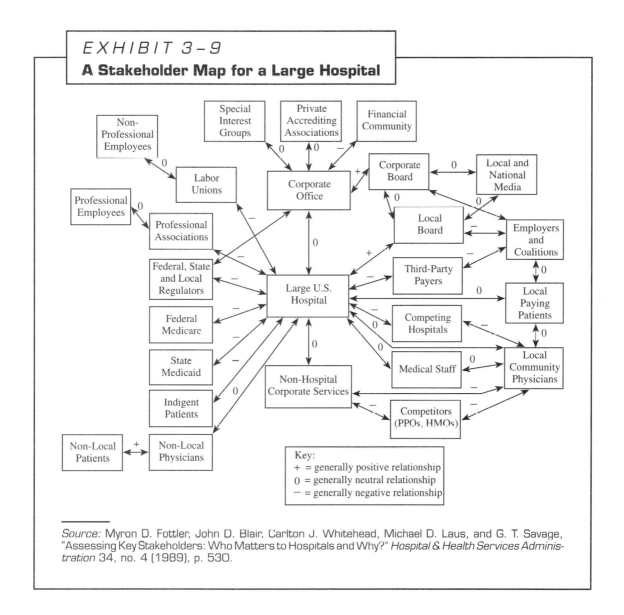

EXHIBIT 3-9

A Stakeholder Map for a Large Hospital

Key:
+ = generally positive relationship
0 = generally neutral relationship
— = generally negative relationship

Source: Myron D. Fottler, John D. Blair, Carlton J. Whitehead, Michael D. Laus, and G. T. Savage, "Assessing Key Stakeholders: Who Matters to Hospitals and Why?" *Hospital & Health Services Administration* 34, no. 4 (1989), p. 530.

Critical Success Factor Analysis

Critical success factor analysis involves the identification and analysis of a limited number of areas within an industry in which the organization must achieve at a high level if it is to be successful. The rationale in critical success factor analysis is that there are five or six areas in which the organization must perform well and, through careful analysis of the environment, it is possible to identify them. In addition, critical success factor analysis may be used to examine new market opportunities.

Typically, once the critical success factors have been identified, several objectives for the organization are developed for each success factor. At that point a strategy may be developed around the objectives. Important in critical success factor analysis is the establishment of linkages among the environment, the critical success factors, the objectives, and the strategy. These linkages are illustrated in Exhibit 3–10.

Scenario Writing and Future Studies

Scenario writing and future studies have been used extensively in environmental analysis. One study showed that over 50 percent of the Fortune 1,000 companies were using scenario analysis.[35] The popularity of scenario analysis is due in large part to the inability of other, more quantitative forecasting methods to predict and incorporate major shifts in the environment and provide a context for strategic

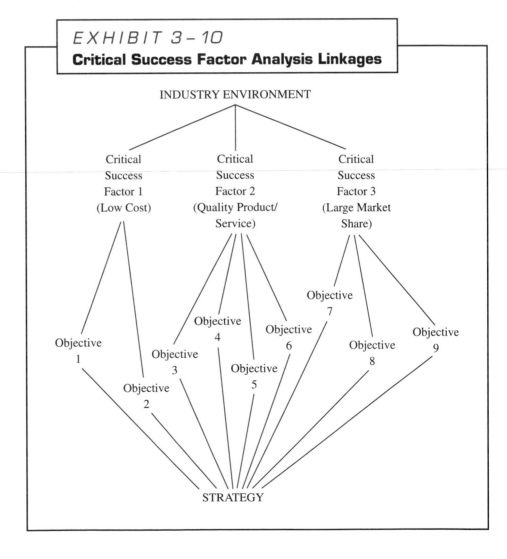

EXHIBIT 3–10
Critical Success Factor Analysis Linkages

thinking. Scenario analysis is an alternative to conventional forecasting that is better suited to an environment with numerous uncertainties or imponderables.

A scenario is a coherent story about the future using the world of today as a starting point.[36] Based on data accumulated in the scanning and monitoring processes, a scenario or narrative that describes an assumed future is developed. The objective of scenarios and future studies is to describe a point of time in the future as a sequence of time frames or periods of time.[37] Scenario writing often requires generous assumptions, and there are few guidelines as to what to include in the scenario.

Alternative Approaches to Scenario Development Two approaches to scenario development are most typical – scenarios involving a single dominant issue and multiple-issue scenarios that incorporate a wide array of key variables into different themes. An example of a dominant issue scenario might involve the impact of AIDS (a single issue) on the strategy of a state health department. Developing a scenario depicting the personal, social, community, economic, and political implications of forecasted increases in AIDS cases will help health department managers decide how (or whether) to redirect the department's strategy to deal with the problem. In contrast, multiple-issue scenarios include the implications of many significant issues. For example, international, national, and state economic, social, regulatory, political, and competitive trends and issues may be combined to depict a reasonable picture (or pictures) of the future as a "backdrop" for a large hospital chain as it considers international and domestic expansion. Alternative possible futures might be named *World Recession, Technological Revolution,* and *Service Proliferation* to provide a strategic context for developing strategy. Either of these approaches to scenario development can vary widely in scope and consequent practicality.[38]

Multiple Scenarios As with the previous international expansion example, in most cases several plausible scenarios should be written. It is an all-too-common mistake to envision only one scenario as the "true picture of the future."[39] Multiple scenarios allow the future to be represented by different cause/effect relationships, different key events and their consequences, different variables, and different assumptions. Most authorities advocate the development of either two or three scenarios. However, to avoid decision makers focusing only on the "most likely" or "most probable" scenario, each scenario should be given a distinctive theme name, such that they appear equally likely.

Multiple scenarios help managers better consider cause and effect relationships. That is, if this environmental event happens (or does not happen), what will be the effect on the organization? The use of multiple scenarios was particularly helpful as organizations considered the probable impact of health care reform legislation on their organizations. Exhibit 3–11 presents a brief summary of five scenarios or alternative futures for health care in the twenty-first century developed by Clement Bezold, executive director of the Institute for Alternative Futures. The scenarios were developed to examine the differences between leadership practices today and the organizational demands that health care leaders will face in the next century. Bezold indicates, "The scenarios were designed to provoke the imagination, raise fundamental questions, and stretch world views."[40]

EXHIBIT 3-11
Five Possible Futures of Health Care

Scenario 1: Continued Growth/High Tech

National health care reform never did occur, but expensive advancing technology and therapeutics, including function enhancing bionics, help health care's share of GNP grow to 17 percent by 2001. Health care providers shift to predicting and then managing illness far earlier and more successfully. For many, poverty and lack of access to health care persist.

Scenario 2: Hard Times/Government Leadership

Recurrent hard times and a political revolt against health care lead to a frugal Canadianlike national health insurance system. Most states follow Oregon in consciously setting priorities. Heroic measures for terminally ill patients decline and a more frugal approach to innovation is adopted. Health care's percentage of GNP is reduced to 11 percent by 2001. Thirty percent of Americans "buy up" to affluent, higher-tech care, and two different systems of health care emerge.

Scenario 3: Buyers' Market

Many thought the 1980s was the decade of health care's entry into the marketplace – that competition would lead to better, less expensive service. What failed during the 1980s worked very well over the next two decades. Markets, including health care, do a much better job of giving consumers a range of high-quality services, delivered in convenient ways, at relatively low cost over the long term, while maintaining a high degree of innovation. These amazing changes are coupled with better social policies to blunt the inequities and lack of access that accompany the stronger market approach.

Scenario 4: A New Civilization

Dramatic changes in the paradigms of science, technology, society, and government hasten health care change. Health care broadens its focus from the individual to the community and the environment. National health care reform favors managed care – particularly social HMOs, which are effective at predicting and often preventing various personal and community health problems. High-tech and alternative therapies are common. Health care consumes 12 percent of GNP by 2001.

Scenario 5: Healing and Health Care

This scenario shares the fundamental characteristics of the "New Civilization" scenario – the same dramatic changes in paradigms of science, technology, society, and government – but with a different emphasis.

EXHIBIT 3-11 cont'd

> In this scenario the role of the spirit and its integration into health care lead to a greater focus on "healing." Health care providers, particularly those running hospitals, take an early and active role in moving health care toward real personal, community, and environmental health, rather than allowing it to continue to simply cure individuals. Poverty, other social problems, and environmental causes of ill health are dealt with more systematically. Health care structures have changed dramatically, merging with a variety of other community organizations. Healing the planet, particularly the environment for our children, is a dominant issue.
>
> ---
>
> *Source:* Clement Bezold, "Five Futures," *Healthcare Forum Journal* 35, no. 3 (1992), pp. 29–42.

Porter's Industry Structure Analysis

Harvard's Michael E. Porter developed a framework for analyzing the external environment through an examination of the competitive nature of the industry. Porter suggested that the level of competitive intensity within the industry is the most critical factor in an organization's environment. In Porter's model, intensity is a function of the threat of new entrants to the market, the level of rivalry among existing organizations, the threat of substitute products and services, the bargaining power of buyers (customers), and the bargaining power of suppliers.[41] The strength and impact of these five forces, illustrated in Exhibit 3–12, must be carefully monitored and assessed.

Threat of New Entrants New entrants into a market are typically a threat to existing organizations because they increase the intensity of competition. New entrants may have substantial resources and often attempt to rapidly gain market share. Such actions may force prices and profits down. The threat of entry of a new competitor into a market depends on the industry barriers. If the barriers are substantial, the threat of entry is low. Porter identified several barriers to entry that may protect organizations already serving a market:

1. existing organization's economies of scale;
2. existing product differentiation;
3. capital requirements needed to compete;
4. switching costs – the one-time costs for buyers to switch from one supplier to another;
5. access to distribution channels;
6. cost advantages (independent of scale) of established competitors; and
7. government and legal constraints.

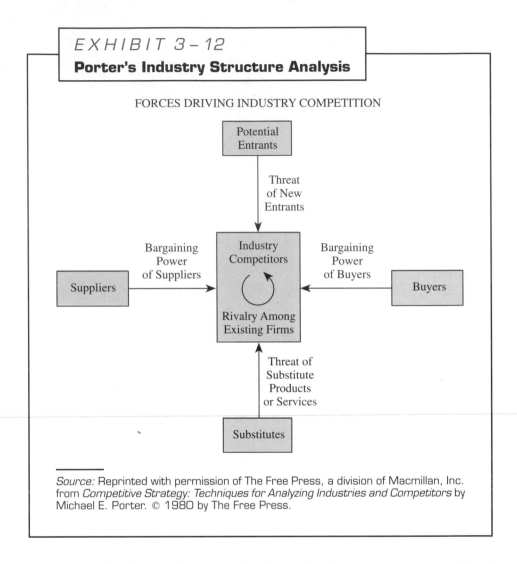

EXHIBIT 3–12
Porter's Industry Structure Analysis

FORCES DRIVING INDUSTRY COMPETITION

Source: Reprinted with permission of The Free Press, a division of Macmillan, Inc. from *Competitive Strategy: Techniques for Analyzing Industries and Competitors* by Michael E. Porter. © 1980 by The Free Press.

These seven barriers may be assessed to determine the current or expected level of competition within an industry.

Intensity of Rivalry Among Existing Organizations Organizations within an industry are mutually dependent because the strategy of one organization affects the others. Rivalry occurs because competitors attempt to improve their position. Typically, actions by one competitor foster reactions by others. Intense rivalry is the result of:

1. numerous or equally balanced competitors;
2. slow industry growth;
3. high fixed or storage costs;
4. a lack of differentiation or switching costs;
5. capacity augmented in large increments;

6. diverse competitors – diverse objectives, personalities, strategies, and so on;
7. high strategic stakes – competitors place great importance on achieving success within the industry; and
8. high exit barriers.

Threat of Substitute Products and Services For many products and services there are a variety of substitutes. These products and services perform the same function as established products. Substitute products limit returns to an industry because at some point consumers will switch to alternative products and services. Usually, the more diverse the industry the more likely there will be substitute products and services.

Bargaining Power of Customers Buyers of products and services attempt to obtain the lowest price possible while demanding high quality and better service. If buyers are powerful, then the competitive rivalry will be high. A buyer group is powerful if it:

1. purchases large volumes;
2. concentrates purchases in an industry;
3. purchases products that are standard or undifferentiated;
4. has low switching costs;
5. earns low profits (low profits force lower purchasing costs);
6. poses a threat of backward integration;
7. has low quality requirements (the quality of the products purchased by the buyer is unimportant to the final product's quality); and
8. has enough information to gain bargaining leverage.

Bargaining Power of Suppliers Much like the power of buyers, suppliers can affect the intensity of competition through their ability to control prices and the quality of materials they supply. Through these mechanisms, suppliers can exert considerable pressure on an industry. Factors that make suppliers powerful tend to mirror those making buyers powerful. Suppliers tend to be powerful if:

1. there are few suppliers;
2. there are few substitutes;
3. the suppliers' products are differentiated;
4. the product or service supplied is important to the buyer's business;
5. the buyer's industry is not considered an important customer; and
6. the suppliers pose a threat of forward integration (entering the industry).

Porter's approach is a powerful tool for assessing the level of competitive intensity within the health care industry. Porter's framework for analyzing the external environment is applied to a nursing home in Exhibit 3–13.

The Diffusion Process

Based on the Battelle Concept (Battelle-Institute, Frankfurt), the diffusion process is a method of studying the "diffusion" of ideas through the external environment.

EXHIBIT 3-13
Using Porter's Industry Structure Analysis

The Hanover House Nursing Home, a skilled nursing facility, used differentiation as its major competitive advantage. In its early years, in a less regulated environment, the home was very profitable. As the facility began to age, and with increasingly stricter regulations for long-term care, profit margins began to deteriorate. The administrators of Hanover House used Porter's Industry Structure Analysis to better understand the forces in their external environment. The following is a summary of their analysis.

Threat of New Entrants

The supply of nursing homes and other long-term-care facilities is currently limited because there is a moratorium on additional beds within the geographic area. Competition is based on price or quality. If the moratorium is lifted, it will remain costly to enter the market because it is highly regulated. The greatest threat as a new entrant (when the moratorium is lifted) will be hospitals attempting to compensate for decreasing occupancy rates. Switching costs are low for hospitals (the same bed can be used for acute care or long-term care). Access to the distribution channel is high as hospitals have many of the required resources, including access to nurses, familiarity with the regulations, and capability to enter quickly (by converting acute-care beds to long-term care).

Intensity of Rivalry Among Existing Organizations

Although there is competition, the long-term-care industry is not fiercely competitive. Hanover House has six competitors – Mary Lewis Convalescence Center, Hillhaven, Altamont Retirement Community, St. Martins in the Pines, Lake Villa, and Kirkwood – that have relatively stable market shares. Because the service has both quality and dollar value, there is the opportunity to differentiate and switching costs are high for the consumer. It is a highly regulated area and, therefore, not a great deal of diversity among competitors is apparent. The long-term-care industry is maturing but remains a rapid growth industry driven by demographic and social trends (the graying of America and the deterioration of the extended family). The most significant factor creating rivalry is the high fixed assets, which make exit difficult and success important.

Threat of Substitute Products and Services

There are few substitute products for nursing home care. Home care is a substitute but an increasingly less available alternative because of the mobility and dissolution of the family unit. Other alternatives include nonskilled homes, retirement housing, and domiciliaries. Increased costs and DRGs have virtually eliminated hospitals as an alternative. On

EXHIBIT 3 – 13 *cont'd*

balance, substitutes do not appear to be a strong force in the nursing home industry.

Bargaining Power of Customers

The power of the customer in the industry is generally high. The major consumer, the government, purchases over 45 percent of nursing home care and regulates reimbursement procedures as well as the industry. Therefore, significant levels of information are available. In addition, for private-pay customers, the purchase represents a significant investment and comparison shopping is prevalent. Product differentiation tends to reduce buying power but relatively low switching costs and government involvement make nursing home care a buyers' market.

Bargaining Power of Suppliers

Because the product is simultaneously produced and consumed in service industries, labor is the major supplier in the nursing home industry. Although Hanover House is unionized, it has maintained good labor relations, and the union is not particularly powerful. Most who work in long-term care have selected the field to satisfy their need to care for others or make a contribution rather than to earn large salaries. Suppliers are not a dominant force in the nursing home industry.

Source: Elaine Asper, "Hanover House Nursing Home," an unpublished case study.

Thus, by studying emerging ideas and values, an environmental early-warning system may be created.[42]

Similar to the product-adoption process discussed in marketing, the Battelle approach traces the adoption of emerging values throughout society. The progression of the "infection" may be measured by the types of people embracing the change:

1. initiator of a change;
2. first group of innovators;
3. early adopters;
4. late adopters;
5. reluctant adopters; and
6. nonadopters.

By systematically observing and plotting values and new ideas through this process, key issues can be identified and monitored, and the major environmental tendencies can be recognized much earlier. For instance, health care organizations assessing the acceptance of surgery centers or freestanding clinics within the service area may use the diffusion process to systematically observe and plot usage of the clinic. Analysis of the diffusion (groups accepting and using the centers and clinics) provides a way to monitor, forecast, and assess the changing pattern of values regarding this type of health care delivery. For example, the diffusion process would be useful in monitoring the growth of group practices without walls described in Chapter 2 (Perspective 2–3).

Selecting the Technique

The intent of environmental analysis is to identify and understand the issues in the external environment. Exhibit 3–14 summarizes the primary focus and advantages and disadvantages of each technique.

EXHIBIT 3–14
Primary Focus, Advantages, and Disadvantages of Environmental Analysis Techniques

Technique	Primary Focus*	Advantage	Disadvantage
Simple Trend Identification and Extension	SMFA	• Simple • Logical • Easy to communicate	• Need a good deal of data in order to extend trend • Limited to existing trends • Does not foster creative thinking
Delphi Technique	SMFA	• Use of field experts • Avoids intimidation problems • Eliminates management's biases	• Members are physically dispersed • No direct interaction of participants • May take a long time to complete
Nominal Group Technique	SMFA	• Everyone has equal status and power	• Structure may limit creativity
Brainstorming	FA	• Fosters creativity • Develops many ideas, alternatives • Encourages communication	• No process for making decisions • Sometimes gets off track
Focus Groups	FA	• Uses experts • Management/expert interaction	• Finding experts • No specific structure for reaching conclusion
Dialectic Inquiry	FA	• Surfaces many subissues and factors	

EXHIBIT 3 – 14   cont'd

Technique	Primary Focus*	Advantage	Disadvantage
		• Conclusions are reached on issues	• Does not provide a set of procedures for deciding what is important • Considers only a single issue at a time • Time consuming
Stakeholder Analysis	SM	• Considers major interdependent groups and individuals • Assures major needs and wants of outside organizations are taken into account	• Emerging issues generated by other organizations may not be considered • Does not consider the broader issues of the general environment
Critical Success Factor Analysis	SFA	• Identifies the factors for success • Directly links external factors with objectives and strategies	• Does not consider emerging trends or issues • Does not consider events in the broader general environment
Scenario Writing	FA	• Portrays alternative futures • Considers interrelated external variables • Gives a complete picture of the future	• Requires generous assumptions • Always a question as to what to include
Porter's Industry Structure Analysis	SMFA	• Provides a structured analysis • Provides extensive checklist of issues	• Does not consider the broader general environment • May be too structured to foster creative thinking
Diffusion Process	SM	• Considers a broad range of issues • Emphasizes data collection • Systematic observation and plotting	• Not industry specific • Little assessment

*S = Scanning
M = Monitoring
F = Forecasting
A = Assessing

The technique selected for environmental analysis will depend on such factors as the size of the organization, the diversity of the products and services, and the complexity and size of the markets (service areas). Organizations that are relatively small, do not have a great deal of diversity, and have well-defined service areas may opt for simple techniques that may be carried out "in-house," such as trend identification and extension, in-house nominal group technique or brainstorming, stakeholder analysis, critical success factor analysis, or Porter's structural analysis. Such organizations may include independent hospitals, HMOs, rural and community hospitals, large group practices, long-term-care facilities, hospices, and county public health departments.

Health care organizations that are large, have diverse products and services, and have ill-defined or extensive service areas may want to use techniques that draw upon the knowledge of a wide range of experts. As a result, these organizations are more likely to set up delphi panels and outside nominal and brainstorming groups. In addition, these organizations may have the resources to conduct dialectics concerning environmental issues, engage in scenario writing, and study the diffusion process. Such techniques are usually more time consuming, fairly expensive, and require extensive coordination. Organizations using these techniques may include national and regional for-profit health care chains, regional health systems, large federations and alliances, and state public health departments.

Ultimately, the technique selected for environmental analysis may depend primarily on the style and preferences of management. If used properly, any of the techniques can provide a powerful tool for identifying, monitoring, forecasting, and assessing environmental issues.

RESPONSIBILITY FOR ENVIRONMENTAL ANALYSIS

In studying the organization of the environmental analysis function, Lenz and Engledow found considerable variety among organizations in the placement of environmental analysis. According to them, "A variety of positions within organizational hierarchies serve as the primary locus of environmental intelligence gathering and interpretation."[43] However, they did identify three administrative models toward which organizations have gravitated. These models were labeled according to the roles they play in the organization. They are the *public policy role* (a group or committee to identify changing public policy issues), the *planning-integrated role* (performing environmental analysis as a part of the planning process), and the *function-oriented role* (performing function-specific analysis).

For the firms exhibiting a public policy role, primary emphasis was placed on the early detection of emerging issues that were suspected to be harbingers of broad-scale shifts in societal attitudes, laws, social norms and roles, and so on.[44] Most units organized in this way had direct access to the top-level power structure of the organization, yet linkages with the strategic planning process were tenuous and in some cases virtually nonexistent. Organizations using the planning-integrated role focused on both general and industry environments. Environmental analysis units using the planning-integrated role contributed significantly to the strategic planning process. Organizations with a function-oriented role concentrated environmental analysis activities on the function and were housed in functional departments.[45] The broad advantages and disadvantages of each of these administrative structures are summarized in Exhibit 3–15. The best approach to organizing the environmental analysis function appears to be to first decide on the specific objectives of the environmental function and then adopt the analysis model most appropriate for the objectives.

ISSUES IN THE HEALTH CARE ENVIRONMENT

The health care industry is faced with many dynamic issues and will have to face a host of new developments in the rapidly changing external environment. Management of health care organizations should assess these issues and others

---

EXHIBIT 3–15

Advantages and Disadvantages Associated with Alternative Environmental Analysis Units

Role	Advantages	Disadvantages
Public Policy	• Direct access to power structure • New perspective for top executives • Stimulates long-term strategic thinking • Access to the "corporate vision"	• Difficulty in establishing legitimacy • No direct planning linkage • Survival depends on "sponsoring executive" • Must compete with strategic planners for top management's attention
Planning-Integrated	• Direct access to strategic planning process • Integration of corporate- and division-level environmental issues • Opportunity to directly influence corporate strategy	• Pressure to become short-range in analysis • Need to conform to planning procedures and formats • Tension between line and staff viewpoints
Function-Oriented	• Environment is more easily defined • Direct input to key strategy decisions • No competition with planning for management attention • Close line – staff interaction	• Restricted environmental focus • Limited prospect for unconventional thinking • Short-term orientation • Requires clear and stable concept of strategy

Source: R. T. Lenz and J. L. Engledow, "Environmental Analysis Units and Strategic Decision-Making: A Field Study of Selected 'Leading Edge' Corporations," *Strategic Management Journal 7*, no. 1 (1986), pp. 69–89.

unique to its situation in order to provide a foundation for understanding the complexity of health care delivery and to furnish a backdrop for developing strategy. An excellent example of identifying environmental issues, recognizing opportunity, and building a strategy around that opportunity has been implemented by Vencor, a for-profit, publicly owned health care organization specializing in long-term catastrophic care. Michael R. Barr, as did HealthSouth's Richard Scrushy (see Perspective 1–7), found a market niche outside of the prospective payment system. He observed that Medicare reimbursed long-term-care hospitals based on cost rather than DRGs. Additionally, cash flow for this type of hospital was enhanced by the Medicare practice of reimbursement while care is being given. A large pool of potential patients existed because traditional hospitals emphasized rapid resolution of the patient's disease and discharge. Also, Barr noted the near absence of competition in the long-term catastrophic-care market. Extending the implications of these developments, identifying the interrelationships between the developments and other factors in the external environment, and developing alternative outcome projections led Barr to form Vencor. Barr understood the significance of these issues and formulated a vision and plan for the future of Vencor.

For the foreseeable future, the health care environment will continue to generate numerous complex issues (see Perspective 3–7). Using a format similar to Exhibit 3–7, some of the major health care issues commonly identified by environmental analysis are listed in Exhibit 3–16. This list of issues, although not exhaustive, provides some insight into the dynamics of the health care environment. In addition, this format provides a usable summary of environmental issues and forces managers to cite specific evidence supporting their beliefs concerning the issues. For instance, the high cost of technology is commonly cited as a health care issue, but what is the specific evidence indicating that it is still an issue or is continuing as an issue? As suggested in Exhibit 3–16, the evidence indicates that high technology costs will continue to be a key issue driving health care strategy. Individual health care managers will have to assess the likelihood that these issues will continue and their impact on individual organizations.

SUMMARY AND CONCLUSIONS

This chapter is concerned with understanding and analyzing the external environment of health care organizations. To be successful, organizations must be effectively positioned within their environment. Organizations involved in making capital allocations, experiencing unexpected environmental changes and surprises from different kinds of external forces, facing increasing competition, becoming more marketing oriented, or experiencing dissatisfaction with their present planning results should engage in environmental analysis.

The general goal of environmental analysis is to classify and organize information flows generated outside the organization. In the process, the organization attempts to detect and analyze current, emerging, and likely future issues. This information is used to develop the vision, mission, internal analysis, and strategy of the organization. In addition, the process should foster strategic thinking throughout the organization.

PERSPECTIVE 3-7
The Genetic Age

Genetic research promises to change the nature of medicine in the next twenty years. Scientists have located genes (bits of DNA) that cause hereditary diseases such as cystic fibrosis as well as common illnesses such as high blood pressure, heart disease, emphysema, and cancer. A missing gene, or a malfunction in one, can cause abnormalities in the production of essential proteins and chemicals.

Currently, over 5,000 scientists are researching genetics worldwide. Much of the research is directed toward mapping DNA and linking diseases to faulty DNA. A convergence of powerful technologies is driving the research, and it is predicted that discoveries will emerge in rapid succession. J. Craig Venter of the National Institutes of Health suggests that there will be twenty to thirty highly significant discoveries a year.

With these discoveries, physicians in the future will be able to detect certain diseases well in advance of their symptoms. Already more than 4,000 genetic disorders have been identified, and tests for dozens of them are now possible. Mi-chael Hayden of the University of British-Columbia suggested that, "We're looking at a totally new form of medicine – preventive medicine." Preventive medicine will take the form of using genes to predict illness and modifying genes (inserting bits of DNA) to prevent its onset.

Genetic mapping and identification of faulty genes will bring a whole new set of ethical considerations to the health care industry, questions such as who will have access to such information, whether individuals will know who has access to their genetic data, and how such data will be used. Will gene testing in the workplace be allowed? With insurance premiums based on risk, will HMOs and other managed-care organizations use gene research to screen out high-risk members? Will the government have to protect the "genetically uninsurable"?

_____

Source: John Carey, Joan O. Hamilton, Laura Jereski, and Emily T. Smith, "The Genetic Age," *Business Week* (May 28, 1990), pp. 68–83; and David Stipp, *Wall Street Journal* (July 5, 1990), pp. B1, B3.

Although the benefits of environmental analysis are clear, there are several limitations. Environmental analysis cannot foretell the future nor can managers hope to detect every change. Moreover, needed information may be impossible to obtain or difficult to interpret, or the organization may not be able to respond quickly enough. The most significant limitation may be managers' preconceived beliefs about what the environment should be like.

This chapter provides a comprehensive description of the external environment for health care organizations. The environment includes organizations and individuals in the general environment (government institutions and agencies, business firms, educational institutions, research organizations and foundations, and individuals and consumers) and organizations and individuals in the health care industry (organizations that plan and regulate, primary providers, secondary

EXHIBIT 3-16

Health Care Environmental Issues of the 1990s

Issue	Evidence
Technology	
High Cost of Technology	• Hospitals spend billions of dollars on capital equipment each year • Spending on equipment is expected to increase 15 percent per year throughout the 1990s • MRI technology costs $2 million, a lithotripter costs $1.5 million
DNA Mapping	• Research links diseases to faulty DNA • There are 1,800 genes already mapped • Five thousand scientists are doing research in genetics • NIH and other agencies are set to spend billions in the next ten years
High-tech Treatments	• Sixteen biotech drugs have been approved by the U.S. Food and Drug Administration, and 132 are in the clinical trial pipeline
High-tech Equipment	• MRI imaging is widespread • Computers have increasing application to health care • Electronic patient record, bedside data entry are possible
Social	
Demand for Access and Quality	• There are 37 million people without health care insurance • Federal and state governments are taking health care reform initiatives • "Outcomes" research is called for • At least seven states have considered universal access legislation and more are expected to investigate it • There are 45 million people enrolled in HMOs in 1993, up 3.6 million from 1992 • Health cost increases are slowing, some HMOs hold increases to less than 5 percent
Disease Trends	• The number of AIDS cases is growing • Cost of individualized care is high • AIDS moves into diverse segments of the population • At least 30,000 cases of multidrug resistant tuberculosis are reported in the United States (72 to 89 percent mortality rates) • A rash of epidemics occur (Washington State *E. coli*, Milwaukee *cryptosporidium*, Four-Corners *hantavirus*)

EXHIBIT 3 - 16 *cont'd*

Issue	Evidence
Aging Population	• Baby boom generation will need increased access to health care • There is a shortage of affordable long-term-care facilities
Focus on Women's Health	• A total of twenty legislative bills have been introduced relating to women's health care issues • Cancer death rates for women are increasing dramatically • The cost of ostcoporosis could be as much as $62 billion by the year 2020 • Women are the fastest growing group with AIDS
Death with Dignity	• Laws and "living wills" are reformed • Suicide machines are being built • Right-to-die legislation is being enacted
Political/Regulatory	
Third-party Payer's Share of Health Care Costs Is Increasing	• Medicare's catastrophic illness total coverage, which called for an individual surtax charge, was repealed • Consumers and government are calling for universal health insurance
Physician Payment Reform	• Medicare Part B payment reforms limiting fees are to be phased-in over five years beginning in 1992
IRS Regulations	• Tax-exempt status and issuance of tax-exempt bonds are increasingly restrained
COBRA	• Antidumping rules and regulations are expanding
National Budget Deficit	• Funds for reasearch are decreasing
Medicare Reimbursement Cuts	• Medicare reimbursements to hospitals are predicted to decrease over the next several years • Outpatient services will increase
Economic	
Increased Pressure to Reduce Health Care Costs	• HCFA estimates health care expenditures will exceed 12 percent of GNP • The United States leads all other industrial nations in health care costs • Length of hospital stay is decreasing • Outpatient visits are increasing (18 percent in some states) • Drinking and smoking are declining in some states

EXHIBIT 3 – 16 cont'd

Issue	Evidence
Personnel Problems	• Exercise and a healthy diet are on the rise • Health care purchasers call for reforms • Business and labor unions are increasingly concerned with health care costs • Nurses and nonphysician personnel are in short supply • There is an oversupply of physicians in urban and suburban areas, an undersupply in rural areas • One-half of the fastest growing occupations are in the health care field
Competitive Managed Care Will Continue to Grow	• Increasing numbers of the population are in managed-care programs
Continued Health Care Industry Restructuring	• Acute care hospital profits rose 23 percent in 1991 and 18 percent in 1992 • 1993 was a record year for health care mergers • New forms of delivery are emerging (integrated health network, group practice without walls, physician/hospital organizations) • Community care networks are emerging • Alliances and networks are growing phenomenally • Average length of hospital stay decreased from 7.3 days in 1990 to 7.1 days in 1992 • Average number of hospital outpatient visits rose from 301 in 1990 to 349 in 1992
Failures/closures Will Continue	• Record numbers of hospital closings each year – between 1980 and 1990, 761 hospitals closed – some experts predict that there will be 50 percent fewer hospitals by 1998 • Many rural hospitals continue to lose money • National Association for Hospital Development estimates 40 percent of the nation's 2,200 acute-care hospitals will be closed or converted to other uses • Emergency rooms close in record numbers • Average hospital occupancy continues to decrease • Nearly one in ten hospitals is in financial difficulty

providers, organizations that represent providers, and individuals and patients). For many health care organizations, much of the environmental analysis may be confined to an immediate service area.

Organizations and individuals in the general and health care environments generate information that may be important to health care organizations. Typically, such information is classified as technological, social, political, regulatory, economic, or competitive. Such a classification system aids in aggregating information concerning the issues and in determining their impact. Sources for environmental information are found both inside and outside the organization and are personal as well as impersonal.

The steps in environmental analysis include scanning to identify signals of environmental change, monitoring identified issues, forecasting the future direction of issues, and assessing organizational implications. Scanning is the process of viewing and organizing external information in an attempt to detect relevant issues that will affect the organization. Monitoring is the process of searching for additional information to confirm or disprove the trend, development, dilemma, or likelihood of the occurrence of an event. Forecasting is the process of extending issues, identifying their interrelationships, and developing alternative projections. Finally, assessing is the process of evaluating the significance of the issues. The information influences the formulation of the vision, mission, internal analysis, and strategy of the organization.

Several methods were discussed to conduct the scanning, monitoring, forecasting, and assessing processes. These methods include simple trend identification and extension, solicitation of expert opinion, stakeholder analysis, critical success factor analysis, scenario writing, Porter's competitor analysis, and the diffusion process.

Finally, several relevant issues in the health care environment were explored. The next chapter will examine the internal environment.

KEY TERMS AND CONCEPTS IN STRATEGIC MANAGEMENT

assessing	**focus groups**	**nominal group technique**
brainstorming	**forecasting**	**(NGT)**
critical success factors	**general environment**	**scanning**
dialectic inquiry	**health care environment**	**scenarios**
diffusion process	**internal environmental**	**service area**
delphi technique	**analysis**	**stakeholder**
external environmental	**monitoring**	**strategic issues**
analysis		**trends**

QUESTIONS FOR CLASS DISCUSSION

1. Why is environmental analysis important for an organization?
2. What are the specific goals of environmental analysis?
3. What are the limitations of environmental

analysis? Given these limitations, is environmental analysis worth the effort required? Why?
4. Why is it important to be able to identify influential organizations in the external

environment? How may these organizations be categorized?

5. Using Exhibit 3–9 as an example, develop an "environmental map" for a health care organization in your metropolitan area or state. On this map show the important health care organizations and indicate what impact they may have on the industry.

6. What four processes are involved in environmental analysis? What are their subprocesses?

7. How does the scanning process create a "window" to the external environment? How does the window concept help in understanding organizations and the types of information they produce?

8. Why is the *process* of environmental analysis as important as the *product?*

9. What are some important technological, social, political, regulatory, economic, and competitive issues that are affecting health care today?

10. Go beyond your immediate data and speculate on the major forces that will affect the delivery of health care in the year 2000.

11. Which of the scenarios in Exhibit 3–11 do you think is most likely? Why? Based on today's available information (trends, issues, dilemma, and so on), develop your own scenario of health care in the twenty-first century.

NOTES

1. Elizabeth Wilson, *Florida Trend* (June 1990), pp. 45–48.
2. A. H. Mesch, "Developing an Effective Environmental Assessment Function," *Managerial Planning* 32 (1984), pp. 17–22.
3. Della de Lafuente, "California Groups Join for Survival," *Modern Healthcare* 23, no. 25 (1993), p. 24.
4. J. J. O'Connell and J. W. Zimmerman, "Scanning the International Environment," *California Management Review* 22 (1979), pp. 15–22.
5. P. T. Terry, "Mechanisms for Environmental Scanning," *Long Range Planning* 10 (1977), pp. 2–9.
6. S. C. Jain, "Environmental Scanning in U.S. Corporations," *Long Range Planning* 17 (1984), pp. 117–128; and Liam Fahey and V. K. Narayanan, *Macroenvironmental Analysis for Strategic Management* (St Paul: West Publishing Company, 1986).
7. Beaufort B. Longest, Jr., *Management Practices for the Health Professional,* 4th ed. (Norwalk, Connecticut: Appleton & Lange, 1990), pp. 12–28.
8. Ibid., p. 23.
9. C. Carl Pegels and Kenneth A. Rogers, *Strategic Management of Hospitals and Health Care Facilities* (Rockville, Maryland: Aspen Publishers, 1988), pp. 35–36.
10. Joseph P. Peters, *A Strategic Planning Process for Hospitals* (Chicago: American Hospital Publishing, 1985), pp. 71–73.
11. Fahey and Narayanan, *Macroenvironmental Analysis for Strategic Management.*
12. James B. Thomas and Reuben R. McDaniel, Jr., "Interpreting Strategic Issues: Effects of Strategy and the Information-Processing Structure of Top Management Teams," *Academy of Management Journal* 33, no. 2 (1990), p. 288.
13. Terry, "Mechanisms for Environmental Scanning," p. 9.
14. Thomas and McDaniel, "Interpreting Strategic Issues," pp. 289–290.
15. W. R. Dill, "The Impact of Environment on Organizational Development," in *Concepts and Issues in Administrative Behavior,* ed. S. Mailick and E. H. VanNess (Englewood Cliffs, New Jersey: Prentice-Hall, 1962).
16. H. Klein and W. Newman, "How to Use SPIRE: A Systematic Procedure for Identifying Relevant Environments for Strategic Planning," *The Journal of Business Strategy* 5 (1980), pp. 32–45.

17. Thomas and McDaniel, "Interpreting Strategic Issues," p. 288.
18. David Burda, "What We've Learned from DRGs," *Modern Healthcare* 23, no. 40 (October 4, 1993), pp. 42–44.
19. Thomas and McDaniel, "Interpreting Strategic Issues," pp. 288–289.
20. Fahey and Narayanan, *Macroenvironmental Analysis for Strategic Management,* p. 39.
21. H. E. Klein and R. E. Linneman, "Environmental Assessment: An International Study of Corporate Practice," *The Journal of Business Strategy* 5 (1984), pp. 66–75.
22. Ibid.
23. "Pediatric Clinics and Surgicenters Widen Market Reach," *Health Care Strategic Management* 8, no. 3 (1990), pp. 4–5.
24. James L. Webster, William E. Reif, and Jeffery S. Bracker, "The Manager's Guide to Strategic Planning Tools and Techniques," *Planning Review* 17, no. 6 (1989), pp. 4–13.
25. Jain, "Environmental Scanning in U.S. Corporations," p. 125.
26. S. Lutz, "Hospitals Reassess Home-care Ventures," *Modern Healthcare* 20, no. 37 (September 17, 1990), pp. 22–30.
27. Ricky W. Griffin and Gregory Moorhead, *Organizational Behavior* (Boston: Houghton Mifflin Company, 1986), pp. 496–497.
28. Ibid., pp. 495–496.
29. "Does Doctor Know Best?" *Newsweek* (September 24, 1990), p. 85.
30. Barbara Karmel, *Point & Counterpoint in Organizational Behavior* (Hinsdale, Illinois: The Dryden Press, 1980), p. 11.
31. Webster, Reif, and Bracker, "The Manager's Guide," p. 13.
32. Ibid.
33. Myron D. Fottler, John D. Blair, Carlton

J. Whitehead, Michael D. Laus, and G.T. Savage, "Assessing Key Stakeholders: Who Matters to Hospitals and Why?" *Hospital & Health Services Administration* 34, no. 4 (1989), p. 527.
34. Ibid., p. 532.
35. R. E. Linneman and H. E. Klein, "The Use of Multiple Scenarios by U.S. Industrial Companies: A Comparison Study, 1977–1981," *Long Range Planning* 16, (1983) pp. 94–101.
36. J. P. Leemhuis, "Using Scenarios to Develop Strategies," *Long Range Planning* 18 (1985), pp. 30–37.
37. Webster, Reif, and Bracker, "The Manager's Guide," p. 13.
38. John M. Venable, Qing Li, Peter M. Ginter, and W. Jack Duncan, "The Use of Scenario Analysis in Local Public Health Departments: Alternative Futures of Strategic Planning," *Public Health Reports* 108, no. 6 (1994), pp. 701–710.
39. Fahey and Narayanan, *Macroenvironmental Analysis for Strategic Management,* p. 39.
40. Clement Bezold, "Five Futures," *Healthcare Forum Journal* 35, no. 3 (1992), p. 29.
41. Michael E. Porter, *Competitive Strategy: Techniques for Analyzing Industries and Competitors* (New York: The Free Press, 1980), pp. 3–33.
42. W. A. Reinhardt, "An Early Warning System for Strategic Planning," *Long Range Planning* 17, no. 5 (1989), pp. 25–34.
43. R. T. Lenz and J. L. Engledow, "Environmental Analysis Units and Strategic Decision-Making: A Field Study of Selected 'Leading Edge' Corporations," *Strategic Management Journal* 7 (1986), pp. 69–89.
44. Ibid.
45. Ibid.

ADDITIONAL READINGS

Ehreth, Jenifer, "Hospital Survival in a Competitive Environment: The Competitive Constituency Model," *Hospital & Health Services Administration* 38, no. 1 (1993), pp. 23–44. This article provides a method for hospital administrators to assess hospital effectiveness in a competitive environment. The author suggests that competition has not been adequately considered in assessing the effectiveness of hospital organizations. A step-by-step procedure is proposed to address the differences in power relations between hospitals, their competition, and their stakeholders. Hospital effectiveness is examined by comparing the hospital to its competition using criteria developed through an understanding of stakeholder goals.

El Sawy, Omar A., and Thierry C. Pauchant, "Triggers, Templates, and Twitches in the Tracking of Emerging Strategic Issues," *Strategic Management Journal* 9, no. 5 (1988), pp. 455–473. This article provides an interesting way of monitoring the external environment through studying the shifts of cognitive frames of reference. The concepts of triggers, templates, and twitches are introduced and operationalized in environmental analysis. The authors demonstrate that examining frame of reference shifts can be more informative than examining the frames themselves.

Fontaine, Sherry J., "Evaluating the Use of Environmental Analysis in Health Care," *Health Care Strategic Management* 5, no. 12 (December 1987), pp. 15–18. The author provides case studies of a community hospital and a teaching hospital to demonstrate how environmental analysis was actually incorporated into the planning process. It was found that environmental analysis was actively utilized in the hospitals' strategic planning efforts. Receiving greatest attention were the economic and sociodemographic environments. The technological and political environments received lesser attention.

The Futurist, published by the World Future Society since 1966 (bimonthly). An association for the study of alternative futures, the World Future Society is a nonprofit educational and scientific organization founded in 1966. This publication is a very readable journal of forecasts, trends, and ideas about the future.

Jackson, Susan E., and Jane E. Dutton, "Discerning Threats and Opportunities," *Administrative Science Quarterly* 33 (September 1988), pp. 370–387. This article provides an innovative methodology for discerning between environmental threats and opportunities. An extensive list of characteristics of both threats and opportunities is presented and discussed.

Mercer, David, ed., *Managing the External Environment* (London: Sage Publications, 1992). This book is a collection of readings concerning the strategic management of an organization's relationship with its external environment. The readings focus on the need to identify and understand the major forces that may shape that environment in the future, and the role of strategic planning in both anticipating change and actively creating a desired future. Articles explore the likely nature of the future, developments in the economic, political, social, and technological environments, and methods for developing strategies.

Schoemaker, Paul J., "Multiple Scenario Development: Its Conceptual and Behavioral Foundation," *Strategic Management Journal* 14 (1993), pp. 193–213. Based on extensive research and a two-year sabbatical with the Planning Group of Royal Dutch/Shell, the author examines the multiple scenario approach as an important corporate innovation in strategic planning. The value of the scenario method is discussed and contrasted with other planning tools. In addition, the circumstances that favor a scenario approach over alternative approaches are identified and behavioral issues associated with its use are explored.

CHAPTER 4

Assessing the Internal Environment

"As healthcare grows from a cottage industry to a near trillion-dollar-a-year industry, there have not been the necessary adjustments in our systems to create smooth-flowing processes. . . . a large part of the problem is the process, or how the work is done."

– Ellen J. Gaucher and Richard J. Coffey

LEARNING OBJECTIVES

After completing this chapter you should:

1. Be able to discuss the importance of internal strengths and weaknesses as they relate to strategic effectiveness.
2. Understand the role quality plays in forming the internal culture of health care organizations.
3. Recognize that quality is an important strength of a health care organization.
4. Be able to discuss the basic concepts and principles of total quality management.
5. Understand the process involved in an internal audit of organizational strengths and weaknesses.
6. Be able to perform an internal audit of organizational strengths and weaknesses for a health care organization.

131

INTRODUCTORY INCIDENT

Running a Hospital as Conducting the Symphony

Richard Graham, CEO of Fairmont General Hospital in West Virginia, believes that running a hospital is like conducting a symphony – a symphony made up of physicians, nurses, trustees, patients, administrators, and community members. Much of Graham's time over the past six years has focused on eliminating conflict among the various members of this orchestra. The extent of the discontentment was highlighted by a bitter seven-month strike by nurses and technical personnel and an almost $3 million operating loss in 1987.

During the past five years, however, the CEO has been involved in a turnaround that began with employee involvement in decision making and building community support for the hospital. Last year, after having addressed major problems including lack of information, inability to collect bills, declining census, loss of medical staff, and low employee morale, the Fairmont General Hospital implemented a continuous quality improvement (CQI) initiative. Graham stated that "Our emphasis here is on a bottom-up process that says if it isn't broke, then break it."

The CQI program began with training on patient orientation followed by an examination of housekeeping, engineering, and nutrition services. All of the hospital's expanded marketing activities were tied to the continuous improvement program. Although hospital turnarounds are always the result of many factors, the results achieved at Fairmont General Hospital are impressive. For 1992, net patient revenues topped $48 million compared to less than $40 million in 1990. Total margin was 4.25 percent, up from .33 percent in 1990, and days in accounts receivable fell from more than ninety-two days in 1990 to less than seventy-four days in 1992.

Source: "Fairmont General: CEO Orchestrates Harmony Among Players," *Hospital & Health Networks* 67, no. 12 (July 20, 1993), pp. 23–24.

FROM EXTERNAL TO INTERNAL CONSIDERATIONS

The external environment is crucially important to successful strategic management. Exhibit 4–1 summarizes the relationship of the internal environment analysis process with the other processes in situational analysis. In Chapter 3, considerable emphasis was placed on the importance of uncontrollable external forces. However, that is only part of the strategic management process. Effectively managing the environment requires an understanding not only of external forces but also internal organizational strengths and weaknesses. Numerous factors determine the internal strengths and weaknesses of health care organizations. Exhibit 4–2 provides a framework for the topics to be discussed in this chapter.

First, organizational culture, and an example illustrating how it can be both a strategic strength and weakness will be examined. (For those who are more concerned with operating culture and its impact on bottom-line performance, a more complete discussion will be presented in Chapter 12.) Next, a process called

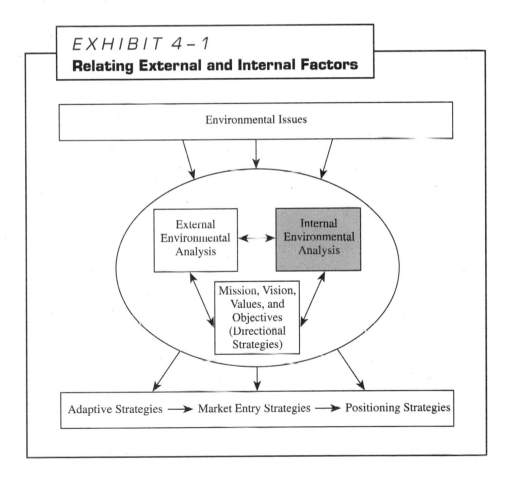

EXHIBIT 4–1
Relating External and Internal Factors

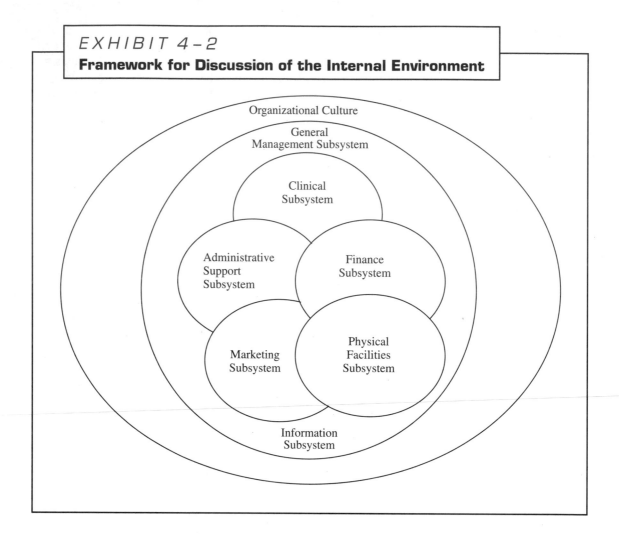

EXHIBIT 4-2
Framework for Discussion of the Internal Environment

Organizational Culture

General
Management Subsystem

Clinical
Subsystem

Administrative
Support
Subsystem

Finance
Subsystem

Marketing
Subsystem

Physical
Facilities
Subsystem

Information
Subsystem

an *internal audit* will be used to assess the strengths and weaknesses of the important functional components or subsystems of health care organizations.

At the heart of the system are the clinical personnel, who are the very foundation of health care organizations. The term *clinical personnel* is used to describe, for example, physicians, nurses, respiratory therapists, and others involved in direct patient care as well as groups that provide direct support to the clinical staff such as pharmacy, pathology, medical laboratories, and rehabilitation services. In addition, important staff functions support the clinicians: marketing, finance, human resources, and so on.

The marketing subsystem, discussed in Chapter 8, includes all the activities necessary to deliver health care services to consumers of all types; the information subsystem will be discussed in Chapter 9. The finance subsystem is involved in acquiring and managing the financial resources needed by health care organizations (Chapter 10). The human resources subsystem encompasses the people required to effectively deliver health services. The human resources subsystem will be examined in greater detail in Chapter 11.

The general management subsystem consists of the people, policies, and systems required to coordinate or "tie together" all the various functions. Finally, the physical facilities of a health care organization influence all aspects of its operations – the capital and operating funds needed, the ease with which clinical and support employees perform their jobs, the marketing plans and strategies, and so on.

These subsystems, along with the culture of the organization, define the internal environment. A substantial amount of attention will be directed toward organizational culture and change in Chapter 12. In this chapter, however, in addition to introducing a basic definition of *culture,* the discussion will focus on the increasingly important aspect of the way people in organizations do their work. This relates to quality or total quality management. Because quality is a state of mind, it is important that all elements of the internal organization be driven by a concern for and consciousness of quality. When this concern is present, quality becomes a critically important internal strength. Before beginning an examination of the internal environment, however, it is important to address the relationship of the internal environment with the external environment.

INTERNAL FACTORS RELATED TO THE EXTERNAL ENVIRONMENT

In his classic book, *Functions of the Executive,* Chester Barnard noted that unless strategic managers possess a commitment to the organization's purpose and understand the capabilities of the organization, the environment has no meaning. Environments are, in fact, so complex that they are simply "mere messes of things" until an understanding of mission and capabilities converts the environment into something meaningful, significant, and interesting.[1] Therefore, we can identify internal strengths and weaknesses only in relation to the external environment. For example, a solo or group medical practice can consider its location a strength only to the extent that other competing practices are not located in the same market area.

Through this process – understanding the opportunities and threats in the external environment and relating them to the organization's internal strengths and weaknesses – strategic managers are able to determine the *distinctive competence* of the organization. Distinctive competence consists of a relatively few things that an organization is able to do quite well. Health care managers need to seriously think about distinctive competence, especially as competition increases with managed-care initiatives. What does our organization do better than anyone else? Depending on the environment, distinctive competence may or may not actually result in a *competitive advantage,* because other health care providers may possess similar attributes. Nevertheless, much of strategic management is a search for distinctive competence and ways to convert such competence into unique competitive advantages.

For example, a children's hospital in a large metropolitan center opened a sports medicine clinic to deal specifically with health problems and injuries of high school athletes. A leading authority on sports injuries was hired, the clinic had a favorable location, and the hospital informed the community of the new facilities and services. Although no one argued that the clinic possessed a distinctive competence in providing medical services to high school athletes, no competitive advantage was gained because numerous other hospitals and clinics were perceived by potential consumers as having adequate sports medicine units. Moreover, personal physicians and local facilities were preferred by schools and families except in the cases of severe injury.

Focusing on Internal Strengths and Weaknesses

The question of identifying an organization's *internal strengths* and *internal weaknesses* is a difficult but essential task for health care managers. The task is difficult because strengths and weaknesses are both objective and subjective as well as absolute and relative. Some strengths possessed by a health care organization are clear by objective standards. For example, the mere presence of one organization in a particular location may provide it with a strategic strength that precludes any other organization from that specific location. Perspective 4–1

PERSPECTIVE 4–1
Competitive Advantage Through Network Formation

One of the most frequently used methods for obtaining a competitive advantage for hospitals and physician practices is the formation of networks that provide patients with a conveniently located array of services. Six physician groups have joined Mercy Healthcare San Diego and the Palomar Pomerado Health System as sponsors of HealthFirst Network, a county-wide health care delivery system. This network is not a merger or a takeover but a community-focused network that includes both primary and acute care sites. The network provides a full range of services from preventive medicine to ambulatory and acute care.

The advantage to patients will be the convenience of its location and the easy access to a full range of services. Insurers who contract with HealthFirst will have, on a county-wide basis, the advantage of a multiple-location, geographically dispersed network. The six physician groups and the health systems involved hope that they can collectively provide services to patients and insurers that will constitute a competitive advantage in a highly competitive market, because an estimated 39 percent of the San Diego market already belongs to prepaid health plans.

Source: "Hospitals and Physicians Form Health Care Network," *Health Care Strategic Management* (August 1993), p. 5.

illustrates an attempt to acquire an important competitive advantage by forming county-wide networks and bringing an array of services to patients in a specific location.

An example of an objective weakness is the health care organization that has used more debt financing for its facilities than its competitors. When the CEO seeks additional money for expansion, the banker makes it clear that the organization already has too much debt, and unless investors are willing to put up additional money, the bank will not loan more funds.

At other times, a strategic strength or weakness may be subjective. Perhaps the administrator of a large hospital believes her medical staff is superior to all others in the area. A look at the qualifications, specialties represented, and services provided does not indicate any substantial differences among the competing hospitals. Despite this, the administrator "has a feeling" that "our staff is thought of as superior." Weaknesses can be subjective as well. The management team may think that the "philosophy" of the board of directors is more conservative than that of other organizations. As a result, the organization may be characterized as "timid" when it comes to taking risks.

Sometimes organizational strengths and weaknesses are absolute. The Mayo Clinic, for example, is known for its excellence and is frequently used as a standard by which other health care organizations are judged. The Johns Hopkins University School of Medicine is recognized worldwide as a leader in medical education.

To illustrate absolute weakness we need only look at the circumstances facing publicly supported indigent care hospitals in view of evolving changes in the health care system. Almost everyone agrees that the future of health care in the United States will involve managed-care systems; and for those individuals who are not employed or for a variety of other reasons are not affiliated with an accountable plan, there will be some type of government-sponsored plan. The goal is to "insure" everyone either through a private or public program, provide everyone access to health care, and give each person as much choice as possible in selecting the provider. Publicly supported indigent care hospitals historically have been providers of last resort. People have come to them because they lack access to other facilities. As a result, the reputation of these hospitals, whether accurate or not, has been of lower quality services, less patient orientation, outdated technology, and deteriorating facilities. This image is considered an absolute weakness as these facilities are forced to become either providers of choice or close their doors.

Finally, strengths and weaknesses may be relative. That is, one long-term care facility may have certain strengths, not in an absolute sense but relative to its competitors. One facility may have limited financial resources in comparison to national averages but considerably more money than any of its competitors. At the same time, a world-renowned academic health center may lose a famous surgeon to a local hospital that is attempting to build a clinical area such as heart transplants. The health center may remain very strong in terms of the services it provides but have a relative weakness with regard to the facility where the surgeon is now located.

As an interesting exercise, Exhibit 4–3 classifies the perceived strengths and weaknesses of a three-physician medical practice in a rural area of the Southwest. Although classifications have been suggested in the exhibit, the problem of precisely categorizing strengths and weaknesses can be illustrated by the fact that total agreement on the precise nature of each item is difficult to obtain.

EXHIBIT 4–3
Classification of Strengths and Weaknesses in a Three-Physician Medical Practice

Strengths/Weaknesses	Elaborations	Classification
Perceived Strengths		
Excellent location for future growth	Located at the intersection of three counties.	*Objective:* Although a rural area, there is a viable population base in the market area. *Relative:* With respect to other medical practices in nonurban areas, this one has the population to support it.
High-quality pediatric services	One of the physicians is a pediatrician.	*Absolute:* None of the other family practices in the area has a pediatrician on staff. *Subjective:* Based on the belief that a pediatrician will automatically provide better pediatric services than an internist.
Image of a caring medical practice	Longevity of doctors, personal treatment and amenities in waiting room, adhered policy of telephone follow-up on visits.	*Subjective:* Perception of caring among patients never documented. *Relative:* Perception, if accurate, can only be assumed relative to competition.
Perceived Weaknesses		
Lack of full range of services. No "one-stop shopping." Visits to multiple specialists sometimes necessary.	Lack of geriatric and pulmonary medicine specialists in a former mining and presently aging community.	*Objective:* Medical specialties of this nature needed in the area. *Relative:* Specialists of this nature available in proximate urban area.

EXHIBIT 4-3 *cont'd*

Strengths/Weaknesses	Elaborations	Classification
Limited number of examining rooms results in increased patient waiting time.	Physical facilities have not been expanded or remodeled in ten years.	*Objective:* Patient waiting time qualitatively greater than at competitors. *Absolute:* Competitive practices have newer and larger facilities.
Practice located in professional space owned by community hospital.	Community hospital in financial trouble and, because of location, practice suspected of being financially troubled as well.	*Subjective:* No objective basis for believing practice is in financial trouble. *Relative:* Hospital space location removes discretion for expanding and remodeling from physicians and places it in the hands of the hospital.

Strategic Effectiveness Requires Adaptability

Regardless of the specific strengths identified, the strategic effectiveness of a health care organization rests on its ability to accomplish two equally important tasks: to operate efficiently in the short run (fiscal year) and to adapt to change over the long run. An overview of the dual problem is illustrated in Exhibit 4–4. In this diagram, time is presented as a continuum labeled *Past* and *Future*. The present can be thought of as a point in time that moves between the past and future. In the present, the goal of management is to efficiently use the organizational resources allocated to it through the budgeting process. This requires that costs be carefully controlled and efforts be made to do things as systematically as possible.

In the future and from outside the health care organization, external forces such as technology, the economy, and regulations emerge that demand that the strategic manager change and adapt to different conditions. Sometimes the ability to adapt requires that the manager sacrifice a degree of short-term efficiency, as when research and development expenditures are made in an attempt to ensure that the latest technologies are available when needed. Or, payments might be made to professional lobbyists to influence legislation in ways the hospital's board of directors believes is desirable. In either case, the money must be spent from the present budget and benefits will not be derived until sometime in the future. The result in the short term is that the operation appears less efficient. Yet this is the type of strategic decision that health care managers must make.

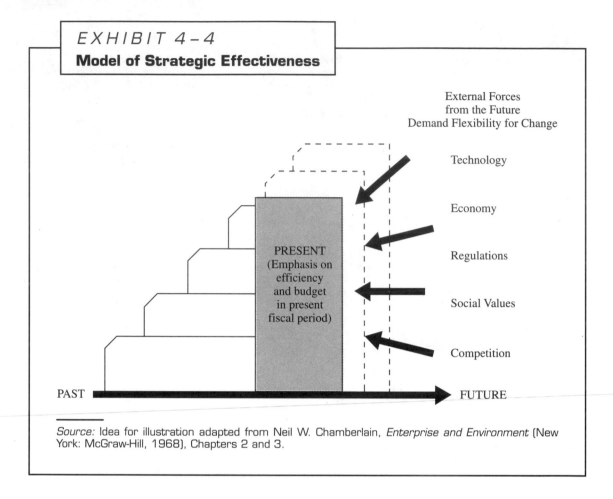

EXHIBIT 4-4
Model of Strategic Effectiveness

External Forces
from the Future
Demand Flexibility for Change

Technology

Economy

PRESENT
(Emphasis on
efficiency
and budget
in present
fiscal period)

Regulations

Social Values

Competition

PAST   FUTURE

Source: Idea for illustration adapted from Neil W. Chamberlain, *Enterprise and Environment* (New York: McGraw-Hill, 1968), Chapters 2 and 3.

The demands for long-term adaptability and flexibility must be carefully weighed against the costs in terms of short-term efficiency.

Efficiency and Health Care

Although it is not the only impetus for controlling costs, the passage of legislation in 1983 placing limits on what Medicare will pay for hospital services caused health care organizations (even those not directly affected by these regulations) to become increasingly concerned about efficiency and cost containment. With prospective pricing and the establishment of diagnostic related groups of procedures, the price (or amount that will be reimbursed for specified procedures) has been "fixed" at specific levels.[2] The result is that if a hospital can provide services for less than the amount reimbursed it can make a profit. If the costs required to deliver services are greater than the amount reimbursed, a loss is incurred. For example, under DRG 459 (nonextensive burn with other operating room procedure) the mandated payment is $7,321. If a hospital can provide this service for $7,000, it earns a profit of $321. If it costs $7,500 to deliver the service, the hospital loses $179.

One effective way to conceptualize how costs are incurred, and consequently how they can be controlled, is to use an activity/cost chain analysis. This activity/ cost chain is used to show the importance of keeping track of the services and products that will ultimately determine how competitive prices will be in the marketplace. An example is provided in Exhibit 4–5.

The key to understanding the *activity/cost chain* is the recognition that the various activities and procedures are what actually add costs to the delivery of products or services. For example, providing a physical examination requires that various activities and procedures be accomplished. Physicians and nurses are needed to take the patient's history, perform different tests, diagnose conditions, and assess results. All of these involve costs.

The examination must take place in a facility that required external capital to build. Because expertise must be purchased in a labor or other type of factor market (nurses, physicians, technicians, suppliers, and so on) and construction funds must be acquired in capital markets, we refer to these as supplier-related activities. The prices of supplier-related resources are determined by uncontrollable external forces, technology, economic conditions, and other elements of the environment as discussed in Chapter 3.

It is likely that the health facility spent money advertising and promoting "executive physicals," and these expenditures must be considered in the overall price of the examination as well. The laboratory tests requested by the physician must be accomplished, records must be accurately maintained, and related services must be rendered. All of these activities add costs that must be covered by the price of the physical examination.

At the extreme right of the chain we encounter external factors, this time at the point of the forward-channel activities, that provide services to patients and clients. Included are any costs that must be assumed to make services more convenient and accessible to the ultimate users and to overcome similar efforts by competitors. Because many patients will have private insurance, the health facility will be involved in billing and otherwise interacting with insurance companies.

Positioned between the supplier-related activities and the forward-channel activities is the internal domain of the health care organization. For simplicity, we have restricted this system to the service production, service marketing, support, and administrative subsystems. When pricing a particular service such as a physical examination or outpatient surgery, the costs associated with each activity must be calculated. To this we add our desired profit level (or excess over costs in the case of not-for-profit organizations) to arrive at a final price for the service.

This illustration clarifies why prospective payment for medical services is so important. When cost-based reimbursement was the rule, health providers could carefully track their costs, add the desired level of profit, and set a price for a service. Because prospective payment sets the price in advance, profits (or any excess of revenues over costs) can be made only when the cumulative costs

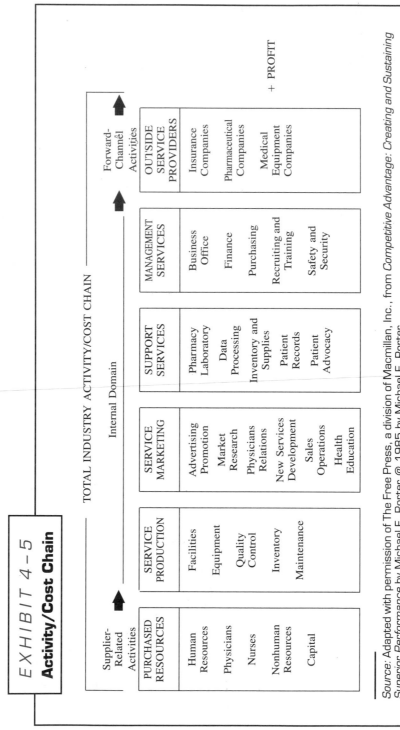

EXHIBIT 4–5
Activity/Cost Chain

TOTAL INDUSTRY ACTIVITY/COST CHAIN

Supplier-Related Activities

Internal Domain

Forward-Channêl Activities

PURCHASED RESOURCES

Human Resources

Physicians

Nurses

Nonhuman Resources

Capital

SERVICE PRODUCTION

Facilities

Equipment

Quality Control

Inventory

Maintenance

SERVICE MARKETING

Advertising Promotion

Market Research

Physicians Relations

New Services Development

Sales Operations

Health Education

SUPPORT SERVICES

Pharmacy

Laboratory

Data Processing

Inventory and Supplies

Patient Records

Patient Advocacy

MANAGEMENT SERVICES

Business Office

Finance

Purchasing

Recruiting and Training

Safety and Security

OUTSIDE SERVICE PROVIDERS

Insurance Companies

Pharmaceutical Companies

Medical Equipment Companies

+ PROFIT

Source: Adapted with permission of The Free Press, a division of Macmillan, Inc., from *Competitive Advantage: Creating and Sustaining Superior Performance* by Michael E. Porter. @ 1985 by Michael E. Porter.

associated with the delivery of a service are less than the preestablished allowable price.

Exhibit 4–6 shows the American Hospital Association index of hospital costs for two years – one ending in March 1992 and the other ending in March 1993 – to illustrate the importance of cost control and operational efficiency. Prices for goods and services purchased by U.S. hospitals increased by 5.9 percent between March 1992 and March 1993 compared to 5.5 percent between March 1991 and March 1992.

For the two years sampled in this exhibit, the largest percentage increases in costs came in the labor component of the marketbasket index even though the rate was down slightly in the most recent year. The nonlabor component, including items such as food, fuel, medical supplies, and pharmaceuticals, although a smaller percentage, increased at more than twice the rate in 1993 compared to 1992. Although the costs of these nonlabor items are often beyond the control of the individual health care organization, they can control the amount of the products actually used. The increase in fuels and utilities was particularly alarming because these costs had actually decreased between 1991 and 1992.

Efficiency and adaptability is a delicate balance that health care managers will always be required to consider in their decision making. The balance they achieve between these two, often competing, demands will be influenced by a number of factors. The changing nature of the health care industry will certainly influence the balance sought and achieved, but internal factors will influence

---

EXHIBIT 4–6

Selected Hospital Costs, March 1992 and March 1993 (figures indicate percentage change over the same period in previous year)

Item	March 1992	March 1993
American Hospital Association Marketbasket Index	**5.5%**	**5.9%**
Labor Component	7.7	7.3
Nonlabor Component	1.7	3.5
Professional Fees	5.9	5.9
Food	0.4	1.1
Fuel and Utilities	−3.9	2.8
Medical Supplies and Pharmaceuticals	3.6	4.2
Administrative Supplies	2.0	2.5
Housekeeping, Maintenance, and Other Supplies	0.1	2.6

Source: AHA News (April 9, 1993), p. 3.

choices as well. Some of these internal factors will relate to the basic "character" or culture of the organization itself.

INTRODUCTION TO ORGANIZATIONAL CULTURE AND TOTAL QUALITY MANAGEMENT

Most managers agree that something characterizes a health care organization's customary way of doing things, the values that most members of the organization share, and the things that must be learned and subscribed to by new members if they are to be satisfied and productive in their jobs. These customary ways of doing things, often referred to collectively as the *culture* of an organization are important in assessing strategic strengths and weaknesses because they can either aid or hinder an organization's response to external opportunities and threats.

Organizational Culture

Organizational culture is an elusive concept that is the subject of considerable controversy in modern management. Some believe it is too "soft" to be taken seriously, although others contend it is a "seminal concept" that cannot be ignored if we are to understand the nature of how health care managers behave strategically as well as operationally.[3]

Unfortunately, managing organizational culture is not an easy task. Although most agree that it is real and affects the accomplishment of organizational goals, there are no widely accepted techniques for measuring and precisely altering culture. Therefore, it is appropriate to begin by understanding as much as possible what actually constitutes organizational culture.

Characteristics of Organizational Culture

Organizational culture is defined as the "implicit, invisible, intrinsic, and informal consciousness of the organization which guides the behavior of individuals and which shapes itself out of their behavior."[4] Less technically, organizational culture is the customary way of doing things. Organizational cultures possess three important characteristics.

Organizational Culture Is Learned The culture of a health care organization is made meaningful by experience. Those who work in an organization gradually accept its expectations. Culture influences all aspects of what goes on in the organization, including how we feel about what we do, how we do our job, what we believe is important to accomplish, and why we think different things are important or unimportant.[5]

For example, consider an organization such as the Mayo Clinic that has a strong culture. Mayo is built on three primary values that permeate its culture and can be traced directly to the founders: (1) pursuit of service rather than profit; (2) concern for the care and welfare of individual patients; and (3) interest by every member of the staff in the progress of every other member.[6] More attention will be given in the next chapter to the importance of core values and guiding principles. However, at this point, it is important to recognize that anyone working at the Mayo Clinic will soon be confronted with these three core values and his or her success will depend to a great extent on how well these values are learned and observed at work.

Organizational Culture Is Shared Some aspects of culture are shared by the members of the organization. Shared understandings and meanings are important because they help employees know how things are to be done. If an employee knows that the culture of the hospital dictates that the patient is all-important, decisions can be made according to this understood value system even when a policy, procedure, or rule is not available in a particular situation.[7]

People who "fit in" at the Mayo Clinic soon find themselves sharing the culture with others. In fact, over the years the chair of the clinic's department of administration has asked residents and others to state what they think makes the Mayo Clinic great. He summarized these into twelve characteristics, three of which (team orientation, special spirit, and trust in those who have "passed the Mayo test") illustrate the importance of sharing basic beliefs for newcomers to become part of the culture.

When the Mayo Clinic made a strategic decision to geographically expand by aggressively establishing a presence in Florida and Arizona, one of the greatest concerns was whether the "Rochester ethic" (culture) could be transferred to the Sunbelt.[8] With different locations in different parts of the country came different lifestyles, traditions, and so on that could have made the sharing of a common culture a significant problem.

Culture Is Objective as Well as Subjective Shared assumptions, meanings, and values are subjective. The objective aspect of organizational culture can be heard and witnessed. Health care organizations are often quite rich in objective culture, which includes the heroes of the organization, the stories told from one generation of employees to another, the ceremonies and rituals of the organization, and so on. These objective and subjective aspects of culture will be discussed in more detail in Chapter 12.

Culture and the Bottom Line The jury is still out on the strategic significance of a strong organizational culture. Organizational cultures such as the one at Mayo do have the potential to inspire aggressive and calculated managerial action whereas a weak culture is likely to do little more than encourage managers to be mere caretakers. Strong cultures build group cohesiveness, and when the other members of the group insist on high levels of performance each individual is encouraged to do his or her best.[9] A surgical team performing complex operations is a good example of how the culture of the group demands that each individual perform at the highest possible level if membership is to be maintained.

Unfortunately, strong cultures can discourage change. When organizations become too committed to "how we do things around here" and "what we believe in," it may be difficult, at least in the short run, to change the culture. Opportunities can be missed and competitive advantages can be lost simply because the culture is so strong that it will not tolerate new ideas and directions. However, as Perspective 4–2 illustrates, organizational cultures, when they encourage key success factors such as patient-centered care, can be positive contributors to the overall success of an organization.

Building a Culture Based on Quality

One of the most often discussed ideas in modern business, health care, and educational circles is *total quality management* (TQM), or *continuous quality improvement* (CQI), or some other variation of the quality theme. Much of the focus has been on various approaches, and the advantages and disadvantages of the ideas presented by different people such as W. Edwards Deming, Philip Crosby, and Joseph Juran. Although each of these individuals has much to offer health care managers, the concern of this discussion is more on creating the "quality-oriented culture." Quality, after all is more a state of mind than any

---

PERSPECTIVE 4–2

A Patient-Oriented Culture Takes Time But Is Worth the Trouble

Technology is wonderful and good food is a tremendous "plus," but when it comes to what makes patients happy or unhappy with their stay in a hospital, it all comes back to the people who provide the care and how they treat the people who receive it. Press, Ganey Associates surveyed almost 140,000 patients from 225 hospitals and found that patient satisfaction may be a good indicator of the overall quality of care people receive in an institution.

Health care organizations such as the Oklahoma City Baptist Medical Center give a copy of each questionnaire filled out by a patient to the head nurse responsible for the patient's care as a reward for high ratings and a valuable technique for highlighting any specific problems that might have been experienced during the hospital stay. Translating a mission and

patient-oriented culture into behaviors is a difficult but rewarding task.

When the culture of a hospital is genuinely "patient centered," certain things seem to happen. A few of the more important are:

- Staff is concerned for the privacy of patients;
- Staff is sensitive to the inconvenience of illness and hospitalization;
- Adequate information is given to the family about the patient's condition;
- Overall the staff is cheerful about calls for assistance;
- Staff takes patient needs and problems seriously; and
- Staff is courteous.

Source: "Human Factor Is What Makes a Hospital with a Heart, Patients Say," *AHA News* (May 18, 1992), p. 5.

particular program or approach. In this sense, quality must be a part of every manager's strategic thinking process and an essential component of organizational excellence.

Quality and Health Care Quality has always been a concern in health care. The driving force for this concern, of course, is the risk to human life when high-quality services are not provided. However, the general approach to improving quality has been one of quality assurance – reviewing medical records after the patient has been seen, assuring protocols have been followed, detecting problems, and, where appropriate, taking corrective actions. In other words, it has been a combination of damage control and risk management.

Although this retrospective approach to quality management is better than nothing, it is not at all in line with modern concepts of TQM. The idea behind TQM is to build quality into everything – not just nurses and physicians but receptionists, technicians, pharmacists, and custodians. The Ford Motor Company motto "Quality Is Job One" captures the idea. In this regard, health care has clearly been behind contemporary trends. As one writer noted, it is "high time for health care to catch up."[10]

Health care is catching up; success stories about total quality in a variety of health care settings support this claim. In 1992 the Joint Commission on the Accreditation of Healthcare Organizations began looking specifically at whether or not quality improvement programs were present in the facilities it accredited. The CEO of Atlantic City Medical Center stated that quality programs increased enthusiasm and commitment more than productivity programs alone and tended to increase output and profitability as much or more. At Rush-Presbyterian-St. Luke's Medical Center, a total quality program, after a three-year implementation period, was judged to increase service, productivity, and employee morale. It was described as a "win/win" process for everyone involved.[11] At the Baptist Medical Center in Columbia, South Carolina, the CEO indicated that as the result of TQM, "we are doing a better job of understanding who our customers are and . . . doing the right things right the first time."[12]

TQM: Some Basic Concepts TQM has been described as a powerful tool for improving the management of health care organizations. It focuses on work processes, applies analytical and behavioral techniques, emphasizes integration of services, and aims to improve both processes and outcomes.[13]

TQM, as noted earlier, is a "state of mind" as well as a comprehensive philosophy for getting better at not just providing better manufactured goods in business, but better services in education, health care, and government. It is never complete, and when working properly all employees, direct care and support personnel, are always in the process of doing a better job. For this reason, TQM is difficult to reduce to a few basic concepts, and any attempt to do so ultimately oversimplifies the idea. However, it is safe to say that most TQM programs share certain characteristics: (1) the need for commitment by top management; (2) extensive communication and training; (3) customer orientation; (4) zero defects and statistical quality control; and (5) continuous improvement.[14] In the following paragraphs, each of these characteristics will be briefly discussed.

Top management commitment and leadership is critical to the success of TQM programs. As will be discussed in Chapter 5, all organizations must have a sense of what they are today, where they want to be tomorrow, and the values they will display and refuse to compromise in the conduct of their affairs. Top management is responsible for articulating and communicating these directional strategies to everyone in the organization. Therefore, it is top management's job to make it clear that high quality is important, that behaviors contributing to improved quality will be rewarded, and that the most important goal of the organization is to determine what are the right things for the organization to do and to do these things right.

Management's task, in short, is to make sure that quality is on the minds of everyone at all times. Although a specific person may be responsible for implementing a TQM program, top management must ultimately champion high quality. Top level leaders must be convinced that quality is the road to success and be able to convince others that they are committed to such quality in everything the organization seeks to accomplish.

Communication and training is an essential part of all successful quality programs. TQM is founded on the idea that everyone is responsible for quality, not just the inspectors and quality assurance personnel. In fact, in a mature and properly functioning TQM program, inspectors are not needed at all. The people doing the work are responsible for their own quality and do not assume that someone else will catch and correct any mistake they might make. Moreover, if the people doing the work are to be responsible for its quality, they must be provided the tools and techniques for monitoring and measuring quality.

Training everyone in quality techniques is an important part of TQM. Through top management leadership and communication, everyone is made aware of the importance of quality, and through training, employees are given the tools to ensure their own work meets high standards. Practically, communication and training are essential to build ownership for the quality program among employees. If employees do not "buy in" it is not likely that they will provide the services patients will have come to expect. For example, when a health care facility advertises its adherence to total quality in all it does, patients will expect to receive excellent services. Frederick W. Smith of Federal Express underscores his belief in employee "buy in" by stating "employee satisfaction is a prerequisite to customer satisfaction."[15] Perspective 4–3 illustrates the importance of total quality management to one hospital.

Customer orientation is not just a marketing concept, it is the very foundation of TQM. One of the problems faced by management attempting to implement TQM in health care is likely to be the argument that patients are not customers in the same sense as people buying automobiles or furniture. Some will go so far as to say that patients cannot make informed judgments about the quality of services because they believe only those properly trained in health care can make such judgments. This, however, has become an increasingly outdated argument and is totally out of step with TQM. Clearly, few people understand the technical aspects of medical science but everyone has some idea about what good quality is when he or she interacts with the health care system. As long as patients (or

PERSPECTIVE 4-3
Central DuPage Hospital Begins TQM

In Winfield, Illinois, the Central DuPage Hospital began a program intended ultimately to redesign and restructure the delivery of health care services. The program is called Operation Improvement. The outcomes expected are a more direct, cost-effective focus on patient care.

In 1991, Central DuPage started a total quality management program in an effort to streamline many of its work processes, improve the quality of services delivered, and reduce costs. Operation Improvement is an integral part of the TQM effort. In the process of "re-engineering" the hospital's work processes, jobs will be realigned, cross training will take place, and there will be a restructuring of the entire delivery system into a more "patient-centered model."

Some of the specific proposals include the use of broadly trained staff members who are capable of providing a variety of services to reduce waiting time and the number of different staff members with whom patients are required to interact. Also, the physical location of services will consider patient convenience. It is expected that the process will take approximately a year and a half to implement but its benefits will continue for many years into the future.

Source: "Central DuPage Hospital Restructures Health Services," *Health Care Strategic Management* (August 1993), pp. 4–5.

a third party representing them) pay the bills in health care, their wishes should be a large part of the quality equation.

In fact, many argue the "customer, or patient, or client, or whatever word is used to identify the receiver of health care services" is the sole judge of quality. This judgment, when it comes to services, operates within five dimensions:[16]

- Tangibles – the appearance of facilities, equipment, and personnel.
- Reliability – the ability to perform accurately and dependably.
- Responsiveness – the "willingness" to provide prompt service.
- Assurance – the ability to convey trust and confidence.
- Empathy – the provision of caring attention.

Organizations devoted to TQM listen to patients. They are close to their customers and ask them regularly what they think and how they were treated then act on the feedback received. They listen carefully to what customers tell them.

Zero defects and statistical quality control are components of TQM, at least informally. The goal to keep defects and problems from developing is accomplished through monitoring performance with modern yet simple statistical techniques that are widely available. Doing things right the first time is the basic principle behind zero defects. Deming maintains that "the central problem of management in all its aspects . . . is to understand better the meaning of variation.''[17] In other words, when people are able to distinguish between normal, routine changes in processes and unusual, abnormal changes that can be attributed to specific causes, quality can be improved and corrections in basic quality problems implemented.[18] If people are to be expected to detect these abnormal changes and act on them, they must be provided the appropriate tools for making such determinations.

Continuous improvement is the ultimate goal of TQM. This idea is the basic philosophy driving much of contemporary management thought. Continuous improvement forces employees and managers to acknowledge that things can always get better and that we can, and should, learn from our experiences. Organizations should look upon their world as an opportunity to learn. Mistakes are looked upon, not as failures, but as learning opportunities. Successes are not monuments to the past, but learning opportunities. Focusing on mistakes and successes helps organizations and employees improve – the ultimate goal of TQM. It has been said that "finger pointing" is the least useful gesture ever created by human beings. In TQM finger pointing and the assignment of blame is not important. Getting better at what we do is the important thing.

Concluding Comments on TQM It is probably not fair or appropriate to discuss TQM without some acknowledgment of the individuals who have championed this important movement and revolutionized the way many managers think and many organizations, in services as well as manufacturing, do their work. At the same time, a detailed discussion of these individuals is not possible. Each quality pioneer's ideas go beyond the obvious and form complete and comprehensive philosophies of the management of work.

W. Edwards Deming, for example, is by far the most influential quality advocate today. He is best known for the way in which he influenced Japanese manufacturing quality and his early rejection by American industry. Deming distinguished between two ways to improve processes – changing the "common causes" and removing the "special causes." Common causes are systemic and shared by all workers. They include things such as poor product design, inferior raw materials, and worn-out machines. Special causes produce nonrandom variations and are the result of individual activities or employees. Worker inattention and lack of skills or training are examples of special causes. Management is responsible for removing the common causes whereas the correction of special causes usually requires someone very close to the actual operation.[19]

Philip B. Crosby, another pioneer, was vice president of ITT before founding his own quality consulting firm. He influenced a number of leading organizations such as Johnson & Johnson and IBM. The Crosby approach is based on the belief that quality improvements will inevitably lead to cost reductions and increases in profitability. Quality thus becomes free or pays for itself through reduced costs and increased profits.[20] The means to increasing quality, in Crosby's view, is zero defects, to be achieved through preventing quality problems from developing.

The final leader who provided much of the foundation of the modern quality movement is Joseph M. Juran, who has been influential in Japan as well as with such American companies as Texas Instruments, Monsanto, and Xerox.[21] Juran focused on quality as "fitness for use" or the extent to which the users of the product or service could count on its ability to do what they expected it to do. This fitness for use involved quality in the design, availability (reliability and ease of maintenance), safety, field use (usability after transportation, storage, and so on), and conformance (match between actual product or service and the design intent). Perhaps the single greatest difference between Juran and Crosby is Juran's implication that zero defects may not be a practical goal if prevention and evaluation costs are greater than the cost of product or service failure.

To be sure, there are differences in the approaches to quality advocated by Deming, Crosby, and Juran. However, all seek continuous improvement in the performance of individuals and organizations. They all challenge managers to look beyond simple quality assurance and inspections. They focus on the importance of the system and the necessity of all employees to assume responsibility for the quality of the work they perform. In fact, Perspective 4–4 confirms that hospitals of different sizes have made significant use of the ideas of all the quality pioneers.

ESTIMATING STRATEGIC CAPACITY

Despite the importance of organizational culture and the growing appreciation of the necessity of continuous improvement, to achieve strategic effectiveness health care organizations must have a means to determine their internal strengths

---

PERSPECTIVE 4–4
Hospitals and the Quality Pioneers

The most widely used quality concepts are those of Deming, Crosby, and Juran. The following table illustrates how the choice of approach differs relative to bed size, teaching orientation, and whether or not the hospital is part of a larger health care system. The smaller hospitals, for exam-

ple, are more likely to use the ideas of Deming and less likely to use the ideas of Juran.

Source: Adapted from "The Quality March: National Survey Profiles Quality Improvement Activities," *Hospital and Health Networks* (December 5, 1993), p. 55. Table used by permission.

Pioneer	6–99 Beds	100–399 Beds	400+ Beds	Teaching	Nonteaching	System Member	System Nonmember
Deming	33.4%	27.6%	19.8%	17.2%	29.4%	28.2%	28.0%
Juran	2.7	4.3	7.2	5.0	4.2	4.2	4.3
Crosby	1.5	1.8	2.7	1.8	1.8	2.0	1.6
More Than One	24.3	25.8	28.1	33.0	24.8	27.7	24.0
Other	14.2	19.6	22.5	19.9	18.2	19.4	17.6
None	24.0	20.9	19.8	23.1	21.5	18.4	24.4

Note: Survey mailed to 5,492 hospitals with a response from 3,303 (60 percent). The responding hospitals were larger (221 vs. 170 bed capacity), teaching (8.8 percent vs. 4.2 percent nonteaching), and system members (41 percent vs. 35 percent system nonmembers).

and weaknesses. To illustrate how this is done, the major functional subsystems of all health care organizations will be examined: clinical, administrative services, physical facilities, finance, marketing, and general management. An evaluation of the adequacy of the organization's information system is an integral part of all these subsystems; therefore it will be addressed as a part of the other subsystems.

Many issues could be discussed with regard to each of these subsystems; therefore, an outline of important questions that should be asked about the organization's strengths and weaknesses in functional area has been developed. The "audit checklist" of strengths and weaknesses will include a review of several key factors:

1. *Staff.* Do we have an adequate staff in terms of both numbers and qualifications for our present activities? Can the staffing base support our expected future development? Do we have the managerial expertise needed to coordinate all the functional areas?
2. *Information and intelligence.* Is the internal information flow relative to clinical operations, administrative services, finance, marketing, and general management sufficient to support day-to-day activities, and do we have a system for obtaining strategic information (intelligence) outside the organization?
3. *Technical capabilities.* Do we have the equipment, facilities, and knowledge necessary to accomplish the tasks required in each functional area?
4. *Synergy.* Are the objectives of the functional areas appropriate to accomplish organizational goals, given the organization's competitive position, resources, and opportunities?

Before beginning, one precautionary note is in order. Checklists and audits are useful tools to guide our thinking. However, it is important to remember that checklists are never exhaustive, and important issues for individual organizations and specific circumstances are omitted even in the most comprehensive audit. Therefore, it is important to remain alert to items and issues that may not be stated explicitly in the checklist of questions.

Evaluating Clinical Capacity

Because of the number and diversity of members of the clinical staff, only selected aspects can be examined in any analysis. One complication is illustrated by examining accreditation standards for different clinician specialists. Because they are constantly undergoing revision, professional assessment of what measures will be used to evaluate the strengths and weaknesses of the *clinical subsystem* has to change as well.

To illustrate, the American Hospital Association *News* (September 10, 1990) contained an examination of the new accreditation standards for nursing services. The Joint Commission on Accreditation of Healthcare Organizations focused on (1) the assessment of patient care needs; (2) competence of the nursing staff; (3) development of organization-wide patient care programs, policies, and procedures by the nurse executive; (4) development of nursing care plans that support innovation and improvement of nursing practice that are consistent with the organizational mission; (5) nurse executive responsibilities in organizational decision making and processes; and (6) evaluation and monitoring of the quality and appropriateness of patient care. Exhibit 4–7 lists the kinds of questions the health care strategist should ask when evaluating the strengths and weaknesses of the clinical staff.

EXHIBIT 4–7
Assessing Clinical Strengths and Weaknesses of the Clinical Operations

Operations Staff

1. Does our medical staff, including physicians, nurses, and technicians, have the recognized qualifications needed to deliver the services provided by our facility?
   a. Do we properly verify and document staff members' qualifications?
   b. Do we have all the specialties needed on our staff? Do we have excess staff in any areas?
   c. Are the morale and performance of our medical staff at an appropriate level in view of our organizational mission?
   d. Do we provide incentives for our professional staff members to remain current in their fields?
2. Do we have a sufficient number of qualified clinical staff members on duty at all times to ensure that patients receive prompt and high-quality care?
   a. Do we have an appropriate number of clinicians on duty at all times who are qualified to verify and act on changes in the condition of patients?
   b. Do we have an appropriate number of qualified clinicians to ensure a safe environment for all patients?
   c. Are our clinical personnel competitively compensated so as to control the level of turnover with regard to voluntary terminations?
   d. Are only professionally qualified clinical specialists assigned to managerial positions in clinical units?
   e. Are professional clinical staff members allowed to exercise their professional judgment on issues relating to patient care without improper influence by administrative considerations?
3. Is there a sufficient number of qualified technicians to provide the appropriate levels of support for professional clinical staff?
   a. Do all technicians meet state licensure/registration or professional certification requirements?
   b. Are provisions made to assure that technicians are current with the latest methods available in their respective fields?
   c. Are appropriately designed and supervised in-service training opportunities available for those individuals who wish to improve their skills on the job?

EXHIBIT 4 – 7   cont'd

Information and Intelligence

1. Do we have satisfactory information-system support for the clinical staff in terms of diagnostic and related systems?
   a. Do we subscribe to or otherwise have access to the data bases needed to deliver high-quality health services?
   b. Do we have the internal information processing capabilities to support the medical staff in delivering high-quality services?
   c. Is our patient record system sufficient to facilitate the work of the medical staff?
2. Are the administrative information systems within and among our clinical departments properly designed and maintained to process both urgent and routine information in a satisfactory manner?
   a. Are patient records and related information available in a form that allows timely decision making?
   b. Is there an established and reliable system for communication between physicians and other clinical personnel?
   c. Are communications properly documented to allow for professional examination and quality control?
3. Do we have established procedures and systems for staying informed about developments in all clinical areas originating outside our own organization?
   a. Do we have proper communication links with relevant organizations outside our organization, such as the state department of public health, the Centers for Disease Control, and so on?
   b. Are we appropriately informed about labor-market conditions and compensation rates in all areas of clinical services?

Technical Capabilities

1. Are our medical diagnosis, treatment, and laboratory technologies current for high-quality treatment of patients?
   a. Do we have difficulty attracting and maintaining the quality and quantity of clinical staff desired because of outdated or insufficient technology?
   b. Do we have technologies available that are no longer needed or not used enough to justify updating and expansion?
   c. Do we anticipate radical new clinical technologies changing the way we diagnose and treat patients in the near future?
2. Are our physical facilities adequate to assure high-quality and comfortable patient care?
   a. Are facilities presently being used for multiple purposes that should be dedicated to single-purpose use?
   b. Are facilities presently dedicated to a single use that could be used for multiple purposes?
   c. Do we have the proper means of monitoring and evaluating high-quality clinical care for our patients?
   d. Do we have the proper facilities and expertise to protect patients and employees from nuclear and other forms of toxic contamination?

EXHIBIT 4-7   cont'd

Synergy

1. Do all areas of our clinical staff understand and share the common goal of high-quality patient care?
   a. Do we have organized efforts to reinforce the importance of the highest standards of professional performance?
   b. Are efforts made to indicate the importance of responding to all organizational stakeholders by the clinical staff?
   c. Are meetings held regularly for members of different clinical specialties to assure that intraorganizational communication occurs at regular intervals?

Source: Audit items adapted from guidelines provided in *Accreditation Manual for Hospitals* (Chicago: Joint Commission on Accreditation of Healthcare Organizations, 1993).

Evaluating Administrative Services Capacity

The effectiveness of the clinical capacity is influenced by the administrative services available to those people who provide direct patient care. Determination of the support available requires an assessment of the *administrative services subsystem* that includes the administrative and clerical support staff and systems. The strategic questions for the administrative staff should relate not just to the acquisition of personnel but to their occupational growth and development through training and career planning. If the support staff is unionized, many of these questions will require different answers. Exhibit 4–8 provides a list of key questions strategic managers should ask relative to an organization's ability to administratively serve those who provide health services.

With regard to the information and intelligence issues, the internal audit must determine the present developmental stage of the information systems supporting medical, administrative, and overall decision-making systems. Another important strategic question is the significance of information for the professional development of the staff. For example, if a health care organization strives to be a leader in the application of service-delivery techniques, its personnel need to be supplied with the information necessary to know what other organizations are doing.

Finally, the technical capabilities of administrative services are important and must be evaluated. As part of this, the pressing question of technology must again be addressed. Few question the importance of technology as it relates to patient diagnosis and treatment. The effectiveness of administratively oriented technologies is important as well. As illustrated in Perspective 4–5, administrative issues such as telecommunications are often fundamental to the support of clinical services technology.

EXHIBIT 4-8

Assessing the Strengths and Weaknesses of Administrative Services

Administrative Staff

1. Does our administrative staff, including managers, clerical support, and the data processing staff, have the recognized qualifications needed to support the delivery of the services provided by our facility?
   a. Do we properly verify, document, and develop staff members' qualifications?
   b. Do we have all the administrative specialists needed on our staff? Do we have excess staff in any areas?
   c. Are the morale and performance of our administrative support staff at an appropriate level in view of our organizational mission?
   d. Do we provide incentives for our administrative staff members to remain current in their fields?
2. Do we have the appropriate support staff to ensure high-quality, cost-effective support for the medical services provided to patients?
   a. Is our collective bargaining (if unionized) or participative decision-making program functioning as well as expected?
   b. Are our wage and benefits programs competitive with other employers in the area?
3. Are our managers properly trained and delegated the authority needed to produce the work demanded?
4. Do we have an effective managerial succession plan for all positions?
5. Is our human resources program effectively recruiting the types of individuals needed in our facility?
   a. Do we have an effective in-service training and development program for employees at all levels?
   b. Do we provide valuable career planning services for employees?

Information and Intelligence

1. Do we have satisfactory information-system support for the administrative staff in terms of automated and modern systems?
   a. Do we subscribe to or otherwise have access to the data bases needed to support the delivery of quality health services?
   b. Do we have the internal information processing capabilities to support the administrative staff in the delivery of quality services?
2. Do we have an effective inventory-control and purchasing-information system?
   a. Are there sufficient information-processing capabilities to satisfy both the service-delivery and administrative requirements?
   b. Is our administrative information system sufficiently understood by all personnel to allow for its effective utilization?
3. Is our human resources management system properly integrated into our management information system?

EXHIBIT 4–8   cont'd

    a. Are personnel actions properly documented and archived?

    b. Are wage and benefits systems integrated into the management information system and accessible by all supervisory and managerial personnel?

4. Is our clinical intelligence system operating effectively for decision making?

    a. Do we provide incentives for our managers and employees to network effectively in community and professional organizations?

    b. Do our in-house library and archives provide operational and administrative developments as well as medical information?

Technical Capabilities

1. Are the latest technologies available to our administrative support staff?

    a. Do we have difficulty attracting administrative staff members because of the unavailability of any specific technologies?

    b. Are technologies available where the usage rate is sufficient to justify updating and enhancing?

2. In addition to documentation of staff qualifications, do we have an adequate quality-control system?

    a. Do we do a good job of making high quality a part of every person's job? In other words, is high quality an integral part of our operating philosophy?

    b. If quality problems develop, do we have the necessary risk management and damage control capabilities in place or available?

Synergy

1. Does our administrative support staff do a good job of interacting with the other line and staff units in the organization?

    a. Does the administrative support staff make the job of the other departments easier to accomplish?

    b. Do the personnel in administrative support genuinely view members of other departments as their customers, who should be served and satisfied?

Evaluating Financial Capacity

An assessment of the strengths and weaknesses of an organization's *financial subsystem* is an integral part of the overall administrative audit. In some cases, because of cost-containment pressures, finance as well as other administrative activities are being decentralized throughout the organization. Regardless of the exact organizational arrangement, finance is an important function for all health care organizations. Exhibit 4–9 provides a list of the types of questions that should be asked when evaluating the strengths and weaknesses of the finance function within the organization.

After determining if the basic skills are available, it is important to evaluate

PERSPECTIVE   4-5

Telecommunications, Physicians, and Cost Savings

Telecommunication technology holds many promises for health care. Unfortunately, many people do not appreciate or are unaware of the potential value of this technology as a cost saver. For over a decade, educational institutions have used it to bring distant students to a teacher at a central location through television. What if physicians could diagnose health problems of people located in a farm community from their office in a major city? It could save millions of dollars in travel costs as well as improving the availability of services for individuals throughout the nation.

An experimental system called the Rural Health Telecommunications Network has been developed on a pilot basis by the Pennsylvania Bureau of Telecommunications. The pilot project, at a cost of $400,000, will have three parts: *telemedicine,* a two-way video and audio system for examination, diagnosis, consultation, and treatment; *teleradiology,* designed to "use telecommunications to practice radiology at a distance" by use of digitized medical images such as X rays and MRIs sent electronically; and *desktop medical conferencing,* using personal computers to operate a teleconference that combines video images, voices, and data. In electronically bringing patients to major medical centers, the network hopes to improve the quality of life in rural areas by making health care services available without physical travel and, in the process, make these rural areas more attractive to physicians because they will be able to easily interact with other professionals.

Source: Brian Miller, "Telecommunications Meets the Doctor," *Government Technology* 6 (August 1993), pp. 34–36.

EXHIBIT   4-9

Assessing Financial Strengths and Weaknesses

The Financial Staff

1. Is our financial staff adequate in terms of qualifications and number to provide the types of services needed to effectively manage a facility of our size and complexity?
2. Are we presently paying for external financial services that we could provide for ourselves given the capabilities of our existing financial staff?
3. Does our financial staff provide executive management with appropriate and timely data that can be incorporated into decision making?
4. Does our financial staff respond adequately to requests for specialized services that aid executive decision making?

EXHIBIT 4-9 cont'd

Information and Intelligence

1. Do we have the appropriate type of financial information system for our organization?
   a. Is the information provided to the appropriate people in a timely manner and in a form that is useful?
   b. Is there a process to ensure that the users of financial data have an input into the design of financial information systems and reports?
   c. Can our financial information system interact easily with the management information system of the organization?
2. Do we have the necessary archival capacity to ensure that we have baseline financial information on our own organization?
3. Do we have the appropriate data bases to ensure that we have the standards for financial performance in our industry?
4. Have we easy access to the archival storage and data bases so as to use them in financial decision making?

Technical Issues

1. Do we have an appropriate degree of financial liquidity to ensure that cash-flow problems do not develop?
   a. Are our liquidity ratios increasing or decreasing? Can we explain any changes that are taking place?
   b How do our liquidity ratios compare to those of similar health care organizations?
2. Is our operating margin (revenues less expenses) increasing or decreasing? Can we explain any changes that are taking place?
   a. How do our expenses compare with similar health care organizations?
   b. How do our revenues compare with similar health care organizations?
3. Are we satisfied with our present financial structure?
   a. Are we using the appropriate degree of financial leverage?
   b. How does our degree of leverage compare with similar health care organizations?
4. Are we achieving a satisfactory rate of financial growth?
   a. Can we obtain the necessary amount of financing to achieve our growth and development goals?
   b. Are we satisfied with our current financial strategies?
5. (If applicable) Are we doing a good job of tax planning?

Synergy

1. Are financial personnel in the department thought of primarily as naysayers who always "throw cold water" on new ideas because "we can't afford them"?
2. Do financial personnel talk and interact with people in other departments to find out what they really need from finance?

the responsiveness of the personnel in finance. For example, an audit of internal financial capabilities requires that the finance department listen to the users of financial data. In other words, how responsive is the financial staff in developing the kinds of reports needed for decision making and providing the information when it is needed?

Next, the quality of the *financial information system* should be examined. It is important to ensure that the financial information system is integrated into the larger management information system. The financial information system needs to be able to store historical data so that managers may track financial trends. In addition, information is needed concerning the performance of similar organizations relative to key indicators. Numerous data bases provide this type of information.

Finally, the technical capabilities of finance are important. The finance function should regularly track, report on, and make recommendations regarding liquidity, earnings, leverage, and other related indicators. Appendix B provides some illustrations of how financial measures of this nature can be developed and used. Only when the decision maker is convinced that the financial information is good and that qualified personnel are monitoring activities can the financial function be considered a true organizational strength and be used effectively in strategic decision making.

Evaluating the Marketing Capacity

The first step in an audit of the strengths and weaknesses of the *marketing subsystem* is an articulation and analysis of the organization's marketing philosophy. Many health care providers behave as if marketing is something the industry should not do. There was a time, not so long ago, when marketing was considered to be unprofessional for those involved in health care delivery. When a hospital or long-term care facility engaged in marketing its services, the activities were frequently referred to as *health education* or *public relations* rather than *marketing*. Exhibit 4–10 provides a list of key questions that health care managers should ask when evaluating the marketing function of a hospital, HMO, nursing home, or other health care organization.

The competitive realities in almost all sectors of health care make marketing an essential part of strategic management. Moreover, when properly performed, marketing aids consumers in making more informed choices about their health and the types of services available. The important point here is that strategic managers need to think carefully about the organization's philosophy concerning marketing before assessing the strengths and weaknesses using the checklist in Exhibit 4–10.

The internal assessment of the marketing staff is particularly important for health care organizations. Because marketing has not been a high priority, marketing activities have been assumed by individuals with little knowledge of the most effective concepts and tools. For the same reason, marketing information and intelligence systems have not been as highly developed as in other industries, and marketing research has been lacking. Therefore, important questions remain

---

EXHIBIT 4-10
Assessing Marketing Strengths and Weaknesses

Marketing Staff

1. Do we have adequately trained and innovative marketing personnel? Are they trained in the most up-to-date marketing tools and concepts?
2. Does our marketing department/function have sufficient input into new services and the promotion of existing services?
3. Do marketing personnel report to the CEO or another high-level administrator?
4. Are marketing personnel effectively interacting and working with operations, research and development, and other personnel?

Information and Intelligence

1. Does our marketing intelligence system provide us with valuable information about our patient base?
   a. Do we know the geographic origin of our patients?
   b. Do we have the information necessary to market our services to potential members of the medical staff and prospective patients? What do we know about the referral patterns of physicians who indirectly send patients to our facility?
2. Do we have the marketing information system necessary to support high-quality market research? If not, do we use the best available outside suppliers?
   a. Does our information system allow us to make accurate revenue forecasts?
   b. Do we have the marketing systems in place that are useful in analyzing the likely acceptance of new services and service delivery techniques?
3. Does our marketing information system provide us adequate data concerning competitive actions? Anticipated actions? Anticipated reactions?
   a. Is the marketing intelligence provided in a timely manner that allows us to develop alternative marketing strategies?
   b. What do we know about the relative market shares for our services mix?
4. What are our capabilities for tracing patient satisfaction levels?
5. Do our marketing systems keep us informed about our reputation in the relevant market area?

Technical Capabilities

1. Have we established attainable market share goals with regard to the services offered?
   a. Do we regularly evaluate market share changes for the services offered? Where are our various services in the service life cycle?
   b. Do we have effective strategies for allocating marketing resources for the various services offered by the organization?
   c. Have we developed an appropriate marketing mix for each market identified?
   d. Do we have a mechanism to generate and screen new service ideas? Do we research and test new service ideas with potential users before introducing them?
   e. Do we periodically review for patient satisfaction with existing services? Add new services? Delete services?
   f. What bases do we have for differentiating the services currently offered?

EXHIBIT 4 – 10 cont'd

2. Do we have satisfactory information about the areas where we have some pricing flexibility?
   a. For those areas where we have pricing flexibility, what is the price elasticity of the service?
   b. For those areas where we do not have control over pricing, are we containing costs?
   c. What is the customer (patient) view of our prices? How do our prices compare with those of our competitors?
3. Should the organization offer services through different channels of distribution (satellite clinics, nursing homes, HMOs, and so on)?
4. What positioning have we selected? Are we adequately supporting that position?
5. Are we doing a good job of promoting our services, staff, and location?
   a. Are all members of the professional and support staff aware of their role in marketing, and do they demonstrate a patient orientation?
   b. Do we have an adequate budget to promote our services, staff, and location?
   c. How do our promotional efforts compare to those of our competitors?
   d. Are there promotional media that we have not used that may be effective in "getting the word out" about our organization?

Synergy

1. Does the marketing function relate effectively with the other units in the organization?
2. Is marketing helpful in providing the research and advice necessary to market services to traditional as well as new groups of patients or clients?

for most health care organizations: "Have we communicated our organization's comparative advantage to the various publics we serve?" "Have we selected a position in the market that is already occupied by another organization?" "Do we have the financial and managerial strengths to take over that position in the market?" "Where do our patients live and work?" "Who are the physicians who refer patients to members of our medical staff?" "How can we make our services and facilities more appealing?"

Evaluating General Management Capacity

Identifying the strengths and weaknesses of the *general management subsystem* of a health care organization is one of the most difficult yet most essential aspects of internal assessment. When assessing general management's capabilities, the fundamental concern is accomplishing the basic management functions of planning, organizing, coordinating, and controlling. As an aid in focusing on these types of issues, examine Exhibit 4–11. It is important to note that all of these functions are facilitated by effective goal setting and coordination.

EXHIBIT 4 – 11
Assessing General Management Strengths and Weaknesses

Management Staff

1. Are our managers committed to planning and strategic management or are they easily diverted into a short-term orientation?
   a. Are managers committed to and practicing goal setting?
   b. Are managers effective communicators of the goals throughout the organization?
   c. Do managers have time to think strategically or are they engaged in continual fire fighting?
2. Are our managers comfortable delegating authority and providing experiences for others to develop decision-making skills?
   a. Do our managers effectively use the staff support available to them?
   b. Are our managers good role models for other members of the organization?
3. Do our managers know and apply the most effective motivation and leadership concepts?
   a. Is the evidence of effective management provided in our absenteeism and turnover rates?
   b. Are our managers effective in their interactions with the medical and support staffs?
4. Have our managers developed and made use of an effective control system?
   a. Do we have an effective budgeting system?
   b. Are we committed to preventive controls?
   c. Are our managers effective at providing positive discipline?
   d. Do managers consistently allocate resources based on contributions to goal attainment?

Information and Intelligence

1. Do our managers encourage effective two-way flows of information (up and down the organization)?
   a. Are employee suggestions seriously considered by managers at all levels?
   b. Do managers encourage innovative behavior and initiative on the part of employees?
2. Are our managers interested in and well informed about what is going on in the health care industry?
   a. Are our managers recognized for their leadership in the profession?
   b. Are our managers recognized in the organization as up-to-date and inspirational leaders?
   c. Do our managers possess and communicate a motivational vision for the organization?

Technical Issues

1. Does our organization have understood goals, procedures, and reward systems?
   a. Do our managers reward performance or loyalty?
   b. Is performance evaluation taken seriously and acted on by our managers?

EXHIBIT 4 – 11   *cont'd*

2. Do we have an organization structure that has been carefully designed and communicated?
   a. Is our organization chart representative of how work should be accomplished in the organization?
   b. Are our job descriptions well conceived and meaningful in assisting employees' understanding of what is expected?
3. Do our managers do an effective job in managing our organizational culture?
   a. Do our managers have a sense of organizational history sufficient to motivate high performance on the part of others?
   b. Do our managers provide good role models for nonmanagerial personnel?
4. Is the organization managed in a way that provides employees with a sense of security and at the same time offers motivation and fulfills a need to serve?

Synergy

1. Are all the general management systems properly designed and implemented to ensure that the different functional subsystems operate as a team rather than as individual units?

Coordinating Specialized Activities Health care organizations produce services by coordinating the human and nonhuman resources at their disposal. This presents particular challenges in health care because of the diverse backgrounds of the people needed to deliver high-quality services.

In the typical hospital, physicians, nurses, administrators, engineers, chaplains, and many other highly trained professionals attempt to work together for the benefit of the patient. In the public health sector, things are equally diverse. There are environmentalists, sanitation specialists, epidemiologists, and rabies-control experts in addition to physicians and nurses. Although the climate created by this diversity is exciting, each person brings his or her own unique way of thinking about, looking at, and doing things. In the absence of intentional managerial actions, this diversity will not result in the efficient delivery of services.

Specialization Provides Many Advantages In the case of health care, where the risks resulting from poor service delivery are high, highly trained personnel are important for risk management and quality control. Often innovation is encouraged because these experts can develop improvements in tasks that would not be possible with less training.

Specialization, however, has its costs both managerially and individually. Sometimes the increased efficiency provided by specialization makes the task less personally rewarding and increases boredom. The daily work of a family practitioner, for example, is frequently more interesting as a very diverse patient base is examined. The specialist in cardiovascular disease, on the other hand, sees a much less diverse group of patients so that the typical day can become more routine and fatiguing. In a very extreme case (such as a person working on a factory assembly line), work may lose its meaning, which can result in absenteeism, turnover, and accidents.

It is important that managers respect the diversity of the work force and at the same time ensure that high-quality services are provided where and when they are needed. In this sense, the strategic capacity of a health care organization to manage its human resources is determined to a great extent by how well employees know and are committed to the goals of the organization.

Goal Setting as a Strategic Tool The importance of goal setting has been a recurring theme in the literature of management. The following chapter will deal specifically with issues of organizational purpose, vision, mission, and objectives – in other words, with strategic goals and goal setting. It is important to emphasize at this point the value of effective goal setting as a tool of strategic management.

In a professionally diverse (specialized) and high-technology environment, clearly stated and communicated goals are important because they enable managers to:

1. Focus the attention of employees and other managers on the really important outcomes required by the organization. These outcomes include quality, compassion, and reasonable profitability, not the number of meetings attended and memoranda written.
2. Help employees and other managers direct the appropriate amount of energy toward different tasks. Energy is spent pursuing a goal in proportion to how well employees accept the legitimacy and importance of the goal. When goals are communicated and reinforced, higher levels of energy are obtained in pursuing them.
3. Provide challenging goals that have been shown to increase an employee's commitment to attaining the goal over longer periods of time.[22]

Perhaps one of the most convincing arguments for the use of goal setting as a tool for strategic management is its importance in building organizational excellence. As the health care environment becomes increasingly competitive, simply being a well-managed hospital, health maintenance organization, or public health department will not be enough to ensure survival and prosperity. Often the difference between being merely well managed and truly excellent is little more than employees knowing what the organization stands for (its philosophy, goals, and so on), accepting the philosophy, and believing they have something to do with determining the future direction of the organization.

When employees know what the goals are, believe in them, and are committed to accomplishing them, patients are made to feel comfortable, employees take pride in their work, and organizational excellence is achieved. The most practical tool managers have for building this important strategic capability of effective coordination, as Chapter 5 will illustrate, is goal setting.

Assessing the Strategic Capacity of the Physical Facilities

The work of health care organizations takes place within a physical setting, referred to as the *health care facility.* The *physical facilities subsystem,* however, includes much more than the shell of the hospital, physician's clinic, long-term care facility, or public health office. Frequently, health care facilities are referred to as *campuses* because they do, in fact, represent a collection of inpatient facilities, professional buildings, parking lots, and pharmacies. The convenience, perceived safety, and overall "friendliness" of a facility can be one aspect of competitive advantage or it can be a significant drain on resources and limit the options an organization has in the future. Exhibit 4–12 provides a checklist for some of the important determinants of an organization's strategic capabilities relative to its facilities.

EXHIBIT 4 – 12
Assessing the Strengths and Weaknesses of the Physical Facility

Facilities Support Staff

1. Does our skilled craft, custodial, and maintenance staff have the proper qualifications and training to support our organizational mission?
   a. Do we properly verify the qualifications and experience of facilities support personnel?
   b. Do we have an efficient mix of skilled craft, custodial, and maintenance personnel?
   c. Are the morale and performance of the physical facilities support personnel adequate to support our organizational mission?
   d. Do we have a regular and systematic method for tracking the morale and performance of physical facilities support personnel?
   e. Do we have an incentive system that rewards high-performing facilities support personnel?
2. Do we have a sufficient level of facilities support personnel to allow adequate staffing on all shifts to support patient and clinical staff needs?
   a. Do our facilities support staff supervisors do a good job of scheduling personnel?
   b. Do we have a facilities support staffing plan that allows us to project resource needs into the immediate future?
   c. Are our facilities support personnel compensated at a level competitive with other employees in the area?
   d. Do we have a competitive benefits package for facilities support personnel?

Information and Intelligence

1. Do we have the information system necessary to provide the facilities support personnel with the information they need to do their jobs?
   a. Do we have an up-to-date specification for all existing facilities and a master plan for future facilities management issues?

EXHIBIT 4 - 12 *cont'd*

    b. Do we have the internal data processing capabilities needed to support the facilities support operations?

    c. Would any available computer hardware (i.e., harsh environment, handheld computers) or software (facility planning templates) aid us in efficiently and effectively utilizing our physical facilities?

2. Is our existing facilities management software adequately designed and updated?

    a. Are we automated to the extent necessary to support our organizational mission?

    b. Are our communications properly documented to provide for efficient and effective work flow and protect us relative to risk management?

    c. Do we have established systems for developing fair and effective priority systems for facilities support work?

Technical Capabilities

1. Are our patient care facilities appropriate to support our organizational mission and strategy?

    a. Do our physical facilities represent a competitive advantage or disadvantage with regard to the medical staff?

    b. How do our patients view the adequacy, cleanliness, and accessibility of our physical facilities?

    c. How do our employees view the adequacy, cleanliness, and accessibility of our physical facilities?

2. Are our physical facilities adequate in light of contemporary environmental and social trends?

    a. Do we check our physical facilities on a regular basis to ensure against the presence of toxic substances?

    b. Are our physical facilities engineered in a manner that makes them accessible to handicapped individuals?

    c. Is accessibility a major consideration in the planning and design of present and future expansion of facilities?

3. Are our physical facilities appropriately located to support our organizational mission and strategy?

    a. Are our facilities secure, to the extent possible and reasonable, from random and systematic crime?

    b. Is our security system directed toward crime prevention as well as damage control?

    c. Are our security personnel properly trained and supported to deal with law enforcement and crime prevention matters?

    d. Do we have adequate parking and other related facilities to support our patients and employees?

    e. Is adequacy of parking and related functions an integral part of all physical facilities planning?

4. Is our facilities utilization rate sufficient to obtain economies of scale?

    a. Are there activities presently done manually that should be automated either for technical or economic reasons?

EXHIBIT 4 – 12   cont'd

> b. Are there areas where multiple usage of facilities would increase the efficiency of space management?
>
> **Synergy**
>
> 1. Does our physical facilities staff understand and appreciate the importance of its role in accomplishing the organizational mission?
>   a. Are facilities support staff involved in planning for the future of the organization?
>   b. Are physical facilities support staff available to personnel throughout the organization to assist in future planning activities?
>   c. Are facility operations a part of the planning of future capital expansion programs?

SUMMARY AND CONCLUSIONS

A variety of topics relating to the internal strengths and weaknesses of health care organizations have been introduced. With the information presented, and that covered in the previous two chapters, it is possible to relate internal strengths and weaknesses to the important external forces that affect an organization.

The nature of organizational cultures was introduced in this chapter because this shared and learned way of doing things can be a strategic strength or weakness, depending on whether it encourages managers and employees to act aggressively and seek new ways of doing things or enslaves them to the past. Organizational culture, as was illustrated, can be strong or weak and can influence a wide range of factors, from leadership styles to organizational politics. The culture can have much to do with the commitment to quality observed in an organization.

Strategically, organizational culture is important because it is a major determinant of how well the organization "fits" within the external environment. The Mayo Clinic culture, which focuses on patients, excellence, and knowledge, would not transfer to environments dedicated specifically to profit maximization, volume generation, or merely adequate levels of quality control. In this sense, there is a close association between organizational and operating cultures. The organizational culture that emphasizes quality and related values has the potential to directly affect operations and the bottom line. The strength of the culture is a factor in changing organizations and ensuring the "strategic fit" necessary for long-term success. The challenges and processes of changing organizational cultures will be examined in more detail in Chapter 12.

The remainder of the chapter concentrated on the staffing, information and intelligence, and technical aspects of the important organizational subsystems or functional areas. The objective was to evaluate a number of dimensions or questions in order to provide a guide for determining whether each function represented an internal strength or weakness.

Although it appears to be excessively operational, this audit has a great deal of strategic importance. Collectively, the strength of the line and staff operations has much to do with the strategic capabilities of any health care organization. A viable health care organization must have highly qualified and dedicated clinical personnel who provide and support direct patient care. This is the front line in the strategic arsenal. However, the clinical personnel must be supported by administrative procedures, systems, and people who make their work easier; marketing approaches and philosophies that provide an adequate patient base; financial stability; and a general management system that coordinates all the diverse units, procedures, and personnel. Finally, work takes place in physical facilities, which may become an important factor in the competitive advantage or disadvantage of a health care organization and influences the satisfaction of employees.

KEY TERMS AND CONCEPTS IN STRATEGIC MANAGEMENT

activity/cost chain
administrative services subsystem
clinical subsystem
common causes
competitive advantage
continuous quality improvement (CQI)

distinctive competence
financial subsystem
general management subsystem
internal strength
internal weakness
marketing subsystem
organizational culture

physical facilities subsystem
special causes
strategic capacity
strategic effectiveness
total quality management (TQM)

QUESTIONS FOR CLASS DISCUSSION

1. Discuss the statement "Internal strengths and weaknesses have meaning only when related to external opportunities and threats."
2. What is the difference between a distinctive competence and a competitive advantage?
3. What is the difference between objective and subjective strengths and weaknesses? What is the difference between absolute and relative strengths and weaknesses?
4. What is an activity/cost chain? What is the importance of this chain to strategic management?
5. Why is the organizational culture considered a key factor in assessing the strategic strengths and weaknesses of a health care organization? How can culture be a strength? How can it be a weakness? How are organizational culture and operational culture related?

6. Do you think the strength of an organization's culture can favorably affect its bottom line? Give an example to support your response.
7. In your opinion, is the total quality movement in health care something that is real and will make an important contribution to patient care or merely another management fad? Support your answer with specific examples.
8. What are the five major characteristics shared by most contemporary approaches to total quality management? Which, if any, of these is most important? Why?
9. In the quality program of Deming, what is the essential difference between common causes and special causes of quality problems? Why is this distinction important?
10. What are the major areas organizations should monitor when assessing the relative strengths and weaknesses of their sub-

systems? Are any of these subsystems more or less important than any others?

11. What is the difference between organizational information and an organizational intelligence system? Which is more important?

12. Why has marketing received less attention in health care than other functions such as finance and operations?

13. Why is the ability to coordinate all the organizational subsystems so important in an evaluation of the strengths or weaknesses of the general management of an organization?

NOTES

1. Chester I. Barnard, *The Functions of the Executive* (Cambridge, Massachusetts: Harvard University Press, 1938), pp. 195–196. See also William G. Scott, *Chester I. Barnard and the Guardians of the Managerial State* (Lawrence: University of Kansas Press, 1992).

2. See S. R. Eastaugh and J. A. Eastaugh, "Prospective Payment System: Steps to Enhance Quality, Efficiency, and Regionalization," *Health Care Management Review* 11, no. 4 (Fall 1986), pp. 37–52.

3. Yvan Allaire and Jean Firsirouto, "Theories of Organizational Culture," *Organizational Studies* 5, no. 3 (1984), pp. 193–226. For other sources on organizational culture see T. E. Deal and A. A. Kennedy, *Corporate Cultures* (Reading, Massachusetts: Addison-Wesley Publishing, 1982); Vijay Sathe, *Culture and Related Corporate Realities* (Homewood, Illinois: Richard D. Irwin, 1985); and Edgar H. Schein, *Organizational Culture and Leadership* (San Francisco: Jossey-Bass, 1985). Also see Malcom J. Morgan, "How Corporate Culture Drives Strategy," *Long Range Planning* 26, no. 2 (1993), pp. 110–118.

4. Christian Scholz, "Corporate Culture and Strategy – The Problem with Strategic Fit," *Long Range Planning* 20, no. 3 (1987), p. 80; and Ralph Stacey, "Strategy as Order Emerging from Chaos," *Long Range Planning* 26, no. 1 (1993), pp. 10–17.

5. H. J. Hagedorn, "Everybody into the Pool: And Other Mysteries Solved by Corporate Culture Detectives," *Across the Board* (October 1984), pp. 26–34. Also see R.

H. Kilmann, M. J. Saxton, and R. Serpa, "Issues in Understanding and Changing Culture," *California Management Review* 28, no. 2 (1986), pp. 87–94.

6. Robert W. Fleming, "Understanding the Mayo Culture," *Medical Group Management* (May/June, 1989), pp. 46–49.

7. B. Z. Posner, J. M. Kouzes, and W. H. Schmidt, "Shared Values Make a Difference: An Empirical Test of Corporate Culture," *Human Resource Management* 24, no. 3 (1985), pp. 293–309.

8. Frederick J. Wenzel, "Corporate Culture: The Silent Governor," *Medical Group Management* (May/June 1989), pp. 33–42.

9. See A. F. Buno, J. L. Bowditch, and J. W. Lewis III, "When Cultures Collide: The Anatomy of a Merger," *Human Relations* 5 (March 1985), pp. 477–500; and D. R. Denison, "Bringing Corporate Culture to the Bottom Line," *Organizational Dynamics* 12 (Autumn 1984), pp. 5–22.

10. D. M. Berwick, A. B. Godfrey, and J. Roessner, *Curing Health Care: New Strategies for Quality Improvement* (San Francisco: Jossey-Bass Publishers, 1990).

11. Marie Sinioris, "The Next Generation of Health Care Quality," *Hospitals* 63 (February 5, 1989), p. 78. Also see Mary T. Koska, "Adopting Deming's Quality Improvement Ideas: A Case Study," *Hospitals* 64 (July 5, 1990), pp. 58–60ff.

12. Thomas W. Nolan, "Understanding Variation," *Quality Progress* (May 1990), p. 70.

13. A. D. Kaluzny, C. P. McLaughlin, and K. Simpson, "Applying Total Quality Management Concepts to Public Health Orga-

nizations," *Public Health Reports* 107, no. 3 (1992), pp. 257–264.

14. Clare Crawford-Mason and Lloyd Dobyns, *Quality or Else* (Boston: Houghton Mifflin Company, 1991).

15. F. W. Smith, "Our Human Side of Quality," *Quality Progress* (October 1990), p. 20.

16. L. L. Berry, "Five Imperatives for Improving Service Quality," *Sloan Management Review* 31 (Summer 1991), pp. 29–38.

17. W. Edwards Deming, *Out of Crisis* (Cambridge, Massachusetts: MIT Press, 1986), p. 20.

18. W. Jack Duncan and Joseph G. Van Matre, "The Gospel According to Deming: Is It Really New?" *Business Horizons* 33 (July/August 1990), pp. 3–9.

19. W. Edwards Deming, *Quality, Productivity, and Competitive Position* (Cambridge, Massachusetts: MIT Center for Advanced Engineering Study, 1982).

20. Philip B. Crosby, *Quality Is Free* (New York: McGraw-Hill, 1979). For elaborations on the fourteen point program, see especially pp. 132–139 and 175–258.

21. Joseph M. Juran and Frank M. Gryna, Jr., *Quality Planning and Analysis* (New York: McGraw-Hill, 1980).

22. For a complete discussion of the relationship between goal setting and performance, see E. A. Locke and G. P. Latham, *A Theory of Goal Setting and Task Performance* (Englewood Cliffs, New Jersey: Prentice-Hall, 1991).

ADDITIONAL READINGS

Bridgers, W. F., *Health Care Reform: The Dilemma and a Pathway for the Health Care System* (St. Louis: G. W. Manning, 1992). This insightful look at health care reform examines the issue of quality in health care from the perspective of accountability. Clearly, this is becoming an increasingly common and useful perspective from which to view the issue of quality.

Gaucher, E. J., and R. J. Coffey, *Total Quality in Healthcare: From Theory to Practice* (San Francisco: Jossey-Bass Publishers, 1993). This book reports shared experiences with the implementation of TQM programs in major medical centers and health care organizations. It includes practical advice for developing an organization that can successfully employ continuous improvement techniques.

Gehani, R. Ray, "Quality Value-Chain: A Meta-Synthesis of Frontiers of the Quality Movement," *Academy of Management Executive* 7, no. 2 (1993), pp. 29–42. A review of the evolution of the quality movement along with discussions of the champions who discovered the new frontiers of quality. It illustrates how each champion has a unique philosophy of quality based on his background and experience.

Hammer, Michael, and James Champy, *Reengineering the Corporation: A Manifesto for Business Revolution* (New York: Harper Business, 1993). By the "father of the reengineering movement" (Hammer), this book provides the essential components of an important trend in the conduct and design of organizational operations. Although acknowledging that TQM and reengineering share many things in common such as concern for the process, important differences are noted.

Johnson, Gerry, "Managing Strategic Change – Strategy, Culture, and Action," *Long Range Planning* 25, no. 1 (1992), pp. 28–36. This article discusses the link among the development of strategy, dimensions of organizational culture, and managerial action. Guidelines are developed for effecting successful strategic and culture change.

Kaluzny, A. D., C. P. McLaughlin, and C. P. Simpson, "Applying Total Quality Management Concepts to Public Health Organizations," *Public Health Reports* 107, no. 3 (1992), pp. 257–264. TQM, in this article, is discussed with specific reference to the public health environment. It is noted that TQM here, as elsewhere, focuses on work processes and applies analytical and behavioral concepts to improve these processes.

Kennedy, M., J. A. Prevost, M. P. Carr, and J. W. Dilley, "A Roundtable Discussion: Hospital Leaders Discuss Quality Improvement Implementation Issues," *Journal of Quality Improvement* 18 (March 3, 1992), pp. 78–97. Hospital executives discuss a series of issues not often addressed in many academic approaches to total quality management – the implementation of programs. It is pointed out that many programs fail, not because they have design flaws, but because the implementation is not successful.

Koska, Mary T., "The Facts Behind Accreditation Success Stories," *Hospitals* (April 5, 1992), pp. 46–47. A discussion of accreditation issues for hospitals. The role of quality and the necessity of integrating quality improvement programs in all aspects of hospital operations are discussed throughout.

Nystrom, Paul C., "Organizational Cultures, Strategies, and Commitments in Health Care Organizations," *Health Care Management Review* 18, no. 1 (1993), pp. 43–49. This study of thirteen health care organizations illustrates how cultural norms and values affect commitment and job satisfaction of managers and executive secretaries. The results show that organizations pursuing a consistent strategy tend to possess strong cultures and weak cultures are associated with inconsistent strategies.

Peters, Tom, *Liberation Management: Necessary Disorganization for the Nanosecond Nineties* (New York: Alfred A. Knopf, 1992). Peters provides a comprehensive discussion of what he believes it takes to be successful in rapidly changing organizational environments. In the world of the future, as painted by Peters, there will be few organizations as we know them today. Most work, in his view, will be conducted by semipermanent networks of people doing "brainwork" in relatively small groups.

CHAPTER **5**

Mission, Vision, and Values

"There is no more powerful engine driving an organization toward excellence and long range success than an attractive, worthwhile, and achievable vision of the future, widely shared."

– Burt Nanus

LEARNING OBJECTIVES

After completing this chapter you should:

1. Understand the relationships among organizational mission, vision, values, key performance areas, and strategic objectives.
2. Appreciate the importance of the manager's role as the "keeper of the organization's vision."
3. Be familiar with the characteristics and components of organizational mission statements.
4. Be able to recognize well-developed mission statements.
5. Recognize the important characteristics of well-conceived organizational vision and values.
6. Recognize the characteristics of key performance areas and strategic objectives.
7. Understand the motivational potential of clearly established and communicated directional strategies.

INTRODUCTORY INCIDENT

**One Hospital That Does Not Allow
Reality to Distort Its Vision**

On paper it is not an encouraging case. The community has an unemployment rate in excess of 10 percent. Seventy-four percent of the high school students drop out, and the median family income is less than $16,000 per year. More than 3,880 cases of AIDS have been reported.

In West Baltimore, Everard O. Rutledge, the president and CEO of Liberty Medical Center, Inc., refuses to allow his vision of the future to be blurred by discouraging statistics. His vision for the 282-bed community hospital includes a $5.5 million urban medical institute to serve as the focal point for community health education and prevention.

Although Liberty Medical Center provides $12 million of uncompensated care per year (second highest in Maryland), Rutledge's vision of the urban medical institute is a place where patients find "one-stop medical shopping" rather than the existing "fractionated care." The medical center plans a number of campaigns, the first of which is against the "clinical killers" – cancer, heart disease, hypertension, diabetes, HIV/AIDS, and substance abuse. All of these killers disproportionately affect the patients at Liberty Medical Center and will require aggressive action to have any real impact. According to Rutledge, "you can't just send people from clinic to clinic to clinic." Paul F. Kelly, outreach coordinator, believes that the "key to outreach is being able to go out to a population that is elusive and be able to drag them back up here."

Source: Farah Kostreski, "MD Hospital Works to Meet Its Community's Health Care Needs," *AHA News* (December 6, 1993), p. 5.

MISSION AND VISION AS DIRECTIONAL STRATEGIES

The basic concepts of strategic management in health care organizations have been introduced, the importance of external factors in the environment have been emphasized, and the methods of assessing strengths and weaknesses developed. Only after managers have completed this series of preliminary activities are they able to carefully look at what the organization really is today and what it should be in the future. The next step is to begin the task of generating and communicating the directional strategies or those decisions that set the fundamental direction for the organization. This means determining what the organization is and its distinctiveness (mission), what it wants to be (vision), and agreeing on the values or guiding principles it will follow and adhere to as the organization moves into the future. Mission and vision are directional strategies. Once identified they allow managers to move to more operational concerns – key performance areas and strategic objectives.

This chapter is about organizational goals or the end results that health care organizations hope to achieve. It is also about values, as discussed in the preceding chapter, because what the organization achieves must always involve a concern for how management accomplishes results as well as the legitimacy of the outcomes. The present chapter's fit into the overall plan of the book is illustrated in Exhibit 5–1.

Mission, vision, values, and strategic objectives are types of organizational goals or desired end results. The mission attempts to capture the organization's

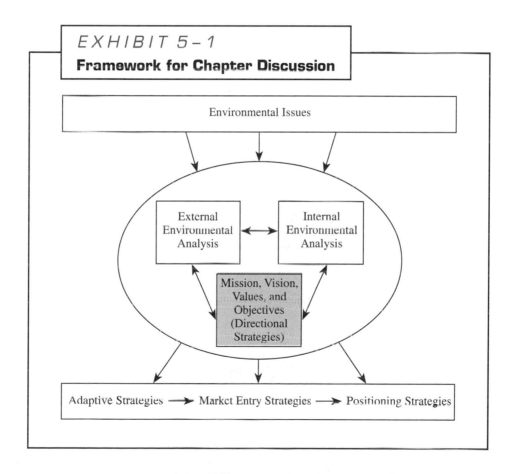

EXHIBIT 5–1

Framework for Chapter Discussion

distinctive purpose or reason for being. The vision is how the managers, employees, physicians, patients, and other interested groups want the organization to be when it is accomplishing its purpose or mission – the hope for the future. Values are the principles (innovation, integrity, teamwork, and so on) that guide decision making and are held dear by members of the organization. These are principles the managers and employees will not compromise while they achieve the mission and pursue the vision.

Once the mission statement is properly conceived it is possible to identify a relatively few key performance areas for the organization. These areas identify the activities that absolutely must be accomplished if the organization is to achieve its purpose and realize its mission. Finally, relative to each key performance area, several strategic objectives are needed to provide tangible performance targets for the organization. The mission is a statement of distinctiveness, the vision is a hope, the values are guiding principles, key performance areas must be accomplished for success, and objectives are specific quantitative desired end results. The conceptual framework for this analysis is summarized in Exhibit 5–2.

ORGANIZATIONAL PURPOSE AND MISSION

Chester Barnard, in *The Functions of the Executive,* stated that only three things are needed to have an organization: (1) communication, (2) a willingness to serve, and (3) a common purpose. The inculcation of the "belief in the real existence

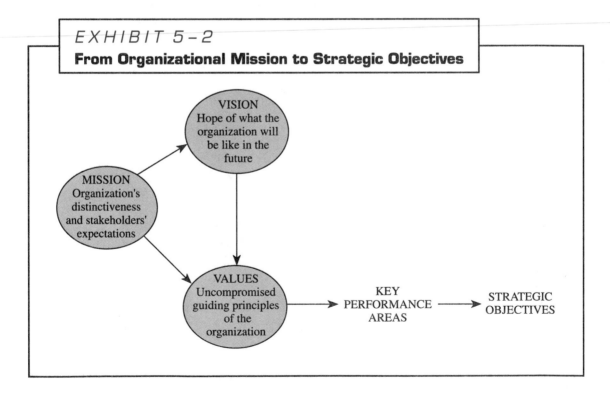

EXHIBIT 5–2
From Organizational Mission to Strategic Objectives

of a common purpose" is, according to Bernard, "the essential executive function."[1] This purpose, among other things, helps managers make sense of the environment. When the purpose of an organization is clearly understood, the complexity of the environment can be reduced and organized in a way that can be analyzed in light of the goals the organization wishes to achieve.[2]

For example, if the CEO of a large managed-care plan looks at all the changes taking place in the organization's macroenvironment, these may appear confusing and overpowering. Can anyone effectively track the changes taking place in the biotechnology, cultural values, and political arenas? However, if the CEO were to focus on only those aspects relating to the elderly such as the aging trend of the population, the increased financial condition of this group of aging people, and selected social values, from the perspective of the mission of the managed-care plan, the task becomes more manageable.

The common purpose (mission) to which Barnard referred is the reason that organizations exist. Some organizations exist to make money for the owners, some are founded to provide health care to indigent patients, others are started to deliver health services in as convenient a way as possible or to provide the care needed by groups of individuals who belong to the same managed-care plan.

Mission: A Statement of Distinctiveness

In the hierarchy of *goals* (end results and organizational plans to accomplish them), the mission is the most general. Although a well-conceived mission is general, it is more concrete than vision. Organizational missions are not expressions of hope. On the contrary, they are attempts to capture the essence of the organizational purpose and commit it to writing.

Unfortunately, mission statements are rarely the true "living documents" that are capable of inspiring high performance. One leading authority on strategic planning stated that most mission statements are "worthless."[3] Surveys of strategic planners in all types of organizations frequently surprise researchers with the relatively small number of organizations that actually have formal mission statements and, of those that do, the few who actually use them. One study of hospital mission statements found that almost 85 percent of the respondents had mission statements but most of the managers who completed the survey did not perceive a high level of commitment to the statement by employees or that individual actions were very much influenced by the mission.[4] A more recent study of state-level departments of public health indicated that more than 90 percent had formal, written mission statements.[5]

Despite the frequency with which formal mission statements are encountered, a great deal of disagreement remains regarding their value and the influence these statements actually have on behavior within organizations. This is unfortunate, because the mission statement is a crucially important part of strategic goal setting. It is the "superordinate goal" that stands the test of time and assists top management in navigating through periods of turbulence and change.[6] It is, in other words, the "stake in the ground" that provides the anchor for strategic planning and management. It must be emphasized, however, that mission statements, even at their best, can never be substitutes for well-conceived and strongly formulated strategies.

An organizational mission is a broadly defined but enduring statement of purpose that distinguishes a health care organization from other organizations of its type and identifies the scope of its operations in product, service, and market (competitive) terms.[7] When formulated correctly and used properly, mission statements force managers in health care organizations to ask a series of questions. The answers radically affect how the organization performs. These questions include:

1. Are we not doing anything new that we should be doing? Perhaps an academic medical center, after analyzing the environment and studying its own strengths and weaknesses, determines that it should purchase a long-term care facility. Historically, the medical center has not been involved in long-term care, but the aging population and the need to train personnel to work with the elderly suggest that the time is right to alter the mission to include long-term care facilities.

2. Are we doing some things now that we should not be doing? The same academic medical center, after proper analysis, may conclude that its burn unit no longer serves the purpose for which it was created and decides that the resources dedicated to the unit could be better used in other ways.

3. Are we doing some things now that we should continue to do, but in a different way? Perhaps the academic medical center concludes that it should continue to provide certain kinds of technician programs to train needed personnel but that it should no longer try to do it in the traditional manner. Perhaps a joint venture with a local junior college, where most of the classroom training could be conducted, would be better for everyone.

Characteristics of Mission Statements

The mission statement definition presented previously highlights several important characteristics. Some of the more important will be illustrated using the mission statement of the Mt. Sinai Hospital Medical Center in Perspective 5–1.

1. *Missions are broadly defined statements of purpose.* Well-formulated mission statements are written and communicated to those involved in doing the work of the organization. They are broad but also, in a sense, specific. That is, mission statements should be vague enough to allow for innovation and expansion into new activities when advisable, yet narrow enough to provide direction.

2. *Mission statements are enduring.* The purpose, and consequently the mission, of an organization does not change often and should be enduring. People are committed to ideas and causes that remain relatively stable over time.

3. *Mission statements should underscore the uniqueness of the organization.* Good missions distinguish the organization from all others of its type.

4. *Mission statements should identify the scope of operations in terms of service and market.* It is important that the mission statement specify what

PERSPECTIVE 5-1

The Mission of Mount Sinai Hospital Medical Center, Chicago

"Mount Sinai Hospital Medical Center is committed to the health and well-being of all those we serve. We accomplish this through: (1) Efficient and compassionate delivery of quality health care to our patients, regardless of their ability to pay; (2) Continuous improvement in the quality of the care and service we provide; (3) Leadership that involves and empowers our local communities in the development, advocacy and implementation of innovative solutions to problems that affect so-cial, economic and individual health and well-being; (4) Education and training of physicians and other health care profes-sionals to ensure the future availability of comprehensive health services for our patients; and (5) Basic and applied research relevant to the health care needs of our communities."

Source: From Generation to Generation: Building A Healthy Family, 1992 Annual Report, Mount Sinai Hospital Medical Center.

business the organization is in (health care) and who it believes are the primary stakeholders.

In the case of Mount Sinai Hospital Medical Center, the mission statement makes it clear that the medical center is a major competitor in the delivery of health care and is committed to the local community. At the same time, the mission precludes Mount Sinai from entering industries such as textiles or heavy manufacturing but allows the center to maintain its options to actively participate in other areas such as home health care, health maintenance organizations, and so on.

Although not in the health care industry, one of America's best known business firms illustrates the enduring nature of a mission. More than two decades after its founder, Thomas Watson, described IBM's purpose, Frank Cary, then chairman, stated: "We've changed our technology, changed our organization, changed our marketing and manufacturing techniques many times, and we expect to go on changing. But through all this change his [Watson's] basic beliefs remain."[8]

This should not imply, however, that the mission will never or should never change. New technologies, demographic trends, and so on, might be very good reasons to rethink the mission of an organization. For example, in view of the graying of the American population Gerber, the leading producer of baby food, has done well to move from the position of "Babies Are Our Business" to consider as well the special dietary demands of an aging population.

These characteristics of mission statements illustrate the essential properties of well-conceived and communicated mission statements. They outline worthy ideals that are not often achieved by strategic managers in business firms or health care institutions. Nevertheless, the mission provides direction. Good mission statements are not easy to write, but fortunately there is general agreement on what they should include.

Components of Mission Statements

There is no single way to develop and write mission statements. The mission, to define the uniqueness of an organization, must highlight those things that constitute this uniqueness. A study of the mission statements of over 200 of the Fortune 500 companies noted eight things that are frequently included.[9] Some of the more important items follow, illustrated with the use of mission statements from a variety of health care institutions.

1. *Mission statements target customers and markets.* Frequently the mission statement provides evidence of the kind of customers or patients the organization seeks to serve and the markets where it intends to compete. The mission statement of a long-term care facility, for example, might make explicit the organization's intent to serve patients with special needs, such as those suffering from Alzheimer's disease, as well as general geriatric patients.

    Perspective 5–2 presents the mission statement of the Children's Hospital of Wisconsin, which emphasizes, as does the name of the institution, that children are the patients the hospital is dedicated to serving. As the only children's hospital in the state, it is clear that patient care, research, and teaching activities all revolve around the unique needs of children.

PERSPECTIVE 5–2

Mission Statement: Children's Hospital of Wisconsin

Children's Hospital of Wisconsin, the only children's hospital in the state of Wisconsin, is an independent, private, not-for-profit regional pediatric center whose mission is to:

1. Provide comprehensive health care services to children appropriate for their special needs;

2. Provide leadership, experience, and expertise as a community and state resource to advocate for the health and welfare of children;

3. Be the center for the education of those requiring experience in the care of children; and

4. Support research activities directed at obtaining new knowledge and a better understanding of the health problems of children.

Source: Public documents of the Children's Hospital of Wisconsin.

2. *Mission statements indicate the principal services delivered by the organization.* A specialized health care organization such as Hospice Care, Inc., would highlight the special services it provides in its mission statement. A less specialized organization such as the Iowa Department of Public Health would have to outline a more comprehensive series of services, as illustrated in Perspective 5–3.

    The Iowa Department of Public Health attempts to fulfill its public health responsibilities to the citizens of Iowa by providing a series of services outlined in the mission statement. Although this list is clearly not comprehensive of the services provided, the department identifies a series of research, regulatory, administrative, and educational services that it intends to provide. This mission statement effectively identifies the department as a research and evaluation unit, an organization that enforces public health laws, an administrator of contracts, and a health promotion and educational organization.

3. *Mission statements specify the geographical area within which the organization intends to concentrate.* This element is most frequently included when there is a regional aspect to the organization's service delivery. A state public health department would clearly confine its area of concern to the state boundaries. The same is true of county and municipal health facilities except where referrals from outside the area constitute a significant part of the total operations. The Baptist Memorial Hospital East was built to serve the rapidly growing population of the East Memphis,

---

PERSPECTIVE 5–3

Mission Statement: Iowa Department of Public Health

The Iowa Department of Public Health exists to promote, protect, and ensure the health and well being of Iowans, and provide for access, quality, and affordability of services. The department promotes health and prevents disease by:

- *Conducting research, planning, and evaluating* as a basis for initiating and revising programs and policies;
- *Assuring compliance* with public health laws through regulation and enforcement;

- *Administering state and local statutory requirements and programs* through direct and contracted services; and
- *Promoting and supporting health and well being* through education and consultation.

<hr width="120">

Source: Iowa Department of Public Health, *1991 Annual Report,* Des Moines.

Tennessee, suburbs to relieve the increasing patient load at the Baptist Memorial Medical Center in downtown Memphis.

4. *Mission statements identify the organization's philosophy.* Frequently the mission of an organization will include statements about unique beliefs, values, aspirations, and priorities. This is often seen in health facilities operated by religious groups.

   Perspective 5–4 shows the mission statement for Wesley Homes. The mission statement is supplemented by an accompanying statement of philosophy. The philosophy statement underscores the organization's commitment to the Judeo-Christian tradition that affirms that aging has a purpose in life and that family and society are strengthened to the extent that elders are valued.

5. *Mission statements include confirmations of the organization's preferred self-image.* The manner in which a health care organization views itself may constitute a uniqueness that should be included in the mission. The mission statement of the South Carolina Department of Health and Environmental Control emphasizes the department's image of itself as the principal advisor on matters of health. In Arkansas, the mission statement of the state health department refers to the department as the "catalyst" to improve health care in the state. In Delaware, the department of public health views itself as a leader and builder of partnerships to improve health.

6. *Mission statements specify the organization's desired public image.* This might manifest itself in statements such as the organization's desire to be a "good citizen" in the communities where its operations are located or a similar concern.

PERSPECTIVE 5–4
Wesley Homes: A Mission Built on a Strong Philosophy

"Our mission is to support the independence and self-esteem of older people wherever they reside . . . to encourage understanding and acceptance of the aging process . . . to strengthen the bonds between older people and their families . . . to enhance people's ability to make responsible decisions about aging . . . to minister to the physical, psychological, social, and spiritual needs of the aging individual . . . to serve as a resource to the community, encouraging healthy aging and effective approaches to care and services . . . to provide charity within our means . . . and to advocate a society that values all ages."

Source: Promotional brochure from Wesley Homes.

The mission statement in Perspective 5–5 of the Health Care Apostolate East Central Province of the Daughters of Charity of Saint Vincent de Paul clearly provides an indication of how the religious community wishes to be viewed by others. In addition, the statement of mission tells everyone how the Daughters of Charity view themselves.

Not every one of the characteristics discussed can be included in a single mission statement. Any particular statement will likely include one or several of these aspects but almost never will all of the components be included. Interestingly, in the study of mission statements previously noted, it was suggested that higher performing organizations generally have more comprehensive mission statements. Moreover, it seemed that components such as organizational philosophy, self-concept, and desired public image were particularly associated with higher performing organizations in the sample studied.

Building a Mission Statement: The Alabama Medicaid Agency

The Alabama Medicaid Agency (ALMA) was originally established in 1973 as a unit in the Department of Public Health. When the agency was founded in 1973, it employed fewer than 100 people. Today, ALMA is a separate unit of government with its own commissioner, almost 600 employees, and a budget of more than $1 billion annually.

PERSPECTIVE 5–5
Mission Statement: Daughters of Charity

The Daughters of Charity extend the healing ministry of Christ wherever they serve in a spirit of humility, simplicity, and charity. In affirming our philosophy, we believe our purposes [mission] are:

- To witness to the good news of Jesus Christ by extending His health ministry to those we serve.
- To promote Christian community among ourselves in the spirit of equality and ecumenism.
- To preserve and protect the rights and dignity of each person we serve. In doing so, we abide by the teachings of the Catholic Church.

- To develop and maintain dynamic organizations that strive for excellence while fostering an environment that reflects concern for the total person.
- To assist individuals in achieving their highest potential through educational endeavors and other programs promoting mental, physical, and spiritual development.
- To promote programs and services that support the family unit.

Source: Daughters of Charity East Central Province, Health Care Apostolate.

Similar to Medicaid agencies in other states, ALMA was formed as part of the federal/state welfare initiative to aid America's poor population and can be traced to the mid-1960s. Under Title XIX of the Social Security Act, each state Medicaid unit is required to provide certain basic services such as hospital inpatient care, hospital outpatient care, laboratory and X-ray services, physicians' services, family planning, and others. States were given the option of providing additional services such as drugs, eyeglasses, physical therapy, dental care, and so on. Due to the diversity of financial resources in different states, the extent and quality of care provided to the poor vary from one location to another. The program is jointly administered by the states and the Health Care Financing Agency (HCFA).

Some of the variation in benefits from one location to another is offset by federal matching dollars that can range from 50 to 83 percent of the state's total Medicaid budget. Historically, in Alabama the federal matching rate has been approximately 75 percent or three to one. This, combined with relatively enthusiastic support from the state legislature has resulted in a well-funded operation for ALMA throughout most of its history.

Soon after the appointment of a new commissioner, it was determined that the agency should carefully examine its mission after two decades of operation and attempt to clearly state its purpose. This statement, it was believed, would be helpful to employees attempting to focus their efforts on the most important priorities and to external groups such as the legislature, the governor's office, and the Department of Public Health. A group of interested administrative and nonadministrative personnel were assembled and began the task of developing a mission statement for the agency.

Prior to actually writing the mission statement, a series of management meetings were held to ensure that there was a desire for and commitment to have a well-understood and widely communicated statement of organizational distinctiveness. Once this was determined, assessments were made of what made the agency successful from the perspectives of employees as well as other key stakeholders. In addition, assessments were made of what these perceptions of success would likely be in the future.

To stimulate some initial thinking on the part of the management group, each person was asked to think about the points noted in Exhibit 5–3. It was recognized that few, if any, members of the management group had been previously involved in writing a mission statement. Exhibit 5–3 was developed to encourage some initial thought without introducing too much structure into the process.

After the management staff had been given time to think about the agency, its distinctiveness in state government, and the likely future it would face, the group met in a planning retreat format. One item on the agenda was to begin, and ideally progress toward, the development of a well-conceived mission statement. At the retreat, the components of the statement were developed with the aid of Exhibit 5–4. This exhibit simply provides a list of the components of a mission statement as discussed previously with space provided for participants to elaborate on their concept of the different components. The final result of the process is illustrated in the mission statement for the agency in Exhibit 5–5.

EXHIBIT 5-3

An Aid for Thinking About Our Mission

1. *The mission of the Alabama Medicaid Agency is to . . .*

   How would you broadly define our purpose? Be sure what you say will be meaningful to the people who work here. Be specific yet broad enough to allow innovation in how things are done, the development of new activities when advisable, and so on. Our purpose should be independent of time – it should be enduring.

2. *We accomplish our unique purpose by . . .*

   What is the scope of our services? This should be meaningful to external stakeholders unaware of the details of our operations as well as employees.

3. *We provide our services to . . .*

   Who are our customers or clients and where are their locations? Do not be limited by the obvious.

4. *The principles we intend to observe in our relationships with customers/clients and stakeholders are . . .*

   What are the standards of conduct to which we are committed? These standards should provide philosophical guides to employee and management behavior in dealing with others and among ourselves.

5. *Our philosophy includes . . .*

   Although our statement of values will list specific guiding principles, the mission statement should underscore or reinforce any particularly important overarching commitments of the agency.

Top-Level Leadership a Must for Mission Development

If a mission statement is to be a "living document," employees must develop a sense of ownership and commitment to the mission of the organization. For this reason, employees should be involved in the development and communication of the mission. However, top-level leadership must be committed if the process is to actually begin. Developing a mission statement is a challenging task. Frequently, attempts are made to formulate "blue sky" statements of constraints and little more. For example, to state that our health maintenance organization is devoted to being a good citizen of the local community and to paying wages and benefits comparable to those of other organizations in the area says little of real value. Realistically, the HMO must be a good citizen and, if it wants employees, its wages and benefits must be competitive.

The role of the chief executive officer in formulating the mission can never be underestimated. Mission statement development is not a task that should be

EXHIBIT 5 – 4

Writing the Components of the Mission Statement

Mission Statement Components	Descriptions [Key Words] About the Agency Mission
1. Target Customer/Clients and Markets	Needy population – Medicaid eligible population. Medicaid recipients and their families.
2. Principal Services Delivered	Preventive and acute medical care, long-term care, health education, and related social services.
3. Geographical Domain of Our Operations	Borders of the state of Alabama.
4. Commitment of Specific Values	Teamwork, cost-effective operations, integrity, caring attitude, high quality of care and service, positive attitude toward change, excellence.
5. Explicit Philosophy	Empowerment of recipients to make informed decisions about their health. Development of equitable partnerships with public and private providers of health services.
6. Other Important Component(s)	Facilitate access to health care and related social services.

EXHIBIT 5 – 5

Mission Statement: Alabama Medicaid Agency

The mission of the Alabama Medicaid Agency is to empower our recipients to make educated and informed decisions regarding their health and the health of their families. We do this by providing a system that facilitates access to necessary, high-quality, preventive and acute medical care, long-term care, and health education and related social services for Medicaid eligible and other needy populations of the state. Through teamwork, we strive to operate and enhance a cost-efficient system by building an equitable partnership with health care providers, both public and private.

Source: Alabama Medicaid Agency Strategic planning retreat.

delegated to the planning staff. Missions should be formulated and approved by the *keeper of the vision*. The CEO, selected line officers, and other key individuals who will be instrumental in accomplishing the mission should have input into the document. Perspective 5–6 summarizes the importance one CEO places on keeping the mission up-to-date while focusing on the organization's fundamental reason for existence.

Of necessity, this process of developing a sense of mission is built with top management leadership. The example of the Alabama Medicaid Agency appears to be simple; however, the actual process was time consuming and complex, with many "drafts" before the final document was produced. The forms helped and can be useful aids to strategic thinking about clients, services, and domain but the development and communication of a well-conceived mission statement is challenging. Although developing a mission statement is not an easy task, it is a necessary one.

PERSPECTIVE 5–6

Fine Tuning the Mission in Light of Changing Conditions

Daniel S. Schechter retired as president of American Hospital Publishing, Inc., in 1993 but he was perceptive enough to recognize that things had changed in the health care industry. One of his final and most significant acts was to administer the name change for the well-respected *Hospitals* magazine to *Hospitals and Health Networks*. For almost sixty years, *Hospitals* had carefully established its reputation as the "single-source" publication for all hospital-based executives by providing analyses that were not available elsewhere to this core audience. However, the health care environment changed radically over the past six decades. It was important for *Hospitals* to remain focused on its mission although at the same time respond to changing conditions.

In view of the emergence and growth of collaborative networks, patient-centered care, health reform, and other changes, *Hospitals* gave way to a new publication *Hospitals and Health Networks*. The mission of the new publication was to reach out to new stakeholders such as physicians, insurers, managed-care executives, vendors, community leaders, patients, and employers while maintaining the core audience of hospital-based executives.

The new name reflects the magazine's expanded mission to help readers: (1) understand the concepts of networks and collaborative management; (2) clarify the issues surrounding integrated-care networks; and (3) learn how hospitals are solving problems of collaboration with others in the health care system.

Source: Daniel S. Schechter, "Hospital and Health Networks: New Name, Expanded Coverage," *AHA News* (February 22, 1993), p. 6.

VISION: HOPE FOR THE FUTURE

The mission is developed from the needs of all the stakeholders or groups who have a vested interest in the success and survival of the organization. As was illustrated in Exhibit 5–2, this includes owners, employees, patients, physicians, the public in the case of government facilities, vendors, and others. Vision, on the other hand, is an expression of hope. It is a description of what the organization will be like and look like when it is fulfilling its purpose.[10]

Origins of Vision

Health care managers acquire vision from an appreciation of the history of the organization, a perception of the opportunities present in the environment, and an understanding of the *strategic capacity* of the organization to take advantage of these opportunities. Exhibit 5–6 provides a picture of the origin of a vision and how it relates to the purpose of the organization.

History and Vision An organization's history is made up of a variety of things that affect the development of vision. The founder's philosophy is important if the organization's inception is sufficiently recent to recall who actually started the hospital, long-term care facility, or home-care agency.

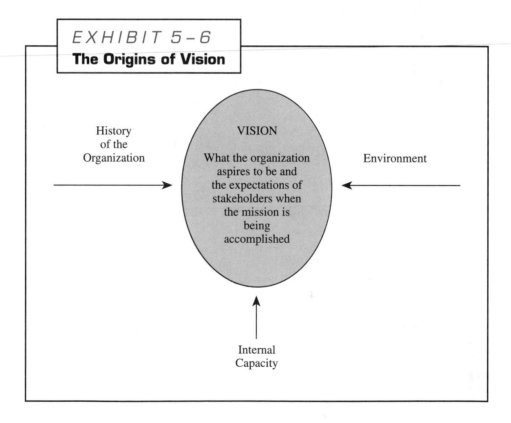

EXHIBIT 5–6
The Origins of Vision

Consider, for example, the Mayo Clinic in Rochester, Minnesota, an organization that is rich in history and tradition. Children's books tell successive generations how a destructive tornado in Rochester one night caused the Sisters of Saint Francis to aid the elder Dr. Mayo in caring for storm victims and encouraged his two sons, Will and Charlie, to follow in their father's footsteps.

The result is a world-famous research, teaching, and patient care facility that continues to thrive and expand far beyond the boundaries of Minnesota. Anyone who hopes to succeed at the Mayo Clinic and understand its unique vision must be aware of the founders and the past.[11] The history of an organization is instrumental in the formation of its image and its vision or hope for what it is capable of becoming.

Vision and the Environment Another important determinant of a manager's vision for an organization is his or her environmental view. Some organizations have "bad" experiences with environmental forces such as the government. Many private physicians and health care managers look at attempts by the government to get involved in setting rates, regulating quality, and so on as unnecessary and unwarranted interventions in private enterprise. When this view is adopted, enemies are seen "out there" in the environment and the vision becomes altered accordingly.[12] The vision is compromised, and lack of accomplishment is blamed on these external forces.

Sometimes the past experiences of organizations and the uncontrollable nature of environmental forces cause managers to engage in strategies that either over or underreact to crises. An interesting example of the interaction of history and environment in the formulation of an organizational vision is the swine flu scare of 1976.

The Public Health Service in the United States has actively stated its vision (hope) that prevention would one day replace the curative approach to health care in this country. In 1976, thirteen recruits in an army camp were diagnosed as having a flu that was "antigenically related" to the flu that killed over half a million Americans in 1918. When one recruit died (after an all-night march against doctors' orders), the Public Health Service and the nation were determined to prevent another flu disaster.[13]

David Spencer, then director of the Centers for Disease Control (CDC), saw the possibility of another outbreak of a killer flu as an opportunity to support the long-standing vision of public health and demonstrate the value of preventive medicine. The Secretary of Health, Education, and Welfare agreed, and President Ford was convinced to initiate an ambitious and widely publicized immunization campaign.

When legal problems developed concerning the vaccine, the manufacturers refused to sell the product because of possible product liability, and the swine flu scare turned into a disaster. Almost everything that could go wrong did go wrong. The goal was commendable, and the strategy for delivering the vaccine was sound. The problem resulted from the strategists' sense of history and their desire to avoid massive fatalities. Many believe the public health strategists overreacted to the threat of swine flu. In addition, they vacillated in their decision making because they allowed their judgment to be excessively influenced by the fear of uncontrollable external factors such as lawsuits if harmful side effects developed from the administration of the vaccine.

Vision and Internal Capacity A manager's vision is also related to the perceived strengths and weaknesses of the organization. An organization that has been successful in making things happen in the past will develop a more ambitious vision. Conversely, an organization that has experienced failures and marginal successes will develop a vision that is less demanding.

The challenge to reconcile vision and internal capacity is illustrated by Senge's integrative principle of creative tension.[14] *Creative tension* comes into play when one develops a view of where we want to be in the future (vision) and tells the truth about where we are now – "current reality." The current reality is greatly determined by our present internal capacity and how this capacity relates to our aspirations. Organizations deal with this creative tension in different ways. If the organization has been successful in the past it may be aggressive about the future and raise its current reality in pursuit of the vision. If it has experienced failure, limited success, or merely has a cautious philosophy, management may choose instead to revise and reduce the vision more in line with current reality.

Managers have visions and organizations gain and lose competitive advantage based on how the vision "fits" the environment and on the strategic capability of the organization to capitalize on opportunities. However, developing a vision is "messy work," and for this reason we will examine more closely what organizational vision actually means.

Health Care Strategists as Pathfinders

The job of building a vision for an organization is frequently referred to as *pathfinding*.[15] When the manager of a health care organization functions as a pathfinder, the focus is on the long run. The goal of the pathfinder is to provide a vision, find the paths the organization should pursue, and provide a clearly marked trail for those who will follow.[16] Pathfinders have an ability to, as Senge notes, create a natural energy for changing reality by "holding a picture of what might be that is more important to people than what is."[17]

Strategic managers are the key to establishing a vision for an organization. A "vision-led" organization is guided by a philosophy to which managers are committed but that has not yet become obvious in the daily life of the organization. The vision-led approach hopes for higher levels of performance that are inspiring although they cannot yet be achieved.[18] A primary role of management under this approach is to clarify goals and priorities and to ensure that they are understood and accepted by employees.

The role of the strategic manager, however, is more than pathfinding. Because, as Barnard noted, executives are responsible for inculcating the purpose into every employee, the manager must also be the "keeper of the vision." This means being a cheerleader and holding on to the vision even when others lose hope. Employees want to believe that what they are doing is important, and nothing convinces employees of the importance of their jobs more than the manager who keeps the inspirational vision before them (especially when things are not going well).

Characteristics of Effective Vision

If vision is really based on hope, it is a snapshot of the future that the health care manager wants to create.[19] For example, the president of the Regional Medical Center in Tennessee stated in the organization's annual report: "Our vision of becoming not just the most respected health care organization in this region but the best public hospital in the United States is a possible dream." Although this vision is short and to the point, it highlights some of the important characteristics of effective visions. It has been said that for an organizational vision to be successful it must be clear, coherent, consistent, have communicative power, and be flexible.[20] Another example of an organization's vision statement is illustrated in Perspective 5–7.

A clear vision is simple. Basic directions and commitments should be the driving forces of a vision, not complex analysis beyond the understanding of most employees. A vision is coherent when it "fits" with other statements including the mission and values. It is consistent when it is reflected in decision-making behavior throughout the organization. A vision "communicates" when it is shared and people believe in the importance of cooperation in creating the future that managers, employers, and other stakeholders desire.[21] Finally, to be meaningful, a vision must be flexible. The future, by definition, is uncertain. Therefore, the effective vision must remain open to change as the picture of the future changes and as the strategic capabilities of the organization evolve over time.

To effectively outline the future and facilitate the pursuit of organizational

---

PERSPECTIVE 5–7

Baptist Healthcare System Vision Statement

We are the provider of choice for a value-driven continuum of health care services through a Christ-centered, not-for-profit health care system undergirded by a commitment to quality that meets the changing needs of patients, physicians, employees, employers, and communities it services in the region encompassing Kentucky.

Source: "Baptist Healthcare System Vision Statement," *Baptist Briefings* (December 16, 1992), p. 1, publication of the Baptist Healthcare System, Louisville, Kentucky.

and individual excellence, visions should possess certain characteristics. The more important ones follow.[22]

1. *Visions should be inspiring, not merely quantitative goals to be achieved in the next performance evaluation period.* In fact, visions are rarely stated in quantitative terms. They are, however, nothing less than revolutionary in character and in terms of their potential impact on behavior.

2. *Visions should be clear, challenging, and about excellence.* There must be no doubt in the manager's mind about the importance of the vision. If the "keeper of the vision" has doubts, those who follow will have even more.

3. *Visions must make sense in the relevant community, be flexible, and stand the test of time.* If the vision is pragmatically irrelevant, it will not inspire high performance.

4. *Visions must be stable, but constantly challenged and changed when necessary.*

5. *Visions are beacons and controls when everything else seems up for grabs.* A vision is important to provide interested people with a sense of direction.

6. *Visions empower our own people first and then the clients, patients, or others we propose to serve.* The vision must first call forth the best efforts of our own people.

7. *Visions prepare for the future while honoring the past.* Effective visions always maintain a sense of where the organization has been and how its past influences where it can go.

8. *Visions come alive in details, not in broad generalities.* Although inspirational visions are generally unconcerned with details, the accomplishment of the vision eventually has to lead to tangible results, whether in health care, business, government or education.

Unfortunately, although many organizations have given substantial attention to writing mission statements, relatively few have written and published vision statements. However, there are some useful aids that can assist managers in thinking about their vision and the direction they desire for the future. For example, Exhibit 5–7 provides some initial considerations as the vision formulation process develops. This exhibit provides a series of questions that are useful to think about in the process of formulating a vision statement.

Although it is not referred to as a vision, the statement of Merck & Company in Perspective 5–8 meets most of the characteristics of a good vision statement. Note how the statement provides an effective agenda for the future. As with our discussion of mission statements, we can use the Merck statement to illustrate how it might have been "built" or how a particular organization might use the form in Exhibit 5–8 to construct an effective vision statement.

A vision is a hope, a picture of what the manager wants the organization to be when it is in the process of fulfilling its purpose. Strategically, visionary leaders are the most important element in the difference between the merely well-managed and the excellent organization.

EXHIBIT 5-7
Thinking About Our Vision

When thinking about the vision for our organization, consider the following points.

1. *As we look toward the future, we believe our organization will/should become* . . .
   If we are successful at everything we are trying to accomplish today, what will our organization look like five years from now?
2. *We want our organization to be "thought of" as* . . .
   What attributes do we most want our organization to achieve? What characteristics should be considered as the essence of organizational excellence in our field of endeavor?
3. *In the future, our employees will have and be seen as* . . .
   What characteristics reflect significant professional achievements in health care and are recognized as reflections of competence by all relevant stakeholders?
4. *The realization of this vision will bring* _____ *to all of us* . . .
   What fundamental, positive changes will occur to us and our stakeholders if we achieve the vision we have set for ourselves?

PERSPECTIVE 5-8
Merck's Agenda for the Future

"We will be the first drug maker with advanced research in every disease category. Our research will be as good as the science being done anywhere in the world. Our drugs won't be used by a single person who doesn't need them. Merck will continue to grow on a steady basis, bringing forth worthwhile products. We will be at the leading edge of concern, making contributions to problems society is struggling with – giving Blacks a more effective role in our economy, righting the sexual imbalances that have existed in the past, and making a contribution to the environment in which we live."

Source: Reprinted from James C. Collins and Jerry I. Porras, "Organizational Vision and Visionary Organizations," *California Management Review* 34, no. 1 (Fall 1991), p. 50.

EXHIBIT 5-8
An Aid to the Development of a Vision Statement

Vision Statement Components	Descriptions (Key Words) in Merck's Vision
1. A Clear Hope (profile) for the Future	"First drug maker with advanced research in every disease category."
2. Challenging and About Excellence	"Research to be as good as the science done anywhere in the world."
3. Inspirational and Emotional	"No one taking the drug who doesn't need it."
4. Empowers Employees First and Clients/customers Second	"Only way these ambitious goals can be achieved is with the full support of all employees."
5. Prepares for the Future	Addresses key social concerns – race and sex discrimination as well as environmental sensitivity.
6. Memorable and Provides Guidance	Use of memorable terms – first, best, and others.

A Cautionary Note: The Problem of Newness

Visionary managers provide their greatest service by making the organization flexible and able to enter new markets, disengage from old ones, and experiment with new ideas. By getting into a new market first, organizations can obtain certain *first-mover* advantages.[23] A reputation for pioneering can be generated and market position can be more easily established when there are no or only a few competitors. Sometimes it is expensive (monetarily and emotionally) for clients and patients to "switch" to other providers once loyalty and mutual trust have been developed.

However, visionary change when directed toward early entry into markets has its disadvantages. This has been referred to as the *liability of newness*. Unfortunately, the innovators often experience pioneering costs. Pioneers make the mistakes that others learn from and eventually correct. First movers face greater uncertainty because the demand for the service has not been verified. Patient and client needs may change and, particularly when large technological investments are required, the first mover can be left with expensive equipment and little demand.

Therefore, it is important that the demand for visionary management be tempered with realistic knowledge of the market, consumers, and other factors that will affect the organization. The rewards often go to the first mover, but the risks are greater.

VALUES AS GUIDING PRINCIPLES

Values are the things organizations and people stand for – the fundamental principles that, along with the mission, make an organization unique. Most often discussions of organizational values relate to ethical behavior and socially responsible decision making. To be sure, these values are extremely important, not just to a single hospital, HMO, or long-term care facility but to society in general.

There are, however, other values that are very specific to particular organizations and the type of behavior that has either characterized its members' behavior in the past or behavior to which members collectively aspire in the future. Total quality management or continuous improvement is, in this sense, a value as is entrepreneurial spirit, teamwork, innovation, and so on. It is important that managers, employees, and key stakeholders understand the values that are expected to drive an organization.

Core values, beliefs, and philosophy seem to be clear during the early stages of an organization's development and become less clear as the organization matures.[24] The distinctive values of the Mayo Clinic were no doubt clearest while the founding brothers were active in its operations. Although values may certainly change over time, it is important, as with mission and vision statements, that organizations reexamine their values, reaffirm them, change them, communicate them, and perhaps commit them to writing for all to see.

Exhibit 5–9 illustrates a particularly well-developed and articulated set of organizational values. Note that this "credo" focuses on what the organization believes are its key responsibilities – to patients, employees, the future, and so on. Throughout the credo are references to motivational terms like *compassion, excellence,* and *respect.* Anyone reading this credo or set of guiding principles can understand the motivational force it might have on employees and the comfort it might give patients who face admission to the facility. The credo ends in a particularly effective manner with the statement of the motto: "Skill, tenderly applied, works wonders."

Not all statements of values or guiding principles are as elaborate as that of the Jewish Hospital of St. Louis. However, they need to be as well conceived. In the case of the credo outlined in Exhibit 5–9, much of the focus is on responsibilities to various stakeholders – physicians, patients, employees, community, and so on. In addition, value statements can be useful in clarifying to employees the specific behaviors that are expected of them as a member of the organization. This was the focus of the Alabama Medicaid Agency when a decision was made to develop a value statement to accompany the organizational mission. The mission statement, presented in Exhibit 5–5, provides direction for the value statement presented in Exhibit 5–10.

EXHIBIT 5–9

Credo of the Jewish Hospital of St. Louis, a Member of BJC Health Systems

"We believe our first responsibility is to our patients. In meeting their needs, we will deliver our services with skill, compassion, and respect for the patient's dignity and privacy, regardless of race, creed, or religious affiliation.

"We will provide superior care across a broad spectrum of medical disciplines, emphasizing the clinical areas in which we have distinctive strengths. We will support that emphasis through the recruitment of outstanding physicians and employees and the provision of state-of-the-art equipment and facilities. We will deliver treatment in the most appropriate setting, whether inpatient, outpatient, or homebound.

"We are responsible to our employees, the men and women who enable us to care for our patients. We respect our employees' dignity, recognize their merit, and value their contributions to Jewish Hospital. We will provide the resources needed to uphold their dedication to excellence.

"We recognize that superior patient care depends on outstanding physicians. We will recruit and support a medical staff that ranks among the best in the nation. Through our affiliation with the Washington University School of Medicine, we will foster the crucial link between medical science and patient care. We believe teaching and research programs enhance the quality of treatment, and we are committed to their advancement.

"Our responsibility to deliver excellent patient care extends beyond our walls to the community. We strive not only to serve the ill but also the healthy. We will serve – to the best of our financial ability – those unable to afford care.

"Our final responsibility is to the future. We will manage our resources in a manner that sustains our ability to serve the community.

"Our future will be built on our Judaic foundation, stressing a dedication to learning and compassion. We best express those values in our motto: Skill, tenderly applied, works wonders."

Source: Promotional material from The Jewish Hospital of St. Louis, a Member of BJC Health Systems.

The management of Medicaid decided that in addition to this statement of organizational values additional reminders were needed to keep the values constantly before employees so they could be readily applied to decision-making situations. The "team for excellence" lapel pin shown in Exhibit 5–11 was developed and distributed to employees when a voluntary commitment was made to the values.

Mission, vision, and value statements are tools for "getting better at what we do." The usefulness for any and all of these statements is the ownership developed on the part of employees and the commitments observed by stakeholders. Framed mission, visions, values, and credos are merely exercises – and futile ones at that – if they are not made real by commitments and actions.[25] The point,

EXHIBIT 5-10

Statement of Values: Alabama Medicaid Agency

We are a *caring* organization and treat our employees, recipients, and providers with respect, dignity, honesty, and compassion.

We understand that to be effective we must be willing to *change*. Therefore, we value new ideas, innovation, and a positive response to change.

We value *integrity* and observe the highest ethical standards and obey all laws and regulations. We pledge to be good stewards of the state's resources entrusted to us.

We are committed to *excellence* and the highest standards of quality in all our activities. We are committed to getting better every day in everything we do.

We value *teamwork*. We encourage team accomplishments over the goals of any one individual. We encourage open discussion of issues, but once a decision is made, commitment is expected from everyone. We understand that the success of our organization relies upon the building and maintenance of effective teams.

EXHIBIT 5-11

Medicaid *Team for Excellence* Pin

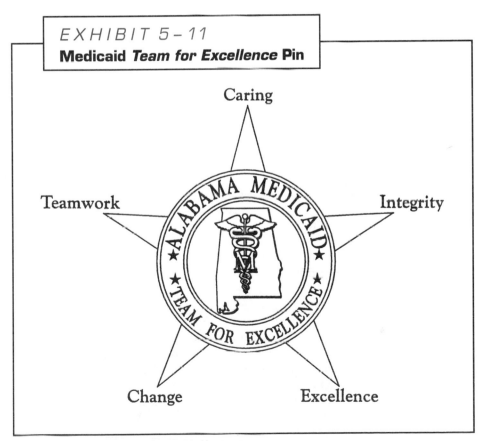

of course, is not to write fancy statements. The point is to motivate and guide employees, managerial and nonmanagerial, to provide high-quality care and respond to external as well as internal customers; it is to distinguish the organization from others in the perceptions of key stakeholders; and it is to let everyone know the organization stands for something important.

These statements and beliefs, as mentioned in Chapter 2, are *directional strategies* that provide the focus and parameters for the more operational strategic objectives. In addition, they provide a means of determining the essential things that must be accomplished if the organization is to be effective.

KEY PERFORMANCE AREAS AND STRATEGIC OBJECTIVES

It is tempting when setting strategic goals to develop as many as possible. Unfortunately, when a large number of goals are established, the task appears to be so great that little progress is made with regard to the really important issues.

Key Performance Areas

Once management is confident that the mission, vision, and values are well formulated, understood, communicated, and expressed in writing, it has to develop a means of focusing on the things that will make the most progress toward accomplishing the vision. The identification of key performance areas is an extremely important step in this process.

Key performance areas or critical success factors highlight those "few key areas of activity necessary for a particular organization to achieve its purpose."[26] It helps to note that these key performance areas represent major commitments for the organization and should not be limited to those things that are easy to measure. If difficult to measure areas are believed to be genuinely critical to success, they should be included as well. They should be as brief and simple as possible because complex descriptions of key performance areas, mission, vision, and values only add confusion to those who must accomplish them. Most management teams find that with careful thought and analysis a few extremely important activities can be identified that absolutely must happen if the organization is to be successful.

Health care management is extremely complex, and many things must happen if the hospital, health maintenance organization, or long-term care facility is to be successful. Key performance areas are often difficult to identify, even for experienced health care executives. The practical matter, however, is that because health care managers are busy; they must find ways to focus on those really important areas that only top management can administer.

A useful exercise to stimulate thinking about the factors that determine success or failure is to put yourself in the position of the chief executive officer. Assume that for some reason you are unconscious or "out of the picture" for a week. When you return, what things would you look for immediately to determine what happened to the organization while you were out of touch? Perhaps it would be the occupancy rate of your hospital's beds. In the public health sector it might be the number of cases of various communicable diseases reported in the state or county during the week. The specifics of what the CEO looks at is not important for our purposes. The important point is that key performance areas are identified by the executive's behavior. We check first on those things we believe make the difference between success and failure.[27]

The things that make the difference can, and often do, vary with the nature of the industry, the stage of a particular organization in its life cycle, and so on. For example, consider three similar yet different group medical practices.[28] The first clinic, a mature medical practice, has been in existence for a number of years and has a good patient base. The second group, in a rural area in a poor state, was highly dependent on government funding. The third, a rapidly growing, relatively new medical practice, needed high levels of cash flow to sustain growth. The key performance areas varied greatly among these group medical practices even though they had many things in common. Finding the factors that make the difference between success and lack of success is a creative and demanding challenge.

To illustrate the importance of this challenge, consider the key performance areas identified by the management of a large local health department. After careful consideration and analysis, the management determined that the success or failure of the organization depended on six key performance areas or critical success factors. These were (1) accurate assessment of community needs; (2) adequate human and nonhuman resources – facilities, staff, financial; (3) clear legal authority; (4) high credibility and favorable image with key stake-holders; (5) state-of-the-art technology for service delivery; and (6) high-quality services.

The department used these identified key performance areas and asked bureau directors to set their objectives for the next fiscal year and for five years into the future, being careful to anchor the objectives into one or more of the key performance areas. To provide focus, each director was asked to set no more than three objectives for each year to ensure that adequate attention was devoted to "making important things happen." Exhibit 5–12 illustrates how the key performance areas were logically related to the department's mission, vision, and values as well as the key performance areas and national health priorities.[29]

Setting Strategic Objectives

Whereas well-developed missions are abstract and provide general direction, strategic objectives are specific and to the point. Strategic objectives should possess the following characteristics:

1. Objectives should be as *explicit* and *measurable* as possible. Objectives should reflect organizational priorities to assist managers in making decisions with regard to the distribution of resources. When formulated in this manner, they provide a basis for control and performance evaluation.[30]

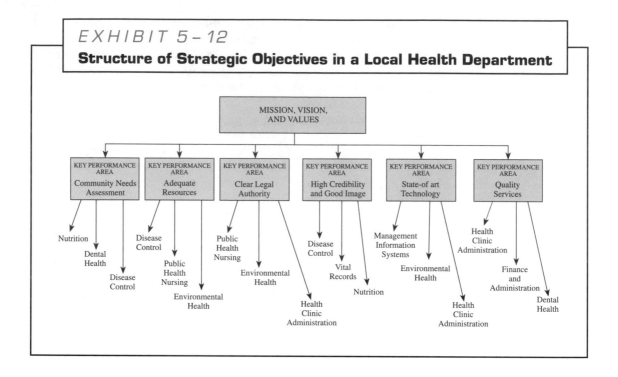

EXHIBIT 5-12

Structure of Strategic Objectives in a Local Health Department

2. Objectives should be *attainable* – challenging yet achievable. Objectives are motivational only if they are feasible. Although a statement of hope (vision) does not have to be achievable to be motivational, an objective that is used eventually for performance appraisal must be feasible or it will lose its motivational impact.

3. Objectives should *relate to the key performance areas* identified by management. Because managers are often tempted to set more objectives than they can properly attend to, it is a good idea to restrict the number of strategic objectives to two or three for each key performance area. Thus, if five key performance areas are identified, managers should focus on a maximum of fifteen objectives for the year rather than be consumed by the "trivial many." This is important for purposes of evaluation. If a single objective identifies more than one output, confusion will result if only part of the objective is accomplished. Good objectives include a time deadline for accomplishment and a budget constraint to make clear the maximum amount of organizational resources to be devoted to their accomplishment.

4. Objectives should be *written*. There should be no confusion about what is to be accomplished, by what date, by whom, and what resources are available to finance the accomplishment.

As a practical matter, few things are more essential for effective management than carefully established and communicated objectives. Objectives are no less important for the 35-bed rural hospital than for the 900-bed research and teaching hospital. In addition to all the other benefits, precise and understood objectives are effective motivators of performance. They focus the attention of employees on important factors, regulate how hard a person actually works, and increase an individual's resolve and persistence.[31]

To illustrate how the strategic objectives of the local health department were tied to key performance areas, a series of strategic objectives have been placed in Exhibit 5–13. For purposes of illustration, one objective has been presented for each of the six key performance areas listed in Exhibit 5–12.

Note that the objectives listed in the second column of the exhibit are carefully anchored into a specific key performance area. This provides focus to individual units, ensures that each unit is making contributions to the overall mission of the department, and communicates what is really important to individuals who may not be continuously involved in the priority setting of the organization.

Although the current baseline data are not provided in this brief example, it should be noted that the objectives established are "attainable" in the period of fiscal year 1994. To have the greatest motivational impact, strategic objectives should be challenging but attainable. Constantly failing to achieve unrealistic objectives is more likely to result in a disregard for goal setting rather than improvement in performance.

The objectives established by the department are measurable. Often it is tempting to substitute trivial yet measurable goals to ensure some outcomes can be successfully achieved. Quantification is an important aspect of strategic objectives and should be insisted on when practical and reasonable. However, managers should not avoid setting strategic goals relative to key performance areas such as employee morale, managerial effectiveness, and patient satisfaction, where measurement is difficult.

In addition to financial and productivity objectives, organizations establish targets for contributions to society. These "public-oriented" objectives are often less easily measured than the objectives just discussed, but they are no less important. Counter to what one might expect intuitively, research has shown that public welfare goals are as important to investor-owned health care organizations as they are to not-for-profit organizations.[32]

The preceding illustration focused on objectives for a single organization. However, one of the greatest lessons in objective setting in health care today can be found in the national priorities established in 1979 with the publication of the surgeon general's *Report on Health Promotion and Disease Prevention,* the revised edition of which is referred to as *Year 2000 Objectives for the Nation.*[33]

National Objectives for Health

The following discussion uses the Year 2000 objectives to illustrate the importance of clear objectives and demonstrates some of the characteristics of objectives

---

EXHIBIT 5-13

Key Performance Areas and Strategic Objectives in a Local Health Department

Key Performance Area	Illustrative Strategic Objective
Community Needs Assessment	Nutrition: To develop a comprehensive plan for ensuring that a minimum of 75 percent of all special populations in the county are informed about food groups and the relationship of wellness activities to cardiovascular disease risks by the end of fiscal year 1994.
Adequate Human and Nonhuman Resources	Environmental Health: To organize and have in place a citizens' advocacy group for the passage of a monetary-fine system on air emissions that will cover all inspection and enforcement costs by the end of fiscal year 1994.
Clear Legal Authority	Environmental Health: To ensure passage of a state law providing legal authority for health department inspection of tattoo and tanning parlors during the 1994 legislative session.
High Credibility and Good Image	Disease Control: To develop and deliver to every health care provider in the county accurate and up-to-date information on how to diagnose and properly report cases of all currently recognized sexually transmitted diseases including genital herpes, hepatitis B, and nongonococcal urethritis by July 1994.
State-of-the-art Technology	Management Information Systems: To complete installation of a geographical information system by the end of fiscal year 1994 including modules for aerial mapping of on-site sewage systems failures.
Quality Services	Finance and Administration: To complete a series of focus groups among internal customers, identify complaints, and initiate corrective actions on no less than 90 percent of identified improvement areas.

---

that we have already discussed. Starting in 1987, the Public Health Service of the Department of Health and Human Services has coordinated a nationwide process to develop national disease prevention and health promotion objectives for the year 2000. If successful, much of the objective setting at state, local, and even organizational levels will be anchored in these statements. Therefore, if the efforts of the Public Health Service are to be successful, it is important that the national objectives exhibit the previously discussed characteristics of good objectives. That is, they should be explicit and measurable, reflect organizational priorities by relating to key performance areas, and be challenging yet attainable so as to motivate high levels of commitment and performance.

Structure of the Year 2000 Objectives The Year 2000 objectives reflect a systematic logic that flows from five specific desired outcomes (called *goals*). These outcomes serve as overall measures of the nation's health. Four high-priority areas were identified and further divided into twenty-one key performance areas (areas where things must happen if the overall health of the nation is to be improved). Objectives were actually established for the twenty-one key performance areas. Finally, from these key performance areas a total of 405 specific, quantitative objectives were formulated.

Some Examples of Objectives To appreciate the nature of the objectives that were actually set, consider an objective in each of two major areas of interest. Both relate to health promotion.

In nutrition, reduce iron deficiency among children ages 1 and 2 to less than 5 percent and among children ages 3 to 4 to less than 2 percent. At the present time, the average iron deficiency level is 9.4 percent for the former group and 3.9 percent for the latter. Iron deficiency is associated with adverse effects on growth and development among children. The effective parts of this objective are (1) the specific populations deserving attention (children ages 1–2 and 3–4) are targeted; (2) the quantitative outcomes are identified (5 percent and 2 percent, respectively); (3) the time period for accomplishing the objective is clear (by the year 2000); and in view of the baseline data (9.4 percent and 3.9 percent) accomplishment of the objective will be challenging yet attainable.

In tobacco use, increase to at least 50 percent the proportion of current smokers age 20 and older who make a serious attempt to quit smoking during the preceding year with one-third or more of these attempts resulting in abstinence for at least three months. Data gathered in 1986 showed that 32 percent of smokers tried to quit and 25 percent of those who quit maintained abstinence for at least three months. Again, the objective is specific, the target group is identified, a schedule is established, and the objective is difficult but attainable. Similar objectives from the health protection priority can be illustrated with an example from occupational safety and health and the prevention priority can be illustrated by an objective relative to maternal and child health.

In occupational safety and health, reduce lost workdays due to on-the-job injuries to no more than 50 per 100 full-time workers. The average was 62.7 days between 1983 and 1987. About 32 million workdays a year were lost due to injury in 1986. A reduction of the magnitude indicated in this objective could significantly increase not only the nation's health but its economic position as well.

In maternal and infant health, reduce the infant mortality rate (deaths of infants under 1 year) to no more than 7 per 1,000 live births. In 1986, this figure was 10.4 deaths per 1,000 live births. The good news is that the rate has been decreasing in recent years. Unfortunately, in spite of the favorable trend, the

United States continues to rank lower than many highly industrialized nations and even some Third World nations in the area of infant mortality.

Finally, under the priority area of system improvements, surveillance and data systems were targeted as particularly important. By 2000, create a system for the rapid transfer of health data among the federal and state agencies that collects and analyzes data to assess progress toward the Year 2000 national health objectives. Unfortunately, baseline data regarding many of the system improvement objectives are not readily available. Although there are some proposed models, no single comprehensive system was in use in 1989. For this reason, some of the least well-formulated objectives in the overall plan relate to the area of system improvement.

As a general rule, however, the majority of the Year 2000 objectives are statements that will be helpful in improving the nation's health. The care with which they have been formulated will help those who must accomplish them to focus their energies. Therefore, one of the primary outcomes associated with good objectives – directing efforts to the really important areas and thereby increasing the likelihood of success – is accomplished.

SUMMARY AND CONCLUSIONS

In this chapter, we covered several important topics. All relate to the outcomes or goals that health care organizations hope to achieve.

First, managers should recognize that strategic planning is a logical process. The goal progression discussed in this chapter illustrates the importance of strategic logic. The mission of the organization drives decision making because it is the organization's reason for existing. The vision provides the hope for the future and the values tell everyone – employees, stakeholders, patients, and so on – how the organization will operate.

Second, a mission alone is not enough. Although the mission is a systematic statement of purpose that distinguishes the organization from all others of its type, such as the care given to patients, physical location of the health care facility, the unusual commitment of physicians to research as well as healing, or any other factor that is important in the minds of those served, it is only the first step. The mission may motivate a few physicians and department managers, but real motivation comes from visionary leadership. The vision is a hope that says how key stakeholders think the organization should look and be like when the purpose is being achieved. Values, as guiding principles, can be powerful motivating forces, as well.

Third, even a well-developed and communicated mission is likely to leave the health care strategist with far too many areas of responsibility, resulting in an impossible task. For this reason, key performance areas must be identified and strategic objectives must be set with regard to each of the performance areas. This helps make the strategist's job feasible. It is likely that most managers in all types of organizations attempt to manage far too many aspects of the job. The logic of this chapter should help managers focus more effectively on those tasks that really make a difference with respect to organizational success.

Finally, management research shows that the existence of specific objectives with deadlines and resource constraints can be extremely motivating. Clearly stated and communicated objectives provide a sense of direction – they specify what managers are expected to accomplish and remove anxiety from those who want to succeed. If managers provide the opportunity to do so, employees generally accept the chance to provide some input into the goals that will ultimately influence, for better or worse, their occupational success or failure.

Well-developed and communicated objectives provide a framework for evaluating how the organization is doing and what might be needed to improve performance. Formulating mission, vision, values, key performance areas, and strategic objectives is often "messy" and unappreciated work. In the end, however, it is an important responsibility of all strategic managers.

KEY TERMS AND CONCEPTS IN STRATEGIC MANAGEMENT

creative tension	**key performance areas**	**pathfinding**
first mover	**goals**	**public welfare goals**
guiding principles	**organizational mission**	**strategic capacity**
keeper of the vision	**organizational vision**	**strategic objectives**

QUESTIONS FOR CLASS DISCUSSION

1. Is it necessary for all organizational mission statements to include the multiple components discussed in this chapter? How do we decide what components to include?

2. What is the relationship among an organization's mission, vision, values, key performance areas, and strategic objectives?

3. Indicate two ways in which an organizational vision is different from other types of organizational goals.

4. Why is the pathfinder's role so important in health care strategic management? Who in the organization is best equipped to fulfill this role and why?

5. Why are values referred to as an organization's guiding principles? In what sense do values constitute a directional strategy for the organization?

6. Who determines the guiding principles of a health care organization? Who should determine these values? What are some guiding principles that you think should be common to all health care organizations? What types of values might, in your opinion, be organization specific?

7. What is a key performance area? How do key performance areas keep us from becoming preoccupied with the "trivial many" factors that can consume a strategic manager's time?

8. Why is it appropriate for an organizational mission to be broad and enduring and strategic objectives to be specific and dynamic?

9. How can health care managers more effectively use goals to stimulate higher levels of performance among all personnel?

10. Think of an organization that you know relatively well and attempt to construct a mission statement in light of the components of missions discussed in this chapter.

11. For the same organization, attempt to write three strategic objectives that possess the characteristics discussed in this chapter.

NOTES

1. Chester I. Barnard, *The Functions of the Executive* (Cambridge, Massachusetts: Harvard University Press, 1938), p. 87.

2. W. Jack Duncan, *Great Ideas in Management: Lessons from the Founders and Foundations of Managerial Practice* (San Francisco: Jossey-Bass, 1989), pp. 117–118.

3. Russell L. Ackoff, "Mission Statements," *Planning Review* 15, no. 4 (July/August 1987), pp. 30–31.

4. C. Kendrick Gibson, David J. Newton, and Daniel S. Cochran, "An Empirical Investigation of the Nature of Hospital Mission Statements," *Health Care Management Review* 15, no. 3 (Summer 1990), pp. 35–46.

5. W. Jack Duncan, Peter M. Ginter, and W. Keith Kreidel, "A Sense of Direction in Public Organizations: An Analysis of Mission Statements in State Health Departments," *Administration & Society* 26, no. 1 (May 1994), pp. 11–27.

6. Perry Pascarella, "Is Your Mission Clear?" *Industry Week* 219 (November 14, 1983), pp. 75–76.

7. John A. Pearce II, "The Company Mission as a Strategic Tool," *Sloan Management Review* 23, no. 2 (Spring 1982), p. 15.

8. For a discussion of the need to regularly reexamine the mission statement, see Lloyd L. Byars and Thomas C. Neil, "Organizational Philosophy and Mission Statements," *Planning Review* 15, no. 4 (July/August 1987), pp. 32–35.

9. John A. Pearce II and Fred David, "Corporate Mission Statements and the Bottom Line," *Academy of Management Executive* 1, no. 2 (1987), pp. 109–116.

10. Perry Pascarella and Mark A. Frohman, *The Purpose Driven Organization* (San Francisco: Jossey-Bass, 1989), p. 23; and Mark Frohman and Perry Pascarella, "How to Write a Purpose Statement," *Industry Week* (March 23, 1987), pp. 31–34.

11. For an example of the rich tradition of the Mayo family, see Marie Hammontree, *Will and Charlie Mayo: Doctor's Boys* (New York: Bobbs-Merrill Company, 1954). For the importance of organizational history in general, see Alan L. Wilkins and Nigel J. Bristow, "For Successful Organization Culture, Honor Your Past," *Academy of Management Executive* 1, no. 3 (1987), pp. 221–229; and Warren Boeker, "Strategic Change: The Effects of Founding and History," *Academy of Management Journal* 32, no. 2 (1989), pp. 489–515. For the importance of founders, see Edgar H. Schein, "The Role of the Founder in Creating Organizational Culture," *Organizational Dynamics* 11 (Summer 1983), pp. 13–28.

12. M. F. R. Kets de Vries and Danny Miller, "Group Fantasies and Organizational Functioning," *Human Relations* 37 (1984), pp. 111–134.

13. An extremely interesting account of the behavior of the Centers for Disease Control, the National Institute for Allergic and Infectious Diseases, and the Food and Drug Administration is presented in Richard E. Neustadt and Ernest R. May, *Thinking in Time: The Uses of History for Decision-Makers* (New York: The Free Press, 1986), pp. 49–51. Public health has continued its concern for vision and hope for the future. In light of health reform, for example, the American Public Health Association has carefully reexamined its vision for the future. See "APHA's Vision: Public Health in A Reformed Health Care System," *The Nation's Health* (July 1993), pp. 9–11.

14. Peter M. Senge, "The Leader's New Work: Building Learning Organizations," *Sloan Management Review* 31 (Fall 1990), pp. 13–14.

15. Robert H. Waterman, Jr., *The Renewal Factor* (New York: Bantam Books, 1987), pp. 222–225.

16. G. B. Morris, "The Executive: A Pathfinder," *Organizational Dynamics* 16 (1988), pp. 62–77.

17. Senge, "The Leader's New Work," p. 8.

18. Richard E. Walton, "A Vision-Led Approach to Management Restructuring," *Organizational Dynamics* 14 (1986), pp. 5–16.

19. James C. Collins and Jerry I. Porras, "Organizational Vision and Visionary Organizations," *California Management Review* 34, no. 1 (1991), pp. 30–52.

20. Ian Wilson, "Realizing the Power of Strategic Vision," *Long Range Planning* 25, no. 5 (1992), pp. 18–28.

21. D. Keith Denton and Barry L. Wisdom, "Sharing Vision," *Business Horizons* (July/August 1989), pp. 67–69.

22. Tom Peters, *Thriving on Chaos* (New York: Alfred A. Knopf, 1988), pp. 401–404.

23. The term *liability of newness* was suggested by James March. However, the most extensive treatment of "first-mover" advantages and disadvantages is presented in Michael E. Porter, *Competitive Advantage* (New York: The Free Press, 1986), pp. 186–191; and in Michael E. Porter, *Competitive Strategy* (New York: The Free Press, 1980), Chapter 10.

24. Collins and Porras, "Organizational Visions and Visionary Organizations," pp. 34–35.

25. For some criticisms of these tools, see George Newman, "Worried About Vision? See an Optometrist," *Across the Board* (October 1992), pp. 7–8; and Colin Coulson-Thomas, "Strategic Vision or Strategic Con: Rhetoric or Reality?" *Long Range Planning* 25, no. 1 (1992), pp. 81–89.

26. John F. Rockart, "The Changing Role of the Information Systems Executive: A Critical Success Factors Perspective," *Sloan Management Review* 24 (Fall 1982), pp. 3–14.

27. For examples, see John F. Rockart and Adam C. Crescenzi, "Engaging Top Management in Information Technology," *Sloan Management Review* 25 (1984), pp. 3–16; and Jeffrey K. Pinto and John E. Prescott, "Variations in Critical Success Factors over the Stages in the Product Life Cycle," *Journal of Management* 14 (1988), pp. 5–18.

28. John F. Rockart, "Chief Executives Define Their Own Data Needs," *Harvard Business Review* (March/April 1979), pp. 87–88.

29. *Promoting Health/Preventing Disease: Year 2000 Objectives for the Nation* (Washington, D.C.: Public Health Service, U.S. Department of Health and Human Services, September 1989).

30. For a discussion of organizational goals and objectives, see Max D. Richards, *Setting Strategic Goals and Objectives,* 2d ed. (St. Paul: West Publishing, 1986).

31. E. A. Locke and G. P. Latham, *Goal Setting for Individuals, Groups, and Organizations* (Chicago: Science Research Associates, 1984).

32. John Kralewski, "Profit vs. Public Welfare Goals in Investor-Owned and Not-for-Profit Hospitals," *Hospital & Health Services Administration* 33, no. 3 (Fall 1988), pp. 312–329.

33. *Promoting Health/Preventing Disease: Year 2000 Objectives for the Nation.*

ADDITIONAL READINGS

Amit, R., and P. J. H. Schoemaker, "Strategic Assets and Organizational Rent," *Strategic Management Journal* 14, no. 1 (1993), pp. 33–46. An interesting examination of the nature of strategic assets in an organization and the manner in which they can and should be deployed. The importance of strategic assets is examined in light of the mission of the organization.

Coulson-Thomas, Colin, "Strategic Vision or Strategic Con: Rhetoric or Reality?" *Long Range Planning* 25, no. 1 (1992), pp. 81–89. This article presents the results of three surveys that attempt to gauge the gap between rhetoric and reality when it comes to formulating organizational missions, visions, and action.

El-Namaki, M. S., "Creating A Corporate Vision," *Long Range Planning* 25, no. 6 (1992), pp. 25–29. An interesting article makes an argument for the importance of having and maintaining a clear corporate vision. The motivational impact of a well communicated vision is discussed and illustrated.

Hamel, G., and C. K. Prahalad, "Strategy as Stretch and Leverage," *Harvard Business Review* 68, no. 3 (1993), pp. 75–84. The originators of the idea of strategic stretch illustrate in this article how the concept of strategic fit may be a significant limitation for the organization. In light of the mission of the organization, the concepts of strategic stretch and leverage may result in higher performance.

Hinterhuber, Hans H., and Wolfgang Popp, "Are You a Strategist or Just a Manager?" *Harvard Business Review* 70, no. 1 (1992), pp. 105–113. This article provides a ten-question profile to assist managers in determining the extent of their strategic orientation. Fundamental to the profile is the manager's vision and philosophy.

Ireland, R. D., and M. A. Hitt, "Mission Statements: Importance, Challenge, and Recommendations for Development," *Business Horizons* 35, no. 3 (1992), pp. 34–42. A critical analysis of mission statements examining both the uses and problems created by mission statements. Recommendations are offered for obtaining the most from missions.

Medley, George J., "WWF UK Creates a New Mission," *Long Range Planning* 25, no. 2 (1992), pp. 63–68. The director of the World Wide Fund for Nature presents in this article a strong case for the development of a sense of mission in all types of organizations. The author also presents a convincing case for revisiting the mission when conditions change.

Nanis, Burt, *Visionary Leadership* (San Francisco: Jossey-Bass Publishers, 1992). This book makes the point that all great leaders have been individuals with a vision. This vision attracted commitment, inspired people to perform at their best, revitalized organizations, and mustered the resources necessary to turn the vision into a reality.

Schoemaker, P. J. H., "How to Link Strategic Vision to Core Capabilities," *Sloan Management Review* 34, no. 1 (1992), pp. 67–81. The critical nature of the clear linkage between the strategic vision of an organization and its core capabilities is discussed with some analysis of how the linkage may become more direct and explicit.

Strategy Formulation

Strategy formulation is concerned with making strategic decisions using the information gathered during the situational analysis. Part 3 has two chapters – Chapter 6 presents the strategic alternatives available to health care organizations and Chapter 7 presents and discusses methods to analyze the alternatives.

Chapter 6 provides a decision logic for strategy formulation and demonstrates that strategic decisions should be made sequentially with each decision more explicitly defining the strategy. Each of the strategy types – directional, adaptive, market entry, and positioning – has several strategic alternatives that may be adopted by health care organizations.

Chapter 7 discusses how to evaluate the strategic alternatives under each type of strategy. These evaluation methods do not make the strategy decision but rather are constructs for helping managers think about the organization and its relative situation. The chapter concludes by illustrating the relationship between the seven strategic decisions and the strategic alternatives.

CHAPTER 6

Developing Strategic Alternatives

"The understanding that underlies the right decision grows out of the clash and conflict of divergent opinions and out of the serious consideration of competing alternatives. . . . Unless one has considered alternatives, one has a closed mind."

– Peter F. Drucker

LEARNING OBJECTIVES

After completing this chapter you should:

1. Understand the decision logic of the strategy formulation process and be able to discuss its steps.
2. Be able to identify the hierarchy of strategies and strategic decisions.
3. Understand the nature of directional strategies, adaptive strategies, market entry strategies, positioning strategies, and operational strategies.
4. Be able to identify the strategic alternatives available to health care organizations.
5. Understand the rationale and advantages and disadvantages of each of the strategic alternatives.

The Columbia/HCA Merger – One of Many Strategic Alternatives Used by the Companies

Although the 1994 merger between Columbia Healthcare Corporation and Hospital Corporation of America (HCA) constitutes one of the most dramatic responses to the health care reform initiatives of the early 1990s, it is but one of a series of strategic alternatives used by both HCA and Columbia over the past several years. The merged company, Columbia/HCA Healthcare Corporation, is the nation's largest private hospital chain, operating 190 hospitals with 42,000 beds in 26 states and 3 hospitals in 2 foreign countries.

Louisville, Kentucky – based Columbia, with annual revenues of over $5 billion, has engaged in an aggressive market development strategy through acquisition strategies since 1987, making it the nation's largest nongovernment hospital chain. Pursuing a product development strategy, Columbia signed an alliance agreement with Medical Care America, the largest outpatient organization in the United States. In addition, Columbia merged with Galen Health Care, the former hospital division of Humana, in a $3.2 billion dollar deal and acquired Basic American Medical. After the mergers, Columbia engaged in enhancement strategies by upgrading facilities and emphasizing quality. In addition, Columbia has pursued vertical integration through managed-care contracts.

Similarly, HCA has used several strategic alternatives over the past ten years. First, HCA used aggressive market development, much of it through acquisition strategies (horizontal integration) of independent hospitals. Despite rapid growth to ownership of 463 facilities, HCA decided bigness was no longer an appropriate approach. In 1984, the company embarked on a retrenchment strategy and divested 104 hospitals to HealthTrust. In 1989, HCA divested Quorum and had just under 150 hospitals. In 1992, HCA divested twenty-eight psychiatric hospitals. After its retrenchment strategy, HCA turned to enhancement strategies – improving management at all levels.

Many types of strategies have been used effectively by this $10 billion health care combination. Which strategies are most appropriate in which situations? Is there a hierarchy of strategies? Which are superordinate and which subordinate? How do organizations select a strategy, especially in turbulent times?

Source: Sandy Lutz and John Burns. "HCA – Columbia Merger Fueling Talk About Prospects for Success," *Modern Healthcare* 23, no. 41 (1993), pp. 2–3 and 6.

STRATEGY FORMULATION

Strategic management and the development of a strategy are essentially parts of a decision-making process – making a choice from several strategic alternatives. Therefore, strategy formulation is not a single decision but rather a series of increasingly more specific decisions. There are several different types of strategies and a decision logic for formulating strategy. In the Introductory Incident, the merger of Columbia and HCA was but one decision in a series of strategic decisions. A merger is not an end in itself. The important strategic question is, "Why did they merge?" What broader strategy were they pursuing that suggested a merger? A merger strategy is a means to a broader strategic end. In addition, what subsequent strategic decisions will have to be made to make the merger (and the broader strategy) successful?

Chapters 6 and 7 discuss the strategy formulation process. This chapter classifies the types of strategies and develops a hierarchy of strategic alternatives available to health care organizations. Chapter 7 discusses methods for analyzing these alternatives to make a strategic choice and develop a strategic plan. In addition, Chapter 7 demonstrates how strategy selection relates to the seven strategic decision areas introduced in Chapter 1. The results of the formulation process constitute a major portion of the strategic plan.

The relationship of strategy formulation to situational analysis and strategic implementation is illustrated in Exhibit 6–1. Situational analysis provides information concerning the external and internal environments that is used in strategy formulation to develop strategic alternatives and select the strategy for the organization. Operational strategies then may be developed to implement the broader organizational strategy. The operational strategies will be discussed in Chapters 8 through 12.

THE DECISION LOGIC OF STRATEGY FORMULATION

Five types of strategies make up the strategy formulation process. Strategy is developed through:

- directional strategies;
- adaptive strategies;
- market entry strategies;
- positioning strategies; and
- operational strategies.

Decisions concerning these strategy types must be made sequentially, with each subsequent decision more specifically defining the activities of the organization. That is, directional strategies must be made first, followed by adaptive strategies and then market entry strategies. Next, the products or services are introduced or reintroduced to the market in a way to be different (or similar to) competitive products (positioning strategies); and finally, specific functional and organization-wide action plans are developed (operational strategies). The decision logic for strategy formulation is illustrated in Exhibit 6–2.

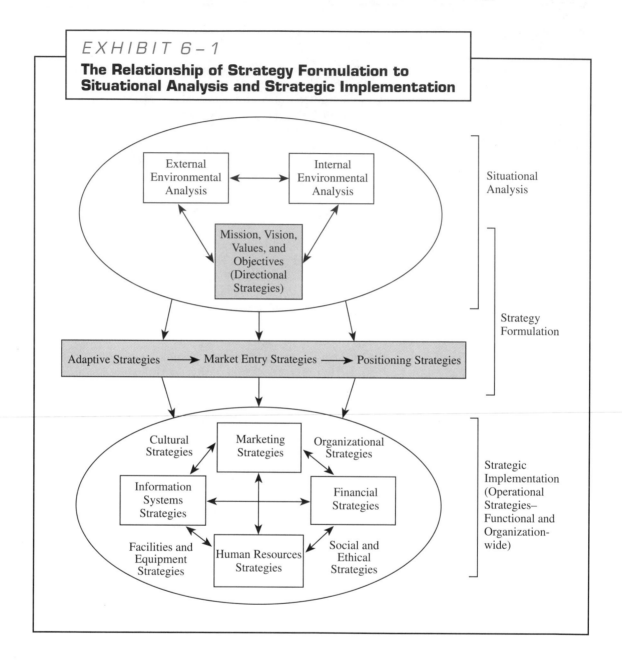

EXHIBIT 6–1

The Relationship of Strategy Formulation to Situational Analysis and Strategic Implementation

As shown in Exhibit 6–2, the organization must first reaffirm or establish and reach consensus on its mission, vision, values, and broad objectives. These decisions set the direction for the organization and as noted in Chapter 5 are referred to as *directional strategies*. Next, the *adaptive strategies* must be identified. These strategies are concerned with the variety of methods available to expand, contract, or maintain (stabilize) operations. The potential

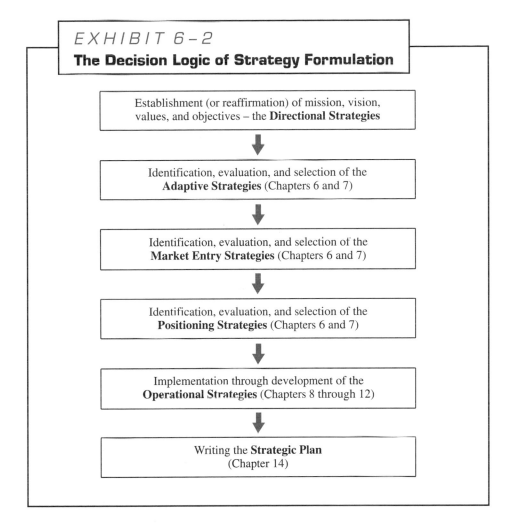

EXHIBIT 6-2

The Decision Logic of Strategy Formulation

Establishment (or reaffirmation) of mission, vision, values, and objectives – the **Directional Strategies**

Identification, evaluation, and selection of the **Adaptive Strategies** (Chapters 6 and 7)

Identification, evaluation, and selection of the **Market Entry Strategies** (Chapters 6 and 7)

Identification, evaluation, and selection of the **Positioning Strategies** (Chapters 6 and 7)

Implementation through development of the **Operational Strategies** (Chapters 8 through 12)

Writing the **Strategic Plan** (Chapter 14)

adaptive strategic alternatives must be evaluated and a specific strategy or combination of strategies adopted. The adaptive strategies outline the major strategic emphasis for the organization to accomplish its mission and objectives – the directional strategies. Third, *market entry strategies* must be identified, evaluated, and specified. Market entry strategies indicate how an adaptive strategy will be carried out or how the market will be entered. Fourth, a positioning strategy must be identified, evaluated, and selected. *Positioning strategies* indicate the place in the market (or buyer's perceptions) of the products and services in relation to other market "players." Finally, *operational strategies,* functional and organization-wide, to carry out the adaptive, market entry, and position strategies, must be identified, evaluated, and selected. The scope and role of the five strategy types are summarized in Exhibit 6–3.

EXHIBIT 6–3

Scope and Role of Strategy Types in Strategy Formulation

Strategy	Scope and Role
Directional Strategies	The broadest strategies set the fundamental direction of the organization by establishing a mission for the organization (Who are we?) and providing a vision for the future (What should we be?). These strategies create an understanding of the philosophy or values and set benchmarks for success – objectives.
Adaptive Strategies	These strategies are more specific than directional strategies and provide the primary methods for achieving the vision of the organization. These strategies delineate how the organization will expand, contract, or stabilize operations.
Market Entry Strategies	These strategies carry out the expansion and stabilization strategies through purchase, cooperation, or internal development. These strategies provide methods for access or entry to the market. Market entry strategies normally are not necessary for contraction strategies.
Positioning Strategies	These strategies position the organization vis-à-vis other organizations within a market. These strategies are market oriented and best articulate the competitive advantage within the market. These strategies may be market-wide or directed to particular market segments.
Operational Strategies	The most specific strategies are developed for the functional areas (marketing, finance, information systems, human resources, and so on) and for the entire organization. Organization-wide strategies include culture, organization, facilities and equipment, ethics and social responsibility, and so on. In combination, these actions must accomplish the positioning, market entry, adaptive, and directional strategies.

After all alternatives have been evaluated, decisions concerning the alternatives within each strategy type have to be made. Then a strategic plan is written. Recall that all decisions are made following a comprehensive situational analysis and should be based on as much information as possible. Before the plan is formalized, it is important to remember that organization-wide understanding of and commitment to the strategies must be developed if they are to be successful.

The choice of a strategic alternative creates momentum or direction for an organization and subsequently shapes its internal systems (organization, technology, information systems, culture, policies, skills, and so on). This momentum is reinforced as managers understand, commit, and make decisions according to the strategy.

Exhibit 6–4 presents a comprehensive schematic or map of the hierarchy of strategic alternatives. The hierarchy represents a multitude of strategic alternatives available to health care organizations. In this context, strategy development should be viewed as a sequential decision-making process – a process of evaluating and selecting from various alternatives. The map not only identifies the alternatives but also the sequential relationships among the strategies. Using Exhibit 6–4, each strategy type and the available alternatives will be discussed in the remainder of this chapter.

DIRECTIONAL STRATEGIES: MISSION, VISION, VALUES, AND OBJECTIVES

Chapter 5 explored mission, vision, values, and objectives and indicated that these elements are part of both situational analysis and strategy formulation. They are a part of situational analysis because they describe the current state of the organization and codify its basic beliefs and philosophy. However, mission, vision, values, and objectives are also a part of strategy formulation because they set the boundaries and indicate the broadest direction for the organization. As a result, these important decisions are referred to as *directional strategies.*

The mission, vision, values, and objectives should provide a sensible and realistic planning framework for the organization. Within this planning framework, more specific strategic alternatives are selected. Therefore, it is important that environmental analysis has been used to identify the current and emerging issues (opportunities and threats) that will affect the success of the organization. Concurrently, management should have carefully analyzed the organization and be attuned to its abilities and capabilities (strengths and weaknesses). Having assimilated and evaluated all this information, management then decides what strategic alternatives are appropriate for the organization.

Because formulation of the mission, vision, values, and objectives provides the broad direction for the organization, directional strategic decisions must be made first. Then the adaptive strategies provide further strategic momentum by specifying product/market expansion, contraction, or stabilization. The adaptive strategies form the core of the strategy formulation process.

ADAPTIVE STRATEGIES

From a practical standpoint, whether the organization should expand, contract, or remain stable is the first decision that must be made once the direction of the organization has been set (or reaffirmed). As shown in Exhibit 6–4, several specific alternatives are available to expand operations, contract operations, or seek stabilization. These alternatives provide the major strategic choices for the organization.

EXHIBIT 6-4

Hierarchy of Strategic Decisions and Alternatives

Directional Strategies → Adaptive Strategies → Market Entry Strategies → Positioning Strategies → Operational Strategies

Directional Strategies
- Mission
- Vision
- Values
- Objectives

Adaptive Strategies

Expansion
- Diversification — Related / Unrelated
- Vertical Integration — Forward / Backward
- Market Development — Geographic / Segmentation
- Product Development — Product Line / Product Enhancement
- Penetration — Promotion / Distribution / Pricing

Contraction
- Divestiture — Total / Partial
- Liquidation — Operations / Assets
- Harvesting — Fast / Slow
- Retrenchment — Personnel / Markets / Products / Assets

Stabilization
- Enhancement — Quality / Efficiency / Innovation / Speed / Flexibility
- Status Quo

Market Entry Strategies

Purchase
- Acquisition
- Licensing
- Venture Capital Investment

Cooperation
- Merger
- Alliance
- Joint Venture

Development
- Internal Development
- Internal Venture

Positioning Strategies

Market-wide
- Cost Leadership
- Differentiation

Market Segment
- Focus/Cost Leadership
- Focus/Differentiation

Operational Strategies

Functional
- Marketing
- Information Systems
- Finance
- Human Resources

Organization-wide
- Culture
- Organization Structure
- Facilities and Equipment
- Ethics and Social Responsibility

Expansion Strategies

If expansion is selected as the best way to perform the mission and realize the vision of the organization, several alternatives are available. Two of the alternatives are corporate level strategies and three are divisional level strategies. The *expansion strategies* include:

- diversification (corporate level);
- vertical integration (corporate level);
- market development (divisional level);
- product development (divisional level); and
- penetration (divisional level).

Corporate-level strategies consider the best mix of semi-autonomous divisions operating in separate markets with distinct products or services. Therefore, corporate-level strategies generally address the current viability and potential of a portfolio of separate businesses (divisions). Corporate strategies are not concerned with one market or product/service, but rather with several "businesses" assembled to fulfill the mission of the organization given the demands of the external environment. Corporate-level strategies address the question, "What business(es) should we be in?" Thus, an integrated health system must consider what portfolio of businesses – acute-care hospital, long-term care, home health, and so on (or businesses outside the health care industry) – best serves the mission of the system. Corporate expansion strategies increase the scope of the organization.

In contrast to corporate strategies, divisional strategies are concerned with a single well-defined market and with a product or service line that serves a specific market or service area. Division-level strategies deal with the question, "How should an organization compete in a given market?" Therefore, division-level strategic alternatives are concerned with an organization's current area of operations and are used by organizations such as SSUs, single-unit hospitals, and small group practices to compete within a service area.

Diversification *Diversification* strategies, in many cases, are selected because markets have been identified outside of the organization's core business that offer potential for substantial growth. Often, an organization that selects a diversification strategy is not achieving its growth or revenue objectives within its current market, and these new markets provide an opportunity to achieve them. There are, of course, other reasons organizations decide to diversify. For instance, health care organizations may identify opportunities for growth in less-regulated markets such as specialty hospitals, long-term care facilities, or managed care.

Diversification is generally seen as a risky alternative because the organization is entering a relatively unfamiliar market or offering a product or service that is different from its current products or services. Organizations have found that the risk of diversification can be reduced if markets and products are selected that complement one another. Therefore, managers engaging in diversification seek synergy between corporate divisions (SBUs or SSUs).

There are two types of diversification: related or concentric diversification and unrelated or conglomerate diversification. Exhibit 6–5 illustrates possible

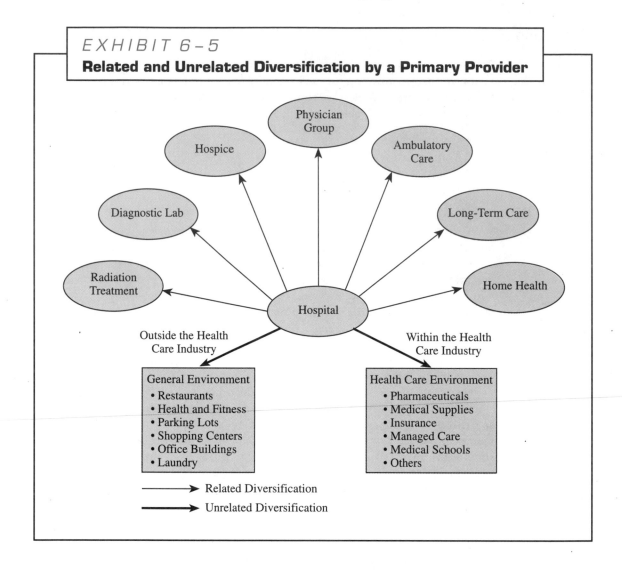

EXHIBIT 6–5
Related and Unrelated Diversification by a Primary Provider

related and unrelated diversification strategies for one type of primary health care organization.

In *related diversification,* an organization chooses to enter a market that is similar or related to its present operations. This form of diversification is sometimes called *concentric diversification* because the organization develops a "circle" of related products. Exhibit 6–6 illustrates the circle of related products for a hospital that is interested in diversifying into another segment of the health care market, the long-term-care market.

The general assumption underlying related diversification is that the organization will be able to obtain some level of synergy (a complementary relationship where the total effect is greater than the sum of its parts) between the production/delivery, marketing, or technology of the core business and the new related

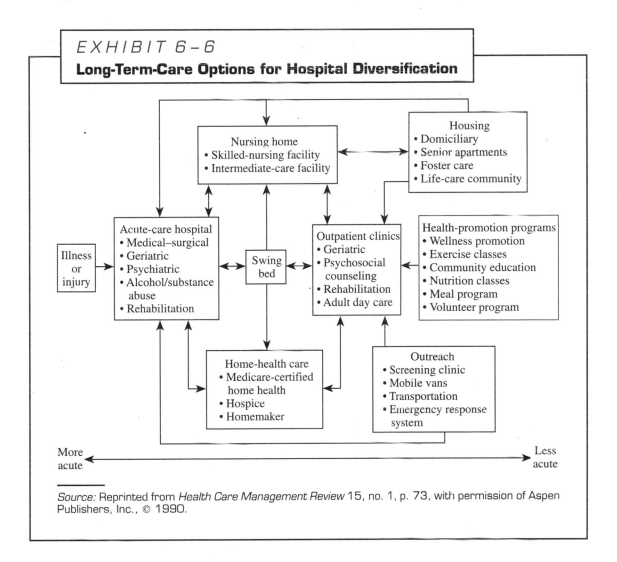

EXHIBIT 6-6
Long-Term-Care Options for Hospital Diversification

Source: Reprinted from *Health Care Management Review* 15, no. 1, p. 73, with permission of Aspen Publishers, Inc., © 1990.

product or service. For hospitals, the two primary reasons for diversifying in the 1990s are to introduce nonacute- or subacute-care services that reduce hospital costs and to offer a wider range of services to large employers and purchasing coalitions through capitated contracts.[1] The movement of acute-care hospitals into skilled-nursing care is an example of related diversification. Related diversification strategies that have been generally profitable and unprofitable are presented in Exhibit 6–7.

On the other hand, in *unrelated diversification,* an organization enters a market that is unlike its present operations. This action creates a "portfolio" of separate products or services. Unrelated diversification, or *conglomerate diversification,* generally involves semi-autonomous divisions or strategic service units. An example of unrelated diversification would be a hospital diversifying into the

---

EXHIBIT 6-7

Most Frequently Reported Profitable and Unprofitable Related Diversification

Profitable	Unprofitable
• Ambulatory surgery	• Crisis intervention
• Chemotherapy/radiation therapy	• Outpatient psychiatric/mental health services
• Rehabilitation program	• Urgent-care/immediate-care centers
• Cardiac rehabilitation conditioning	• Geriatric assessment/consultation/case management
• Outpatient respiratory therapy	• Geriatric day care
• Durable medical equipment	• Home-delivered meals
• In-home infusion therapy	• Health screening services
• In-home physical therapy	• Immunization services
• In-home extended therapy service	• Occupational health services
• In-home respiratory care	• School health exams
• Outpatient radiology	• Wellness programs
• Outpatient CT scan	• Disease counseling
• Outpatient nuclear magnetic resonance or magnetic resonance imaging	• Community health lectures
• Outpatient ultrasound	• Family planning; parenting and sibling education
• Outpatient hematology/biochemistry lab	• Hospice
• Outpatient neurological diagnostic services	• Intermediate-care/skilled-nursing facility
• Outpatient cardiovascular diagnostic services	• Hospital-sponsored primary-care group practice
• Outpatient nuclear medicine	

Source: Stephen M. Shortell, Ellen Morrison, and Susan Hughes, "The Keys to Successful Diversification: Lessons from Leading Hospital Systems," *Hospital & Health Services Administration* 34, no. 4 (Winter 1989), p. 476. Health Administration Press, Ann Arbor, MI. © 1989, Foundation of the American College of Healthcare Executives.

---

operation of a restaurant, parking lot, or medical office building. In such a case, the new business is unrelated to health care although it may be complementary (synergistic) to the provision of health services. Unrelated diversification, however, has been generally unsuccessful in generating revenue for acute-care hospitals as illustrated in Perspective 6–1.

Vertical Integration   A *vertical integration* strategy is a decision to grow along the channel of distribution of the core operations. Thus, a health care organization

PERSPECTIVE 6-1
Unrelated Diversification Difficult for Hospitals

In the 1980s hospitals were buying dude ranches in Montana and bottling companies in Ohio. They were expanding into janitorial services, catering firms, condominiums, travel agencies, and health clubs. Unrelated diversification was intended to spread risks or develop new sources of revenues to support acute-care operations; however, many of the diversified businesses have been divested or liquidated as losing money or not in the best interests of a health care organization. Some unrelated diversifications broke even or were marginally profitable, but they did not justify the diversion of executive time. Many hospital administrators lacked the skills to manage these non-acute-care businesses. In addition, boards of trustees questioned the additional capital needed by these diversified businesses and wondered when they would become profitable.

In the 1990s, health care organizations are more apt to employ related diversification to create or move into a new market or vertical integration to manage the health of a population. Simply owning an asset to increase revenue has not been an effective strategy. Often related diversification and vertical integration are achieved through collaboration or joint ventures with similar providers.

Source: Jay Greene, "Trying a New Line? Diversifier Beware" and "Diversification, Take Two," *Modern Healthcare* 23, no. 39 (1993). pp. 28–32.

may grow toward suppliers or toward patients. When an organization grows along the channel of distribution toward its suppliers (upstream) it is called *backward vertical integration.* When an organization grows toward the consumer or patient (downstream) it is called *forward vertical integration.*

Vertical integration can reduce costs and enhance an organization's competitive position. Reductions may occur through lower supply costs and better integration of the "elements of production." With vertical integration, management can better ensure that supplies are of the appropriate quality and delivered at the right time. For instance, some hospitals have instituted technical educational programs because many health professionals (the major element of production in health care) are in critically short supply.

A decision to vertically integrate further commits an organization to a particular product or market and therefore management must believe in the long-term viability of the product/service and market. As a result, the opportunity costs of vertical integration must be weighed against the benefits of other strategic alternatives such as diversification. Examples of vertical integration would be a hospital chain acquiring one of its major medical products suppliers (backward integration) or a drug manufacturer moving into drug distribution (forward integration).

Whether a strategic alternative is viewed as vertical integration or related diversification may depend on the objective or intent of the alternative. For instance, when the primary intent is to enter a new market in order to grow, the decision is to diversify. However, if the intent is to control the flow of patients to various units, the decision is to vertically integrate. Thus, a decision by an acute-care hospital to acquire a skilled-nursing unit may be viewed as related diversification (entering a new growth market) or vertical integration (controlling downstream patient flow).

In the area of supplying patients to various health care units, several patterns of vertical integration may be identified.[2] In Exhibit 6–8, an inpatient acute-care facility is the strategic service unit or core technology that decides to vertically integrate. Example 1 is a hospital that is not vertically integrated. The hospital admits and discharges patients from and to other units outside the organization. Example 2 is a totally integrated system in which integration occurs both upstream and downstream. In this case, patients flow through the system from one unit to the next, and upstream units are viewed as "feeder" units to downstream units.

Example 3 represents a hospital that has vertically integrated upstream. In addition, more than one unit is involved at several stages of the integration. For instance, there are two wellness/health promotion units, three primary-care units, and three urgent-care units. The dashed line represents the receipt of patients via external or market transfers. Example 4 illustrates a multihospital system engaged in vertical integration. Three hospitals form the core of the system, which also contains three nursing homes, two rehab units, a home health unit, three urgent-care facilities, three primary-care facilities, and a wellness center.

Finally, a quirk of the health care system is illustrated in Example 5. Some health care systems are closed systems with fixed patient populations entirely covered through prepayment. Thus, whereas in the second example, the health care organization is vertically integrated, in the fifth example, patients are a part of the system. This insurance function is shown as an additional unit and identified by the letter *i* in the example. An example of a forward vertical integration opportunity is illustrated in Perspective 6–2.

Market Development *Market development* is a divisional strategy used to enter new markets with present products or services. Specifically, market development is a strategy designed to achieve greater volume, through geographic (service area) expansion or by targeting new market segments within the present geographic area. Typically, market development is selected when the organization is fairly strong in the market (often with a differentiated product), the market is growing, and the prospects are good for long-term growth. A market development strategy is strongly supported by the marketing, financial, information system, organizational, and human resources functions. An example of a market development strategy would be a chain of outpatient clinics opening a new clinic in a new geographic area (present products and services in a new market).

Product Development *Product development* is the introduction of new products to present markets (geographic and segments). Typically, product development takes the form of product enhancements and product line extension. Product

EXHIBIT 6-8

Patterns of Vertical Integration Among Health Care Organizations

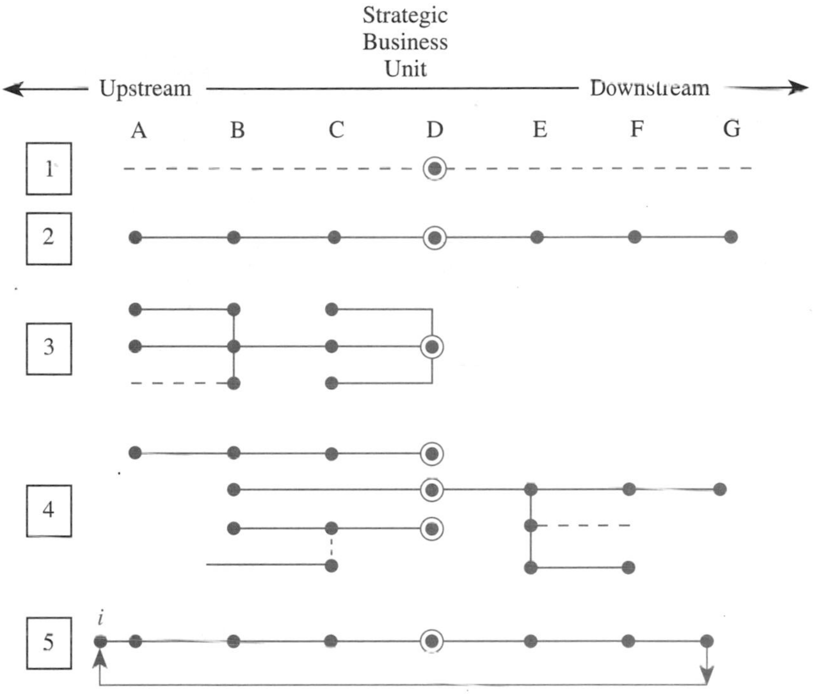

A = wellness/health promotion unit
B = primary care unit
C = urgent care unit
D = hospital (inpatient acute care unit)
E = skilled nursing unit
F = rehabilitation unit
G = home health unit

Solid lines depict fully internal transfers

Dashed lines depict market or external transfers

Source: Adapted from Stephen S. Mick and Douglas A. Conrad, "The Decision to Integrate Vertically in Health Care Organizations," *Hospital & Health Services Administration* 33, no. 3 (Fall 1988), p. 351. Health Administration Press, Ann Arbor, MI. © 1988, Foundation of the American College of Healthcare Executives. As adapted from K. R. Harrigan, "Formulating Vertical Integration Strategies," *Academy of Management Review* 9, no. 4 (1984), pp. 638–652.

development should not be confused with related diversification. Related diversification introduces a new product category (though related to present operations), whereas product development may be viewed as refinements, complements, or natural extensions of present products. Product development strategies are common in large metropolitan areas where hospitals vie for increased market share

---

PERSPECTIVE 6-2
Forward Vertical Integration for Nursing Homes

An emphasis on community-based home care and an increase in long-term care insurance has opened new markets for many nursing homes. David R. Banks, chairman, president, and chief executive officer of Beverly Enterprises, which operates four nursing centers and more than 800 nursing homes, has indicated that vertical integration into home health care would be a logical step for Beverly. Banks pointed out that home care expansion is a logical step for large nursing home chains because it creates a new market for patients discharged from their subacute- and specialty-care facilities. Forward vertical integration is appealing to nursing home management because it creates a continuum of care where consistent care may be provided. In addition, the skills required to treat patients in nursing homes are readily transferable to the home market plus population trends suggest a growing and stable market.

Source: Eric Weissenstein and John Burns, "Long-Term Care to Evolve," *Modern Healthcare* 23, no. 39 (1993), p. 13.

---

within particular segments of the market, such as cancer treatment and open-heart surgery. Another good example of product development is in the area of women's health. Many hospitals have opened clinics designed to serve the special needs of women in the present market area.

Penetration An attempt to better serve current markets with current products or services is referred to as a *market penetration* strategy. Similar to market and product development, *penetration* strategies are used to increase volume and market share. A market penetration strategy is supported by aggressive functional strategies, particularly within the marketing function. Market penetration is centered on promotional, distribution, and pricing strategies and often includes increasing the number of salespersons, increasing advertising, offering sales promotion, or increasing publicity efforts.

An example of a penetration strategy is Baptist Medical Center's (BMC) response to the expansion of the prestigious Mayo Clinic into the Jacksonville, Florida, area. BMC believed that it was unlikely that the Mayo Clinic would compete in pediatric care. Therefore, BMC capitalized on its major strength and initiated an aggressive adaptive/penetration strategy in pediatric care. To enhance availability to the market, BMC formed alliances (a market entry strategy) to develop a regional children's health center. BMC allied with the 450-bed University Medical Center, the University of Florida Health Science Center in Gainesville, and the Nemours Foundation of Wilmington, Delaware (a source of competition in the past). In addition, BMC opened a new $45 million children's hospital. BMC has supported this strategy with extensive promotion to inform the public of its strategic emphasis.[3] An additional example of both penetration and product development used to turn around a failing hospital is provided in Perspective 6–3.

The various expansion strategies, their relative risks, and their rationales are summarized in Exhibit 6–9.

Contraction Strategies

Contraction strategies decrease the size and scope of operations either at the corporate level or divisional level. Contraction strategies include:

PERSPECTIVE 6–3

Memorial Hospital Uses Penetration and Product Development Expansion Strategies

Memorial Hospital, a ninety-nine-bed, county-run hospital in Palestine, Texas, engaged in penetration and product development strategies as well as some internal enhancement strategies to turn around declining revenues. For example, its penetration strategies included cafeteria discounts for senior citizens, free health screenings, and monthly get-acquainted luncheons. In addition, product development included:

- a community education program run by a nurse who began compiling information on heart and lung disease,
- education programs for women on breast self-examination,
- a mobile unit staffed by a nurse and three assistants to offer health and education outreach to groups and employers covering a five-county area,
- recruitment of specialty physicians,
- purchase of new technology (product development/enhancement),
- six centers of excellence, including heart and laser surgery, and
- a sports medicine center that provides services to high school athletes

in surrounding counties (product development/market development).

Underlying the penetration and product development strategy was the belief that the strategies would strengthen Memorial's relationship with its community. As the hospital's administrator indicated, "If we're out there all the time giving people blood pressure checks and offering them literature on sports medicine or laser surgery, then they will begin to think of Memorial Hospital when they get sick." The strategy has paid off. Visits to the emergency department have risen from about 500 a month in 1989 to about 1,100 in 1992. In addition, operating income rose from $242,000 in 1990 to nearly $3 million in 1992; total margin improved from 1.94 percent in 1990 to 14.1 percent in 1992, and days of cash on hand went from five days to fifty-three days.

Source: Frank Cerne and Rhonda Bergman, "Into the Black: 1993 Hospital Turnaround Contest Winners," *Hospitals & Health Networks* 67, no. 14 (1993), pp. 20–30.

Strategy	Relative Risk	Rationale
Related Diversification	Moderate	• Pursuit of high-growth markets • Entering less-regulated segments • Cannot achieve current objectives • Synergy is possible from new business • Offset seasonal or cyclical influences
Unrelated Diversification	High	• Pursuit of high-growth markets • Entering less-regulated segments • Cannot achieve current objectives • Current markets are saturated or in decline • Organization has excess cash • Antitrust regulations prohibit expansion in current industry • Tax loss may be acquired
Backward Vertical Integration	High	• Control the flow of patients through the system • Scarcity of raw materials or essential inventory/supplies • Deliveries are unreliable • Lack of materials or supplies will shut down operations • Price or quality of materials or supplies variable • Industry/market seen as profitable for long period
Forward Vertical Integration	High	• Control the flow of patients through the system • Faster delivery required • High level of coordination required between one stage and another • Industry/market seen as profitable for long period
Market Development (geographic and segmentation)	Moderate	• New markets are available for present products • New markets may be served efficiently • Expected high revenues

EXHIBIT 6-9   cont'd

Strategy	Relative Risk	Rationale
		• Organization has cost leadership advantage • Organization has differentiation advantage • Current market is growing
Product Development (product line and product enhancement)	Moderate	• Currently in strong market but product is weak or product line incomplete • Market tastes are changing • Product technology is changing • Maintenance or creation of differentiation advantage
Penetration (promotion, distribution, and pricing)	Moderate	• Present market is growing • Product/service innovation will extend market of product life cycle • Expected revenues are high • Organization has cost leadership advantage • Organization has differentiation advantage

- divestiture (corporate level),
- liquidation (corporate level),
- harvesting (divisional level), and
- retrenchment (divisional level).

Divestiture *Divestiture* is a contraction strategy in which an operating strategic service unit is sold off as a result of a decision to permanently and completely leave the market despite its current viability. Generally, the business to be divested has value and will continue to be operated by the purchasing organization. A good example of a divestiture strategy is American Medical International's (AMI) decision to sell its four acute-care Swiss hospitals to Klinik Hirslanden AG of Zurich, Switzerland, for $169 million. These hospitals will continue to be operated by Klinik Hirslanden. This decision was part of a strategy by AMI to divest itself of all the company's overseas operations.[4]

Within the past decade, the strategy of "unbundling" (divesting by a hospital of one or more of its services) has become common. Thus, hospitals are divesting noncore services previously performed internally. Typical services and products produced in a hospital that are not necessarily part of the core bundle of activities include laboratory, pharmacy, X ray, physical therapy, occupational therapy, and dietary services.[5] In addition, "hotel" services (laundry, housekeeping, and so on) formerly performed by hospitals are contracted to outsiders. Exhibit 6–10 shows contract hotel services used by hospitals and the reason these services are out-sourced. Even medical services in such specialty areas as ophthalmology are increasingly being performed outside the hospital in "surgi-centers" and may be candidates for divestiture.

Divestiture decisions are made for a number of reasons. An organization may need cash to fund more important operations for long-term growth, or the division/SSU may be seen as not achieving management's objectives. For AMI, the cash generated by the sale of its overseas operations was used to reduce long-term debt.

Some practical guidelines for the divestiture of services are presented in Exhibit 6–11. If eight or more responses support reinvesting, the organization should continue with the activity; however, if eight or more support divestiture, consideration should be given to selling the service. If the responses are relatively even, significant modifications in the service should be considered.

Liquidation *Liquidation* involves selling the assets of an organization. The assumption underlying a liquidation strategy is that the unit cannot be sold as a viable and ongoing operation. However, the assets of the organization (facilities, equipment, and so on) still have value and may be sold for other uses. Organizations, of course, may be partially or completely liquidated.

Common reasons for adopting a liquidation strategy include bankruptcy, the desire to dispose of nonproductive assets, and the emergence of a new technology that results in a rapid decline in the use of the old technology. For instance, upon leaving a market, an aging hospital building may be sold for its property value or an alternative use. In a declining market, a liquidation strategy may be a long-term strategy to be carried out in an orderly manner over a period of years.

Harvesting A *harvesting* strategy is selected when the market has entered long-term decline. The reason underlying such a strategy is that the organization has a relatively strong market position but industry-wide revenues are expected to decline over the next several years. Therefore, the organization will "ride the decline," allowing the business to generate as much cash as possible but at the same time it will invest no new resources.

In a harvesting strategy, the organization attempts to reap maximum short-term benefits before the product or service is eliminated. Such a strategy allows the organization an orderly exit from a declining segment of the market by planned downsizing. Harvesting has not been widely used in health care but will be more frequently encountered in the 1990s as markets mature and organizations exit various segments. For instance, some regional hospitals that have developed rural hospital networks have experienced difficulty in maintaining their commitment to health care in small communities. The twenty-bed hospitals frequently found in rural networks tend to struggle financially because of a lack of support from both specialists and primary-care physicians, an aging population, and flight of

EXHIBIT 6 – 10
Contract Services Used by Hospitals

Hotel Service	Percent of Health Facilities Contracting the Service 1991	Percent of Health Facilities Contracting the Service 1992
Laundry	14.6	17.0
Housekeeping	13.1	14.2
Dietary	*	11.9
Food Service	13.5	10.8
Security	7.8	9.1
Plant Operations/ Maintenance	4.5	5.1
Groundskeeping	5.1	3.7
Any Hotel Service	29.7	36.0

*Data not available

Why Contract for Hotel Services?

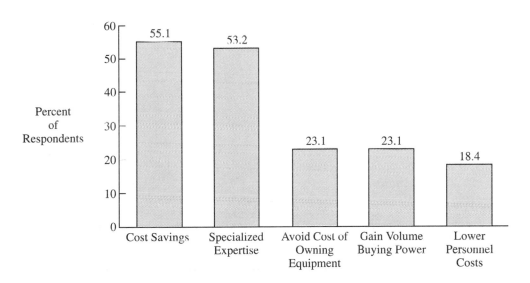

Note: Results are based on a survey of 1,185 health facility respondents
Source: 1993 Contract Service Survey, American Hospital Publishing, Inc. Chicago, Reported in Health Facilities Management 6, no. 8 (1993), p. 84.

EXHIBIT 6 – 11

Guidelines for Divestiture of Services

	Reinvest	Divest
1. Were the actual financial results equal to or better than those anticipated in the strategic plan?	Yes	No
2. Has the organization been in operation less than 18 months?	Yes	No
3. Is there at least an example of a known profitable operation of approximately the same size as your operation?	Yes	No
4. If utilization targets have not been achieved, what is the reason?	Not achieved, but still reasonable	Overestimated
5. Is your payer mix the same as or better than you expected?	Yes	No
6. Is this a high fixed-cost operation with excess capacity?	Yes, could increase utilization without adding much expense	No, expanding services means adding expenses
7. Can you quantify spin-off benefits to the system?	Yes	No
8. Can you identify any real competitive advantages this service has in the marketplace?	Yes	No
9. Can you identify specific management actions that can reverse the losses?	Yes	No
10. Is this a mature product or market?	No	Yes
11. Would you use your own money to invest in this venture?	Yes	No

Source: Adapted from Jay Greene, "A Strategy for Cutting Back," *Modern Healthcare*, August 18, 1989, p. 29, developed by the Society for Healthcare Planning and Marketing, American Hospital Association.

the young to urban areas. Twenty-bed rural hospitals are probably in a long-term decline with little hope for survival. On the other hand, fifty-bed hospitals have managed to maintain or improve their financial position because of effective physician recruitment, good community image, and the continued viability of the communities themselves. Therefore, regional hospitals with rural networks may have to employ a harvesting strategy for the twenty-bed hospitals while using one of the development or stabilization strategies for the fifty-bed and larger hospitals.

Retrenchment A *retrenchment* strategy is a response to declining profitability usually brought about by increasing costs. The market is still viewed as viable, and the organization's products and services continue to have wide acceptance. However, costs have risen as a percentage of revenue, putting pressure on profitability.

Retrenchment typically involves a redefinition of the target market, selective cost elimination, and asset reduction. Retrenchment is directed toward reduction in personnel, the range of products/services, or the geographic market served and represents an effort to reduce the scope of operations.

Over time, organizations may find that they are overstaffed given the level of demand. As a result, their costs are higher than those of competitors. When market growth is anticipated, personnel are added to accommodate the growth, but during periods of decline, personnel positions are seldom eliminated. A reduction in the staff members who have become superfluous or redundant is often central to a retrenchment strategy.

Similarly, in an attempt to "round-out" the product or service line, products and services are added. Over time, these additional products and services may tend to add more costs than revenues. In many organizations, less than 20 percent of the products account for more than 80 percent of the revenue. Under these circumstances, retrenchment may be in order.

Finally, there are times when geographic growth is undertaken without regard for costs. Eventually, managers realize they are "spread too thin" to adequately serve the market. In addition, well-positioned competitors are able to provide quality products and services at lower costs because of their proximity. In this situation, geographic retrenchment (reducing the service area) is appropriate.

In many cases, a retrenchment strategy is implemented after periods of aggressive market development or acquisition of competitors. For example, in the early 1990s, HealthTrust employed a retrenchment strategy after having acquired 104 of HCA's hospitals. The retrenchment strategy reduced HealthTrust's hospitals from 104 to 92.

The various contraction strategies, their relative risks, and their rationales are summarized in Exhibit 6–12.

Stabilization Strategies

Often organizations pursue *stabilization strategies* when management believes the past strategy has been appropriate and few changes are required in the target markets or the organization's products and services. Stabilization does not necessarily mean that the organization will do nothing, but rather that management believes the organization is progressing appropriately. There are two stabilization strategies: enhancement (divisional) and status quo (divisional).

EXHIBIT 6-12
Rationales and Relative Risks of Contraction Strategic Alternatives

Strategy	Relative Risk	Rationale
Divestiture	Low	• Industry in long-term decline • Cash needed to enter new, higher-growth area • Lack of expected synergy with core operation • Required investment in new technology seen as too high • Too much regulation
Liquidation	Low	• Organization can no longer operate • Bankruptcy • Trim/reduce assets • Superseded by new technology
Harvesting	Low	• Late maturity/decline stage of the product life cycle • Considering divestiture or downsizing • Short-term cash needed
Retrenchment (personnel, markets, products, assets)	Moderate	• Market has become too diverse • Market is too geographically spread out • Personnel costs are too high • Too many products or services • Marginal or nonproductive facilities

---

Enhancement When management believes that the organization is progressing toward its vision and objectives but needs to "do things better," an *enhancement strategy* may be used; expansion or contraction of operations is not appropriate but "something needs to be done." Typically, enhancement strategies take the form of quality programs (CQI, TQM) directed toward improving organizational processes or cost-reduction programs designed to render the organization more efficient. In addition to quality and efficiency, enhancement strategies may be directed toward innovative management processes, speeding up the delivery of the products or services to the customer, and adding flexibility to the design of the product or services (market-wide customization).

Many times after an expansion strategy, an organization engages in stabilization/enhancement strategies. This was the case for Columbia Healthcare after its acquisition of Galen Health Care (see the Introductory Incident). After the $3.2 billion acquisition, Columbia initiated enhancement strategies directed toward upgrading facilities, improving its ability to evaluate clinical results, and reducing overhead costs. To help physicians make more cost-effective decisions, Columbia installed a new computer system that allowed them to look at clinical results on personal computers in their offices to compare the types of drugs, tests, and treatments that other physicians used for similar diagnoses. In addition, Columbia initiated enhancement strategies to reduce purchasing costs and improve quality. Despite its size, speed remained a strategic priority for Columbia.[6]

Status Quo A *status quo strategy* is based on the assumption that the market has matured and periods of high growth are over. Often, the organization has secured an acceptable market share and managers believe the position can be defended against competitors. This strategy is sometimes referred to as a *maintenance strategy*.

In a status quo strategy, the goal is to maintain services at current levels. However, additional resources may be required. Management attempts to prolong the life of the product or service for as long as possible. Environmental influences affecting the decline of the products or services should be carefully analyzed to determine when decline is imminent. An example of this strategy would be a full-service hospital investing heavily in marketing to prevent market share erosion for inpatient services.[7] Typically, organizations attempt a status quo strategy in some areas while engaging in market development, product development, or penetration in others to better utilize limited resources. For instance, a hospital may attempt to hold its market share (status quo) in slow-growth markets such as cardiac and pediatric services and attempt market development in higher growth markets such as intense, short-term rehabilitation care (renal dialysis, ophthalmology, or intravenous therapy, for example).

In mature markets, industry consolidation occurs as firms attempt to add volume and reduce costs. Therefore, managers must be wary of the emergence of a single dominant competitor that has achieved a significant cost differential. A status quo strategy is appropriate when there are two or three dominant providers in a stable market segment, because in this situation, market development or product development may be quite difficult and extremely expensive. The various stabilization strategies, their relative risks, and their rationales are summarized in Exhibit 6–13.

MARKET ENTRY STRATEGIES

The selection of the expansion or stabilization strategies from among the adaptive strategic alternatives dictates that the next decision to be made is which of the *market entry strategies* should be used. If a contraction adaptive strategy is selected, normally there is no market entry decision and market entry strategies are not used. The expansion strategies specify entering or gaining access to a new market, and the stabilization strategies call for obtaining new resources. Therefore, the next important decision that must be made for these strategies concerns how the organization will enter or develop the market.

There are three ways to enter a market. As illustrated in Exhibit 6–4, an organization can use its financial resources and *purchase* into the market, team with other organizations and use *cooperation* to enter a market, or use its own

EXHIBIT 6-13

**Rationales and Relative Risks of
Stabilization Strategic Alternatives**

Strategy	Relative Risk	Rationale
Enhancement (quality, efficiency, innovation, speed, and flexibility)	Low	• Organization has operational inefficiencies • Need to lower costs • Need to improve quality • Improve internal processes
Status quo	Low	• Maintain market share position • Maturity/late maturity stage of the product life cycle • Product/market generating cash but has little potential for future growth • Extremely competitive market

resources and *develop* its own products and services. It is important to understand that market entry strategies are not ends in themselves but serve a broader aim – the adaptive strategies. Any of the adaptive strategies may be carried out using any of the market entry strategies but each one makes different demands on the organization.

Purchase Strategies

Purchase market entry strategies allow an organization to use its financial resources to enter a market quickly, thereby initiating the adaptive strategy. There are three purchase market entry strategies: acquisition, licensing, and venture capital investment.

Acquisition *Acquisitions* are entry strategies to grow through the purchase of an existing organization, a unit of an organization, or a product/service. Thus, acquisition strategies may be used to carry out both corporate and divisional strategies. The acquiring organization may integrate the operations of the newly acquired organization into its present operations or may operate it as a separate business/service unit. Acquisitions offer a method for quickly entering a market or securing a needed channel member to improve or secure distribution. It is usually possible to assess the performance of an organization before purchase and thereby minimize the risks through careful analysis and selection. However, even a small acquired organization can be difficult to integrate into the existing culture and operations. Often it takes several years to "digest" an acquisition or to combine two organizational cultures.

Acquisition of a direct competitor is called *horizontal integration.* Horizontal integration is a method of obtaining growth within a market by purchasing direct competitors rather than using internal operational/functional strategies to take market share from competitors. Typically, organizations select horizontal integration for rapid geographical expansion or acquisition of a new technology.

Much of the growth of the for-profit hospital chains has been via a market development/acquisition/horizontal integration strategy. For example, Epic Healthcare Group used a horizontal integration strategy to rapidly enter the for-profit hospital market when it acquired thirty-six hospitals from American Medical International. In the past two decades, diversification and vertical integration through acquisition have been key entry strategies for initiating rapid market growth by health care organizations as well as by non-health care businesses. An example of vertical integration through acquisition is Aurora Health Care's acquisition of physician groups examined in Perspective 6–4.

PERSPECTIVE 6–4
Vertical Integration Through Acquisition

Many experts believe that physicians must be an integral part of a fully integrated health care system. Therefore, as part of a vertical integration strategy, Aurora Health Care in Milwaukee is converting itself from a multihospital system into an integrated delivery system by acquiring primary physician group practices. Seven-hospital Aurora created Aurora Medical Group (an SSU) to coordinate its acquisition and management of physician group practices. The Aurora Medical Group owned three group practices and nineteen clinics. A total of 116 primary-care and specialist physicians were employed with plans to add additional group practices. Donald Nestor, Aurora's senior vice president and chief financial officer indicated, "We think that we can offer lower cost and more convenient service locations in an integrated system approach." Complete physician/hospital integration has another benefit – it can reduce transactional or per-unit costs, which enhances their competitive position in managed-care contracting.

In addition to practice management assistance, Aurora pays for employed physicians' malpractice insurance and provides extensive benefit and pension programs. Intangible benefits for the physicians includes less frequent on-call status and greater control over their schedules. Creating an integrated delivery system that includes physicians has higher start-up costs than developing a physician/hospital organization (PHO) through contracts with an independent practice. However, Aurora believes that not only will long-term costs be lower but the organization will be better positioned for managed competition than those that deal with physicians as independent practitioners.

Source: Jay Green, "Physician Groups Key to Success at Milwaukee System," *Modern Healthcare* 23, no. 28 (1993), p. 30.

Licensing Acquiring a technology or product through *licensing* avoids the risks of technology or product development and may be viewed as an alternative to acquiring a complete company. License agreements provide rapid access to proven technologies and reduce the financial risk to the organization. However, the licensee usually does not receive proprietary technology and is dependent on the licensor for support and upgrade. In addition, the up-front dollar costs may be high. Typical of licensing is CareMap Corporation, which licenses operations software to hospitals.

Venture Capital Investment *Venture capital investments* offer an opportunity to enter or "try out" a market while keeping risks low. Typically, venture capital investments are used to become involved in the growth and development of a small organization that has the potential to develop a new or innovative technology. By making minority investments in young and growing enterprises, organizations have an opportunity to become close to and possibly later enter into new technologies.[8] As part of a strategy to transform a struggling hospital alliance into a multibillion dollar concern, American Healthcare Systems (AmHS) used venture capital investments. AmHS operates two venture capital funds that have invested $45 million in emerging medical companies.[9]

Cooperation Strategies

Probably the most used and certainly the most talked about strategies of the 1990s are cooperation strategies. Many organizations have carried out adaptive strategies – particularly diversification, vertical integration, product and market development strategies – through cooperation strategies. Cooperation strategies include mergers, alliances, and joint ventures.

Merger *Mergers* are similar to acquisitions; however, in mergers two organizations combine through mutual agreement to form a single new organization, often with a new name. Increasing market share and eliminating competitors to improve patient volume and profitability are the primary reasons for many recent hospital mergers. For example, when The Penrose Health System and St. Francis Health System, both in Colorado Springs, Colorado, were consolidated through a national merger of the health care operations of Sisters of Charity Health Care Systems, Inc., of Cincinnati, Ohio, and Franciscan Healthcare Corporation of Colorado Springs, the Penrose – St. Francis Healthcare System consolidation set as its objectives:

- greater efficiency in the delivery of health care services;
- reduction in duplication of services;
- improved geographic dispersion;
- increased service scope;
- restraint in pricing increases; and
- improved financial performance.[10]

As in acquisitions, a major difficulty in a merger is the integration of two separate organizational cultures. Mergers offer a more difficult problem than acquisitions because a totally new organization must be forged. In an acquisition, the dominant culture remains and subsumes the other. In a merger, a totally new organizational culture (the way we do things) must be developed. In the Penrose – St. Francis consolidation, with changes in the organization structure, governance, senior and middle management, service mix, product mix, and outside relationships, management realized that merging two distinctly different corporate cultures would be a challenge. Therefore, at Penrose – St. Francis a great deal of time was spent in communications at all levels in the organization. Medical staff and employees were engaged in a reformulation of the vision, mission, and statement of the shared values of the new organization. Work groups met and planned how to effectively and efficiently meet the needs of patients. Internal and external communications were given top priority.[11] Even with such efforts, merging the organization cultures will take years to complete.

Mergers and acquisition continue to be a major market entry strategy for health care organizations. An environment conducive to large health care combinations, institutional coordination, demands for efficiency, and the continuum of care (seamless care) has fostered many of these mergers and acquisitions. As a result, 1993 was a record year for large mergers and acquisitions. Perspective 6–5 presents a list of the largest mergers and acquisitions during the year.

Alliance Strategic *alliances* are loosely coupled arrangements among existing organizations that are designed to achieve some long-term strategic purpose not possible by any single organization.[12] They are an attempt to strengthen competitive position while maintaining the independence of the organizations involved. Strategic alliances are cooperative agreements that go beyond normal company-to-company dealings but fall short of merger or full partnership.[13]

Strategic alliances, although not mergers, have many of the same problems – previously unrelated cultures have to learn to cooperate rather than compete; numerous "sessions" are required to determine what will be shared, what is proprietary, and how to balance the two; and efforts made to maintain cooperation over time within such a "loose" cooperative effort. On the other hand, alliances offer several opportunities such as learning from each other, having access to expertise not currently "owned" by the organization, strengthening market position, and directing competitive efforts toward others instead of each other.

In health care, the term *alliance* has been used to refer to the voluntary organization that hospitals joined for access to a resource that was knowledgeable about the changing environment including rapidly advancing technology and to achieve economies of scale in purchasing. Alliances provide hospitals with the benefits of being part of a multihospital system, yet allow them to exist as freestanding, self-governing institutions. It is estimated that by the year 2000, 50 percent of hospitals will be members of alliances.[14] Examples of some major hospital alliances include American Healthcare Systems (AmHS), SunHealth Alliance, Voluntary Hospitals of America (VHA), and University Hospital Consortium.

More recently, as the environment becomes more unpredictable and reform efforts appear to be directed toward increased integration, a number of health

PERSPECTIVE 6 – 5

1993 – A Boom Year for Health Care Mergers and Acquisitions

February. Two Des Moines hospitals, Iowa Methodist and Iowa Lutheran, announced that they will merge to become the state's largest health system.

May. Denver's two largest providers, P/SL Healthcare System and Swedish Medical Center, announced plans to merge.

June. The largest hospital system in Missouri was created when Christian Health Services and Barnes-Jewish in St. Louis approved a merger.

July. Humana agreed to buy Group Health Association, a health maintenance organization, in a $50 million transaction.

July. After rejecting an offer from Abbey Health Groups, Lifetime Corporation agreed to a bid from Olsten Corporation in a $2.2 billion deal that created the nation's largest home health care company.

August. Horizon Healthcare Corporation, a long-term-care provider, made an $85 million bid for the twenty-hospital Greenery Rehabilitation Group.

September. American PsychManagement and Preferred Health Care agreed to a $425 million merger to form the nation's largest managed behavioral health program.

September. Health Net and Qual-Med agreed to merge in a $775 million deal that created California's largest for-profit managed-care operation with 1.1 million enrollees.

September. Abbey Healthcare Group agreed to buy Total Pharmaceutical Care for $197 million in one of the year's largest home-infusion provider deals.

September. Columbia Hospital Corporation and Galen Health Care merged in a $3.2 billion deal, forming the nation's largest investor-owned hospital chain, Columbia Healthcare Corporation.

October. Quorum completed its purchase of Charter Medical Corporation's ten acute-care hospitals for $340 million.

October. Columbia Healthcare Corporation and Hospital Corporation of America announced a $5.7 billion deal to merge into a 190-hospital for-profit-chain.

November. Shareholders approved a $6 billion swap of stock and cash in a merger of pharmaceutical giant Merck & Company with drug distributor and marketer Medco Containment Services.

November. Surgical Care Affiliates completed a hostile bid for the nation's largest surgery center operator, Medical Care America, to form a 146-center chain.

November. American Management and OrNda HealthCorp agreed to merge in a $400 million deal that created a thirty-six-hospital chain with more than $1 billion in revenues.

December. HealthSouth Corporation agreed to buy twenty-eight rehabilitation hospitals and forty-five outpatient rehabilitation centers from the Santa Monica – based National Medical Enterprises for $300 million. The purchase will give HealthSouth 265 facilities in thirty-two states, Canada, and the District of Columbia.

Source: "1993 – A Boom Year for Healthcare Mergers and Acquisitions." *Modern Healthcare* 23, no. 48 (1993), p. 6.

care providers have been seeking strategic alliances. Many primary providers have turned to alliances as vehicles for providing services, soliciting physician loyalty, and reducing their investment in operations.[15] Strategic alliances between physicians and hospitals must be anchored in their common purpose – improving patient care. The physicians involved may not concur with the hospital in its management of facilities, staffing, and so forth. In addition, conflict may emerge as hospitals diversify into areas that compete more directly with the physicians' own clinics, ambulatory care centers, and diagnostic centers. Finally, although the hospital would prefer to have many qualified physicians admitted to the staff (who could refer more patients), allied physicians would prefer to limit credentialing of outside physicians.

Health Care reform and the pressures of a rapidly changing environment have initiated some unique alliances. Perspective 6–6 is the press release for one such alliance between a public hospital and a religious hospital that previously were intense competitors. The third major hospital in the area was not consulted nor invited to participate. In Columbia, South Carolina, four hospitals – a Baptist, a Catholic, and two public hospitals – have agreed to participate in the Midlands Partnership for Community Health. It has undertaken three major joint projects: helping fund the relocation of the Columbia Free Clinic to a larger site, adding staff to the local AIDS consortium, and conducting a community health assessment. Although the hospitals are collaborating on some projects and hoping to do more, they are still competitive.[16]

Joint Venture When projects get too large, technology too expensive, or the costs of failure too high for a single organization, joint ventures are often used.[17] A *joint venture* is the combination of the resources of two or more separate organizations to accomplish a designated task. A joint venture may involve a pooling of assets or a combination of the specialized talents or skills of each organization. The most common organizational forms used in health care joint ventures are:

- Contractual agreements. Two or more organizations sign a contract agreeing to work together toward a specific objective.
- Subsidiary corporations. A new corporation is formed, usually to operate nonhospital activities.
- Partnerships. A formal or informal arrangement in which two or more parties engage in activities of mutual benefit.
- Not-for-profit title-holding corporations. Tax legislation enacted in 1986 allowed not-for-profit organizations to form tax-exempt title-holding corporations providing significant benefits to health care organizations engaged in real estate ventures.[18]

With the dynamic health care environment, hospitals engage in joint ventures to lower costs and improve and expand services. Joint ventures can be an innovative way to generate revenues, supplement operations, and remain competitive.[19] Through the mid-1990s, the most common use has been hospital/physician joint venture. Hospital/physician joint ventures were popular in the 1980s because

Joint statements similar to the following by Ed Schlicksup, president and CEO of Mercy Hospital, Inc., and Harry A. Nurkin, president and CEO of Charlotte-Mecklenburg Hospital Authority, announcing a strategic alliance, have become common in the health care industry:

The management of Mercy Health Services, parent corporation of Mercy Hospital and Mercy Hospital South, and the Charlotte-Mecklenburg Hospital Authority, parent company of Carolinas Medical Center and University Hospital, have agreed to form a collaborative relationship. This relationship will further position both organizations as a fully integrated health care delivery network.

This network will consist of hospitals and physicians working together for the purpose of (1) enhancing the quality of health care provided to citizens of this region, (2) providing the most cost-effective, efficient continuum of care, and (3) better addressing the health care needs of under-served citizens.

Under this agreement, both Mercy and the Hospital Authority will remain independent and retain their legal and organizational identity. CMHA will continue as a "Hospital Authority" and the Mercy Hospitals will continue as Catholic hospitals, sponsored (owned and operated) by the Sisters of Mercy of North Carolina, located in Belmont. The Sisters will continue their 87-year role with Mercy Health Services.

The collaborative relationship will be managed by a new organization which is governed by a board whose members are appointed by CMHA and Mercy. The new organization will be a jointly owned operating company. The role and responsibilities of the new organization will be defined, although it is expected that it will manage and coordinate joint activities of CMHA and Mercy. Harry A. Nurkin, will act as Chief Executive Officer of the entity, with President Ed Schlicksup serving as Chief Operating Officer.

"We are excited about this new endeavor," said Ed Schlicksup, President of Mercy Hospital, Inc. "We believe collaboration for the delivery of health care is proactive and positive. And, after careful review, we have concluded that the Charlotte-Mecklenburg Hospital Authority and Mercy will make good teammates."

Harry Nurkin, President of CMHA, added, "Our two health care systems are very compatible in terms of programs and services, values, and mission. Yet, this collaboration will still offer consumers a variety of health care choices."

Representatives of Mercy and CMHA will begin work immediately to finalize details of the collaboration, which will be presented to their respective boards for approval.

they allowed the hospital to preempt physicians as competitors and, at the same time, stabilized their referral base. Joint ventures with hospitals increased physicians' profitability. In the early 1990s, physicians entered joint ventures with hospitals to protect their incomes and autonomy whereas hospitals were motivated to form joint ventures as a means of controlling medical care costs and gaining influence over physician utilization of hospital services. Changes in third-party payer methods have created competition based on price, and joint ventures have been created to give hospitals the capability to reduce costs and compete more effectively.[20] An example of market development using the joint venture is presented in Perspective 6–7.

Development Strategies

Organizations may enter new markets by using internal resources. This entry strategy takes the form of internal development or internal ventures.

Internal Development *Internal development* uses the existing organizational structure and personnel to generate new products or services or distribution strategies. Internal development may be most appropriate for products or services that are closely related to existing products or services. As demonstrated in Perspective 6–8, product development through internal development is common in the pharmaceutical industry.

Internal Ventures *Internal ventures,* on the other hand, set up a separate, relatively independent entity within the organization. Internal ventures may be most appropriate for products or services that are unrelated to the current products or services. Diversification and vertical integration through internal

---

PERSPECTIVE 6–7
HMOs Use Joint Venture to Expand Market

Three New England health maintenance organizations, Tufts Associated Health Plans, Healthsource, and Health New England, put together a joint venture that will create a network of 8,500 physicians and 65 hospitals providing coverage to over 400,000 enrollees in Maine, Massachusetts, New Hampshire, and Rhode Island. The joint venture is called Managed Care Network of New England and offers point-of-service health coverage (self-referral) to large employers. In joining together, the joint venture partners will mutually benefit by appealing to regional employers. Dr. Harris Berman, Tufts's president and chief executive officer, indicated that the joint venture will enable companies to provide seamless managed care to their employees on a regional basis through one administrator.

Source: Paul J. Kenkel, "HMOs Join to Blanket New England," *Modern Healthcare* 23, no. 29 (1993), p. 6.

PERSPECTIVE 6-8
Internal Development Strategies in Pharmaceuticals

Many pharmaceutical companies such as Merck & Co., Hoffmann – La Roche, Inc., Genentech, and Rhone – Poulenc Rorer have pursued product development adaptive strategies through internal development market entry strategies. A pharmaceutical company depends on its R&D department to develop new products (drugs). These departments are supported by massive budgets because the average development cost for a single new drug is estimated to be around $360 million, and a drug on average takes twelve years to develop. For example, Merck spent approximately $1.6 billion on R&D in 1993, second in the industry to Hoffmann – La Roche, Inc. As a result, Merck developed the broadest product line in the industry, with sixteen drugs that each brought in more than $100 million in revenue per year. Dependence solely on product development can be risky if the company cannot produce a steady stream of new products. Merck had 27 percent annual earnings growth throughout the 1980s and early 1990s as a result of the steady stream of

new internally developed products such as Vasotec, a drug to control hypertension, and Mevacor, a cholesterol reducer. In the mid-1990s, however, growth slowed substantially because of a lack of success with new product developments. Genentech had a similar "dry spell" during the early 1990s. Some experts believe that the decrease in new products was a result of a slowdown in advances in Merck's traditional chemistry-based research and an organizational culture that became too centralized and bureaucratic. To offset a lack of new product development, Merck engaged in product line extension/market segmentation strategies by developing a line of generic drugs to appeal to health-maintenance organizations and third-party payers such as insurance companies and corporate benefit plans that threaten to replace physicians as the drug industry's chief customers.

Source: Joseph Weber, "Merck Is Showing Its Age," *Business Week* (August 23, 1993), pp. 72–74.

development or internal ventures usually take considerably longer to establish than through acquisition.

The major advantages and disadvantages of the market entry strategies are summarized in Exhibit 6–14.

POSITIONING STRATEGIES

Having selected the adaptive strategies and market entry strategies, managers must decide how the products and services will be positioned vis-à-vis competitors' products and services. An organization must consciously position its products and services within a market through one of the market-wide or market segment positioning strategies. Products and services may be positioned through the adoption of one of the generic positioning strategies. Michael Porter proposes three

EXHIBIT 6-14
**Advantages and Disadvantages
of Market Entry Strategies**

Market Entry Strategy	Major Advantages	Major Disadvantages
Acquisition	• Rapid market entry • Image already established	• New business may be unfamiliar to parent • Takes a long time to assimilate organization's culture • New management team may be required • High initial cost
Licensing	• Rapid access to proven technology • Reduced financial exposure	• Not a substitute for internal technical competence • Not proprietary technology • Dependent on licensor
Venture Capital Investment	• Can provide window on new technology or market	• Alone, unlikely to be a major stimulus of growth
Merger	• Uses existing resources • Retains existing markets and products	• Takes a long time to merge cultures • Merger match often difficult to find
Alliance	• Fills in gaps in product line • Creates efficiencies (e.g., purchasing power) • Reduces competition in weak markets • Focuses growth in critical areas	• Potential for conflict between members • Limits potential markets/products
Joint Venture	• Technological/marketing joint ventures can exploit small/large organizational synergies • Spreads distribution risks	• Potential for conflict between partners • Objectives of partners may not be compatible
Internal Development	• Uses existing resources • Organization maintains a high level of control • Presents image of developing (growth) organization	• Time lag to breakeven tends to be long • Unfamiliarity with new markets • Obtaining significant gains in market share against strong competitors may be difficult
Internal Venture	• Uses existing resources • May enable organization to hold a talented entrepreneur • Isolates development from organization's bureaucracy	• Mixed record of success • Organization's internal climate often unsuitable

generic strategies that may serve as basic positioning strategies. These generic strategies are cost leadership, differentiation, and focus.[21] Exhibit 6–15 presents Porter's concept of generic strategies.

Market-wide Strategies

Market-wide strategies position the products and services of the organization to appeal to a wide audience. These products and services, therefore, are not specifically tailored to the particular needs of any special segment of the population. As shown in Exhibit 6–15, differentiation and cost leadership are industry-wide or market-wide positioning strategies.

Cost Leadership *Cost leadership* is a positioning strategy designed to gain an advantage over competitors by producing a product or providing a service at a lower cost than competitors' offerings. The product or service is often highly standardized to keep costs low. Cost leadership allows for more flexibility in pricing and relatively greater profit margins.

Cost leadership is based on economies of scale in operations, marketing, and

---

EXHIBIT 6 – 15
Porter's Matrix

Strategic Advantage

		Uniqueness Perceived by the Customer	Low Cost Position
Strategic Target	Market-wide (broad)	DIFFERENTIATION	OVERALL COST LEADERSHIP
	Particular Segment Only (narrow)	FOCUS	

Source: Reprinted with permission of The Free Press, a division of Macmillan, Inc. from *Competitive Strategy: Techniques for Analyzing Industries and Competitors* by Michael E. Porter. © 1980 by The Free Press.

administration and the use of the latest technology. Cost leadership may be used effectively as the generic strategy for any of the adaptive strategies and seems particularly applicable to the primary providers segment of the health care industry. As Porter suggests, "Cost leadership requires aggressive construction of efficient-scale facilities, vigorous pursuit of cost reduction from experience, tight cost and overhead control, avoidance of marginal customer accounts, and cost minimization in areas such as R&D, service, sales force, advertising, and so on."[22] Therefore, in order to use cost leadership, an organization must be able to develop a significant cost advantage and have a reasonably large market share.

An industry segment where cost leadership is being used successfully is in the area of long-term care. Long-term-care facilities are a "thin-margin business" in which profit margins range from approximately 1.2 percent to 1.7 percent. In this industry, older facilities are at a competitive disadvantage relative to new facilities. However, long-term-care facilities that have been able to drive costs down while maintaining quality have enjoyed higher margins. In addition, many of these facilities have been upgraded to be more efficient and have instituted tight cost controls. Advertising has been used to keep occupancy above 95 percent, which is often required in the industry to be profitable.

Differentiation *Differentiation* is a strategy to make the product or service different (or appear so in the mind of the buyer) from competitors' products or services. Thus, consumers see the service as unique among a group of similar competing services.

The product or service may be differentiated by emphasizing quality, a high level of service, ease of access, convenience, reputation, and so on. There are a number of ways to differentiate a product or service, but the attributes that are to be viewed as different or unique must be valued by the consumer. Therefore, organizations using differentiation strategies rely on brand loyalty (reputation or image), distinctive products or services, and the lack of good substitutes.

The most common forms of differentiation in the health care industry have been based on quality and image. Many acute-care hospitals emphasize and promote quality care as the difference between them and other hospitals in their service area. Similarly, a "high-tech" image is often the basis for differentiation among health care organizations. Affiliation with a medical school, performing the most sophisticated procedures, or using the latest (often expensive) technology may promote the image of "the best possible care."

Market Segment Strategies

As shown in Exhibit 6–15, market segment strategies are directed toward the particular needs of a well-defined market segment and often are called focus strategies. A *focus strategy* identifies a specific, well-defined "niche" in the total market that the company will concentrate on or pursue. Because of its attributes, the product or service or the organization itself may appeal to a particular niche within the market. A focus strategy may involve tailoring the product or service to meet the special needs of the segment the company is trying to serve. Focus strategies may be based on cost leadership (cost/focus) or differentiation (differentiation/focus).

Because of the complexity of medicine and the industry, focus strategies are quite common in the health care industry. Just as physicians have had to specialize, the institutions within the field have tended to focus on specialized segments. Examples of focus strategies are rehabilitation hospitals, psychiatric hospitals, ambulatory-care centers, Alzheimer's centers, and so on. These specialty hospitals are further positioned based on cost leadership or differentiation.

Each of the generic strategies results from an organization making consistent choices on product/services, markets (service areas), and distinctive competencies – choices that reinforce each other. Exhibit 6–16 summarizes the choices appropriate for each generic strategy. Exhibit 6–17 presents the advantages and disadvantages of each of the positioning strategies.

OPERATIONAL STRATEGIES

As was shown in Exhibit 6–4, both functional and organization-wide operational strategies are developed to support the higher level strategies. Functional-level

---

EXHIBIT 6 – 16
Product/Market/Distinctive Competence Choices and Generic Competitive Strategies

	Cost Leadership	Differentiation	Focus
Product Differentiation	LOW (by price)	HIGH (by uniqueness)	LOW TO HIGH (price or uniqueness)
Market Segmentation	LOW (mass market)	HIGH (many market segments)	HIGH (only one or a very few segments)
Distinctive Competence	OPERATIONS AND MATERIALS MANAGEMENT	RESEARCH AND DEVELOPMENT/ MARKETING	ANY KIND OF DISTINCTIVE COMPETENCE

EXHIBIT 6-17
Advantages and Disadvantages of Positioning Strategies

Positioning Strategy	Major Advantages	Major Disadvantages
Cost Leadership	• Provides clear competitive advantage • Provides clear market position • Provides opportunities to spend more than competition	• Must obtain large volume • Product/service must be standardized • Product/service may be viewed as low quality
Differentiation	• Product/service viewed as unique • Often viewed as high quality • Greater control over pricing	• Often difficult to adequately differentiate product or service • Product/service may be higher priced
Focus	• Appeals to specialized market • May develop good relations with market	• Market may be small • Expansion of market may be difficult

---

strategies are developed within departments (marketing, information systems, finance, human resources, and so on) and organization-wide strategies are developed across all functions (culture change, reorganization, facilities upgrades, social responsibility actions). Both functional and organization-wide operational strategies are the means for implementing directional, adaptive, market entry, and positioning strategies. These strategies are complete strategies and have situational analysis, strategy formulation, strategic implementation, and strategic control stages as well. Each major function within the organization develops an "implementation" strategy and for major strategic shifts, there will be organization-wide strategies as well.

The major areas for which functional strategies must be developed include marketing, finance, information systems, and human resources. The functional strategies must be linked to the higher level strategies. Chapters 8 through 11 examine the functional strategies appropriate for each of the higher level strategies. Typical organization-wide operational strategies may include changing the organizational culture, reorganization, upgrading facilities and equipment, and social responsibility initiatives. These strategies are addressed in Chapter 12.

COMBINATION STRATEGIES

No single strategy alone may be appropriate for an organization and, therefore, *combination strategies* are often used, especially in large, complex organizations. For example, an organization may concurrently divest itself of one of its divisions and engage in market development in another. Similarly, a strategy may have several phases. It may be necessary to "string together" several strategic alternatives as phases or elements to implement a broader strategic shift. In a two-phase strategy, an organization may employ a retrenchment strategy in phase one and an enhancement strategy in phase two.

The strategic alternative or set of alternatives should be selected that best meets the requirements of the external environment, the capabilities of the organization, and the mission, vision, values, and objectives of management. As illustrated in Exhibit 6–18, top management's vision often extends through several strategic alternatives or phases. Such vision helps provide long-term continuity for the entire management team. However, management must be aware that, in a dynamic environment, circumstances may change and later phases may have to be modified or revised to meet the needs of the unique and changing situation. Strategic management is a continuous process of assessment and decision making.

The decision logic for the formulation of the strategic plan was illustrated in Exhibit 6–2. At this point, it would be useful to return to Exhibits 6–2 and 6–4 to review the complete strategy formulation process. In addition, as a review, Exhibit 6–19 provides summary definitions and examples of all of the strategic alternatives.

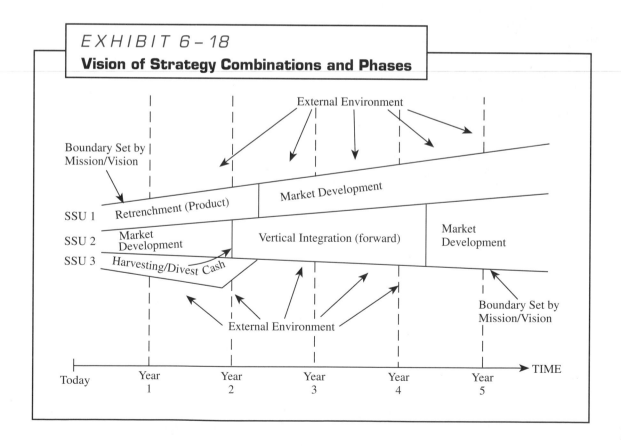

EXHIBIT 6 – 18
Vision of Strategy Combinations and Phases

EXHIBIT 6-19

Definition and Examples of the Strategic Alternatives

Strategy	Definition	Example
Adaptive Strategies		
Related Diversification	Adding new related product or service categories. Often requires the establishment of a new division.	Sun Healthcare, a long-term-care chain, purchases Mediplex Group, specializing in subacute care. The principal reason for the purchase was to enter a growth market.
Unrelated Diversification	Adding new unrelated product or service categories. Typically requires the establishment of a new division.	The University of Alabama Medical School owns a motel.
Forward Vertical Integration	Adding new members along the distribution channel (toward a later stage) for present products and services or controlling the flow of patients from one institution to another.	Merck & Company (pharmaceuticals) purchases Medco Containment Services (mail-order drug distributor).
Backward Vertical Integration	Adding new members along the distribution channel (toward an earlier stage) for present products and services or controlling the flow of patients from one institution to another.	San Angelo Texas Community Hospital moves into the wellness market by developing a fitness center open to those aged 50 and over in the community.
Market Development	Introducing present products or services into new geographic markets or to new segments within a present geographic market.	National Health Plans, a subsidiary of National Medical Enterprises, targets various regions of California for market expansion.
Product Development	Improving present products or services or extending the present product line.	San Pedro (California) Peninsula Hospital expands its psychiatric program by establishing a therapy program for elderly patients who require little or no hospitalization.

EXHIBIT 6 – 19　cont'd

Strategy	Definition	Example
Penetration	Seeking to increase market share for present products or services in present markets through marketing efforts (promotion, distribution, price).	Integrated Medical Systems is trying to increase its market share of automated communications between physicians' offices and health care delivery organizations through industry advertising.
Divestiture	Selling an operating business unit or division to another organization. Typically, the business unit will continue in operation.	Baxter International divests its $675 million diagnostics manufacturing business.
Liquidation	Selling all or part of the organization's assets (facilities, inventory, equipment, and so on) to obtain cash. The assets may be used by the purchaser in a variety of ways and businesses.	MedCare HMO is liquidated by the state of Illinois.
Harvesting	Taking cash out while providing few new resources for a business in a declining market. Sometimes referred to as "milking" the organization.	Many state health departments are planning harvest strategies for primary-care services if comprehensive health reform is passed. Health departments will slowly harvest these services as private providers assume patient loads.
Retrenchment	Reducing the scope of operations, redefining the target market and selectively cutting personnel, products and services, or service area (geographic coverage).	National Medical Enterprises streamlines its psychiatric hospital division by cutting personnel and three regional divisional offices.
Enhancement	Seeking to improve operations within present product or service categories through quality, efficiency, innovation, speed, and flexibility	AMI Brookwood initiates a complete reorganization to ensure that all activities revolve around the patient.

EXHIBIT 6 – 19 *cont'd*

Strategy	Definition	Example
Status Quo	Seeking to maintain relative market share within a market.	VA Hospitals call for steady state until specifics of health care reform are clearer.
Market Entry Strategies		
Acquisition	Strategy to grow through the purchase of an existing organization, a unit of an organization or a product/service.	HealthTrust – the hospital company announced a $1 billion acquisition of Epic Healthcare Group.
Licensing	Acquiring an asset (technology, market, equipment, etc.) through contract.	Medicaid waivers are licenses for providers (often health departments) to perform certain services for the Medicaid Agency.
Venture Capital Investment	Financial investment in an organization in order to participate in its growth.	American Healthcare Systems (AmHS) invests $45 million in emerging medical companies.
Merger	Combining two (or more) organizations through mutual agreement to form a single new organization.	Summit Health (California) merges with OrNda (Tennessee) and American Healthcare Management (Pennsylvania).
Alliance	Formation of a formal partnership.	Rural Huntington (Indiana) Memorial Hospital signs a clinical affiliation agreement with urban Lutheran Hospital of Indiana (Fort Wayne) to share clinical services.
Joint Venture	Combination of the resources of two or more organizations to accomplish a designated task.	Tufts Associated Health Plans, Healthsource, and Health New England create a point-of-service network.
Internal Development	Products or services developed internally using the organization's own resources.	Swedish Covenant Hospital of Chicago develops a 37,000 square foot health and fitness center out of their cardiac rehabilitation program.

EXHIBIT 6 – 19 cont'd

Strategy	Definition	Example
Internal Venture	Establishment of an independent entity within an organization to develop products or services.	Columbia University's College of Physicians and Surgeons establishes a center for alternative and complementary medicine.
Positioning Strategies		
Cost Leadership	Low cost/price strategy directed toward entire market.	HealthSouth Rehabilitation Corporation is a cost and price leader in rehabilitation.
Differentiation	Development of unique product/service features directed toward the entire market.	Holy Cross Medical Center of Mission Hills, California, opens a regional cancer center where patients receive treatments in private or semiprivate cabana-type rooms equipped with televisions, video cassette recorders, and other audio equipment. Other support therapies include accupressure, art, yoga, and pain management.
Focus – Cost Leadership	Low cost/price strategy directed toward a particular market segment.	Presbyterian Hospital of Charlotte, North Carolina, offers $35 mammograms. Presbyterian is targeting women over 35 years of age.
Focus – Differentiation	Development of unique product/service features directed toward a particular market segment.	AMI's St. Francis Hospital in Memphis plans to convert forty-two beds to subacute care targeting patients not sick enough to stay in the hospital but not ready to go home.

SUMMARY AND CONCLUSIONS

This chapter introduced a hierarchy of strategic alternatives. There are several types of strategies, and within each type, several strategic alternatives are available to health care organizations. In addition, there is a sequential decision logic in the strategy formulation process. First, directional strategies must be articulated through the organization's mission, vision, values, and objectives. Second, adaptive strategies must be identified, evaluated, and selected. The adaptive strategies are the central part of the strategy formulation process and delineate how the organization will expand, contract, or stabilize operations. Expansion strategies include diversification, vertical integration, market development, product development, and penetration. Contraction strategies include divestiture, liquidation, harvesting, and retrenchment. Finally, the stabilization strategies include enhancement and status quo.

The third type of strategic decision concerns the market entry strategies. The expansion and stabilization strategies call for a method to carry out the strategy in the marketplace. Therefore, some method for entering or gaining access to that market is required. Market entry strategies include acquisitions and mergers, internal development and internal ventures, alliances and joint ventures, licensing, and venture capital investments. Any of the market entry strategies may be used to carry out an adaptive strategy.

The fourth type of strategy is the positioning strategy. Positioning strategies relate consumers' perceptions of products and services vis-à-vis competitors. These positioning strategies, often called *generic strategies,* include cost leadership and differentiation, which are market-wide strategies, and focus, which is a market segment strategy. Each of the generic strategies places different demands upon the organization and requires unique competences.

Finally, operational strategies were discussed. Operational strategies are developed within the organization's functional departments (marketing, finance, human resources, and so on). Often there are organization-wide strategies (changing the organization's culture, reorganization, and so on) as well. Functional and organization-wide strategies are developed to implement the higher level strategic alternatives. These strategies and their linkage with the higher level strategies are discussed in Chapters 8 through 12.

It is unlikely that a single strategy will suffice for an organization. Several strategic alternatives may have to be adopted and used in combination. For instance, one product may require market development whereas another may require harvesting. Similarly, one division may be positioned as a cost leader and another may be pursuing differentiation. In addition, several strategic alternatives may be seen as phases or sequences in a broader strategic shift.

Chapter 7 will present methods for evaluating the strategic alternatives presented in this chapter and demonstrate how the seven strategic decisions are linked to the formulation process.

KEY TERMS AND CONCEPTS IN STRATEGIC MANAGEMENT

acquisition	expansion strategy	merger
adaptive strategy	focus	operational strategy
alliance	forward vertical integration	organization-wide strategy
backward vertical integration	functional strategy	penetration
	generic strategies	positioning strategy
combination strategy	harvesting	product development
concentric diversification	horizontal integration	related diversification
conglomerate diversification	internal development	retrenchment
contraction strategy	internal venture	stabilization strategy
cost leadership	joint venture	status quo
differentiation	licensing	unrelated diversification
directional strategy	liquidation	venture capital investment
diversification	market development	vertical integration
divestiture	market entry strategy	
enhancement strategy	market penetration	

QUESTIONS FOR CLASS DISCUSSION

1. Describe the elements of the strategy formulation process.
2. What five types of strategies make up the strategy formulation process? Describe the role each plays in developing a strategic plan.
3. Why are the directional strategies both a part of situational analysis and strategy formulation?
4. Name and describe the expansion strategies. Name and describe the contraction strategies. Name and describe the stabilization strategies. Which of the adaptive strategies are corporate and which are division level? Under what conditions may each be appropriate?
5. Why does the selection of the strategic alternative(s) create "direction" or "momentum" for the organization?
6. Which of the adaptive strategic alternatives is selected most frequently by for-profit chains? Provide some examples of such strategies.
7. What is the difference between related diversification and product development? Provide examples of each.
8. Describe vertical integration in terms of patient flow.
9. Explain the difference between an enhancement strategy and a status quo strategy.
10. How is market development different from product development? Penetration? Provide examples of each.
11. Compare and contrast a divestiture strategy with a liquidation strategy.
12. How might a retrenchment strategy and a penetration strategy be linked together? What are some other logical combinations of strategies?
13. Which of the market entry strategies provides for the quickest entry into the market? Slowest?
14. Explain Porter's generic strategies. How do they position the organization (products and services) in the market?
15. How do functional strategies support higher level strategies?
16. What are combination strategies? How may a combination of strategies be related to vision?
17. Work through Exhibit 6–4, Hierarchy of Strategic Decisions and Alternatives, for several organizations with which you are familiar. Practice selecting different alternatives under each strategy type.

NOTES

1. Jay Greene, "Diversification, Take Two," *Modern Healthcare* 23, no. 28 (1993), pp. 28–32.
2. Stephen S. Mick and Douglas A. Conrad, "The Decision to Integrate Vertically in Health Care Organizations," *Hospital & Health Services Administration* 33, no. 3 (Fall 1988), p. 352.
3. E. Gardner, "Baptist Uses Expansion Alliances to Bypass Mayo Jacksonville Beachhead," *Modern Healthcare* (August 13, 1990), pp. 34–36, 38, 39.
4. "AMI to Sell Four Swiss Hospitals for $169 Million," *Modern Healthcare* (April 30, 1990), p. 6.
5. Mick and Conrad, "The Decision to Integrate Vertically," p. 348.
6. Sandy Lutz, "Columbia on the Fast Track," *Modern Healthcare* 23, no. 36 (1993), pp. 10–15.
7. Charles L. Breindel, "Nongrowth Strategies and Options in Health Care," *Hospital & Health Services Administration* 33, no. 1 (Spring 1988), p. 42.
8. Edward B. Roberts and Charles A. Berry, "Entering New Businesses: Selecting Strategies for Success," *Sloan Management Review,* (Spring 1985), p. 7.
9. Jay Green, "AmHS' Retiring CEO Trout Cites Turnaround as Top Accomplishment," *Modern Healthcare* 23, no. 36 (1993), p. 18.
10. Sharon Roggy and Ron Gority, "Bridging the Visions of Competing Catholic Health Care Systems," *Health Care Strategic*
11. *Management* 11, no. 7 (1993), pp. 16–19.
11. Ibid.
12. Howard S. Zuckerman and Arnold D. Kaluzny, "Strategic Alliances in Health Care: The Challenges of Cooperation," *Frontiers of Health Services Management* 7, no. 3 (1991), p. 4.
13. Michael E. Porter, *The Competitive Advantage of Nations* (New York: The Free Press, 1990), p. 65.
14. Arnold Kaluzny and Howard Zuckerman, "Strategic Alliances Ensure TQM's Full Potential," *Healthcare Executive* 8, no. 3 (May/June 1993), p. 33.
15. Sandra Pelfrey and Barbara A. Theisen, "Joint Ventures in Health Care," *Journal of Nursing Administration* 19, no. 4 (April 1989), p. 39.
16. Kathryn S. Taylor, "Columbia, SC," *Hospitals & Health Networks* 67, no. 21 (November 5, 1993), p. 45.
17. Roberts and Berry, "Entering New Businesses," p. 6.
18. Pelfrey and Theisen, "Joint Ventures in Health Care," pp. 39–41.
19. Ibid., p. 42.
20. Donna Malvey, "Hospital–Physician Joint Ventures: Unstable Strategies for a Rapidly Changing Environment," Unpublished Working Paper, School of Health Related Professions, University of Alabama at Birmingham (1994).
21. Michael E. Porter, *Competitive Strategy* (New York: The Free Press, 1980) p. 35.
22. Ibid.

ADDITIONAL READINGS

Files, Laurel A., "Strategy Formulation in Hospitals," *Health Care Management Review* 13, no. 1 (1988), pp. 9–16. This article reviews the art and practice of strategy formulation in hospitals. It provides a clear definition of strategy formulation, identifies and discusses elements that influence the determination of strategy, and reviews the current state of strategic planning in hospitals.

Fottler, Myron D., Howard L. Smith, and H. J. Muller, "Retrenchment in Health Care Organizations: Theory and Practice," *Hospital & Health Services Administration* 31 (1986), pp. 29–43. This article analyzes retrenchment strategies in health care organizations by comparing recommendations for retrenchment in the health care literature with the actual practices of health care executives.

Fox, Wende L., "Vertical Integration Strategies: More Promising Than Diversification," *Health Care Management Review* 14, no. 1 (1989), pp. 49–56. The author indicates that diversifying into businesses outside of traditional health care services has been disappointing. The core or traditional business has been forced to subsidize the diversification venture. An alternative is to strengthen the core business through vertical integration. The author describes vertical integration, explores its benefits for the health care industry, and provides a rationale for growth through vertical integration.

Graham, Judith, "Diversified Hospitals Review Plans After Some Bumpy Ride," *Modern Healthcare* (August 14, 1987), pp. 30–40. This is an excellent article concerning the movement toward hospital diversification that occurred in the 1980s. The article reviews the rationale underlying the diversification strategies and discusses the lessons learned from the difficulties of diversification. The article provides considerable insight into diversification strategies through the experiences (case studies) of several health care systems.

Luke, Roice D., "Local Hospital Systems: Forerunners of Regional Systems?" *Frontiers of Health Services Management* 9, no. 2 (1992), pp. 3–51. Professor Luke examines one of the central health care delivery system issues of the 1990s–the development of local hospital systems (LHSs). Local hospital systems are combinations of two or more hospitals in the same company and located in or around the same metropolitan area. Such systems are vertically integrated and provide an integrated continuum of health and health-related services for a population of patients over time. This comprehensive article presents a detailed examination of 402 of these systems. LHSs seem to offer great potential for achieving the cost, quality, and access benefits that are often attributable to regional systems.

Yuan, Gao, *Lure the Tiger out of the Mountains: The Thirty-six Stratagems of Ancient China* (New York: Simon and Schuster, 1991). The book provides a summary of thirty-six general strategies developed by ancient Chinese military leaders and tacticians, politicians, merchants, philosophers, writers, and even ordinary people. The thirty-six stratagems are of practical use to anyone and were developed over five millennia of wars, coups d'état, court intrigues, economic innovations, and competition. The thirty-six stratagems teach a way of thinking and means of understanding other people's behavior and for analyzing all types of situations. The stratagems' historical and legendary origins are traced through ancient tales and anecdotes illustrating their use.

CHAPTER 7

Evaluation of Alternatives and Strategic Choice

"If the grand strategy is correct, any number of tactical errors can be made and yet the enterprise proves successful."
– General Robert E. Woods (1879–1969)
President, Sears, Roebuck & Company

LEARNING OBJECTIVES

After completing this chapter you should:

1. Understand the rationale underlying the various decision tools used to evaluate strategic alternatives.
2. Be able to discuss, evaluate, and select appropriate adaptive strategic alternatives for a health care organization.
3. Be able to discuss, evaluate, and select appropriate market entry strategic alternatives.
4. Be able to discuss, evaluate, and select appropriate positioning strategic alternatives.
5. Understand the role of the functional and organization-wide operational strategies.
6. Understand the interrelationship and importance of the seven strategic decisions.

A phenomenon of the 1990s has been the combining of health care delivery with the payment for health care. Many commercial insurers are forming partnerships with providers and in some cases are becoming directly involved in the delivery of medical services through the development of primary-care clinics. This trend is occurring because in pursuing their separate missions, insurance and managed-care businesses understand that value is not going to be simply paying claims or selling policies; value will be developed by having some level of control over the provider network. Insurance carriers understand that provider networks will control the flow of patients (claims) and costs; however, health systems need the actuarial skills, ability to assess risk, processing capacity, pricing (rate setting) methodologies, and management and marketing expertise of carriers. This has led to vertical integration and product development adaptive strategies by both the large insurance companies and health care providers. But, which market entry strategy will be most effective in carrying out their mission and adaptive strategies?

Joint Venture?

Some providers have formed joint ventures with insurers rather than develop an insurance product from scratch primarily because of cost considerations and the belief that changes in the health care environment will create excess capacity in the insurance field. One example of using joint venture as an entry strategy is the joint venture between Mutual of Omaha Companies and Community Health Vision. The three hospitals and four contractual partners of Community Health Vision will become the primary providers of services for Mutual of Omaha's ExclusiCare HMO.

Merger?

Merger is another strategy that insurers are pursuing to become more closely aligned with the direct delivery of patient care. For example, Prudential Insurance Company of America merged its 165,000-member HMO in Chicago with three health plans affiliated with Rush-Presbyterian-St. Luke's Medical Center. The merger enabled Prudential to gain direct access to Rush's staff-model HMO and its eighteen medical offices staffed by 120 primary-care physicians.

Internal Venture?

The market may be entered through internal development or internal ventures. For instance, Aetna Life Insurance Company, through its subsidiary Aetna Professional Management Corporation, opened five primary care centers in Atlanta, the first of at least twenty HealthWays Family Medical Centers the company will open in five markets – Atlanta, Charlotte, Chicago, Dallas/Fort Worth, and Washington/Baltimore. Aetna may enter as many as twenty different areas spending up to $2 billion. The centers are open to any patients, including members of Aetna's health plans, and are staffed by Aetna-employed physicians.

Acquisition?

Experts agree that a major third-party payer may be interested in purchasing an entire provider network in a certain market or, quite possibly, an entire multimarket hospital system (such as Columbia Healthcare Corporation). Acquisition of a multimarket hospital system would provide outright control of provider networks in a number of markets.

Strategy: Radical Change in a Relatively Short Period of Time

The combining of these consumer services will significantly change the nature of the industry in a relatively short period of time. In an increasingly turbulent environment, a variety of models of integrating finance and delivery of services will emerge; some will succeed and others will fail. But which? Are the adaptive strategies appropriate? What factors should be considered in adopting the market entry strategy?

Source: Frank Cerne, "Learning by Merging," *Hospitals & Health Networks* 67, no. 22 (1993), pp. 30–32.

EVALUATION OF THE ALTERNATIVES

How did managers of the insurance companies discussed in the Introductory Incident decide on their strategy? Are their adaptive strategies appropriate? Which market entry and positioning strategies will best support their selected adaptive strategies? Several methods may be used in the determination of the appropriate strategic alternatives for each type of strategy (adaptive, market entry, and positioning). All of these methods incorporate the results of external and internal analyses, which in turn have been conducted within the context of the directional strategies – mission, vision, values, and objectives. In using these selection methods, all of the strategic alternatives discussed previously should be available for consideration.

The methods for evaluating and selecting strategic alternatives are actually constructs or frameworks for helping managers think about the organization and its relative situation. These constructs allow health care managers to consciously balance organizational motives with community health needs. Thus, market share and revenue issues may be seen in a context of providing health and well being to "real people." However, none of the methods provides a definitive answer to the question of appropriate strategy. None of the methods *makes* the strategic choice. Rather, the methods categorize and demonstrate the relationships inherent in the situation. The various methods help to structure the thought processes of decision makers.

Although the evaluation methods fine-tune the manager's perspective and organize thinking, ultimately, the manager must make the decision. Managers need to understand the risks, make judgments, and commit the organization to some course of action. Therefore, the evaluation methods cannot be used to obtain "answers," but rather to gain perspective and insight into a complex relationship between organization and environment. There is no right answer. As Peter Drucker has pointed out: "It is a choice between alternatives. It is rarely a choice between right and wrong. It is at best a choice between 'almost right' and 'probably wrong' – but much more often a choice between two courses of action neither of which is probably more nearly right than the other."[1]

EVALUATION OF THE ADAPTIVE STRATEGIES

As discussed throughout Chapter 6, once the directional strategies have been developed, consideration is given to the adaptive strategies. The adaptive strategies are central to the strategy formulation process and are the broadest interpretation of the directional strategies. This level of strategic decision making specifies whether the organization wants to grow (expansion), become smaller (contraction), or remain about the same (stabilization). In addition, the method to accomplish expansion, contraction, or stabilization (diversification, divestiture, enhancement, and so on) must be formulated.

Several constructs help managers think about adaptive strategic decisions. However, as expressed previously, these constructs help show relationships of the organization to its markets and competitors, they do not make the decision. Methods to evaluate the adaptive strategies include:

- a threats, opportunities, weaknesses, and strengths (TOWS) matrix;
- product life cycle analysis;
- portfolio analysis;
- extended portfolio matrix analysis;
- strategic position and action evaluation (SPACE); and
- program evaluation.

For the most part, any of these methods may be used to evaluate the adaptive strategic alternatives for all types of health care organizations – for-profit as well as not-for-profit. As illustrated in Perspective 7–1, the strategic thinking requirements and resultant strategies are often quite similar for both profit and nonprofit institutions.

Because strategy formulation is a process of "fitting" the organization to its environment, each of these evaluation methods uses the organization's external opportunities and threats and internal strengths and weaknesses (Chapters 3 and 4) as inputs to the process. The opportunities, threats, strengths, and weaknesses constitute the *strategic assumptions* on which the strategy will be grounded. Although the strategic assumptions are based on extensive information gathering and analysis, managers cannot always be certain that the assumptions are correct. Therefore, it is often useful to have more than one set of likely strategic assumptions, particularly regarding the external environment. This provides several "backdrops" or contexts for the formulation process and facilitates strategic thinking. Depending on the environmental analysis method used, several sets of simple trend, expert opinion, stakeholder, critical factor, scenario, industry structure analysis, or diffusion (see Chapter 3) assumptions may be generated to evaluate strategy. For example, in evaluating the adaptive strategic alternatives several possible scenarios about the external environment (see Exhibit 3–11) or industry structure analyses (Exhibit 3–13) may be used as a basis for evaluating

---

PERSPECTIVE 7–1
For-Profits and Not-for-Profits Pursue Similar Strategies

Of particular significance in the development of hospital systems is the blurring of differences between investor-owned systems and not-for-profit systems. With the exception of large public hospital systems (and even here the distinctions are fading), the not-for-profit systems are behaving more like investor-owned systems in terms of increasing attention given to balance sheets, the external environment, and competitive strategies. Not-for-profit systems have adopted corporate models, established for-profit subsidiaries, and narrowed the profitability gap when compared to investor-owned systems. Meanwhile, the role of the large investor-owned system has been diminishing. Recognizing

that health care is a local business and that survival depends on dominance in local and regional markets, investor-owned systems are no longer focusing on national competition. Instead, they are pursuing growth strategies similar to not-for-profit systems. Investor-owned systems are concentrating on smaller local and regional markets and are abandoning markets where they are poor competitors. These systems have streamlined, reorganized and refinanced, plus divested themselves of unprofitable acquisitions.

Source: Donna Malvey, Ph.D. candidate, Health Services Administration, University of Alabama at Birmingham.

alternatives. Different strategic assumptions can provide the basis for contingency plans should the assumptions be wrong or change over time.

TOWS Matrix

Within a framework provided by the mission, vision, values, and objectives, the internal and external factors may be combined to develop and evaluate specific adaptive strategic alternatives using a *TOWS* (threats, opportunities, weaknesses, strengths) *matrix.*[2] As illustrated in Exhibit 7–1, the internal strengths and weaknesses of the organization are summarized on the horizontal axis and the external environmental opportunities and threats are summarized on the vertical axis.

EXHIBIT 7–1
TOWS Matrix

	List Internal Strengths 1. 2. 3. 4.	List Internal Weaknesses 1. 2. 3. 4.
List External Opportunities 1. 2. 3. 4.	**4** **Future Quadrant** • Related diversification • Vertical integration • Market development • Product development • Penetration	**2** **Internal Fix-it Quadrant** • Retrenchment • Enhancement • Market development • Product development • Vertical integration • Related diversification
List External Threats 1. 2. 3. 4.	**3** **External Fix-it Quadrant** • Related diversification • Unrelated diversification • Market development • Product development • Enhancement • Status quo	**1** **Survival Quadrant** • Unrelated diversification • Divestiture • Liquidation • Harvesting • Retrenchment

Source: Adapted from Heinz Weihrich, "The TOWS Matrix: A Tool for Situational Analysis," *Long Range Planning* 15, no. 2 (1982), p. 60.

The TOWS matrix indicates four strategic conditions that the organization may encounter. Adaptive strategic alternatives may be developed by matching the organization's strengths with external opportunities, strengths with threats, weaknesses with opportunities, and weaknesses with threats.

Adaptive strategic alternatives are suggested by the interactions of the four sets of variables. In this example, the primary concern is the adaptive strategic alternatives, but this analysis could also be applied to the development of any type of strategy.[3] In practice, particularly in open discussion sessions, some of the alternatives developed through the TOWS matrix may be adaptive, market entry, positioning, or operational.

The Survival Quadrant An organization faced with significant internal weaknesses and external threats is in a difficult position. Because the organization must attempt to minimize both weaknesses and threats, this quadrant is often referred to as the *survival quadrant*. Obviously, the organization must respond to this situation with an explicit strategy. Adaptive alternatives that may be pursued by an organization in this situation include unrelated diversification (if financial resources are available), divestiture, liquidation, harvesting, and retrenchment. For instance, a PPO may have the internal weaknesses of declining enrollments and an image of declining quality in the face of growing external threats from HMOs, AHPs, and industry-wide consolidation. Such conditions may suggest retrenchment.

The Internal Fix-It Quadrant The second quadrant indicates that managers should attempt to minimize internal weaknesses and maximize external opportunities. Typically, an organization will recognize an external opportunity but have internal weaknesses that prevent it from taking advantage of the opportunity. Therefore, this quadrant is referred to as the *internal fix-it quadrant*.

If actions are taken to strengthen the organization (often an operational-level strategy), it may be able to pursue the opportunity. Strategies in this quadrant may require two phases (a combination strategy): first, fixing the internal weakness and, second, pursuing the opportunity. Strategic alternatives that are frequently selected in this quadrant (after fixing the weakness) include retrenchment, enhancement, market development, product development, vertical integration, and related diversification. For example, a for profit hospital may have an external opportunity to enter an attractive new market but presently lacks the financial resources to do so. After addressing this weakness (perhaps by selling additional stock), the opportunity may be pursued (market development).

The External Fix-It Quadrant In this quadrant, the organization recognizes that it has significant strengths but that it must deal with external environmental threats. Therefore, managers must attempt to maximize the organization's strengths and minimize the external threats. This quadrant may be referred to as the *external fix-it quadrant*. As in the internal fix-it quadrant, strategies in this quadrant may require two phases. Strategies that are often employed in this quadrant include related and unrelated diversification, market development, product development, enhancement, and status quo. For instance, an investor-owned, skilled-nursing home with internal strengths of strong management, financial resources, and customer loyalty may encounter the external threat of a powerful new competitor planning to enter the service area. The nursing home may use a preemptive strategic response by engaging in status quo in the skilled-nursing home segment while using related diversification into domiciliaries and retirement communities to expand its presence in the total market.

The Future Quadrant This quadrant represents the best situation for an organization. The organization tries to maximize its strengths and take advantage of external opportunities. Therefore, this quadrant may be referred to as the *future quadrant* because it represents the strategies that the organization will adopt for future growth. Strategies in this quadrant lead from the strength of the organization and use its internal resources to capitalize on the market for its products and services.[4] Typical strategic alternatives that might be selected in this quadrant include related diversification, vertical integration, market development, product development, and penetration. For example, a metropolitan hospital with the internal strengths of access to technology, economies of scale in purchasing, and capable management may be presented with an external opportunity to initiate affiliations with several rural or specialty hospitals and thus create a more extensive referral system for the hospital (vertical integration). See Perspective 7–2 for the major reasons that the health care industry has engaged in vertical integration in the 1990s.

Product Life Cycle Analysis

Product life cycle (PLC) *analysis* can be useful in selecting strategic alternatives based on the principle that all products and services go through several distinct

---

PERSPECTIVE 7-2
Reasons for Vertical Integration in the 1990s

The health care industry is rushing toward vertical integration just when some other industries are moving away from vertical integration. Integrated health care systems are being formed and consolidated to:

- Compete with other integrated systems and managed care organizations in the delivery of high-quality care to enrollees and other patients;
- Give providers enough market clout to force managed-care organizations to renegotiate contracts that are more favorable to them; and
- Dominate markets so that providers and their managed-care components will be virtually free of meaningful competition.

Source: Donald E. L. Johnson, "Integrated Systems Face Major Hurdles, Regulations," *Health Care Strategic Management* 11, no. 10 (1993), pp. 2–3.

phases or stages. These stages relate primarily to the changing nature of the marketplace, the product-development process, and the types of demands made on management. In evaluating product life cycles, the evolution of industry sales and profits (or a surrogate for sales such as the number of subscribers, hospital visits, or competitors) is tracked over time. This evolution will have strategic implications for the organization. A typical product life cycle and the attributes of each stage are presented in Exhibit 7–2.

Products and services have an introductory stage during which sales are increasing but profits are negative at first and then may rise slowly. In this stage,

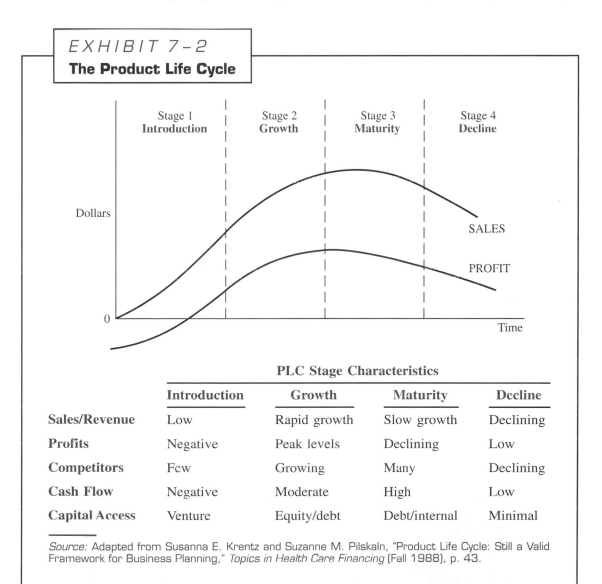

EXHIBIT 7–2
The Product Life Cycle

PLC Stage Characteristics

	Introduction	Growth	Maturity	Decline
Sales/Revenue	Low	Rapid growth	Slow growth	Declining
Profits	Negative	Peak levels	Declining	Low
Competitors	Few	Growing	Many	Declining
Cash Flow	Negative	Moderate	High	Low
Capital Access	Venture	Equity/debt	Debt/internal	Minimal

Source: Adapted from Susanna E. Krentz and Suzanne M. Pilskaln, "Product Life Cycle: Still a Valid Framework for Business Planning," *Topics in Health Care Financing* (Fall 1988), p. 43.

there are few competitors, prices are usually high, promotion is informative about the product category, and there are limited distribution outlets. In the growth stage, sales and profits are both increasing and, as a result, competing organizations enter the market to participate in the growth. During this stage, prices are still high but may begin to decline, promotion is directed toward specific brands, and there is rapid growth in the number of outlets.

The maturity stage of the PLC marks the end of rapid growth and the beginning of consolidation. In addition, market segmentation (defining narrower and narrower segments of the market) occurs. In this stage, prices have stabilized or declined, price promotion becomes common, and distribution is widespread. In the decline stage, total revenues and profits for the product or service are declining and will likely continue to decline over the long term. An article describing the PLC for health maintenance organizations is reproduced in Perspective 7–3.

PERSPECTIVE 7–3

The Product Life Cycle Concept Applied to Health Maintenance Organizations

An excellent example of the PLC phases and the different sources of capital available in the four phases is the health maintenance organization (HMO) industry.[1-3]

HMOs had an extremely long phase 1, or development period. The first HMO prototype, the Ross-Loos Clinic in Los Angeles, became operational in 1929. Forty years later, in 1970, there were only thirty-three HMOs in the United States, serving approximately 3 million enrollees. The early HMOs were generally not-for-profit.

The boost that pushed HMOs from development into growth included the passage of the Health Maintenance Organization and Resources Act of 1973,[4] which provided development funding of over $350 million over ten years. This was, in essence, a form of venture capital. Additionally, the market for HMOs was expanded with the passage of the HMO Act Amendments, which resulted in acceptance of federal qualifications.

In addition to the federal funding for development and growth, HMOs sought additional capital in the early 1980s. One method to accomplish this was to convert from a not-for-profit to a for-profit HMO. U.S. Health Care Systems, Inc. (then known as HMO of Pennsylvania), converted to for-profit status in 1981 and obtained a venture capital investment of $3 million from Warburg, Pincus and Co., Inc. Within two years of converting, in 1983, U.S. Health Care Systems, Inc., became the first HMO to offer stock to the public and raised $25 million in two public offerings. Other HMOs followed suit, and for several years HMOs were the darlings of Wall Street as record growth and earnings were reported. Not-for-profit HMOs also sought additional capital to fund growth. Also in 1983, Kaiser – Permanente Medical Care Program, the country's largest HMO, offered $75 million in tax exempt bonds. By 1983, there were 280 HMOs serving some 12 million enrollees.

Signs of the shift to phase 3 were typified by the acquisition of Health-America

Corporation by Maxicare Health Plans, Inc., in late 1986. In many parts of the country HMOs were changing hands as the returns began to decrease and the phase 2 entrepreneurs and investors pulled out. Wall Street's view of HMOs also calmed down as the price – earnings multiples on HMO stocks fell from 16 times 1986 (forecast) earnings to 13 times 1987 (forecast) earnings. Even a market favorite, U.S. Health Care, fell from a 1986 multiple of 25 to a 1987 multiple of 19.[5]

Some hospital providers sought to enter the industry. Recognizing that development would require too much time and investment, organizations such as the Voluntary Hospitals of America entered into joint ventures with insurance companies seeking to merge insurance and health provider skills. Insurance companies also invested in HMOs. Prudential continued with its own internal development, whereas others such as Travelers Corporation purchased HMOs in early 1986. Insurance companies have the available capital from other sources to fund a long-term commitment. From a business perspective, there is also a health insurance product decision involved.

The phase 3 shakeout among HMOs will continue. In the long term, as with other sectors of the insurance business, the margins generated by HMOs will be small. It will be those organizations with well managed, cost-effective operations that will be able to succeed.

Even with its limitations, the PLC is a useful tool for business planning. It provides a framework for assessing existing activities as well as new lines of business. The decomposition and critical review of market characteristics in conjunction with the PLC can serve as a guideline for strategy development. A PLC framework is particularly useful for product, marketing, and management strategies. It can also clarify access and types of capital available and the intrinsic PLC risk.

In the consideration of new lines of business, a PLC analysis can help to answer not only whether an activity is attractive for the organization, but also which way is best to enter the market. Historically, hospitals have always developed the businesses or services that they offer. However, development makes sense only if the business is in phase 1 or 2 of the life cycle. If the hospital chooses to enter a phase 3 business, it is usually better to joint venture the business with an experienced party or acquire an existing provider.

References

1. National Industry Council for HMO Development, *The Health Maintenance Organization Industry Ten Year Report, 1973–1983: "A History of Achievement, A Future with Promise,"* Washington, D.C.: National Industry Council for HMO Development, 1985.
2. U.S. Department of Health and Human Services, Office of Health Maintenance Organizations, *The 1983 Investor's Guide to Health Maintenance Organizations,* Contract No. 240-81-0051, Washington, D.C.: Touche Ross & Co., 1983.
3. Graham, J., "Initial Public Offerings Slow as HMOs Fail to Extract Substantial Profits," *Modern Healthcare* 16, no. 13 (1985), p. 62.
4. 42 U.S.C. §300e.
5. Graham, "Initial Public Offerings Slow as HMOs Fail to Extract Substantial Profits."

Source: Susanna E. Krentz and Suzanne M. Pilskaln, "Product Life Cycle: Still a Valid Framework for Business Planning," *Topics in Health Care Financing* 15, no. 1 (Fall 1988), pp. 47–48. Used with permission of Aspen Publishers, Inc., © 1988.

There are two important questions for strategy formulation when using product life cycles: "In what stage of the life cycle are the organization's products and services?" "How long are the stages (and the life cycle itself) likely to last?"

Stage of the Product Life Cycle By determining the stage in the product life cycle for a product or service, management may formulate a strategic response and determine the level of resources to be committed to a particular product or service. Exhibit 7–3 shows logical strategic alternatives for each stage of the product life cycle.

Length of the Product Life Cycle The relevance of the strategies shown in Exhibit 7–3 depends on management's perception of the timing of the cycle. Products and services that management determines have lengthy stages (or a long PLC) will require dramatically different strategies than those management concludes have short stages or a short PLC. For instance, extensive vertical integration may be justified in the growth stage and even in the mature stage of the PLC if the cycle is judged to be a long one. However, the investment in and commitment to the product required in vertical integration may not be justified when the PLC is viewed as being relatively short.

EXHIBIT 7–3

Strategic Choices for Stages of the Product Life Cycle

Stage 1
Introduction

- Market development
- Product development

Stage 2
Growth

- Market development
- Product development
- Penetration
- Vertical integration
- Related diversification

Stage 3
Maturity

- Market development
- Product development
- Penetration
- Enhancement
- Status Quo
- Retrenchment
- Divestiture
- Unrelated diversification

Stage 4
Decline

- Divestiture
- Liquidation
- Harvesting
- Unrelated diversification

Determining the PLC Stage and Its Length To determine the stage of the PLC, management must use a great deal of judgment. Total industry revenues and profits may be monitored as an initial indicator. In addition, information obtained in external environmental analysis concerning technological, social, political, regulatory, economic, and competitive change is valuable in assessing both the current stage and the expected length of the cycle.

The usefulness of product life cycles can be seen in tracking hospital outpatient and inpatient revenue trends. As shown in Exhibit 7–4, there has been a significant reduction in hospital inpatient revenues since 1985. This decline can be attributed largely to a shift to less costly services, efforts by public and private payers to contain their outlays for health care, and hospital efforts to contain or reduce staff and beds. As a result, outpatient visits and revenues have been on the increase. Therefore, for hospitals, it appears that inpatient services have reached the mature or even decline stage of the PLC, whereas outpatient services appear to still be in a growth stage. Administrators of a hospital who are considering product/service mix decisions may initiate a status quo or harvesting strategy for inpatient services and engage in a market development strategy for outpatient

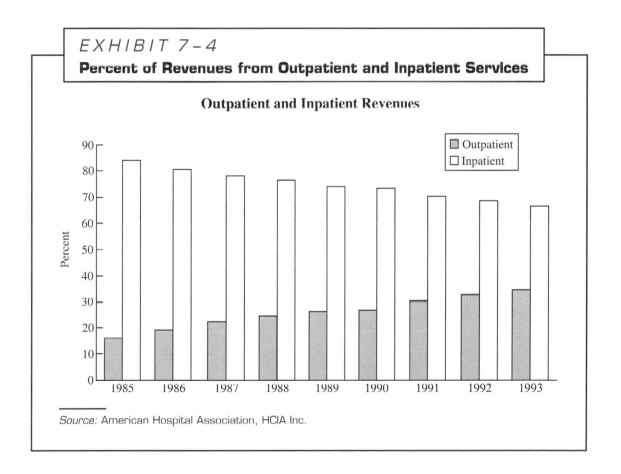

EXHIBIT 7–4
Percent of Revenues from Outpatient and Inpatient Services

Outpatient and Inpatient Revenues

Source: American Hospital Association, HCIA Inc.

services (or related diversification into outpatient services). In addition, hospital administrators should continue to monitor, forecast, and assess these trends because new forces in the environment could change the life cycles or create entirely new life cycles.

The product life cycle may be represented by tracking the number of competitors. For example, Exhibit 7–5 shows the growth in the number of preferred provider organizations (PPOs). It appears from this exhibit that PPOs have progressed through the introduction and growth stages and are entering the mature stage of the PLC. Therefore, for PPOs, we might anticipate fewer competitors entering the market, further market segmentation, industry consolidation, and an emphasis on price. Organizations in this market will most likely adopt aggressive market development and penetration strategies or enhancement strategies (quality and efficiency). Smaller PPOs will probably begin to leave the market, be acquired by a larger competitor, or secure a strong niche position within a market segment.

Some experts suggest that if PPOs persist as discounted fee-for-service arrangements with less utilization review than HMOs, they might quickly enter the decline stage of the product life cycle. The principal reason for the decline will be that PPOs have been less effective than HMOs in containing costs and the quality of care often varies widely from provider to provider. However, the

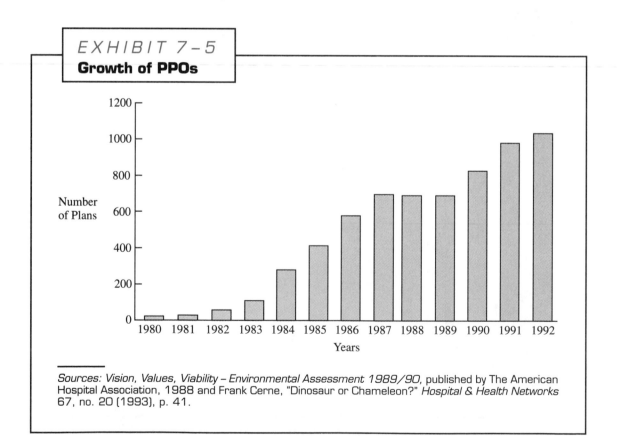

EXHIBIT 7–5
Growth of PPOs

Sources: *Vision, Values, Viability – Environmental Assessment 1989/90,* published by The American Hospital Association, 1988 and Frank Cerne, "Dinosaur or Chameleon?" *Hospital & Health Networks* 67, no. 20 (1993), p. 41.

product life cycle may be extended (or new PLC created) as happened in the early 1990s, if PPOs begin to incorporate more complex utilization management techniques, assume risks, ensure quality and patient satisfaction, create specialty products such as centers of excellence or exclusive provider organizations (EPOs) to segment risks, and deliver specific patient services at specific prices (diversification and product development).[5] One PPO that is making the transition is USA Health Network, the largest single-source PPO in the nation. USA Health Network is developing EPOs to share risks with providers who agree to provide services at a set price. The arrangement financially rewards physicians who consistently provide good outcomes.[6]

Portfolio Analysis

Portfolio analysis, popularized by the Boston Consulting Group (BCG), has become a fundamental tool for strategic analysis. The market position of the health care organization as a whole or its separate programs can be examined in terms of its share of the market and the rate of industry growth.[7] As illustrated in Exhibit 7–6, the traditional BCG portfolio analysis matrix graphically portrays differences among the various products and services (Stars, Cash Cows, Problem Children, and Dogs) in terms of relative market share and market growth rate.

Relative market share is defined as the ratio of a SSU (strategic service unit) to the market share held by the largest rival organization. The midpoint of the horizontal axis is usually set at .50, which corresponds to a SSU whose market share is half that of the leading provider. Thus, all SSUs that are smaller than the largest competitor would have values of less than 1; only the largest SSU would have a value of 1.

Growth rate is usually measured by the changes in level of gross patient service revenues or by population or service utilization growth (e.g., admissions or inpatient days).[8] Classification as high, medium, or low may be determined through comparison with national or regional health care growth figures, the prime rate, return on alternative investments, or the stage in the product life cycle.[9]

An example of portfolio analysis for one institution is illustrated in Exhibit 7–7. Service lines in the upper left quadrant such as women's services, geriatrics, cardiology and so on, have high market growth and a relatively high market share (and most likely high profitability). These services are the most attractive for the institution and should be provided additional resources and encouraged to grow (and become cash cows). Services in the upper right-hand quadrant (neurology/neurosurgery, G.I./urology, emergency services, and so on) over time will move into the stars quadrant or the dogs quadrant. It is important to nurture the services that will most likely move to the stars quadrant. Services such as psychiatry, vascular surgery, pediatrics, and so on have low growth rates as well as a low relative market share (and most likely low profitability) and may be targets for contraction strategies. However, in health care some dogs quadrant services may be slated for stabilization or even expansion because of community needs. Cash cow services (plastic surgery and substance abuse) have achieved high market share but the growth rate has slowed. These services should generate excess cash that may be used to develop stars and problem children services.

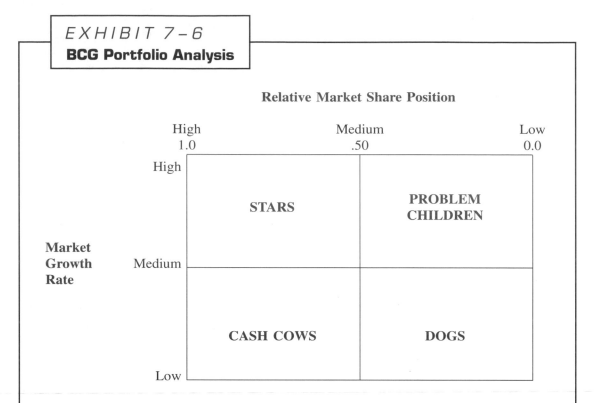

EXHIBIT 7–6
BCG Portfolio Analysis

Stars

Products and services that fall in this quadrant (high market growth and high market share) represent the organization's best long-run opportunity for growth and profitability. These products and services should be provided resources. Market development, product development, penetration, vertical integration, and related diversification are appropriate strategies for this quadrant.

Cash Cows

Products and services in this quadrant have low market growth (probably in maturity or decline stages of the PLC) but the organization has a high relative market share. These products and services should be maintained but should consume few new resources. For strong cash cows, appropriate strategies are status quo, enhancement, penetration, and related diversification. For weak cash cows, strategies may include retrenchment, harvesting, divestiture, and perhaps liquidation.

Problem Children

Problem children have a low relative market share position, yet compete in a high-growth market. Managers must decide whether to strengthen the products in this quadrant with increased investment through market development or product development or get out of the product/service area through harvesting, divestiture, or liquidation. A case may also be made for retrenchment into specialty niches.

EXHIBIT 7-6   cont'd

Dogs

These products and services have a low relative market share position and compete in a slow- or no-growth market. These products and services should consume fewer and fewer of the organization's resources. Because of their weak position, the products or services in this quadrant are often liquidated or divested or the organization engages in dramatic retrenchment.

EXHIBIT 7-7

BCG Portfolio Analysis for a Health Care Institution

Relative Market Share Position

	High	Medium	Low
High	Women's Services Geriatrics Cardiology/Cardiovascular Oncology Pulmonary Orthopedics	Neurology/Neurosurgery G.I./Urology Emergency Services Ambulatory Surgery, Adult Ambulatory Surgery, Pediatrics	
Medium	Plastic Surgery Substance Abuse	Psychiatry Vascular Surgery Pediatrics E.N.T. Ophthalmology General Medicine	
Low			

Market Growth Rate

Source: Adapted from Doris C. Van Doren, Jane R. Durney, and Colleen M. Darby, "Key Decisions in Marketing Plan Formulation for Geriatric Services," *Health Care Management Review* 18, no. 3 (1993), pp. 7–20.

Extended Portfolio Matrix Analysis

Although the BCG matrix may be used by health care organizations, portfolio analysis must be applied with care. For example, health care organizations typically have interdependent programs such as orthopedics and pediatrics, that make

SSU definition difficult. Additionally, underlying the BCG matrix is an assumption that high market share means high profitability and that profits may be "milked" to benefit other programs with growth potential. In health care organizations, however, it is quite possible to have a high market share and no profit. For example, because of reimbursement restrictions, a high number of Medicare patients may cause a physician practice to be unprofitable. Similarly, programs such as obstetrics, pediatrics, neonatal intensive care, and psychiatry may have high market share but be unprofitable.[10]

The profitability issues suggest that portfolio analysis for health care organizations might better utilize an *extended portfolio matrix analysis* that includes a profitability dimension. The profitability dimension is measured by high or low profitability according to positive or negative cash flow or return on invested capital. The expanded matrix is presented in Exhibit 7–8.

Shining Stars Shining stars have high market growth (typically in the early stages of the PLC), a high market share, and high profitability. This quadrant

EXHIBIT 7–8
Expanded Product Portfolio Matrix

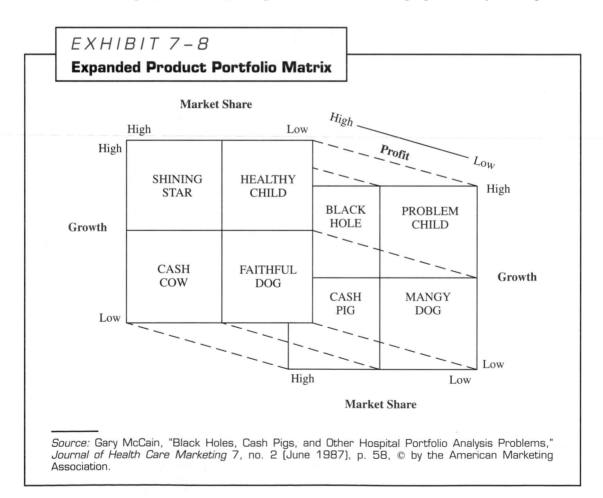

Source: Gary McCain, "Black Holes, Cash Pigs, and Other Hospital Portfolio Analysis Problems," *Journal of Health Care Marketing* 7, no. 2 (June 1987), p. 58, © by the American Marketing Association.

represents the best situation for an organization; however, it is likely that high profitability will attract competitors. Therefore, aggressive enhancement or product development will be required; market development may be difficult because of the already high market share. In addition, the organization will want to consider vertical integration and related diversification.

Cash Cows Cash cow products and services have low market growth but a high market share and high profitability. In this situation, the organization has a dominant position in the market (perhaps 100 percent) and further growth is unlikely. Again, the high profitability may attract competition, and the organization may have to defend its market share. Thus, strategies should be directed toward maintaining market dominance through enhancement. If the PLC is viewed to be long, the organization may want to engage in vertical integration or related diversification.

Healthy Children In this quadrant, products and services have high market growth, a low market share, and high profitability. This quadrant demonstrates that there are situations in which it is possible to have a low share of the market and be profitable (at least in the short term or through segmentation). This situation is potentially attractive to the organization, which may be able to move the product or service into the shining star and, ultimately, cash cow quadrant. These products and services will require investment to nurture them and gain relative market share. Strategies may include market development, product development, penetration, and vertical integration coupled with strong functional support.

Faithful Dogs In this situation, the products and services have low market growth and a low market share, but have been profitable. For example, many hospital services involve less-dominant units showing slow growth. But if they are profitable, such units make a positive contribution to the overall health of the hospital.[11]

For faithful dogs, managers must assess if increased market share will add to profitability. For instance, if profitable segments can be identified, it may be more advantageous to withdraw from broader markets, concentrate on a smaller segment, and maintain profitability. In such situations, a status quo or retrenchment strategy may be appropriate. If profitability is likely to decline over time, a harvesting or divestiture strategy may be employed.

Black Holes Black hole products and services have high growth and a high market share but low profitability. Not all high-growth, high-share programs are profitable in health care. For instance, costly technological equipment may make an organization the sole provider of a service whose high cost cannot be recovered from individual patients. However, such services may contribute to the overall image of the organization and increase the profitability of other services.

Nevertheless, having a high share for a service that is low or negative in profitability is quite disturbing. There must be a concentrated effort to reduce costs (enhancement strategy) or to add revenue without adding costs to such a program (a functional-level strategy). "When circumstances prevent a service from generating most of its own cash inflow, it becomes a 'black hole' – a collapsed star sucking in light (profit or cash) – rather than shining and generating cash or profits."[12]

If a black hole product or service cannot be made into a shining star, it is likely to become a cash pig. Therefore, enhancement and retrenchment strategies may be most appropriate. In addition, functional strategies should be employed to reduce costs and increase revenue.

Problem Children Low-share, high-growth, and low-profitability products and services present both challenges and problems. Some of the products and services represent future shining stars and cash cows although others represent future black holes and mangy dogs. Management must decide which products and services to support and which to eliminate. For supported products, market development with strong functional commitment is appropriate. For products that management does not feel can become shining stars, divestiture and liquidation are most appropriate.

Cash Pigs In this quadrant, products and services have a high or dominant share, are experiencing low growth, and have low profitability. Health care cash pigs are likely to be those well-established SSUs with dominant shares that once were considered to be cash cows. Typically, they have well-entrenched advocates in the organizational hierarchy who support their continuance.[13]

A possible solution to the cash pig problem is to cut costs and raise prices. Therefore, aggressive retrenchment may be required. This strategy may allow the organization to give up the market share to find smaller, more profitable segments and thus create a smaller cash cow.

Mangy Dogs Products and services with low growth, a low share, and poor profit have a debilitating effect on the organization and should be eliminated as soon as possible. In this situation, it appears that other providers are better serving the market. Probably the best strategy at this point is liquidation, as it will be difficult to find a buyer for products and services in this quadrant.

Strategic Position and Action Evaluation

Strategic position and action evaluation *(SPACE)*, an extension of two-dimensional portfolio analysis (BCG), is used to determine the appropriate strategic posture of the organization. By using SPACE, the manager can incorporate a number of factors into the analysis and examine a particular strategic alternative from several perspectives.[14]

SPACE analysis suggests the appropriateness of strategic alternatives based on factors relating to four dimensions: industry strength, environmental stability, the organization's competitive advantage, and the organization's financial strength. The SPACE chart and definitions of the four quadrants are shown in Exhibit 7–9. Listed under each of the four dimensions are factors to which individual numerical values ranging from 0 to 6 can be assigned. The numbers are then added together and divided by the number of factors to yield an average. The averages for environmental stability and competitive advantage each have the number 6 subtracted from them to produce a negative number. The average for each dimension is then plotted on the appropriate axis of the SPACE chart and connected to create a four-sided polygon. Factor scales for each dimension are presented in Exhibit 7–10, which has been filled in for a typical regional hospital. The resulting

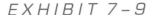

EXHIBIT 7-9

Strategic Position and Action Evaluation (SPACE) Matrix

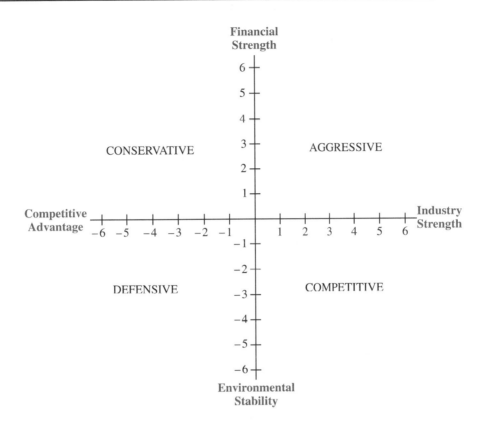

Aggressive Posture

This posture is typical in an attractive industry with little environmental turbulence. The organization enjoys a definite competitive advantage, which it can protect with financial strength. The critical factor is the entry of new competitors. Organizations in this situation should take full advantage of opportunities, look for acquisition candidates in their own or related areas, increase market share, and concentrate resources on products having a definite competitive edge.

Competitive Posture

This posture is typical in an attractive industry. The organization enjoys a competitive advantage in a relatively unstable environment. The critical factor is financial strength. Organizations in this situation should acquire financial resources to increase marketing thrust, add to the sales force, extend or improve the product line, invest in productivity, reduce costs, protect competitive advantage in a declining market, and attempt to merge with a cash-rich organization.

EXHIBIT 7-9　cont'd

Conservative Posture

This posture is typical in a stable market with low growth. Here, the organization focuses on financial stability. The critical factor is product competitiveness. Organizations in this situation should prune the product line, reduce costs, focus on improving cash flow, protect competitive products, develop new products, and gain entry into more attractive markets.

Defensive Posture

This posture is typical of an unattractive industry in which the organization lacks a competitive product and financial strength. The critical factor is competitiveness. Firms in this situation should prepare to retreat from the market, discontinue marginally profitable products, aggressively reduce costs, cut capacity, and defer or minimize investments.

Source: Alan J. Rowe, Richard O. Mason, Karl E. Dickel, and Neil H. Snyder, *Strategic Management: A Methodological Approach*, 3d ed. (Reading, Massachusetts: Addison-Wesley Publishing Company, 1989), pp. 145–150. © 1989 by Addison-Wesley Publishing Company. Reprinted with permission of the publisher.

shape of the polygon can be used to identify four strategic postures – aggressive, competitive, conservative, and defensive. The quadrant with the largest area is suggested as the most appropriate general strategic position.

The factor scales shown in Exhibit 7–10 are for a California-based regional hospital system specializing in health services for the elderly and chemically dependent. As illustrated in Exhibit 7–10, this hospital system is operating in a fairly turbulent environment with many competitive pressures and many technological changes (environmental stability axis). However, the hospital's industry segments (industry strength axis) show good growth potential, which attracts strong competition. Increasing competition requires increased investment in new facilities and technology. The hospital still has a competitive advantage (competitive advantage axis) derived from early entry into the market, and it has been able to retain customer loyalty because of high-quality service. However, the hospital's financial position (financial strength axis) is weak because it financed new facilities through a substantial amount of debt. Its liquidity position has eroded and cash flow continues to be a problem.

Which of the adaptive strategic alternatives is most appropriate for this regional system? The dimensions for this organization are plotted on the SPACE matrix shown in Exhibit 7–11, which demonstrates that the hospital is competing fairly well in an unstable but attractive industry segment. This organization cannot be too aggressive because it has few financial resources and the environment is a bit unstable. Therefore, it should adopt a competitive posture.

It is important to remember that the SPACE chart is a summary display; each factor should be analyzed individually as well. In particular, factors with very high or very low scores should receive special attention.[15] Exhibit 7–12 examines various possible strategic profiles that may be obtained in a SPACE analysis, and Exhibit 7–13 shows the adaptive alternatives for each strategic posture.

EXHIBIT 7–10
Strategic Position and Action Evaluation Factors

Factors Determining Environmental Stability

Technological changes	Many	0	①	2	3	4	5	6	Few
Rate of inflation	High	0	①	2	3	4	5	6	Low
Demand variability	Large	0	1	2	3	④	5	6	Small
Price range of competing products/services	Wide	0	①	2	3	4	5	6	Narrow
Barriers to entry into market	Few	0	1	2	③	4	5	6	Many
Competitive pressure	High	0	1	②	3	4	5	6	Low
Price elasticity of demand	Elastic	0	1	2	3	④	5	6	Inelastic
Other: _____	_____	0	1	2	3	4	5	6	_____

Average − 6 = <u>−3.7</u>

Critical factors

<u>Fairly turbulent environment; strong competition; many technological changes.</u>

Comments

<u>Necessary to maintain financial stability because of turbulence in the environment; demand in market segments relatively stable; protect market niche against competition.</u>

Factors Determining Industry Strength

Growth potential	Low	0	1	2	3	④	5	6	High
Profit potential	Low	0	1	2	3	4	⑤	6	High
Financial stability	Low	0	1	②	3	4	5	6	High
Technological know-how	Simple	0	1	2	3	4	⑤	6	Complex
Resource utilization	Inefficient	0	1	2	3	④	5	6	Efficient
Capital intensity	High	0	1	②	3	4	5	6	Low
Ease of entry into market	Easy	0	①	2	3	4	5	6	Difficult
Productivity, capacity utilization	Low	0	1	2	3	4	⑤	6	High
Other: <u>Flexibility, adaptability</u>	Low	0	1	2	3	4	⑤	6	High

Average <u>3.7</u>

Critical factors

Good growth and profit potential; strong competition.

EXHIBIT 7 – 10 cont'd

Comments

Very attractive industry segment, but strong competition; degree of capital intensity increasing.

Factors Determining Competitive Advantage

Market share	Small	0	1	②	3	4	5	6	Large
Product quality	Inferior	0	1	2	3	4	5	⑥	Superior
Product life cycle	Late	0	1	2	③	4	5	6	Early
Product replacement cycle	Variable	0	1	2	3	④	5	6	Fixed
Customer/patient loyalty	Low	0	1	2	3	④	5	6	High
Competition's capacity utilization	Low	0	1	2	3	④	5	6	High
Technological know-how	Low	0	1	2	3	④	5	6	High
Vertical integration	Low	0	1	②	3	4	5	6	High
Other: _____	_____	0	1	2	3	4	5	6	_____

$$\text{Average} - 6 = \underline{-2.4}$$

Critical factors

Market share low; product/service quality very good.

Comments

The organization still enjoys slight competitive advantage because of quality and customer loyalty; can be expected to diminish, however, because of improving performance of competitive organizations.

Factors Determining Financial Strength

Return on investment	Low	0	1	2	3	④	5	6	High
Leverage	Imbalanced	0	①	2	3	4	5	6	Balanced
Liquidity	Imbalanced	⓪	1	2	3	4	5	6	Balanced
Capital required/capital available	High	0	①	2	3	4	5	6	Low
Cash flow	Low	0	①	2	3	4	5	6	High
Ease of exit from market	Difficult	0	1	2	3	④	5	6	Easy
Risk involved in business	Much	0	①	2	3	4	5	6	Little
Other: Inventory turnover	Slow	0	①	2	3	4	5	6	Fast

$$\text{Average} \quad \underline{1.6}$$

Critical factors

Very little liquidity; too much debt.

Comments

Financial position very weak; cash inflow has to be increased in order to improve liquidity; outside financing difficult because of high leverage.

Source: Alan J. Rowe, Richard O. Mason, Karl E. Dickel, and Neil H. Snyder, *Strategic Management: A Methodological Approach,* 3d ed. (Reading, Massachusetts: Addison-Wesley Publishing Company, 1989), pp. 148–149. © 1989 by Addison-Wesley Publishing Company. Reprinted with permission of the publisher.

The regional hospital system examined previously was plotted into a competitive profile. Accordingly, the most appropriate strategic alternatives are penetration, market development, product development, status quo, or enhancement, with the most likely being enhancement. The hospital should continue to differentiate itself but must rectify its financial position because an unstable environment may place unanticipated demands on the organization that will require an additional infusion of capital. In light of its financial problems, the hospital may have to pursue its objectives (for example, market development) through a cooperation market entry strategy. As pointed out in Perspective 7–4, a cooperation strategy – joining a network – may be important in an environment where health care systems, continuums, and referral networks are the key to market development and penetration. In the end, the adaptive and market entry strategic decisions are inextricably linked.

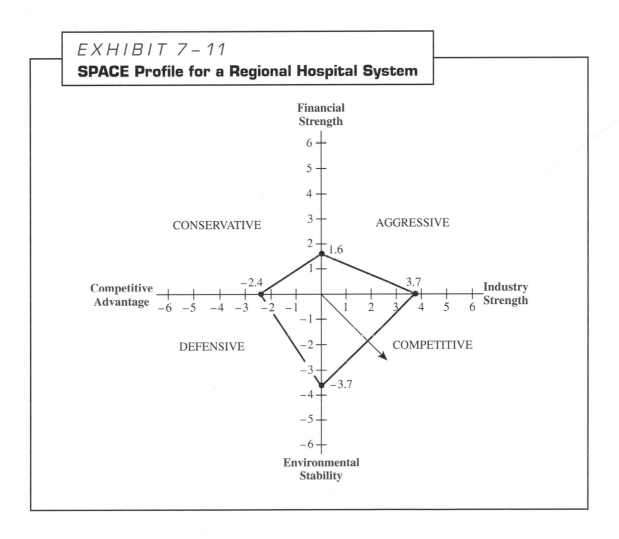

EXHIBIT 7–11
SPACE Profile for a Regional Hospital System

EXHIBIT 7-12
SPACE Strategy Profiles

AGGRESSIVE PROFILES

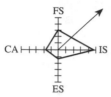

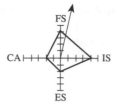

A financially strong organization that has achieved major competitive advantages in a growing and stable industry segment

An organization whose financial strength is a dominating factor in the industry segment

CONSERVATIVE PROFILES

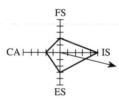

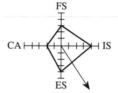

An organization that has achieved financial strength in a stable industry segment that is not growing; the organization has no major competitive advantages

An organization that suffers from major competitive disadvantages in an industry segment that is technologically stable but declining in revenue

COMPETITIVE PROFILES

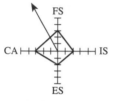

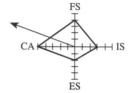

An organization with major competitive advantages but limited financial strength in a high-growth industry segment

An organization that is competing fairly well in an industry segment where there is substantial environmental uncertainty

DEFENSIVE PROFILES

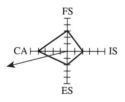

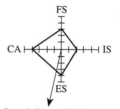

An organization that has a very weak competitive position in a negative-growth, stable but weak industry segment

A financially troubled organization in a very unstable and weak industry

Source: Adapted from a summary by Fred R. David, *Strategic Management,* 2d ed. (Columbus, Ohio: Merrill Publishing Company, 1989), p. 216, of Alan J. Rowe, Richard O. Mason, and Karl E. Dickel, and N. H. Snyder, *Strategic Management: A Methodological Approach* (Reading, Massachusetts: Addison-Wesley Publishing Company, 1982), p. 155. © 1989 by Addison-Wesley Publishing Company. Reprinted with permission of the publisher.

EXHIBIT 7–13
Strategic Alternatives for SPACE Quadrants

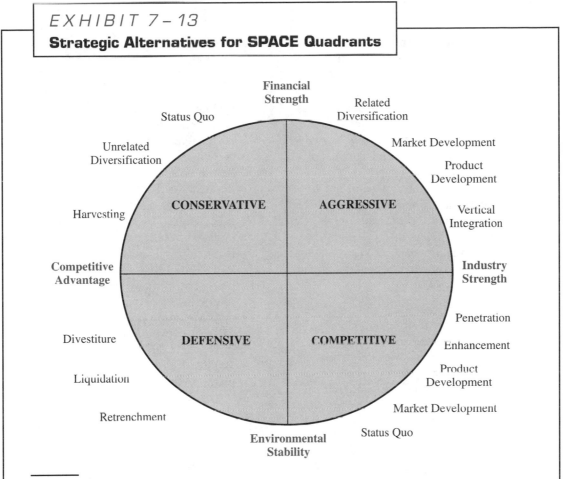

Source: Adapted from Alan J. Rowe, Richard O. Mason, Karl E. Dickel, and Neil H. Snyder, *Strategic Management: A Methodological Approach,* 3d ed. (Reading, Massachusetts: Addison-Wesley Publishing Company, 1989), p. 157. Reprinted with permission of the publisher.

Program Evaluation

Program evaluation is especially useful in organizations where market share, industry strength, and competitive advantage are not particularly important or not relevant. Such organizations are typically not-for-profit, state and federally funded institutions such as state and county public health departments, state mental health departments, Medicaid agencies, community health centers, and public community hospitals. Even though these organizations are public and not-for-profit, they should develop explicit strategies and evaluate the adaptive strategic alternatives open to them. Although TOWS and a form of portfolio analysis may be used to evaluate

PERSPECTIVE 7–4

Joining a Health Network Is a High-Stakes Decision for a Specialty Hospital

Regardless of their area of expertise, specialty hospitals – rehabilitation, pediatrics, psychiatry, or others – face questions over network involvement as they consider their futures in the changing delivery system. However, the stakes are high for specialty providers because patients are more seriously ill and often require a greater concentration and coordination of health care services. What factors should specialty hospitals consider in deciding whether to become a part of an integrated health care network?

• Specialty providers generally draw patients from large, regional referral bases. Restricting themselves to a single network may not allow for an adequate number of referrals. If faced with a choice, would referring physicians keep their patients locally or send them to the specialty hospital?

• The more unique the services in their markets or regions, the more specialty hospitals may want to leave the door open to provide some services to several networks. Could other providers easily replicate some or all of our services in competing networks or health care plans, thus increasing the competition?

• Good location, high quality, and ef-

ficiency increases options for the specialty hospital and increases the desirability of the services provided by the specialty hospital.

• Networks desiring to close down their own specialty unit to eliminate duplication of services may pressure the specialty hospital for exclusive association. Do emerging networks already have the capacity or capability for the specialty?

• Are the traditions, mission, and values of the specialty hospital compatible with the network?

• Will capitation (a part of a managed care network) put the specialty hospital at a disadvantage?

• Will there be a loss of organizational identity and autonomy by joining the network?

• Will referrals decline if the hospital is not part of a health care network? What is the relationship to referring physicians? How strong are those links?

• Are links to other parts of the health care continuum important and provided as a part of the network?

Source: Kevin Lumsdon, "Specialty Gamble," *Hospital & Health Networks* 67, no. 21 (1993), pp. 32–36.

public health programs,[16] evaluation methods that consider increasing revenue and market share may be inappropriate or difficult to use.

Public and not-for-profit institutions typically maintain any number of programs funded through such sources as state appropriations, federal grants, private donations, fee for service, and so on. In a public health department, such programs might include HIV/AIDS education, disease surveillance, disease control, immunizations, food sanitation inspection, on-site sewage inspection, and many more. Usually, these programs have been initiated to fill a health care need within the community that has not been addressed through the private sector. These "health care gaps" have occurred because of federal or state requirements for coordination and control of community health and because of the large number of individuals without adequate health care insurance or means to pay for services.

Within the context provided by an understanding of the external environment, internal environment, and the directional strategies, these nonprofit institutions must chart a future through a set of externally and internally funded programs. The set of programs maintained and emphasized by the organization constitutes the adaptive strategy. The degree to which they are changed (expansion, contraction, stabilization) represents a modification of the adaptive strategy. Therefore, the fundamental question is, "Does our current set of programs effectively and efficiently fulfill our mission and our vision for the future?" This question may be addressed through a process of program evaluation. Two program evaluation methods that have been used successfully are needs/capacity assessment and program priority setting.

Needs/Capacity Assessment The set of programs in not-for-profit organizations such as public health departments essentially are determined by (1) community need and (2) the organization's capacity to deliver the program to that community. Of course, some programs may be mandated by law such as disease control, disease surveillance, and the maintenance of vital records (birth and death records). However, the assumption is that the legislation is a result of an important need and, typically, the mandate is supported by nondiscretionary or categorical funding (funding that may be used for only one purpose). Therefore, in developing a strategy for a public health organization or not-for-profit organization serving the community, community needs must be assessed, as well as the organization's ability (capacity) to address the needs.

Community need is a function of (1) clear *community* requirements (environmental, sanitation, disease control, and so on) and *personal* health care (primary care) gaps, (2) the degree to which other institutions (private and public) fill the identified health care gaps, and (3) public/community health objectives. Most not-for-profit institutions enter the health care market to provide services to those who otherwise would be left out of the system. Despite health care reform efforts, these gaps are likely to remain for some time. Through community involvement, community assessments such as those carried out by the Centers for Disease Control (CDC) and political pressure, health care gaps are identified. These gaps exist because there are few private or public institutions positioned to fill the need. Where existing institutions are willing and able to fill these gaps, public and not-for-profit organizations should probably resist entering the market. In addition, public and community health objectives must be considered when developing strategy. National, state, and community objectives such as the Year 2000 Objectives should be included as a part of a community needs assessment.[17]

Organization capacity is the organization's ability to initiate, maintain, and enhance its set of adaptive strategy programs. Organization capacity is composed of (1) funding to support programs, (2) other organizational resources and skills, and (3) the program's fit with the mission and vision of the organization. Availability of funding is an important part of organization capacity. Many programs are supported with categorical funding and accompanying mandates (program requirements dictated by a higher authority, usually federal or state government). Often, however, local monies supplement federal and state funded programs. For other programs, only community funding is available. Thus, funding availability is a major consideration in developing strategy for public and not-for-profit organizations. In addition, the organization must have the skills, resources, facilities, management, and so on to initiate and effectively administer the program. Finally, program strategy will be dependent upon the program's fit with the organization's mission and vision for the future. Programs outside the mission and vision will be viewed as luxuries, superfluous, or wasteful.

Exhibit 7–14 presents the adaptive strategic alternatives indicated for public organizations as they assess community needs and the organization's capacity to fill the identified needs. Where the community need is assessed as high (significant health care gaps, few or no other institutions addressing the need, and the program is a part of the community's objectives) and the organization's capacity is assessed as high (adequate funding, appropriate skills and resources, and fit with mission/vision), then the organization should adopt one of the expansion adaptive strategies (upper right-hand quadrant). Appropriate strategies might include vertical integration, related diversification, product development, market development, and penetration. When the community need assessment is low (no real need, the need has abated, need is now being addressed by another institution, or the need does not fit with community objectives), but organization capacity is high (adequate funding, appropriate skills and resources, and fit with mission/vision), there should be an orderly redistribution of resources, suggesting contraction and stabilization adaptive strategies (upper left-hand quadrant). Contraction strategies should be given priority as the community need diminishes; however, phasing out a program may take some time or the uncertainty concerning the changing community needs may dictate stabilization in the short term. Appropriate adaptive strategies include status quo, related diversification, retrenchment, and harvesting.

Where community needs have been assessed as low (no real need, the need has abated, need is now being addressed by another institution, or the need does not fit with community objectives) and the organization has few financial or other resources to commit to programs (low organization capacity), one of the contraction adaptive strategies should be adopted (lower left-hand quadrant). These strategies include harvesting, retrenchment, divestiture, and liquidation. When community needs have been assessed as high but organizational capacity is low, stability and contraction strategies are appropriate (lower right-hand quadrant). Stability strategies should be given priority because of the high community need but, as resources dwindle or funding is reduced, contraction may be required. Appropriate adaptive strategic alternatives include status quo, enhancement, retrenchment, and harvesting. As resources become available, programs in this

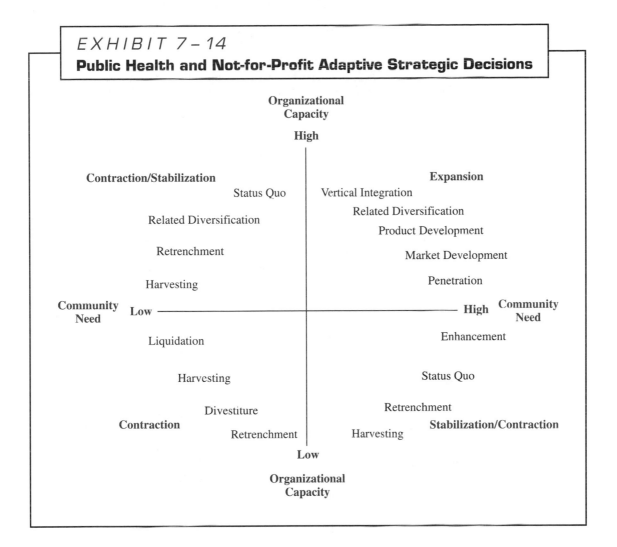

EXHIBIT 7-14
Public Health and Not-for-Profit Adaptive Strategic Decisions

quadrant will move to the upper left-hand quadrant and more aggressive (expansion) strategies may be selected.

Program Priority Setting The second method of developing adaptive strategies for public programs involves ranking programs and setting priorities. This process is significant because community needs (both the need itself and the severity of the need) are constantly changing and organizational resources, in terms of funding and organization capacity, are almost always limited. Invariably more programs have high community need than resources are available. Therefore, the most important programs (and perhaps those with categorical funding) may be expanded or stabilized. The organization must have an understanding of which programs are the most important, which should be provided incremental funding, and which should be the first to be scaled back if funding is reduced or eliminated.

The nature and emphasis on programs is the central part of strategy formulation in many public and not-for-profit organizations. However, a problem in ranking these programs is that typically all of them are viewed as "very important" or "essential." This is particularly true when using Likert or Semantic Differential scales to evaluate the programs. Therefore, it is necessary to develop evaluation methods that further differentiate the programs. The Q-sort method has proven helpful in differentiating the importance of programs.

Q-sort is a ranking procedure that forces choices along a continuum in situations where the difference between the choices may be quite small. The *program Q-sort evaluation* is particularly useful when experts may differ on what makes one choice preferable over another. By ranking the choices using a Q-sort procedure, participants see where there is wide consensus (for whatever reasons used by the experts) and have an opportunity to discuss the choices for which there is disagreement (and, hopefully, reach greater consensus).

The Q-sort is a part of *Q-methodology,* a set of philosophical, psychological, statistical, and psychometric ideas oriented to research on the individual. Q-sort evaluation helps overcome the problem of ranking all programs as very important by forcing a ranking based on some set of assumptions. Therefore, the Q-sort is a way of rank-ordering objects (programs) and then assigning numerals to subsets of the objects for statistical purposes. Fred N. Kerlinger, in *Foundations of Behavioral Research,* characterized the Q-sort as "a sophisticated way of rank-ordering objects."[18]

Q-sort focuses particularly in sorting decks of cards (in this case each card representing a program) and in the correlations among the responses of different individuals to the Q-sorts. Kerlinger reports good results with as few as forty items (programs) that have been culled from a larger list, but usually greater statistical stability and reliability results from at least sixty items and not more than one hundred.[19]

For ranking an organization's programs, only the first step in using Q-methodology is used – the Q-sort. In the Q-sort procedure, each member of the management team is asked to sort the organization's programs into categories based on their perceived importance to the organization's mission and vision. To facilitate the task, the programs are printed on small cards that may be arranged (sorted) on a table. To force ranking of programs, managers are asked to arrange the programs in piles from most important to least important. The best approach is that the number of categories be limited to nine and the number of programs to be assigned to each category be determined in such a manner as to ensure a normal distribution.[20] Therefore, if a public health department had forty-nine separate programs that management wished to rank (culled from a larger list of programs), they may be sorted as shown in Exhibit 7–15. Notice that, to create a normal distribution (or quasi-normal), 5 percent of the programs are placed in the first pile or group, 7.5 percent in the second group, 12.5 percent in the third, and so on. In this case, there are two programs in the first group, four programs in the second group, six in the third, and so on.

Depending in which group it is placed, each program is assigned a score ranging from 1 to 9 where 1 is for the lowest and 9 is for the highest ranked programs. The score indicates an individual's perception of that program's importance to the mission and vision of the organization. A program profile is developed by averaging individual members' scores for each program.

Based on the results of the Q-sort, programs may be designated for expansion, contraction, or stabilization. For the public health programs in Exhibit 7–15, food sanitation and epidemiology, sewage planning and operation, sexually transmitted disease (STD) control, and so on might be earmarked for expansion. Cancer prevention, lodging/jail inspection, injury prevention, and so on might be slated for stabilization, whereas plumbing inspection, hearing aid dealer board regulation, and animal control may be marked for contraction. The Q-sort procedure works well using several different sets of strategic assumptions. For example, the programs may be sorted based on different scenarios.

EVALUATION OF THE MARKET ENTRY STRATEGIES

Once an expansion or stabilization (enhancement) adaptive strategy is selected, one or more of the market entry strategies must be used to break into or capture more of the market. All of the expansion adaptive strategies require some activity to reach more consumers with the products and services. Similarly, enhancement stabilization strategies indicate that the organization must undertake to "do better" what it is already doing, which requires market entry analysis. Contraction strategies are methods to either rapidly or slowly leave markets and therefore do not require a market entry strategic decision.

The market entry strategies include acquisition, licensing, venture capital investment, merger, alliance, joint venture, internal development, and internal venture. Any one (or several) of these strategies may be used to enter the market; however, mergers and alliances have received most of the media attention in the 1990s. Mergers and alliances are the principal cooperation strategies. As depicted in Perspective 7–5, consolidation seems to be proceeding at a fairly steady pace.

The specific market entry strategy or strategies considered to be appropriate depends upon (1) the internal skills and resources of the organization, (2) the external conditions, and (3) the objectives of the organization. Each of these three areas should be scrupulously evaluated in the selection of the appropriate market entry strategy.

Internal Requirements Each of the market entry strategies requires somewhat different internal skills and resources (Exhibit 7–16). Before selecting the appropriate market entry strategy, a review of the internal strengths and weaknesses (Chapter 4) should be undertaken. If the required skills and resources are available, the appropriate market entry strategy may be selected. On the other hand, if they are not present, another alternative should be selected or a combination strategy of two or more phases should be adopted. The first phase would be directed at correcting the weakness prohibiting selection of the desired strategy, and the second phase would be the initiation of the desired market entry strategy. For

EXHIBIT 7–15
Department of Public Health Q-Sort Results*

Most Important	Next Most Important	Next Most Important	Next Most Important	Next Most Important	Next Most Important	Next Most Important	Next Most Important	Next Most Important
5%	7.5%	12.5%	15%	20%	15%	12.5%	7.5%	5%
Food Sanitation 8.0	Sewage Planning and Operation 7.22	Immunization 6.99	Seafood Sanitation 6.11	Cancer Prevention 4.88	Microbiology 4.44	Administrative Support 3.99	Medicaid and Community Based Waiver 3.33	Hearing Aid Dealer Board Regulation 1.88
	STD Control 7.22	Tuberculosis Control 6.88	Infection Control 5.77	Lodging/Jails Inspection 4.88	Home Health 4.22	Vector Control 3.99		
	Milk Sanitation 7.0	Licensure and Certification 6.77	Health Education 5.66	Injury Prevention 4.77	Quality Assurance 4.11	Dental Health 3.87	Swimming Pools 3.11	
			Family Planning 5.66	Disaster Preparedness 4.77	Primary Care Support 4.11			
		Newborn Screening 6.62	Child Health 5.55	Public Health Nursing 4.75	School Health Education 4.0	Diabetes 3.77		
Epidemiology 8.0	HIV/AIDS Planning and Control 7.0	Health Statistics 6.44	Emergency Medicine 5.50	Lead Assessment 4.62	WIC 4.0			
			Radiation Control 5.44	HMO Regulation 4.55	Vital Records 4.0	Indoor Air Quality 3.66	Adolescent Health 2.66	
				Hypertension 4.55				
		Solid Waste 6.33	Maternity 5.22	Mycobacteriology 4.55	Serology 4.0	Public Health Social Work 3.44	Plumbing Inspection 2.55	Animal Control 1.44

*Program name and mean score in each box

example, Perspective 7–6 suggests some reasons a merger may be difficult for two-hospital towns.

External Conditions The next consideration in the selection of the market entry strategy is the evaluation of the environment. A review of the external environmental opportunities and threats and supporting documentation (Chapter 3) should provide information to determine which of the market entry strategies is most appropriate. Exhibit 7–17 provides a list of representative external conditions appropriate for each of the market entry strategies.

PERSPECTIVE 7–5
Hospital Mergers, Consolidations, and Acquisitions

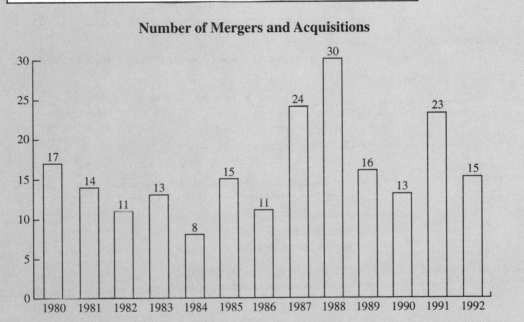

Number of Mergers and Acquisitions

As shown in the chart, there have been an average of sixteen mergers annually in the period from 1979 through 1992. Fredric Entin, the American Hospital Association's senior vice president and general counsel indicated, "Until the last couple of years, mergers were undertaken by individual institutions for reasons specific to their situations. Now, consolidation is an industry-wide strategy." In the thirteen-year period from 1979 to 1992, there have been 210 mergers. Entin expects the pace of mergers, consolidations, and acquisitions to accelerate throughout the rest of the 1990s.

Source: American Hospital Association, in John Morrissey, "Number of Hospital Mergers Slips in '92, Expected to Rise for '93," *Modern Healthcare* 23, no. 51 (1993), p. 3.

EXHIBIT 7 – 16
Internal Requirements for the Market Entry Strategies

Market Entry Strategy	Required Internal Skills and Resources
Acquisition	• Financial resources • Ability to manage new products and markets • Ability to merge organizational cultures and organizational structures • Rightsizing capability for combined organization
Licensing	• Financial resources (licensing fees) • Support organization to carry out license • Ability to integrate new product/market into present organization
Venture Capital Investment	• Capital to invest in speculative projects • Ability to evaluate and select opportunities with a high degree of success
Merger	• Management willing to relinquish or share control • Rightsizing capability • Agreement to merge management • Ability to merge organizational cultures and organizational structures
Alliance	• Lack of competitive skills/facilities/expertise • Desire to create vertically integrated system • Need to control patient flow • Coordinative board/skills • Willing to relinquish/share control
Joint Venture	• Lack of a distinctive competency • Additional resources/capabilities are required
Internal Development	• Technical expertise • Marketing capability • Operational capacity • Research and development capability • Strong functional organization • Product/service management expertise
Internal Venture	• Entrepreneur • Entrepreneurial organization • Ability to isolate venture from the rest of the organization • Technical expertise • Marketing capability • Operational capacity

---

PERSPECTIVE 7-6
Small Market Mergers

Following the consolidation trend occurring in the 1990s, pressures of health reform, and decreasing inpatient days, hospitals are merging in many cities and towns where there are only two hospitals. Many experts believe 200-bed hospitals have a much better chance of surviving than smaller hospitals. Therefore, rather than have two hospitals fight for their share in a small market, the hospitals are merging. Although these mergers often make economic and operational sense, the mergers have run into difficulty. The following reasons may inhibit a merger in small markets and should be considered carefully when considering such mergers.

- Fear of antitrust intervention,
- Risk of physician resistance,
- Chief executive officer and trustees fear loss of control or job,
- Conflicting organizational cultures,
- Unwillingness to give up control,
- Competitor not perceived as a threat, and
- Financial concerns or disparity between the two hospitals.

Source: Sandy Lutz, "Mergers: Two-Hospital Towns Try Togetherness," *Modern Healthcare* 23, no. 49 (1993), pp. 39–44.

Organizational Objectives Along with the internal and external factors, organizational objectives play an important role in evaluating the appropriate market entry strategies (see Perspective 7–7). As shown in Exhibit 7–18, internal development and internal ventures offer the greatest degree of control over the design, production, operations, marketing, and so on of the product or service. On the other hand, licensing, acquisition, mergers, and venture capital investment offer the quickest market entry. Alliances and joint ventures offer relatively quick entry with some degree of control. The trade-off between speed of entering the market and organizational control over the product or service must be assessed by management in light of organizational objectives.

EVALUATION OF THE POSITIONING STRATEGIES

After the market entry strategies have been selected, the products or services must be positioned within the market using the generic positioning strategies of cost leadership, differentiation, or focus. All of the expansion, contraction, and stabilization strategies require explicit positioning strategies and operational strategies. As pointed out in Chapter 6, products and services may be positioned market-wide or for a particular market segment. Cost leadership and differentiation are used as market-wide strategies or they are used to focus on a special segment of the market.

EXHIBIT 7-17

External Conditions Appropriate for Market Entry Strategies

Market Entry Strategy	Appropriate External Conditions
Acquisition	• Growing market • Early stage of the product life cycle or long maturity stage • Attractive acquisition candidate • High volume economies of scale (horizontal integration) • Distribution economies of scale (vertical integration)
Licensing	• High capital investment to enter market • High immediate demand for product/service • Early stages of the product life cycle
Venture Capital Investment	• Rapidly changing technology • Product/service in the early development stage
Merger	• Attractive merger candidate (synergistic effect) • High level of resources required to compete
Alliance	• Market demands complete line of products/services • Market is weak and continuum of services is desirable • Mature stage of product life cycle
Joint Venture	• High capital requirements to obtain necessary skills/expertise • Long learning curve in obtaining necessary expertise
Internal Development	• High level of product control (quality) required • Early stages of the product life cycle
Internal Venture	• Product/service development stage • Rapid development/market entry required • New technical, marketing, production approach required

---

Presence in a market requires that the products and services be positioned vis-à-vis competing products and services. Similar to the other strategy types, positioning depends upon the strengths and weaknesses of the organization and the opportunities and threats in the external environment. In other words, how a product or service is positioned depends on the organization's capability and the competitive situation. Therefore, the positioning strategies must be selected based on their required organizational skills, resources, and structure, as well as environmental risks. For example, it would be difficult for an

William L. Dowling, vice president of planning and development at Sisters of Providence Health System, Seattle, discusses the reasons the system started HMOs in Oregon and Washington.

We wanted to rationalize the flow of payment into the delivery system and be able to turn around and rationally allocate resources internally. With the aggregate dollars, we can decide to allocate more beds to long-term care or pay a nurse to provide well-baby care. If the hospital and physicians are being paid independently, this is difficult to do. For instance, you could have both DRGs and fee-for-service payments, which create different incentives.

As a Catholic-sponsored system, we are committed to serving all segments of the community. We use the HMO to that end. For instance, the health plans that contract with us may decide they don't want Medicaid enrollees. With our own health plan, we can reach out to poor and rural areas. We've invited federally qualified clinics that service needy populations to be providers in our HMOs. Many of these clinics are too small to be at risk by themselves.

The HMO is an important tool for bringing market perspective into an organization. We can learn how to be more cost-effective in the delivery of patient care. We are directly dealing with those footing the bill for health care and must listen to them. The HMO collects intelligence and brings it into the organization.

The HMO helps providers gear up to deliver managed care. Providers see the need for clinical treatment protocols and work out clinical interfaces between primary care physicians and specialists. It allows comprehensive data to be gathered, not just data from one provider. Then we can look at entire episodes of treatment for given conditions and profile cost-effective treatment regimens. The HMO is a tool for both assessing and evaluating care. For instance, it enables us to look at immunization levels and flag services that need to be delivered. It's a powerful educational tool.

Source: Terese Hudson, "Learning by Doing," *Hospitals & Health Networks* 87, no. 22 (1993), pp. 36–37.

urban public community hospital dependent on limited county funding to be positioned as the high technology (differentiation) hospital in the region. Conversely, a well-funded hospital using the latest technology most likely would not be positioned as the cost leader.

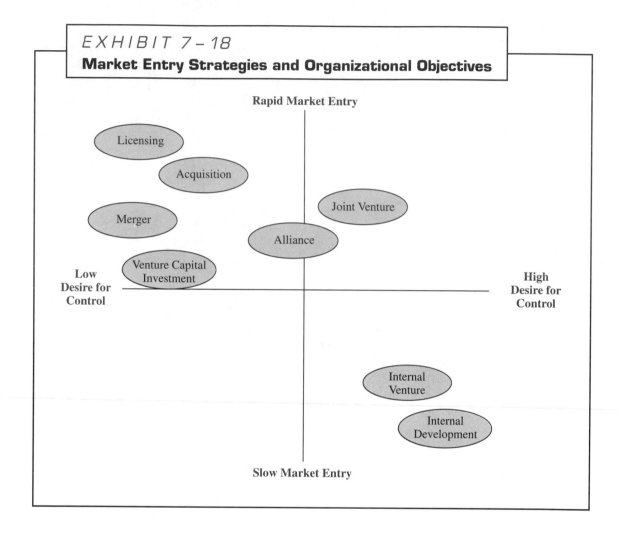

EXHIBIT 7 – 18
Market Entry Strategies and Organizational Objectives

Rapid Market Entry

Licensing

Acquisition

Joint Venture

Merger

Alliance

Venture Capital Investment

Low Desire for Control

High Desire for Control

Internal Venture

Internal Development

Slow Market Entry

Internal Requirements Exhibit 7–19 presents the internal requirements for each of the positioning strategies. In order for an organization to use a cost leadership strategy, it must have or develop the ability to achieve a real *cost* advantage (not price) through state-of-the-art equipment and facilities and low-cost operations. This competitive advantage must be maintained through tight controls and emphasis on economies of scale. Differentiation requires the ability to distinguish the product or service from other competitors. Typically, this will require technical expertise, strong marketing, a high level of skills, and an emphasis on product development. A focus strategy is directed toward a particular segment of the market; however, either cost leadership or differentiation may be used. Therefore, the required skills are the same for a market segment and for market-wide strategies. It is important that organizations adopting a focus strategy stay in

---

EXHIBIT 7 – 19

Internal Requirements for the Positioning Strategies

Generic Strategy	Skills and Resources	Organizational Requirements
Cost Leadership	• Sustained capital investment and access to capital • Process engineering skills • Intense supervision of labor • Products and services that are simple to produce in volume • Low-cost delivery system	• Tight cost control • Frequent, detailed control reports • Structured organization and responsibilities • Incentives based on meeting strict quantitative targets
Differentiation	• Strong marketing abilities • Product/service engineering • Creative flair • Strong capability in basic research • Reputation for quality or technological leadership • Long tradition in the industry or unique combination of skills • Strong cooperation from channels	• Strong coordination among functions in R&D, product/ service development, and marketing • Subjective measurement and incentives instead of quantitative measures • Amenities to attract highly skilled labor, scientists, or creative people
Focus	• Combination of the preceding skills and resources directed at a particular strategic target	• Combination of the preceding organizational requirements directed at a particular strategic target

Source: Adapted from Michael E. Porter, *Competitive Strategy: Techniques for Analyzing Industries and Competitors* (New York: The Free Press, 1980), pp. 40–41.

---

close communication with their market so that specialized needs may be fully addressed and changes in the segment carefully monitored.

External Conditions Each of the generic strategies has its own external risks that must be evaluated by the organization (Exhibit 7–20). Perhaps the biggest risk for cost leadership is technological change. Technological change in processes may allow competitors to achieve cost advantages. Technological change in product or service may result in differentiation of the product that make the cost leader's product less desirable. The most significant risks for the differentiator

---

EXHIBIT 7–20

External Risks Associated with Positioning Strategies

Generic Strategy	External Risks
Cost Leadership	• Technological change that nullifies past investments or learning • Low-cost learning by industry newcomers or followers, through imitation or through their ability to invest in state-of-the-art facilities • Inability to see required product or marketing change because of the attention placed on cost • Inflation in costs that narrow the organization's ability to maintain sufficient price differential to offset competitors' brand images or other approaches to differentiation
Differentiation	• The cost differential between low-cost competitors and the differentiated firm too great for differentiation to hold brand loyalty; buyers therefore sacrifice some of the features, services, or image possessed by the differentiated organization for large cost savings • Buyers' need for the differentiating factor diminishes, which can occur as buyers become more sophisticated • Imitation narrows perceived differentiation, a common occurrence as the industry matures
Focus	• Cost differential between broad-range competitors and the focused organization widens to eliminate the cost advantages of serving a narrow target or to offset the differentiation achieved by focus • Differences in desired products or services between the strategic target and the market as a whole narrows • Competitors find submarkets within the strategic target and out-focus the focuser • Focuser grows the market to a sufficient size that it becomes attractive to competitors that previously ignored it

Source: Adapted from Michael E. Porter, *Competitive Strategy: Techniques for Analyzing Industries and Competitors* (New York: The Free Press, 1980), pp. 45–46.

---

is that emphasis on differentiation pushes costs too high for the market or that the market fails to see, understand, or appreciate the differentiation. There are risks, also, for the organization adopting a focus strategy. Often, the focuser is dependent on a small segment that may diminish in size or purchasers may turn to the broader market for products or services. Movement toward market-wide products and services will occur if the differences in cost or differentiation become blurred.

Perspective 7–8 provides an example of a hospital system that used a focus/differentiation strategy in a highly saturated market (eighteen major hospitals in a medium-sized market). In addition, the Perspective demonstrates that the adaptive, market entry, and positioning strategies must be linked together.

THE SEVEN STRATEGIC DECISION AREAS

The seven strategic decision areas (discussed in Chapter 1) in combination with the directional strategies, adaptive strategies, entry strategies, and positioning strategies make up the general strategy of the organization and form the basis for the operational strategies. These decision areas are mission, customer mix, product mix, service area, goals and objectives, competitive advantage, and outside relationships.

PERSPECTIVE 7–8
Eastern Health Systems: Anatomy of Growth

As Somerset Maugham said, "For the complete life, the perfect pattern includes old age as well as youth and maturing." Eastern Health Systems, Inc. (EHS), a not-for-profit health care organization, has taken Maugham's dictum to heart as it strives to assure its own long-term success. EHS, pursuing an expansion adaptive strategy, has vertically integrated its operations to offer services for patients literally from cradle to grave. Although centered around vertical integration, the EHS expansion strategy has included diversification, product development, market development, and penetration strategies.

EHS's new acute-care full-service hospital, Medical Center East, includes labor/delivery/recovery rooms as well as several intensive care units. Contiguous to the hospital are the Cancer and Diabetes Clinics and office buildings for the physicians on staff. The Apothecary, operated by Eastside Ventures, Inc., is a for-profit subsidiary of EHS and has space in the hospital as well as a freestanding location.

Additionally, Eastside Ventures, Inc. serves a multitude of health care business needs from medical consulting and media management to construction, workers' compensation programs, and grounds maintenance.

One of the company's goals is to meet all the health care needs of older adults. Therefore, in addition to the hospital, Medical Center East, and a Physician Information Line that provides the names of area specialists, EHS, through its Health Services East, Inc., (HSE) subsidiary, turned one of its older hospitals into Lake Villa, an independent and assisted-living facility. HSE Home Care Services will send the needed health care workers to the home of a patient if care in the home is preferred. If the patient requires a private nurse, Private Duty Nursing provides one-on-one nursing 24-hours a day, seven days a week. The Hospice, another HES Home Care Service, provides care in the home for the terminally ill. Respite Care is available at Lake Villa in case a primary homecare giver must be out of town or needs a break. In addition, Lakeview Nursing Home, Inc., a skilled nursing facility, is available should the older adult require a more intense level of care.

If an older adult already has living accommodations, the Friendship Center Adult Day Care Program provides assistance for adults during the day only. Active older people can join HSE Goldenagers, which provides members with fellowship, field trips, volunteer services, and discounts at local retail establishments. The HSE Goldenagers also market the Emergency Response Program that provides a device attached to a necklace to be used to signal for emergency personnel if the need arises.

Through its Eastside Ventures, Inc., subsidiary, EHS provides durable medical equipment delivered to the patient at the hospital or at home. Should a patient need help with home repairs, Eastside Ventures Construction Services provides home renovations or it can build physicians' offices. The Apothecary at Medical Center East is a full-service pharmacy. The Diabetes Clinic offers all patients the convenience of complete facilities and evaluation processes, from dental care, eye evaluations, and podiatry service, to pulmonary, vascular, and cardio/vascular studies, and includes the most technologically advanced

radiology tests. For any patients unable to drive, transportation is provided to doctor and dentist appointments or to the Friendship Center by the MCE Shuttle Care.

EHS provides community education programs. It has opened the Wellness Place in a local shopping mall to provide blood screenings, blood sugar tests, and blood pressure checks for free or at low cost. The Liz Moore Low Vision Center caters to the older adult by providing educational materials and referrals for people with poor vision and training on the use of low-vision equipment. Finally, the Woman's Resource Center at Medical Center East provides informational brochures or videotapes and has registered nurses and other health care professionals available to speak to civic groups on a wide variety of topics.

Thus, instead of diversifying into other "sectors," EHS's strategy appears to be one of vertical integration, both upstream and downstream from its hospital core. Given the changing demographics of the United States, EHS's decision to integrate all services, especially those for the older adult, seems to be a good strategy for future success.

Source: Terrie Reeves, Ph.D. candidate, Health Services Administration, University of Alabama at Birmingham. Adapted from Eastern Health Systems, Inc., publications.

At this point, we should be able to develop the major portion of a strategic plan. Specifying the adaptive strategic alternative, the entry and positioning strategy, and each of the seven strategic decision areas creates a framework and clear direction for the development of specific operational (implementation) plans. Operational strategies, which will complete the plan, are developed separately. An example of such a framework (expanded from Exhibit 1–7) is presented in Exhibit 7–21.

SUMMARY AND CONCLUSIONS

Several strategic alternatives are available to health care organizations. It is important that the organization has a process in place for understanding the internal and external environments and methods for evaluating strategic alternatives. This chapter has provided the methods for evaluating strategic alternatives – adaptive strategies, market entry strategies, and positioning strategies. In addition, these

---

EXHIBIT 7–21
Rancho Los Amigos Medical Center Strategy

Adaptive Strategies
Market development and product development

Market Entry Strategy
Internal Development

Positioning Strategy
Focus/Differentiation: High-quality and innovative services in the evaluation and treatment of severely disabled persons.

Strategic Decision Areas

1. *Mission.* The mission of Rancho Los Amigos Medical Center is to maximize the performance, function, and mobility of each of our patients and to afford them the greatest possible opportunity for achieving independence in the activities of daily living.
2. *Customer Mix.* Those with congenital and acquired disabilities from Los Angeles County, Southern California, the nation, and other nations.
3. *Product Mix.* Surgical services, rehabilitation nursing, children's services, patient progress conferences, physical therapy, occupational therapy, pathokinesiology, communication disorders therapy, spinal injury service, recreation therapy, rehabilitation engineering, and other related services.
4. *Service Area.* Primarily Los Angeles County and Southern California, but can draw nationally and internationally.
5. *Goals and Objectives.*
   - Maintain and improve traditionally high level of patient care;
   - Reduce dependence on financial support from public funds;
   - Foster innovation; and
   - Upgrade and replace facilities.

EXHIBIT 7 – 21   cont'd

6. *Competitive Advantage.*
   - Image;
   - High-quality services;
   - Excellent, widely recognized staff;
   - County support; and
   - Emphasis on management and financial management.
7. *Outside Relationships.*
   - Excellent relationship with the County of Los Angeles;
   - Established board of directors from large, locally based organizations;
   - Medical school affiliation;
   - Received high commendations from both the Joint Commission on Accreditation of Hospitals (JCAH) and the Commission on Accreditation of Rehabilitation Facilities (CARF).

Operational Support Strategies (Discussed in Chapters 8 through 12)

- *Marketing:* Aggressive marketing emphasizing image, high quality, and sensitivity to the needs of patients.
- *Finance:* Strong financial management and a capital improvement program to fund new facilities (medical/industrial campus).
- *Organization and Staffing:* Strong research program, unique interdisciplinary team approach, diverse and ongoing professional education programs, and an emphasis on people.

Source: Rancho Los Amigos Medical Center publications.

strategies have been translated into the seven strategic decisions that provide the basis and direction for development of the operational strategies.

There are a number of methods for deciding which of the adaptive strategic alternatives is most appropriate for an organization. The TOWS (threats, opportunities, weaknesses, and strengths) matrix, product life cycle analysis, portfolio analysis, the SPACE (strategic position and action evaluation) analysis, and program evaluation were examined in considerable depth. Using these methods, managers can classify internal and external factors to gain perspective on which adaptive strategic alternative or combination of alternatives is most appropriate.

Once the most appropriate adaptive strategy (or combination of adaptive strategies) has been selected, a market entry strategy must be selected. Expansion and stabilization strategies are initiated through one or more of the entry strategies. Entry strategies include acquisition, licensing, venture capital investment, merger, alliance, joint venture, internal development, and internal venture. The organization's internal skills and resources, the external conditions, and the organization's objectives will determine which of these strategies is most appropriate.

After the market entry strategy has been selected, positioning strategies should be evaluated and selected. Positioning strategies include cost leadership, differentiation, and focus. The most appropriate positioning strategy may be selected through an evaluation of the internal skills and resources of the organization and the external conditions.

After decisions have been made concerning the adaptive strategies, market entry strategies, and positioning strategies, the strategic plan must be further articulated and communicated throughout the organization by way of the seven strategic decision areas. These areas include mission, customer mix, product mix, service area, goals and objectives, competitive advantage, and outside relationships.

Chapters 8 through 12 discuss various operational strategies. Chapter 8 will address strategic implementation through marketing strategies.

KEY TERMS AND CONCEPTS IN STRATEGIC MANAGEMENT

BCG portfolio analysis
extended portfolio matrix analysis
needs/capacity assessment

product life cycle analysis
program evaluation
program priority setting
program Q-sort evaluation

SPACE analysis
strategic assumptions
TOWS matrix

QUESTIONS FOR CLASS DISCUSSION

1. Explain how external opportunities and threats may be combined with internal strengths and weaknesses to develop adaptive strategic alternatives.
2. Using the TOWS matrix, what adaptive strategic alternatives might be appropriate for each quadrant?
3. Describe the product life cycle. How is it useful for thinking about the adaptive strategy of a health care organization?
4. Why is the length of the product life cycle important for strategy formulation?
5. What adaptive strategic alternatives are indicated for each stage of the product life cycle?
6. Is portfolio analysis useful for developing adaptive strategic alternatives for health care organizations?
7. Explain the rationale for expanding the traditional BCG portfolio matrix.
8. Identify appropriate adaptive strategic alternatives for each quadrant in the expanded portfolio matrix.
9. Explain the strategic position and action

evaluation (SPACE) analysis. How may adaptive strategic alternatives be developed using SPACE?
10. Why should program evaluation be used for public health and not-for-profit institutions in the development of adaptive strategies?
11. What are the critical factors for determining the importance of programs within a public health organization?
12. Why should public health and not-for-profit organizations set priorities for programs?
13. Describe program Q-sort. Why would an organization use program Q-sort?
14. How are market entry strategies evaluated? What role do speed of market entry and control over the product or service play in the market entry decision?
15. How may the positioning strategic alternatives be evaluated?
16. Why are the seven decision areas important in the formulation of the strategic plan?

NOTES

1. Peter F. Drucker, *Management: Tasks, Responsibilities, Practices* (New York: Harper and Row Publishers, 1974), p. 470.
2. Heinz Weihrich, "The TOWS Matrix: A Tool for Situational Analysis," *Long Range Planning* 15, no. 2 (1982), pp. 54–66.
3. Ibid., p. 61.
4. Ibid.
5. Frank Cerne, "Dinosaur or Chameleon?" *Hospitals & Health Networks* 67, no. 20 (1993), pp. 41–43.
6. Ibid.
7. Robin E. Scott MacStravic, Edward Mahn, and Deborah C. Reedal, "Portfolio Analysis for Hospitals," *Health Care Management Review* (Fall 1983), p. 69.
8. Gary McCain, "Black Holes, Cash Pigs, and Other Hospital Portfolio Analysis Problems," *Journal of Health Care Management* 7, no. 2 (June 1987), p. 56.
9. Ibid., pp. 56–57.
10. MacStravic, Mahn, and Reedal, "Portfolio Analysis for Hospitals," p. 70.
11. McCain, "Black Holes, Cash Pigs," p. 60.
12. Ibid., p. 61.
13. Ibid., p. 62.
14. Alan J. Rowe, Richard O. Mason, Karl E. Dickel, and Neil H. Snyder, *Strategic Management: A Methodological Approach,* 3rd ed. (Reading, Massachusetts: Addision-Wesley Publishing Company, 1989), p. 143.
15. Ibid., p. 145.
16. Peter M. Ginter, W. Jack Duncan, Stuart A. Capper, and Melinda G. Rowe, "Evaluating Public Health Programs Using Portfolio Analysis," *Proceedings of the Southern Management Association,* Atlanta (November 1993), pp. 492–496.
17. *Healthy Communities 2000 Model Standards: Guidelines for Community Attainment of the Year 2000 National Health Objectives,* 3rd ed. (Washington D.C.: American Public Health Association, 1991); and *Healthy People: National Health Promotion and Disease Prevention Objectives* (Washington, D.C.: U.S. Department of Health and Human Services, Public Health Service, 1991).
18. Fred N. Kerlinger, *Foundations of Behavioral Research* (New York: Holt, Rinehart and Winston, Inc., 1973), p. 582.
19. Kerlinger, *Foundations of Behavioral Research,* p. 584.
20. J. Block, *The Q-Sort Method in Personality Assessment and Psychiatric Research* (Palo Alto, California: Consulting Psychologist Press, 1978), p. 137.

ADDITIONAL READINGS

Arndt, Margarete, and Barbara Bigelow, "Vertical Integration in Hospitals: A Framework for Analysis," *Medical Care Review* 49, no. 1 (1993), pp. 93–115. Over the past several years, hospitals have vertically integrated into activities along all stages of production. However, the motives for vertical integration are not well understood. The authors make the case that early and late adopters of vertical integration act for different reasons. Early adopters seek economic and marketing advantages whereas late adopters seek to maintain their legitimacy by adopting a structure that is prevalent in the environment, even when the economic effects are unknown.

Desai, Harsha B., and Charles R. Margenthaler, "A Framework for Developing Hospital Strategies," *Hospital & Health Services Administration* (May 1987), pp. 235–248. This article provides a practical strategic management approach that addresses short-term operational issues, long-term survival issues, and profitability. Several analysis methods for developing strategic alternatives, including the BCG matrix, the General Electric –

McKinsey matrix, and Arthur D. Little's Cycle Approach, are discussed.

Hurley, Robert E., "The Purchaser-Driven Reformation in Health Care: Alternative Approaches to Leveling Our Cathedrals," *Frontiers of Health Services Management* 9, no. 4 (1993), pp. 5–35. The author suggests that a reconfiguration of the health care delivery system is underway, engineered by aggressive purchasers. The once widely held view that provider-sponsored integrated firms represent the ideal health care system is being challenged by purchasers contracting with provider networks. These alternative approaches to restructuring delivery systems are examined and appraised.

Miller, Robert H., and Harold S. Luft, "Managed Care: Past Evidence and Potential Trends," *Frontiers of Health Services Management* 9, no. 3 (1993), pp. 3–37. The authors indicated that enrollment in network-based managed-care plans has grown rapidly, raising questions concerning the impact of different types of managed-care plans on health care use, expenditure, and quality of care. The authors found that staff- and group-model HMOs lowered utilization and expenditure relative to fee-for-service plans while maintaining quality. The conclusions concerning the new forms of managed-care are not as clear. The authors speculate on the future trends of managed-care networks.

Size, Tim, "Managing Partnerships: The Perspective of a Rural Hospital Cooperative," *Health Care Management Review* 18, no. 1 (1993), pp. 31–41. Cooperatives, alliances, coalitions, consortia, and networks seek collaborative approaches to common challenges. The author presents management principles that have been learned over the past thirteen years by a rural hospital cooperative. The eight fundamental principles for effective partnership include (1) mutual trust, (2) commitment, (3) participants needed, (4) involvement in planning, (5) understanding the big picture, (6) participants affect their own future, (7) accountability up front, and (8) appeals process for decisions.

Walker, Lawrence R., and Michael D. Rosko, "Evaluation of Health Care Service Diversification Options in Health Care Institutions and Programs by Portfolio Analysis: A Marketing Approach," *Journal of Health Care Management* 8, no. 1 (March 1988), pp. 48–59. This article describes portfolio analysis and its use in evaluating health care diversification options. Portfolio analysis is demonstrated through a case study.

PART 4

Strategic Implementation: Operational Strategies

Strategic implementation deals with putting strategies to work. Implementation requires that the coordinated efforts of marketing, information systems, human resources, and finance be directed toward the accomplishment of the organization's mission and its vision for the future. Strategic marketing (Chapter 8), strategic information systems (Chapter 9), strategic financial planning (Chapter 10), and strategic human resources (Chapter 11) are examined in greater detail.

Chapter 12 discusses the organization-wide operational strategies that undergird the implementation strategies. Organizational culture, organization structure, facilities and equipment, and ethics and social responsibility are a backdrop for the entire organization's decision making regardless of the direction charted by different strategies.

In the final analysis, implementation is critical. Situational analysis may be sophisticated and impressive. Strategy formulation may be creative and even brilliant. However, if strategies are poorly implemented, little is likely to change, and the process of strategic management will contribute nothing to the success of the organization.

CHAPTER 8

Strategic Marketing

"Even if you're on the right track, you'll get run over if you just sit there."
— *Will Rogers*

LEARNING OBJECTIVES

After completing this chapter you should:

1. Be able to define marketing and its role in health care organizations.
2. Understand the movement from a services-oriented to a selling-oriented to a marketing-oriented organization.
3. Understand the interrelationships among the various customers for health care and be able to identify an appropriate target market for a health care provider.
4. Understand the role of strategic marketing within the strategic management process.
5. Understand the role marketing plays in the situational analysis.
6. Link the various marketing strategies to the health care organization's directional, adaptive, market entry, and positioning strategies.

INTRODUCTORY INCIDENT

MammaCare at Presbyterian Hospital

Presbyterian Hospital developed a strategy to increase the number of women who have life-saving mammograms (and encourage women to experience Presbyterian Hospital's service and caring attitude) – a good strategy when women make the health care decisions for their families 70 percent of the time. Presbyterian's marketing strategy contained an identifiable target market – women primarily 35 years and older who want the assurance of mammography without having to take the time and pay the price of a doctor visit for referral. The marketing mix was designed to meet the needs of that target market.

In addition to promoting the program, Presbyterian cut the price for its self-referral mammography program. Presbyterian's $35 price was the lowest in the region – as much as $42 lower. Prices at other hospitals and clinics ranged from $39 to over $77 with an average of slightly over $50.

The service was offered at four locations: the hospital, the central city office area, south of the city in a high socioeconomic area, and north of the city in a similar area. Parking is free. In addition, Saturday hours were added making it more convenient.

Specially trained staff aided in completing insurance claims. Women staffed the facilities and could accurately describe the process to those who came for the procedure. The facilities were decorated with living room furnishings and had no appearance of a hospital. The strategy has exceeded expectations in its first year of operation.

Source: Conversations and correspondence with Henry Bostic, director of marketing, Presbyterian Hospital.

Because of its customer focus, marketing is the first type of operational strategy to be discussed. However, as illustrated in Exhibit 8–1, the planning and coordinating of the operational strategies in marketing, information systems, finance, and human resources actually have to be done concurrently to achieve synergy in accomplishing organizational objectives.

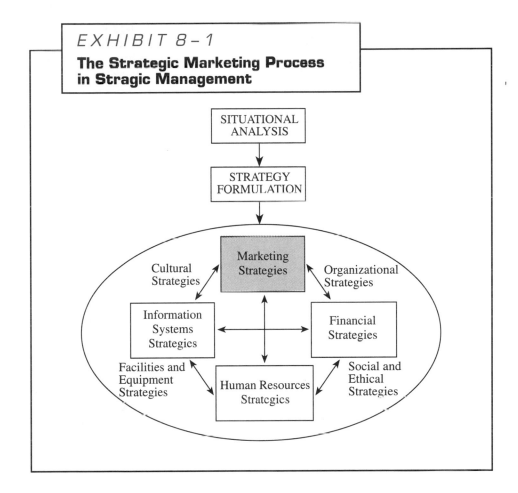

EXHIBIT 8-1

**The Strategic Marketing Process
in Stragic Management**

WHAT IS HEALTH CARE MARKETING?

Marketing is often defined as an exchange process where customers buy goods and services and the selling company accomplishes its objectives at a profit. Therefore, marketing has been viewed by some health care providers as unprofessional, inappropriate, or even as "crass commercialism." Before 1970 the demand for hospital beds was greater than the supply, but the prospective payment system and DRGs, health maintenance organizations and preferred provider organizations, and an increasing concern about rising health care costs prompted some health care providers to think differently about marketing.

Broadened Definition for Health Care

Philip Kotler and Sidney J. Levy, in their classic article in the *Journal of Marketing,* advocated that the concept of marketing should be broadened beyond the traditional definition.[1] In its broadest sense, marketing is a process of providing want-satisfying goods and services in exchange for value. Rather than the traditional business definition of profit, value for health care providers might be dollars that are exchanged for the health services provided. This "value" might be used to provide an emergency room, staff a hospital, or buy the latest equipment. For health care, value might be the "psychic" value of "doing something for someone else" as perceived by a volunteer or donor. There are two parties to the health care exchange, and both the user or consumer (buyer) and the provider (seller) must receive benefits.

The Uniqueness of Marketing Services

Marketing services is not the same as marketing automobiles, beer, or computers. It is important to differentiate between *services* and *service.* "Competitors commonly offer the same services and different service."[2] In the early 1980s, when marketers began differentiating between physical goods and services, Len Berry defined a *good* as an object, a device, or a thing; a *service* was defined as a deed, a performance, or an effort.[3]

The differences between goods and services are based on intangibility, inseparability, perishability, and variability. A good can be picked up, inspected, put in a bag to be taken home, and stored until it is needed. Services, in contrast, are intangible. There are no samples to feel, try out, or return if the purchase is unsatisfactory. Because physical goods do contain some elements of service and services contain some physical components, marketers think of products (the inclusive term used to mean goods, services, or ideas) as ranging along a goods/services continuum. As indicated in Exhibit 8–2, most primary health care providers (hospitals, physicians, hospices, and so on) would be located further to the

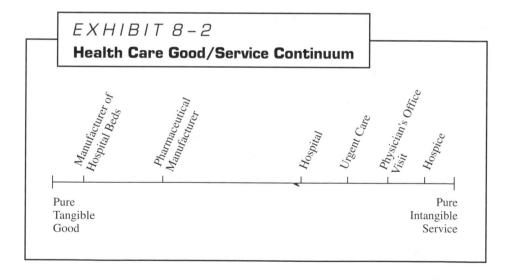

EXHIBIT 8–2
Health Care Good/Service Continuum

Manufacturer of Hospital Beds

Pharmaceutical Manufacturer

Hospital

Urgent Care

Physician's Office Visit

Hospice

Pure Tangible Good

Pure Intangible Service

right on the continuum. Secondary providers, such as pharmaceutical manufacturers, would be further to the left on the continuum.

Services are generally inseparable; production and consumption occur simultaneously. An appointment is made, and then a physician is physically present to ask questions, examine, and make a diagnosis for the patient who participates in the process. Because services are inseparable, they cannot be inventoried and are therefore perishable. Even when a clinic has no appointments scheduled during some hours, the facility, staff, and so on are still available. Therefore, an important task of health care providers is to match services availability with services demand. Finally, services are, in many regards, more heterogeneous than physical goods, resulting in greater variability. Quality of care varies from physician to physician, nurse to nurse, and so on in the same practice or hospital. Moreover, the quality of care from the same physician or nurse will vary from day to day. People-based services (as opposed to machine-based services) are very difficult to standardize.

France and Grover have suggested that several other differences translate into unique marketing problems for health care services:

1. Health care is probably the most intangible service because the consumer cannot sample it before the purchase and usually cannot evaluate it after "consumption."
2. The mismatch between consumer expectations and actual delivery may be greater for the health care product because of the uniqueness of individual diagnosis, response to medications, and treatment; in addition, the multiplicity of health care professionals that the patient interacts with results in greater variation in quality of care.
3. The demand for a health care product is less predictable, although some possibilities exist to better control usage. For example, incentives can be offered to induce physicians to perform elective surgery in the afternoons and over weekends when the operating room is virtually unused.
4. Distinguishing the decision maker from the consumer may be more involved for the health care product as the physician often recommends specific hospitals, long-term-care facilities, home-care agencies, therapists, and others to the patient who customarily – but not always – follows that advice.
5. Frequently, the patient does not directly pay for the health care service.[4]

Although services, and health care services in particular, have a number of differences when compared to physical products, they have many more similarities. The basic approach to marketing does not change. Health care organizations, as services providers, need to understand and adopt marketing practices if they are to survive in today's competitive environment.

DEVELOPING A MARKETING-ORIENTED PHILOSOPHY

Competition, consumerism, and cost containment are mandates for health care professionals to think about marketing. Competition has increased across the range of health care providers. Empty beds or an empty waiting room provide constant reminders. The high costs of health care in the 1990s have led to a mandate for reform and demands for hospitals and other health care delivery systems to be more responsive to patient needs. Development of HMOs, PPOs, and EPOs through employers have either limited choices or consumers have to pay more for health care. Government, business, and other third-party payers have demanded cost containment. The influence of government legislation, insurance, business, and others in the environment have propelled health care providers to develop a marketing-oriented philosophy. Typically, an organization moves through two stages before adopting a marketing orientation.

The Services (Production) Orientation

In the early days, health care professionals and health care administrators focused on delivery of health care or a *services (production) orientation*. If a new piece of equipment meant better care for a patient or was requested by a physician, it was purchased. If a community was without a hospital, money was raised, taxes were assessed, and a hospital was built. This was the time of a services orientation – provide more health care, better, and faster.[5] Because health care organizations were dominated by professionals whose primary commitment was to their own professional practice, managers tended to be services (production) oriented. They were concerned with filling a preconceived number of beds or with the number of patients seen or the number of procedures or tests that had been administered. Emphasis was on quality of delivery, as perceived by the professional. Needs, as perceived by the patients, received little consideration. After all, "What did the patient know about health care?"

Interestingly, the overbuilding of hospitals and medical schools and the increasing costs associated with this orientation led to more intense competition. Many beds remained empty causing communities to have to contribute more and more resources to maintain the local hospital. Physicians attempted to draw new patients by opening satellite offices.

The Selling Orientation

Because of empty beds, health care professionals began to try to "sell" the community on using the local hospital – a *selling orientation*. Since the inception of hospital marketing in the 1970s, the focus has been on the promotional component of marketing rather than the entire strategy. Marketing was equated with advertising. The focus was on short-term results: "What can be done to fill more beds?"

At about the same time, physicians were being graduated from medical schools in record numbers and chose to move to major cities to fulfill the promise of the good life, only to find extreme competition for patients. Some doctors began attempting to "sell" to patients by advertising. Others, however, were appalled that their colleagues would participate in such activities. Many health care professionals claimed that "marketing" did not work.

Marketing is not merely advertising in various media. It entails determining the appropriate customer (target market), designing services that will satisfy that customer, pricing the service at a level that is acceptable to the customer yet will allow the organization to survive, and developing a plan to make the service available where the customer wants or is able to obtain it. Once these activities have been completed, the information about the service has to be made available to the potential customers. Only then does advertising become involved.

The Marketing Orientation

The *marketing orientation* focuses on the premise that customer wants and needs have to be met for the health care organization to survive. If hospitals or extended-care facilities treat patients as bodies on which a certain number of procedures are to be performed in a given day without regard for patient preferences or doctors feel that bedside manner makes no difference because of medical training and skill, patients can and will find alternatives. Patients feel they have a right to be treated with respect and have their questions answered.

Today, outside forces are focusing greater attention on patient satisfaction – the net result of a successful marketing effort. Total quality management or continuous quality improvement use patient satisfaction as a key indicator of success, and satisfying patients is becoming more difficult because of reduced lengths of stay, heavier workloads for hospital personnel, and more critical and demanding patients.[6]

The marketing orientation focuses on customer needs as determined by the customer. As Peter Drucker so aptly stated, "The aim of marketing is to know and understand the customer so well that the product or service fits him and sells itself."[7]

Marketing is in part a "state of mind." It is a willingness to always think of the client or patient first, recognizing that when the patient is satisfied, other organizational goals can be realized as well. Patient-centered care, a relatively new approach by hospitals, clinics, and physician practices, reorients the entire organization around the patient rather than functions or departments. In a survey by *Hospitals* and ServiceMaster Company, nearly half of the hospitals that responded indicated that they were either planning to or already implementing patient-centered care programs. More than 90 percent of the existing programs are three years old or less.[8] Perspective 8–1 outlines the patient-centered care approach implemented by one hospital.

It makes little sense to spend thousands of dollars developing a marketing strategy to increase the patient load of a private physician's practice or long-term facility while ignoring basic "antimarketing" behavior among employees. For example, the same physicians who are often willing to pay for marketing studies fail to see that patients are being lost every day because of the way they have been treated by the receptionist, nurse, or doctor, or because of excessive waiting

---

PERSPECTIVE 8–1
Patient-Focused Care

Trinity Regional Hospital has one of the nation's most advanced patient-focused care programs. The 200-bed, not-for-profit hospital is the only hospital in Fort Dodge, Iowa. Trinity recognized that it had to change to prepare for the new health care environment.

The reorientation to patient-centered care was controlled by a steering committee of upper-level executives and fourteen mid-level managers. Radical restructuring eliminated one administrative level and realigned the hospital's units into three care centers. The family center includes obstetrics, pediatrics, psychiatry, chemical dependency, and recreational therapy. Preadmission testing, anesthesia, skilled care, radiology, and laboratory services are housed in the surgery center. The medicine center entails the emergency room, inten-

sive care, cardiac rehabilitation, renal services, cardiopulmonary, and pharmacy.The result is a streamlined organization where most procedures occur on the nursing floors.

The objective was to focus on patients' convenience rather than departments, functions, or stations. Patients no longer are transported to various locations for blood tests, EKGs, and so forth. Cross-trained nurses perform most of these activities from admission to lab testing, often in the patient's room. The goal is to cut the number of people the average patient sees during a typical one-week stay from fifty-seven to ten or fifteen.

Source: "Patient-Focused Care," *Strategies for Healthcare Excellence* (September 1993), pp. 1–9.

---

time. Other health care organizations have similar non-patient-oriented activities that need to be investigated and changed.

Few organizations, whether for-profit or not-for-profit, health care or manufacturing, have managed to truly adopt the philosophy of a customer orientation. In a 1991 study published in the *Journal of Health Care Marketing,* Naidu and Narayana concluded that only about 20 percent of hospitals are marketing oriented.[9] Most organizations pay lip service to the concept and then cannot understand why marketing does not work. A major underlying factor of a marketing orientation is that money will be spent to determine what customers actually want. Often time-consuming and expensive marketing research is needed to identify the customer and his or her needs and wants. If marketing takes its rightful place at the center of provider decision making and focuses on the customer, it can have a significant impact on many of the important factors affecting cost[10] and profitability.[11] Critical care mapping is one of the current areas of interest for many hospitals because of its potential to reduce the length of stay and inpatient costs. Although most hospitals are making extensive efforts to include a variety of the providers of health care in the development processes they must be cautioned to include the patient, as indicated in Perspective 8–2.

PERSPECTIVE 8-2
Critical Paths Improve Health Care, Reduce Costs

The concept of critical paths emerged in health care about a decade ago as a nursing and case management initiative at the New England Medical Center in Boston. The term was borrowed from engineering project management and applied to the clinical setting. Sometimes called *care mapping,* four questions anchor the concept: (1) What is required by each discipline to bring patients with similar diagnoses to realistic outcomes? (2) What is the best way to produce that work? (3) Who is accountable for those outcomes? (4) How can we restructure care so that this happens more consistently?

The project team developed a one-page tool containing the clinical interventions and a time line that became the critical path. Hospitals and health networks use the critical path to analyze outcomes and variances. Most who have implemented the process report improvements in quality and efficiency as well as cost savings and improved teamwork. Many predict that because of health care reform, critical path analysis will escalate.

Caregivers have been asked and are involved in developing these critical paths, but what about the patients? "If there's been a limitation to what most hospitals are doing, it's been a process driven primarily by nursing and primarily on the inpatient frame. In many cases they haven't done much to engage physicians in the process, or perhaps more important, to engage patients in the design process,"

says Jonathan (Jack) Lord, M.D., executive vice president for SunHealth Alliance in Charlotte, North Carolina.

Emory University's Crawford Long Hospital in Atlanta has incorporated patient input into the design of a "picture path" that illustrates for patients and their immediate families what to expect. Patients scheduled for coronary artery bypass surgery are given a picture path when they come for preoperative tests. It tells them what to expect on each day during the course of their inpatient stay. Experienced patients are asked to help develop new patient pathway materials.

If research is not done on the level of patient satisfaction with critical paths, it has the potential to become one more area where patients feel things are done to them and they perceive that the health care organization's concern is just moving a body through its process – only faster. Health care organizations must find out if critical care paths or care mapping is valued by their customers. Although physicians may develop an appreciation for the concept because of the documentation of outcomes, they are not the only "customer" involved. Patients may have different perceptions and they – not their doctors – need to be asked about their attitudes and feelings.

Source: Kevin Lumsdon and Mark Hagland, "Mapping Care," *Hospitals & Health Networks* 67, no. 20 (October 20, 1993), pp. 34–40.

In the McDermott, Franzak, and Little study of medium- and large-size hospitals that related marketing activities and profitability, they found that market intelligence activities, such as surveying the general public, evaluating performance against marketing objectives, evaluating effectiveness of marketing expenditures, and analyzing competitors' strengths and weaknesses were positively related to profitability. In addition, an integrated, team-oriented approach (reorganizing to speed the flow of resources across departments, involving other department heads in the marketing planning process, sharing competitor information with other departments, and organizing interdepartmental teams to call on potential customers) was positively related to profitability.[12]

IDENTIFYING THE HEALTH CARE CUSTOMER

One of the difficulties with health care marketing is that there are many, very diverse "customers" to satisfy in the market. When an organization identifies its customer as "the market" or "everyone," it is clear that the managers do not understand marketing. Eventually, every organization realizes that if you try to satisfy everybody you will end up satisfying nobody very well. You cannot "be everything to everybody."

Health care organizations by nature have some inherent specializations: long-term care, emergency medicine, oncology, dermatology, and so on, that determine who the customer will be. Yet within these specializations are customers with varying needs, wants, and desires.

Segmentation is the process of identifying recognizable groups that make up the market and then selecting a group as the target market. Several groups may be targeted, but each one requires different marketing activities to achieve customer satisfaction. Exhibit 8–3 illustrates the many customers for a hospital and the segments a physician (one of the hospital's customers) may consider. The process of segmentation for a general practice would be more challenging than for an oncology practice, which is more specialized, but many segments can be identified among cancer patients – those with leukemia, skin cancer, lung cancer, and so on. Specialization of the hospital, nursing home, or physician's practice would be a first step in the segmentation process, but other demographic, psychographic, geographic, and benefits factors must be considered as well.

Physicians

Physicians are a major target for marketing efforts because they recommend other health care providers for their patients. Estimates are that physicians control 80 percent of health care costs as they prescribe pharmaceuticals and medical equipment and determine hospitalization and diagnostic and surgical procedures. Doctors are an important customer base for hospitals because almost all patients are admitted by physicians who have staff privileges at the hospital. If physicians choose not to admit patients to a given hospital, the hospital will have no patients. Thus, major efforts have been undertaken by hospitals to "market" to physicians through personal selling, provision of new products (facilities, equipment, pro-

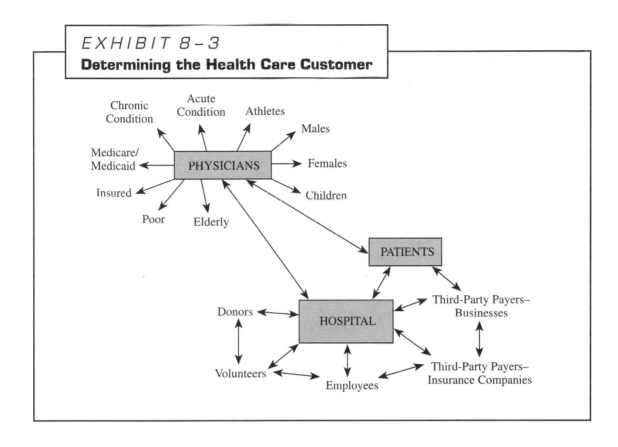

EXHIBIT 8-3
Determining the Health Care Customer

grams, and so on) that the physicians want, improved locations, advertising, and referral services.

Physicians use a referral system when patients need care outside their expertise. With the abundance of specialists, physicians are learning that marketing to other physicians is also important. Because a long-term-care facility is often recommended by a physician, nursing homes, rehabilitation centers, home health care organizations, and others have targeted physicians with their marketing efforts. Typically the patient or responsible caregiver chooses a facility from the group recommended by the physician. If a health care provider is not in the suggested group, there is little chance a patient will consider it.

Patients

The patients themselves are customers. However the buyer/seller relationship of traditional exchange processes has to be modified in much of health care because the patient has a professional dependency on the doctor. Most people have no knowledge of medical terminology nor the complexity of medical diagnosis or care and cannot accurately evaluate the medical care provided. Hence patients are dependent on the professional.

At one time, patients would never have questioned their doctor's choice of a hospital. Today, a patient whose physician does not have privileges at the hospital of the patient's choice, may change physicians. In a national study by Professional Research Consultants and American Hospital Publishing, Inc., more than 42 percent of the participants said they would change physicians to be admitted to the hospital they preferred.[13] When considering maternity care, 58 percent of pregnant women select a hospital before choosing a physician.[14] In addition, as third-party payers and the popular press have encouraged consumers to seek "second opinions" before having surgery, patients' preferences for a particular hospital have become part of the decision making process. Moreover, the physician who performed the original diagnosis may not be the physician who continues the patient's care.

A variety of marketing efforts have been directed to patients. Advertising has been used to communicate with patients concerning the benefits (satisfaction) available from the health care provider. However, the services offered must be carefully developed to satisfy consumers before advertising will be effective. Public relations activities, such as heart transplant recipient reunions, health fairs, baby fairs, and others, provide additional opportunities to make information available to the public.

Third-Party Payers

Third-party payers (insurance companies and employers) are customers as well and must be satisfied that the health care provider is efficiently treating patients or their considerable financial influence will dictate that patients go elsewhere. For example, because of their dissatisfaction with escalating health care costs, Hershey Foods Corporation and Xerox Corporation have developed their own systems to contain health care costs. Through price incentives employees are "encouraged" to participate in the HMOs determined by the corporation to be the most efficient at providing quality care. The employees can choose other HMOs but they pay a higher portion of their health care costs to do so. Perspective 8–3 describes the Hershey Foods Corporation program. Personal selling is important in the HMO, PPO, and EPO market – not only between the HMO, PPO, or EPO and employers but also between employers and employees. Not all employees are pleased with the increasing restrictions on their health care choices.

Xerox's HealthLink monitors the satisfaction of its enrollees on a constant basis. Employees can select from a variety of HMOs but those that Xerox has determined provide the highest quality care and customer satisfaction at the lowest cost are designated as "HealthLink" HMOs and are offered at no cost to the employee. To participate in other programs the employee has to pay higher premiums and copayments. Xerox holds the HMO to specific stated standards. If the specific target (designated satisfactory percentage) for childhood immunizations or mammograms or blood pressure checks is not achieved in a given year by an HMO in HealthLink, it may not be a participant in the future.

As payers, insurance companies (and managed-care organizations) are a major customer of nursing homes, hospitals, and others. If they are not satisfied with

---

PERSPECTIVE 8-3

Hershey Foods Corporation Develops a Point-of-Service Network

Hershey Foods provides health care benefits to over 12,000 employees nationwide, approximately 6,000 of which are in the area of Hershey, Pennsylvania. As with other businesses, Hershey's health care costs have escalated significantly. The corporation paid $35 million in 1991, and projections were that costs would increase 14 percent in 1992 and 15 percent in 1993. Rather than cutting coverage or raising premiums, Hershey developed its own point-of-service (POS) provider network of hospitals and physicians.

Hershey did not invite any interested hospitals or physicians to "sign up" to provide care, instead the company spent two years gathering and studying information on the costs and outcomes of fifty-five DRGs at twenty-three hospitals in central Pennsylvania. Hershey was fortunate to have access to data from the Pennsylvania Health Care Cost Containment Council (PHC[4]), which required every hospital in the state to install software that generated reports containing severity of illness scores for all patients. A team of consultants investigated lengths of stay, rates for mortality and morbidity, C-sections, back surgery, and inappropriate admissions.

The team determined that 14 percent of the procedures Hershey covered in 1990 were unnecessary. From this information the team ranked the hospitals on criteria based on 70 percent quality and 30 percent cost. In addition to quality and cost, ease of access was used to select nine area hospitals. Over 180 primary care physicians and 800 specialists were selected based on having privileges to practice at the selected hospitals plus analysis of physician performance from Capital Blue Cross and Pennsylvania Blue Shield.

Hershey employees select a network physician and are referred to network specialists. They can go to out-of-network physicians by paying higher copayments and deductibles. After six months, more than one-fourth of the 6,000 Hershey, Pennsylvania, area employees have joined the POS plan. Hershey hopes to have all employees on the POS or other HMO plans within the next few years.

Source: Jim Montague, "Low Fat, Low Cost," *Hospitals & Health Networks* 67, no. 15 (August 5, 1993), pp. 76, 78.

---

the quality of care or the charges for procedures, they can use their considerable clout to make changes. If the insurance company's customers (the patients) are not happy with the health care provided, the company will react as well.

Others

State health departments actively compete with other agencies for public funding. It is important that the community (the health department's customer) and the legislators (elected representatives for the general public) are aware of and understand the services provided by the health department. If the general public is not aware of the needs being met (benefits provided), government funding will be very difficult to obtain. Similarly, hospitals and other health care providers have community, state, and federal regulatory groups and funding agencies to satisfy.

Not-for-profit health care organizations have contributors and volunteers whose needs must also be satisfied. Contributors want to feel that their donations are to a worthwhile organization and that they can make a difference. As seen in Exhibit 8–4, a Red Cross blood donation advertising campaign has successfully appealed to the need to make a difference.

Volunteerism is an important part of the not-for-profit health care organization's ability to appear less "institutional" and more caring and friendly. Patients appreciate the volunteers who are common in many not-for-profit hospitals and extended-care facilities. Because of the increased number of women in the work force, the ranks of volunteers have thinned, and many organizations compete for their time. Volunteers' needs must be satisfied if they are to continue to contribute.

Another group that has to be considered are current and potential employees of the organization. Because of the shortages in health care professions (current and projected), recruiting becomes a marketing activity aimed at satisfying the needs of potential employees, not just at the time of hiring, but over their careers as well. Retention of the best and brightest has the potential to ease the marketing effort, especially in people-based services.

The impact of a change in marketing strategy to one group must be assessed in terms of the potential impact on other groups. Critical care mapping, although viewed favorably by hospital administration and nurses, is often less enthusiastically supported by physicians. It has to be demonstrated to them that it brings better efficiency and outcomes for the patient and may actually free them up to spend more time on the more difficult cases.[15]

Because there are many diverse customers to serve, a coordinated effort must be directed toward the various customers of health care institutions. When a specific group of customers is identified, it is called the *target market*. Each target market requires different marketing efforts and activities to successfully satisfy the group. As illustrated in the discussion of customers, health care organizations, by their very nature, have a number of target markets to satisfy. Therefore, strategic marketing has an important role to play in the organization.

MARKETING IN THE STRATEGIC MANAGEMENT PROCESS

Specific marketing inputs to the situational analysis are presented in Exhibit 8–5. Although marketers are involved in scanning all the components of the external environment, they focus on market analysis, competitive analysis, and customer analysis. Internally marketers attempt to maintain a customer-oriented focus when assessing the strengths and weaknesses of the various facets of the organization. Specific internal marketing activities are reviewed under Internal Environment in Exhibit 8–6, but it would be helpful to review Exhibit 4–10 Assessing Marketing Strengths and Weaknesses as well. Finally, marketing people should be involved in development of mission, vision, values, and corporate objectives.

EXHIBIT 8–4
Red Cross Advertisement

When you give blood
you give another birthday,
another anniversary,
another day at the beach,
another night under the stars,
another talk with a friend,
another laugh,
another hug,
another chance.

American Red Cross

Please give blood.

Council

Source: The American Red Cross, Cabot Communications, and The Advertising Council.

EXHIBIT 8–5

Marketing Input to the Situational Analysis

Situational Analysis	Marketing Input to Situational Analysis
External Environment	
Market Analysis	Determine actual size, forecast potential; estimate rate of growth, market profitability, cost structure, distribution patterns, critical success factors
Customer Analysis	Forecast demand from current and new customers, analyze lost customers; study diffusion of innovation, customer buying behavior and motivation; uncover unmet needs, benefits sought, brand loyalty of segments, price sensitivity, purchasing patterns, intensity of distribution required, information needs of customers; identify sources of information and media usage patterns, demographic and socioeconomic trends
Competitive Analysis	Identify generic, specific, service, brand competition; estimate strength of each competitor in terms of finances, profitability, management; determine market share, competitor size, growth rate; identify number of substitutes; compare product quality, customer service, comparative advantage, brand loyalty, length/ breadth/depth of product line, distribution, pricing levels and flexibility, advertising and promotion, public relations activity, amount of positive and negative publicity; segmentation for each direct competitor and selected indirect competitors
Internal Environment	
Marketing	Develop/evaluate the marketing strategy – segmentation and target market(s) identified; product positioning strategy; image development; usage rates; pricing strategy; advertising, personal selling, sales promotion, publicity; distribution strategy. Measure against objectives – sales growth, market share increase, profitability by product, share of mind, sales efficiency, customer complaints and compliments, accuracy of forecasts
Mission, Vision, Values, and Objectives	Ensure an understanding of customer, services, competitor; focus on customer orientation; include personal ethic, customer and employee expectations; participate in development of corporate objectives; develop marketing objectives to accomplish corporate objectives

---

EXHIBIT 8-6
Strategic Marketing Input to Strategic Management

Hierarchy of Strategic Decisions	Strategic Marketing Input
Directional Strategies	
Mission	Ensure understanding of the customer, services, and competition
Vision	Focus on customer orientation
Values	Include personal ethic, customer and employee (internal customer) expectations
Objectives	Participate in developing corporate objectives; development of marketing objectives to accomplish corporate objectives
Adaptive Strategies	
Expansion	
Diversification Related	Assist in identifying products, services needed to fill in the line of current offerings
Vertical Integration – Forward	Identify customers that if acquired, would enable the health care organization to satisfy customers even more
Market Development	Identify unserved segments and geographic areas; analysis of size; predict level of achievable penetration; analysis of extent of competition
Product Development	Identify new products/services to add to the line; analysis of profit potential; extent of competition
Penetration	Enhance current products/services – greater differentiation; increase promotion – advertising, personal selling, public relations, sales promotion; reduce price; increase distribution
Contraction	
Divestiture	Recommend products/services no longer satisfying current customers for divestiture; identify buyers, suggest ways to enhance the offering to make it more saleable; assist in determining a fair market value
Liquidation	Recommend products/services no longer satisfying current customers for liquidation
Harvesting	Recommend products/services no longer meeting organization objectives but still satisfying some current customers; recommend appropriate phase-out time

EXHIBIT 8-6   cont'd

Hierarchy of Strategic Decisions	Strategic Marketing Input
Retrenchment	Recommend areas where limiting the scope or product line will turn around the organization's ability to profitably satisfy customers
Stabilization	
Enhancement	Identify product/service features to improve customer acceptance, provide greater differentiation; improve comparative advantage
Status Quo	Recommend product enhancement activities; increase promotion, reduce price, or increase distribution to maintain position, market share, or revenues
Market Entry Strategies	
Purchase	
Acquisition	Recommend organizations/products/services to acquire based on ability to integrate and then market the acquired entity; analyze market share, position, comparative advantage, profitability of potential acquiree
Licensing	Recommend attractive licenses to purchase based on fit with current products/services; analyze benefits of licensing versus internal development to enhance the product line; analyze profitability, comparative advantage, market share with and without licensed product/service
Cooperation	
Merger	Analyze fit with current products/services; assess whether increased size will lead to a dominant or more significant position in the market; if the merger is with a cash-rich entity detail how the added capital can enhance current products/ services
Alliance	Analyze fit with current products/services; assess whether alliance will lead to a dominant or more significant position in the market
Joint Venture	Analyze anticipated market share, position, dominance, and profitability of new products/services developed in cooperation with another organization; is it worth the cost in lost control?

EXHIBIT 8-6 *cont'd*

Hierarchy of Strategic Decisions	Strategic Marketing Input
Development	
Internal Development	Direct traditional marketing activities – select the appropriate target market(s) and develop the product, price, promotion, and distribution to satisfy it
Internal Venture	Contribute intrapreneurial marketing person to the team
Positioning Strategies	
Market-wide	
Cost Leadership	Design or redesign product to be cost efficient but meet quality standards of customers; lower price or increase value; promote position selected; match distribution with selected position
Differentiation	Study market to determine relative positioning perceived by customers; analyze competitors' image and positioning; understand our image and positioning; identify positioning we want; develop marketing strategy to develop the image and positioning desired to achieve comparative advantage
Market Segment	
Focus – Cost Leadership	Determine segment for concentration, design or redesign product to be cost efficient but meet quality standards of customers; lower price or increase value; promote position selected; match distribution with selected position
Focus – Differentiation	Determine segment for concentration; determine if it is large enough to be profitable; study market to determine relative positioning perceived by customers; analyze competitors' image and positioning; understand our image and positioning; identify positioning we want; develop marketing strategy to achieve the image and positioning desired to achieve comparative advantage
Operational Strategies	
Functional – Marketing	Direct traditional marketing – select the appropriate target market(s) and develop the product, price, promotion, and distribution to satisfy it

In addition, the senior marketing executive for the health care organization should be involved in all levels of strategic management as illustrated in Exhibit 8–5. However, the greatest contribution from strategic marketing usually occurs in carrying out the positioning and operational strategies.

The *strategic marketing process* starts by conducting a thorough situational analysis (covered in Chapters 3 and 4), contributing to and understanding the organization's mission, vision, and objectives (covered in Chapter 5), and contributing to and understanding marketing's role in the organization's adaptive, market entry, and positioning strategies (covered in Chapters 6 and 7).

The next phase is to develop marketing objectives that will contribute to accomplishing the corporate objectives. Finally, marketing strategies are developed as part of the strategic implementation process. Marketing strategies occur at the operational level as functional strategies to be implemented by marketing management.

Prior to developing marketing strategies, the health care organization has to undertake a situational analysis that includes its market definition, the important environmental factors, and the competition that exists in the defined market. The market, environmental factors, and competition are instrumental in determining the best strategic marketing alternatives.

Situational Analysis

In developing a marketing strategy, health care providers must understand their current situation in the market. How well are they satisfying the various customers they currently serve? Are competitors better meeting customer needs? What new needs will occur in the near future that should be in the planning stages today? Frequently, the necessary information is not available, and marketing research must be conducted to understand patient satisfaction, medical staff satisfaction, competitive offerings, and so on. Often it is important to collect data from patients and staff who do not use (or occasionally use) the facility as well as current users.

From a marketing perspective, the key to developing a situational analysis that will assist in providing the organization with strategic direction lies in determining the market definition. The question "What business are we in?" needs to be answered in customer terms. The customer's needs and wants must be identified and understood in the first stage of the situational analysis.

Market Definition The health care provider's market definition can be deduced from the mission statement and is central to identifying the market to be served. A market consists of those prospective buyers who are willing and able to purchase the organization's offering. Marketers use a variety of methods to arrive at a definition of the market. Identifying the market has important implications for strategic planning and thus a great deal of effort is expended to accurately define the market served.

Few in marketing would use a single method or criteria to identify the market, because if an aspect of the health care organization's services is not addressed it may be an open invitation to competitors to enter the market or it may indicate a vulnerable position that a competitor could attack. Some health care providers, by their very nature, define the market. For instance, community hospitals, regional hospitals, county public health departments, and so on, serve specific market service areas.

One way to define the customer served is by the *scope* of the health care provider. The customer groups served (or *not* served) are identified geographically, demographically, or by benefit desired. Geographic scope or service area could be defined in terms of the number of miles in a radius around a physician's office that represents the distance patients would travel to see the doctor. Obviously, the willingness to travel will vary from patient to patient depending on the physician's reputation, referrals from other physicians and friends, access, parking, and proximity to the patient's home or place of work. The scope could be a city, county, or regional area, as defined by many hospitals. Some health care providers (particularly for-profit hospitals and nursing home chains) have determined that they want to be national in scope, although others have set goals to be international in scope.

Demographic scope might be defined by age (children's hospitals, elderly care), sex (birthing centers, mammography clinics, and so on), religion (Catholic, Presbyterian, or other denominational hospitals), and other specific, identifiable, and quantitative characteristics of the population. Scope that is defined by benefits sought must be expressed as benefits that customers want, not benefits that health care professionals want. Some patients want to use the same physician that the "stars" use. The benefit sought is prestige. Some patients want to be admitted to a specific hospital that is known to have performed the necessary procedure most frequently. The perceived benefit is risk reduction through experience. The hospital that has performed the most heart-lung transplants is considered to be the most experienced. Some patients want to be admitted to the hospital that is known for having the latest technology or the most up-to-date equipment. The benefit sought is risk reduction through advances in technology.

The market served can be defined by the segment of the general population that the health care provider has decided to serve. Examples would include specialization in specific procedures (open heart surgery, hernias, burns, and so on) or diseases (diabetes, cancer, cystic fibrosis, and so on).

Distinctive competence assets can be used to define the market. A distinctive competence is something that the health care provider does better than others. Johns Hopkins Hospital is known for its research and experimentation in bone marrow transplants for leukemia patients. The Shouldice Hospital in Toronto, Canada, is known worldwide for its competence in hernia-repair surgery. To maintain distinctive competence is a never-ending pursuit as competitors identify, improve, and adopt new ideas, services, and benefits to better satisfy customers.

An asset is something the health care provider has that is stronger than others can possess. An example would be a hospital located in a densely populated, built-up area. No other hospital would be able to build at that location. Another example would be for a physician practice or clinic to have a world renowned physician as a partner. For either a distinctive competence or an asset, the consumer has to perceive the benefit. That perception is formed in light of what customers know or think they know about competitive offerings.

As was indicated previously, most organizations use many different factors to attempt to accurately define the market served. Exhibit 8–7 illustrates how Hospice, Inc., used multiple factors to define its market. Perspective 8–4 illustrates the diversity of factors that could be used to define the newly flourishing subacute-care market.

Customer Analysis Segmentation, or the process of investigating the defined market to identify specific subgroups, has in fact been done by hospitals and physicians. When a hospital determines how many private, semiprivate, and ward rooms should be constructed, the number should be based on the expected demand for each type of room in the given community. Information such as major employers, general income levels, previous history, and so on should be investigated and then a number of each type of room determined.

Physicians segment the market, in part, by their choice of office location.

EXHIBIT 8–7

Defining the Market for Hospice, Incorporated

Scope

Hospice is a nonprofit organization dedicated to caring for terminally ill patients and their families.

Geographic:	Major metropolitan areas.
Demographic:	Primarily elderly (over age 65), any income level, educated, independent living arrangements (at least prior to illness), extended family.
Benefit Sought:	Quality of life in the remaining days of life.

Segmentation

Terminally ill (cancer patients, heart/lung disease, AIDS, and so on), usually involving a great deal of pain.

Distinctive Competencies

Care for the patient in the surroundings the patient prefers as well as care for the entire family; team approach to care (experts who provide guidance to the family as care givers).

Growth Direction

Market Development – Hospice is attempting to enter more communities with the current "product."

PERSPECTIVE 8-4

Segmentation for Subacute Care

Subacute care, sometimes termed the *middle ground* of health care, provides services for those patients who no longer require inpatient acute care, but need a higher level of care than can be provided in a skilled nursing facility or at home. There are multiple ways to segment this market that includes diverse post-acute care and rehabilitation services. An organization could select one or a combination of services to offer. Some examples for each of the three major categories follow:

Diagnosis

- Acute-care injuries such as from accidents
- Post-acute-care treatment after surgery
- Rehabilitation after accident, surgery, or illness
- Chronic illness (AIDS, cancer)
- Stroke victims
- Ventilator-dependent patients

Length of Stay Range

- Short term (for example, three to thirty days)
- Intermediate (thirty to ninety days)
- Long term (over ninety days but less than two years)

Treatment Needs

- Medical/nursing care from low to moderate to high level
- Rehabilitation for medical condition from good to moderate to limited potential for improvement
- Rehabilitation for functional (daily living) improvement from good to moderate to limited potential
- Comprehensive care from medical/nursing to rehabilitation

Any of the generic strategies could be applied to subacute care. For example, Community Psychiatric Centers has created a new subacute subsidiary, Transitional Hospitals, that will focus on ventilator-dependent patients. Transitional Hospital in Atlanta has selected complex medical cases – those discharged from intensive care – and treats them at a lower cost. Several of the largest nursing home chains, such as Beverly Enterprises and Hillhaven Corporation, have added chronically ill subacute care to their services. Living Centers of America, another long-term-care organization, decided to offer infusion therapy, wound care, and rehabilitation services.

Source: John Burns, "Subacute Care Feeds Need to Diversify," *Modern Healthcare* 23, no. 51 (December 13, 1993), pp. 34–36, 38.

Unfortunately, this is not often a planned process as most doctors do not study the demographics of the area where they plan to locate. Segmentation, and the subsequent selection of specific segments to satisfy, leads to more effective and efficient marketing.

Marketing research firms or consultants can be hired to gather information about a market. Secondary data that have already been collected by someone else can also be used by the health care organization. Although this type of data has the advantage of being quickly available at little or no cost, the information often does not answer the specific questions the health care organization wants addressed. For example, census data by ZIP code may be available and sufficient for some purposes, but for other, more complex marketing decisions concerning new service offerings, office location, and so on, primary research may be necessary. Primary data are collected for the organization's own use, so it should answer specific questions. The disadvantages of primary data collection are the high cost and the length of time it takes to generate the information. Perspective 8–5 illustrates the importance of looking beyond the numbers when doing marketing research.

Patient records, a form of secondary data, can provide a great deal of information about such things as percentage of patients whose stay is covered by third-

---

PERSPECTIVE 8–5

Marketing Research for Health Care Organizations Needs to Look Beyond Statistics

It is important for health care organizations to go beyond traditional data bases and health status indicators to understand their patients and markets. Census data and morbidity and mortality data lack the richness of research that asks consumers how they feel about health care. Focus groups, household interviews, questionnaires, town meetings, and informal gatherings provide qualitative data lacking in traditional assessments of community needs.

"The kind of information you collect in a more informal consumer survey is truly more useful," according to Jeffrey C. Bauer, Ph.D. of The Bauer Group in Hill Rose, Colorado. "It includes people's perceptions, their gut-level feelings about health care – things that don't show up in data bases. You can analyze data all day and all night and never really know what people's preferences would be."

Stanford University Hospital used psychographic profiling to illustrate that different health care personality "types"

rate the same services differently. Two personality types that dominate Stanford University Hospital's service area tend to rate room accommodations, nursing, and physician care lower than other health care personality types, regardless of the hospital used. An attitude and behavior shared by these two groups is their propensity to gather health care information in order to choose from health care alternatives. According to Frederick Navarro, marketing research manager at Stanford, "This information has shown the hospital the importance of understanding its customers' needs and wants, and that simply trying to provide more services is not the whole answer."

Source: Jill L. Sherer, "Assessment Data Evaluated," *Hospitals & Health Networks* 67, no. 14 (July 20, 1993), p. 38; and Frederick Navarro, "Psychographic Research Enhances Community Profile," *The AHSM Academy Bulletin* (January 1993), p. 7.

party payers, addresses, repeat business (if a mother comes to the hospital for her second delivery, which facility was used for the first?), and so on. To delve into individuals' attitudes toward health care at a particular practice, clinic, or hospital, it may be necessary to conduct such primary research as surveying previous patients, potential patients, and nonpatients (those who use a competitor). Focus groups (usually a group of ten to fifteen individuals who come together for an hour or two to discuss issues presented by an impartial moderator) have enlightened many administrators and physicians as to how consumers perceive the hospital, long-term-care facility, or practice.

Exhibit 8–8 provides a listing of general questions that should be answered in analyzing the customers for a health care organization.

Competitive Analysis In previous times when there were not enough doctors, hospitals, or nursing home beds, health care providers did not have to be concerned about competition. With the current oversupply, most physicians and hospitals

---

EXHIBIT 8–8

Suggested Questions for Customer Analysis

Segmentation

Who uses the health care?
Who buys the health care?
Who are the most frequent users?
Who are the biggest purchasers?
Who should be using the health care but is not?
How is the market currently segmented for health care?
How should the market be segmented?

Customer Motivation

What motivates the individual to use health care?
What aspects of the offered service are really important to the consumer?
What goal is the consumer seeking?
What changes will occur or are likely to occur in consumer motivation to use health care?

Unmet Needs

Are consumers currently satisfied with the health care available to them?
Are there problems with the health care delivery system?
Are there unmet needs of which consumers may not be aware?

Source: Adapted from David A. Aaker, *Strategic Market Management* (New York: John Wiley & Sons, 1984), pp. 50–51.

as well as other kinds of health care providers are competing for patients. To develop an effective marketing strategy, it is important to identify which health care institutions are direct competitors and which are indirect competitors.

Competition occurs at various levels in the environment, as illustrated in Exhibit 8–9. The most general level of competition is termed *generic competition.* Consumers have a need for health care, which can be satisfied by a variety of health care providers. At the generic level, those providers might include hospitals, clinics, urgent care centers, a physician's office, home health care, and so on.

Specific competition would include "like kind" providers of health care. Exam-

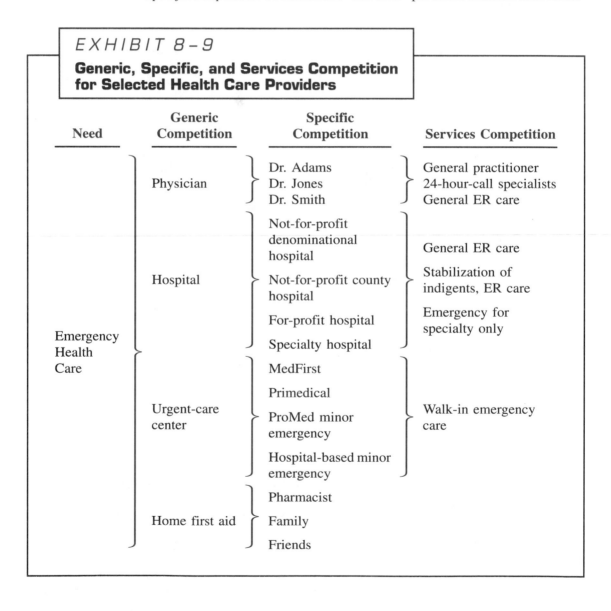

EXHIBIT 8–9
Generic, Specific, and Services Competition for Selected Health Care Providers

Need	Generic Competition	Specific Competition	Services Competition
Emergency Health Care	Physician	Dr. Adams Dr. Jones Dr. Smith	General practitioner 24-hour-call specialists General ER care
	Hospital	Not-for-profit denominational hospital Not-for-profit county hospital For-profit hospital Specialty hospital	General ER care Stabilization of indigents, ER care Emergency for specialty only
	Urgent-care center	MedFirst Primedical ProMed minor emergency Hospital-based minor emergency	Walk-in emergency care
	Home first aid	Pharmacist Family Friends	

ples include hospitals that compete directly for both patients and physicians, nursing homes that compete, physicians in the same specialty who compete, and so on. *Services competition* occurs at the product level. Emergency rooms, delivery rooms, surgery, and so on, are examples of some of the services offered by a hospital.

The most specific level would be *brand competition.* Although most hospitals and other health care providers have not branded the services they offer, a few have, and panelists of *TrendWatch* expect branding to increase albeit at a slow pace.[16] Consumers select a health care institution based on image and reputation. Brands offer consistency of quality. Consumers will use health care brands to help in decision making. Recognizing the benefit of brands, American Health Care Group has purchased several physician practices in various cities with a clear goal to "develop a consistency in image so that some sort of brand recognition would occur."[17]

"New Life," a psychiatric service for Christians, is a brand of product offered by Western Medical Center in Anaheim, California. Other wings of the medical center offer different products. "Free Home Care" is a brand of Olsten Health Care Services, Inc., a home health care agency. When a patient uses Olsten's services as a result of a hospital referral, the hospital builds up credits for days of care that it can use to provide home health care for other patients who cannot afford it and lack insurance or other benefits to pay for it. "CareBank" is a similar product offered by CareTeam Management Services, Inc. "CarePaths" and "CareMaps" are registered brand names for competing products that provide critical path analysis for specific medical procedures.

Competition must be identified in terms of quantity and quality. There may be many providers of health care in a given region, but they will not all be of the same quality. It is important that the strategic marketing manager accurately identify the competition to develop a sustainable competitive advantage.

Primary competitors offer the same or very similar services and would be considered to be direct competition. *Secondary competitors* provide some of the same services, but may be worse (or better) at it or they may be further away (more distant) from the service area. This type of competition is more indirect. Tertiary competitors offer an alternative or substitute product; they are indirect competitors. For example, if a nursing home is full, home health care might be used as a substitute until space becomes available in a nursing home.

Because competition is identified in customers' terms, it is often necessary to conduct marketing research to identify the competition from the customer's point of view rather than the provider's point of view. A few questions to recent maternity patients could determine the competition for the OB/GYN service of a hospital: "Which hospitals did your physician recommend? If the hospital you selected had been full, where would you have gone for delivery? Which hospitals did you consider? Which hospitals did you visit? Why did you choose this hospital for your baby's delivery? How satisfied were you with the experience? Would you choose the same hospital for the birth of your next child?"

Understanding consumers' perceptions and their evaluation of a health care organization's image is essential for the institution's long-term survival and prosperity. Image can be defined as the aggregate of beliefs, attitudes, impressions, and ideas that people have for something. A consumer's image of a health care organization is based on his or her perception of that organization in relationship to other competitors in the environment. It is a function of the health care organization's strategies, how they are implemented, and how the consumer perceives the organization.

Images are formed from past experiences, word-of-mouth, and marketing communications. Image is important for health care organizations to ensure strong public support, favorable legislation, tax breaks, outside funding, and a supply of volunteers. Whether management is concerned with relating to prospective or current patients, physicians, employees, volunteers, boards of trustees, government agencies, or special interest groups, image management is crucial to the strategic management process.

Javalgi, Whipple, McManamon, and Edick used a correspondence analysis approach to understand the image of Lake Hospital System's (LHS) two hospitals (LakeEast and LakeWest) in relation to the fourteen other hospitals in the Northeast Ohio area.[18] The study asked consumers (through telephone interviews) to identify the hospitals that had certain features. Thirteen features were studied including expert emergency treatment, heart disease prevention and treatment, rehabilitation services, cancer treatment, call-in health information services, women's health services, laser surgery, outpatient services, doctors keeping up with medical advances, staff giving personal attention, special programs for seniors, offering community programs, and advanced technological equipment. The image map (Exhibit 8–10) created through analysis of responses was used to develop strategy.

The results of the image study enabled the LHS strategic planners to assess the hospitals' competitive positions by comparing consumer perceptions with the results of an internal analysis of clinical strengths and weaknesses. For the strong programs that did have an external image associated with LHS (special programs for seniors), new markets were created and communications activities were increased. To reduce the likelihood of losing consumers to competitors in areas of perceived clinical weaknesses, LHS undertook defensive measures (cancer treatment, women's health services, outpatient services) by first strengthening the products and then increasing communications about the services at LHS. Although LHS was perceived favorably as a hospital system known for offering community programs, more internal resources had been expended to implement strategies to increase technological capabilities. It was clear from the study that management had not successfully communicated the high tech availability at the hospital. Armed with the information of how consumers viewed the hospitals, management developed strategies to live up to its image in the community and develop clearer positioning strategies.[19]

Strategically managed health care organizations, which are usually larger, more comprehensive, and in a more competitive situation, would use additional means such as Porter's model of competitive analysis (covered in Chapter 6) to review the situation. Porter's model is particularly useful to determine the provider's positioning relative to competition. Once the marketing manager is satisfied

EXHIBIT 8-10
Image Map for Lake Hospital System

```
community programs                    |
   LHS      call-in                   | FACTOR 2
            information               |
         LAKEWEST                     |

                                      |                              heart
programs for                          |                              disease
seniors                               |
   LAKEEAST                           |    rehabilitation
                                      |    services
                                      |              CLEVELAND
                                      |              CLINIC    cancer
                                      |                        treat-
                                      |                        ment
         emergency                    |              technological
         treatment                    |              equipment
--------------------------------------+------------------------------------
                                      |                          FACTOR 1

   outpatient   EUCLID                |
   services     women's               |         UNIVERSITY
                health                |

   RICHMOND MERIDIA                   |
   HEIGHTS      METRO                 |
                HEALTH                |
      personal                        |
      attention    HURON              |
                   ROAD               |       laser surgery
   HILLCREST                          |
          ST. VINCENT                 |     doctors keep up

      GEAUGA  ST. LUKE'S  | MT. SINAI
   GENEVA                             |
```

How to Read the Image Map

Cleveland Clinic is most closely associated with cancer treatment, heart disease prevention and treatment, and having advanced technological equipment.

Meridia Health System hospitals (Euclid, Huron Road, and Hillcrest) are closely associated but their image as a system is not distinguishable from the images of Metro-Health, Richmond Heights, and St. Vincent. Euclid has the most distinct image in the quadrant for outpatient services and women's health.

LakeEast and LakeWest are perceived as a cohesive hospital system with a distinct image but not for high technological equipment.

Source: Rajshekhar G. Javalgi, Thomas W. Whipple, Mary K. McManamon, and Vicki L. Edick, "Hospital Image: A Correspondence Analysis Approach," *Journal of Health Care Marketing* 12, no. 4 (December 1992), pp. 34–39.

that the situation has been thoroughly analyzed, the marketing objectives must be determined.

Marketing Objectives

Marketing objectives are not set in a vacuum. A hierarchy of objectives exists, as indicated in Chapter 5. Therefore, after the situational analysis, a review of the organization's mission and objectives are the starting point for determining the marketing objectives. If the marketing objectives are achieved, they should help the organization accomplish its overall objectives. Marketing objectives typically include revenues, market share, growth, innovation, and public responsibility.

Revenues Merely setting an objective for the dollar amount of money that should come into the health care organization can be shortsighted, because the outflow of money is a major consideration. Moreover, the revenue objective should be tied to a growth (or status quo) objective. An example of a marketing revenue objective would be: to generate revenues of $12,500,000 by year end holding expenses to budgeted amounts.

Market Share Market share objectives are tricky because the percentages are based on the quantity and quality of competitors in the selected "market." In the hospital software market, the top five vendors account for over 44 percent of the market. The leader, at 12.3 percent market share, has 1,454 applications. For any one application, the market share figures would be much different.[20]

A local community hospital could say that it has 100 percent share of the market (town) where it is located. But the important question is, "How many people leave town for their medical care?" Therefore, hospitals use a variation of market share based on occupancy rates or bed census data.

Growth Growth is usually set as a percentage over the previous year in terms of revenue, market share, or census rates. Growth for growth's sake is not always desirable, which is sometimes a difficult lesson to learn. Almost any organization can reach growth objectives, but what will the cost be? Often, remaining the same size and increasing profitability is a more important objective.

Innovation Innovation objectives could include new services to be offered, speeding service delivery, or being the leader in developing or offering new technology.

Public Responsibility Most not-for-profit hospitals, nursing homes, hospices, and so on have publicly mandated social responsibility objectives, but many for-profit providers have also included public or social responsibility in their objectives. For example, some hospitals aim to serve a certain percentage of indigent patients or to return a certain amount of money to the community in the form of health benefits.

STRATEGIC IMPLEMENTATION THROUGH MARKETING

No position of leadership lasts forever. Every health care organization that succeeds at differentiation serves as a model for new competitors.[21] The dynamic health care market and ever-changing technology mean that no competitive advantage can be sustained in the long run without a great deal of thought and effort. To further complicate the strategic process, the long run itself is becoming shorter as the rate of change becomes increasingly rapid.

There is no single established way in which a health care organization can assure success; rather, a number of possibilities exist. As discussed in previous chapters, the organization determines its directional strategies through mission, vision, and objectives; adaptive strategies determine whether the organization strives for growth or stabilization, or manages contraction. Positioning strategies are based on cost leadership, differentiation, and focus. Marketing is involved with accomplishing each of these strategies in a number of different ways as illustrated in Exhibit 8–11.

EXHIBIT 8 – 11
Summary of Marketing Implementation Strategies

Strategic Alternatives	Marketing Strategies and Tactics
Adaptive Strategies	

Expansion/Market Penetration	• Product enhancement
	     Improve quality of service
	     Faster service delivery
	     Technological innovation
	     Reliability
	 • Reduce price
	 • Increase promotion
	 • Make services more available in current market area

Expansion/Market Development	• New service areas near current area • New service areas beyond current area • Innovative delivery sites
Expansion/Product Development	• New products/services lines • Expansion within product lines • Increase product variations
Contraction/ Decrease Scope	• Reduce product lines • Reduce number of offerings within the lines • Reduce the number of product variations

EXHIBIT 8 – 11 cont'd

Strategic Alternatives	Marketing Strategies and Tactics
Contraction/Decrease Service Area	• Close entire facilities • Close units/wings • Limit promotional efforts to smaller geographic area • Only offer some services in a limited geographic area
Contraction/ Demarketing of Services	• Educate to reduce demand • Promote alternatives as superior • Be less customer oriented

Stabilization/ Enhancement	• Less aggressive use of:
	    Increased differentiation
	    Improved quality
	    Reduced price
	    Increased promotion

Stabilization/ Status Quo	• Maintain product quality, service, and reliability • Monitor competitive prices and maintain current position • Monitor competitive promotional activities, maintain "share of mind"

Positioning Strategies

Market-wide/ Cost Leadership	• Lowest cost • Best value • Highest cost
Market-wide/ Differentiation	• Be first • Be best • Be unique • Be most prestigious • Position against the leader • Position against competitors • Promote your position

Market Segment/ Cost Leadership	• For a specific segment be:
	    Lowest cost
	    Best value
	    Highest cost

Market Segment/ Differentiation	• For a specific segment:
	    Be first
	    Be best
	    Be unique
	    Be most prestigious
	    Position against the leader
	    Position against competitors
	    Promote your position

Adaptive/Expansion Strategies

Markets are often defined for expansion opportunities, as discussed in Chapter 6. Market penetration, market development, and product development are implemented through marketing strategies.

Expansion/Market Penetration Market penetration attempts to improve revenues or market share by better satisfying current customers with current products. *Product enhancement* (modifying the product to make it more appealing to the target market) is a fundamental component of market penetration strategies, although pricing, promotion, and distribution are used as well.

Improved quality of service is one way to increase market penetration. Most health care providers like to think they can enhance their institution on the basis of the service they offer to their various customers. "Quality" is frequently used in discussions by health care providers, but they do not determine what quality is. The consumer's perception of what constitutes quality will be used to judge it. To the consumer, quality is achieved only when the service meets or exceeds expectations.[22]

Realistically, quality can be perceived by the consumer only from other environmental cues, because few people have the expertise to actually judge competent medical care. Thus, friendly nurses, clean and pleasant surroundings, prompt response to patient call buzzers/lights and questions, convenient hours of operation, and so on are used to judge quality for many hospitals, long-term-care providers, and private practices.

Individual consumers are not the only health care customers to judge quality, however. Physicians and other health care professionals are more likely to judge the quality of an institution by assessing equipment, physicians who are currently on staff (or who have staff privileges), the competence of the nursing staff, and the organization and leadership provided by the nonmedical staff.

Strategies can be formulated to improve (expansion strategy) or maintain (stabilization strategy) quality over time. When quality is allowed to deteriorate, whether planned (contraction) or unplanned, use of the facility will eventually decline. A hospital's emergency room is generally a cash user but can increase admissions by 25 percent or more. If a community hospital's emergency room is using cash and does not lead to at least some increase in admissions, it might be neglected and allowed to deteriorate over time; and it is likely that this perception of deterioration would carry over to the rest of the institution. To avoid this unplanned side effect, it might be better to face the issue squarely. Many CEOs overlook the role that the public relations staff can play in relating the appropriate message to the community.[23] In the case of a community hospital, public meetings could be held to demonstrate to the citizens that the hospital cannot afford to provide quality emergency care and, with group consensus, decide to close the unit (contraction).

Faster service delivery can be used to increase penetration. Consumers are increasingly impatient. They value their time and will not wait for service.[24] Horror stories about such things as long waits in the emergency room and sick patients being left in wheelchairs outside the X ray room are shared with family and friends. To avoid negative word-of-mouth communication, hospitals need to think about service delivery. To "speed service delivery" does not mean to do things faster, but to rethink why the delays occur and correct the underlying reasons. Faster responsiveness can develop into a sustainable competitive advantage.

Waiting time in physicians' offices represents another opportunity. One busy professional calls the doctor on the morning of his appointment and politely informs the receptionist that it is his policy to wait no longer than fifteen minutes for the doctor. He then inquires as to the doctor's current schedule. If the doctor is behind for whatever reason and the caller would have to wait longer than fifteen minutes, he reschedules the appointment. If it happens more than once, he changes doctors. Most people understand emergencies, but when a doctor's staff consistently overschedules so that patients have long waiting times, many will find a new physician.

Another way a health care organization may improve patients' or potential patients' perception that it provides quality care is to educate them about some of the special diagnostic capabilities and treatment expertise the hospital or clinic offers. To pursue expansion through technological innovation, large sums of money must be available as breakthroughs in medical equipment are costly. The price for new technology generally decreases over time, but to maintain technological innovation as a competitive strategy, financial resources must continue to be accessible to purchase new equipment as soon as it becomes available. This represents an example of the importance of the marketing/finance interface. Communicating information about the new technology to patients is another necessary and expensive part of maintaining technological innovation as a competitive advantage.

Reliability, or standardization to achieve consistent quality, is another differentiating strategy. Service reliability is a goal for most health care organizations. Services are difficult to standardize because the consumer participates in the simultaneous production and consumption of services, and as previously indicated, the human beings involved in health care delivery (patient, doctor, nurse, and so on) are not capable of performing in the same way every time they might encounter the same situation. However, a prescribed routine known to all can achieve some level of consistency in admitting or new patient procedures, preop preparation, and so on.

Many freestanding urgent-care facilities have attempted to standardize procedures, thereby providing the additional benefit of "avoiding long emergency room waiting time." However, the procedures that are more unusual and do not fit the standards are often sent on to the more sophisticated hospital emergency rooms.

When demand is elastic, reducing the price generally increases the demand. In the competitive environment of the 1990s, the health care organization may be able to grow by reducing the price. Certainly this is true if the customer is a third-party payer. As exemplified by Hershey and Xerox, price is one of the important factors for providers that become options for their employees; however, quality must be maintained at acceptable levels. As deductibles and copayments have become more common, consumers are asking more frequently about price.

Demand for health care services may be expanded by advertising, personal selling, sales promotion, and publicity (promotion). There is limited demand for some health care services. For example, an individual needs only one appendectomy. However, that individual may tell several others about his or her experiences with the lab technician, physician, hospital, nurse, and so on. Therefore, health care organizations wanting to expand through market penetration might develop a newsletter for previous patients to encourage them to return when the need arises for some other type of procedure. A hospital's image, in part, is developed by the communications it develops and makes available in its community. By increasing the number of times potential patients receive that message, the more likely they are to remember it when the need for health care arises.

Greater availability of services in the current market area can increase penetration. A health care provider might relocate within the current service area to improve convenience for consumers or increase parking, or furnish another examining room. A pharmaceutical company that increased the intensity of distribution (sold the products to more retail locations in the service area) would increase availability. A long-term-care facility that added beds in another nearby facility would be expanding distribution as well. The health care organization is trying to grow *within* the service area.

Expansion/Market Development When expansion is outside the "normal" service area to new markets, the organization has selected a market development strategy. This may be accomplished by using purchase or cooperation market entry strategies. However, if a development strategy has been selected, marketing will be involved to implement expansion through internal development. Specific areas for a new location have to be identified through market research. Competitive activity in the area has to be monitored, and an exact site located. Some health care organizations have reached an optimum size in the current location and to grow they will need another facility. Decisions have to be made concerning location near the current facility or further away. More distant facilities can bring in entirely new customers, but sometimes interaction of clinical staff, managers, and so on becomes far more difficult.

A location that is attractive because of its proximity to patients' homes and work is a valuable asset, especially if other health care providers cannot duplicate the location. Because people do not want to travel great distances for most health care, demographic studies of population are an important part of choosing a location for a facility. Satellite offices and hospital branches have become increasingly important in order to be available where patients want to receive care. Although satellite offices/hospitals do not typically cut costs for the organization, they do cut costs for the patient, which can lead to an increased market share and improved efficiency for the health care provider.

Some hospitals are finding it worthwhile to establish education centers in shopping malls. These centers can enhance a hospital's reputation by demonstrating its commitment to provide easily accessible outpatient care and increase the hospital's visibility, which can lead to increased bed census rates and economies of scale.[25]

Mobile units are another method of achieving the optimum in health care delivery. Long practiced by the Red Cross to gain more blood donations, other institutions are using movable diagnostic equipment to be closer to patients. Approximately 200 mobile mammography units are in operation in the United States to increase women's use of this excellent but expensive tool.[26]

Once the decision has been made to expand the service area, promotion becomes important to build awareness for the new facility. If the organization has a definite image it can be carried to the new site as was the case when the Mayo Clinic opened another office in Jacksonville, Florida. If the organization has a less well-developed image, it will need to invest in promotional activities. Advertising can inform consumers of the opening and services offered. Personal selling will be important to inform third-party payers in the area. Publicity may be garnered with the proper planning.

Expansion/Product Development Offering new services that satisfy customer needs can be an opportunity. The first hospitals that offered a physician referral service met the needs of two of their consumers – patients and physicians. The hospital that developed the referral service first could use it as a differentiating strategy. When others copy the new service with a similar "me too" offering, there is less opportunity to differentiate. Although it is good to have a quality offering, it is better still to have a quality offering, be the first to offer it, and tell everyone about it.[27]

Product development can occur through expansion of the width, length, or depth of the health care organization' offerings. *Product line width* refers to the number of product lines offered. For a hospital, programs such as oncology, pediatrics, cardiology, orthopedics, and obstetrics represent product lines. If obstetrics were to expand into infertility treatment and childbirth classes in addition to its usual labor and delivery services, the line has been lengthened. The *product line depth* is increased if "natural childbirth" were added to regular and C-section childbirth services.[28]

Adaptive/Contraction Strategies

The scope of the market often has to be narrowed when there are limited resources, whether financial, natural, or human. The shortage of health professionals in some areas has caused hospitals to have to close wings until the necessary number of nurses, physical therapists, and so on could be recruited. Generally, the scope is broadened (multisystem hospitals) with successes over time as additional resources become available and economies of scale can be achieved.

Contraction/Decrease Scope Because of decreasing revenues, personnel, or available space a health care organization may decide to serve fewer customers. When the Chicago hospitals eliminated emergency room service they were decreasing the scope. When Dade County Florida OB/GYN doctors refused to delivery babies because of the high cost of malpractice insurance, they decreased the scope of their practices to gynecology patients only.

Contraction/Decrease the Service Area A health organization can withdraw from the market by closing, selling, or merging. Entire facilities can be closed or selected units or wings can be closed. Careful analysis of the contribution margin of the facility, unit, or wing should be undertaken before the decision is announced. In the long run, all hospital costs have to be covered and provide a satisfactory return to survive. However, in the short run, incremental costs are important.[29]

Promotional efforts should be limited to a smaller geographic area or indicate the current services mix. If the services mix has been reduced, a positive, proactive campaign should be initiated. For example, few consumers object to having more attention from the physician or easier accessibility to him or her, when the physician decides to accept no new patients. If the long-term-care facility decides to accept only Alzheimers patients, many families would be pleased with this contraction in services.

Contraction/Demarketing of Services One hospital administrator conferred with a consultant about the hemorrhaging costs of the emergency department (ED). The consultant's advice was *demarketing* the ED by maintaining insufficient staff, closing the parking lot next to the ED, and reducing housekeeping activities so that it became dirty. This is demarketing at its worst. In actuality, demarketing attempts to educate to reduce demand (when toddlers have a temperature over 102° for longer than 24 hours bring them to the ED), shift demand by pointing out the benefits of alternatives (no long waits at the medical center next door to the hospital), or place less emphasis on total customer satisfaction (longer waits). The health care organization that engages in demarketing through education and stressing the superiority of alternatives will not infuriate consumers and cause them to develop negative attitudes toward all services offered by the provider.

Adaptive/Stabilization Strategies

There are times when a health care provider is best served by maintaining its current place in the market. A hospital, nursing home, or physician might not be in a financial position to try to grow its service area. Sometimes, aggressive strategies on the part of one health care provider may "raise the stakes" so much that all of the providers in a community would be negatively affected. At other times, because of intense competition, an organization will have to engage in market penetration-type strategies simply to maintain its market share.

Stabilization/Enhancement Strategies In a dynamic health care environment the organization often has to develop new products or enhance current products to maintain its position in the market. Pricing needs to be monitored to make sure that it remains in line with other "like" competitors and promotional activities have to be maintained in relation to its competition. If the organization strives for evolutionary change or incremental growth it may not upset the "balance" in an otherwise stable industry. If one organization begins to aggressively develop new products, offensively price, and step up promotion, its more aggressive expansion efforts will be noticed by its competition and retaliation may occur.

Stabilization/Status Quo To maintain status quo may be extremely challenging. Typically, health care organizations that select stabilization strategies perceive their own particular environment as "stable" and that they need not make significant changes to maintain their market share and revenues or that they have restricted capital and cannot aggressively pursue growth strategies. Most of the expansion strategies can be used less aggressively to achieve stabilization.

Implementation Strategies May Occur in Phases or Concurrently Riverside Health System illustrates concurrent and phases of strategic implementation (Perspective 8–6). Based on its mission, the hospital system engaged in contraction of its inpatient acute care as it focused on prevention. Then expansion strategies were carried out through product development, market development, and market penetration.

Market-wide Positioning Strategies Through Cost Leadership

Being the low-cost producer in the service area can be a significant competitive advantage. It allows the organization to make many more choices in terms of such things as product quality and development, expansion of the service area, increasing awareness of the organization through paid media, pricing, and profitability. In health care, low cost strategies must be selected carefully because few people want to think that they are receiving "cheap" (poor quality) care. Although cost leadership strategies are generally associated with having low costs that can be translated into low prices, a high-price strategy can effectively position an organization as a high-quality health care provider. However, the consumer must perceive that the benefits (aesthetically pleasing surroundings, attentive care, latest technology, and so on) are worth the high price.

Reduced Overhead This strategy is usually selected when an organization is mature. Overhead generally consists of rent, utilities, and other expenses that would occur even if there were no patients. It can also include administrative salaries, insurance, and other costs that are ongoing.

It might be that the health care provider invested too much in overhead during times of growth. Many organizations are quick to add employees and facilities when times are good but they rarely cut back when times are difficult. The result is excessive overhead. One way for a hospital to reduce overhead is to close off a wing or eliminate an infrequently used department. Sometimes spending *more* money can reduce overhead, as when a physician moves to a newer building with a more energy-efficient heating and cooling system.

Control Raw Materials Access to factors of production can provide a competitive advantage in terms of price as well as availability. When the Carolinas Medical Center (Charlotte, North Carolina) was having difficulty recruiting nurses, the administration decided to develop a school of nursing. By reducing or eliminating the cost of tuition to those students who would agree to practice nursing at the center after graduation, Carolinas Medical Center gained much more control over a hospital's major factor in services production – its nurses.

PERSPECTIVE 8-6
From Mission to Marketing Strategy

Riverside Health System made a commitment to a vision of prevention-driven health care more than a decade ago. The organization stated as its mission, "The only reason for our existence is to improve the health status of the community we serve." Management believed that preserving the illness-based model of care no longer was useful.

Riverside's first commitment to prevention was to obtain a failing racquet club and turn it into a fitness center. The racquet club was donated for the tax write-off and in 1982 Riverside's first wellness and fitness center was opened. Over the next ten years, four more centers were opened, each one in a different geographic location, with the specific groups living in those areas as its targets. Over 20,000 paying members have made the effort profitable, including the finances to improve, replenish, and update the center's personnel, equipment, facilities, programs, and services.

The five wellness and fitness centers have become the core business, the "heart" of Riverside's health care system, linking a variety of components from hospitals to home health care. Riverside embraced the shift from sick care to well care by making its wellness and fitness centers the building blocks for its health care delivery system. Members have annual health risk assessments to turn up indications of new conditions that may require physician intervention. Management expects this information to become a data base of wellness information that will

eventually link all points of care and enable Riverside to offer proactive rather than reactive care. For example, it will indicate which members should be called to remind them that it is time for a blood cholesterol check, mammogram, prostate exam, or other diagnostic.

Riverside has committed to health and wellness so completely that it has formed a joint venture with Blue Cross – Blue Shield of Virginia to form Peninsula Health Plan to provide care on a capitated basis. It is management's hope that those who join and use the centers will be entitled to lower insurance premiums and eventually lower costs for other types of care.

Twenty thousand members did not join Riverside's wellness and fitness centers without a well-conceived marketing strategy. Not only did each fitness center have to have its own specific decor and activities for an identified target market, but each had to become "known" in its community and pricing had to be high enough to cover costs and maintain Riverside's image yet reasonable enough for people to afford. Although some are recuperating patients covered by third-party payers, most of Riverside's wellness and fitness members pay out of pocket. Riverside's vision of maintaining wellness rather than sick care is being implemented through an effective marketing strategy.

Source: M. Caroline Martin, "Working out for the Best," *Healthcare Forum Journal* 36, no. 6 (November/December 1993), pp. 57–63.

Reduced Labor Costs This appears to be a very difficult strategy to implement for today's health care organizations. As with other service industries, health care is labor intensive. In addition, the industry requires skilled labor. With the shortage of trained personnel, wages and salaries are going up rather rapidly. Moreover, certification standards for qualified personnel must be met. Thus, certification standards, shortages of skilled labor, and wage inflation make it very difficult to reduce labor costs. Rather than focus on reducing the costs of labor, greater emphasis must be placed on proper scheduling. By better matching consumer demand and labor availability, costs can be reduced.

Redesign of the Offering Another strategy is to change the product offered so that it becomes less costly, but no less desirable. An extended-care facility that enjoys an excellent reputation in the community for cleanliness, good food, and competent and sympathetic caregivers could probably reduce the square footage in patients' rooms – and thereby reduce the cost of construction, heating/cooling, and maintenance – without harming its image.

Automation Labor-intensive services are difficult to automate, but not impossible. Blood pressure checks have been automated. Additionally, a finger stick for routine blood work could be automated by using a machine, but would the public accept a machine instead of a nurse? In another service industry, many bankers held on to their belief that consumers would want to talk to a real person when cashing checks or depositing money. Those banks that were the first to automate with teller machines have been very profitable. Can similar results be achieved in health care?

In addition, monitoring and data entry for patient records are increasingly done through automation in many hospitals. Although not yet common, individual patient stations instead of a larger nurses' station are the technology of the future.

Increased Government Subsidy Many not-for-profit hospitals, extended-care facilities, hospices, and so on, are subsidized by city, county, state, or federal government. Those that have done a good job of keeping the public and the lawmakers informed of the benefits they provide often have an easier time obtaining increased subsidies.

No Frills In this strategy, all "extras" are eliminated from the services, through a rather direct approach that tells consumers from the beginning that there will be no frills and in return they will receive a lower price. Home health care offered by a hospital seems to fit this strategy. On the other hand, for many who are admitted to a large hospital ward, few "frills" are perceived. Caution has to be exercised in positioning "no frills" so that the patient perceives that only the "extras" have been eliminated. Otherwise the perception may be of poor quality care.

Combination of Low Cost and High Quality Most managers believe that high quality always leads to higher costs. More expensive facilities, more staff, more customized (personalized) services, and so on do usually cost more. But by offering higher cost services only to consumers that prefer it, overall costs can actually be reduced by moving along the experience curve and achieving economies of scale (brought about by increased market share). Accurate assessment of demand, careful planning, and increased expertise (actual movement along the experience curve) are crucial to the successful implementation of a high-quality/low-cost strategy.

Market-wide Positioning Strategies Through Differentiation

Differentiation is typically used in reference to a product offering that is superior to competitive offerings in quality, prestige, features, value, performance, convenience in use, reliability, or service. Brand names are important in differentiating the product. For example, only the Mayo Clinic can use the name. Location (distribution) can be a differentiating feature if the health care organization has a convenient location with easy access to parking in a pleasant, or at least safe, area. Price is usually higher because of the "extra" features, prestige, and so on. Promotion, particularly advertising, is the way health care organizations inform their customers that the facility *is* different from others. Those hospitals, long-term facilities, and physicians that have invested heavily in developing patient-centered care have to inform consumers that it is available.

Several hospitals are differentiating on the basis of "efficient care." This product is offered to customers who "want not only high quality hospital care, but also physicians who can provide the quick route to health."[30] They want a physician who has enough clinical experience and judgment to reduce the amount of unnecessary tests, drugs, and days in the hospital. Not overwhelmingly adopted, efficient care has met some obstacles that in today's health care reform environment may be diminishing.

Using Differentiation Strategies Some caution must be exercised in selecting any of the differentiation strategies. Differentiation will not work when the superior attribute highlighted is meaningless or unimportant to the consumer. Additionally, if the health care provider has a differentiating attribute that provides benefits but consumers do not know about it, there is no advantage. For example, a new technology is used to better diagnose a patient's problem, but the patient is unconscious when the equipment is used. The patient will not perceive the benefit unless he or she is told that the hospital cares enough to purchase the wonderful, new equipment that works so much faster (or is less intrusive, or whatever the benefit may be).

Providing "quality care" has been overused by so many health care organizations as a differentiation strategy that it is virtually meaningless. In addition, how many patients can judge quality of care? When severity-adjusted mortality and morbidity data become available to more consumers, will they use it to judge quality of care?

If the health care organization does not appear to provide quality care only those who have no choice will use it. It is important for health care managers to realize that there is a cost in not providing quality in the delivery of health care – including lawsuits. Furthermore, costs are associated with doing things incorrectly. Consider a hospital or nursing home billing statement that contains errors. Not only is there the cost of finding the error and redoing the statement, there is also the cost of losing a positive consumer attitude and perhaps a patient.

Positioning Strategies Through Market Segment Focus

Sometimes called *niche strategies, focus strategies* are often implemented when an organization has limited resources. The organization does not compete across the board, but in selected areas. The market definition is narrowed to identify a select group to serve. Enough resources can then be devoted to that customer group to achieve some degree of prominence or even dominance. In addition, increased specialization may lead to development of greater understanding and satisfaction on the part of the particular group targeted, which may in turn increase usage and loyalty.

Market scope is easily (and often preferably) narrowed when a large enough set of customers will be satisfied by a specific benefit. For example, some centers of excellence are marketing their expertise nationally, providing significant cost savings and improved outcomes despite the patient having to travel to fairly distant cities. Perhaps the best example of this is the Shouldice Hospital in Toronto. Shouldice treats only one illness – inguinal hernias – and attracts patients from all over Canada, the United States, and Europe. It succeeds with this very narrow scope because its services are highly efficient and of the highest quality. Patients who have had the Shouldice method for hernia repair have reoccurrences at 0.5 percent – the lowest in the world.[31]

A sharply focused strategy has the benefit of being difficult for the competition to attack. Yet at the same time such a strategy often restricts the organization's ability to grow. Take, for example, the case of EMI, which made only CAT scanners. The company was plagued by its inability to field enough service people. To avoid expensive downtime for the machine, quick response by service personnel was necessary. Larger competing firms, selling broad product lines that included CAT scanners and other diagnostic equipment, could support bigger and better trained service staffs, resulting in faster response times for repair work.[32]

Focused Cost Leadership Strategies　All of the previously discussed cost leadership strategies can be focused on a given segment. Being the low-cost producer in a segment rather than the entire market still provides an opportunity for developing a sustainable competitive advantage.

Focused Differentiation Strategies　A *focused product* is one part of a product line. Rather than attempting to offer a complete product line, which usually includes some mangy dogs and underperforming cash cows, the organization offers only a part of a product line. Usually an organization will focus on a product in which it has greater expertise and in which it believes some economies of scale may be achieved with a smaller product line. Because there is less of a "one-stop shopping" orientation, the product does need to differentiate itself from competition as it may be less convenient to obtain.

A birthing center has selected a focus or niche strategy based on the *segment* served. Another example is a nursing home that focuses on Alzheimer's patients. Within all nursing homes in a community, it may be differentiated on the basis of the Alzheimer's care offered; however, if other long-term or home-care organizations offer the service, differentiation is required.

Most community hospitals use *geography* as part of their strategy. They serve a specific geographic market and are the only hospital in the area. The private practice of an individual physician who attempts to find a convenient location for patients with no other similar type physicians located nearby uses a geographic area differentiation focus strategy as well. As the practice develops and flourishes, a second office may be opened that extends the geography.

Low-share markets are those that are not of sufficient size to interest the larger health care providers. A hospital or physician practice that specializes in less common diseases can satisfy a smaller market extremely well and thereby capture virtually all of the patients with that disease. This strategy can be more profitable than trying to capture a very small part of a larger market that includes many large and knowledgeable competitors. This strategy emphasizes profitability rather than size or growth.

IMPLEMENTING THE STRATEGY

Once the general implementation strategy has been selected, marketing management's task is to translate the generalities of the strategy into meaningful distinctions for consumers. The selected strategy becomes the marketing strategy when a target market is selected and a *marketing mix* is developed to meet the target market's needs. As shown in Exhibit 8–12, the elements of the marketing mix – product, price, distribution (location of delivery), and promotion – must be designed and coordinated to present the competitive advantage to the targeted consumers. The answers to each of the questions posed in the exhibit would be different depending on which marketing implementation strategy had been selected – differentiation, cost leadership, or focus.

Once the target market is identified and the marketing mix determined, the marketing strategy should provide the sustainable competitive advantage and serve as the cornerstone for making decisions. In addition, it should be reviewed on a periodic basis to make sure the organization's competitive advantage still exists and is desired by consumers. When competitive pressure is increasing, revenue is decreasing or static in what should be a time of growth, or the excess of revenues over expenses is declining, health care managers must reassess whether the competitive advantage is still meaningful to consumers.

The market naturally works to cut the competitive advantage of a leader by technological and environmental changes that erode protective barriers. Additionally, competitors learn how to imitate the leader and negate or equalize the competitive advantage. The organization itself may not take action to protect its

EXHIBIT 8 – 12
Concurrent Decisions Involved in Developing a Marketing Strategy

Target Market: Of the identified market segments, which one or ones should we satisfy?

Product: Which health care services shall we offer? What position in the market can we capture? Should our service offering be given a brand name?

Price: What shall we charge for our services? Can we cover the cost of indigent care in prices set for others?

Promotion: Shall we advertise? If so, where and in what media? How much shall we spend? Shall we create a special public relations event? Should we hire a salesperson?

Place: Where shall we locate? Should we establish additional facilities? Where?

position.[33] This passive reaction may occur because the organization does not perceive a threat from competitors or the threat is dismissed as unimportant. Sometimes an organization does not respond because any action is considered to be detrimental to the organization's overall strategy.

An organization can engage in defensive moves to thwart prospective challengers.[34] One defensive move is to signal intentions to defend a position. If a smaller hospital announces its intention to build specialized labor/delivery rooms, a larger competitor in the region could increase its advertising budget to promote its already in-place specialized maternity care. It has signaled that it will defend its position.

Others will attempt to foreclose avenues for attack, as when a large group practice adds previously uncovered specialties to provide comprehensive care. "Raising the stakes" is another way to combat competition. A hospital that purchases high-tech diagnostic equipment that no other hospital in the area can afford is raising the stakes.

Finally, a competitor can attempt to reduce the attractiveness of the market by using the mass media, which has covered health care extensively. For example, a number of articles have been written about the financial and personal difficulties faced by home health care organizations. Potential entrants to the industry may find it less attractive if they are exposed to a number of such articles or commentary in the mass media.

The final step in implementing any strategy should be assessment or control. The marketing audit looks at all marketing activities to determine if there are areas where marketing could be improved, if the marketing effort is supporting the organization's mission, goals, and strategic objectives, and if the results of the marketing effort were as planned.[35] The marketing audit is a part of organizational control, which Chapter 13 investigates more thoroughly.

SUMMARY AND CONCLUSIONS

Marketing is relatively new to most health care organizations. This chapter traced the evolution of acceptance that most organizations follow from a production orientation through a selling orientation to a marketing orientation. The basics of a marketing-oriented health care provider include customer satisfaction, an integrated marketing effort, and the provision of value for both parties in the exchange process.

A variety of health care customers – including physicians, patients, third-party payers, volunteers, employees, and so on – were discussed and their interdependence illustrated. Patients have to be admitted to a hospital by a physician; third-party payers influence physician choice, length of stay, and so on; volunteers and employees may also be patients; government entities interpret the need for additional health care subsidies from the public.

Because of the competition and complexity in the market, health care providers must implement strategic marketing to survive. The strategic marketing process involves determining the market served, analyzing the situation (including customers, competitors, and environmental factors), reviewing the organization's mission and objectives, setting marketing objectives, and determining marketing strategy.

The chapter illustrates how the directional, adaptive, market entry, and positioning strategies are implemented through marketing strategies. Marketers are intricately involved in strategic management of the health care organization. Marketing strategies are implemented through decisions concerning the selected target market and the appropriate marketing mix – product, price, distribution, and promotion – to satisfy that market.

The next chapter discusses strategic information systems.

KEY TERMS AND CONCEPTS IN STRATEGIC MANAGEMENT

demarketing	marketing mix	selling orientation
differentiation	marketing orientation	service
focus (niche) strategy	positioning	services
generic competition	primary competition	services competition
health care consumer	product line length	services (production)
low-cost strategy	product line width	orientation
market definition	product line depth	specific competition
market share	scope	strategic marketing process
marketing	secondary competition	target market

QUESTIONS FOR CLASS DISCUSSION

1. Why have health care providers been forced to think about marketing?
2. What "clues" could you identify that would indicate whether a health care organization is really applying the marketing concept?
3. How does the marketing of a service differ from the marketing of a physical product (good)?
4. Explain the strategic marketing process. How does it fit within strategic management?
5. Discuss the various ways that health care providers can define the market that they want to serve.
6. Why is it important to understand the organization's direct and indirect competitors?
7. Explain how you would select between a differentiating, focus, or cost leadership positioning strategy for a nursing home in New York City and for one in Butte, Montana.
8. How would you recommend the CEO of a local hospital differentiate itself from others in the area?
9. Name several ways that marketing can implement adaptive strategies for growth.
10. Does marketing have a role to play in the market entry strategies? Explain your answer.

NOTES

1. Philip Kotler and Sidney J. Levy, "Broadening the Concept of Marketing," *Journal of Marketing* 33, no. 1 (January 1969), pp. 10–15.
2. Valarie A. Zeithaml, A. Parasuraman, and Leonard L. Berry, *Delivering Quality Service* (New York: The Free Press, 1990), p. 11.
3. Leonard L. Berry, "Services Marketing Is Different," *Business* (May–June 1980), pp. 24–30.
4. Karen Russo France and Rajiv Grover, "What Is the Health Care Product?" *Journal of Health Care Marketing* 12, no. 2 (June 1992), p. 32.
5. For a more in-depth study of health care organizations and their movement toward a marketing orientation, see Robert Stensrud and Barbara Arrington, "Marketing-Oriented Organizations: An Integrated Approach," *Health Progress* (March 1988), pp. 86–89, 95.
6. Les J. Hauser, "Hospitals Must Advance Beyond Advertising to True Marketing," *Modern Healthcare* 23, no. 6 (February 8, 1993), p. 25.
7. Peter F. Drucker, *Management: Tasks, Responsibilities, Practices* (New York: Harper and Row, 1973), p. 64.
8. Jill L. Sherer, "Putting Patients First,"

Hospitals 67, no. 3 (February 5, 1993), p. 14.

9. G. M. Naidu and C. L. Narayana, "How Marketing Oriented Are Hospitals in a Declining Market?" *Journal of Health Care Marketing* 2, no. 1 (1991), p. 30.

10. Dan F. Duda, "Marketing Must Turn Savage," *Modern Healthcare* (April 16, 1990), p. 50.

11. Dennis R. McDermott, Frank J. Franzak, and Michael W. Little, "Does Marketing Relate to Hospital Profitability?" *Journal of Health Care Marketing* 13, no. 2 (Summer 1993), pp. 18–25.

12. Ibid.

13. "Smart Consumers Present a Marketing Challenge," *Hospitals* (August 20, 1990), pp. 42–47.

14. "It's a Woman's Market . . . ," *Hospitals & Health Networks* 67, no. 18 (September 20, 1993), p. 30.

15. Kevin Lumsdon and Mark Hagland, "Mapping Care," *Hospitals & Health Networks* 67, no. 20 (October 20, 1993), p. 39.

16. "Franchised, Branded Services Rapidly Increasing," *TrendWatch* 3, no. 4 (Fall 1993), p. 2.

17. George Anders, "McDonald's Methods Come to Medicine as Chains Acquire Physicians' Practices," *Wall Street Journal* (August 24, 1993), p. B-1.

18. Rajshekhar G. Javalgi, Thomas W. Whipple, Mary K. McManamon, and Vicki L. Edick, "Hospital Image: A Correspondence Analysis Approach," *Journal of Health Care Marketing* 12, no. 4 (December 1992), pp. 34–39.

19. Ibid.

20. Charles J. Austin, *Information Systems for Health Services Administration* (Ann Arbor, Michigan: AUPHA Press, 1992), p. 108. To calculate market share an individual organization's revenues are divided by the total revenues for the market. Other alternatives to revenue market share can be calculated such as share of occupied beds (the number of adjusted occupied beds compared to the total number of beds available in a community, state, nation, or world) or "share of mind" interpreted as the percent of the target market that recalls the health care organization's name or what it is known for without prompting.

21. George S. Day, *Market Driven Strategy: Processes for Creating Value* (New York: The Free Press, 1990), p. 163.

22. For an excellent discussion of quality in service organizations, see Valarie A. Zeithaml, A. Parasuraman, and Leonard L. Berry, *Delivering Quality Service* (New York: The Free Press, 1990).

23. For further information, see Julie Johnsson, "Survey: Many CEOs Overlook PR Staff's Role in Strategic Planning," *Hospitals* 66, no. 17 (September 5, 1992), pp. 34–40.

24. For suggestions on how to speed up health care service delivery, see Dan Beckham, "Making Speed a Priority," *Marketing to Doctors* 5, no. 11 (November 1992), pp. 1–3.

25. "Education Centers Are Subtle Marketing Tools," *Hospitals* (September 20, 1989), p. 76.

26. Mary Wagner, "Mobile Mammography Tries to Enhance Its Image, Revenue Through Strategic Ties," *Modern Healthcare* (January 8, 1990), p. 78.

27. Al Ries and Jack Trout, *Positioning: The Battle for Your Mind* (New York: McGraw-Hill, 1981), p. 22.

28. For a more thorough discussion of expansion of the product line, see France and Grover, "What Is the Health Care Product?" pp. 31–38.

29. For greater understanding of incremental cost analysis, see Shahram Heshmat, "The Role of Cost in Hospital Pricing Decisions," *Journal of Hospital Marketing* 6, no. 1 (1991), pp. 155–161.

30. Jon A. Chilingerian, "New Directions for Hospital Strategic Management: The Market for Efficient Care," *Health Care Management Review* 17, no. 4 (Fall 1992), pp. 73–80.

31. Ibid., p. 79.

32. Day, *Market Driven Strategy,* p. 202.

33. Ibid., p. 213.

34. For further discussion of defensive posi-

tioning, see Day, *Market Driven Strategy,* Chapter 8.

35. Ellen Pearson, "Marketing Audit Reveals Holes and Opportunities," *Health Care Strategic Management* 8, no. 7 (July 1990), pp. 17–18.

ADDITIONAL READINGS

Brown, Montague, *Health Care Marketing Management* (Gaithersburg, Maryland: Aspen Publishers, 1992). This book is a collection of articles published in *Health Care Management Review.* Of the twenty-two articles included, sixteen were published before 1988, requiring that the reader be aware of the changes that have occurred in health care since that time. Articles are organized into three sections marketing management issues; media relations, advertising, and patient satisfaction; and marketing concepts and approaches – and a number are authored by leaders in the field.

Heskett, James L., W. Earl Sasser, Jr., and Christopher W.L. Hart, *Service Breakthroughs – Changing the Rules of the Game* (New York: The Free Press, 1990). When service providers consistently meet or exceed the consumer's expectations, the organization has created a service breakthrough. Although this book uses many business examples, some health care examples are included and the chapter on managing demand and supply is directly applicable to health care organizations that have little capability to predict demand.

Hillestad, Steven G., and Eric N. Berkowitz, *Health Care Marketing Plans: From Strategy to Action,* 2d ed. (Gaithersburg, Maryland: Aspen Publishers, 1991). The authors provide a step-by-step approach to setting and achieving objectives, a strategy grid for determining competitive actions, a list of key questions to use in conducting an external and internal analysis, and a sample marketing plan. The focus is on integrating marketing strategy and marketing tactics. An excellent resource for those new to health care marketing.

Kotler, Philip, and Roberta N. Clarke, *Marketing for Health Care Organizations* 2d ed. Englewood Cliffs, New Jersey: Prentice-Hall, 1995. This book is an adaptation of Philip Kotler's marketing management text used in many graduate-level marketing courses. The original work provides extensive coverage of marketing and serves as a comprehensive resource for students. This volume is the same basic text with health care examples throughout.

Pol, Louis G., and Richard K. Thomas, *The Demography of Health and Health Care* (New York: Plenum Press, 1992). This is an extremely useful book for health care marketers because it applies demographic concepts and methods to the understanding of health care delivery. The use of minicases and "implications for health care" sections provide examples. There is an excellent review of secondary data sources with discussion of the strengths and weaknesses of each. The book is ideal for a marketer who is new to health care marketing and can serve as a reference to the experienced health care marketer.

CHAPTER 9

Strategic Information Systems

"Information is a strategic weapon."
— *Unknown*

After completing this chapter you should:

1. Be able to define strategic information and its role in health care organizations.
2. Understand the importance of strategic information in strategic management.
3. Understand the importance of information in situational analysis.
4. Be able to explain how a strategic information system can be a competitive advantage for a health care organization.
5. Be able to relate change in the way work is done through new ways of thinking and doing to understand the impact of information on this process.
6. Explain how information systems and electronic data interchanges link various internal and external constituencies of health care organizations.
7. Identify the strategic issues facing strategic information systems managers in health care organizations.

In 1989, long before there was such heated discussion about health care reform, Memorial Sloan-Kettering recognized the need to do something about the escalating documentation that was driving up administrative costs (estimated to be 25 percent of hospital costs). The world's largest private facility for comprehensive cancer care, Memorial Sloan-Kettering determined that an investment in document imaging technology would help to control administrative costs and enhance the quality of patient care.

The center's imaging system, called *OSCAR* for optical system controlling administrative records, was designed to read, use, store, and retrieve patient records. First used for accounts receivable, the system has been expanded to medical records. The technology paid for itself in twenty-two months. In addition, the center was able to reduce its staff by nearly 9 percent ($330,000 annually), cut the microfilm and media budget ($140,000 annually), and reduce space requirements ($115,000 annually). Most important, the automation and reengineering of the work processes increased productivity by 20 percent.

The key benefits include enhanced quality of patient care and service, improved cash flow (for both accounts receivable and accounts payable), streamlined record processing, reduced administrative costs and overhead, enhanced continuous quality improvement, and an improved the hospital's competitive position. The current goal is to automate all patient medical records to improve turnaround time for health care practitioners and others in related areas with simultaneous and immediate access to patent charts from all points of patient entry and to compress the record completion process. Currently the data base can be accessed from 1,600 terminals including external systems at Empire Blue Cross and Blue Shield and the National Electronic Insurance Corporation's claims processing network.

The OSCAR system contains two scanners, ninety-five workstations, four optical libraries, a tri-density tape server, and a fax server, used in conjunction with WorkFlo software from FileNet Corporation. Currently the center is evaluating imaging technology for human resources applications and physician billing and accounts payable.

Can these impressive cost savings be duplicated at other facilities? Is doing more work faster through technology the answer to reducing health care administrative costs? Can information and technology be combined to reduce costs and improve patient care for health care organizations other than hospitals?

Source: John McBride, "Memorial Sloan-Kettering Cures Paperwork Problems with Document Imaging," *Computers in Healthcare* (December 1993), pp. 38–40.

Information must be considered a tool of strategic management just like marketing, human resources, or financing. Used to its fullest capabilities, the information system is a strategic weapon. "Information, intelligently used, and information systems, carefully planned, can be great assets to the health services manager."[1] A *strategic information system* (SIS) has been defined as one that is any combination of computers, workstations, software systems, and communications technology used to gain competitive advantage.[2] In contrast, traditional information support systems focus on improved efficiency. This chapter describes how health care organizations can effectively use strategic information systems to not only improve the direct care of patients but also improve the organization's ability to compete.

THE IMPORTANCE OF INFORMATION IN STRATEGIC MANAGEMENT

For strategic management to successfully direct the organization to accomplish its mission and vision, information is essential. Exhibit 9–1 reinforces the importance of information in development of strategic management. Information can be generated through the information system; by management's reading of newspapers, professional association newsletters, and journals; and by word-of-mouth, to name a few sources. However, properly planned and implemented, the information system is the most critical source. "In order for health services organizations to effectively use information technology to gain strategic advantage, two conditions (among others) are essential: (1) information systems planning must be guided by the strategic directions of the organization, and (2) information systems managers must think, plan, and act in *strategic* rather than *technical operational* ways."[3] According to Applegate, Mason, and Thorpe, operational planning requires specific detailed information that is internal to the organization and is used repeatedly

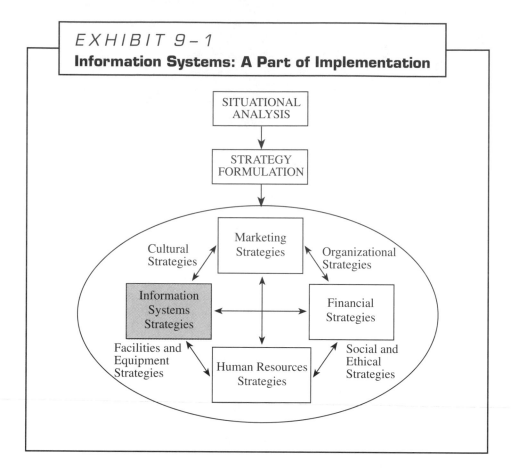

EXHIBIT 9-1
Information Systems: A Part of Implementation

(e.g., day, date, and time of emergency room admissions to the hospital). Strategic planning requires a broad range of data from a variety of diverse sources, both external and internal to the organization, and focuses on the development of relationships and analysis of trends.[4] In actuality, a fair amount of strategic internal information is available in the organization's operational systems; however, without proper planning it may not be accessible. For example, internal billing statements could provide outcomes research data on the efficacy of drugs and medical devices for various surgeries – if the system was planned to allow capturing of all billing information by the procedure. By use of outcomes data, competitive positioning could be developed or enhanced.

Information is vital to the strategic management process of situational analysis. The process of monitoring the external environment for threats and opportunities and the methodologies to do so were covered extensively in Chapter 3. Chapter 4 discussed the assessment of the internal environment. Exhibit 9–2 summarizes the areas of greatest contribution to situational analysis by strategic information systems.

EXHIBIT 9-2

Information Systems Input to Situational Analysis

Situational Analysis	Information Systems Input to Situational Analysis
External Environment	
Economic	Monitor and provide information on the economy and aspects that affect the health care organization
Regulatory	Access databases that provide the latest information on regulatory changes from national, state, and local governments and regulatory groups; convert it to useful information
Competitor Analysis	Develop a database of competitive activity to include market share, revenues, costs, profitability, productivity, services offered, number of employees, and so on
Market Analysis	Develop a database of the market – its size, changes, potential, rate of growth, profitability, cost structure, critical success factor measures
Customer Analysis	Develop a database that profiles current customers and usage patterns, previous customers; match demographics of the area with customer profiles to predict future usage
Internal Environment	
Information Systems	Assess the information provided to marketing, finance, accounting, human resources, clinical/medical staff, administrative staff, executive staff, and facilities against goals
Mission, Vision, Values, and Objectives	
	Identify whether SIS can be a competitive advantage; provide information on customers, services, competition; provide information that can empower the vision; include personal ethic; confidentiality of patient information; participate in developing corporate objectives by providing historical and projected future information; develop strategic information systems objectives to accomplish corporate objectives

---

Situational Analysis

The application of information technology to situational analysis to collect, analyze, and manipulate data is well documented. According to Peter Drucker,

"Information is data endowed with relevance and purpose. Converting data into information thus requires knowledge."[5] Information systems specialists have to know and understand the technology of data organization, storage, retrieval, and manipulation and use their knowledge to convert the data into information for various organizational purposes, one of which is situational analysis. The general environment as well as the health care environment has to be monitored in terms of social, regulatory, political, economic, competitive, and technology changes as was illustrated in Exhibit 3–1. Although information is the basis for decision making in strategic management, there are additional specific and identified roles that it can serve.

Scanning the Information Technology Environment It is important to note that the field of *information technology* should be incorporated into situational analysis as well as the more traditional areas of the economy, competition, and so on. Although it is only one area of situational analysis, it is important because of the rapid changes occurring in information technology over the past three decades in hardware, software, and telecommunications plus the high costs committed to providing information for the organization. "In addition, each application and technology decision is both enabling and constraining – it opens some doors and closes others."[6] For example, information system decisions made today will affect the organization's ability to respond to changes in motion video, voice, and document imaging in the near future. Errors in judgment are costly in terms of both time and money.

Environmental scanning should forewarn the organization and allow time to plan for an orderly transition to new software if, for example, a vendor goes out of business or decides to stop marketing (and supporting) the software purchased by the health care organization. If the health care organization has developed proprietary programs (software developed in-house), it still has to know what is available because competition may choose to purchase it.

Developing Competitive Advantage

In today's fast paced environment, health care professionals are searching for any competitive advantage that might be available. An important contribution of strategic information systems in strategic management is developing competitive advantage through decision support systems and improved customer service levels. Examples of information systems that increase market share, raise profitability, add value to products, and change the competitive position of an organization have many CEOs reexamining the role of information technology in their corporate strategy.[7]

Decision Support Systems *Decision support systems* (DSSs) attempt to take vast quantities of unorganized data and turn them into useful information for managers to make better decisions. Although DSSs have been available in health care for some time, they have been unknown, mistrusted or ignored.[8] DSSs involve organizing the data, selecting the models that will analyze the data, and interpreting the output. It is not sufficient simply to provide the reports to the decision maker. Sometimes there is a need to interpret and clarify the data relative to the assumptions that were used. Because decision support systems attempt to investigate *future* activities, the assumptions will be critical. The organization that can design a DSS that is pertinent, relatively accurate, and timely will have developed a competitive advantage. "Inappropriate use and interpretation of decision support models can be dangerous, but appropriate use of these models can be a powerful tool in the hands of an informed decision maker."[9]

Improved Customer Service Levels Competitive advantage can be created through improved response times – the time it takes to call up a patient's record, the speed with which the pharmacy can reorder a drug, or the ability to quickly access a data base for incidence of disease. Another competitive advantage could be in the quantity of data handled and stored in a shorter period of time with greater accuracy. These superior "service levels" can become the organization's opportunity to differentiate itself from others in its field. Perspective 9–1 describes the frustration of one company when its supplier would not provide timely information to help the organization control its health care costs and its decision to develop the information in-house.

Service levels have to be developed based on customer expectations. Internally, customers (other organizational users of information technology) negotiate with the information specialists based on costs and benefits to determine the level of service that will be provided. Another customer-oriented measure is the number of transactions completed per hour. Users understand and can compare this measure of performance. They can then compute the time to complete the processing and determine the time to complete their own job. Externally, service levels are determined by customer expectations and competition. Service levels must be expressed in the customers' terms. Response time is how long the customer has to wait for information at the terminal, not the processing time of the central processor.

Once a service level has been established as satisfactory it still has to be reviewed periodically, because there are changes in hardware and software as well as competitive activity. Any deterioration of service levels, whether response speed or number of transactions, should be carefully monitored and corrected before it negatively affects users. This requires considerable attention to long-range planning to maintain a competitive advantage by forecasting when additional increments of information technology resources will be necessary and to bring them on-line at the appropriate time. Providing customers what they want and need is a dynamic process.

A supplier can develop competitive advantage by the degree and duration of training. Users will need training and support to solve the problems they encounter (or create). In addition, a user-friendly system may encourage use.

Finally, a sophisticated information system has become the competitive advantage in many industries. For example, in the pharmaceutical and hospital supply industries, those organizations with an automated order entry and distribution system are more competitive than those without. Hospitals and other health care organizations have realized the value of just-in-time (JIT) ordering to reduce

Self-Insured Company Develops Its Own Health Information System

First National Bank of Chicago was tired of being charged extra for specific information it requested from its vendor and the delays in gaining access to the information. First Chicago, provider of insurance coverage for 15,000 employees and 1,700 retirees, was trying to control corporate health costs but was "stymied" by lack of information. So in 1987 it developed Occupational Medical and Nursing Information (OMNI) to monitor claims and utilization data.

Described as a "work in progress," the initial investment of $125,000 for consulting fees, hardware, and software plus $35,000 annually for consulting, software licenses, and other costs has paid off for First Chicago. Through ready access to its own utilization data, the company was able to identify specific health services that were "out of line" with local norms. Maternity costs, mental health, and cardiovascular health were targeted.

Because of the high number of young, women employees, the bank attributed almost 15 percent of its indemnity claims to maternity costs. First Chicago's C-section rates were 29 percent compared to 23 to 25 percent in the region. To reduce the number of unnecessary C-sections and improve prenatal and neonatal health, First Chicago began a series of on-site prenatal classes. For the women who attended the classes, only 19 percent had C-sections and the delivery claims averaged $2,500 less.

Average length of stay for First Chicago's major diagnostic groups for mental health were too high compared to other similar populations. The utilization firm was not holding down costs. First Chicago resumed managing mental health care in-house. In-house activities reduced the number of days of inpatient psychiatric care from 158 per 1,000 workers to 80 per 1,000 workers.

Cardiovascular care was targeted as a wellness area that could save the bank money and improve the health of workers. Prior to its attention, one-third of workers with high blood pressure were under a doctor's care. After screenings and wellness programs, 80 percent of those with high blood pressure are under a doctor's care and the percentage of claims resulting from cardiovascular disease has dropped from 9 percent to 6 percent in three years.

According to Wayne Burton, M.D., vice president, and medical director for First Chicago, "The value of an in-house data system is the ability to evaluate everything we are doing as a medical unit in health promotion and prevention programs." He pointed out that a single year of data is not that valuable, but that OMNI has been in operation for five years and "that data is pretty good" but will be better when there is ten years of data.

Source: Dan Wise, "To Control Costs, First Chicago Controls the Data, Too," *Business and Health* (Mid-March 1993), pp. 26–27, 31.

storage costs and release space for other uses. In many situations, electronic data interchange is mandatory to just "stay in the game" and compete. For expansion strategies, information that is cutting edge is required.

To satisfy customers, provide a quality product, and do it with great cost efficiencies, today's health care managers need the most current information to make decisions affecting the long-term viability of their organizations. Many community and urban hospitals have closed because they could not manage costs. A variety of additional reasons can be noted, but accurate information could have assisted the manager – if with nothing else at least when the operation should have been closed to minimize the losses.

Information Technology as a Catalyst for Change

Many top managers have looked upon information systems as a necessary aspect of company operations but did not recognize the impact on the traditional "bottom line." According to Sprague and McNurlin that view is changing, and "information technology can be used strategically as a catalyst for fundamentally revamping ways of doing business – ways that were appropriate for slower, paper-based processes but impede speedier computer-based operations."[10]

Rather than evolutionary thinking, health care organizations need to respond in terms of revolutionary thinking. Organizational processes tend to evolve over time (evolutionary thinking). Mead Corporation has identified the analogy of "cow paths" to clarify the revolutionary thinking that must occur to achieve the best benefits of information systems.[11] Cows in covering the distance from the pasture to the barn, follow meandering paths as they avoid obstacles and rough terrain. Even after the obstacles have been removed, the cows continue to follow the old meandering path rather than create a new, more direct route. The organization often does the same by attempting to more efficiently "follow the path" rather than rethinking the processes. Old assumptions must be questioned.

Information technology can be used as a catalyst for change to not only improve automated processes but also to improve the way work is performed. This may lead to restructuring the organization or to support for greater external linkages, including strategic alliances or other partnering activities. The on-line world of the future will allow far greater fluidity in organizational structure. Work teams will come together and disband as needed. Individuals will control what they do while managers think for the future.

Total Quality Management Forces Strategic Thinking Total quality management incorporates this same type of revolutionary thinking. Rather than focusing on improving speed and accuracy of information processing and reports, TQM is oriented to new ways of thinking and performing operations. In a 1990 *Harvard Business Review* article, Michael Hammer discussed this reengineering process for business and clinical situations. He identified seven principles for organizational reengineering:[12]

1. *Organize around outcomes, not tasks.* The old ways are task oriented – one person works on one file at a time to generate one bill for one patient. By focusing on the desired outcome, people consider new ways to accomplish the work.
2. *People who use the output should perform the process.* Why should purchasing order IV tubing when the emergency department runs low? With approved vendors, safety stock numbers, and order quantities determined, the information system can order IV tubing when the emergency department reaches a predetermined level.
3. *Include information processing in the "real" work that produces the information.* Those who produce the information should also process it. This eliminates the overspecialization where one group collects the data and another processes it, reducing errors and time. Patient bedside data entry would be an example. Rather than having a written patient chart with dictated physician input given to another individual in another location to enter and transcribe the data at another time (impeding the timeliness of information), nurses, physicians, and others enter data as they examine, prescribe, and document decisions for the patient's care.
4. *Treat geographically dispersed resources as if they were centralized.* By using networks and systems, organizations can achieve economies of scale and at the same time offer flexibility and responsiveness.
5. *Link parallel activities rather than integrate them.* By coordinating similar kinds of work while it is in process rather than after completion, better cooperation can be fostered and the process accelerated.
6. *Let "doers" be self-managing.* By putting decisions where the work is performed and building in controls, organizations can eliminate layers of managers. Expert systems can aid the "doers" in decision making.
7. *Capture information once and at its source.* Because of on-line capabilities, the information can be shared everywhere it is needed after it has been entered.

Perspective 9–2 provides information on some of the software that is being developed to "reengineer" information about patients.

Reorganizing Based on New Ways of Thinking Once the work has been redesigned because of revolutionary thinking, the old organization structure may need to be reassessed. In the centralized form of organization, the decisions are made at the top and directed down the hierarchy. Middle-level managers are expected to apply the policies determined by top managers to the work they and their subordinates perform. In decentralized organizations, middle-level managers have relative autonomy to do what they consider appropriate "to get the work done."

Although few organizations operate at these extremes, centralized control operates most effectively when the environment is relatively stable and the work is homogeneous. Decentralized control is most effective when the environment is dynamic and the work is very different, requiring creativity on the part of lower level managers. Information systems can blend these extremes and modify

Bedside Data Entry – A Reality for Some Health Care Organizations

First Data Corporation has begun marketing "First Empower" software to hospitals nationwide. The software uses a personal or handheld computer for data entry. Although that in itself is not revolutionary, the use of the personal computer to retrieve all known information about a patient from multiple sources is going to revolutionize health care delivery.

With First Empower, physicians can highlight a patient's name with a mouse or a light pen. They can access information from the hospital, their office, car, or home. Once a patient is selected from the list on the first screen, a second screen appears with the patient's photograph and a variety of choices: lab tests, X ray results, current diagnosis, current and past prescribed pharmaceuticals, and so on. If the physician wants to view X rays, the screen illustrates a human body with dots. A dot at the chest and knee indicate those places where X rays have been taken for the patient. When the dot is touched with a light pen, the X ray is displayed on the screen. There is no need to call to radiology to have someone find the last X ray taken and then wait for someone to deliver it or travel to view it. The time savings are readily apparent.

First Data has invested three years and $30 million in development of its software. A First Empower system costs a small hospital between $600,000 and $800,000 and a larger hospital might spend $5 million. With government and insurers looking for ways to reduce administrative costs and the Joint Commission on Accreditation of Healthcare Organizations investigating requirements for information sharing through computers, the industry is expected to grow as much as 15 percent per year.

Competitive products have been developed by Shared Medical Systems Corporation, HBO & Company, Cerner Corporation, and IBAX Health Systems, a joint venture between Baxter International and IBM.

3M and Intermountain Health Care in Idaho, Utah, and Wyoming have been installing the HELP system since 1988. Although not an electronic patient record, it uses expert systems technology to warn physicians about drug interaction hazards and ordered drugs that are inconsistent with the diagnosis. Intermountain estimates that it has saved $1.2 million per year on this aspect alone. In addition the hospital saves $1 million a year by having leased telephone lines for its own network. Within each facility all computers tie into local area networks. Intermountain spends about 2 percent of its operating budget on information systems, which is about the national average for hospitals.

Source: Conversations and correspondence with Larry Ferguson, president and chief quality officer, First Data Corporation, and Elizabeth Gardner, "Computers, Networks Help Intermountain Integrate," *Modern Healthcare* 23, no. 29 (July 19, 1993), pp. 30–31.

the organization on an as needed basis. In other words, the organization becomes more fluid, responding to change as it occurs.

In his information systems – oriented book *Shaping the Future,* Peter Keen predicted eight events to occur by the mid-1990s. Several of the events are the results of information technology impacting the organizational structure.

1. Every large firm in every industry will have from 25 to 80 percent of its cash flow processed on-line.
2. Electronic data interchange will be the norm.
3. Point-of-sale and electronic payments will be core services.
4. Image technology will be an operational necessity.
5. Work will be distributed, and reorganization will be commonplace.
6. Work will increasingly be location independent.
7. Electronic business partnerships will be standard.
8. Reorganizations will be frequent, not exceptional.[13]

Information Linkages Through Electronic Data Interchange

Several trends are occurring that will bring about greater information linkages or electronic communication both internally and externally. In the internal context, the linkages can improve efficiency and lower costs. For example, inventory control and billing can be linked through an automated updating process. Any time a drug, special diet, medical device, or other item is prescribed or ordered for a patient, the inventory can be automatically adjusted and the cost of the item added to the patient's bill and reimbursement filing forms. Internal linkages between departments, including the management of information systems must be planned for in the strategic management process.

This same system can be expanded externally through interorganizational linkages to automatically reorder from specified suppliers to keep sufficient safety stock on hand. Thus, advanced order entry systems in the health care industry can reduce ordering costs for both the customer and the supplier. Suppliers are linking with their customers to electronically process ordering. Third-party payers are linked with health care providers for billing and reimbursement procedures. Government regulators are linking for documentation and research purposes. Finally, as health care organizations form strategic alliances, they will need to be linked and information technology will be heavily involved. There is some discussion that the Joint Commission on Accreditation of Healthcare Organizations is readying requirements for a minimum level of information sharing that can be accomplished only through a computer.[14]

The success of these interorganizational systems depend on eight characteristics according to Sprague and McNurlin:

1. *Interorganizational systems require partners.* There has to be a willingness for two or more parties to cooperate.
2. *Standards play a key role.* For linkages to be successful in the future, the programs and processes developed today should be easily expandable to

other links whether they are community, regional, state, industry, national, or international.

3. *Education is important.* The more advanced information technology partner will pull the others along through education.

4. *Third parties are often involved.* They operate as electronic intermediaries to facilitate the flow of information.

5. *The work must be synchronized.* A change in any one of the cooperating systems has to be coordinated with all the others.

6. *Work processes are often reevaluated.* When electronic ordering is implemented, paper invoices can be eliminated and payments made without an invoice.

7. *Technical aspects are not the major issue.* Relationship issues are the key to making interorganizational systems work.

8. *Efforts often cannot be secretive.* By using standards the cooperating organizations have to be involved in the ongoing development of the standards.[15]

Many organizations are using *electronic data interchange* (EDI) for standard business transactions. Many health care organizations, particularly physicians' practices, are still operating at the lowest level of computer-to-computer linkage; however, some organizations are reaching the second level of applications-to-applications linkage (ordering to billing). Few organizations have achieved the third level of process-to-process linkage. At this point in time, EDI provides the greatest potential when standard transactions require accuracy and make it easier for the customer to buy. In the future, less standardization will be required as processes are used.

Time Value of Information

A time value is associated with information. The reduction in time required or improved timeliness of delivery of information can be developed into a competitive advantage. Anyone who has had to wait for results of tests until they can be read by the specialist knows the cost of time. Emergency medical services understand the time value of information. They work in a time-based environment. Telecommunications will play an increasing role in time-valued operations.

The major time-related factors for information technology include response time to serve customers; time-based competitive differentiation; efficiency in inventory, ordering, and out of stocks; and eliminating distance as a barrier.

IMPORTANCE OF STRATEGIC INFORMATION SYSTEMS

Organizations of all sizes have come to rely on computers. From small private physician practices to the largest hospital systems, computers have enabled information to be collected, stored, and manipulated for payroll and billing, diagnostics (both clinical and managerial), records management, facilities control, and decision making. Because information transfer is required among all the major functional areas of the health care organization, an integrated information system (one where the various departments/functional areas can communicate and share information) is superior. In a 1993 study by Hewlett-Packard Company and the Healthcare Information and Management Systems Society, more than one-half of the 571 hospital information system specialists surveyed indicated that connecting with outside facilities including physicians' offices, clinics, HMOs, and others was one of the driving forces in hospital computerization. Over 60 percent indicated that integrating existing systems was a top priority.[16] Perspective 9–3 reviews one hospital's efforts at integrating its information system. An integrated approach requires great effort in a rapidly changing environment such as health care.

Rapidly Changing Environment

Because of the potential changes in the regulatory environment, many health care organizations are using market entry strategies such as alliances, mergers, and so on. Multi-institutional health care systems must communicate across institutions as well as within institutions. Communication is particularly important for vertically integrated health care organizations. All of these linkages require increasingly sophisticated information technology and expanded strategic information systems.

PERSPECTIVE 9–3
Strategic Plan Is First Step In Information System Revamping

Lehigh Valley Hospital, an 830-bed regional trauma center, was in need of an information system makeover. End-user departments had selected a variety of hardware and software for their individual department needs. As a result they could not share information, and a barrier was created that was less than optimum in terms of providing excellent health care. In addition, overhead costs were rising.

The first step, a strategic plan, identified three main functional areas that required interdepartmental communications: PCMA that includes patient care, management and accounting, and laboratory; FSS that includes financial systems for human resources and accounting; and DSS for decision support services that includes reporting capabilities and executive information systems. A wide area network (WAN) was developed that served as the "glue" for the entire system, which included two hospitals, a data center, several off-campus buildings, and numerous end-user workstations throughout the system.

By eliminating the need for redundant hardware and wiring and reducing the number of changes (moves), the universal terminal is expected to save the hospital $3 million, which more than offsets the cost of the network. The system has streamlined operations, lowered overhead, and improved patient care.

Source: Joel A. Gaddy, "Enterprise-wide Network Eliminates 'Tower of Babel,'" *Computers in Healthcare* (May 1993), pp. 35–36.

Information technology has played a part in many aspects of change in health care delivery. *Medical informatics* is the term used to describe the technology associated with the organization and management of information in support of patient care, medical information, and medical research.[17] For example, collecting the data on the number of C-sections by hospital by physician nationwide has allowed researchers to determine that it may be practice patterns rather than clinical evidence dictating that a patient give birth by C-section rather than vaginal delivery. That information, in combination with the general public's perception of "excessive costs," has affected the number of C-sections performed. In the past, that data could have been collected but the process would have taken so long that it would have been meaningless by the time it became available. Thus technology allows information to be generated and evaluated faster, causing an increase in the speed with which events occur and the pace with which managers and organizations have to respond.

Federal government reform efforts are causing changes in the health care environment as well, dictating the need for more information to make informed decisions. It appears that health care reform will focus on increased clinical accountability, efficiency of administrative and other operations, and detailed knowledge of costs. Managed care and capitation force health care managers to understand every cost decision and the resulting implications.

Some states have legal requirements that hospitals provide information on admissions, discharges, lengths of stay, and so on to the public. Federal and state regulations determine specific information that must be collected, but there is still some uncertainty over the format for the information when it is submitted electronically. Perspective 9–4 provides information on the Workgroup for Electronic Data Interchange, an industry-led, government sponsored group investigating electronic submission of health care data.

In addition, federal and state governments specify the length of time that records must be maintained and housed. In the recent past, all electronic medical records systems were required to have paper backup. Optical disk manufacturers were required to prove that their storage medium would contain data for at least twenty-five years before they could be used to store medical records. Fortunately, these requirements are changing almost as rapidly as the environment.

Quantity of Information Generated and Stored

In health care organizations, the sheer quantity of information generated and the requirements that much of it be maintained over time has elevated the importance of strategic information systems. Health care providers must maintain meticulous records that document a patient's ailment (from his or her perspective), the physician's diagnosis, and the recommended course of treatment. This information is used by a variety of reimbursement sources, including insurance companies, the federal government (Medicare patients), state government (Medicaid patients), and an individual's records for reimbursement and taxes. In addition, it may be used in malpractice cases, research studies, outcomes measurement, and so on. Every time the patient is admitted to the hospital or a long-term-care facility that

PERSPECTIVE 9–4

Workgroup for Electronic Data Interchange

In 1991, the Secretary of Health and Human Services, Dr. Louis Sullivan, convened three industry-led workgroups to investigate reducing the administrative costs of health care. The Workgroup for Electronic Data Interchange (WEDI) was co-chaired by the president of Blue Cross and Blue Shield Association and the president of The Travelers Insurance Company. It included a fifteen-member steering committee and a staff of fifty.

The major committee recommendations include:

1. Define and adopt a standard format for core financial transactions such as enrollment, eligibility, claims submission, and payment and remittance advice through the American National Standards Institute (target: 4Q 1993).

2. Of the Category I industry participants (major public and private payers, hospitals, major employers and self-insured plans, pharmacies, and clinics and group practices of twenty or more professionals), 95 percent should implement electronic data interchange (EDI) by 4Q 1994. Of the Category II participants (remaining health care payers, providers, employers and self-insured plans, and pharmacies), 85 percent should implement EDI directly or through a clearinghouse by 4Q 1996.

3. WEDI should submit periodic reports to DHHS, and if percentage goals are not being met, appropriate legislation should be pursued to support the voluntary initiatives.

4. Public and private payers should provide incentives for increased use of EDI. Suggestions included no- or low-cost software and maintenance support, quick payment incentives, cost/benefit analyses, and so on. Informational partnership should be encouraged to reduce the development, transitional, and operating costs of EDI.

5. To facilitate the necessary initial investment by small or rural Category II providers and small employers, WEDI recommended that Congress provide tax incentives.

6. Develop a unique identifier system for all participants in the health care system by 4Q 1993.

7. Develop accreditation standards for clearinghouses that include minimum performance standards to protect the business, confidentiality, and security of EDI customers by 4Q 1994.

8. Congressional action to protect consumer confidentiality and privacy rights.

Other recommendations included industry commitment to fund further investigation and development of a variety of task forces to facilitate the adoption of EDI.

Source: Workgroup for Electronic Data Interchange, *WEDI Report to the Secretary of U.S. Department of Health and Human Services* (Washington, D.C.: U.S. Department of Health and Human Services, 1992).

information is expanded as nurses and a variety of technicians add to the physician's documentation of the patient's care.

Information Systems Affect Health Care Delivery

Several additional factors occurring in the health care environment affect the increasing use of information technology. Examples include an increased focus on quality from the customer's perspective; concern over the environment; consumers' abilities and increasing expectations to use computers; acceleration of the development process for new technology; the ability to provide sophisticated health care away from the hospital; and so on. The focus on quality has caused management to examine and redesign many processes to improve organizational performance. Information systems themselves are used in the redesigning of work.

Children learn to operate computers in their toys and become skilled in programming without noticing. It takes somewhat greater effort for adults, but most people have learned to use an automatic teller machine. There is the opportunity to teach patients how to access and check their health care billing information through the telephone or use at-home medical diagnostic equipment such as diabetes and oxygen monitoring or even ordering prescription drugs through telephone access to the pharmaceutical company's internal information system.

Alteration of the Service Area Expansion of the traditional delivery area is occurring through information technology by use of video diagnostics, the information highway, and so forth. Shortened product development time and product life cycles underscore the need for timely information. The development of lightweight powerful computers have enabled many health care professionals to work outside the traditional confines of the hospital. Home health care is expanding rapidly because of the ability to access, through a modem, any patient information and add to the data base keeping it current.

Point-of-service (POS) *systems* are heavily computer dependent. Kaiser Permanente, one of the largest HMOs, provides health care services on a prepaid basis exclusively to enrollees. Competitive pressures are forcing Kaiser to give enrollees the option of receiving services from non-Kaiser physicians.[18] U.S. Healthcare, Inc., based in Pennsylvania, offered point-of-service options to its enrollees and grew 13 percent. "Information systems can and do influence competitive measures. Systems are competitive tools."[19] Without massive communication capabilities, POS systems could not be offered. Overall, enrollment in point-of-service HMOs grew 50 percent in 1992 to 6 percent of HMO enrollment. Although they have to pay somewhat more, consumers prefer POS options because they have greater choice. Within the industry there is some doubt that point-of-service options will continue because of increasing cost pressures.[20]

Alteration at the Point of Delivery Information technology is pervasive. Most nursing stations have workstations, and bedside computers are predicted to be the way of the future. These computers will be interconnected via local area networks to large sophisticated mainframes. The technology is expandable to all health care settings including physicians' offices, hospitals, long-term-care facilities, public health departments, and others. In addition, all the patient's health information could be portable after being recorded on a magnetic strip affixed to a plastic card. According to Frenzel, "The penetration of electronic information processing into the fabric of human activity will continue unabated into the foreseeable future."[21] However, the electronic patient record that assists in patient care, billing, and so on, is somewhat more challenging to develop than most people envision (see Perspective 9–5).

PERSPECTIVE 9-5
Designing an Automated Patient Record Is More Challenging Than It Appears

First, there is no agreement on what this automated record should be called. Several alternatives are being used: computer-based record, computerized patient record, electronic patient record, or electronic medical record. Next, there is no agreement over what it means. The National Academy of Sciences' Institute of Medicine (IOM) defined the computer-based patient record (CPR) as "an electronic patient record that resides in a system specifically designed to support users by providing accessibility to complete and accurate data, alerts, reminders, clinical decision support systems, links to medical knowledge, and other aids."

Although a number of vendors have electronic patient record software, none of the systems is as sophisticated as that described by IOM. Components of computer-based patient records exist, but only as components. Examples include *Oacis* by Bell Atlantic, *PowerChart* by Cerner Corporation, *Ulticare* by Health Data Sciences, *TDS 7000* by TDS Healthcare Systems Corporation, and *3M HELP Patient Care System* by 3M Corporation.

The technology will become available (predictions are an IOM-type electronic record by the turn of the century), but it will be expensive and, more important, it will require significant changes in the way clinicians process orders and test results and document medical care. The new CPR should not merely automate the existing medical record but emerge as the next generation of records, which are clinically focused and patient centered. A clinically focused record might provide visual summaries of a patient's diagnosis, treatment, and response to treatment over time in just one screen or it could alert one physician to other medications prescribed by a different physician that could cause problems in combination. A record would be patient centered if it contained all the patient's medical history including pertinent information on number of hospital admissions with outcomes, relatives' medical problems, immunization record, allergies, insurance coverage, and so on. Then the patient would not have to repeat this information to the admissions personnel, residents, nurses, and physicians, to name just a few.

PERSPECTIVE 9-5 _cont'd_

Paper records are bulky, sometimes are lost, and have to be maintained after the patient's discharge. In addition, searching paper records for comparative clinical data is very labor intensive. For example, if a physician wanted to know how many patients had allergic reactions to a certain drug, a medical records information specialist would have to search, find, and review the records of patients with the same diagnosis. Next, all charts would have to be read to see which patients were prescribed the drug and which of those patients had an allergic reaction. Ideally an electronic patient record system should be able to accumulate that information in seconds, resulting in vast improvements in treatments and outcomes.

For CPR to flourish three essential tools have to be developed: (1) cost-efficient data entry, (2) standard medical nomenclature, and (3) a medically intelligent computer system that is capable of dealing with narrative-type free text. The patient record includes many pertinent medical facts. Some of the information may be a single word that provides information: single, white, female, 25 years old. Other information is more complex such as "had radical hysterectomy for cervical cancer two years ago, severe back pain for the past week, admitted to determine cause of back pain." If a clinical fact contains modifiers – _radical_ hysterectomy, _severe_ back pain – the system has to be able to distinguish the variation. The system is required to distinguish the more than 144,000 different primary medical terms plus their synonyms and modifiers. Fortunately, physicians are trained to customize their medical terms quite precisely, although they do not necessarily write or dictate in the same way. For example, some physicians might record "dizziness of three days duration," others might record "severe intermittent dizziness," and still others "severe, intermittent dizziness of three days duration." According to Elmer Gabrieli, M.D. and president of Electronic Health Care Records Research, the fact that there are only 144,000 different medical concepts means that medical narrative text is computerizable. Two further challenges that he advocates are important for electronic records: facilitating retrieval of clinical facts and providing compatibility among data banks. Retrieving clinical facts will allow for outcomes studies, both limited (highly specialized as in rare disease or few patients) and extensive (common occurrences or broad based). In addition, compatibility will encourage physicians, hospitals, HMOs, researchers, and others to participate in providing data and making use of those studies. All of this is possible, claims Dr. Gabrieli, if the encoding of medical terms is identical and patient confidentiality is protected. Finally, standardization will be important to provide longitudinal compatibility, comparability, and compression (much information presented in a "tight" format for easy viewing).

Source: Rhonda L. Bergman, "In Pursuit of the Computer-Based Patient Record," _Hospitals and Health Networks_ 67, no. 18 (September 20, 1993), pp. 43–44, 46, 48; and Elmer R. Gabrieli, "Aspects of a Computer-Based Patient Record," _Journal of American Health Information Management Association_ 64, no. 7 (July 1993), pp. 70–82.

Alteration of the Industry An *information highway* is expected to electronically connect all hospitals before the turn of the century. Moynihan and Norman developed a model of the complex myriad of information flows for health care providers (Exhibit 9–3). Although integration of health facilities is occurring rapidly under the predictions of looming health care reform, health care is an $800 billion cottage industry.[22] When more and more health care organizations can access each other or come under one umbrella through the information highway, those outside the system will be at a distinct competitive disadvantage.

Financial Commitment

Purchasing sophisticated computers and telecommunications equipment is a major financial commitment for most organizations. Developing software and training personnel add to the high cost of information systems. Thus, there are long-term consequences to decision making. Management must incorporate information requirements into its vision of the future and consider future needs in current

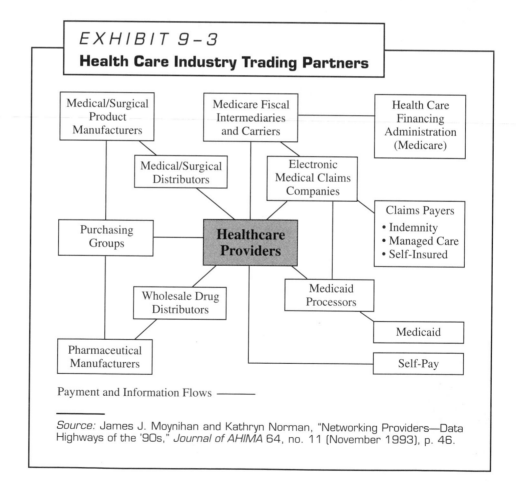

EXHIBIT 9–3
Health Care Industry Trading Partners

Payment and Information Flows ———

Source: James J. Moynihan and Kathryn Norman, "Networking Providers—Data Highways of the '90s," *Journal of AHIMA* 64, no. 11 (November 1993), p. 46.

information technology purchasing. To convert an information system is a monumental, time-consuming, and expensive task; it is far better to prepare for the future. However, because of the rapidly changing technology in the field, the future is extremely difficult to predict.

IMPORTANCE OF PLANNING

Strategic management has at its core planning for the future. This long-term plan is articulated through the mission, vision, and objectives of the organization as discussed in previous chapters. The attainment of many of these objectives will be determined by the quality and efficiency of the information system. Therefore, when organizational planning occurs, information systems planning should be incorporated.

Sprague and McNurlin suggest that the goal for information systems should be "to improve the performance of people in organizations through the use of information technology."[23] Information technology managers would need to keep abreast of changes in technology in the areas of processors, storage devices, telecommunications, operating systems, communications software, programming tools, vendor application software, systems management tools, and others to assess the ways that information technology can improve the performance of people.

Critical success factors (CSFs), a concept developed by John Rockart of the Sloan School of Management at MIT in the late 1970s, define information needs of top managers. "CSFs identify those areas where things must go right; they are the executive's necessary conditions for success."[24] The CSF method can help organizations identify information systems that need to be developed. Rockart identified four major areas to investigate for critical factors: the industry, the organization itself, the environment, and temporal organizational factors (requiring intense attention for a short period of time). He further divided CSFs into either monitoring or building types. Monitoring CSFs keep track of ongoing operations (patient billing, ordering of pharmaceuticals, and so on). Building CSFs are those operations determined by the manager as important to bring about change within the organization.[25]

Critical success factors can be incorporated into the strategic planning process by listing the corporate objectives and identifying factors that are critical for accomplishing the objectives. Then several measures need to be identified for each objective. Hard, factual data is the easiest to identify; the qualitative information such as opinions, perceptions, and hunches is more challenging and requires greater persistence to identify the underlying sources of information.

Information systems planning and organizational systems planning are becoming increasingly linked. However, in some cases, especially where information has a great deal of time value, information systems may *lead* organizational strategy to develop competitive advantage.

Most information systems are developed in a "piecemeal" fashion; add-ons abound. The laboratory and radiology departments, for example, are two areas that developed computer-based information systems early. However, in many hospitals one cannot communicate with (access) the other. The results are problems with inefficiencies, duplication of work, lack of access, and difficulty of use. Because of a focus on crisis-type problem solving, strategic information planning often is pushed aside to attend to the current critical problem of the day. Charles J. Austin, in *Information Systems for Health Services Administration,* advocates a specific planning process for information systems that starts with a review of the organization's mission and major strategic objectives for the next five years. The entire process is outlined in Exhibit 9–4.

INFORMATION TECHNOLOGY STRATEGIC ISSUES

Several strategic issues are driving information technology. First, routine transaction processing is relatively the norm across organizations. Only minimal future gains in cost reduction and speed of processing are possible. "In a sense the playing field has been leveled as far as transaction processing is concerned."[26] Because most of the benefits of routinized transaction processing have been achieved, time and resources will be directed to more innovative uses of information technology. Specifically, there has been greater emphasis on using information technology to accomplish organizational goals and objectives rather than using it to reduce costs.

Information Technology Positions the Organization

Information technology is being used to analyze competition (through such models as that suggested by Michael Porter discussed in Chapter 3) and develop competitive advantage. The belief that information has time value dictates that speed can provide competitive advantage. On-line systems for patient data bases can provide speed of access to many different users plus offer the added benefit of requesting the data from the patient just a single time. Time can be an asset internally as well as externally. Externally, response time to customers, markets, and changing market conditions can be sources of competitive advantage. Internally, time is of value in planning, implementing, and controlling.

Properly conceived information systems can provide enormous advantages to their owners. "Advances in technology shape the products and services of the future and offer opportunity for innovative organizations to increase their value in the stream of economic activity."[27] Information technology is particularly important because of its pervasiveness in the processes leading to advances in most other industries. Advances in information technology have a compounding effect on other technological advances across the spectrum.[28]

Resistance to Information Technology

When increased emphasis is placed on information technology, not all organizational participants are enthusiastic. There is a normal resistance to change and particularly in the art of practicing medicine. Many providers focus on computers detracting from personal relationships in health care delivery rather than the

EXHIBIT 9–4

Strategic Information Systems Planning Process Flowchart

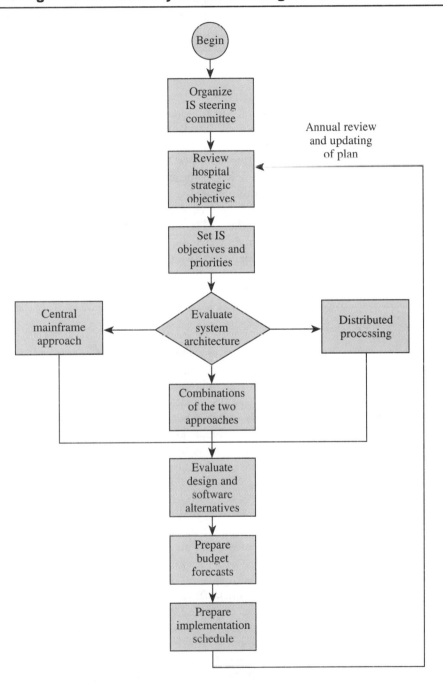

Begin

Organize IS steering committee

Review hospital strategic objectives

Annual review and updating of plan

Set IS objectives and priorities

Evaluate system architecture

Central mainframe approach

Distributed processing

Combinations of the two approaches

Evaluate design and software alternatives

Prepare budget forecasts

Prepare implementation schedule

Source: Charles J. Austin, *Information Systems for Health Services Administration* (Ann Arbor, Michigan: AUPHA Press, 1992), p. 53.

increased speed, accuracy, and convenience that computers can provide in the clinical setting. In addition, many feel that the high costs of increasing information technology may have an impact on the budget in such a way that other areas in the health care organization are denied important allocations.

Financial Implications

Financial considerations are an important strategic issue because although the cost of information technology in terms of speed per function is declining, the total dollar costs of these new systems are increasing. The costs of hardware are declining (if the organization does not continually upgrade in terms of capacity and speed), but the costs of software are increasing. Another cost is associated with recruiting, hiring, training, and retaining skilled personnel for information technology. These professionals extend their knowledge to the data to make information available to others. They use sophisticated equipment that is constantly changing, and as an employment category, they are in demand. The hiring organization needs to understand the needs of this group of people, who are typically working under pressure, to have the opportunity to work on the newest equipment and to be constantly exposed to new technology.

Preserving Privacy of Patient Records

Data security is a particularly important component of the information system for health care organizations. According to consultant Dale Miller, "A primary application of information technology, the computer-based patient record, will be found at the heart of the next generation of health care information systems."[29] With this forecast of increased emphasis on the computer-based patient record and concerns about security for all electronic information, strategic managers should be planning to protect the patient's right to privacy.

An individual's diagnosis and treatment are confidential, and the data should be protected. The *Manual for Accreditation* published by the Joint Commission of Healthcare Organizations has been revised to include a chapter on information management that specifies security requirements. Court decisions in lawsuits have confirmed the patient's right to privacy and have held health care organizations and their managers liable for preserving that privacy.

Passwords and limited access should be implemented and properly used. Information systems professionals cite poor password management, the sharing of passwords among physician/office staff members, unattended but logged-in terminals, improper disposal of printed reports, and similar problems as the major threats to security. However, information systems professionals often do not monitor their own department's violations.

Information technologists are exposed to legal action if they allow unlimited and unrecorded access to patient information by systems managers, network managers, and programmers as they test or back up the system; allow vender access; or have inadequate controls with network connections. "Ideally, no person should be aware of confidential patient information without the knowledge and authorization of the patient. The publicity about patient confidentiality and privacy affords an excellent opportunity for CIOs [chief information officers] to include information security in the strategic plans for systems and networks."[30]

INFORMATION SYSTEMS CONTRIBUTION TO STRATEGIC MANAGEMENT

Information systems managers provide a significant amount of information for strategic management as illustrated in Exhibit 9–5. Although by no means an

---

EXHIBIT 9–5
Strategic Information Systems Input to Strategic Management

Hierarchy of Strategic Decisions	Strategic Information Systems Input
Directional Strategies	
Mission	Identify whether SIS can be a competitive advantage, provide information on customers, services, competition
Vision	Provide information that can empower the vision
Values	Include personal ethic, confidentiality of patient information
Objectives	Participate in developing corporate objectives by providing historical and projected future information; develop strategic information systems objectives to accomplish corporate objectives
Adaptive Strategies	
Expansion	
Diversification – Related	Provide information about current products/services gaps; financial information on ability to acquire; analysis of competitive activity
Diversification – Unrelated	Provide financial information on ability to acquire; analysis of competition and profitability in new area
Vertical Integration – Forward	Provide financial information on ability to take over customers; analysis of competition and profitability
Vertical Integration – Backward	Provide financial information on ability to take over suppliers; analysis of competition and profitability
Market Development	Access to data bases of information on developing markets, underserved markets, and unserved markets; provide information for analysis of competition and profitability

EXHIBIT 9 – 5   cont'd

Hierarchy of Strategic Decisions	Strategic Information Systems Input
Product Development	Provide information on usage of current products; market share; analyze information on competitive offerings and potential profitability of new services
Penetration	Provide information about services that are not meeting objectives and require additional marketing effort and those that are exceeding objectives to capitalize on customer demand
Contraction	
Divestiture	Provide information on services, facilities, equipment, etc. not meeting objectives over time for a divestiture decision; provide information to determine a fair market value
Liquidation	Provide information on services, facilities, equipment, etc. not meeting objectives over time to liquidate; provide information to determine remaining investment
Harvesting	Provide information on services, facilities, equipment, etc. not meeting objectives for eventual phase-out
Retrenchment	Provide information on personnel costs/productivity for determining optimum size of labor force; provide information to assess market profitability for decisions about markets and services to eliminate; provide information for analysis of costs/benefits of facilities, equipment, and other assets
Stabilization	
Enhancement	Provide information on competitive activity; compare with the organization's own results
Status Quo	Provide information on competitive activity; compare with the organization's own results
Market Entry Strategies	
Purchase	Provide information on the organization's ability to purchase; expected future profitability; scan for potential purchases
Cooperation	Provide information on profitability (risk) of cooperating organization(s); determine if there is information system compatibility
Development	Provide information systems specialist to better delineate any information systems needs of the new development

EXHIBIT 9–5 *cont'd*

Hierarchy of Strategic Decisions	Strategic Information Systems Input
Positioning Strategies	
Market-wide	
Cost Leadership	Provide continuous information on market share, competitor costs and prices, and productivity for the market
Differentiation	Provide continuous information on market share, patient satisfaction with current services, consumer preferences, competitive offerings, changing demographics, and so on for the entire market
Market Segment	
Focus – Cost Leadership	Provide continuous information on market share, competitor costs and prices, and productivity for the identified market segment
Focus – Differentiation	Provide continuous information on market share, patient satisfaction with current services, consumer preferences, competitive offerings, changing demographics, and so on for the identified market segment
Operational Strategies	
Functional – Information Systems	Plan, develop, and maintain information systems (hardware, software, telecommunications, EDI) for clinical, administrative, and executive decision support
Organization-wide – Structure	Provide flexibility to organizational structure because availability and use of information systems allows the organization to opt for centralized or decentralized operations (or vice versa) depending on the number of individuals and units involved in decision making
Organization-wide – Facilities and Equipment	Enhance efficiency and productivity of various subsystems within the facility (such as energy, scheduling of housekeeping, maintenance of equipment) by improving monitoring and control
Control	
	Provide the information of "control" that measures performance and compares performance against the objectives; identify areas in need of management attention

exhaustive list of information input to strategic management, it is evident from reading through the exhibit that information permeates the strategic management process. In addition, other implementation strategies are affected by having good information. Specifically, operational strategies in marketing, human resources, and finance benefit from an effective information system. The information specialist has to be able to work with multiple constituencies including the administration, the clinical staff, and the operating departments.

Apart from the input to strategic management, the strategic information system itself is affected by the organization's choice of directional and adaptive strategies.

Expansion Strategies

In most growth situations, the information system should grow as rapidly as the health care organization. Rather than hiring new employees for the information system department, rapid growth is often times addressed by *outsourcing* or by using consultants (especially if the need is perceived to be of short-term duration or an extremely specialized situation). By using outsourcing or consultants, capital is not tied up in computer equipment, freeing the health care organization to invest in facilities and equipment more directly related to patient care.

Outsourcing generally means that an outside organization is hired to be "staff" and is paid by the hour. It can refer to buying or adapting hardware and software or codeveloping a system. Purchasing requires an excellent working knowledge of which vendor's products can meet the organization's needs and perform as stated, and vendor pricing strategies. This can be a time-consuming activity.

Outside consultants, familiar with the health care information systems industry, can save the organization time and money. Estimates are that costs of hospital information systems consultants exceeded $300 million or $50,000 per hospital in 1990.[31] Many health care organizations have purchased systems in the past that did not meet expectations. Consultants can save a health care organization millions of dollars by helping it avoid making a mistake in an information technology purchase. Consultants should be hired when the expertise is not available in-house or the expertise will be needed for a short period of time or the CEO can afford the expertise for only a short period of time. Consultant services include selection and evaluation of information systems, contract negotiations, implementation support, systems testing, documentation, telecommunication/networking, interface support, cost justification, and so on. To gain the best results with consultants Elizabeth Ball suggests: check the references of information system consultants, strive to avoid a learning curve (hire consultants that have had experience doing what needs to be done), agree to estimated due dates and check points, and require weekly status reports.[32] Consulting costs can escalate rather rapidly if not carefully managed.

Contraction Strategies

Downsizing of the information systems area is expected with mergers, alliances, and so on, as considerable duplication exists. In addition, increasingly limited resources affects the information system as it does other areas of the health care organization. Because health care organizations exist to provide care to patients, developing a sophisticated information system when contraction strategies are being implemented detracts time and money away from organization goals. Rather than maintaining information system specialists, outsourcing could be used in contraction strategies because the health care organization pays on an as-needed basis. It does not guarantee that the costs will be less, however.

Stabilization Strategies

Rightsizing is a term that could be applied to stabilization strategies for information systems. If a health care organization decides to pursue a steady course in terms of market share, revenues, and so on, it does not necessarily follow that it should maintain the status quo in terms of information systems. Status quo is not possible without information to know what is going on in the general environment as well as the health care environment.

SUMMARY AND CONCLUSIONS

Strategic information systems are changing health care delivery by providing information for situational analysis and development of competitive advantage. Decision support systems provide information for better clinical decision making as well as improving timeliness and accuracy of administrative information (billing, inventory control, third-party reimbursements, cost data, and so on).

Information systems are a catalyst for change in a health care organization because they assist in quality improvements and reengineering many aspects of delivery of care. Electronic data interchange will occur through the information highway that enables all health care facilities to communicate electronically. This increase in linkages can accelerate efficiencies as the organization quickly and accurately communicates with internal and external constituencies.

Planning for strategic information systems is important because of the rapid changes in information technology, the quantity of information generated and stored in health facilities, the high cost and time commitment to any change in the SIS, and the change it causes in health care delivery — alteration of the service area, alteration at the point of delivery with bedside data entry, and alteration of the industry through the information highway.

SIS affects and interacts with every department in a health care organization. At the same time, it is an independent department similar to others in the organization and has to determine how its operational strategies support the strategic plan. The next chapter discusses implementation strategies for finance.

KEY TERMS AND CONCEPTS IN STRATEGIC MANAGEMENT

decision support system (DSS)

electronic data interchange (EDI)

information highway

information technology

medical informatics

outsourcing

point-of-service (POS) system

strategic information system (SIS)

QUESTIONS FOR CLASS DISCUSSION

1. Explain the impact of decision support systems on provision of direct patient care (clinical decision making).
2. How can a strategic information system (SIS) be used to develop competitive advantage?
3. Explain how SIS is a catalyst for change as it changes.
4. Why is EDI important for vertically integrated health care organizations?
5. Does an information system differ for internal linkages versus external linkages?
6. Explain your plan for an electronic patient record.
7. What changes are information systems bringing to health care?
8. Why is planning for SIS important?
9. Discuss the impact of SIS on the directional, adaptive, and operational strategies of a health care organization.

NOTES

1. Charles J. Austin, *Information Systems for Health Services Administration,* 4th ed (Ann Arbor, Michigan: AUPHA Press, 1992), p. 7.
2. Ibid.
3. Ibid., p. 299.
4. Lynda M. Applegate, Richard O. Mason, and Darryl Thorpe, "Design of a Management Support System for Hospital Strategic Planning," *Journal of Medical Systems* 10 (1986), pp. 82–83.
5. Peter F. Drucker, "The Coming of the New Organization," *Harvard Business Review* (January/February 1988), p. 45.
6. Peter G. Spitzer, "A Comprehensive Framework for I/S Strategic Planning," *Computers in Healthcare,* 14, no. 5 (May 1993), p. 28.
7. David D. Moriarty, "Strategic Information Systems Planning for Health Service Providers," *Health Care Management Review* 17, no. 1 (Winter 1992), p. 85.
8. Homer H. Schmitz, "Decision Support: A Strategic Weapon," in *Healthcare Information Management Systems,* ed. Marion J. Ball, Judith V. Douglas, Robert I.

O'Desky, and James W. Albright (New York: Springer-Verlag, 1991), pp. 42–48.
9. Ibid., p. 47.
10. Ralph H. Sprague, Jr., and Barbara C. McNurlin, *Information Systems in Practice,* 3rd ed. (Englewood Cliffs, New Jersey: Prentice-Hall, 1993), p. 69.
11. Ibid., p. 31.
12. Michael Hammer, "Reengineering Work: Don't Automate, Obliterate," *Harvard Business Review* (July/August 1990), pp. 104–112.
13. Peter G. W. Keen, *Shaping the Future: Business Design Through Information Technology* (Boston: Harvard Business School Press, 1991), p. 111.
14. John Morrissey, "Time to Put Info System in Order?" *Modern Healthcare* 23, no. 47 (November 22, 1993), p. 64.
15. Sprague and McNurlin, *Information Systems in Practice,* pp. 94–96.
16. Elizabeth Gardner, "Hospitals on the Road to Data 'Highways,'" *Modern Healthcare* (June 7, 1993), p. 32.
17. R. A. Greenes and E. H. Shortliffe, "Medical Informatics: An Emerging Academic

Discipline and Institutional Priority," *Journal of the American Medical Association* (February 1990), pp. 1114–1120.

18. Paul J. Kenkel, "Kaiser Planning to Boost Point-of-Service Options," *Modern Healthcare* 23, no. 38 (September 20, 1993), p. 38.

19. Sprague and McNurin, *Information Systems in Practice,* p. 68.

20. "Point-of-Service: Transitional Product or Here to Stay?" *HMO Magazine* (March/April 1993), pp. 49–51.

21. Carroll W. Frenzel, *Management of Information Technology* (Boston: boyd & fraser, 1992), p. 17.

22. James J. Moynihan and Kathryn Norman, "Networking Providers – Data Highways of the '90s," *Journal of AHIMA* 64, no. 11 (November 1993), p. 42.

23. Sprague and McNurin, *Information Systems in Practice,* p. 14.

24. Frenzel, *Management of Information Technology,* p. 27.

25. Ibid.

26. Ibid., p. 41.

27. Ibid., p. 57.

28. Ibid.

29. Dale Miller, "Preserving the Privacy of Computerized Patient Records," *Healthcare Informatics* 10, no. 10 (October 1993), p. 72.

30. Ibid., p. 73.

31. Bill W. Childs, "Consulting: State of the Art," in *Healthcare Information Management Systems,* p. 319.

32. Elizabeth E. Ball, "Maximizing the Benefits of Using Consultants," in ibid., pp. 326–330.

ADDITIONAL READINGS

Abrami, Patrick F., and Janice Jones, *Bringing Computers to the Hospital Bedside: An Emerging Technology* (New York: Springer Publishing Company, 1990). This book provides six case studies of varying degrees of success in using computers at the bedside. It includes a discussion of the types of technology available, the views of health care professionals in using bedside data entry, and a method to document the benefits. Three hospitals using bedside data entry are evaluated using the proposed method to document results.

Austin, Charles J. *Information Systems for Health Services Administration,* 4th ed. (Ann Arbor, Michigan: AUPHA Press, 1992). An excellent resource for managers and students, this book covers the fundamentals of information systems in health care organizations. It is comprehensive and pertinent. Regular revisions (this is the fourth edition), keep the information current.

Ball, Marion, J., Judith V. Douglas, Robert I. O'Desky, and James W. Albright, *Healthcare Management Information Systems* (New York: Springer-Verlag, 1991). This collection of articles on information systems contains some excellent papers for strategic managers. In addition to chapters such as "Decision Support: A Strategic Weapon," "Methods and Models for Planning Strategically," and "Information Systems: A Competitive Advantage for Managing Healthcare," there are two excellent pieces on evaluating and selecting information systems consultants.

DeLuca, Joseph, and Owen Doyle, *Health Care Information Systems: An Executive's Guide for Successful Management* (Chicago: AHA Publishing, 1991). This book addresses the needs of administrators and senior managers who have no technical background but who have responsibilities for planning, implementing, and managing computer technology.

Ferrand, Dominique J., Michel Chokron, and Colin M. Lay, "An Integrated Analytic Framework for Evaluation of Hospital Information Systems Planning," *Medical Care Review* 50, no. 3 (Fall 1993), pp. 327–366. Ferrand and her colleagues provide a very different way for hospitals to evaluate their information systems planning. Most work on the topic has been functionalist based or politically based. They advocate a system that measures *outputs* and whether they help or hinder users (stakeholders) of the information generated.

CHAPTER 10

Strategic Financial Systems

"The emerging health care debate, it seems clear, will force Americans to confront basic questions of life, death, and economics in a way they rarely have before."
— *Erik Eckholm*

LEARNING OBJECTIVES

After completing this chapter you should:

1. Understand the relationship between overall strategic plans and strategic financial planning.
2. Be able to discuss the strategic financial implications of adaptive strategies relating to expansion, and stabilization.
3. Be able to discuss the necessity to finance the market entry strategies associated with expansion and stabilization.
4. Understand the advantages and disadvantages associated with different methods of financing market entry strategies.
5. Be able to evaluate the effectiveness of different methods of implementing financial strategies.
6. Appreciate the importance of integrating financial strategies into the strategic management process.

INTRODUCTORY INCIDENT

Venturing into Related Health Services

Sutter Surgery Centers in Sacramento, California, wanted to combine the "very best elements" of its expertise in outpatient surgery and the expertise of EJ Financial Enterprises in home infusion and home-care services. To do this, the two companies decided to pool $20 million to finance the startup of a new company that will offer all these services. Sutter Surgery Centers will own and operate four surgery centers (three in California and one in Arizona) and will continue to operate four Sacramento-area surgery centers through a subsidiary, Sutter Ambulatory Care Corporation. EJ Financial Enterprises will own 51 percent of the venture, which is projected to earn $30 million this year.

Sutter has also acquired the Visiting Nurses Association of Sacramento, which operates skilled-nursing and retirement facilities in Northern California. All of these moves are part of a "rapid expansion plan" designed to establish an integrated health care delivery system. These acquisitions will accomplish a number of goals including the extension of Sutter's geographical reach throughout Northern California and parts of Arizona. The joint venture is a means of providing the capital necessary to accomplish the expansion strategy.

Source: Della de Lafuente, "Sutter Joint Venture Envisions Integrated Care," *Modern Healthcare* 23, no. 5 (February 1, 1993), p. 14.

Sutter Health is an example of an organization that is attempting to engage in a rapid expansion strategy through the acquisition of related services. This outpatient surgical center, on its own, might have difficulty obtaining the capital it needs to acquire home infusion and skilled-nursing services without a joint venture with another company. EJ Financial Enterprises of Chicago agreed that Sutter's expansion plans represented an opportunity, and a cooperative enterprise was developed.

This chapter is about strategic financial management in health care organizations. More specifically, it is about the strategic financial implications of the overall strategic management process. It will not deal with broader issues of national or public policy aspects of health care financing. Although it is true that the way health care services are financed greatly influences decision making, this is basically a public policy issue and beyond the scope of this text.

The concern here begins at another level in the overall model that has been followed throughout this book. As illustrated in Exhibit 10–1, the focus of this chapter is on financial considerations at the level of strategic implementation. Although only one part of the strategic plan, it is an important element. The financial function is an aid to the overall strategic plan rather than its driving force. Without adequate financial planning, the organization's strategic plan has little practical meaning. At the same time, strategic thinking should not be limited by finances alone. To do so would unnecessarily limit the vision of creative health care managers.

Overall strategic decisions are influenced by the quality and quantity of financial resources. In this chapter we will investigate the strategic management of financial resources. Appendix B provides some additional details on specific aspects of financial analysis.

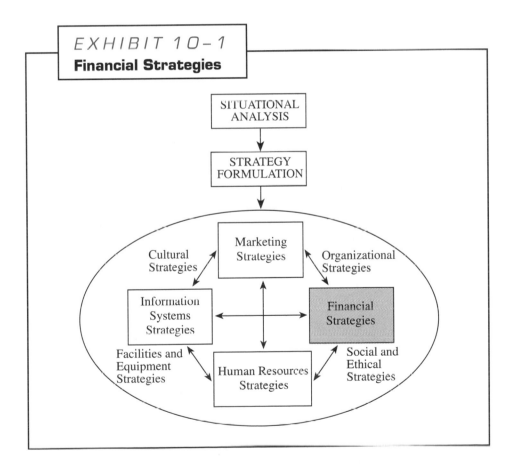

EXHIBIT 10–1
Financial Strategies

- SITUATIONAL ANALYSIS
- STRATEGY FORMULATION
- Cultural Strategies
- Marketing Strategies
- Organizational Strategies
- Information Systems Strategies
- Financial Strategies
- Facilities and Equipment Strategies
- Human Resources Strategies
- Social and Ethical Strategies

INTEGRATING STRATEGIC PLANNING AND FINANCIAL PLANNING

Financial planning is important for all health care organizations. Because a large part of what an organization hopes to accomplish with sound strategic management is to "propel the organization from the present to a predetermined desired future," there must be some idea as to whether the financial resources are capable of taking the organization where it wants to go.[1] *Strategic financial planning* is a type of reality check, because without it there is no way of knowing if the goals are even feasible.[2]

Strategic Planning and Financial Planning Linkages

The financial strategies of an organization should contribute to the accomplishment of its directional strategies. They should be consistent with the mission and values and support the vision. Financial plans should fit logically into the clearly defined pattern of strategic decisions.

It is important that all aspects of financial planning maintain a consistent and logical relationship with the strategic plan. Exhibit 10–2 illustrates a *continuum of refinement* that demonstrates this type of relationship. This continuum highlights the proper relationship that should exist between strategic financial planning and budgeting.[3]

Note that the first two stages of the process relate specifically to strategic concerns. This avoids the conflict that frequently develops in financial planning between strategic planners, who correctly see budgets as being driven by the organization's overall strategic plan and the strategic financial plan, and budgetary

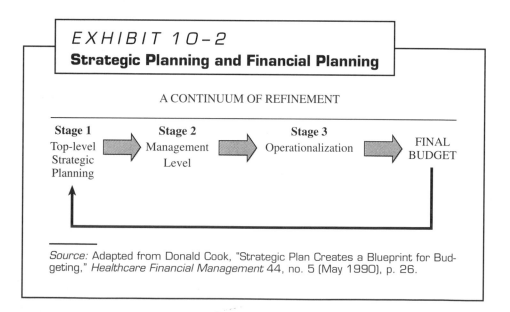

EXHIBIT 10–2
Strategic Planning and Financial Planning

A CONTINUUM OF REFINEMENT

Stage 1 → **Stage 2** → **Stage 3** → FINAL BUDGET
Top-level Strategic Planning   Management Level   Operationalization

Source: Adapted from Donald Cook, "Strategic Plan Creates a Blueprint for Budgeting," *Healthcare Financial Management* 44, no. 5 (May 1990), p. 26.

planners, who see strategic plans as being driven by unit and departmental budgets. In this continuum of refinement, it is not until Stage 3 that the budget becomes operationalized or is converted into the familiar revenue and cost projections that represent the output of the *budgetary financial planning* process.

This method focuses on the strategic plan and has the advantage of being more efficient, because lower-level managers who are responsible for developing specific budgetary requests gain the benefit of knowing how the budget relates to the total strategic plan. Budgeting then becomes a refining process for the overall plan rather than a compilation of isolated decisions provided by each department. The individuals actually making department-level decisions see how their choices relate to overall financial strategies and the strategic plan.

Strategic Financial Planning

There are several important steps in successful strategic financial planning:[4]

1. Establish specific financial performance objectives that are directly linked to the directional strategies of the organization.
2. Compare the return and cost of strategic alternatives to assist in determining overall priorities.
3. Evaluate the costs of different financing options.
4. Assess the financial impact of alternative pricing and marketing strategies.
5. Provide comparative financial data for capital investment alternatives, and present alternatives in a way that is useful for decision-making purposes.

This brief list demonstrates that the role of strategic financial planning is to assist in the accomplishment of directional strategies by providing accurate analyses and evaluations of the financial implications of alternative strategic options.

Although financial considerations can be one of the primary elements of strategic performance, they should not be allowed to reduce the organization's vision.[5] At times, the hostile financial environment facing health care organizations appears overwhelming. Insurance companies set their own reimbursement schedules and refuse to pay full charges, capital markets are in disarray causing interest-rate projections to be virtually impossible, and private donors are reluctant to pledge support for deserving projects. Perspective 10–1 provides an illustration of the importance of doing the right thing strategically even though the financial implications are not entirely certain.

No one would debate the truth of all these uncertainties and more. However, the vision of a health care organization is, as noted in Chapter 5, a hope of what the organization will and should be at some time in the future. Strategic managers should not allow financial considerations to make them so timid that they fail to strive for the full potential of the organization.

For an example, consider the need to carefully integrate, not just strategic, operational, and budgetary financial planning but also the strategic, operational, and budgetary plans of different health care providers in a single health network. The affiliation of Christian Health Services, Barnes Hospital, and Jewish Hospital in St. Louis was initiated to consolidate services and planning while allowing the three

---

PERSPECTIVE 10–1
Reasons for Transforming Hospitals Go Beyond Financials

Advocates of patient-centered care believe it will be cost effective but at the same time they stress that the reasons for moving hospitals in this direction go beyond financial considerations. They believe it is strategically the right thing to do. The president of Mid-Columbia Medical Center in Oregon stated that they moved to patient-centered care because "it is the correct way to treat patients." The executive director of the Vanderbilt University Hospital and Clinic in Nashville, Tennessee, stated that they were convinced the "traditional hospital structure was not working" so that moving in the direction of patient-centered care was the right direction.

A survey by *Hospitals* found that 42 percent of the hospitals implementing patient-centered care were uncertain about its financial impact. Because startup costs are significant, it is not surprising that many of the hospitals moving toward patient-centered care are financially healthy institutions. Only 7 percent of the respondents estimated that patient-centered care would cost them less than $50,000, and 26 percent thought it would cost more than $1 million. Almost 60 percent expected savings to be primarily in the area of labor costs, 51 percent thought it would come through combining departments, and 23 percent expected to obtain savings by eliminating departments. All indicated that changes of this nature will be difficult but will ultimately prove to be a sound strategy.

Source: H. J. Anderson, "New Planning Models: Reasons for Transforming Hospital Go Beyond Financials," *Hospitals* (February 5, 1993), pp. 20–22.

---

involved organizations to maintain separate identities. As with other affiliations, however, the extent to which this structure is successful will depend to a great degree on how the organizations can integrate their strategic and financial planning to most effectively deploy and allocate the resources at their disposal.[6]

An Integrative View

One way to illustrate the integration of strategic planning and financial planning is with the aid of Exhibit 10–3. Numerous long-term consequences are involved when an organization provides the health services called for in its mission. As hospitals, long-term-care facilities, physicians' practices, and so on, provide services for patients, facilities depreciate, technologies evolve and need updating, and fund balances accumulate or become depleted. The result is that organizations need to grow, diversify, vertically integrate, modernize facilities, and expand. Alternatively, some organizations will be faced with contraction, divestiture, and even liquidation.

All of these long-term consequences create the need for long-term, strategic, financial decisions. New financial resources will be required under some circum-

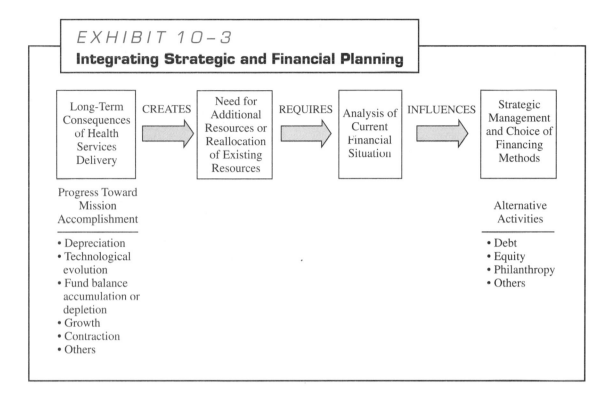

EXHIBIT 10-3
Integrating Strategic and Financial Planning

Long-Term Consequences of Health Services Delivery — CREATES → Need for Additional Resources or Reallocation of Existing Resources — REQUIRES → Analysis of Current Financial Situation — INFLUENCES → Strategic Management and Choice of Financing Methods

Progress Toward Mission Accomplishment

- Depreciation
- Technological evolution
- Fund balance accumulation or depletion
- Growth
- Contraction
- Others

Alternative Activities

- Debt
- Equity
- Philanthropy
- Others

stances and correction of resource misallocations will be required under others. It is not unusual for strategic decision makers to be faced with the tasks of obtaining new financial resources and reallocating existing resources at the same time. This is particularly true in view of the fact that financing alternatives are greatly influenced by the external factors taking place in the economic environment.

Historically, for example, strategic financial decision makers have made capital budgeting decisions assuming the continuation of the specialty-driven, hospital-based model. Under this assumption, major sources of revenue result from income from operations, depreciation, acquisition of debt, and philanthropy. As an interesting exercise consider the issues that could emerge when different scenarios of health care delivery are examined from the perspective of their financial impact. For example, what would the mix of revenue sources be assuming only three simple financing arrangements such as fee for service, contracting, and capitation rates?[7] The relationship between adaptive strategies and the financial strategies to accomplish them will form the basis for the remainder of this discussion.

A FRAMEWORK FOR FINANCING STRATEGIC DECISIONS

To accomplish the adaptive strategies of expansion, contraction, or stabilization a variety of strategic financial actions can be considered as illustrated in Exhibit 10–4. For example, expansion through diversification, vertical integration, market

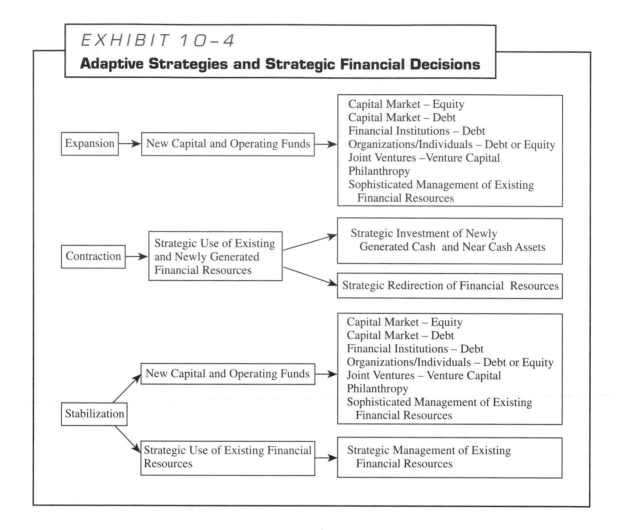

EXHIBIT 10-4
Adaptive Strategies and Strategic Financial Decisions

development, or product development can be accomplished by acquiring, merging, or entering into cooperative alliances or joint ventures with other organizations or individuals. The primary financial strategies required to support these decisions involve the acquisition of new capital and operating funds. A survey of 290 hospital chief financial officers revealed that the most commonly identified sources of funding for capital projects were cash reserves, tax-exempt bond issues, equipment leasing, and bank or other financial institution loans. The most frequently financed projects were renovations, acute-care facilities, medical office buildings, and outpatient centers (see Exhibit 10–5).

Stabilization strategies directed toward enhancement of facilities, equipment, quality of services, and so on will often require new capital and operating funds. For example, an organization may have to acquire new property and relocate in its efforts to change the image held by physicians who might join its staff and

EXHIBIT 10-5

Sources of Financing and Projects Financed

Projected Funding Sources	Percentage of Respondents	Projected Projects to Be Financed	Percentage of Respondents
Cash Reserves	56.9	Renovations	44.5
Tax-Exempt Bonds	23.1	Acute Care Facility	20.7
Equipment Leasing	13.8	Other	16.6
Bank/Institutional Loan	11.7	Medical Office Building	14.1
Other	4.5	Outpatient Center	12.4
Equipment Rental	2.4	Parking Facility	9.7
Private Equity Placement	1.0	Diagnostic Imaging Center	8.6
Taxable Bond Issue	1.0	Long-Term-Care Facility	5.2
Private Debt Placement	1.0	Rehabilitation Facility	3.8

Source: Survey results reported in "Hospitals Exhibit Caution in Spending," *Health Systems Review* 26 (January/February 1993), pp. 32–34.

the patients who might use its facilities. New technology may be demanded as well for this change in image or for significant improvement of services. Therefore, expansion and stabilization frequently make it necessary for health care organizations to enter the capital market or make arrangements to borrow money from one or more financial institutions. Joint ventures are often financed by attracting other individuals such as physicians to invest in promising ideas or equipment along with the hospital. Organizations with sufficient financial resources may even act as venture capitalists for promising new ideas.

Another avenue of funding available to many health care organizations is private philanthropy. Organizations with long histories of service to a particular area or ones that are particularly well known for their good works can, and frequently do, attract gifts from individuals who wish to be a part of the organization's future. Sometimes these gifts are restricted and must be used for specific purposes; although many times the gifts can be used at the discretion of the organization.

Contraction strategies require equally challenging financial decision making. Divestiture, liquidation, and harvesting converts financial resources, at least temporarily, into cash or near cash assets. This forces the decision maker to consider alternative uses of the funds and ensure that the funds are appropriately invested until they are needed for other uses. Contraction requires careful reevaluation and possible redirection of the use of financial resources. For example, a hospital experiencing financial distress, after careful analysis, might decide that its emergency room is too expensive to continue to operate in view of limited demand by the community. The high level of specialized staffing for around the clock operations is a financial burden that cannot be justified economically. The decision to close the emergency room would temporarily free financial resources that could be allocated to more profitable areas and relieve some of the pressure on the hospital.

Because it is a moving target, stabilization strategies directed toward maintaining the status quo may require additional capital. Stabilization demands that health care managers effectively and efficiently use existing and newly generated financial resources. In view of all these factors, a series of financial issues will be discussed in terms of their relationship to adaptive and market entry strategies. These factors are:

- capital acquisition – equity and debt,
- other forms of debt acquisition,
- fund raising and philanthropy, and
- effective investment and management of financial resources.

Capital Acquisition – Equity and Debt

There are two major reasons why capital investments are significant financial challenges. First, they involve large sums of money. Second, they relate to long time periods. The larger sums cause greater exposure to financial risks, and the longer time period commits management to actions that are not easily altered.[8]

Capital investments are extremely important to health care organizations because the industry is so "capital intense." State-of-the-art medical equipment is essential to the delivery of quality medical care, and this type of equipment is very expensive. The inability or unwillingness of a hospital to obtain the most advanced technology can result in a loss of medical staff, patients, reputation, and ultimately, market share.[9]

One alarming trend is that since 1980 the capital/expense ratio (the ratio of capital expenses to all expenses) has increased for hospitals. Several factors account for this increase including lower occupancy rates that have reduced operating expenses but not capital expenses, new capital investments for outpatient care at the expense of the more traditional inpatient aspect of the hospital business, and the age of many physical plants that require greater investment in capital improvements.[10] In 1993, capital expenses for acute-care community hospitals accounted for 8.4 percent of all expenses. Although this was significantly below the 55 percent accounted for by labor and benefits costs, capital expenditures represented the single largest nonlabor related expense.[11]

The risks associated with capital investments have resulted in caution with regard to large and long-term expenditures. Surveys of hospital chief financial officers (CFOs) indicated that, although most saw the capital markets improving, they were extremely cautious in terms of their plans to increase capital financing. More than half of the CFOs indicated that their hospitals planned increases in expenditures for equipment during 1993; however, the number planning such expenditures was significantly below the number planning to make such expenditures in 1992. The same was true relative to acquisition of property.[12]

All of these examples illustrate that the ability of a health care organization to effectively manage its capital investments is an important strategic strength. Management of capital investments requires an understanding of such specific techniques as the time value of money and the benefits of collecting income streams as soon as possible to take advantage of reinvestment opportunities. In addition, it requires the ability to use suitable financial management concepts, such as discounted cash flows and other techniques that are necessary to evaluate long-term capital projects.

Acquiring Equity Funds In the health care industry, *equity funding* comes from several sources. Financing mergers, acquisitions, and other market entry strategies may require that private health care organizations issue new stock or pursue increased investment from existing owners. If a health care organization is closely held, it may be built with personal investments from physicians and other interested investors who see an opportunity for a good return on their money. If it is a larger facility, it may have the ability to raise its funds by *going public* and offering equity (shares of stock) to investors throughout the region or nation. In many cases, joint ventures between a health care organization and physicians or other firms represent equity investments. Equity funding may also be obtained through the reinvestment of profits.

The attractiveness of issuing new stock to finance expansion, however, depends to a great extent on how well health care stocks are performing relative to other stocks and related investments. Perspective 10–2 compares the performance of a sample of health care stocks with the Dow Jones Industrial Average and the Standard & Poor's 500 for one month and one year time periods. During this particular time, health care stocks performed significantly worse than either the Dow Jones Average or the Standard & Poor 500. This, however, has not always been the case.

As in any industry, some areas of health care may perform well while other areas perform poorly. One analysis looked at the performance of different health care stocks during 1992. The results were interesting. The price of for-profit hospital stocks dropped approximately 6 percent from 1991 values whereas the price of managed-care stocks increased more than 60 percent during the same period. Long-term-care facility stocks increased slightly over 30 percent but outpatient service stocks dropped 33 percent. Price differences were attributed to the uncertainty created by discussions of health care reform and how such reform might affect various segments of the health care industry.[13] Even more impressive was the fact that seven of the ten top performing health care stocks during 1992 were HMOs. The HMOs among the top twenty overall performing health care stocks obtained price increases averaging 86 percent.[14]

If top management decides to pursue equity funding from the public, it is necessary to weigh some important advantages and disadvantages. Some of the more important pros and cons of going public are presented in Exhibit 10–6.

By going public, it is possible that equity capital can be raised at stock prices that are high multiples of earnings, resulting in large amounts of capital in exchange for relatively few shares of stock. The fewer the number of shares

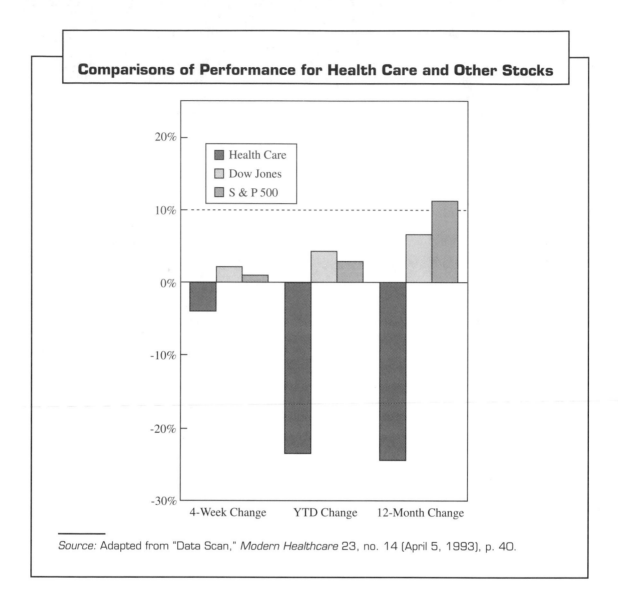

Comparisons of Performance for Health Care and Other Stocks

Legend:
- ■ Health Care
- □ Dow Jones
- ■ S & P 500

Categories: 4-Week Change, YTD Change, 12-Month Change

Source: Adapted from "Data Scan," *Modern Healthcare* 23, no. 14 (April 5, 1993), p. 40.

translates into less dilution of the original investors' ownership. However, this apparently low cost of equity financing can be deceptive. Underwriting costs are usually high, and the clerical costs of providing proper documentation as well as the loss of control by the present owners can be costly. This option is chosen, however, for reasons other than cost. Successfully going public usually makes it easier to raise equity capital in the future. Moreover, the improved equity position enables the organization to obtain additional debt funding based on the increased owners' equity.

EXHIBIT 10-6

Advantages and Disadvantages of Going Public

Advantages	Disadvantages
• Raises capital at lower cost. • Keeps control in hands of insiders if they purchase additional shares. • Maintains leveraging potential. • Increases ability to obtain more equity. • Retains shareholders' liquidity. • Makes acquisition easy.	• Makes disclosure of information necessary. • Dilutes insiders' control. • Costs to underwrite. • Reduces original investors' percentage of ownership. • Lessens ownership control in decision making. • Increases taxes.

Source: Adapted from G. B. Shields and G. C. McKann, "Raising Health Care Capital Through the Public Equity Markets," *Topics in Health Care Financing* 12, no. 3 (Spring 1986), pp. 38–40.

Acquiring Debt When funds are needed for expansion strategies, it is possible to reach the capital market through *debt financing*. Long-term debt in the form of tax-exempt health care bonds increased significantly in 1993 primarily because of low interest rates. Health care bond volume in the second quarter of 1993 was almost $9 billion or 62 percent above the same period in 1992. In the third quarter of 1993, New York City Health and Hospital Corporation issued $550 million in tax-exempt bonds, Grady Memorial Hospital in Atlanta issued $336 million, and at least three other health care organizations issued bonds worth approximately $200 million each.[15] Long-term debt in the form of tax-exempt bonds has been the largest single source of capital funds for hospitals over the past two decades. To qualify for the federal tax exemption, bonds are issued by a state or local authority and the health care facility leases the financed assets from the authority, which holds the title until the indebtedness is repaid.[16]

In the third quarter of 1993, 176 health care bond issues were sold for a total of $6.77 billion or an increase of a little over 35 percent from the previous year.[17] Fixed-rate bonds were the most popular form of debt financing because of the extremely favorable interest rates. The favorable interest rates were not only the result of conditions in the capital markets but also were directly related to the financial condition of the organization seeking the funds. In the latter case, it has been difficult for health care organizations to acquire extremely high ratings from agencies such as Standard & Poor's Corporation. For example, in 1992, the median profit margin of not-for-profit hospitals acquiring an A rating on proposed bond issues was 6.2 percent compared to only 5.1 percent in 1989. Overall, health care finance experts observed that, to obtain the high bond ratings, stronger financial performance was needed to offset the increasing uncertainty

PERSPECTIVE 10-3
Upgrades and Downgrades for Hospital Bonds

Late in 1993, four tax-exempt hospital bonds valued at over $279 million were upgraded by Moody's Investor Services. Some of the most important were OSF Healthcare Systems in Illinois (from A to A1), Michigan Health Care Corporation (from B to B1), St. Catherine Hospital in Kansas (from Ba1 to Baa), and Foote Memorial Hospital in Minnesota (from A to A1). This was the third time in the past four quarters that Moody's upgrades exceeded its downgrades. According to Moody's officials, there was a belief in the company that the health care industry had stabilized to an extent necessary to justify the upgrades. This was a great contrast to the past several years when downgrades outnumbered upgrades.

The collapse of the New Jersey hospital-reimbursement system in 1992 caused Standard & Poor's to downgrade nine hospital bond issues in that state alone affecting $350 million in debt during the second quarter. However, Standard & Poor's upgrades during the third quarter outpaced downgrades by a margin of 8 to 5. Standard & Poor's upgraded sixteen issues totaling $400 million and downgraded ten issues totalling $300 million. The majority of the downgrades were small hospitals in highly competitive markets that experienced drops in admissions and consequently financial performance. Despite favorable recent experiences, experts predict that downgrades may be even more common in the future as reimbursement and competitive pressures increase.

Source: "Moody's Upgrades Six Hospital Bonds; Eleven Standard & Poor's Ratings Up, Forty-Six Down," *AHA News* (April 19, 1993), p. 3; "Hospital-Bond Upgrades Outpace Downgrades in 3rd Quarter," *AHA News* (October 18, 1993), p. 3.

in the industry.[18] Perspective 10–3 illustrates that despite the increasing uncertainty in the health care environment, many hospitals have actually been able to upgrade the ratings of their bonds.

In the case of long-term debt, whether in the form of tax-exempt bonds, FHA-insured or conventional mortgages, or public taxable bonds, it is important to consider several issues before committing to this form of financing. The cost of long-term debt is determined by the coupon rate or the amount that must be paid to borrow the necessary money. In addition, costs are involved in issuing the debt. If the debt is privately held by a relatively few investors, the costs can be greatly reduced. However, if the bond issue is made to the public, certificates must be printed, information must be supplied to regulating authorities, the underwriters' spread must be paid, and sometimes reserve funds in the form of an escrow account must be maintained to minimize the public's risk.

Risk is an important consideration. To a great extent, the coupon or interest rate that must be paid reflects the perceived risk by the investors. However, the organization that issues the long-term debt must consider the risks as well. If debt is issued at a time when interest rates are very high, it may be desirable to build in a "call feature" whereby the debt can be refinanced when interest rates are lower. Despite a prepayment fee being charged, it may be beneficial to call in the debt if interest rates drop significantly.

Another aspect of risk is the ability of the organization to service the debt. If revenues are not available to pay the interest in a timely manner and retire the debt, closure is possible. For example, Standard & Poor's lowered the bond rating of the Eden Hospital Medical Center in California because of a rapid decline in the hospital's admissions, its erratic financial performance, and limited flexibility. The 234-bed hospital was adversely affected by Kaiser Permanente's increased penetration into its historical market. Between 1987 and 1993, the hospital reported over $2 million in operating losses, and the prospects for reducing expenses were not encouraging. The hospital was highly leveraged with a 67 percent debt-to-capitalization ratio. With the prospects for difficulty in debt servicing, the bond rating was reduced.[19]

In deciding whether to use long-term debt, strategic managers are favorably influenced by the fact that control over operations and decision making can be maintained better than with equity financing. Although it is true that creditors can require restrictive covenants that reduce flexibility and control, the organization's ability to obtain financing for a promised return without having to broaden participation in decision making is attractive.

Other Forms of Debt Acquisition

Health care organizations may prefer to deal with a single financial institution rather than numerous individuals and underwriters in the capital market. In such a case, funds can be obtained from banks or other financial institutions. Alternatively, *private offerings* may be placed that can provide funds faster and with fewer regulatory requirements than public offerings.

Regency Health Services, a skilled nursing facility chain, offered $50 million of convertible subordinated debentures to retire slightly over $8 million in debt and used the remainder to establish additional subacute-care units and expand its pharmacy operations. The plan was to place the debt privately and allow the debentures that were due to mature in 2003 to be converted to Regency common stock.[20]

National Medical Funding Corporation raised $100 million in a private placement of health care receivables-based securities with Prudential Insurance Company of America. This is National Medical Funding's largest single health care receivables-backed transaction to date. The money is expected to be used to provide working capital for acute-care hospitals, psychiatric facilities, nursing homes, large clinics, and other health care providers.[21]

Other interesting and promising financing arrangements are being developed in a effort to offset the increased competition, pressure on profit margins, and related difficulties faced by companies that supply the goods and services needed by health care organizations. Manufacturers of imaging equipment have abandoned using one or a relatively few standard financing packages in an effort to maintain the viability of the market. Some have added to their finance staffs and charged them to work with hospital strategic planners to create customized financing programs.[22] This creates many possibilities that could aid in the financing of high technology medical equipment.

These examples, although not exhaustive, illustrate some of the sources health care organizations have used to obtain capital and operating funds. The attractiveness of debt financing, of course, is influenced primarily by interest rates. Because rates have been at all time lows during the early 1990s, debt financing has been particularly appealing.

Fund Raising and Philanthropy

During a time when capital markets are uncertain, when there is public resistance to tax increases (some of which might eventually assist health care organizations), and when a host of other problems complicate long-term financing, *philanthropy* is being "rediscovered" and pursued seriously by many health care organizations. Because of the need for earnings, the cost of public offerings, and the desire of many health care organizations to retain their tax-exempt status, private philanthropy has become more important as a source of funds in health care. In 1992, health-related not-for-profit organizations received over $10 billion in charitable contributions. Exhibit 10–7 illustrates how charitable contributions were distributed in 1992.

During 1992, donations to hospitals increased approximately 6.3 percent to about $1.89 billion. Although equal to the 1990 level, it was below the $1.99 billion received in 1989. Donations to health care taken as a whole increased approximately 5.79 percent over 1991. Overall, giving was up by 6.41 percent with donations to environmental causes increasing more than any other single area. Perhaps the most interesting, yet disturbing, trend is that, although giving by individuals, foundations, and bequests all increased, corporate giving during 1992 actually dropped by almost 4 percent.[23]

These trends, taken in the larger context of changing tax laws, suggest an increasingly difficult, complex, and competitive environment for corporate donations to health care in the future. On one hand, there is a positive trend – since 1989 corporations have increased their giving to health and human services. In 1989, this accounted for only 29.9 percent of corporate gifts; in 1992, the percentage had increased to 31.3 percent. However, education accomplished more, moving its percentage from 38.2 percent to 42 percent.[24] The disturbing point, however, is the projections made by corporations regarding the future of their giving in light of expected tax changes. For example, one survey indicated that although approximately 42 percent of the corporate respondents thought the tax law changes would increase their giving, the remaining respondents forecasted either some or significant decreases in their donations to all causes.[25]

Private individual, corporate, and foundation gifts will remain an important source of funds for health care organizations. As with many other areas of activity, fund raising is more competitive than ever. Educational, religious, and environmental organizations are actively seeking and acquiring funds. In the future, hospitals and other health care organizations will be pressured to become even more aggressive and innovative just to maintain their historical share of available gifts.

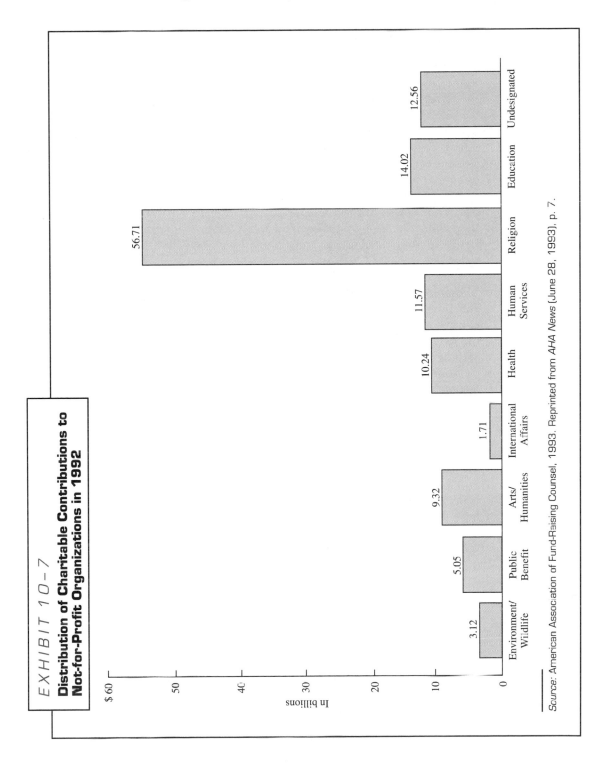

EXHIBIT 10-7

Distribution of Charitable Contributions to Not-for-Profit Organizations in 1992

Source: American Association of Fund-Raising Counsel, 1993. Reprinted from *AHA News* (June 28, 1993), p. 7.

Effective Management of Financial Resources and Investment

Prior to pursuing the acquisition of new capital and operating funds, a careful examination of the utilization of existing financial resources should be conducted. Moreover, some strategic alternatives might actually be able to be funded through the better utilization of existing financial resources. For example, if the leadership of a hospital determines that enhancing quality demands significant increases in training expenditures, the funds for training might be acquired by reducing the amount in the cash account, more carefully managing and reducing inventories, or similar actions.

Some decisions may actually provide organizations with excess cash and near cash assets, at least temporarily. Divesting of parts of an organization or liquidating major pieces of equipment will provide financial resources that must be carefully invested to ensure the highest possible returns or reallocated in some systematic manner.

Managing Financial Resources   Health care organizations constantly face financial problems and the need to develop innovative ways to increase revenues, control costs, and thus increase profitability. Even in not-for-profit organizations, the extent to which income exceeds costs is an important measure of financial viability.

Although not-for-profit organizations do not make profits as such, they do attempt to generate a surplus of revenues over expenses and thereby develop a fund balance or, at the very least, make enough income to cover costs. Not-for-profit health care organizations may not be as focused on the bottom line as for-profit organizations but cost containment and revenue generation remain important and often critical issues. Therefore, all types of health care managers must carefully evaluate how effectively revenue-earning assets are used.[26]

In fact, much of strategic financial management relates to what is sometimes called the *financial management paradox*. This dilemma is derived from the fact that, in the management of financial resources, decision makers are forced to choose between two appealing outcomes: liquidity or profitability (excess of income over expenses). The great challenge for financial managers is to balance the organization's need to pay bills when due (liquidity) and the need to keep assets earning additional funds (profitability).

Liquidity relates to the speed and convenience with which noncash assets can be converted into cash. If the hospital's accounts receivable are current (no more than thirty days old), there is a high likelihood that they will be collected. Thus, they are considered to be very liquid because they can be converted quickly into cash. The older the accounts are, the less likely collection will occur, and therefore the less liquid are the assets. Perspective 10–4 provides some information on the trend in hospital receivables.

The most liquid asset is cash. However, holding cash in the hospital safe or in a checking account at the local bank further illustrates the financial management dilemma. If the health care organization holds the cash in the safe, it earns no interest and is not profitable. Managers could put the cash into a savings account,

Accounts receivables can be a serious problem for hospitals and adversely affect the balance between liquidity and profitability. If hospitals finance excessively high levels of receivables, funds are tied up that might produce greater returns in alternative opportunities. At the end of 1992, it took hospitals about seventy-one days to collect payments, down from almost seventy-five days in 1991.

Uncollectables dropped as well. At the beginning of 1992, uncollectables had showed steady increases but the trend was reversed at the end of the year. In the fourth quarter, uncollectables dropped to 5.2 percent of gross revenues compared to over 6 percent earlier in the year. A corresponding reduction in receivables that took ninety days or longer to collect occurred.

Earlier in the year, 29.5 percent of the receivables took ninety days or longer to collect but by year end it dropped to 27.8 percent.

Industry observers believed these trends were accounted for by a tougher financial environment that made the management of working capital assets more essential. Regardless of the financial environment, the result is that increasing collections makes funds available for alternative, and perhaps more profitable, uses.

Source: Judith Nemes, "Receivables Due Continue to Decline," *Modern Healthcare* 23, no. 5 (February 1, 1993), p. 8; and "Amount of Hospital Uncollectables Decline Slightly," *AHA News* (February 1, 1993), p. 3.

use it to build more inventory, or purchase a specialized piece of medical equipment. Although these actions have the potential to generate profits, they also place cash assets into a less-convertible (less-liquid) state.

In not-for-profit organizations, the need for liquidity is as important as it is in any for-profit organization. Salaries must be paid at the end of each week and vendors demand payment for supplies placed in inventories within thirty days in not-for-profit as well as for-profit settings. Therefore, although the not-for-profit health care organization does not specifically have the bottom-line profit figure to direct decision making, it must get the best return it can on its reserves and resources to accumulate funds to replace equipment, purchase new technologies, and so on.

In view of this everpresent conflict, paradox, or dilemma, the financial manager is required to constantly weigh the advantages and disadvantages of actions based on the impact each will have on liquidity and profitability. Although no attempt will be made to examine the details of assessing the financial management of a health care organization, the following section attempts to provide more insight into this challenging area.

Information concerning key indicators of financial strength and weakness must be obtained and used in decision making. In analyzing key indicators, it is important to look at two types of measures. The first relates to how the organization compares with other similar organizations in the same industry. The second relates to how the measures for an organization are changing over time; that is, what trends can be identified for our own hospital, health department, or long-term-care facility?

Health care organizations customarily use a variety of measures to evaluate their financial capabilities. Two of these measures have been introduced. The first was liquidity, a measure of an organization's ability to convert its assets to cash and near-cash assets. As previously noted, high liquidity implies that the organization is able to take all its assets and convert them into cash in a short time. Certain assets, such as petty cash, are perfectly liquid. Inventories and accounts receivable, depending on their age, are somewhat liquid and can be converted into cash by collecting the receivables or finding a buyer for them. Often this conversion does not result in a dollar-for-dollar exchange but the funds received are usually close to the dollar value. Many not-for-profit facilities have to plan for uncollectables from indigent and uninsured patients.

The second measure was profitability (or, in the case of not-for-profit organizations, the extent to which income exceeds expenses). A customary measure of profitability is operating income divided by revenues. Further, the net profit margin and rate of return on investments are useful profitability measures. Perspective 10–5 illustrates how for-profit hospitals performed relative to other health

---

PERSPECTIVE 10–5

For-Profit Hospital Income Drops in 1993

The profits of for-profit hospitals dropped a dramatic 58 percent in 1993. The drop was largely the result of losses in the psychiatric services market according to industry observers. Managed care, on the other hand, showed impressive increases. The adjusted year-to-date profit figures compiled by WDI Capital, Inc. for 1994 follow.

Health Care Organization	Profit Increase Over 1993 (Percent)
Managed Care	+70
Long-Term Care	+33
Home Health	−7
Rehabilitation	−17
Outpatient Services	−39
Hospitals	−58

Source: "For-Profit Hospitals' Income Drops: Report," *AHA News* (February 14, 1994), p. 4.

care organizations during 1993. This can be extremely useful information in assessing the relative performance of an organization.

Three additional areas should be investigated: leverage, growth, and activity levels. As a measure of financial strength *leverage* relates to the choices strategic decision makers have made between debt and equity. The leverage of a health care organization indicates how much of its capital is borrowed compared to the amount invested by owners. Leverage is most often measured by the debt-to-equity ratio, or the result obtained when total debt is divided by stockholders' equity. When the health care organization is not owned by private investors, different measures such as fund balances must be substituted for stockholders' equity.

Growth measures are important factors in attempting to assess the financial strengths and weaknesses of a health care organization. Financial indicators of growth document the organization's progression in terms of its development in important areas such as revenues generated, contributions to fund balances, price/earnings ratio of the stock, and so on.

Finally, *activity measures* are important. These measures relate to how the management of the organization "turns over" certain assets such as inventories, receivables, and even beds in some cases. Often, tracking the age of accounts receivable to determine an average collection period is used as one important measure of activity.

Decision makers usually look at comparative financial data for the industry as well as measures of liquidity, profitability, leverage, growth, and activity that apply to their own specific organizations to suggest the types of financial goals that might be achieved in a particular planning period. Frequently, it is necessary to use a variety of data bases such as the Financial Analysis Service of the Healthcare Financial Management Association or the Strategic Operating Indicators, which provides sixty key indicators of hospital financial performance by city, region, bed size, bond rating, and so on.[27]

The liquidity versus profitability paradox and the assessment of financial strength have obvious implications for day-to-day operations, but the strategic implications are less obvious. However, it is important to remember that strategy and operations are closely linked. For example, the liqudity of a health care organization, in addition to providing some measure of how well current assets and liabilities are managed, will also influence the degree to which additional debt can be acquired from financial institutions. Moreover, the current financial strength of an organization determines to a great extent how aggressive it can be in entering new markets, what entry strategies it might use in introducing new services, and the extent to which it can invest in the latest medical technologies.

Effectively Managing Cash Flow One of the more difficult problems faced by health care organizations is the effective management of cash flow. Increasingly, all organizations have recognized that it is not enough to be profitable or to grow at a rate equal to or better than others in the industry.[28] The inflow of cash must be related to the outflow. That is, certain things such as salaries, rent, and utility bills must be paid by a particular date, and most health care organizations must plan carefully so that sufficient cash is on hand when needed. Although the organization may have large billings to patients, if payment has not been received, it will be forced to borrow to meet obligations at the end of the month. This involves extra expenses and is simply not good financial management. Therefore, cash-flow management is an important measure of the organization's financial capability.[29]

Cash flow is managed through a combination of two actions.[30] The first is to accelerate cash inflows by converting accounts receivable to cash at the earliest possible time (get payments in the bank as fast as possible, impose a service charge on late payments, and provide incentive discounts for early payment). Accounts receivable are often singled out for special attention in improving cash flow because they constitute one of the more complex problems facing health care organizations. Unlike most business firms, health care organizations routinely deal with third-party payers such as Blue Cross, private health insurance companies, and federal and state governments. Often the necessity to file the proper forms (in the format dictated by each of the many third-party payers) and related logistical problems delay payment to health care providers.

Organizations, including hospitals and physicians practices, sometimes sell their accounts receivable to companies that specialize in collecting the accounts. This provides an earlier inflow of cash for the organization. Customarily, the purchasers buy the accounts for some percentage of their value and make a return on the collections.

When the accounts receivable become old and less likely to be collected, a collection agency may be employed to assist. Hospitals give collection agencies more business than any other industry according to the American Collectors Association. These agencies collect about 22 cents on every dollar – these are first-party bills that are typically four-to-six months old. About 25 cents on the dollar is collected for physician practices but almost 28 cents on the dollar is collected for other health care organizations such as HMOs and long-term-care facilities. For comparison purposes, the highest collection rate is about 38 cents on the dollar for legal firms. Commercial organizations get about 25 cents; utilities, 18 cents; and bank cards, less than 6 cents on the dollar. In return, the collection agency keeps from 20 to 35 percent of what they collect.[31]

Some companies such as Principal Residential Advisors buy bad debts of hospitals and physician practices. First-party accounts receivable that are four to six months and older may be considered uncollectable and sold for whatever can be obtained in the market place. Fraser Memorial Hospital, for example, sold Principal Residential Advisors over $1 million in bad debts for 4.7 cents on the dollar. Principal, in turn, sold the portfolio to United Asset Recovery for $52,000, kept 25 percent of the proceeds and gave Fraser Memorial Hospital the remaining $39,000. Although the recovery from the original amount was small, the hospital believed taking what it could get for these accounts was a better alternative than attempting to collect them or turning them over to a standard collection agency.[32]

The second approach to cash-flow management is to delay cash outflows as long as possible. This can be done by paying bills at the latest date possible to receive discounts, centralizing the payables function to ensure that procedures for avoiding early payments are followed, and keeping payroll funds in interest-bearing accounts as long as possible. Studies show that most employees wait a day or so before cashing their salary checks; therefore, with the proper data, an organization can probably keep payroll funds in interest-bearing accounts a few days longer and still cover salary checks when they are presented for payment.

Budgeting and Financial Planning Planning is key to effective financial management and a crucial factor in estimating the ability of an organization to take strategic actions. An effective budgeting system is a health care organization's means of identifying the most efficient use of resources and the primary control mechanism to ensure that resources are used effectively.[33]

An effective budgeting system can assist an organization in accomplishing one of the most difficult strategic tasks facing managers: reallocating resources away from the less beneficial to the more beneficial programs. A variety of approaches to budgeting can be used in health care organizations. Which is the most appropriate will depend to a great extent on how the organization generates its support. If the health organization is supported by private investors, available corporate budgetary systems will likely apply. On the other hand, if the organization is publicly supported, techniques used effectively in government, such as zero-base budgeting and planning/programming/budgeting systems, may be more applicable.[34]

Managing Operations One important source of financial resources is the better management of existing operations. If operations can be improved, work can be accomplished with fewer employees, collections can be made sooner, and the demand for external funding can be reduced.

Fortunately, new management techniques such as *reengineering* have the potential to greatly reduce billing cycles and collection times. One interesting case illustration is that of Maricopa Medical Center in Phoenix, which completed a year-long redesign of its finance department. In fiscal year 1992, Maricopa Medical Center had a $20 million loss on net patient revenues of slightly over $116 million. With the aid of Andersen Consulting, the medical center redesigned every major business function in finance, admitting, and patient registration in an effort to streamline the work. Exhibit 10–8 illustrates how the Medicaid billing process was streamlined.[35]

The important benefit from this reengineering project was improved use of existing financial resources so that more resources were available for alternative uses. Before reengineering, almost twenty activities were required to bill Medicaid. The process took from one to two months to complete. After reengineering, less than ten activities were required and the process could be completed in twelve to twenty-five days. Reengineering of this type can save considerable sums when the costs of the personnel required for the less-efficient process are included in the savings picture. This issue of saving funds through the more efficient and effective use of human resources highlights another important area that must be considered in any systematic strategic decision making.

Strategic financial management is an important aspect of strategic management in health care organizations. Financial resources must reinforce the overall

EXHIBIT 10–8

Reengineering the Medicaid Billing Process at Maricopa Medical Center

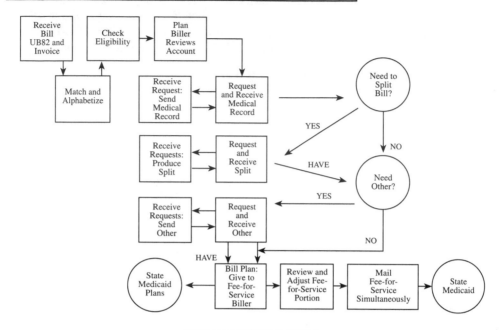

BEFORE REENGINEERING
RANGE 30–60+ DAYS

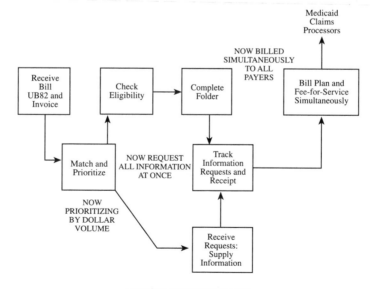

AFTER REENGINEERING
RANGE 12–25 DAYS

Source: Adapted from Judith Nemes, "Reconfiguring the Finance Department," *Modern Healthcare* 23, no. 7 (February 15, 1993), p. 60.

strategies of the organization or managers will be continuously frustrated in their ability to accomplish planned strategies. Exhibits 10–9 and 10–10 are included to provide a summary of the role finance and strategic financial management play in the overall situational analysis and strategic management of health care organizations.

SUMMARY AND CONCLUSIONS

In this chapter the financial implications of the adaptive strategies of expansion, contraction, and stabilization were discussed. It was initially noted that, although

---

EXHIBIT 10–9
Financial Input to the Situational Analysis

Situational Analysis	Financial Input to Situational Analysis
External Environment	
Financial Analysis	Determine the condition of financial markets including financial aspects of the economic environment, interest rate trends and projections, assessment of trends in philanthropic giving, determination of likely sources of funds other than customary financial institutions
Competitive Financial Analysis	Comparison of financial data on competitors and potential competitors; analysis of financial strength of industry and various market segments; comparative financial ratios and industry standards for financial growth, liquidity, and activity measures
Financial Market Analysis	Determine the purchasing capabilities of potential customers and the credit status of groups of potential customers in present and potential industries and locations
Internal Environment	
Finance	Develop indicators of present financial strength; evaluate the strategic financial capacity of the organization; determine the degree to which the organization is capable of financing different strategies from internally generated sources
Mission, Vision, Values, and Objectives	Ensure management understands the financial requirements for present and future operations; determine financial implications of possible changes in organizational mission; establish financial benchmarks and objectives to accomplish organizational mission and vision

---

EXHIBIT 10–10

Strategic Financial Management Input to Strategic Management

Hierarchy of Strategic Decisions	Financial Input
Directional Strategies	
Mission	Ensure understanding of financial requirements for building and maintaining organizational distinctiveness
Vision	Determine ways of obtaining financial resources necessary to accomplish the organization's hope for tomorrow
Values	Include clarification of importance of personal ethics and organizational responsibility in financial decision making
Objectives	Participate in the formulation of organizational objectives; develop financial objectives to support accomplishment of organizational objectives
Adaptive Strategies	
Expansion	
Diversification – Related and Unrelated	Assist in obtaining the funds necessary to finance the movement into related and unrelated services; assess the relative advantages of expanding existing operations or moving into related and unrelated areas; determine the relative mix of different sources of capital
Vertical Integration – Forward and Backward	Assist in obtaining the funds necessary to finance the movement into backward and forward operations; assess the relative financial advantages of diversification and vertical integration; determine the relative mix of different sources of capital
Market Development	Identify the sources of funds available for expanding the underserved geographical areas and market segments; determine the relative mix of different sources of capital
Product Development	Evaluate the financial costs and benefits of different services that have been identified as possible additions to the service mix
Penetration	Assess the availability of funds to support greater service differentiation, fuel promotional activities and other marketing efforts. Evaluate the effect of aggressive pricing strategies

EXHIBIT 10–10 cont'd

Hierarchy of Strategic Decisions	Financial Input
Contraction	
Divestiture	Ensure the effective financial management of temporary excess funds until additional investment opportunities are located; focus on effective utilization of existing and newly generated financial resources through divestment activities
Liquidation	Ensure the effective financial management of funds generated through liquidation of assets; evaluate alternative investment opportunities for financial resources generated from liquidation strategy
Harvesting	Financial management of funds generated; evaluation of alternative uses of financial resources made available by harvesting
Retrenchment	Evaluate and recommend areas where the greatest use of financial resources can be utilized in view of the more limited scope of operations
Stabilization	
Enhancement	Identify sources of financial resources to be used in enhancement programs; assess the financial impact of alternative enhancement activities – quality programs, training and development, and so on
Status Quo	Ensure effective financial management of existing resources
Market Entry Strategies	
Purchase	
Acquisition	Evaluate the financial viability of target organizations; assess the organization's ability to finance the acquisition; recommend the appropriate sources of capital
Licensing	Evaluate the financial impact of creating additional competition through the licensing process versus the potential gains from a licensing arrangement; assess the opportunities and financial impact of expanded licensing agreements
Cooperation	
Merger	Examine and evaluate the financial condition of the merger target; assess the financial impact of the addition of the target organization to the present organization's service line; evaluate the consolidated financial strength of a new and larger organization

EXHIBIT 10-10 cont'd

Hierarchy of Strategic Decisions	Financial Input
Alliance	Evaluate the financial condition of partner(s); assess the financial synergies likely to result from cooperation
Joint Venture	Assess the potential financial benefits and costs from entering a joint venture; consider the financial implications of association with a joint partner; evaluate the possibility of financial gains from additional joint venture arrangements
Development	
Internal Development	Assess the availability of financial resources to support the proposed internal development activities

Positioning Strategies

Market-Wide	
Cost Leadership	Evaluate the impact of a cost leadership strategy relative to the earnings goal of the organization; suggest ways of increasing efficiency in the use of financial resources without sacrificing quality of financial services
Differentiation	Evaluate the financial impact of potential increases in costs resulting from differentiation relative to the projected increases in revenues resulting from differentiation efforts
Market Segment	
Focus – Cost Leadership	Project the potential financial effects of cost leadership activities, expected increases in efficiency, and resulting effects on revenues for a given segment
Focus – Differentiation	Project the potential financial effects of increasing differentiation – expected cost increases relative to forecasted revenue increases for a given segment

Operational Strategies

Functional – Finance	Ensure that financial operations are as efficient and effective as possible; assess the orientation of financial personnel to the internal customers of the organization; develop the strategic financial plan to support the mission and strategies of the organization

financial resources are important reality checks to strategic decision making, the vision of management should not be limited by the financial resources available. Because vision is a hope for the future, it may be necessary to acquire more and different types of financial resources if future aspirations of the organization and its key stakeholders are to be achieved.

The argument was made that the strategic management of financial resources should be carefully integrated into the overall strategic management of health care organizations. Attention should be given to ensure that strategic financial planning is an integral part of overall strategic management.

Expansion strategies such as diversification and vertical integration frequently require additional financial resources. Implementation will require investigation of the different options for obtaining capital. A few of the more important sources of new capital are equity, debt, raising philanthropic funds from individuals or organizations, and more efficient use of existing financial resources.

Contraction strategies make different demands on financial resources. A health care organization that divests itself of existing programs, harvests the benefits of present operations, or liquidates parts of its business will likely find itself, at least temporarily, with excess funds in a liquid state. These overly liquid financial resources will have to be invested until more profitable long-term uses can be implemented. Stabilization strategies such as enhancing existing operations, services, and facilities require a great deal of expertise in the management of the steady state.

Financial resource strategies must be consistent with adaptive strategies and address the realities created by their implementation. Financial resources are one of the important "enablers" that determine to a great extent the success of decision makers in realizing the vision of the organization.

KEY TERMS AND CONCEPTS IN STRATEGIC MANAGEMENT

activity measures	**equity funding**	**financial management**
budgetary financial planning	**growth measures**	**paradox**
cash flow	**leverage**	**going public**
comparative financial data	**liquidity**	**strategic financial planning**
continuum of refinement	**philanthropy**	
debt financing	**profitability**	

QUESTIONS FOR CLASS DISCUSSION

1. What relationship does financial resource planning have to strategic planning? Should financial resource capabilities determine the aspiration levels of a health care organization? Explain your answer.

2. What are the important differences between budgetary and strategic financial planning? Which is more important? Explain your response.

3. Explain what is meant by the term *continuum of refinement*. Why is this concept important to effective financial planning in health care organizations?

4. What are the primary differences in the financial strategies needed for expansion, contraction, and stabilization? Which type of adaptive strategy is most difficult to implement from a financial perspective? Why?

5. List some of the primary advantages and

disadvantages of "going public." If you were the chief financial officer of a large health care organization, what advice would you give the CEO about going public to raise operating funds? Under what specific conditions would you advise in favor of a public offering?

6. Health care organizations are sometimes able to attract philanthropic funds from individuals and organizations to finance capital expansion. What are the advantages and disadvantages of using this type of funding to accomplish growth plans?

7. Why is it important to relate stakeholder relations and the need for philanthropic fund raising on the part of health care organizations? Do you think philanthropic gifts will become more or less important in the future as a source of funding? Explain your answer.

8. How are financial growth measures different from financial activity measures? Which is more important in assessing the financial strength of a health care organization? Why?

9. Briefly explain the financial management paradox. Provide an illustration of this dilemma in the health care setting.

10. How can the profitability needs of health care organizations be balanced with their unique mission to see to the health care needs of all people regardless of ability to pay?

NOTES

1. R. D. Stier and C. L. Pugh, "The Strategic Linkage of Marketing and Finance," *Healthcare Forum Journal* 20, no. 2 (April 23, 1989), p. 37.

2. J. C. Folger, "Integration of Strategic, Financial Plans Vital to Success," *Healthcare Financial Management* 43, no. 1 (January 1989), pp. 22–32.

3. Donald Cook, "Strategic Plan Creates a Blueprint for Budgeting," *Healthcare Financial Management* 44, no. 5 (May 1990), pp. 21–25.

4. Adapted from Dale Anderson, "Impact of Strategic Financial Planning in the Health Care Industry," *Topics in Health Care Financing: Strategic Financial Planning* 11, no. 3 (Summer 1985), pp. 1–16.

5. A. E. Glenesk, "Six Myths that Can Cloud Strategic Vision," *Healthcare Financial Management* 44, no. 5 (May 1990), pp. 38–43.

6. Frank Cerne, "Balancing Complex Choices," *Hospitals & Health Networks* (June 20, 1993), pp. 28–30.

7. Robert Saunders, J. J. Mayerhofer, and W. J. Jones, "Strategic Capital Planning Scenarios for the Future," *Healthcare Financial Management* 48, no. 4 (April 1993), pp. 50–55.

8. J. H. Arnold, "Assessing Capital Risks: You Can't Be Too Conservative," *Harvard Business Review* 64, no. 5 (September/October 1986), pp. 113–121.

9. Larry Malcolmson, "CFOs Put the Squeeze on the Hospital's Big Ticket Purchases," *Healthcare Financial Management* 40, no. 8 (August 1986), pp. 23–26.

10. William O. Cleverley, "Assessing Present and Future Capital Expense Levels Under PPS," *Healthcare Financial Management* 40, no. 9 (September 1986), pp. 62–72.

11. "Data Scan," *Modern Healthcare* 23, no. 16 (April 19, 1993), p. 44.

12. Frank Cerne, "CFOs Are Cautious About Capital Outlays," *AHA News* (November 2, 1992), p. 1.

13. "Health Reform Affects Hospital and Managed Care Stocks," *AHA News* (January 25, 1993), p. 3.

14. Judith Nemes, "Healthcare Stocks: Some Bright Spots in a Cloudy Year," *Modern Healthcare* 23, no. 5 (February 1, 1993), p. 47.

15. "Health Care Financings Surge in 2nd Quarter of 1993," *AHA News* (July 12, 1993), p. 3.

16. William O. Cleverley, "Capital Formation," in *Handbook of Health Care Ac-*

counting and Finance, 3rd ed., vol. 2, ed William O. Cleverley (Rockville, Maryland: Aspen Publishers, 1989), pp. 803–821.

17. "Low Interest Rates Fuel Bond Sales in First Quarter," *Modern Healthcare* 23, no. 15 (April 12, 1993), p. 64; "Health Care Financings Surge: Bond Issues Totaled $6.7 Billion in Third Quarter of 1993," *AHA News* (October 18, 1993), p. 3.

18. Judith Nemes, "S & P's 'A' Rating Plays Hard to Get for Hospitals," *Modern Healthcare* 23, no. 7 (February 15, 1993), p. 24.

19. "S & P Downgrades California Hospital," *Modern Healthcare* 23, no. 11 (March 15 1993), p. 50.

20. "Skilled Nursing Chain Files for Offering of $40 Million," *Modern Healthcare* 23, (February 15, 1993), p. 74; and "Regency Health Finishes Debenture Sale," *Modern Healthcare* 23, no. 15 (April 12, 1993), p. 65.

21. "Receivables-Backed Securities Raise $100 Million," *Modern Healthcare* 23, no. 15 (April 12, 1993), p. 66.

22. Michael Sullivan, "Manufacturers, Hospitals Cooperate on Imaging Equipment Acquisition," *Healthcare Financial Management* 47, no. 10 (October 1993), pp. 38–42.

23. "Donations to Hospitals Rose by 6.3 Percent Last Year, but Arts Funds Saw Only a Small Increase," *Chronicle of Philanthropy* (June 1, 1993), p. 21; and "Contributions in 1992: Charities Get 6 Percent Increase," *Chronicle of Philanthropy* (June 1, 1993), p. 1.

24. "Corporate Giving to Charities Dropped in 1992, First Decrease in Twenty Years," *Chronicle of Philanthropy* (September 1, 1993), p. 8.

25. "Charities Hope Tax Law Causes Surge of Giving by the Wealthy," *Chronicle of Philanthropy* (September 7, 1993), p. 32.

26. L. C. Gapenski, W. B. Vogel, and Barbara Langland-Orban, "The Determinants of Hospital Profitability," *Hospital & Health Services Administration* 38, no. 1 (Spring 1993), pp. 63–80; and W. B. Vogel, Bar-

bara Langland-Orban, and L. C. Gapenski, "Factors Influencing High and Low Profitability in Hospitals," *Health Care Management Review* 18, no. 2 (1993), pp. 15–26.

27. William O. Cleverley, "How Boards Can Use Comparative Data in Strategic Planning," *Healthcare Executive* 4, no. 17 (May 6, 1989), pp. 32–33.

28. William O. Cleverley and R. K. Harvey, "Profitability: Comparing Hospitals Results with Other Industries," *Hospital Financial Management* 44, no. 3 (March 1990), pp. 42–52.

29. C. E. Chastain and S. T. Cianciolo, "Strategies in Cash-Flow Management," *Business Horizons* 29, no. 5 (May/June 1986), pp. 65–73.

30. "Portfolio Reoptimization Improves Cash Flow," *Hospitals* (April 20, 1986), pp. 55–56.

31. For more details and trends, see T. J. Kincaid, "Selling Accounts Receivable to Fund Working Capital," *Healthcare Financial Management* 47, no. 4 (April 1993), pp. 27–31.

32. Lisa Scott, "Firm Offers to Sell Bad Debts to Highest Bidder," *Modern Healthcare* 23, no. 6 (February 8, 1993), p. 34. The discussion of accounts receivable collections is adapted from this article.

33. F. Hahimoro, A. Bell, and S. Marshment, "A Computer Simulation Program to Facilitate Budgeting and Staffing Decisions in an Intensive Care Unit," *Critical Care Medicine* 15, no. 1 (1987), pp. 256–259.

34. For some useful examples, see S. Duncombe and R. Kinney, "Agency Budget Success: How It Is Defined by Budget Officials in Five Western States," *Public Budgeting and Finance* 7, no. 1 (1987), pp. 24–37; and V. B. Lewis, "Reflections on Budgeting Systems," *Public Budgeting and Finance* 8, no. 1 (1988), pp. 4–19.

35. Judith Nemes, "Reconfiguring the Finance Department," *Modern Healthcare* 23, no. 7 (February 15, 1993), pp. 51–64.

ADDITIONAL READINGS

Bazerman, Max H., *Judgment in Managerial Decision Making* (New York: John Wiley & Sons, Inc., 1994). This book is a comprehensive review of the decision-making process with a focus on the importance of judgment. It provides a convincing argument that the purely quantitative aspects of decision making should not limit the vision of managers and organizations.

Gapenski, L. C., "Capital Investment Analysis: Three Methods," *Healthcare Financial Management* 47, no. 8 (August 1993), pp. 60–66. Three cash flow and discount rate methods are discussed that can be used to conduct capital budgeting analysis. These methods include net operating cash flow, net cash flow to investors, and net cash flow to equity holders.

Miller, Gerald J., "What Is Financial Management? Are We Inventing A New Field Here?" *Public Administration Review* 54, no. 2 (March/April 1994), pp. 209–213. This article relates a comprehensive review of eleven books dealing with financial management in the public sector. The author illustrates what he believes is a fundamental conflict among three primary views of financial management—those of the economist, the accountant, and the budget executive.

Newton, R. L., "Measuring Accounts Receivable Performance: A Compliance Method," *Healthcare Financial Management* 47, no. 5 (May 1993), pp. 33–36. Nonperforming assets such as accounts receivable are cited as financial problems for hospitals. Discussion of the costs imposed by accounts receivable is presented along with a description of three components of cost that must be considered if the true picture of accounts receivable is to be understood.

O'Leary, Meghan, "Reinventing the Heal," *CIO Magazine* 6, no. 7 (February 1993), pp. 1–5. A team saw opportunities to reduce a hospital's $200 million operating expenses by 5 to 10 percent with the creation of patient-focused care teams. The teams handled 80 percent of all patient-care needs in their departments and improved coordination and quality of care.

Rogers, M. M., and K. Rothe, "Integrating Capital Budgeting Techniques," *Health Care Strategic Management* 11, no. 2 (February 1993), pp. 7–10. A practical model is presented that requires the integration of clinical, fiscal, and strategic elements to reach informed capital investment choices.

CHAPTER 11

Strategic Management
of Human Resources

"It's really up to leaders to pull the group together, get the best talent out of that
group, get the group thinking about the greatest possibilities, and think how each
person can contribute as a leader."

– William H. Gates
Microsoft Corporation

LEARNING OBJECTIVES

After completing this chapter you should:

1. Understand the relationship between strategic human resources management and overall strategic management of health care organizations.
2. Be able to discuss the human resources implications of adaptive strategies
   relating to expansion, contraction, and stabilization.
3. Be able to discuss the decisions necessary to provide appropriate human
   resources for market entry strategies associated with expansion and stabilization.
4. Be able to evaluate different methods of implementing human resources
   strategies.
5. Appreciate the importance of integrating human resources strategies into
   the strategic management process.

INTRODUCTORY INCIDENT
The Real Work of Job Redesign

One employee, not impressed by the transformation of work for the twenty-first century, was heard to say that reorganization is the "illegitimate child of the need to justify ten people doing fifteen other peoples' jobs, and the need to show a profit." This statement illustrates what some people think about new forms of human resources management known variously as job redesign or work transformation. Among the most critical are nurses who argue that shifting traditional nursing duties to less skilled aides has and will adversely affect the quality of patient care. The president of the California Nurses Association criticized one management consulting firm in the *Wall Street Journal* by stating that: "They're out selling cost-savings models that have been used in the industrial sector. The problem is they look at the patient as a bunch of parts, rather than as a whole human being."

Work transformation advocates, on the other hand, although stating that they understand the concern of nurses, believe that changing the role and responsibilities of nurses may actually improve the quality of patient care. A study by the Hay Group titled *The Nursing Crisis, Short-Term Strategies and Long-Term Solutions,* found that 52 percent of a nurse's time is devoted to tasks that do not require professional knowledge. By shifting such tasks to less skilled aides, nurses would be free to practice what they are actually trained to do. Patients should be the beneficiaries, not the victims.

Source: "Work Transformation Creates a More Rewarding Role for Nurses," *Hospitals & Health Networks* 68, no. 7 (April 5, 1994), p. 51.

Health care organizations are faced with many conflicting demands. For example, the public continues to encourage health care organizations to be innovative, provide high-quality services, increase access, and contain costs. Often these desires are in conflict and at times they are mutually exclusive. To illustrate the magnitude of the problem, consider how human resources management strategies relate to the three adaptive strategies of health care organizations.[1] Exhibit 11–1 shows the place of human resources in the overall model followed through-

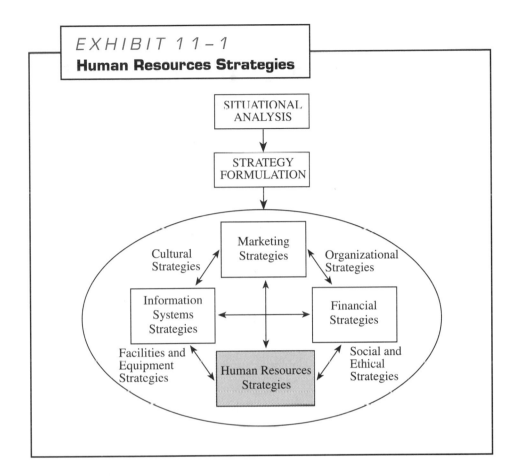

EXHIBIT 11–1
Human Resources Strategies

SITUATIONAL ANALYSIS

STRATEGY FORMULATION

Cultural Strategies

Marketing Strategies

Organizational Strategies

Information Systems Strategies

Financial Strategies

Facilities and Equipment Strategies

Human Resources Strategies

Social and Ethical Strategies

out this book. Human resources strategies and implications are outlined in Exhibit 11–2.

Cost-reduction strategies require a particular type of human resources management system. The emphasis is on carefully designing and defining jobs that contribute to efficiency. Performance appraisal systems emphasize short-term results that directly affect quantified goals. Because jobs are narrowly defined, career paths tend to be equally narrow. Under a cost-reduction strategy, nurses enter the organization as nurses, do their jobs, and retire as nurses or perhaps nurse supervisors. The same is true of engineers and financial administrators. There is relatively little training and development because of the expense required and the uncertainty of a direct payoff.

When the focus is on quality, the human resources management strategy must change. Jobs tend to remain relatively fixed and narrow, but the "experts" or specialists have more input into how their jobs should be done in order to improve quality. Although appraisals tend to be short-term and oriented toward

---

EXHIBIT 11-2
Strategic Human Resources Decisions

Cost-Reduction Strategy

1. Stable job descriptions that allow little room for confusion.
2. Narrowly designed jobs and narrow career paths that encourage specialization and efficiency.
3. Short-term, results-oriented performance appraisals.
4. Close monitoring of market pay levels in compensation decisions.
5. Minimal levels of employee training and development.

Quality-Enhancement Strategy

1. Fixed and explicit job descriptions.
2. High levels of employee participation in matters relating to the job itself.
3. Mix of individual and group performance appraisals that emphasize short-term results.
4. Egalitarian treatment of employees with some employment guarantees.
5. Extensive and continuous training and development.

Innovation Strategy

1. Jobs that require interaction and coordination among groups of individuals.
2. Performance appraisals that reflect long-run, group-based achievements.
3. Jobs that allow employees to develop skills that can be used in other parts of the organization.
4. Compensation that emphasizes internal equity rather than external markets.
5. Pay rates that tend to be lower but that allow employees flexible compensation packages.
6. Broad career paths that encourage employees to develop wide arrays of skills.

Source: Adapted from R. S. Schuler and S. E. Jackson, "Linking Competitive Strategies with Human Resource Management Practices," *Academy of Management Executive* 1 (August 1987), p. 213. Used by permission of the authors.

specific results, more emphasis is placed on group performance. Because high-quality demands the latest information, there is a high commitment to training and development.

Innovative competitive strategies require innovative human resources management strategies. They must focus on job designs that require close interaction and coordination among groups of individuals. Job descriptions in innovative organizations tend to be less specific to allow employees to develop multiple skills. In addition, these "loose" job descriptions allow for broader career paths and encourage individuals to move to where they are needed most in the organization. Although pay levels are not always high, compensation programs emphasize equity among group members and flexibility so that employees can design their own compensation packages to the extent possible.

SOME SPECIAL HUMAN RESOURCES CHALLENGES IN HEALTH CARE

Health care organizations present a number of unique human resources management challenges. One of the most difficult problems facing hospitals, long term care facilities, and HMOs relates to the different skill levels required to accomplish an organization's mission. Simultaneously motivating and retaining physicians, plumbers, engineers, nurses, electricians, and the janitorial staff can be a human resources manager's nightmare. Research has shown that human resources management issues such as recruiting, staffing, evaluation, and training and development are directly affected by strategic choices at both the corporate and SSU levels.[2]

Managing Occupational Diversity

The art of effectively managing professionals despite their occupational diversity is essential in health care organizations.[3] Some professionals (nurses, laboratory scientists, and hospital-based physicians) are salaried, and others are independent such as private physicians with hospital staff privileges.

The changes and projected changes taking place in the health care environment make it difficult to predict precisely which health related human resources will be demanded most in the future. Experts agree that health related personnel will continue in high demand although they may be demanded in different types of organizations. For example, as hospitals downsize, many of those displaced will find employment in managed-care organizations, long term care facilities, and so on.

One area that has received too little attention is the retention of employees once they are employed. By focusing more on retention, a health care organization can reduce the necessity of competing directly for scarce human resources. A comprehensive study of employee retention in health care organizations suggested the following five-part program for retaining valued employees.[4]

1. *Pay for productivity.* Health care organizations of all types are attempting to reduce personnel costs. Accomplishing this objective will require that

the most productive employees be retained and rewarded for exceptional performance that leads to significant productivity improvement.

2. *Employee development.* Employees, especially professionals, view their current jobs from the perspective of career development. Effective staffing strategies demand that employees be given incentives and rewards for continuing their professional development.

3. *Matching goals.* Beginning with initial recruitment, increased attention is needed to ensure that individual and organizational goals match. One effective motivator, as noted in Chapter 5, is to constantly keep the vision and purpose of the organization before all employees and do everything possible to ensure that the vision and purpose are related to individual aspirations.

4. *Voicing dissatisfaction.* To keep valued employees, health care managers should provide opportunities for people to voice dissatisfactions rather than allow an atmosphere of fear and intimidation to develop.

5. *Reward loyalty.* Although longevity is not necessarily related to performance, those employees who remain loyal to the organization over the long term should be recognized and rewarded.

Special Staffing Problems Relating to Physicians

The strategic decisions of health care organizations are always affected to some extent by the staffing strategies designed to ensure an adequate supply of physicians. Because physicians ultimately determine whether a patient will be admitted to a particular hospital, human resources managers must focus a great deal of attention on physician recruitment and retention.[5] Frequently, staff physicians are given minimum income guarantees, relocation expenses, and even initial signing bonuses. Non-hospital-based physicians are sometimes given equally appealing incentives to admit patients to a particular hospital, such as favorable rental fees in professional office buildings and opportunities to spread some of the cost of insurance over a larger base. Despite their best efforts, however, hospitals continue to fall behind group practices and HMOs relative to physician reimbursement, as illustrated in Perspective 11–1.

One of the more innovative and elaborate strategies used to attract and retain physicians is the hospital/physician joint venture. This represents a type of partnership in which the private physician and the hospital decide to jointly purchase expensive equipment, buildings, or laboratory facilities. The advantage to the hospital is that the physician has a mutual interest in the success of the venture and the organization because of his or her cooperative investment. The physician benefits from the funds made available by the hospital.

Emphasizing the Unique Mission of Health Care

The public health sector is likely to continue to experience a competitive disadvantage relative to the private sector in terms of money and benefits. Even in the for-profit health care sector, there are dedicated personnel whose attraction to

PERSPECTIVE 11–1

Keeping Hospitals Competitive for Physicians

Group practices are maintaining the lead over hospitals in terms of the salaries paid to physicians. During 1992, total cash compensation paid to salaried group practice physicians increased by 11 percent. Compensation to salaried physicians working in hospitals dropped by 3 percent during the same period. The total compensation paid to staff physicians in HMOs increased by 9 percent. It was estimated that during 1993, hospitals planned to increase the compensation of their physicians 4.8 percent whereas group practices planned increases of 5 percent and HMOs planned to raise physician pay by 4.5 percent.

Hospitals simply have not kept pace with other types of health care providers when it comes to physician pay. Experts suggest that it will be increasingly difficult to recruit and retain staff physicians in hospitals as the competition increases for their services in other types of health care organizations.

Source: David Burda, "Hospitals Begin to Lose Ground in Physician Pay," *Modern Healthcare* 23, no. 5 (February 15, 1993), p. 65.

the field goes beyond monetary rewards alone. If the personnel shortages among health professionals are to be properly addressed by strategic decision makers, it will be necessary to focus on some of the "strategic uniquenesses" of health care that were discussed in Chapter 5.

Some of these important unique characteristics of the health care field can be effectively used as "currencies" to attract and retain professional employees.[6] The term *currency* is used in this context to describe any type of resource that can be exchanged for something else of value. In this case, the question becomes, what of a strategic or long-term nature can the health care organization offer that might give it an advantage in attempting to attract scarce resources in the labor market? Some examples might be:

1. *Inspiration-related currencies.* Health care professionals can be offered the vision of being involved in a unique type of work that helps other people. Public-sector employees can be offered the vision of offering unique services to people regardless of their ability to pay. Excellence, the opportunity to do important things well, and the moral correctness of providing health services to everyone are important inspiration-related currencies as well.

2. *Task-related currencies.* Health care strategists can offer unique attractions to health professionals by giving them opportunities to learn new and challenging technologies and by offering resources that encourage professionals to obtain the educational and work experiences that will allow them to remain up-to-date in their profession.

3. *Position-related currencies.* Health care organizations can recognize professionals for high levels of performance and provide opportunities for networking that will give them visibility and recognition beyond a single organization.
4. *Relationship-related currencies.* Being a part of a highly professional environment can offer unique opportunities for interaction with other individuals who share similar interests and vision.
5. *Personal-related currencies.* Perhaps the greatest currency of all is the strategic manager's ability to offer professionals an important return on the time and energy they have invested in preparing for a career of service. The return includes gratitude, a sense of ownership, freedom from bureaucratic hassles, and affirmation of the basic service-oriented values that attracted them to the profession initially.[7]

This "strategic reorientation" away from a salary- and benefits-driven recruitment and motivation philosophy could do much to attract and retain the kinds of health care professionals who are capable of providing the high-quality services desired in both private and public health care organizations. Certainly, compensation rates must be reasonable and equitable. However, we increasingly recognize the truth in the statement: "The difference between employees who perform well and those who do not is not how much they are paid but how they are treated."[8] Specifically, with respect to professional employees it is clear that meaningful products from their labor, freedom to use personal judgment, time to do quality work, and challenge are the primary motivators of high performance.[9]

HUMAN RESOURCES DECISIONS IN ADAPTIVE STRATEGIES

Adaptive strategies require human resources decisions. Expansion, contraction, and stabilization demand an ongoing evaluation of governance and organizational structures. In addition, they demand that specific actions be taken to ensure human resources are employed in an efficient and effective manner, as illustrated in Exhibit 11–3. Expansion requires different human resources actions, depending on the specific positioning strategy employed.

Expansion strategies such as related diversification will make it necessary to recruit new personnel with skills and talents similar to those already in the organization. Unrelated diversification and backward and forward vertical integration will create the need for human resources with skills and talents different from those presently employed. The necessity of recruiting, hiring, and leading individuals with different skills and talents is a major reason that these strategies are "riskier" than related diversification. Any one of these strategies requires the merger of similar or dissimilar organizational cultures, which presents another human resources challenge.

Contraction involves different human resources management skills. Incentives must be devised to encourage employees to find other jobs or retire earlier than

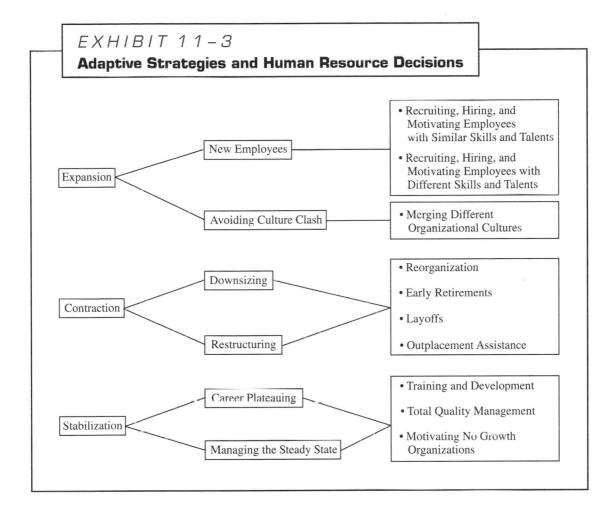

EXHIBIT 11-3
Adaptive Strategies and Human Resource Decisions

anticipated. For some, layoffs may be necessary, and the organization will be forced to determine its responsibility in assisting displaced employees to find alternative employment opportunities. At times, health care organizations may assist employees by retraining them for different tasks that will be needed as contraction takes place.

Stabilization strategies almost always require training and development activities. Enhancement strategies through total quality management programs involve significant commitments to continuous learning on the part of the individual and the organization. Status quo requires the challenging task of keeping people motivated in the face of career plateauing, and so on. In view of this, several issues such as hiring and recruiting, early retirement, layoffs, reorganization, and training development as strategic concerns will be discussed in the remainder of this chapter.

Human Resources Considerations During Expansion

In discussing the various choices and their implications, we will make frequent reference to Exhibit 11–3, which summarizes the more important aspects of human resources implications of the different strategic alternatives. Organizations go through a number of stages in their life cycles. Although there are many theories and even more labels for the different stages, most agree that organizations experience growth, maturity, and decline.[10] The magnitude of change required on the part of health care organizations in each stage will depend on how prepared they are to deal with the different strategic, organizational, and human resources management problems of each phase of the organizational life cycle. Exhibit 11–4 provides an example of the *growth-preparedness matrix* and illustrates how different changes are needed under different conditions.

If the organization is in the mature stage, the primary focus is on efficiency. An organization such as a general hospital with a reasonably long history generally

---

EXHIBIT 11–4
Growth Preparedness Matrix

		High Organizational Preparedness	Low Organizational Preparedness
Life-Cycle Stage	Growth	EXPANSION	DEVELOPMENT
	Maturity		
		EFFICIENCY	REDIRECTION
	Decline		

Organizational Preparedness

Source: Idea adapted from the growth-readiness matrix originally presented in C. A. Lengnick-Hall and M. L. Lengnick-Hall, "Strategic Human Resources Management: A Review of the Literature and a Proposed Typology," *Academy of Management Review* 13 (July 1988), p. 461.

has its services well defined and the human and nonhuman resources to deliver the services efficiently in place. The hospital may not, however, be prepared for rapid growth. If new opportunities develop (such as expansion into psychiatric hospitals) that present the potential for significant growth, the organization must be prepared to take advantage of the opportunity for expansion. Organizational changes will be required to accommodate the increased size and diversity of the organization. Staffing and human resources management strategies will require similar changes.

Diversification and Vertical Integration More attention has probably been devoted to related and unrelated diversification than to any other strategic alternatives.[11] Diversification, as noted in Chapter 6, is selected as a strategic alternative when management believes that markets outside the organization's core operations offer significant growth opportunities. Theoretically, diversification is chosen to improve performance by entering new and promising areas or to reduce the risk of having "all our eggs in one basket." Some evidence suggests that there is indeed a trade-off between risk and performance.[12] That is, the more an organization engages in unrelated diversification to avoid financial risk, the less likely it is that it will obtain high levels of performance in overall operations because of potential organizational and human resources management problems. This seems to occur so consistently in health care organizations that strategic managers frequently end up divesting unrelated operations to concentrate more on what they know best – health care.[13] Perspective 11–2 suggests the trend for divesting wellness centers has not been as great as originally thought.

One study of 570 hospitals that belong to eight hospital systems found four primary practices that distinguished the successful from the unsuccessful organizational diversifications.[14] These *best practices,* as they were called, involved (1) a diversification plan that was closely linked to physicians' interests; (2) plans that were strategically driven and focused on the markets to be served; (3) new services that were different from the acute-care inpatient services already offered but close enough to benefit from present expertise and past experience; and (4) market entry at an opportune time. In other words, the most successful diversification experience has occurred when the strategy was deliberate and planned, recognized the reality of dependence on physician acceptance, took advantage of experience and expertise, and was well timed. The necessity of physician acceptance as well as the importance of individual experience and expertise illustrates the importance of human resources implications for the successful implementation of strategies.

Although diversification and integration are two very different strategic choices, they require similar types of organizational and human resources management responses. In these illustrations, one underlying fact is clear: when diversification or integration is selected as a strategic alternative, the potential exists that organizational size and diversity will increase as will the demand for more specialized human resources management services.

Moreover, to ensure that organizations are structured properly and human resources management is coordinated, certain types of transaction costs between

---

PERSPECTIVE 11–2

Hospital and Wellness Centers: An Uneasy Association?

At one time, wellness programs were considered unproductive and unprofitable. Despite the claims that wellness centers and programs are on the decline, a Gallup Poll and the growth of the Association of Hospital Health and Fitness Centers indicate the opposite. The importance of preventive medicine, rehabilitation, and wellness concepts under current health care reform proposals suggests that wellness centers may, in fact, be important diversification opportunities for hospitals as they face more and more competition for traditional, acute-care services.

Memberships in well-developed fitness centers indicate a growing public awareness of exercise, nutrition, and healthy lifestyle as a means of assuming personal responsibility for preventive care.

John McCarthy, president of the Association of Quality Clubs, advocates the importance of providing high-quality fitness and wellness centers as well as an environment that is enjoyable.

Observers indicate that hospitals are building and purchasing health and fitness centers to provide rehabilitative services and preventive medicine programs in a nonhospital environment. By pulling the rehabilitation and preventive medicine services out of the hospital and repositioning them in health-club environments, hospitals have noticed an improved community image.

Source: A. J. Kania, "Hospital Health and Fitness Centers Promote Wellness," *Health Care Strategic Management* 11, no. 6 (June 1993), pp. 1 and 18.

---

and among the different organizations and organizational units must be taken into account. These transaction costs are the costs associated with handling market or interunit transfers within an organization, such as the transfer prices charged by the hospital-owned laundry that provides services for a number of other facilities.[15] The costs associated with this type of operation are not always evident on the financial statements of the organization. For example, the costs of recruiting laundry staff as well as the administrative costs associated with motivating and leading individuals in the laundry must be considered. As noted earlier under occupational diversity, the needs and skills of laundry workers are quite different from the needs and skills of nurses and physicians. This requires skillful management, and the costs of providing this attention should be carefully monitored so that the true costs of diversification and integration are known.

When a hospital decides to enter the long-term-care market, it ventures outside its area of relatively short-term acute care. For this reason, organizational and human resources management problems are likely. As size increases, there is likely to be pressure to add another functional unit to specialize in long-term care. In addition, special organizational units may be needed to deal with domiciliary housing, health promotion programs, outreach efforts such as alcohol and substance abuse programs, and other forms of rehabilitation. Recruitment, performance appraisal, training and development, compensation, and employee relations become more complex. New services and new clients require different specialists. The typical hospital does not have an established network to effectively recruit specialists in the newer fields nor sufficient knowledge of the work to evaluate the performance with confidence. In addition, there is little understanding of the training and development needs of the new professional staff and limited information about compensation customs.

The acquisition of new technologies, different medical services, and additional health care professionals greatly complicates the staffing or human resources management function. Once these new types of resources are identified and employed, it is necessary to review and probably revise the performance-appraisal system to ensure that the new employees are fairly evaluated and compensated. The increasing diversity of the skills required by the organization makes employee relations more difficult to develop and maintain. Professional and occupational jealousies and conflict place tremendous demands on human resources personnel and line managers.

There is increasing need for "managed-care" specialists within all types of health care organizations, from hospitals to home health care providers. The ultimate goal of managed care is to provide quality medical services at reasonable costs. This requires an entire array of health professionals who have clinical training and experience as well as a "head for business." To be successful, managed-care firms "need to combine business astuteness with medical knowledge and medical understanding."[16]

Whether to centralize or decentralize human resources management is a question that must be addressed. Centralization occurs when a single human resources management unit is established to develop staffing and related policies, recommend evaluation procedures, and ensure that all regulatory requirements are met. If the human resources management activities are delegated more to the individual functional units and the central human resources staff provides only overall management support, decentralization has occurred.

One illustration is the divisional structure put in place when Methodist Medical Center, a 465-bed medical center in St. Joseph, Missouri, merged in the early 1980s with the 205-bed St. Joseph Hospital to form Heartland Health System. Specialized units were added to provide an organizational home for the new services provided and to combine these new services with those already available to clients. In addition to the physician and service changes, Heartland developed a divisionalized structure with services relating to the elderly, rehabilitation, and chronic diseases located in the Heartland Center. The Heartland Samaritan Center for Human Development specialized in addiction recovery and mental health. By establishing these specialized, relatively autonomous units, decision making for specialized care could take place at the level closest to the patient.[17]

In organization structures such as Heartland's, human resources management and staffing activities are usually very decentralized, and the challenge is to ensure that excessive duplication of administrative functions does not take place. Because the divisions are relatively autonomous, it is tempting for each one to have its own human resources, data processing, and accounting units. Thus, the trade-off is important – those activities that are truly unique to the SSU should be focused at that level with only oversight at the corporate level, whereas those activities that do not relate specifically to the SSU should be centralized to achieve economies of scale.

Finally, it is important to remember that whenever a health care organization grows, diversifies, or integrates through acquisitions or mergers, there is potential for *culture clash*. Different organizations, which may have been former competitors, have different histories, missions, and traditions. The combined organizations do not "fit" together without effort. A new mission and vision must be conceived and communicated. The importance of achieving synergy is paramount.[18] In April 1991, the Sioux Valley Hospital and New Ulm Medical Clinic in Minnesota merged, completing a process that had been started several years earlier. Before the merger, the organizations were going in different directions, and no effort was made to coordinate actions or policies. To build the kind of "oneness" required for future success, great care was taken to foster the development of a single culture to avoid any form of culture clash.[19]

When organizations are combined, there is considerable concern about what happens to the employees in the acquired health care organization. One study found that 75 percent of the executives in acquired industrial firms were gone after five years.[20] Because health care has been growing so rapidly, the outlook appeared to be somewhat better. Despite the fact that jobs might have been eliminated in one organization, there have been opportunities in others. However, in light of economic pressures, health care may become more similar to industrial firms.

Human Resources and Other Expansion Strategies In health care, there are a number of hybrid organizational arrangements that have strategic implications for health care organizations and are used in many cases as means of facilitating expansion. Some of these arrangements, such as pooled purchasing and facility management groups, are not new. Others are not only new but innovative.

Hybrid organizational arrangements involve two or more independent organizations that combine to pursue common interests.[21] These organizations are commonly referred to as *quasi-firms* because they are composed of highly autonomous organizations loosely coupled to achieve long-term strategic purposes. Some of these arrangements are very familiar in the health care sector. Preferred provider organizations (PPOs), independent practice associations (IPAs), and some health maintenance organizations (HMOs) are quasi-firms.[22]

Although quasi-firms have a variety of structures, they all share one important characteristic: They are the result of cooperative expansion strategies. In each case, strategists make a decision to cooperate rather than compete, even if the cooperation is relatively uncoordinated, to take advantage of certain perceived long-term advantages.[23] These arrangements can vary from extremely tight and formal legal arrangements to relatively "loose" group practices "without walls" similar to that implemented by Premier Medical Group, P.C., in Denver, Colorado.

This type of practice allows physicians to centralize many support functions such as data processing and human resources, develop a more powerful marketing strategy, and experience a number of other economies of scale while preserving the autonomy and practice style of each physician.[24]

All of these cooperative expansion strategies have important human resources implications. For example, physicians and hospitals sometimes decide to "pool" their resources to pursue an opportunity neither is prepared to pursue alone. These internal corporate joint ventures (ICJVs) are unique in that the parties remain independent and invest their own money although the activity takes place within the organizational structure and is subject to the governance of the overarching health care organization.

One study examined fifty-three hospitals and their physicians who initiated such arrangements. The goals of the ICJVs were to expand primary-care services to the community, increase referrals within the group, and increase the hospital's market share of admissions.[25] This analysis of ICJVs offered several important insights for organization structure and human resources management. First, hospitals and their boards of directors assumed responsibility for the ICJVs' performance and maintained the right to make policy decisions relative to operations. Each ICJV, however, was established as an organizational entity with its own bylaws, mission statement, and strategic goals. The organizational unit was staffed internally and thereby maintained a great deal of operational autonomy. Finally, the ICJVs annually negotiated with the hospital to determine compensation levels and the range of services to be rendered.

Pragmatically, the ICJV possesses many of the characteristics of a SSU in the divisionalized form of organization. In fact, the study cited previously pointed out one of the often unanticipated problems that can develop when such a "division" is given autonomy not afforded to others. Initially, there was a significant amount of staff resistance to the establishment of the ICJVs. Some insiders feared that the new ventures would compete with the hospital for patients, beds, and services. Others simply had a philosophical disagreement with the hospital over forming such associations.

The primary human resources issues are related to the ICJV's ability to develop its own management team, marketing strategies, and budgetary controls. Some of these, of course, could be centralized and provided by the larger administrative infrastructure already in place in the hospital. However, it is important to provide as much operational autonomy as possible for the ICJV or it becomes nothing more than a SSU of a single organization.

Organizational alliances are more common, loosely coupled arrangements. These cooperative groups consist of three or more hospitals (or other health care organizations) that pool their resources to achieve strategic objectives.[26] Cooperative expansion strategies (joint ventures, quasi-firms, alliances, and so on) avoid some of the more troubling organizational and human resources management problems because the loosely coupled organizations remain autonomous. However, there are issues of organizational governance that must be considered. In the case of a group purchasing alliance, provisions for policy making and representation of the individual member organizations must be addressed. At the same time, because a staff will be required to manage the day-to-day operations, understandings must be reached about the extent of each person's authority.

To this point, we have examined appropriate organizational/human resource management responses to expansion strategies. Although the problems are difficult and demanding, expansion is always more fun to manage than maturity and decline. During maturity, the emphasis is on efficiency. Human resources management practices must be constantly refined and improved to ensure that things are done in the best way at the least cost. However, organizations do not always successfully manage maturity, and markets erode and even disappear. Therefore, it is important for the strategic health care manager to also understand how to manage the organizational and human resources aspects during market contraction.

Contraction and Human Resources

In Chapter 6, several contraction strategies such as divestiture and liquidation were discussed. Although terms such as divestiture and liquidation imply financial actions (see Perspective 11–3), they have important human resources implications in the form of restructuring and reorganizing, early retirements, layoffs, and so on.

Specifically, in the case of divestiture or liquidation, recruitment for new personnel to fill essential positions is extremely difficult. It is not easy to attract

---

PERSPECTIVE 11–3
Healthcare International's New Beginning as HealthVest

In 1991, Healthcare International filed for bankruptcy protection. After two years of legal battles, the U.S. Bankruptcy Court in Austin, Texas, approved HealthVest's plan for reorganizing Healthcare International and its hospitals. Under the plan, HealthVest, a real-estate investment trust created by Healthcare International in 1986 will consolidate with its former parent. HealthVest stockholders will own 96 percent of the new company and Healthcare International's subordinated bondholders will own the remaining 4 percent. The plan, of course, is subject to the approval of the IRS because the government has more than $5 million of tax claims against the company.

The excitement created by the reorganization is echoed by a spokesperson for HealthVest who stated, "This is a very important time for the company. It's a new beginning for the company, the employees, and the stockholders." Sometimes organizations can emerge from difficult times, preserve jobs, and begin again.

Source: "HII Reorganization Plans OK'ed: New Beginning for Health Vest," *AHA News* (November 8, 1993), p. 3.

qualified applicants who might assist in turning the organization around when less-essential employees are being terminated. Recruitment is difficult (if not impossible) in times of organizational decline. Employee relations are difficult as well. It is a challenge to maintain morale and productivity in the midst of organizational decline even though compensation, training and development, and appraisal activities may be simplified.

Expansion may be fun, but it is certainly not easy to manage, and when problems develop, expansion can rapidly turn into organizational decline and contraction. For example, much of the early enthusiasm of the Sutter plan discussed in the introductory incident was reduced when Omni Health Plan, a 55,000-member HMO and member of the "Sutter family" reported a loss of more than $2 million. This type of change illustrates the difficulty involved in directing the "strategic thrust" of an organization such as Sutter and the overall diversification strategy.[27]

More serious, however, are the human resources decisions that require actual layoffs of personnel. These decisions, sometimes referred to as *downsizing* or *rightsizing*, can come in a variety of forms. Cost-driven downsizing takes place when health care organizations remove a specific number of employees from the payroll to reduce costs by a certain percent or absolute amount. Targeted restructuring takes place when particular parts of the organization such as the emergency room are eliminated or people in a certain department are laid off. Downsizing may also take place through attrition, hiring freezes, and so on.[28] Chicago's Rush-Presbyterian-St. Luke's Medical Center, for example, eliminated 220 positions through a combination of attrition, consolidation of jobs, and a layoff of 85 employees to "decelerate the increase in prices."[29]

The human resources implications of downsizing and layoffs for those who lose their jobs are obvious. However, it is important to note that reorganizations can carry implications for the performance of the organization. A study by E. C. Murphy, Ltd., a New York–based research and consulting firm, found that hospitals that reduce staff for financial reasons are up to four times more likely to experience increases in patient morbidity and mortality. The study examined the staffing structures of 281 general acute-care hospitals and the work practices of more than 72,000 health care workers and concluded that hospitals that make across-the-board staff reductions of 7.6 percent or more for financial reasons were 400 percent more likely to experience increases in patient death or injury.[30] Unless general work practices, such as reengineering, are combined with staff reductions, organizations simply have fewer people doing inefficient operations. The adverse effects on patient care are worse than before the downsizing.

An example of one organization that has attempted to downsize through personnel reductions is National Medical Enterprises. NME announced in mid-1993 that it would restructure its operations for the second time in less than two years. The plan was to reduce overhead by $20 million by merging all of NME's diverse holdings into a single "hospital division." Eventually NME sold off its rehabilitation hospitals to HealthSouth. Originally the majority of the savings were expected to come from staff reductions. Most of the reductions were expected to be in the corporate headquarters. These layoffs were in addition to the 183 layoffs announced previously by NME.[31]

Another way of dealing with the human resources aspects of downsizing is provided by the Ohio Valley Health Services and Education Corporation (OVHS& E). This three-hospital system in northern West Virginia and eastern Ohio has been attempting to deal with the human resources aspects of a downsizing strategy designed to reduce its work force by approximately 15 percent since 1987. OVHS&E operates about 1,000 licensed beds in a region characterized by a large elderly population, high unemployment, and significant outmigration.[32]

In an attempt to avoid widespread layoffs, OVHS&E initiated several actions, including a system-wide hiring freeze, incentives for early retirement, delays in scheduled salary increases, and so on. Although the effects of such measures complicate employee relations, they have the positive impact of alerting everyone to the seriousness of the problem.

Once it was evident that the attempts to avoid layoffs would not be successful, the reductions were planned to have the least-disruptive effect on the organization and its personnel. To maintain morale and productivity, management decided that reductions would not be across the board. Instead, the reductions were minimized in those areas where services showed evidence of increased utilization, had growth potential, and contributed in a unique way to the accomplishment of the hospital's mission. Decision makers continued to follow the operational needs of units after the layoff plan was implemented to ensure that adjustments could be made if unanticipated problems developed for any department or function.

A more dramatic case of contraction (closure after merger into a larger system) is provided by Woodruff Hospital in Cleveland, Ohio.[33] The acquiring organization made provisions to rehire more than 40 percent of the initially displaced personnel, and because of the market area, almost all personnel eventually found comparable employment. Unfortunately, before the final merger was completed, year-long negotiations with another hospital were terminated and employees were not kept informed about the differences in the proposals under discussion. The result was that the agreements of the final merger were very different (especially in regard to the effect on personnel) than what had been communicated originally to employees.

The direct short-term effects on personnel were quite significant. Almost half of the employees blamed the closing of Woodruff on poor management and a majority did not believe they had been adequately informed or prepared for the closing. Three-quarters of those who lost jobs indicated that the closing was an extremely stressful experience. The greatest problems were considered to be tangible loss of wages and a sense of not belonging. The long-term effects, however, appeared less dysfunctional although about one-quarter of the terminated employees reported being unemployed at the time of the follow-up study about four months later. Of those who had been reemployed, 50 percent had obtained similar-level jobs, 30 percent had lower-level jobs, and about 20 percent had actually received promotions.

Strategically, the process of managing organizational degeneration is challenging and difficult. Studies of organizational decline (including bankruptcy and liquidation) show certain patterns. Decision makers tend to become paralyzed by the events and indecisive about what to do to prevent further decline. When they do act, the actions are often wrong. For example, managerial imbalances develop when executive-level decision makers from critical functional areas such as nursing, medicine, marketing, and finance are replaced by individuals with less knowledge concerning these critical functions.[34] Additional ill-advised actions include an excessive focus on centralization of control and efficiency measures at a time when innovation is needed.[35] At no other time are decision makers more likely to focus exclusively on short-term solutions to serious and recurring problems.

Effective management of organizational contraction demands clear and courageous decision making. The environment created by decline makes the quest for excellence difficult if not altogether impossible. Uncertainty characterizes the organization and insecurity can increase the likelihood of reductions in the quality of services delivered. The challenges to the effective management of organizational decline are great. If a turnaround is to be achieved, inspiration as well as good decision making is crucially important. Perhaps more than anything, honest and timely communication is needed to reduce as much as possible the uncertainty and insecurity faced by the very people who must perform if the organization is to survive.

Managing Stabilization Strategies

The benefits of systematically managing the human resources dimension under expansion and contraction strategies are somewhat obvious. The need for carefully managing stabilization strategies is equally important, if not as obvious.

When an organization reaches a point in its life cycle where it is no longer growing, it must work extremely hard to keep from contracting. Strategic decision makers may adopt a conservative strategy, such as managing the steady state or status quo. As was noted in Chapter 6, the assumption underlying this strategy is that the expansion phase of the organization's evolution is over, maturity has been achieved, and that acceptable market shares have been attained. Relative to human resources strategies, the goal is likewise conservative. The organization attempts to replace personnel with employees of similar skills and training and works to keep existing personnel up-to-date and technologically prepared to perform their jobs at high levels of effectiveness.

Stabilization can present an opportunity to enhance current levels of operation. The stage of organizational development can be looked on as a temporary "breather" and preparation can commence for the next period of growth. Or, decision makers can simply think of stabilization in a dynamic sense and recognize that they must work hard just to maintain their current position. In this case, they may choose to enhance their facilities, improve the quality of their services, increase the speed with which they respond to patients and make decisions, and create new and better ways of doing things.[36] Human resources strategies are important to support any attempt at enhancement because ultimately it is the employees that must improve quality, innovate, and work faster if things are to improve.

In Chapter 4, total quality management was discussed as a means of continuously improving operations.[37] In the remainder of this chapter quality will again be examined from the perspective of enhancing and improving organizational effectiveness.

Organizational Enhancement Through Human Resources Strategies

Exhibit 11–5 provides an overview of some specific ways in which the total quality management and continuous improvement philosophies can be implemented relative to human resources considerations.[38] Overall, as the top portion

---

EXHIBIT 11–5
Human Resource Issues and TQM

Human Resources Characteristics (corporate culture)	Traditional Paradigm (individualism, profits, autocratic, specialization)	TQM Paradigm (teamwork, autonomous work groups, coaching, customer/patient focus)
Communication	Top Down	Multidimensional
Voice and Involvement	Employment at Will	Due Process, Quality Circles, Attitude Surveys
Job Design	Industrial Engineering Focus	Cross Functional, Empowerment, Innovation
Training	Job Related and Technical	Continuous Learning, Problem Solving Skills
Performance Measurement and Evaluation	Individually Focused	Team Focused
Rewards	Individual Merit	Team Merit
Health and Safety	Treat Problems	Prevent Problems
Recruitment, Promotion, Career Development	Supervisor Driven	Driven by Contribution to Team Effort

Source: Adapted from Richard Blackburn, "Total Quality and Human Resources Management: Lessons from Baldrige Award – Winning Companies," *Academy of Management Executive 7*, no. 3 (August 1993), p. 51.

of the exhibit illustrates, the traditional culture paradigm based on individualism, autocratic leadership, profits, and productive efficiency is replaced with collective efforts (teamwork), cross-functioning rather than specialized work groups, coaching and enabling, and a focus on customer/patient satisfaction. Human resources management plays an important role in achieving this culture change.

Organizational communication, traditionally viewed as top down, is encouraged to become multidimensional – top down, bottom up, lateral, or some other combination. Employment at the pleasure of management gives way to due process in disciplinary matters, quality circles, and employee attitude surveys. Job design based on industrial engineering concepts moves to autonomous work teams that facilitate innovation and better ways of doing things. Training is oriented more toward continuous development and problem solving and less toward traditional technical skills–oriented learning. Performance measurement and evaluation are based less on individual attainment, financial focus, and supervisory grading and more on team accomplishments, customer satisfaction outcomes, and service delivery. Rewards likewise are less individual in character and more team oriented. In recognition of the contemporary realities facing health care organizations, health and safety issues are more preventive in character and less problem focused. Finally, hiring, promotion, and career development revolves less around the judgment of supervisors and more on group input. Downsizing and maturity cause career development to be horizontal and less hierarchical.

Enhancement through a focus on quality is significantly changing all types of industries and health care organizations are becoming increasingly involved in this movement. Numerous organizations have attempted to develop approaches that uniquely fit their situation. Regardless of the characteristics, it is important for an organization to develop a benchmark based on the best practices of the industry. In fact, as Perspective 11–4 illustrates, information is an important aspect in all attempts to verify quality differences among health care providers. This is what SunHealth Alliance did with regard to its quality program.

An Example of Quality Enhancement

SunHealth Alliance is a network of 250 hospitals located primarily in the Southeastern United States and Texas.[39] Fifteen of the hospitals have participated in pilot projects designed to enhance the primary processes involved in health care delivery. None of the participating hospitals were direct competitors and members of the medical, technical, and administrative staffs agreed to work together and share best practices. The general process consisted of four steps – planning, data collection and analysis, identification of best practices, and implementation.

Despite the promise held by the adoption of the best practices identified through benchmarking, most of the teams at SunHealth had problems implementing the improvements. Most best practices required changes from established ways of doing things and were resisted. Empowering nurses to do certain things they had not done previously, for example, was resisted by some of the physicians. However, many of the best practices were implemented and significantly reduced the waiting time for many patients. The teams that were most successful in getting

---

PERSPECTIVE 11–4

Quality Programs and Data Dissemination

The Greater Cleveland Hospital Association is concerned that the area has an estimated excess of 2,500 to 4,000 patient beds. Some believe scoring well on Cleveland's quality-information program will be the key to survival. A spokesperson for the association believes that local businesses will look at the quality data when deciding where to send their employees for hospital care.

The quality program's hospital data is provided to businesses and the public and is expected to be instrumental in shifting patient flow to hospitals with high quality and low cost scores and may eventually cause less efficient providers to close. The project, known as Cleveland Health Quality Choice, is expected to initially have its greatest impact on hospitals that score as anticipated on quality but with higher costs. Hospitals of this type are expected to see a drop in managed-care contracts with businesses. In an area with excess beds, a single facility need not lose much business to make a difference.

The new measurement system, called CHOICE (Cleveland hospital outcomes indicators of care evaluations) is based on outcomes associated with heart attacks, congestive heart failure, stroke, pneumonia, and chronic-obstructive lung disease. Hospital officials appear to have confidence in the accuracy of the measures. The quality information systems show whether hospitals perform at, above, or below predicted levels relative to patient satisfaction; length of stay for general medical, intensive care, and general surgical services; and in mortality for general medical and intensive care units.

Source: Geri Aston, "Quality Program Spurs Hospitals to Identify and Solve Problems," *AHA News* (June 7, 1993), pp. 1ff.

---

their ideas approved were the ones that did the most professional job justifying, supporting, and presenting their ideas to upper management. This illustrates the benefits that can be obtained by enhancing existing processes and focusing on services that can be rendered to external and internal customers. Unfortunately, not everyone is convinced that total quality management programs have resulted in high rates of return for the investments they require as illustrated in Perspective 11–5. In Chapter 12 an attempt will be made to examine several actions that can further enhance operations such as better facilities management and attention to the organization structure.

This concluding section of the chapter has discussed many of the human resources implications of different strategies in health care organizations. Human resources provide important reality checks to strategic decisions in health care organizations. If the human resources necessary to support today's mission and tomorrow's vision are not developed, strategies will not be realized. Exhibits 11–6 and 11–7 assist in summarizing some of the ways in which human resources contribute to situational analysis and the overall strategic management of health care organizations.

Chi Systems of Ann Arbor, Michigan, argues that, although 4,500 hospitals have spent millions of dollars on total quality management programs, most have not realized their financial goals. Much of the skepticism relates to the inability to measure whether the programs have been successful. For example, the idea behind much of TQM is to save money by reducing duplication, improving processes, and eliminating waste. Results of this nature are difficult to identify, and the dollars saved are difficult to calculate. However, the University of Michigan Medical Center projects a net gain of about $17 million in incremental benefits over costs during the past five years as the direct result of TQM. According to reports, nineteen of twenty-one quality improvement projects showed a positive benefit equal to or greater than the costs involved.

Source: Jill L. Sherer, "Hospitals Question the Return on Their TQM Investment," *Hospitals and Health Networks* 68, no. 7 (April 5, 1994), p. 63.

EXHIBIT 11-6

Human Resources Input to Situational Analysis

Situational Analysis	Human Resources Input
External Environment	
Analysis of Human Resources	Assess elements of macroenvironment that possess human resources implications: availability of adequately trained work force; socioeconomic status of present and potential employees; cultural diversity
Competitive Human Resources Analysis	Evaluate available pool of employees relative to competitive organizations; carefully assess critical human resources areas such as nursing and physicians
Internal Environment	
Human Resources	Assess present strength relative to human resources; inventory existing skills relative to mission and vision for the future; evaluate succession planning activities
Mission, Vision, Values, and Objectives	Ensure management understands the human resources requirements for present and future operations; determine human resources implications of possible changes in organizational mission; establishment of human resources benchmarks and objectives to accomplish organizational mission and vision

EXHIBIT 11-7

Human Resources Management Input to Strategic Management

Hierarchy of Strategic Decisions	Human Resources Input
Directional Strategies	
Mission	Ensure understanding of human resources requirements for building and maintaining organizational distinctiveness
Vision	Determine ways of obtaining human resources necessary to accomplish the organization's hope for tomorrow
Values	Include clarification of importance of personal ethic and organizational responsibility in human resources decision making
Objectives	Participate in the formulation of organizational objectives; develop human resources objectives to support accomplishment of organizational objectives
Adaptive Strategies	
Expansion	
Diversification – Related and Unrelated	Assess available human resources pool relative to similar skills needed for related diversification; build network to assist in obtaining the unfamiliar skills needed for unrelated diversification; evaluate advantages of decentralized versus centralized human resources operations
Vertical Integration – Forward and Backward	Build a network to obtain the unfamiliar skills needed to staff vertically integrated operations; evaluate advantages of decentralized versus centralized human resources operations
Market Development	Identify the sources of human resources needed for expanding the underserved geographical areas and market segments; determine the incremental human resources needed to support market development
Product Development	Evaluate present human resources and assess the additions needed to support service development activities
Penetration	Assess the availability of human resources needed to support greater service differentiation, staff promotional activities, and marketing efforts

EXHIBIT 11-7   cont'd

Hierarchy of Strategic Decisions	Human Resources Input
Contraction	
Divestiture	Assess the capacity of the organization to absorb human resources displaced by divestiture; evaluate the organization's commitment to assisting displaced employees with outplacement efforts; evaluate any acquiring organization's commitment to provide opportunities for existing employees
Liquidation	Evaluate the organization's responsibility to displaced employees; consider the use of outplacement services; assess the organization's capacity to absorb employees from liquidated operations; evaluate acquiring organization's willingness to continue employment of present human resources
Harvesting	Initiate efforts to retrain employees presently in areas of harvesting; develop a program to offer retraining opportunities to employees desiring such services and outplacement opportunities for those who do not
Retrenchment	Evaluate and recommend areas where greatest use of human resources can be achieved despite more limited scope of operations; evaluate the capacity of the organization to absorb employees displaced by retrenchment activities
Stabilization	
Enhancement	Identify specific training and development activities needed to support enhancement efforts
Status Quo	Ensure effective management of human resources
Market Entry Strategies	
Purchase	
Acquisition	Assess the human resources of the target organization; evaluate the target organization's culture relative to present organizational culture and plan for any expected culture clash; evaluate the ability of the organization to absorb the human resources of the acquired organization
Licensing	Negotiate the precise relationship and responsibilities to employees of other organizations as part of a licensing agreement

EXHIBIT 1 1 – 7   *cont'd*

Hierarchy of Strategic Decisions	Human Resources Input
Cooperation	
Merger	Assess the possibility of culture clash from merging of organizations; evaluate advantages of decentralized versus centralized human resources operations and any possible human resources synergies from the merger
Alliance	Evaluate the human resources condition of the partner(s); assess human resources synergies likely to result from cooperation; precisely state the reciprocal responsibilities of cooperating organizations to employees of all organizations
Joint Venture	Consider the combined human resources capabilities of joint venture partners for possible synergies; evaluate the human resources that will be needed to support the venture but are not currently available in either partner to the venture
Development	
Internal Development	Assess the availability of human resources to support the proposed internal development activities
Positioning Strategies	
Market-wide	
Cost Leadership	Assess the human resources implications of cost leadership – particularly any temporary or permanent displacement of employees resulting from efficiency measures; assist employees that may be displaced by efficiency measures
Differentiation	Consider whether different types of human resources will be required for increased differentiation efforts; plan for acquisition of any human resources needed to support the differentiation strategy
Market Segment	
Focus – Cost Leadership	Project the potential human resources effects of cost leadership activities and expected increases in efficiency
Focus – Differentiation	Project the potential human resources effects of increasing differentiation; assess the pool of human resources needed for increased differentiation relative to those currently available

EXHIBIT 11-7   cont'd

Hierarchy of Strategic Decisions	Human Resources Input
Operational Strategies	
Functional – Finance	Ensure that human resources operations are as efficient and effective as possible; assess the orientation of human resources personnel to the internal customers of the organization; develop the strategic human resources plan to support the mission and strategies of the organization

SUMMARY AND CONCLUSIONS

This chapter discussed the human resources implications of expansion, contraction, and stabilization. It is important that human resources planning be carefully integrated into the overall strategic management process of health care organizations. However, the vision of management should not be limited by the existing quantity or quality of human resources. Human resources, like financial resources, are important "enablers" and reality checks but not the sole determinate of what a health care organization should aspire to become as evidenced by the vision of its leaders.

Expansion strategies such as diversification and vertical integration frequently require additional and different types of human resources. If expansion strategies such as related diversification are adopted, the new employees may possess the same skills and training as present employees. Unrelated diversification and vertical integration, on the other hand, will require employees with different skills and training. This is one of the primary risk factors for expansion, as little may be known about how to manage and lead these new types of employees.

Contraction strategies make different demands on human resources. Human resources implications of contraction strategies are particularly threatening because they often mean downsizing, layoffs, early retirements, and alternative career paths for devoted and loyal employees. Although there are no easy solutions to contraction strategies when it comes to human resources, a convincing argument can be made that systematic planning can sometimes eliminate the need to take extremely radical actions and allow time for employees to find alternative careers and employment.

Stabilization strategies such as enhancing existing operations and improving the quality of services have a direct impact on human resources. Reengineering processes demand that traditional ways of doing things be altered and improved. Those who have devoted years to learning how to succeed under existing systems may find reengineering, redesign, and work transformations almost as threatening as layoffs. Total quality management offers an appropriate option for enhancing operations and improving services. However, although total quality management has become an increasingly popular method for enhancing operations, some believe that data remain too limited to assess the success or failure of TQM and related techniques.

KEY TERMS AND CONCEPTS IN STRATEGIC MANAGEMENT

benchmarking	**inspiration-related**	**reengineering**
best practices	**currencies**	**relationship-related**
culture clash	**occupational diversity**	**currencies**
growth-preparedness	**personal-related currencies**	**task-related currencies**
matrix	**position-related currencies**	

QUESTIONS FOR CLASS DISCUSSION

1. Why do you think job redesigns and work transformations are so threatening in health care organizations? Do you think employees in industrial organizations are more or less threatened by these measures? Why or why not?

2. Can human resources strategies be effectively implemented without addressing the issue of organizational culture? How is culture related to job redesign and work transformations?

3. What relationship does human resources planning have to strategic planning? Should human resources capabilities determine the aspiration levels of a health care organization? Explain your answer.

4. Why is it important to avoid allowing the quantity and quality of present human resources to determine the vision of a health care organization? What is the proper role of human resources when planning for the future?

5. What are the primary differences in the human resources strategies needed for expansion, contraction, and stabilization? Which type of adaptive strategy is most difficult to implement from a human resources perspective? Why?

6. Is total quality management really worth the investment it takes in terms of time, money, and energy? What do you see as the primary problem involved in evaluating the effectiveness of TQM?

7. What type of adaptive strategy is most likely to benefit from systematic benchmarking and the consequent development of best practices? Why did you select this strategy?

NOTES

1. R. S. Schuler and S. E. Jackson, "Linking Competitive Strategies with Human Resource Management Practices," *Academy of Management Executive* 1, no. 3 (August 1987), pp. 207–219.

2. Ibid., p. 213.

3. J. A. Raelin, "An Anatomy of Autonomy: Managing Professionals," *Academy of Management Executive* 3, no. 3 (August 1989), pp. 216–228.

4. H. L. Smith and Richard Discenza, "Developing a Framework for Retaining Health Care Employees," *Hospital Topics* 67, no. 3 (May/June 1989), pp. 26–32.

5. David Burda, "And What Is Your Bid for this Loyal Admitter? Please, Don't Hold

Back," *Modern Healthcare* 20, no. 2 (January 15, 1990), pp. 22–27ff.

6. For an innovative application of the currency metaphor, see A. R. Cohen and D. L. Bradford, *Influence Without Authority* (New York: John Wiley & Sons, 1990), Chapter 4.

7. Ibid., p. 79.

8. J. S. Livingston, "Pygmalion in Management," *Harvard Business Review* 65, no. 5 (September/October 1987), p. 118.

9. W. H. Griggs and S. L. Manring, "Money Isn't the Best Tool for Motivating Technical Professionals," *Personnel Administrator* 37, no. 6 (June 1985), pp. 63–78; and Ralph Katz, ed., *Managing Professionals in Innovative Organizations* (Cambridge, Massachusetts: Ballinger Publishing Company, 1988).

10. For a summary of organizational life cycles in general, see R. E. Quinn and Kim Cameron, "Organizational Life Cycles and Shifting Criteria of Effectiveness: Some Preliminary Evidence," *Management Science* 29, no. 1 (January 1983), pp. 33–51.

11. V. Ramajujam and P. Varadarajan, "Research on Diversification: A Synthesis," *Strategic Management Journal* 10, no. 6 (November/December 1989), pp. 523–551. For a debate on the pros and cons for diversification in health care, see Jeffrey A. Alexander and Beaufort B. Longest, Jr., "Diversification in Health Care: Point and Counterpoint," *Strategic Issues in Health Care Management,* ed. W. J. Duncan, P. M. Ginter, and L. E. Swayne (Boston: PWS-Kent Publishing Co., 1992), pp. 11–33.

12. Yegmin Chang and Howard Thomas, "The Impact of Diversification Strategy on Risk-Return Performance," *Strategic Management Journal* 10, no. 5 (May/June 1989), pp. 271–284.

13. J. R. Williams, B. L. Paez, and L. Sanders, "Conglomeration Revisited," *Strategic Management Journal* 9, no. 5 (September/October 1988), pp. 403–414.

14. S. M. Shortell, Ellen Morrison, and Susan Hughes, "The Keys to Successful Diversification: Lessons from Leading Hospital Systems," *Hospital & Health Services Administration* 34, no. 4 (Winter 1989), pp. 471–492.

15. S. S. Mick and D. A. Conrad, "The Decision to Integrate Vertically in Health Care Organizations," *Hospital & Health Services Administration* 33, no. 3 (Fall 1988), pp. 345–359, and S. S. Mick, "Explaining Vertical Integration in Health Care: An Analysis and Synthesis of Transaction-Cost Economics and Strategic Management Theory," in S. S. Mick and Associates, eds., *Innovations in Health Care Delivery* (San Francisco: Jossey-Bass, 1990), pp. 207–240.

16. R. C. Harnett, "Managed Health Care Needs Its Own Kind of Specialists," *HealthWeek* 4, no. 21 (June 11, 1990), p. 73.

17. See L. C. Kruse, "Heartland Health System: Merged Hearts and Minds," *Healthcare Executive Briefings* (May/June 1989), pp. 3–4.

18. J. W. Hunt, "Changing Pattern of Acquisition Behavior in Takeovers and the Consequences for the Acquisition Process," *Strategic Management Journal* 11, no. 1 (January 1990), pp. 69–78.

19. Bill Siwicki, "Hospital, Clinic Merger Proves Advantageous, Perhaps Prophetic," *Healthcare Financial Management* 48, no. 4 (April 1993), p. 26. See also "Developing a Collaborative Culture in a Hospital Setting," *Health Care Strategic Management* 11, no. 1 (January 1993), pp. 7–10.

20. Caren Siehl, Dayle Smith, and Ann Omura, "After the Merger: Should Executives Stay or Go?" *Academy of Management Executive* 4, no. 1 (February 1990), pp. 50–60. See also J. E. Gutknecht and J. B. Keys, "Mergers, Acquisitions, and Takeovers: Maintaining Morale of Survivors and Protecting Employees," *Academy of Management Executive* 7, no. 3 (August 1993), pp. 26–36.

21. Bryan Byrys and D. B. Jemison, "Hybrid

Arrangements as Strategic Alliances: Theoretical Issues in Organizational Combinations," *Academy of Management Review* 14, no. 2 (April 1989), pp. 234–249.

22. Roice Luke, J. W. Begun, and D. D. Pointer, "Quasi-Firms: Strategic Interorganizational Forms in the Health Care Industry," *Academy of Management Review* 14, no. 1 (January 1989), pp. 9–19.

23. B. B. Longest, Jr., "Interorganizational Linkages in the Health Sector," *Health Care Management Review* 15, no. 1 (1990), pp. 17–28.

24. D. L. Schryver, G. A. Niederman, and B. A. Johnson, "Establishing a Group Practice Without Walls," *Health Care Strategic Management* 11, no. 1 (January 1993), pp. 18–21.

25. S. M. Shortell and E. J. Zajac, "Internal Corporate Joint Ventures: Development Processes and Performance Outcomes," *Strategic Management Journal* 9, no. 6 (November/December 1988), pp. 527–542.

26. H. S. Zuckerman and T. A. D'Aunno, "Hospital Alliances: Cooperative Strategy in a Competitive Environment," *Health Care Management Review* 15, no. 2 (1990), pp. 21–30. See also Douglas Gregory, "Strategic Alliances Between Physicians and Hospitals in Multihospital Systems," *Hospital & Health Services Administration* 37, no. 2 (Summer 1992), pp. 247–258.

27. P. J. Kenkel, "Omni Health Plan Loss Casts Shadow on Sutter," *Modern Healthcare* 23, no. 14 (April 5, 1993), p. 13.

28. "Hospital-Staff Downsizing Can Have Effect on Patient Mortality and Morbidity," *AHA News* (November 8, 1993), p. 3.

29. Geri Aston, "Employees Bear Brunt of Hospital Push to Streamline Operations," *AHA News* (August 2, 1993), pp. 1 and 5.

30. "Hospital-Staff Downsizing Can Have Effect on Patient Mortality," p. 3.

31. Judith Nemes, "NME Sees Big Savings Through Realignment," *Modern Healthcare* 23, no. 14 (April 5, 1993), p. 12.

32. This case is based on information obtained from A. D. Mullaney, "Downsizing: How One Hospital Responded to Decreasing Demand," *Health Care Management Review* 14, no. 3 (1989), pp. 41–48.

33. This case is based on information from M. K. Petchers, Sandra Swanker, and M. K. Singer, "The Hospital Merger: Its Effect on Employees," *Health Care Management Review* 13, no. 4 (1988), pp. 9–14.

34. R. A. D'Aveni, "The Aftermath of Organizational Decline: A Longitudinal Study of the Strategic and Managerial Characteristics of Declining Firms," *Academy of Management Journal* 32, no. 3 (September 1989), pp. 577–605.

35. M. D. Fottler, H. L. Smith, and H. J. Muller, "Retrenchment in Health Care Organizations: Theory and Practice," *Hospital & Health Services Administration* 31, no. 3 (Fall 1986), pp. 29–43.

36. K. M. Eisenhardt, "Speed and Strategic Choice: Accelerating Decision Making," *Planning Review* 20, no. 5 (September/October 1992), pp. 30–32.

37. Bryan Dieter and Doug Gentile, "Improving Clinical Practices Can Boost the Bottom Line," *Healthcare Financial Management* 47, no. 9 (September 1993), pp. 38–40. See also T. H. Davenport, "Need Radical Innovation and Continuous Improvement? Integrate Process Reengineering and TQM," *Planning Review* 22, no. 3 (May/June 1993), pp. 6–12.

38. R. J. Schonberger, "Is Strategy Strategic? Impact of Total Quality Management on Strategy," *Academy of Management Executive* 6, no. 3 (August 1992), pp. 80–87.

39. Information for this case was obtained from T. R. V. Davis and M. S. Patrick, "Benchmarking at the SunHealth Alliance," *Planning Review* 21, no. 1 (January/February 1993), pp. 28–31ff.

ADDITIONAL READINGS

Bergman, Rhonda, "Reengineering Health Care," *Hospitals & Health Networks* 68, no. 3 (February 5, 1994), pp. 28–36. A discussion of a new management tool that is expected to transform processes and raise important discussions in health care organizations. This article reports on the potential applications and problems of reengineering as it moves from purely industrial to health care applications.

Boje, David M., and Robert F. Dennehy, *Managing in the Postmodern World: America's Revolution Against Exploitation* (Dubuque, Iowa: Kendall/Hunt Publishing, 1993). A wide-ranging discussion of diverse topics in management with interesting stories that illustrate important lessons for leaders in modern organizations. The book provides a number of useful concepts to managers of all types of organizations.

Bowman, James S., "At Last, An Alternative to Performance Appraisal: Total Quality Management," *Public Administration Review* 54, no. 2 (March/April 1994), pp. 129–136. An argument is made in this article that performance appraisal's focus on assessing and changing individual behavior is misguided. In contrast, TQM stresses improvements in work process rather than individual employee performance. A series of scenarios for the future of quality management is discussed.

Carson, K. D., P. P. Carson, C. W. Roe, J. P. Authement, and R. Yallapragada, "Increasing the Effectiveness of Healthcare Managers," *Hospital Topics* 71, no. 3 (Summer 1993), pp. 16–19. This article deals with the problems associated with clinic operations that are geographically separated from general administration. Physical distance creates communication barriers and inhibits psychological attachment. Specific intervention strategies are offered for correcting dysfunctional behaviors in these health care settings.

Hammer, Michael, and James Champy, *Reengineering the Corporation: A Manifesto for Business Revolution* (New York: Harper Business, 1993). This manifesto is an authoritative guide by the originator of the reengineering concept on how to create new types of organizations. The authors discuss the approaches used for reengineering at Bell Atlantic, Taco Bell, and Hallmark Cards.

Gehani, R. R., "Quality Value-Chain: A Meta-Synthesis of Frontiers of Quality Movement," *Academy of Management Executive* 7, no. 2 (May 1993), pp. 29–42. An interesting analysis of some of the quality pioneers such as Ishikawa and Taguchi and how they compare with champions of quality in the United States – Deming, Juran, and Crosby.

Goold, Michael, and Kathleen Luchs, "Why Diversify? Four Decades of Management Thinking," *Academy of Management Executive* 7, no. 3 (August 1993), pp. 7–25. This article reviews the logic that has advocated diversification during a four-decade period in management thought. It provides an interesting historical perspective on this key expansion strategy in the industrial sector.

Longest, B. B., Jr., Kurt Darr, and J. S. Rakich, "Organizational Leadership in Hospitals," *Hospital Topics* 71, no. 3 (Summer 1993), pp. 11–15. In the dynamic environment faced by hospitals, leaders must respond to diverse community needs and stakeholder expectations. Leadership in this environment is particularly complex. An integrative view of leadership is presented and determinants of success are discussed.

Manz, Charles C., and Henry P. Sims, Jr., *Business Without Bosses: How Self-Managing Teams Are Building High-Performing Companies* (New York: John Wiley & Sons, 1993). Self-managing teams provide a means of increasing productivity that is consistent with new and developing leadership philosophies in all types of organizations. This book provides many examples and organizational experiences on the use of self-managing teams.

Nystrom, P. C., "Organizational Cultures, Strategies, and Commitments in Health Care Organizations," *Health Care Organization Review* 18, no. 1 (1993), pp. 43–49. Cultural elements such as norms and values affect organizational commitment and job satisfaction for managers and executive secretaries according to this study of thirteen health care organizations. Results show that organizations pursuing a consistent strategy possess strong cultures whereas inconsistent strategies produce weak cultures.

Watson, Gregory H., *Strategic Benchmarking: How to Rate Your Company's Performance Against the World's Best* (New York: John Wiley & Sons, 1993). A quality executive with Xerox and one of the pioneers of benchmarking tells, from firsthand experience, some of the benefits and promises of benchmarking as a strategic tool. The author shares many of his insights and advice for improving organizational performance at all levels.

Organization-wide Strategies

"Healthcare, like industry, can no longer afford the maxim, 'if it isn't broke, don't fix it.' Rather, 'if it isn't perfect, make it better,' is becoming the credo of leading hospitals."

— *Michael Everett and James C. Brent*

LEARNING OBJECTIVES

After completing this chapter you should:

1. Be able to discuss the differences between organizational cultures that contribute to long-term high performance and those that do not.
2. Understand seven factors that relate to building a culture based on organizational excellence.
3. Appreciate the importance of changing organizational culture as an element in implementing strategic change.
4. Understand the relationship between organization structure, culture change, and the implementation of different strategies.
5. Be able to discuss the primary areas of facilities management and their impact on organizational strategies.
6. Understand the importance of ethical and social responsibility constructs in health care organization strategic management.

INTRODUCTORY INCIDENT

Culture Change at Ciba-Geigy

In 1986, a warehouse fire at Sandoz, a major competitor of Switzerland's largest chemical and pharmaceutical group, greatly changed the way Ciba-Geigy does business. The fire resulted in the release of 30 tons of toxic chemicals in the Rhine River at Basle. Although Ciba-Geigy had nothing to do with the spill, the resulting public outcry highlighted the magnitude of resentment toward the chemical industry to company officials. Management's response was a comprehensive culture change program known as *Vision 2000.*

Vision 2000 was designed to assist the company in better understanding the external environment in which it operates and in changing internal operations in a way that aids in appropriately responding to external economic, social, and political changes. Vision 2000 began with a new set of corporate values based on "striking a balance" between the company's economic, social, and environmental responsibilities and the prosperity of the enterprise. All business units (three "pillar" businesses – pharmaceuticals, agriculture chemicals, and additives – and four "growth" businesses – over-the-counter compounds, diagnostics, vision care, and composite materials) were given the charge to reduce their environmental impact, save resources, meet all environmental standards, reduce waste and dispose of what is left in the most environmentally responsible manner, and strengthen environmental consciousness at all levels of the organization. All products were placed in highly autonomous business units where initiative and innovation were emphasized. Ciba-Geigy hopes that, over time, the public will come to view the company as very socially responsible, and employees will demonstrate the creativity and initiative necessary to be competitive in all the areas of company operations.

Source: Carol Kennedy, "Changing the Company Culture at Ciba-Geigy," *Long Range Planning* 26, no. 1 (1993), pp. 18–27.

Implementing strategies is a complex, time-consuming task. More than one frustrated executive has thought "It's been rather easy for us to decide where we wanted to go. The hard part is to get the organization to act on the new priorities."[1] Implementation presumes that organizations have done a good job of formulating directional, adaptive, market entry, and positioning strategies. In addition, it presumes that the functional strategies necessary to support the overall strategy have been developed. However, for most health care organizations, more is needed. Organization-wide strategies such as initiatives to change the organization's culture, reorganize operations to more effectively support new and emerging strategies, upgrade equipment and facilities, and develop and implement philosophies that ensure the organization's fit into the prevailing social and culture realities must be developed. These organization-wide strategies are the focus of this chapter. The relationship of organization-wide strategies to the overall model of strategic management is illustrated in Exhibit 12–1.

The purpose of this chapter is to illustrate four important organization-wide

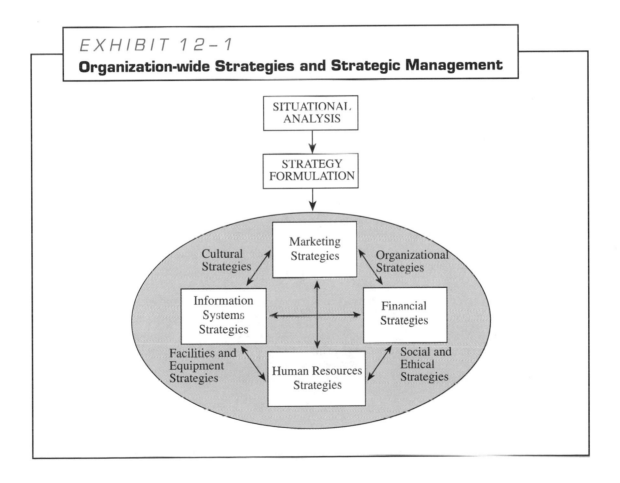

EXHIBIT 12–1

Organization-wide Strategies and Strategic Management

SITUATIONAL ANALYSIS

STRATEGY FORMULATION

Cultural Strategies

Marketing Strategies

Organizational Strategies

Information Systems Strategies

Financial Strategies

Facilities and Equipment Strategies

Human Resources Strategies

Social and Ethical Strategies

strategies needed to support strategic management of health care organizations. These are culture changes emphasizing organizational excellence, organizational structure changes to support the move toward excellence, appropriateness of equipment and facilities, and responsible decision making in an ethical and social context. The importance of these organization-wide strategies is illustrated by the Ciba-Geigy experience in the Introductory Incident. The culture and structure of the company had to be altered in line with external economic, social, and political changes. Strategic change initiates a wide range of related changes in order for implementation to be successful.

ORGANIZATIONAL EXCELLENCE AND CULTURE

Many organizations in health care, business, education, and government are very good at achieving their mission. In a competitive enterprise, an organization has to be good in terms of efficiency and effectiveness or it will not survive. In the public sector, unless an organization does at least a satisfactory job at what taxpayers created it to do, it will not survive. The result is that many organizations do a very good job of accomplishing their purpose. Many hospitals admit and discharge patients with respectable mortality rates. Hundreds of public health clinics see patients without making them wait so long that they become frustrated and leave. Thousands of pharmacies fill the prescriptions of millions of customers every day without making serious mistakes. Even though literally millions of organizations around the world do an adequate job, perhaps even a commendable job, at accomplishing their mission, relatively few are truly excellent. In health care, organizations such as the Mayo Clinics or physician practices that treat patients as real customers are remarkably few.

Why is this? What is the difference between very good and truly excellent organizations? The answer, according to Tom Peters and Nancy Austin in *A Passion for Excellence,* is that excellence is at the margin. Many organizations consistently operate at the 80 to 90 percent level. However, excellent organizations consistently operate at 95 percent or better. Excellence is a "game of inches."[2] Excellence is consistently working a few percentage points above the competition with regard to patient services, innovation, teamwork, and other areas of importance.

In this chapter, one view of organizational excellence will be presented and the argument made that excellence, to a great extent, begins with the culture of the organization. Culture permeates the environment for organizational activities. Therefore, to successfully bring about strategic change and foster excellence something must be known about how to build, change, and maintain organizational culture.

Changing Organizational Culture

In Chapter 4 the characteristics of organizational culture were introduced and discussed. It was noted that culture is important in determining the internal capabilities of an organization. Culture may be supportive of efforts to improve organizational performance or it may actually resist changes that alter the accepted ways of doing things. If the latter occurs, the implementation process will require modification of the culture. Although culture change is difficult, it is an important factor in moving the organization toward high performance. Perspective 12–1 illustrates the importance of a culture emphasizing cooperation and teamwork for the success of a community care network.

Developing Adaptive Cultures

Kotter and Heskett reviewed much of the literature on organizational culture and studied numerous organizations in an attempt to understand the relationship between an organization's culture and its long-term performance.[3] They found that the strength of an organization's culture and its "fit" with the demands of the external environment only partially explained the culture/performance relationship. Instead, adaptive cultures or those cultures that assisted in anticipat-

---

PERSPECTIVE 12–1
Community Care Networks and Health Care Cultures

In Petoskey, Michigan, a hospital, a physicians' group practice, and a community mental health center joined together to provide complete mental-health services to the surrounding rural area. In Franklin, New Hampshire, a hospital collaborated with social service agencies, civic groups, and churches to create a community wellness center. In New Ulm, Minnesota, a hospital and a medical clinic decided to share a single medical record system, maintenance and security departments, and a system of medical-waste disposal and to cooperate in recruiting physicians to the area.

Community care networks, many believe, represent a unique type of "health reform." Individual providers work with a variety of other organizations to increase access and control costs. Despite these lofty goals, networks are not easy to build and they are even harder to maintain.

American culture encourages competition among groups with similar goals and often complicates cooperation. This competitive culture has resulted in a great deal of "redundancy" in the health care and human services systems. System sharing and network building could be effective means of reducing costs and ensuring access. The success of these promising efforts, however, relies on the development of a common vision among cooperating groups to effect the needed culture changes. Community care networks are built on a belief in teamwork, responsible leadership, a commitment to innovation, and a determination to constantly seek ways to inspire better care for patients.

Source: R. J. Davidson, "Community-Care Networks," *National Forum* 68 (Summer 1993), pp. 39–40.

ing and adapting to environmental changes were associated with superior performance over the long run.[4]

An *adaptive organizational culture* is one that allows for reasonable risk taking, builds on trust and a willingness to allow people to fail, and exhibits leadership at all levels.[5] In organizations with adaptive cultures everyone, regardless of position, is encouraged to initiate changes that are in the best interests of patients, employees, and managers. The fear of failure is reduced by tolerating creative, and sometimes risky, efforts to make the organization a better place to work and more responsive to all stakeholders.

Assessing the receptivity of an organization to any proposed strategy is an important step in implementation. This assessment requires investigation of both the subjective and objective dimensions of culture. Many of the subjective aspects can be inferred from the understood distinctiveness of the organization (the mission), the hope that the members have for the future (the vision), and the principles they hold dear in accomplishing the mission (the values). There is, however, a more objective side of culture that leaders can observe and use to gain insights into the culture of the organization.

Culture and Heroes Much can be learned about an organization by observing its *cultural heroes.* Portraits of former chairs of boards of directors, famous physicians who have been members of the medical staff, and others who have made unique contributions to the development of the organization's growth and reputation are often displayed in the board room of hospitals. State and local health departments frequently and proudly display former health officers. Many organizations will feature pictures and stories about the employee of the month or employees of the year as well as individuals who performed meritorious acts or services. Heroes provide important artifacts of an organization's culture and suggest how receptive it might be to new strategic directions. The heroes are the role models. What does the organization portend to recognize in its heroes? Are the heroes those people who were merely loyal for many years or did they really make things happen and challenge the organization and its members to higher levels of achievement? Sometimes culture change requires a change of heroes.

Rites, Ceremonies, and Organizational Culture Rites and ceremonies that are preserved and honored in organizations can reveal a great deal about the culture. *Rites* are elaborate and dramatic sets of activities designed to perpetuate, reward, or punish behaviors in an organization. *Ceremonies* are systems of rites connected into a single occasion or event.[6] Health care organizations, similar to other industries, require that members "get their tickets punched" before they are allowed to become "true members" of the work group or progress to higher levels of responsibility. These *rites of passage,* such as spending time in both line and staff units, working the midnight shift, and so on, provide useful information about the organization, help members appreciate the contributions of others, and show that the new person can "take it."

A common *rite of integration* is the welcoming reception for new residents or the hospital's orientation program for new employees. Elaborate ceremonies are used to reward performance and recognize outstanding service (i.e., award banquets and retirement dinners). Just as role models show what the organization values, so do its rites and ceremonies. The message these events convey should be observed carefully as new and different strategies are implemented and culture changes are required.

One study of a rehabilitation unit in a Veterans Administration hospital found that rites and ceremonies were used to build and maintain the strength of the culture itself, which was considered to be particularly high performing. New employees were required to attend staff meetings (*staffings,* as they were called) where core values of teamwork, intergroup cooperation, and concern for clients were discussed, demonstrated, and emphasized. *Parting ceremonies* were held along with "roasts" for residents who were rotating out of the unit. Interviews with members of the unit confirmed that these rites and ceremonies effectively "bonded members to one another and helped build confidence and trust."[7]

Rites and ceremonies, however, do more than bond members to one another and the organization. They indoctrinate and socialize newcomers as well as communicate the behaviors existing members believe are instrumental to success. In addition, they reduce anxiety and uncertainty. Thus, they imply a great deal about what actions will be needed to successfully implement proposed strategies. If they "glorify" retirement, changing the way people do things will be difficult. If they celebrate the performance of those who constantly work to make the organization better, people will be more willing to try something new and different.

A Specific Implementation Problem To illustrate, consider the case of hospital mergers. Sometimes a merger failure can be traced directly to differences in the cultures of the merging organizations.[8] Reflecting on the merger of HealthWest Foundation and Lutheran Hospital Society Corporation into a new organization called UniHealth, one executive noted that the merger was successful because both parties recognized that their cultures, although similar, were not identical. Therefore, a great deal of attention was devoted to working out potential problems before the merger actually went into effect.

The most common problem in any merger, according to the president of Centra Health, Inc. (Virginia), is the lack of a common vision. The development and acceptance of a common vision is particularly difficult to accomplish when cultures are different.[9]

Culture, Leadership, Politics, and Implementation If organizational culture is to be used as an implementation tool in strategic management, health care leaders will have to work to understand its potential advantages and disadvantages and be willing to change the culture when necessary. To successfully do this, several intentional acts on the part of management are necessary:[10]

1. *Learn the history of the organization.* Older hospitals and health care organizations have more traditions. Where the history is recognized as important, managers can use the traditions to motivate and maintain high levels of performance. One health care executive assigned a person to each of the eight decades of the hospital's history to highlight the accomplishments, heroes, and significant events in each period. During the

review, old timers were visibly moved and newcomers reported feeling a part of the hospital for the first time.[11]

2. *Reinforce existing cultural patterns.* Health care managers can be important symbolic leaders. The successful leader should understand the history of the organization so its best features can be reinforced through various actions and activities, such as the way managers dress, the meetings they call and attend, and so on. One hospital executive reinforced the organization's commitment to cost containment by moving to a very spartan office in the basement. This action was tangible evidence of a commitment to cost control at the highest level.

3. *Change and reshape culture.* Health care organizations must be careful to avoid becoming enslaved to their culture, yet they must also avoid jumping into new directions without assuring some stability for those who find security in a well-established culture. At Vanderbilt University Hospital and Clinic, nurses were experiencing low levels of morale and productivity. Examination of the situation led managers to believe the root of the problem was over a decade old. When the hospital moved to its new facilities, some of the old symbols were lost – the sycamore trees outside the windows and the interaction that was possible in the old facility. Once the issue surfaced and changes were made to preserve what was possible of the old environment in the new facility, performance and morale improved dramatically.

The manner in which things are accomplished in an organization frequently reflects the political climate that the culture fosters. When physicians, nurses, managers, and support personnel view the ultimate purpose of the organization to be providing high-quality, cost-effective health services, their actions are coordinated toward the accomplishment of organizational goals. When individuals and departments are concerned only with their own well-being, distrust develops and power politics enters the strategic picture.

The tactics of organizational politics are familiar.[12] The laboratory personnel describe simple tests in complicated terms that only they understand. In this manner, they control important information that others depend on for decision making. Computer specialists often do precisely the same thing. Physicians attempt to win the budget struggle by arguing that their budget request has more to do with high-quality patient care than sound business practices. Managers, in a similar manner, formulate decisions in terms of administrative issues to win the negotiations. They argue that the organization's very survival depends on following administrative leadership.

Sometimes, when one group in the organization is not strong enough to "win," a coalition is formed with another unit.[13] The maintenance staff and clerical employees may threaten to join a union if their demands are not met. Office personnel and technicians may join together to increase their power relative to the nursing staff. The nurses enlist the assistance of their accrediting agency to ensure that their wishes receive consideration before those of the administrative staff.

The degree to which informal political behavior is encouraged and tolerated in an organization is an important element of its culture. If winning through intimidation has been a part of the organizational history, the tactic will continue to be employed unless an incentive is provided for a different type of behavior. This type of political culture, where members have been allowed to hinder new ideas and innovation, greatly complicates the implementation of new strategies.

Building Organizational Excellence As noted previously, organizational excellence is a difficult concept to define but it is relatively easy to identify in an organization. In excellent organizations, all people – managers, employees, and customers – are treated better than in other organizations. Excellent organizations are rarely taken by surprise when the external environment changes and they insist on quality in everything they do. They are the first to introduce new products and services, and they innovate in the way they manage their operations.

Building excellence in organizations often means looking first at the existing culture and asking how well a particular hospital or HMO compares to the standard provided by the recognized industry leaders. In the following section, a model will be developed around seven factors that have been shown to be key elements in the development of organizational excellence.

A Model of Organizational Excellence

Exhibit 12–2 illustrates factors that are instrumental in developing an organizational culture that fosters excellence. The factors are shown in no particular order

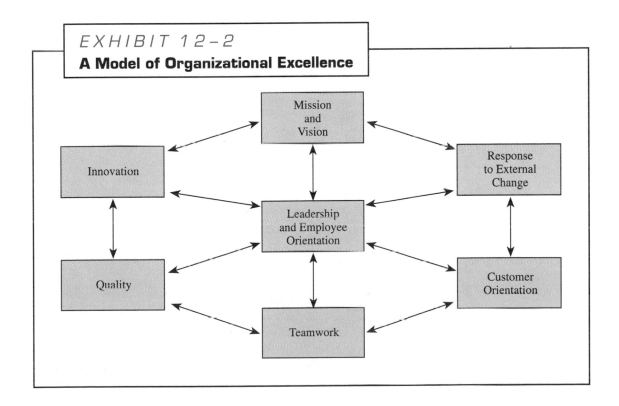

EXHIBIT 12–2
A Model of Organizational Excellence

Mission and Vision

Innovation

Response to External Change

Leadership and Employee Orientation

Quality

Customer Orientation

Teamwork

because all are important to organizations that aspire to be the best they can be and maintain sustained competitive advantage over the long run. Although it is true that none of the factors is more important than any other, it is important to note that the three factors in the center of the exhibit, mission/vision, leadership, and teamwork, are fundamental to the development and maintenance of the other factors. The "centrality" of these factors will become apparent in this discussion.

A Sense of Mission and Vision   Chapter 5 was devoted to a detailed discussion of mission, vision, and values in health care organizations. Little more will be said at this point except that an organization's mission is the critical starting point toward excellence. There must be a well-communicated understanding of why the organization exists. Not only must the mission be understood, it should be shared. Employees and managers should look upon the mission statement as a living document that genuinely describes "what we are all about" and follow it on a daily basis. Perspective 12–2 illustrates how one well-known sponsor

---

PERSPECTIVE 12–2
Where Health Care Is Free – By Design

There is a place where health care is free to all who need it. No patients are sent bills. To be admitted, the prospective patient needs only to show that the receipt of care in other hospitals would create an excessive financial burden on the family. Some facilities do not require proof of financial need although this is an increasing problem because the patients served by the Shriners come from a population that increasingly has no medical insurance. In 1977, about 13 percent of the nation's children did not have insurance. Today, that figure has increased to 18 percent.

The Shriners and Scottish Rite children's hospitals across the nation operate through philanthropy and some third-party reimbursement. The hospitals specialize in niches such as burn care and orthopedics. Each one shares a sense of mission and vision that makes them unique phenomena in the health care industry. It is a system where, as one recruit stated, "They give you a reason to be a part of it."

The Shriners and Scottish Rites children's hospitals operate on fixed budgets and there are fewer perks for employees than in other types of facilities. One administrator noted that she did not have a company car or country club membership but she had less bureaucracy and fewer problems with billing and paperwork.

Some suggest that there will not be a need for Shriners and Scottish Rites hospitals under health reform because everyone will have access to care. The Shriners, however, are not convinced. Advocates cite the case of Canada with its national health care system. Even there, the Shriners hospital in Montreal is needed. According to one spokesperson, "As long as there are children, there will be a need for Shriners hospitals."

Source: "Free for All," *Modern Healthcare* (September 20, 1993), pp. 34–36.

of health care services keeps its focus on its unique role within the system of care.

It is important that employees and managers understand where the organization is going. It is extremely important that everyone believes that people are thinking about and providing for the future. Moreover, there should be an appreciation that the organization "stands for something" (its fundamental values). Mission, vision, and values are the building blocks of organizational culture. If people are to be expected to creatively adapt to change, they must understand what the organization is, where it is going, and what it stands for through good times and bad.

Leadership and Employee Orientation In excellent organizations, leadership is exhibited at all levels, not just in the executive suite. People willingly take responsibility to ensure that jobs are accomplished. Leaders make sure employees and colleagues know that they care about them as people and understand the importance of everyone to accomplish the organizational mission. In excellent organizations there is an understanding that leadership is different from management. Management is an important element in the success of any health care organization. Plans have to be made, budgets prepared, work coordinated, and performance evaluated. These are critical ingredients of efficiency and problem solving. Managers are responsible primarily for ensuring that things are done consistently and that organizational members have a sense of order and an idea of where they are in the pursuit of organizational goals.

However, management, as important as it is, is not leadership. Leadership involves setting direction or creating a vision, enfranchising people in decision making, building coalitions that get things done, and inspiring and motivating others.[14] Whereas management is concerned with order and efficiency, leadership is concerned with change, movement, and doing things in different, and ideally better, ways.

Leadership is stewardship not ownership.[15] It implies that people setting the direction care about the success of the organization and the welfare of its members. Although leadership is critical at all levels, *strategic leadership* involves skillfully developing and communicating the mission, vision, and values of the organization. This must be done inspirationally if it is to motivate high levels of performance. The necessity of this inspirational communication sometimes causes problems in organizational settings that have historically valued "management-oriented communication" that is precise, rational, analytical, and often graphically presented.

The "language of leadership" is often very different from management-oriented communication.[16] Conger notes that the language of leadership can be divided into two parts. The first is *framing* – defining in a meaningful way to others the mission of the organization for today along with the vision for the future and the higher purposes it hopes to fulfill. The focus is on the importance and necessity of the mission, the heroic behavior that makes it happen, and the importance of the organization succeeding at what it was designed to do (its purpose).

The second aspect of the language of leadership is *rhetorical crafting*. This, when done well, is what makes the language of leadership inspirational. Metaphors as well as analogies are used to bring a genuine "alikeness" between the leader and those who are listening. Great orators and some political leaders are highly skilled at inspiring people to do the impossible, think about the unthinkable, and make things happen where others have failed.

In reality, leadership is more than communication. It is also *role modeling*. Words are important and metaphors can inspire, as can tales of superhuman accomplishments. In the real world of health care organizations, actions speak louder than words. If leaders are to inspire others, they must be prepared to model the valued behaviors. This is what Eire Chapman tried to do as president of Riverside Methodist Hospital in Columbus, Ohio.[17] Every month Chapman puts on the uniform of the housekeeper, nurse aide, parking attendant, or dietary employee and conducts "walkabouts" to find out what it is like to be that kind of employee at Riverside Methodist. Chapman's counterparts in other health care organizations wondered how the busy executive could afford the time to do these jobs. He did not understand how they "could afford not to do them."

A president who comes in at midnight and attends the parking lot, cleans the floors, and talks to people on their own terms sends a powerful message. It disarms charges that "they [management] do not understand how it is to be in the trenches and do not care about average employees." Chapman says, "The CEO does not take care of patients, the CEO takes care of people who take care of patients." This is an important responsibility and requires dedicated strategic leadership.

What do the framing, rhetorical crafting, and management walkabouts achieve? In a word, they *empower* people to do their jobs. Empowerment makes available more of the creative resources of an organization. It activates and energizes people in their individual quest for excellence.

To empower others, strategic decision makers need to be sure several things take place.[18] First, employees must be properly trained to do their jobs and make decisions. Second, employees have to share the vision and understand where the organization is going. Third, it is important to share values and beliefs about the things that are important and how things should be done. Next, the benefits of the culture change that result from empowerment must be shared. Finally, leaders have to demonstrate faith and trust in fellow employees. This means tolerating reasonable risk taking. The benefits of empowerment will not occur unless everyone knows new ideas can be expressed and new ways of doing things are encouraged.

The results of empowerment can be significant in terms of individual and organizational performance. When people are encouraged to depend on their own creative solutions to problems, they assume greater ownership of the organization's success or failure. This causes them to use their own time and the organization's resources more effectively in the accomplishment of goals. In other words, everyone assumes responsibility for the organization's performance. Everyone becomes a leader.[19]

Organizations benefit from the empowerment of people. Resources and talents are better utilized. People develop and become better able to exercise even more responsibility. Everyone assuming greater responsibility improves operations with fewer layers of management and less overhead. In the extreme, the entrepreneurial spirit replaces the bureaucratic mentality.[20] The changes in the organizational culture made possible by everyone demonstrating leadership and by organizations that care about and encourage employees to grow personally and professionally are limited only by the collective imagination of the entire group.

The motivational power of this type of culture change is illustrated by one woman's experience. An accomplished communications specialist, she was hired to ensure the organization's vision was communicated to 20,000 employees. She arrived on the job with few instructions and little support. Realizing that she needed office equipment, clerical support, and so on, she approached the CEO and asked for the needed resources. The CEO responded in a way that taught an important lesson about empowerment: "You are an executive director with signature authority to run your operation. I trust you. That is why we hired you for that position. Go and do it." The new employee was energized, motivated, and determined to make good things happen because of the trust that had been placed in her.[21]

Thinking and Working as Teams Teamwork is a characteristic of excellent organizations. Very little is accomplished in complex health care settings without the involvement of teams. Yet, there is widespread "failure to cooperate." In many organizations members of individual clinical units are divided by personal agendas that prevent them from being real team players.[22] Entire departments such as nursing and the clinical laboratory have ongoing conflicts, physicians may horde operating room time, egos may interfere with a group practice realizing its full potential, and so on.

It is not uncommon for top leadership to discover after spending time, energy, and resources on strategic planning that the hospital, health department, or family planning center simply does not have a culture that is capable of implementing the strategies. Usually the tasks required for implementation demand that people work together as teams and accomplish work in a cooperative manner. Team building, therefore, is usually a prerequisite to or integral part of the implementation process. It is rarely enough to simply point out the necessity of working as a team. The culture of an organization must be altered.

Researchers have observed that groups pass through four stages in their progression to becoming a team. This evolution is descriptive of the way an organization's culture changes to one that fosters teamwork.[23] In the *forming* stage, members of the organization who are experienced at working and being rewarded as individuals begin to "test the water" of teamwork. Many will not like it and some will resist efforts to become real team players. Inexperienced team players are highly dependent on other things during this stage – leaders, more experienced team members, and the guidelines (rules and regulations on which team interaction is built). Organizationally, changes are needed to move members beyond this state. Top level support and leadership is critical at this point to avoid attempts by many to stop "all these meetings" and get back to the real work.

Storming is the second stage of change as individuals move toward becoming team players and as organizations move toward accepting the group concept. The team development evolution is analogous to the "rebelliousness of youth." Earlier converts may come to genuinely question the wisdom of moving to a team-oriented culture and become less zealous. Those who were never true believers may take the loss of enthusiasm and natural conflicts as an opportunity to sabotage the process. This is a critical point in the development of a team-oriented culture. At this time it is important to showcase some "small victories" of the power of group performance.

For example, a public hospital's pharmacy department had experienced ongoing conflict between registered pharmacists and pharmacy technicians. The pharmacists believed the technicians unnecessarily complained about the condescending way they were treated by the "professionals." The technicians believed the pharmacists, as a group, thought they were "too good" to perform certain routine tasks and, by refusing to do so, reduced the services delivered to the patients.

A joint working group of pharmacists and technicians implemented a "put yourself in my shoes" program whereby pharmacists and technicians switched roles for two hours a week. Although the technicians could not perform specific tasks legally requiring a registered pharmacist, the two groups designated allowable activities and once a week put themselves in the role of the other party. Pharmacy supervisors report that a new understanding has developed between pharmacists and technicians and the two groups are working more as a team. In addition, this small victory has received attention by other groups in the hospital that are considering implementing a similar program in their areas.

The third stage in the evolution of a team-oriented culture is *norming*. During this stage the desired cohesion begins to develop. More people become believers in the power of team performance. Fewer people engage in social loafing and teams become the norm.[24] Members become more willing to work – even enthusiastic – about working in teams. Cooperation becomes the natural way of doing things. The challenge relative to the small victories taking place during the earlier storming stage is to find ways to make sure the good ideas and improvements are adopted and become the "norm."

The final stage of team development is *performing*. Groups in this stage become mature and develop into high performing teams. There is an established structure and the purpose and role of the team are well understood by all its members. At the organizational level, the cultural transition is complete. The organization is structured around teams and problems to be resolved rather than the more traditional departmental functions. The emphasis is on results to be achieved and the common good of the team.

The quest for excellence within organizations involves a commitment to teams. Realistically, they are difficult to form – especially in organizational cultures built on and proud of their commitment to individualism. However, merely envisioning the potential power of a team can cause a leader to become a believer and an advocate. Teams can achieve tasks that individuals can only dream about and teams can provide a feeling of satisfaction and accomplishment to equal that of individual achievement when the culture recognizes and rewards the group. It has been stated that: "The opportunity for increased performance [in teams] is too great to let misunderstanding, inexperience, uncertainty, or false assumptions – or even past team failures – stand in the way."[25] Teams are essential to excellence in organizations.

Innovation, Culture, and Excellence Excellent organizations are creative and innovative in the way they do things. Not only do they develop truly new products and services, they adopt creative ways from other organizations to solve problems. Unfortunately, innovativeness is not easy to instill within organizations. Typically, established rules and regulations are designed to ensure things are done consistently rather than creatively. Organization structures often place people in boxes and provide no incentive to assist others to improve through intergroup cooperation. The result is a culture that places greater value on conformity than innovation. "Trying to be more innovative," according to Schein, "will not help if the corporate culture and employees are not open to the process – organizations [if they wish to be innovative] must change the way managers and employees think."[26]

Many people, when thinking of inventions and innovations, think only of radical new discoveries – microprocessors, improved imaging technologies, or beta blockers for heart disease. Most ideas, even the ones that make a tremendous difference in the way organizations deliver their services, take place incrementally and over a relatively long period of time.[27] The organization must often be patient in its attempts to encourage people to think and act in different ways and people must support each other when innovations are not successful. Trying to improve through innovation assumes that many, perhaps most, ideas will not be successful. However, as the CEO of the Allegheny Health Systems noted, "The heroes and heroines of tomorrow will have failed their way to success."[28] The people who make a difference in organizations are willing to try something new when the odds of success seem reasonable or the potential gains are sufficient to justify even extreme risks.

Health care is typically described as an innovative industry. Hardly any sector of the economy can match the technological progress made in areas such as genetics, surgery, pharmaceuticals, and materials engineering. Less visible but no less important are process or managerial innovations taking place that have encouraged new ways of doing things and improved patient services.[29]

The University of Michigan Hospitals introduced a pilot program to encourage managerial innovation. Suggestions for change could cover any area of the hospital and, if selected, the individual submitting the idea would be given an opportunity to implement the plan and offered a mentor to assist in the implementation. Rejected proposals were returned with comments and encouragement to develop the idea further or pursue the idea through different routes. In the initial evaluation stage, ten of approximately forty proposals were selected and implemented, resulting in cost reductions and better service delivery.[30]

One of the Innovation Awards given by the Ford Foundation and the Harvard University Kennedy School of Government illustrates the importance of service improvement innovations in public health. The Monroe Maternity Center in Madisonville, Tennessee, was designed to provide improved services to maternity patients through an innovative alliance between nurse midwives and local physicians. After almost a decade of operation, the center was nearly self-supporting and proving to be a cost-effective alternative to traditional hospital deliveries. For example, Medicaid maternity bills at the center were less than $2,000 compared to $3,000 to $5,000 in local hospitals. In addition, convenient access was provided to a broader range of patients in this area of Appalachia.[31]

Other examples include these: waiting time has been reduced in innovative ways in health clinics, the rate of "no-shows" has been dramatically decreased through relatively simple employee suggestions, and school-based clinics have made access to services available in creative ways to teenagers not willing or able to go to traditional providers of medical services. When innovations occur, two things seem to be present – an organizational culture that encourages everyone to think and share ideas plus a *champion of change,* a person who is determined to overcome all odds, all bureaucratic barriers, and all naysayers to shepherd the new idea into reality.

Normal organizational inertia means that very few new and creative things will happen in organizations of any type if a champion does not foster change. People have the new ideas and the knowledge to implement them. Therefore, whether innovative thinking is adopted depends on some person or group that champions the idea and overcomes resistance.[32] It is important to identify and nurture these people to ensure a steady flow of new ideas. Exhibit 12–3 provides a summary of selected characteristics possessed by individuals who emerge as champions of change.

Individuals who champion change are willing to take reasonable risks. Although the organization may take risks in adopting new services and methods, individuals take risks in advocating new ways of doing things. Even in the best organizations, dangers are associated with trying new things – especially if the new things do not work. It is much safer to do things according to policy guidelines and avoid "rocking the boat." This, however, is not how champions operate. Champions are innovative people, discontent with operating "according to policy" when there are better ways of doing things. This does not mean that they are renegades who consistently engage in clandestine actions, merrily violating all the organization's rules and regulations. Sometimes they do violate the rules but they may be successful in developing a convincing justification for the value of their ideas and involving others in the implementation of new ideas.[33]

Champions, whether in the executive suite or in the operating room, are natural leaders because of their ability to articulate the vision of what "might be." They are confident, perhaps even overly optimistic and have little doubt that their ideas better enable the organization to accomplish its mission. And, perhaps most important, they are persistent. All people have a spark of creativity and innovativeness. A few can effectively articulate the vision they have for their ideas; however, most of these fall away when their ideas are questioned and rejected. Champions persist. They keep the pressure on to rethink ways of doing things and are always available to discuss their own pet projects.

Finally, the role of strategic managers relative to champions of change is to nurture and protect them. They may appear aggressive and time consuming but

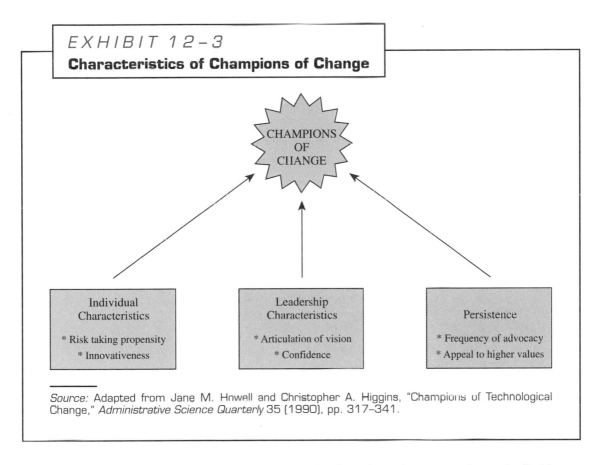

EXHIBIT 12-3
Characteristics of Champions of Change

CHAMPIONS
OF
CHANGE

Individual Characteristics	Leadership Characteristics	Persistence
* Risk taking propensity	* Articulation of vision	* Frequency of advocacy
* Innovativeness	* Confidence	* Appeal to higher values

Source: Adapted from Jane M. Howell and Christopher A. Higgins, "Champions of Technological Change," *Administrative Science Quarterly* 35 (1990), pp. 317–341.

they are the "fresh air" that organizations depend on to continuously find better ways of doing things. Exhibit 12–4 provides a process for the care and nurturing of champions.

Top executives must create a culture based on autonomy and variety in job experiences to ensure that champions have the knowledge and freedom necessary to innovate. In addition, they have to develop a vision that incorporates innovation and is supportive of innovative actions. This is done, to a great extent, by sponsoring individuals who demonstrate the ability to be creative, protecting them from "static" in the organization, and running interference for them when policies and rules become oppressive. Finally, it is important to recognize that organizations make heroes of someone. If creative ideas and innovation are recognized and rewarded, champions become the heroes and others look to them as role models. If people who "do their jobs" and "stay out of trouble" are the heroes, they will become the role models. Recognition and reward for creative ideas will dictate the rate of idea generation in the hospital, HMO, or physician's office.

Quality and Continuous Improvement Quality was discussed in Chapter 4 as one of the aspects of the internal environment that influences the organization's

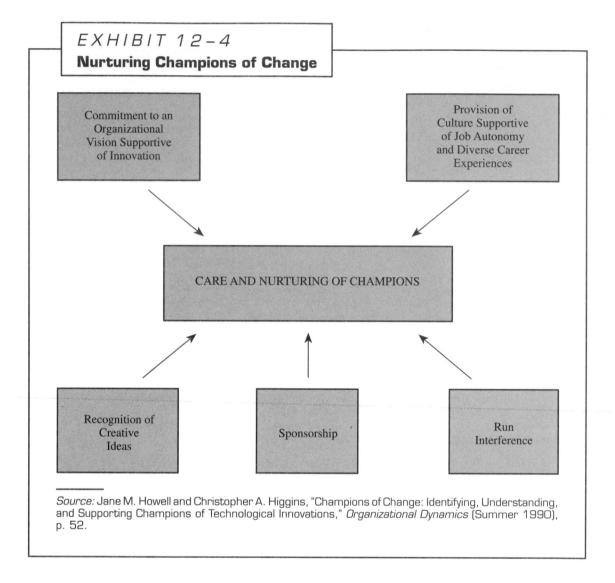

EXHIBIT 12-4
Nurturing Champions of Change

Commitment to an Organizational Vision Supportive of Innovation

Provision of Culture Supportive of Job Autonomy and Diverse Career Experiences

CARE AND NURTURING OF CHAMPIONS

Recognition of Creative Ideas

Sponsorship

Run Interference

Source: Jane M. Howell and Christopher A. Higgins, "Champions of Change: Identifying, Understanding, and Supporting Champions of Technological Innovations," *Organizational Dynamics* (Summer 1990), p. 52.

strategic capacity. An obsession with quality is a characteristic of excellent organizations. However, quality will not be discussed in detail at this point except to say that an organizational culture based on excellence focuses on continuous improvement. Excellent organizations always expect more of themselves than they did last year or even last month.[34] This process of "raising the hurdle" is important to ensure that the organization and all its members continuously move toward being the best they can be. The image of quality that is developed in this manner frequently translates into a tangible competitive advantage in the marketplace.[35]

Making sure that quality is ever present in the thoughts and actions of all employees, at all levels, at all times, demands attention from leaders. Peters and

Austin summarized it accurately in their statement that quality is "about care, people, passion, consistency, eyeball contact, and gut reaction."[36] Quality does not just happen. It must be reinforced and nurtured if it is to survive. There is no resting with regard to quality. It is, as one strategist has observed, "a race without a finish line."[37]

Response to External Change Excellent organizations appreciate the importance of external factors, develop ways of assessing their importance, and change the way they do things when external factors demand responses. Often they see change as an opportunity and make adjustments before change is required. Excellent organizations are still surprised occasionally by external events but they are consistently better able to deal with change than their "ordinary competitors." Waterman notes that some organizations are "continuously adapting . . . to the shocks and prosper from the forces that decimate their competition. They move from strength to strength, adjusting to crises that bedevil others in their industry."[38]

One characteristic that excellent organizations seem to share is the expectation that the organization will develop ways to deal with the changes taking place around it. Sometimes the methods are formal; sometimes they are little more than an effort on the part of top-level leadership to get people involved in informally communicating about changes taking place in their areas of interest. Perspective 12–3 illustrates some of the technologies strategic leaders in health care believe will have the greatest potential for improving the quality of service delivery.

More formal techniques are being utilized by many health care organizations. One example of a more formal approach is the state department of public health that convened a group of its own employees to function as "in-house experts" to scan and monitor the external environment for events taking place in their areas of expertise that might affect the department's operations over the next five years.[39] This strategic thinking task force included members who became knowledgeable monitors in areas such as health care technology, environmental issues, political and legislative affairs, economic trends, and disease control. The objective was to keep the health officer informed about developing trends that should be incorporated into planning activities. This process was useful in developing ways of classifying external events as opportunities and threats and thereby developing action plans to assist in avoiding threats and taking advantage of opportunities.[40]

The point is clear from the standpoint of excellence. Excellent organizations know how important it is for them to "fit" into the environment and match internal strengths and weaknesses to the demands of the forces beyond their control. A key action to ensure that the organization fits the environment is to muster all the internal expertise possible toward responding to external change.

Customer/Patient Orientation In health care organizations as in business firms, government agencies, or universities, there are two types of customers: the *external customer,* patient, student, or citizen – the person who pays the bills; and the *internal customer.* Internal customers are colleagues within the organization that rely on someone or some other unit to accomplish a task. Nursing, for example,

Keeping up with Technology

Leaders are constantly involved in strategic thinking. Technology is one of the areas that is of greatest strategic concern to health care executives. One survey of American Hospital Association leaders indicated that they believed the technologies highlighted in the following bar chart had the greatest potential for improving the quality of health care in the United States. The numbers indicate the percentage of respondents identifying each technology.

In the chart, CDSS = clinical decision support systems; MM = multimedia – images, patient data, and voice communications in a single terminal; HHC = handheld computers; and TM = telemedicine – real-time conferences, X rays sent over telephone lines and personal computers, and others.

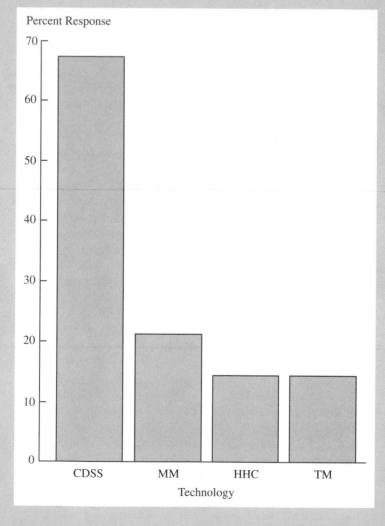

Source: "Health Care Fact," *AHA News* (July 5, 1993), p. 7.

is an internal customer of the medical records department because nurses depend on medical records to properly maintain patient records. Pharmacy relies on data processing, and everyone depends on the services of the payroll department.

Chapter 8 focused on the external customer. It is important to recognize, however, that many, perhaps most, employees of hospitals, universities, and even business firms never interact with a patient, student, or citizen. However, everyone has a customer and excellent organizations know this well. Organizational cultures that emphasize the importance of serving all customers and "making their jobs easier rather than making our jobs easier" are striving toward true excellence.

There is an emerging emphasis on the importance of the patient as a customer in health care organizations. Many organizations are making, or have made, the transition from the point where, as one IBM executive noted, "service is no longer a 'problem' but a business strategy."[41] Excellent organizations seem to understand better than others the true importance of a satisfied customer and focus their energies at all levels to accomplishing this goal.

Perhaps a more difficult concept to communicate is the importance of internal customers. As already noted, competitive environments demand high levels of teamwork. Sometime the difference between one long term care facility, HMO, or ambulatory care center in the mind of a potential patient or staff member is very small. Perhaps it is little more than how they are treated by the receptionist when they arrive for a visit, how their bill is handled by the business office, or how the nurse treats their friends and neighbors who have come for a visit. This "margin of excellence" often has much to do with the team spirit that exists among staff members. For example, if nurses are frustrated because the personnel department treated them with annoyance when a question was raised about a different deduction on a paycheck or disgusted with pharmacy because "they can't get my orders right," the margin of excellence will not exist.

If customer orientation is to be an organizational strategy or factor of excellence, all members of the organization need to think of one another as customers. The point is not how to best design an order request field in a computer screen to "make data processing's or pharmacy's job easier." The challenge should be "how to design this field, menu, or screen so as to make the nurse's job easier." The nurse interacts with the patient and should be assisted in every way possible to serve the patient more effectively.

Exhibits 12–10 and 12–11 at the end of this chapter summarize the importance of culture in the situational analysis and as an input to strategic management.

MAKING THE STRUCTURE RESPONSIVE TO THE STRATEGY

Although there has been justified controversy over whether strategic changes cause changes in the organizational structure or vice versa, there is general agreement that changes in one of these important factors almost always requires changes in the other. One of the most important organization-wide implementation strategies, therefore, is the consistent pattern of decisions that leads to a structure that will encourage and facilitate the overall strategic change. If organizations are to foster innovation and risk taking, the structure must relax control and delegate decision-making authority to the point that employees can activate the rapid responses necessary to take advantage of opportunities detected in the environment. If management hopes to encourage leadership at all levels, the "distance" between managers and employees must be reduced and the upper levels of leadership must be accessible enough to ensure everyone knows and understands the mission and vision of the hospital, health department, or HMO. Often, when a particular philosophy of organization has been in place for a considerable length of time, changes in the structure will necessitate culture changes similar to those discussed earlier.

As environmental issues provide incentives for changes in the organization and the culture becomes receptive to accomplishing the organizational mission in new and innovative ways, pressure inevitably increases for changes in the structure of the hospital, HMO, or long term care facility. Hierarchical organizations with tight operational controls are barriers to team building, innovation, and empowerment. Therefore, one important organization-wide strategy for strategic change is making the structure more responsive.

Components of Organizations

Organizations have many component parts, but for purposes of this discussion, only three of the more important will be discussed. These components are governing boards, management, and the operating core.

Governing Boards Boards of directors or boards of trustees in all types of organizations are responsible for making policies or establishing the general guidelines under which the organization will operate. In health care, as in other industries, there are different types of governing boards. *Philanthropic governing boards* are service oriented and concerned primarily with spanning the boundary between the health care organization and the community. These boards are larger and more diverse to gain as much community representation as possible. The inclusion of different types of stakeholders is important and requires that board members be selected from among business leaders, physicians, local politicians, consumers of health care services, and so on.

Corporate governing boards are more involved in strategic planning as well as policy making. This type of board is smaller and composed of individuals who possess expertise that will aid the organization in accomplishing its goals.[42] Membership diversity is important, but less so than the actual skills possessed by the members.

The current trend in health care organizations is toward the corporate board. To a great extent, this is the result of the increasingly competitive environment facing health care organizations and the need for expertise in dealing with the complexities of the economic environment.[43] For example, in the late 1980s Middlesex Hospital in Middletown, Connecticut, consisted of nine separate corporations and was governed by a board of twenty-one members. The terms of the board had no limit. The hospital was operating at a deficit and the morale of the employees was extremely low. Middlesex was losing the competitive battle. In an effort to turn the situation around, the senior management of the facility was reduced, the nine corporations were reduced to one parent corporation with three subsidiaries, and the size of the board was reduced to twelve. Limits were placed on the length of time board members could serve in an effort to ensure a continuous supply of new ideas.[44] The results have been impressive. In 1992, operating income was $3.7 million compared to less than $500,000 two years earlier.

This experience supports the findings of research on boards of directors, which suggests that when profound or radical organizational change confronts a hospital, the corporate board is more likely to effect a positive response. Philanthropic boards, on the other hand, are more likely to be associated with either no change or negative responses to profound changes.[45] As a specific case in point, it was found that the boards of directors in health care organizations undergoing corporate restructuring, defined as the "segmentation of [the organization's] assets and functions into separate corporations to reflect specific profit, regulatory, or market objectives," tended to become less philanthropic and more corporate in composition and the way they operated.[46]

Other research has provided additional information about various types of governing boards in health care organizations. When compared to boards of directors of successful high-technology firms, for example, it was found that governing boards in a sample of multihospital health care systems were almost twice as large (eleven to fifteen members).[47] In fact, boards are frequently too large to be effective aids in decision making, and where the goal is stakeholder representation, board members often know so little about health care that CEOs are forced to spend a great deal of their time informing and educating lay members. Perspective 12–4 provides some opinions of selected CEOs regarding their needs and responsibilities relative to board members.

One final study examined the issue of outside directors in large investor-owned health care organizations. Four major subsamples were examined, including hospitals, elder-care organizations, HMOs, and alternative-care facilities such as psychiatric clinics and ambulatory-care centers.[48] This study found that, in general, governing boards of health care organizations were composed of more outside than inside members.

Outside representatives were primarily physicians, financial professionals, attorneys, and academics. The inclusion of physicians was found to be particularly significant in terms of bottom-line performance. It was suggested that this resulted primarily from the fact that the presence of physicians on governing boards enhanced the support of the medical community to improve the market share and quality.

Although it is dangerous to generalize, some inferences can be drawn from the research on governing boards in health care organizations. First, when health care organizations are profit oriented, their boards take on more corporate characteristics. They tend to be smaller, to compensate members for service, to select members for specific expertise, to involve the CEO as a voting member and make him or her formally accountable to the board, and to require the participation

PERSPECTIVE 12–4
What Board Members Need to Know

Keith Baldwin, CEO of the Samaritan Hospital in Moses Lake, Wisconsin, believes that trustees "must understand how reimbursement scenarios being discussed will affect hospitals." Leo M. Henikoff, M.D., CEO of Rush-Presbyterian-St. Luke's Medical Center in Chicago, however, believes that "although it's important to look for people with financial experience, I sure wouldn't populate my board with them." Peter E. Makowski, CEO of the Riverside (California) Community Hospital, maintains that hospital management must remain flexible when putting together its board. Financial expertise on the part of board members is important, but so are strategic planning expertise, an understanding of medical staff issues, and community needs.

The more informed trustees are, the more likely they are to be valuable, contributing members of the board. It is the responsibility of the CEO to provide board members with continuing opportunities to learn and experience more about the nature of the health care environment. These more informed trustees, according to Makowski, are likely to "challenge the heck" out of management and expect them to stay on top of things. However, that is the role of the board, and the organization will benefit from such involvement.

Source: J.L. Sherer, "CEOs: Trustees Need Financial Savvy," *Hospitals* (March 20, 1993), p. 62.

of board members in strategic decision making. From the perspective of the board member, the motivation may be to provide a valuable service, but board membership may be an important source of income as well.

In not-for-profit health care organizations, governing boards tend to display characteristics more in line with the philanthropic model. They are generally large (in fact, too large to be effective aids in strategic decision making), do not compensate the members, select members primarily as stakeholder representatives, and do not hold the CEO formally accountable for performance. In this case, the primary motivation for board membership is service and recognition.

The future of board composition and responsibility is difficult to predict. However, one thing appears certain, the role of the board is changing and likely to change even more in the face of radical changes in the environment of health care.[49]

Management The role of the board of directors is to make policy. The role of professional management personnel such as presidents, hospital administrators, and directors of long term care facilities is to implement policies. Boards of directors are representatives of the stakeholders, and as such, they attempt to identify the desires of stakeholders and translate those desires into policy statements.

Managers are responsible to the board for effective policy implementation. The board, for example, may develop a policy relating to the degree of risk a multisystem health care organization may assume in financing expansion into other services. The job of management is to ensure the organization experiences only that degree of risk exposure expressed in the policy. Conforming to that policy may require specific choices such as issuing stock rather than engaging in long-term borrowing. Once strategic choices are made, management's responsibility is to develop appropriate operational strategies to implement the strategic choices.

Strategic management has traditionally focused on top management, particularly the CEO. This individual is considered the person most responsible for scanning and influencing the environment, developing adaptive strategies, and managing key constituencies.[50] Unfortunately, the exclusive focus on the CEO's role in strategic management has implied that middle management has little or no involvement in determining the strategic direction of the organization. In recent times, organizations have made a greater effort to involve large numbers of employees and managers in strategic planning through a process similar to that outlined in Chapter 14.

Admittedly, the primary responsibility of middle management is strategy implementation. However, certain strategic directions require middle-management leadership. Middle management, for example, is a particularly key resource in the development of employee commitment to the organizational mission and vision. The increasing importance of quality as a strategic objective and middle management's role in keeping this objective before all employees is a good example.[51] As noted in Chapters 4 and 5, quality has become an important "value" to which employees at all levels can be committed, and middle managers are in the best position to encourage and reinforce this commitment.

Another important area in which middle management ought to be involved is in the redefinition of organizational vision. Grand strategies and futuristic visions are important for health care organizations. If the vision is to become meaningful to nurses, pharmacists, medical laboratory technicians, and others, middle- and first-line managers must take the lead in redefining the organizational vision in terms that are meaningful to departments and work groups. Finally, with regard to building involvement and commitment to service and quality, middle managers are in the best position to appeal to the social and economic motives important to health care employees.

The Operating Core Operational-level personnel are responsible for accomplishing the tasks required by the policies of the board and derived from the strategic choices and action plans of management. This organizational level will be directly and immediately affected by strategic decisions such as selling off a series of specialty hospitals or engaging in a contractual arrangement with an independent laboratory.

Operational-level personnel are in many ways the "heart" of the health care organization. This is particularly true of the clinical personnel, who are involved in direct patient care. This is the reason why the "clinical subsystem" and other aspects of internal operations were assigned such importance in the audit of internal strengths and weaknesses in Chapter 4. As a result of this earlier discussion, the examination here will be necessarily brief.

Organizing for Strategic Change

In a classic study of General Motors, Standard Oil of New Jersey, Sears and Roebuck, and duPont, Alfred Chandler documented the way in which an organization's structure must respond to its strategy.[52] Chandler's analysis focused on the developmental stages of an organization (its life cycle) ranging from the initial problems of accumulating and organizing resources to entering new and different markets. Through each change in strategy, organizational changes were required to facilitate the new strategic demands on the firms.

The organizational life cycle is only one way of relating strategy to structure. Another approach is based on the interaction of three important variables – client homogeneity, service diversity, and organizational size. These variables are defined as follows:[53]

1. *Client homogeneity.* How similar are the patients, clients, or customers the organization serves? If different adaptive strategies are being considered (such as moving from related to unrelated diversification or vertical integration) will the differences in the new clients be sufficient to demand a new organizational structure? The more dissimilar the clients (low homogeneity), the more likely is the need for organizational units specifically designed and staffed to deal with them.
2. *Services diversity.* Again, the more diverse the services offered (high), the more likely is the need for units that specialize in particular services with the relevant types of specialists to provide them. If a highly diversified health care organization decides to divest unrelated operations such as parking decks, will the concentration back on related health care activities allow a simplification of the organization structure?
3. *Size of the organization.* This may or may not be related to the stage of the organizational life cycle. The important question here is whether the organization is large enough (adequate or inadequate) to take advantage of economies of scale if it is divided into departments or autonomous units.

To illustrate the relationship between an organization's directional strategy, organizational structure, and culture change, consider the case of the University Hospital Pharmacy Department. The department is used here as the "unit of analysis" because specific changes were being made in the directional strategies of the department, and the director had committed to an eighteen month program designed to change the culture in line with the new strategic direction. A change in organizational structure was, therefore, an important element in overall strategic change.

Changing the Structure of a Hospital Pharmacy

University Hospital is part of a large academic medical center with more than 1,000 beds in its various core and affiliated facilities. The hospital, like most health care organizations, has attempted to deal with the changing environment by initiating a number of strategic changes. For example, an attempt has been made to downsize the scale of operations and reduce the organizational distance between patient-care workers and formal leaders while maintaining high levels of service. The overall thrust of the strategy to restructure operations has been to provide more autonomy to patient care personnel and encourage innovation to find better ways of delivering needed health services. Implementation efforts have involved the initiation of total quality management concepts and attempts to reorganize operations in ways that decentralized decision making when feasible or advisable.

The hospital pharmacy (original organizational structure illustrated in Exhibit 12–5) is a critical part of hospital operations because the quality of the medical care delivered in the hospital depends, to a great extent, on the accurate dispensing and timely delivery of medications to patients when and where they are needed. In addition, University Hospital's patient population is a mix composed of some of the most seriously ill patients in the region. Many have life-threatening illnesses, some are undergoing treatment with experimental drugs, and a number are prescribed controlled substances.

The goal of the pharmacy, therefore, is to deliver the right drugs to patients at the right time, with a very high level of accuracy, and to pay particular attention to controlled substances so that they are accounted for and secured at all times. Some important organizational characteristics of the hospital pharmacy are shown in Perspective 12–5.

Previously, the overall decentralization philosophy of the medical center and hospital has been endorsed by the Department of Pharmacy. The pharmacists are highly trained through advanced residencies (many hold pharmacy doctorates), and ongoing professional training and development are expected. The pharmacy technicians, who provide vital support to the departmental operations, are carefully selected and trained so that they are capable of assuming increased levels of responsibility. However, there remains the requirement for high levels of quality control in light of the department's mission to maximize the accuracy of its services and minimize incidents of control problems. These potentially conflicting demands presented the director of pharmacy with a dilemma when it came to the restructuring of the department. Although there were no visible problems or signs of impending problems, the director wanted to be sure that the department's highly successful structure, designed for another very different time in the hospital's history, was still appropriate.

Strategy and Structure Before any attempt was made to alter the organization structure, a number of interviews were held with key stakeholders of the department. Physicians throughout the hospital, general nurses as well as intensive-

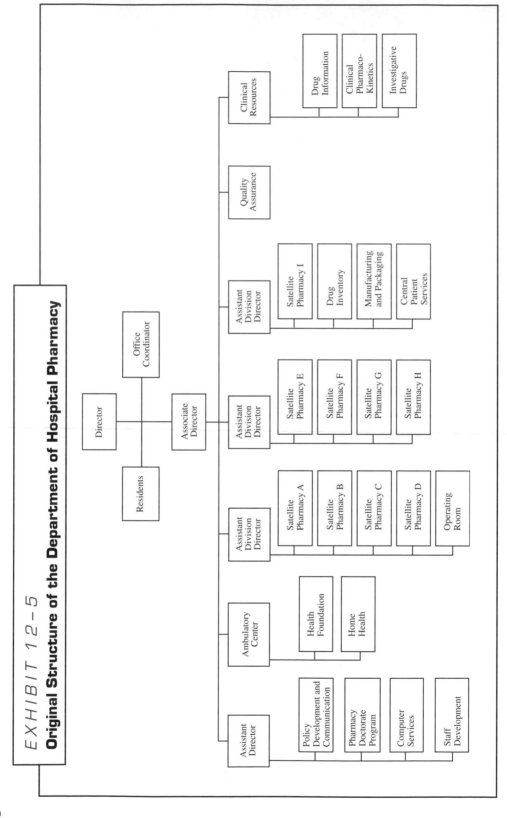

EXHIBIT 12-5
Original Structure of the Department of Hospital Pharmacy

PERSPECTIVE 12-5
Characteristics of the Hospital Pharmacy

The Department of Pharmacy could be characterized as follows: (1) the organizational life cycle is in the maturity stage, having achieved significant growth over the past two decades; (2) client homogeneity is low, with patients receiving services ranging from routine and non-life threatening surgery to complicated procedures such as bone marrow and heart transplants; (3) service diversity is high, with pharmacists engaged in a wide range of activities from routine dispensing of medications to manufacturing, compounding, and packaging drugs as well as kinetic consultations with physicians; and (4) the department is large by most hospital standards, with more than 200 employees, half of whom are professionally trained, registered pharmacists.

In addition to the direct support of the patient care personnel, the pharmacy is responsible for the development of the hospital's drug policies. The pharmacy advises clinical personnel about new and developing drugs, assists physicians in keeping up to date on the latest developments through its drug information center, and assists in ensuring the most cost-effective medications are used in light of the needs of the individual patients.

---

care-unit nurses, representatives of related services such as dietetics, patients, and others were asked to identify any organizational or communication problems they experienced with the department. In addition, the director named an internal task force to serve as a "reality check" for different organizational configurations and to provide suggestions for improving services.[54]

A number of possible organizational structures were developed, evaluated, and rejected. Careful consideration of the mission of the hospital and the department, the important values that govern departmental operations, and the vision of where pharmacy should be in the future suggested that the only way to achieve the goal of moving decision making as close as possible to actual patient care was to develop a series of relatively autonomous small professional practices in the department. The director believed that, for high level professional services to be maintained in an environment that valued cost-efficiency, every member of the department had to assume responsibility for working better every day. All leaders had to develop a "department-wide" view of operations. The director's responsibility was to create an environment where taking reasonable risks in the interest of getting better was tolerated and where team and departmental performance was more important than the performance of a single individual or small group.

The result of the thoughts, analysis, and discussion is illustrated in Exhibit 12-6. The structure is developed around a series of "strategic practice units" that effectively operate as strategic service units. This structure appears to have the potential to make the department respond more effectively to the demands

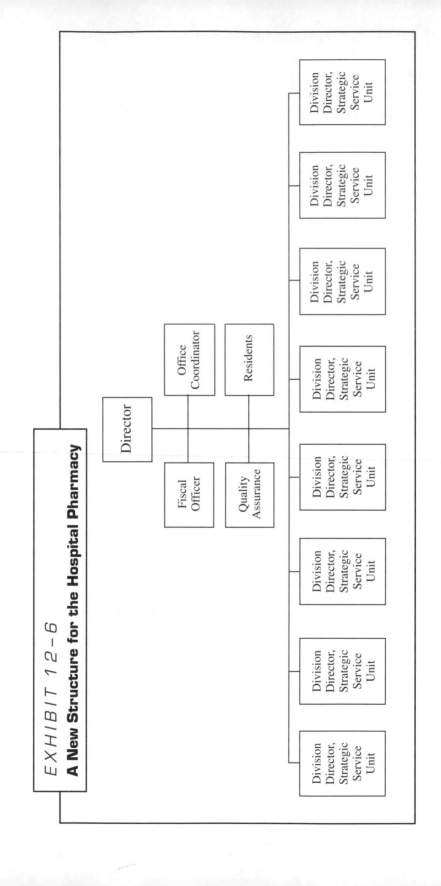

EXHIBIT 12-6
A New Structure for the Hospital Pharmacy

Director

Fiscal Officer

Office Coordinator

Quality Assurance

Residents

Division Director, Strategic Service Unit

Division Director, Strategic Service Unit

Division Director, Strategic Service Unit

Division Director, Strategic Service Unit

Division Director, Strategic Service Unit

Division Director, Strategic Service Unit

Division Director, Strategic Service Unit

Division Director, Strategic Service Unit

created by the strategic direction of the medical center and the hospital, although it created new and unique challenges.

Ensuring the Culture Change Although the structure has been developed, much work remains to implement the operation of the strategic practice units. Many of the members of the department and most of the leadership learned pharmacy and pharmacy management in an environment that was very different from that of today.

For this new organization structure to succeed, significant culture change will be needed. First, with the movement to decentralized operations through the strategic practice units will be a corresponding need to ensure everyone is involved with the development of the department's mission, vision, and values and that there is a general "buy-in" by as many members as possible.

Second, pharmacists and technicians will no longer be able to assume that all the leadership will be exercised by the formal managers. To be successful, this structure requires that everyone at all levels assumes the responsibility necessary to accomplish the department's mission. In addition, there must be teamwork among the practice units; empire building and protection of turf will ensure failure. Finally, it is important that the director and division directors develop an environment in the organization whereby new ideas and ways of doing things are encouraged. Collectively, these changes will lead to a departmental culture that can successfully deal with the new and different structure.

Although the division directors have their own specific areas of responsibility, under the new organizational philosophy, they are expected to have a department-wide perspective. The question is always to be, "Is it best for the department?" rather than, "Is it best for my unit or division?" This structure, along with the continued recruitment and development of outstanding pharmacists and technicians, should prepare the hospital pharmacy for many future challenges, such as the increasing trend toward outpatient services and the traditional hospital pharmacy's role in this changing way of doing things. The organization structure is assessed as part of the internal environment for situational analysis and contributes to strategic management. This will be illustrated in Exhibits 12–10 and 12–11 at the end of this chapter.

STRATEGIC FACILITIES MANAGEMENT

Facilities management is the broad term used to delineate the management of the physical environment of the health care organization. It is the "shell" in which health care is delivered. Although the departments or areas included in facilities management vary by institution, it generally includes such diverse areas as design and construction of new facilities and renovation of older facilities, technology management, operations and maintenance, clinical engineering, environmental services, safety and security, materials management, and food service. Each component affects the health care organization's ability to implement its strategy.

Health facilities management is an area of increasing concern to top management of health care organizations for a variety of reasons. One of the most important is the changing technology that has fostered tremendous growth in the number and kind of alternative delivery systems requiring different strategies for success. Freestanding outpatient clinics, ambulatory (same day) surgery centers, diagnostic and imaging centers, and others are challenging traditional inpatient health care delivery. To survive, hospitals have altered their strategies to expand vertically and horizontally or to diversify into these new delivery systems. However, each type is subject to entirely different design needs for buildings as well as different regulatory guidelines – a challenge for the facilities manager.

These integration and diversification strategies have caused the facilities and related support systems to increase in complexity and cost, another reason why top management has an increased interest in facilities management. With the advent of PPS, controlling costs within areas supervised by facilities management became critically important. Pressure mounts to increase efficiencies and deliver more cost-effective support without impeding the quality of patient care.

Facilities support delivery of quality patient care. Facilities management can identify activities that will lead to continuous improvements in the quality of patient care. "Patient satisfaction can be enhanced by a well-designed and well-maintained facility, the quality of foodservice, and the general courteousness and service orientation of all employees."[55] However, patient-centered care is straining financial resources as significant remodeling must be undertaken to implement the strategy. In addition, with rapidly changing technology, a convenient location and sufficient space are needed to put new diagnostic equipment, for example, a new PET scanner. Will the hospital choose to sell its older scanning equipment (the MRI? the CT scan?) or add on to the facility to house the new equipment?

Another reason for the importance of facilities management within strategic management is that the physical aspects of the health care organization are the first encountered by patients, visitors, and employees. If the health care facility is difficult to find, parking is limited and challenging to navigate, and the outside environment is unmanicured and ill-kept, it presents an image of an institution that does not care. It may have the best caregivers and the latest technology inside the building, but most people will not give it a chance if they have a choice to go elsewhere. The organization's strategy will surely fail.

Designing a Health Care Facility

A variety of components are to be considered in the design of a health care facility: medical technology, the full range of medical procedures from routine exams to complicated life-saving activities, medical staff, sanitation, prevention of injury, economics, patients, and visitors. From the patients' perspective, the facility includes "curb appeal," ease of access to the main entrance, ease of parking, ease of *wayfinding* (finding the department, room, diagnostic area, or other area where the patient is expected), comfort, and convenience. Designing the facility with the human experience in mind recognizes that people's perceptions of health care are multidimensional; the facility helps them define the care they receive. Sending a "we care" message cannot stop with the staff but must be designed into the facility itself.[56] As illustrated in Perspective 12–6, many facility planning activities are not anchored by the organizational mission.

When the health care organization decides on a high-tech, a high-touch, or some other strategy, the facility provides the first impression. The design, layout, color scheme, and so on should reflect the desired image to improve the implementation of the strategy. "Unlike the quality of medical care, health facility design

---

PERSPECTIVE 12-6
New Construction Fails to Meet the Organizational Mission

Although health care organizations invest millions of dollars in new construction and renovation of facilities, some of them fail to fulfill the organization's mission or meet the community's health care needs. Robert Levine, a New York architect who specializes in health care facilities, identifies pitfalls to be avoided:

1. *A reluctance to invest time and resources in long-range planning and to view construction as a process.* A master site plan should be developed in conjunction with the organization's strategic plan. "Patching" can lead to more expensive delivery and a lack of competitiveness in pricing under capitation.

2. *An overwhelming desire to please key constituencies.* Facilities designed around the preferences of physicians, executives, or regulators usually turn out to be extravagant experiments.

3. *Faith in autocracy.* If top management consults with no others because of the time it takes or the lack of control over the "product" when others offer input, resistance to the new project, mistakes in design, and lowered morale are likely.

4. *Clinging to the past by retaining inefficient facilities.* By converting obsolescent space into other uses, the health care organization usually ends up with new obsolete space that not only can be expensive to renovate but loses the goodwill of the physicians or community. However, with buildings of historical significance to the community, it is wise to try to maintain at least part of the structure.

5. *Resistance to the sensitive probing that accompanies facilities planning.* Facilities planners need to know the processes, flow, and activities that will be incorporated into the new space. The management and clinical teams should be prepared to expect difficult questions from the planners and should realize the benefit for the facilities plan.

6. *The push for a quick fix to a complex issue.* "Quick fixes" are not usually cost-effective. Better to plan, revise the plan, and plan some more.

Source: Robert H. Levine, "Knowing Where Misconceptions Lurk Can Reduce Construction Mistakes," *Modern Healthcare* 22, no. 44 (November 2, 1992), p. 18.

is something that can readily be understood and judged, for better or worse, by the public."[57]

The quality of the health care environment has ramifications beyond its image, however. Research has shown that the design of the facility, its color scheme, arrangement of furniture, availability of windows, music, and accommodation for family members contribute to a patient's progress toward recovery.[58] Any way that the facility can relieve stress, not only for patients but also the health care staff, is an organizational strength. Patients and visitors have needs for wayfinding, physical comfort, regulation of social contact (privacy and personal space), and symbolic meaning (the sights, sounds, and smells that blend into the total image of a caring place).[59]

Technology Affects Facilities

Effective technology management is an integral part of strategic management and should be approached in a systematic way. Because health care technology changes rapidly, is costly, and often requires changes in the facility, it must be assessed and carefully planned for in order to operate the facility at its greatest potential. Physicians generally want the latest technology – using the "latest" provides prestige with colleagues and patients and may save more lives or provide less discomfort to patients – but there may be questions about how many lives will be saved and how much the discomfort will be lessened. In the dynamic environment of the 1990s, costs and benefits are being assessed before decisions are made to purchase new technology.

According to Berkowitz and Swan, technology decisions involve technology assessment, planning, acquisition, and management.[60] They advocate that a committee assess requests for new and emerging technology alongside the capital budget requests for new and replacement technology. The committee should report to senior hospital management and should set mission-based, strategic priorities for new, emerging, and replacement technologies. Many hospitals do not incorporate into the budget the costs of redesigning and "space" for new technology, nor do they investigate ways to reduce maintenance, insurance, and outside service contract costs. The planning process has to take into account competitive institutions' plans for acquisition of new and emerging technology as well as assessing services offered by competitors.

Clinical engineering (sometimes called *biomedical engineering*) is a relatively new department in most health care organizations. Its responsibilities include applying engineering technology to diagnostic and treatment devices used by health care facilities through testing, maintaining, and repairing equipment; training; consultation with clinical staff concerning capabilities, efficiencies, and accuracies of equipment; environmental testing; and incident and recall investigations that involve diagnostic or treatment equipment. The number and sophistication of technologies within health care institutions has increased significantly in the past decade. From 1980 to 1991, the number of diagnostic or treatment devices per occupied bed in an acute care facility went from 1.5 to nearly 7.[61] Because of the expertise required for such a large variety of equipment, some health care organizations use outside service contracts for some or all of their technological equipment.

Risk management is an important part of diagnostic equipment testing. Testing standards are implemented by a number of governmental and regulatory agencies. Equipment failures and user errors must be documented, and for some equipment they must be reported for further follow-up.

Operations and Maintenance

The goal of the department responsible for the physical plant and its internal machinery (often referred to as *engineering and maintenance department*) is to operate the physical plant in an efficient, cost-effective manner and to ensure the maximum comfort and safety of the facility's patients, visitors, and employees. Mechanical systems (including heating, ventilating, and air-conditioning systems; plumbing; fire protection; and the medical gas system) and electrical systems make up about 40 percent of the nonequipment construction cost of a new or replacement facility, and it is not unusual that they would account for 50 percent of the cost.[62] In addition, these systems have very high operating costs compared to similar systems in other types of facilities. In part this is because of the many regulations by federal, state, and local governments and codes and guidelines by regulatory agencies such as the Department of Health and Human Services and the Joint Commission on Accreditation of Healthcare Organizations.

Physical plant and equipment ranked seventh or eighth in studies of hospital administrators' problem areas in 1948, 1961, 1963, and 1978; in 1990 it moved to the fifth most challenging problem area, jumping ahead of department functioning and community relations.[63] Mechanical and electrical systems are rarely noticed by patients, visitors, and employees – unless something is not working properly. Although the engineering and maintenance department does not deal directly with patient care in the facility, virtually every aspect of its operation has some indirect effect on the care of the facility's patients, visitors, and staff. The physical environment supports the efforts of the health care professionals to provide excellent care to patients.[64]

Additional Facilities Management Areas

The value of an *environmental services* department (sometimes called *housekeeping, facilities maintenance, domestic services,* or *janitorial services*) is immediately evident to everyone who enters the health care facility.[65] In addition to keeping the facility clean, this group is typically responsible for laundry, groundskeeping, minor maintenance, pest control, and waste management.

Security of patients, visitors, and staff, as a responsibility of the health care organization, has been verified repeatedly in the court system. The liability as a result of inadequate or negligent security, coupled with the negative impact of theft, pilferage, and waste, represents a serious threat to health care organizations.[66] Safety is another area that is potentially a threat to health care organizations.

Exhibit 12–7 illustrates some of the safety issues in a typical health care organization.

Materials management includes the acquisition, warehousing, inventory, distribution and transportation, and processing of supplies and equipment. Materials management has a significant impact on health care organizations both in terms of operations and finances. Studies have consistently shown that ordering, procuring, storing, moving, and using supplies consume up to 45 percent of a hospital's operating budget. This percentage includes the time that clinical and support staff are handling supplies; the supplies themselves are 13 to 23 percent of the operating budget.[67] The goal for most materials managers in health care organizations today is to achieve greater efficiency and cost-effectiveness without sacrificing the quality of patient care. Standardization of items and purchasing procedures, minimum inventory, enhanced purchasing through vendor management or cooperative buying groups, and on-line purchasing are being used to achieve the goal.

Food service is another area of health that has undergone significant change in the past decade. Increased knowledge about diet and health has increased the demand for nutritionists for health care facilities. In addition, patients are not the only consumers of food service. Family and visitors of the patient and employees of the facility are important sources of revenue. Thus, cafeterias, vending, coffee

EXHIBIT 12-7
Safety Threats for a Health Care Organization

Accidents

Disasters

Infectious Waste

Exposure to Chemicals

Regulatory Inspections

Potential Threats

Fires

Theft

Low Employee Morale

Malpractice Suits

Union Grievances

Source: Linda F. Chaff, "Safety," in *Effective Health Care Facilities Management,* ed. V. James McLarney et al. (Chicago: American Hospital Publishing, 1991), p. 63.

shops, and others are important because they generate additional profit for the health care organization.

Facilities management provides input to the situational analysis, as will be illustrated in Exhibit 12–10. The health care organization's physical environment or "facilities" is an important aspect to strategic management, as will be summarized in Exhibit 12–11.

ETHICAL AND SOCIAL RESPONSIBILITIES OF HEALTH CARE ORGANIZATIONS

By their very nature, hospitals, physicians, nurses, and other health professionals seek to help people. Most not-for-profit public health care organizations that provide service for those who cannot pay for it have long been involved in operating with social responsibility. If not-for-profit private or for-profit health care organizations have not paid attention to their broader social responsibility, fundamental questions will have to be addressed before decisions are made on strategy, objectives, and programs that will be recommended. "Historical attitudes about competition, lack of profit motive, and not-for-profit status have both helped and hindered the health services system."[68] The absence of economic incentives has contributed to public health services organizations feeling good about themselves because they were doing good rather than concentrating on performing well and efficiently. Many of the private and for-profit organizations have performed well but have not focused on social responsibilities beyond their particular customers.

As health care has moved more toward the competitive model and more health care organizations are operated as "businesses," the concept of social responsibility must be investigated and given considerable attention by management. Governmental bodies established during the 1970s underscore that the national policy officially recognizes the environment, employees, and consumers to be significant and legitimate stakeholders. For executives, the question has become how to balance commitments to owners and their obligations to an ever-broadening group of stakeholders who claim both legal and ethical rights.

Archie Carroll, in a *Business Horizons* article, viewed these social responsibilities in a pyramid as illustrated in Exhibit 12–8.[69] First and foremost, the organization was created as an economic entity to provide goods and services to societal members at a "profit" (enough revenues to cover costs and survive). Next, organizations are legal entities and required to fulfill laws and legal obligations established by the lawmakers. The next level, ethical responsibilities, embodies the standards, norms, or expectations that employees, customers, and shareholders in the community-at-large regard as fair. Ethical responsibilities go beyond what is legally acceptable. They reflect a higher standard of performance than that currently required by law.

Philanthropic responsibilities encompass those activities that respond to society's expectations that the organization be a good community citizen, including actively engaging in acts or programs to promote human welfare or goodwill. Philanthropy is thus more discretionary or voluntary on the part of organizations, although there is a societal expectation that all organizations provide it. Many

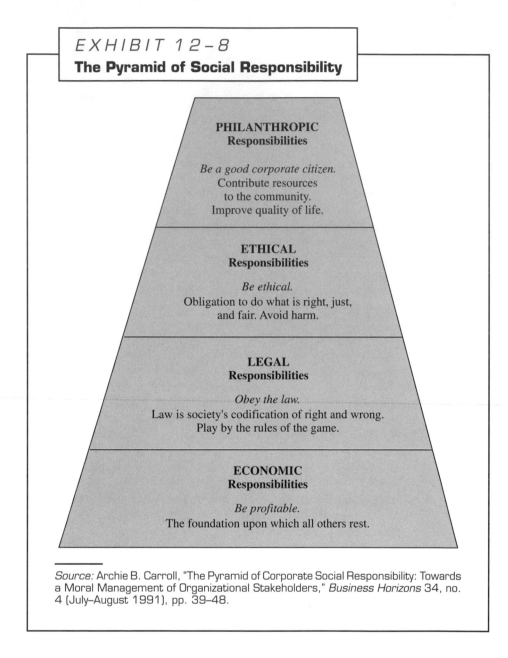

EXHIBIT 12–8
The Pyramid of Social Responsibility

PHILANTHROPIC
Responsibilities

Be a good corporate citizen.
Contribute resources
to the community.
Improve quality of life.

ETHICAL
Responsibilities

Be ethical.
Obligation to do what is right, just,
and fair. Avoid harm.

LEGAL
Responsibilities

Obey the law.
Law is society's codification of right and wrong.
Play by the rules of the game.

ECONOMIC
Responsibilities

Be profitable.
The foundation upon which all others rest.

Source: Archie B. Carroll, "The Pyramid of Corporate Social Responsibility: Towards a Moral Management of Organizational Stakeholders," *Business Horizons* 34, no. 4 (July–August 1991), pp. 39–48.

health care organizations have made significant commitments to fulfilling philanthropy goals. For example, Bristol-Myers Squibb began a corporate program over twenty years ago to provide life-saving drugs to those who cannot afford to pay for the necessary pharmaceuticals (see Perspective 12–7).

Stakehoder management has been defined as the process by which managers reconcile their own organization's objectives for "profit" with the claims and

---

PERSPECTIVE 12-7

Bristol-Myers Squibb Company Access Programs for the Medically Indigent

More than twenty years ago Bristol-Myers Squibb began its access program for the company's anticancer medications. In more recent years the company added its anti-AIDS therapy and all its cardiovascular therapies. According to Dr. Isadore M. Pike, vice president of Medical Affairs for Bristol-Myers Oncology Division, "As the world's foremost manufacturer of anticancer drugs, our responsibility is not only to supply physicians with the most current information on drug therapies but also provide these life-saving drugs for those patients who cannot afford them. We believe in equal access to the best therapy for all patients, regardless of their ability to pay."

For patients who cannot afford to pay, an enrolled physician (there are over 19,000 enrolled nationwide) calls a toll-free number at the Bristol-Myers Squibb Access Program. Reimbursement counselors help secure financial assistance for people with cancer, AIDS, or cardiovascular disease through third-party payment programs for which the patient may qualify. If none is available, Bristol-Myers Squibb will provide any of the company's sixteen anticancer drugs, VIDEX anti-AIDS therapy, or eighteen cardiovascular drugs free of charge for as long as the patient needs it.

In the past five years, over 8,500 cancer patients have been provided oncology drugs. In 1990, Bristol-Myers made VIDEX available free of charge to over 23,000 AIDS patients. The cardiovascular program was started in 1992 and has already benefited more than 5,000 people. Most of the people involved are the unprotected elderly on a fixed income, workers who are not protected by employer-purchased health insurance, those who fall outside the criteria for government assistance or who lack pharmaceutical coverage and cannot afford the necessary medication.

Source: Correspondence and conversations with Isadore M. Pike, M.D., vice president for medical affairs, Bristol-Myers Oncology Division, Bristol-Myers Squibb Company.

---

expectations being made on it by various stakeholder groups.[70] Of course, the challenge of stakeholder management is to ensure that the firm's primary stakeholders achieve their objective while other stakeholders are also satisfied. It is a legitimate and desirable goal for management to pursue to protect the organization's long-term survival.

Social Responsibility Stakeholders

Health care organizations have ethical and social responsibilities to at least five different stakeholders or constituencies: owners/shareholders, employees, customers, suppliers, and the general public.[71] As was pointed out in Chapter 1, these various stakeholders affect the organization and the organization affects the stake-holders. The owners of a health care organization are often the public who, through contribution of their tax dollars and financial and time donations, expect the organization to survive and provide the services that are needed for the community. Thus, there is an inherent social responsibility for the organization to generate more revenues than costs in order to survive and serve the community. Publicly owned, for-profit organizations, whether health care organizations or others, have a legal and social responsibility to their shareholders to manage the investment of those shareholders in a manner that provides return.

In health care organizations, employees are an important constituency group, and strategies must take them into consideration. Employees have a right to be treated fairly and to expect that the strategy choice will not disadvantage them, or if hardship cannot be avoided, they receive proper notice and as much guidance as possible. Employees have a right to work in as safe an environment as possible and be treated with dignity and respect.

Health care organizations have a particular ethical responsibility to their customers to provide the service in the best way that they can. If the health care organization makes mistakes – as it will because humans deliver health care – the organization that admits its mistakes and makes every effort to correct them will be respected for its ethical conduct. "Anecdotal evidence suggests that patients and families can understand that mistakes occur and things do go wrong. Organizations that acknowledge this fact and do all they can to make things right are much better served than those that circle the wagons and make a last ditch stand."[72] A guiding question perhaps is, "How would you like to be treated if you were in the situation?"

The ethical considerations for the public- or community-at-large include being a good citizen as well as participating in community activities to maintain the health and safety of the community. In the 1990s, health care reform is receiving significant attention. Many aspects of reform deal with ethical and social responsibility issues – the "right" to health care, death and dying, and so on. There are no easy answers when resources are finite and needs are infinite.

Strategic Management and Ethical and Social Responsibility

"The manager is the organization's conscience."[73] Management is responsible for managing the enterprise. The CEO is responsible for management. Therefore, all ethical considerations start with the CEO. His or her perception of ethics determines whether and how strategy is linked to ethical behavior. "A company that truly cares about ethics and corporate social responsibility is proactive rather than reactive in linking strategy and ethics."[74] The ethical organization does not deal with unethical suppliers or employees. The products and services are safe for customers to use. An ethical organization recruits and hires employees who are ethical as well.

Health care organizations must consider ethical and social responsibilities, and their orientation should be reflected in the organization's mission, vision, values, policies, and procedures. Without proper forethought, the organization may become governed by the events rather than governing the events. The organization's philosophy affects its strategic planning as the organization's views of its social responsibility are incorporated into the mission statement. The development of the mission is the responsibility primarily of the organization's governing body; however, the implementation is based on the responsibility of senior management. A difficult balance is to be achieved between social responsibility and economic performance.

An organization defines its mission based on its vision and philosophy and determines by what means its mission will be achieved. "This exercise *prospectively* resolves conflicts among competing but legitimate ends."[75] As discussed in Chapter 5, mission statements may contain ethical positions or include the philosophy of the organization. An organization is most effective when it is built on shared values or a common culture, as discussed in Chapter 4. Adequately communicated to and accepted by the staff, a goal as simple as "getting the caring back into curing" could reap great rewards for the organization through increased efficiency, better care, and improved relations with employees and the community.

In addition to mission and vision, some health care organizations have a statement of philosophy. A *statement of philosophy* should include some reference to the organization's relationship with patients, staff, community, and other institutions. By answering questions about the health care organization's relationship to its community, the organization can pose important questions to itself on its role prospectively. Although this is a useful exercise in developing organizational philosophy, it also provides an opportunity for introspection and staff involvement in creating a corporate culture. Major differences in moral philosophies inhibit cooperative efforts.

Organizations have philosophies that are value laden, and individuals have a personal ethic. When the personal ethics of the individuals are concurrent with the organization's philosophy, there are few problems. When they differ, the personal ethic is often subsumed to the organizational philosophy because the individual does not wish to lose his or her job, but this dissonance causes considerable discomfort. To be an effective leader, an individual should maintain certain elements of a personal ethic. One way to judge whether an action is ethical is to look at what is being contemplated and ask a series of questions as to how others would view this activity. "If you don't get caught, it's OK" is not an ethical position. In addition, ethics should be applicable to everyone in the organization. If the manager at the top says one thing and does another, it will be translated by all employees as an acceptable thing to do. Further, if goals are stated but rewards are different from the goals, the employees have no ethical dilemma – they will do what is rewarded.

If not identified and handled early, ethical problems can multiply into culture-deteriorating events that can threaten the organization's survival. Many managers are uncomfortable dealing with ethical problems. They do not believe that they are responsible, they are not sure they know how to recognize ethical problems, and they do not believe they have the skills to solve such problems. Sometimes managers consider ethics to be the purview of the clinical staff, yet ethical dilemmas have an administrative aspect in health care organizations.

Managers are problem solvers. Developing problem-solving skills is an important part of management education, and solving ethical problems is really an extension of basic problem-solving skills. Ethical problems are solved in the same manner as other managerial problems. That is, there is an awareness of the problem, gathering of facts, evaluating the various alternatives, selecting the best alternative, and evaluating the results. Implementation of the solution is an important part in ethical dilemmas.

Guidance for Managers

Steiner and Steiner prepared a list of guidelines that are applicable to health care organizations. Although not every topic included in Exhibit 12–9 is appropriate

---

EXHIBIT 12-9
Guidelines for Organizational Social Responsibility

1. Think carefully about the organization's social responsibilities.
2. If applicable, make full use of tax deductibility laws through contributions – when profit margins permit.
3. Share the social costs of the community when it is possible to do so without jeopardizing the organization's competitive or financial position.
4. Concentrate action programs on limited objectives. No single organization can remake the entire social system, culture, or government. But an organization can make a difference in a single community or with a single objective or a single activity.
5. Concentrate action programs on areas strategically related to the present and perspective functions of the organization – begin close to home and deal with what appears to be the most urgent areas of concern that in some way can be related to the organization.
6. Facilitate employee actions that can be taken as individuals rather than representatives of the organization – free them to do good deeds but do not force them.
7. An organization can do many things that are socially responsible as well as profitable, if not in monetary terms at least in improved image in the community.
8. Actions taken in the name of social responsibility should enhance the economic strength of the organization.
9. Take socially responsive actions continuously. Plan for it.
10. Examine carefully before proceeding responsibly. Investigate the community's needs, weighing the contribution the organization can make, the risk involved, and the potential benefits to both the organization and society.

Source: Adapted from George A. Steiner and John F. Steiner, *Business, Government, and Society* (New York: Random House, 1980).

for every health care organization, the list stimulates thinking about social responsibilities.

The major source of guidance for managers within their organizations are the individual's ethics supplemented by the codes of his or her professional group and the organization's philosophy. In addition, specific policies and management committees and task forces help identify and solve administrative ethical problems. Conflict of interest is the most often reported administrative ethical problem confronting health services organizations. *Conflict of interest* occurs when a person owes duties to two or more persons or organizations and meeting a duty to one of them causes derogation of duty to another.[76]

For example, conflict of interest occurs when a member of the hospital or long-term-care facility board of trustees is also a major stockholder or CEO of a supplier of goods and services to that organization. Another administrative ethical issue is *fiduciary duty,* defined as a relationship that exists whenever confidence and trust on one side result in superiority or influence on the other. The health care organization's governing body members (trustees) are fiduciaries. It is their ethical duty to avoid using their position for personal gain, and they must act only in the best interests of the health care organization. A major conflict of interest occurs when physicians and health care organizations participate in prepaid plans, where the institution benefits by minimizing the cost of caring for the patient although that may not be in the patient's best interest. This dilemma will become increasingly important as health care reform efforts succeed at developing more managed care.

One of the major ethical dilemmas for health care organizations today is how to allocate health care resources. Some people believe that every individual has a right to health care. At the other end of the continuum are people who believe that access to health care is not a right guaranteed by society but a privilege. A middle ground that many people subscribe to is that routine, basic services ought to be available to all people. Where to draw the line is a political decision and depends on society's willingness to provide the resources needed. As our country debates health care reform, what we are really trying to do is to decide where to draw the line, how much we can afford to spend on health care, and what services will be available to all.[77] For the health care manager, allocation of resources is a difficult decision because resources are limited. Should the health care organization purchase new technology that will significantly help a limited number of people or should it hire more nurses to staff the emergency room that would help many people incrementally?

Consider the following example. The CEO of a successful hospital was approached by a physician who had recently attended a seminar on a new outpatient procedure that was stated to be quick and profitable. However, the procedure was still considered experimental, and some authorities considered it to be of questionable value. The physician wanted to offer this new procedure and promote it through a media campaign. The CEO was faced with a dilemma. Should the health care organization promote an experimental, perhaps unnecessary, service that would add profits to the hospital? In actuality, because the CEO decided against the new procedure, the physician contracted with a freestanding surgical center and the promotion was extremely successful. Because of this ethical issue, the hospital lost a source of revenue plus the physician's good will. The CEO had to decide whether the price was worth it.[78]

The starting point for determining a decision on this issue would be to review the organizational philosophy and mission. If this health care organization's mission included leading edge technology, it would be expected that not every new technology would be successful. Therefore, expectations of patients who go to this hospital would be that the procedures might be experimental. However, if the mission was to serve patients in need, then the health care organization should use its resources to improve the general health of the population that it serves. Yet the hospital lost the opportunity for additional profits that could have been used to provide other services. There are no easy answers.

Have a Plan for Ethics

Health care executives can develop and implement a comprehensive, long-term initiative in organizational ethics according to David Perry, a former consultant of the Ethics Resource Center in Washington, D.C. He advocates that organizations first assess the organizational values and vulnerabilities to misconduct. Find out what kinds of ethical issues employees really face in their day-to-day jobs. Not only does it highlight what the code of ethics should cover, it also enlightens management to the kinds of problems that employees within the organization face.

For example, management, through goal-setting practices, often develops incentives and reward systems that may not encourage ethical conduct because employees perceive that something other than what is stated is rewarded. Although it may be stated that quality and safety are paramount, if employees in practice are rewarded only for cutting costs, employee values will be directed toward cost cutting.[79]

Second, create opportunities for management to discuss organizational values and risks. Management has to reach a consensus on the high-priority issues as well as the action plans that need to be implemented within an ethical construct. Employees need to understand that an ethics program is not merely a temporary fad but a long-term commitment. Therefore, organizational values, risks, and ethics should be discussed freely and frequently. Third, develop and communicate clear standards of conduct. A written code of ethics can be created or revised that relates to management systems and practices. It should affirm a basic set of organizational values, establish ground rules, provide illustrations and guidelines in some of the gray areas that are pertinent for a particular organization, and explain how employees can obtain further information and counsel without fear of retaliation.

Finally, refine management systems and practices to support the ethics program. In other words, when management develops the mission and strategic goals at the top departmental and individual level – including incentive and reward systems, performance appraisals, and disciplinary practices – they need to be evaluated according to whether they reinforce the ethics program. Ethics is not a one-shot attendance at a program or reading the code of conduct. Ethics has to be incorporated into the organization's basic culture and operating values.

"When the entire organization operates on treating customers, suppliers, and employees fairly and honestly, there is nothing but benefit to be gained for the overall reputation and success of the organization."[80]

Code of Ethics

The basic goal of a *code of ethics* is to guide the behavior and decisions of people who want to do the right thing but may need guidance in determining what that is. The American College of Healthcare Executives has had a code of ethics since 1939, just six years after its founding. The current code was adopted in 1993 and is included as Perspective 12–8. The emphasis is on ethical issues in

---

PERSPECTIVE 12–8
American College of Healthcare Executives Policy on Ethics

Statement of the Issue:

A number of factors have contributed to the growing concern in healthcare organizations with ethical and bioethical issues: pressures to lower costs, scarcer financial resources, advances in medical technology, decisions near the end of life, and increased patient demands, to name just a few. Increasingly, executives of healthcare organizations are being called upon to resolve these serious ethical conflicts, but they cannot and should not make these decisions alone. Healthcare organizations should have vehicles, such as an ethics committee, a set of written policies, and/or a staff ethicist, to assist in the decision-making process. In this way, demands from patients or their families, physicians, the government, special interest groups, and the community can all be weighed and balanced, and the decision-making process can reflect these multiple interests.

The Joint Commission on Accreditation of Healthcare Organizations has also recognized the ethical issues present in the healthcare setting. The commission's

"Accreditation Manual for Hospitals" now requires accredited hospitals to have in place "mechanism(s) for the consideration of ethical issues arising in the care of patients and to provide the education to care givers and patients on ethical issues in healthcare."

Simply stated, ethics can be defined as the application of a person's values in decision-making situations. These values are derived from a number of sources – family background, religious training, social interaction, education, and employment experiences. In addition, an individual's ethics are often impacted by societal boundaries such as state and federal laws and business practices. And, of course, any value system is always subject to change.

Policy Position:

The American College of Healthcare Executives supports the development in healthcare organizations of mechanisms to deal with general ethical and bioethical issues and decisions. Further, the College supports and encourages its affiliates, as executives of healthcare organizations and as leaders in their communities, to play an active role in developing organizational ethical guidelines, policies, and/or committees.

Decision-making mechanisms should also be ones that can deal with a variety of ethical concerns – medical, social, and financial. The most obvious examples include providing assistance and counsel on care for the terminally ill, care for the critically ill and/or handicapped newborns, organ transplantation, patients' right to refuse treatment, and providing support for patients and family members. However, more abstract issues should also be addressed such as the allocation of scarce resources, the fair distribution of benefits and burdens, and the rights of individual patients in relation to other patients and to society. These mechanisms, ideally, should allow for the just distribution of power, the protection of human rights, and security for the weak and the vulnerable.

As leaders in their respective organizations, healthcare executives have a primary role in the development and operation of these organizational ethical mechanisms. The effectiveness of such a process should be of personal as well as professional concern to the manager since it is his or her responsibility to act as facilitator and advocate in upholding the values of the organization, safeguarding the rights of patients, and promoting a full and fair discussion of the issues. In addition, it is the healthcare executive who assists others in the organization in reaching a consensus on value-laden questions.

While other healthcare personnel, such as physicians, nurses, social workers, etc., often consider ethical decisions individually on a case-by-case basis, it is the executive's task to also consider the implications for the community in general and society at large in any ethical decision-making situa-

tion. To effectively perform this task, the healthcare executive must work with the trustees of the organization to establish clear ethical standards that will serve as guidelines in their decision making.

The exact form of decision-making mechanisms may vary. For example, if it is an ethics committee, it might include some or all of the following types of persons: physicians, nurses, managers, trustees of the healthcare organization, social workers, attorneys, patient and/or community representatives, and the clergy. All of these individuals have a unique perspective in discussing current and anticipated ethical problems, as well as in considering possible solutions and outcomes. It is the task of the executive to facilitate this discussion, and it is also his or her responsibility to ensure that no one person or group controls the process.

Other mechanisms to advance ethical decision making include the establishment of agreed upon ethical standards, education of trustees, staff, physicians, and suppliers regarding these standards, and the provision of forums for open discussion of ethical issues.

As technology advances and as financial resources shrink, ethical and bioethical dilemmas will likely become an increasing element in the decision-making process in healthcare organizations. No one policy will be effective in every organization. Each organization, under the leadership of its executives, must develop its own processes and procedures for discussing and dealing with these sensitive issues.

Approved by the Board of Governors of the American College of Healthcare Executives, Aug. 6, 1993.

Source: American College of Healthcare Executives. Used with permission.

management, including conflict of interest, confidentiality, governing body/medical staff relations, resource allocation, and the manager's personal ethical behavior. A variety of other codes and groups, as summarized in Perspective 12–9, help managers with ethical dilemmas.

PERSPECTIVE 12–9
Resources for Ethical and Social Responsibility

Patient Bills of Rights

A variety of organizations, including the American Hospital Association, American Medical Association, the Joint Commission on Accreditation of Healthcare Organizations, the Department of Veteran's Affairs, and the American Civil Liberties Union have developed patient bills of rights. They have in common the patient's right to confidentiality and consent. There is considerable variation thereafter, but the objective is to point out that patients have rights and must be consulted. The information that patients provide must be kept confidential. The bills of rights reflect the law, but a patient bill of rights is not legally binding.

Professional Codes of Ethics

Self-regulation is one of the factors that differentiates the learned professions – law, medicine, and others. They require members to adopt a code of ethics, complete competency requirements, and determine sanctions. The different professional organizations have expressed guidelines for those who violate the organization's "rules." Membership, the rules, and sanctions are all governed by members of the profession. Licensure statutes (enacted in each state) are reviewed by members of the profession that the statutes are designed to regulate. This gives ethical considerations determined by the profession the force of law. Breaching them could lead to license suspension or revocation. It is important to note that this has not been done with great enthusiasm or frequently.

There are codes for physicians written by the American Medical Association, nurses written by the American Nurses Association, health care executives written by the American College of Healthcare Executives, nursing home administrators written by the American College of Health Care Administrators, hospitals by the American Hospital Association, and nursing facilities covered by the American Healthcare Association. In addition to ethical codes developed by the various professional associations, nearly all clinical groups are regulated by state laws.

Institutional Review Boards

Institutional review boards (IRBs) are required by the Department of Health and Human Services and the Food and Drug Administration as well as the Environmental Protection Agency, the National Science Foundation, and the Consumer Product Safety Commission when human subjects participate in experimentation. Health care organizations that receive grant funds for research and use human subjects must use an institutional review board. Acceptable IRBs have a minimum of five members, who are expected to have varying backgrounds (at least one member must have professional interests that are nonscientific) and who are capable of reviewing research proposals and activities of the type commonly performed by the organization.

Institutional Ethics Committees

Institutional ethics committees (IECs) have no specific guidelines. Sometimes these groups are responsible to the organization's administration, sometimes they report to the governing board, and sometimes to the clinical staff.[1] Generally they are used for administrative issues as well as biomedical ethical issues. Because there is such a variety in the activities that this group might undertake, each IEC should develop a statement of its ethics, derived from the organizational philosophy and mission. In some institutions, the IECs have a very limited scope – they answer questions about the terminally ill, specifically whether to continue life support. These so-called god squads help determine when life support should be withdrawn and the patient declared dead. Typically, most IECs have a broader role and have undertaken activities such as developing do not resuscitate (DNR) orders and patient consent policies as well as educational programs.

Infant Care Review Committees

Infant care review committees (ICRCs) have become more common since the enactment in 1984 of federal legislation that directs the Department of Health and Human Services to encourage their establishment within health care facilities, especially those with tertiary-level neonatal care units. ICRCs specialize in the biomedical ethical problems of infants with life-threatening conditions. Recom-

mended membership includes a practicing physician who specializes in infants including pediatricians, neonatologists, pediatric surgeons, or others; a practicing nurse; a hospital administrator; a social worker; a representative of a disability group; a lay community member; and a member of the facility's medical staff, who should serve as chair. DHHS recommends that these committees have adequate staff support including legal counsel; procedures to ensure that hospital personnel and patient families are fully informed of its existence, functions, and 24-hour availability; that it inform itself of pertinent legal requirements and procedures, including state laws; and that it maintain records of its deliberations and summary descriptions of the cases considered and their disposition.[2]

Advanced Directives

Individuals have requested a variety of advanced directives.

Living wills, based on state statutes, are acceptable in forty-two states.[3] Patients must rely on the willingness of caregivers to accept such documents. In general, the laws recognize a patient's right to instruct physicians to withhold or withdraw life-sustaining procedures. The problem arises in that the patient must have completed all documentation at a time when he or she was mentally competent, and in some states patients must reaffirm the living will at the time of their terminal illness (which may not be possible). Problems continue to surface concerning living wills: how to determine the patient's mental status, establishing the presence of a terminal illness, and determining whether the patient

PERSPECTIVE 12-9   cont'd

comprehends the effect of what is being done.

Durable power of attorney provides for someone else, typically a family member or the individual's attorney, to act in their behalf concerning withdrawing or withholding life support.

Do not resuscitate orders should be applied based on policies determined by the health care organization that affirm the right of patients to provide direction to their caregivers regarding the aggressiveness of life-saving efforts.

[1]For further discussion of institutional ethics committees, see Judith Wilson Ross, et al., *Health Care Ethics Committees: The Next Generation* (Chicago: American Hospital Publishing, 1993).
[2]Department of Health and Human Services, "Services and Treatment for Disabled Infants: Model Guidelines for Health Care Providers to Establish Infant Care Review Committees," *Federal Register* 50, no. 72 (April 15, 1985), p. 14893.
[3]Kurt Darr, *Ethics in Health Services Management*, 2nd ed. (Baltimore: Health Professions Press, 1991), p. 187.

Guiding Principles for Health Care Organizations

Robert Goldman believes that four ethical principles apply to health care organizations: (1) put the patient's welfare first, (2) avoid unnecessary services, (3) maintain high standards of honesty and accuracy, and (4) be accountable to the public. He believes that health care marketing efforts must reflect the highest ethical standards because health care customers lack the knowledge needed to make truly educated choices. "Patients must come before profits if the hospital is to profit."[81]

Other Ethical Considerations

"Strategy ought to be ethical."[82] A phrase often used is "no money, no mission" to justify an organization's termination of care provided for those who cannot afford to pay for it. Hospitals with large amounts of uncompensated care have to manage the organization so that it offers some services that have better reimbursements (such as rehabilitation and cosmetic surgery) as a way to offset losses. More fiscally sound hospitals must ask themselves whether they are meeting a general duty under the principle of justice to offer unprofitable but needed services that benefit the wider community.

Technology is central to the ethical and legal problems about death and dying that have arisen. New technology may solve some problems but it is likely to create other dilemmas as it is to solve existing problems. Most death and dying issues for the very old and very young would not even be under consideration were it not for technology.

Several marketing activities have ethical components. True marketing attempts to satisfy customer needs. To know what those needs are, marketers study information about consumers and try to project and predict what their needs will be. Need is subjective. For example, with all the clinical evidence that is available, why would a woman request a radical mastectomy when her physician indicates that it is not necessary? More than likely, for her, the worry and concern about reoccurring cancer would change her life. With the radical mastectomy, she may feel better in control. Are we to tell her she is wrong?

Reasonable people can reach different conclusions as to what patients need and whether the demand that arises from that need should be met by the health care system. Should people be denied elective procedures such as cosmetic surgery simply because other people judge such procedures as trivial or because what they seek to correct is not life threatening? This level of infringement on individual autonomy is greater than the public is likely to accept at this point in history.[83]

Managers have an ethical duty to ensure the confidentiality of all patients' medical records. This means a health care organization that uses its patients for a mailing list is violating confidentiality if they select heart patients, for example. To be ethically safe, all past patients would have to be sent the same mailing.

Managers who are responsible for health care teaching institutions have a major ethical concern with *consent.* When a patient requests a specific physician to do surgery, signs a consent form for that physician to do the surgery, and then a resident actually performs the surgery, the patient may be justifiably angry. Patients have a right to know. They need to be thoroughly informed of any experimental procedures and give permission for the physician to perform these procedures or to have someone else perform the procedures under the physician's guidance.

Managers often think that they have no responsibility in decisions concerning death and dying because these are "clinical matters." Doubtlessly, physicians are prime decision makers in this area but health care organization managers must be knowledgeable and participate in policy development and implementation to guide physicians within the context of their health care organizations. A major problem is how we define death and when we are willing to terminate life. This includes beginning of life issues with infants born with severe disabilities and end of life issues for the elderly as well as individuals who have been irrevocably harmed to where they cannot expect to ever come out of a persistent vegetative state.

Ethical and social responsibilities permeate the entire organization. When management is involved in situational analysis, the way competitors, the market, and customers are perceived will be reflective of the organization's ethical and social perspective, as illustrated in Exhibit 12–10. (For space reasons the words *ethical* and *social responsibilities* have been incorporated into *ethics.*) Exhibit 12–11 includes many examples of the inputs of "ethics" into strategic management.

EXHIBIT 12–10

Organization-wide Input to Situational Analysis

Situational Analysis	Organization-wide Input
External Environment	
Cultural/Social Environment	Assess the changing environment that will affect employees, consumers, and other stakeholder values, preferences, morality, and attitudes; assess the implications for the organization's culture, structure, and social responsibilities
Technological Environment	Evaluate changing general environment and health care environment technologies for potential impact on the organization especially in terms of purchasing new technology
Legal/Regulatory Environment	Monitor any changes in the legal and regulatory environment that would require organizational change, especially in facilities management and clinical operations
Competitive Environment	Determine the changing trends in organization structures in the health care industry, especially among highly successful organizations; project the implications for organization culture for any surfaced trends; assess the facilities, equipment, food service, and other operations of competitors, including, if possible, their plans for technology or property acquisitions or changes in methods of operation; evaluate the ethical and social implications of competitive activity
Market Analysis	Assess changing consumer attitudes relative to the organization's cultural and structural abilities to respond: does the organization foster a culture of respect for consumers and a passion for continuous monitoring and responding to their needs? What technologies and services do consumers expect access to in our facility? Does the physical setting, comfort, cleanliness, safety, food service, and so on meet consumers' expectations? Are shifts in ethical and social expectations occurring among our consumers?
Internal Environment	
Culture, Structure, Facilities, Ethics	Audit and track the organization culture relative to key factors such as mission/vision/values, leadership, teamwork, consumer orientation, capacity to respond to external change, innovation, and quality; assess the present organization structure and its ability to foster an organization culture that fosters excellence; determine the appropriateness of present facilities to provide excellent services; ensure ethical and social considerations are incorporated into the decision-making process at all levels and evaluate the organization's progress in internalizing ethical and social values

EXHIBIT 12–10   cont'd

Situational Analysis	Organization-wide Input
Mission, Vision, Values, and Objectives	
	Culture: Develop specific programs for communicating present mission/vision/values/objectives as well as changes in all of these elements
	Structure: Ensure the organization structure is consistent with the values proposed in the mission and vision of the organization and carried throughout the culture
	Facilities: Determine the commitment of the organization to providing an excellent physical environment for health care delivery including attractive, clean, and comfortable surroundings for patients, guests, and employees; current and well-maintained technology; safe and nutritious food; and others; communicate this commitment to all stakeholders
	Ethics: Ensure the mission/vision/values/objectives are ethically consistent, socially responsible, accurately reported, and fairly applied

EXHIBIT 12–11

Organization-wide Input to Strategic Management

Hierarchy of Strategic Decisions	Organization-wide Input
Directional Strategies	
Mission	*Culture:* Ensure culture is consistent with stated mission
	Structure: Determine that present structure complements mission
	Facilities: Determine facilities needed to accomplish mission
	Ethics: Ensure mission is morally and socially acceptable
Vision	*Culture:* Communicate changes needed in culture to achieve the organization's hope for the future
	Structure: Initiate structural alterations needed to support the vision
	Facilities: Determine appropriate facilities to realize the vision
	Ethics: Ensure the vision incorporates morality and social responsibility

EXHIBIT 12-11 *cont'd*

Hierarchy of Strategic Decisions	Organization-wide Input
Values	*Culture:* Ensure that the culture is supportive of the stated values *Structure:* Ensure structure facilitates stated values *Facilities:* Physical environment should facilitate values *Ethics:* Ensure that values are consistent with prevailing views of community morality and social responsibility
Objectives	*Culture:* Assess the ease with which objectives can be accomplished within present cultural constraints *Structure:* Determine if the present structure inhibits accomplishment of objectives *Facilities:* Determine if objectives require new or remodeling of facilities *Ethics:* Ensure objectives complement ethical and social responsibility values

Adaptive Strategies	
Expansion Strategies	
Diversification — Related and Unrelated	*Culture:* Suggest cultural changes needed for expansion into related areas and the suitability of culture for entering unfamiliar areas of operation *Structure:* Determine the most appropriate way to organize the expanded related or unrelated operations *Facilities:* Evaluate the adequacy of existing facilities for expansion into related areas and new and different kinds of facilities for unrelated operations *Ethics:* Determine if there are any ethical traps in present areas or unknown ethical mine fields in unrelated areas
Vertical Integration — Forward and Backward	*Culture:* Determine the cultural changes needed for entering unfamiliar areas of operation *Structure:* Assess the changes that will be required for managing vertically integrated operations *Facilities:* Recommend changes for expansion into vertically integrated operations *Ethics:* Determine if unique ethical risks are associated with expansion into vertically integrated operations
Market Development	*Culture:* Facilitate cultural changes needed to expand into new market segments and geographic areas *Structure:* Define and implement structural changes needed to effectively manage new market segments and areas

EXHIBIT 12–11   cont'd

Hierarchy of Strategic Decisions	Organization-wide Input
	Facilities: Construct and equip new facilities for new markets and areas *Ethics:* Analyze potential ethical dangers of market development
Product Development	*Culture:* Evaluate the organization culture's capacity to develop and deliver new services *Structure:* Determine and implement changes in the organization structure needed to manage new services *Facilities:* Assess adequacy of existing facilities to develop and deliver new services *Ethics:* Analyze possible ethical dangers of developing and delivering new services
Penetration	*Culture:* Assess the organization culture's receptivity to measures necessary to expand through penetration activities (i.e., advertising) *Structure:* Analyze the capacity of the present structure to absorb the functions needed to reinforce the penetration strategy *Facilities:* Determine any new facilities needed to support penetration efforts *Ethics:* Evaluate contemporary ethical and social responsibility attitudes relative to promotion and other efforts required for penetration
Contraction Strategies	
Divestiture	*Culture:* Assess the impact of divestiture on current and desired organizational culture *Structure:* Recommend structural changes to implement after divestiture *Facilities:* Analyze alternative uses and markets for any facilities and equipment no longer needed after divestiture *Ethics:* Evaluate the ethical and social implications of divestiture actions on individuals and the community – will the divested services still be available in the community?
Liquidation	*Culture:* What effect will liquidation of all or parts of the organization have on the culture of the surviving parts? *Structure:* Determine the changes in structure after liquidation *Facilities:* Analyze the market for the assets that will be liquidated *Ethics:* Determine the effect of the liquidation on the health of the community

EXHIBIT 12-11   cont'd

Hierarchy of Strategic Decisions	Organization-wide Input
Harvesting	*Culture:* Assess the effects of harvesting (short range) on the organization's culture *Structure:* Assess possible ways in which structural streamlining can facilitate the goals of harvesting *Facilities:* Project the effect of harvesting on the need for and the value of facilities and equipment *Ethics:* What will be the effect of a harvesting strategy on the health of individuals and the community?
Retrenchment	*Culture:* Assess the impact of retrenchment on current and desired organization culture *Structure:* Evaluate streamlining of the organization structure as a reinforcement to retrenchment *Facilities:* If facilities are "cut back" during retrenchment, can the organization catch up in the future? *Ethics:* Analyze possible ethical and social implications of retrenchment
Stabilization Strategies	
Enhancement	*Culture:* Communicate the necessity of an organization culture that values and rewards enhancement efforts *Structure:* Evaluate the contribution changes in structure can make to efficiency of operations and improvement in services delivery *Facilities:* Determine contributions to enhance efficiency and quality *Ethics:* Highlight the ethical and social desirability of enhancement efforts
Status Quo	*Culture:* Evaluate the actions needed to maintain a positive culture in a no-growth environment *Structure:* What organizational changes should be deferred in light of the commitment to the status quo? *Facilities:* Emphasis on maintenance and repair of current facilities and equipment *Ethics:* Ensure that no ethical or social issues arise from the conscious decision to commit to the status quo
Market Entry Strategies	
Purchase	
Acquisition	*Culture:* Assess the cultural compatibility of the target organization and the willingness of the existing culture to absorb the acquired operations

EXHIBIT 12-11   cont'd

Hierarchy of Strategic Decisions	Organization-wide Input
	Structure: Evaluate the relative advantages of centralized versus decentralized operations of the newly formed organization *Facilities:* Determine the contribution acquired facilities and equipment can make to the new organization *Ethics:* Assess the ethical and social implications of the acquisition
Licensing	*Culture:* Evaluate licensing in light of historical modes of operating and project needed changes in organization culture *Structure:* Develop a structure to incorporate a new way of doing business *Facilities:* Determine how and when the organization can use the facilities of others *Ethics:* Evaluate ethical and social perceptions of licensing agreements
Cooperation	
Merger	*Culture:* Determine how to avoid culture clash among individuals of the merging organizations *Structure:* Evaluate the structural changes needed to ensure maximum synergies from the merger *Facilities:* Analyze synergies of facilities and equipment of merging organizations *Ethics:* Consider the ethical and social implications of the merger
Alliance	*Culture:* Assess the receptivity of aligning parties to a cooperative culture *Structure:* Evaluate any structural changes needed to facilitate alliance *Facilities:* Determine any facilities and equipment not currently available needed to ensure success of the alliance *Ethics:* Analyze any possible adverse ethical and social implications of cooperation
Joint Venture	*Culture:* Assess the cultural receptivity of both parties to the joint venture *Structure:* Determine organization changes needed to ensure success of the joint venture *Facilities:* Analyze the facility needs versus those needed for the success of the joint venture

EXHIBIT 1 2 – 1 1 *cont'd*

Hierarchy of Strategic Decisions	Organization-wide Input
	Ethics: Analyze any possible adverse ethical and social implications of the joint venture
Development	
Internal Development	*Culture:* Determine the capacity of the organization culture to encourage, reinforce, and tolerate internal development *Structure:* Determine organizational components that should be added or deleted to facilitate the success of internal development *Facilities:* Ensure that facilities are available that will be needed to support internal development *Ethics:* Assess ethical and social implications of an internal development strategy
Positioning Strategies	
Market-wide	
Cost Leadership	*Culture.* Assess the present culture's interpretation of a cost leadership strategy and the efficiency measures needed to achieve it *Structure:* Assess structural changes that could contribute to cost efficiencies *Facilities:* What can facilities management contribute to increase cost efficiencies? *Ethics:* Evaluate ethical and social implications of actions taken to attain cost leadership
Differentiation	*Culture:* Analyze the tolerance of the present culture to actions designed to differentiate services *Structure:* Evaluate the structural changes that may be necessary to effectively manage more differentiated services *Facilities:* How much differentiation of facilities will be required to differentiate services? *Ethics:* Evaluate ethical and social implications of a differentiation strategy
Market Segment	
Focus – Cost Leadership	*Culture:* Assess the present culture's interpretation of a focused cost leadership strategy and the efficiency measures needed to achieve it *Structure:* Assess structural changes that would be necessary to support or reinforce this strategy

EXHIBIT 12-11   *cont'd*

Hierarchy of Strategic Decisions	Organization-wide Input
	Facilities: What can facilities management contribute to increase cost efficiencies? *Ethics:* Evaluate ethical and social implications of actions taken to attain cost leadership for a given segment
Focus – Differentiation	*Culture:* Analyze the tolerance of the present culture to actions designed to further differentiate services for a specific segment *Structure:* Evaluate the structural changes that may be necessary to effectively manage differentiated services for one segment *Facilities:* How will differentiation of services impact facilities? *Ethics:* Evaluate ethical and social implications of a differentiation strategy focused on one segment
Operational Strategies	
Functional – Organization-wide	*Culture:* Ensure that an organization culture exists that will facilitate the strategy of choice *Structure:* Ensure that the appropriate organization structure is in place to facilitate the selected strategy *Facilities:* Determine the facilities that are necessary to accomplish the organization's mission *Ethics:* Incorporate ethical and social concerns in all strategic decision making

SUMMARY AND CONCLUSIONS

In this chapter four important organization-wide strategies were examined – organizational culture, organization structure, physical facilities, and ethical and social responsibility. These strategies have two things in common – they are directed at the entire organization and they are critically important in the implementation of the directional, adaptive, and market entry strategies. In other words, the organization-wide strategies discussed in this chapter are designed to support strategic management.

If excellence is to be achieved, the culture of the organization must support and reinforce an understanding of the mission and vision, the emergence of leadership at all levels, teamwork, responsiveness to external change, innovation, quality, and a passion for patient service. Adaptive cultures allow for reasonable risk-taking behavior. Although adaptive cultures are not easy to build and maintain, successful organizations seem to be especially good at sensing those things in their history that should be preserved while readily modifying others in light of changing conditions.

One of the most important yet difficult changes to make is in an organization's structure. Organization structures often become a symbol of what makes an organization successful. People become comfortable with "where they fit" and established reporting arrangements. As a result, efforts to change the organization chart is often seen as a threat to be resisted. In reality, however, organization structures must be changed if any significant improvements are to be made in the organization's culture. An organization chart is one of the most cherished "artifacts" of culture because it defines communication and authority patterns. If employees are expected to exercise leadership, assume responsibility for things not normally in their job descriptions, and assume reasonable risks, the organization will have to be less hierarchical and authority driven.

Another important element of an organization's culture is its physical facilities. These facilities are more accurately thought of as the "shell" within which health care is delivered. It includes the total physical environment. The way in which facilities are designed and maintained says much about the culture and values of an organization. Physical facility strategies need to consider more than the design and construction of general and special purpose buildings. A comprehensive physical facilities strategy includes operations and maintenance, security, materials management, and others that can enhance or detract from the health care organization's strategy.

The final organization-wide strategy discussed in this chapter was the ethical and social responsibilities of health care organizations. Ethical and socially responsible decision making is an important element in strategic management. In Chapter 1, strategic management was referred to as a "philosophy" or system of thinking that values adjusting the organization in whatever ways are necessary to fit the external environment. Fitting the organization to the ethical and social values of the larger society is essential to success in the health care environment.

Although it is recognized that ethical and social commitments of strategic leaders in organizations are, to a large extent, based on personal background, religious convictions, and experiences, there are useful aids to encourage ethical and socially responsible strategic decision making. For example, it is important to have a plan for ethical behavior. These plans are often greatly facilitated by the existence of recognized codes of ethical behavior for health care managers

KEY TERMS AND CONCEPTS IN STRATEGIC MANAGEMENT

adaptive organizational cultures	**consent**	**fiduciary duty**
ceremonies	**corporate boards of directors**	**forming (stage of group development)**
champions of change	**cultural heroes**	
clinical engineering	**empowerment**	**framing**
code of ethics	**environmental services**	**materials management**
conflict of interest	**ethics**	**norming (stage of group development)**
	facilities management	

organization-wide strategies
performing (stage of group
    development)
philanthropic boards of
    directors

rhetorical crafting
rites
role modeling
social responsibility
statement of philosophy

storming (stage of group
    development)
strategic leadership
wayfinding

QUESTIONS FOR CLASS DISCUSSION

1. Why are there so few excellent organizations? What are some of the excellent organizations you can identify? What is it that makes each one excellent?
2. Why is culture change so difficult to effect in health care organizations? What are some ways leaders could make culture change easier?
3. What are some of the actions that can be taken to make work groups functions more as teams? Why is teamwork so hard to build in organizations? What role do mission, vision, and values play in building teamwork?
4. What is the difference between leadership and management? From the perspective of strategy implementation, which is more important? Why?
5. Which do you think changes first, strategy or structure? After formulating your answer and making your case, argue the opposite position.
6. What are the primary differences between corporate and philanthropic boards of directors? Why do you think corporate boards are becoming increasingly popular in health care organizations?

7. Why is facilities management an increasing concern for strategic management?
8. How do facilities affect a health care organization's strategy?
9. Do you think the "environment" has an impact on a patient's recovery time?
10. Who is responsible for ethical acts and practices within the health care organization?
11. What stakeholders have ethical and social responsibility claims on the organization?
12. How are ethical problems similar to other managerial problems? How are they different?
13. Explain how a statement of philosophy instills a sense of ethics into an organization's culture.
14. Explain how a "conflict of interest" might arise in a health care organization. How would you prevent conflicts of interest?
15. Discuss the process you would initiate to introduce a greater emphasis on ethics in a health care organization.
16. What are the four ethical principles that apply to health care organizations?

NOTES

1. S. W. Floyd and Bill Wooldridge, "Managing Strategic Consensus: The Foundation of Effective Implementation," *Academy of Management Executive* 6 (November 1992), p. 27.
2. Tom Peters and Nancy Austin, *A Passion for Excellence: The Leadership Difference* (New York: Random House, 1985), p. 46.
3. John P. Kotter and James L. Heskett, *Corporate Culture and Performance* (New York: The Free Press, 1992).

4. Ibid., p. 44.
5. For a more detailed discussion of adaptive cultures see R. H. Kilmann, M. J. Saxton, R. Serpa, and Associates, *Gaining Control of the Corporate Culture* (San Francisco: Jossey-Bass, 1985), p. 356. Also see P. J. Frost, L. F. Moore, M. L. Louis, C. C. Lundberg, and Joanne Martin, eds., *Reframing Organizational Culture* (Newbury Park, California: Sage Publications, 1991).

6. For a detailed discussion, see M. M. Trice and J. M. Beyer, "Studying Organizational Culture Through Rites and Ceremonies," *Academy of Management Review* 9, no. 4 (December 1984), pp. 653–669.

7. W. Jack Duncan, "Organizational Culture: 'Getting A Fix' On An Elusive Concept," *Academy of Management Executive* 3, no. 3 (August 1989), p. 232.

8. Examples used in this section were adapted from Sally Berger and Susan K. Sudman, "Merging Cultures: Successful CEOs Read Warning Signs," *Healthcare Executive* 5, no. 2 (March/April 1990), pp. 21–23.

9. Susan Cartwright and C. L. Cooper, "The Role of Culture Compatibility in Successful Organizational Marriage," *Academy of Management Executive* 7, no. 2 (May 1993), pp. 57–70.

10. Examples used in this section were adapted from Terrence E. Deal, "Healthcare Executives as Symbolic Leaders," *Healthcare Executive* 5, no. 2 (March/April 1990), pp. 24–27.

11. A. L. Wilkins and J. J. Bristow, "For Successful Organizational Culture, Honor Your Past," *Academy of Management Executive* 1, no. 3 (August 1987), pp. 221–229.

12. Robert L. Kuhn, *Creativity and Strategy in Mid-Sized Firms* (Englewood Cliffs, New Jersey: Prentice-Hall, 1989), pp. 193–194.

13. Ian C. McMillan and Patricia E. Jones, *Strategy Formulation: Power and Politics*, 2d ed. (St. Paul: West Publishing, 1986), pp. 60–62.

14. John P. Kotter, *A Force for Change* (New York: The Free Press, 1990).

15. M. DuPree, "What Is Leadership?" *Planning Review* 18, no. 4 (July/August 1990), pp. 14–15ff.

16. This discussion of the "language of leadership" is from Jay A. Conger, "Inspiring Others: The Language of Leadership," *Academy of Management Executive* 5, no. 1 (1991), pp. 31–45.

17. Paula Eubanks, "CEO Walkabouts Get Firsthand Look at Employee Problems," *Hospitals* (May 5, 1990), pp. 50–51.

18. Jeffrey Gandz, "The Employee Empowerment Era," *Business Quarterly* 55 (Autumn 1990), pp. 74–79.

19. For examples see Terry Catchpole, "Empowering Part-Time Workers," *Industry Week* (March 16, 1992), pp. 18–24, and M. A. Verspej, "When Workers Get New Roles," *Industry Week* (February 3, 1992), p. 11.

20. W. J. Rinke, "Winning Management: Doing More with Less," *Supervisory Management* (June 1991), p. 4; and Michael Yate, "Delegation: The Key to Empowerment," *Training and Development Journal* (April 1991), pp. 23–24.

21. J. F. McKenna, "Smart Scarecrows: The Wizardry of Empowerment," *Industry Week* (January 1990), pp. 8–19.

22. The term *failure of cooperation* was used by Michael L. Dertouzos, Richard K. Lester, and Robert M. Solo in the report of the MIT Commission on industrial productivity entitled *Made in America: Regaining the Productive Edge* (New York: Harper Perennial, 1989), Chapter 7. It identified one of the primary reasons American firms are having difficulty competing on a global scale.

23. These stages are discussed in G. M. Parker, *Team Players and Team Work: The New Competitive Business Strategy* (San Francisco: Jossey-Bass, 1990), Chapter 6. The stages were originally presented in B. W. Tuckman, "Developmental Sequence in Small Groups," *Psychological Bulletin* 63 (1965), pp. 384–399.

24. W. Jack Duncan, "Translations: Why Some People Loaf in Groups and Some People Loaf Alone," *Academy of Management Executive* 8, no. 3 (1994), pp. 79–80.

25. J. R. Katzenbach and D. K. Smith, *The Wisdom of Teams: Creating the High-Performance Organization* (Boston: Harvard Business School Press, 1993), p. 263.

26. Edgar H. Schein, "Corporate Culture Is the Real Key to Creativity," *Business Month* (May 1989), p. 73.

27. D. M. Schroeder, "A Dynamic Perspective on the Impact of Process Innovation

upon Competitive Strategies," *Strategic Management Journal* 11, no. 1 (January 1990), pp. 25–42. Also, see S. R. Quinn, "Supporting Innovation in the Workplace," *Supervision* (February 1990), p. 3.

28. Michael Bice, "Corporate Culture Must Foster Innovation," *Hospitals* (November 1990), p. 58.

29. For discussions of innovation in health care and the public sector, see Norman Cates, "Intrapreneurial Models and Applications for Hospitals and Health-Related Organizations," *Society for the Advancement of Management Advanced Management Journal* (Summer 1987), pp. 41–45; and W. H. Agor, "Intrapreneurship and Productivity," *The Bureaucrat* (Summer 1989), pp. 41–44.

30. E. Marszalek-Gaucher and V. D. Elsenhans, "Intrapreneurship: Tapping Employee Creativity," *Journal of Nursing Administration* 18 (December 1988), pp. 20–22.

31. Eileen Shanahan, "The Mysteries of Innovative Government," *Governing* (October 1991), pp. 35–53.

32. Ari Ginsberg and Eric Abrahamson, "Champions of Change and Strategic Shifts: The Role of Internal and External Change Advocates," *Journal of Management Studies* 28 (March 1991), pp. 173–190.

33. Jane M. Howell and Christopher A. Higgins, "Champions of Change," *Business Quarterly* (Spring 1990), pp. 31–36.

34. D. J. Daniel and W. D. Reitsperger, "Linking Quality Strategy with Management Control Systems: Empirical Evidence from Japanese Industry," *Accounting, Organizations, and Society* 16 (1991), pp. 601–618.

35. G. L. Clark, P. F. Kaminski, and D. R. Rink, "Consumer Complaints: Advice on How Companies Should Respond Based on An Empirical Study," *Journal of Services Marketing* 6 (1992), pp. 41–50.

36. Peters and Austin, *A Passion for Excellence,* p. 98.

37. K. W. Harrigan, "Ensuring Quality is Job 1 at Ford," *Business Quarterly* 54 (1989), p. 97.

38. R. H. Waterman, Jr., *The Renewal Factor* (New York: Bantam Books, 1987), p. xii.

39. P. M. Ginter, W. J. Duncan, and S. A. Capper, "Keeping Strategic Thinking in Strategic Planning: Macro-Environmental Analysis in a State Department of Public Health," *Public Health* 106 (1992), pp. 253–269.

40. W. J. Duncan, P. M. Ginter, and S. A. Capper, "Identifying Opportunities and Threats in Public Health," *European Journal of Public Health* 3 (1993), pp. 54–59.

41. Frank Rose, "Now Quality Means Service Too," *Fortune* 123 (April 22, 1991), p. 108.

42. J. A. Alexander, L. L. Morlock, and B. D. Gifford, "The Effects of Corporate Restructuring on Hospital Policymaking," *Health Services Research* 23, no. 2 (1988), pp. 311–338; and A. R. Kovner, "Improving Hospital Board Effectiveness: An Update," *Frontiers in Health Services Management* 6 (Spring 1990), pp. 3–27.

43. S. M. Shortell, "New Directions in Hospital Governance," *Hospital & Health Services Administration* 34, no. 1 (Spring 1989), pp. 7–23.

44. Frank Cerne and Rhonda Bergman, "Into the Black: 1993 Hospital Turnaround Contest Winners," *Hospitals & Health Networks* (July 20, 1993), pp. 28–30.

45. M. L. Fennell and J. A. Alexander, "Governing Boards and Profound Organizational Change," *Medical Care Review* 46 (Summer 1989), pp. 157–187.

46. J. A. Alexander and L. L. Morlock, "CEO-Board Relations Under Hospital Corporate Restructuring," *Hospital & Health Services Administration* 33, no. 3 (Winter 1988), p. 436.

47. A. L. Delbecq and S. L. Gill, "Developing Strategic Direction for Governing Boards," *Hospital & Health Services Administration* 33, no. 1 (Spring 1988), pp. 25–35.

48. R. A. McLean, "Outside Directors: Stakeholder Representation in Investor-Owned Health Care Organizations," *Hospital & Health Services Administration* 34, no. 1 (Spring 1989), pp. 25–38.

49. Terese Hudson, "Change Is Not an Option," *Hospitals* (January 20, 1993), pp. 36–41.

50. H. S. Zuckerman, "Redefining the Role of the CEO: Challenges and Conflicts," *Hospital & Health Services Administration* 34, no. 1 (Spring 1989), pp. 25–38. For an additional discussion of the role of the CEO, see Stephen C. Harper, "The Challenges Facing CEOs: Past, Present, and Future," *Academy of Management Executive* 6, no. 3 (August 1992), pp. 7–25.

51. A. D. Kaluzny, "Revitalizing Decision Making at the Middle Management Level," *Hospital & Health Services Administration* 34, no. 1 (Spring 1989), pp. 39–51.

52. A. D. Chandler, Jr., *Strategy and Structure* (Cambridge, Massachusetts: MIT Press, 1962).

53. Adapted from J. R. Montanari, C. P. Morgan, and J. S. Bracker, *Strategic Management: A Choice Approach* (Chicago: Dryden Press, 1990), Chapter 6.

54. Additional details on this case can be found in Herman L. Lazarus and W. Jack Duncan, "Organizational Integrity and Integrity in Organizations," *American Journal of Hospital Pharmacy* (in press).

55. V. James McLarney, Preface, *Effective Health Care Facilities Management* (Chicago: American Hospital Association Publishing, 1991), p. xiv.

56. Janet R. Carpman and Myron A. Grant, *Design That Cares: Planning Health Facilities for Patients and Visitors,* 2d ed. (Chicago: American Hospital Publishing, 1993).

57. Ibid., p. 19.

58. R. S. Ulrich, "Effects of Interior Design on Wellness: Theory and Recent Scientific Research," *Health Care Interior Design* 3 (1991), pp. 97–109.

59. Carpman and Grant, *Design That Cares,* pp. 9–10.

60. David A. Berkowitz and Melanie M. Swan, "Technology Decision Making," *Health Progress* 74, no. 1 (January/February 1993), pp. 42–47.

61. Gary D. Slack, "Clinical Engineering," in *Effective Health Care Facilities Management,* ed. V. James McLarney et al. (Chicago: American Hospital Publishing, 1991), p. 16.

62. Hugh O. Nash, Jr., James Robin Barrick, Edward Spivey Lipsey, Jr., and Branton B. Blount, "Engineering and Maintenance," in ibid., p. 1.

63. Augustine O. Agho and Stacey T. Cyphert, "Problem Areas Faced by Hospital Administrators," *Hospital & Health Services Administration* 37, no. 1 (Spring 1992), p. 78.

64. Ibid.

65. Aralee Scardina, "Environmental Services," in *Effective Health Care Management Facilities,* p. 29.

66. Sherman G. McGill, Jr., "Security," in ibid., p. 58.

67. Patrick E. Carroll, Clarence W. Daly, and Jamie C. Kowalski, "Materials Management," in ibid., p. 97.

68. Kurt Darr, *Ethics in Health Services Management,* 2d ed. (Baltimore: Health Professions Press, 1991), p. 231.

69. Archie B. Carroll, "The Pyramid of Corporate Social Responsibility: Towards a Moral Management of Organizational Stakeholders," *Business Horizons* 34, no. 4 (July–August 1991), pp. 39–48.

70. Ibid.

71. For a discussion of the impact of social responsibility on various constituencies see Arthur A. Thompson, Jr., and A. J. Strickland, III, *Strategic Management Concepts and Cases* (Homewood: Richard D. Irwin Company, 1992), pp. 46–50; and George A. Steiner, John B. Miner, and Edmond R. Gray, *Management Policy and Strategy,* 2d ed. (New York: Macmillan Publishing Company, 1992), Chapter 5.

72. Darr, *Ethics in Health Services Management,* p. 144.

73. Ibid., p. 2.

74. Thompson and Strickland, *Strategic Management,* p. 49.

75. Darr, *Ethics in Health Services Management,* p. 44.

76. Ibid., p. 95.

77. The state of Oregon has pioneered this effort in the United States. Current litera-

ture on the Oregon Plan abounds. Oregon identifies the specific medical procedures that will be paid for by the state based on its available budget. The people of Oregon have been heavily involved in "drawing the line" for their state.

78. Robert L. Goldman, "Practical Applications of Health Care Marketing Ethics," *Healthcare Financial Management* 47, no. 3 (March 1993), p. 47.

79. David L. Perry, "Keys to Creating an Effective Ethics Program," *Healthcare Executive* 8, no. 2 (March/April 1993), p. 26.
80. Ibid.
81. Goldman, "Practical Applications of Healthcare Marketing Ethics," p. 46.
82. Thompson and Strickland, *Strategic Management*, p. 48.
83. Darr, *Ethics in Health Services Administration*, p. 223.

ADDITIONAL READINGS

Belasco, James A., and Ralph C. Stayer, *Flight of the Buffalo: Soaring to Excellence, Learning to Let Employees Lead* (New York: Warner Books, 1993). This book calls for managers to act less like managers of past eras (the lead buffalo), who charge ahead in fits and starts urging others to follow. They suggest instead that managers "lead the journey" by developing flexible organizations and focus on encouraging everyone to see to the needs of those whom the organization is supposed to serve.

Friedman, Emily, *Choices and Conflict: Explorations in Health Care Ethics* (Chicago: American Hospital Publishing, Inc., 1992). Twenty-eight essays and articles are included in this book on health care ethics. Not focused exclusively on hospitals or physicians, topics range from rationing, dilemmas in the patient-provider relationship, ethics and the health care professional, and bioethics to the individual seeking fairness in society.

Frize, Monique and Michael Shaffer, "Clinical Engineering in Today's Hospital," *Hospital & Health Services Administration* 36, no. 2 (Summer 1991), pp. 288–299. Costs of providing maintenance and repair in-house versus external contracting is just one of the topics covered in this focused article. Investment in technology is so high today that health care organizations need to make specific efforts to buy wisely, train users for correct operation of the equipment, and provide preventive maintenance, according to the authors.

Garrett, Thomas M., Richard J. Klonoski, and Harold W. Baillie, "American Business Ethics and Healthcare Costs," *Healthcare Management Review* 18, no. 4 (1993), pp. 44–50. This article looks at the breakdown of business ethics as it applies to health care – particularly fraud and the abuse of insurance, waste, and distortions in the market. The authors believe that there is substantial fraud and abuse of health insurance on the part of both providers and patients, perhaps as much as $75 billion per year. The authors conclude with several suggestions that may have some impact on business ethics in health care costs.

Hickman, C. R., *Mind of A Manager, Soul of a Leader* (New York: John Wiley & Sons, 1992). A useful book for clearly distinguishing between leadership and management. The focus is on a constructive analysis of the strengths and weaknesses of both leadership and management. It underscores the necessity of leaders and managers for the successful functioning of organizations.

Hiller, Marc D., *Ethics and Health Administration: Ethical Decision Making in Health Management* (Arlington, Virginia: Association of University Programs in Health Administration, 1986). Hiller's book is academic in presentation. He discusses definitions and basic theory before dealing with specific issues confronting health administrators from a theoretical perspective. It is ideal for a doctoral student in health administration.

Lemieux-Charles, Louise, "Ethical Issues

Faced by Clinicians/Managers in Resource-Allocation Decisions," *Hospital & Health Services Administration* 38, no. 2 (Summer 1993), pp. 267–286. This article investigates the ethical issues faced by clinicians/managers when making decisions related to resource allocation and utilization at a Canadian teaching hospital. The ethical issues that occurred throughout the discussions included fairness, concern with preventing harm, consumer/patient choice, balancing needs of different groups of patients, conflict between financial incentives and patient needs, and professional autonomy. The findings suggest that decentralizing resource allocation and utilization decisions does raise ethical issues for clinicians/managers and that a better understanding of these issues can be obtained using an interdisciplinary perspective including nurse managers, physician managers, and managers from other professional groups.

Lumsdon, Kevin, "Form Follows Function," *Hospitals,* February 5, 1993, pp. 22–26. This article builds the case for careful planning to develop a patient-centered facility. Design of patient rooms, nursing stations, and flow of activities are different in a facility dedicated to patient-centered care.

Morgan, Gareth, *Imagination: The Art of Creative Management* (Newbury Park, California: Sage Publications, 1993). An argument is made that imagination is a new way of thinking, a way of organizing, and a fundamental skill of successful managers. Managers need to rethink their roles and review their traditional ways of doing things. This book helps in addressing these new ways of doing things.

Nutt, P. C., and R. W. Backoff, "Transforming Public Organizations with Strategic Management and Strategic Leadership," *Journal of Management* 19 (Summer 1993), pp. 299–347. This article uses strategic management and strategic leadership as means to transform public organizations. Attention is given to the manner in which transformational or radical change should be carried out in public organizations.

Robertson, P. J., D. R. Roberts, and J. I. Porras, "Dynamics of Planned Organizational Change," *Academy of Management Journal* 36, no. 4 (June 1993), pp. 619–634. This article attempts to evaluate the validity of a model of planned organizational change. Support was found for the model and recommendations for future research in the field are provided.

Rosen, E. D., *Improving Public Sector Productivity: Concepts and Practice* (Newbury Park, California: Sage Publications, 1993). The public is insisting that public organizations, health and nonhealth, become more accountable for their operations. A useful book for public sector health managers, it will encourage thinking about new and more productive ways of operating.

Ross, Judith Wilson, John W. Glaser, Dorothy Rasinski-Gregory, Joan McIver Gibson, and Corrine Bayley, *Health Care Ethics Committees* (Chicago: American Hospital Publishing, 1993). This book is more like a manual to start an ethics committee, validate current ethics committee practices, or assist new committee members. It has samples of an ethics committee plan for a year, format for minutes, attendance and other policy letters, questionnaires for committee members, and a variety of assessment instruments. It has sufficient detail to satisfy most needs.

Sheridan, J. E., "Organizational Culture and Employee Retention," *Academy of Management Journal* 35, no. 4 (December 1992), pp. 1036–1056. A study of the retention of graduate accountants in public accounting firms using cultural variables. It was estimated that cultural variables resulted in more than $6 million difference in human resource costs between firms that had different cultural values.

Stein, Howard, "Organizational Psychohistory," *Journal of Psychohistory* 21 (Summer 1993), pp. 97–114. A unique look at the problems associated with culture change and the way it can be managed in nonbusiness organizations. The author provides insights into the challenges and difficulties associated with changing organizational cultures.

Taylor, Kathryn S., "Construction Change: Strong Strategic Plans Can Help Hospitals Keep Facility Plans in Line," *Hospitals & Health Networks* 67, no. 16 (August 20, 1993), pp. 37–39. The dramatically changing health care environment demands that organizations change the way they plan for facilities. Hospitals have to be able to revise plans to meet the changing needs of their communities. Through the use of strategic planning, some of the problems can be avoided as hospitals design outpatient services facilities to complement their inpatient activities.

Controlling and Creating the Strategy

Part 5 completes the strategic management process with chapters that discuss strategic control and a comprehensive strategic plan. Chapter 13, "Control of the Strategy," illustrates that the strategic management process must be monitored, evaluated, and adjusted when necessary. A framework for controlling the strategy is presented with questions for validating the strategic assumptions, as well as the directional, adaptive, market entry, positioning, and operational strategies.

The last chapter pulls the entire strategic management process together through a complete and comprehensive example. Chapter 14 chronicles the year-long strategic management experience of the Indiana State Department of Health. Each of the strategic management processes is described in detail along with the actual methods used and the results achieved. This chapter demonstrates the actual use of the concepts presented in this text and the practicality of their application.

Control of the Strategy

"A strategy that cannot be evaluated in terms of whether or not it is being achieved is simply not a viable or even useful strategy."

– C. H. Roush and B. C. Ball

LEARNING OBJECTIVES

After completing this chapter you should:

1. Understand the nature of control and be able to discuss why health care organizations need strategic control.
2. Be able to discuss the relationship between planning and control.
3. Understand the characteristics of effective control in health care organizations.
4. Describe and discuss a practical framework for controlling organizational strategies.
5. Determine the need for evolutionary change or revolutionary change.
6. Understand that the type of strategic change is determined by management's assessment of the urgency of strategic issues and the capability of the organization to deal with these issues.
7. Be able to identify and discuss organizational mechanisms for implementing strategic control.
8. Understand the role of contingency planning in strategic control.

University Hospital in London, Ontario, has inaugurated a strategic management system that incorporates the organization's mission statement and strategic direction into departmental activities. The new system weaves any change in mission and direction into ongoing operations. In addition, the strategic management system is supported by a great deal of participation from hospital staff, and strong emphasis is placed on coordination, implementation, evaluation, and strategic controls.

Previously, management had few strategic controls and, as a result, planning was disjointed and uncoordinated. For instance, few department heads set objectives with the hospital's strategy or mission in mind. Some department heads even set their objectives prior to the establishment of corporate objectives. A more comprehensive, better coordinated approach was needed.

Changes in the strategic management system involved installing strategic controls within the planning system, including mechanisms to assure well-coordinated and well-integrated corporate and departmental objectives, and periodic evaluation and revision of the objectives and strategy. The new planning cycle begins when the corporate group evaluates past performance, determines strategy, and reevaluates corporate objectives and the mission statement. Major changes in strategic direction occur through a series of meetings, retreats, or other consensus-building activities. These meetings, which include personnel from throughout the organization, provide management a means to correct or change the organization's strategy.

Once strategic changes and corporate objectives have been identified, department managers and corresponding corporate heads determine which corporate objectives apply to the departments and negotiate resource needs. Implementation is coordinated through the setting of corporate priorities and funds availability, thus assuring that inadvertent changes in strategic direction will not be made at the department level.

Performance appraisals provide one method for evaluating the effectiveness of the new planning process. Performance at all levels in the organization is measured against predetermined objectives. The linkage of individual performance objectives and corporate objectives serves two purposes. First, it provides a more coordinated approach to the setting of objectives, and second, it helps every employee realize that his or her actions make a real difference in the achievement of the mission. Other measures of effectiveness are primarily subjective and include evaluations by departmental managers, corporate executives, and ad hoc committees.

By installing strategic controls in the planning process, University Hospital has enhanced planning coordination and comprehensiveness. Department managers benefit because they no longer set their objectives independent of the organization as a whole. University Hospital's president, Patrick Blewett, believes a primary benefit of this process will be its motivating effect on the people in the organization.

Source. Sharon White, "Corporate Objectives and the Planning Process," *Dimensions* (February 1990), pp. 18–20, 42.

THE NATURE OF STRATEGIC CONTROL

The control process may be applied at any level in an organization. For instance, *operational control* focuses on controlling individual performance, work groups, or specific processes such as operations, inventory, scheduling, and so on. These types of controls are necessary and a part of the overall control of an organization. Strategic control is much broader and is an important part of the strategic management process. *Strategic control* provides top management a means of determining whether the organization is performing satisfactorily and an explicit process for refining or completely altering the strategy.

Strategic control is an inherent part of situational analysis and strategy formulation and difficult to separate from them. Generally, control involves agreeing upon objectives, measuring performance, evaluating performance against the objectives, and taking corrective action, if necessary. More specifically, *control* is defined as a combination of components that act together to ensure that the level of actual performance comes as close as possible to a set of desired performance specifications.

A *strategic control system* is a system to support managers in assessing how well the organization's strategy compares to its progress in the accomplishment of its goals and, when discrepancies are detected, to support areas that need attention.[1] Therefore, the strategic control system monitors, evaluates, and adjusts the strategic implementation (the operational strategies), the strategy itself (directional, adaptive, market entry, and positioning strategies), and the situational analysis processes (validates the strategic assumptions). The relationship of strategic control to these processes is shown in Exhibit 13–1.

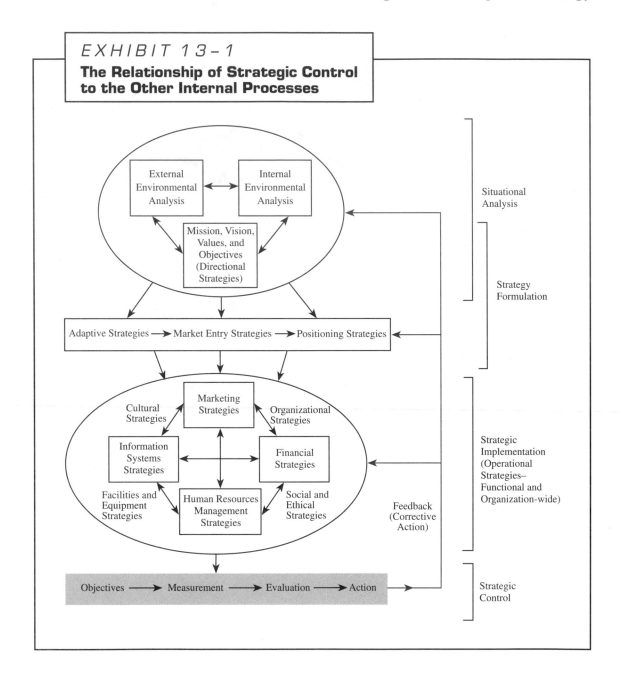

EXHIBIT 13–1

The Relationship of Strategic Control to the Other Internal Processes

The Need for Control

The need for strategic control is a logical extension of the need for strategy. A compelling case can be made for the establishment of an explicit strategic control system within organizations. Specifically, strategic control systems:

1. provide a means to coordinate the efforts of everyone in the organization;
2. motivate managers to achieve objectives;
3. provide an early detection system that indicates when strategic assumptions are wrong or when environmental conditions have changed; and
4. provide a method for management to intervene to correct an ineffective or inefficient strategy.[2]

Agreement by management on the objectives and how those objectives will be measured helps to coordinate the efforts of everyone in the organization. Although objectives are a part of the planning process and were discussed in Chapter 5, they are part of the control process, as well. Objectives not only provide standards of performance but also suggest a means for the evaluation of performance. Therefore, objectives should be clear, precise, and measurable. These attributes provide direction for a coordinated effort, establish explicit measures of progress, and point out where corrective action may be required.

As indicated in the Introductory Incident, objectives and the subsequent evaluation of progress toward those objectives motivate employees. The control system assigns individual responsibility for the accomplishment of objectives and bases individual reward on the achievement of organizational goals. Thus, the control system provides the personal incentives that align individual and organizational objectives and motivates managers to devote their best efforts to achieving the organization's objectives.[3]

Management may have formulated a strategy based on an erroneous assumption, or it may have correctly matched the strategy with environmental conditions, but those conditions may have changed. The strategic control system, as it monitors the progress of the organization, should provide early warning signals that something may be wrong. If the organization is not making progress toward achieving its objectives, the strategic control process will call for additional investigation. This process may reveal the faulty reasoning of the past or the new environmental conditions that impair the strategy.

Even the best-laid plans will sometimes fail or need major adjustments. The control system provides a method for managers to evaluate the strategy and initiate required changes. As indicated in Exhibit 13–1, such changes may be directed toward the operational, market entry, or positioning strategies in the form of strategic adjustments (evolutionary change) or at the directional or adaptive strategies in the form of strategic change (revolutionary change). By monitoring performance and identifying deviations from agreed upon objectives, the strategic control system provides the signals that trigger management intervention in the selection, adjustment, or implementation of the strategy.

Many hospitals in the nation are carefully reevaluating their missions to be sure they have not "abandoned the values" that have been traditional in health care. One particular area is the importance of recognizing the community as a key stakeholder. Some observers fear that as health care organizations become more cost conscious and technologically intense, the needs of the community will be lost. The Greater Southeast Community Hospital in Washington, D.C., was awarded the Foster G. McGaw Prize for Community Service for its intentional efforts to reassess its mission and involvement in community activities.[4] As a starting point for strategic control, the process outlined in Perspective 13–1 is useful.

The Concept of Control

Organizational control systems, whether operational or strategic, have several fundamental elements. These elements include setting objectives or predetermined standards, measuring actual performance, comparing the objectives or standards with actual performance, determining the reason for deviations, and taking corrective action, if necessary.

As illustrated in Exhibit 13–2, the control system forms a feedback or self-correcting loop to assure a steady state. Such feedback provides information to assure that progress is being made toward achieving objectives. All control

PERSPECTIVE 13–1
The Strategy Checkup

Managers of health care organizations want to know if their organizations are moving in the right direction or if changes in the strategy are necessary. The assumptions made just a few years ago and the strategies based on them are likely to be invalid. The "strategy checkup," as a broad approach to assess the strategy, provides a starting point for the strategic control process in health care organizations. The checkup is designed to surface signals that suggest further analysis may be needed or to trigger a more in-depth investigation.

The six steps of the strategy checkup are:

1. Articulate the current strategy (there must be agreement as to the current strategy and supporting assumptions).
2. Assess how the current strategy has worked (determine how successfully the organization has met its goals).
3. Assess the current environment (validate the assumptions on which the current strategy is based).
4. Determine consequences of retaining the current strategy (project how the organization will fare in the future if the current strategy is maintained and environmental trends persist).
5. Look for gaps in the current strategy (identify additional opportunities or threats for the organization).
6. Prepare an assessment of the strategy (synthesize the information produced from the previous five steps and prepare a summary).

Source: Gary B. Hirsch, Lawrence M. Butler, and Martin S. Klein (Institutional Strategy Association, Inc.), "The Strategy Checkup: How Healthy Is Your Strategic Plan?" *Trustee* (January 1990), pp. 10, 17.

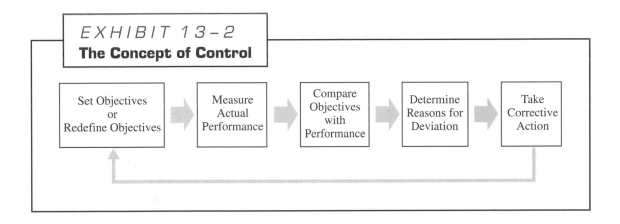

EXHIBIT 13-2
The Concept of Control

Set Objectives or Redefine Objectives → Measure Actual Performance → Compare Objectives with Performance → Determine Reasons for Deviation → Take Corrective Action

systems have standards, periodically measure progress, make comparisons to the objectives, determine the problems, and take corrective action.

The Characteristics of Control

It is impossible, as well as undesirable, to control everything in an organization. In addition, too much emphasis on control can discourage the exploration of new opportunities and dampen innovation. Therefore, in order to be effective, it is important that organizational controls have certain characteristics. For controls to be effective, they should:

- be based on accurate, relevant, and timely information,
- be directed at controlling only the critical elements,
- be flexible,
- be cost-effective,
- be simple and easy to understand,
- be timely, and
- emphasize the exceptions.

All types of control require information; control will be only as good as the information on which it is based. Care should be taken that the information managers use to assess performance is accurate, relevant to the element being controlled, and current (the latest information available). Strategic control relies primarily on information obtained through external and internal environmental analyses. This information is used to test management's assumptions and assess the organization's performance.

When the president and CEO of Memorial Health Services in Southern California first accepted the position, he discovered that no system-wide information was available to aid in making or monitoring overall strategic decisions. The flagship hospital, Long Beach Memorial Medical Center, was spending more than $7 million on its automated information system but progress was extremely slow. This "crisis in confidence over technology" was solved only by top-level leadership. The development of effective system-wide strategies required accurate and timely information from all areas and only top executives had the authority and leadership to obtain it.[5]

Control should be directed at only a few critical elements. Typically, for any process only three or four results must occur for the process to be effective. Management must identify and control these essential results. Broadly, the central factor for strategic control is the overall performance of the organization through the appropriateness of the strategy.

Control systems should be both flexible and cost-effective. An overzealous application of controls can lead to excessive dogmatism, which may inhibit the real objective of control. Hence, controls should not determine decisions; rather, managers should be allowed to make decisions within acceptable boundaries. Control can be time consuming and costly. Therefore, the fewer and more economical the controls, the better is the control system. In strategic management, planning processes and control processes are closely aligned or identical, so flexibility must be an inherent characteristic.

Controls need to be simple and easy to understand. Controls that are overly complex or difficult to apply are often ignored or applied incorrectly. Therefore, management should work to keep controls simple. In addition, control systems need to alert management to possible deviations early in the process. Signals of danger after significant damage has occurred are not effective. Generally, strategic control processes are simply a review of the planning process. Furthermore, this review is accomplished periodically so that deviations may be identified and discussed as early as possible.

Finally, control systems should emphasize the exceptions. Managers can never monitor all the activities within their areas of responsibility at all times. For this reason, controls are effective when they highlight exceptional or out-of-control activities. Strategic controls should alert managers that the organization's mission, vision, values, objectives, strategy, or strategic implementation are not appropriate, effective, or efficient.

A FRAMEWORK FOR THE CONTROL OF THE STRATEGY

The logic underlying strategic control is to evaluate the organization's strategy and make changes if necessary. This is the same fundamental logic underpinning the general concept of control shown in Exhibit 13–2. The steps of the strategic control model are compared with the general concept of control in Exhibit 13–3. Strategic control provides a more explicit framework for controlling the strategy and determining whether revolutionary or evolutionary change is needed.

Establish Performance Standards

Significantly, the strategic management internal processes (situational analysis, strategy formulation, and strategic implementation) generate the objectives and standards of the organization. Thus, planning and control are inherently intertwined. The development of the directional strategies (mission, vision, values,

EXHIBIT 13-3
The Concept of Control and a Framework for Strategic Control

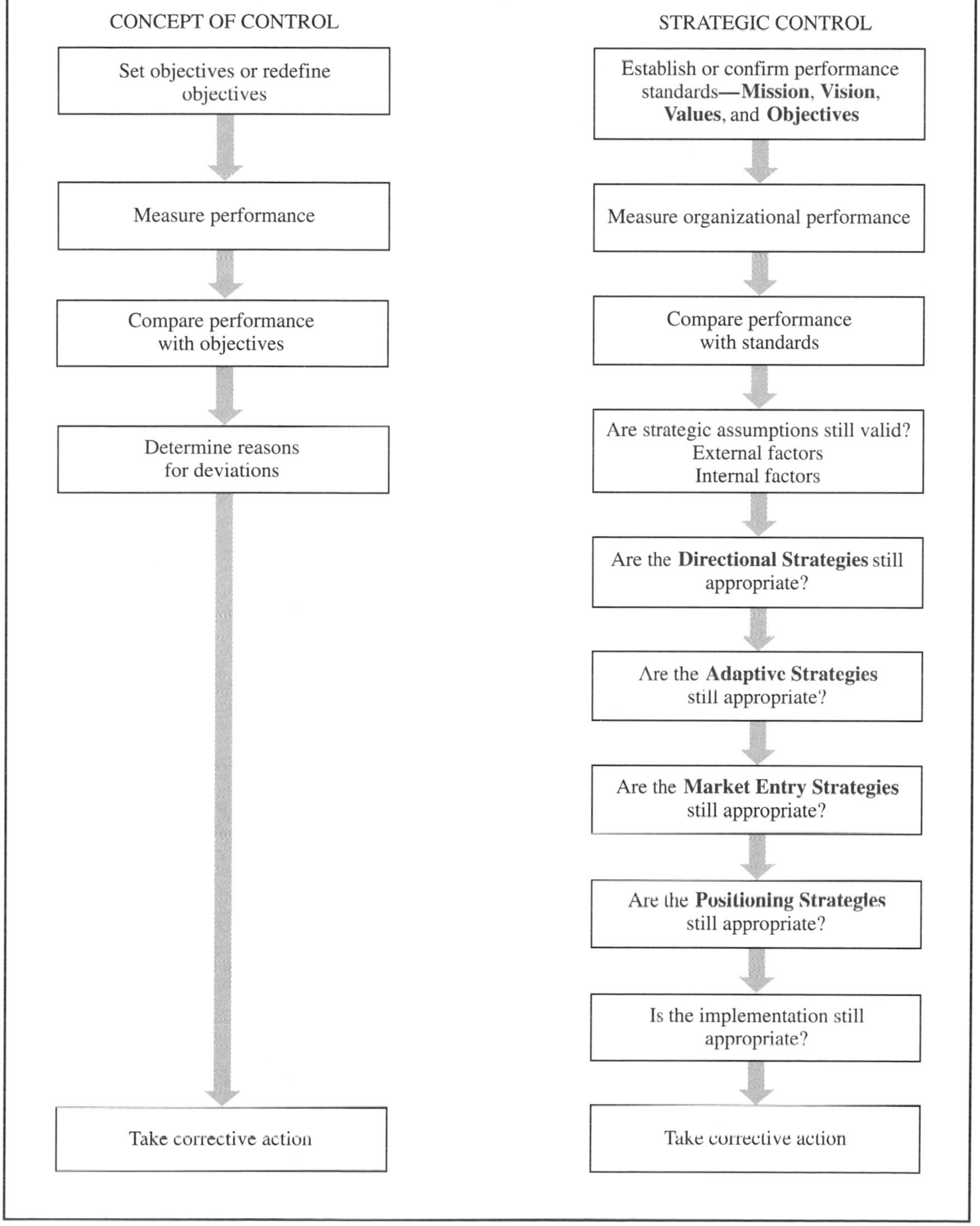

CONCEPT OF CONTROL

Set objectives or redefine
objectives

↓

Measure performance

↓

Compare performance
with objectives

↓

Determine reasons
for deviations

↓

Take corrective action

STRATEGIC CONTROL

Establish or confirm performance
standards—**Mission**, **Vision**,
Values, and **Objectives**

↓

Measure organizational performance

↓

Compare performance
with standards

↓

Are strategic assumptions still valid?
External factors
Internal factors

↓

Are the **Directional Strategies** still
appropriate?

↓

Are the **Adaptive Strategies**
still appropriate?

↓

Are the **Market Entry Strategies**
still appropriate?

↓

Are the **Positioning Strategies**
still appropriate?

↓

Is the implementation still
appropriate?

↓

Take corrective action

and objectives) establish the broadest standard for comparison with organizational performance. Similarly, the adaptive, market entry, and positioning strategies, developed through an analysis of the external and internal environments of the organization, must be supported by explicit operational objectives. These planning elements provide the starting point for strategic control.

The standards of performance (evaluation criteria) for control will vary with the strategy of an organization. For example, an organization pursuing a retrenchment adaptive strategy would have different standards of performance than an organization pursuing market development. Managers must decide which objectives are most appropriate for their particular circumstances.

Frequently, the way in which outcomes are measured and monitored can actually change the character of the service. Blue Choice of Rochester, New York, developed procedures for measuring the quality of medical services provided by HMOs. Employers such as Eastman Kodak could then use the data when entering into HMO agreements. The knowledge that such monitoring takes place can significantly affect the care provided by an individual HMO by requiring HMO managers to include objective quality considerations in their strategic decision making.[6]

Measure Organizational Performance and Compare

As discussed in Chapter 2, internal factors, external factors, and performance factors exert pressure for change on organizations. Organizational performance factors are the clearest indicators that the strategy is performing well or poorly. As a result, negative organizational performance provides significant insight and incentive to take corrective action if the strategy is not meeting expectations.

Qualitative and quantitative performance measures are commonly used to gauge the performance of an organization. For mission, vision, and values, the measures of performance are largely qualitative. Managers must match the actions of the organization to the templates provided by the statements of mission, vision, and values, which is why it is important that they be clearly stated and communicated throughout the organization.

The most commonly used quantitative measures of performance are financial ratios and market standing. Typically, these performance measures are related directly to the objectives of the organization. Although perhaps not the best measures, financial ratios and measures of market standing are relatively easy to obtain and widely used to evaluate and compare organizations.

Commonly used financial ratios include:

- return on investment (ROI),
- return on equity (ROE),
- profit margin,
- debt to equity,
- earnings per share,
- revenue growth, and
- asset growth.

Commonly used market standing measures include:

- overall market share,
- share of the target market, and
- market share as a percentage of the market leader.

These ratios and measures may be used to assess the performance of an organization by comparing the present period with previous periods, comparing the organization with similar competing organizations, and comparing organizational measures with industry averages. In addition to financial and market standing measures, patient satisfaction measures are influencing strategic decisions, as illustrated in Perspective 13–2.

Peter Drucker has suggested using a mix of quantitative and qualitative measures of performance. Drucker indicates that five measures can provide a clear picture of performance for most organizations:

1. *Market standing.* Is the share increasing? Is it increasing, decreasing, or remaining the same in particular submarkets and niches?
2. *Innovative performance.* Are there new products in growth areas?
3. *Productivity.* How much value has been added per resource input?
4. *Liquidity and cash flow.* Can the organization generate adequate cash to sustain operations?
5. *Profitability* (revenue over expenses). Is there adequate return to the organization, investors, owners, and so on?[7]

PERSPECTIVE 13-2
Patient Satisfaction Data – A Valuable Control Tool

According to a study by Cooper Research, a Cincinnati-based health care research firm, nearly 95 percent of hospitals use some form of patient satisfaction measurement. Of the few that do not systematically survey patients, one-half indicated that they plan to implement a patient satisfaction program in the next twelve months. The study showed that hospital executives use the patient satisfaction information:

- to measure hospital services,
- for planning and decision making,
- for individuals' work performance reviews,
- to help guide or make organization changes,
- to measure total quality management programs,
- as input to executive compensation decisions,
- to help gauge the quality assurance program, and
- as part of requirements by the Joint Commission on Accreditation for Healthcare Organizations, stipulating that hospitals make patient information available.

Source: John Burns, "Patient Satisfaction Data a Valuable Tool for Most Hospital Execs – Survey," *Modern Healthcare* 23, no. 49 (1993), p. 54.

Determine the Reasons for Deviations

The fundamental question in strategic control is, "Why has the organization's performance not met the previously established performance standards?" In the model for strategic control presented in Exhibit 13–3, efforts to determine the reasons for deviations from performance expectations are directed toward three areas. Strategic managers must determine if there have been or should be changes in the strategic assumptions (external and internal factors), in the organizational strategy (directional, adaptive, market entry, or positioning strategies), or in strategic implementation (operational strategies).

Strategic control is concerned with an evaluation of the strategic assumptions. Hence, the key question is, "Are the assumptions that underlie the strategy still valid?" The selection of the organization's strategies (Chapters 6 and 7) is based on conclusions concerning the opportunities and threats in the external environment and the internal strengths and weaknesses of the organization. If these factors have changed, operational strategies may be inappropriate, the organizational strategy may need altering, or the mission may no longer be appropriate (although this is rare). Therefore, strategic evaluation and control is concerned with validating the *basis* for the strategy, as well as the strategy itself.

Strategic control provides a means of validating and adjusting the organization's strategy. Therefore, in addition to validating the strategic assumptions, the strategic control process must be concerned with three other areas:

1. The validity of the organization's directional strategies – determining if the mission is still valid and the assumptions underlying the vision, values, and objectives are still valid;
2. The appropriateness of the organization's adaptive, market entry, and positioning strategies – determining if the current strategy is correct and moving the organization toward its objectives and mission; and
3. The effectiveness and efficiency of the operational strategies – determining if the functional and organization-wide strategies (strategic implementation) are making the appropriate contribution.

Take Corrective Action

The purpose of strategic control is to assure that the organization has the appropriate strategies and is performing as expected. The strategic control process should identify any deviations in these areas so that management may take the necessary corrective action. In strategic control, revision is directed toward:

- directional strategies – mission, vision, values, and objectives;
- adaptive strategies – expansion, contraction, or stabilization;
- market entry strategies – purchase, cooperation, or development;
- positioning strategies – market-wide or market segment; or
- operational strategies – functional and organization-wide (implementation) strategies.

The scope of corrective action in strategic control is conceptually illustrated in Exhibit 13–4. The controlled elements in strategic management should be few enough in number to allow management to focus specifically on them. These

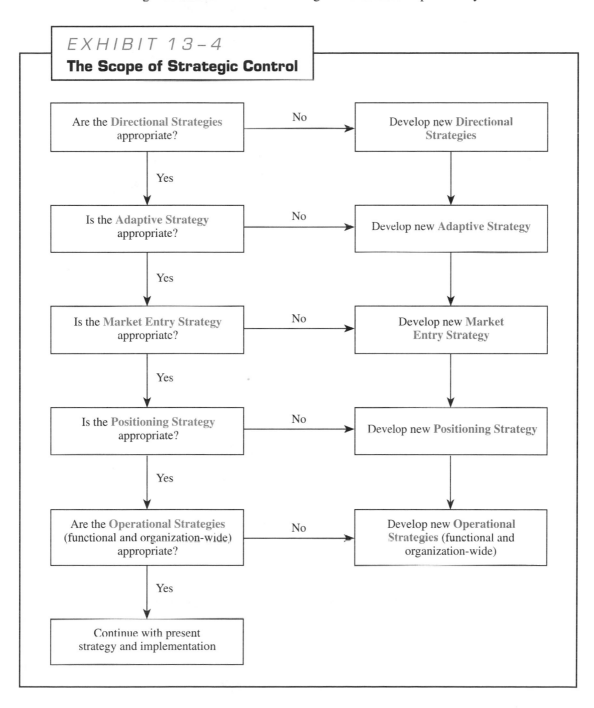

EXHIBIT 13-4
The Scope of Strategic Control

Are the **Directional Strategies** appropriate? — No → Develop new **Directional Strategies**

Yes ↓

Is the **Adaptive Strategy** appropriate? — No → Develop new **Adaptive Strategy**

Yes ↓

Is the **Market Entry Strategy** appropriate? — No → Develop new **Market Entry Strategy**

Yes ↓

Is the **Positioning Strategy** appropriate? — No → Develop new **Positioning Strategy**

Yes ↓

Are the **Operational Strategies** (functional and organization-wide) appropriate? — No → Develop new **Operational Strategies** (functional and organization-wide)

Yes ↓

Continue with present strategy and implementation

elements form a hierarchy, with change occurring relatively rarely at the top and more frequently farther down the hierarchy. Additionally, a change in one element will likely call for a change in every element below it. For example, a change in directional strategies will probably necessitate a change in the adaptive, market entry, and positioning strategies, as well as the operational strategies. Similarly, if the directional strategies are seen as appropriate but the adaptive strategy must be changed, then all subsequent strategies will require modification. A careful assessment of each element is required to determine any need for change.

DETERMINING THE NEED FOR CHANGE

Strategic evaluation and control decisions are perhaps the most important decisions managers will have to make. Strategic control decisions *change* the organization – its rules, procedures, policies, strategies, philosophy, and direction. Major organizational change is often frustrating and always disruptive. Therefore, decisions to make changes in these fundamental elements of the organization must not be taken lightly. Such changes may take years to implement and may affect the success or failure of the organization.

As suggested in the model of strategic control presented in Exhibit 13–3, the key to controlling the strategy is the process of identifying and evaluating deviations to determine if strategic change is required. Therefore, it is necessary to validate the existing strategic assumptions, the strategic alternatives, and strategic implementation. This process is referred to as *strategic issue diagnosis (SID)*. As defined in Chapter 3, strategic issues are those trends, events, or developments that have the potential to influence the organization's strategy. Through the SID process, strategic issues are detected and interpreted. The understanding formed in SID creates the momentum for strategic change. Much of the control process outlined in Exhibit 13–3 is actually a process for identifying and diagnosing issues that are relevant to strategic change.

Jane Dutton and Robert Duncan depict strategic issue diagnosis as an iterative, cyclical process (Exhibit 13–5). The SID process has two major parts: strategic issues recognition and strategic issues assessment. Recognition of issues may be a part of the normal activities of the organization or it may occur as a part of the formal strategic planning and control process. Issues assessment involves determining the urgency of taking action on the issue and the feasibility of dealing with the issue.[8] On the basis of these assessments, momentum for change is created and the forces for organizational responses are set into place. These responses may be radical (revolutionary) change or incremental (evolutionary) change.[9]

An example of the strategic issue diagnosis process may be seen in the actions of many urban hospitals in response to the alarming trends in medical emergencies. Nationwide, there has been a fivefold increase in medical emergencies over the past several years, many due to violence and drugs. These patients are causing severe financial strain for hospitals because trauma patients consume vast amounts of resources and the majority of these victims have no health insurance. As

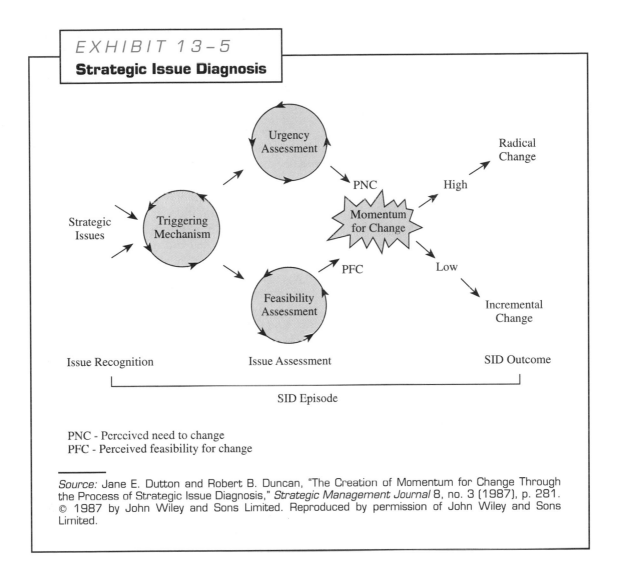

EXHIBIT 13-5
Strategic Issue Diagnosis

PNC - Perceived need to change
PFC - Perceived feasibility for change

Source: Jane E. Dutton and Robert B. Duncan, "The Creation of Momentum for Change Through the Process of Strategic Issue Diagnosis," *Strategic Management Journal* 8, no. 3 (1987), p. 281. © 1987 by John Wiley and Sons Limited. Reproduced by permission of John Wiley and Sons Limited.

management monitors the rise in trauma cases and the rising costs (losses) for the hospitals, a serious strategic issue is identified and evaluated.

For many of Chicago's hospitals, this issue has been assessed as extremely urgent, because continued losses are threatening the very survival of several of the institutions. For instance, Chicago's seven trauma centers together lose $10 million to $12 million annually. Several of these hospitals believe that the only way to deal with the issue is to leave the trauma network. As a result, there has been momentum for change in Chicago's health care system. Four hospitals have left the trauma network: the 543-bed University of Chicago Hospital, the 272-bed Louis A. Weiss Memorial Hospital, the 567-bed Foster G. McGaw Hospital (the teaching facility of Loyola University of Chicago), and the 649-bed Michael

Reese Hospital and Medical Center.[10] These institutions are engaging in both revolutionary and evolutionary change.

Issue Recognition – Triggering Mechanisms

The strategic control process encourages decision makers to actively engage in methods to recognize, isolate, and understand emerging strategic issues. As in the other strategic management processes, issue identification and evaluation are decision-making processes. These decisions are difficult and require the weighing of a mix of quantitative data, qualitative information, opinions, weak signals, and so on. For instance, in one hospital a patient-complaint feedback system was used to detect the need for changing the existing philosophies and the means to improve the delivery of health care services.[11] In addition, health care strategic information systems are becoming more sophisticated and are aiding management in detecting weak signals of change. In many cases, health care executives can access the mainframe computer through personal computers at their desks and evaluate financial and competitive trends.

Although it may be supported with a great deal of data, determining whether the organization has deviated or should deviate from the current strategy will, in the end, require management's best judgment. Clearly, there can be no hard-and-fast rules for deciding whether evolutionary change, revolutionary change, or a change in the fundamental values of the organization is required.

A series of questions for each element of the strategic control model will be useful in detecting and evaluating emerging strategic issues. In addition, these questions are useful in generating discussion among concerned managers. These questions often call for judgments and opinions regarding the appropriateness of strategic change. This approach is used in Exhibit 13–6, beginning with validating the strategic assumptions.

Validating the Strategic Assumptions The strategic plan is based on an analysis of the external and internal environments. These analyses provide the basic beliefs or assumptions that management holds concerning external opportunities and threats and internal strengths and weaknesses. Therefore, validating the strategic assumptions involves determining whether issues in the external and internal environments have changed and to what extent.

Exhibit 13–6 provides a series of questions designed to surface signals of new perspectives regarding these assumptions. The first section examines management's understanding of the external environment and the effectiveness of the strategy. The second part explores the internal demands of the strategy and the relationship of the organization to its environment. These questions may be used by the board of directors, planning staff, or management itself as a beginning point to validate the assumptions underlying the strategy. Such an "audit" may indicate the emergence of new external or internal factors that will affect the organization and suggest areas where additional information will be required in future planning efforts. As suggested in Perspective 13–3, current, accurate information may mean survival for many health care organizations. Questions

EXHIBIT 13-6

Questions for Validation of the Strategic Assumptions

	Yes/No	Evaluation

External Environment

1. Is the strategy acceptable to the major constituents?
2. Is the strategy consonant with the competitive environment?
3. Do we have an honest and accurate appraisal of the competition? Have we underestimated the competition?
4. Does the strategy leave us vulnerable to the power of a few major customers?
5. Does the strategy give us a dominant competitive edge?
6. Is the strategy vulnerable to a successful strategic counterattack by competitors?
7. Are the forecasts on which the strategy is based really credible?
8. Does the strategy follow that of a strong competitor?
9. Does the strategy pit us against a powerful competitor?
10. Is our market share sufficient to be competitive and generate an acceptable amount of profit?
11. Is the strategy subject to government response?
12. Is the strategy in conformance with the organization's moral and ethical codes of conduct?

Internal Environment

13. Does the strategy really fit management's values, philosophy, know-how, personality, and sense of social responsibility?
14. Is the strategy identifiable and understood by all those in the organization?
15. Is the strategy consistent with the internal strengths, objectives, and policies?
16. Is the strategy divided into appropriate substrategies that interrelate properly?
17. Are the operational strategies in conflict?
18. Does the strategy exploit the strengths and avoid the major weaknesses of the organization?
19. Is the organizational structure consistent with the strategy?
20. Is there sufficient capital to support the strategy?
21. What are the financial consequences associated with the allocation of capital to the strategy?
22. Is the strategy appropriate with respect to the physical plant?
23. Are there identifiable and committed managers to implement the strategy?
24. Do we have the necessary skills among both managers and employees to successfully carry out the strategy?

Source: Adapted by permission of Macmillan Publishing Company from George A. Steiner, John B. Minor, and Edmund R. Gray, *Management Policy and Strategy*, 2d ed. © 1982 by Macmillan Publishing Company. (New York: Macmillan Publishing Co., Inc., 1982), pp. 240–241.

PERSPECTIVE 13-3
Information Means Survival

Health care providers that develop data bases concerning service use and cost patterns will be better prepared to survive in a cost-competitive future. Providers must have a means to track utilization and cost trends, evaluate costs of service, offer discounted prices to large volume consumers, and make up the difference elsewhere. Uwe Reinhardt, professor of political economy at Princeton University's Woodrow Wilson School of Public and International Affairs, suggests providers could learn a lesson from the airline industry. He indicated: "both have high fixed costs, low incremental costs in the short run, a lot of human services, and highly skilled labor. Airlines have huge computation centers where price strategists figure out prices per seat. When you take off on a flight, that plane's seats have been carefully sold. Initially, so many were blocked out for 'supersavers.' If there are a lot of empty coach seats left, the strategists release more seats into 'supersaver.' You have very skillful day-to-day price discrimination for each aircraft. Hospital administrators have to play this game too, only much more sharply."

Source: Kevin Lumsdon, "Researchers Say Cost Data Spells Survival for Hospitals," *Healthcare Financial Management* (January 1990), p. 48.

concerning the external environment may reveal that a group practice knows far too little about the views of its major constituents (stakeholders), or the existence of new competitors and their strategies, or how well the current strategy is understood and implemented by members of the practice. A validation (or invalidation) of the strategic assumptions provides a basis for controlling the strategy.

Controlling Revolutionary Change – Directional and Adaptive Strategies
Strategic control at this level is not a matter of keeping the organization on track, but rather one of deciding if a completely new track or approach is warranted. Managers must decide if conditions require a change in the organization's fundamental strategies. Lorange, Morton, and Ghoshal have called this decision *controlling the strategic leap.* They suggest:

> Here the challenge is to reset the trajectory of the strategy as well as to decide on the relative levels of thrust and momentum for the new strategic direction. The critical underlying assumptions that underpin the strategy are no longer viable, and the rules that govern the strategy must be redefined. This situation involves a mental leap to define the new rules and to cope with any emerging new environmental factors. Such a recalibrating of strategy requires a personal liberation from traditional thinking, an ability to change one's mindset, and confront the challenge of creating advantage out of discontinuity. The question now is how to achieve a quantum leap in one's strategy to capitalize on emerging environmental

turbulence. One must proceed by redefining the rules rather than by clinging to the unrealistic hope that the old rules are still valid.[12]

After the organization's performance has been compared with its objectives and standards and the strategic assumptions have been evaluated, the directional strategies should be reevaluated. The objective of this process is to determine if the mission, vision, values, and objectives are still appropriate. Exhibit 13–7 provides several questions that will aid managers in their thinking concerning the appropriateness of the organization's directional strategies.

As suggested in this exhibit, decisions to change an organization's mission, vision, values, and objectives are complex and involve many variables. This control process calls into question the fundamental activities and direction of the organization: "Are we not doing anything new that we should be doing? Are we doing some things now we should not be doing?"

A number of major tertiary-care hospitals are faced with the problem of whether to continue as highly specialized centers of excellence or to diversify and expand into new markets more akin to general trends in the industry.[13] For example, the growth of the outpatient sector of the health care industry may alter the traditional mission of some health care organizations (see Perspective 13–4). Further, a decision to alter the basic mission or vision of the future of the institution could mean becoming a multihospital system with all the opportunities as well as the demands and risks. Generally, there is competition from other institutions

---

EXHIBIT 13–7
Questions for the Evaluation of the Directional Strategies

	Yes/No	Evaluation

1. Are we not doing anything new that we should be doing?
2. Are we doing some things now we should not be doing?
3. Are we doing some things now we should continue to do but do in a different way?
4. Do our mission and vision allow for innovation?
5. Do our mission and vision allow for expansion?
6. Is our mission relatively enduring?
7. Are our organization's mission and vision unique in some way?
8. Is our scope of operations clear (market, products/services, customers, geographic coverage)?
9. Do our mission, vision, and objectives fit the needs of our stakeholders?
10. Do our fundamental values and philosophy still make sense?
11. Is the image of the organization what it should be?

PERSPECTIVE 13-4
Health Care's Future in Outpatient Alternatives

Several analysts are predicting that the inpatient sector of the health care industry has matured and only nominal growth is forecast. Instead, future growth opportunities are in outpatient alternatives. Will acute-care hospitals have to change their mission, objectives, or strategy? Will hospitals have to redefine their vision?

Health care is being pushed outside the hospital by technology and research. Increasingly, physicians are able to use diagnostic and therapeutic technologies in their offices. In the future, it is conceivable that coronary complications requiring open-heart surgery will be treated through drug therapy and other noninvasive methods. Both examples indicate the magnitude of change affecting hospitals and the impact on their traditional missions.

The hospital of tomorrow may resemble its original likeness as it becomes smaller, with a core of services for chronic and highly intensive services. In many ways, it will resemble a critical-care unit — a place of last resort.

Is this a realistic, plausible future for hospitals? Is it something hospital CEOs should consider? What does it mean for the hospital industry?

Source: Barrett L. Boehm and Susan M. Murray, "Healthcare's Future Found in Outpatient Alternatives," *Modern Healthcare* 20, no. 9 (February 26, 1990), p. 24.

---

offering similar specialized services. Technological changes are allowing procedures that formerly were performed in a hospital to take place in nonhospital settings. As other hospital systems diversify in an attempt to develop new and successful markets, the board of directors will ask, "Why aren't we doing the same?"

Concurrently and counter to the impetus for diversification are the strong financial and administrative requirements for maintaining state-of-the-art technology and specialization in a single institution rather than draining off resources for other hospitals in a system. In addition, specialization may suggest strengthening areas of excellence by developing strong feeder institutions and expanding the organization's proven markets.[14]

Perhaps the best approach for controlling the directional strategies is to place the CEO's vision for the future, the existing mission statement, statement of values, and the organization's general objectives next to the questions in Exhibit 13–7 and ask the board of directors or trustees and the executive management team to freely discuss and reach a consensus on each question. This process will either validate the existing mission, vision, values, and objectives or generate momentum for a change. This process invites clarification, understanding, and reinforcement of exactly "what this organization is all about."

Changes in the adaptive strategy also create revolutionary change. As suggested in Chapter 2, such revolutionary change is relatively rare in stable environments but somewhat more frequent in dynamic environments. Signals that the basic strategy for the organization needs to be changed will have serious long-term consequences for the organization. The questions presented in Exhibit 13–8 are helpful in surfacing such signals for the adaptive strategies, and they provide a starting point for discussion of the appropriateness of the organization's adaptive

---

EXHIBIT 13-8
Questions for Evaluation of the Adaptive Strategies

	Yes/No	Evaluation

1. Has the adaptive strategy been tested with appropriate analysis, such as return on investment and the organization's ability and willingness to bear the risks?
2. Does the adaptive strategy balance the acceptance of minimum risk with the maximum revenue potential?
3. Is the payback period acceptable in light of potential environmental change?
4. Does the strategy take the organization too far from its current products and markets?
5. Is the adaptive strategy appropriate for the organization's present and prospective position in the market?
6. Is the strategy consonant with the product life cycle as it exists or as the organization has the power to make it?
7. Is the organization rushing a revolutionary product or service to market?
8. If the adaptive strategy is to fill a currently unfilled niche in the market, has the organization investigated whether the niche will remain open long enough to return the capital investment?
9. Have the major forces inside and outside the organization that will be most influential in ensuring the success of the strategy been identified and evaluated?
10. Are all the important assumptions on which the strategy is based realistic?
11. Has the strategy been tested with appropriate analytical tools?
12. Has the adaptive strategy been tested with appropriate criteria, such as past, present, and prospective economic, political, and social trends?

Source: Adapted from George A. Steiner, John B. Minor, and Edmund R. Gray, *Management Policy and Strategy,* 2d ed. (New York: Macmillan Publishing Co., 1982), pp. 240–241.

strategy. The assumption underlying Exhibit 13–8 is that the mission, vision, values, and general objectives are still appropriate but that the organization's adaptive strategy should be questioned.

A recalibration of the strategy and the challenge of creating advantage out of discontinuity were faced by Comprehensive Care Corporation (CompCare), the largest provider of chemical-dependency programs to hospitals. CompCare's board approved a major retrenchment strategy as a result of increased competitive pressures, hospital cost cutting, and a failed merger attempt. The CEO of Comp-Care indicated, "We determined that we didn't have time to consider further alternatives. We needed to reassert full control and start doing things ourselves."[15] CompCare was indeed, engaging in revolutionary change.

Controlling Evolutionary Change – Market Entry, Positioning, and Operational Strategies If the directional and adaptive strategies of the organization appear to be appropriate, then the market entry, positioning, and supporting functional and organization-wide strategies (operational strategies) must be examined to determine if they are still appropriate. This type of change represents an evolutionary alteration or a strategic adjustment. Thus, strategic control at this level focuses on maintaining a particular strategic direction while coping with environmental turbulence and change. Lorange, Morton, and Ghoshal referred to this type of control as *controlling the strategic momentum* and expanded: "The basic continuity of the business is still credible, and one can hence speak of an extrapolation of the given strategy, even though a lot of operational changes may be taking place. The challenge here is to manage the buffeting of the given strategy and to maintain the strategy on course."[16]

Exhibit 13–9 presents questions for the evaluation of the market entry strategies. Evaluation of the effectiveness of the market entry strategies provides insight into how well the adaptive strategies are being carried out in the marketplace. Exhibit 13–10 provides questions for the evaluation of the positioning strategies. The adaptive strategies and market entry strategies may be appropriate but if the product or service is not positioned effectively the organization may not achieve its objectives.

Each of the functional strategies and organization-wide strategies should be examined separately to determine whether management has correctly defined the role of these strategies in supporting the organization's overall strategy. In addition, management must determine whether the functional and organization-wide strategies are well integrated and support one another.

For instance, a diversification strategy may be appropriate but refinements are called for in marketing, financing, or clinical operations. Scott and White Corporation of Temple, Texas, which owns the 415-bed Scott and White Memorial Hospital, has found unrelated diversification into a hotel and restaurant across the street from its campus to be successful, but the complex has required some operational and positioning modifications.

The questions listed in Exhibit 13–11 provide a format for examining and controlling the operational strategies. These questions should be applied to each of the functional areas supporting the strategy (marketing, finance, human resources,

---

EXHIBIT 13-9

Questions for Evaluation of the Market Entry Strategies

	Yes/No	Evaluation

1. Have adequate financial resources been allocated to enter the market?
2. Does management understand the important market forces?
3. Does management understand the unique requirements of the market entry strategy (purchase, cooperation, development)?
4. Is the market entry strategy the best way to accomplish the adaptive strategy?
5. Is the market entry strategy compatible with the adaptive strategy?
6. Does the selection of the market entry strategy affect the ability of the organization to effectively position its products/services in the market?
7. Is the market entry strategy compatible with the positioning strategy?
8. Is the market entry strategy the most appropriate way to achieve the mission, vision, and objectives of the organization?
9. Is the market entry strategy consonant with the values of the organization?
10. Does the market entry strategy place unusual strains on any of the functional areas?
11. Have new stakeholder relationships developed as a result of the market entry strategy (customers, vendors, channel institutions, and so on)?
12. Has the relationship between the desire and need for rapid market entry been properly analyzed?
13. Has the desired and appropriate level of control over the products and services been achieved?
14. Have the trade-offs between costs and control been properly analyzed?

---

information systems, and so on) as well as the organization-wide initiatives. The logic underlying these questions is that the organization's strategy is fundamentally sound but the organization's performance in carrying out the strategy may not be as effective or efficient as possible.

EXHIBIT 13–10
Questions for Evaluation of the Positioning Strategies

	Yes/No	Evaluation
1. Is the product or service positioned appropriately in the market?		
2. Can the organization use one of the other generic positioning strategies?		
3. Is the positioning strategy appropriate considering the external opportunities and threats?		
4. Will the market forces allow for the selected positioning?		
5. Is the positioning strategy best suited to capitalize on the organization's strengths and minimize its weaknesses?		
6. Is the positioning of the organization's products and services unique in the marketplace?		
7. Is the positioning strategy defensible against new players trying to position in a similar fashion?		
8. Is the positioning strategy compatible with the market entry strategy?		
9. Does the positioning strategy provide the appropriate image for the organization?		
10. Is the positioning strategy sustainable?		
11. Is the appropriate distribution channel being used?		
12. Is the current promotional strategy appropriate?		
13. Is the pricing strategy appropriate?		

McKinsey's 7-S Framework McKinsey & Company has developed a model, known as the *7-S framework,* used to evaluate the implementation of the strategy.[17] The McKinsey model may be used to assess all of the elements in the "determining the reasons for deviation" stage of the strategic control model. Additionally, the 7-S framework provides a model for testing the "strategic fit" or the match between the strategy and the organization. As illustrated in Exhibit 13–12, the elements of this model are strategy, structure, systems, style, staff, shared values, and skills.

The basic premise underlying the model is that all seven of these variables must fit with one another if strategy is to be successfully implemented. Thus, all of the elements must be "pulling in the same direction" if the organization is going to reach its full potential. Examination of the strategic fit of these elements provides a workable checklist for evaluation of the implementation capabilities and efforts of the organization. A health care organization in which the seven

---

EXHIBIT 13-11
Questions for Evaluation of Strategic Imlementation

	Yes/No	Evaluation

1. Overall, can the strategy be implemented in an efficient and effective manner?
2. Has the organization's overall stratcgy been well communicated to all members of the functional areas of the organization?
3. Is there a high level of commitment to the strategy within the functional unit?
4. Has the functional area developed a realistic strategic plan to implement the overall strategy?
5. Is the functional strategy appropriate for the position in the market?
6. Has the functional strategy been well communicated to all of the members of the functional areas of the organization?
7. Is there a system of communications and control that best supports the organization's strategy?
8. Does the functional area have the managerial and employee capabilities required to successfully implement the organization's strategy?
9. Does the functional area have the resources required for successful implcmcntation of the strategy?
10. Is the organization's culture appropriate for the overall strategy?
11. Are the facilities and equipment up-to-date and appropriate to carry out the overall strategy?
12. Does the organization structure help facilitate the overall strategy?
13. Does the organization have the appropriate social and ethical relationships with its communities?
14. Is there a better way to implement the organization's overall strategy?
15. Is the timing of implementation appropriate in light of what is known about market conditions, competition, and so on?
16. Has the strategy been tested with appropriate criteria, such as performance indicators?

Source: Adapted from George A. Steiner, John B. Minor, and Edmund R. Gray, *Management Policy and Strategy,* 2d ed. (New York: Macmillan Publishing Co., Inc. 1982), pp. 240 241.

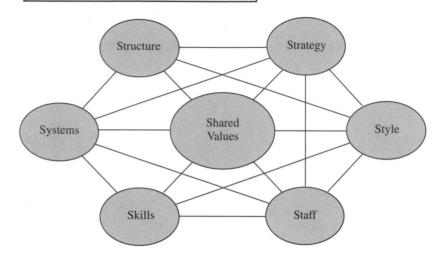

EXHIBIT 13–12
McKinsey 7-S Framework

Strategy

A coherent set of actions aimed at gaining a sustainable advantage over competition, improving position vis-à-vis competitors, or allocating resources.

Structure

The organization chart and accompanying documentation that show who reports to whom and how tasks are both divided up and integrated.

Systems

The processes and flows that show how an organization gets things done from day to day (information systems, capital budgeting systems, service delivery systems, quality control systems, and performance measurement systems all would be good examples).

Style

Tangible evidence of what management considers important by the way it collectively spends time and attention and uses symbolic behavior. It is not what management says that is important; it is the way management behaves.

Staff

The people in an organization. Here it is very useful to think not about individual personalities but about corporate demographics.

EXHIBIT 13 – 12 *cont'd*

Shared Values

The values that go beyond, but might well include, simple goal statements in determining corporate destiny. To fit the concept, these values must be shared by most people in the organization.

Skills

A derivative of the rest. Skills are those capabilities that are possessed by an organization as a whole as opposed to the people in it. (The concept of corporate skill as something different from the aggregate of the skills of the people in it seems difficult for many to grasp; however, some organizations that hire only the best and the brightest cannot get seemingly simple things done while others perform extraordinary feats with ordinary people.)

Source: Reprinted from Robert H. Waterman, Jr., "The Seven Elements of Strategic Fit," *Journal of Business Strategy* 2, no. 3 (Winter 1982), pp. 69–73. (New York: Warren, Gorham & Lamont) © 1982 Warren, Gorham & Lamont, Inc. Used with permission.

variables are pulling together is Allegheny General Hospital (AGH) of Pittsburgh. Exhibit 13–13 demonstrates the high level of excellence that can be achieved when strategy, structure, systems, style, staff, shared values, and skills are complementary.

EXHIBIT 13 – 13

McKinsey 7-S Model Applied to Allegheny General Hospital

Allegheny General Hospital (AGH) is a 714-bed tertiary-care hospital in Pittsburgh, Pennsylvania. AGH has been cited as the top hospital in an extremely competitive market that includes such formidable tertiary-care competitors as 500-bed Mercy Hospital of Pittsburgh, 583-bed Presbyterian–University Hospital, 729-bed St. Francis Medical Center, and 452-bed Western Pennsylvania Hospital. How can AGH excel in one of the nation's most sophisticated health care markets? Allegheny seems to have found the correct strategic fit.

Strategy

Through strategic planning, AGH has identified its strategy: Establish Allegheny General Hospital as *the* regional referral center in Pennsylvania for tertiary-care services. AGH offers specialized patient care, teaching, and research.

EXHIBIT 13-13 cont'd

Structure

AGH has a medical school affiliation with Medical College of Pennsylvania, located in Philadelphia, and maintains Allegheny Singer Research Institute, which has a $30 million annual research budget to conduct research in eighteen clinical areas.

Systems

AGH has a system of objectives and strategies to guide the hospital's progress. The organization maintains advanced systems for matching specialists with referring physicians, medical staff development plans, and clinical services development plans to guide decisions about new services and technology. AGH engages in financial planning and has supportive budgeting systems as well as plant and equipment replacement plans. In addition, AGH has created a system of hospital-wide productivity measures and quality targets.

Style

Management at Allegheny is direct and aggressive. Management has clear objectives and pursues them vigorously. Management is externally oriented, attempting to understand and respond to the region's health care needs. Management also has an internal orientation and emphasizes efficiency. Management is highly committed to being the best hospital in the region.

Staff

AGH has 4,000 employees, including 565 medical staff members, 1,221 registered nurses, and 132 practical nurses. AGH conducts a residency program for third- and fourth-year students of the Medical College of Pennsylvania. The medical school affiliation helps AGH attract highly sought-after specialists who want to teach as well as practice medicine. AGH has a medical staff development plan that weighs the medical needs in the community with the ability of the hospital's current staff to meet those needs.

Shared Values

The medical staff and employees value excellence, the highest level of technology, and community involvement. The emphasis at AGH is on supporting employees through development programs and gain-sharing programs.

Skills

AGH has many specialists, specialty services, and high-tech procedures. AGH has been highly successful in its ability to entice primary-care physicians to refer patients to specialists on the hospital staff. AGH is highly skilled at marketing its services to both the public and referring physicians. Thirty-five people work in the corporate communications department, whose objective is to make primary-care physicians aware of the specialty services and to help its specialists make contact with referring physicians. Allegheny performs a variety of highly specialized procedures, including heart, liver, kidney, pancreas, and single-lung transplants. AGH offers specialized training to its nurses.

Source: David Burda, "Allegheny: A Tertiary Titan with All the Right Moves," *Modern Healthcare* (February 12, 1990), pp. 50–58.

Issue Assessment – Urgency and Feasibility

As illustrated in Exhibit 13–5, once strategic issues have been identified (triggered), decision makers attempt to understand the degree of issue urgency and feasibility. *Issue urgency* is the perceived cost of not taking action or the importance of taking action on an issue. Management's greater perception of the need for change arises from pressures from the external and internal environments as well as organizational performance.

Issue feasibility, on the other hand, is the perception that the means for resolving the issue are available and accessible. Management's perception of feasibility arises primarily from the assessment of the capabilities and resources of the organization. Both urgency and feasibility assessments are largely subjective or judgmental in nature.

Impetus for Strategic Change

Management's assessment of the urgency and feasibility of change creates a momentum for change in the strategy. The momentum for change is the level of effort and commitment managers are willing to devote to action designed to resolve an issue. Where effort and commitment are high, strategic managers are willing and motivated to consider radical responses to emergent issues. Where momentum is low, more conservative changes will likely be made.[18]

The matrix in Exhibit 13 14 shows the link between urgency and feasibility assessments in strategic issue diagnosis and likely organizational responses. For the most part, when managers assess urgency and feasibility to be low, decision makers are unconcerned with resolution. For low urgency/low feasibility issues the impetus to take action is lacking. Where urgency is assessed as low but the feasibility is viewed as high, change will likely be initiated but only at an opportune time for the organization. Management is in no hurry but will move to address the issue in time. Such movements are likely to be evolutionary changes. Low urgency/high feasibility assessments may lead to further modification in implementing a strategy already in place.

An assessment of strategic issues that results in a belief that the issue has high urgency and low feasibility may result in a number of responses, including:

- ignoring or minimizing the issue,
- adjusting current scanning/monitoring or control mechanisms,
- more intensive research,
- preparing to defend against the change, or
- ousting the decision makers.[19]

Often management is frustrated with the organization's inability to respond to the issue in this situation. Thus, management may choose to ignore the issue (and hope it will go away), adjust the scanning or control to obtain new types of information, attempt to obtain more information, or simply remove the decision makers because of their inability to deal with the situation (this is the fate of many a baseball manager who faces high urgency – the need to win, especially

EXHIBIT 13-14
Issue Urgency, Feasibility, and Organizational Response

Assessments of Feasibility

	Low	High
Low	NO RESPONSES	OPPORTUNISTIC RESPONSES
High	COPING, OUSTING RESPONSES	REORIENTING RESPONSES

Assessments of Urgency

Source: Jane E. Dutton and Robert B. Duncan, "The Creation of Momentum for Change Through the Process of Strategic Issue Diagnosis," *Strategic Management Journal* 8, no. 3 (1987), p. 281 © 1987 by John Wiley & Sons Limited. Reproduced by permission of John Wiley & Sons Limited.

late in the season – and low feasibility – a poor team). If the issue is viewed as extremely urgent, management may prepare to defend itself against the change to minimize the impact.

Where the assessment of urgency is high and the assessment of feasibility is high, the greatest momentum for change is generated. Urgency and feasibility combine to produce more radical change involving reorientation of the organization. In this case a change in strategy (revolutionary change) is most likely (and probably most appropriate). As discussed in the earlier example, the Chicago hospitals participating in the trauma network viewed the urgency of the issue as extremely high because their financial viability was threatened. In addition, the hospitals' managers believed their ability to deal with the situation was high. Therefore, the hospitals formulated and implemented exit strategies rather quickly.

HealthCare Compare Corporation became the nation's largest independent utilization-review company with annual gross revenues of more than $31 million. However, several strategic issues had emerged (see Perspective 13–5).

ORGANIZATIONAL MECHANISMS FOR STRATEGIC CONTROL

The mechanisms for strategic control are integrated into the managerial processes, procedures, style, and technologies of the organization; strategic control is not a separate process imposed on an organization. Rather, strategic control is an

---

PERSPECTIVE 13–5
Assessing the Need for Strategic Change

HealthCare Compare Corporation had to assess several strategic issues that had emerged. Which issues were urgent? Which should be addressed?

1. Earnings for the most recent fiscal year were disappointing at $1.95 million, down from $2.3 million the year before.
2. In 1988 the company acquired Affordable Health Care Concepts, a utilization-review and preferred provider organization; however, Affordable Health Care was losing money.
3. Key clients left when some members of management resigned to start their own company.
4. HealthCare Compare sued over a noncompete clause in the former employees' contracts and won, but the suit took management attention away from the business.
5. HealthCare Compare's membership growth slowed. Compare did not attract new clients as anticipated.
6. HealthCare Compare was fully staffed and spent money to attract new clients who failed to purchase the service.

7. Doctors have indicated that they do not like to be second guessed, and there are many questions concerning how much money utilization reviews actually save.
8. A study by the National Academy of Sciences' Institute of Medicine indicated that third-party reviews do not appear to be changing the long-term rate of increase in physician-recommended treatments.
9. Some employers who saw short-term moderation in benefit expenditures were seeing a return to the previous high-cost trends.
10. Many utilization-review firms had reduced inpatient-care costs but the savings had been at least partially offset by increases in outpatient-care costs and administrative expenses.

Were these "urgent issues"? Could the organization effectively deal with these issues? Was it time for a change in strategy? Revolutionary or evolutionary?

Source: Erich Kirshner, "HealthCare Compare's Star Is Beginning to Fade," *HealthWeek* (November 20, 1989), pp. 36–37.

inherent part of the organization and the way it operates. Strategic control should be regarded as a normal and necessary part of what the organization and its managers do. Moreover, control is not an end in itself, but is incorporated into managerial processes to make the processes themselves more effective and efficient. A good example of the integration of control is found in the model of strategic management that serves as a framework for this text. Control is part of the process, not separate from it. Strategic management without an inherent control element is a meaningless activity unrelated to the real world.

Types of Organizational Controls

It is easier to identify and discuss strategic control systems if they are classified by type or category. Doz and Prahalad identified three types of strategic control mechanisms: data management mechanisms, management mechanisms, and conflict resolution mechanisms.[20]

Data Management Mechanisms Data management mechanisms include the information system, strategic management processes (situational analysis, strategy formulation, and strategic implementation), performance measurement, resource allocation procedures, and budgeting procedures. These processes exercise strategic control by providing management with information concerning competitive conditions and organizational performance. Thus, information received by management forms the basis for the organization's strategy and objectives and for their control.

It is apparent that the organization's information systems are extremely important in controlling the strategy. Great effort should be made to ensure that the appropriate information is obtained concerning the external environment and that the information reaches decision makers in a useful form and timely manner. Similarly, the internal information systems need to be designed to provide management with decision-making information, not just data. Ultimately, the quality of management's decisions rests on the quality of the information it receives and understands.

Management Mechanisms Strategic control is exercised by managing the managers. Through the setting of objectives, the performance appraisal process, the compensation program, and so on, managers' actions are coordinated toward agreed-upon organizational objectives. Such controls become part of the operating procedures and culture (shared values) of the organization.

As health care managers manage their organizations, one of the most powerful strategic controls has been the emphasis on quality. In health care, quality has proven to be a winning strategy. As Heskett, Sasser, and Hart expressed in their book on services breakthroughs, "The mark of an outstanding service organization is the continued effort it devotes to widening the gap between itself and its major competitors on both service quality and productivity (efficiency). The effort is both diligent and persistent, almost crusade-like in nature."[21]

Other writers have observed that a strong management commitment to service quality energizes and stimulates an organization to improved service performance.[22] In these types of organizations, quality becomes the central value. Peter Drucker has called this type of control "the strategy of doing better what we already do well."[23] The emphasis on quality is apparent in all strategic decisions because the underlying consideration for the mission, objectives, strategy, and so on is, "How will it affect the quality of the services we offer?" Thus, as illustrated in Perspective 13–6, outcomes management and quality programs can work well together. Managers assess qualitative objectives, strategies, and implementation by asking, "What have we contributed in the past three years that made a difference?" and "What do we plan to contribute?"[24] In health care, merely good service may not be good enough to differentiate the organization from other organizations (or good enough for the patient). Quality-oriented organizations value doing the right thing, even when it is inconvenient or costly.

Conflict Resolution Mechanisms Conflict resolution creates strategic and administrative integration between diverse organizational groups (division- and corporate-level units). Thus, formal and informal task forces, boards of directors or trustees, committees, ad hoc groups, and retreats facilitate a shared understanding of environmental conditions, organizational capabilities, vision and mission, objectives, and strategies.

University Hospital in London, Ontario, introduced in the Introductory Incident, demonstrates the use of all three categories of strategic control. Strategic control was introduced into the organization by modifying the strategic planning

---

PERSPECTIVE 13–6
Compass and Rudder

Powerful management control may be exerted through combining outcomes management (OM) and continuous quality improvement (CQI). Because they are based on different assumptions and have different orientations, these management control mechanisms have been referred to as the *compass* (OM) and the *rudder* (CQI). OM is viewed as the compass because outcomes measures provide specific direction, and CQI is thought of as the rudder because it helps steer the organization efficiently toward that destination.

Outcomes management begins with the assumption that once managers know the outcomes of health care and organizational processes, they can develop guidelines for those processes. CQI assumes that quality improvement results from improving processes. Because OM's focus is on outcomes – patient as well as organizational – it serves as the basis for setting objectives. CQI works to improve outcomes by reducing variation and complexity in the process. CQI makes it possible to measure outcomes. Only when a process is stable can the capability of the process be measured.

Source: James L. Reinertsen, "Outcomes Management and Continuous Quality Improvement: The Compass and Rudder," *Quality Review Bulletin* 19, no. 1 (1993), pp. 5–7.

process to include the establishment and integration of objectives, performance measurement, resource allocation, and budgeting. Individual departments and managers themselves were evaluated using a performance appraisal system tied to the strategy and objectives of the organization. Formal and informal meetings, committees, and retreats evaluated strategy and reached consensus on planning assumptions and effectiveness. Strategic control had become an inherent part of University Hospital's managerial processes.

Levels of Strategic Control

Boards of directors or trustees are being used increasingly for strategic control, particularly in multihospital systems. Reliance on boards of directors of system-owned hospitals for strategic control has been effective where member hospitals have high degrees of autonomy over the organization of their services, services are diverse, member hospitals are geographically dispersed, and systems are large or newly formed.[25]

Peter Lorange has suggested a more explicit approach to strategic controls. He proposes establishing strategic controls at the corporate, division, and operational levels of the organization. In addition to tracking the key assumptions on which the strategy is based, for each level he suggests establishing:

- strategic objectives (objectives of the corporate and division strategy),
- strategic programs and milestones (the tasks and timetable by which the strategic objectives will be accomplished),
- strategic budgets (resources for strategic programs), and
- operating budgets (resources for support programs).[26]

Performance for each of the control areas must be evaluated and action taken as appropriate. Such a strategic control effort will help assure coordinated organizational effort both vertically and horizontally throughout the organization.

CONTINGENCY PLANNING AS STRATEGIC CONTROL

Contingency planning may be incorporated into the normal strategic management process and provide for strategic control. *Contingency plans* are alternative plans that are put into effect if the strategic assumptions change quickly or dramatically or if organizational performance is lagging. Thus, if the organization unexpectedly reaches a strategic pressure point, plans are already in place that provide management with a course of action until further analysis can be undertaken. The more turbulent, discontinuous, and unpredictable the external environment, the more likely it is that unexpected or dramatic shifts will occur and the greater is the need for contingency planning.

Strategic plans are based on the events and trends that management views as most likely (the strategic assumptions). However, these events may not occur, or trends may weaken or accelerate far faster than management anticipated. Therefore, contingency plans are normally tied to key issues or events occurring or not occurring. For instance, if management has based the strategy on an expanding economy but is presented with clear evidence that the economy is slipping into a recession, contingency plans may be activated. Similarly, the announcement that a major competitor is leaving the market may present an opportunity that initiates contingency plans for market development. Such contingency planning forces managers to think in terms of possible outcomes of the strategy.

An example where contingency plans may be developed is in the area of home health care. Many hospitals have viewed home health care as a fertile area for diversification. However, the home medical-equipment segment of the business is quite volatile because of major changes in Medicare reimbursement policies (home medical-equipment businesses traditionally have relied on Medicare reimbursements for at least half of their revenues). As a result, hospitals have seen profit margins from medical equipment units decline and some have incurred substantial losses.[27] A hospital may formulate a strategic plan for its home medical-equipment business based on the knowledge that federal government proposals call for dramatic cuts in spending. Therefore, a hospital that has diversified into this segment of the market may also formulate a contingency strategy to divest its home medical-equipment operations if new restrictive legislation is enacted or if profit margins continue to erode. On the other hand, home health infusion therapy is growing despite its restricted reimbursement from Medicare. Many hospitals perceive that home care in general will be a necessary part of their strategy to develop a continuum of care. In addition, health care reform may significantly improve reimbursement for all aspects of home care.

In providing a strategic control for organizations, Linneman and Chandran suggested that effective contingency planning involves a seven-step process:

1. Identify both favorable and unfavorable events that could possibly derail the strategy or strategies.
2. Specify trigger points. Calculate a likely timetable for contingent events to occur.
3. Assess the impact of each contingent event. Estimate the potential benefit or harm for each contingent event.
4. Develop contingency plans. Be sure that contingency plans are compatible with current strategy and economically feasible.
5. Assess the counterimpact of each contingency plan. That is, estimate how much each contingency plan will capitalize on or cancel out its associated contingent event. Doing this will quantify the potential value of each contingency plan.
6. Determine early warning signals for key contingent events. Monitor the early warning signals.
7. For contingent events with reliable early warning signals, develop advance-action plans to take advantage of the available lead time.[28]

STRATEGIC CONTROL – A NEW BEGINNING

The model of strategic management introduced in Chapter 2 presented strategic control as the last stage of the model. However, control is an inherent part of all the strategic management processes, and indeed, strategic management itself is an attempt to control the future of the organization. Managers exercise the explicit process of control as they consider the reasons for strategic change.

There is a valid argument that strategic control is the first stage of strategic management. Strategic control addresses making changes in what the organization is currently doing. Perhaps the best explanation is that strategic management is logically a circular process, and all of its processes are continuous. For instance, situational analysis is not halted so that strategy formulation may begin. Both are continuous and affect one another.

Nevertheless, strategic control provides the momentum for change, and change is a fundamental part of survival. Because managers understand the relationship between change and survival, there have been many management approaches to changing organizations (see Perspective 13–7). As health care managers control and change their organizations, they chart new courses into the future. In effect, they create new beginnings, new chances for success, new challenges for employees, and new hopes for patients. Therefore, it is imperative

---

PERSPECTIVE 13–7
What Are These?

1950s	1960s	1970s
• Theory "Y" • Management by Objectives • Quantitative Management • Diversification	• Managerial Grid • T-Groups • Matrix Management • Conglomeration • Centralization/ Decentralization	• Zero-Based Budgets • Participative Management • Portfolio Management • MBAs
1980s	**1990s**	**2000s?**
• Theory Z • One-Minute Managing • Organization Culture • Intrapreneuring • Downsizing • MBWA (Management by Wandering Around) • TQM/CQI	• Strategic Thinking • Customer Focus • Quality Improvement • Reengineering • Benchmarking	

Management fads? Management techniques? Management fads is usually the flippant answer. However, each of these management approaches was a genuine attempt to change and improve the organization – to focus efforts, improve the quality of the products and services, to improve employee morale, to do more with less, to put meaning into work, and so on. Some of the approaches worked better than others; some stood the test of time and others did not. Yet, it would be too harsh to simply dismiss them as fads or techniques. The goals for all of these management approaches were to control and shape the organization – to make it better, to make it an excellent organization. One of the things that has distinguished all of these "fads" is the enthusiasm and commitment they have engendered among managers and workers. For many, these approaches have significantly increased the meaning of work – no small accomplishment in a era in which people are increasingly hungry for meaning. And certainly organizations need to create meaning.[1]

When management approaches such as these fail, it is usually because they become an end in themselves. Managers lose sight of the real purpose of the approach and the process becomes more important than the product. Managers start working for the approach rather than letting the approach work for them.

Important Thoughts for the Future

What will be the "management fads" of the next decade? Will you be a part of these attempts to make the organization better or will you simply dismiss them as fads? Perhaps benchmarking, quality improvement, or strategic thinking will turn your organization around. One of these approaches may help make your organization truly excellent or save it from decline.

Is strategic management just another fad? Will it stand the test of time? If strategic management becomes an end in itself, if the process does not foster and facilitate thinking, it will not be useful. However, if the structured process helps managers think about the future and guide their organizations through this turbulent decade, strategic management will have succeeded.

[1] J. Daniel Beckham, "The Longest Wave," *Healthcare Forum Journal* 36, no. 6 (November/December 1993), pp. 78, 80–82.

that health care managers understand the changes taking place in their environment and not simply be responsive to them, but strive to create the future. Health care managers must see into the future and create new visions for success.

SUMMARY AND CONCLUSIONS

Strategic control is an integral part of the strategic management process. Strategic control helps managers determine the relevance of the organization's strategy and assess its progress toward achieving objectives. Where progress is not satisfactory, managers must take corrective action.

Strategic control is a major part of coordination within an organization and can help motivate employees to achieve organizational objectives. In addition, strategic control provides managers a means to make major changes in the direction and strategy of the organization.

Generally, the control process has five elements: (1) setting objectives or standards, (2) measuring performance, (3) comparing objectives with performance, (4) determining the reasons for deviation, and (5) taking corrective action. To be effective, this process should be based on accurate information, focused on controlling only the critical elements, flexible, cost-effective, simple, timely, and emphasize the exceptions.

Strategic control is broader than just operational control but it has the same underlying logic. Specifically, strategic control is directed toward controlling the strategic assumptions (perceived opportunities, threats, strengths, weaknesses); directional and adaptive strategies (revolutionary change); and the market entry, positioning and operational strategies (evolutionary change).

Both qualitative and quantitative performance measures are used to evaluate an organization's performance. Typically, qualitative measures are used in controlling the strategy. However, a number of quantitative measures provide management with signals or indicators of organizational performance. These indicators are primarily financial and marketing oriented.

To determine a need for strategic change, managers engage in strategic issue diagnosis. Strategic issue diagnosis involves the recognition of issues that will influence the strategy. Once strategic issues have been identified, management must assess their urgency and the feasibility of the organization to deal with them. The combination of urgency and feasibility will indicate management's willingness and commitment to initiate strategic change (momentum for change). This momentum may result in radical (revolutionary) or incremental (evolutionary) change.

Judgment and opinion must be used to determine the relevance of the strategy and progress toward organizational goals. To aid in the identification and evaluation of strategic issues, a series of questions designed to trigger analysis and discussion may be used.

Mechanisms for strategic control are integrated into the policies, procedures, and practices of management. These mechanisms are typically found within data management, management of managers, and the conflict-resolution methods of the organization. Therefore, strategic planning, the information system, resource-allocation procedures, performance-appraisal procedures, boards of directors or trustees, retreats, and so on are inherently strategic evaluation and control mechanisms of the organization. In addition, contingency planning (developing alternative strategic plans) is an effective strategic control. Typically, contingency plans are initiated when change occurs more rapidly than expected or when unexpected events render the current strategy inappropriate.

KEY TERMS AND CONCEPTS IN STRATEGIC MANAGEMENT

contingency planning	issue feasibility	strategic control
control	issue urgency	strategic control systems
controlling the strategic leap	operational control	strategic issue diagnosis (SID)
controlling strategic momentum	organizational performance standards of performance	7-S framework
	strategic assumptions	

QUESTIONS FOR CLASS DISCUSSION

1. Define *strategic control.* Why is it important that managers establish strategic control within their organizations?
2. How are strategic planning and strategic control related? Can you distinguish control from planning?
3. What are the fundamental elements of control? Do all organizational control systems have these elements?
4. What are the characteristics of effective control?
5. Strategic control is concerned most with what three areas?
6. What are the steps involved in strategic control of a health care organization?
7. What part do judgment, opinion, beliefs, and values play in strategic control?
8. How is organizational performance measured? Are the measures of performance for health care organizations different from the measures for business organizations?
9. What is strategic issue diagnosis? What are its elements? Is it a part of strategic control?
10. What are an organization's strategic assumptions? How may the strategic assumptions be evaluated?
11. Is it possible to determine if the mission, vision, and values of an organization are valid? How can we approach this determination?
12. How can revolutionary and evolutionary change be strategically controlled? What organizational mechanisms facilitate controlling the strategy?
13. What is the McKinsey 7-S framework? What is the purpose of the framework? Is it a practical strategic control tool?
14. How does management's assessment of issue urgency and the feasibility of the organization to deal with the issue combine to influence strategic change?
15. What is contingency planning? How may contingency planning be viewed as strategic control?

NOTES

1. Peter Lorange, Michael F. Scott Morton, and Sumantra Ghoshal, *Strategic Control* (St. Paul: West Publishing Company, 1986), p. 10.
2. Michael Goold and John J. Quinn, "The Paradox of Strategic Controls," *Strategic Management Journal* 11, no. 1 (January 1990), p. 44.
3. Ibid.
4. Thomas W. Chapman, "Rediscovering Abandoned Values," *Health Management Quarterly* 12, no. 2 (1990), pp. 20–23.
5. Stephen L. Ummel and Sheldon I. Dorenfest, "Complex Information Systems Option: How One CEO Triumphed," *Healthcare Executive* 5, no. 1 (January/February 1990), pp. 25–27.
6. Carolyne K. Davis and Frederick B. Abbey, "Keeping Score Alters the Game," *Health Management Quarterly* 11, no. 2 (1989), pp. 6–9.
7. Peter F. Drucker, "If Earnings Aren't the Dial to Read," *The Wall Street Journal* (October 30, 1986), p. 15.

8. Jane E. Dutton and Robert B. Duncan, "The Creation of Momentum for Change Through the Process of Strategic Issue Diagnosis," *Strategic Management Journal* 8, no. 3 (1987), pp. 279–295.

9. Ibid.

10. Lynn Wagner, "Hospitals Feeling Trauma of Violence," *Modern Healthcare* (February 5, 1990), pp. 23–32.

11. Sara Carmel, "Patient Complaint Strategies in a General Hospital," *Hospital & Health Services Administration* 35, no. 2 (Summer 1990), pp. 277–288.

12. Lorange, Morton, and Ghoshal, *Strategic Control,* p. 11.

13. Gerald E. Sussman, "CEO Perspectives on Mission, Healthcare Systems, and the Environment," *Hospital & Health Services Administration* 30, no. 1 (Spring 1985), pp. 27–29.

14. Ibid.

15. Karen Southwick, "Ailing CompCare Retrenches," *HealthWeek* 3, no. 22 (November 6, 1989), pp. 1, 64.

16. Lorange, Morton, and Ghoshal, *Strategic Control,* p. 11.

17. Robert H. Waterman, Jr., "The Seven Elements of Strategic Fit," *Journal of Business Strategy* 2, no. 3 (Winter 1982), pp. 69–73.

18. Dutton and Duncan, "Creation of Momentum for Change," p. 287.

19. Ibid., pp. 287–288.

20. Y. Doz and C.K. Prahalad, "Headquarter Influence and Strategic Control in MNCs," *Sloan Management Review* 22, no. 4 (Fall 1981), pp. 15–29.

21. James L. Heskett, W. Earl Sasser, Jr., and Christopher W. L. Hart, *Service Breakthroughs: Changing the Rules of the Game* (New York: The Free Press, 1990), p. 112.

22. Valarie A. Zeithaml, A. Parasuraman, and Leonard L. Berry, *Delivering Quality Service: Balancing Customer Perceptions and Expectations* (New York: The Free Press, 1990), p. 3.

23. Peter F. Drucker, *Managing the Non-Profit Organization* (New York: Harper Collins Publishers, 1990), p. 60.

24. Ibid., p. 62.

25. R. D. Kosnik, "Coordination and Control in Multi-Hospital Systems: The Role of Boards of Directors," *Academy of Management Proceedings,* 1987, pp. 91–95.

26. Peter Lorange, ed., *Implementation of Strategic Planning* (Englewood Cliffs, New Jersey: Prentice-Hall, 1982); and Peter Lorange, "Monitoring Strategic Progress and Ad Hoc Strategic Modification," in *Strategic Management Horizons,* ed. J. Grant (Greenwich, Connecticut: JAI Press, 1988).

27. Sandy Lutz, "Hospitals Reassess Home-Care Ventures," *Modern Healthcare* (September 17, 1990), pp. 23–30.

28. Robert Linneman and Rajan Chandran, "Contingency Planning: A Key to Swift Managerial Action in the Uncertain Tomorrow," *Managerial Planning* 29, no. 4 (January/February 1981), pp. 23–27.

29. J. Daniel Beckham, "The Longest Wave," *Healthcare Forum Journal* 36, no. 6 (November/December 1993), pp. 78, 80–82.

ADDITIONAL READINGS

Bates, Donald, L., and John E. Dillard, Jr., "Wanted: A Strategic Plan for the 1990s," *Journal of General Management,* 18, no. 1 (1992), pp. 51–62. The authors provide an excellent framework for evaluating and controlling the strategic plan. The framework includes a series of penetrating questions grouped under the topics of mission statement, desired future position, industry analysis – historical understanding, industry analysis – future expectations, industry critical success factors, gap analysis, external environment, competitor analysis, strengths and weaknesses, industry/market superiority, organization critical success factors, strategy development, implementation, and strategic response.

Bell, Ralph, "Laying the Groundwork for a

Smooth Transition to TQM," *Hospital Topics* 71, no. 1 (1993), pp. 23–26. The author provides some general background on quality programs and presents the seven deadly diseases that inhibit effective management, quality, and service. A method for enabling health care managers to move their "structured and bureaucratic" systems toward effective TQM programs is discussed.

Bender, A. Douglas, Susan S. Geoghegan, and Carla J. Krasnick, "Planning and Teamwork: Critical Health Delivery Issues," *Medical Group Management Journal* 37, no. 4 (July/August 1990), pp. 30–35. This article illustrates an effective means of "closing the planning loop" by asking three important questions: Where do we want to go? How do we work together to get there? How do we know how we are doing?

Brown, Montague, and Barbara P. McCool, "Health Care Systems: Predictions for the Future," *Health Care Management Review* 15, no. 3 (Summer 1990), pp. 87–94. An identification of some of the issues that will demand the attention of strategic decision makers in health care organizations. Issues of quality, accountability, and regionalization will be particularly pressing.

Dutton, Jane E., and Robert B. Duncan, "The Influence of the Strategic Planning Process on Strategic Change," *Strategic Management Journal* 8, no. 2 (1987), pp. 103–116. This paper discusses how an organization's strategic planning process affects the strategic issues that capture decision maker's attention. The authors suggest that modifications in the planning process may need to be made as the addition of specific processes or systems for strategic issue management foster changes in the array of strategic issues identified by management. The authors further hypothesize that the design of the planning process systematically affects the occurrence and success of strategic change efforts.

Griffith, John R., "Principles of the Well-Managed Community Hospital," *Hospitals & Health Services Administration* 34, no. 4 (Winter 1989), pp. 457–470. Five principles for the effective management of community hospitals are presented. Of particular importance to this chapter is the need to carefully integrate planning and control activities and the need to use rewards to reinforce desired performance.

Levitt, Theodore, "The Thinking Manager," *Health Management Quarterly* 12, no. 2 (1990), pp. 6–9. For managers of rapidly changing health care organizations, the ability to think and constantly "rethink" their decisions is essential for success.

Linder, Jane C., "Outcomes Measurement in Hospitals: Can the System Change the Organization?" *Hospital & Health Services Administration* 37, no 2 (1992), pp. 143–166. Many management experts believe that improved outcomes measures will provide an opportunity to correct many of the problems with health care delivery. This article explores whether implementing an outcomes measurement system in a hospital compels this kind of change. Despite its potential, the study shows that hospitals found it difficult to improve the quality of care or their internal practices for thirty-one hospitals that implemented a market-leading outcomes measures system.

Strasser, Stephen, Lea Aharony, and David Greenberger, "The Patient Satisfaction Process: Moving Toward a Comprehensive Model," *Medical Care Review* 50, no. 2 (1993), pp. 219–248. This article provides a comprehensive model of the patient satisfaction process. The article reviews the theoretical work on patient satisfaction, presents the underlying principles of the proposed model, examines the model's component parts and linkages, discusses the model and its limitations, and suggests how the model may be used as a guide for future research and interpreting past research findings.

CHAPTER 14

Creating the Strategic Plan: An Example

"All men can see these tactics whereby I conquer, but what none can see is the strategy out of which victory is evolved."

– Sun-tzu
4th century B.C. Chinese military strategist

LEARNING OBJECTIVES

After completing this chapter you should:

1. Understand how the steps in the strategic planning process logically fit together.
2. Be able to apply the appropriate analysis methods to develop an actual strategic plan.
3. Be able to use the methods and approaches discussed in the preceding chapters creatively – adapting them to facilitate your understanding of situational analysis, strategy formulation, implementation, and control.
4. Understand the complete model of strategic management.
5. Be able to develop a comprehensive strategic plan for an actual organization or an organization presented in a case study.
6. Be able to think strategically.

After being appointed state health commissioner of the Indiana State Department of Health (ISDH), John C. Bailey, M.D., reviewed the plans and organization of the Department of Health and decided that a major strategic planning effort was required to better establish the role of the public health department in Indiana and to set the future direction for the department. In addition, it was Bailey's belief that the changing health care environment – and changing role of public health – would require a new direction for public health and a new way of operating. He believed that the organization had not dealt with change very well and over the years had grown far too bureaucratic to be effective in a rapidly changing environment.

Bailey believed that strategic management would provide an understanding of the trends and issues that the Department of Health would have to address in the next several years and that the process would be instrumental in developing a course of action for the department. Therefore, Dr. Bailey committed to engage in a year-long strategic planning effort that would provide a foundation for determining the future direction of the department. It was Bailey's belief that everyone should be a part of strategic management, and therefore, he invited participation by employees from throughout the department and all organizational levels. He envisioned that the year-long process would provide the basis for ongoing strategic management of the organization.

Although poised to begin, several questions remained. What was the best way to initiate the process? How should it be organized? What was the best approach? Who should facilitate the planning effort? Would this be a worthwhile endeavor or merely a long exercise? Did people have the time to participate?

DEVELOPING A STRATEGIC PLAN

Some health care organizations have extensive experience in strategic management and developing strategic plans. However, as suggested in the Introductory Incident, other organizations may have had little experience with strategic management, or when they have developed a strategic plan, it was little used and ended up gathering dust on a shelf. Regardless of the level of expertise, strategic management requires a thorough understanding of the situation; developing, analyzing, and selecting strategic alternatives (formulation); implementing the strategy; and controlling the strategy.

Using the strategic management model presented in Chapter 2 (refer to Exhibit 2–1) plus the methods and approaches discussed throughout the book, this chapter illustrates development of a comprehensive strategic plan for the Indiana State Department of Health (ISDH). Each stage of the strategic management process as well as the various methods and approaches used are examined in detail. A summary of the ISDH strategic plan is included at the end of the chapter. The summary is an important element of the strategic plan and serves as a ready, easy to use decision-making reference for managers.

In some instances it will be apparent that the methods presented in previous chapters may have been modified to meet the particular needs of the ISDH. It is important to realize that each organization is unique and the methods and approaches presented in this book cannot be applied blindly; rather, they must be understood in terms of the objectives of the organization and the logic of the situation. Managers must always make a method or approach *work* for them, not work for the method. When working through a process, if a method or approach is not contributing to greater understanding, then it should be modified to better serve the organization's needs or abandoned in favor of an approach that does contribute to improved effectiveness in reaching a decision. Remember, a manager's job is to *think*. After studying the previous chapters, you should be familiar with the theories and concepts of strategic management. Now it is time to *apply* the theories and concepts to think strategically.

ORGANIZATION OF THE PROCESS

Because the ISDH had not engaged in agency-wide strategic management for a number of years, the department utilized outside facilitators familiar with strategic management to facilitate the process and help build an internal capacity for future strategic management efforts. The role of the facilitators was to provide guidance in the process and work directly with Joe Hunt, the director of the Office for Policy Coordination. The director was responsible for coordination of the strategic management activities throughout the agency, development of the written strategic plan, and development of future strategic management activities. A brief profile of the director of the Office for Policy Coordination is presented in Perspective 14–1.

It is often difficult for "outsiders" to independently develop the strategy of an organization. It takes a significant amount of time to understand any organization – its mission, values, tasks, culture, and so on. In addition, if people from all levels of the organization are involved in the development, the strategy will be better and ultimately is more likely to be accepted. On the other hand, outsiders can be excellent facilitators, examine sensitive issues, and provide more objective opinions.

Wide participation in the strategic management effort by personnel throughout the agency was believed to be essential. Therefore, employees from all levels and all functional specialties within the organization were to be included in the process. A task force structure with five working groups was adopted to carry out the important tasks of strategic management. Each group had about twenty members. Thus, at the outset, approximately one hundred employees were involved in the process. In addition, the executive staff, composed of the deputy commissioner and the assistant commissioners, supported and guided the process. Nancy C. Blough, deputy state health commissioner, was a particularly enthusiastic supporter of the process and ensured that the process kept on schedule. The work groups and their general responsibilities are presented in Exhibit 14–1 and a profile of Blough is provided in Perspective 14–2.

As an additional aid in organizing the strategic management process, a milestone chart was developed (Exhibit 14–2). The milestone chart helped everyone visualize the entire process and the interrelationships of the individual elements. In addition, the milestone chart highlighted specific priorities and the appropriate sequence for accomplishing the required tasks.

SITUATIONAL ANALYSIS

As shown on the milestone chart, the first five months of the strategic management process were spent in developing the situational analysis. By thoroughly examin-

EXHIBIT 14-1

ISDH Strategic Management Organization

Strategic Planning Steering Committee

- Program Evaluation
- Critical Success Factor Analysis
- Affirm Mission and Vision
- Set Strategic Objectives
- Set Functional-Level Strategies
- Unique Position (Competitive Advantage)
- Set Stakeholder Relations

Task Force for External Environmental Assessment

Opportunities/Threats Identification

- Health Care Environment
- Political/Regulatory Environment
- Technological Environment
- Social/Cultural Environment
- Economic Environment

Stakeholder Analysis
- Indiana Citizens
- County Health Departments
- Indiana Health Centers
- Indiana Primary Health Care Association
- State Medical Association
- Indiana Family and Social Services
- IU School of Nursing
- IU School of Medicine
- IU School of Law
- Indiana State Legislature
- Employee Union

Indiana Trends
- Demographic
- Social/Cultural
- Political

Task Force for Internal Environmental Assessment

Strengths/Weaknesses Identification

- Organizational Culture
  Mission/Vision
  Leadership
  Teamwork
  Quality
    Service
    Process
  Innovation
    Service
    Management
  Client Orientation
    External Clients
    Internal Clients
  Response to External Change
- Financial Subsystem
- Information and Outreach Subsystem
- Human Resources, Staffing, and Physical Facilities Subsystems

Task Force for Mission, Vision, and Values

Mission Formulation

Vision Formulation

Critical Success Factor Identification

Task Force for Strategy Implementation

Organization-wide Strategies

- Mission/Vision
- Leadership
- Teamwork
- Quality
    Service
    Process
- Innovation
    Service
    Management
- Client Orientation
    External Clients
    Internal Clients
- Response to External Change

Work with Steering Committee to Develop Functional-level Strategies

PERSPECTIVE 14–2

Profile of Nancy C. Blough, J.D., Deputy State Health Commissioner

Nancy C. Blough is an attorney and was appointed deputy state health commissioner at the Indiana State Department of Health in 1992. Her responsibilities include overseeing the day-to-day operations of the Public Health Quality Assurance, Prevention & Community Health and Planning and Information Commissions. Prior to her appointment as deputy state health commissioner, Blough served as assistant commissioner of public health services. In addition, she was an executive assistant to the state health commissioner, providing both legal and policy advice. Prior to working at the State Department of Health, she held the title of equal employment opportunity manager for the Indiana Department of Highways.

Blough received both her undergraduate degree in public administration and doctorate of jurisprudence from Indiana University. She is a certified mediator in the state of Indiana and currently is enrolled in the Masters of Business Administration program at Indiana University. She is a member of the local bar association, the American Bar Association, and the National Association of Health Lawyers. In addition, she serves as an advisor to the Law, Medical, and Health Institute associated with Indiana University School of Law and is a member of the Indiana Environmental FORUM.

ing the external environment, internal environment, and the mission, vision, values, and critical success factors, the ISDH's unique situation was brought into perspective. The information gathered during the situational analysis phase was then used to provide the basis for strategy formulation.

General Situation and Background

The citizens of Indiana are very independent and generally do not favor government "interference." The population's "home rule" attitude has limited the influence of state and federal government and created an unusual operating environment. To understand the setting of the ISDH and its unique set of circumstances, it is helpful to review Perspective 14–3, which contains general information concerning the state of Indiana. In addition, the governance of the state and the structure of the ISDH are important to understand the situation.

County Governance Most county governments have two governing bodies, a board of commissioners and a county council. The board of commissioners serves as the executive and legislative bodies of county government. The county council serves as the fiscal body. Counties in Indiana have home rule authority as granted

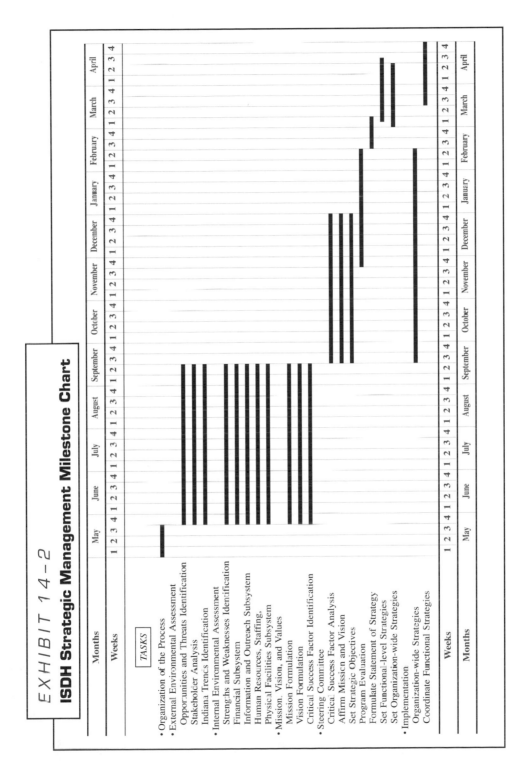

EXHIBIT 14-2
ISDH Strategic Management Milestone Chart

The midwestern territory known as Indiana entered the Union on December 11, 1816, as the nineteenth state. The citizens of Indiana consider themselves to be "typically American." The capital of the state, Indianapolis, lies at the geographic center of Indiana and at the "crossroads of America." The state itself is rectangular, with a maximum length of 280 miles and a breadth of 160 miles. In land area, Indiana is the thirty-eighth largest state.

Economic Base

Of the land in Indiana, 70 percent is devoted to agriculture. Corn and soybeans are the state's primary cash crops. In addition, wheat, oats, tobacco, hay, rye, apples, and peaches contribute meaningfully to the economy. However, service industries account for 60 percent of the gross state product. The northwest portion of the state is a major industrial area fostered by the close proximity to industrial centers in Chicago, Detroit, and Toledo. Iron, steel, and petroleum products are major manufacturing outputs. Other manufactured products include aluminum, chemicals, clay products, furniture, and automotive parts. On a national basis, Indiana is a major producer of pharmaceuticals, manufactured housing, and musical instruments.

Population

In 1990 the population of Indiana was approximately 5.5 million. However, the population growth rate is slowing. From 1980 to 1990 the growth rate was 1 percent. In addition, the population of Indiana is getting older. In 1990, about 13 percent of the population was 65 years or older as compared to 12 percent in 1986. About 9 percent of the population is nonwhite.

Education

Indiana has thirty-four colleges or universities. In 1990, about 76 percent of the population age 25 years and older had an educational attainment of high school graduate or higher. About 16 percent attained a level of bachelor's degree or higher.

State Spending

Marion County, including the capital city of Indianapolis, is governed by a mayor/council form of government. All other counties are governed by a board of county commissioners. In 1988, the state had total general expenditures of $8.4 billion. On a per capita basis, it ranked thirty-seventh among the states. The major categories of state expenditures included $3.66 billion for education, $1.48 billion for public welfare, $903 million for highways, $604 million for health and hospitals, and $117 million for the management of natural resources.*

Health

High-priority statewide health needs that have been identified and are being actively addressed include high-risk pregnancies, child abuse/neglect, unintentional injuries, older adults, environmental health, and the medically underserved. The ten leading causes of death in 1990 were diseases of

PERSPECTIVE 14-3 cont'd

the heart, cancer, cerebrovascular diseases, pneumonia, other chronic obstructive pulmonary diseases, diseases of the arteries, diabetes mellitus, motor vehicle accidents, accidents excluding motor vehicle accidents, and suicide.

Selected Sociodemographic Indicators

Indicator	Indiana	United States
Population	5,556,000	245,803,000
Population Density (per/square mile)	154.6	69.4
Number of Counties	92	3,139
Median Age	31.3	31.7
Percent Below Poverty Level	12%	14%
Percent Rural Population	36%	26%
Percent White Population	91.2%	83.1%
Percent Nonwhite Population	8.8%	16.9%
Median Years of Education	12.4	12.5

Source: Public Health Practice Program Office, Division of Public Health Systems, Centers for Disease Control, *Profile of State and Territorial Public Health Systems: United States, 1990,* U.S. Department of Health and Human Services, Public Health Service, Centers for Disease Control, Atlanta, Georgia (December 1991), p. 121.
*Abstracted from *The Travel Guide,* Mobile Oil Corporation, Prodigy Interactive Personal Service, 1993; *Academic American Encyclopedia,* Grolier Electronic Publishing, Inc., Prodigy Interactive Personal Service, 1993; and *Statistical Abstract of the United States,* 111th ed. (Washington, D.C.: U.S. Bureau of the Census), p. 289.

in Title 36 of the Indiana code, which specifies that counties have the powers granted by law and other powers necessary or desirable to conduct county affairs.[1]

The Indiana State Department of Health The Indiana State Department of Health is a freestanding, independent state agency. The state health commissioner, John C. Bailey, M.D., serves as the chief executive officer of the department and as the secretary of the eleven-member executive board of the state board of health. Perspective 14–4 provides a profile of Bailey. The commissioner is appointed by and serves at the pleasure of the governor. As chief executive officer, the commissioner is responsible for overall management of the ISDH. The executive board of the state board of health is composed of eleven individuals, who are appointed by the governor. The executive board is responsible for providing policy advice and guidance for the ISDH.[2] An organization chart for the ISDH is presented in Exhibit 14–3.

An important role of the ISDH staff members is to function as consultants to staff members of local (county) health departments within the state. In addition,

PERSPECTIVE 14–4

**Profile of John C. Bailey, M.D.,
Indiana State Health Commissioner**

John C. Bailey, M.D., was appointed by Governor Bayh to the Executive Board of the Indiana State Department of Health in 1989, and he became state health commissioner in November 1990. As state health commissioner, he oversees the agency operations and serves as Secretary of the eleven-member executive board.

Bailey graduated from the Indiana University School of Medicine and did his residency in internal medicine at St. Vincent Hospital and the Indiana University Medical Center in Indianapolis. After serving as a U.S. Army Medical Corps artillery surgeon in Vietnam, Bailey returned to the I.U. School of Medicine in 1970 for a United States Public Health Service Trainee Fellowship in cardiology. Subsequently he was appointed as research associate and then senior research associate at the Krannert Institute of Cardiology in Indianapolis and promoted to professor at the I.U. School of Medicine. Bailey's twenty-year career encompasses widely published scientific research, professional consultantships, academic appointments, private practice, and public service.

there is a division of local support services whose staff are assigned on a geographical basis to work directly with local health departments. These staff members provide both technical and management consultative services. Interaction between state and local public health agencies in Indiana is highly decentralized. Under this arrangement, local governments somewhat independently operate and finance their own local health departments.[3]

Indiana has ninety-six local health departments: ninety county, one multi-county, and five city health departments (see Exhibit 14–4). According to state law, the ISDH is the "superior agency" to each of the local health departments. In this capacity the ISDH is charged with the responsibility for recording the appointments of local health officers and overseeing the programs and activities of the local health departments; however, staff members of local health departments are employed and supervised by the local jurisdiction. The number of staff members for a local health department ranges from 1 to 550.[4]

Because of the quasi-autonomy of the local health departments, public health services vary widely from county to country depending upon local funding and the decisions of the commission and county council. Therefore, services provided in one county may not be provided in a contiguous county, or these services may be carried out in a different manner or with varying levels of enthusiasm. In general, the services offered by the local health departments may be classified as (1) assessment, (2) policy development, and (3) assurance activities. Exhibit 14–5 provides a list of these services and identifies the number of local health departments that provide each service in Indiana.

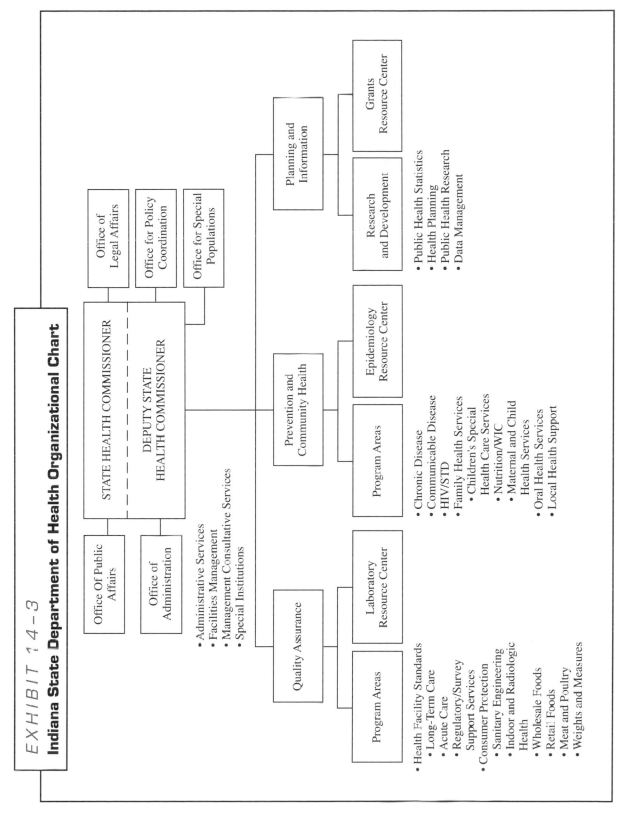

EXHIBIT 14-3

Indiana State Department of Health Organizational Chart

STATE HEALTH COMMISSIONER

DEPUTY STATE HEALTH COMMISSIONER

Office of Public Affairs

Office of Administration

Office of Legal Affairs

Office for Policy Coordination

Office for Special Populations

- Administrative Services
- Facilities Management
- Management Consultative Services
- Special Institutions

Quality Assurance

Program Areas

- Health Facility Standards
  - Long-Term Care
  - Acute Care
  - Regulatory/Survey Support Services
- Consumer Protection
  - Sanitary Engineering
  - Indoor and Radiologic Health
  - Wholesale Foods
  - Retail Foods
  - Meat and Poultry
  - Weights and Measures

Laboratory Resource Center

Prevention and Community Health

Program Areas

- Chronic Disease
- Communicable Disease
- HIV/STD
- Family Health Services
  - Children's Special Health Care Services
  - Nutrition/WIC
  - Maternal and Child Health Services
- Oral Health Services
- Local Health Support

Epidemiology Resource Center

Planning and Information

Research and Development

- Public Health Statistics
- Health Planning
- Public Health Research
- Data Management

Grants Resource Center

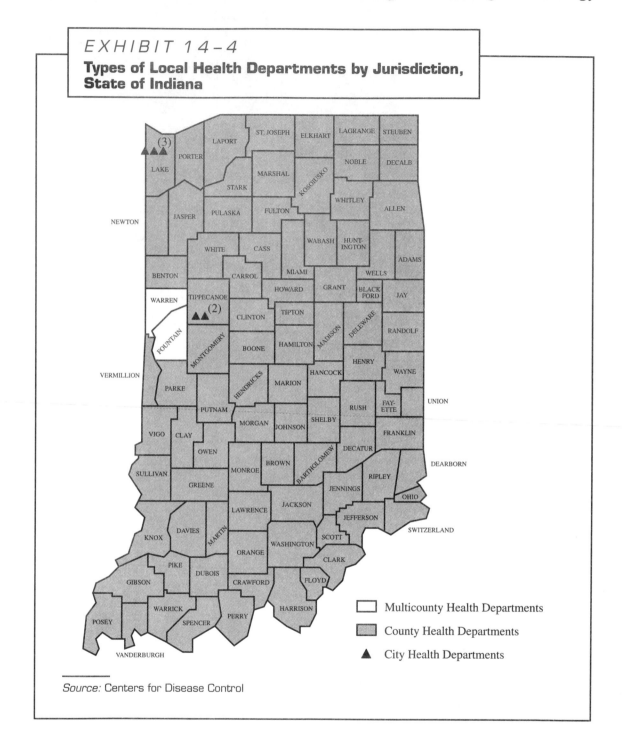

EXHIBIT 14–4

Types of Local Health Departments by Jurisdiction, State of Indiana

Multicounty Health Departments

County Health Departments

▲ City Health Departments

Source: Centers for Disease Control

EXHIBIT 14-5
Services Provided by Local Health Departments

Services	Number of Departments Providing Each Service
Assessment Activities	
Data Collection/Analysis	
Behavioral Risk Assessment	13
Morbidity Data	38
Reportable Diseases	71
Vital Records and Statistics	89
Epidemiology/Surveillance	
Chronic Diseases	38
Communicable Diseases	85
Policy Development	
Health Code Development and Enforcement	51
Health Planning	49
Priority Setting	21
Assurance Activities	
Inspection	
Food and Milk Control	67
Health Facility Safety/Quality	21
Recreation Facility Safety/Quality	30
Other Facility Safety/Quality	8
Licensing	
Health Facilities	6
Other Facilities	63
Health Education	56
Environmental	
Air Quality	41
Hazardous Waste Management	50
Individual Water Supply Safety	76
Noise Pollution	9
Occupational Health and Safety	12
Public Water Safety	51
Radiation Control	17
Sewage Disposal Systems	87
Solid Waste Management	61
Vector and Animal Control	76
Water Pollution	65
Personal Health Services	
AIDS Testing and Counseling	22
Alcohol Abuse	3

EXHIBIT 14-5 cont'd

Services	Number of Departments Providing Each Service
Child Health	61
Chronic Diseases	50
Dental Health	9
Drug Abuse	6
Emergency Medical Service	4
Family Planning	16
Handicapped Children	53
Home Health Care	45
Hospitals	2
Immunizations	89
Laboratory Services	17
Long-term Care Facilities	1
Mental Health	4
Obstetrical Care	11
Prenatal Care	29
Primary Care	5
Sexually Transmitted Diseases	26
Tuberculosis	75
WIC (women, infant, children) Program	30

Note: 94 of 96 local health departments reported.
Source: Public Health Practice Program Office, Division of Public Health Systems, Centers for Disease Control, *Profile of State and Territorial Public Health Systems: United States, 1990,* (Atlanta: U.S. Department of Health and Human Services, Public Health Service, Centers for Disease Control, 1991), pp. 121–122.

Within this setting and without a great deal of strategic management experience, the Indiana State Department of Health began its determined effort to incorporate strategic management into the administrative philosophy of the organization. The process used closely followed the model of strategic management discussed in Chapter 2. The first phase of the process involved situational analysis – environmental analysis, internal analysis, and the development of mission, vision, and values.

External Environmental Analysis

The department had to understand and respond to external opportunities and threats because they represent the fundamental issues that would spell success or failure. The specific objectives that guided the Task Force for External Environmental Assessment included:

- Classify and order information generated outside of the department;
- Identify and analyze current important issues that will affect the department;
- Detect and analyze the weak signals of emerging issues that will affect the department;
- Speculate on the likely future issues that will have significant impact on the department;
- Provide organized information for the development of the department's vision, mission, objectives, and strategy; and
- Foster strategic thinking throughout the department.

External analysis for the ISDH was carried out in two phases. First, stakeholder analysis was used to identify the relationships of the ISDH with other organizations. Second, the department used trend/issue identification and analysis to focus on the issues considered to be most important.

Stakeholder Analysis An enthusiastic Task Force identified over 250 stakeholder groups and organizations, 12 of which were considered to be central to the department's mission. These key stakeholders are identified in the stakeholder map shown in Exhibit 14–6. Stakeholder analysis was selected because of the belief that these outside organizations would be in a good position to suggest areas of excellence within the ISDH and areas for improvements. Further, the stakeholders had important perspectives on the changing economic, social, and political environment of Indiana and the future role that the ISDH should play.

Interviews with the twelve stakeholder groups were conducted to determine the general purpose or mission of the stakeholder and the nature of the relationship of the stakeholder to the ISDH. Results of the interview process are presented in Exhibit 14–7.

The conclusions of the stakeholder analysis were that relations with stakeholders were generally positive although relations were sometimes strained between the ISDH and the local health departments. There was a high level of cooperation with other agencies and the members generally understood the reciprocal relationship between their agency and the ISDH. Most of the agencies wanted an even closer working relationship with the ISDH.

The major deficiency in stakeholder relations was with the county health departments. As indicated in the background section, the quasi-autonomous county health departments deliver most public health services. That is, the county health departments actually provide the services such as food inspections, immunizations, health code enforcement, and so on. The ISDH creates policy and supports the activities of the counties. However, the relationship between the counties and state was not always viewed positively. Often counties saw the ISDH as bureaucratic, nonresponsive, and inappropriately staffed to serve the needs of the counties.

Trend/Issue Analysis In an effort to identify the major trends and issues, the External Environmental Assessment Task Force was divided into five subcommit-

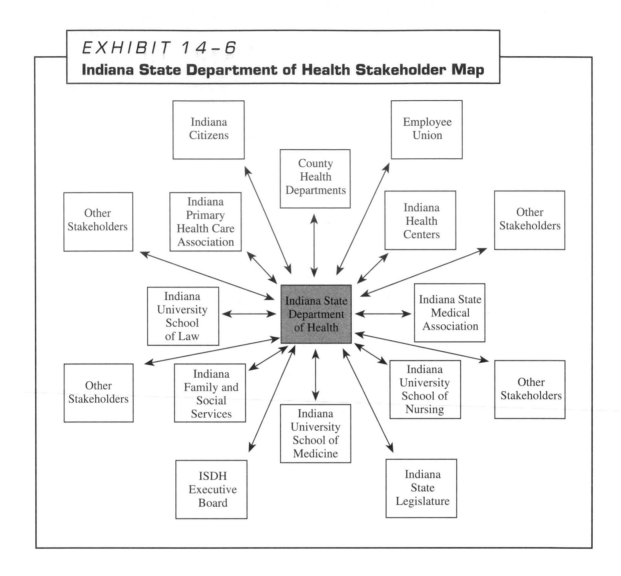

EXHIBIT 14-6
Indiana State Department of Health Stakeholder Map

tees, corresponding to the five "environments" that the ISDH believed represented the major classifications of the public health environment in Indiana:

- health care,
- political/regulatory,
- technological,
- social/cultural, and
- economic.

Each subcommittee was given the responsibility of gathering information, using internal/external and personal/nonpersonal sources of data to identify key trends and issues within its category. The data gathering strategy used in trend and issue identification is conceptualized in Exhibit 14–8.

EXHIBIT 14-7

Indiana State Department of Health Stakeholder Relationships

Stakeholder	General Purpose/Mission	Nature of the Relationship
Indiana Citizens	To achieve health and happiness	The medically underserved depend on ISDH for clinical services; entire community depends on department for prevention and protection
County Health Departments	To deliver public health services such as clinical services, permits, inspections, birth and death certificates, and so on, at the county level	Provide for the direct delivery of public health in Indiana; policy guidance from the state-level organization; rely on state expertise and advice; little financial dependence; semi-autonomous, county departments prefer to stay independent (home rule) but also need the expertise of the state
Indiana Health Centers	To provide health services to those, who because of poverty or location in rural areas, do not have access to affordable health care; emphasis is on farm workers	ISDH provides many important regulatory functions and contracting opportunities for Indiana Health Centers
Indiana Primary Health Care Association	To provide family care to the underserved through health centers/clinics, advocacy, data analysis, and so on	Cooperative agreement with ISDH; have a similar mission, want to maintain a close relationship
Indiana Medical Association	Professional association to represent state physicians; provides licensure services as well as lobbying activities	ISDH has important regulatory functions and collects useful epidemiology and vital statistical data; both organizations tend to be on the same side of the lobbying issues; Indiana Medical Association would like to see more mutual efforts to communicate with ISDH

EXHIBIT 14-7   *cont'd*

Stakeholder	General Purpose/Mission	Nature of the Relationship
Indiana Family and Social Services	To protect and serve families in need of human services resources or support, including family and children, mental health, Medicaid, aging, and rehabilitative services	Similar mission to serve the public; clients overlap; would prefer more communication with ISDH
ISDH Executive Board	To provide advice from different perspectives to facilitate the highest quality of strategic decision making in ISDH	Board composed of a panel of relevant experts willing to volunteer time and assistance to ISDH
Indiana University School of Nursing	To provide undergraduate and graduate education, the largest nursing school in the United States	ISDH is seen as a key player in the debates concerning nursing practice and licensure; School of Nursing wants statutes changed to allow independent nursing practices
Indiana University School of Medicine	To ensure the highest quality of medical education, contribute to medical research, and provide health services	Participation in joint research ventures; reciprocal assistance to ISDH when mutually beneficial
Indiana University School of Law	To provide high levels of teaching, research, and service to the legal community and citizens of Indiana	Some limited participation in mutually beneficial joint activities
Indiana State Legislature	To provide informed governance to citizens of Indiana through enlightened and responsive legislation	Primary funding agency of ISDH; ISDH directly assists through contribution to the legislature's health care agenda
Employee Union	To represent department employees	Membership of approximately 20 percent of department employees

After the initial data gathering activity, the External Environmental Assessment Task Force decided that the trends and issues identified by the various subcommittees should be classified by (1) *scope* (national, state, or county issues) and (2) *strength* (current, emerging, or speculative issues). To illustrate the classifi-

---

EXHIBIT 14-8

External Environmental Task Force Data Gathering Strategy

	Personal Sources		Nonpersonal Sources	
Subcommittee	Internal Experts	External Stakeholders	Internal Department Studies	External Data Bases, Libraries
Economic Environment				
Social/Cultural Environment				
Political/Regulatory Environment				
Competitive Environment				
Technological Environment				
Health Care Environment				

---

cations, the economic environment is shown in Exhibit 14–9. A conceptualization of the process for the entire external environment is presented in Exhibit 14–10. Overall, the external environment for the ISDH was viewed as having five major categories or environments, each with national/state/county and current/emerging/speculative issues. This organization of the process helped members of the task force to better focus data gathering and evaluation.

Using this approach, each subcommittee identified numerous (over fifty) national, state, and county; current, emerging, and speculative issues. However, the subcommittees concluded that many of the issues were trivial or would have little direct impact upon the department. Furthermore, only the most important issues ultimately could be addressed by the strategic plan. Therefore, each subcommittee reduced the list to ten or fewer trends/issues by assessing the importance of the impact of the trends and issues on the ISDH. Subsequent discussions and combination of some issues resulted in a total of thirty-four environmental issues (Exhibit 14–11).

To verify the validity of the trends and issues identified by the subcommittees of the External Environment Task Force, 317 external stakeholders (including

EXHIBIT 14-9

Classifications of the Economic Environment

		Scope of the Issue		
		National	**State**	**County**
Issue Strength	**Current**	• No growth in total economy results in less tax revenue • Increasing hospital and nursing home closures	• No growth in total economy results in less tax revenue • Twelve percent of households earn less than $10,000	• Continued shortage of health care workers in rural areas
	Emerging	• Less health insurance benefits offered by employers • Limited funding for public health	• Less discretionary money for the average Indiana citizen • Limited funding for public health	• Limited funding for public health
	Speculative		Increasing hospital and nursing home closures	

the administrators of the ninety-six local health departments) were surveyed. The stakeholders were asked to evaluate each of the thirty-four trends and issues as being *very important, important, less important,* or *not important.* In addition to the stakeholders, the External Environmental Assessment Task Force evaluated the trends and issues using the same instrument. Mean scores for each trend were calculated, and stakeholder and task force results were compared. The trends and issues rated as very important (mean scores above 3.38) for both groups are presented in Exhibit 14–12.

After considerable discussion concerning the survey result, the task force decided that the views of the stakeholders *and* the task force should be considered by combining several of the important individual trends and issues under broader headings. The total number of trends and issues could be reduced yet still retain the subtlety of the individual factors considered important by both groups. By collapsing the trends and issues under broader headings, eight significant areas were identified (Exhibit 14–13). Note that twenty-five of the original thirty-four

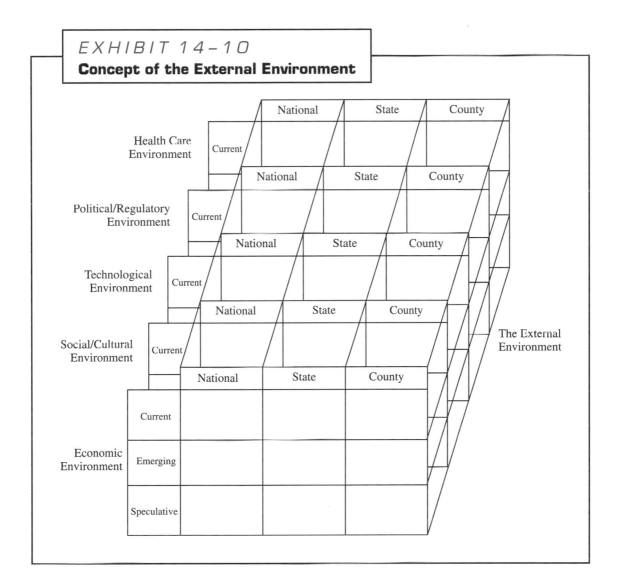

EXHIBIT 14-10
Concept of the External Environment

issues were subsumed under the eight broad headings. It was felt that this approach provided general areas of focus for the ISDH, but retained the necessary detail to guide the strategy.

It was the belief of the task force that each of the eight trends and issues represented both opportunities and threats for the ISDH. To highlight this belief, the task force began identifying the implications of the opportunities and threats for each of the eight issues. The points identified were the initial thoughts of the task force and designed to stimulate strategic thinking of the steering committee

EXHIBIT 14-11
Trends/Issues by Environmental Classification

Economic Environment	Code	Social/Cultural Environment	Code	Health Care Environment	Code	Technological Environment	Code	Political/Regulatory Environment	Code
No growth in total economy with less tax revenue	E-1	Increasing ethnic/racial diversity	S-1	Increasing long-term-care needs for those with chronic disease	HC-1	Inadequate support by ISDH in some technical areas	T-1	Impact of health care reform	PR-1
12 percent of households earn less than $10,000	E-2	Increasing number of single heads of households	S-2	Increasing need for collaboration between public and private providers	HC-2	Increasing awareness of environmental health problems (lead, water, food safety, PCBs, etc.)	T-2	Increasing emphasis on the measurement of health care outcomes	PR-2
Fewer health insurance benefits offered by employers	E-3	Increasing emphasis on women's health	S-3	Inadequate access to health care within the state	HC-3	State bureaucracy which does not facilitate procurement of latest technoloy	T-3	Increasing number of federal and state mandates	PR-3

E		S		HC		T		PR	
E-4	Less discretionary money for the average Indiana citizen	S-4	Increasing concern for gender/racial/sexual discrimination	HC-4	Increasing need for emphasis on prevention (communicable diseases, smoking, substance abuse, etc.)	T-4	Low budget allocations for the procurement of technology	PR-4	Increasing influence of special interest groups on health policy
E-5	Continued shortage of health care workers in rural areas	S-5	Increasing amount of violence (child abuse, rape, etc.)	HC-5	Medicaid reform	T-5	Low image of ISDH as a technology leader	PR-5	Increasing demand for cooperation between state and local health departments
E-6	Increasing hospital and nursing home closures	S-6	Increasing number of homeless	HC-6	Increasing number of senior citizens	T-6	Increasing number of new required lab tests and procedures	PR-6	Increasing demand for community-based services
E-7	Limited funding for public health	S-7	Increasing amount of substance abuse	HC-7	Increasing need for primary care in rural settings			PR-7	Increasing need for cooperation among community, state, and federal agencies

EXHIBIT 14-12

Trends/Issues Rated as Important by Stakeholders and Task Force Members

Trends with Means Greater Than 3.38 for Stakeholders but Not External Task Force	Code	Trends with Means Greater Than 3.38 for Both Stakeholders and External Task Force	Code	Trends with Means Greater Than 3.38 for External Task Force but Not Stakeholders	Code
No growth in total economy with less tax revenue	E-1	Limited funding for public health	E-7	Inadequate access to health care within the state	HC-3
Fewer health insurance benefits offererd by employers	E-3	Increasing amount of violence (child abuse, rape, etc.)	S-5	Inadequate support by ISDH in some technical areas	T-1
Increasing amount of substance abuse	S-7	Increasing need for emphasis on prevention (communicable diseases, smoking, substance abuse, etc.)	HC-4	Low budget allocations for the procurement of technology	T-4
Increasing number of federal and state mandates	PR-3	Medicaid reform	HC-5		
Increasing need for collaboration between public and private providers	HC-2	Impact of health care reform	PR-1		
		Increasing demand for community-based services	PR-6		
		Increasing need for cooperation among community, state, and federal agencies	PR-7		

as well as the entire department. The implications of the trends and issues for the ISDH are conceptualized in Exhibit 14–14.

Internal Environmental Analysis

The general objective of the internal environmental analysis at the ISDH was to provide the steering committee with an assessment of the strengths and weaknesses of the major operating systems as discussed in Chapter 4. These included the culture of the organization as well as the financial, human resources, information, and physical facilities subsystems (marketing was determined not to be a major system of the department). The specific objectives of the Internal Environmental Assessment Task Force included:

- Identify the key organizational subsystems that collectively determine the strategic capability of the department (i.e., culture, finances, information, human resources, physical facilities);

EXHIBIT 14-13
External Environment Significant Trends/Issues

Trend/Issue	Codes
• Impact of Health Care Reform	
Impact of health care reform	PR-1
Medicaid reform	HC-5
Increasing need for primary care in rural settings	HC-7
Continued shortage of health care workers in rural areas	E-5
• Need for Cooperation-Based Strategies	
Increasing need for cooperation among community, state, and federal agencies	PR-7
Increasing need for collaboration between public and private providers	HC-2
Increasing demand for cooperation between state and local health departments	PR-5
Increasing demand for community-based services	PR-6
• Limited Funding for Public Health	E-7
Increasing number of federal and state mandates	PR-3
No growth in total economy with less tax revenue	E-1
Fewer health insurance benefits offered by employers	E-3
• Increasing Amount of Violence (child abuse, rape, etc.)	S-5
• Increasing Need for Emphasis on Prevention (communicable diseases, smoking, substance abuse, etc.)	HC-4
• Access/Care for Special Populations	
Inadequate access to health care within the state	HC-3
Increasing ethnic/racial diversity	S-1
Increasing emphasis on women's health	S-3
Increasing concern for gender/racial/sexual discrimination	S-4
Increasing numbers of homeless	S-6
Increasing numbers of senior citizens	HC-6
• External Technological Advancements	
Inadequate support by ISDH in some technical areas	T-1
Low budget allocations for the procurement of technology	T-4
Increasing awareness of environmental health problems (lead, water, food, safety, PCBs, etc.)	T-2
Low image of ISDH as a technology leader	T-5
• Increasing Amount of Substance Abuse	S-7

EXHIBIT 14-14

Significant Trends/Issues as Opportunities and Threats

Trend/Issue	Opportunities for Action	Threats from No Action
Impact of Health Care Reform	More emphasis placed on core public health – assurance, policy development, and assessment	Major populations remain without access to health care; no meaningful provisions for rural populations
Need for Cooperation-Based Strategies	Integrated health care initiatives; public and private partnerships; state and counties share common goals; higher level of community-based services	Health care remains fragmented and inconsistent throughout the state
Limited Funding for Public Health	Emphasis on efficiency and essential services	Decline in community health; provision of fewer services; lag in technology; lower level of cooperation between state and counties
Increasing Amount of Violence	New programs directed toward vulnerable populations; education; counseling safety; etc.	Continued increase in violence; fewer intervention services
Increasing Need for Emphasis on Prevention	More emphasis on core public health; improved community health	Breakdown in disease control, epidemiology
Access/Care for Special Populations	Special population programs designed to meet specialized needs	Increasing large segments of the population without access; inadequate health care
External Technological Advancements	Upgrade of technology – lab, computers, etc.	Low image of ISDH remains; inefficiency; public turns to other organizations for technology-based services
Increasing Amount of Substance Abuse	New programs for substance abuse – education, etc.	Continued rise in substance abuse among more populations

- Isolate the organizational systems and analyze the strengths and weaknesses associated with each;
- Analyze the results of the organizational excellence questionnaire administered to all members of the department;
- Identify specific strengths and weaknesses of the department relative to each key organizational subsystem;
- Recommend, based on the findings of the analysis, actions for maintaining strengths and eliminating weaknesses; and
- Foster strategic thinking throughout the department.

Operationally, the Internal Environmental Assessment Task Force decided to form four groups – organizational culture, finance, information systems, and human resources. At the first meeting, the information systems group was redefined as the *information and outreach* group to highlight the importance and uniqueness of the department's communication with external organizations and the public. The human resource group became the *human resource, staffing, and physical facilities* group.

Assessing the Organizational Culture The organizational culture group assessed the culture of the ISDH with the aid of a self-administered questionnaire. The questionnaire had sixty-one items designed to obtain the opinions of the department's 900 employees regarding the seven items discussed in Chapter 12 (mission/vision, service and managerial innovation, leadership and employee orientation, responsiveness to external change, teamwork, external and internal customer/client orientation, and quality).[5] All items on the organizational excellence questionnaire were stated in positive terms, with response scales ranging from *strongly disagree* to *strongly agree*. In addition to the sixty-one questions, respondents were provided an opportunity to elaborate on any responses through open-ended comments. More than 500 usable questionnaires were returned.

The open-ended comments were used, in conjunction with the objective responses, to discover problems or potential problems. For example, although most of the employees were familiar with the mandated purpose or mission of the ISDH, they were not sure about the department's vision or its direction over the next five years. (It should be noted that these responses were obtained during the health care reform debate, and there was a great deal of uncertainty about the future direction of health care, in general, and public health, in particular.) In addition, the belief of most employees was that changes in the purpose and vision by the leadership in the department were not effectively communicated.

Relative to innovation, the respondents did not believe that the department was a highly creative organization. Open-ended comments indicated that respondents perceived a great deal of innovation was limited because of regulatory mandates and excessive policies and procedures imposed on all state agencies. However, respondents believed that new ways of doing things were *valued* by department leadership and that individuals were allowed to try new ways of doing things without excessive fear of punishment for failure.

Leadership and employee orientation was a particularly troublesome area as reported on the questionnaire. It received the second lowest evaluation of all factors and indicated a need for substantial attention by top management. There was a widespread belief that top leadership was excessively distant from the operational level of the department, that leaders were not as concerned as they should be about the welfare of employees, and that management was too concerned with political pressures to the detriment of key public health priorities. Much of the discontent, no doubt, resulted because the employees had not had a wage increase in three years and the recently enacted state budget virtually assured no raises for two more years.

The highest ranked factor was the department's ability to deal with external changes. Although this area was perceived as needing improvement, open-ended comments indicated that most employees believed that the ISDH was aware of changing forces in the external environment, had some means of monitoring and forecasting trends, and generally responded to environmental changes.

Teamwork was not ranked very high by employees. There was a belief that most employees were more concerned with their individual jobs and the welfare of their work units than with the overall success of the department. As a result, people sometimes protected rather than shared information, made decisions based on the welfare of their unit rather than the ISDH, and did not work effectively as teams. Competition among work groups was perceived to be more common than cooperation.

The items on the customer/client orientation section of the questionnaire were designed to assess employee responses to both external *and* internal customers. Relatively few of the ISDH employees, except for those in vital records and similar units, interacted regularly with external customers. Each employee, however, had a number of internal customers – ISDH employees who relied on other ISDH employees to successfully accomplish their jobs.

Considerable agreement existed that employees respected and responded to external and internal customer needs. On the other hand, there was the belief that rules and regulations were more important to many than a true devotion to serving customers. Additionally, it was thought that many people attempted to make their own jobs easier by hiding behind rules and regulations rather than trying in every practical way to facilitate responsiveness to all customers. Consensus was clear that everyone could do more to improve customer orientation.

Finally, concern for quality was widespread in the department. It was generally agreed that employees were professional, well trained for what they did, and committed to public service. However, respondents often indicated that high levels of service quality were not adequately emphasized or rewarded; that the hiring, retention, and promotion policies were not based on the quality of services provided; and that the general work environment made high levels of quality difficult to ensure.

In summary, the results of the questionnaire indicated a perceived need for improvement in all seven areas. There was a need to more clearly state and communicate the future direction of the department to all employees and reduce as much as possible the excessive policies that frustrated many managers and nonmanagerial employees in completing their jobs in the most effective manner. In addition, more managers needed to exercise leadership and encourage teamwork.

Financial Subsystem As previously noted, finance was a particularly serious problem for the ISDH (as well as other state agencies). State employees had not been able to maintain their real incomes, and programs and facilities reflected the deteriorating financial situation. In an attempt to isolate the most important strategic considerations, the financial assessment group examined the present, past, and projected future financial resources, interviewed financial personnel at other Midwestern state health departments, and conducted internal interviews and surveys.

Before beginning with the specific analysis, the financial situation of the ISDH was placed in perspective based on what was happening in other states in the region. In the year immediately prior to the beginning of the strategic planning process, Illinois and Michigan reduced their public health work force and Ohio endured about an 11 percent decrease in public health funding.

During the five years prior to the initiation of the strategic planning process, the ISDH's proportion of annual state appropriations was relatively fixed at less than 1 percent of the state general fund. According to the Public Health Foundation, this level of funding placed Indiana as forty-nine out of the fifty states in per capita funding for public health. As illustrated by Exhibit 14–15, state general funds for all purposes increased about 9 percent in 1990 and gradually declined to an increase of a little over 3 percent by 1993. By comparison, the ISDH appropriations from the general fund in 1990 were about 3 percent over 1989. However, 1993 funding was about the same as 1992 funding. It is clear that increases in state general funds have declined significantly over the past five years and that, of the smaller increases, public health has received increasingly smaller shares.

The one bright spot in the ISDH funding picture can be inferred from Exhibit 14–16. During the past five years when actual budget receipts (not appropriations) from the state general fund were virtually level, the department's federal funding increased significantly. In 1989, for example, the ISDH received approximately $63 million in federal funds. This amount increased to more than $90 million in 1993.

With this general background, the group proceeded with its assessment of financial strengths and weaknesses (see Exhibit 14–17). Relative to financial strengths, the group identified three important aspects of the financial operations that were favorable. The first was the ISDH's ability to attract federal funds. Over the five-year period immediately preceding the initiation of the strategic planning process and during a period when state funding was almost level, federal funds increased by 45 percent. Second, although not a strength in an absolute sense, the fact that the ISDH had not been forced to reduce its public health work force as had its sister states of Illinois and Michigan was certainly a relative strength. Finally, the Finance Division had apparently developed a strong internal customer orientation. A survey of internal users conducted by the division indi-

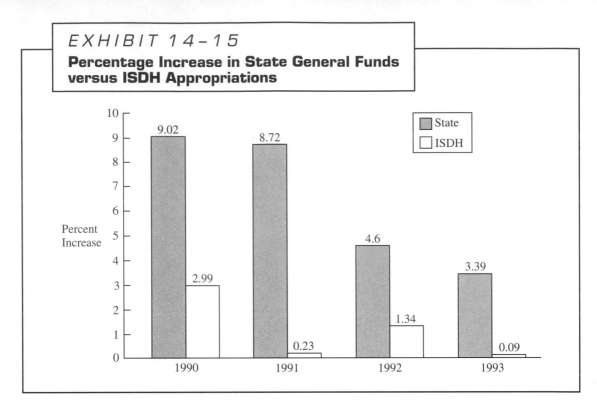

EXHIBIT 14-15

Percentage Increase in State General Funds versus ISDH Appropriations

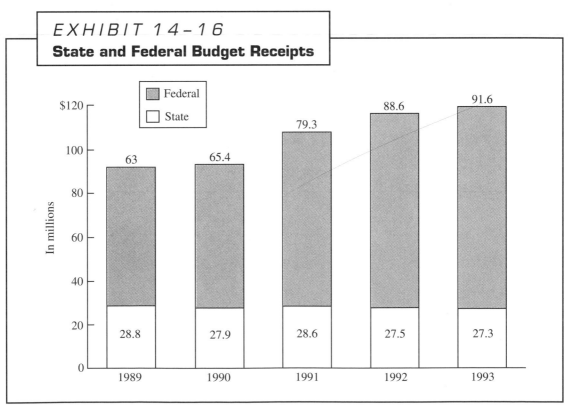

EXHIBIT 14-16

State and Federal Budget Receipts

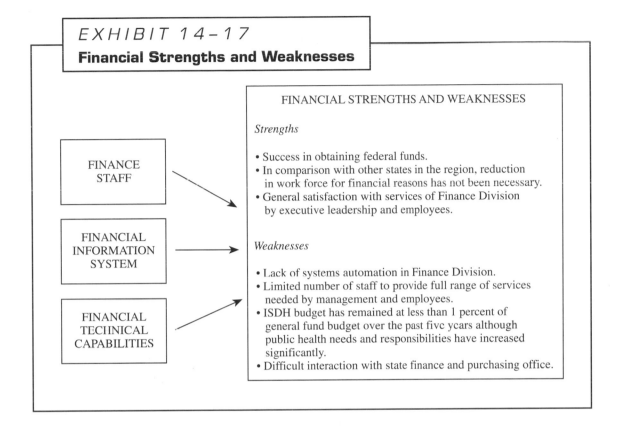

EXHIBIT 14-17

Financial Strengths and Weaknesses

FINANCIAL STRENGTHS AND WEAKNESSES

Strengths

- Success in obtaining federal funds.
- In comparison with other states in the region, reduction in work force for financial reasons has not been necessary.
- General satisfaction with services of Finance Division by executive leadership and employees.

Weaknesses

- Lack of systems automation in Finance Division.
- Limited number of staff to provide full range of services needed by management and employees.
- ISDH budget has remained at less than 1 percent of general fund budget over the past five years although public health needs and responsibilities have increased significantly.
- Difficult interaction with state finance and purchasing office.

FINANCE STAFF

FINANCIAL INFORMATION SYSTEM

FINANCIAL TECHNICAL CAPABILITIES

cated that virtually everyone who responded was satisfied with the manner in which the payroll, travel reimbursements, and similar services were accomplished. There were a number of suggestions concerning how purchasing, contract development, and budget support activities could be improved, and the division developed action plans for addressing the problems that surfaced.

The group identified four important financial weaknesses. First, although industry, state governments, and health care were moving toward increased automation and computerization, the Finance Division had not "kept up" technologically. Personal computers were available only to do the work of the division. Moreover, the capability for on-line assistance with financial services was extremely limited, representing a significant restriction on the staff's ability to provide needed services, particularly in the area of budget development and administration.

In real terms, the decline in funding for the department over the past five years had not reduced public expectations and demands for public health services. As a result, despite a period of extremely limited funding, services had increased, making the financial plight of the ISDH even more critical. Finally, much of the criticism regarding the delays in purchasing resulted from an inability to "get things through" the centralized state purchasing system. Although this was to a great extent beyond the control of the division, it caused frustration for everyone and the finance division often had to take the blame.

Information and Outreach Subsystems   The information systems analysis was divided into two major components. The first related to internal information systems and information resources, and the second related to external or outreach information. Information concerning these key subsystems was obtained by a survey of internal "users" of information resources as well as interviews with selected external stakeholders of the department. The analysis of this information resulted in the significant strengths and weaknesses listed in Exhibit 14–18.

The analysis of the information and outreach subsystems indicated that the department had several important strengths when compared to other state agencies and other organizations. The individuals in Management Information Systems (MIS) and the Office of Communications were resourceful and able to accomplish a great deal despite limited resources. The department was fortunate to have

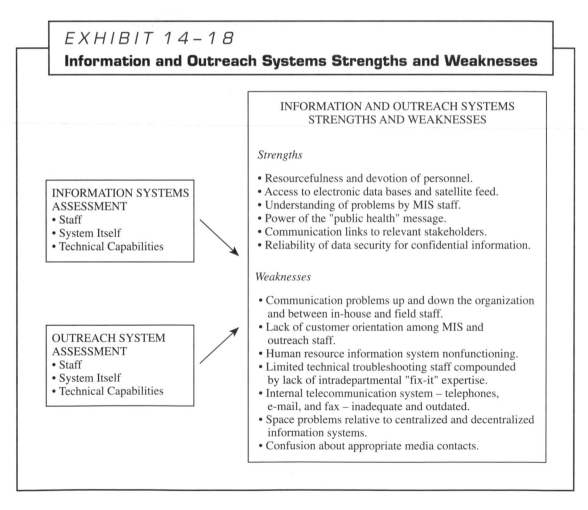

EXHIBIT 14–18
Information and Outreach Systems Strengths and Weaknesses

INFORMATION AND OUTREACH SYSTEMS
STRENGTHS AND WEAKNESSES

Strengths

• Resourcefulness and devotion of personnel.
• Access to electronic data bases and satellite feed.
• Understanding of problems by MIS staff.
• Power of the "public health" message.
• Communication links to relevant stakeholders.
• Reliability of data security for confidential information.

Weaknesses

• Communication problems up and down the organization and between in-house and field staff.
• Lack of customer orientation among MIS and outreach staff.
• Human resource information system nonfunctioning.
• Limited technical troubleshooting staff compounded by lack of intradepartmental "fix-it" expertise.
• Internal telecommunication system – telephones, e-mail, and fax – inadequate and outdated.
• Space problems relative to centralized and decentralized information systems.
• Confusion about appropriate media contacts.

INFORMATION SYSTEMS
ASSESSMENT
• Staff
• System Itself
• Technical Capabilities

OUTREACH SYSTEM
ASSESSMENT
• Staff
• System Itself
• Technical Capabilities

found the resources that enabled it to interface with a large number of useful electronic data bases. In addition, a "satellite feed" made it possible to communicate electronically with locations throughout the nation and the world.

Internally, it was perceived that the MIS staff understood the problems of the overall system and that the Office of Communications used the power of the "public health message." That is, external communications focused on those issues that captured the interest of the citizens relative to public health issues in Indiana. The department was considered to be well prepared to assure security over confidential information.

The group identified some generally agreed-on weaknesses in the information and outreach areas that needed attention. First, there was a lack of consistently effective communication up and down the organization as well as with external groups. There was substantial confusion about the protocol for contact and communication with the media. Some of this was attributable to the lack of external and internal customer/client orientation on the part of both MIS and the Office of Communications. It was agreed that the human resources information system was nonfunctioning and did little, if anything, to help mangers and employees with personnel matters. There was no parity in the internal distribution of information processing resources and the internal telecommunications infrastructure – telephone system, e-mail, and fax – was inadequate and unreliable. The central MIS could not afford to employ the human resources necessary to keep all the hardware and software operating on a timely basis, and computer expertise to temporarily "fix" things until help arrived was inadequate. There was inadequate physical space for effective hardware operations not only for centralized MIS but also for the individual work units.

Overall, the picture relative to the information and outreach systems was consistent. The devotion and hard work of the individuals at all levels had made the systems work adequately despite severely limited resources. In the process, however, the staff of both the Management Information Systems and the Office of Communications processing units had become internally oriented and lost sight of the importance of identifying and serving all their relevant customers/clients.

Human Resources, Staffing, and Physical Facilities Assessment In attempting to gauge the quality, quantity, and distribution of these resources, the group assigned to assess these factors employed several data gathering methods, including employee surveys and interviews with management and nonmanagement staff members. This information was used to formulate the departmental strengths and weaknesses as listed in Exhibit 14–19.

The basic human resources, staffing, and physical facilities infrastructure were primary concerns of the employees of the department. Again, it was perceived that colleagues – managerial and nonmanagerial – were committed to the success of the department and to public health in Indiana. Because of this devotion, loyalty, and hard work, the department was able to accomplish a great deal with relatively little in terms of resources. From a physical facilities perspective, a significant strength was the department's location adjacent to Indiana's primary academic medical center.

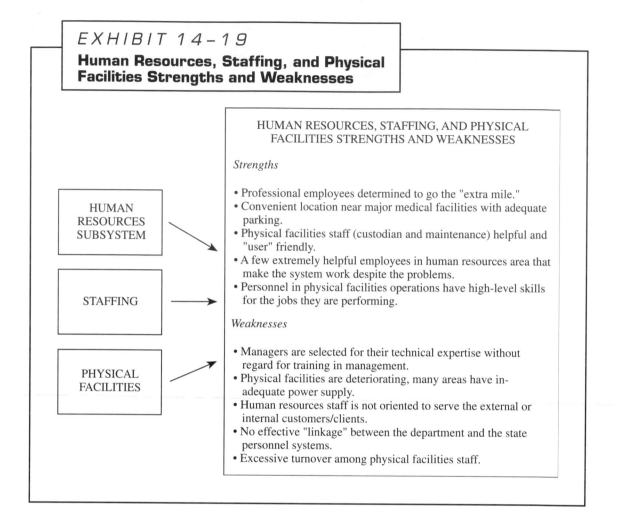

EXHIBIT 14-19

Human Resources, Staffing, and Physical Facilities Strengths and Weaknesses

HUMAN RESOURCES, STAFFING, AND PHYSICAL
FACILITIES STRENGTHS AND WEAKNESSES

Strengths

- Professional employees determined to go the "extra mile."
- Convenient location near major medical facilities with adequate parking.
- Physical facilities staff (custodian and maintenance) helpful and "user" friendly.
- A few extremely helpful employees in human resources area that make the system work despite the problems.
- Personnel in physical facilities operations have high-level skills for the jobs they are performing.

Weaknesses

- Managers are selected for their technical expertise without regard for training in management.
- Physical facilities are deteriorating, many areas have inadequate power supply.
- Human resources staff is not oriented to serve the external or internal customers/clients.
- No effective "linkage" between the department and the state personnel systems.
- Excessive turnover among physical facilities staff.

HUMAN RESOURCES SUBSYSTEM

STAFFING

PHYSICAL FACILITIES

There were, however, a number of weaknesses in the human resources, staffing, and physical facilities infrastructure. As is the case with many high-technology organizations, people were promoted to management positions based on their technical expertise rather than their existing or potential management skills. Further compounding this problem was that, when the managers were placed in these new jobs, little management training was provided. The result was often good public health technicians and scientists who were frustrated and unremarkable managers. The results of the frustration were often felt by those they managed.

There was widespread concern over the inadequacy of the physical facilities. Air quality, ventilation, storage space, and power supply were not adequate for the quality of work expected of employees. More than a few employees suggested that the department would probably "fail" its own health inspections. Finally, as with MIS and the Office of Communications, it was believed that the human resources staff was not properly oriented to serve either external or internal customers/clients.

Mission, Vision, and Values

The ISDH determined early in its strategic planning process that the formulation of directional strategies, similar to assessment of the external and internal environments, had to come from consensus building among as many employees (managerial and nonmanagerial) as possible. Therefore, it was decided to form a task force to address the formulation of the departmental mission and vision, to suggest the values that would become the basis for decision making, and to develop an initial list of critical success factors for the department. The general objectives of the task force included:

- Generate and develop consensus for a clear, concise statement of the department's primary clients, principal services, geographical domain, philosophy, and desired public image;
- Incorporate these items in a clear, concise statement of the mission of the Indiana State Department of Health;
- Reach a consensus on a challenging, exciting, and inspiring statement of vision (hope) of the ISDH;
- Review the results of the external environment, organizational culture, and internal environmental assessments and suggest a series of critical success factors for the department; and
- Foster strategic thinking throughout the department.

Drafting the Mission and Vision Statements To assist in developing a draft of the ISDH mission statement, the group decided to use the general template presented in Exhibit 5–4. This template is reproduced and adapted to the ISDH in Exhibit 14–20. The components of a mission statement are listed in the first column and the descriptions and key words summarized by the task force are presented in the second column. The descriptive key words were obtained through interviews with personnel from all functions and levels throughout the agency. After listing the key words and descriptions relative to each component, the draft mission statement was developed.

The same process, except that only senior managers were interviewed, was used to develop the vision statement for the ISDH (Exhibit 14–21). The group decided not to develop a separate value statement for the department because values such as respect for all individuals, quality, trust, concern, ethical standards, and so on, were integral parts of both the mission and vision statements. The drafts of the mission and vision statements provided a clear picture for stakeholders, clients, and employees of what the department viewed as its current purpose or reason for existing as well as its hope for the future. The mission provided a sense of "what is" and the vision statement created a clear picture of the possibilities of what "might be" or "could be" when the mission was being accomplished to the mutual benefit of all citizens of Indiana. These draft statements were forwarded to the steering committee for discussion, revision, and adoption.

EXHIBIT 14-20
Components of the ISDH Mission Statement

Mission Statement Components	Descriptions (Key Words) About ISDH's Mission
1. Target Customer/Clients and Markets	People in Indiana – especially those in need, as identified by measures of health and economic status.
2. Principal Services Delivered	Training and technical assistance, prevention and health education programs, surveillance and analysis of health data, policy development, and planning and evaluation.
3. Geographical Domain of Operations	Borders of Indiana.
4. Commitment of Specific Values	Respect for the individual, quality services, innovation, personal integrity, trust, concern, and high ethical standards.
5. Explicit Philosophy	Proactive leadership through the application of public health sciences and epidemiology and the quest for efficiency of operations.
6. Other Important Component(s)	Recognition of interdependence with the larger world.

From Mission and Vision to Critical Success Factors Having achieved some consensus concerning what the department is today (mission) and its vision for the future, the task force proceeded to formulate critical success factors. A careful review of the mission and vision, the external environmental analysis, the organizational excellence questionnaire, and the internal environmental assessment resulted in the formulation of a draft of six critical success factors that the task force members believed *absolutely must* happen if the department were to be successful:

1. *Public health work force.* Become the employer of choice for public health professionals and support staff rather than employer of last resort.
2. *Communications.* Improve expertise with internal communication as well as with external stakeholders.
3. *Funding.* Secure adequate and stable funding.
4. *Collaboration.* Expand and improve the network of collaborative relationships with local health departments and other relevant public and private agencies.

> ### *EXHIBIT 14-21*
> ### **Components of the ISDH Vision Statement**
>
> | Vision Statement Components | Descriptions (Key Words) in ISDH's Vision |
> |---|---|
> | 1. A Clear Hope for the Future | A future where communities, local health agencies, and the private sector cooperate to increase the span of healthy life for all Hoosiers, reduce the disparities among segments of the population, and assure access to preventive services for all people. |
> | 2. Challenging and Concerns Excellence | Strive for excellence, display initiative, and demonstrate achievement. |
> | 3. Inspirational and Emotional | Forging alliances with public and private sectors to ensure timely, cost-effective, public health interventions with primary commitment to local health departments. |
> | 4. Empowers Employees First and Clients/Customers Second | Value employees. |
> | 5. Prepares for the Future | Catalyst for progress that will result in healthier people and a healthful environment. |
> | 6. Memorable and Provides Guidance | Memorable terms – catalyst for progress, public health leader in the Hoosier state, core values integral to public health, innovation, and so on. |

5. *Service quality.* Improve quality of services from the viewpoint of external clients and internal clients.
6. *Organizational focus.* Concentrate on professionalism and scientifically identified causes of disease, prevention, disability, and premature death.

Similar to the mission and vision statements, the draft of critical success factors was regarded as a starting point for organization-wide discussion and forwarded to the steering committee for revision and finalization.

STRATEGY FORMULATION

Based on the results of the situational analysis, the ISDH began the process of finalizing the directional strategies and developing adaptive, market entry, and positioning strategies. These decisions (strategies) would set the course into the future for the ISDH.

Results of the internal analysis suggested that regardless of strategy, the agency needed to create a more participative decision-making environment and foster teamwork. Therefore, it was decided that the steering committee, responsible for coordinating strategy formulation, and the implementation task force could begin their work concurrently. As illustrated in Exhibit 14–22, the activities of these groups were divided into two phases, which allowed some implementation activities to proceed in parallel with strategy formulation activities.

EXHIBIT 14–22
Strategic Decision-Making Phase

	Steering Task Force	Implementation Task Force
Phase I	• Understand information gathered, analyzed, and summarized by the task forces • Finalize external issues, internal strengths and weaknesses, and mission, vision, and critical success factors • Set strategic objectives for the organization (based on external analysis, internal analysis, and mission, vision, and critical success factors) • Develop the statement of strategy • Develop the adaptive, market entry, and positioning strategies • Work with unit managers and develop unit-specific implementation actions for the strategic objectives	• Set objectives for cultural change using the seven-factors of excellence plus critical success factors • Develop organization-wide implementation actions to achieve the objectives • Develop milestone charts for implementation • Submit objectives and actions to steering task force for review and suggestions • Make final recommendations to management concerning cultural change
Phase II	• Coordinate implementation of actions developed in Phase I • Coordinate activities of implementation committee • Aid programs in developing implementation work plans • Ensure implementation is proceeding as planned	• Develop organization-wide implementation actions for objectives developed by the steering task force • Coordinate organization-wide and unit specific implementation action plans

In Phase I, the steering committee finalized the directional strategies (mission, vision, and strategic objectives) and developed the adaptive, market entry (if necessary), and positioning strategies. In Phase II, the steering committee coordinated implementation (development and implementation of the operational or program strategies). The steering committee objectives included:

- Review and confirm the external opportunities and threats and internal strengths and weaknesses;
- Finalize the mission, vision, and critical success factors;
- Specify the set of programs and services that will achieve the mission and vision;
- Operationalize the critical success factors with clear and concise strategic objectives (later called *agency goals*) to provide direction for departmental operations;
- Coordinate the development of the adaptive, market entry, and positioning strategies;
- Coordinate the development of program implementation work plans; and
- Foster strategic thinking throughout the department.

Meanwhile, the implementation task force in Phase I formulated organization-wide strategies directed toward improving the organization culture and in Phase II developed organization-wide strategies to support the strategic objectives that had been developed by the steering committee. This approach provided adequate time for strategic thinking and yet allowed the strategic management process to proceed at two levels. In addition, this approach kept a large number of people involved, maintained the momentum of the project, and helped ensure an atmosphere of change.

The Directional Strategies

The initial responsibility of the steering committee was to review the external environmental issues, internal capabilities, and the draft of directional strategies that were developed, analyzed, and summarized by the three task forces. From this review the committee set out to finalize the directional strategies.

Finalizing the Mission and Vision The first task of the steering committee was to finalize the mission and vision statements initially developed by the mission, vision, and values task force. After considerable discussion, interviews with members of all of the task forces, and discussion throughout the agency, the mission and vision statements were revised. The final statements appear in Exhibits 14–23 and 14–24. Because of the criticality of these statements, it was essential that the steering committee members and the ISDH executive staff play a part in shaping and approving the statements. However, it was believed that the original spirit of the documents should be maintained because they were developed through wide participation throughout the organization.

Finalizing the Critical Success Factors The next task of the steering committee was to review and finalize the critical success factors developed by the mission,

---

EXHIBIT 14-23
Indiana State Department of Health Mission Statement

The Indiana State Department of Health (ISDH) is dedicated to promoting health and wellness among people in Indiana through planning, prevention, service, and education. The ISDH serves to help people attain the highest level of health possible. The ISDH is a proactive leader and collaborator in assessment, policy development, and assurance, based on science, innovation, and efficiency.

ISDH affirms that health includes physical, mental, and social well-being, and is dependent on economic and environmental factors, access to health care, and individual responsibility and choice. Although the ISDH primarily serves people within Indiana's geographic boundaries, we recognize our interdependence with the larger world.

To achieve our mission, the ISDH supports:

- Training and technical assistance,
- Disease prevention and health education programs,
- Epidemiology for surveillance and analysis of health data for intervention and program evaluation,
- Development of policies and regulations to optimize health,
- Planning and evaluation,
- Staff recruitment and development to accomplish our mission, and
- Collaboration with the public, local health departments, governmental agencies, the scientific community, and special populations.

The ISDH is dedicated to quality service, innovation, respect for every individual, affirmative action, personal integrity, trust, and high ethical standards.

---

vision, and values task force. Again, input and discussion concerning the critical success factors were solicited from all divisions and levels of the ISDH. There was a great deal of agreement that the critical success factors generated by the mission, vision, and values task forces were important, but the committee believed that one factor (organizational focus) should be expanded and that further rationale or explanation of each factor would help clarify and provide focus for subsequently setting organizational objectives. The revised critical success factors and rationale are presented in Exhibit 14–25.

Developing Agency Goals (Strategic Objectives) Strategic objectives (called *agency goals* by the ISDH) were developed for each of the critical success factors presented in Exhibit 14–25. The steering committee believed that it was better to have a few well-defined goals rather than a long list of objectives that would be impossible to accomplish in view of resource limitations. Therefore, it was decided that one agency goal relative to each critical success factor would be developed. A great deal of effort was put into making the goals simple and

---

EXHIBIT 14-24
Indiana State Department of Health Vision Statement

The Indiana State Department of Health is committed to act as a catalyst for progress that will result in healthier people in a healthful environment.

As a public health leader in the Hoosier State, the department will incorporate strategic management to implement a core set of values that are integral to public health. We will translate science and technology into action to safeguard the public's health. We will apply innovative, sound, and reasonable solutions to traditional public health challenges and emerging issues. At the same time, we will retain that which is good with public health in the state. We will expand knowledge through epidemiology and applied research on health and environmental issues.

The department recognizes its tie with other health and human service agencies to respond to global, national, state, and local public health concerns. We will forge alliances with public and private sectors to ensure that timely, cost-effective, public health interventions are planned and implemented. We will strengthen our commitment to collaborate with local health departments.

Our employees are our most valuable resource. We will provide an environment in which our employees strive for excellence, display initiative, and demonstrate achievement. Our employees will continue to promote health; work to prevent diseases, disability, and premature death; and help to assure access to health care for all populations.

This vision of the future is one in which the Indiana State Department of Health, communities, local health agencies, Special Institutions, and the private sector across the state cooperate to develop plans, programs, and resources. It guides our work to increase the span of healthy life, to reduce health disparities among different populations, and to assure access to preventive services for all.

---

straightforward. Specific activities were developed for each goal to guide program areas in the types of actions needed to achieve the agency goals. Individual programs could then develop their own set of objectives with the ISDH goals and actions as an "anchor." The logic of the process used to develop each of the agency goals for the ISDH is illustrated in Exhibit 14–26.

The exhibit demonstrates how the mission, vision, external, and internal environmental factors identified in the data gathering stage of the strategic planning process relate to the development of the work force (a critical success factor), which in turn translates into an agency goal (strategic objective) and actions to orient, train, and develop. In the example, the mission underscores "support for staff recruitment and development" and the vision statement emphasizes the value placed on employees. The data from the external environmental analysis indicated that relevant public health technologies will continue to develop and require increasingly qualified and committed personnel. Finally, if the ISDH is

EXHIBIT 14-25
Critical Success Factors and Rationale

Work Force: The ISDH must provide a working environment and resources that will attract and retain qualified staff members and empower them to achieve or exceed agency goals. The working environment will support responsive personnel policies, competitive compensation, adequate training, advancement opportunities, trust, sensitivity to diversity, and efficiency, innovation, and excellence.

Communication: The ISDH must communicate effectively both internally with employees and externally with local, state, and federal public health agencies and other stakeholders. Communication must accurately and consistently reflect the mission, vision, and activities of the agency.

Funding: The ISDH must establish funding priorities, pursue innovative strategies to obtain adequate, stable financial resources for ensuring that fundamental public health services are available, and monitor use of funds to achieve established objectives.

Collaboration: The ISDH must expand and improve internal teamwork and external partnerships with local health departments and other local, state, and federal public and private organizations to promote public health.

Service: The ISDH must maintain a client orientation and assure the quality of all services for internal and external clients.

Leadership: The ISDH must be a visible, active, and persistent advocate on behalf of its employees and public health. This leadership must be based on efficiency, innovation, respect for the individual, and science. Leadership qualities will be recognized and promoted at all levels of the agency.

Management: The ISDH must implement a process that plans and sets priorities within the constraints of available resources and in the context of strategic thinking. Management processes must promote interprogram coordination and cooperation to achieve agency goals.

Data and Information: The ISDH must acquire and use timely and accurate data to assess needs, develop policy, and assure quality services. The data and information acquired must be shared with all people who need it to carry out their responsibilities.

to be successful, agency staff will have to understand the directional strategies, the interrelationship of programs, their individual roles, and the expectations of the organization. Only when the department has a reputation for providing ongoing training and development opportunities and employees believe they are more important than policies, rules, and procedures will the department be able to further develop highly qualified personnel. Exhibit 14–27 presents agency goals and illustrates their relationship to the critical success factors.

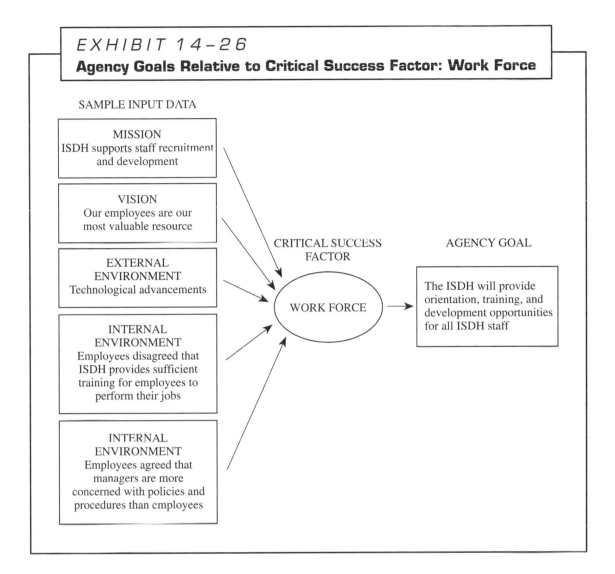

EXHIBIT 14-26
Agency Goals Relative to Critical Success Factor: Work Force

SAMPLE INPUT DATA

MISSION
ISDH supports staff recruitment and development

VISION
Our employees are our most valuable resource

EXTERNAL ENVIRONMENT
Technological advancements

INTERNAL ENVIRONMENT
Employees disagreed that ISDH provides sufficient training for employees to perform their jobs

INTERNAL ENVIRONMENT
Employees agreed that managers are more concerned with policies and procedures than employees

CRITICAL SUCCESS FACTOR

WORK FORCE

AGENCY GOAL

The ISDH will provide orientation, training, and development opportunities for all ISDH staff

The Adaptive Strategies

On completion of the directional strategies (mission, vision, and objectives), the steering committee began to develop a statement of strategy and the adaptive strategies (the fundamental strategies for the organization). After reviewing the methods for analyzing the adaptive strategies (TOWS, portfolio approaches, PLC, SPACE, and so on), the steering committee decided that program evaluation would provide the best results. Because of the not-for-profit nature of the agency, funding from state appropriations and grants, and the program orientation of the ISDH, the steering committee thought that both approaches to program evaluation – program priority setting and needs/capacity assessment – would best facilitate strategic thinking within the agency. Program priority setting was used to

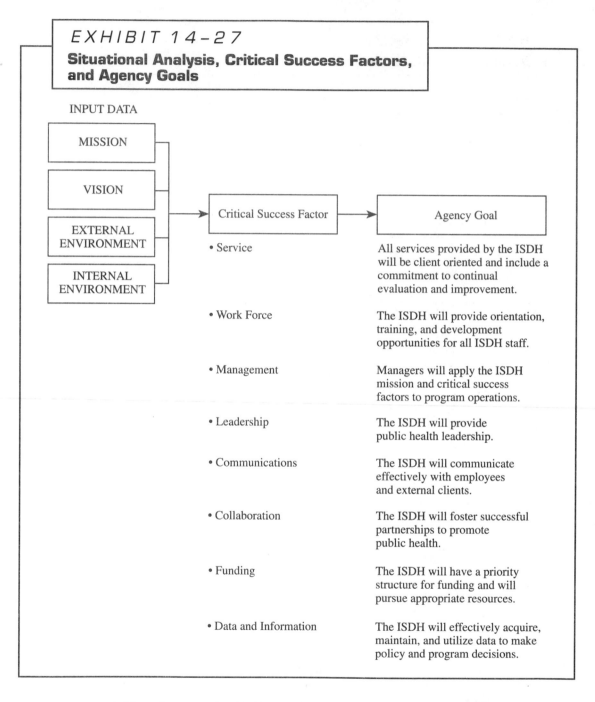

EXHIBIT 14-27
Situational Analysis, Critical Success Factors, and Agency Goals

INPUT DATA

MISSION

VISION

EXTERNAL ENVIRONMENT

INTERNAL ENVIRONMENT

Critical Success Factor	Agency Goal
• Service	All services provided by the ISDH will be client oriented and include a commitment to continual evaluation and improvement.
• Work Force	The ISDH will provide orientation, training, and development opportunities for all ISDH staff.
• Management	Managers will apply the ISDH mission and critical success factors to program operations.
• Leadership	The ISDH will provide public health leadership.
• Communications	The ISDH will communicate effectively with employees and external clients.
• Collaboration	The ISDH will foster successful partnerships to promote public health.
• Funding	The ISDH will have a priority structure for funding and will pursue appropriate resources.
• Data and Information	The ISDH will effectively acquire, maintain, and utilize data to make policy and program decisions.

initiate the strategic thinking process and needs/capacity assessment was used to corroborate the results of program priority setting.

Program Priority Setting Joe Hunt, the director of the Office of Policy Coordination, with the aid of the steering committee and executive staff developed a complete listing of the programs of the ISDH. Seventy-three separate ISDH programs were identified (see Exhibit 14–28). The steering committee decided to use the Q-sort method to set priorities for the department's programs. Further, the steering committee believed that several different perspectives of program priorities would enhance

---

EXHIBIT 14-28
Indiana State Department of Health Programs

1. MCH: Indiana Family Helpline
2. MCH: Genetic Diseases/Newborn Screening
3. MCH: Childhood Lead Poisoning Prevention Program
4. MCH: Prenatal Substance Use Prevention Program
5. MCH: Adolescent Health
6. Children's Special Health Care Services
7. Nutrition/WIC Program
8. Oral Health Services (includes fluoridation and sealants)
9. Epidemiology Resource Center
10. Management Information Systems
11. Health Planning
12. Health Planning: Certificate of Need
13. Health Planning: Hospital Financial Disclosure
14. Public Health Research
15. Public Health Research: County Needs Assessment
16. Public Health Statistics
17. Public Health Statistics: Vital Records
18. Public Health Statistics: Birth Problems Registry
19. Grants Resource Center
20. Office of Legal Affairs
21. Local Health Support: (Local Health Department Coordination and Liaison Activities)
22. MCH: Family Planning Program
23. Office for Policy Coordination
24. Office for Special Populations: Disability Concerns
25. Office for Special Populations: Interagency Council for Black and Minority Health
26. Office of Public Affairs: Health Education
27. Health Education: Film Library
28. Health Education: Library
29. Office of Public Affairs: Media Relations
30. Office of Public Affairs: Photographer
31. Office of Public Affairs: Print Shop
32. Office of Administration: Administrative Services
33. Office of Administration: Correspondence Center
34. Office of Administration: Finance
35. Office of Administration: Purchasing

EXHIBIT 14-28   cont'd

36. Office of Administration: Human Resources
37. Facilities Management: Safety Programs Coordination
38. Facilities Management: Environmental Services
39. Facilities Management: Physical Plant
40. Facilities Management: Security
41. Facilities Management: Asset Service Center
42. Office of Administration: Management Consultive Services
43. MCH: Breastfeeding Promotion Program
44. Health Facility Standards: Long-Term Care Program
45. Health Facility Standards: Regulatory/Survey Support Services
46. Acute Care Services: Hospital, Lab, ASC, Home Health Inspections
47. Laboratory Support Services
48. HIV/STD Program: CTS/STD Program (sexually transmitted disease control)
49. HIV/STD Program: HIV Prevention Activities
50. HIV/STD Program: Clinical Data and Research
51. Communicable Disease Program: Immunization, TB Control, General Communicable Disease Control
52. Chronic Disease Program: Injury Control Program
53. Chronic Disease Program: Renal Program, Cancer Registry, PHBG Activities, Antitobacco Activities
54. MCH: Pregnancy Risk Assessment Monitoring System (PRAMS)
55. Family Health Services: Women's Health
56. MCH: Prenatal Care, Primary Care/Managed Care, School-Based Clinics
57. Consumer Services: Retail Food Division
58. Consumer Services: Meat and Poultry
59. Manufactured Food Section
60. Consumer Services: Weights and Measures
61. Wholesale Food Division
62. Wholesale Food Division: Milk
63. Sanitary Engineering: Residential Sewage Disposal Section
64. Sanitary Engineering: Vector Control Group
65. Environmental Health Laboratory
66. Sanitary Engineering: Plan Review Section
67. Disease Control Laboratory
68. Indoor and Radiologic Health
69. Consumer Health Laboratory
70. Office for Special Populations: Rural Health Initiative
71. Sanitary Engineering: Environmental Health Section
72. MCH: Healthy Pregnancy/Healthy Baby Campaign
73. MCH: Sudden Infant Death Syndrome Project (SIDS)

strategic thinking. Therefore, two groups – the executive staff and a group of middle-level managers – were asked to "sort" the ISDH's programs.

To provide a context for evaluating the programs, all of the Q-sort participants were provided and were familiar with the results of the external environmental analysis, internal environmental analysis, and the revised mission, vision, critical success factors, and agency goals. In addition, because the prospects of health care reform (both industry evolution and legislation) was such a dominant environmental theme, three possible scenarios for health care reform were developed as a backdrop for sorting the programs. These scenarios are presented in Exhibit 14–29.

The executive staff believed that given the environmental forces, any of the scenarios was possible for the short term, but that in the long term scenario one –

EXHIBIT 14-29
Health Care Reform Scenarios

Scenario I: *Return to Core Public Health.* In this scenario comprehensive health care reform legislation is passed that provides some form of health insurance for everyone. Thus, individuals who formerly relied on public health agencies and emergency rooms for primary care, now have access (through their insurance) to private providers. In addition, providers have found it advantageous to serve this population. Under this assumption, the private sector would assume virtually all of the personal primary care responsibilities. The department would emphasize data collection, monitoring, health promotion, education, regulation, assessment, environmental health, disease control, research, and policy leadership. In this situation, the department's focus would be almost exclusively on community health issues rather than the provision of personal primary care.

Scenario II: *Core Public Health Plus Special Care Needs.* In this scenario health care reform is passed; however, because of high costs, major gaps in coverage remain. Under this assumption, most treatments and special populations would be covered by the private sector; however, significant "gaps" in coverage will continue. The only source of care for these populations or treatments will be in the public sector. In this scenario, the department would emphasize community health (core public health) but would continue to provide primary health care for special populations and treatments not covered under any type of (revolutionary or evolutionary) health care reform.

Scenario III: *Health Care Reform Bogs Down.* In this scenario no significant health care reform legislation is passed. Even the evolutionary restructuring of the health care industry has left major "gaps" for significant populations and treatments. Under this assumption, any type of health care reform fails to significantly change the ratio of people without access to primary care. Primary care may even be expanded under this assumption as the Health Department plays a larger role in ensuring access. In this scenario, the department would emphasize community health and the provision of primary care about equally.

Return to Core Public Health – was most likely. Exhibit 14–30 illustrates the short- and long-term views of the committee. Therefore, Q-sort participants were asked to sort the ISDH's programs three times, based on the strategic assumptions embodied in the three scenarios. Q-sort results for the executive staff for each scenario are presented in Exhibits 14–31 through 14–33. In addition to the executive staff, twelve middle- and upper-level managers sorted the agency's seventy-three programs. The Q-sort results of the twelve managers were quite similar to those of the executive staff. Both sets of Q-sort rankings were used in subsequent deliberation of strategy. After considerable discussion of the different scenarios, the executive staff chose to use the results of Q-sorts according to the second scenario – health care reform would not be *fully* implemented in the next two to five years but that there would be some type of reform.

Needs-Capacity Assessment To corroborate the results of the program priority setting process by the executive staff and managers throughout the agency, four members of the executive staff, including Joe Hunt and the deputy commissioner, Nancy Blough, independently made a needs/capacity assessment. The four members of the executive staff evaluated each of the agency's seventy-three programs

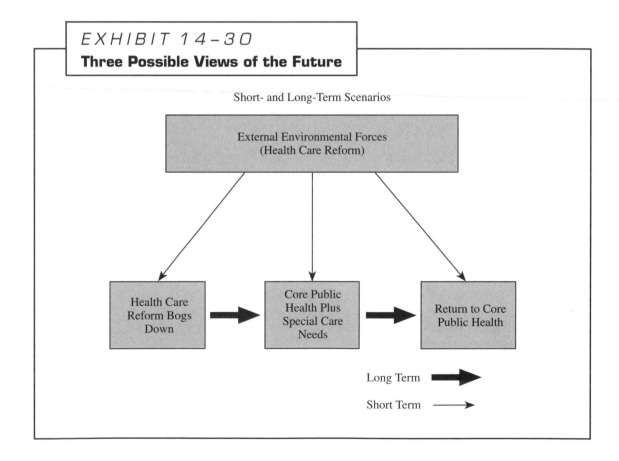

EXHIBIT 14–30
Three Possible Views of the Future

Short- and Long-Term Scenarios

External Environmental Forces
(Health Care Reform)

Health Care Reform Bogs Down

Core Public Health Plus Special Care Needs

Return to Core Public Health

Long Term

Short Term

EXHIBIT 14-31

Executive Staff Q-Sort Results: Scenario One – Return to Core Public Health

Most Important	Next Most Important	Next Most Important	Next Most Important	Next Most Important	Next Most Important	Next Most Important	Next Most Important	Next Most Important
				(5) MCH: Adolescent Health 5.38				
				(20) Legal Affairs 5.38				
				(61) Wholesale Food 5.38				
				(69) Consumer Health Lab 5.38				
			(19) Grants Resource Center 5.75	(58) CS: Meat and Poultry 5.25	(63) SE: Residential Sewage 4.75			
			(2) MCH: Genetic Disease 5.63	(64) SE: Vector Control 5.25	(70) OSP: Rural Health 4.75			
		(52) CDP: Injury Control 6.5	(36) OA: Human Resources 5.63	(22) MCH: Family Planning 5.13	(71) SE: Environmental Health 4.75	(56) MCH Program 4.13		
		(53) Chronic Disease 6.5	(46) ACS: Health Inspections 5.63	(25) OSP: Minority Health 5.13	(47) Lab Support Services 4.63	(38) FM: Environment Services 4.0		
		(48) CTS/STD 6.38	(8) Oral Health Services 5.5	(50) HIV/STD Clinical Data 5.13	(1) MCH: Family Helpline 4.38	(73) MCH: SIDS 4.0		
		(72) MCH: Healthy Pregnancy 6.25	(11) Health Planning 5.5	(55) FHS: Women's Health 5.13	(32) OA: Administrative Services 4.38	(43) MCH: Breastfeed Promotion 3.88		
	(17) PHS: Vital Records 7.5	(7) Nutrition/WIC 6.13	(29) OPA: Media Relations 5.5	(18) PHS: Birth Problems Registry 5.0	(41) FM: Asset Service 4.38	(24) OSP: Disability Concerns 3.75	(6) Child Special Services 3.38	
(9) Epidemiology Resource Center 7.85	(49) HIV Prevention 7.38	(67) Disease Control Lab 6.13	(45) HFS: Regulatory/Support 5.5	(23) Policy Coordination 5.0	(35) OA: Purchasing 4.25	(37) FM: Safety Programs 3.75	(60) CS: Weights and Measures 3.38	(27) HE: Film Library 2.0
(21) Local Health Support 7.85	(16) Public Health Statistics 7.25	(44) HFS: Long-Term Care 6.0	(57) Retail Food 5.5	(34) OA: Finance 5.0	(39) FM: Physical Plant 4.25	(40) FM: Security 3.75	(42) OA: Consultive Services 2.63	(28) HE: Library 1.88
(10) Management Information 7.63	(15) PHR: County Assessment 7.13	(14) Public Health Research 5.88	(3) MCH: Lead Poisoning 5.38	(65) Environmental Health Lab 5.0	(54) MCH Pregnancy Risk 4.25	(68) Indoor Radiologic Health 3.75	(12) HP: Certificate of Need 2.25	(33) OA: Correspond Center 1.75
(51) Communicable Disease 7.63	(26) OPA: Health Education 6.5	(62) WFD: Milk 5.88	(4) MCII: Prenatal Substance 5.38	(59) Manufactured Food 4.88	(66) SE: Plan Review 4.25	(13) HP: Financial Disclosure 3.63	(31) OPA: Print Shop 2.13	(30) OPA: Photographer 1.38

Note: Mean scores are the result of forced choice and therefore indicate only relative position rather than absolute value of a program.

EXHIBIT 14-32

Executive Staff Q-Sort Results: Scenario Two – Core Public Health Plus Special Care Needs

Most Important	Next Most Important	Next Most Important	Next Most Important	Next Most Important	Next Most Important	Next Most Important	Next Most Important	Next Most Important
				(8) Oral Health Services 5.13				
				(20) Legal Affairs 5.13				
				(34) OA: Finance 5.13				
				(45) HFS: Regulatory/ Support 5.13				
			(52) CDP: Injury Control 5.88	(55) FHS: Women's Health 5.13	(23) Policy Coordination 4.75			
			(5) MCH: Adolescent Health 5.75	(57) Retail Food 5.13	(61) Wholesale Food 4.75			
		(15) PHR: County Assessment 6.63	(56) MCH Program 5.75	(58) CS: Meat and Poultry 5.13	(65) Environmental Health Lab 4.63	(41) FM: Asset Service 4.25		
		(6) Child Special Services 6.5	(11) Health Planning 5.63	(3) MCH: Lead Poisoning 5.0	(47) Lab Support Services 4.5	(38) FM: Environmental Services 4.13		
		(48) CTS/STD 6.5	(26) OPA: Health Education 5.63	(24) OSP: Disability Concerns 5.0	(59) Manufactured Food 4.5	(54) MCH Pregnancy Risk 4.13		
		(70) OSP: Rural Health 6.5	(19) Grants Resource Center 5.5	(18) PHS: Birth Problems Registry 4.88	(63) SE: Residential Sewage 4.5	(40) FM: Security 4.0		
	(17) PHS: Vital Records 7.5	(67) Disease Control Lab 6.38	(36) OA: Human Resources 5.5	(46) ACS: Health Inspections 4.88	(64) SE: Vector Control 4.0	(73) MCH: SIDS 4.0	(13) HP: Financial Disclosure 3.25	
(21) Local Health Support 8.0	(53) Chronic Disease 7.38	(2) MCH: Genetic Disease 6.25	(44) HFS: Long-Term Care 5.5	(50) HIV/STD Clinical Data 4.88	(71) SE: Environmental Health 4.5	(37) FM: Safety Programs 3.88	(60) CS: Weights and Measures 3.13	(27) HE: Film Library 1.88
(51) Communicable Disease 7.88	(16) Public Health Statistics 7.13	(72) MCH: Healthy Pregnancy 6.25	(4) MCH: Prenatal Substance 5.25	(69) Consumer Health Lab 4.88	(32) OA: Administrative Services 4.38	(66) SE: Plan Review 3.88	(42) OA: Consultive Services 2.5	(33) OA: Correspond Center 1.88
(9) Epidemiology Resource Center 7.75	(7) Nutrition/ WIC 7.0	(14) Public Health Research 5.88	(29) OPA: Media Relations 5.25	(1) MCH: Family Helpline 4.75	(35) OA: Purchasing 4.38	(43) MCH: Breastfeed Promotion 3.63	(12) HP: Certificate of Need 2.25	(30) OPA: Photographer 1.63
(10) Management Information 7.63	(49) HIV Prevention 6.75	(25) OSP: Minority Health 5.88	(62) WFD: Milk 5.25	(22) MCH: Family Planning 4.75	(39) FM: Physical Plant 4.25	(68) Indoor Radiologic Health 3.5	(31) OPA: Print Shop 2.0	(28) HE: Library 1.5

Note: Mean scores are the result of forced choice and therefore indicate only relative position rather than absolute value of a program.

EXHIBIT 14–33

Executive Staff Q-Sort Results: Scenario Three – Health Care Reform Bogs Down

Most Important	Next Most Important	Next Most Important	Next Most Important	Next Most Important	Next Most Important	Next Most Important	Next Most Important	Next Most Important
				(20) Legal Affairs 5.25				
				(69) Consumer Health Lab 5.25				
				(26) OPA: Health Education 5.13				
				(29) OPA: Media Relations 5.13				
			(5) MCH: Adolescent Health 5.88	(46) ACS: Health Inspections 5.13	(58) CS: Meat and Poultry 4.63			
			(2) MCH: Genetic Disease 5.75	(57) Retail Food 5.13	(61) Wholesale Food 4.63			
		(56) MCH Program 7.0	(3) MCH: Lead Poisoning 5.75	(62) WFD: Milk 5.13	(63) SE: Residential Sewage 4.63	(41) FM: Asset Service 4.13		
		(6) Child Special Services 6.75	(4) MCH: Prenatal Substance 5.75	(1) MCH: Family Helpline 5.0	(47) Lab Support Services 4.5	(32) OA: Administrative Services 4.0		
		(48) CTS/STD 6.75	(14) Public Health Research 5.75	(23) Policy Coordination 5.0	(59) Manufactured Food 4.5	(73) MCH: SIDS 4.0		
		(72) MCH: Healthy Pregnancy 6.63	(19) Grants Resource Center 5.75	(45) HFS: Regulatory Support 5.0	(65) Environmental Health Lab 4.5	(39) FM: Physical Plant 3.88		
	(7) Nutrition/WIC 7.25	(16) Public Health Statistics 6.38	(55) FHS: Women's Health 5.63	(34) OA: Finance 5.0	(54) MCH Pregnancy Risk 4.38	(13) HP: Financial Disclosure 3.75	(68) Indoor Radiologic Health 3.25	
(51) Communicable Disease 8.25	(10) Management Information 7.25	(67) Disease Control Lab 6.38	(22) MCH: Family Planning 5.5	(8) Oral Health Services 4.88	(64) SE: Vector Control 4.38	(38) FM: Environmental Services 3.75	(60) CS: Weights and Measures 2.75	(27) HE: Film Library 1.88
(9) Epidemiology Resource Center 7.5	(15) PHR: County Assessment 7.13	(70) ONP: Rural Health 6.13	(44) HFS: Long-Term Care 5.5	(24) OSP: Disability Concerns 4.88	(71) SE: Environmental Health 4.38	(40) FM: Security 3.71	(12) HP: Certificate of Need 2.5	(33) OA: Correspond Center 1.88
(53) Chronic Disease 7.5	(17) PHS: Vital Records 7.13	(25) OSP: Minority Health 6.0	(11) Health Planning 5.38	(50) HIV/STD Clinical Data 4.88	(43) MCH: Breastfeed Promotion 4.25	(37) FM: Safety Programs 3.5	(42) OA: Consultive Services 2.38	(28) HE: Library 1.5
(21) Local Health Support 7.38	(49) HIV Prevention 7.0	(52) CDP: Injury Control 5.88	(36) OA: Human Resources 5.38	(18) PHS: Birth Problems Registry 4.75	(35) OA: Purchasing 4.13	(66) SE: Plan Review 3.38	(31) OPA: Print Shop 2.0	(30) OPA: Photographer 1.5

Note: Mean scores are the result of forced choice and therefore indicate only relative position rather than absolute value of a program.

based on their perceptions of the community need for the program and the capacity of the agency to meet that need (using the assumptions underlying scenario two). The programs were rated as *very high, high, low,* or *very low* for both community need and organizational capacity. Mean scores were calculated and the program number (as shown in the list of programs in Exhibit 14–28) was plotted on a needs/capacity grid. Results of this process are presented in Exhibit 14–34.

The needs/capacity assessment generally corroborated the results of the priority setting Q-sorts and provided additional perspective to program priority. Based on these evaluative tools, the executive staff began discussions on programs that needed to be expanded, stabilized, or contracted (adaptive strategies). For example, programs with high community need but low organization capacity and a "high" Q-sort ranking might be marked for expansion. Programs with low community need, high capacity, and a "low" Q-sort ranking could be considered for contraction.

Developing the Statement of Strategy Based on the results of the program priority setting and needs/capacity assessment, an adaptive strategy was developed. The adaptive strategy was viewed as a process of evolving the agency toward a desired profile or portfolio of programs. The makeup of that profile was influenced by the strategic assumptions (external issues, internal issues, and mission, vision, and objectives). Dominant in the strategic assumptions was the belief that, in the *long term,* health care reform would be successful and the agency would move toward more community or core public health (scenario one) activities. However, it was the belief of the steering committee and executive staff that, in the *short term,* special populations and certain medical treatments would be "uncovered" and the health department would have to remain in (or enter) those segments (scenario two). Therefore, the ISDH adaptive strategy was characterized as moving slowly and carefully toward more community health but assuring personal health needs as long as gaps in coverage remained. With this strategy, managers would have to be able to shift resources from personal health care to community health as health care reform progressed.

With this understanding of the changing environment, the following statement of strategy emerged from discussions of the executive staff concerning the program adaptive, market entry, and positioning strategies.

> Within the scope of the mission and vision, the ISDH's strategic directions will be expansion in core public health areas with an emphasis on assessment (data collection, epidemiology), policy development, and assurance (health promotion, disease control). The expansion strategies will be primarily market development (expanding the service population), product development (improving or extending current services), and penetration (increasing the ISDH role in the particular service). The ISDH will use contraction strategies in personal health programs where community need is decreasing or where other providers are available and in other programs where there is duplication of effort or where consolidation could offer enhancement in the quality and timeliness of service. Stabilization/enhancement strategies, emphasizing quality improvement and efficiency, will be used for all other programs.

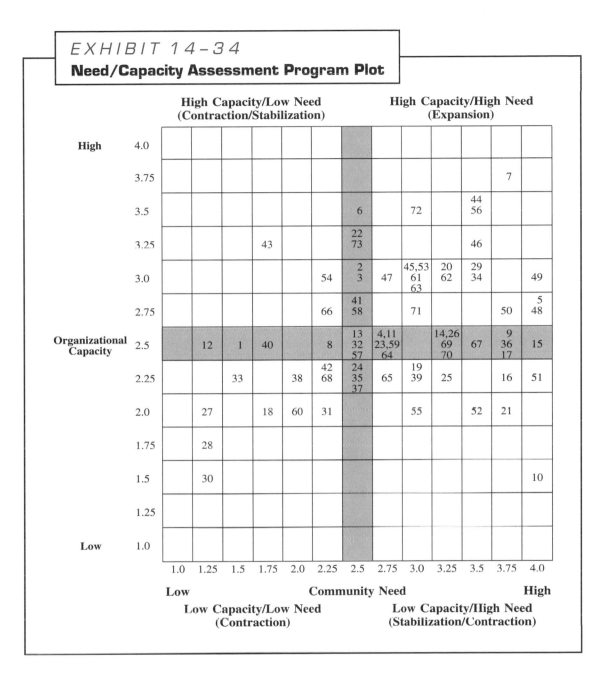

EXHIBIT 14–34
Need/Capacity Assessment Program Plot

Translating Program Evaluation into Program Adaptive Strategies Given the view of the future and selected strategy, the executive staff believed that the agency's portfolio of programs might be enhanced through the addition of new programs that addressed anticipated community health needs or health care reform gaps. Therefore, several new programs were proposed and discussed. The importance of programs was evaluated in relation to the ISDH's existing programs.

However, after discussing the results of the program priority setting and the needs/ capacity assessment and the likely nature of health care reform, it was determined that no new programs would be initiated at this time. The discussion of the results of program evaluation convinced the executive staff that the ISDH must continue to aggressively manage its programs to meet changing external needs. Within this context and because of the consistency of the results of the strategic analysis, the agency's programs were grouped under the broad categories of expansion, stabilization, and contraction. The following program rationales were developed through extensive discussions by the executive staff and steering committee.

The programs marked for expansion emphasized improving data collection and epidemiology, health promotion, and disease control. Expansion of these programs was consistent with the view that health care reform would begin to substantively affect public health in the next two to three years. The role of public health as a source of information for needs assessment, program evaluation, and epidemiology would, therefore, increase. In addition, a national emphasis on outcomes of care will require extensive data on the results of all types of health care. This data will have to be of high quality to support the tracking of disease in the population and to link health problems to the health care system.

Health promotion will be essential for improving the health of the populations and contributing to long-term cost control. Keeping people healthy longer will save money in earlier years of life and result in a healthier older adult population. Public health agencies are uniquely situated to provide, support, and encourage health promotion through direct service, community-based programs, and through education and encouragement to health providers.

Disease control is a traditional public health program. Effective disease reporting and case follow-up are critical to health care reform. The early identification of disease outbreaks will enable health care services, both individual and community based, to be targeted to early intervention and control.

The majority of the ISDH programs were identified as candidates for stabilization. Stabilization meant that these programs had a departmental commitment to maintain the present level of resources. Stabilization, however, did not mean that these programs were expected to remain unchanged. For instance, these programs could focus on improved quality of services, efficiency, or development of different services with the same resources (enhancement). The specific alternative for each program would be developed by the program director in consultation with the appropriate assistant commissioner or office director. The ISDH was to maintain a strong commitment to these programs as part of assuring quality service to meet identified needs.

Stabilization was to be the adaptive strategy for regulatory and support programs. Health promotion programs that had experienced significant growth in resources in the past few years were identified for stabilization. These programs faced changing needs. Stabilization assured the basic level of resources but allowed programs to select different uses of these resources to meet current and changing needs.

A few programs were identified for contraction. These programs were generally still important to the ISDH but their roles may have diminished or may have been completed, in part, by action in other programs. The essential functions would be maintained while activities that were not critical to the ISDH would be eliminated. Resources in these programs would be redirected according to an implementation work plan to areas of higher priority. These programs also had an opportunity to redefine their role within the agency to contribute to high-priority activities or to enhance the way they fulfilled their responsibilities. The programs identified for contraction included library, film library, Renal Disease Program, video/graphics/photography, the Sudden Infant Death Syndrome (SIDS) Project, and the correspondence center.

In addition to services and service population decisions concerning expansion, stabilization, or contraction, the executive staff believed that program managers should understand the agency's resource commitment to the various programs. For each program, the executive staff evaluated funding and staffing needs as expand, stable, or contract. A summary of the results of this process indicating strategies for funds, staff, market development, and product/service development strategies for the ISDH programs are presented in Exhibit 14–35, which shows the portfolio of the ISDH programs and the "directions" for future growth.

To provide program managers with a clearer idea of how expansion, stabilization, and contraction could be accomplished, specific definitions and examples for program expansion, stabilization, and contraction strategies were developed. These definitions were the ISDH's (public health) adaptations of traditional market development, product development, penetration, and enhancement strategies. The

---

EXHIBIT 14–35
Program Strategies

Program	Funds	Staff	Market Development	Product/Service Development
Office of Public Affairs				
Health Education	Stable	Stable	Expand	Expand
Health Education: Film Library	Contract	Contract	Expand	Expand
Health Education: Library	Contract	Contract	Contract	Stable/Contract
Office of Public Affairs: Media Relations	Stable	Stable	Stable	Expand
Office of Public Affairs: Video/ Graphics/Photo	Stable/ Contract	Contract	Expand	Expand
Office of Public Affairs: Print Shop	Stable	Stable	Stable	Expand
Office of Administration				
Office of Administration: Administrative Services	Stable	Expand	Expand	Expand
Office of Administration: Correspondence Center	Contract	Contract	Contract	Contract
Office of Administration: Finance	Expand	Expand	Expand	Expand
Office of Administration: Purchasing	Expand	Expand	Expand	Expand

EXHIBIT 14-35   *cont'd*

Program	Funds	Staff	Market Development	Product/Service Development
Office of Administration: Human Resources	Expand	Expand	Expand	Expand
Facilities Management: Safety Programs Coordination	Stable	Stable	Expand	Expand
Facilities Management: Environmental Services	Stable	Stable	Expand	Expand
Facilities Management: Physical Plant	Expand	Stable	Expand	Expand
Facilities Management: Security	Stable	Stable	Stable	Stable
Facilities Management: Asset Service Center	Stable	Stable	Stable	Expand
Office of Administration: Management Consultive Services	Expand	Expand	Expand	Expand
Office of Legal Affairs				
Office of Legal Affairs	Stable	Stable	Stable	Stable
Office for Policy Coordination				
Office for Policy Coordination	Expand	Expand	Expand	Expand
Office for Special Populations				
Special Populations: Disabilities	Stable	Stable	Expand	Expand
Office for Special Populations: Black and Minority Health	Expand	Expand	Expand	Expand
Rural Health Initiative	Expand	Expand	Expand	Expand
Quality Assurance Commission				
Consumer Protection:				
Retail Food Division	Stable	Stable	Stable	Stable
Meat and Poultry	Stable	Stable	Stable	Stable
Manufactured Food Section	Stable	Stable	Stable	Stable
Consumer Services: Weights and Measures	Stable	Stable	Stable	Stable
Wholesale Food Division	Stable	Stable	Stable	Stable
Milk	Stable	Stable	Stable	Stable
Residential Sewage Disposal	Stable	Stable	Stable	Stable
Vector Control Group	Stable	Stable	Expand	Expand
Plan Review Section	Stable	Stable	Stable	Stable
Indoor and Radiologic Health	Stable	Stable	Stable	Stable
Environmental Health Section	Stable	Stable	Stable	Stable
Health Facilities Standards:				
Long-Term Care Inspections	Stable	Stable	Stable	Stable
Survey Support Services	Stable	Stable	Stable	Stable
Acute Care Services	Stable	Stable	Stable	Stable
Laboratory Resource Center:				
Laboratory Support Services	Stable	Stable	Stable	Stable
Environmental Health Lab	Stable	Stable	Stable	Stable
Disease Control Lab	Expand	Stable	Stable	Stable
Consumer Health Lab	Stable	Stable	Stable	Stable

EXHIBIT 14-35   *cont'd*

Program	Funds	Staff	Market Development	Product/Service Development
Prevention and Community Health Commission				
Chronic Disease:				
Injury Control Program	Stable	Stable	Expand	Expand
Renal Program	Contract	Contract	Contract	Contract
Cancer Registry	Expand	Expand	Expand	Expand
PHBG Supported Activities	Stable	Expand	Expand	Expand
Antitobacco Activities	Stable	Stable	Expand	Expand
Communicable Disease:				
Communicable Disease Program	Expand	Expand	Expand	Expand
IIIV/STD:				
CTS/STD Program	Expand	Stable	Expand	Expand
HIV Prevention Activities	Expand	Stable	Expand	Expand
HIV/STD Clinical Data and Research	Stable	Stable	Expand	Expand
Family Health Services:				
Family Health Services: Women's Health	Expand	Stable	Expand	Expand
Maternal and Child Health:				
MCH: Family Helpline	Stable	Stable	Expand	Stable
MCH: Genetic Disease/ Newborn Screening	Stable	Stable	Expand	Expand
MCH: Childhood Lead Program	Stable	Expand	Expand	Expand
MCH: Prenatal Substance Abuse Program	Stable	Stable	Expand	Stable
MCH: Adolescent Health	Expand	Expand	Expand	Expand
MCH: Family Planning Program	Stable	Stable	Expand	Stable
MCH: Breastfeeding Promotion Program	Stable	Stable	Expand	Expand
MCH: Pregnancy Risk Assessment Monitoring System (PRAMS)	Stable	Stable	Expand	Expand
MCH: Prenatal Care, Primary Care/Managed Care, School-Based Clinics	Stable/ Expand	Stable	Expand	Expand
MCH: Healthy Pregnancy/ Healthy Baby Campaign	Stable	Stable	Expand	Expand
MCH: Sudden Infant Death Syndrome Project (SIDS)	Contract	Contract	Expand	Stable
Children's Special Health Care Services:				
Children's Special Health Care Services	Stable	Stable	Expand	Expand
Nutrition/ WIC Program:				
Nutrition/WIC	Stable	Stable	Expand	Expand
Oral Health Services:				
Oral Health	Stable	Stable	Expand	Stable

EXHIBIT 14-35   cont'd

Program	Funds	Staff	Market Development	Product/Service Development
Epidemiology Resource Center:				
EpiResource Center	Expand	Expand	Expand	Expand
Local Health Support:				
Local Health Support	Expand	Expand	Expand	Expand
Planning and Information Services Commission				
Management Information	Expand	Expand	Expand	Expand
Health Planning	Stable	Stable	Expand	Expand
Health Planning: Certificate of Need	Stable	Stable	Stable	Stable
Health Planning: Hospital Financial Disclosure	Stable	Stable	Expand	Expand
Public Health Research	Expand	Expand	Expand	Expand
County Health Needs Assessment	Stable	Stable	Expand	Expand
Public Health Statistics	Expand	Expand	Expand	Expand
Vital Records	Stable	Stable	Expand	Expand
Public Health Statistics: Birth Problems Registry	Expand	Expand	Expand	Expand
Grants Resource Center	Stable	Stable	Expand	Expand

definitions and examples (see Exhibit 14–36) provided program managers a starting point for developing specific program strategies.

Market Entry Strategies and Positioning Strategies

Generally, the market entry used by the ISDH programs was internal development. However, the health care reform environment presented the ISDH with opportunities to use cooperation strategies, particularly alliances, for new and future programs. Because of the nature of the ISDH, most of the programs were positioned as market segment (focus) strategies.

STRATEGIC IMPLEMENTATION: OPERATIONAL STRATEGIES

Although it was understood that there would be some overlap and duplication with the efforts of the steering committee, Phase I of strategic implementation began concurrently with strategy formulation. The objectives of the implementation task force included:

- Review and discuss the internal strengths and weaknesses;
- Develop goals and action plans for each of the seven organizational excellence factors;
- Develop specific organization-wide action plans to achieve the strategic objectives; and
- Foster strategic thinking throughout the department.

EXHIBIT 14-36

Definitions for Expansion, Stabilization, and Contraction – ISDH Statement of Strategy

The ISDH Statement of Strategy identifies the ISDH commitment of resources to support services and a commitment to the levels and types of the services. These commitments are described as expansion, stabilization, or contraction. The following definitions help explain what the ISDH means by the commitment to expand, stabilize, or contract resources and services.

Expansion of resources is a commitment by the ISDH to identify and allocate additional funding or staff to selected programs. The source of funds can include:

- Grant funds,
- New general fund appropriations,
- Possible fee-supported dedicated funds,
- Redirection of current funding, or
- Funds from collaborative efforts with other agencies.

The sources of personnel could include:
- New staff supported by grant funds,
- Reassignment of current staff,
- Staff available through collaborative efforts with other agencies,
- Federal assignees, or
- Students.

Expansion of programs includes both changes in service population and in the characteristics of the services offered. Expansion of service population can be achieved by:

- Increasing the number of people eligible for a service who actually use the service,
- Serving new population groups not currently targeted either by geographic area or new categories of population,
- Developing collaborative efforts with ISDH/other programs to increase the number of people served, or
- Increasing program efficiency to enable the program to serve more people with the same funding and staffing levels.

Expansion of services can include:

- Developing new service offerings such as screening or data reports,
- Changing the current service or offering the service in different ways to increase the range of services offered, or
- Developing collaborative efforts with ISDH/other programs to develop new services or expand the scope of services offered.

Stabilization of resources means that the current allocation of funding and staff will remain the same for the next fiscal year. Managers will develop work plans to match the resource level to program expectations.

EXHIBIT 14-36   cont'd

Stabilization of programs means that the level of services offered will remain the same. This does not necessarily mean maintaining the status quo. Each program manager is expected to review programs for possible enhancements such as improved efficiency or quality. Enhancements within stabilization can include:

- Work process streamlining to improve efficiency,
- Quality improvement for services provided,
- Focusing on customer service aspects of care to increase client satisfaction with services,
- Redefining the way services are provided within stable resources, or
- Changing the service mix to meet higher priority needs within stable resources.

Contraction of resources will be accomplished over the next fiscal year. Contraction strategies include:

- Readjusting work flow to reduce resources needed to provide the same service,
- Improving efficiency to reduce resources needed to provide the same service,
- Shifting staff to higher priority activities, with appropriate training for new responsibilities,
- Eliminating or shifting surplus vacant positions to complete work,
- Shifting equipment to higher priority activities, or
- Sharing positions between two programs to support activities in both.

Contraction of programs means that a program will stop offering a service or reduce the amount of services offered. Contraction strategies include:

- Eliminating unnecessary services,
- Developing collaborative relationships with ISDH/other programs to assume responsibility for part of the work conducted by your unit,
- Reducing the units of service available through evaluation of requests for service and providing only those services essential to community need, or
- Arranging for another agency to assume responsibilities for a service currently offered by the ISDH.

Managers, working with their assistant commissioners or office directors, will develop specific steps to implement the Statement of Strategy. These steps will become each ISDH program's work plan for the next year.

Organization-wide Strategies

Three related organization-wide implementation strategies were initiated by the ISDH – organization-wide cultural changes (based on the seven factors of excellence), agency goals and implementation priorities, and reorganization of the agency.

Changing the Culture Phase I of the implementation was directed toward changing the culture of the agency (an organization-wide strategy). The implementation task force formed seven subcommittees to address the seven factors of excellence thought to be important in shaping the culture of the organization. Each subcommittee was asked to identify a few targeted short-term activities or "quick victories" that would make an immediate impact on "the way work is done" in the excellence area assigned to it. The quick victories were considered important in fixing well-defined, short-term problems and in assuring employees that the strategic management process was progressing. In addition to the quick victories, the subcommittees developed strategies that clearly addressed less-well-defined, long-term cultural problems.

Agency Goals and Implementation Priorities Phase II of strategy implementation involved a translation of the agency goals into organization-wide actions incorporating the overall strategy into the operations of the individual programs. Specific organization-wide actions (agency implementation priorities) were developed for each of the eight agency goals. Recall that these goals were tied directly to the critical factors for success and were viewed as essential for development of the entire organization. The implementation actions accomplish the agency goals, which in turn address the critical success factors. The critical success factors, agency goals, actions items, and implementation dates are presented in the agency-wide work plan in Exhibit 14–37.

Reorganization In addition to the organization-wide cultural initiatives and agency goals, the ISDH made several changes to the organization structure to better accomplish the strategy. One of the strategic objectives was to further promote public health by working more closely with community health organizations. Therefore, an entirely new commission (Community Health Services) was created to focus on community health needs including local health support services, institutions, and consumer protection.

Because health policy as a core public health function would be critical, given the ISDH's strategy, the Office of Policy was expanded to include research

EXHIBIT 14-37
Agency-wide Work Plan

Critical Success Factor	Agency Goals	Action Items	Target Date
Service: The ISDH must maintain a client orientation and assure the quality of all services for internal and external clients.	All services provided by the ISDH will be client oriented and include a commitment to continual evaluation and improvement.	All areas will have a customer service plan by October 1994.	October 1994
		All areas will conduct baseline assessments of customer satisfaction by December 31, 1994, driven from customer service plan. (MIS will assist with design and nonduplication.)	December 1994

EXHIBIT 14–37   *cont'd*

Critical Success Factor	Agency Goals	Action Items	Target Date
Work Force: The ISDH must provide a working environment and resources that will attract and retain qualified staff members and empower them to achieve or exceed agency goals. The working environment will support responsive personnel policies; competitive compensation; adequate training; advancement opportunities; trust; sensitivity to diversity; and efficiency, innovation, and excellence.	The ISDH will provide orientation, training, and development opportunities for all ISDH staff.	ISDH will have a training options packet for all employees by June 1994 designed by the training task force with input from executive staff and Human Resources.	June 1994
		Managers will evaluate employee training needs and make recommendations to each employee regarding training needs by his or her next annual review.	Annually
		By August 1994, Human Resources will develop and deliver a comprehensive staff orientation to all new employees.	August 1994
Management: The ISDH must implement a process that plans and sets priorities within the constraints of available resources, in the context of strategic thinking. Management processes must promote interprogram coordination and cooperation to achieve agency goals.	Managers will apply the ISDH mission and critical success factors to program operations.	Managers will develop work plans based on at least three` agency goals by August 1994.	August 1994
		Managers will incorporate mission, vision, and critical success factors into employee job descriptions by December 1994.	December 1994
		Managers will do personal assessment of their training needs by October 1994.	October 1994
Leadership: The ISDH must be a visible, active, and persistent advocate on behalf of its employees and public health. This leadership must be based on efficiency, innovation, respect for the individual, and science. Leadership qualities will be recognized and promoted at all levels of the agency.	The ISDH will provide public health leadership.	Executive staff will establish criteria that define leadership by June 1994.	June 1994
		Executive staff will create an enhanced recognition program including leadership by September 1994.	September 1994
		Health Reform think tank will develop transition plans for ISDH to assist in outlining Indiana's plan by December 1994.	December 1994
Communication: The ISDH must communicate effectively both internally with employees and externally with local, state, and federal public health agencies and other stakeholders. Communication must accurately and consistently reflect the mission, vision, and activities of the agency.	The ISDH will communicate effectively with employees and external clients.	By June 1994, the ISDH will implement a communication plan designed by the Office of Public Affairs with input from program areas.	June 1994
		By December 1994, program areas will develop strategies to implement the communication plan in their program.	December 1994

EXHIBIT 14-37   *cont'd*

Critical Success Factor	Agency Goals	Action Items	Target Date
Funding: The ISDH must establish funding priorities and pursue innovative strategies to obtain adequate, stable financial resources for ensuring that fundamental public health services are available and monitor use of funds to achieve established objectives.	The ISDH will have a priority structure for funding and will pursue appropriate resources.	Executive staff will design a system for priority setting of projects and funding for the agency annually.	End of each March
		Grants Resource Center will identify three funding opportunities for programs listed for expansion annually.	End of each August
		Designated program areas that are listed for expansion will develop at least one new grant application or alternative funding stream based on priorities set by executive staff annually.	End of each December
Collaboration: The ISDH must expand and improve internal teamwork and external partnerships with local health departments and other local, state, and federal public and private organizations to promote public health.	The ISDH will foster successful partnerships to promote public health.	Executive staff, with program input, will identify agency-wide collaboration projects that match mission, vision, and critical success factors by the end of each January.	End of each January
		Managers will meet with at least two different program areas and form or improve internal partnerships.	December 1994
		Program areas will identify all existing external collaborative efforts by September 1994.	September 1994
		Grant applications to ISDH must support strategies consistent with mission, vision, and critical success factors for the agency.	Immediately – ongoing
		A strategic plan for strengthening local health departments' relationship with ISDH will be in place by December 1994.	December 1994
Data and Information: The ISDH must acquire and use timely and accurate data to asess needs, develop policy, and assure quality services. The data and information acquired must be shared with all people who need it to carry out their responsibilities.	The ISDH will effectively acquire, maintain, and utilize data to make policy and program decisions.	Management Information Services will have a data-base architecture plan that describes data sources and relationships by December 1994.	December 1994
		Managers will validate the data and information service needs assessment conducted by Management Information Services by May 1994.	May 1994
		Management Information Services will create a policy-setting work group on data needs by May 1994.	May 1994 – ongoing

and grant efforts so that grants could be linked to outcomes research. In addition, the name was changed to the Office of Policy and Research to reflect its new emphasis. Finally, the role of the Quality Assurance Commission was expanded. This commission would work with program areas throughout the agency to incorporate quality assurance into the programs. In addition, this commission would be responsible for continuing the strategic planning process and integrating the quality program into the strategic planning process. Joe Hunt assumed the leadership role in this endeavor. The new Indiana State Department of Health organization chart is shown in Exhibit 14–38.

Functional Strategies

Functional areas in the ISDH are the programs (programmatic areas such as health education, meat and poultry, vector control plus support services such as human resources, finance, planning, and so on). Therefore, it was up to the program directors and their staffs to develop the functional implementation strategies. As shown in Exhibit 14–39, situational analysis had produced three organizational change initiatives – a change in strategy (statement of strategy), strategic objectives and implementation priorities, and cultural change initiatives. Although there were organization-wide strategies for implementation of the strategic objectives and cultural change, program directors were expected to address all three organizational change initiatives in their program work plans (see Exhibit 14–39). Therefore, in addition to the organization-wide implementation actions, program directors developed specific work plans to carry out their respective expansion, stabilization, or contraction adaptive strategies plus address the strategic objectives and implementation priorities and cultural change within their respective programs. Development of the work plans generally followed the flowchart of activities shown in Exhibit 14–40. An example of a typical work plan developed for one of the ISDH programs is presented in Exhibit 14–41.

STRATEGIC CONTROL

A strategic control system monitors, evaluates, and adjusts the situational analysis processes, the strategy itself, and strategic implementation as appropriate. Therefore, the ISDH set out to formalize the control process so that progress toward the strategy could be maintained. Realizing that the strategic management process itself was a strategic control, Joe Hunt began to institutionalize the strategic management process. A formal year-long schedule for strategic planning events including environmental analysis, internal analysis, reassessing the mission, vision, critical success factors, strategy formulation, and so on was developed.

The executive staff played a key role in guiding the agency. Therefore the staff was provided with questions for validation of the strategic assumptions; questions for the evaluation of the directional strategies, adaptive strategies, market entry strategies, and positioning strategies; and questions for the evaluation of strategic implementation. These questions served as an additional strategic control and to foster strategic thinking.

In addition to the strategic management process, the implementation dates specified in the agency work plan (Exhibit 14–37) and the individual program

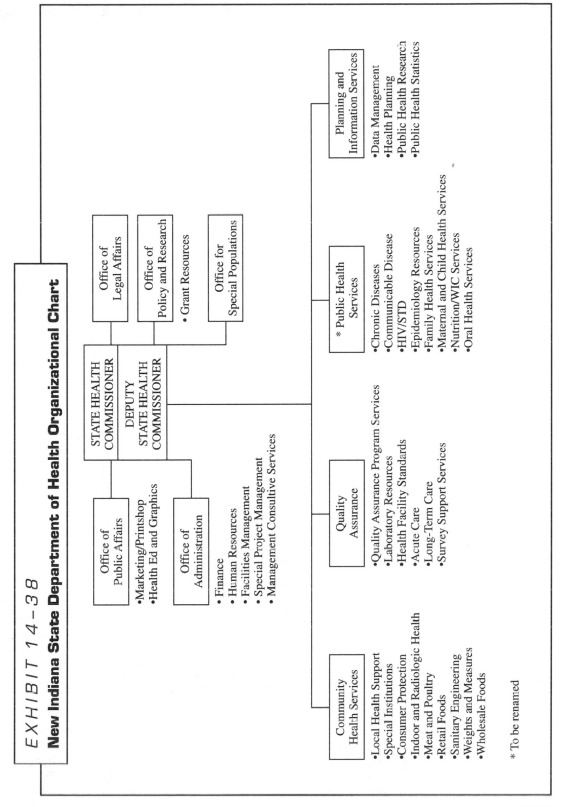

EXHIBIT 14-38

New Indiana State Department of Health Organizational Chart

STATE HEALTH COMMISSIONER

DEPUTY STATE HEALTH COMMISSIONER

Office of Legal Affairs

Office of Policy and Research
• Grant Resources

Office for Special Populations

Office of Public Affairs
• Marketing/Printshop
• Health Ed and Graphics

Office of Administration
• Finance
• Human Resources
• Facilities Management
• Special Project Management
• Management Consultive Services

Community Health Services
• Local Health Support
• Special Institutions
• Consumer Protection
• Indoor and Radiologic Health
• Meat and Poultry
• Retail Foods
• Sanitary Engineering
• Weights and Measures
• Wholesale Foods

Quality Assurance
• Quality Assurance Program Services
• Laboratory Resources
• Health Facility Standards
• Acute Care
• Long-Term Care
• Survey Support Services

* Public Health Services
• Chronic Diseases
• Communicable Disease
• HIV/STD
• Epidemiology Resources
• Family Health Services
• Maternal and Child Health Services
• Nutrition/WIC Services
• Oral Health Services

Planning and Information Services
• Data Management
• Health Planning
• Public Health Research
• Public Health Statistics

* To be renamed

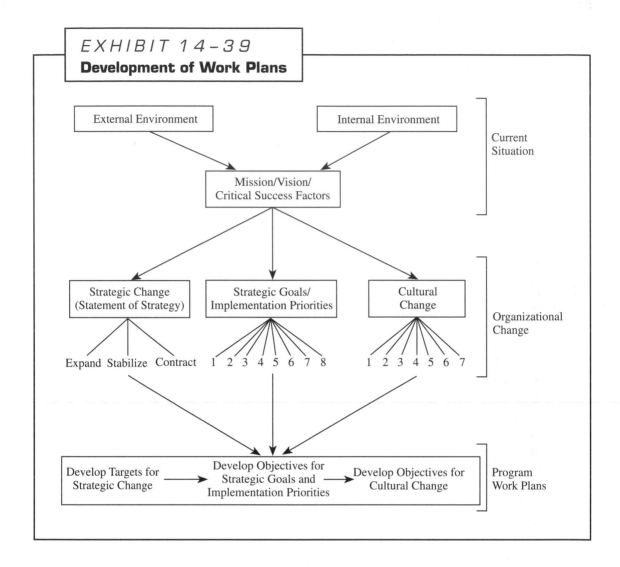

EXHIBIT 14-39
Development of Work Plans

work plans (Exhibit 14–41) were to be monitored and evaluated periodically. As an additional part of the integration of operations into the strategic management process, performance evaluations (both personal and program) were specifically tied to the accomplishment of the strategy.

SUMMARY OF THE STRATEGIC MANAGEMENT PROCESS

The summary of the strategic plan brings the process together into a single document that provides a quick reference and serves as a guide for decision making. Oftentimes these documents are proprietary (confidential) because of the competitive environment. However, this is not a problem for the ISDH. Therefore, the summary was communicated to all personnel and other stakeholders including the public. The summary of the ISDH strategic plan is presented in Exhibit 14–42.

EXHIBIT 14-40

Development of Implementation Work Plans

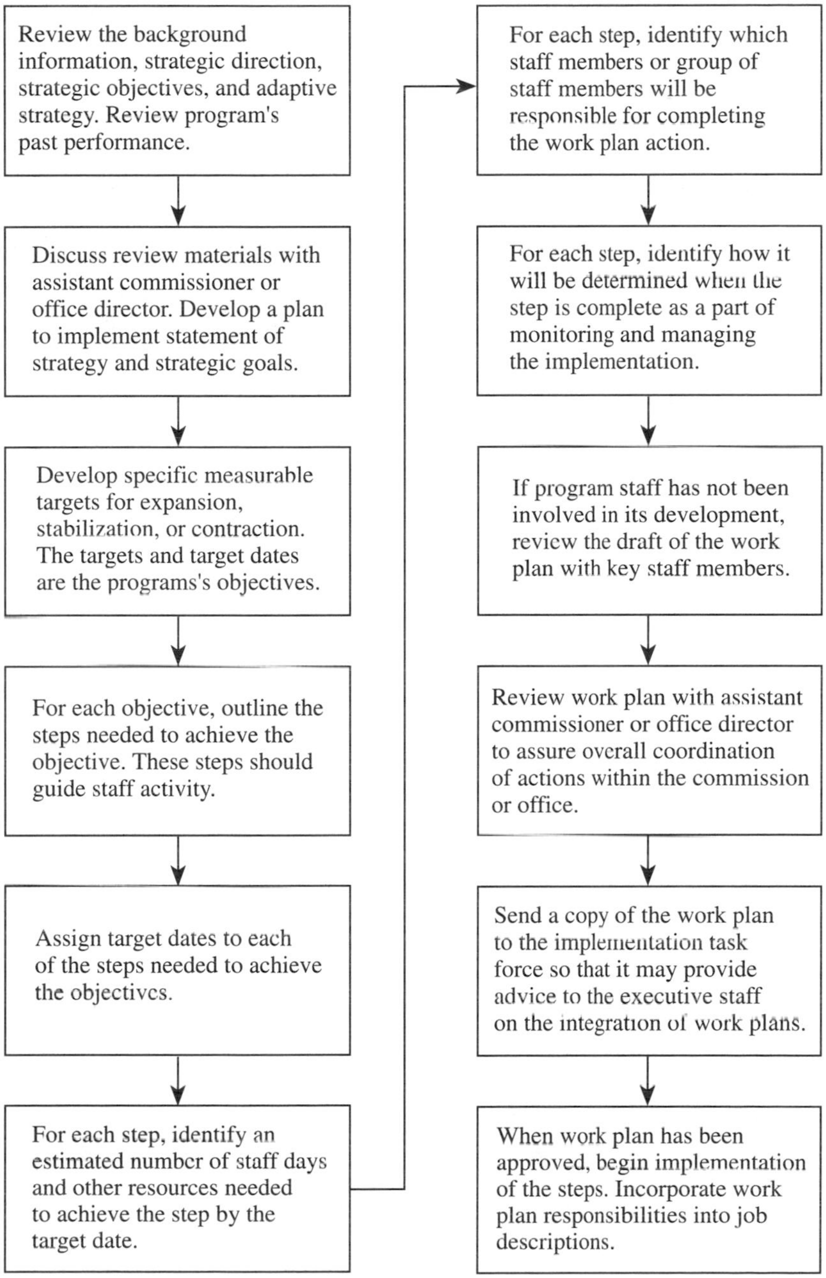

Review the background information, strategic direction, strategic objectives, and adaptive strategy. Review program's past performance.

Discuss review materials with assistant commissioner or office director. Develop a plan to implement statement of strategy and strategic goals.

Develop specific measurable targets for expansion, stabilization, or contraction. The targets and target dates are the programs's objectives.

For each objective, outline the steps needed to achieve the objective. These steps should guide staff activity.

Assign target dates to each of the steps needed to achieve the objectives.

For each step, identify an estimated number of staff days and other resources needed to achieve the step by the target date.

For each step, identify which staff members or group of staff members will be responsible for completing the work plan action.

For each step, identify how it will be determined when the step is complete as a part of monitoring and managing the implementation.

If program staff has not been involved in its development, review the draft of the work plan with key staff members.

Review work plan with assistant commissioner or office director to assure overall coordination of actions within the commission or office.

Send a copy of the work plan to the implementation task force so that it may provide advice to the executive staff on the integration of work plans.

When work plan has been approved, begin implementation of the steps. Incorporate work plan responsibilities into job descriptions.

EXHIBIT 14-41

Typical Work Plan for Children's Special Health Care Services (slated for stabilization): Children's Special Health Care Services Program Goals

I. Promote the delivery of high-quality, family-centered services to children with special health care needs.

II. Stress efforts that emphasize early evaluation, prevention of regression in health status, promotion of maximum function, and community-based services.

III. Promote systems development to improve the organization and delivery of services for children with special health care needs.

IV. Develop, promote, and improve the standards of care for children with special health care needs.

V. Provide culturally relevant care coordination and case management for children with special health care needs.

VI. Facilitate accomplishment of program mission statement.

Sample Work Plan for Goal I – Promote the delivery of high-quality, family-centered services to children with special health care needs – and dates for completion.

A. Outreach Plan (Communication, Management)
   1. Develop plan for outreach efforts.   April 30
   2. Present plan to advisory council.   September 30
   3. Begin implementation of outreach plan.   April 30

B. Health Care Reform (Leadership)
   1. Keep up to date with the status of health care reform. Ongoing
   2. Present to director as necessary, the impact of health care reform
      on: April 30
      a. Children with special health care needs.
      b. Division of CSHCS.
      c. Impact of FSSA's system.
   3. Present quarterly to staff the changes in health care reform. April 30

C. Part H Liaison (Collaboration)
   1. Work with director of Part H by meeting quarterly to assure all
      needs of children with special health care needs are met. April 30
   2. Continue to work on the Interagency Memorandum of
      Agreement PL 99-457 to assure collaboration between agencies. June 30
   3. Develop plan to pay for diagnostic services and enroll children
      in CSHCS.   April 30

EXHIBIT 14-41 *cont'd*

D. Interagency Agreements (Collaboration, Leadership)
1. Assign staff to assure Medicaid interagency agreement is implemented. April 30
2. Assign staff to assure completion and implementation of the interagency agreement between OPIN and CSHCS. April 30
3. Assign staff to assure completion and implementation of the interagency agreement between FSSA and CSHCS in regards to MMIS project. April 30
4. Assign staff to assure completion and implementation of the interagency agreement between Shriners Hospital and CSHCS. September 30
5. Assign staff to assure completion and implementation of the interagency agreement between Part H and CSHCS. June 30

E. Credentials (Service)
1. Develop policy to assure applications are processed in allowed time frames. June 30
2. Develop quality assurance system to assure credentials are processed appropriately. June 30
   a. Data input.
   b. Medical eligibility.
   c. Financial eligibility.
3. Cross train assigned staff. June 30

F. Provider Relations (Communication, Leadership)
1. Assure all providers understand the program expectations by mailing a provider update at least quarterly. April 30
2. Assign staff to respond to provider inquiries. March 31
3. Develop a plan to work with the multiple providers for outreach. April 30
4. Implement a plan, reporting status to division director monthly. June 30
5. Develop plan to assure 90 percent of providers for CSHCS program sign provider agreement in collaboration with EDS. April 30
6. Implement plan, reporting status to division director monthly. June 30
7. Work with EDS to develop CSHCS portion of provider manual. June 30
8. Create a position for provider relations. April 30

G. Primary-Care Linkage (Service)
1. Develop policy to assure all new children enrolled in the program are linked to a primary-care physician within 45 calendar days of their approval. April 30
2. Develop policy that allows participants to change primary-care physicians when requested. June 30
3. Collect and analyze data for those participants declining the primary-care linkage. June 30
4. Develop list of data needs for tracking primary care linkage. April 30

EXHIBIT 1 4 – 4 1   *cont'd*

H. Specialty Care Linkage (Service)
   1. Develop policy to assure all children who need a specialist are
      linked to a specialty care provider.   April 30
   2. Assure 90 percent of all children needing linkage are linked to
      a specialty care physician by monthly report from tracking
      system.   May 31

I. Dental-Care Linkage (Service)
   1. Develop policy to assure all children who are eligible to receive
      dental care are linked to a dentist.   April 30
   2. Assure 90 percent of all children who are eligible to receive
      dental care are linked to a dentist through monthly report from
      tracking system.   June 30

J. Staff Development/Training (Work Force)
   1. Analyze the training needs assessment and develop plan for
      staff training.   May 31
   2. Develop staff training schedule to include coding training,
      medical terminology training, and prior authorization training.   May 31
   3. Provide claims staff training quarterly.   March 31/
                                                                              ongoing

K. Caseworker Training/Billback (Collaboration/Funding)
   1. Develop relationship with FSSA by meeting quarterly with
      FFSA staff regarding case worker issues.   June 30
   2. Negotiate an agreement for billback system for CSHCS
      applications completed by case workers.   June 30
   3. Track case worker inquiries, report/respond quarterly.   April 30
   4. Develop informational letter quarterly to be sent to the case   April 30/
      workers explaining policy changes within the program.   ongoing

L. Parent Manual (Communication)
   1. Develop parent manual for all families interested in the program.   June 30
   2. Consult OPIN on the development of the manual.
   3. Distribute parent manual to all participants in the program.   September 30

M. SSDD Outreach (Collaboration)
   1. Meet with SSDD staff to develop outreach plan.   March 31
   2. Begin implementation of outreach program.   June 30

N. Multi-agency Review Meeting (Collaboration)
   1. Assign appropriate staff to attend review of applications for
      alternative or residential services.   March 31
   2. Assure all information is transferred.   June 30

EXHIBIT 14-42
Strategic Plan Indiana State Department of Health June 1994

Strategic Assumptions

External Environment		Internal Environment	
External Opportunities	**External Threats**	**Internal Strengths**	**Internal Weaknesses**
• Health care reform	• Health care reform	• Professional employees	• Management skills
• Need for cooperation	• Limited funding	• Data bases/satellite	• Physical facilities/space
• New emphasis on prevention	• Increasing violence	• Awareness of problems	• Some personnel turnover
• Care for special populations	• Technological advancements	• Public health message	• Human resources department
• Technological advancements	• Substance abuse	• Stakeholder communication	• Internal communications
• Increasing violence		• Data security	• Customer orientation
• Substance abuse		• Federal funding record	• Telecommunication system
			• Limited staff in some areas
			• Limited/level state funding
			• Some agency relations

Our View of the Future: Core Public Health Plus Special Care Needs

Health care reform will be passed; however, because of high costs, major gaps in coverage will remain. Under this assumption, most treatments and special populations will be covered by the private sector; however, significant "gaps" in coverage will continue. The only source of care for these populations or treatments will be in the public sector. The department will emphasize community health (core public health) but will continue to provide primary health care for special populations and treatments not covered under any type of (revolutionary or evolutionary) health care reform.

ISDH Mission

The Indiana State Department of Health (ISDH) is dedicated to promoting health and wellness among people in Indiana through planning, prevention, service, and education. The ISDH serves to help people attain the highest level of health possible. The ISDH is a proactive leader and collaborator in assessment, policy development, and assurance, based on science, innovation, and efficiency.

ISDH affirms that health includes physical, mental, and social well-being and is dependent on economic and environmental factors, access to health care, and individual responsibility and choice. Although the ISDH serves people primarily within Indiana's geographic boundaries, we recognize our interdependence with the larger world.

To achieve our mission, the ISDH supports:

- Training and technical assistance,
- Disease prevention and health education programs,
- Epidemiology for surveillance and analysis of health data for intervention and program evaluation,
- Development of policies and regulations to optimize health,
- Planning and evaluation,
- Staff recruitment and development to accomplish our mission, and
- Collaboration with the public, local health departments, governmental agencies, the scientific community, and special populations.

The ISDH is dedicated to quality service, innovation, respect for every individual, affirmative action, personal integrity, trust, and high ethical standards.

ISDH Vision

The Indiana State Department of Health is committed to act as a catalyst for progress that will result in healthier people in a healthful environment.

As a public health leader in the Hoosier State, the department will incorporate strategic management to implement a core set of values that are integral to public health. We will translate science and technology into action to safeguard the public's health. We will apply innovative, sound, and reasonable solutions to traditional public health challenges and emerging issues. At the same time, we will retain that which is good with public health in the state. We will expand knowledge through epidemiology and applied research on health and environmental issues.

The department recognizes its tie with other health and human service agencies to respond to global, national, state, and local public health concerns. We will forge alliances with public and private sectors to ensure that timely, cost-effective, public health interventions are planned and implemented. We will strengthen our commitment to collaborate with local health departments.

Our employees are our most valuable resource. We will provide an environment in which our employees strive for excellence, display initiative, and demonstrate achievement. Our employees will continue to promote health; work to prevent diseases, disability, and premature death; and help to assure access to health care for all populations.

This vision of the future is one in which the Indiana State Department of Health, communities, local health agencies, Special Institutions, and the private sector across the state cooperate to develop plans, programs, and resources. It guides our work to increase the span of healthy life, to reduce health disparities among different populations, and to assure access to preventive services for all.

Critical Success Factors	Strategic Objectives and Statement of Strategy
Work Force: The ISDH must provide a working environment and resources that will attract and retain qualified staff and empower them to achieve or exceed agency goals. The working environment will support responsive personnel policies; competitive compensation; adequate training; advancement opportunities; trust; sensitivity to diversity; and efficiency, innovation, and excellence. *Communication:* The ISDH must communicate effectively both internally with employees and externally with local, state, and federal public health agencies and other stakeholders. Communication must accurately and consistently reflect the mission, vision, and activities of the agency. *Funding:* The ISDH must establish funding priorities, pursue innovative strategies to obtain adequate, stable financial resources for ensuring that fundamental public health services are available, and monitor use of funds to achieve established objectives. *Collaboration:* The ISDH must expand and improve internal teamwork and external partnerships with local health departments and other local, state, and federal public and private organizations to promote public health. *Service:* The ISDH must maintain a client orientation and assure the quality of all services for internal and external clients. *Leadership:* The ISDH must be a visible, active, and persistent advocate on behalf of its employees and public health. This leadership must be based on efficiency, innovation, respect for the individual, and science. Leadership qualities will be recognized and promoted at all levels of the Agency. *Management:* The ISDH must implement a process that plans and sets priorities within the constraints of available resources and in the context of strategic thinking. Management processes must promote interprogram coordination and cooperation to achieve agency goals. *Data and Information:* The ISDH must acquire and use timely and accurate data to assess needs, develop policy, and assure quality services. The data and information acquired must be shared with all people who need it to carry out their responsibilities.	*Strategic Objectives:* All services provided by the ISDH will be client oriented and include a commitment to continual evaluation and improvement. The ISDH will provide orientation, training, and development opportunities to all ISDH staff. Managers will apply the ISDH mission and critical success factors to program operations. The ISDH will provide public health leadership. The ISDH will communicate effectively with employees and external clients. The ISDH will foster successful partnerships to promote public health. The ISDH will have a priority structure for funding and will pursue appropriate resources. The ISDH will effectively acquire, maintain, and utilize data to make policy and program decisions. *Statement of Strategy:* Within the scope of the mission and vision, ISDH's strategic directions will be expansion in core public health areas with an emphasis on assessment (data collection, epidemiology), policy development, and assurance (health promotion, disease control). The expansion strategies will be primarily market development (introducing new services), product development (improving current services or extending current services), and penetration (increasing the ISDH role in the particular service). The ISDH will use contraction strategies in personal health programs where community need is decreasing or where other providers are available and in other programs where there is duplication of effort or where consolidation could offer enhancement in the quality and timeliness of service. Stabilization/enhancement strategies, emphasizing quality improvement and efficiency, will be used for all other programs.

Expansion Strategies	Stabilization Strategies	Contraction Strategies
Data Collection/Epidemiology	Data Collection/Epidemiology	Library
Epidemiology Resource Center	Hospital Financial Disclosure	Renal Disease Program
Management Information	Vital Records	Sudden Infant Death Syndrome
Services	Pregnancy Risk Assessment	(SIDS) Project
Public Health Statistics	Monitoring System	Correspondence Center
Public Health Research	County Health Needs	Film Library
Birth Problems Registry	Assessment	Video/Graphics/Photography
Cancer Registry	HIV/STD Clinical Data	
	Research	
Health Promotion		
MCH: Adolescent Health	Health Planning	
Black and Minority Health	Health Promotion	
Initiatives	Family Helpline	
Chronic Disease Programs	Prenatal Substance Abuse	
Through Preventive Health	Program	
Block Grant	Nutrition/WIC	
Rural Health Initiative	Oral Health	
Childhood Lead Program	Family Planning Program	
HIV Prevention Activities	Breastfeeding Promotion	
Women's Health	Program	
	Health Education	
Disease Control	Injury Control	
CTS/STD Program	Antitobacco Program	
Communicable Disease	Maternal and Child Health	
Program	Prenatal Care, Primary Care/	
	Managed Care, School-	
Policy Development/	Based Clinics	
Collaboration/Support	Healthy Pregnancy/Healthy	
Local Health Support	Baby	
Policy Coordination		
Administrative Services	Regulation	
Human Resources	Long-Term-Care Inspection	
Finance	Survey Support Services	
Purchasing	Acute Care Services	
Physical Plant	Retail Food Division	
Management Consultive	Meat and Poultry	
Services	Manufactured Food Section	
	Wholesale Food Division	
	Milk	
	Weights and Measures	
	Residential Sewage Disposal	
	Plan Review Section	
	Indoor and Radiological Health	
	Certificate of Need	
	Disease Control	
	Vector Control Group	
	Consumer Health Laboratory	
	Disease Control Laboratory	
	Environmental Health	
	Laboratory	
	Environmental Health Section	
	Personal Health Services	
	Children's Special Health Care	
	Needs	
	Genetic Disease/Newborn	
	Screening	
	Policy Development/	
	Collaborative/Support	
	Grants Resource Center	
	Office of Legal Affairs	
	Special Populations:	
	Disabilities Program	
	Media Relations	
	Print Shop	
	Safety Programs	
	Environmental Services	
	Security	
	Asset Services Center	
	Laboratory Support Services	

The ISDH strategic management process and resulting strategic plan were developed through wide participation throughout the organization. The process was often frustrating, controversial, difficult, and time consuming. However, through the conflict created by the process, employees openly explored the important issues confronting the ISDH, reached a consensus on the definition of public health in Indiana, and established the direction public health will take within the state. As the ISDH gains in strategic management experience, its view of the future will become even more focused and its strategy more well defined. The ISDH had taken its first certain steps into the future. Those steps are accompanied by a clear destination and detailed guide map – the ISDH strategic plan.

NOTES

1. Public Health Practice Program Office, Division of Public Health Systems, Centers for Disease Control, *Profile of State and Territorial Public Health Systems: United States, 1990,* (Atlanta: U.S. Department of Health and Human Services, Public Health Service, Centers for Disease Control, 1991), p. 121.
2. Ibid., pp. 121–122.
3. Ibid.
4. Ibid.
5. Early development of the underlying factors for the questionnaire can be examined in W. Jack Duncan, Peter M. Ginter, and Stuart A. Capper, "Excellence in Public Administration: Four Transferable Lessons from the Private Sector," *Public Productivity and Management Review* 14 (Spring 1991), pp. 227–236.

PART **6**

Appendices

Analyzing Strategic Health Care Cases

How do managers learn to make strategic decisions in health care organizations? The most obvious way, and maybe the most valuable if the opportunity is available, is to work your way up the organization and observe how senior executives deal with strategic issues. Then, when the opportunity presents itself, combines what you have learned from others and your own management philosophy and do the best you can. Unfortunately, such mentoring is not practical in most rapidly changing organizations.

Even if this approach were feasible, it would be very risky, and business firms, hospitals, health maintenance organizations, long-term-care facilities, and other organizations trust important strategic decision making only to the most "seasoned managers." As a result, cases have been successfully used as a method to give aspiring managers opportunities to make strategic decisions without "betting the organization" on the outcome. In other words, cases offer an opportunity to deal with real decisions in a low-risk environment.

Cases contain situations actually faced by managers in health care organizations documented in a way that makes them useful in training decision makers. The decisions required to solve cases represent a wide range of complexity so that no two are addressed in exactly the same manner. In the following discussion, one method of case analysis is presented. This approach, illustrated in Exhibit A–1, offers a process or way of thinking about cases rather than prescribing the only way to approach the task of case analysis. Exhibit A–1 is the model or outline used throughout the book to direct thinking about strategic management in health care organizations. The model can be effective in thinking about analyzing cases as well. This approach to case analysis is useful because it is a logical method of decision making.

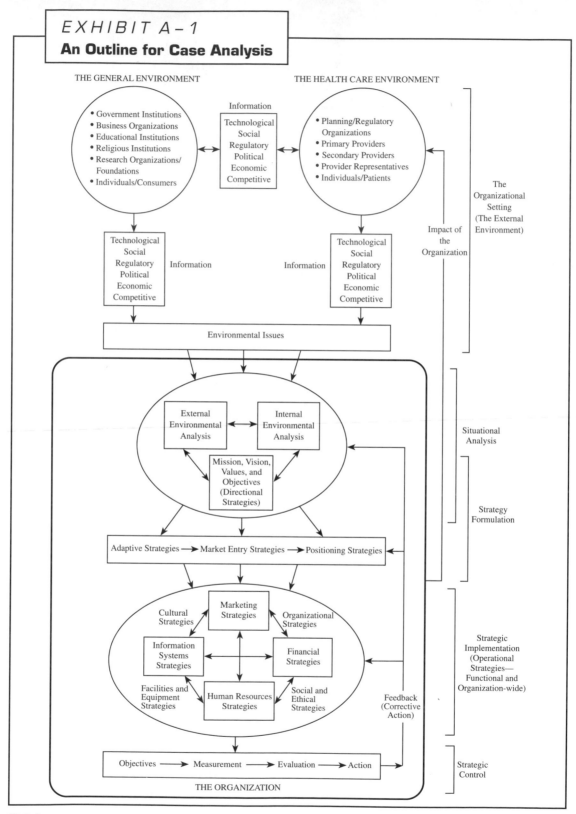

EXHIBIT A-1
An Outline for Case Analysis

THE GENERAL ENVIRONMENT

THE HEALTH CARE ENVIRONMENT

- Government Institutions
- Business Organizations
- Educational Institutions
- Religious Institutions
- Research Organizations/ Foundations
- Individuals/Consumers

Information

Technological
Social
Regulatory
Political
Economic
Competitive

- Planning/Regulatory Organizations
- Primary Providers
- Secondary Providers
- Provider Representatives
- Individuals/Patients

The Organizational Setting (The External Environment)

Technological
Social
Regulatory
Political
Economic
Competitive

Information

Information

Technological
Social
Regulatory
Political
Economic
Competitive

Impact of the Organization

Environmental Issues

External Environmental Analysis

Internal Environmental Analysis

Mission, Vision, Values, and Objectives (Directional Strategies)

Situational Analysis

Strategy Formulation

Adaptive Strategies → Market Entry Strategies → Positioning Strategies

Cultural Strategies

Marketing Strategies

Organizational Strategies

Information Systems Strategies

Financial Strategies

Facilities and Equipment Strategies

Human Resources Strategies

Social and Ethical Strategies

Feedback (Corrective Action)

Strategic Implementation (Operational Strategies— Functional and Organization-wide)

Objectives → Measurement → Evaluation → Action

Strategic Control

THE ORGANIZATION

644

First, it is important to understand the economic, social, technological, and political environments facing the industry and organization. After developing a knowledge of these aspects of the general environment it is possible to progress to the specifics of the health care industry. Next, as many facts as possible should be gathered about the environment of the organization under examination. This may be a hospital, health maintenance organization, public health agency, or long-term-care facility. At this point it is important to relate the strategic capabilities of the organization to the external environment. To do this, a thorough and objective analysis of internal strengths and weaknesses is required. It is also necessary to understand the unique culture of the organization, its mission, and its strategic objectives.

Once the situation analysis is complete, strategic alternatives can be generated as possible solutions to the problems identified in the case. This is the strategy formulation stage and is an important part of solving strategic management in health care cases.

When the strategic direction is determined based on the unique "fit" between the organization's internal strengths and weaknesses and the external opportunities and threats, the capabilities of the various subsystems such as marketing, finance, operations, and so on must be evaluated. These subsystems will determine, to a great extent, the likelihood that a particular strategy will be implemented.

Finally, the effectiveness of the chosen strategic alternative must be evaluated. Because of the nature of case analysis, this aspect of strategic control is not always possible. However, at least some thought must be given to the likely outcomes resulting from different strategic choices.

Although the approach outlined here is logical, it is important to remember that each case should be approached and appreciated as a unique opportunity for problem solving. The organization, environment, and situation make every case different.

CASES: REAL AND IMAGINED

Many different types of cases are used in strategic management texts. Sometimes cases are invented to illustrate a specific point. Usually these appear as "Ajax Hospital and Medical Center" or some similar name. Other cases are real but disguised. A writer may, for example, have information from an organization such as the Mayo Clinic or Massachusetts General Hospital but for some reason has been requested not to use the name of the institution.

The best cases, like those in this book, are real and undisguised. Cases such as HealthSouth, SunHealth Alliance, University of Texas at Tyler Medical Center, New England Health Plan, Calumet Community Hospital, and so on are real organizations. Of course, less well-known cases also have been selected because of the important issues they present to prospective managers. Sometimes the issues presented are not even problems. Often the greatest challenge facing an organization is recognizing and acting on an opportunity rather than solving a problem.

Cases that have obvious solutions upon which everyone agrees are not good decision making aids. Managers in health care organizations rarely face decisions where the solution is self-evident to everyone. This does not mean that there are no good and bad answers or solutions in case analysis. However, the evaluation of a case analysis as good, better, or best is often based more on the approach and logic employed than the precise recommendation offered.

CASES, STRATEGIC MANAGEMENT, AND HEALTH CARE

Cases add realism that is impossible to achieve in traditional lecture classes. Realism results from the essential nature of cases, although we may complain that cases fail to provide all the information necessary for decision making. The complaint is valid because cases rarely give us everything we need. However, decision makers in health care organizations never have all the information they want or need when they face strategic decisions. Risks must be taken in case analysis just as in actual decision making.

Risk Taking in Case Analysis

Decisions about the future involve uncertainty. Strategic decision making, because it is futuristic and involves judgment, is particularly risky. Decision making under conditions of uncertainty requires that means be devised for dealing with the risks faced by managers. Cases are valuable aids in this area because they allow us to practice making decisions in low-risk environments. A poor case analysis may be, and should be, embarrassing but at least it will not result in the closure of a hospital. At the same time, the lessons learned by solving cases and participating in discussions will begin to build problem solving skills.

Unfortunately, many future health care decision makers are not familiar with how to analyze cases. Customarily, prospective managers learn how to succeed as students by taking objective examinations, writing occasional term papers, and crunching numbers on a computer but they seldom solve real case problems. For this reason this appendix has been included – not to prescribe how all cases should be solved but to offer some initial direction on how to "surface" the real issues presented in the cases.

Solving Case Problems

Solving a case is much like solving any problem. First, the issues are defined, information is gathered, alternatives are generated, evaluated, selected, and implemented. Although the person solving the case seldom has the opportunity to implement a decision, he or she should always keep in mind that recommendations must be tempered by the limitations imposed on the organization in terms of its human and nonhuman resources. As the success or failure of the recommendations are analyzed, lessons are learned that can be applied to future decision making.

ALTERNATIVE PERSPECTIVES: PASSION OR OBJECTIVITY

Different hypothetical roles can be assumed when analyzing cases. Some prefer to think of themselves as the chief executive or administrator in order to impose a perspective on the problems presented in the case. This provides the case analyst the liberty of becoming a passionate advocate of a particular course of action. Others prefer to observe the case from the detached objectivity of a consultant who has been employed by the organization to solve a problem.

Either perspective can be assumed but the first offers some unique advantages. Because there are no absolutely correct or incorrect answers to complex cases, the most important lesson to learn is why managers behave as they do, why they select one alternative in preference to all others, and why they pursue specific strategies under the conditions presented in the case. Becoming the manager, at least mentally, helps us learn the lessons case histories have to teach.

Consider the case of Memorial Hospital in Palestine, Texas. In 1987, a community, for-profit facility was opened as a competing hospital. Memorial, at the time, was a 99-bed county-run hospital losing $200,000 a month. Most of Memorial's medical staff "jumped ship" and affiliated with the new for-profit hospital. When a new administrator arrived in 1988, the future seemed dark indeed.[1]

The new administrator tried a number of things to restore financial viability to the hospital. The county was convinced to transfer governance to an independent foundation along with $1 million of liabilities. Memorial even discounted its outpatient programs by offering surgical procedures at a price one-third below the prevailing rate. Still, no one came.

To solve this case from the administrator's perspective, it is important to "get inside" the decision maker's head. Feel the frustration of "not being able to give medical services away" in today's environment. What could be done? How can the hospital ever be saved?

The passion and frustration of the administrator suggests why some prefer to assume the objective posture of a consultant. Not being in the trenches can sometimes suggest alternatives that cannot be seen by those directly involved in making the payroll and paying the bills. The consultant's perspective allows the student to step back, look at what patients and physicians are actually telling the hospital by their unwillingness to come at any reasonable price. Perhaps specific programs must be offered to special populations in the community. Certainly, medical staff relations must be improved. The fun and excitement of case analysis is enhanced by assuming the decision maker's role. The options, however, can often be expanded through a more objective and detached outlook.

HOMEWORK: AN ESSENTIAL ASPECT OF CASE ANALYSIS

Effective case analysis begins with data collection. This means carefully reading the case, rereading it, and sometimes reading it yet again. Rarely can anyone absorb enough information from the first reading of a comprehensive case to adequately solve it. Therefore, collect information and make notes about details as the case unfolds.

Getting Information

The information required to successfully solve a case comes in two forms. The first type of information is given as part of the case and customarily includes things such as the history of the hospital, long-term-care facility, or home health care agency, how it is organized, its management, and its financial condition. This is the easy part because the author of the case has done the work.

Occasionally, a case will include information about the industry and maybe even some problems shared by competing firms. If the case involves a chain of long-term-care facilities, a health maintenance organization, or a pharmaceutical company, the industry must be thoroughly understood before looking at specific problems.

A second type of information is "obtainable." This information is not provided in the case or by the instructor but available from secondary sources in the library in familiar magazines and related publications. Obtainable secondary information helps us understand the nature of the industry, the competition, and even some managers, past and present, who have made an impact on the industry. Examples of sources of obtainable information are given in Appendix D.

If the case does not include industry information, the instructor may expect the class to do some detective work before proceeding. Find out what is happening in the industry and learn enough about trends to position the problems discussed in the case in a broader health care context. The culture of the organization or the style of the chief executive officer may also constitute relevant information.

Threats and Opportunities

From the very first reading start to list the strategic threats and opportunities facing the organization. When a threat is discovered mark it for more detailed examination. Are the threats financial? Do the primary issues appear to be those of human resources, capital investment, or marketing? Perhaps there are few, if any, apparent threats. The strategic issue facing the organization may be an opportunity to be exploited or at least investigated.

For example, the trend in the health care industry toward managed care has created some interesting problems, and opportunities, for drug companies. Managed care often means larger buyers of pharmaceutical products and larger buyers mean that greater discounts must be given to compete effectively. In attempts to maintain profits while offering larger and larger discounts, drug companies began to announce layoffs of personnel. Merck and Company, the world's largest pharmaceutical firm, stated that it would eliminate over 2,000 jobs and at the same time announced it would purchase Medco Containment Company and enter the mail order drug market. Industry trends can create problems and opportunities, almost simultaneously.

ANALYZING THE PRESENT SITUATION

After getting a fix on the mission and the initial impressions of the major strategic issues in the case, the next step is to understand where the organization, the industry, and the decision makers are at the time a strategic decision is needed. This is called *situational analysis* because we must understand the circumstances and the environment facing the organization if good decisions are to result from our analysis.

Selected Aspects of Situational Analysis

Situational analysis is one of the most important steps in analyzing a case. The list below highlights some of the important areas that should be included in this stage of case analysis.

1. The environment of the health care organization.
    A. Size. What is the size of and growth trends in the industry?
    B. Nature of the competition. How many direct competitors are there, and is the competition increasing or decreasing? What are the relative market shares of the different competitors? If the case involves a long-term-care facility, look at Exhibit A–2 and consider the increasing share of this market accounted for by chains.[2] What implications would this have for individual long-term-care facilities not affiliated with a national chain?
    C. Macroenvironmental factors. What are the prevailing economic conditions, regulatory philosophies, lifestyle and demographic factors, and

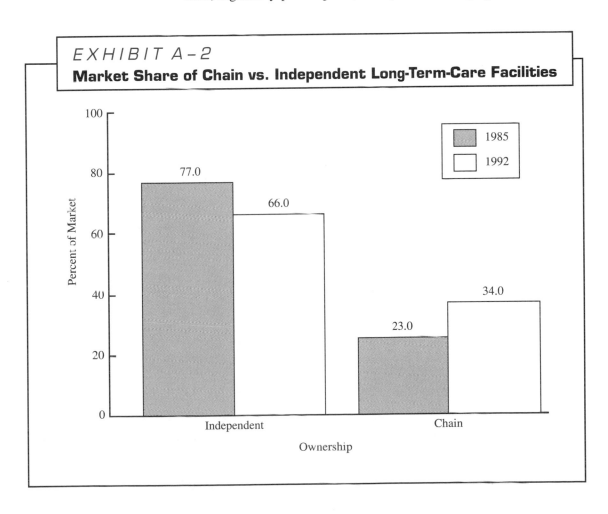

EXHIBIT A–2
Market Share of Chain vs. Independent Long-Term-Care Facilities

technological forces that are likely to influence strategic decision making in health care? What is the industry's and the organization's history with respect to labor/management relations?

2. The market.

A. Customers. Who are the organization's primary customers – patients, elderly residents of long-term-care facilities, the home-bound ill? To what extent are the patients or customers loyal to the organization's services? Is price the major determinant in the purchasing decision of patients? Will patients and clients travel and be otherwise inconvenienced to obtain the organization's services?

B. Services. Does the organization offer a full range of services? Is the present service mix complementary or does the organization compete with itself in some areas? Could the overall level of business be significantly increased if selected new services were added?

C. Geography. Is the market for the organization's services geographically concentrated?

D. Marketing. How sophisticated are the organization's clients/patients in terms of their buying habits and processes? What does this tell management about advertising and promotion?

E. Demographics. Are market segments easily identified? Are different strategies for each feasible or advisable?

3. The organization.

A. Mission. Does the organization have a clear sense of mission? Is there a mission statement and is it communicated to those responsible for accomplishing it? Are there well-developed and communicated long- and short-range objectives? Does the organization have the human and nonhuman resources necessary to accomplish its mission?

B. Culture. What do we know about the culture of the organization? Will the culture allow innovation or are management and employees bound to past ways of doing things?

C. Marketing strategies. How sophisticated is the organization in terms of its marketing? Has serious thought been given to a promotion strategy? Has the appropriate channel(s) of distribution been identified and utilized? How flexible are the organization's marketing policies? When was the last time management tried something innovative in the area of marketing? More important perhaps, has the organization ever done any serious marketing of its services?

D. Finance. Are the financial resources needed to compete available or is the organization undercapitalized, too highly leveraged or not leveraged enough? How do the key financial ratios of this organization compare with others in the industry and region?

Note that Chapter 4 provides an extensive checklist of the kinds of questions that should be asked with regard to the various organizational subsystems that will be needed for effective strategy implementation.

Threats, Opportunities, Strengths, and Weaknesses

Once the situation has been reviewed, a better evaluation of the opportunities and threats facing the organization can be made. Moreover, we must be able to look objectively at the hospital or long-term-care facility and ask, "Given the organization's apparent strengths and weaknesses how do we take advantage of our opportunities and avoid the dangers in the environment?" An effective way of asking these questions is with the use of a simple two-by-two chart listing the threats, opportunities, strengths, and weaknesses. Exhibit A-3 presents an example of how these can be organized.

EXHIBIT A-3
Threats, Opportunities, Strengths, and Weaknesses for a Hospital

INTERNAL STRENGTHS	INTERNAL WEAKNESSES
1. Existing expertise	1. Little experience with long-term-care facilities
2. Reputation for quality service	2. Large amount of debt used to finance hospital
3. Adaptive medical and support staff	3. Proposed acquisition will not overcome adverse financial ratios
EXTERNAL OPPORTUNITIES	**EXTERNAL THREATS**
1. Relaxation of certificate of need (CON) regulations	1. Attraction of new competition
2. Emerging medical technology	2. Rising interest rates
3. Favorable demographic indicators	3. Uncertain long-term-care facility market

To illustrate how to relate threats, opportunities, strengths, and weaknesses, suppose in the case that you are presently studying the administrator of a large general hospital is evaluating an opportunity to purchase a regional long-term-care chain and thereby diversify the services offered to existing patients. An environmental analysis confirms that there will be increasing needs for long-term-care beds in the future. The population is aging in this country and long-term-care facilities are generally not meeting present or forecasted needs. Moreover, as Exhibit A–2 illustrates, the long-term-care market is being controlled more and more by chains rather than independent operators. Of course, the administrator realizes that she is not the only executive aware of the aging trend and anticipates significant competition from other organizations.

The administrator believes that the hospital has a number of internal strengths. It has, for example, a reputation for high-quality and price-competitive services. In addition, it has a medical and administrative staff with proven records of flexibility in responding to new ventures. The hospital has always been able to go into the labor market and get the number and quality of employees needed – even in the highly competitive market for nurses.

The administrator does worry about the hospital's ability to easily enter the nursing home market even with the purchase of the regional chain. Few members of the management team have any experience with long-term care and only a few are really experienced dealing with elderly patients' unique demands and needs. Moreover, a review of the hospital's financial statements raises serious doubts about its ability to absorb the additional debt financing needed to purchase the long-term-care chain. Financially, the chain does not offer the kind of strength that would overcome an excessive degree of financial leverage.

In addition, the recent trend in interest rates has been upward so that even if funds could be borrowed, the expense involved would be substantially more than the board of directors would want to pay. Through an examination of the threats, opportunities, strengths, and weaknesses (Exhibit A–3), the administrator can make a more informed decision.

Purpose or Mission of the Organization

Peter Drucker says that anyone who wants to "know" a business must start with understanding its purpose or mission.[3] If a mission statement is included in the case, does it serve the purpose of communicating to the public why the organization exists? Does it provide employees with a genuine statement of what the organization is all about?

Mission statements provide valuable information, but they may leave much to be inferred and even imagined. Missions are broad, general statements, outlining what makes the organization unique. When the mission is understood, a number of things are known that will help in arriving at a good solution to the case.

As discussed in Chapter 5, a good mission should answer a series of questions. When you read the assigned case, ask if you know enough about the organization's mission to confidently speculate about the following:[4]

1. Who are the customers? The customers may be children, older adults, women, or patients in the hospital. This group or these groups must be identified before any serious strategic analysis of the organization can be initiated.
2. What are the organization's principal services? Does the organization have unique experience and expertise in home health care, rehabilitation services, psychological counseling, open-heart surgery, or some other area of specialization?
3. Where does the organization intend to compete? Is the case about a small group medical practice that competes in only one local market or is it a regional or national force in the delivery of health care services?
4. Who are the competitors? Is the case about an academic research and teaching hospital with a few well-known competitors or does the hospital operate in a market along with other rural hospitals? In other words, how much competition is actually present in the market(s) where the organization competes or intends to compete?
5. What is the preference of the organization with regard to its public image? If the long-term-care facility wants to be perceived in certain ways it may have to limit its options when defining and solving strategic issues. Is it, for example, important to the home's leadership that it be regarded as a uniquely "caring" or "affordable" citizen of the community or is the mere fact that it creates a large number of jobs sufficient?
6. What does the organization want to be like in the future? Does the information in the case indicate that the organization wants to continue to operate as it does at the present time or does it wish to expand its markets and services offered or, even change its own basic operating philosophy?

If a formal mission statement is not presented in a case, it is important to attempt to construct one from the information given.

Objectives: More Specific Directions

Mission statements are broad and provide general direction. Objectives should be specific and explicitly point to where the organization is expected to be at a particular time in the future. Sometimes the case will indicate what the health care organization plans to achieve in the next year, where it hopes to be in three years, or even its five year objectives. As with mission statements, if the objectives are not explicitly stated, there is a need to speculate about them, because they will be the standards against which the success or failure of a particular strategy will be evaluated.

When constructing or modifying hospital or other health care organization objectives, be sure they are as measurable as possible. This is important so that decision makers can use them as a reflection of organizational priorities and as a way of determining how to set their own personal and professional priorities. Make sure that the objectives are motivational and inspirational, yet feasible and attainable. Moreover because strategic management is futuristic, and no one can predict the future with complete accuracy, objectives should always be adaptable to the changing conditions taking place in the organization and in the industry. Sometimes an organization will have to face a major strategic problem simply because it was unwilling to alter its objectives in light of changing conditions in the industry.

As a test of understanding of the case and the health care organization under examination, before attacking problems, reflect on what an initial reading of the case reveals about the mission and objectives of the organization:

- Identify two or three of the primary values of the organization and speculate about the type of objectives it would like to accomplish. How important, for example, is the quality as well as the quantity of medical services delivered by the organization?
- Speculate about the indicators that should be used to judge whether or not the values are being realized and objectives are being accomplished. Is there an adequate means of professional review and evaluation to ensure outcomes are really achieved and that the basic values are not simply given lip service?
- Are the aspirations of the organization's managers realistic in view of the competition and the organization's strengths and weaknesses?
- Are the objectives being pursued consistent with what you understand to be the mission of the organization?

If the questions raised cannot be easily answered, reread the case yet again.

FINDING PROBLEMS AND OPPORTUNITIES

Situation analysis is designed to surface present and potential problems. In case analysis, problems include not only the usual idea of a "problem" but also situations where things may be working well but improvements are possible. As noted previously, the "problem" may actually be an opportunity that can be capitalized on by the organization if it acts consciously and decisively.

When we analyze things carefully, patterns can be detected and discrepancies between what actually is and what ought to be become more apparent. In other words, fundamental issues, not mere symptoms, begin to emerge.

Looking for Real Causes Not Symptoms

It is important to realize that the things observed in an organization and reported in a case may not be the "real" or essential problems and opportunities. Often what we observe are the symptoms of more serious core problems. For example, increasing interest rates and cash flow discrepancies appear to be problems in many case analyses. In reality, the problem is the fundamental absence of adequate financial planning. The lack of planning is simply manifested as a cash flow problem and increasing interest rates certainly complicate cash flow.

Frequently, hospitals conclude that they have operational problems in the area of marketing when bed occupancy rates decline. Someone may suggest that the marketing department is not doing a good job in convincing physicians to use the hospital. Sometimes people will complain that the hospital is not spending enough on promotion. The real problem, however, might be fundamental changes in the demographics of the market area or an outdated services mix that no amount of promotion will overcome. In organizations as complex as health care facilities, problems may have more than a single cause, so do not be overly confident when a single, simple reason is isolated. In fact, the suggestion of a simple solution should increase rather than decrease skepticism.

Getting to core problems requires that information be carefully examined and analyzed. Often quantitative tools can help. Financial ratio analysis of the exhibits included in the case will sometimes be helpful in the identification of the real problems. Appendix B illustrates how financial analysis and information can be used to identify core problems in an organization.

In arriving at the ultimate determination of core problems, case analysis should never be "paralyzed by analysis" and waste more time than is necessary on identifying problems. At the same time premature judgments about problem areas should not be made because of the risk of missing the "real" issues.

Always review the obtainable sources of data before moving to the next step. One general guideline is that when research and analysis cease to generate surprises the analyst can feel relatively, but not absolutely, sure that adequate research has been conducted and the core problems have been identified.

The threat and opportunity discovery process should not become myopic. There may be a tendency on the part of individuals interested and experienced in accounting and finance to see all problems in terms of accounting and finance. A physician approaching the same case will likely focus on the medical implications. This is too limited a view for effective strategic decision makers. Strategic analysis is the work of "general managers" or those who effectively transcend a single function.

Successful case analysis depends on correctly identifying issues. Insistence on approaching case analysis exclusively from the viewpoint of one's own expertise and training is not likely to produce an accurate overall picture of the situation facing the organization nor is this approach likely to improve the organization's performance.

Never accept information, either given or obtained, at face value. The ratios on a hospital's financial statements may look strange, but are they? Before jumping to such a conclusion, look at the financial ratios in a historical perspective. Even better, look at the history (as well as similar ratios) of other hospitals of the same nature during the same time period.

Identifying Important Issues

Once the problems are identified they must be precisely stated and the selection defended. The best defense for the selection of the core problem is the data set used to guide the problem discovery process. The reasons for selection of the problems and issues should be briefly and specifically summarized along with the supportive information on which judgments have been based.

The problem statement stage is not the time for solutions. Focusing on solutions at this point will reduce the impact of the problem statement. If the role of consultant has been assumed, the problem statement must be convincing, precise, and logical to the client organization, or credibility will be reduced. If the role of the strategic decision maker has been selected you must be equally convincing and precise. The strategic decision maker should be as sure as possible that the correct problems have been identified in order to pursue the appropriate opportunities. After all, the manager will be the one responsible for ensuring things actually happen and strategies are implemented.

The statement of the problem should relate only to those areas of strategy and operations where actions have a chance of producing results. The results may be either increasing gains or cutting potential losses. Long- and short-range aspects of problems should be identified and stated. In strategic analysis, the emphasis is on long-range problems rather than merely patching up emergencies and holding things together.

It is important to keep in mind that most strategic decision makers can deal with only a limited number of issues at a single time. Therefore, identify key result areas that will have the greatest positive impact on organizational performance.

ANALYSIS

When the problem(s) in the case are satisfactorily defined it must be analyzed. This involves (1) developing a theoretical perspective, (2) generating alternative solutions or actions, and (3) evaluating the alternatives.

Developing a Perspective

One of the most serious mistakes made in case analysis is to attempt analysis inside a "theoretical vacuum." Although strategic management is not highly theoretical compared to other areas of management, it is important that the problems be defined and opportunities be evaluated according to some consistent theoretical perspective.

Are the problems the kind that cash flow analysis can assist in solving? Are the strategic issues facing the firm problems of leadership, organization, or control? It might be that problems concerning lack of revenue growth are really problems of not responding adequately to patient needs – the lack of a marketing orientation. In the past, health care organizations have tended to disregard the importance of the "strategic decision" to focus on patients.

Many revenue short falls could be resolved with the use of the relatively simple marketing philosophy. A proper theoretical perspective, for example, might suggest that patients are less concerned with the location of a clinic than they are with how they are treated when they arrive.

Alternative Actions and Solutions

If the job of obtaining and organizing information has been done well, the generation of alternatives will be a challenging yet attainable task. To investigate options, the given and obtained information must be matched with what is known about financial analysis, statistics, marketing, and management so that actions that are promising, feasible, and consistent with the mission can be generated.

Good alternatives possess specific characteristics. They should be *practical* or no one will seriously consider them. Alternative courses of action that are too theoretical or abstract to be understood by those who have to accomplish them are not useful. Alternatives should be *carefully stated* with a brief justification as to why they are useful ways of solving at least one of the core problems in the case.

Alternatives should be *specific*. Relate each alternative to the core problem it is intended to address. This is a good check on your work. If the alternatives generated do not directly address core problems, ask how important they are to the case analysis.

Finally, alternatives should be *usable*. A usable alternative is one that can be reasonably accomplished within the constraints of the financial and human resources available to the organization. Alternatives should be ones that can be *placed into action* in a relatively short period of time. If it takes too long to implement a proposed solution, it is likely that the momentum of the recommended action will be lost. Of course, implementation should always take place in light of potential long-range effects of shorter term decisions.

After the alternatives have been generated and listed, each one must be (1) evaluated in terms of the core problems and key result areas isolated in the prior analysis, (2) evaluated in terms of its relative advantage or disadvantage compared to other possible solutions to core problems, and (3) justified as a potentially valuable way of addressing the strategic issues found in the case.

Evaluating Alternatives

Alternatives should be evaluated according to both quantitative and qualitative criteria. Financial analysis provides one basis for examining the impact of different courses of action. However, a good alternative course of action is more than merely the one with the highest payoff. It may be that the culture of the organization cannot accommodate some of the more financially promising alternative courses of action.

For example, an established policy and practice in the organization may tolerate no more than a certain percentage of debt financing. Although the financial analysis illustrates that additional debt is a low-cost way to finance expansion, top management can be expected to reject the level of debt required, which will make other options necessary. On the more qualitative side, a hospital with a reputation for avoiding layoffs at all costs could be expected to reject any strategic alternative that involves closing part of the facility and reducing staff.

Once the alternatives have been evaluated, one must be selected. At this point it is *absolutely essential* to completely understand the criteria upon which the selection is being made and the justification for the criteria. Sometimes the key to identifying the criteria is in the case itself. The chief executive officer may have clearly stated the basis on which decisions are to be made.

At other times it is necessary to look outside to what is going on in the industry. Is competition for services so fierce that capital investment decisions are likely to radically affect our ability to compete with other organizations? If so, should the hospital intentionally postpone short-term actions to ensure sufficient resources are dedicated to the modernization of facilities and the purchase of up-to-date technologies to improve the chances of long-range growth and development?

Action Planning

Once the strategic alternative(s) has been selected, an action plan is required. Action planning moves the decision maker from the realm of strategy to operations. Now the question becomes, "How do we get all this done in the most effective and efficient way possible?"

The task of case analysis does not require that the student implement a decision in a real firm. However, because our alternatives must be "implementable" it is necessary that thought be given to how each alternative would actually be put into action. This is called *action planning* and requires three important steps for each recommended alternative. First, the decision maker must decide what activities are needed to accomplish the alternative action. This involves thinking through the process and outlining all the steps that will be required.

Next, the list of required activities should be carefully reviewed and tasks should be grouped into logical patterns. Those that relate to accounting go into one group, medical service delivery activities go into another, and financial activities go into a third. Each itemized activity must be placed into such a group and any activities that do not fit neatly into the existing organization should be placed in another category of miscellaneous tasks. (If this "other" list is too long it may suggest that the structure of the organization needs revision.)

Finally, the responsibility for accomplishing the different groups of tasks must be clearly assigned to the appropriate individuals in the organization. Although this is not always possible in case analysis, it is important that consideration be given to how, in a real organization, the recommendations would be accomplished. If, in the process of thinking about getting the different activities completed, it becomes apparent that the organization lacks the resources or the structure to accomplish the recommendations, other approaches should be proposed.

The process of action planning should never be neglected. Organizations sometimes spend large amounts of money and resources developing strategic plans only to discover that they are not prepared to implement them in an effective manner.

MAKING RECOMMENDATIONS

Making good recommendations is a critical aspect of successful case analysis. If recommendations are theoretically sound and justifiable, people will pay attention to them. If they are not, little is likely to result from all the work done to this point.

One effective method for presenting recommendations is to relate each one to organizational strengths. Or, if necessary, a recommendation can illustrate how it assists in avoiding known weaknesses. If the organization has sufficient financial strength, the recommendations should highlight how each alternative will capitalize on the strong financial condition. If, on the other hand, the marketing resources are limited, it will be important to avoid recommendations that rely on resources that are not available.

It will be particularly useful to ask the following questions when making recommendations:

1. Does the health care organization have the financial resources needed to make the recommendation work?
2. Does the organization have the personnel to accomplish what will be required by each recommendation?
3. Does the organization have the controls needed to monitor whether or not the recommendations are being accomplished?
4. Is the timing right to implement each recommendation? If not, when will the timing be right? Can the organization afford to wait?

FINALIZING THE REPORT

The preparation and presentation of the case report is the final part of case analysis. The report can be either written or oral depending on the preference of the instructor. Although the form is slightly different, the goal is the same – to summarize and communicate in an effective manner what the analysis has uncovered. This final section will provide only a brief outline of how to construct and present a case report. Appendix C deals with oral presentations in greater detail.

Decision making is the intended result of the report. The analysis must be complete but the emphasis should be on making the entire report brief enough that people will read it and at the same time comprehensive enough to ensure no major factors are overlooked that might adversely affect the decision. A brief outline of the important sections of a case analysis report follows.

Executive Summary

One of the most important things a case can teach prospective managers is how to organize and present ideas in a short, concise, pervasive manner. Always keep in mind that the reader is a busy person who needs information about the case. At the same time, the reader wants the essential facts quickly.

One of the most important parts of a written case report is the executive summary. This brief section (usually one page and rarely more than two pages) functions as an abstract. Its purpose is to force the writer to carefully evaluate what is really important in all the accumulated facts and data and to familiarize the reader with the organization and the industry.

The executive summary should clearly state the major problems and opportunities facing the organization. The outline of strategic issues should be followed by a list of recommendations and a brief justification for each. This summary will allow the reader to quickly see what has been done and help the reader see the logic in the following report. In addition, it forces the analyst to think about the organization's problems and formulate recommendations in a direct manner rather than hiding them away in the body of the case report.

Body of the Case Report

The body of the case analysis should be broken into several sections. The first section should report what you found in the *situational analysis*. What is the state of the organization today? What type of industry is it in, and what is happening with regard to the competition?

The *strategic problems* should be introduced after the situational analysis. In this section, the three to five most important strategic issues facing the firm should be listed and a justification provided for the inclusion of each. Consideration should also be given to the operational strengths and weaknesses inside the organization and how they relate to the basic strategic problems.

It is a particularly good practice when matching the strategic issues and the organization's strengths and weaknesses to think about the structure and the personnel. When the strategic issues are presented, it will be useful to outline them in terms of the functional areas of the organization most critical for the implementation of the recommendation. Therefore, the body of the report should include careful consideration of the production, financial, marketing, information processing, and human resources implications of the different recommended courses of action.

This final point is particularly important. All strategic actions must ultimately be accomplished by people. Therefore, the action plan for accomplishing recommended courses of action should include an audit of the individual capabilities required to ensure the actions are taken. Who will be responsible for getting each of the recommendations accomplished? Is this individual likely to have the skills required to complete the task? If not, what actions will be necessary before the recommendation is fully implemented?

In view of the strategic *problems* and the operational condition of the organization, the *alternative* courses of action can now be generated and listed. Each of the alternatives can then be *evaluated*. When the evaluation is complete, the *recommendations* should be presented in considerable detail and particular attention should be given to the problem of *implementation*. When writing a formal case analysis remember the following points:

1. Do a professional job of designing and preparing the report. Get a good typist or be sure you use a word processor with a good ribbon or cartridge. If graphs and related tabular material are used, make sure the figures are drawn well, the words are spelled correctly, and the tables are neat. Face it, nothing is going to affect the creditability of your analysis more than how it looks! One misspelled word can destroy the confidence of the reader in the entire report.
2. Put yourself in the reader's place. It takes only a little extra effort to anticipate potential problems for those who read the analysis. The more problems that can be eliminated, the more favorable the ultimate evaluation will be. Make the sections as short as possible. Use subheadings to make the reading more interesting.
3. Get the reader interested and never lose the initiative. It is a good idea to use a hard hitting or witty introduction to create a favorable initial impression. The careful use of charts, tables, and other visual aids is well worth the time, energy, and expense.

Always provide a list of sources that might be useful to decision makers so they can follow up on points made in the body of the report. Do not attempt to impress the professor with the length of the reading list used in compiling the references. To the contrary, find some very good sources that apply to the case analysis and list these valuable sources in a way that any reader who wishes to do so can follow up on them.

It is particularly helpful to abstract the most useful sources. This will not do away with the reader's need to review the sources, but it will help him or her decide precisely which sources need to be read in greater detail.

CONCLUSIONS

Case analysis is an art. There is no one precise way to accomplish the task. Adapt the analysis to the case problem under review. The thing to keep in mind is that case analysis is a logical process that involves (1) understanding the organization, industry, and environment; (2) clearly defining strategic problems and opportunities; (3) generating alternative courses of action; (4) analyzing, evaluating, and recommending the most promising courses of action; (5) and providing at least some consideration of the operational aspects of how and by whom the recommendations will be accomplished.

The work of case analysis is not over until all these stages are completed. Often a formal written report or oral presentation of the recommendations is required. Case analysis and presentation should always be approached and accomplished in a professional manner. Case problems provide a unique opportunity to integrate all you have learned about decision making and direct it toward specific problems and opportunities faced by real organizations. It is an exciting way to gain experience and decision-making skills. Take it seriously and develop your own, systematic, and defensible way of solving management problems.

NOTES

1. Frank Cerne and Rhonda Bergman, "Memorial Hospital: Rebuilding Physician, Community Support," *Hospital and Health Networks* (July 20, 1993), pp. 20–22.
2. "Chains Put on New Face Ahead of Looming Reform," *Modern Healthcare* 23, no. 14 (April 5, 1993), pp. 30–32.
3. Peter F. Drucker, *Management: Tasks, Responsibilities, and Practices* (New York: Harper and Row, 1974).
4. John Pearce, II and Fred David, "Corporate Mission Statements: The Bottom Line," *Academy of Management Executive* (May 1987), pp. 109–116.

ADDITIONAL SOURCES OF INTEREST

Edge, Alfred G., and Denis R. Coleman, *The Guide to Case Analysis and Reporting,* 3d ed. (Honolulu System Logic, 1986).

Ronstadt, Robert, *The Art of Case Analysis,* (Dover, Massachusetts: Lord Publishing, 1980).

Financial Analysis for Health Care Organizations

by Mahmud Hassan

The purpose of this appendix is to explain some basic concepts of finance as they relate to health care. Finance in health care does not require a different methodology but it does occur in a different context. Unlike most other sectors of the economy, the health industry is composed of both for-profit and not-for-profit organizations. In addition, it is extremely technology dependent and heavily regulated by the government. These special characteristics of the industry have prompted the development of innovative ways to survive and grow financially.

To analyze the financial health of a hospital, long term care, or other health care organization, you need to understand how to read the financial statements. The income statement and balance sheet are the two most important financial reports of an organization. Not-for-profit organizations do not produce income statements, but they may prepare balance sheets. In this appendix, we will compute financial ratios, net income, and other financial performances for Memorial Hospital, a for-profit hospital company, for the years 1993 and 1994. The detailed financial statements are available in the *Annual Report* of Memorial Hospital. Copies of these statements are shown in Exhibits B–1 and B–2 (the notes that accompany the statements can be found in the *Annual Report* and are an integral part of the financial statements).

As previously mentioned, not-for-profit organizations are not required to prepare balance sheets or income statements. However, some not-for-profit health care organizations do prepare balance sheets to satisfy requirements of the Securities and Exchange Commission (SEC) and the rating agencies (Moody's or Standard & Poor's) when they borrow money by selling bonds. For example, University Hospital (a not-for-profit organization) borrowed money in 1994 from

EXHIBIT B–1

Consolidated Statement of Income (in thousands of dollars except per share results)

	1992	1993	1994
Revenues	$2,973,643	$3,435,397	$4,087,994
Operating expenses	2,340,178	2,786,230	3,401,884
Depreciation and amortization	180,197	195,651	209,469
Interest expense	154,156	145,938	138,477
Interest income	(30,923)	(46,064)	(60,570)
	2,643,608	3,081,755	3,689,260
Income before income taxes	330,035	353,642	398,734
Provision for income taxes	147,196	126,602	142,747
Income before extraordinary items and cumulative effect of a change in accounting principle	182,839	227,040	255,987
Extraordinary loss on early extinguishment of debt, net of income tax of $9,597	—	(16,133)	—
Cumulative effect on prior years of a change in accounting principle for retirement plan actuarial gains, net of income tax of $9,645	—	16,214	—
Net income	$ 182,839	$ 227,121	$ 255,987
Earnings per common share:			
Income before extraordinary item and cumulative effect of a change in accounting principle	$1.86	$2.30	$2.56
Extraordinary loss on early extinguishment of debt	—	(.16)	—
Cumulative effect on prior years of a change in accounting principle for retirement plan actuarial gains	—	.16	—
Net income per share	$1.86	$2.30	$2.56

EXHIBIT B-2

Memorial Hospital Consolidated Balance Sheet
(in thousands of dollars except per share amounts)

	1993	1994
Assets		
Current assets		
Cash and cash equivalents	$140,202	$105,340
Marketable securities	106,490	79,104
Accounts receivable less allowance for loss of		
$157,505—1994 and $110,909—1993	507,141	616,210
Inventories	69,786	80,632
Other current assets	104,788	133,615
Total current assets	928,407	1,014,901
Property and equipment, at cost		
Land	168,761	177,275
Buildings	1,678,685	1,759,959
Equipment	1,086,374	1,211,401
Construction in progress (estimated cost to complete		
and equip after August 31, 1994—$114,000)	41,729	57,719
Gross fixed assets	2,975,549	3,206,354
Less accumulated depreciation	987,790	1,154,868
Net fixed assets	1,987,759	2,051,486
Investments of insurance and health plan subsidiaries	315,875	462,541
Other assets	189,921	167,646
Total assets	$3,421,962	$3,696,574
Liabilities and common stockholders' equity		
Current liabilities		
Trade accounts payable	$107,666	$115,338
Salaries, wages, and other compensation	82,184	95,760
Other accrued expenses	173,956	229,201
Medical claims reserves	141,773	194,925
Income taxes	95,475	106,241
Long-term debt due within one year	32,680	35,045
Total current liabilities	633,734	776,510
Long-term debt	1,210,618	1,140,366
Deferred credits and other liabilities	422,993	452,722

EXHIBIT B–2 cont'd

	1993	1994
Common stockholders' equity		
Common stock, 16 2/3¢ par; authorized 200 million shares; issued and outstanding 98,438,852 shares—1994 and 97,886,147 shares—1993	16,314	16,406
Capital in excess of par value	233,898	243,398
Other adjustments	(11,047)	(11,029)
Retained earnings	915,452	1,078,201
Stockholders' equity	1,154,617	1,326,976
Total liabilities and stockholders' equity	$3,421,962	$3,696,574

the capital market by selling bonds. It had to prepare a balance sheet for three years, 1991 through 1993, to have its bonds rated. The balance sheet for University Hospital is shown in Exhibit B–3. Publicly traded for-profit hospitals are required by their charters to produce balance sheets and income statements each year. As mentioned earlier, we will analyze the financial statements of Memorial Hospital in this appendix.

The contents of balance sheets vary by company depending on the nature of the business and the type of ownership. The balance sheet of Memorial contains some information regarding investments in subsidiaries, while the not-for-profit University Hospital reported a trust fund in its balance sheet. Not-for-profit organizations show their equity share as a fund balance. For University Hospital, the amount of equity investment in 1993 was nearly $185 million, as shown in Exhibit B–3 under "fund balance." All other items in Exhibit B–3 are comparable with those in Exhibit B–2.

Financial ratios for University Hospital can be computed using the same formulas as shown for Memorial Hospital, but some financial ratios will require information from income statements. Because not-for-profit hospitals do not prepare income statements, the ratios for days in accounts receivable, average payment period, days' cash on hand, times interest earned, debt service coverage, operating margin, markup, return on assets, and so on, cannot be computed for University Hospital.

In addition to the analysis of the income statement and balance sheet, we have provided an analysis of the cost of capital. This is an important topic for the health care industry because of its dependence on technology and because of reimbursement issues involving third-party payers.

EXHIBIT B-3
University Hospital Balance Sheet

	Fiscal Year Ended September 30		
	1991	1992	1993
Assets			
Current assets			
Cash and short-term investments	$5,768,785	$7,184,131	$2,084,610
Accounts receivable	51,415,071	40,085,497	53,338,410
Inventory	1,518,012	2,097,327	2,677,247
Prepaid expenses and other current assets	6,971	0	0
Total current assets	58,708,839	49,366,955	58,100,267
Property, plant, and equipment	171,270,793	197,572,904	212,140,823
Less accumulated depreciation	61,175,801	72,626,040	85,433,535
Net property, plant, and equipment	110,094,992	124,946,864	126,707,288
Capital fund	23,233,852	26,730,346	20,657,000
Trustee funds	6,992,981	6,731,182	7,034,719
Total assets	$199,030,664	$207,775,347	$212,499,274
Liabilities and fund balance			
Current liabilities			
Accounts payable	$2,684,893	$3,911,504	$2,638,836
Accrued salaries	462,326	663,161	1,084,692
Advances from third-party payers	1,051,000	0	0
Deferred revenue	61,561	85,554	85,554
Current portion of long-term debt	2,022,140	2,068,744	1,659,565
Other current liabilities	69,623	17,038	561,853
Accrued interest expense	983,277	805,688	768,511
Total current liabilities	7,334,820	7,551,689	6,799,011
Long-term debt	21,792,410	21,525,786	19,866,221
Fund balance	169,903,434	178,697,872	185,834,042
Total liabilities and fund balance	$199,030,664	$207,775,347	$212,499,274

THE INCOME STATEMENT

Income statements are prepared by proprietary hospitals for the computation of net profit and incurred tax. (A not-for-profit hospital is not required to prepare an income statement but it may choose to do so to keep its various constituencies informed. The IRS does require "informational reports" to be filed for not-for-profit organizations generating over $25,000 in revenue.)

The income statement shows all revenue receipts and expenditures during a year. Receipts are usually shown as gross revenue and net revenue. Net revenue is equal to gross revenue minus any uncollectibles such as contractual allowances, bad debt, charity care, and business discounts. In the case of Memorial, the net revenue for 1994 was (all figures for Memorial are in thousands of dollars):

Net revenue: $4,087,994

Memorial does not report gross revenue or uncollectibles.

Operating expenses represent selling, general, and administrative expenses.

Operating expense: $3,401,884

Depreciation and amortization are noncash expenses (there is no cash payment for these items, but a company uses them as expense items to compute taxable income) due to wear and tear or decline in the useful life of an asset. Depreciation can be on a straight-line basis or an accelerated basis. For straight-line depreciation, the assumption is that there will be equal wear and tear on the asset each year of its useful life. Accelerated depreciation assumes the wear and tear is high during initial years and declines over time.

Depreciation and amortization: $209,469

Interest expense is the amount paid to creditors on the total amount of debt the organization holds.

Interest expense: $138,477

Interest income is computed by subtracting dividends and capital gains from the investment income. In the case of Memorial, this amount is a positive quantity for 1994 and hence entered as a negative quantity in the expense category (see Exhibit B–1).

Interest income: $60,570

Income before income taxes can be computed by subtracting operating expense, depreciation, amortization, interest expense, and interest income from net revenue.

Income before income taxes: $398,734

Provision for state and federal taxes is computed at the statutory rate (35.8 percent for Memorial) on the income before income taxes.

Provision for income taxes: $142,747

Net income is computed by subtracting provision for income taxes and other adjustments from the income before taxes.

Net income: $255,987

THE BALANCE SHEET

A balance sheet is a statement of the financial status of an organization at a particular point in time (date). It is divided into two sides: assets are shown on the left side and liabilities and owners' equity are shown on the right side. Assets are divided into current assets and fixed assets. Current assets include cash, marketable securities, accounts receivable (less uncollectibles), inventories, and other current assets. Marketable securities are short-term government securities. Other current assets include prepaid expenses such as insurance premiums, advertising charges for the next year, and so on.

In the case of Memorial in 1994:

Cash and cash equivalents:	$105,340
Marketable securities:	79,104
Accounts receivable less uncollectibles:	616,210
Inventories:	80,632
Other current assets:	133,615
Total current assets:	1,014,901

In this case, cash equivalents include investments in securities with a maturity of three months or less.

Fixed assets are land, buildings, equipment, and construction in progress.

Land:	$177,275
Buildings:	1,759,959
Equipment:	1,211,401
Construction in progress:	57,719
Gross fixed assets:	3,206,354

Accumulated depreciation is the sum of all the depreciation expenses (as found in the income statement) since the inception of the organization.

Accumulated depreciation: $1,154,868

Net fixed assets are computed by subtracting the accumulated depreciation from the gross fixed assets.

Net fixed assets: $2,051,486

Memorial shows investments in its subsidiaries in a separate category:

Investments in insurance and health plan subsidiaries:	$462,541
Other assets:	167,646
Total assets:	$3,696,574

On the other side of the balance sheet, liabilities include current liabilities, long-term liabilities, and other liabilities. Current liabilities are accounts payable, salaries, wages and other compensation payable, other accrued expenses, medical claim reserve, income taxes payable, and that portion of long-term debt due within one year. Other accrued expenses include any other unpaid amounts; medical claim reserves include outstanding claims from Memorial's insurance business.

Total current liabilities: $776,510

All debts not due within one year are listed under long-term debt.

Long-term debt: $1,140,366

Owners' equity includes the value of common stock outstanding (at par value), the value of the stocks in excess of par value, other adjustments in the value of stocks, and retained earnings. For not-for-profit hospitals, the owners' equity is represented by a fund balance. Retained earnings is the accumulated net income minus the amount of the dividends paid to shareholders.

Owners' equity: $1,326,976

FINANCIAL RATIOS

Thus far, different items on the income statement and balance sheet of Memorial have been explained. Now we can proceed with the computation of different financial ratios that are used to evaluate the financial health of an organization. The four types of financial ratios usually computed are liquidity ratios, capital/structure ratios, activity ratios, and profitability ratios.

Liquidity ratios consist of different measures of liquidity (how rapidly a noncash asset can be converted into cash without losing its value) and the cash position of an organization; capital/structure ratios include measures of leverage (the amount borrowed compared to the amount invested by owners) and equity (investment or ownership). Different types of efficiency measures are included in the activity ratios, and a variety of profitability measures (the extent to which income exceeds expenses) are included in the profitability ratios. Each of these four types of ratios are computed and described. The first example is for 1994 and the second example is for 1993.

Liquidity Ratios *

Current Ratio

$$\frac{\text{current assets}}{\text{current liabilities}} = \text{current ratio} \qquad \frac{1,014,901}{776,510} = 1.31 \qquad \frac{928,407}{633,734} = 1.46$$

Current ratio is one of the most widely used financial ratios. It represents the firm's ability to pay current financial obligations out of current assets. A

---

*In thousands of dollars except for ratios.

higher value of current ratio is better than a lower value. A value of 1.31 in 1994 means that for every dollar of current liability, Memorial has $1.31 in current assets. The value declined from 1.46 in 1993. This means that Memorial's liquidity (ability to pay financial claims) deteriorated in 1994. It is possible for a firm with a high current ratio to experience payment problems if its current assets are not available in liquid form (cash or short-term investments) in time to meet the current obligations. A large current ratio may also imply idle cash, too much investment in inventory, or bad collection policies resulting in large accounts receivable. To verify the possibility that a high current ratio may indicate overinvestment in current assets or a high number of days in accounts receivable, the current-asset turnover and inventory ratios should be analyzed. Hospitals with low current ratios can reduce the probability of short-term liquidity problems by carrying larger balances of liquid assets.

Quick Ratio

$$\frac{\text{current assets less inventory}}{\text{current liabilities}} = \text{quick ratio}$$

$$\frac{934,269}{776,510} = 1.20$$

$$\frac{858,621}{633,734} = 1.35$$

The quick ratio is a more stringent test of liquidity than the current ratio. A higher quick ratio implies a better liquidity position for the organization. However, because it includes accounts receivable, a high value could indicate a bad collection policy, and a low quick ratio is not necessarily indicative of a future liquidity problem. For example, a large accounts payable (due to construction) might result in a lower quick ratio, but the construction accounts payable does not require payment from the current assets. It is paid out of construction-in-progress assets. In the case of Memorial, the quick ratio declined from 1.35 in 1993 to 1.20 in 1994. This says that Memorial can pay off its current liabilities from its current assets without liquidating inventory, even though the quick ratio declined between 1993 and 1994.

Acid Test Ratio

$$\frac{\text{cash plus marketable securities}}{\text{current liabilities}} = \text{acid test ratio}$$

$$\frac{184,444}{776,510} = 0.24 \qquad \frac{246,692}{633,734} = 0.39$$

The acid test ratio is the most stringent test of liquidity. It measures the firm's ability to pay its current liabilities out of cash and marketable securities only. A high value is a good indication of a favorable liquidity position, although a very high value may imply too much idle cash and inefficient investment-portfolio management. The primary source of funds for paying current liabilities is usually collections from accounts receivable. Firms with large variances in collection of accounts receivable should maintain higher levels of cash and short-term investments, which would result in a higher acid test ratio. Memorial's acid test ratio declined from 0.39 in 1993 to 0.24 in 1994. This means that in 1994 Memorial could pay off $0.24 of every dollar of its current liabilities from its cash and marketable securities. An increase in the quick ratio and a decrease in the acid test ratio indicate an increase in the days in the accounts receivable ratio.

Days in Accounts Receivable Ratio

$$\frac{\text{net accounts receivable}}{\text{net revenue}} \times 365 = \text{days in A/R ratio}$$

$$\frac{616,210}{4,087,994} \times 365 = 55.00 \qquad \frac{507,141}{3,435,397} \times 365 = 53.88$$

This ratio represents the average collection period. The value for this ratio provides a measure of the average time that receivables are outstanding. A value of 55 in 1994 implies that a patient discharged from a Memorial hospital pays the bill on the 55th day from the date of his or her discharge. High values imply a longer collection period and thus a greater sum in accounts receivable. An increase in the number of days in the collection period may result in a shortage of cash. The short-term solution would be to borrow or to liquidate a part of the investment portfolio. A continuing increase in the collection period would require an increase in operating margin or equity financing. To reduce the A/R collection period, the health care organization might improve management of the business office and improve third-party payer relationships.

Average Payment Period Ratio

$$\frac{\text{current liabilities}}{\text{operating expenses} - \text{depreciation}} \times 365 = \text{average payment period ratio}$$

$$\frac{776,510}{3,401,884 - 209,469} \times 365 = 88.78$$

$$\frac{633,734}{2,786,230 - 195,651} \times 365 = 88.29$$

The average payment period ratio is the counterpart to the days in accounts receivable ratio. The average payment period provides a measure of the average time that elapses before current liabilities are paid. A high value for this ratio indicates a liquidity problem. Low values for this ratio may not always imply a good liquidity position; they might simply be due to a change in policy. For example, changing payroll from biweekly payments to weekly payments will decrease the value for this ratio. A very low value for this ratio might also indicate poor cash management, including poor investment-portfolio management. In both 1993 and 1994, Memorial took about 89 days to pay off its current liabilities.

Days' Cash-on-Hand Ratio

$$\frac{\text{cash } + \text{ marketable securities}}{\text{operating expenses } - \text{ depreciation}} \times 365 = \text{days' cash-on-hand ratio}$$

$$\frac{184{,}444}{3{,}401{,}884 \, - \, 209{,}469} \times 365 = 21.09$$

$$\frac{246{,}692}{2{,}786{,}230 \, - \, 195{,}651} \times 365 = 34.76$$

Days' cash-on-hand ratio measures the number of days of average cash expenses that a firm maintains in cash and marketable securities. A high value for this ratio implies a greater ability to meet short-term financial obligations. However, high values for the days' cash-on-hand ratio are not always in the best interest of the organization. They may imply overinvestment in liquid assets that have a very low rate of return.

An increase in days in accounts receivable ratio may be associated with a reduction in the days' cash-on-hand ratio. If the increase in days in accounts receivable ratio is permanent, some alternative financing may be necessary. In 1994, Memorial had 21 days of operating expenses in cash and marketable securities.

Capital-Structure Ratios

Equity Ratio

$$\frac{\text{fund balance or stockholders' equity}}{\text{total assets}} = \text{equity ratio}$$

$$\frac{1{,}326{,}976}{3{,}696{,}574} = 0.36 \qquad \frac{1{,}154{,}617}{3{,}421{,}962} = 0.34$$

The equity ratio measures the proportion of total assets that have been financed with equity. High values for this ratio imply that a greater amount of equity relative to debt has been used to finance the total assets. Creditors usually consider this a sign of good financial health because it means less debt and therefore less likelihood of insolvency.

A high equity ratio does not always imply solvency. Poor profitability may result in a cash-flow problem that weakens the liquidity position. Equity financing of 100 percent is not desirable because it increases the cost of capital. In practice, some mix of debt and equity is used to finance an organization's total assets. In 1994, Memorial invested $0.36 of its own funds in every dollar of total assets. The remaining $0.64 came from borrowed funds.

Long-Term Debt-to-Equity Ratio

$$\frac{\text{long-term debt}}{\text{fund balance or stockholders' equity}} = \text{long-term debt-to-equity ratio}$$

$$\frac{1,140,366}{1,326,976} = 0.86 \qquad \frac{1,210,610}{1,154,617} = 1.05$$

Long-term debt and equity are permanent capital because they are not repaid within one year. A higher ratio implies a greater amount of external capital in the form of debt relative to equity. This is viewed unfavorably by creditors, although a high long-term debt-to-equity ratio may not prohibit future debt financing (nor does a low ratio guarantee a favorable credit line). The ability to repay debt, rather than the amount of debt, is the important issue. A high long-term debt-to-equity ratio can be risky for an organization if it has high and stable values for debt service coverage (loan payments) and low times-interest-earned ratios. In 1994, Memorial had $0.86 in long-term debt for every dollar of its own fund. The value had declined somewhat in 1994 from $1.05 in 1993. This is an indication of a more favorable financial condition for Memorial in 1994.

Fixed-Asset Financing Ratio

$$\frac{\text{long-term debt}}{\text{net fixed assets}} = \text{fixed-asset financing ratio}$$

$$\frac{1,140,366}{2,051,486} = 0.56 \qquad \frac{1,210,618}{1,987,759} = 0.61$$

The fixed-asset financing ratio measures the extent of long-term debt invested in fixed assets. A high value is considered by creditors to be an indicator of future debt repayment problems. The numerator of the ratio represents a future demand for cash and the denominator is the source to generate that cash in the form of depreciation charges. In 1994, 56 percent of Memorial's net fixed assets were funded by long-term debt.

High values for the fixed-asset financing ratio are associated with low equity financing and high long-term debt-to-equity ratios. The risk of insolvency due to a high value of the fixed asset ratio can be partially offset by achieving high values for the times-interest-earned and the high debt service coverage ratios.

Times-Interest-Earned Ratio

$$\frac{\text{excess of revenues over expenses} + \text{interest expense}}{\text{interest expense}} = \text{times-interest-earned ratio}$$

$$\frac{686,110 + 138,477}{138,477} = 5.95 \qquad \frac{649,167 + 145,938}{145,938} = 5.45$$

The times-interest-earned ratio measures the ability of a firm to pay its interest expense obligation. The higher the value, the better is the financial ability of the firm to pay its interest obligation. Note that this ratio does not measure the ability of the firm to repay the principal. Therefore, it is important to consider both the times-interest-earned and debt service coverage ratios when evaluating a firm's ability to pay its total debt obligation (interest expense plus principal payment).

Debt Service Coverage Ratio

$$\frac{\text{excess of revenues over expenses + depreciation + interest}}{\text{principal payment + interest expense}} = \frac{\text{debt service}}{\text{coverage ratio}}$$

$$\frac{686{,}110 + 209{,}469 + 138{,}477}{63{,}980 + 138{,}477} = 5.11$$

$$\frac{649{,}167 + 195{,}651 + 145{,}938}{256{,}387 + 145{,}938} = 2.46$$

(*Note:* Principal payments for 1994 and 1993, respectively, are $63,980 and $256,387. These are not shown in the financial statements here but are provided in the detailed cash-flow statements shown in Memorial's 1994 *Annual Report.*)

The debt service coverage ratio measures the firm's ability to pay its total debt obligation (both interest and principal). High values are considered favorably by creditors. However, this interpretation could be misleading in some cases, especially in the early years of a capital-expansion program when debt principal is not yet due but the depreciation expense has started. In this situation, the times-interest-earned and the fixed-asset financing ratios are better measures of the debt repayment ability of a firm.

It is important to maintain a high debt service coverage when new debt financing is being considered. The ability to attract debt capital with favorable terms may be related to past debt service coverage ratios.

Activity Ratios

Asset Turnover Ratio

$$\frac{\text{total revenue}}{\text{total assets}} = \text{asset turnover ratio}$$

$$\frac{4{,}087{,}994}{3{,}696{,}574} = 1.11$$

$$\frac{3{,}435{,}397}{3{,}421{,}962} = 1.00$$

The asset turnover ratio measures the dollar amount of revenue generated per dollar of investment. This is a measure of efficiency. Higher values for this ratio imply better usage of the available resources. In 1994, Memorial generated $1.11 in revenue for every dollar invested in assets. This ratio should not be the only criterion of efficiency because the age of the plant affects this ratio rather significantly. As the plant gets older, the book value of the asset, net of depreciation, gets smaller, resulting in a higher asset turnover ratio. The point is that the age of the plant needs to be considered when analyzing asset turnover ratios.

Fixed-Asset Turnover Ratio

$$\frac{\text{total revenue}}{\text{net fixed assets}} = \text{fixed-asset turnover ratio}$$

$$\frac{4,087,994}{2,051,486} = 1.99 \qquad \frac{3,435,397}{1,987,759} = 1.73$$

This ratio computes dollars of revenue generated for each dollar of investment in fixed assets. The items included in fixed assets are land, buildings, equipment, and furniture. It represents those assets not intended for sale that are used over and over again to provide the services of the hospital or other health care organization. High values for the fixed-asset turnover ratio are usually regarded as a positive indication of operating efficiency.

The fixed-asset turnover ratio is also likely to be affected by the age of the plant, as in the case of the asset-turnover ratio. The fixed-asset turnover ratio decreases immediately after an expansion or replacement program.

Current-Asset Turnover Ratio

$$\frac{\text{total revenue}}{\text{current assets}} = \text{current-asset turnover ratio}$$

$$\frac{4,087,994}{1,014,901} = 4.03 \qquad \frac{3,435,397}{928,407} = 3.70$$

The current-asset turnover ratio measures the dollars of revenue generated per dollar of investment in current assets. The lower the investment in current assets and the higher the current-asset turnover ratio, the more efficient is the organization. This does not imply that the investment in current assets should be cut to a minimum; that would cause delivery of services to be impaired, which would create severe short-term operating problems.

A high value for the current-asset turnover ratio is better than a low value, but a lower value might be the result of an expansion program during which the hospital holds more liquid assets. A low or high value for the current-asset turnover ratio can be further investigated and diagnosed by analyzing the days' cash-on-hand ratio, the days in accounts receivable ratio, and the inventory turnover ratio.

Inventory Turnover Ratio

$$\frac{\text{total revenue}}{\text{inventory}} = \text{inventory turnover ratio}$$

$$\frac{4,087,994}{80,632} = 50.70 \qquad \frac{3,435,397}{69,786} = 49.23$$

An inventory turnover ratio measures the dollars of revenue generated per dollar of investment in inventory. A higher value for this ratio indicates operating efficiency because the organization is not tying up a lot of money in inventory. Customer service (being out-of-stock) is not considered, however.

A hospital using just-in-time (JIT) inventory management would have a high inventory turnover ratio. Other reasons for low investment in inventory (resulting in a high inventory turnover ratio) include geographic location, access to suppliers, nonavailability of quantity discounts, and so on.

Profitability Ratios

Deductible Ratio

$$\frac{\text{gross revenue} - \text{net revenue}}{\text{gross revenue}} = \text{deductible ratio}$$

(Memorial does not report gross revenue.)

The deductible ratio measures the proportion of gross revenue that is not expected to be realized due to contractual allowances, bad debts, charity care, volume discounts, and so on. In the hospital industry, this ratio is very important because of the widespread presence of contractual allowances for insurers, HMOs, PPOs, and charity care to indigent patients. From a profitability point of view, increasing values of the deductible ratio result in lower profitability. A high deductible ratio may not imply poor profitability if the organization has high markup or a large amount of nonoperating revenue (philanthropic donations).

The deductible ratio should be closely monitored against changes in the collection process, reimbursement management, or the organization's charity care policy.

Markup Ratio

$$\frac{\text{gross revenue}}{\text{operating expenses}} = \text{markup ratio}$$

(Memorial does not report gross revenue.)

The markup ratio measures the multiples by which prices are set above expenses. Higher numbers for this ratio imply a higher price per dollar of expenses and the likelihood of achieving greater profitability. If a high markup ratio is associated with a high deductible ratio, then the hospital may not be any better off. Hospitals with relatively old plants and a high debt-to-principal payment schedule may need to maintain relatively high markup ratios. However, if markups are too high, the hospital may lose patients and eventually become insolvent. If it is too low, then the hospital may also become insolvent. The markup ratio is directly related to the operating margin ratio, the return on total asset ratio, the return on equity ratio, the debt service coverage ratio, and the times-interest-earned ratio. An increase in prices may improve profitability but, depending on the third-party payer mix, it may also increase the deductible ratio, driving profitability downward.

Operating Margin Ratio

$$\frac{\text{net income}}{\text{total revenue}} = \text{operating margin ratio}$$

$$\frac{255{,}987}{4{,}087{,}994} = 0.06 \qquad \frac{227{,}040}{3{,}435{,}397} = 0.07$$

This ratio is a measure of profitability. Alternative measures of profitability include return on total assets or return on equity. A low operating margin is not necessarily an indication of poor profitability if the hospital has significant nonoperating revenue from investment income, philanthropic donations, or any other sources. Improvement in the operating margin usually results in higher working capital, which in turn improves liquidity ratios.

Operating Margin Price-Level Adjusted Ratio

$$\frac{\text{net income} + \text{depreciation} - \text{price-level depreciation}}{\text{total revenue}} = \begin{array}{c}\text{operating margin} \\ \text{price-level} \\ \text{adjusted ratio}\end{array}$$

$$\frac{255{,}987 + 209{,}469 - 242{,}984}{4{,}087{,}994} = 0.05$$

$$\frac{227{,}040 + 195{,}651 - 219{,}129}{3{,}435{,}397} = 0.06$$

(*Note:* The age of the plant in 1994, as computed earlier, is six years. This indicates that investments in plant assets were made in 1988. Price-level depreciation is defined as the amount of annual depreciation expressed in the year of the investment. In this case, because the investments were made in 1988, the annual depreciation of 1993 and 1994 should be expressed in the 1988 dollar. According to the *Survey of Current Business,* the purchasing power of the dollar declined to 0.88 and 0.84 in 1993 and 1994, respectively, using 1988 as the reference year. Thus, a dollar in 1988 is worth only $0.88 in 1993 and $0.84 in 1994 due to inflation. The Consumer Price Index (CPI) for 1993 and 1994 was 1.12 and 1.16, respectively, using 1988 as the reference (base) year. The price-level depreciation for 1993 and 1994 is computed as the product of annual depreciation expenses and the CPI of each year.)

This ratio is the same as the operating margin ratio except the depreciation expenses are adjusted for inflation. When equipment is purchased, a depreciation schedule is developed that identifies the future deductions from the operating revenue for the depreciation expense. The dollar values posted are based on the year the equipment was acquired. Because of inflation, those posted dollar values can be worth less than the original estimate. Therefore, the operating margin should be computed to reflect the inflation-adjusted depreciation, not the originally estimated depreciation.

The higher the inflation, the higher is the inflation-adjusted depreciation, and hence the lower is the operating margin in the price-level adjusted ratio. In 1994, Memorial's operating margin ratio was 6 percent but after the depreciation expense was adjusted for inflation, the operating margin dropped to 5 percent.

Return on Total Assets (ROA)

$$\frac{\text{net income}}{\text{total assets}} = \text{return on total assets}$$

$$\frac{255{,}987}{3{,}696{,}574} = 0.07$$

$$\frac{227{,}040}{3{,}421{,}962} = 0.07$$

The return on total assets measures the amount of net income earned per dollar of investment in total assets. It is a measure of profitability. This ratio is affected by the age of the plant. A hospital with a relatively old and largely depreciated plant may show a higher return on assets ratio. If the hospital is planning a major replacement, this high profit rate may be misleading for creditors.

Return on Equity (ROE)

$$\frac{\text{net income}}{\text{fund balance or shareholders' equity}} = \text{return on equity}$$

$$\frac{255{,}987}{1{,}326{,}976} = 0.19 \qquad \frac{227{,}040}{1{,}154{,}617} = 0.20$$

This ratio, like the return on assets ratio, measures the extent of profitability but uses return on equity investment instead of total assets. Many analysts consider the return on equity as the primary test of profitability. Unless a satisfactory return on equity is generated, the hospital may find it very difficult to raise future equity capital by selling new shares. Not-for-profit hospitals may not be very interested in analyzing this ratio.

A high return on equity may not imply sound financial health, because the organization might have huge debt and earned the profit on monthly debt-financed (leased) assets. Further analysis of the return on equity ratio compared to the return on assets ratio would indicate the effect of debt-financed assets. If replacement needs are expected to be financed from operating income, the return on total assets ratio may be a better indicator of profitability than the return on equity ratio.

Other Financial Information

Age of the Facility

$$\frac{\text{accumulated depreciation}}{\text{depreciation expense}} = \text{age of the facility}$$

$$\frac{1{,}154{,}868}{209{,}469} = 5.51 \qquad \frac{987{,}790}{195{,}651} = 5.05$$

This is a very crude formula to estimate the age of the plant in years. It is more reliable using straight-line depreciation than accelerated depreciation. With the accelerated depreciation method, this formula tends to underestimate the age of newer plants and overestimate the age of older plants. When inflation is occurring, the formula underestimates the age of the plant because the annual depreciation expense increases with inflation.

Working Capital

$$\text{current assets} + \text{current liabilities} = \text{working capital}$$

$$\$1{,}014{,}901 + 776{,}510 = \$1{,}791{,}411$$

$$\$928{,}407 + 633{,}734 = \$1{,}562{,}141$$

The amount of working capital, defined as current assets plus current liabilities, is very important for an organization in its day-to-day operations. An organization's liquidity depends on the amount of working capital.

Net Working Capital

$$\text{current assets} - \text{current liabilities} = \text{net working capital}$$

$$\$1{,}014{,}901 - 776{,}510 = \$238{,}391$$

$$\$928{,}407 - 633{,}734 = \$294{,}673$$

Many analysts want to find out the net liquidity position (net working capital) of an organization. Net liquidity is computed by subtracting current liabilities from the current assets. If the organization were to pay its current obligations (current liabilities), how much working capital would be left? The answer is the net working capital.

The duPont System

Return on assets can be increased by a higher profit margin or higher asset turnover. To observe the dominant factors in return on assets, some analysts compute return on assets as the product of profit margin and asset turnover. Recall that the profit margin or operating margin ratio was computed as net income divided by total revenue and the asset turnover ratio was defined as total revenue divided by total assets. This can be written:

$$\text{return on assets}_{(\text{duPont})} = \frac{\text{net income}}{\text{total revenue}} \times \frac{\text{total revenue}}{\text{total asset}}$$

The return on assets computed in this manner is called the *duPont System* because it was developed by the duPont Company. This ratio can also be used to compute return on investment (ROI).

In the case of Memorial, the ROI using the duPont System for 1993 and 1994 were:

$$1993_{(\text{duPont})} \frac{227{,}040}{3{,}435{,}397} \times \frac{3{,}435{,}397}{3{,}421{,}962} = 0.07$$

ROI

$$1994_{(\text{duPont})} \frac{255{,}987}{4{,}087{,}994} \times \frac{4{,}087{,}994}{3{,}696{,}574} = 0.07$$

Limitations of Ratio Analysis

The financial ratios we have discussed provide valuable information concerning the financial health of an organization. We computed different ratios for Memorial for two consecutive years, which indicates changes in financial performance by the organization. However, every ratio can also be compared with national or regional averages that are available annually from the Financial Analysis Service (FAS) of the Healthcare Financial Management Association (HFMA). These national or regional averages are called the *standards* of the industry. An individual hospital's ratios are compared with these standards and financial performances are evaluated. If a hospital is older or newer than the rest of the hospitals in the region, then comparing its financial ratios with the regional averages is not quite as meaningful. Financial ratios reflect the activities of the firm in the past year or years. However, financial ratios do not reflect strategic planning by the hospital. It is possible that a hospital is going through a structural change to achieve future benefits, which would affect many of the ratios. Thus, the long-term planning of the hospital must be considered as well as the financial ratios. Using financial ratios alone may give the wrong signal to analysts.

The presence of severe inflation in the early or later years of a trend analysis makes the analysis less reliable. Values for the financial ratios also depend on the accounting practices and policies of the organization. For example, the value of investment in inventory depends on the valuation policies of the organization (first in, first out or last in, first out), the depreciation policies (straight-line or accelerated), which in turn determine the value of net assets, and so on. To the extent these policies vary, financial ratios will also vary

COST OF CAPITAL

When hospitals borrow money, they have to pay interest on the debt. If a hospital chooses to use its own funds for the acquisition or replacement of an asset, an opportunity cost is associated with that decision, called *the cost of equity*. In many cases, some combination of debt and equity is used to finance a capital investment. The weighted average cost of capital (WACC) is derived as an average cost of debt (k_d) and cost of equity (k_e). (A numerical example follows later in the section.)

$$\text{WACC} = Dk_d + (1 - D)k_e$$

where D is the ratio of debt to assets.

Some insurers reimburse hospitals on a cost basis so that a portion of the cost of debt (k_d) is considered a pass through. Assuming M is the proportion of cost-based reimbursement, the cost of debt is $(1 - M)k_d$. Some insurers pay on a cost-plus basis to for-profit hospitals where the payment above the cost represents some agreed upon (or at least known) return on equity. For-profit hospitals pay taxes on income at the current tax rate (t_c). Interest payments by for-profit hospitals work as a tax shield because tax liability decreases with an increase in interest payments. However, for-profit organizations have to pay taxes on any return they earn on their equity investment. Assuming k_e^m as the return on equity and m' as the proportion from the payer that uses the cost-plus basis, then the WACC for not-for-profit (np) and for-profit (fp) can be written as:

$$\text{WACC}_{np} = D(1 - M)k_d + (1 - D)K_e$$

$$\text{WACC}_{fp} = D(1 - M)(1 - t_c)k_d + (1 - D)(k_e - m'[1 - t_c]k_e^m)$$

COST OF DEBT

To compute the cost of debt (k_d), data must be collected on the types and amount of debt and the corresponding interest rates for different hospitals over several years. For each year, a weighted average cost of debt can be computed using the individual debt information. Assume that the cost of debt (k_d) for not-for-profit and for-profit hospitals in 1993 is 5.4 percent and 7.5 percent, respectively. Further assume that the proportion of payers who pay cost based *(M)* are 10 percent and 8 percent for not-for-profit and for-profit hospitals, respectively. The effective corporate tax rate (t_c) for the for-profit hospitals in 1994 is assumed to be 22 percent.

The cost of debt for the not-for-profit and for-profit hospitals can then be computed as

$$\text{Not-for profit cost of debt} = (1 - M)k_d$$

$$= (1 - 0.10)5.4$$

$$= 4.86 \text{ percent}$$

$$\text{For-profit cost of debt} = (1 - M)(1 - t_c)k_d$$

$$= (1 - 0.08)(1 - 0.22)7.5$$

$$= 5.38 \text{ percent}$$

The cost of debt is usually available from the for-profit hospital's annual reports. The cost of debt for not-for-profit hospitals is usually lower than for the for-profit hospitals. The reason is that the not-for-profit hospitals use tax-exempt revenue bonds to borrow money from the capital market.

COST OF EQUITY

Cost of equity can be estimated using the capital asset pricing model (CAPM). The expected rate of return on the share of equity i, $E(R_i)$, depends on the expected return on a market portfolio $E(R_m)$ and a risk-free bond rate R_f. Specifically,

$$E(R_i) = R_f + \beta_i[E(R_m) - R_f]$$

$$\text{where } \beta_i = \text{Cov}(R_i, R_m)/\text{Var}(R_m)$$

The expected rate of return on the share of i is the sum of the risk-free rate of return plus a risk premium. To compute the risk premium, $\beta_i[E(R_m) - R_i]$, we need an estimate of β_i for the hospital industry. Assume the β_i of the for-profit and not-for-profit hospitals is 1.41 and 1.46, respectively. Value line estimates beta of different companies on a periodic basis. The rate of return of the efficient market portfolio $E(R_m)$ and the risk-free rate of return R_f for 1993 are assumed to be 8.5 percent and 5.4 percent, respectively. These rates of return are available in the University of Chicago's Center for Research in Security Prices (CRSP) files.

Now, applying the CAPM equations, we can estimate the cost of equity for 1993 as

$$\text{For-Profit } E(R_i) = 5.4 + 1.41\ (8.5 - 5.4)$$

$$= 9.77 \text{ percent}$$

$$\text{Not-for-profit } E(R_i) = 5.4 + 1.46\ (8.5 - 5.4)$$

$$= 9.92 \text{ percent}$$

Note that cost of equity is greater than cost of debt. This makes sense because equity holders are residual claimants of the property in the case of bankruptcy. They take more risks; hence, the cost of equity is greater than the cost of debt.

WEIGHTED AVERAGE COST OF CAPITAL

Assuming the debt-to-asset ratio, D, for for-profit and not-for-profit hospitals is 0.53 and 0.48, respectively, the weighted average cost of capital (WACC) for 1993 can be estimated as

$$\text{WACC}_{np} = (0.48)(4.86) + (1 - 0.48)(9.92)$$

$$= 7.49 \text{ percent}$$

$$\text{WACC}_{fp} = (0.53)(5.38) + (1 - 0.53)(9.77)$$

$$= 7.44 \text{ percent}$$

REIMBURSEMENT UNDER THE PROSPECTIVE PAYMENT SYSTEM

On October 1, 1983, Medicare started reimbursing hospitals for inpatient nonphysician services under a DRG-based prospective payment system (PPS). Several types of hospitals were exempt from this DRG-based payment system, including psychiatric, rehabilitation, childrens, and long-term-care hospitals. About 500 DRGs have been identified from the International Classification of Diseases, 9th Revision, Clinical Modification (ICD-9-CM). Total payments made to a hospital under Medicare include two components: (1) prospective payment and (2) reasonable cost payment. Prospective payment is further divided into operating payment and capital payment. (Effective October 1, 1992, Medicare began using prospective payments for capital payments. Prior to this date, capital payments were paid on a reasonable cost basis.) Reasonable cost payment includes direct medical education costs, kidney acquisition costs, and outpatient costs.

Each of the DRGs has been assigned a weight to indicate the relative resource requirement to provide the service. For example, DRG 103 (heart transplant) has a weight of 14.0323 and DRG 320 (kidney and urinary tract infection) has a weight of 1.0002. This means that DRG 103 is about fourteen times more expensive than DRG 320. When the Health Care Financing Administration (HCFA) announced a nationwide payment for labor and nonlabor component of the operating payment every hospital in the country was preassigned a wage index for the labor component. Reimbursement for a particular DRG is computed as follows:

$$\text{Reimbursement} = \text{DRG weight} \times [(\text{ labor amount} \times \text{wage index })\\ + (\text{ nonlabor amount })]$$

The reimbursement may be further increased by an additional payment to cover the costs of indirect medical education, disproportionate share, and outlier payments. Teaching hospitals incur additional costs due to extra laboratory and other teaching demonstrations. The allowance for indirect medical education covers these additional costs. Hospitals that treat a large percentage of Medicare and Medicaid patients receive an additional payment under PPS. This additional payment is referred to as a disproportionate share payment. The outlier payments are additional payments for patients who use an unusually large amount of resources indicated by either a long length of stay or cost.

The capital component of the prospective payment that began on October 1, 1992, has a ten year phase-in period, blending federal and hospital components of payments. The hospital component of the capital costs include interest, depreciation, and lease costs. Taxes and insurance are also considered capital costs if they are related to capital assets. There is a federal payment for capital costs that is similar to the national rates for labor and nonlabor costs discussed earlier.

PHYSICIAN REIMBURSEMENT UNDER THE RESOURCE-BASED RELATIVE VALUE SCALE

Beginning January 1992, Medicare started paying physicians using a resource-based relative value scale (RBRVS). Physician services are categorized into approximately 7,000 different codes using the current procedural terminology (CPT). Resource-based relative value (RBRV) has three components: (1) a work unit that represents physician time, level of stress, and skill; (2) a unit of practice expense representing the costs of support personnel and office expense; and (3) a unit of cost that represents the cost of malpractice insurance.

The level of RBRV for a particular CPT code is obtained by adding the products of each of the three components and multiplying the RBRV by a conversion factor, determined by the Health Care Financing Administration each year. The products of the three factors are generated by multiplying the work unit, practice cost expense, and malpractice insurance cost by the regional cost index for each. The regional cost index is based on the difference in costs geographically as well as the inflation rate.

In Exhibit B–4 the Medicare's RBRV reimbursement for an office visit is computed. The physician's level of work depends on the predetermined CPT

EXHIBIT B-4

Physician Reimbursement for an Office Visit in San Francisco, 1993

1. Relative Value

Physician's work (based on CPT code)	1.19	
× Cost index	× 1.038	
Adjusted value		1.235
Practice expense (based on CPT code)	0.55	
× Cost index	× 1.303	
Adjusted value		0.717
Malpractice insurance (based on CPT code)	0.06	
× Cost index	× 1.370	
Adjusted value		0.082
Total value		2.034

2. Conversion factor (determined by HCFA each year)   × 31.25
3. Medicare's office visit reimbursement $63.57

---

codes. The example is for a CPT designated "mid-level" office visit (other options would include minimum-level and extensive office visits) for a San Francisco physician in 1993. The $63.57 reimbursement is significantly less than what the physician charged self-pay or insured patients. For this reason, many physicians limit the number of Medicare patients they accept; too many patients paying below practice costs means they close the practice.

ADDITIONAL REFERENCES

Asper, Elaine, and Mahmud Hassan. "The Impact of PPS Legislation on the Systematic Risk of Hospitals." *Journal of Economics and Finance* 17, no. 3 (Fall 1993), pp. 121–135.

Cleverley, William O., and Paul C. Nutt. "The Decision Process Used for Hospital Bond Rating—And Its Implications." *Health Services Research* 19, no. 5 (December 1984), pp. 615–637.

Cleverley, William O., and W. H. Rosegay. "Factors Affecting the Cost of Hospital Tax-Exempt Revenue Bonds." *Inquiry* 19 (Winter 1982), pp. 317–326.

Sloan, Frank A., Joseph Valvona, Mahmud Hassan, and Michael A. Morrisey. "Cost of Capital to the Hospital Sector." *Journal of Health Economics* 7, no. 1 (March 1988), pp. 25–45.

Presenting Information Orally in the Health Care Field

by Gary F. Kohut and Carol M. Baxter

The techniques for communicating information orally are similar whether you are presenting to a group of your peers, your supervisor, a group of community leaders, or members of the health care profession. At any time you might be called on to present a proposal to accept a new treatment, give a report to persuade higher management to adopt a new policy, or present a marketing status report. Regardless of the audience or the type of presentation, effective oral communication involves three major steps: planning, organizing, and delivering the subject matter.

PLANNING THE PRESENTATION

Three issues must be considered in the planning step: determine the purpose of your presentation, evaluate your audience, and consider the logistics involved in the presentation.

Purpose

Oral presentations are generally divided into two broad categories: informative and persuasive. Informative presentations generally are meant to convey information or ideas. Persuasive presentations involve "selling" an idea, product, or service to an audience. Included in the informative category are progress reports, instructions, and explanations. For example, you may give a progress report to your supervisor detailing your efforts on an assigned project, or you may give similar information to a small group if it is a team-related task. On the other hand, you may be directing a group of volunteers in a fund-raising effort, and as coordinator you may inform them about their responsibilities.

Many presentations in the health care field are instructional. For example, you might instruct individuals on how to operate a Magnetic Resonance Imaging (MRI) device, how to administer a new drug, or how to complete a new form required by Blue Cross/Blue Shield.

Explanatory presentations are also common in the health care industry. For example, you may be asked to explain features of a planned hospital wing to members of the media. Other examples of explanatory presentations include informing family members of a patient's condition and orienting new employees about the policies of a health care facility.

The second category, persuasive presentations, includes proposals and requests. For example, you may have to make a persuasive presentation to get authorization to purchase an expensive piece of equipment. Or, you may present a proposal to your supervisor to conduct market research about outpatients.

The best way to ensure that your purpose is clear is to write out a thesis or statement of purpose. This statement focuses the entire presentation. In other words, it serves the same purpose as a rudder of a ship: to keep you on course. Two examples of thesis statements follow:

- Today I will explain how to operate the (particular piece of equipment).
- I propose that we begin accepting patients from Monroe County for three reasons.

Once you have decided on the purpose of your presentation, you will need to know something about your audience.

Audience Analysis

Audience analysis is critical to ensuring that your information is accepted. Many presentations might be well delivered, but they fail because speakers do not anticipate audience reaction. You need to consider such characteristics as the size of the group, their level of knowledge about your subject, their interest in the material, their attitude and predispositions toward the subject, and their organizational relationship to you. For example, if your audience consists of five people, select a site that is small and personal when you present the information. If your audience is large, make sure all members can both hear and see the information you are presenting.

Although individuals within the health care industry tend to be very well educated, their technical expertise is usually very specific. Therefore, when planning a presentation, you must ask, "What does this audience already know about this subject?" Never assume that your audience is as knowledgeable about the topic as you are. You may want to ask yourself the following questions: What information will I use to impress my audience? Will I employ technical data, demonstrations, or statistical comparisons? Whatever information you use, care should be taken to reach your intended audience. This is particularly true when presenting ideas to lay people, who generally know much less about the material than health care professionals. Choose your vocabulary and your examples to meet the audience's needs. Within the industry, people tend to have high interest in their respective areas but may have less interest in subjects that affect them less directly. Lay people are often especially interested in their own health but may be easily confused about the technical details.

Every audience is unique. All audience members have different perceptions based upon personal experiences, which influence their attitudes about any subject. Understanding these predispositions will prevent your making bold assumptions that may offend the audience. For example, if your audience consists of people 60–75 years old, avoid any current slang lest you appear flippant and uncaring. Similarly, if your audience consists of young adults, avoid examples that they cannot understand because they have not experienced them. Because experience is such an important factor in understanding perceptions, you would not use the same explanations and examples with an audience of parents as with a childless audience. Good questions to ask when analyzing an audience are, What does this group want/need from me? and How can I give that to them?

Logistics

Before you can organize your presentation, you must consider some logistical concerns such as length and location. How much time will you need to give your presentation? Sometimes you have no control over how long you will speak, you are given a specific amount of time. In such cases, it is imperative that you stay within your time limit. When the time is exceeded, the audience becomes less receptive to your ideas. When given some choice over the length of a presentation, most speakers take too much time. Remember that it is difficult to hold people's attention beyond 20–30 minutes. To improve effectiveness, speakers need to watch the audience for verbal and nonverbal feedback to evaluate whether their message is being comprehended.

You also need to know where you will make the presentation. Will the presentation be made in an office, a conference room, a large auditorium, a fellowship hall, or a cafeteria? The location of your presentation will determine the kind of delivery and the types of visual aids you will use, as well as how you set up the room. Some guidelines for setting up your speaking site are as follows:

1. Arrange seating so that every member of your audience can see you and hear you. The horseshoe arrangement is preferred if the room and size of the audience will allow for it.
2. Check the lighting, heating/cooling and noise level of the site to ensure that your audience will be comfortable. Avoid high traffic areas that may cause your audience to be distracted.
3. Check any equipment you intend to use to be sure that it can be easily viewed or heard by your audience. Remember, if anything can go wrong, it generally will. Therefore, try to anticipate any problems before they occur.

ORGANIZING THE PRESENTATION

In an oral presentation your audience will probably not have the opportunity to refer to written material about your topic. Therefore, you must structure the information so that it is very easy to understand the first time it is heard. Every effective presentation has an introduction, a body, and a conclusion.

Introduction

Individuals tend to remember the beginning and end of presentations. For this reason, an introduction has to fulfill three major purposes: (1) gain attention, (2) establish rapport or goodwill with the audience, and (3) introduce the audience to the topic. The more specifically a speaker states what he or she will present, the easier it will be for the audience to follow the main ideas. Some types of introductions include the following:

1. *A reference to the event or occasion.* "On Wednesday, October 12, Health Care Delivery Systems treated our 10,000th patient. Although this is only year 2 of our operation, we cannot rest on our laurels. We need to build a strategic plan for the next decade. That is what I'd like to talk about today."

2. *A brief story that relates to the topic.* "On May 18 John Miller survived complications from an automobile accident the night before. Medical personnel at Our Lady of Mercy Hospital diagnosed his condition and the potential for complications with an X787 scanner. This presentation will review the life saving qualities of this miracle of modern science and its sales potential for the coming year."

3. *A quotation by a recognized authority on the subject.* "The Surgeon General of the United States has recommended that we reduce our fat intake by 40 percent. Three out of four Americans have too much fat in their diets. This serious problem is one of many reasons why we need to begin our health awareness program."

4. *A rhetorical question (a thought-provoking question to which you do not expect an answer from the audience).* "What would happen if we could no longer obtain the raw materials to produce Zenterol? I am going to show you how we can obtain a viable substitute for that raw material."

5. *An academic question (a question that requires the audience to participate by answering the question or getting involved by raising their hands).* "How many of you have been hospitalized in the past year? (pause for an audience response) If you have, you know the importance of having a family physician. Today, I'm going to talk about what qualities consumers are looking for in a family physician."

6. *A startling statement (it may or may not be a statistic).* "If our costs continue to increase over the next three years at the rate they have been over the last decade, we will have to increase our initial office consultation charge to $200. Today, I will present five strategies for reducing costs in . . ."

7. *A personal story.* "Seven years ago I suffered from a serious disease. Locatril was prescribed to treat my illness. I'm happy to say that I am fully recovered and owe much of my recovery to this miracle drug. Locatril was just one of the drugs we developed in the last decade. We continue to add new products. This presentation will preview two of them: Daconaise and Zacarin."

Once you have successfully chosen an attention-getting statement, tell the audience the purpose of your presentation by communicating your thesis statement. Although the introduction is designed to get the audience to think about the topic, you must be sure that they understand what you intend to do. Ask yourself, What do I want to accomplish in this presentation? Your statement about what you want to do is the thesis statement or statement of purpose.

The attention span of an audience varies from one occasion to the next. To keep your audience attuned to what you are saying, it is beneficial to preview the main points of your presentation. For example, if your presentation is instructional, you may tell the audience that there are four major steps in administering the new procedure. Likewise, if you are giving a persuasive presentation, you may want individuals to contribute to a particular cause by briefly mentioning three main reasons. Later, during the body of the presentation, you will develop each of these points in more detail.

Body

In our discussion of the introduction, we suggested that you preview the information for your audience. In the body, you will develop each point that was previewed. Some methods of developing the main points or key ideas are as follows:

1. Use statistics or other facts,
2. Describe personal experiences,
3. Cite quotations or expert testimony,
4. Employ examples (real or hypothetical), or
5. Use comparisons, contrasts, or analogies to things the audience already knows.

Whatever method you choose to employ, smooth transitions are the key aspect of organization. A link must be established between one idea or issue and another so the audience sees the relationship. This link may take the form of a short summary that simply states that a new point will now be discussed or contrasts what has just been presented with that which is to follow. Another technique is the repetition of key words or phrases for emphasis. Some examples include:

- "The new product, Daconil, differs from our earlier products in three ways . . ."
- "Now for the second difference . . ."
- "Also . . ."
- "To begin . . ."
- "Finally . . ."

Conclusion

The end of your presentation should contain a brief summary of the main points of your presentation. Do not introduce any new information in your conclusion lest you appear unfinished. If some action is expected from the audience, the speaker's expectations should be made clear and easy to follow. Too often, speakers just trail off with a "That's all. Thank you very much" ending. Whatever the specific nature of your conclusion, it should clearly communicate that the speaker is ending.

A presentation can have an excellent introduction and body and yet not be effective. Good speakers must leave a favorable impression on the minds of the audience. They can accomplish this by having an effective conclusion. Conclusions can be developed in a number of ways:

1. Use a summary of your main points,
2. Ask the audience to take some action (such as getting an annual mammogram if they are over age 50), or
3. Recall the earlier story or anecdote used in the introduction and elaborate on it.

Now that you have planned the content of your presentation, you must find ways to enhance it further.

Visual Aids

Because we are a visually oriented society, we expect to see as well as hear information. Therefore, effective speakers will attempt to show as well as tell the audience their points. Research indicates that audiences remember only 10–20 percent of what they hear but 80 percent of what they see. Remember that your audience must understand the material that is being presented to remember it. Visual aids help maintain audience attention and involvement. Two broad categories of visual aids are available to enhance presentations. One category, direct viewing visuals, includes such things as real objects, models, flip charts, diagrams and drawings, photographs, and handouts. The second category, projected visuals, includes transparencies, slides, and videotapes.

Several factors must be considered in selecting the appropriate visual aid. Some of these are:

1. *The constraints of the topic.* For example, if you were explaining to a group of lay people how microsurgery is performed on a hand, you would not use a flip chart because it would be ineffective. Also, you would probably not show a videotape of the surgery being performed because the sight of blood may upset some individuals. Instead, you might use a model of the hand. On the other hand (no pun intended), a videotape might be very effective in teaching surgeons how to perform the procedure.
2. *The availability of the equipment.* If the speaking site does not have an overhead projector, you would not be able to use transparencies. Similarly,

if the site does not have any outlets, the use of any projected visual is prohibited.

3. *The cost of the visual.* If your budget is very small, a transparency or a handout may be preferable to the more elaborate types of visuals such as slides or videotapes.

4. *The difficulty of producing the visual.* If, for example, you have only three days to prepare for your presentation, it may be impossible to assemble a scale model of a proposed hospital addition, but you may be able to make a transparency from architects' drawings. Look for ways to simplify the visual aid. Nothing should appear on it except the content relevant to the specific ideas. Audiences may get irritated if they are told that there is something important on the visual aid that they cannot see. For example, lettering on a visual aid should be large enough for everyone to see.

Once you have prepared the content of your presentation and planned your visual aids, you are ready to practice the delivery of your material. There is no substitute for saying the presentation aloud to hear whether you stumble over a phrase or use too many fillers such as "you know" or "OK."

DELIVERING THE PRESENTATION

A well-prepared speaker will have analyzed the audience, developed the opening statement, organized the presentation, and developed appropriate visual aids. What about actually giving the presentation? Several methods for delivering material to an audience are available to a speaker and each has its respective use. The four methods of delivery are (1) impromptu, (2) manuscript, (3) memorized, and (4) extemporaneous. *Impromptu delivery* refers to speaking spontaneously on the topic. This type is generally inappropriate for technical or complex material. Obviously, you may forget critical information if the presentation has not been carefully planned. Impromptu delivery is often used at social occasions such as retirement dinners where you may be asked to toast the retiree. Another example is a professional meeting where you are asked to "sit in" for someone who was going to introduce a speaker but was called out because of an emergency.

Manuscript delivery requires that the speaker read from prepared text. This type of delivery is ineffective in most presentations because audiences generally prefer more eye contact; they also dislike being read to. However, manuscript delivery is a must in one particular situation: when a crisis has occurred in the organization. For example, if someone receives the wrong medication and dies in a hospital, the media will immediately "look for the story." The spokesperson for the hospital should never deliver the information in an impromptu manner. Rather, the response should be carefully prepared and read to the media by the public relations director because any misstatement in such a situation could result in litigation against the organization.

Memorized delivery is self-explanatory, and in most cases it should be discouraged. Memorized presentations usually do not sound natural but rather "canned" because the pitch of the voice is higher than a conversational pitch. This type of delivery is appropriate in situations where the presentation will be only a few minutes long. Examples would be introducing a speaker or "saying a few words" about someone leaving the organization.

Extemporaneous delivery is the preferred approach for most presentations. This type of delivery requires that the speaker talk in a conversational tone with the audience and use notes or an outline periodically to ensure that all the information is covered. Some people have recommended following a precise outline while others have identified the benefits of note cards to deliver a presentation. Each person must find what works best for him or her. Although notes can be a valuable resource for a speaker, they can easily become a psychological crutch. To make sure that they do not become a crutch, remember to use notes only when absolutely necessary. Delivery helps build the speaker's credibility in the eyes of an audience.

Credibility

Credibility refers to the confidence an audience has in a speaker. Several factors determine credibility: enthusiasm, expertise, and trustworthiness. These qualities work in a synergistic manner to give a speaker credibility. *Enthusiasm* is projected through tone of voice, eye contact, and energy. Obviously, the major ways speakers can display these characteristics are by believing in the subject and acting as if they enjoy conveying the information. *Expertise* is conveyed through the accuracy of your information, the amount of experience you have had with the subject, and the confidence with which you speak. *Trustworthiness* refers to whether or not the speaker is biased. Clearly, consistency in conveying information over a period of time is important to establish trust with an audience.

One factor that detracts from credibility is excessive nervousness. Most speakers are nervous but they have learned techniques for handling this extra energy so that there are few outward signs of anxiety. Several techniques are recommended for managing speech anxiety:

1. Avoid medications that will dry out your mouth and produce more anxiety;
2. Practice deep breathing exercises just before speaking to reduce your anxiety;
3. Reduce tension by squeezing your hand into a fist and releasing it, tensing your leg muscles and releasing them, or stretching your facial muscles with exaggerated expressions;
4. Avoid alcohol as a means of relaxation because it only exacerbates the problem, if you have "dry mouth" take a glass of water to the podium;
5. Avoid milk products just before speaking because they thicken the saliva and make it difficult to pronounce words;
6. Rehearse your presentation aloud so that you are comfortable and confident with the material; and
7. Get a good night's sleep – just before falling asleep, visualize yourself making an outstanding presentation.

Speech anxiety is difficult to see unless it is obvious in your nonverbal communication. Therefore, monitor your nonverbal behavior by videotaping and critiquing your presentation before it is to be delivered.

Nonverbal Communication

Nonverbal communication enhances or detracts from the credibility you have worked to establish. Several dimensions of nonverbal communication include kinesics or how people use their bodies, proxemics or how people use space to communicate, and paralanguage or how people use their vocal qualities to communicate information.

Gestures and eye contact are two of the most important types of kinesic behavior. Speakers are rarely credible to an audience when they stand rigidly behind a podium, grasp it as a continuous crutch, and seldom look at the audience. Similarly, poor posture, hands in your pockets, reading your notes word for word, and playing with objects such as pens and pointers lessen your impact.

Speakers who recognize that space communicates will use it appropriately. If your audience is very small, it may be better to sit with them rather than stand and deliver the presentation formally. Also, when communicating unfavorable information, it may be better to stand close to the audience or even touch them as a way of communicating sincerity and understanding.

Aspects of the voice that affect credibility include volume, rate, pitch, speed, and tone. The quality of the voice such as raspiness or nasal whine communicates images to the audience; however, it is relatively difficult to change this. On the other hand, tone and pitch are more easily addressed. For example, a person who speaks in a monotone can make it seem less so by varying the volume of some words. Though the speaker has not changed the tone, the audience believes there are variations. Pitch is often associated with nervousness because it is governed by one's breathing patterns. High pitch comes from shallow breathing that creates nasal sounds whereas low pitch is characterized by deeper breathing and the sound comes from the mouth rather than the nose. Speakers are encouraged to start speaking in the lowest pitch they can achieve, because the lower pitch is more credible in our culture.

Visual Aids and Delivery

Although visual aids enhance presentations, poor use of them can actually detract from effective delivery. Some guidelines for using visual aids are as follows:

1. Talk to the audience, not your visual aid. Avoid having your back to any part of the audience while speaking.
2. Show the visual aid only when talking about it because the audience may look at it and be distracted from what you are saying. For example, if you are using transparencies, cover the parts not being discussed; uncover only the information you are talking about at that moment.

3. Refrain from removing the visual before the audience has had an opportunity to digest the material. Also, avoid talking about the visual aid after you have put it aside.

4. Use enough visual aids to make your points, but do not use so many that the audience tires of trying to look at all of them.

HANDLING QUESTIONS FROM YOUR AUDIENCE

The question-and-answer period at the end of your presentation can help reinforce key points and gain acceptance of your ideas. To make the most of this time, consider the following guidelines:

1. Allow for sufficient time to answer questions from an audience. Always maintain control of the situation. Have a designated time limit for questions and answers.

2. Ask for questions in a positive way. You may start off by stating "Who has the first question?" If no questions are asked, you could ask yourself a question. For example, you could say, "I'm often asked . . ." then supply the answer. Then you could follow with, "Are there any other questions?"

3. If the questions being asked cannot be heard by the entire audience, repeat it for the rest of the group.

4. Look at the entire audience when you are answering a question. You must remember that you are addressing not just the person who asked the question, but an entire audience.

5. Do not allow one person to ask all the questions. Look around the room and involve others in the audience.

6. Keep your answers concise and to the point; do not give another speech. You do not want to lose your audience with an overly long response to a simple question.

7. Avoid evaluating a question by saying "That's a good question." Such a response may inadvertently be telling others that their questions are not good.

8. Cut off the rambling questioner politely. If a person gets up and starts to make a speech without getting to a question, when he or she pauses to take a breath, interrupt with, "Thanks for your comment. Next question." Then look to the other side of the room.

9. Watch your nonverbal communication when answering questions. For example, pointing a finger at the audience, putting your hands on your hips, or raising your voice above the pitch of the presentation may give the appearance of authoritarianism and rudeness.

10. Look for the unexpected and plan ahead as much as possible. Anticipate questions from your audience and formulate answers. Never lose your temper as you respond to someone who is trying to make you look bad.

Your presentation does not end when you finish your speech. This period is important to your overall presentation success, so prepare intelligently for the session and consider appropriate strategies for handling any difficult situations. If you follow with an effective question-and-answer period, the presentation will be remembered long after the audience has left.

CLOSING COMMENTS

To ensure an effective presentation, a speaker should make sure that everyone involved has the same purpose for the presentation. Once the purpose has been clearly established, the speaker must conduct an audience analysis, select an introduction, and organize visual aids. A strong summary or conclusion can help the presentation end on a high note. If appropriate, a speaker should also schedule sufficient time for questions at the end of the presentation.

With the fast pace of today's world, having the skills and the ability to present your point of view in a convincing manner is essential to conveying your concerns and ideas and reaching your goals. Presenting information orally is a challenging task. However, if you follow the guidelines we have suggested, your presentation will not only be rewarding for your audience, but you will also experience greater satisfaction for a job well done.

Information Sources for Health Care Administration

In case analysis it is often useful to perform at least part of the situational analysis by investigating secondary data. Although the cases in this text have about as much information as the decision maker had at the time, further information could be obtained. However, it is wise to check with your professor as to his or her preference for your investigating the organization through library research. Some professors want students to use only the information provided in the case, but others insist that students investigate the organization and the industry using additional materials. Still others want students to research the organization but only up to the time of the decision in the case.

Some students believe that a successful approach to case analysis is to find an article about the organization and the decision that was made and then write up the decision that was implemented as the "correct" solution to the case. However, knowing what the organization did may prejudice your thinking and limit your ability to develop a creative solution. Consider this question: If the organization had the opportunity to do it over, would management implement the same decision? If the results were impressive, a student might be tempted to say yes. But would a different decision have yielded even greater benefits?

As an aid to locating information, sources that are typically available in university libraries, along with a brief description of each, are listed. This non-exhaustive list is organized by abstracts, bibliographies, dictionaries, directories, electronic data bases, financial data, handbooks and guides, indexes, industry information, journals, loose-leaf services, newspaper and periodical indexes, statistical sources, and guides to sources not described. It suggests sources that might be used by a student or health care professional in a situational analysis.

ABSTRACTS

Abstracts of Health Care Management Studies
Ann Arbor: Health Administration Press for the Cooperative Information Center for Health Care Management Studies, School of Public Health, University of Michigan (quarterly).

This publication is focused primarily on the delivery of health care and provides abstracts of materials recently published on management, public policy, and planning.

Excerpta Medica
Amsterdam: Excerpta Medica (ten issues per year, with semiannual accumulations).

An international abstracting service, this publication can be used as a general index as well as a specialized resource because it covers all aspects of health care.

Health Planning and Services Research: An Abstract Newsletter
Springfield, Virginia: National Technical Information Service (weekly).

This newsletter contains information on health services and facilities use; health personnel requirements, use, and education; health-related costs; and methods of funding.

Hospital Abstracts
London: Her Majesty's Stationery Office (monthly).

The organization and management of hospitals are covered in this publication through listings of both books and periodicals. Abstracts are listed according to subject and relate to all aspects of hospital administration as well as specific publications of Great Britain's Ministry of Health.

Medical Care Review
Ann Arbor: Bureau of Public Health Economics, School of Public Health, University of Michigan (monthly).

Abstracts from articles as well as entire journal articles are included in this monthly review of the literature. Federal and state legislation is an added feature.

Standard & Poor's Industry Surveys
New York: Standard & Poor's Corporation (quarterly).

This source contains a wealth of data for sixty-nine major domestic industries. Examples include health care, leisure time, computer and data processing equipment, liquor, and photography.

BIBLIOGRAPHIES

The Administrator's Bookshelf
Denver: Medical Group Management Association (annually).

Health care administration is the primary focus of this bibliography. Books and periodical articles are included.

Administrator's Collection
Chicago: American Hospital Association (annually).

This is a listing of publications on all aspects of health administration. The materials are arranged by subject categories and there is an additional listing for periodicals.

A Business Information Guidebook
By Oscar Figueroa and Charles Winkler, New York: AMACOM, 1980.

A reference book that provides direction for business people, consultants, students, or anyone seeking information on available markets, competition, and financing.

Business Information Sources, Rev. Ed.
By Lorna M. Daniells, Berkeley: University of California Press, 1985.

This guide provides a selected, annotated list of books and reference sources for businesses (including the health care industry).

Encyclopedia of Business Information Sources, 7th ed.
By James Woy, Detroit: Gale Research Company, 1988.

This is a bibliographic guide to approximately 20,000 citations, covering about 1,000 subjects. It contains abstracting and indexing services, almanacs and yearbooks, bibliographies, directories, financial ratios, online data bases, periodicals and newsletters, price sources, research centers and institutes, statistics sources, trade associations, and professional societies. The health industry is included.

Federal Information Sources in Health and Medicine: A Selected Annotated Bibliography
By Mary G. Chitty, New York: Greenwood Press, 1988.

Annotates approximately 1,200 government publications and 100 data bases from 90 federal agencies, institutes, and information centers. An appendix gives addresses of the federal agencies and other departments. The index gives all pertinent information about each title. The annotated subject bibliography is divided by types of publications.

Current Management Resources for Health Care Professionals, 2nd ed.
Elaine C. Foster, Editor, Chicago: American Hospital Association, 1985.

This bibliography of health services administration sources is intended for the professional in the health care field. It includes abstracts.

Health Administration and Organization
By Cortus T. Koehler, Monticello, Illinois: Vance Bibliographies, 1980.

A comprehensive listing of pertinent sources in the administration and organization of hospitals and other health care institutions is included in this bibliography.

Medical Books and Serials in Print: An Index to Literature in the Health Sciences
New York: Bowker (annual).

A listing of books and other materials in the medical and allied health sciences fields currently available from publishers is included in this index.

Health Care Administration: A Guide to Information Sources
By Dwight A. Morris and Lynne D. Morris, Detroit: Gale Research Company, 1978.

This basic annotated guide includes listings of associations, libraries, audiovisual sources, and publishers in health care as well as graduate schools offering majors in health care administration.

Public Health Administration Monographs, 1970–1987
By Mary Vance, Monticello, Illinois: Vance Bibliographies, 1988.

This source combines information in the public administration field as well as the health administration area. It is noteworthy because of the time span covered.

Where to Find Business Information: A Worldwide Guide for Everyone Who Needs the Answers to Business Questions, 2nd ed.
By David M. Brownstone and Gorton Carruth, New York: John Wiley & Sons, 1982.

This book contains a descriptive list of over 5,000 sources of current business information, concentrating on periodic publications and services such as magazines, newsletters, and computerized data bases.

COMPUTERIZED INFORMATION SERVICES

Many of these electronic data base services are available to "members" who have paid a membership or subscriber fee and then are charged for access time. Although the electronic data bases are expensive to use, they have the advantage of speed and comprehensiveness.

ABI/Inform
Louisville, Kentucky: UMI/Data Courier.

All phases of business management and administration are indexed in this on-line information service. ABI/Inform is the largest and oldest data base of bibliographical information. Over 680 business periodicals are indexed as well as the major health care administration journals. A 150-word summary is included for each article. The data base covers from 1971 to the present.

Health Planning and Administration
Bethesda, Maryland: U.S. National Library of Medicine.

Contains references to nonclinical literature on all aspects of health care planning, management, human resources, and licensure and certification. References are compiled from the *Hospital Literature Index* and *Medline.*

Health Periodicals Data Base
Foster City, California: Information Access Company.

This is a full-text data base that provides references to journals covering the entire range of health issues.

Medline
Bethesda, Maryland: U.S. National Library of Medicine.

This database is the major source for information in the biomedical literature. All aspects of medicine are included. Although most of this data base is devoted to developments in medical science, many economic, finance, and administrative sources are included.

Nursing and Allied Health
Glendale, California: Cumulative Index to Nursing and Allied Health Literature Corporation.

Over 300 English-language journals are included in this data base. All disciplines in nursing and allied health are included and citations are provided from *Index Medicus* as well as other sources.

Business Periodicals Index
New York: H. W. Wilson Co.

This data base, available on CD-ROM, contains the same information as the hard copy version previously described.

CompuServe
Columbus, Ohio: CompuServe, Inc.

An on-line data base, CompuServe offers a variety of services through a time-sharing computer system. Terminal access to the service can be made through the TYMNET system. Two distinct services are offered by CompuServe: Micronet and CompuServe Information Services (CIS). Micronet is designed for those who are familiar with programming and software. CompuServe is menu-driven and provides access to newspapers and specific topics such as finance, entertainment, communications, and so on.

Dow Jones News/Retrieval
New York: Dow Jones & Co., Inc.

Subscribers to this data base can obtain the latest price quotations (no delay) for more than 6,000 stocks traded on nine different exchanges. It also allows for text searches for up-to-date news from the Dow Jones News Service Wires, the *Wall Street Journal, Barron's,* and the *Washington Post.*

InfoTrac
Forest City, California: Information Access Company.

Available on CD-ROM, InfoTrac indexes articles from 1,100 business and general interest periodicals and newspapers.

The Source
Source Telecomputing Corporation.

Also known as "America's information utility," The Source is a data base service of Source Telecomputing Corporation. By dialing a Source access number and supplying a password, subscribers gain access to hundreds of data bases. Some of the files included in The Source are United Press International (UPI), *New York Times* News Summary, Aware Financial Services, and Business and Finance.

Standard & Poor's Corporate Descriptions
New York: Standard & Poor's Compustat Services, Inc.

More than 9,000 publicly held U.S. corporations are included in this data base, which is available on CD-ROM. Descriptions include corporate background, income account and balance sheet figures, and stock and bond data.

DICTIONARIES

Encyclopedia and Dictionary of Medicine, Nursing, and Allied Health, 2nd ed.
By Benjamin F. Miller and Claire B. Keane, Philadelphia: Saunders Publishing, 1978.

This dictionary can be used by the lay person as well as the professional. The appendix lists sources for educational materials and a list of agencies concerned with health.

The New American Medical Dictionary and Health Manual, 5th ed.
By Robert E. Rothenberg, New York: New American Library, 1988.

This all in one handbook, dictionary, and manual provides information on health in general and special sections on relevant topics such as the elderly and their special needs.

Dictionary of Health Services Management, 2nd ed.
Thomas C. Timmerick, Editor, Owings Mills, Maryland: National Health Publishing, 1987.

Health services administration, organization, and management terms are defined in this book. Special treatment is given to hospital information.

DIRECTORIES

American Hospital Association Guide to the Health Care Field
Chicago: American Hospital Association (annually).

This guide is a central reference for information on health care institutions, on the AHA, on organizations and agencies in the health care field, and on national hospital statistical data. The information is divided into sections with each section providing definitions and explanatory information.

Medical and Health Information Directory, 2nd ed.
Detroit: Gale Research Company, 1980.

Provides locator information on agencies, institutions, associations, and companies concerned with health care at the state and national level. The directory is a useful resource for locating organizations concerned with different aspects of health care.

FINANCIAL INFORMATION

Almanac of Business and Industrial Financial Ratios
By Leo Troy, Englewood Cliffs, New Jersey: Prentice-Hall (annually).

This source provides selected financial ratios for key U.S. industries including a variety of health care organizations.

Annual Reports
Washington, D.C.: RC Publications, Inc. (biennially).

Most libraries maintain a file of annual reports for *Fortune* 500 and other public firms.

Directory of Corporate Affiliation
Skokie, Illinois: National Register Publishing Co. (annually with bimonthly supplements).

The directory lists 3,500 U.S. parent companies with their domestic and foreign divisions, subsidiaries, and affiliates, as well as 35,000 "corporate children" and their parent companies. Five bimonthly publications update personnel changes, acquisitions, address changes, and so on.

Financial Analyst's Handbook
By Sumner Levine, Homewood, Illinois: Dow Jones-Irwin, 1975.

The handbook is in two volumes. Volume 1 contains methods, theory, and portfolio management. Volume 2 contains discussions by specialists for a variety of industries. The orientation is toward economic, social, marketing, regulatory, taxation, accountancy, and other topics considered to be of significance to the industries included.

Financial Research Associates' Financial Studies of Small Business
Arlington, Virginia: Financial Research Associates (annually).

Most industry data is provided for larger business operations. FRA publishes ratios and norms for small businesses with total capitalization that is less than $1 million.

Industry Norms and Key Business Ratios
New York: Dun & Bradstreet Credit Services (annually).

Over 800 different types of business operations are included. Key industry ratios (including the common ROA, ROI, ROE, current ratio, quick ratio, and so on plus some less common such as current liabilities to net worth, total liabilities to net worth) and industry norms are presented.

Q-File
St. Petersburg, Florida: Q-Data Corp., 1982.

An extensive microfiche file, this source contains corporate annual reports and 10-K reports for firms listed on the New York Stock Exchange (NYSE) or the American Stock Exchange (AMEX), and for public firms traded over-the-counter (OTC). The master index and updates are usually available in printed form in a loose-leaf binder as well as on microfiche.

Robert Morris Associates' Annual Statement Studies
Philadelphia: Robert Morris Associates (annually).

Robert Morris is an association of bank lenders that publishes composite financial data (activity, profitability, liquidity, market price ratios, and so on) for nearly 300 lines of business representing manufacturers, wholesalers, retailers, providers of services (including health care), and contractors. Financial ratios are computed for each industry included.

HANDBOOKS AND GUIDES

Health Services Administration: Education and Practice
By Karen M. Lorentz, St. Louis: W. H. Green, 1988.

This basic guide and text would be beneficial to any new professional to the health care field. Recent developments in the education of health administrators is the primary focus of this guide.

The Health Care Supervisor's Handbook, 2nd ed.
By Norman Metzger, Rockville, Maryland: Aspen Systems Corporation, 1982.

The handbook addresses the complex and varied responsibilities of today's health care supervisor. Features include sample supervisor evaluations, a leadership questionnaire, and a description of the leadership selection process.

Human Resource Management in the Health Care Sector: A Guide for Administrators and Professionals
By Amarjit S. Sethi, New York: Quorum Books, 1989.

Health facilities, personnel management in the health services field, and hospital administration are all topics in this new and important addition to the health administration literature. This guide would be very useful to the practicing administrator.

A Guide to Health Data Resources
By Ira D. Singer, Millwood, Virginia: Center for Health Affairs Project HOPE, 1985.

This guide offers descriptions of resource documents on health care that have been published by public and private sector organizations in the United States. Complete bibliographic information is given for each item. An added feature is a general description as well as an abridged table of contents when applicable.

Administrator's Handbook for Community Health and Home Care Services, 3rd ed.
By Anne S. Smith, New York: National League of Nurses, 1988.

This specialized book would be useful to nurses as well as other health administrators. Publication includes discussions of strategic planning, marketing, management, and evaluation of community and home health care services.

The White Labyrinth: A Guide to the Health Care System
By David B. Smith, Ann Arbor, Michigan: Health Administration Press, 1986.

This detailed analysis of the health care delivery system includes external environmental issues shaping financial and regulatory providers, an in-depth account of the structural shifts in health care delivery, and a presentation of the health care system's operational issues. It is organized into sections that include figures and tables as part of the text.

Hospital Health Promotion
By Neil Sol, Champaign, Illinois: Human Kinetics Books, 1989.

This book represents a strategic approach to hospital health promotion and is designed to make health care administrators aware of the current and future importance of marketing. Divided into six parts, Part 3 offers a "how-to" strategy for program development, management, marketing, selling, and delivery.

Health Statistics: A Guide to Information Sources
By Freida Weise, Detroit: Gale Research Company, 1980.

This inclusive resource annotates and evaluates the references cited in the following areas: natality and mortality, marriage and divorce, morbidity, health care facilities, health personnel, use of health services, health care costs and expenditures, health professions, education, and population characteristics.

INDEXES

Cumulative Index to Nursing and Allied Health Literature
Glendale, California: Seventh Day Adventist Hospital Association (five per year with annual accumulations).

This index is not limited to nursing journals. Health care delivery and other special topics are also included.

Hospital Literature Index
Chicago: American Hospital Association (quarterly, with annual and quinquennial accumulations).

This is a major index service providing information about hundreds of health journals. It is arranged by author and subject. Cumulative indexes are published periodically.

Business Index
Forest City, California: Information Access Company (monthly).

This source is available on 16-mm computer-output microfilm for viewing on a microfilm reader, which provides more rapid availability and more complete accumulation of information. Over 375 business periodicals are indexed, as well as acquisitions, mergers, and corporate promotions from the *New York Times* and the *Wall Street Journal*.

Business Periodicals Index
New York: H. W. Wilson Co. (monthly).

BPI is a cumulative index to English-language periodicals pertaining to business. Approximately 300 periodicals are indexed primarily by subject. Articles about a company are indexed under the name of the company. Volumes are issued monthly, with a cumulative quarterly update and a cumulative annual update published.

Funk and Scott (F & S) *Index of Corporations and Industries*
Cleveland: Predicasts, Inc. (annually).

F & S is an excellent source to locate information concerning specific industries and companies. It indexes business related journals, some newspapers, trade publications, newsletters, and loose-leaf services. This index is divided into two sections, industry and company. The industry section is arranged by SIC number; the company section is arranged alphabetically by company name. To identify the SIC code for an industry, check the *Standard Industrial Classification Manual* usually kept at the reference desk at most libraries.

New York Times Index
New York: The New York Times Company (semimonthly).

Published semimonthly with quarterly updates and a yearly cumulative issue, the *NY Times Index* abstracts news and editorial matter classified by appropriate subject, geographic, organization, and personal name headings. Entries are by subject whenever possible and are alphabetized.

Wall Street Journal Index
New York: Dow Jones & Company.

This index covers articles published in the *Wall Street Journal.* There are two sections: general news, where articles concerning various subjects are arranged alphabetically, and corporate news, where articles about companies are arranged by company name.

HEALTH CARE AND MANAGEMENT JOURNALS

Academy of Management Executive
Ada, Ohio: Academy of Management (quarterly).

Academy of Management Journal
Ada, Ohio: Academy of Management (quarterly).

Academy of Management Proceedings
Ada, Ohio: Academy of Management (annually).

Academy of Management Review
Ada, Ohio: Academy of Management (quarterly).

Administrative Science Quarterly
Ithaca, New York: Cornell Graduate School of Business (quarterly).

American Journal of Hospital Pharmacy
Philadelphia: Philadelphia College of Pharmacy and Science (monthly).

American Journal of Public Health
Washington, D.C.: American Public Health Association (monthly).

Annual Review of Public Health
Palo Alto, California: Annual Reviews, Inc. (annually).

Business Horizons
Bloomington, Indiana: Indiana University School of Business (bimonthly).

California Management Review
Berkeley: University of California at Berkeley School of Business (quarterly).

Computers in Health Care
Englewood, Colorado: Cardiff (monthly).

Education and the Health Professions
Beverly Hills, California: Sage Publications (quarterly).

Emergency Health Services Review
New York: Haworth Press (quarterly).

Frontiers of Health Services Management
Ann Arbor, Michigan: Health Administration Press (quarterly).

Harvard Business Review
Boston: Harvard University, Graduate School of Business Administration (bi-monthly).

Hastings Center Report
Briarcliff Manor, New York: Hastings Center Studies (bi-monthly).

Health Affairs
Chevy Chase, Maryland: People-to-People Health Foundation, Inc. (quarterly).

Health Care Executive
Chicago: American College of Healthcare Executives (six per year).

Health Care Financing Review
Baltimore: U.S. Department of Health and Human Services, Health Care Financing Administration (quarterly).

Health Care Forum Journal
San Francisco: Healthcare Forum (bimonthly).

Health Care Management Review
Frederick, Maryland: Aspen Publishers, Inc. (quarterly).

Health Care Strategic Management
Ann Arbor, Michigan: Chi Systems (monthly).

Health Care Supervisor
Frederick, Maryland: Aspen Publishers, Inc. (quarterly).

HMQ (Hospital Management Quarterly)
Evanston, Illinois: American Hospital Supply Corporation (quarterly).

Healthcare Computing & Communications
Littleton, Colorado: Health Data Analysis (monthly).

Healthcare Financial Management
Westchester, Illinois: Healthcare Financial Management Association (monthly).

Health Marketing Quarterly
Binghamton, New York: Hawthorne Press, Inc. (quarterly).

Health Policy
Amsterdam, Netherlands: Elsevier Science Publishers (nine per year).

Health Progress
St. Louis: Catholic Health Association of the United States (ten per year).

Health Services Management Research
Harlow, England: Longman Group, UK (three per year).

Health Services Research
Ann Arbor, Michigan: Health Care Administration Press (bimonthly).

Home Health Care Services Quarterly
Binghamton, New York: Haworth Press, Inc. (quarterly).

Hospice Journal
Binghamton, New York: Haworth Press, Inc. (quarterly).

Hospital Capital Finance
Chicago: American Hospital Association (monthly).

Hospital Forum
San Francisco: Association of Western Hospitals (bimonthly).

Hospital & Health Services Administration
Chicago: Foundation of the American College of Healthcare Executives (quarterly).

Hospital Topics
Sarasota, Florida: Hospital Topics (bimonthly).

Hospital Trustee
Ottawa, Canada: Canadian Hospital Association (bimonthly).

Hospitals & Health Networks
Chicago: American Hospital Publishing, Inc. (quarterly).

Inquiry
Chicago: Blue Cross/Blue Shield (quarterly).

International Journal of Health Planning and Management
Essex, England: John Wiley & Sons (quarterly).

International Journal of Health Services
Amityville, New York: Baywood Publishing Company (quarterly).

Journal of Allied Health
Chicago: College of Associated Health Professions, University of Illinois (quarterly).

Journal of Ambulatory Care Management
Frederick, Maryland: Aspen Publishers, Inc. (quarterly).

Journal of Ambulatory Health Management
Netherlands: Swet and Zeithinger BV (quarterly).

Journal of Ambulatory Health Marketing
Binghamton, New York: Haworth Press, Inc. (quarterly).

Journal of American Health Policy
Washington, D.C.: Faulkner & Gray (bimonthly).

Journal of the American Medical Association
Chicago, Illinois: American Medical Association (weekly).

Journal of Business Strategy
New York: Warren, Gorham, and Lamont (six per year).

Journal of Emergency Medical Services
Solana Beach, California: JEMS Publishing (monthly).

Journal of General Management
Sussex, England: Braybrooke Press, Ltd. (quarterly).

Journal of Health Administration Education
Arlington, Virginia: Association of University Programs in Health Administration (quarterly).

Journal of Health Care Marketing
Chicago: American Marketing Association (quarterly).

Journal of Health Economics
Amsterdam, Netherlands: North Holland (quarterly).

Journal of Health & Human Resources Administration
Montgomery, Alabama: Southern Public Administration Education Foundation (quarterly).

Journal of Health Politics, Policy and Law
Durham, North Carolina: Duke University (quarterly).

Journal of Health and Social Behavior
Washington, D.C.: American Sociological Association (quarterly).

Journal of Long Term Care Administration
Alexandria, Virginia: American College of Health Care Administrators (quarterly).

Journal of Management
Bloomington, Indiana: Indiana University School of Business (quarterly).

Journal of Management Studies
Oxford, England: Basil Blackwell, Ltd. (annually).

Journal of Medical Practice Management
Baltimore, Maryland: Williams & Wilkins (quarterly).

Journal of Medical Systems
New York: Plenum Press (quarterly).

Journal of Mental Health Administration
Washington, D.C.: Association of Mental Health Administrators (semi-annually).

Journal of Nursing Administration
Philadelphia: J. B. Lippincott, Co. (monthly).

Journal of Public Health Policy
Burlington, Vermont: Journal of Public Health Policy (quarterly).

Journal of Rural Health
Kansas City, Missouri: National Rural Health Association (semi-annually).

Law, Medicine & Health Care
Boston: American Society of Law and Medicine (bimonthly).

Long Range Planning
Tarrytown, New York: Pergamon Press, Inc. (six per year).

Management International Review
Wiesbaden, Germany: Journal of International Business (quarterly).

Medical Care
Philadelphia: J. B. Lippincott Co. (monthly).

Medical Care Review
Ann Arbor, Michigan: Health Administration Press (quarterly).

Medical Group Management
Denver, Colorado: Medical Group Management Association (bimonthly).

Milbank Quarterly
New York: Blackwell Publishers (quarterly).

Mobius
Berkeley: University of California Press (quarterly).

Modern Health Care
Chicago: Crain Communications, Inc. (weekly).

New England Journal of Medicine
Waltham: Massachusetts Medical Society (weekly).

Nursing Administration Quarterly
Rockville, Maryland: Aspen Systems (quarterly).

Planning Review
Oxford, Ohio: International Society for Strategic Management and Planning (bimonthly).

Public Health Reports
Rockville, Maryland: U.S. Public Health Service (bimonthly).

Social Science and Medicine
Tarrytown, New York: Pergamon Press, Inc. (bimonthly).

Strategic Management Journal
Sussex, England: John Wiley & Sons, Ltd. (eight per year).

Topics in Health Care Financing
Frederick, Maryland: Aspen Publishers, Inc. (quarterly).

Trustee
Chicago: American Hospital Association (monthly).

U.S. Healthcare
Lakewood, Colorado: Health Data Analysis, Inc. (monthly).

LOOSE-LEAF SERVICES

Health Administration: Laws, Regulations and Guidelines
Towson, Maryland: National Health Publishing Limited Partnership.

Direct federal regulation of the health care industry is covered in this service, which provides current updates of federal regulation of the health care industry.

Hospital Law Manual
Germantown, Maryland: Aspen Systems.

This unique set of books has separate volumes for use by health administrators as well as attorneys. Topics are conveniently organized according to subject. All sections are periodically updated with recent developments in health care law.

INDUSTRY INFORMATION

Economic Census
Washington, D.C.: U.S. Government Printing Office.

The U.S. Bureau of the Census publishes an economic census every five years in years that end in 2 or 7. This government document includes manufacturers, retail, wholesale, service, construction, transportation, and mineral industries. The data include number of establishments, value of shipments or sales, cost of materials, employment, and payroll, arranged by line of business.

Forbes Magazine
New York: Forbes, Inc. (monthly).

Annually *Forbes* publishes a special issue (in January) that reviews the performance of major American industries and ranks the identified firms by profitability and growth.

Fortune Magazine
New York: Time-Warner, Inc. (biweekly).

Annually the *Fortune 500* is published in May that reviews the performance of the 500 largest industrials in the United States; the Services 500 is published in June and the International 500 is published in August.

Statistical Abstracts of the United States
Washington, D.C.: U.S. Government Printing Office (annually).

A standard summary of statistics on the social, political, and economic organizations in the United States, this source includes data from many statistical publications, both governmental and private. Emphasis is on national data, but regional, state, and metropolitan data is also included.

Survey of Current Business
Washington, D.C.: U.S. Government Printing Office.

This publication provides up-to-date leading economic indicators, as well as general business indicators, and analyses for selected industries.

U.S. Industrial Outlook
Washington, D.C.: U.S. Government Printing Office (annually).

Industries are profiled along with forecasts for industry activity for the next decade.

SOURCES OF FINANCIAL INFORMATION

Moody's Manuals
New York: Moody's Investors Services, Inc. (annually).

A subsidiary of Dun & Bradstreet, *Moody's* publishes manuals annually in five areas: industrial, bank and finance, public utility, transportation, and OTC (over-the-counter) industrial. Detailed financial information is provided for companies that represent investment opportunities. The information for the industries includes location and history of the firm, type of business, property, reserves, subsidiaries, officers, directors, annual meetings, balance sheets and income statements for several years, earnings, dividends, loans, debts, securities issued, market prices of securities, and related data. Similar information, tailored to other types of organizations, is provided in the different manuals. Each manual is updated by the loose-leaf *News Reports*.

Standard & Poor's Corporation Services
New York: Standard & Poor's Corporation.

Standard & Poor's lists corporations and other organizations offering investment opportunities. Information is arranged alphabetically by company and includes capitalization, corporate background, financial statements, properties, officers, stock data, numbers of stockholders, price range of securities, dividends, and other data.

Value Line Investment Survey
New York: A. Bernard (weekly).

Although this source is designed to guide the private investor, professional analysts, corporate executives, purchasing agents, and sales managers, it does provide timely information on corporate developments and analysis of financial position as well as a brief industry overview. More than 1,500 companies in a variety of industries are covered in the weekly publication. Data include a ten-year statistical history of the firms in the *Survey,* estimates of the next three to five years' sales, estimates of quarterly sales, earnings, and dividends.

STATISTICAL SOURCES

Hospital Statistics
Chicago: American Hospital Association (annual).

This detailed statistical compendium presents current and trend data about hospitals in the United States. The tables are compiled from a survey response. Data are arranged according to geographic area, type of organization reporting, and services provided. It also offers comprehensive statistics on the number of hospitals, beds, and patients.

Facts at Your Fingertips: A Guide to Sources of Statistical Information on Major Health Topics, 6th ed.
Hyattsville, Maryland: U.S. Department of Health and Human Services, National Center for Health Statistics, 1982.

Many sources of statistical information on major health topics are listed in this publication. It provides citations for individual sources and also includes information on persons to contact with phone numbers and addresses.

Standard Medical Almanac, 2nd ed.
Chicago: Marquis Academic Media, 1979.

A periodically updated publication with an overall focus on health personnel and health services statistics. Divided into six parts, this publication covers human resources, budgeting, licensure, facilities management, general health care, and federal information. There are also three separate indexes: subject, organization, and geographic.

APPENDIX E

Bibliography for Health Care Researchers and Strategists

Ackerman, F. K., III. "The Movement Toward Vertically Integrated Regional Health Systems." *Health Care Management Review* 17, no. 3 (Summer 1992), pp. 81–88.

Agho, A. O., and S. T. Cyphert. "Problem Areas Faced by Hospital Administrators." *Hospital & Health Services Administration* 37, no. 1 (Spring 1992), pp. 131–135.

Akin, B. V., L. Rucker, F. A. Hubbell, R. W. Cygan, and H. Waitzkin. "Access to Medical Care in a Medically Indigent Population." *Journal of General Internal Medicine* 4 (May/June 1989), pp. 216–220.

Alexander, J. A. "Adaptive Change in Corporate Control Practices." *Academy of Management Journal* 34, no. 1 (March 1991), pp. 162–193.

Alexander, J. A., and T. L. Amburgey. "The Dynamics of Change in the American Hospital Industry: Transformation or Selection?" *Medical Care Review* 44, no. 2 (Fall 1987), pp. 279–321.

Alexander, J. A., B. L. Lewis, and M. A. Morriscy. "Acquisition Strategies of Multihospital Systems." *Health Affairs* 4, no. 3 (Fall 1985), pp. 49–66.

Alexander, J. A., and L. L. Morlock. "CEO-Board Relationships Under Hospital Corporate Restructuring." *Hospital & Health Services Administration* 33, no. 4 (Winter 1988), pp. 435–448.

Alexander, J. A., L. L. Morlock, and B. D. Gifford. "The Effects of Corporate Restructuring on Hospital Policymaking." *Health Services Research* 23, no. 2 (June 1988), pp. 311–338.

Alexander, J. A., and M. A. Morrisey. "Hospital-Physician Integration and Hospital Costs." *Inquiry* 25, no. 3 (Fall 1988), pp. 388–401.

Alexander, J. A., and M. A. Morrisey. "Hospital Selection into Multihospital Systems." *Medical Care* 26, no. 2 (February 1988), pp. 159–176.

Alexander, J. A., M. A. Morrisey, and S. M. Shortell. "Effects of Competition, Regulation, and Corporatization on Hospital-Physician Relationships." *Journal of Health and Social Behavior* 27 (1986), pp. 220–235.

Alexander, J. A., and T. G. Rundall. "Public Hospitals Under Contract Management." *Medical Care* 23, no. 3 (March 1985), pp. 209–219.

Alter, C. "An Exploratory Study of Conflict and Coordination in Interorganizational Service Delivery Systems." *Academy of Management Journal* 33, no. 3 (1990), pp. 478–502.

Amara, R., J. I. Morrison, and G. Schnid. *Looking Ahead at American Health Care.* Washington, D.C.: McGraw-Hill Book Company, Health Information Center, 1988.

American Hospital Association. *Vision, Environmental Values, Viability Assessment 1989–1990.* Chicago: American Hospital Association, 1988.

Amit, R., and P. J. H. Schoemaker. "Strategic Assets and Organizational Rent." *Strategic Management Journal* 14 (1993), pp. 33–46.

Anders, G. "McDonald's Methods Come to Medicine as Chains Acquire Physicians' Practices." *Wall Street Journal* (August 24, 1993), p. B-1.

Ansoff, H. I., and E. J. McDonnell. *Implementing Strategic Management,* 2d ed. Englewood Cliffs, New Jersey: Prentice-Hall, 1990.

Arndt, M., and B. Bigelow. "Vertical Integration in Hospitals: A Framework for Analysis." *Medical Care Review* 49, no. 1 (1993), pp. 93–115.

Arnold, R. J., and L. M. DeBrock. "Competition and Market Failure in the Hospital Industry: A Review of the Evidence." *Medical Care Review* 43, no. 2 (Fall 1986), pp. 253–292.

Atchison, T. A. *Turning Health Care Leadership Around: Cultivating Inspired, Empowered, and Loyal Followers.* San Francisco: Jossey-Bass, 1990.

Austin, C. J. *Information Systems for Health Services Administration.* Ann Arbor, Michigan: AUPHA Press, 1992.

Autrey, P., and D. Thomas. "Competitive Strategy in the Hospital Industry." *Health Care Management Review* 11, no. 1 (Winter 1986), pp. 7–14.

Barsky, A. "A Radical Prescription for Hospitals." *Harvard Business Review* 66, no. 3 (May/June 1988), pp. 100–104.

Bates, D. L., and J. E. Dillard, Jr. "Wanted: A Strategic Planner for the 1990s." *Journal of General Management,* 18, no. 1 (1992), pp. 51–62.

Baysinger, B., and R. E. Hoskisson. "The Composition of Boards of Directors and

Strategic Control: Effects on Corporate Strategy." *Academy of Management Review* 15, no. 1 (January 1990), pp. 72–87.

Beam, H. H. "Strategic Discontinuities: When Being Good May Not Be Enough." *Business Horizons* 33, no. 4 (July/August 1990), pp. 10–14.

Beckham, D. "Making Speed a Priority." *Marketing to Doctors* 5, no. 11 (November 1992), pp. 1–3.

Beckham, J. D. "The Longest Wave." *Healthcare Forum Journal* 36, no. 6 (November/December 1993), pp. 78, 80–82.

Bell, R. "Laying the Groundwork for a Smooth Transition to TQM." *Hospital Topics* 71, no. 1 (1993), pp. 23–26.

Berkowitz, D. A., and M. M. Swan. "Technology Decision Making." *Health Progress* 74, no. 1 (January/February 1993), p. 42–47.

Berry, L. L. "Five Imperatives for Improving Service Quality." *Sloan Management Review* 31 (Summer 1991), pp. 29–38.

Berry, L. L. "Services Marketing Is Different." *Business* (May/June 1980), pp. 24–30.

Berwick, D. M. "Health Services Research and Quality of Care: Assignments for the 1990s." *Medical Care* 27, no. 8 (August 1989), pp. 763–771.

Berwick, D. M., A. B. Godfrey, and J. Roessner. *Curing Health Care: New Strategies for Quality Improvement.* San Francisco: Jossey-Bass, 1990.

Bezold, C. "Five Futures." *Healthcare Forum Journal* 35, no. 3 (1992), p. 29.

Bezold, C. "The Future of Health Care: Implications for the Allied Health Professions." *Journal of Allied Health* 18, no. 5 (Fall 1989), pp. 435–458.

Biendon, R. J. "The Public's View of the Future of Health Care." *Journal of the American Medical Association* 259, no. 24 (1985), pp. 3587–3593.

Bigelow, B., and M. Arndt. "Ambulatory Care Centers: Are They a Competitive Advantage?" *Hospital & Health Services Administration* 36, no. 3 (Fall 1991), pp. 351–363.

Bigelow, B., and J. F. Mahon. "Strategic Behavior of Hospitals: A Framework for Analysis." *Medical Care Review* 46, no. 3 (Fall 1989), pp. 295–311.

Blair, J. D., and M. D. Fottler. *Challenges in Health Care Management: Strategic Perspectives for Managing Key Stakeholders.* San Francisco: Jossey-Bass, 1990.

Blair, J. D., G. T. Savage, and C. J. Whitehead. "A Strategic Approach for Negotiating with Hospital Stakeholders." *Health Care Management Review* 14, no. 1 (Winter 1989), pp. 13–23.

Blair, J. D., C. R. Slaton, and G. T. Savage. "Hospital-Physician Joint Ventures: A Strategic Approach for Both Dimensions of Success." *Hospital & Health Services Administration* 35, no. 1 (Spring 1990), pp. 3–26.

Blair, J. D., and C. J. Whitehead. "Too Many on the Seesaw: Stakeholder Diagnosis and Management for Hospitals." *Hospital & Health Services Administration* 33, no. 2 (Summer 1988), pp. 153–166.

Blumenthal, D., and B. R. Berenson. "Health Care Issues in Presidential Campaigns." *New England Journal of Medicine* 321, no. 13 (September 28, 1989), pp. 908–912.

Bodenheimer, T. "The Fruits of Empire Rot on the Vine: U.S. Health Policy in the Austerity Era." *Sociology, Science and Medicine* 28, no. 6 (1989), pp. 531–538.

Boeker, W. "Strategic Change: The Effects of Founding and History." *Academy of Management Journal* 32, no. 3 (September 1989), pp. 489–515.

Boles, K. E., and J. K. Glenn. "What Accounting Leaves out of Hospital Financial Management." *Hospital & Health Services Administration* 31, no. 2 (Summer 1986), pp. 8–27.

Borys, B., and D. B. Jemison. "Hybrid Arrangements as Strategic Alliances: Theoretical Issues in Organizational Combinations." *Academy of Management Review* 14, no. 2 (April 1989), pp. 234–249.

Boscarino, J. A., "Hospital Wellness Centers: Strategic Implementation, Marketing, and Management," *Health Care Management Review* 14, no. 2 (Spring 1989), pp. 25–29.

Bowman, E. H., and D. Hurry. "Strategy Through the Option Lens: An Integrated View of Resource Investments and the Incremental-Choice Process." *Academy of Management Review* 18, no. 4 (October 1993), pp. 760–782.

Bracken, J., J. Calkin, J. Sanders, and A. Thesen. "A Strategy for Adaptive Staffing of Hospitals Under Varying Environmental Conditions." *Health Care Management Review* 10, no. 4 (Fall 1985), pp. 43–53.

Breindel, C. L. "Nongrowth Strategies and Options in Health Care." *Hospital & Health Services Administration* 33, no. 1 (Spring 1988), pp. 37–45.

Bridgers, W. F. *Health Care Reform: The Dilemma and a Pathway for the Health Care System.* St. Louis: G. W. Manning, 1992.

Brown, M. "The 1990s: Just Around the Corner." *Health Care Management Review* 13, no. 2 (Spring 1988), pp. 81–86.

Brown, M. *Health Care Marketing Management.* Gaithersburg, Maryland: Aspen Publishers, 1992.

Brown, M., and B. P. McCool. "High-Performing Managers: Leadership Attributes for the 1990s." *Health Care Management Review* 12, no. 2 (Spring 1987), pp. 69–75.

Brown, M., and B. P. McCool. "Vertical Integration: Exploration of a Popular Strategic Concept." *Health Care Management Review* 11, no. 4 (Fall 1986), pp. 17–19.

Broyles, R. W., and B. J. Reilly. "Physicians, Patients, and Administrators: A Realignment of Relationships." *Hospital & Health Services Administration* 33, no. 1 (Spring 1988), pp. 5–14.

Buller, P. F., and L. Timpson. "The Strategic Management of Hospitals: Toward an Integrative Approach." *Health Care Management Review* 11, no. 1 (Spring 1986), pp. 7–13.

Burns, L. R. "Matrix Management in Hospitals: Testing Theories of Matrix Structure and Development." *Administrative Science Quarterly* 34, no. 2 (June 1989), pp. 349–368.

Burns, L. R., R. M. Andersen, and S. M. Shortell. "The Impact of Corporate Structures on Physicians Inclusion and Participation." *Medical Care* 27, no. 10 (October 1989), pp. 967–982.

Burns, L. R., and D. P. Thorpe. "Trends and Models in Physician-Hospital Organization." *Health Care Management Review* 18, no. 4 (Fall 1993), pp. 7–20.

Byars, L. L., and T. C. Neil. "Organizational Philosophy and Mission Statements." *Planning Review* 15, no. 4 (July/August 1987), pp. 32–35.

Cantrell, L. E., Jr., and J. A. Flick. "Physician Efficiency and Reimbursement: A Case Study." *Hospital & Health Services Administration* 31, no. 4 (Winter 1986), pp. 43–50.

Carpman, J. R., and M. A. Grant. *Design That Cares: Planning Health Facilities for Patients and Visitors,* 2d ed. Chicago: American Hospital Publishing, 1993.

Carroll, A. B. "The Pyramid of Corporate Social Responsibility: Towards a Moral Management of Organizational Stakeholders." *Business Horizons* 34, no. 4 (July–August 1991), pp. 39–48.

Carroll, P. E., C. W. Daly, and J. C. Kowalski. "Materials Management." In *Effective Health Care Facilities Management,* ed. V. James McLarney. Chicago: American Hospital Publishing, 1991.

Carson, K. D., P. P. Carson, C. W. Roe, J. P. Authement, and R. Yallapragada. "Increasing the Effectiveness of Healthcare Managers." *Hospital Topics* 71, no. 3 (Summer 1993), pp. 16–19.

Cartwright, S., and C. L. Cooper. "The Role of Culture Compatibility in Successful Organizational Marriage." *Academy of Management Executive* 7, no. 2 (May 1993), pp. 57–70.

Casalou, R. F. "Total Quality Management in Health Care." *Hospital & Health Services Administration* 36, no. 1 (Spring 1991), pp. 134–146.

Chaffee, E. E. "Three Models of Strategy." *Academy of Management Review* 10, no. 1 (January 1985), pp. 89–98.

Chang, Y., and H. Thomas. "The Impact of Diversification Strategy on Risk-Return Performance." *Strategic Management Journal* 10, no. 3 (May/June 1989), pp. 271–284.

Chilingerian, J. A. "New Directions for Hospital Strategic Management: The Market for Efficient Care." *Health Care Management Review* 17, no. 4 (Fall 1992), pp. 73–80.

Choi, T., R. F. Allison, and F. Munson. "Impact of Environment on State University Hospital Performance." *Medical Care* 23, no. 7 (July 1985), pp. 855–871.

Chow, C. W., K. M. Haddad, and K. Wong-Boren. "Improving Subjective Decision Making in Health Care Administration." *Hospital & Health Services Administration* 36, no. 2 (Summer 1991), pp. 191–210.

Christianson, J. B., M. Shadle, M. M. Hunter, S. Hartwell, and J. McGee. "The New Environment for Rural HMOs." *Health Affairs* 5, no. 1 (Spring 1986), pp. 105–121.

Christianson, J. B., S. M. Sanchez, D. R. Wholey, and M. Shadle. "The HMO Industry: Evolution in Population Demographics and Market Structures." *Medical Care Review* 48, no. 1 (Spring 1991), pp. 3–46.

Clement, J. P. "Corporate Diversification: Expectations and Outcomes." *Health Care Management Review* 13, no. 2 (Spring 1988), pp. 7–13.

Clement, J. P. "Does Hospital Diversification Improve Financial Outcomes?" *Medical Care* 25, no. 10 (October 1987), pp. 988–1001.

Clement, J. P. "Vertical Integration and Diversification of Acute Care Hospitals: Conceptual Definitions." *Hospital & Health Services Administration* 33, no. 1 (Spring 1988), pp. 99–110.

Clement, J. P., T. D'Aunno, and B. L. M. Poyzer. "The Financial Performance of Diversified Hospital Subsidiaries." *Health Services Research* 27, no. 6 (February 1993), pp. 741–763.

Cleverley, W. O. "How Boards Can Use Comparative Data in Strategic Planning." *Healthcare Executive* 4, no. 3 (May 6, 1989), pp. 32–33.

Cleverley, W. O. "Three Ways to Measure A Strategic Plan's Viability." *Healthcare Financial Management* 31, no. 1 (January 1989), pp. 63–69.

Cleverley, W. O. "Is a Leveraged ESOP a Possibility for the Voluntary Hospital?" *Hospital & Health Services Administration* 33, no. 3 (Fall 1988), pp. 385–405.

Cleverley, W. O. "Promotion and Pricing in Competitive Markets." *Hospital & Health Services Administration* 32, no. 3 (Fall 1987), pp. 329–341.

Cleverley, W. O. "Strategic Financial Planning: A Balance Sheet Perspective." *Hospital & Health Services Administration* 32, no. 3 (Fall 1987), pp. 1–20.

Cleverley, W. O. "Financial Policy Formation: Principles for Hospitals." *Hospital & Health Services Administration* 30, no. 1 (Spring 1985), pp. 29–42.

Cleverley, W. O., and R. K. Harvey. "Critical Strategies for Successful Rural Hospitals." *Health Care Management Review* 17, no. 1 (Winter 1992), pp. 27–33.

Cleverley, W. O., and R. K. Harvey. "Competitive Strategy for Successful Hospital Management." *Hospital & Health Services Administration* 37, no. 1 (Spring 1992), pp. 53–69.

Coddington, D. C., D. J. Keen, K. D. Moore, and R. L. Clark. *The Crisis in Health Care: Costs, Choices, and Strategies.* San Francisco: Jossey-Bass, 1990.

Coddington, D. C., and K. D. Moore. *Market-Driven Strategies in Health Care.* San Francisco: Jossey-Bass, 1987.

Coddington, D. C., L. E. Palmquist, and W. V. Trollinger. "Strategies for Survival in the Hospital Industry." *Harvard Business Review* 63, no. 3 (May/June 1985), pp. 129–138.

Coile, R. C., Jr. "Re-Visioning Health Care." *Health Management Quarterly* 11, no. 4 (1990), pp. 2–3.

Collins, J. C., and J. I. Porras. "Organizational Vision and Visionary Organizations." *California Management Review* 34, no. 1 (1991), pp. 30–52.

Conger, J. A. "Inspiring Others: The Language of Leadership." *Academy of Management Executive* 5, no. 1 (February 1991), pp. 31–45.

Conrad, D. A., S. S. Mick, C. W. Madden, and G. Hoare. "Vertical Structures and Control in Health Care Markets: A Conceptual Framework and Empirical Review." *Medical Care Review* 45, no. 1 (Spring 1988), pp. 49–100.

Cook, D. "Strategic Plan Creates a Blueprint for Budgeting." *Healthcare Financial Management* 44, no. 5 (May 1990), pp. 21–25.

Costello, M. M. "Caution: Business Opportunity Ahead." *Hospital & Health Services Administration* 31, no. 4 (Winter 1986), pp. 19–31.

Coulson-Thomas, C. "Strategic Vision or Strategic Con: Rhetoric or Reality?" *Long Range Planning* 25, no. 1 (1992), pp. 81–89.

Counte, M. A., G. L. Glandon, D. M. Oleske, and J. P. Hill. "Total Quality Management in a Health Care Organization: How Are Employees Affected?" *Hospital & Health Services Administration* 37, no. 4 (Winter 1992), pp. 503–518.

Coyne, J. S. "A Financial Model for Assessing Hospital Performance: An Application to Multi-Institutional Organizations." *Hospital & Health Services Administration* 31, no. 2 (Summer 1986), pp. 28–40.

Coyne, J. S. "A Comparative Financial Analysis of Multi-Institutional Organizations by Ownership Type." *Hospital & Health Services Administration* 30, no. 4 (Winter 1985), pp. 48–63.

Crawford-Mason, C., and L. Dobyns. *Quality or Else.* Boston: Houghton Mifflin Company, 1991.

Culhane, D. P., and T. R. Hadley. "The Discriminating Characteristics of For-Profit versus Non-For-Profit Freestanding Psychiatric Inpatient Facilities." *Health Services Research* 27, no. 2 (June 1992), pp. 177–194.

Cyphert, S., and J. Rohrer. "A National Medical Care Program: Review and Synthesis of Past Proposals." *Journal of Public Health Policy* (Winter 1988), pp. 456–471.

D'Aunno, T. A., R. Hooijbert, and F. C. Munson. "Decision Making, Goal Consensus, and Effectiveness in University Hospitals." *Hospital & Health Services Administration* 36, no. 4 (Winter 1991), pp. 505–523.

D'Aunno, T. A., and H. S. Zuckerman. "A Life-Cycle Model of Organizational Federations: The Case of Hospitals." *Academy of Management Review* 12, no. 3 (July 1987), pp. 534–545.

D'Aunno, T. A., and H. S. Zuckerman. "The Emergence of Hospital Federations: An Integration of Perspectives from Organizational Theory." *Medical Care Review* 44, no. 2 (Fall 1987), pp. 323–343.

D'Aveni, R. A. "The Aftermath of Organizational Decline: A Longitudinal Study of the Strategic and Managerial Characteristics of Declining Firms." *Academy of Management Journal* 32, no. 3 (September 1989), pp. 577–605.

Daniel, D. J., and W. D. Reitsperger. "Linking Quality Strategy with Management Control Systems: Empirical Evidence from Japanese Industry." *Accounting, Organizations, and Society* 16 (1991), pp. 601–618.

Darr, K. *Ethics in Health Services Management,* 2d ed., Baltimore: Health Professions Press, 1991.

Davenport, T. H. "Need Radical Innovation and Continuous Improvement? Integrate Process Reengineering and TQM." *Planning Review* 22, no. 3 (May/June 1993), pp. 6–12.

Davis, T. R. V., and M. S. Patrick. "Benchmarking at the SunHealth Alliance." *Planning Review* 21, no. 1 (January/February 1993), pp. 28–31ff.

Day, G. S. *Market Driven Strategy: Processes for Creating Value.* New York: The Free Press, 1990.

Delbecq, A. L., and S. L. Gill. "Developing Strategic Direction for Governing Boards." *Hospital & Health Services Administration* 33, no. 1 (Spring 1988), pp. 25–35.

Desai, H. B., and C. R. Margenthaler. "A Framework for Developing Hospital Strategies." *Hospital & Health Services Administration* 32, no. 2 (Summer 1987), pp. 235–248.

Drucker, P. F. *Managing the Nonprofit Organization.* New York: Harper Collins Publishers, 1990.

Duncan, W. J., "When Necessity Becomes a Virtue: Do Not Get Too Cynical About Strategy," *Journal of General Management* 13, no. 2 (Winter 1987), pp. 29–43.

Duncan, W. J., P. M. Ginter, and S. A. Capper. "Identifying Opportunities and Threats in Public Health." *European Journal of Public Health* 3 (1993), pp. 54–59.

Duncan, W. J., P. M. Ginter, and W. K. Kreidel. "A Sense of Direction in Public Organizations: An Analysis of Mission Statements in State Health Departments." *Administration & Society* 28, no. 1 (May 1994), pp. 11–24.

Dutton, J. E., and S. J. Ashford. "Selling Issues to Top Management." *The Academy of Management Review* 18, no. 3 (July 1993), pp. 397–428.

Dutton, J. E., and R. B. Duncan. "The Creation of Momentum for Change Through the Process of Strategic Issue Diagnosis." *Strategic Management Journal* 8, no. 3 (May/June 1987), pp. 279–295.

Dutton, J. E., and R. B. Duncan. "The Influence of the Strategic Planning Process on Strategic Change." *Strategic Management Journal* 8, no. 2 (March/April 1987), pp. 103–116.

Dutton, J. E., and S. E. Jackson. "Categorizing Strategic Issues: Links to Organizational Action." *Academy of Management Review* 12, no. 1 (January 1987), pp. 76–90.

Dutton, J. E., and E. Ottensmeyer. "Strategic Issue Management Systems: Forms, Functions, and Contexts." *Academy of Management Review* 12, no. 2 (April 1987), pp. 355–365.

Dwore, R. B., and B. P. Murray. "Hospital Administrators in a Market Environment: The Case of Utah." *Hospital & Health Services Administration* 32, no. 4 (Winter 1987), pp. 493–508.

Dychtwald, K., and M. Zitter. "Developing a Strategic Marketing Plan for Hospitals." *Healthcare Financial Management* 42, no. 9 (September 1988), pp. 42–46.

Eastaugh, S. R. "Hospital Specialization and Cost Efficiency: Benefits of Trimming Product Lines." *Hospital & Health Services Administration* 37, no. 2 (Summer 1992), pp. 223–235.

Eastaugh, S. R. "Hospital Strategy and Financial Performance." *Health Care Management Review* 17, no. 3 (Summer 1992), pp. 19–31.

Eastaugh, S. R., and J. A. Eastaugh. "Prospective Payment System: Steps to Enhance Quality, Efficiency, and Regionalization." *Health Care Management Review* 11, no. 4 (Fall 1986), pp. 37–52.

Ehreth, J. "Hospital Survival in a Competitive Environment: The Competitive Constituency Model." *Hospital & Health Services Administration* 38, no. 1 (Spring 1993), pp. 23–44.

El Sawy, O. A., and T. C. Pauchant. "Triggers, Templates and Twitches in the Tracking of Emerging Strategic Issues." *Strategic Management Journal* 9, no. 5 (September/October 1988), pp. 455–474.

El-Namaki, M. S. S. "Creating a Corporate Vision." *Long Range Planning* 25, no. 6 (1992), pp. 25–29.

Enthoven, A. "The History and Principles of Managed Competition." *Health Affairs,* Supplement (1993), pp. 24–48.

Enthoven, A., and R. Kronick. "A Consumer-Choice Health Plan for the 1990s." *New England Journal of Medicine* 320, no. 1 (January 5, 1989), pp. 29–37.

Enthoven, A., and R. Kronick. "A Consumer-Choice Health Plan for the 1990s." *New England Journal of Medicine* 320, no. 2 (January 12, 1989), pp. 94–101.

Erickson, G. M., and S. A. Finkler. "Determinants of Market Share for a Hospital's Services." *Medical Care* 23, no. 8 (August 1985), pp. 1003–1018.

Fahey, L., and V. K. Narayanan. *Macroenvironmental Analysis for Strategic Management,* 2d ed. St. Paul: West Publishing Company, 1986.

Fallon, R. P. "Not-for-Profit ≠ No-Profit: Profitability Planning in Not-for-Profit Organizations." *Health Care Management Review* 16, no. 3 (Summer 1991), pp. 47–61.

Fennell, M. L., and J. A. Alexander. "Governing Boards and Profound Organizational Change in Hospitals." *Medical Care Review* 46, no. 2 (Summer 1989), pp. 157–187.

Fennell, M. L., and J. A. Alexander. "Organizational Boundary Spanning in Institutionalized Environments." *Academy of Management Journal* 30, no. 3 (September 1987), pp. 456–476.

Ferrand, J. D., M. Chokron, and C. M. Lay. "An Integrated Analytic Framework for Evaluation of Hospital Information Systems Planning." *Medical Care Review* 50, no. 3 (Fall 1993), pp. 327–366.

Fetter, R. B., and J. L. Freeman. "Diagnosis Related Groups: Product Line Management Within Hospitals." *Academy of Management Review* 11, no. 1 (January 1986), pp. 41–54.

Files, L. A. "Strategy Formulation in Hospitals." *Health Care Management Review* 13, no. 1 (Winter 1988), pp. 9–16.

Findelstein, S. "Power in Top Management Teams: Dimensions, Measurement, and Validation." *Academy of Management Journal* 35 (1992), pp. 505–538.

Floyd, S. W., and B. Wooldridge. "Managing Strategic Consensus: The Foundation of Effective Implementation." *Academy of Management Executive* 6 (November 1992), pp. 27–35.

Folger, J. C. "Integration of Strategic, Financial Plans Vital to Success." *Healthcare Financial Management* 43, no. 1 (January 1989), pp. 22–32.

Folger, J. C. "Strategic Plans Provide Lasting Solutions to Rural Crisis." *Healthcare Financial Management* 44, no. 4 (April 1990), pp. 25–30.

Fontaine, S. J. "Evaluating the Use of Environmental Analysis in Health Care." *Health Care Strategic Management* 5, no. 12 (December 1987), pp. 15–18.

Fosler, R. S. "Demographics of the 90s: The Issues and Implications for Public Policy." *Vital Speeches of the Day* 55 (1989), pp. 572–576.

Foster, J. T. "Hospitals in the Year 2000: A Scenario." *Frontiers of Health Services Management* 6, no. 2 (Winter 1989), pp. 3–29.

Fottler, M. D., J. D. Blair, C. J. Whitehead, M. D. Lau, and G. T. Savage. "Assessing Key Stakeholders: Who Matters to Hospitals and Why?" *Hospital & Health Services Administration* 34, no. 4 (Winter 1989), pp. 525–546.

Fottler, M. D., R. L. Phillips, J. D. Blair, and C. A. Duran. "Achieving Competitive Advantage Through Strategic Human Resources Management." *Hospital & Health Services Administration* 35, no. 3 (Fall 1990), pp. 341–364.

Fottler, M. D., and L. J. Repasky. "Attitudes of Hospital Executives Toward Product Line Management: A Pilot Survey." *Health Care Management Review* 13, no. 3 (Summer 1988), pp. 15–22.

Fottler, M. D., H. L. Smith, and H. J. Muller. "Retrenchment in Health Care Organizations: Theory and Practice." *Hospital & Health Services Administration* 31, no. 3 (Fall 1986), pp. 29–43.

Fox, I., and A. Marcus. "The Causes and Consequences of Leveraged Management Buyouts." *Academy of Management Review* 17, no. 1 (January 1992), pp. 62–85.

Fox, W. L. "Vertical Integration Strategies: More Promising than Diversification." *Health Care Management Review* 14, no. 3 (Summer 1989), pp. 49–56.

France, K. R., and R. Grover. "What Is the Health Care Product?" *Journal of Health Care Marketing* 12, no. 2 (June 1992), pp. 32–45.

Fredrickson, J. W. "Effects of Decision Motive and Organizational Performance Level on Strategic Decision Processes." *Academy of Management Journal* 28, no. 4 (December 1985), pp. 821–843.

Fredrickson, J. W., ed. *Perspectives on Strategic Management.* New York: Harper Business, 1990.

Fredrickson, J. W., and T. R. Mitchell. "Strategic Decision Processes: Comprehensiveness and Performance in an Industry with an Unstable Environment." *Academy of Management Journal* 27, no. 2 (June 1984), pp. 399–423.

Frenzel, C. W. *Management of Information Technology.* Boston: boyd & fraser publishing company, 1992.

Friedman, B., and S. M. Shortell. "The Financial Performance of Selected Investor-Owned and Not-for-Profit System Hospitals Before and After Medicare Prospective Payment." *Health Services Research* 23, no. 2 (June 1988), pp. 237–267.

Friedman, E. *Choices and Conflict: Explorations in Health Care Ethics.* Chicago: American Hospital Publishing, 1992.

Frize, M., and M. Shaffer. "Clinical Engineering in Today's Hospital." *Hospital & Health Services Administration* 36, no. 2 (Summer 1991), pp. 288–299.

Frost, P. J., L. F. Moore, M. L. Louis, C. C. Lundberg, and J. Martin, eds. *Reframing Organizational Culture.* Newbury Park, California: Sage Publications, 1991.

Gabler, J. M. "Information Systems: A Competitive Advantage for Managing Healthcare." In Marion J. Ball, Judith V. Douglas, Robert I. O'Desky, and

James W. Albright, eds., *Healthcare Information Management Systems.* New York: Springer-Verlag, 1991.

Gabrieli, E. R. "Aspects of a Computer-Based Patient Record." *Journal of AHIMA* 64, no. 7 (July 1993), pp. 70–82.

Gallupe, R. B., A. R. Dennis, W. H. Cooper, J. S. Valacich, L. M. Bastianutti, and J. F. Nunamaker, Jr. "Electronic Brainstorming and Group Size." *Academy of Management* 35, no. 2 (June 1992), pp. 350–369.

Gapenski, L. C. "Capital Investment Analysis: Three Methods." *Healthcare Financial Management* 47, no. 8 (August 1993), pp. 60–66.

Gapenski, L. C., W. B. Vogel, and B. Langland-Orban. "The Determinants of Hospital Profitability." *Hospital & Health Services Administration* 38, no. 1 (Spring 1993), pp. 63–80.

Garnick, D. W., H. S. Luft, J. C. Robinson, and J. Tetreault. "Appropriate Measures of Hospital Market Areas." *Health Services Research* 22, no. 1 (April 1987), pp. 69–89.

Garrett, T. M., R. J. Klonoski, and H. W. Baillie. "American Business Ethics and Healthcare Costs." *Healthcare Management Review* 18, no. 4 (1993), pp. 44–50.

Gay, E. G., J. J. Kronenfeld, S. L. Baker, and R. L. Amidon. "An Appraisal of Organizational Response to Fiscally Constraining Regulation: The Case of Hospitals and DRGs." *Journal of Health and Social Behavior* 30 (1989), pp. 41–55.

Gehani, R. R. "Quality Value-Chain: A Meta-Synthesis of Frontiers of the Quality Movement." *Academy of Management Executive* 7, no. 2 (1993), pp. 29–42.

Gehrt, K. C., and M. B. Pinto. "Assessing the Viability of Situationally Driven Segmentation Opportunities in the Health Care Market." *Hospital & Health Services Administration* 38, no. 2 (Summer 1993), pp. 243–265.

Gersick, C. J. G. "Revolutionary Change Theories: A Multilevel Exploration of the Punctuated Equilibrium Paradigm." *Academy of Management Review* 16, no. 1 (January 1991), pp. 10–36.

Giardina, C. W., M. D. Fottler, R. M. Schewchuk, and D. B. Hill. "The Case for Hospital Diversification into Long-Term Care." *Health Care Management Review* 15, no. 1 (Winter 1990), pp. 71–82.

Gibson, C. K., D. J. Newton, and D. S. Cochran. "An Empirical Investigation of the Nature of Hospital Mission Statements." *Health Care Management Review* 15, no. 3 (Summer 1990), pp. 35–46.

Gill, S. L., and S. S. Meighan. "Five Roadblocks to Effective Partnerships in a Competitive Health Care Environment." *Hospital & Health Services Administration* 33, no. 4 (Winter 1988), pp. 505–520.

Gillock, R. E., H. L. Smith, and N. F. Piland. "For-Profit and Nonprofit Mergers: Concerns and Outcomes." *Hospital & Health Services Administration* 31, no. 4 (Winter 1986), pp. 74–84.

Ginn, G. O., and G. J. Young. "Organizational and Environmental Determinants of Hospital Strategy." *Hospital & Health Services Administration* 37, no. 3 (Fall 1992), pp. 291–302.

Ginsberg, A. "Measuring and Modeling Changes in Strategy: Theoretical Foundations and Empirical Directions." *Strategic Management Journal* 9, no. 6 (November/December 1987), pp. 559–575.

Ginsberg, A., and E. Abrahamson. "Champions of Change and Strategic Shifts: The Role of Internal and External Change Advocates." *Journal of Management Studies* 28 (March, 1991), pp. 173–190.

Ginsberg, A., and A. Buchholtz. "Converting to For-profit Status: Corporate Responsiveness to Radical Change." *Academy of Management Journal* 33, no. 3 (September 1990), pp. 445–477.

Ginter P. M., W. J. Duncan, and S. A. Capper. "Keeping Strategic Thinking in Strategic Planning: Macro-Environmental Analysis in a State Department of Public Health." *Public Health* 106 (1992), pp. 253–269.

Ginter, P. M., W. J. Duncan, S. A. Capper, and M. G. Rowe. "Evaluating Public Health Programs Using Portfolio Analysis." *Proceeding of the Southern Management Association,* Atlanta, November 1993, pp. 492–496.

Ginter, P. M., W. J. Duncan, W. D. Richardson, and L. E. Swayne. "Analyzing the Health Care Environment: 'You Can't Hit What You Can't See.' " *Health Care Management Review* 16, no. 4 (Fall 1991), pp. 35–48.

Ginter, P. M., A. C. Rucks, and W. J. Duncan. "Characteristics of Strategic Planning in Selected Service Industries and Planner Satisfaction with the Process." *Management International Review* 29, no. 2 (1989), pp. 66–74.

Ginter, P. M., A. C. Rucks, and W. J. Duncan. "Planners' Perceptions of the Strategic Management Process." *Journal of Management Studies* 22, no. 6 (1985), pp. 581–596.

Ginzberg, E. "Health Personnel: The Challenges Ahead." *Frontiers of Health Services Management* 7, no. 2 (Winter 1990), pp. 3–20.

Ginzberg, E. "Medical Care for the Poor: No Magic Bullets." *Journal of the American Medical Association* 259, no. 22 (1988), pp. 3309–3311.

Giola, D. A., and K. Chittipeddi. "Sensemaking and Sensegiving in Strategic Change Initiation." *Strategic Management Journal* 12, no. 6 (September 1991), pp. 433–448.

Glenesk, A. E. "Six Myths That Can Cloud Strategic Vision." *Healthcare Financial Management* 44, no. 5 (May 1990), pp. 38–43.

Goldberg, J., and H. J. Martin. "Control and Support: What Physicians Want from Hospitals." *Hospital & Health Services Administration* 35, no. 1 (Spring 1990), pp. 27–37.

Goldman, R. L. "Practical Applications of Health Care Marketing Ethics." *Healthcare Financial Management* 47, no. 3 (March 1993), pp. 47–54.

Goldsmith, J. "A Radical Prescription for Hospitals." *Harvard Business Review* 67, no. 3 (May/June 1989), pp. 104–111.

Goodstein, J., and W. Boeker. "Turbulence at the Top: A New Perspective on Governance Structure Changes and Strategic Change." *Academy of Management Journal* 34, no. 2 (June 1991), pp. 306–330.

Goody, B. "Defining Rural Hospital Markets." *Health Services Research* 28, no. 2 (June 1993), pp. 183–200.

Goold, M., and K. Luchs. "Why Diversify? Four Decades of Management Thinking." *Academy of Management Executive* 7, no. 3 (August 1993), pp. 7–25.

Goold, M., and J. J. Quinn. "The Paradox of Strategic Controls." *Strategic Management Journal* 11, no. 1 (January 1990), pp. 40–50.

Gould, S. J. "Macrodynamic Trends in Health Care: A Distribution and Retailing Perspective." *Health Care Management Review* 13, no. 2 (Spring 1988), pp. 15–22.

Gourley, D. R., and M. E. Moore. "Marketing and Planning in Multihospital Systems." *Hospital & Health Services Administration* 33, no. 3 (Fall 1988), pp. 331–344.

Govindarajan, V. "Implementing Competitive Strategies at the Business Unit Level: Implications of Matching Managers to Strategies." *Strategic Management Journal* 10, no. 3 (March/April 1989), pp. 251–269.

Gray, B. H. "Why Nonprofits? Hospitals and the Future of American Health Care." *Frontiers of Health Services Management* 8, no. 4 (Summer 1992), pp. 3–32.

Greaf, W. D. "Public Hospital Strategic Planning: Does it Differ From Voluntary, Not-For-Profit Hospital Strategic Planning?" *Health Care Management Review* 13, no. 3 (Summer 1988), pp. 7–14.

Greer, C. R., and T. C. Ireland. "Organizational and Financial Correlates of a Contrarian Human Resource Investment Strategy." *Academy of Management Journal* 35 (1992), pp. 956–984.

Gregory, D. "Strategic Alliances between Physicians and Hospitals in Multihospital Systems." *Hospital & Health Services Administration* 37, no. 2 (Summer 1992), pp. 247–258.

Greifinger, R. B., and M. S. Bluestone. "Building Physician Alliances for Cost Containment." *Health Care Management Review* 11, no. 4 (Fall 1986), pp. 63–72.

Griffith, J. R. "Voluntary Hospitals: Are Trustees the Solution?" *Hospital & Health Services Administration* 33, no. 3 (Fall 1988), pp. 295–309.

Grim, S. A. "Win/Win: Urban and Rural Hospitals Network for Survival." *Hospital & Health Services Administration* 31, no. 1 (Spring 1986), pp. 34–46.

Gupta, A. K. "SBU Strategies, Corporate-SBU Relations, and SBU Effectiveness in Strategy Implementation." *Academy of Management Journal* 30, no. 3 (September 1987), pp. 477–500.

Gutknecht, J. E., and J. B. Keys. "Mergers, Acquisitions, and Takeovers: Maintaining Morale of Survivors and Protecting Employees." *Academy of Management Executive* 7, no. 3 (August 1993), pp. 26–36.

Hall, R. "A Framework Linking Intangible Resources and Capabilities to Sustainable Competitive Advantage." *Strategic Management Journal* 14, no. 8 (November 1993), pp. 607–618.

Halseth, M. J., and J. R. Paul. "The Coming Revolution in Information Systems." *Computers in Healthcare* 13, no. 11 (November 1992), pp. 43–44.

Hambrick, D. C. "Some Tests of the Effectiveness and Functional Attitudes of Miles and Snow's Strategic Types." *Academy of Management Journal* 26, no. 1 (March 1983), pp. 263–279.

Hambrick, D. C., I. C. MacMillan, and D. L. Day. "Strategic Attributes and Performance in the BCG Matrix: A PIMS-Based Analysis of Industrial-Product Business." *Academy of Management Journal* 25, no. 3 (September 1982), pp. 510–531.

Hamel, G., and C. K. Prahalad. "Strategy as Stretch and Leverage." *Harvard Business Review* 68, no. 3 (1993), pp. 75–84.

Hammer, M. "Reengineering Work: Don't Automate, Obliterate." *Harvard Business Review* (July/August 1990), pp. 104–112.

Hammer, M., and J. Champy. *Reengineering the Corporation: A Manifesto for Business Revolution.* New York: Harper Business, 1993.

Harper, S. C. "The Challenges Facing CEOs: Past, Present, and Future." *Academy of Management Executive* 6, no. 3 (August 1992), pp. 7–25.

Harrell, G. D., and M. F. Fors. "Planning Evolution in Hospital Management." *Health Care Management Review* 12, no. 1 (Winter 1987), pp. 9–22.

Harrington, C., R. J. Newcomer, and T. G. Moore. "Factors that Contribute to Medicare HMO Risk Contract Success." *Inquiry* 25, no. 2 (Summer 1988), pp. 251–262.

Harris, C., L. L. Hicks, and B. J. Kelly, "Physician-Hospital Networking: Avoiding a Shotgun Wedding." *Health Care Management Review* 17, no. 4 (Fall 1992), pp. 17–28.

Hart, S. L. "An Integrative Framework for Strategy-Making Processes." *Academy of Management Review* 17, no. 2 (April 1992), pp. 327–351.

Hax, A. C. "Redefining the Concept of Strategy and the Strategy Formation Process." *Planning Review* 18, no. 3 (May/June 1990), pp. 34–40.

Healthy Communities 2000 Model Standards: Guidelines for Community Attainment of the Year 2000 National Health Objectives, 3rd ed. Washington D.C.: American Public Health Association, 1991.

Healthy People: National Health Promotion and Disease Prevention Objectives. Washington, D.C.: U.S. Department of Health and Human Services, Public Health Service, 1991.

Henderson, J. C., and J. B. Thomas. "Aligning Business and Information Technology Domains: Strategic Planning in Hospitals." *Hospital & Health Services Administration* 37, no. 1 (Spring 1992), pp. 71–87.

Herbert, T. T., and H. Deresky. "Generic Strategies: An Empirical Investigation of Typology Validity and Strategy Content." *Strategic Management Journal* 9, no. 2 (February 1987), pp. 135–147.

Herzlinger, R. E. "The Failed Revolution in Health Care – The Role of Management." *Harvard Business Review* 67, no. 3 (May/June 1989), pp. 95–103.

Heshmat, S. "The Role of Cost in Hospital Pricing Decisions." *Journal of Hospital Marketing* 6, no. 1 (1991), pp. 155–161.

Heskett, J. L., W. E. Sasser, Jr., and C. W. L. Hart. *Service Breakthroughs – Changing the Rules of the Game.* New York: The Free Press, 1990.

Higgins, C. W., and E. D. Meyers. "Managed Care and Vertical Integration: Implications for the Hospital Industry." *Hospital & Health Services Administration* 32, no. 3 (Fall 1987), pp. 319–327.

Hiller, M. D. *Ethics and Health Administration: Ethical Decision Making in Health Management.* Arlington, Virginia: Association of University Programs in Health Administration, 1986.

Hillestad, S. G., and E. N. Berkowitz. *Health Care Marketing Plans: From Strategy to Action,* 2d ed. Gaithersburg, Maryland: Aspen Publishers, 1991.

Hinterhuber, H. H., and W. Popp. "Are You a Strategist or Just a Manager?" *Harvard Business Review* 70 (January/February 1992), pp. 105–113.

Hitt, M. A., R. E. Hoskisson, and J. S. Harrison. "Strategic Competitiveness in the 1990s: Challenges and Opportunities for U.S. Executives." *Academy of Management Executive* 5, no. 2 (May 1991), pp. 23–33.

Hitt, M. A., R. E. Hoskisson, and R. Nixon. "A Mid-Range Theory of Interfunctional Integration, Its Antecedents and Outcomes." *Journal of Engineering and Technology Management* 10 (1993), pp. 26–40.

Hoskisson, R. E., and R. A. Johnson. "Corporate Restructuring and Strategic Change: Effect on Diversification Strategy and R&D Intensity." *Strategic Management Journal* 13 (1992), pp. 625–634.

Huff, A. S., and R. K. Reger. "A Review of Strategic Process Research." *Journal of Management* 13, no. 2 (Summer 1987), pp. 211–236.

Hughes, W. L., and S. Y. Soliman. "Short-Term Case Mix Management with Linear Programming." *Hospital & Health Services Administration* 30, no. 1 (Spring 1985), pp. 61–71.

Hunter, S. S. "Marketing and Strategic Management: Integrating Skills for a Better Hospital." *Hospital & Health Services Administration* 32, no. 2 (Summer 1987), pp. 205–217.

Hurley, R. E. "The Purchaser-Driven Reformation in Health Care: Alternative Approaches to Leveling Our Cathedrals." *Frontiers of Health Services Management* 9, no. 4 (1993), pp. 5–35.

Hutchinson, R. A., K. E. White, and D. P. Vogel. "Development and Implementation of a Strategic Planning Process at a University Hospital." *American Journal of Hospital Pharmacy* 46 (May 1989), pp. 952–957.

Ireland, R. D., and M. A. Hitt. "Mission Statements: Importance, Challenge, and Recommendations for Development." *Business Horizons* 35 no. 3 (1992), pp. 34–42.

Ireland, R. D., M. A. Hitt, R. A. Bettis, and D. A. DePorras. "Strategy Formulation Processes: Differences in Perceptions of Strengths and Weaknesses Indicators and Environmental Uncertainty by Managerial Level." *Strategic Management Journal* 8, no. 4 (July/August 1987), pp. 469–485.

Jackson, S. E., and J. E. Dutton. "Discerning Threats and Opportunities." *Administrative Science Quarterly* 33, no. 3 (September 1988), pp. 370–387.

Jacobson, C. K. "A Conceptual Framework for Evaluating Joint Venture Opportunities Between Hospitals and Physicians." *Health Services Management Research* 2, no. 3 (Summer 1989), pp. 204–212.

Jacobson, R. "The 'Austrian' School of Strategy." *Academy of Management Review* 17, no. 4 (October 1992), pp. 782–807.

Jaeger, B. J., A. D. Kaluzny, and K. Magruder-Habib. "A New Perspective on Multiinstitutional Systems Management." *Health Care Management Review* 12, no. 4 (Fall 1987), pp. 9–19.

James, K. "Process and Culture Impediments to Health Care Innovation." *Hospital & Health Services Administration* 35, no. 3 (Fall 1990), pp. 395–407.

Javalgi, R. G., T. W. Whipple, M. K. McManamon, and V. L. Edick. "Hospital Image: A Correspondence Analysis Approach." *Journal of Health Care Marketing* 12, no. 4 (December 1992), pp. 34–39.

Jerrell, S. L. "Strategic Adaptation by Community Mental Health Centers." *Academy of Management Proceedings* (August 1986), pp. 87–90.

John, J., and A. R. Miller. "Strategic Planning for Nursing Homes: A Market Opportunity Analysis Perspective." *Health Care Management Review* 14, no. 4 (Fall 1989), pp. 11–19.

Johnson, D. E. L. "Health-Care Futurists Face New Scenarios in Planning." *Health Care Strategic Management* 6, no. 6 (June 1988), pp. 2–3.

Johnson, E. A. "Ethical Considerations for Business Relationships of Hospitals and Physicians." *Health Care Management Review* 16, no. 3 (Summer 1991), pp. 7–13.

Johnson, E. A. "The Competitive Market: Changing Medical Staff Accountability." *Hospital & Health Services Administration* 33, no. 2 (Summer 1988), pp. 179–187.

Johnson, G. "Managing Strategic Change—Strategy, Culture, and Action." *Long Range Planning* 25, no. 1 (1992), pp. 28–36.

Johnson, R. A., R. E. Hoskisson, and M. A. Hitt. "Board of Director Involvement in Restructuring: The Effects of Board Versus Managerial Controls and Characteristics." *Strategic Management Journal* 14, Special Issue (1993), pp. 33–50.

Jones, K. R., and S. G. Sloate. "Academic Health Center Hospitals: Alternative Responses to Financial Stress." *Health Care Management Review* 12, no. 3 (Summer 1987), pp. 83–89.

Jones, S. B., M. K. DuVal, and M. Lesparre. "Competition or Conscience? Mixed-Mission Dilemmas of the Voluntary Hospital." *Inquiry* 24, no. 2 (Summer 1987), pp. 110–118.

Jones, W. "Letting Technology Dictate Design." *Health Care Strategic Management* 6, no. 11 (November 1988), pp. 10–12.

Judge, W. Q., and C. P. Zeithaml. "An Empirical Comparison Between the Board's Strategic Role in Nonprofit Hospitals and in For-Profit Industrial Firms." *Health Services Research* 27, no. 1 (April 1992), pp. 47–64.

Kaluzny, A. D. "Revitalizing Decision Making at the Middle Management Level." *Hospital & Health Services Administration* 34, no. 1 (Spring 1989), pp. 39–51.

Kalunzy, A. D., L. M. Lacey, R. Warnecke, D. M. Hynes, J. Morrisey, L. Ford, and E. Sondik. "Predicting the Performance of a Strategic Alliance: An Analysis of the Community Clinical Oncology Program." *Health Services Research* 28, no. 2 (June 1993), pp. 159–182.

Kaluzny, A. D., C. P. McLaughlin, and C. P. Simpson. "Applying Total Quality Management Concepts to Public Health Organizations." *Public Health Reports* 107, no. 3 (1992), pp. 257–264.

Kaluzny, A., and H. S. Zuckerman. "Strategic Alliances Ensure TQM's Full Potential." *Healthcare Executive* 8, no. 3 (May/June 1993), p. 33.

Kaluzny, A. D., and H. S. Zuckerman. "Strategic Alliances: Two Perspectives for Understanding Their Effects on Health Services." *Hospital & Health Services Administration* 37, no. 4 (Winter 1992), pp. 477–490.

Kamath, R. R., and J. Elmer. "Capital Investment Decisions in Hospitals: Survey Results." *Health Care Management Review* 14, no. 2 (Spring 1989), pp. 45–56.

Keen, P. G. W. *Shaping the Future: Business Design Through Information Technology.* Boston: Harvard Business School Press, 1991.

Kellinghusen, G., and K. Wubbenhorst. "Strategic Control for Improved Performance." *Long Range Planning* 23, no. 3 (1990), pp. 30–40.

Kennedy, M., J. A. Prevost, M. P. Carr, and J. W. Dilley. "A Roundtable Discussion: Hospital Leaders Discuss Quality Improvement Implementation Issues." *Journal of Quality Improvement* 18 (March 3, 1992), pp. 78–97.

Kiernan, M. J. "The New Strategic Architecture: Learning to Compete in the Twenty-First Century." *Academy of Management Executive* 7, no. 1 (February 1993), pp. 7–21.

Kimberly, J. R., and E. J. Zajac. "Strategic Adaptation in Health Care Organizations: Implications for Theory and Research." *Medical Care Review* 42, no. 2 (Fall 1985), pp. 267–302.

Klein, H. E., and R. E. Linneman. "Environmental Assessment: An International Study of Corporate Practices." *Journal of Business Strategy* (1984), pp. 69–77.

Kotabe, M., and E. P. Cox, III. "Assessment of Global Competitiveness: Patent Applications and Grants in Four Major Trading Countries." *Business Horizons* 36, no. 1 (1993), pp. 57–64.

Kotler, P., and R. N. Clarke. *Marketing for Health Care Organizations.* Englewood Cliffs, New Jersey: Prentice-Hall, 1987.

Kotler, P., and S. J. Levy. "Broadening the Concept of Marketing." *Journal of Marketing* 33, no. 1 (January 1969), pp. 10–15.

Kotter, J. P., and J. L. Heskett. *Corporate Culture and Performance.* New York: Free Press, 1992.

Kovner, A. R., and M. J. Chin. "Physician Leadership in Hospital Strategic Decision Making." *Hospital & Health Services Administration* 30, no. 4 (Winter 1985), pp. 64–79.

Kralewski, J. E., R. Feldman, B. Dowd, and J. Shapiro. "Strategies Employed by HMOs to Achieve Hospital Discounts." *Health Care Management Review* 16, no. 1 (Winter 1991), pp. 9–16.

Kralewski, J., G. Gifford, and J. Porter. "Profit vs. Public Welfare Goals in Investor-Owned and Not-for-Profit Hospitals." *Hospital & Health Services Administration* 33, no. 3 (Fall 1988), pp. 311–329.

Kropf, R., and A. J. Szafran. "Developing a Competitive Advantage in the Market for Radiology Services." *Hospital & Health Services Administration* 33, no. 2 (Summer 1988), pp. 213–220.

Leebov, W., and G. Scott. *Health Care Managers in Transition.* San Francisco: Jossey-Bass, 1990.

Lemieux-Charles, L. "Ethical Issues Faced by Clinicians/Managers in Resource-Allocation Decisions." *Hospital & Health Services Administration* 38, no. 2 (Summer 1993), pp. 267–286.

Lengnick-Hall, C. A. "Innovation and Competitive Advantage." *Journal of Management* 18, no. 2 (1992), pp. 399–429.

Levitz, G. S., and P. P. Brooke. "Independent versus System-Affiliated Hospitals: A Comparative Analysis of Financial Performance, Cost, and Productivity." *Health Services Research* 20, no. 3 (August 1985), pp. 315–339.

Liedtka, J. M. "Formulating Hospital Strategy: Moving Beyond a Market Mentality." *Health Care Management Review* 17, no. 1 (Winter 1992), pp. 21–26.

Linder, J. C. "Outcomes Measurement in Hospitals: Can the System Change the Organization?" *Hospital & Health Services Administration* 37, no. 2 (Summer 1992), pp. 143–166.

Linder, J. C. "Outcomes Measurement: Compliance Tool or Strategic Initiative?" *Health Care Management Review* 16, no. 4 (Fall 1991), pp. 21–33.

Longest, B. B., Jr. "Interorganizational Linkages in the Health Sector." *Health Care Management Review* 15, no. 1 (Winter 1990), pp. 17–28.

Longest, B. B., Jr., K. Darr, and J. S. Rakich. "Organizational Leadership in Hospitals." *Hospital Topics* 71, no. 3 (Summer 1993), pp. 11–15.

Lubatkin, M., and R. C. Rogers. "Diversification, Systematic Risk, and Shareholder Return." *Academy of Management Journal* 32, no. 2 (June 1989), pp. 454–465.

Luft, H. S., J. C. Robinson, D. W. Garnick, R. Hughes, S. J. McPhee, S. Hunt, and J. Showstack. "Hospital Behavior in a Local Market Context." *Medical Care Review* 43, no. 2 (Fall 1986), pp. 217–251.

Luke, R. D. "Local Hospital Systems: Forerunners of Regional Systems?" *Frontiers of Health Services Management* 9, no. 2 (1992), pp. 3–51.

Luke, R. D. "Spatial Competition and Cooperation in Local Hospital Markets." *Medical Care Review* 48, no. 2 (Summer 1991), pp. 207–237.

Luke, R. D., and J. W. Begun. "Strategic Orientations of Small Multihospital Systems." *Health Services Research* 23, no. 5 (December 1988), pp. 597–618.

Luke, R. D., and J. W. Begun. "The Management of Strategy." In S. M. Shortell and A. D. Kaluzny, eds., *Health Care Management,* pp. 463–491. New York: John Wiley & Sons, 1988.

Luke, R. D., J. W. Begun, and D. D. Pointer. "Quasi Firms: Strategic Interorganizational Forms in the Health Care Industry." *Academy of Management Review* 14, no. 1 (Winter 1989), pp. 9–19.

Lumsdon, K. "The 1990s: A Time for Developing Creative Financial Vision." *Healthcare Financial Management* 43, no. 10 (October 1989), pp. 19–30.

Lynn, M. L., and D. P. Osborn. "Deming's Quality Principles: A Health Care Application." *Hospital & Health Services Administration* 36, no. 1 (Spring 1991), pp. 111–120.

MacStravic, R. S. "A Customer Relations Strategy for Health Care Employee Relations." *Hospital & Health Services Administration* 34, no. 3 (Fall 1989), pp. 397–411.

MacStravic, R. S. "Market and Market Segment Portfolio Assessment for Hospitals." *Health Care Management Review* 14, no. 3 (Summer 1989), pp. 25–32.

MacStravic, R. S. "Product-Line Administration in Hospitals." *Health Care Management Review* 11, no. 1 (Winter 1989), pp. 35–43.

MacStravic, R. S. "The Patient as Partner: A Competitive Strategy in Health Care Marketing." *Hospital & Health Services Administration* 33, no. 1 (Spring 1988), pp. 15–24.

Manheim, L. M., S. M. Shortell, and S. McFall. "The Effect of Investor-Owned Chain Acquisitions on Hospital Expenses and Staffing." *Health Services Research* 24, no. 4 (October 1989), pp. 461–484.

Manton, K. G., M. A. Woodbury, J. C. Vertrees, and E. Stallard. "Use of Medicare Services Before and After Introduction of the Prospective Payment System." *Health Services Research* 28, no. 3 (August 1993), pp. 269–292.

Marszalek-Gaucher, E., and R. J. Coffey. *Transforming Healthcare Organizations.* San Francisco: Jossey-Bass, 1990.

McCain, G. "Black Holes, Cash Pigs, and Other Hospital Portfolio Analysis Problems." *Journal of Health Care Management* 7, no. 2 (June 1987), pp. 56–64.

McCue, M. J. "A Profile of Preacquisition Proprietary Hospitals." *Health Care Management Review* 13, no. 4 (Fall 1988), pp. 15–24.

McCue, M. J., and R. W. Furst. "Financial Characteristics of Hospitals Purchased by Investor-Owned Chains." *Health Services Research* 21, no. 4 (October 1986), pp. 515–527.

McCue, M. J., T. McCue, and J. R. C. Wheeler. "An Assessment of Hospital Acquisition Prices." *Inquiry* 25, no. 2 (Summer 1988), pp. 290–296.

McCue, M. J., and Y. A. Ozcan. "Determinants of Capital Structure." *Hospital & Health Services Administration* 37, no. 3 (Fall 1992), pp. 333–346.

McDermott, D. R., F. J. Franzak, and M. W. Little. "Does Marketing Relate to Hospital Profitability?" *Journal of Health Care Marketing* 13, no. 2 (Summer 1993), pp. 18–25.

McDermott, S. "The New Hospital Challenge: Organizing and Managing Physician Organizations." *Health Care Management Review* 13, no. 1 (Winter 1988), pp. 57–61.

McDevitt, P. "Learning by Doing: Strategic Marketing Management in Hospitals." *Health Care Management Review* 12, no. 1 (Winter 1987), pp. 23–30.

McFall, S. L., S. M. Shortell, and L. M. Manheim. "HCA's Acquisition Process: The Physician's Role and Perspective." *Health Care Management Review* 13, no. 1 (Winter 1988), pp. 23–34.

McGill, S. G. Jr. "Security." In *Effective Health Care Facilities Management,* ed. V. James McLarney. Chicago: American Hospital Publishing, 1991.

McKinney, M. A., A. D. Kaluzny, and H. S. Zuckerman. "Innovation Diffusion Networks in Multihospital Systems and Alliances." *Health Care Management Review* 16, no. 1 (Winter 1991), pp. 17–23.

McLafferty, S. "The Geographical Restructuring of Urban Hospitals: Spatial Dimensions of Corporate Strategy." *Social Science & Medicine* 23, no. 10 (1986), pp. 1079–1086.

McLarney, V. J., ed. *Effective Health Care Facilities Management.* Chicago: American Hospital Publishing, 1991.

McLean, R. A. "Outside Directors: Stakeholder Representation in Investor-Owned Health Care Organizations." *Hospital & Health Services Administration* 34, no. 1 (Spring 1989), pp. 255–268.

McMahon, L. F., R. B. Fetter, J. L. Freeman, and J. D. Thompson. "Hospital Matrix Management and DRG-Based Prospective Payment." *Hospital & Health Services Administration* 31, no. 1 (Spring 1986), pp. 62–74.

Mechanic, D. "America's Health Care System and Its Future: The View of a Despairing Optimist." *Medical Care Review* 50, no. 1 (Spring 1993), pp. 7–47.

Mechanic, D. "Changing Our Health Care System." *Medical Care Review* 48, no. 3 (Fall 1991), pp. 247–260.

Medley, G. J. "WWF UK Creates a New Mission." *Long Range Planning* 25, no. 2 (1992), pp. 63–68.

Mercer, D., ed. *Managing the External Environment.* London: Sage Publications, 1992.

Meyer, R. H., M. N. Mannix, and T. F. Costello. "Nursing Recruitment: Do Health Care Managers Gear Strategies to the Appropriate Audience?" *Hospital & Health Services Administration* 36, no. 3 (Fall 1991), pp. 447–453.

Michael, J. G., and D. C. Hambrick. "Diversification Posture and Top Management Team Characteristics." *Academy of Management Journal* 35 (1992), pp. 9–37.

Mick, S. S., and Associates. *Innovations in Health Care Delivery.* San Francisco: Jossey-Bass, 1990.

Mick, S. S., and D. A. Conrad. "The Decision to Integrate Vertically in Health Care Organizations." *Hospital & Health Services Administration* 33, no. 3 (Fall 1988), pp. 345–360.

Milakovich, M. E. "Creating a Total Quality Health Care Environment." *Health Care Management Review* 16, no. 2 (Spring 1991), pp. 9–20.

Miller, D. "Preserving the Privacy of Computerized Patient Records." *Healthcare Informatics* 10, no. 10 (October 1993), p. 72.

Miller, D. "Relating Porter's Business Strategies to Environment and Structure: Analysis and Performance Implications." *Academy of Management Journal* 31, no. 2 (June 1988), pp. 280–308.

Miller, R. H., and H. S. Luft. "Managed Care: Past Evidence and Potential Trends." *Frontiers of Health Services Management* 9, no. 3 (1993), pp. 3–37.

Miner, J. B. "The Validity and Usefulness of Theories in an Emerging Organizational Science." *Academy of Management Review* 9, no. 2 (April 1984), pp. 296–306.

Mintzberg, H. "The Design School: Reconsidering the Basic Premises of Strategic Management." *Strategic Management Journal* 11, no. 3 (March/April 1990), pp. 171–195.

Mohr, R. A. "An Institutional Perspective on Rational Myths and Organizational Change in Health Care." *Medical Care Review* 49, no. 2 (Summer 1992), pp. 233–255.

Molinari, C., L. L. Morlock, J. A. Alexander, and C. A. Lyles. "Hospital Board Effectiveness: Relationships Between Governing Board Composition and Hospital Financial Viability." *Health Services Research* 28, no. 3 (August 1993), pp. 357–377.

Montgomery, C. A., B. Wernerfelt, and S. Balakrishnan. "Strategy Content and the Research Process: A Critique and Commentary." *Strategic Management Journal* 10, no. 2 (March/April 1989), pp. 189–197.

Morefield, F. L. "Combining EDI and the Electronic Patient Record: The Information Infrastructure That Is Needed for Healthcare." *Journal of AHIMA* 64, no. 11 (November 1993), pp. 56–61.

Morgan, M. J. "How Corporate Culture Drives Strategy." *Long Range Planning* 26, no. 2 (1993), pp. 110–118.

Moriarty, D. D. "Strategic Information Systems Planning for Health Service Providers." *Health Care Management Review* 17, no. 1 (Winter 1992), pp. 85–90.

Morlock, L. L., and J. A. Alexander. "Models of Governance in Multihospital Systems." *Medical Care* 24, no. 12 (December 1986), pp. 1118–1135.

Morlock, L. L., J. A. Alexander, and H. M. Hunter. "Formal Relationships Among Governing Boards, CEOs and Medical Staffs in Independent and System Hospitals." *Medical Care* 23, no. 12 (December 1985), pp. 1193–1213.

Morrisey, M. A., and J. A. Alexander. "Hospital Acquisition or Management Contract: A Theory of Strategic Choice." *Health Care Management Review* 12, no. 4 (Fall 1987), pp. 21–30.

Moynihan, J. J., and K. Norman. "Networking Providers – Data Highways of the '90s." *Journal of AHIMA* 64, no. 11 (November 1993), p. 42.

Mullaney, A. D. "Downsizing: How One Hospital Responded to Decreasing Demand." *Health Care Management Review* 14, no. 3 (Summer 1989), pp. 41–48.

Muller, H. J., and H. L. Smith. "Retrenchment Strategies and Tactics for Healthcare Executives." *Hospital & Health Services Administration* 30, no. 3 (Fall 1985), pp. 31–43.

Mullner, R. M., R. J. Rydman, D. G. Whites, and R. F. Rich. "Rural Community Hospitals and Factors Correlated with Their Risk of Closing." *Public Health Reports* 104, no. 4 (July/August 1989), pp. 315–325.

Murphy, R. F. "Venture Profile Analysis." *Hospital & Health Services Administration* 30, no. 4 (Winter 1985), pp. 80–95.

Murray, V. V., and T. D. Jick. "Taking Stock of Organizational Decline Management: Some Issues and Illustrations From an Empirical Study." *Journal of Management* 11, no. 3 (September 1985), pp. 111–123.

Nackel, J. G., and I. W. Kues. "Product-Line Management: Systems and Strategies." *Hospital & Health Services Administration* 31, no. 2 (Summer 1986), pp. 109–123.

Naidu, G. M., and C. L. Narayana. "How Marketing Oriented Are Hospitals in a Declining Market?" *Journal of Health Care Marketing* 2, no. 1 (1991), pp. 30–42.

Nanis, B. *Visionary Leadership.* San Francisco: Jossey-Bass Publishers, 1992.

Nash, H. O., Jr., J. R. Barrick, E. S. Lipsey, Jr., and B. B. Blount. "Engineering and Maintenance." In *Effective Health Care Facilities Management,* ed. V. J. McLarney. Chicago: American Hospital Publishing, 1991.

Navarro, V. "The Arguments of a National Health Program: Science or Ideology." *International Journal of Health Services* 18, no. 2 (1988), pp. 179–188.

Navarro, V. "Why Some Countries Have National Health Insurance, Others Have National Health Services, and the U.S. Has Neither." *Social Science and Medicine* 18, no. 9 (1989), pp. 887–898.

Nayyar, P. R. "Performance Effects of Information Asymmetry and Economics of Scope in Diversified Service Firms." *Academy of Management Journal* 36, no. 1 (February 1993), pp. 28–57.

Newman, G. "Worried About Vision? See an Optometrist." *Across the Board* 19 (October 1992), pp. 7–8.

Nutt, P. C. "How Top Managers in Health Organizations Set Directions That Guide Decision Making." *Hospital & Health Services Administration* 36, no. 1 (Spring 1991), pp. 57–75.

Nutt, P. C. "Identifying and Appraising How Managers Install Strategy." *Strategic Management Journal* 8, no. 6 (January/February 1987), pp. 1–14.

Nutt, P. C. "Tactics of Implementation." *Academy of Management Journal* 29, no. 2 (June 1986), pp. 230–261.

Nutt, P. C., and R. W. Backoff. *Strategic Management of Public and Third Sector Organizations: A Handbook for Leaders.* San Francisco: Jossey-Bass Publishers, 1992.

Nutt, P. C., and R. W. Backoff. "Transforming Public Organizations with Strategic Management and Strategic Leadership." *Journal of Management* 19 (Summer 1993), pp. 299–347.

Nystrom, P. C. "Organizational Cultures, Strategies, and Commitments in Health Care Organizations." *Health Care Management Review* 18, no. 1 (Winter 1993), pp. 43–49.

O'Leary, M. "Reinventing the Heal." *CIO Magazine* 6, no. 7 (February 1993), pp. 1–5.

Oliver, C. "Strategic Responses to Institutional Processes." *Academy of Management Review* 16, no 1 (January 1991), pp. 145–179.

Oliver, C. "Determinants of Interorganizational Relationships: Integration and Future Directions." *Academy of Management Review* 15, no. 2 (April 1990), pp. 241–265.

Ozcan, Y. A., and R. D. Luke. "A National Study of the Efficiency of Hospitals in Urban Markets." *Health Services Research* 27, no. 6 (February 1993), pp. 719–739.

Parkhe, A. "Strategic Alliance Structuring: A Game Theoretic and Transaction Cost Examination of Interfirm Cooperation." *Academy of Management Journal* 36, no. 4 (August 1993), pp. 794–829.

Parry, M., and A. E. Parry. "Strategy and Marketing Tactics in Nonprofit Hospitals." *Health Care Management Review* 17, no. 1 (Winter 1992), pp. 51–61.

Pearce, J. A., II, and F. David. "Corporate Mission Statements and the Bottom Line." *Academy of Management Executive* 1, no. 2 (May 1987), pp. 109–116.

Pearson, E. "Marketing Audit Reveals Holes and Opportunities." *Health Care Strategic Management* 8, no. 7 (July 1990), pp. 17–18.

Pegels, C. C., and K. A. Rogers. *Strategic Management of Hospitals and Health Care Facilities.* Rockville, Maryland: Aspen Publishers, 1988.

Pelfrey, S., and B. A. Theisen. "Joint Ventures in Health Care." *Journal of Nursing Administration* 19, no. 4 (April 1989), pp. 39–42.

Penrod, J. I. "Methods and Models for Planning Strategically." In M. J. Ball, J. V. Douglas, R. I. O'Desky, and J. W. Albright, eds., *Healthcare Information Management Systems.* New York: Springer-Verlag, 1991.

Perry, D. L. "Keys to Creating an Effective Ethics Program." *Healthcare Executive* 8, no. 2 (March/April 1993), p. 26.

Petchers, M. K., S. Swanker, and M. K. Singer. "The Hospital Merger: Its Effect on Employees." *Health Care Management Review* 13, no. 4 (Fall 1988), pp. 9–14.

Peteraf, M. A. "The Cornerstones of Competitive Advantage: A Resource-based View." *Strategic Management Journal* 14, no. 3 (March 1993), pp. 179–191.

Peters, J. P. *A Strategic Planning Process for Hospitals.* Chicago: American Hospital Publishing, 1985.

Peters, T. *Liberation Management: Necessary Disorganization for the Nanosecond Nineties.* New York: Alfred A. Knopf, 1992.

Pettigrew, A. M. *The Management of Strategic Change.* Oxford: Basil Blackwell, 1987.

Pettigrew, A. M., E. Ferlie, and L. McKee. *Shaping Strategic Change.* London: Sage Publications, 1992.

Pickett, G. "Local Public Health and the State." *American Journal of Public Health* 79, no. 8 (August 1989), pp. 967–968.

Pickett, G. "The Future of Health Departments: The Governmental Presence." *Annual Review of Public Health* 9, no. 1 (1988), pp. 298–322.

Pitts, T. "The Illusion of Control and the Importance of Community in Health Care Organization." *Hospital & Health Services Administration* 38, no. 1 (Spring 1993), pp. 101–109.

Pointer, D. D. "Offering-Level Strategy Formulation in Health Services Organizations." *Health Care Management Review* 15, no. 3 (1990), pp. 15–23.

Pointer, D. D., J. W. Begun, and R. D. Luke. "Managing Interorganizational Dependencies in the New Health Care Marketplace." *Hospital & Health Services Administration* 33, no. 2 (Summer 1988), pp. 167–177.

Pointer, D. D., and J. Zwanziger. "Pricing Strategy and Tactics in the New Hospital Marketplace." *Hospital & Health Services Administration* 31, no. 4 (Winter 1986), pp. 5–18.

Pol, L. G., and R. K. Thomas. *The Demography of Health and Health Care.* New York: Plenum Press, 1992.

Prahalad, C. K., and G. Hamel. "The Core Competence of the Corporation." *Harvard Business Review* 68, no. 3 (May/June 1990), pp. 79–91.

Priem, R. L. "Top Management Team Group Factors, Consensus, and Firm Performance." *Strategic Management Journal* 11, no. 6 (1990), pp. 469–478.

Provan, K. G. "Environmental and Organizational Predictors of Adoption of Cost Containment Policies in Hospitals." *Academy of Management Journal* 30, no. 2 (1987), pp. 219–239.

Provan, K. G. "Organizational and Decision Unit Characteristics and Board Influence in Independent versus Multihospital System-Affiliated Hospitals." *Journal of Health and Social Behavior* 29, no. 3 (September 1988), pp. 239–252.

Rakich, J. S. "The Canadian and U.S. Health Care Systems: Profiles and Policies." *Hospital & Health Services Administration* 36, no. 1 (Spring 1991), pp. 25–42.

Rakich, J. S., and K. Darr. "Outcomes of Hospital Strategic Planning." *Hospital Topics* 66, no. 3 (1988), pp. 23–27.

Ramajujam, V., and P. Varadarajan. "Research on Diversification: A Synthesis." *Strategic Management Journal* 10, no. 6 (November/December 1989), pp. 523–551.

Reed, R., and M. Reed. "CEO Experience and Diversification Strategy." *Journal of Management Studies* 26 (June 1989), pp. 251–270.

Reeves, P. N. "Issues Management: The Other Side of Strategic Planning." *Hospital & Health Services Administration* 38, no. 2 (Summer 1993), pp. 229–241.

Reisler, M. "Business in Richmond Attacks Health Care Costs." *Harvard Business Review* 63, no. 1 (January/February 1985), pp. 145–155.

Reynolds, J. X. "Using DRGs for Competitive Positioning and Practical Business Planning." *Health Care Management Review* 11, no. 3 (Summer 1986), pp. 37–55.

Rhyme, L. C. "The Relationship of Strategic Planning to Financial Performance." *Strategic Management Journal* 7, no. 5 (September/October 1986), pp. 423–436.

Ries, A., and J. Trout. *Positioning: The Battle for Your Mind.* New York: McGraw-Hill, 1981.

Roberts, C. C. "Getting to Hospitals of the Year 2000: Evolution or Revolution?" *Frontiers of Health Services Management* 6, no. 2 (Winter 1989), pp. 35–40.

Robertson, P. J., D. R. Roberts, and J. I. Porras. "Dynamics of Planned Organizational Change." *Academy of Management Journal* 36, no. 3 (June 1993), pp. 619–634.

Robinson, R. K., G. Franklin, and R. L. Fink. "Sexual Harassment at Work: Issues and Answers for Health Care Administrators." *Hospital & Health Services Administration* 38, no. 2 (Summer 1993), pp. 181–195.

Rogers, M. M., and K. Rothe. "Integrating Capital Budgeting Techniques." *Health Care Strategic Management* 11, no. 2 (February 1993), pp. 7–10.

Rood, D. L. "Beyond Synoptics and Incrementalism: Interpretivism and the Social Construction of Reality." In D. F. Ray, ed., *Southern Management Proceedings,* November 1988, pp. 377–379.

Rosen, E. D. *Improving Public Sector Productivity: Concepts and Practice.* Newbury Park, California: Sage Publications, 1993.

Rosenberger, H. R., and K. M. Kaiser. "Strategic Planning for Health Care Management Information Systems." *Health Care Management Review* 10, no. 1 (Winter 1985), pp. 7–17.

Rosenstein, A. H. "Hospital Closure or Survival: Formula for Success." *Health Care Management Review* 11, no. 3 (Summer 1986), pp. 29–35.

Ross, J. W., J. W. Glaser, D. Rasinski-Gregory, J. M. Gibson, and C. Bayley. *Health Care Ethics Committees.* Chicago: American Hospital Publishing, 1993.

Sahney, V. K., and G. L. Warden. "The Quest for Quality and Productivity in Health Services." *Frontiers of Health Services Management* 7, no. 4 (Summer 1991), pp. 2–40.

Sapienza, A. M. "Imagery and Strategy." *Journal of Management* 13, no. 3 (Fall 1987), pp. 543–555.

Saunders, R., J. J. Mayerhofer, and W. J. Jones. "Strategic Capital Planning Scenarios for the Future." *Healthcare Financial Management* 48, no. 4 (April 1993), pp. 50–55.

Savage, G. T., J. D. Blair, M. J. Benson, and B. Hale. "Urban-Rural Hospital Affiliations." *Health Care Management Review* 17, no. 1 (Winter 1992), pp. 35–49.

Savage, G. T., T. W. Nix, C. J. Whitehead, and J. D. Blair. "Strategies for Assessing and Managing Organizational Stateholders." *Academy of Management Executive* 5, no. 2 (May 1991), pp. 61–75.

Scardina, A. "Environmental Services." In *Effective Health Care Management Facilities,* ed. V. James McLarney. Chicago: American Hospital Publishing, 1991.

Schauffler, H. H., and T. Rodriguez. "Managed Care for Preventive Services: A Review of Policy Options." *Medical Care Review* 50, no. 2 (Summer 1993), pp. 153–198.

Schmitz, H. H. "Decision Support: A Strategic Weapon." In M. J. Ball, J. V. Douglas, R. I. O'Desky, and J. W. Albright, eds., *Healthcare Information Management Systems.* New York: Springer-Verlag, 1991.

Schoemaker, P. J. H. "Multiple Scenario Development: Its Conceptual and Behavioral Foundation." *Strategic Management Journal* 14, no. 3 (March 1993), pp. 193–213.

Schoemaker, P. J. H. "How to Link Strategic Vision to Core Capabilities." *Sloan Management Review* 34, no. 1 (1992), pp. 67–81.

Scholz, C. "Corporate Culture and Strategy – The Problem with Strategic Fit." *Long Range Planning* 20, no. 8 (August 1987), pp. 80–90.

Schonberger, R. J. "Is Strategy Strategic? Impact of Total Quality Management On Strategy." *Academy of Management Executive* 6, no. 3 (August 1992), pp. 80–87.

Schwartz, G. F., and C. T. Stone. "Strategic Acquisitions by Academic Medical Centers." *Health Care Management* 16, no. 2 (Spring 1991), pp. 39–47.

Schwenk, C. "A Meta-Analysis of the Comparative Effectiveness of Devil's Advocacy and Dialectical Inquiry." *Strategic Management Journal* 10, no. 3 (May/June 1989), pp. 303–306.

Scott, W. R. "The Organization of Medical Care Services: Toward an Integrated Theoretical Model." *Medical Care Review* 50, no. 3 (Fall 1993), pp. 271–302.

Selbst, P. L. "A More Total Approach to Productivity Improvement." *Hospital & Health Services Administration* 30, no. 3 (Fall 1985), pp. 85–96.

Senge, P. M. "The Leader's New Work: Building Learning Organizations." *Sloan Management Review* 32 (Fall 1992), pp. 7–22.

Sharon, R., and R. Gority. "Bridging the Visions of Competing Catholic Health Care Systems." *Health Care Strategic Management* 11, no. 7 (1993), pp. 16–19.

Shelton, N. "Competitive Contingencies in Selective Contracting for Hospital Services." *Medical Care Review* 46, no. 3 (Fall 1989), pp. 271–293.

Sheridan, J. E. "Organizational Culture and Employee Retention." *Academy of Management Journal* 35, no. 6 (December 1992), pp. 1036–1056.

Shortell, S. M. "Revisiting the Garden: Medicine and Management in the 1990s." *Frontiers of Health Services Management* 7, no. 1 (Fall 1990), pp. 3–32.

Shortell, S. M. "New Directions in Hospital Governance." *Hospital & Health Services Administration* 34, no. 1 (Spring 1989), pp. 7–23.

Shortell, S. M. "The Evolution of Hospital Systems: Unfulfilled Promises and Self-Fulfilling Prophesies." *Medical Care Review* 45, no. 2 (Fall 1988), pp. 177–214.

Shortell, S. M., M. A. Morrisey, and D. A. Conrad. "Economic Regulation and Hospital Behavior: The Effects on Medical Staff Organization and Hospital-Physician Relationships." *Health Services Research* 20, no. 5 (December 1985), pp. 597–628.

Shortell, S. M., E. M. Morrison, and B. Friedman. *Strategic Choices Facing American Hospitals: Managing Change in Turbulent Times.* San Francisco: Jossey-Bass, 1990.

Shortell, S. M., E. M. Morrison, and S. Hughes. "The Keys to Successful Diversification: Lessons from Leading Hospital Systems." *Hospital & Health Services Administration* 34, no. 4 (Winter 1989), pp. 471–492.

Shortell, S. M., E. M. Morrison, S. L. Hughes, B. Friedman, J. Coverdill, and L. Berg. "The Effects of Hospital Ownership on Nontraditional Services." *Health Affairs* 5, no. 4 (Winter 1986), pp. 97–111.

Shortell, S. M., E. M. Morrison, and S. Robbins. "Strategy Making in Health Care Organizations: A Framework and Agenda for Research." *Medical Care Review* 42, no. 2 (Fall 1985), pp. 219–266.

Shortell, S. M., and E. J. Zajac. "Internal Corporate Joint Ventures: Development Processes and Performance Outcomes." *Strategic Management Journal* 9, no. 6 (November/December 1988), pp. 527–542.

Shrivastava, P. "Rigor and Practical Usefulness of Research in Strategic Management." *Strategic Management Journal* 8, no. 1 (January/February 1987), pp. 77–92.

Sieveking, N., and D. Wood. "Hospital CEOs View Their Careers: Implications for Selection, Training, and Placement." *Hospital & Health Services Administration* 37, no. 2 (Summer 1992), pp. 167–279.

Simmons, J. "Integrating Federal Health Care Resources at the Local Level." *Hospital & Health Services Administration* 34, no. 1 (Spring 1989), pp. 113–122.

Simon, J. K., and B. A. Cohen. "Reorganization/Diversification: Six Years Later." *Health Care Management Review* 14, no. 4 (Fall 1989), pp. 77–84.

Siu, A. L., E. A. McGlynn, H. Morgenstern, M. H. Beers, D. M. Carlisle, E. B. Keeler, J. Beloff, K. Curtin, J. Leaning, B. C. Perry, H. P. Selker, W. Weiswasser, A. Wisenthal, and R. H. Brook. "Choosing Quality of Care Measures Based on the Expected Impact of Improved Care on Health." *Health Services Research* 27, no. 5 (December 1992), pp. 619–650.

Size, T. "Managing Partnerships: The Perspective of a Rural Hospital Cooperative." *Health Care Management Review* 18, no. 1 (1993), pp. 31–41.

Slack, G. D. "Clinical Engineering." In *Effective Health Care Facilities Management*, ed. V. James McLarney. Chicago: American Hospital Publishing, 1991.

Smith, C. T. "Strategic Planning and Entrepreneurism in Academic Health Centers." *Hospital & Health Services Administration* 33, no. 2 (Summer 1988), pp. 143–152.

Smith, C. T. "Hospital Management Strategies for Fixed-Price Payment." *Health Care Management Review* 11, no. 1 (Winter 1986), pp. 21–26.

Smith, D. B. "One More Time: What Do We Mean by Strategic Management?" *Hospital & Health Services Administration* 32, no. 2 (Summer 1987), pp. 219–233.

Smith, D. B., and J. L. Larson. "The Impact of Learning on Cost: The Case of Heart Transplantation." *Hospital & Health Services Administration* 34, no. 1 (Spring 1989), pp. 85–97.

Smith, D. G., and J. R. C. Wheeler. "Strategies and Structures for Hospital Risk Management Programs." *Health Care Management Review* 17, no. 3 (Summer 1992), pp. 9–17.

Smith, H. L., and N. F. Piland. "Does Planning Pay Off? A Look at the Experience of New Mexico's Rural Hospitals." *Hospital Topics* 71, no. 1 (1993), pp. 27–35.

Smith, H. L., N. F. Piland, and M. J. Funk. "Strategic Planning in Rural Health Care Organizations." *Health Care Management Review* 17, no. 3 (Summer 1992), pp. 63–80.

Snell, S. A. "Control Theory in Strategic Human Resource Management: The Mediating Effect of Administrative Information." *Academy of Management Journal* 35, no. 2 (June 1992), pp. 292–327.

Sobczak, P. M., M. D. Fottler, and D. Chastagner. "Managing Retrenchment in French Public Hospitals: Philosophical and Regulatory Constraints." *International Journal of Health Planning and Management* 3, no. 1 (January 1988), pp. 19–34.

Sofaer, S., and R. C. Myrtle. "Interorganizational Theory and Research: Implications for Health Care Management, Policy, and Research." *Medical Care Review* 48, no. 4 (Winter 1991), pp. 371–409.

Solovy, A. "Health Care in 1990s: Forecasts by Top Analysts." *Hospitals* 63 (July 20, 1989), pp. 34–46.

Spiegel, A. D., and H. H. Hyman. *Strategic Health Planning: Methods and Techniques Applied to Marketing and Management.* Norwood, New Jersey: Ablex Publishing, 1991.

Sprague, R. H., Jr., and B. C. McNurlin. *Information Systems in Practice,* 3rd ed. Englewood Cliffs, New Jersey: Prentice Hall, 1993.

Stacey, R. "Strategy as Order Emerging from Chaos." *Long Range Planning* 26, no. 1 (1993), pp. 10–17.

Starkweather, D. B., and J. M. Carman. "The Limits of Power in Hospital Markets." *Medical Care Review* 45, no. 1 (Spring 1988), pp. 5–48.

Stein, H. "Organizational Psychohistory." *The Journal of Psychohistory* 21 (Summer 1993), pp. 97–114.

Steiner, G. A., J. B. Miner, and E. R. Gray. *Management Policy and Strategy,* 2d ed. New York: Macmillan, 1992.

Stevens, R. A. "The Hospital as a Social Institution, New-Fashioned for the 1990s." *Hospital & Health Services Administration* 36, no. 2 (Summer 1991), pp. 163–173.

Stier, R. D., and C. L. Pugh. "The Strategic Linkage of Marketing and Finance." *Healthcare Forum Journal* (March/April 1989), p. 37.

Strasser, S., L. Aharony, and D. Greenberger. "The Patient Satisfaction Process: Moving Toward a Comprehensive Model." *Medical Care Review* 50, no. 2 (1993), pp. 219–248.

Sullivan, J. M. "Health Care Reform: Toward a Healthier Society." *Hospital & Health Services Administration* 37, no. 4 (Winter 1992), pp. 519–532.

Sussman, G. E. "CEO Perspectives on Mission, Healthcare Systems, and the Environment." *Hospital & Health Services Administration* 30, no. 2 (Summer 1985), pp. 21–34.

Sutton, R. I. "The Process of Organizational Death: Disbanding and Reconnecting." *Administrative Science Quarterly* 32, no. 4 (December 1987), pp. 542–569.

Swett, J. N. "Reconstitution of the Not-for-Profit Hospital: New Ethics, New Equity." *Hospital & Health Services Administration* 30, no. 3 (Fall 1985), pp. 20–30.

Sykes, C. S., Jr. "The Role of Equity Financing in Today's Health Care Environment." *Topics in Health Care Financing* 12, no. 3 (1986), pp. 1–3.

Thakur, M., W. English, and W. Hoffman. "Cost Containment in Small Hospitals: Targeting Strategies Beyond This Decade." *Hospital & Health Services Administration* 31, no. 3 (Fall 1986), pp. 34–44.

Thomas, A. S., R. J. Litschert, and K. Ramaswamy. "The Performance Impact of Strategy-Manager Coalignment: An Empirical Examination." *Strategic Management Journal* 12 (1991), pp. 509–522.

Thomas, J. B., D. J. Ketchen, Jr., L. K. Trevino, and R. R. McDaniel, Jr. "Developing Interorganizational Relationships in the Health Sector." *Health Care Management Review* 17, no. 2 (Spring 1992), pp. 7–19.

Thomas, J. B., and R. R. McDaniel, Jr. "Interpreting Strategic Issues: Effects of Strategy and the Information-Processing Structure of Top Management Teams." *Academy of Management Journal* 33, no. 2 (June 1990), p. 288.

Thompson, A. A., Jr., and A. J. Strickland, III. *Strategic Management Concepts and Cases.* Homewood, Illinois: Richard D. Irwin Company, 1992.

Topping, S., and M. D. Fottler. "Improved Stakeholder Management: The Key to Revitalizing the HMO Movement?" *Medical Care Review* 47, no. 3 (Fall 1990), pp. 365–393.

Topping, S., and S. R. Hernandez. "Health Care Strategy Research, 1985–1990: A Critical Review." *Medical Care Review* 48, no. 1 (Spring 1991), pp. 47–89.

Trautwein, F. "Merger Motives and Merger Prescriptions." *Strategic Management Journal* 11, no. 4 (1990), pp. 283–295.

Traxler, H., and T. Dunaye. "Emerging Patterns in Transitional Care." *Health Affairs* 6, no. 2 (Summer 1987), pp. 57–68.

Tucker, L. R., and R. A. Zaremba. "Organizational Control and Marketing in Multihospital Systems." *Health Care Management Review* 16, no. 1 (Winter 1991), pp. 41–56.

Turner, B. R. "Future Role of Academic Medical Centers." *Health Care Management Review* 14, no. 2 (Spring 1987), pp. 73–77.

Tushman, M. L., W. H. Newman, and E. Romanelli. "Convergence and Upheaval: Managing the Unsteady Pace of Organizational Evolution." *California Management Review* 29, no. 1 (Winter 1986), pp. 29–44.

Tuttle, W. C., N. F. Piland, and H. L. Smith. "The Evolving Role of Health Care Organizations in Research." *Hospital & Health Services Administration* 33, no. 1 (Spring 1988), pp. 47–56.

Ulrich, R. S. "Effects of Interior Design on Wellness: Theory and Recent Scientific Research." *Health Care Interior Design* 3 (1991), pp. 97–109.

Venable, J. M., Q. Li, P. M. Ginter, and W. J. Duncan. "The Use of Scenario Analysis in Local Public Health Departments: Alternative Futures of Strategic Planning." *Public Health Reports* 108, no. 6 (1994), pp. 701–710.

Vessey, J. T. "The New Competitors: They Think in Terms of 'Speed to Market.'" *Academy of Management Executive* 5, no. 2 (May 1991), pp. 23–33.

Vladeck, B. C. "Health Care Leadership in the Public Interest." *Frontiers of Health Services Management* 8, no. 3 (Spring 1992), pp. 3–26.

Vogel, W. B., B. Langland-Orban, and L. C. Gapenski. "Factors Influencing High and Low Profitability Among Hospitals." *Health Care Management Review* 18, no. 2 (Spring 1993), pp. 15–26.

Vraciu, R. A. "Hospital Strategies for the Eighties: A Mid-Decade Look." *Health Care Management Review* 10, no. 4 (Fall 1985), pp. 9–19.

Vraciu, R. A., and J. Harkey. "Strategies for Small Community Hospitals Operating in the Shadow of a Medical Center." *Health Care Management Review* 17, no. 4 (Fall 1992), pp. 65–72.

Walker, L. R., and M. D. Rosko. "Evaluation of Health Care Service Diversification Options in Health Care Institutions and Programs by Portfolio Analysis: A Marketing Approach." *Journal of Health Care Management* 8, no. 1 (March 1988), pp. 48–59.

Walsh, J. P., and R. D. Kosnik. "Corporate Raiders and Their Disciplinary Role in the Market for Corporate Control." *Academy of Management Journal* 36, no. 4 (August 1993), pp. 671–700.

Watson, D., and L. Strasen. "The Integration of Respiratory Therapy into Nursing: Reorganization for Improved Productivity." *Hospital & Health Services Administration* 32, no. 3 (Fall 1987), pp. 369–398.

Webster, J. L., W. E. Reif, and J. S. Bracker. "The Manager's Guide to Strategic Planning Tools and Techniques." *Planning Review* 17, no. 6 (1989), pp. 4–13.

Weiner, A. J., and J. A. Alexander. "Hospital Governance and Quality of Care: A Critical Review of Transitional Roles." *Medical Care Review* 50, no. 4 (Winter 1993), pp. 375–409.

Weinstein, B. M. "Situation Analysis and Strategic Development in a Public Hospital." *Hospital & Health Services Administration* 31, no. 4 (Winter 1986), pp. 62–73.

Welge, W. L. "Managed Care Is Limited by the Information System." *Topics in Health Care Financing* 19, no. 2 (Winter 1992), pp. 23–32.

Westley, F. R. "Middle Managers and Strategy: Microdynamics of Inclusion." *Strategic Management Journal* 11, no. 5 (1990), pp. 337–352.

Wheeler, J. R. C., T. M. Wickizer, and S. M. Shortell. "Hospital-Physician Vertical Integration." *Hospital & Health Services Administration* 31, no. 2 (Summer 1986), pp. 67–80.

Wheeler, K. E., and T. Porter-O'Grady. "Barrell Technology: A Strategic Factor in Hospital Planning." *Health Care Management Review* 10, no. 2 (March/April 1985), pp. 55–63.

White, S. L., and T. N. Chirikos. "Measuring Hospital Competition." *Medical Care* 26, no. 3 (March 1988), pp. 256–262.

Whitehead, C. J., J. D. Blair, R. R. Smith, T. W. Nix, and G. T. Savage. "Stakeholder Supportiveness and Strategic Vulnerability: Implications for Competitive Strategy in the HMO Industry." *Health Care Management Review* 14, no. 3 (Summer 1989), pp. 65–76.

Widra, L. S., and M. D. Fottler. "Determinants of HMO Success: The Case of Complete Health." *Health Care Management Review* 17, no. 2 (Spring 1992), pp. 33–44.

Widra, L. S., and M. D. Fottler. "Survival of the Hospital Emergency Department: Strategic Alternatives for the Future." *Health Care Management Review* 13, no. 3 (Summer 1988), pp. 73–83.

Wiersema, M. F., and K. A. Bantel. "Top Management Team Demography and Corporate Strategic Change." *Academy of Management Journal* 35, no. 1 (March 1992), pp. 91–121.

Wilke, C. L. F., and T. Choi. "Changing Criteria for Hospital Acquisitions." *Health Care Management Review* 13, no. 3 (Summer 1988), pp. 23–34.

Williams, J. R. "How Sustainable Is Your Competitive Advantage?" *California Management Review* (Spring 1992), pp. 29–51.

Williams, J. R., B. L. Paez, and L. Sanders. "Conglomeration Revisited." *Strategic Management Journal* 9, no. 5 (September/October 1988), pp. 403–414.

Wilson, I. "Realizing the Power of Strategic Vision." *Long Range Planning* 25, no. 5 (1992), pp. 18–28.

Wodinsky, H. B., D. Egan, and F. Markel. "Product Line Management in Oncology: A Canadian Experience." *Hospital & Health Services Administration* 33, no. 2 (Summer 1988), pp. 221–236.

Wood, D. J. "Corporate Social Performance Revisited." *The Academy of Management Review* 16, no. 4 (October 1991), pp. 691–718.

Yip, G. S. "Who Needs Strategic Planning?" *Journal of Business Strategy* 6, no. 2 (Fall 1985), pp. 30–42.

Young, G., R. I. Beekun, and G. O. Ginn. "Governing Board Structure, Business Strategy, and Performance of Acute Care Hospitals: A Contingency Perspective." *Health Services Research* 27, no. 4 (October 1992), pp. 543–564.

Young, J. P. "Pawns or Potentates: The Reality of America's Corporate Boards—An Interview with Jay W. Lorsch." *Academy of Management Executive* 4, no. 4 (1990), pp. 85–87.

Yuan, G. *Lure the Tiger out of the Mountains: The 36 Stratagems of Ancient China.* New York: Simon & Schuster, 1991.

Zahra, S. A., and S. S. Chaples. "Blind Spots in Competitive Analysis." *Academy of Management Executive* 7, no. 2 (May 1993), pp. 7–28.

Zajac, E. J., and M. H. Bazerman. "Blind Spots in Industry and Competitor Analysis: Implications of Interfirm (Mis)perceptions for Strategic Decisions." *Academy of Management Review* 16, no. 1 (January 1991), pp. 37–56.

Zeithaml, V. A., A. Parasuraman, and L. L. Berry. *Delivering Quality Service.* New York: The Free Press, 1990.

Zelman, W. N., and D. L. Parham. "Strategic, Operational, and Marketing Concerns of Product Line Management." *Health Care Management Review* 15, no. 1 (1990), pp. 29–35.

Zentner, R. D., and B. D. Gelb. "Scenarios: A Planning Tool for Health Care Organizations." *Hospital & Health Services Administration* 36, no. 2 (Summer 1991), pp. 211–222.

Zuckerman, H. S. "The Strategies and Autonomy of University Hospitals in Competitive Environments." *Hospital & Health Services Administration* 35, no. 1 (Spring 1990), pp. 103–120.

Zuckerman, H. S. "Redefining the Role of the CEO: Challenges and Conflicts." *Hospital & Health Services Administration* 34, no. 1 (Spring 1989), pp. 25–38.

Zuckerman, H. S., and T. A. D'Aunno. "Hospital Alliances: Cooperative Strategy in a Competitive Environment." *Health Care Management Review* 15, no. 2 (Spring 1990), pp. 21–30.

Zuckerman, H. S., and A. D. Kaluzny. "Strategic Alliances in Health Care: The Challenges of Cooperation." *Frontiers of Health Services Management* 7, no. 3 (Spring 1991), pp. 3–23.

PART 7

Cases in the Health Care Sector

The U.S. Health Care System: Thinking Strategically in a Turbulent Environment

INTRODUCTION

The U.S. health care system is undergoing significant change, changes generally referred to as *health care reform*. Reform essentially means changes in the way we allocate health care resources. However, it is unclear what the specific changes will be; which, if any, of these changes will actually take place; and when they would occur if they do. Therefore, to have some environmental basis to evaluate the organizationally specific strategic management cases that follow, this chapter will attempt three things.

First, the chapter will provide a brief snapshot of the U.S. health care system as it exists today. This will include a description of the providers of service, the payers for service, the products and services provided, and the users of the products and services. Second, the chapter will describe major components of the health care reform proposals that many analysts believe will become a permanent part of a revised U.S. health care system. Finally,

This Health Services Note was prepared by Stuart A. Capper of the University of Alabama at Birmingham. It is intended as a basis for classroom discussion rather than to illustrate effective or ineffective handling of an administrative situation. Used with permission from Stuart Capper.

the chapter will posit three brief alternative scenarios for the shorter term outcomes of the health care reform initiative. With these alternative scenarios in mind, specific trends in the health care environment will be suggested that are likely to continue regardless of which scenario becomes reality. Part of your job, as you analyze the cases, will be to evaluate the uncertainties, determine their importance for the specific issues to be resolved in the case, and then, propose and defend the actions that you think are strategically justified.

A DESCRIPTION OF THE CURRENT U.S. HEALTH CARE SYSTEM

As prelude to a discussion of the current health care system, the following briefly describes some of the most significant historical events since World War II that have contributed to the evolution of the U.S. health services sector:

1940s Introduction of antibiotics, penicillin, and sulfonamides gave physicians their first effective therapies for treating infectious diseases. These drugs accelerated the shift from infectious diseases to chronic diseases as the chief source of mortality.

1946   Passage of the Hill-Burton Act for Health Facilities Construction—the first major involvement by the federal government in a national program to allocate resources to health services. Over the next thirty years, the program provided billions of dollars in construction subsidies primarily to hospitals. Between 1940 and 1980, community hospital beds per capita increased 40 percent, although some areas of the country, such as the East South Central Region, experienced as much as a threefold increase.[1]

1950s   Development of modern anesthesiology—introduction of synthetic agents for anesthesia that lead to significantly reduced risks in surgery especially for higher-risk patients.

1960s   Extension of the adult lifespan—an increase of about two years per decade during each decade subsequent to the 1950s. This represented a significant change as life expectancy had been increasing due to decreases in infant deaths. Now life expectancy is increasing due to years added at the end and middle of life.

1963   Passage of the Health Professionals Education Assistance Act—projections of a shortage of physicians and other health personnel led to the passage of this program to encourage increased training of health professionals. Between 1960 and 1985, forty-one new medical schools opened in the United States, a 48 percent increase. Between 1960 and 1988, the number of first-year enrollees in U.S. medical schools more than doubled.[2] The number of physicians in active practice rose from 14.0 per 10,000 population in 1960 to 23.46 per 10,000 population in 1990.[3]

1964   Surgeon General's *Report on Smoking and Health* identified cigarette smoking as one of the primary preventable causes of morbidity and premature death.

1965   Passage of Medicare and Medicaid—the Social Security Amendments of 1965 marked the first large-scale federal initiative to provide health insurance for major segments of the population. The elderly, and to some extent the poor, became beneficiaries of congressionally-mandated health insurance programs. Between 1967 and 1991, total expenditures for Medicare enrollees increased from $4.74 billion to $121.34 billion. During approximately the same period, per capita payments for enrollees increased thirteenfold from $217 to $2,869.[4]

1972   Passage of Social Security Amendments—in 1972 Congress attempted to link payments to health services providers for services to federal beneficiaries to compliance with federally mandated planning decisions. These amendments also created Professional Standards Review Organizations (PSRO), the first direct intervention by the federal government into medical practice by mandating the creation of "standards of care."[5]

1975   In Goldfarb vs. Virginia Bar, 421 U.S. 713 a Supreme Court decision effectively removed the traditional "learned professions" exemption from antitrust laws. Professional practices are not immune from price-fixing restrictions and professional associations could not mandate bans on professional advertising.

1983 Passage of Social Security Amendments created the prospective payment system (PPS) for hospital services to Medicare beneficiaries. This significantly changed the financial incentives for health care providers. Between 1980 and 1990, the number of days of care in short-stay hospitals for Medicare enrollees dropped from 4,016 per 1,000 enrollees to 2,783 per 1,000 enrollees.[6] Payments to hospitals for federal Medicare beneficiaries changed from price per day, established retrospectively on a cost-plus basis, to a prospectively established fixed fee per case. Although the rate of increase in hospital expenditures for the total population decreased significantly in the first half of the 1980s, from a rate of 13.9 percent to 6.8 percent, the most recent figure for 1991 indicates a rate of increase of 11.8 percent.[7]

1989 Passage of the Omnibus Budget Reconciliation Act of 1989 (OBRA89) that included the mandate from Congress for Medicare to change the method used to pay physicians beginning in 1992. Up to this time, physicians were paid by Medicare on the basis of "customary, prevailing, and reasonable (CPR) fees. Payment for a service was limited to the lowest of (1) the physician's billed charge for the

service, (2) the physician's customary charge for the service, or (3) the prevailing charge for the service in the community. In OBRA89 Congress mandated the move to a Medicare Physician Fee Schedule built upon a resource-based relative value scale (RBRVS), limitations on the amount physicians may charge above the fee schedule payments, and volume performance standards.[8]

Health Care Expenditures

One way to describe the U.S. health care system is in terms of its economic size. Since 1960, the percentage of the U.S. gross domestic product (GDP) devoted to health expenditures has more than doubled. In 1970, national health expenditures were 7.4 percent of GDP. By 1990, they had reached 12.2 percent of GDP. If current projections are realized, health care expenditures will represent 18.1 percent of GDP by the year 2000 (see Exhibit 1.1).

It is important to recognize that this tripling of the percentage of GDP devoted to health care is occurring during a period when the total U.S. economy itself has grown dramatically. Between 1960 and 1990, the GDP increased ninefold from $513.4 billion to $5.522 trillion. Hence, health services have been acquiring an increasingly significant proportion of a rapidly growing domestic resource pie.[9]

One result of this accelerated rate of growth in health care expenditures has been the change over time in the relative size of the health care sector as compared to other major sectors of the U.S. economy. In 1960, the health services sector was $11.5 billion of a total GNP of $515.3 billion. (The U.S. Bureau of Economic Analysis is in the process of making a transition to a more frequent use of GDP rather than GNP. Because this process is not

EXHIBIT 1.1
National Health Expenditures, Selected Years 1970–2010

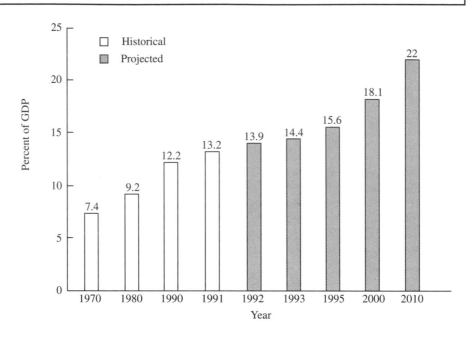

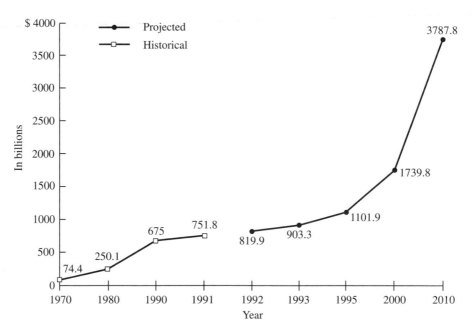

Source: Adapted from S. T. Burner, D. R. Waldo, and D. R. McKusick, "National Health Expenditure Projections through 2030," *Health Care Financing Review* 14, no. 1 (Fall, 1992), Table 7, p. 14; and National Center for Health Statistics, *Health United States 1992* (Hyattsville, Maryland: United States Public Health Service, 1993), Table 114, p. 160.

complete, some of the information presented in this case is relative to GDP whereas other information is relative to GNP. The primary difference between these two indicators of economic growth is that GDP is the total output of goods and services produced by labor and property located in the United States while GNP is output attributable to all labor and property supplied by United States residents.) Numerous sectors of the economy were larger in dollar terms than health services, including the combined category of agriculture, forestry, and fisheries that was nearly twice as large as the health services sector. Also larger than health services were mining, primary metals manufacturing, machinery manufacturing, food products, transportation, electric gas and sanitary utilities, real estate, and the federal government (see Exhibit 1.2).

By 1987, the situation had significantly changed; health services made up $223.7 billion of a $4.5 trillion dollar GNP. The only

sector of the economy that remained larger than health services was real estate. Health services had become larger than the entire federal government. In addition, a sector such as agriculture, forestry, and fisheries, which had been twice the size of the health services sector, was now less than half its size. The relationship of the health services industries to other sectors of the U.S. economy has been significantly altered by the extraordinarily rapid growth in expenditures for health care products and services. Even rapid growth in other sectors of the economy has been no match for the explosive growth in health.

Many reasons have been postulated for the rapid increases in health care expenditures over the past thirty years. One series of studies by the Health Care Financing Administration (HCFA) attempted to categorize and quantify factors affecting the growth of health expenditures.[10] These studies documented that the average annual percent change in personal health

---

EXHIBIT 1.2
Selected Sector Breakdown of GNP, 1960 vs. 1987 (amounts in billions, current dollars)

	1960	1987
Total Gross National Product	$515.3	$4526.7
Health Services	11.5	223.7
Agriculture, Forestry, and Fisheries	21.7	94.9
Mining	12.8	85.4
Primary Metals Manufacturing	12.1	36.4
Machinery Manufacturing	13.2	81.2
Gas, Electric, and Sanitary Services	13.3	136.4
Food Products	16.4	74.0
Transportation	23.4	150.8
Real Estate	54.1	519.3
Federal Government	24.8	181.3

Source: U.S. Bureau of Economic Analysis, *National Income and Product Accounts of the United States, 1929–1982*, p. 252; and U.S. Bureau of the Census, *Statistical Abstract of the United States, 1990*, Table 641, p. 426.

care expenditures during the period 1960 through 1990 was 11.3 percent. Three primary factors were identified as contributing to this growth rate. First, changes in the U.S. population accounted for 10 percent of the increase in expenditures. The U.S. population is aging, and older Americans use more health care products and services than younger residents. For example, in 1990, payments per Medicare enrollee age 65 or 66 averaged $1,854. Payments for Medicare enrollees 85 and over averaged $3,962.[11]

The second factor identified in the HCFA studies was intensity, defined as changes in the amount of services used or the kinds of supplies and services used. For example, a new diagnostic modality, magnetic resonance imaging (MRI), has improved the ability to visualize internal soft tissue. This method has not replaced the traditional X ray. Rather, often it is used in addition to other methods and thus increases the intensity of service provided. It was estimated that changes in intensity accounted for 33 percent of the growth in health care expenditures between 1960 and 1990.

By far the most significant factor identified by HCFA as affecting the growth in personal health care expenditures was price increases. Prices were estimated to have contributed 57 percent of the increase in expenditures during this thirty-year period. The ability to significantly raise prices while providing increasingly larger volumes and more varied types of services suggests that normal market forces have not been available to contain health care costs. As will be discussed in a later section of this chapter, regulation to enhance market forces in health care is a primary strategy suggested for reform of the U.S. health care system.

Providers of Health Care Products and Services

Americans are spending more on health care to buy products and services from a diverse group of professionals and organizations that represent one of the participant groups in the health services sector. Collectively called *health care providers,* a variety of individuals and organizations are delivering health care.

Physicians. In terms of national expenditures for health services, physicians make up the largest single professional service component of the health services sector. Payments to physicians accounted for 19 percent of total health services expenditures in 1990. By contrast, dental services, the next largest professional service component, accounted for 5 percent of total expenditures.

Physicians are the only professionals in the health services sector who are broadly licensed to perform any medical service. Thus, they have significant influence over the allocation of most health care resources. For example, hospitals, which account for the largest single category of health care expenditures, are not licensed to provide health services independent of physician oversight. By the same token, the vast majority of prescription drug use is controlled by physician decisions. Hence, although this chapter will describe a number of different categories of health care providers, it is important to recognize that physician decisions control the allocation and use of most of the dollars that are expended on health services.

An important trend in the provision of physician services has been the rapidly increasing number of physicians in the United States. In 1960, U.S. medical schools graduated 5,553 new M.D.s. By 1980, the United States graduated 15,135 new physicians.[12] One effect of the increasing physician supply can be seen in the trend in the number of people in the United States per active physician. In 1970, there were 641 people for each active physician. By 1985, the ratio had decreased to 455. It is projected that by the year 2000, there will be only 372 people for each active physician in the United States (see Exhibit 1.3).

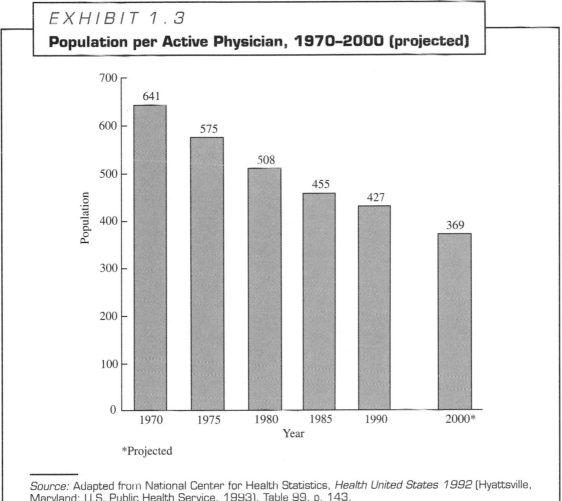

EXHIBIT 1.3

Population per Active Physician, 1970–2000 (projected)

*Projected

Source: Adapted from National Center for Health Statistics, *Health United States 1992* (Hyattsville, Maryland: U.S. Public Health Service, 1993), Table 99, p. 143.

Other Professionals. As previously stated, the only other professional category that is individually significant in terms of health expenditures is dentists. In 1990, dental services accounted for approximately 5 percent of total national health expenditures. Although expenditures for dentists services grew 7.6 percent between 1989 and 1990, overall expenditures for health services grew at a 10.5 percent rate during the same period. This general pattern has been the case since the 1960s, and as a consequence, dental services have decreased from 7 percent of total expenditures in 1965 to the current 5 percent. Private insurance coverage for dental services has been expanding. However, very little dental care is paid for from public sources.[13]

Other licensed professionals who often practice and bill independently include podiatrists, optometrists, private-duty nurses, chiropractors, and others (see Exhibit 1.4). In 1990, the services of these other professionals ac-

EXHIBIT 1.4

Selected Health Professionals in Active Practice for 1970, 1980, 1989

	1970	1980	1989
Physicians (nonfederal)	290,862	409,480	542,480
Dentists	95,700	121,240	144,000
Optometrists	18,400	22,330	25,500
Podiatrists	7,110	8,880	11,950
Veterinarians	25,900	36,000	49,300

Source: Adapted from National Center for Health Statistics, *Health United States 1991* (Hyattsville, Maryland: U.S. Public Health Service, 1992), Table 99, p. 247.

counted for approximately the same percentage of total health care expenditures as dentists, about 5 percent. However, unlike the pattern in dentist services, other professionals have seen their portion of the national health care dollar increase from 2 percent in 1965 to the current 5 percent.

Hospitals. The largest single component of the health services dollar pays for hospital care. Approximately 38 percent of all health care expenditures were for hospital services in 1990. The hospital sector uses several different methods to categorize participants. For example, hospitals are classified by ownership, size (in numbers of beds), or type of services (long-term vs. short-term, children's, mental, or burn care). Of the 5,675 short-stay hospitals in the United States in 1991, one commonly used categorization method based primarily on ownership indicates that nonfederal, not-for-profit hospitals are the largest segment at 56 percent (see Exhibit 1.5).

The number of hospitals in the United States has been declining. In 1980, there were 6,229 short-stay hospitals. By 1989, this number had decreased to 5,808; a decline of over 400 hospitals. In addition, the stock of short-stay hospital beds declined over this time period by more than 65,000 beds. The decrease in the hospital bed supply appears to be related directly to declines in inpatient hospital use. Despite the decrease in the number of available hospital beds, hospital occupancy rates in the United States have declined. In 1980, the average occupancy rate for short-stay hospitals was 75.6 percent. By 1991, this rate had fallen to 66.4 percent.[14]

Hospitals have little direct control over their utilization. Hospitals can be characterized as the inpatient environment for physicians' services. As previously mentioned, hospitals are not licensed to provide health care services independent of physician oversight. Only a licensed physician (and, to a limited extent dentists and podiatrists) can admit a patient to a hospital.

Nursing Homes. Nursing home services accounted for 8 percent of total health care expenditures in 1990. This is a significant increase over the 1960s, when nursing homes generally accounted for about 4 percent of total expenditures.

Between 1976 and 1986, the supply of nursing home beds increased from 1.292 mil-

EXHIBIT 1.5
U.S. Hospitals by Ownership, 1990

	General Hospitals	Psychiatric	All Others
Nongovernment, Not-for-Profit	3,085	82	117
Investor-Owned, For-Profit	693	292	56
Local Government	1,420	9	8
State Government	94	28	9
Federal Government	305	1	3
Total	5,720	412	193

Source: American Hospital Association, Hospital Statistics (Chicago: American Hospital Association 1991–92), Table 2A, pp. 8–9.

lion beds to 1.616 million beds. However, this increase in nursing home bed supply was no match for the rapid rise in the number of U.S. residents 85 years of age and over. The oldest old are the heaviest users of nursing home beds. In 1976, there were 681 beds per 1,000 residents 85 years of age and older. By 1986, that ratio had decreased to 582 per 1,000.[15]

Drugs and Medical Supplies. The drug and medical supply industry is represented by major international corporations such as Burroughs-Wellcome, Merck, Johnson & Johnson, and American Home Products. The portion of the domestic health care dollar devoted to products from these suppliers has declined. In 1960, drugs and medical supplies accounted for 16 percent of total health care expenditures. By 1991, this portion had decreased to 8 percent. However, because of the rapid growth in total health care expenditures, the decrease still represents a fourteenfold increase in non-inflation-adjusted dollars expended on drugs and sundries from $4.336 billion to $60.9 billion in the same time period.[16]

The elderly consume the largest share of prescription drugs. By one estimate using 1977

data, people age 65 and over use three times as many prescription drugs as all other age groups. The Health Care Financing Administration estimated that the 12 percent of the population who are elderly accounted for 35 percent of expenditures on prescription drugs in 1988.[17]

Vision Products and Medical Appliances. This category represents approximately 2 percent of total health care expenditures. This percentage has held relatively constant since the mid-1970s. In 1990, sightly over $13.3 billion was spent on products of this type.

Government Public Health Activities. Government public health activities do not fit neatly into any individual category within the health services sector. Public health is a provider of personal health services, a payer for services, a regulator of service providers, and a source of health-related research. Federal, state, and local governments all conduct public health activities. Services provided by this industry include immunizations, health facility licensure, collection and reporting of vital health statistics, environmental health-related regulation, disease vector control, and others. However, immunizations are the only consistently provided service. The provision of other public health services varies significantly. Although 92 percent of all local health departments provide immunizations, 71 percent conduct facility licensure, and only 60 percent are involved in control of water pollution.[18] Government public health activities have accounted for about 3 percent of total national health expenditures since the early 1980s. These expenditures are included in the provider discussion because, on a national basis, most of these dollars are used to deliver personal health services (see Exhibit 1.6).

Medical and Other Health Related Education. Although the provider groups just described account for the vast majority of all health service expenditures (see Exhibit 1.7), the education of health professionals should be considered because of its impact on the future direction of provider services.

Medical education is conducted primarily in the 126 public and private academic health sciences centers (AHSC) in the United States.

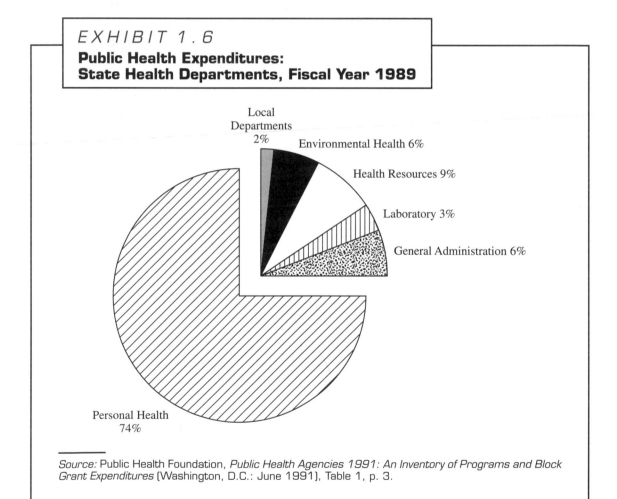

EXHIBIT 1.6

**Public Health Expenditures:
State Health Departments, Fiscal Year 1989**

Local Departments 2%

Environmental Health 6%

Health Resources 9%

Laboratory 3%

General Administration 6%

Personal Health 74%

Source: Public Health Foundation, *Public Health Agencies 1991: An Inventory of Programs and Block Grant Expenditures* (Washington, D.C.: June 1991), Table 1, p. 3.

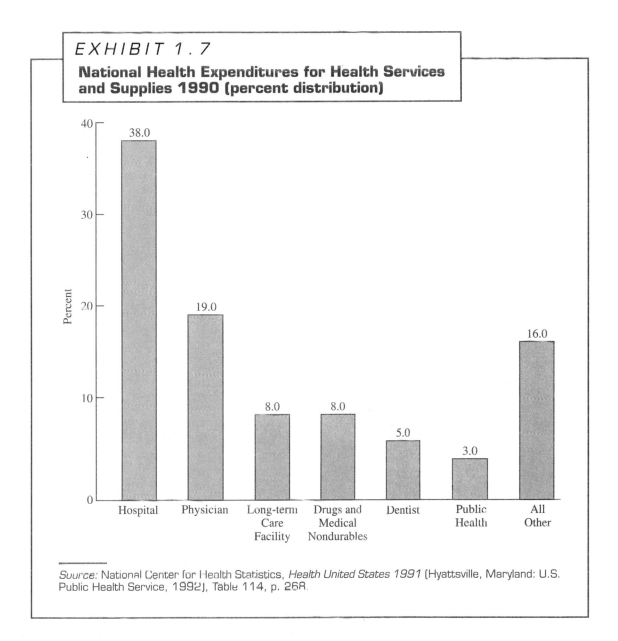

EXHIBIT 1.7

National Health Expenditures for Health Services and Supplies 1990 (percent distribution)

Source: National Center for Health Statistics, *Health United States 1991* (Hyattsville, Maryland: U.S. Public Health Service, 1992), Table 114, p. 268.

All AHSCs contain a medical school, affiliated teaching hospital, and at least one other health professional education program. Although all U.S. trained M.D.s are educated within one of the AHSCs, another fifteen schools of osteopathic medicine graduate over 1,500 physicians per year. In 1990, the AHSCs and schools of osteopathy graduated nearly 17,000 new physicians. This is more than double the number of graduates in 1960. Exhibit 1.8 presents trends in enrollment for selected health occupations.

EXHIBIT 1.8
Enrollment in Selected Health Occupation Schools, 1979–80 and 1989–90

	Number of Students		
Profession	**1979–80**	**1989–90**	**1991–92**
Medicine			
Allopathic	63,800	65,016	65,602
Osteopathic	4,571	6,615	7,012
Podiatry	2,531	2,397	2,247
Dentistry	22,486	16,198	15,715
Optometry	4,500	4,723	4,743
Veterinary Medicine	7,803	8,456	8,440
Registered Nurses	239,486	201,458	237,598

Source: National Center for Health Statistics, *Health United States 1991* (Hyattsville, Maryland: U.S. Public Health Service, 1992), Table 104, p. 254.

Payers for Health Care Products and Services

Another important component of the health services sector are those agencies, organizations, and individuals that provide payment for health care products and services.[19] In general, health service payer organizations can be dichotomized into those in the private sector and those in the public sector.

Private Payers for Health Services. Various categories of payment from individual households in the United States make up the largest single payer component. In 1991, individual households paid $247 billion of the $729 billion expended on health services and supplies. Households pay for health services through four primary mechanisms: (1) direct out-of-pocket health spending by individuals; (2) various premiums paid by employees and the self-employed into the Medicare hospital insurance trust fund; (3) premiums paid by individuals to the Medicare supplemental medical insurance trust fund; and (4) the employee-paid share of private health insurance premiums and individual health insurance policy premiums (see Exhibit 1.9).

Payments made by private businesses accounted for 28 percent of all expenditures for health services and supplies in 1991. Of this $205 billion, $153 billion was spent by employers for private health insurance premiums. These premiums were paid for both traditional indemnity types of insurance and, to an increasing degree, for employer self-insurance programs. In addition, private employers contributed nearly $33 billion into the Medicare hospital insurance trust fund and another $17.5 billion for workers' compensation and various forms of disability insurance. A small portion of the private expenditures ($2.4 billion) was made for in-house company-provided health services (see Exhibit 1.10).

The final category of private payments for health services and supplies is nonpatient reve-

---

EXHIBIT 1.9

Individual Household Payers: Expenditures for Health Services and Supplies, 1970, 1980, 1985, 1991 (in billions)

	1970	1980	1985	1991
Individual out-of-pocket spending	$25.6	$59.5	$94.4	$144.3
Employee and self-employed contributions and voluntary premiums paid to Medicare hospital insurance trust fund	2.4	12.0	24.0	39.9
Premiums paid by individuals to Medicare supplemental medical insurance trust fund	1.0	2.7	5.2	10.7
Employee share of private health insurance premiums and individual policy premiums	6.0	16.6	30.0	52.2
Total	$35.0	$90.8	$153.6	$247.0

Source: Adapted from C. A. Cowan and P. A. McDonnell, "Business, Households, and Governments: Health Spending, 1991," *Health Care Financing Review* 14, no. 3 (Spring 1993), Table 1, p. 228.

EXHIBIT 1.10

Private Business Payers: Expenditures for Health Services and Supplies, 1970, 1980, 1985, 1991 (in billions)

	1970	1980	1985	1991
Private employer share of private health insurance premiums	$9.8	$47.9	$83.9	$152.7
Private employer contributions to Medicare hospital insurance trust fund	2.1	10.5	20.3	32.8
Workers' compensation and temporary disability insurance medical benefits and administration	1.4	5.1	7.8	17.5
Industrial in-plant health services	0.3	0.9	1.4	2.4
Total	$13.6	$64.4	$113.4	$205.4

Source: Adapted from C. A. Cowan and P. A. McDonnell, "Business, Households, and Governments: Health Spending, 1991," *Health Care Financing Review* 14, no. 3 (Spring 1993), Table 1, p. 228.

nue. Nonpatient revenues accounted for about 3 percent of expenditures for health services and supplies in 1991, a percentage unchanged for over a decade. Nonpatient revenues include such sources as philanthropy, hospital gift shops, parking lots, and cafeterias. Although the dollar amount of philanthropy for health services has been steadily increasing, the role of philanthropy in terms of all payments for health services and supplies is becoming less significant. Philanthropy has increased from one-half billion dollars in 1965 to $3.3 billion in 1987. However, in terms of percent of total payments, philanthropy has decreased from a 1.3 percent share in 1985 to less than 0.7 percent in 1987.[20]

Public Payers for Health Services. Public expenditures from all levels of government accounted for 35 percent of the payments for health services and supplies in 1991. The largest portion of these public payments, $133.8 billion, was from the federal government through its various health services programs. Revenue sources for these programs include general revenue contributions, federal employer contributions, and interest income.

The collected monies are allocated to Medicare, which makes payments for the elderly and certain classes of disabled individuals; the federal portion of Medicaid payments, which provide health services for some poor individuals; the health services system of the Veterans Administration, which operates 171 VA medical centers throughout the United States with a budget in excess of $11 billion;[21] the Indian Health Service, which provides health care services to Native Americans; and an extensive military health service operated by the various branches of the U.S. armed services through the Department of Defense. Department of Defense health programs accounted for expenditures of $12.8 billion in 1991.

State and local governments contributed in excess of $120 billion to total payments for health services and supplies in 1991. In addition to health services programs provided directly by these governmental entities, this figure includes state and local government contributions to private health insurance programs for their employees as well as their contributions as employers to the Medicare hospital insurance trust fund (see Exhibit 1.11).

EXHIBIT 1.11

Public Payers: Expenditures for Health Services and Supplies, 1970, 1980, 1985, 1991 (in billions)

	1970	1980	1985	1991
Federal government net health services and supplies spending	$10.4	$42.6	$68.9	$133.8
Local and state government net health services and supplies spending	8.5	34.2	59.3	120.7
Total	$18.9	$76.8	$128.2	$254.5

Source: Adapted from C. A. Cowan and P. A. McDonnell, "Business, Households, and Governments: Health Spending, 1991," *Health Care Financing Review* 14, no. 3 (Spring 1993), Table 1, p. 228.

Integrating Payers and Providers. Some organizations will be considered in the payer group for the purposes of this chapter that do not actually pay for health services. Rather they manage resources in some way for organizations that are payers. Many of these payment management firms market their services as a means to control the cost of health care for the client. Due to the very dynamic nature of the health services market, there are numerous variations on the cost containment or cost management theme and these types of organizations continue to evolve.

Blue Cross and Blue Shield programs in the various states most often are thought of as health insurance organizations. They do in fact sell traditional indemnity insurance plans; however, much of their business revolves around their role as an administrator for the self-insurance programs of large- and medium-sized corporations. In 1989, a majority of employer health plans were self-funded. Fully 84 percent of companies with 10,000 or more employees were self-insured.[22] The Blue Cross organization will act as a "third-party administrator" and, for a fee, will adjudicate claims, disburse payments, account for funds, and provide utilization management services for a self-insurance program of an employer. In this role, Blue Cross is not itself a payer, but rather the manager of resources for a payer organization.

Utilization management services provided by Blue Cross and other health resource management organizations include such methods as preadmission certification programs, individual case management programs, mandatory second surgical opinion programs, concurrent utilization review, discharge planning programs, retrospective review programs, and denial of payment policies. Although generally considered to be cost control techniques, these methods are evolving to encompass quality and medical appropriateness considerations. Health services research studies have suggested that 20 to 40 percent of hospital admissions may be inappropriate.[23] Other studies

have suggested that these methods have a mixed record of success in controlling costs or appropriate use of health services. Preadmission certification and retrospective review coupled with denial of payment have been shown to produce statistically significant reductions in hospital admissions, inpatient days used, and payments.[24]

Other examples of health resource management organizations include preferred provider organizations (PPO) and certain types of health maintenance organizations (HMO). In many cases, these organizations are technically not providers of services in that they employ no providers, nor are they the actual payers for services. They are mechanisms between the providers and the payers that attempt to "manage the care" provided on behalf of the health service consumer and payer. Staff model HMOs do employ providers and hence can be considered actual provider organizations. Although staff models are a small percentage of HMOs, accounting for less than 12 percent of enrollment in 1992, enrollment in staff models has recently begun to grow rapidly, increasing 41 percent during the first half of 1992.[25] Total enrollment in all types of HMOs in 1992 was over 43.7 million; an increase of 8.3 percent from 1991.[26] In 1992, an estimated 121.8 million individuals had access to PPO networks through their employers.[27]

Products of the Health Services Sector

Within those organizations that conduct health policy research, such as the federal Agency for Health Care Policy Research, the academic health sciences centers, and the Blue Cross Association, a great deal of interest continues in better defining the products of the health services sector. This interest relates to concerns for improving the payment methods for health care and the need for improving methods to judge the quality of health services. It is difficult to negotiate a price or judge the quality of a product you cannot define. If traditional marketplace methods based on competition are to allocate health care resources, then these are fundamental concerns for all participants in this market.

The most well-known outcome of this research is a patient categorization method known as *diagnosis related groups* (DRGs).[28] This method currently is used by the Health Care Financing Administration (Medicare) to define the products of the hospital sector so that a price for each product can be prospectively determined. Before DRGs, each patient's care was considered to be so unique that hospitals were paid on the basis of an after-the-fact accounting of the costs. This method was known as *retrospective cost-based payment.* DRGs allowed a before-the-fact determination of the average cost for a category of care and hence a prospectively determined payment for that category. Over the next decade, refinements for and alternatives to this type of product definition may surface.

For the purpose of this health services industry analysis, the following very broad definitions for the products of this economic sector are provided. These definitions have been structured to provide an introduction to health services products in a manner that demonstrates the relationship between health care products and outcomes for individual health care consumers. The link between the structures and processes of medical care and the outcomes for individual patients is often very tenuous. Efforts to strengthen this linkage are an important research focus in the attempt to better define the health care product. Products of the health services industries can be considered to be any good or service that is used to:

1. *Describe the current state of an individual's physiology.* X ray machines, X ray film, and the interpretation of an X ray procedure are goods and services used to describe the current state of an indi-

vidual's physiology. An X ray of a hand may be used to determine whether or not a pain in that hand is due to a damaged bone. The X ray procedure does not prevent, correct, or relieve the pain. It is used to help describe the physiological state that may be the underlying cause of the pain.

2. *Correct a deranged physiology.* Otitis media (an inflammation of the middle ear) is an example of deranged physiology that, if left untreated, can lead to serious complications. The derangement generally can be completely corrected through the use of sulfonamides or antibiotics. These substances and the services of a clinician to choose the most appropriate therapy, are products that can correct a deranged physiology.

3. *Relieve pain, discomfort, or disability caused by deranged physiology.* Anti-inflammatory agents are often used to reduce the pain and discomfort associated with degenerative joint disease (osteoarthritis). The drugs do not correct or necessarily even slow the progression of the disease. They do, however, temporarily relieve the symptoms of the deranged physiology.

4. *Prevent or slow the derangement of human physiology.* Various vaccines, such as the oral polio vaccine, are produced and consumed because they are known to prevent infection in humans by agents that will derange an otherwise healthy physiology. Other products, such as coronary artery bypass graft surgery, will slow the progression of a physiologic derangement, but do not correct the disease process. A bypass graft moves blood around a blocked coronary artery to provide oxygen to the heart muscle. It does not correct the disease process that led to the blockage of the artery.

Users of Health Care Products and Services

The use of health care goods and services is not uniform throughout the U.S. population. An individual's use of health services is influenced by various sociodemographic characteristics such as age, sex, educational attainment, place of residence, and insurance status. For example, a survey by the Agency for Health Care Policy and Research estimated that 85.3 percent of the total population used some health product or service in 1987. However, one's age and insurance status appears to have a meaningful impact on the use of health care. For those individuals 65 and older with only Medicare Insurance, 86.7 percent used some health service. If, on the other hand, you had Medicare and private insurance, the use of some health service increased to 95.3 percent. Contrast this with a child between the ages of 6 and 17 who had no health insurance of any kind during the entire year. Only 59.2 percent of these individuals used some health care product or service during 1987.[29]

Where you live in the United States appears to influence your use of health care services. Individuals who live in the Northeast are much more likely to spend a day in the hospital than people in the West. On an age-adjusted basis, residents of the South used hospital days in 1991 at a rate of 670.3 days per 1,000 population while the rate for residents of the West was 414.2 days per 1,000 population. This is a 38 percent difference in the use of hospital days between these two geographic areas of the United States.[30]

Gender has an impact on use of health services. In 1991, women had a higher rate of physician contacts than men. Women had an average of 6.3 physician contacts during that year while men averaged only 4.9 physician contacts. Additionally, men waited longer periods of time between physician contacts. Over 15 percent of men had waited at least

two years between physician contacts while only about 8 percent of women waited this length of time.[31] Gender influences use of health services in other ways. For example, females were over 41 percent more likely to have an operation during an inpatient hospital stay than males.[32]

Individual behaviors can influence the need for and use of health care goods and services. The single largest risk factor for mortality in the United States is cigarette smoking. Over 400,000 deaths per year are attributable to cigarette smoking. The likelihood of being a smoker is directly related to levels of education. Men who did not graduate from high school are almost three times more likely to be smokers as male college graduates. About 42 percent of men who did not finish high school smoked in 1990 while only 15 percent of male college graduates smoked during that year.[33]

REFORMING THE U.S. HEALTH CARE SYSTEM

The issues involved in changing the allocation of health care resources in the United States have been described as massively complex. It is unquestionably true that any significant alteration in the way we allocate the resources of such a large component of our economy will have unforseen effects. Therefore, predicting how reform will evolve is, at best, risky. However, national initiatives to reform health care provision are likely to include some of the following components.

Control of Biased Risk Selection

Studies of health care expenditures have suggested that in a given year, the top 1 percent of high-cost patients account for 30 percent of total costs.[34] Obviously, health insurers who can avoid selling coverage to these high cost patients significantly reduce their financial risk. Consequently, several methods are commonly used by insurers to avoid covering such individuals. These methods include restrictions on coverage for preexisting conditions, cancellation of coverage for small groups with high utilization, refusal to renew coverage for persons developing chronic conditions, and the requirement that a person seeking to purchase health insurance provide evidence of good health before becoming insured.

Use of these biased risk selection methods has decreased risk for the insurance industry but made it difficult for many individuals and small groups to obtain health insurance at a price comparable to that afforded large groups. It is likely that health care reform will include specific reforms of the health insurance market. Although there are many different proposals, most would limit the insurers ability to use methods such as those just described to limit risk.

A Minimum Benefits Package

Most health care reform proposals discuss some type of minimum benefits package. This could be a most difficult political issue because the details of such a package have important consequences not only for the kinds of services that will be provided, but also for the incomes of various providers and the costs that will ultimately have to be met.

One example of a minimum benefits package that currently exists is the Medicare Program. By private health insurance standards, this is not a generous benefits package. The vast majority of Medicare beneficiaries carry some type of supplemental insurance. If a more generous minimum package is mandated in national health reform, there would have to be changes to several large federal entitlement programs such as Medicare that would significantly increase federal costs. For example, Medicare does not cover prescription drugs. Some proposed minimum benefits packages

cover prescription drugs. Hence Medicare coverage may, by law, have to increase.

Providers of all types obviously are interested in the definition of this minimum benefits package. Although it is unlikely that exclusion from the minimum benefits package would eliminate the provision of a good or service entirely, it could significantly decrease the use of excluded products and therefore reduce the income of the provider. On the other hand, goods and services that are included could see increased use. Health promotion and disease prevention services have traditionally been excluded by many types of health insurance programs. Some proponents believe that broader access to these programs could significantly lower health care costs.[35] It is likely that many goods and services, such as preventive services, pharmaceuticals, and others will be debated in depth as a minimum benefits package is negotiated.

It is important to recognize that specifying a minimum benefits package that must be offered does not guarantee universal access to that minimum set of services. Universal access is a separate issue that is not resolved by mandating a set of minimum benefits. It is unclear whether the fundamental goal of health reform is to increase access or provide universal access. It is also unclear whether we are talking about access to insurance coverage for a minimum set of health care goods and services or access to the health care goods and services themselves. In other words, do we mean fiscal access or physical access? Although some type of minimum benefits package likely will be specified in law or regulation, the precise level and type of access that reform will guarantee is not apparent.[36]

Changes to Tax Policy

A third component that is likely to be included in any health reform legislation is some changes to the federal tax code. Changes to the tax code will enter the debate both as a method for raising the revenue needed to fund expanded access to the health care system and as a necessary step to correct incentives for overuse of health care resources.

How the government will obtain the funds to pay for health care expansion varies under different proposals for health care reform. The details of any changes to the federal tax laws could have important redistributional effects. Some proposals will recommend increases in "sin taxes" such as taxes on cigarettes or alcohol. It has been argued that increasing the price of substances known to have negative health consequences will decrease their use and thereby lower both negative health outcomes and decrease the costs for medical care used to treat these health problems.[37] Further, to some extent, such taxes redistribute the costs of health care to those undertaking the risky health behaviors.

More extensive redistributional effects are projected with other proposed tax changes such as limiting the exclusion of employer payments for worker health insurance from the employee's taxable income. At present, no employer payments for health insurance are included in employees' taxable income. It has been suggested that this artificially lowers the cost of health insurance for the employee and reduces the incentive to choose cost-effective services. The extent of this "tax subsidy" of employer-paid health insurance premiums is estimated by one source to be nearly $37 billion for 1994.[38] Changes to tax policy that would include the employer paid health insurance premium in the employees taxable income may decrease the number of individuals with employer-sponsored health insurance and reduce the breadth of covered services for those continuing to have employer-sponsored health insurance.[39] Given the magnitude of additional expenditures required in any meaningful reform of the health care system, changes to federal tax policies are likely.

Control of Health Care Costs

More than any other factor, the rising costs of the U.S. health care system have brought health care reform to the center of the national policy debate. It appears unlikely that any reform proposal will be enacted that does not describe how it will control these escalating costs. Of course, describing the mechanism that will provide cost control and having that mechanism actually work and produce results are two different things.

Fundamentally, there are two philosophical viewpoints concerning the government's role in dealing with the costs of health care. The first view suggests that the health care market is different than other markets and not subject to the same market forces that guide the price, quality, and distribution of other services. Therefore, to ensure equitable and efficient distribution of health care goods and services, the government must step in and allocate health care resources through "command and control" regulation of the market.

The second viewpoint holds that health care goods and services do respond to the normal forces of the marketplace. Studies by the Rand Corporation and others have suggested that consumers would be responsive to changes in the price of health services.[40] However, through government interventions in the past, we have distorted the health care market and caused it to behave inefficiently. Therefore, the role of government should be to correct the marketplace distortions and protect and enhance competition in the health care market. The marketplace should then be allowed to allocate health care resources.

It is likely that health care reform will contain elements of both viewpoints. Regardless of which viewpoint predominates, cost control measures will have to address both the prices charged for services and the volume of services used. Command and control methods have traditionally done this by fixing prices through regulation and monitoring utilization through prospective or retrospective utilization review. The Medicare prospective payment system (PPS) is an example of such a price-fixing method.

Marketplace methods have been suggested that would encourage competition among capitated programs. Capitated plans compete on the basis of a prenegotiated price for a defined set of services. The capitated plan receives a set payment for a beneficiary regardless of the amount of health care the individual consumes. For the plan to remain financially healthy, it must manage the health care its enrollees receive. Hence, volume controls are said to be built in by the incentives inherent in a capitated program. Price control is maintained by the marketplace competition among plans.

Because the total cost of health care is a function of the price per unit of service and the amount of service consumed, successful reform is likely to contain regulatory or market incentive mechanisms to control cost through control of both price and volume. How either of the two philosophical views will deal with the information problems associated with judging the quality of health care services is unclear.

CONTINUING TRENDS IN THE HEALTH CARE ENVIRONMENT

Substantive reform of the U.S. health care system may or may not take place. However, as is true in any sector of the economy, markets anticipate change. That is, individuals and organizations with economic interests in the health care sector will not wait for changes to occur to protect their interests and to try to position themselves to benefit from change. Rational strategic positioning is taking place and will continue to take place along a number of dimensions in the health care market regardless of the outcome of federal initiatives to "reform" health care.

We believe that a number of trends will continue within the health care environment. These trends should continue to evolve regardless of the success or failure of health care reform at the national level. National initiatives could effect the rate of change, but the direction to the trends and their meaning for strategic thinking in health care organizations should remain intact.

To illustrate this point, what precedes a discussion of these health care environmental trends is a brief description of three alternative scenarios for the outcome of the health care reform movement. Read these scenarios and keep them in mind as you read and think about the environmental trends that follow. Remember that other macro-environmental forces are at work that propel these trends independent of national measures to change the market for health care products and services.

Three Scenarios for Health Care Reform

Scenario I: Universal Access – Health Care Reform Succeeds. In this scenario, comprehensive health care reform legislation is passed providing some form of comprehensive health insurance for everybody. Thus, individuals who were formally "medically indigent" and relied on emergency rooms and public modes of care now have access to private providers. In addition, the private sector has found it advantageous to serve this population and to compete fiercely on price for the benefit package defined in the legislation. Well-organized managed-care competitors rapidly arise, and large group purchasing cooperatives that control the premiums for tens of thousands of beneficiaries are set up covering the vast majority of the U.S. population.

Scenario II: Reform Is Passed – However Problems Rapidly Arise. In this scenario, comprehensive health care reform legislation is passed, but problems with implementation arise immediately. Political battles in numerous states over the design of purchasing cooperatives slows the implementation dramatically, and the federal government must use its authority to mandate this process in many states. Many cooperatives are unable to meet their cost targets and the "National Health Board" steps in to use its "backstop" mechanisms that shift dollars from providers to employers. Many providers are caught off-guard by these processes and difficult financial decisions become the norm. Some provider groups go out-of-business and many providers scramble to find a new comfortable organizational home.

Scenario III: The Legislative Process on Health Care Bogs Down – No Reform. In this scenario, the thousands of health care special interest groups have a field day on Capitol Hill. No health care reform legislation is passed in the first two years of debate, and the momentum is no longer there. Substantive legislated reform seems to be dead for the near future.

Trends in the Health Care Environment

Regardless of which of these scenarios becomes fact, several trends in the health care environment should continue. These trends are not independent and a substantive change in the direction of one trend will have impact on the other trends as well.

Continued Evolution and Market Share Expansion for "Managed Health Care." Managed-care organizations such as health maintenance organizations and preferred provider organizations have been mentioned previously in this chapter. These managed-care systems will continue to evolve and gain market share.

Managed-care programs continue to attract new enrollees. HMOs provided medical care for 16.6 percent of the U.S. population in 1992 (an increase from 13.9 percent at the end of 1989). This trend is likely to continue because managed care programs have demonstrated an ability to lower expenses over time while continuing enrollment growth. Significantly, some of this reduction in expenses appears to be coming in the area of costs for physician services. Physician services are the largest single expense item for HMOs. In 1991, large HMOs recorded a 9 percent drop in the median cost per member for physician services, however, smaller HMOs registered a 10 percent increase.[41]

In addition to market share gains for the managed care industry, it is likely that these organizations will continue to evolve. One probable evolutionary trend is the continuation of industry consolidation. Although HMOs continued to increase their number of enrollees, the actual number of HMOs has been decreasing (see Exhibit 1.12). Undoubtably experimentation will continue within these organizations concerning the design of their provider networks and the contract provisions they offer as well as significant entrepreneurial activity to establish new managed-care programs. However, the basic trend should be toward consolidation of enrollees in fewer, large managed-care programs.

As the trend toward consolidation continues, there is a high probability that there will be changes in the way physicians are paid by these organizations. Managed-care programs will compete for enrollees on the bases of both price and quality. However, at least for the foreseeable future, it will be much easier for a purchaser to compare price rather than quality. Hence, price comparisons are likely to be the first line of competition. Because physician services are the largest single expense for managed care programs, attention to the control of this expense will likely increase. Although most managed care programs now pay physicians on a discounted fee basis, straight salary arrangements may become increasingly common.

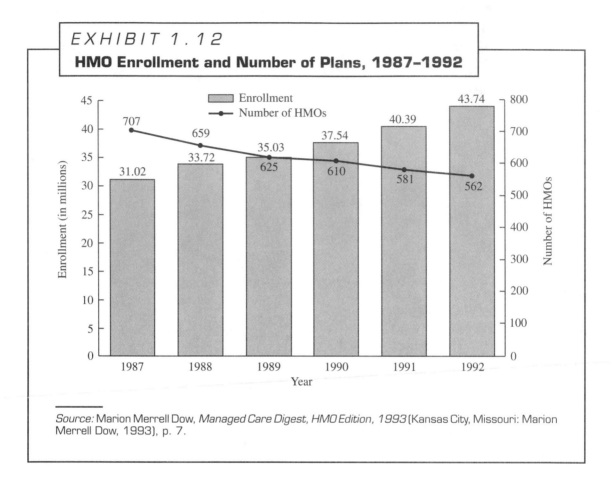

EXHIBIT 1.12

HMO Enrollment and Number of Plans, 1987–1992

Source: Marion Merrell Dow, *Managed Care Digest, HMO Edition, 1993* (Kansas City, Missouri: Marion Merrell Dow, 1993), p. 7.

Increasing Supply of Physicians. A second health care environmental trend that is likely to continue is the increasing supply of physicians. This trend makes changes to physician payment methods even more probable. Although the fact that the number of physicians in active practice will significantly increase in the years ahead is not in question, there is debate about whether or not this increased supply will actually create a physician surplus. Some analysts suggest that increasing numbers of people with health insurance, plus the aging of the population and rapidly evolving medical technology will more than create enough increased demand to offset the increased supply of physicians. However, increasing concern about the effectiveness of therapies as well as increasing demand for efficiency will limit the impact of these countervailing trends. It is likely that the supply of physicians will increase relative to demand, and that this trend will have its impact on both the geographic distribution of physician services and the cost of physician services. However, any excess supply will not be shared evenly by all physician specialties. The demand for primary-care services is expected to increase.[42]

Increased Demand for Primary-Care Physician Services. A third trend that is likely to continue regardless of any national initiative on health care reform is the increasing demand for primary-care physician services. Increasing numbers of enrollees in managed-care programs require increasing numbers of primary-care physicians to "manage" the interactions of these enrollees with other health care providers. This demand will be further heightened by the increasing competition among managed-care organizations. As the competitive environment increases, the current practice of physicians affiliating with several different managed-care networks is likely to end. Large, economically powerful managed-care networks may offer only exclusive contracts to physicians to increase their competitive positions. Hence, the demand for efficient, high-quality primary-care physicians should increase.

This trend toward increasing demand for primary-care physicians has significant implications for U.S. medical schools. Pressures on medical schools to rapidly increase the proportion of primary-care specialists they produce is mounting. In addition, the schools are beginning to anticipate a demand from currently active non-primary-care specialists for retraining in primary-care specialties. Only about 25 percent of active physicians are in the primary-care specialties of general practice, family practice, internal medicine, or pediatrics. This percentage has actually decreased slightly since 1970, when 27 percent of active physicians considered themselves in a primary-care specialty.[43]

Consolidation and Closure of Acute-Care Hospitals. Activity to reform the U.S. health care system is likely to increase a decade-long trend in the hospital sector toward reduced capacity. The total number of acute care hospital beds has been decreasing since the mid-1980s, and the actual number of U.S. hospitals of this type began to decline even earlier. Despite decreasing capacity, acute-care hospitals remain severely underutilized. In 1985, the overall occupancy for acute care hospitals was approximately 66 percent. Although beds-in-

service have decreased by over 85,000 since 1985, the occupancy rate in 1991 remained essentially the same[44] (see Exhibit 1.13).

Trends toward alternatives to expensive inpatient hospital services will likely continue. In addition, hospitals will face increasing price pressures. The cost of maintaining unused capacity will become a significant competitive disadvantage. Therefore, reduction of acute-care bed capacity will continue. As clients who are less severely ill are treated in the outpatient environment, the severity of patients remaining as inpatients rises. Severely ill patients require more intensive and sophisticated services. Small or financially weak institutions are unlikely to be able to provide this level of care. Recent research has demonstrated that financially troubled hospitals try to survive by reducing their rate of investment in technology.[45] Hence, their ability to attract admissions will continue to erode. Thus the increasing number of severely ill inpatients will contribute to continuation of the trend toward closure and consolidation. Since 1980, nearly 1,000 U.S. hospitals have closed or merged.[46]

Increased Availability of Quality Information on a Provider-Specific Basis. As was mentioned in the discussion of trends in managed care, for the near future, organizations that manage the provision of care will compete for enrollees primarily on the basis of price. The ability to measure and communicate comparative information on quality is weak. However, major public and private initiatives are underway to improve access to quality information for the health care consumer. Given that care for the individual client will continue to be managed by physicians and that physicians will continue to allocate the vast majority of health care resources, these initiatives must concentrate on developing comparative quality information on a physician-specific basis.

The trend toward consolidation of larger numbers of enrollees in fewer managed-care programs will increase the development of the

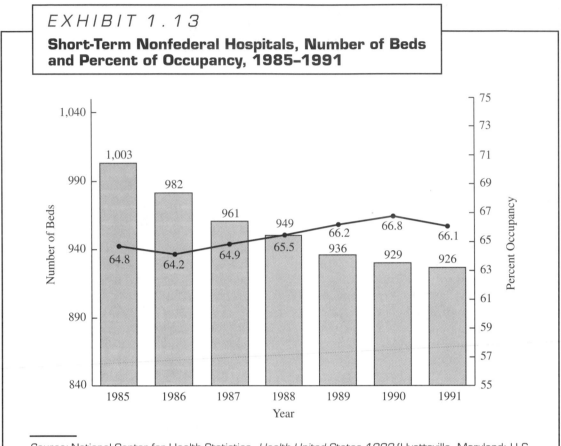

EXHIBIT 1.13

Short-Term Nonfederal Hospitals, Number of Beds and Percent of Occupancy, 1985–1991

Source: National Center for Health Statistics, *Health United States 1992* (Hyattsville, Maryland: U.S. Public Health Service, 1993), Table 107, p. 153.

trend toward physician-specific quality information. Very large populations are necessary to provide the statistical power to evaluate professional services as diverse as medical care. Previously, very few groups had an enrollment large enough to generate comparative data on providers. The useful information that could be generated was based only on the most common services. A recent report in *Health Care Financing Review* stated, "Compared with health systems where there is a single payer, United States data are divided among many insurers, making it virtually impossible to pro-

duce comprehensive provider or beneficiary profiles."[47] As managed-care organizations grow and consolidate, the ability to produce provider specific profiles will increase, and this information will become more available for individual consumers and large purchasers.

CONCLUSION

This chapter began by noting that significant change is the fundamental characteristic that describes the U.S. health care environment at this time. The chapter ends by discussing a number of trends in this environment that should continue regardless of how other changes in health care evolve. In other words, a turbulent environment does not mean that strategic thinking and planning cannot take place. Rather, in such an environment, the ability to think strategically and identify relevant trends becomes one of the most critical processes for organizational growth and survival. Although it is true that change creates opportunities for success, it is equally true that the opportunities must be identified and the organization positioned to create the potential to succeed.

NOTES

1. National Center for Health Statistics, *Health United States 1992* (Hyattsville, Maryland: U.S. Public Health Service, 1993), Table 110, p. 156.
2. P. Jolly, J. Y. Krakower, R. Beran, and D. Williams, "U.S. Medical School Finances," *Journal of the American Medical Association* 264, no. 7 (August 15, 1990), pp. 27–54.
3. *Health United States 1992*, Table 100, p. 143.
4. Ibid., Tables 138 and 139, pp. 185–186.
5. G. J. Ammase, S. A. Law, R. E. Rosenblatt, and K. R. Wing, *American Health Law* (Boston: Little, Brown and Company, 1990), p. 526–527.
6. *Health United States 1992*, Table 140, p. 187.
7. S. W. Letsch, H. C. Lazenby, K. R. Levit, and C. A. Cowan, "National Health Expenditures, 1991," *Health Care Financing Review* 11, no. 4 (Winter 1992), p. 19.
8. Physician Payment Review Commission, *Annual Report to Congress 1991* (Washington, D.C., March 1991), x–xiii.
9. *Health United States 1992*, Table 114, p. 160.
10. Office of National Health Statistics, Office of the Actuary, "National Health Expenditures, 1990," *Health Care Financing Review* 13, no. 1 (Fall 1991), pp. 29–54.

11. *Health United States 1992*, Table 139, p. 186.
12. R. H. Ebert and S. S. Brown, "Academic Health Centers," *The New England Journal of Medicine* 308, no. 20 (May 19, 1983), pp. 1200–1207.
13. Office of National Cost Estimates, "National Health Care Expenditures, 1988," *Health Care Financing Review* 11, no. 4 (Summer 1990), pp. 1–41.
14. *Health United States 1992*, Table 107, p. 153.
15. Ibid., Table 113, p. 159.
16. Ibid., Table 116, p. 162.
17. Office of National Cost Estimates, "National Health Expenditures, 1988," p. 14.
18. Centers for Disease Control and Prevention, *Profile of State and Territorial Public Health Systems: United States, 1990* (Washington, D.C.: U.S. Department of Health and Human Services, December 1991, pp. 8–9.
19. Data on payers is excerpted from Cathy A. Cowan and Patricia A. McDonnell, "Business, Households, and Governments: Health Spending, 1991," *Health Care Financing Review* 14, no. 3 (Spring 1993), pp. 227–248.
20. K. R. Levit, M. S. Freeland, and D. R. Waldo, "Health Spending and Ability to Pay: Business, Individuals, and Government," *Health Care Financing Review* 10, no. 3 (Spring 1989), pp. 1–11.
21. W. J. Hollingsworth and P. K. Bandy, "The Role of Veterans Affairs Hospitals in the Health Care System," *New England Journal of Medicine* 322, no. 36 (June 28, 1990), pp. 1851–1857.
22. Blue Cross, Blue Shield Association, Environmental Analysis, 1990, p. 40.
23. A. L. Sui, F. A. Sonnenberg, W. G. Manning, G. A. Goldberg, E. S. Bloomfield, J. P. Newhouse, and R. H. Brook, "Inappropriate Use of Hospitals in a Randomized Trial of Health Insurance Plans," *New England Journal of Medicine* 315, no. 20 (November 13, 1986), pp. 1259–1266.
24. R. M. Scheffler, S. D. Sullivan, and T. H. Ko, "The Impact of Blue Cross and Blue Shield Plan Utilization Management Pro-

grams, 1980–1988," *Inquiry* 28 (Fall 1991), pp. 263–275.

25. Marion Merrell Dow, *Managed Care Digest Update Edition 1992* (Kansas City, Missouri: Marion Merrill Dow, 1992), pp. 8 and 9.

26. Marion Merrell Dow, *Managed Care Digest HMO Edition 1993* (Kansas City, Missouri: Marion Merrill Dow, 1993), p. 4.

27. Marion Merrell Dow, *Managed Care Digest PPO Edition 1993* (Kansas City, Missouri: Marion Merrill Dow, 1993), p. 2.

28. R. B. Fetter, Y. Shin, J. L. Freeman, R. F. Averill, and J. D. Thompson, "Case Mix Definition by Diagnosis Related Groups," Working Paper #40, Yale School of Organization and Management.

29. D. Lefkowitz and A. Monheit, "Health Insurance, Use of Health Services, and Health Care Expenditures," National Medical Expenditure Survey Research Findings 12, Agency for Health Care Policy and Research, Public Health Service, December 1991, p. 9.

30. *Health United States 1992,* Table 83, p. 122.

31. Ibid., Tables 78 and 79, pp. 117–118.

32. Ibid., Table 88, p. 129.

33. National Center for Health Statistics, *Health United States 1991* (Hyattsville, Maryland: U.S. Public Health Service, 1992), p. 24.

34. M. L. Berk and A. C. Monheit, "The Concentration of Health Expenditures: An Update," *Health Affairs* (Winter 1992), pp. 145–149.

35. J. F. Fries et al., "Reducing Health Care Costs by Reducing the Need and Demand for Medical Services," *The New England Journal of Medicine* 329, no. 5 (January 29, 1993), pp. 321–325.

36. United States Congress, Office of Technology Assessment, *An Inconsistent Picture: A Compilation of Analyses of Economic Impacts of Competing Approaches to Health Care Reform by Experts and Stakeholders,* OTA-H-540 (Washington, D.C.: U.S. Government Printing Office, June 1993), p. 70.

37. M. Grossman, J. L. Sindelar, J. Mullahy, and R. Anderson "Alcohol and Cigarette Taxes," *Journal of Economic Perspectives* 7, no. 4 (Fall 1993), pp. 211–222.

38. United States Congress, Joint Committee on Taxation, *Estimates of Federal Tax Expenditures for Fiscal Years 1994–1998,* as cited in United States Congress, Office of Technology Assessment, *An Inconsistent Picture,* pps. 37–38.

39. Employee Benefits Research Institute "EBRI Issue Brief: Health Care Reform, Managed Competition and Beyond," no. 135 (March 1993), pp. 18–21.

40. For an excellent discussion of marketplace allocation of health care resources, see Michael A. Morrisey, *Price Sensitivity in Health Care: Implications for Health Care Policy* (Washington, D.C.: NFIB Foundation, 1992).

41. Marion Merrell Dow, *Managed Care Digest Update Edition 1992,* pp. 3–4.

42. D. A. Kindig, J. M. Cultice, and F. Mullan, "The Elusive Generalist Physician: Can We Reach a 50 Percent Goal?" *Journal of the American Medical Association* 270, no. 9 (September 1, 1993), pp. 1069–1073

43. *Health United States 1992,* Table 100, p. 144.

44. Ibid., Table 107, p. 153.

45. S. Q. Duffy and B. Friedman, "Hospitals with Chronic Financial Losses: What Came Next?" *Health Affairs* (Summer 1993), pp. 151–163.

46. Milt Freudenheim, "Hospitals Begin Streamlining for a New World in Health Care," *The New York Times* (June 20, 1993).

47. N. De Lew, G. Greenberg, and K. Kinchen, "Special Report, A Layman's Guide to the United States Health Care System," *Health Care Financing Review* 14, no. 1 (Fall 1992), p. 157.

The SunHealth Alliance: Making a Real Difference

"Our benchmarking program *has* received a lot of coverage in the media," said Ben Latimer, president and chief executive officer of SunHealth. "The alliance hospitals participating in that 1992 study found that the fastest hospitals moved the Emergency Room patient to the doctor in 30 minutes or less while the slowest hospitals took nearly 90 minutes to move the patient. If you're the patient, that's a considerable difference. Having identified the factors that can speed up the process, we are helping other alliance hospitals implement changes."

"The Emergency Room benchmarking study is just one example – and a good one – of what we do to try to help our hospitals fulfill their missions. That's why SunHealth was founded in 1969 and we are still operating that way today," Ben Latimer pointed out.

Currently we're developing a Physician Practice Management Institute and the Clinical Resources Management Initiative. They're both in response to what we see as the needs of our partners in today's uncertain environment. We also have to decide what we should be doing in terms of helping our partners with managed care and the likelihood of capitation. Managed care was investigated by SunHealth – and all the other alliances. Because a fair amount of risk was involved SunHealth decided not to develop a managed care program. We felt that our partner organizations preferred to become part of integrated systems and preferred provider organizations rather than having SunHealth set up and assume the risk for managed care. That may change as we see how the reform initiatives unfold.

"There are several other important issues facing our alliance," Ben said.

We're evaluating whether we should change our status from a for-profit corporation to a cooperative structure. Two of the other major alliances – Voluntary Hospitals of America (VHA) and Premier – have become cooperatives. American Healthcare Systems (AmHS) has remained as a for-profit corporation and University Hospital Consortium (UHC) has a nonprofit status.

We'd like to grow, but not at the cost of sacrificing quality. One way we could get larger is to require our

This case was prepared by Linda E. Swayne, Peter M. Ginter, and W. Jack Duncan. It is intended as a basis for classroom discussion rather than to illustrate effective or ineffective handling of an administrative situation. Used with permission from Linda Swayne.

partners to belong only to SunHealth Alliance and set a specific amount of purchasing that is required. But then we have to decide if we will require partners to disassociate if they don't meet these requirements and whether we would pay them a "market value" for their shares and how we would determine that market value.

He continued, "Some experts have referred to alliances as dinosaurs in these reform-minded times, but I think SunHealth will continue helping our partners improve the health of the communities they serve. We are committed to making a real difference in the health of the people who live in our region."

HISTORY

In 1969, SunHealth was founded as Carolinas Hospital and Health Services, Inc. (CHHS), by the state hospital associations of North Carolina and South Carolina as a freestanding, not-for-profit, shared services corporation. The South Carolina Hospital Association (SCHA) had contacted The Duke Endowment, a major foundation, to determine whether it had any interest in helping SCHA set up something similar to a California program – the Commission for Administrative Services to Hospitals (CASH). In the mid-1960s, hospitals cooperated more than they competed, and CASH and other similar organizations were emerging to assist with planning and applying industrial and management engineering techniques to hospitals to become more efficient.

Although receptive, The Duke Endowment leadership was concerned that the twenty or so hospitals in South Carolina were too few to be able to develop such a program. In addition, they knew that a similar group was underway in North Carolina. The Duke Endowment proposed one organization with a board of directors comprising hospital CEOs

from both states. The two Carolinas had many commonalities, including culture, social structure, and economy. The hospital communities were similar in philosophy and maintained close ties. In addition, The Duke Endowment was chartered to improve higher education and health care in both North Carolina and South Carolina. Through cooperation of the two states' hospital associations and The Duke Endowment, CHHS was formed. The Duke Endowment saw an opportunity to leverage its grants to benefit more hospitals in the two states.

The original governing board had three executives of hospitals from each state, the CEOs of the two state hospital associations, plus Duke Endowment representatives. D. Kirk Oglesby, Jr., CEO of Anderson Area Medical Center in Anderson, South Carolina, was the first chairman of the board. The two state hospital association CEOs developed the plan and bylaws for the organization. Dr. John Canada, a professor at North Carolina State University, put together a proposal for introducing management engineering and management education for the hospitals. Canada took the responsibility for finding the first staff. According to Ben Latimer, "He considered a number of folks, I understand, but he had some contact with Dr. Harold Smalley at Georgia Tech who suggested that I be considered. I met with the eight-member board and was fortunate to be selected by that group."

Ben Latimer Assumed Leadership of CHHS

Ben W. Latimer earned a BME degree from Georgia Tech University in 1962 and then worked for somewhat over a year at Procter & Gamble in the Department of Industrial Engineering as a management trainee. He returned to Georgia Tech and studied under Dr. Harold Smalley, one of the pioneers in applying industrial engineering and quantitative analysis techniques to health care. (The term *management engineering* was more acceptable to hospital administrators and physicians and thus was used in health care.) Just before he completed the Master of Science degree in industrial engineering, Latimer was recommended by Smalley for a position with Methodist Hospital in Memphis, Tennessee. There he worked on improving staffing and scheduling, particularly in the area of nursing. He realized early on that management techniques would be interwoven with the newly developing computer technology and management information systems. Although satisfied with the progress he was making in introducing management engineering at Methodist Hospital, he was intrigued by the opportunity at CHHS.

"Though independent of direct hospital association control or ownership, CHHS did serve *in effect* as the associations' operational arm for some services developed or wanted by them for hospital members," wrote Ben Latimer and Pat Poston in a 1976 *Topics in Health Care Financing* article. As an example, they cited group purchasing that was researched and developed by the South Carolina Hospital Association but operationalized by CHHS. He continued, "However, CHHS was never limited to implementing only those activities assigned it by the associations. In fact, CHHS operated as an expansion-minded company and would assess user needs and organize services to meet those needs."

"This organizational model was especially applicable to states in which size, density, and health care patterns precluded the existence of enough mid-sized hospitals to support shared services economically," commented Ben. "In addition, the separate but 'associated' corporation provided additional benefits – services could cross state lines, we had to be cost effective in order to survive, we had greater flexibility to recruit and pay employees differently than the associations, we could provide some services that associations were not able to provide, and members did not pay 'dues' but rather membership fees plus fees for the services that they selected."

He continued,

The first service provided was management engineering known originally as the Carolinas Hospital Improvement Program or CHIP. It was designed to move hospital administration toward developing strategies for quality improvement and cost containment. It included such things as work and cleaning schedules and management education because most hospital administrators were educated in various health professions and had to learn management skills "on the job." For the CHIP program, all the development support came from the Duke Endowment. But as that was followed by other programs in the biomedical engineering and clinical engineering areas, the W. K. Kellogg Foundation supported our efforts as did the Kate B. Reynolds Health Care Trust.

We used foundation support for development funds to establish new programs, however, each service we added was designed to be self-supporting. If the service was not good enough that the member hospitals weren't willing to pay for it, then it was not continued.

The Growing Alliance Expanded Beyond the Carolinas

When Carolinas Hospital and Health Services was originally developed, the support from the Duke Endowment and the composition of the governing board dictated that it was a service organization for the two Carolinas. "It never crossed our mind to serve anyone other than North and South Carolina," commented Ben. He continued, "In the mid-1970s the question was first raised about offering services beyond our two states. The board decided that it would not harm the current partners and would allow for a larger staff that would have the opportunity to gain more from a broader representation of health organizations, and there would be broader forums for development and expansion." SIGMA was a for-profit division created to provide the various CHHS services to not-for-profit organizations primarily outside the two Carolinas. "We selected a different name for this division because it was hard to offer 'Carolinas' Hospital and Health Services to places like Tennessee and Virginia," Ben Latimer said. SIGMA later was phased out as full membership was offered to hospitals outside the Carolinas.

He continued,

It was also about this time that the board decided to expand its membership beyond hospital CEOs. The first non-CEO board member was from academia, but currently we have members from academia, business, law, and medicine. Each one of these areas has value for our board, but I think it is particularly important to work closely with the medical community – to have the perspective of the physician on the board.

Up until the mid-1970s, CHHS served all sizes of hospitals in the Carolinas. Because of our location and the mix of hospitals in the area, most people probably thought we only served small and medium sized hospitals. Some of the large hospitals – those with 400-plus beds – thought they had more in common with other large-sized hospitals across a broader region. So we formed The Sun Alliance which corresponded loosely with the geographic area of the Southeastern Hospital Conference. We [CHHS] provided services for Sun Alliance.

CHHS Became SunHealth Alliance

"Eventually we determined that having two separate organizations was not beneficial. On the advice of Dr. Howard Zuckerman, a consultant from the University of Michigan, we merged the two organizations into SunHealth Corporation in 1985." The planning consultants laid out the concept of a regional health services network and encouraged the development of a network organization that in effect mirrored the composition of the hospital industry in the region – small community hospitals, large hospital systems, university hospitals, public hospitals, and so on. Given that the purpose of SunHealth was to provide health services to a large share of the population in the region, the consultants encouraged alignment of hospitals corresponding to actual patient flow patterns among facilities and physicians.

The large hospitals formerly in Sun Alliance became 1,000 share (four-unit) partners. Smaller hospitals became 250 share (one-unit) partners but could petition and purchase additional shares to become a four-unit partner. Originally 1,000 shares cost the hospital $100,000 and 250 shares cost $25,000. Today, because the value of the shares has increased and additional capital is needed for development and refinements, the costs have gone up. The price of stock for 1,000 shares is $150,000 and for 250 shares is $37,500.

Stock is held in SunHealth Corporation. SunHealth Enterprises, as a wholly owned subsidiary of SunHealth Corporation, is the operational arm and manages the provision of services (see Exhibit 2.1 for the SunHealth corporate structure). The board and management of SunHealth did not want the organization to be thought of as an "investment vehicle designed to return earnings," but rather as a service organization to help partners fulfill their missions. *Partner* was consciously selected to be used when referring to shareholder hospitals to constantly remind all involved par-

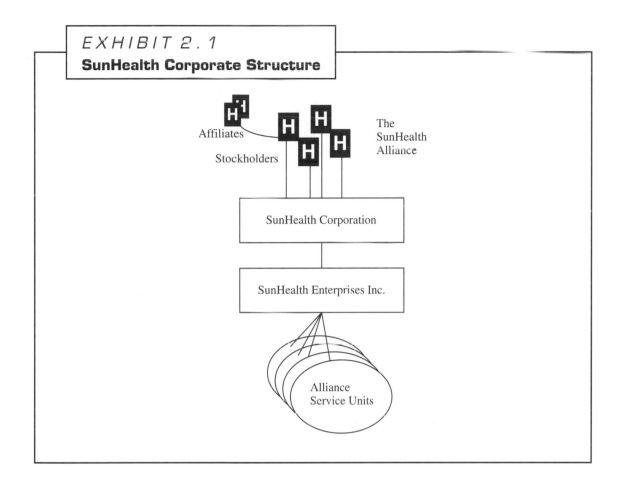

EXHIBIT 2.1

SunHealth Corporate Structure

Affiliates

Stockholders

The SunHealth Alliance

SunHealth Corporation

SunHealth Enterprises Inc.

Alliance Service Units

ties that SunHealth is a shared alliance where partners work together to share risk and improve health care.

SunHealth Today

Approximately 520 employees at SunHealth Enterprises provide services to SunHealth's 151 partners. The partners provide over $23 billion worth of health services annually through 272 hospitals that account for nearly 70,000 licensed beds. Located primarily in fifteen southeastern and south central states, hospital bed-size of partners varies as illustrated in the following table:

Number of Adjusted Occupied Beds[1]	Percent of Partners
1–199	34.2
200–299	32.2
300–399	10.7
400–499	12.1
Over 500	10.7

SunHealth has clearly stated its mission and vision (see Exhibit 2.2). SunHealth believes that a committed group of not-for-profit hospitals and health care organizations, serving a homogeneous region, can be catalysts in

---

EXHIBIT 2.2
SunHealth Alliance Mission and Goals

Our Mission: The Tasks Ahead

We as the alliance's core organization are charged with carrying out the commitments below, *with and through our partners:*

- *Collecting and sharing information and experience* about new and better ways to organize, operate, and manage hospital and health services.
- Creating "new and better ways" through *research, development, and testing.*
- *Supporting the installation and implementation* of "new and better ways" through SunHealth-provided services such as consulting, group purchasing, information sharing, and the provision of specialized staff to hospitals.

Our Goals: The Achievements Sought

- To increase the capability of each hospital in our alliance to better perform its mission and roles.
- To increase the combined capability of alliance hospitals to serve more of the region's people, in terms of the number of hospitals in the alliance, their locations, and their service capabilities.
- To improve health services for people in our region by improving the capabilities of our alliance hospitals and linkages among them.
- To make demonstrated contributions to the way health services are organized, managed, and operated.

---

combination with physicians on their medical staffs in leading the reformation of health services. According to Ben Latimer,

> Regardless of the pace of national or state reform legislation, it seems likely that a number of events are going to occur or continue. First, the financial risk of providing care will continue to shift to providers. Second, the "design" of health care will relate more and more to the bundled benefit packages that large payers, such as companies, purchasing alliances, and government, pay for. Third, cooperation among hospitals and physicians will be necessary in order to produce and contract for high-value health services. Fourth, the structure of hospital-physician collaboration and managed care activities will vary widely. And last, a sound positioning strategy for the hospitals and SunHealth Alliance is to focus on service as well as structure . . . that is designing and implementing integrated health care systems that fit the local environment.

He continued, "Therefore, we are putting great emphasis on initiatives through which hospitals and physicians come together to provide clinical services of superior value for their communities and payer-customers. We think value means efficacy and quality of clinical outcome for those served, satisfaction of those served, and cost effectiveness in terms of price-to-outcome. Because one part of value is cost effectiveness, SunHealth is providing support for partner organizations and affiliated physicians that want to manage the financial risk of providing care under fixed payment arrangements."

SunHealth has been extremely successful in serving its partners' needs and remaining financially strong, as evidenced by its key indicators and comparisons of its hospitals with other hospitals nationally and regionally (Exhibit 2.3). Purchasing volume was $1.5 billion for FY1992 or $28,253 per adjusted occupied bed. Purchasing incentives of $1.9 billion plus $16.6 million in vendor dividends were credited to partner organizations in FY1992.

Requirements for Membership

SunHealth Alliance offers membership to hospitals that meet the following criteria:

1. A candidate must be a tax-exempt organization engaged principally in the operation, directly or through an affiliated entity, of a not-for-profit hospital with total assets of $5 million or more;
2. It must not be contract managed by an entity other than one that is controlled by or under common control with the member; and
3. It must have approval in accordance with board policies and procedures.

In terms of recruiting for new partners in the Alliance, priority is given to (1) hospital organizations in population areas not served by existing partners, (2) those readily able to hold equity interest, and (3) those demonstrating interest in existing alliance activities and commitment to improve region-wide health care delivery.

A new partner is evaluated on the basis of the characteristics it conveyed in its management team, relationship with other providers (competing and cooperative), recommendations from existing members, and the candidate's objectives in seeking network membership. SunHealth uses the term *multi-hospital system* to refer to partners who operate

multiple hospital facilities in different service areas. The term *emerging integrated health-care system* is used to refer to those partners that operate acute-care hospitals but have related (diversified and nondiversified) hospital services.

Because of its regional orientation, The SunHealth Alliance (more so than other major alliances in the country) is composed of diverse segments of membership, including public, general, denominational, rural, community, not-for-profit, and regional referral hospitals plus academic medical centers that serve patients from throughout the world. Some of the implications of this diversity among members has been reflected in the establishment of membership criteria and requirements. Although members share some objectives in networking, their local strategies are typically diverse. Some members, constrained by law, organizational relationships, or philosophy, cannot make certain types of institutional commitments. For example, public general hospitals and tax-district hospitals are subject to public bidding. Denominational, university, and foundation-operated hospitals are subject to systems or organizational investment requirements for purchasing.

A partner's rights may be terminated if that shareholder fails to continue to meet the technical eligibility requirements such as: loses its tax exemption, is no longer engaged in the operation of a not-for-profit hospital, becomes acquired or contract managed by a nonrelated organization, or fails to pay its approved assessment.

SunHealth's primary service area is defined as the fifteen-state region on the southern side of a line from Maryland to Texas. SunHealth's concentration of hospitals in near proximity in some states, as well as the kind of activities SunHealth partners engage in, make sensitivity to antitrust considerations more important to SunHealth than to some other alliances whose members are more widely dispersed.

EXHIBIT 2.3
SunHealth Key Financial Indicators

Key Indicator	FY1991	FY1992	FY1993
Current ratio	2.4	2.2	1.9
Total assets	$14.2 million	$16.4 million	$18.3 million
Total shareholder equity	$8.8 million	$9.5 million	$9.8 million
Book value per share	$123.98	$130.68	$131.00
Enrollment of alliance	141	145	149

Comparisons of SunHealth Hospitals with Other Health Care Institutions:

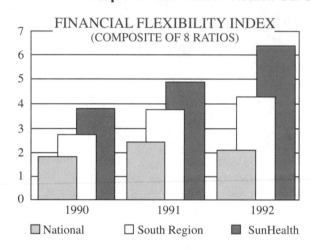

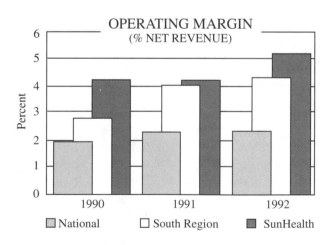

Source: HFMA Reports and Company Records

SUNHEALTH'S GOALS AND BENEFITS FOR PARTNERS

SunHealth's overarching goal is supporting partners to achieve their goals. "I think that our support is one of the things that distinguishes SunHealth from other multihospital organizations and arrangements," said Latimer. "We are so committed to helping our partners reach their goals. We do that through a variety of means:

- Collecting and sharing information and experience,
- Creating new and better ways through research, development, and testing, and

- Supporting the installation and implementation of new and better ways at alliance hospitals."

SunHealth has formalized its beliefs in a statement of responsibilities for SunHealth to its partners. In turn, it expects partners to have a commitment to SunHealth Alliance. The partners developed and voted to accept a list of responsibilities that they have to the alliance (see Exhibit 2.4).

One of the major benefits of involvement with SunHealth is networking and benchmarking among partners. According to Latimer, "We spend a great deal of time developing standards and comparisons, not only among

---

EXHIBIT 2.4
SunHealth Responsibilities

SunHealth Alliance's Responsibilities to Its Partners

1. SunHealth Alliance provides all partners with direct representation in alliance governance and governance functions such as planning and policy making.
2. SunHealth Alliance will safeguard the confidentiality of partner-specific information, releasing such information to others only if the partner has given specific permission or such disclosure is required by law or regulation.
3. SunHealth will protect the competitiveness of partners in the alliance by offering alliance membership to hospital organizations in primary service areas in which there is no existing SunHealth partner; the alliance nor any of its board committees will seek or participate in any arrangements which would prevent a health care institution from providing services as it may elect in any service area.
4. SunHealth will provide services and program access to any facility or unit owned, managed, or leased by a partner with service fees calculated in accordance with prevailing policy.
5. SunHealth services or programs that have limited capacity will be offered to alliance partners first.
6. SunHealth services and programs are available to partners on an "as needed," voluntary participation basis.
7. SunHealth will make decisions in regard to service development and operation on the basis of meeting the needs of all partners or important segments of the partnership. SunHealth will strive for optimization through effective planning, marketing, and operations within the parameters of its purposes and board policies.
8. SunHealth will actively maintain communications with partners concerning alliance issues, activities, and plans and will provide direct liaison representation and support for area-wide networking efforts.

EXHIBIT 2.4   cont'd

9. SunHealth will respond to the best of its ability and resources to a partner CEO's call for assistance in any emergency, operational or management crisis, or other situation requiring immediate external support.

Responsibilities of Partners to the SunHealth Alliance

1. Active participation in planning and policy making of the alliance through attendance at meetings of the governing parent board, regional network meetings, and CEO roundtables.
2. A representation in alliance education exchange and development programs including the willingness to serve on task forces and committees, sending pertinent personnel to various educational sessions, and exchanging information freely with peers.
3. Cooperating with the alliance by providing information that will be collectively used by the alliance.
4. Work toward developing the alliance across the region by participating in clusters and developing and networking with other health care institutions in the partner's region.
5. Actively communicate participation in SunHealth Alliance by using the alliance logo and generally making others aware of the partner's involvement with SunHealth Alliance.
6. Partners are prohibited from using information obtained through alliance activities in any way that would be detrimental to SunHealth interests or partner interests.
7. Partners should give equal consideration to SunHealth programs and services in competition with alternatives, communicate to SunHealth the reasons that a SunHealth program or service was not selected after evaluation, and actively participate in SunHealth programs including group purchasing and other services programs such as consulting, education, etc.

our own partners and our own region but often nationally. Sometimes the same surgical procedure [operation] varies from one hospital to the next. We benchmark the process and determine if there is a difference in the recovery rates or the discharge rates and make available the information to partners."

The overall purpose of the alliance is to make a real difference in the health care provided to the population of the region, by providing an increasing share of such health care through alliance partner organizations that (by virtue of their own characteristics, their interaction with each other, and the availability of alliance services) are able to deliver health care at levels of quality, price, and access that are superior to the services delivered by others, and improve the health status of their communities.

SERVICES PROVIDED FOR PARTNER HOSPITALS

Early Services Oriented Toward Improving Efficiency

The impact of the prospective payment system (implemented in 1983) on hospitals caused considerably more concern with improving efficiency. Because hospitals were reimbursed at a predetermined level for each diagnosis related group, those hospitals that could provide the service at a cost below the reimbursement rate had greater revenues over costs and thus greater flexibility. The hospital could choose to spend the money on expansion, development of new services, new technology, and so on. Therefore, Carolinas Hospital and Health Services served the hospital members by helping them to increase efficiency.

After CHIP, Carolinas Hospital Engineering Support Services (CHESS) was the next service CHHS offered. It was established to assess and provide feedback on the rapidly emerging new health care technologies. CHIP and CHESS were followed shortly by group purchasing developed in the mid-1970s to offset inflation, the money crunch, and cost justification requirements. SunHealth does not actually purchase or warehouse items that partners need. Rather it negotiates terms and conditions to ensure the quality of goods and services plus seeks value-added arrangements.

To provide the best in quality and price, SunHealth developed "corporate partnerships" in the mid-1980s with a small number of selected companies. SunHealth Alliance partners purchase approximately $1.5 billion annually, encouraging vendors to provide an array of value-added offerings as well as an excellent price. Purchasing includes medical and surgical supplies, dietary products, pharmaceuticals, medical imaging products, capital equipment, and laboratory supplies. According to Latimer, "We go beyond trading volume for price. With our corporate partners we want to work closely together for our mutual benefit. Some of our corporate partners are Johnson & Johnson, Abbott Labs, duPont, Juran, and General Medical."

Management Services: A Life Saver for Some Hospitals

The CHHS Management Services (MS) division was created in 1974. It became apparent

that the smallest hospitals in the region were not taking advantage of the shared services offered by CHHS because they were too small to attract or pay skilled managers who understood the value being offered by CHHS. "We called it the 'management gap.' These organizations had a need for management depth but they had insufficient resources – financial or otherwise – to attract a high level manager or specialized management staff," said Latimer.

The CHHS/MS program was envisioned as providing full management without ownership. For a fee, CHHS/MS provided complete day-to-day management of the institution although the hospital's board of trustees, acting in the community's behalf, retained legal responsibility for all assets, liabilities, policy making, and budgets. Thus the trustees were hiring an executive department (provided by CHHS) rather than one person as an administrator. According to Ben Latimer, "Its implementation marked an advancement from the provision of functional services supporting a hospital management's efforts to the actual provision of management itself."

Initiated with support from the Duke Endowment, original projections were that CHHS would manage five to six hospitals at the end of the three-year development period. However, in just seven months CHHS was managing five hospitals. The management service fee was based on a percentage of gross patient revenue, although CHHS retained the option of setting a flat fee for smaller hospitals where a percentage was not reasonable. According to Ben Latimer, "The fee included the salary of the in-hospital director and was considerably lower than the fees charged by most investor-owned contract management organizations. Although most for-profit companies charged 7 to 10 percent of gross revenue, we charged 2 to 4 percent. The added benefit was that our charge included the administrator's salary *plus* provided access to all CHHS shared services."

By April 1979, CHHS was providing management for thirteen hospitals, ranging in size from 35 to 185 licensed beds. Profit performance improved in nine of the hospitals from an average loss of $3.89 per day to a gain of $6.47 for the first full year of CHHS/MS management.

In 1989, SunHealth was managing twenty-two hospitals, which varied in size from less than 100 beds to over 500 beds. The number was down from a high of thirty-five hospitals a few years earlier. SunHealth began rethinking its commitment to management of a few hospitals. Latimer stated, "We thought about getting back to our mission—helping our partner hospitals improve the health in their communities. There was a perception among some partners and some staff that we were spending too much time with these few contract-managed hospitals. Also, we realized that our four-unit partners could provide this same kind of help as well as we could. By the end of 1993 the program was phased out. However, most of the hospitals were retained either as partners or affiliates of partners."

Consulting and Other Services

SunHealth's consulting unit has been in operation for more than twenty years. A variety of consulting services allows hospitals to increase their efficiency in both administrative and clinical areas. Consulting expertise includes nursing management, financial management, cost management, decision support, quality management, telecommunications, materials management, facilities management, human resources management, productivity management, health care planning (both strategic and operational), managed care issues, information systems, and medical staff services.

"Each consulting service provided partners with new techniques or new services not previously employed to maximum benefit in typical hospitals in the region," Ben said. As SunHealth was better able than individual hospitals to locate, recruit, and compensate scarce

technical and professional personnel, these programs made staff expertise available economically on a shared basis.

Partner hospitals can obtain support services that assist in the planning, development, operation, and management of integrated managed-care programs, including contract evaluation and negotiation. The SunHealth staff can provide assistance to hospitals in strategic consulting and health care planning services designed to strengthen alliance members as market leaders and improve interactions among hospitals, physicians, patients, and payers.

SunHealth joins with a variety of outside organizations to assist in the planning, development, and management of more specialized areas such as malpractice, general liability and workers' compensation insurance services, mental health, addictive disease and rehabilitation service, financial management consulting, human resources consulting, executive and physician search, medical claims collection, housekeeping, dietary plan operations and laundry management, electronic claims processing, employee health benefits, and utilization review services.

"Technology assessment is one of our newer services," said Lattimer. "It provides assistance in selection, operation, maintenance, and repair of new technology – a huge expense for our partners." Exhibit 2.5 contains details of technology assessment programs.

SunHealth's two newest activities, the Physician Practice Management Institute and the Clinical Resources Management Initiative are in the development phases. Exhibit 2.6 contains details of these new services. A comprehensive listing of services is included as Exhibit 2.7.

A service that SunHealth has deliberately chosen *not* to provide is lobbying. SunHealth supports the American Hospital Association for lobbying efforts in Washington and usually the state hospital associations throughout its service area.

EXHIBIT 2.5

Technology Assessment Division of SunHealth Enterprises

The SunHealth Technology Assessment Program was extended as an added-value service to the alliance members in November 1991. Two imaging specialists, two biomedical specialists, and one technology assessment specialist share a support staff for a total of 8.5 individuals with one director. The Technology Assessment Division of SunHealth has as its program objective: "To provide accurate, objective information to SunHealth Alliance hospital managers and staff to assist in solving problems related to the acquisition and/or implementation of medical technology."

The various areas covered include capital equipment, clinical procedures, pharmacy and biotechnology, laboratory nursing, dietary strategic planning, facility consulting, and management consulting. Activities of the program include assessment reports on major technology, white papers on various aspects of technology, technological consulting for equipment planning and evaluation, and capital equipment support through specification development, proposal evaluation, and technical data sources.

Equipment evaluated over the past year include CT scans, surgical lasers, MRIs, ultrasound, cardiac catheter labs, infusion pumps, breast needle biopsies, patient monitoring, PET scans, and others.

The goal for FY92 is to produce six assessment reports on specific topics, including monitors, lasers, teleradiology, nuclear medicine, CFCs, and ultrasound. White papers will include topics such as the CT market, the ultrasound market, the electrosurgery market, PET overview, and PET versus MRI comparisons in addition to pulmonary function market and autologous blood transfusions.

The group offers periodic technology news briefs and *Technology Horizons,* a quarterly newsletter distributed to partners. In addition, Technology Assessment sponsors or supports two SunHealth technology-related educational seminars. For FY92, Nuclear Medicine Trends and Technologies and Digital Image and Information Management seminars were offered. The goal is to provide four seminars annually. The group is developing a data base of major technologies owned and used by alliance partners to provide reference for those partners who have not yet implemented the specific technology. In addition, the group would like to investigate overlapping service areas and possible joint ventures between partners.

The reports to be completed in FY93 include ones on MRI, mammography, nuclear medicine, bedside terminals, Holter monitoring, surgical lasers, laser cameras, and multi-channel infusion pumps. To get feedback on operations, the group is collecting data concerning utilization by hospital size, by region of the country, and through focus groups and questionnaires sent to CEOs and technology assessment recipients.

Technology assessment provides telephone consultation at no charge to partners as the goal is to enhance this service and increase utilization. Partners are charged on a per-day basis for consulting when members of technology assessment provide on-site analysis and expertise.

The program is relatively new and is still building awareness among partners. Competitors include MD Byline, which provides services to some SunHealth hospitals on a fee-for-service basis.

EXHIBIT 2.6
SunHealth's Newest Services

Physician Practice Management Institute

SunHealth has outlined three main strategies to improve and integrate clinical services over the next three years:

1. Create a foundation for collaboration by hospitals and physicians in providing care and promoting healthiness through activities that strengthen hospital-physician relations.
2. Position physicians to operate in an at-risk environment, in much the same way that SunHealth currently helps position hospitals to provide high-value components of health benefit plans – improve efficiency, decrease overhead, and enhance management skills.
3. Link effective clinicians and high-value providers of inpatient and procedural services over time for the following purposes – selling the "bundle of services" at a set price, determining the best site for patient access to services, and carrying out the processes that result in clinical outputs and outcomes.

SunHealth has made a commitment to expand the array and number of services provided to partners to help them build collaborative relationships with physicians and to physicians associated with partner organizations to help them cope with the changes in the health care environment and increase their capabilities as high-value providers. In addition, SunHealth will provide expertise to help partners develop new health care delivery strategies in collaboration with physicians, including building integrated health systems.

The vision is that the Physician Practice Management Institute will become the resource for physicians allied with SunHealth partner organizations for expertise, education, and training and collegial support for continuous improvement of clinical services. For the partner, the institute will offer assistance in recruiting physicians, increasing medical staff effectiveness, and improving the utilization of clinical resources. Customer groups for the institute include (1) physicians including solo practitioners; group practice physicians; physicians who direct or practice within medical service organizations (MSOs), physician-hospital organizations (PHOs), and health maintenance organizations (HMOs); members of the medical staffs of partner organizations particularly chiefs of staff and department heads; physician executives; (2) business management staff of physician practices and MSOs, PHOs, and HMOs; and (3) partner organizations' medical staff leaders and liaisons as well as physician executives.

The shift from fee-for-service to fixed pricing alternatives requires change for physicians and partner organizations. It is the purpose of the Physician Practice Management Institute to facilitate that change. Physician practices that are affiliated with SunHealth partner organizations are eligible for membership. Additional benefits include group purchasing, a help desk for practice management questions, access to discounted educational opportunities, a quarterly newsletter, opportunities to participate in SunHealth benchmarking studies, a referral service, an annual forum, and comparative reports for operational and performance indicators.

EXHIBIT 2.6   cont'd

Clinical Resources Management Initiative

The Clinical Resources Management Initiative includes developing and testing methods, tools, and resources to design integrated sets of services for defined populations across the continuum of services. The initiative invites two or more partner hospital organizations to volunteer to be coleaders and learning laboratories.

The overall goal for the initiative is to refine planning and management processes for designing, performing, and improving the clinical care path (path of service for community health improvement). The goal is to define paths in such a way that market and community expectations are better met, clinical resources are effectively used to achieve the best outcomes, and the financial risk of providing care is better managed.

The Clinical Resources Management Initiative is a way to integrate various tools and methods that incrementally improve health care but collectively could have synergistic results. For example, integration of marketing planning, managed care, quality management, outcomes measurement, benchmarking, process management, and reengineering will offer synergy to the organizations willing to devote the effort to combine all the processes into an integrated whole.

EXHIBIT 2.7
SunHealth's Comprehensive Services

Administration/Management
- Management Consulting
- Management Engineering Services
- Productivity Management
- Productivity INSIGHT
- Productivity Education Services
- Benchmarking
- Quality Management
- Quality Assurance
- Telecommunications Consulting
- Physician/Clinic Practice Management Consulting
- Health Care Planning Services
  Business planning and feasibility studies
  Internal and environmental assessments
  Market research
  Strategic planning

  Functional planning
  Annual education forum
  Affiliation network development
- Hospital Information Exchange
- Educational Activities for Department Heads and Executive Staff
- Small Hospital Affiliation Programs
- Pre-JCAHO Survey and Assistance

Finance
- Business Office Consulting
- Financial Feasibility Consulting
- Strategic Financial Planning
- Capital Financing and Cash Management
- Operating and Capital Budgeting
- Medical Practice Valuations/Set-Up
- Third-Party Reimbursement Consulting

EXHIBIT 2.7   *cont'd*

- Certificate of Need Review and Preparation
- Review Rate Maximization
- IRS Regulations Compliance Review

Cost Management
- Human Resources Audit
- Case-Mix Management Consulting
- Comparative Cost Management Data Base
- Severity of Illness Methodology
- Decision Support System
- DRG Profitability and Consumption Analysis

Human Resources
- Human Resources Audit
- Wage and Salary Administration Services
- Executive Compensation Consulting and Survey
- Employee and Management Wage Survey
- Employee Attitude Survey
- Fringe Benefit Survey
- Criteria-Based Job Descriptions and Performance Appraisals
- Gainsharing

Nursing
- Nursing Organizational Audit
- Patient Acuity System Development and Review
- Nursing Management System – VISION
- Costing Nursing Services
- Management Training and Development
- Organizational Analysis
- Standards of Care
- Recruitment and Retention
- Specialized Departmental Studies

Clinical Studies
- Medical Equipment Maintenance and Repair

- Clinical Engineering Department Management
- Automated Maintenance Management System
- Clinical Engineering Consulting
- Medical Imaging Glassware and Replacement Parts
- Refurbishing and Used Medical Equipment
- Clinical Engineering Department Support Services
- BMET Technical Training
- Medical Equipment Insurance

Facilities
- Safety Management
- CFC Compliance
- ADA Compliance
- Maintenance Management Support
- Maintenance Management Evaluation
- Energy Management
- JCAHO and Code Compliance Consulting
- Microprocessor-Based Maintenance Management Systems
- Hazardous Materials Management
- Computer-Aided Design Systems – CAD
- Facilities Evaluation and Small Project Design

Insurance Services
- Hospital Professional Malpractice
- Hospital General Liability
- Workers' Compensation
- Directors and Officers Liability
- Group Employee Life Insurance
- Hospital Property
- Health Benefit Stop Loss

Materials Management
- Materials Management Audit
- Materials Management Department Management
- Group Purchasing

EXHIBIT 2.7 cont'd

- Materials Management Information Systems
- Inventory Management
- Departmental Supply Management
- Patient Charge Systems
- Materials Distribution Assessment
- Product Standardization and Evaluation
- Capital Equipment Planning and Selection
- Computerized Purchasing Order Entry System – SunHealth Buy Line

Pharmacy
- Pharmacy Management Consulting
- Pharmacy Department Management Services

Laboratory
- Comprehensive Group Purchasing
- Equipment Packaging
- Comparative Laboratory Data Base
- Laboratory Pricing Services

Dietary
- Dietary Management Consulting
- Dietary Pricing Services

Data Processing
- Information Systems Assessment
- HIS Planning and Selection Assistance

Managed Care
- Direct Contracting
- Contract Negotiation, Implementation, and Monitoring
- Network Marketing
- Pricing Strategy Review and Development

- Comparative Charge Information
- Managed Care Position Planning

Medical Staff Services
- Physician Recruitment Planning and Assistance
- Physician Practice Assessment
- Medical Staff Personnel Assessment
- Medical Staff Development Appraisal
- Annual Forum and Periodic Skills Seminars
- Resource Inventory
- Management Education
- Physician Purchasing

Additional Services Available Through Corporate Partnerships
- Electronic Claims Processing
- Medical Claims Collection
- Executive and Physician Search
- Housekeeping, Dietary, Plant Operations, and Laundry Management
- Capital Equipment, Consumables, Dietary, and Pharmaceutical Purchasing Programs
- Mental Health Inpatient/Partial Hospitalization Contract Management
- Inpatient and Outpatient Medical Rehabilitation Services Contract Management
- Healthcare Opinion Research
- Employee Health Benefit Utilization Review
- Patient Severity Measurement Systems

OPERATIONS

The SunHealth Alliance is an alliance of not-for-profit hospitals and health care organizations that works to improve and strengthen health care at all levels. The fifteen-state region is divided into eight regional offices, each served by a regional vice president (see Exhibit 2.8 for a map of partner locations and Sun-Health corporate offices and regional offices). Participating organizations range in size from 80 beds to 1,600 beds. Some partners are teaching institutions, renowned nationwide for their technological advances. Others are respected public general and community medical centers. Still others are multihospital systems in their own right, organized to serve the health care needs of a wide geographic area.

SunHealth is an organization whose membership is open to not-for-profit hospitals that are either one-unit or four-unit partners, depending on size and level of financial commitment to SunHealth Alliance. SunHealth is totally owned by the health care organizations that are partners in the alliance. The organization of SunHealth Alliance includes a board of directors (the parent board) comprising a representative from *every* partner hospital as a voting member and a sixteen-member executive committee (governing board) elected by the parent board. The Executive Committee includes ten elected partner CEOs, Ben Latimer as the CEO of SunHealth Enterprises, and five at-large members from health care, business, finance, and law (Exhibit 2.9).

The executive committee has operations, planning, and finance working committees. In addition, there are several other permanent and ad hoc committees, including major advisory boards such as the Alliance for Quality advisory board and the Medical Staff Directors advisory board. The Alliance for Quality advisory board includes members from a variety of areas such as administration, physicians, nurses, corporate partners, and others. Additionally, committees study specific hospital areas such as pharmacy, dietary, capital equipment, technology, and more.

"Alliances are part coop and part entrepreneurial," stated Ben Latimer. First organized as a 501(c)(3) tax-exempt corporation, the service orientation of programs allowed the government to push for a 501(e), shared-services cooperative. The 501(e) status was resisted because it did not allow for development and retention of earnings. He continued,

> Because of the retention of earnings limitations and other considerations that we felt would hamper our growth, we eventually decided to become a traditional, taxable stock corporation. However, our stock can only be owned ' y not-for-profit hospitals—501(c)(3) or governmental equivalents. We no longer can receive grants from foundations as we did in the early days, but our partners can and—with our help—frequently do.
>
> Our services offered to partners must be of sufficient value to be used by the hospitals without resorting to mandates or dues. In essence, we have had to be self-sufficient, including generating some surplus so that we can develop new programs or improve existing programs that are of benefit for our partners.

Partners are charged for the consulting and clinical technology services they use in three different ways. One is the per diem rate or a fixed amount per "expert day." Another is a per project charge: "We quote a charge to carry out the project and if the quote is off we have to absorb the loss or if it comes in under the quote, it is to our advantage," Latimer explained. The third way is a continuing service arrangement. "We place a full-time industrial engineer in the hospital to manage a department. The hospital reimburses us for the compensation of the individual."

Purchasing incentives are offered to part-

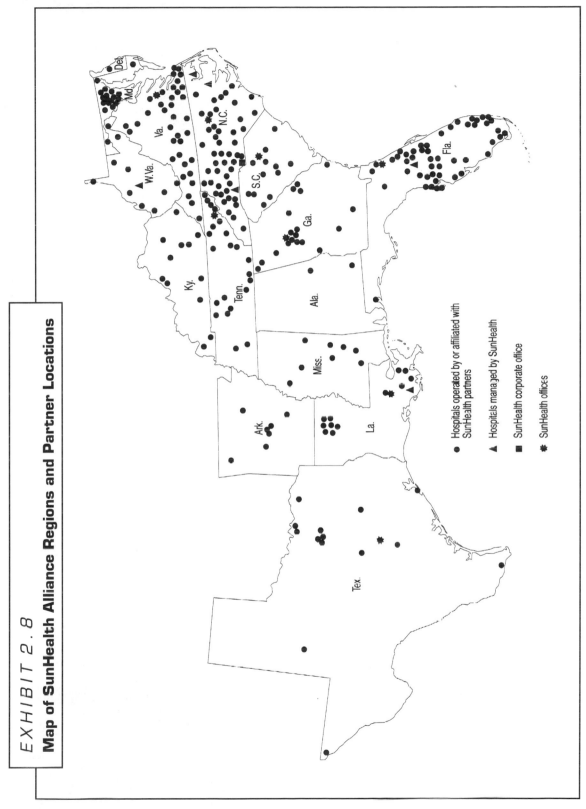

EXHIBIT 2.8
Map of SunHealth Alliance Regions and Partner Locations

- ● Hospitals operated by or affiliated with SunHealth partners
- ▲ Hospitals managed by SunHealth
- ■ SunHealth corporate office
- ✱ SunHealth offices

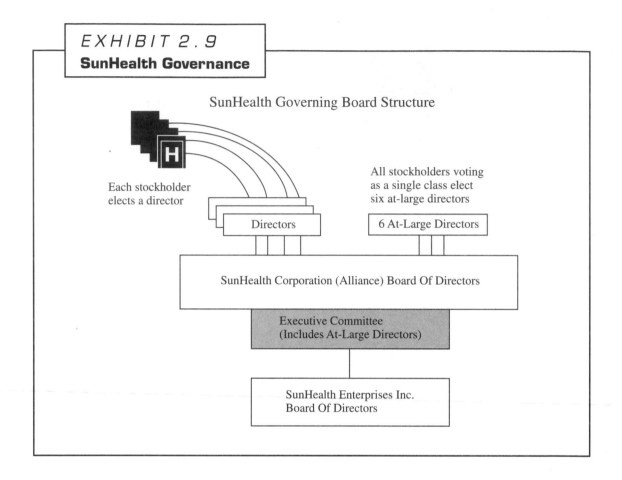

EXHIBIT 2.9
SunHealth Governance

SunHealth Governing Board Structure

Each stockholder elects a director

All stockholders voting as a single class elect six at-large directors

Directors

6 At-Large Directors

SunHealth Corporation (Alliance) Board Of Directors

Executive Committee
(Includes At-Large Directors)

SunHealth Enterprises Inc.
Board Of Directors

ners in the form of credits against the partner's annual alliance service fee of $19,000 for a one-unit partner and $30,000 for a four-unit partner. Ben Latimer related, "Financial incentives are offered in those situations that are likely to produce financial results. For example, volume purchasing achieves greater savings for the alliance; the savings are returned to partners through rebating of the service fees. Other services, such as consulting, are offered purely on a fee-basis as volume usage does not generate discounts."

In addition, there are recognition incentives. Up to four institutions may receive The SunHealth Alliance Pacesetter Award, presented annually to institutions in recognition of the innovative use of network resources. The SunHealth Service to Alliance Award is an individual award to recognize the contributions of a CEO or other partner hospital representative that advances the alliance's purposes and programs. Up to three CEOs and three other representatives may receive the award each year.

In some instances, SunHealth partners find it effective to work in small groups, known as *clusters.* In addition to facilitating distribution for materials management, the geographically based groups are suited to collecting and sharing data as well as creating special interest projects. Generally within geographic proximity to one another, they can come together to focus on various topics and provide superiority for partner institutions. "The Florida cluster has been particularly effective," Latimer said.

The *Alliance Update* is a periodic communication from Ben Latimer and his staff that provides information of importance to the partner CEOs. In addition, specifically targeted publications are sent to purchasing departments or clinical engineering units or nursing units. Partner "roundtables" bring together partners from around the network for a day of exchange on various topics. CEOs who have faced similar problems offer advice. It is a "no-threat" environment and provides a sounding board for new ideas to improve efficiency and service. "This used to occur at state hospital association meetings, but as the competitiveness of hospitals has increased that kind of exchange diminished," Lattimer said.

COMPETITION

Although CHHS/SunHealth was one of the earliest alliances, several others emerged in the late 1970s and early 1980s as a response by independent hospitals and regional health care systems to the perceived threat of "super-meds" – the huge, for-profit hospitals that were expected to become national health care systems and significantly alter health care in the United States. Alliances were supposed to offer independent members the same buying clout and economies of scale enjoyed by national systems plus the opportunity to contract with employers as part of a national health care delivery network.[2] For a variety of reasons many independent hospitals belong to more than one alliance or purchasing group. Nationally hospitals belong to an average of 2.8 purchasing groups, although in New York and Pennsylvania, they belong to four buying organizations.[3]

The super-meds that experts predicted would dominate the health care landscape by the 1990s have not materialized. When they did not emerge as predicted, the alliances adjusted to changing conditions by generally adopting one of two strategies. Either they concentrated on serving a wide range of needs for a narrowly defined set of hospitals or they concentrated on providing a few services to a large number of diverse health care organizations. Two of the largest alliances, AmHS and VHA have tightened their focus over the past two years and offer fewer services to their members.

"VHA is the alliance that is most similar in mission and philosophy to SunHealth," Ben Latimer recounted. "However, VHA is nationally focused and we are oriented to our general fifteen-state region." He continued, "Individual hospitals in the SunHealth Alliance may occasionally work with VHA hospitals to develop an effective provider network in a region. They do that on their own, not connected to SunHealth."

Ben continued, "UHC's members usually hold membership in another alliance. We have several university hospitals as partners and they have expressed to us that they do not expect to change."

"There was a time in the mid-1980s that we actually became a shareholder in AmHS for a short period of time." Ben explained,

> VHA and Aetna were having conversations about joining together to create a national HMO brand name. AmHS wanted to counterbalance that strong association with one of its own. AmHS offered SunHealth Alliance, Yankee Alliance, Adventists System, and several others an opportunity to develop a national brand name approach to the market through Provident Insurance Company. They only required that SunHealth buy one share of AmHS stock to be a part of the enterprise. We purchased a share as it seemed to be a low-risk opportunity.

However, we decided fairly quickly it was not for us. Subsequently, AmHS decided that members of its alliance should be required to do all their purchasing through AmHS and the deal with Provident fell through. We withdrew, as did the Adventists who decided to join with us.

He continued, "Premier is not often a direct competitor of SunHealth, and we do collaborate with them in some service areas."

"Competition is in a state of flux," he concluded. "And it's not just limited to other alliances. Of the groups, systems, and alliances, American Healthcare Systems, Voluntary Hospitals of America, University Hospital Consortium, and Premier Alliance are similar to SunHealth in that they are more than purchasing groups." In addition to these five 'major' alliances, there are other organizations that have impact in the industry. Columbia-HCA Healthcare Corporation is large and offers many services to the 190 hospitals it owns.[4] Aetna, Provident, and Blue Cross have established divisions that are similar to alliances.[5]

Industry Competitors

Within the industry there are over 200 purchasing groups. However, a purchasing group differs from an alliance in that there is usually no financial or leadership commitment to the purchasing group. An alliance expects member organizations to participate in its governance, sharing information, and assisting other members as well as paying membership fees. Of the five major alliances in the United States, AmHS and VHA are about twice the size of SunHealth and SunHealth is about twice the size of Premier and UHC.

American Healthcare Systems, located in San Diego, California, restricts its membership to hospital systems. AmHS was founded in 1984 by merging two previous alliances, Asso-

ciated Health Systems and United Health Care Systems. Its board is composed of forty CEOs of the shareholder systems, which operate more than 1,000 hospitals in forty-seven states.[6]

In January 1987, AmHS adopted a new strategic plan that called for eliminating programs that directly involved the alliance in health care delivery and expanding services that could best be offered on a national scale.[7] AmHS turned over control of six PPOs to member systems and aborted a plan to develop a national PPO network because it felt that members would do a better job of delivering health care in regional markets. AmHS concentrates on group purchasing, pooled insurance, market information development, and investment programs. AmHS maintains the AmHS Institute, a political action group in Washington, D.C., to lobby on issues affecting not-for-profit health care systems. It offers no management consulting services because its members are large hospital systems that have the capacity to deal with most of their day-to-day management problems.[8]

In the summer of 1989, AmHS initiated a program to improve member compliance in some group purchasing programs.[9] The compliance improvement program encouraged members to participate at specified levels. Shareholders were rewarded for total compliance in the program with up to 10 percent of annual dividends. Shareholders falling below specified levels were penalized. The eventual goal was 100 percent compliance, which would result in higher returns on investments for members. If a purchasing group cannot guarantee commitment from its members, it has no bargaining leverage. It is not only the number but the commitment that vendors desire.

University Hospital Consortium, located in Oakbrook, Illinois, was started in 1980 by several CEOs of university hospitals. University Hospital Consortium targets a specific group of hospitals, those owned by universities and whose staffs are controlled by medical schools. It began a group purchasing program in 1984 to provide university institutions increased clout in purchasing pharmaceuticals, insurance, supplies, and services. In 1993, UHC surpassed $1 billion in group purchases on behalf of its members. Sixty-five university hospitals in the United States are members of UHC.[10] According to Samuel Schultz II, Ph.D., vice president for information services at UHC, the organization has grown so much because its member hospitals are "in dire straights."[11] General university funding has been severely restricted across the United States during this period of a weakened economy. University hospitals, as part of the university, have been affected as well.

University hospitals tend to see their mission to be on the cutting edge of health care as they see patients, gather data, and perform research. Thus, they have specific needs for the very newest technology and in fact are often involved with developing that technology. Many academic health centers face the dilemma of being the site not only where new drugs and technologies are first used but also where the cost ramifications first emerge. Therefore UHC is very involved in cost and reimbursement assessments. UHC does not offer consulting services for investments in technology or services designed to acquire patients such as managed care. Services currently include group purchasing, materials management, a national traveling nurse placement service, a nurse recruiting service, risk-management insurance services, and information sharing services.[12]

New strategic goals recently formulated for UHC include an aggressive quality agenda with a dozen programs in management reengineering and quality of care plus development of tools for members to perform market assessments.[13] A major growth area is development of information services for clinical and technology assessment. UHC serves as a clearing house for information on new technology and

is setting up information sharing systems that will assist member hospitals in clinical research by sharing outcomes information. UHC is developing a Clinical Information Network – a vehicle for collecting members' clinical, financial, and administrative data to investigate quality of care and resource management issues.[14] The ability to share data among academic centers whose I/S (information system) architecture varies from archaic paper systems to PC LANs to minis to mainframes to client-server setups is a challenging task but one that is being tackled at UHC.

Voluntary Hospitals of America, located in Irving, Texas, is the nation's largest hospital alliance in number of beds. It was founded by thirty hospitals in 1977 and has grown to include 483 members and more than 900 hospitals at the end of 1993.[15] In 1989, VHA Enterprises divested a variety of business activities that were considered strategically less valuable: VHA Physician Services that offered physician bonding products; VHA Capital; VHA Consulting Services, sold to Arthur Andersen & Co., Chicago; VHA Long-Term Care and VHA Physician Placement Services to their respective managements; and VHA Diagnostic Services to a group of outside investors.[16]

At that time, VHA renewed its emphasis on managed care. "We're probably the only alliance that is appropriately in the managed care business on a national level, because we have the broadest national presence," according to Bruce Brennen, VHA's vice president for communication.[17] VHA retained 50 percent stake in Partners National Health Plans, a joint venture with Aetna Life Insurance Company of Hartford, Connecticut. With substantially over 2 million members enrolled in thirty-three states, Partners is the third largest managed care program in the United States (Kaiser Permanente is the largest). Brennen said that VHA was keeping its managed care operations because it helped hospitals in local markets and would be strategically important in the future. About 90 percent of VHA members were involved with Partners, which operated a number of PPOs and HMOs.[18] However, by the end of 1993, VHA sold its 50 percent share to Aetna.[19]

Premier Health Alliance (formerly Premier Hospital Alliance), located in Westchester, Illinois, has limited its membership to community-teaching hospitals. It was founded in 1983 by seventeen hospitals and in 1993 had 156 members.[20] Originally they did not plan to grow because of their focus on community-teaching hospitals. Premier offers a wider range of services to its members than other alliances that serve a broader constituency as their member hospitals have similar needs and wants and the group is small enough that the staff can maintain personal contact with each hospital. Premier services fall into three areas: services that save hospitals money directly, such as group purchasing and investment programs; services that enhance the member's market share, such as home care, imaging, and physician bonding; and information sharing services.[21] Premier has seventy programs, which are evaluated continuously. A program that has not met its expectations is marked and studied to see if it should be dropped. Between seven and twelve programs are dropped in a year, but at least that many are added. Premier is expanding its managed-care consulting and management services for its members.[22]

The Future of Alliances

Not all hospital CEOs are satisfied with alliances.[23] They perceive a number of disadvantages and shortcomings (Exhibit 2.10). The primary disadvantage reported is that programs do not meet the needs of individual hospitals. The larger is the alliance, which is good for purchasing volume, the more challenging it becomes to tailor services that meet the needs of individual partners.

For alliances to survive, they have to think strategically for their members, be financially sound, and provide the desired services. Specific factors that are important for alliances to survive include:

1. The ability to drive compliance;
2. The ability to provide successful, comprehensive services beyond purchasing;
3. The willingness to take risks and be creative in finding solutions for their members;
4. Homogeneity in alliance members;
5. The ability to provide value-added services to both members and vendors;
6. The ability to focus on the "top-down sell" (meaning hospital CEO involvement); and
7. The ability to implement at the local level.[24]

According to John A. Henderson, president of SMG Marketing Group, a health care consulting organization, "The past several years have seen significant changes in the focus, direction, and strategies of many group purchasing organizations as they have tried to attract new customers and retain existing clients."[25] Henderson believes that group purchasing has gone through an important evolution. In the past, hospitals belonged to many groups and as a result had divided loyalties. With several different options to consider in each product area, they often chose selectively from the contracts of several groups, a practice known as *cherry picking*. "Hospitals that continue to pick and choose from group purchasing contracts are deceiving themselves; they are not getting the best prices and probably costing their institutions money," said Henderson. However, he believes this practice is coming to an end.

Because of the complexity of current agreements, it is becoming increasingly difficult for hospitals to determine the real value of individual contracts. Hospitals more often are finding that their best strategy is to make a commitment to the group that they believe

EXHIBIT 2.10

**Concerns of CEOs with Health Care Alliances:
What do you see as the most significant disadvantages
or shortcomings in hospital alliances today?**

	Number of Respondents
Programs do not meet individual hospital needs	31
Membership too expensive	30
Limits freedom of control	27
Too bureaucratic or cumbersome	24
Lack of consensus or commitment by membership	19
Unable to measure cost/benefit	18
Not focused on purpose or too many services	17
Disorganized, inexperienced, or ineffective management	13
Does not deliver what is promised	8
Competition among hospitals	7
Not enough meetings or contact	3
Financial problems	3
Not enough services	2

Note: Based on a poll of 250 CEOs
Source: Professional Research Consultants, in Howard Larkin, "Alliances: Changing Focus for Changing Times," *Hospitals* 63 (December 20, 1989), p. 38.

can best meet their needs on an overall basis – price is not the only criterion. Hospitals may not be able to assess the actual value of group purchasing contracts because they have to weigh the value of available services such as inventory management, electronic data interchange, in-service programs, and remote order entry.

Manufacturers' attitudes toward groups are changing, as well.[26] Vendors are becoming more selective in their dealings. They are targeting groups that can best deliver compliance and market share. This selectivity may prompt some manufacturers to refuse to sign contracts with certain groups if they cannot deliver the business in return for price concessions. As a result, some groups may have to close. This makes it even more important for hospitals to

develop an understanding of which groups can best serve their needs. The consequence of not understanding a group's direction is that a hospital will pay higher prices for the products and services it purchases, which could mean clinical and competitive obsolescence.[27]

In the past, the core service provided was group purchasing and the savings from that program alone were expected to cover the cost of being a member. Because super-meds no longer pose a strategic threat and it is generally recognized that health care was and continues to be primarily a local and regional business, not-for-profit alliances are at a crucial strategic crossroad.[28] They are struggling to satisfy rising expectations and provide tangible value to their often diverse memberships. Sandwiched between trade associations and multihospital systems, facing aggressive competition from the proliferation of shared service and group purchasing, not-for-profit alliances are searching for unique identities and strategies that provide a sustainable competitive advantage for their members. Some alliances are criticized by their members because they are trying to do too much – trying to be all things to all members and consequently exceling in few endeavors. There has been a preoccupation with growing without first developing a strategic focus. The diversity of needs and interests among members of an alliance make consensus building, setting priorities, and strategic planning efforts very difficult. The alliance that survives will be the one that achieves value for its member organizations.

Gerald McManis believes that successful alliances will:

1. Develop and communicate a concise vision for the future and clearly state long-term strategy and objectives;
2. Establish a member network that shares the vision and has a good structural fit with the alliance's strategy;
3. Implement programs and services that capitalize on the unique competence of the organization and its membership;
4. Operate a lean, professionally managed organization, concentrating on adding real value for members, not simply its own growth and self-perpetuation; and
5. Build long-term relationships with members based on trust, commitment, and value.[29]

McManis believes that national alliances will continue to rely on economies of scale in group purchasing, shared data systems, off-the-shelf marketing programs, and other services.[30] Regional alliances will become more like business entities and less like associations. In many cases, they will link local health care systems in natural markets for regional referrals. Increased regional emphasis may be the answer as selling has become more complex. In addition, the adoption of standards for various supplies is challenging if the alliance is nationally oriented. In other words, standards are difficult to implement across the United States, but somewhat easier in a region.[31]

Mergers and consolidations are going to cause problems for alliances. For example, in the recent merger in St. Louis, Christian Health Services belonged to AmHS, Barnes to VHA, and Jewish to Premier Hospitals Alliance. Management for the new CHS/Barnes-Jewish decided to remain with VHA to purchase needed products and services for its thirteen hospitals, seven long-term-care, and twenty alternative health care sites. The decision definitely rearranged buying power within the alliances.

Network growth may eliminate the need for purchasing alliances. Some networks may grow large enough to buy on their own or at least become a different type customer. Alliances may need to add alternative-site members to grow – clinics, long-term-care facilities, and so on. Among purchasing groups, alternative site members increased 27.5 percent, but hospital membership only grew 1.2 percent.[32]

Ben Latimer's observation on the future of alliances is telling, "If the top management of the alliance keeps the needs of members foremost rather than seeking a place unto themselves, alliances have a long-term future."

LOOKING TOWARD THE FUTURE OF THE SUNHEALTH ALLIANCE

The SunHealth Alliance has avoided some problems of other alliances by concentrating its presence in the South, Southeast, and Middle Atlantic states. "The most common element we share is a common market," said Latimer. Therefore, SunHealth concentrates on programs that enable partners to work together, including consulting to develop PPOs, shared marketing staff, and programs to serve ultimate delivery sites, such as group purchasing for physicians.

In the early 1990s, The SunHealth Alliance became a force for information exchange and development of quality programs and services. Its Alliance Exchange concept – introduced in 1992 – continues to play an important role in the alliance's strategic plan. The goal of Alliance Exchange is to foster information and experience sharing among alliance hospitals and employees, at all levels. Information is gleaned and transferred from data bases, management information systems, comparative reporting, newsletters, consultants, help desks, reference sources including Alliance Fax Exchanges, literature searches, interlibrary loan materials, hospital peer committees, task forces, and educational forums.

Regarding the promotion of quality programs and services at alliance hospitals, The SunHealth Alliance in the early 1990s developed a special partnership with Juran Institute in Wilton, Connecticut. Together, Juran, Sun-Health, and several corporate partners formed the Alliance for Quality to encourage continuous improvement efforts in partner hospitals, foster the exchange of information and experience among partner hospitals, and actively work to improve health care in the region.

"For us to focus on survival of the acute care hospital is wrong," Ben Latimer emphatically stated. "Success will be increasing the health status of our partners' communities without acute care. It is our task to help our partners achieve this paradigm shift and deliver care – wellness promotion as well as illness care – in new ways that lead to improved health status."

NOTES

1. Adjusted occupied bed (AOB) is computed by multiplying total annual patient care revenues by the average twelve-month census and dividing by total annual inpatient revenues:

$$AOB = \frac{\begin{array}{c}\text{total annual}\\ \text{patient care revenues}\\ \times \text{ average 12-month census}\end{array}}{\begin{array}{c}\text{total annual}\\ \text{inpatient revenues}\end{array}}$$

2. Gerald L. McManis, "Not-for-Profit Alliances Need to Focus on Value," *Modern Healthcare* (October 15, 1989), p. 20; and Howard Larkin, "Alliances: Changing Focus for Changing Times," *Hospitals* 63 (December 20, 1989), pp. 34–38.
3. "Group Purchasing Evolution," *Modern Healthcare* (September 27, 1993), p. 52.
4. Mariann Caprino, "Merger Flurry Hits Health Care, Related Industries," *The Birmingham News* (December 26, 1993), p. A-2.
5. Lisa Scott, "Group Purchasing Evolution," *Modern Healthcare* 23, no. 39 (September 27, 1993), pp. 49, 52, 58–59.
6. Jay Greene, "Trout Announces His Intent to Retire from Top AmHS Spot," *Modern Healthcare* 23, no. 34 (August 23, 1993), p. 4.
7. Larkin, "Alliances: Changing Focus for Changing Times," pp. 34–35.
8. Ibid., p. 37.
9. Howard Larkin, "Alliances Argue Merits of Compliance Incentives," *Hospitals* 63 (December 20, 1989), p. 37.
10. Membership information was provided by University Hospital Consortium corporate offices in a telephone interview January 7, 1994.
11. Carolyn Dunbar, "A New Era Dawns for the University Hospital Consortium," *Computers in Healthcare* 13, no. 13 (December 1992), pp. 32.
12. Ibid., p. 34.
13. Ibid.
14. Ibid.
15. Current membership information was supplied by VHA corporate offices in a telephone interview on January 7, 1994.
16. Larkin, "Alliances: Changing Focus for Changing Times," p. 35.
17. Ibid.

18. Ibid.
19. Information supplied in a telephone interview January 7, 1994.
20. Membership information was provided by the corporate offices of Premier Alliance in a telephone interview on January 7, 1994.
21. Larkin, "Alliances: Changing Focus for Changing Times," p. 35.
22. "Collaborative Efforts Enhance Program Development," *Health Care Strategic Management* 11, no. 2 (February 1993), p. 23.
23. Larkin, "Alliances: Changing Focus for Changing Times," p. 37.
24. John A. Henderson, "Hospitals Should Reassess Group Purchasing," *Modern Healthcare* (March 10, 1989), p. 80.
25. Ibid.
26. Ibid.
27. Ibid.
28. Ibid.
29. McManis, "Not-for-Profit Alliances," p. 20.
30. Ibid.
31. Scott, "Group Purchasing Evolution," p. 59.
32. Ibid., p. 58.

InterMark: Designing UNICEF's Oral Rehydration Program in Zambia

The setting sun gave a pink tone to the Washington skyline across the Potomac as the jets glided over the river to National Airport in early August 1991. Allison Boyd enjoyed the view, but her thoughts were far away. For weeks she had been occupied with the children of Zambia. As a project manager for InterMark, an international consulting firm, she had been working on UNICEF's oral rehydration program for reduction of diarrheal disease in Zambia for the past six months. Her final recommendations were due in a week.

United Nations International Children's Emergency Fund (UNICEF) contracted with InterMark to recommend how UNICEF should spend its funds in the next three years to reduce the incidence of diarrheal disease primarily through increased use of oral rehydration salts (ORS). UNICEF spent $87,000 in 1991 to import ORS donated to the Ministry of Health for free distribution to hospitals and clinics. It was willing to spend between $87,000 and $113,000 annually for purchase of ORS or

alternative programs if it could be shown that their program objectives were likely to be met. The two major objectives were to substantially reduce infant and child deaths and illnesses associated with diarrheal disease and have a high likelihood of sustainability after three years when the aid is no longer available.

The assignment had been interesting and challenging. Two, month-long visits provided a large amount of information for her recommended program to increase the appropriate use of ORS in Zambia. Allison was expected to provide written recommendations and make a presentation to the UNICEF staff.

ZAMBIA

The Republic of Zambia (formerly Northern Rhodesia) attained independence from Britain in 1964. Zambia is situated on an elevated plateau in South-Central Africa with a population of 8 million in 1990 and an area of 752,614 sq. km., slightly larger than the state of Texas (see Exhibit 3.1). As a land-locked country it is dependent on either its neighbors or air transport for links with the outside world.

For many years, the mining of copper dominated the Zambian economy, although its contribution had declined significantly in recent years. The agricultural sector received the

This case was prepared by Ronald Stiff from the University of Baltimore. It is intended as a basis for classroom discussion rather than to illustrate effective or ineffective handling of an administrative situation. Copyright © by the *Case Research Journal* and Ronald Stiff. Used with permission from Ronald Stiff and the *Case Research Journal*.

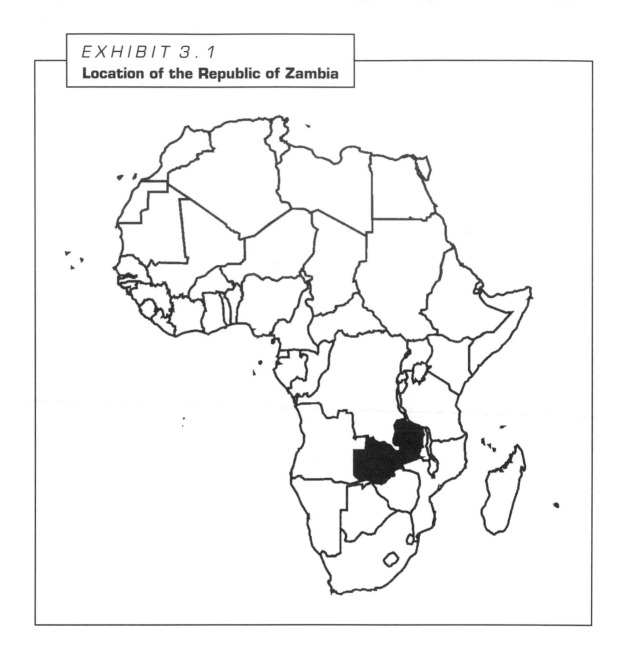

EXHIBIT 3.1
Location of the Republic of Zambia

active support of the government and international donors, but did not achieve its potential and agricultural exports have declined. The per capita GNP, which stood at US $290 in 1988, placed it in the low income economies as defined by the World Bank (eighteenth poorest worldwide). Per capita GNP was expected to be as low as US $150 or K10,500[1] per capita in 1991. Many households earned less than K2,800 per month.

Health Expenditures and Status

In 1986 the government spent K250 per capita for health care. Estimation of morbidity (illnesses) and mortality (deaths) levels and trends were uncertain in many developing countries, including Zambia, because of problems with the quality of measurements. The national infant mortality rate fell from around 130 deaths per 1,000 in the mid-1950s to about 120 in the mid-1960s, and thence to about 115 in the early 1970s. This was considerably higher than the infant mortality rate in the twenty-five highest income countries which was nine in 1988. Correspondingly, the proportion of children dying between birth and their fifth birthday (childhood mortality) fell from 22 percent to 20 percent and thence to 19 percent, respectively where it remained through 1991. One of every five children died before reaching age 5.

The national figures were within the general range of other countries in central and southern Africa. These statistics concealed regional differentials in mortality that had implications for the effective delivery of health programs. Childhood mortality estimates for the 1960s showed a clear general pattern of highest mortality in the rural provinces, lowest mortality in the two most urbanized provinces, and an intermediate level in Southern province. The infant mortality rate for that period ranged from 82 (Copperbelt) to 175 (Eastern), giving a national average of 121.

Allison analyzed the most current Zambian statistical reports and grouped the Zambian provinces into three regions to evaluate geographical differences (Exhibit 3.2). She noted that the central provinces, along the main rail line, were far more urbanized than the provinces she grouped as northeastern and northwestern. The lower population densities and less developed road systems in these areas made delivery of health care services challenging. Allison wondered if UNICEF had the resources to achieve widespread distribution of ORS in both rural and urban regions.

This pattern fit well with what was known of background factors such as income levels, general economic development, nutrition, education, and fertility levels. The leading causes of mortality at Zambia's health centers in 1981 were: measles (26 percent), pneumonia (14 percent), malnutrition-anemia (14 percent), malaria (10 percent), and diarrheas (10 percent). The leading causes of outpatient morbidity in children under 15 years were respiratory illnesses, malaria, diarrhea, and injuries, most of which were preventable. Diarrhea cases for children under 15 years of age at health centers are shown in Exhibit 3.3.

Public Sector Health Services. Most patients received free medical care through the Ministry of Health, missionary, military, or mining company facilities. The medical facilities existing in 1988 are given in Exhibit 3.4; the estimated number of health care providers in Exhibit 3.5.

Private Sector Health Services. There were several private medical practitioners, primarily seeing patients in Zambia's capital, Lusaka. In addition, approximately 10,000 traditional healers provided services throughout the country. It was estimated that as many as nine out of ten patients sought help from "traditional" healers before coming for "scientific" treatment; some continued traditional medicine while hospitalized. The cost of the traditional healer's consultation fees could be greater than that paid to private medical doctors for the same symptoms.

DIARRHEA CAUSES AND TREATMENT

Diarrhea results from consuming contaminated food or water. The percentage of Zambian households supplied with piped water and sewage systems declined in the later half of the 1980s. In 1991, about 50 percent of the total population had access to water defined as "rea-

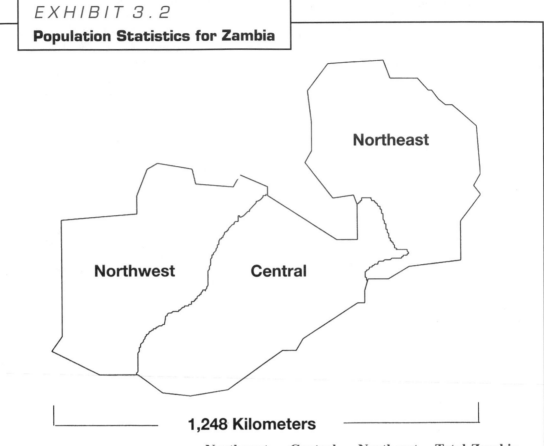

EXHIBIT 3.2
Population Statistics for Zambia

1,248 Kilometers

	Northwest	Central	Northeast	Total Zambia
Population	990,643	4,459,486	2,368,318	7,818,447
Percent of population	12.8%	57.0%	30.2%	100%
Number under 5 years	200,704	903,492	479,821	1,584,017
Area (Sq Km)	252,000	232,000	268,000	752,000
Population density/Sq Km	4	19	9	10
Urban	20.8%	68.4%	17.7%	48%
Population per physician – 1988	12,926	17,380	23,449	15,544
Expected births	49,037	220,744	117,232	387,013
Births in medical units – 1988	27.7%	37.2%	21.7%	31.3%

Notes: Analysis combines Zambian provinces as Northwest: North-Western and Western; Central: Central, Copperbelt, Lusaka, and Southern; Northeast: Eastern, Luapula, and Northern. All 1990 except as noted.
Source: Country Profile, Republic of Zambia: 1989–1990, Central Statistical Office: Lusaka; *Bulletin of Health Statistics: 1978–1988,* Ministry of Health, Health Information Unit: Lusaka; *Monthly Digest of Statistics: January 1991,* Central Statistical Office: Lusaka.

EXHIBIT 3.3
Diarrhea Cases in Health Centers for Children Under 15 Years of Age

1986	805,880
1987	758,151
1988	842,142

Source: Bulletin of Health Statistics; 1987–1988. Ministry of Health, Health Information Unit, Republic of Zambia.

EXHIBIT 3.4
Medical Facilities

Hospitals	
Government	42
Mission	29
Mines	11

Clinics: Rural	
Government	643
Mission	64

Clinics: Urban	
Government	142
Mines	75
Total	1,006

Source: Bulletin of Health Statistics: 1987–1988. Ministry of Health, Health Information Unit, Republic of Zambia.

EXHIBIT 3.5
Health Care Providers

Physicians	500
Clinical officers	1,100
Nurses	5,250
Midwives	1,135
Health assistants	531
Community health workers	983

Source: Bulletin of Health Statistics: 1987–1988. Ministry of Health, Health Information Unit, Republic of Zambia.

sonably" safe by World Health Organization standards.

Diarrhea was one of the most critical health problems in Zambia. For children under 5 years of age, who constituted over 18 percent of the total population, diarrhea was a leading cause of morbidity and mortality. In 1992, diar-rhea accounted for up to 13.5 percent of total admissions, 19.2 percent of total out patient visits, and 13.2 percent of total deaths in rural health centers. It was responsible for 7.8 per-cent of total admissions, 17.3 percent of total outpatient visits, and 8.6 per cent of total deaths in the hospitals.

Management of diarrhea cases involves restoring and maintaining fluids by oral rehy-dration and in a few cases, intravenous therapy. Often, improving or maintaining nutritional status by appropriate feeding (including breast-feeding) during and after diarrhea, as well as treating fevers and other complications with drugs, is necessary. The most effective treat-ment is drinking oral rehydration salts, as rec-ommended by the World Health Organization and UNICEF. ORS contains three essential salts (the formulation of ORS has some simi-larities to sports drinks such as Gatorade®). Contents of a typical packet is shown in Exhibit 3.6. At the onset of diarrhea weak tea and juice are often given to children, but a correctly prepared salt-sugar solution is better. ORS is, however, by far the most effective means of establishing rehydration. Health care educators consider it essential that parents understand that a dehydrated infant could die in less than twenty-four hours and learn how to provide the child with the best available rehydration

```
┌─────────────────────────────┐
│    EXHIBIT 3.6              │
│    Example, One-Liter       │
│    ORS Packet               │
└─────────────────────────────┘
```

ORAL
REHYDRATION SALTS

Each sachet contains the equivalent of:

Sodium chloride:	3.5 g.
Potassium chloride:	1.5 g.
Trisodium citrate, dihydrate:	2.9 g.
Glucose anhydrous:	20.0 g.

DIRECTIONS
Dissolve in ONE LITER of drinking
water.

To be taken orally –
Infants – over a 24 hour period
Children – over an 8 to 24 hour period,
according to age or as otherwise
directed under medical supervision.

CAUTION: DO NOT BOIL
SOLUTION

MANUFACTURER

Jianas Bros., Packaging Co.
Kansas City, Missouri, U.S.A.

```
┌─────────────────────────────┐
│    EXHIBIT 3.7              │
│    Typical Sequence Leading │
│    to Diarrhea Deaths       │
└─────────────────────────────┘
```

1. Low per capita income
2. Low protein diet
3. Malnourishment
4. Poor sanitation
5. Air or water infection
6. Diarrhea episode
7. Dehydration
8. Diarrhea death

solution. Parents should be educated to recognize serious cases requiring that the child be taken to a trained health care provider.

Diarrhea produces severe dehydration especially damaging to the health of infants. The typical sequence leading to diarrhea deaths is shown in Exhibit 3.7 and factors to reduce diarrheal deaths at each stage in this sequence are given in Exhibit 3.8. In this sequence, ORS does not stop diarrhea but reduces dehydration by replacing fluids and electrolytes. Use of antidiarrheal drugs, such as kaolin, codeine, or activated charcoal can cause severe life-threatening reactions in young children because these drugs do not reduce dehydration. Some pharmacists encouraged use of these drugs either because they were not educated in the use of ORS or they wanted to sell products that were higher priced than ORS.

Health care educators believed that ideal communications directed to parents should include these informational items:

- Diarrhea, any diarrhea, is a potentially serious illness for children.
- A child who has diarrhea should receive appropriate and sufficient fluids and food while diarrhea persists and should receive extra fluids and food after an episode of diarrhea for a period equal to the duration of the illness.
- The caretakers of a child with diarrhea should observe and monitor the child for danger signs, persistence of diarrhea, and the presence of blood in the stool.
- Children with these danger signs must be taken for appropriate medical treatment as soon as possible.

NEED AND DEMAND FOR ORS

Without high quality health statistics, determining the need and demand for ORS was difficult. Over 842,000 new cases of diarrhea

---

EXHIBIT 3.8

Factors Reducing Diarrhea Deaths at Each Stage

1. Better distribution of national income
   - Increase national productivity
   - Additional donor aid in cash and materials
2. Add soya to mealy meal (cornmeal)
3. Add kapenta (fish) to mealy meal
4. Effective sewage system
   - Use of latrines
   - Proper disposal of the stools of young children
   - Pure water
   - Boiled water
5. Increase persons immunized
   - Breast feeding
   - Washing hands
   - Well cooked foods
   - Increase AIDS prevention programs
6. IV solutions
   - Manufactured oral rehydration solutions
   - Increased availability of health centers
   - Effectively trained health care professionals and parents
   - Home prepared oral rehydration solutions
   - Home prepared fluids

---

in children under 15 years of age were treated at hospitals or health centers in 1988. Many cases did not receive pre-admission care. Additionally, the population under age 5 was in-

creasing at a rapid rate. More than 400,000 births were expected with as many as 100,000 to new mothers, who were unlikely to understand the proper care of sick infants because virtually no pre-natal education was provided. It was estimated that there were about five episodes of diarrhea in each of the 1.6 million children under 5 years of age each year; at least one-third of these required ORS. There were at least 1 million more cases in older children and adults each year. Effective treatment required about two liters of ORS. Treating these cases with ORS would require 6 million one-liter packets or the equivalent in packets of other sizes. (In Zambia, ORS was supplied as concentrated salts requiring the user to mix with the correct quantity of water.) Only about half of this supply was available either through free distribution at health clinics or hospitals or for sale in the marketplace.

The actual demand for ORS was somewhat less than this estimate due to the difficulties in obtaining ORS and limited consumer awareness of its benefits. ORS supplied at no cost through hospitals and health centers by the Ministry of Health had limitations due to shortages, the distance and time involved in obtaining the ORS from these sources, and frequent long waiting lines for health care services. In addition, it was estimated that 25 percent of the population lay outside a 12-kilometer radius of a health clinic or hospital. Marketplace distribution was often ineffective because some segments of consumers were unable to pay for the ORS or unaware of its benefits. As with most products, demand varied with the price charged.

The need for education was extensive as many parents with children under 15 years of age were not knowledgeable about oral rehydration therapy. Adult literacy in 1985 was reported to be 67 percent. Allison thought that literacy was likely to be lower than reported because the average years of schooling was only 2.6 years.

ANALYSIS OF CONSTRAINTS

Some constraints present in the general economic and social environment applied specifically to a diarrheal disease control program – constraints to the supply or use of ORS by mothers. Other constraints applied more broadly to delivery of all primary health care service, but had a direct bearing on the potential success of the program.

General Environment

Although Zambia had the most highly urbanized population in sub-Saharan Africa, about 60 percent of the population lived in rural areas, where there were few points of population concentration. Household contact between mothers and the health system were common for the 75 percent of parents who lived within 12 kilometers of clinics (average of five contacts per year for children under 1 year of age), however, contact was far less likely for those who lived further away. Distribution of ORS packets was expensive and delays were frequent in many rural areas where the transportation infrastructure was weak.

Cash available in households for purchases of ORS, radio batteries, public transport, and even "mealy meal" (the local term for corn meal, the major food staple) was scarce. The typical high-end expenditures for traditional medical treatment were generally between K70 and K350 for a routine course of treatment. Many households had monthly incomes of K2,800 or less. This highlighted the need for education about the most cost-effective medical treatments such as ORS for diarrhea.

A large proportion of female-headed households existed in rural areas as a result of male labor migration to urban communities in search of higher wages. The approximately 25 percent of rural households headed by females were those most likely to be at the bottom of the income scale. Because these mothers needed to produce income, they were less likely to have time to seek health services, obtain health education, or provide health care at the onset of diarrhea. These households were less likely to participate in or benefit from a diarrheal rehydration program because of financial and time constraints.

Health System Constraints

The general health system constraints in Zambia consisted of shortages of staff, shortages of supplies, inadequate support measures, and lack of appropriate supervision at all levels. Field supervision suffered from shortages of staff and inadequate provision of transportation. The large percentage of attrition found among trained community health workers and other peripheral workers was considered by Allison to be the result of infrequent or non-existent supervisory visits. It was likely that workers at remote Rural Health Clinics felt isolated in any case, but to never have any contact with the supervisor encouraged high employee turnover. Ideally, the supervisor's role included in-service training, checking on procedures, reinforcement, and encouragement – all vital for good performance. This support was especially needed for the distant workers.

Drastic cuts in the Ministry of Health budget made it unlikely that it could buy enough drugs, limiting expenditures to essential hospital supplies. It was likely that the Ministry of Health would encourage donor assistance for ORS rather than supporting an oral rehydration therapy program directly or by instituting a patient fee for drugs or services. Allison thought that UNICEF would be required to play a larger role than the Ministry of Health during the next three years.

Constraints Specific to Control of Diarrheal Disease

Allison visited hospitals and clinics with UNICEF physicians and observed inadequacies in diagnosis and treatment of diarrhea by all categories of health workers. There was a lack of awareness of the vital importance of oral rehydration therapy in clinical management and home use for early prevention of dehydration. Health workers said that diarrheal disease was not strongly emphasized in their education, suggesting a need for refresher courses.

The doctor or clinical officer often delegated to the nurse the dispensing of ORS and instructing the parent. This put the therapy in the hands of the nurse who may not have the same degree of therapeutic credibility as the doctor or clinical officer (physician's assistant). Similarly, pharmacists might be the ones to instruct mothers and might recommend less effective treatment methods than oral rehydration therapy either through lack of education or a desire to make profits on more expensive drugs which were often less effective or even harmful.

ORS could be manufactured either as a premixed solution or as a powdered concentrate in packets to be mixed with water by the consumer. Although premixed ORS had the advantages of being sterile and mixed in the correct proportions, it was significantly more expensive than using packets – as much as eight times more expensive per treatment. Because this discouraged purchase, packets received considerably wider use than premixed solutions in developing countries.

ORS in packets required careful mixing. Ideally the solution was to be prepared using the correct amount of boiled water. Use of unboiled water, however, was unlikely to cause serious problems because it is likely that the patient has been using the unboiled water previously and has developed a resistance to most impurities. Mixtures that were too diluted were less effective than correctly prepared solutions. The most serious mixing problem was excessive concentrations of salts which could lead to severe illness and even death in infants.

Mixing instructions for ORS were complicated because there was no standardized single measuring container. For example, no standard one-liter bowl was commonly available although there were a large number of 500 ml. cups. Once a standard packet size was selected, mothers could still become confused by having to use combinations of measuring containers.

Because ORS was not readily available throughout the health system, mothers needed to know how to prepare home-mixed solutions. The occasional unavailability of either salt or sugar made home preparation problematic, this was compounded by the frequent unavailability of mixing containers or teaspoons and the lack of consumer knowledge of oral rehydration therapy. Incorrect formulations were harmful to children, especially infants.

Information provided to the mother when oral rehydration therapy was promoted did not state that ORS was not designed to stop the diarrhea. ORS maintains hydration through the disease course. Diarrhea often runs its course if the child is kept hydrated and there is not a serious underlying cause. This must be described carefully to the mother or father so that rapid cessation of the diarrhea was not expected. Unfortunately, if such information was not provided, parents who believed oral rehydration therapy should stop the diarrhea might not only end the therapy when diarrhea did not cease immediately, but also would be unlikely to employ oral rehydration therapy in future diarrheal episodes.

PROGRAM ALTERNATIVES

Allison considered several interrelated questions to increase the use of oral rehydration therapy with ORS. These included how to ensure a reliable supply of ORS, what method of distribution would be effective in reaching consumers, what method of packaging should be encouraged, what training health care professionals need in the use of ORS, and what method would be best to promote ORS therapy with consumers.

Supply Alternatives

The major supply of ORS was from the Swedish International Development Agency that supplied one-liter packets of ORS in essential drug kits to the 707 rural health clinics monthly. Each sealed kit included 150 one-liter packets. As a result the supply of ORS was greater in some rural health clinics than in urban areas. There was no inventory control in place to balance supply and demand between the rural health clinics. Consequently, there could be several months supply at some clinics whereas others had no stock. The Swedish International Development Agency was considering an increase in the ORS to 200 packets in each kit next year. In addition, they considered supplying some stocks at the district level for reallocation to clinics on an as-needed basis, developing methods to reallocate inventories, and distributing to urban clinics. Allison was concerned that the Swedish International Development Agency's policies of free distribution were likely to have an effect on the motivation of private manufacturers and distributors of ORS.

UNICEF remained the most likely donor for additional ORS supplies. It could agree to help the Ministry of Health by continuing to donate imported one-liter packets. In the past year 1.2 million one-liter packets were donated at a total imported cost of US$87,000—about K5 per packet. Or UNICEF had the option of supporting production by subsidizing the production of ORS packets by local manufacturers. UNICEF has done this in two countries (Haiti and Indonesia) by paying the local producers the equivalent of the imported cost of packets.

The major constraint to this type of arrangement in Zambia was the high cost of the locally produced ORS packets. The approximate cost breakdown for local manufacturing of one-liter packets of ORS is given in Exhibit 3.9.

Packets were produced for free distribu-

EXHIBIT 3.9
Local Manufacturing Costs for One-Liter Package of ORS

Materials	K3.58	
Labor	0.80	
Direct costs		4.38
Factory overhead	1.10	
Production cost		5.48
Company overhead	1.33	
Cost		6.81
Profit margin	1.19	
Manufacturing selling price		K8.00

Notes: Costs are based on an annual production volume of 2 million packets. Retail price is higher due to markups. Costs for smaller packets are identical except that materials cost is less per packet.
Source: Company interviews.

tion at health clinics and hospitals through the Ministry of Health by the government-owned company, General Pharmaceutical Ltd., and at various times for sale in the private sector by Cadbury Schweppes' Zambian operations and the Zambian firms, Gamma Pharmaceuticals and Interchem. A UNICEF grant of K7 million (estimated at half the total cost of setting up ORS manufacturing for 2 million annual packet production) helped supply the equipment necessary for General Pharmaceutical to manufacture up to 2 million packets per year. General Pharmaceutical produced 1.4 million one-liter packets under the brand name "Madzi-a-moyi" (Water for Life) in the past year, but General Pharmaceutical Ltd. ceased production due to the high cost of imported raw materials and packaging.

A small amount of the General Pharmaceutical production was sold through about one hundred government owned pharmacies for K6 to K10. Although this price appears to be less than the manufacturer's cost, it resulted from these packets being produced in 1990 when the kwacha had not devalued to its current level. The retail price was expected to be higher if they resumed production.

Gamma Pharmaceuticals and Interchem each had the capacity to manufacture 2 million packets of either one-liter or 250 ml. per year. Neither was producing ORS. Gamma used its machine to produce other products and Interchem had not been able to use its Korean-made machine for two years because of a failed part. Distribution of drug products was either through deliveries to sales agents in the Copperbelt and Livingstone, or to general merchandise wholesalers who came to Lusaka to purchase ORS. There was some direct distribution to pharmacies and other outlets in Lusaka.

The manufacturer's costs and prices were expected to be approximately the same for either manufacturer. Additional production capacity was expected to cost about K14 million for each 2 million units produced per year for either one-liter or 250 ml. packet sizes. However, long delays were experienced in supplying equipment to General Pharmaceutical due to shipping delays, building construction problems, and the need to install a three-phase electrical supply. Interchem's parent company was evaluating replacing the current machine.

Cadbury Schweppes had recently received Ministry of Health approval to market orange flavored ORS in 250 ml. packets using the brand name Oresa (Oral REhydration SAlts). They had manufactured 500,000 packets; 40,000 had been distributed directly to chemists (drug stores) to test market acceptance. The remainder was in inventory. The manufacturer's price was K12 with a suggested retail price of K15. Some chemists, however, charged K18. Flavored ORS was neither encouraged nor discouraged by the World Health Organization, although, at one time they op-

posed flavored ORS due to its potential for unnecessary use and its increased cost relative to unflavored ORS. On the other hand, 300 ml. soft drink bottles such as Coke, Fanta, and Torino were widely available in Zambia for mixing 250 ml. ORS (many were distributed by Cadbury). Research at the University Teaching Hospital showed that children, even at very young ages, were more willing to drink flavored ORS and, as a result, consumed more total fluids than when given unflavored ORS. Cadbury Schweppes had the capacity to produce 18 million packets a year in one shift which was also used to produce powdered Kia-Ora, a children's drink (similar to Kool-Aid®). These could be either 250 ml. flavored or one-liter unflavored. The cost of unflavored ORS was expected to be about the same as for other local manufacturers. The per packet cost of 250 ml. flavored ORS was slightly more than that of one-liter of unflavored. In addition, Cadbury could supply either flavored or unflavored ORS in bulk packages for hospitals and health clinics.

Flavored ORS has been imported in limited quantities. Small quantities of Rehidrat,® from Searle, were available in lemon-lime 250 ml. packets for K30. Any ORS imported for resale, however, was subject to a 100 percent import duty under import substitution laws. An additional 200,000 to 400,000 packets were supplied annually by the Red Cross, churches, and other non-government organizations.

Cadbury was the only firm that had the potential to produce ORS in bottles. It was expected that the cost for 250 ml. bottles would be about the same as for soft drinks; K40 per bottle including a K20 bottle refund. Thus a two liter treatment would cost the consumer K320 without refund and K160 if bottles were returned; considerably more than the cost of buying packets.

Considering the low incomes of many target consumers, a need existed to price ORS to be affordable; this approach might be impossible without some type of subsidy. An ORS price subsidy to manufacturers or importers could create a financial burden that is unlikely to be sustainable over time. In the short-term UNICEF might use the value of the raw materials as a subsidy or provide promotional or educational services for branded products. Another option was for industry to offer a modest price to low-income consumers and still create revenues to help pay program costs by charging a much higher price for a different, more "modern" product aimed at higher-income consumers.

Distribution

Even if there was substantial donor support for free ORS distribution through clinics and hospitals, there was a need for other modes of access to ORS as well as a need to promote home-mix solutions. The commercial sector in Zambia offered several possibilities.

As a normal business practice in Zambia, a manufacturer established the recommended consumer price for his product. Trade discounts based on the recommended consumer price were 20 percent to retailers and 20 percent to trade channel members.

Allison conducted interviews with the general manager or the marketing manager of the major organizations that expressed an interest in distributing ORS. Each reached a large number of retail outlets as shown in Exhibit 3.10.

Gamma Pharmaceutical. Gamma Pharmaceutical, which started activities in 1984, manufactured pharmaceutical products for the Zambian market and for export. It sold products to private pharmacies, government and industry health facilities, and retail outlets including supermarkets. Gamma had a fleet of six delivery trucks and one van and two sales agents. Gamma was a sound, fast-growing company with a strong production and marketing team.

EXHIBIT 3.10
Potential Distribution Outlets for ORS

	Outlets
Gamma Pharmaceutical	1,000
Interchem	1,000
Cadbury Schweppes	5,000
Lyons Brooke Bond	2,200
Colgate & Palmolive	8,000

Interchem. Interchem manufactured a variety of pharmaceutical products. In addition to distributing ORS, their Marketing Manager was interested in resuming production. They needed to either repair their existing packaging machine or purchase a new one. It was not certain that repair parts were available from the Korean supplier. A new machine would cost K14 million.

Cadbury Schweppes. Cadbury Schweppes was a major producer of soft drinks, drink syrups, and other consumer packaged goods. Cadbury distributed its products direct to their retail outlets. Cadbury was evaluating flavored ORS and deciding if they should introduce Oresa throughout Zambia. They had about 460,000 packets in inventory and could begin production of additional packets within a month.

Lyons Brooke Bond. Lyons Brooke Bond, Zambia, formerly a Lever Brothers company, was an independent firm incorporated in Zambia. Lyons Brooke Bond manufactured and distributed processed food products. The Managing Director of the company had shown an interest in distributing ORS, although it did not handle any pharmaceutical products.

Colgate & Palmolive. Colgate, one of the largest distributors in Zambia, had five sales agents, four delivery vans, five freight trucks, and more than ten large wholesalers. Colgate & Palmolive manufactured and distributed personal care and hygiene products.

Evaluation of Distribution Alternatives

Allison's review of distribution capabilities in Zambia offered several options in terms of cost-effectiveness, marketing opportunities, sustainability, and possible future self-sufficiency. Although historically the bulk of ORS had been distributed at no cost by non-profit organizations, the commercial firms in Zambia could be enlisted in the implementation of an ORS program. These firms had strong experience in marketing, sound management capabilities, financial stability, and well-developed infrastructures that allowed them to access thousands of retail outlets. They were interested in participating in a marketing program as both good corporate citizens and as a potentially profitable business. Allison believed that these firms had a good understanding of the marketing environment in Zambia and their existing distribution channels could provide an effective method of distributing ORS. One or more firms could be encouraged to make a long-term financial commitment to supplying ORS.

However, she felt that there were several problems in encouraging increased participation by local manufacturers and distributors. Would the market price to consumers be too high to encourage appropriate use? Is the market large enough to encourage sufficient participation of manufacturers and distributors? Would free distribution by the government and other organizations reduce the private sector's interest in entering the market? Finally, would an oversupply be created as a result of competition which would lead to either reduced quality control or withdrawals from the market by manufacturers and distributors?

Packaging

The form of packaging had significant implications for correct use of ORS. ORS could be packaged as a premixed solution in bottles or cardboard containers or as powdered salts in foil packets.

Premixed ORS.

PROS:
> ORS is sterile.
> Correct concentration of ORS.
> Less intense consumer education required for preparation.
> Cadbury could produce in bottles.

CONS:
> Only one firm had the capacity to produce bottles.
> As much as eight times more expensive per treatment to the consumer than packets.
> Requires more space in delivery vehicles and on store shelves.
> Use of bottles requires deposit and return system due to limited supply of bottles in Zambia.
> No Zambian firm could produce cardboard containers suitable for ORS.
> Use of cardboard increases waste and litter.

Packets. It was felt that simple, consistent messages were needed in promotion of ORS packets and the associated training and education efforts. A single packet size was likely to be most effective; risk of confusion among mothers was possible if more than one packet size was available. Two packet sizes were possible for wide-spread production and distribution – 250 ml. or one liter. The following are the pros and cons:

250 ML. PACKET

Pros:

> Soft drink bottles of 300 ml. were widely available and could be used for 250 ml. packets. Soft drinks were sold for K40 per bottle, including a K20 bottle refund.
>
> Tea cups of 250 ml. were widely available.

Cons:

> Half a million one-liter packets were available in the distribution system.
>
> Imported ORS was generally available in one-liter packets.
>
> Changes in syrup bottle sizes could occur. If parents mixed 250 ml. packets in one-liter containers, ORS was less effective.

ONE-LITER PACKET

Pros:

> At least 500,000 existed in the supply system.
>
> UNICEF's imported cost was less than that of local manufacturer's price.
>
> UNICEF one-liter packets could be purchased in emergency shortages.
>
> Cups of 500 ml. were widely available.

Cons:

> The variety of cup sizes available at retail outlets was increasing with many cups of non-standard size available.
>
> If parents mixed one-liter packets in 300 ml. bottles, vomiting and serious heart and nervous problems could result, especially in younger children.

A key question was when local production could begin. Another important issue was whether local production would provide a substantial, reliable supply of acceptable quality. If production was delayed or unreliable, UNICEF or another supplier would have to fill the gap with one-liter packets.

TRAINING OF HEALTH CARE PROFESSIONALS

Physicians, nurses, clinical officers, pharmacists, and traditional healers in their regular treatment and advice set the standards for medical care. If these professionals did not understand and have confidence in oral rehydration therapy it was unlikely that they would establish oral rehydration as the standard treatment for diarrhea in Zambia.

Physicians needed training in appropriate clinical management of infants and children with diarrhea. Physicians needed to go beyond statements of symptoms as a basis for prescribing treatment for diarrhea. This included a patient history, an examination, and therapeutic management. Because physicians are opinion leaders, special efforts were desirable at the beginning of a program to inform them about oral rehydration therapy through seminars and refresher training courses.

Diarrhea Training Units

Diarrheal training units had been effective in training health care workers in other developing countries; however, only one existed in Zambia. The purpose of diarrheal training units was to develop the skills and confidence of physicians and nurses so they could give proper therapy to children with diarrhea. Those participants who attended clinical training developed skills in assessing and managing diarrhea. They learned to treat simple and complicated cases and how to communicate these skills to mothers and colleagues.

Experience suggested that a three- to five-day training course was needed to be effective. This approach made training expensive. Also, some professionals found it difficult to leave their responsibilities for the required period. Because diarrheal training units emphasized individual and practical teaching, only relatively small numbers of professionals could be trained at any time. In effective diarrheal training units, the number of participants ranged from five to fifteen. In addition, the need to have enough diarrhea cases of various types for each trainee to handle meant that some diarrheal training units could be run only during the rainy season.

The only diarrheal training unit in Zambia was a World Health Organization funded unit at the University Teaching Hospital in Lusaka that trained doctors and nurses. Allison felt that additional diarrheal training units could be effective, but their costs needed to be evaluated. Costs involved in training are included in Exhibit 3.11.

PROMOTION

There were an estimated 3 million radios in Zambia and two broadcasting stations; both were state owned. *Radio Mulungushi,* a very popular station, was primarily urban; *Radio Zambia* was primarily rural. There were as many as 250,000 television sets and one state-operated television station (operating from 5 P.M. to midnight weekdays with longer hours on the weekend). There were seven major languages; therefore it was considered critical to advertise in English plus several other languages to reach the population effectively. A media rate card is provided in Exhibit 3.12.

Message Content

A major challenge for ORS advertising was to persuade consumers that restoring the child's activity and preventing dehydration was a sufficient reason for using the product. Most communications/promotions efforts had chosen to avoid negative messages such as "oral rehydration therapy does not stop diarrhea" or "antidiarrheals do not stop diarrhea," although both are factual. Programs have chosen to address these issues in other ways such as in scientific seminars for physicians or changes in national drug policies.

A second major challenge was not only to stimulate sales of the product, the traditional goal of advertising, but also to emphasize the correct mixture and utilization of ORS. ORS product advertising should include brand-specific advertising from the beginning for maximum effectiveness, but generic advertising may also be appropriate within the same campaign.

THE SUSTAINABILITY ISSUE

Any donor program is considered sustainable when the flow of benefits from the program can be maintained or enhanced when donor funding ceases. Thus, sustainability does not refer to each activity undertaken as part of a control of diarrheal disease program, but refers to the lasting impact of the program. Seen in

---

EXHIBIT 3.11
Local Costs in Kwacha

Cost per Unit per Year

Land Cruiser Truck (4WD)	K1,200,000
Annual Fuel and Maintenance	300,000
Driver	30,000

Trainers (If Full Time with Program)

Physician	72,000
Public Health Nurse	36,000
Public Health Trainer	36,000
Training Materials For Health Care Persons	120
For Parents	10
Jugs (one-liter)	100
Measuring Spoons	30
Mugs (250 ml)	15
"Banana" Cups (500 ml)	35
Posters—each	500

Source: Interviews with health education professionals.

EXHIBIT 3.12
Basic Media Rates for Zambia, 1 December 1990 (gross rates include 20 percent sales tax)

Television		Radio	
Time Slot	**Rate for 1 Ad**	**Time Slot**	**Rate for 1 Ad**
Prime Time		A Time	
60 sec	K12,000	60 sec	K1,800
45 sec	9,600	45 sec	1,500
30 sec	6,000	30 sec	1,200
15 sec	3,600	15 sec	900
7 sec	3,000	B Time	
A Time		60 sec	K1,440
60 sec	K9,600	45 sec	1,200
45 sec	6,600	30 sec	900
30 sec	4,200	15 sec	720
15 sec	3,000	C Time	
7 sec	2,160	60 sec	K1,080
B Time		45 sec	780
60 sec	K6,000	30 sec	720
45 sec	6,600	15 sec	540
30 sec	3,600		
15 sec	1,800		
7 sec	1,200		

TV Time Distributions

Prime Time	18:55 to 20:00
A Time	07:00 to 11:00
	20:00 to 23:00
B Time	06:00 to 07:00
	15:00 to 18:55
	23:00 to Close

Radio Time Distributions

A Time	05:00 to 08:00
	12:00 to 14:00
	16:30 to 22:00
Weekend	05:00 to 22:00
B Time	08:00 to 12:00
	14:00 to 16:30
	22:00 to 23:00
Weekend	22:00 to 23:00
C Time	23:00 to Close
Weekend	23:00 to 24:00

Press — One Centimeter Down by One Column Wide

Times of Zambia	K100.80
Zambia Daily Mail	70.87

Source: Zambia National Broadcasting Company Rate Card, 1991.

this perspective, the global smallpox eradication program achieved the ultimate in sustainability – the target population continues to receive the health benefits resulting from the eradication of the disease. Ultimately, the goal of any diarrheal disease program is a sustained reduction in morbidity and mortality from diarrhea.

There are various levels at which diarrheal disease program activities take place including strategies that have shorter or longer term impacts on diarrhea. For example, the installation of a water and sewer system would be likely to have a larger impact on diarrhea morbidity and mortality than an advertising campaign promoting oral rehydration therapy use. However, this is a longer term, considerably more expensive solution. Allison knew that multiple actions were possible, but it was not possible to do everything and solve all of the problems. One solution would be seeking ways to ensure that mothers and health workers maintained appropriate case management practices (oral rehydration therapy use being one of them) after the initial program investment had been made. More directly yet, one might concentrate on ways to sustain the resource base for program activities such as training, information systems, ORS production and distribution, or any other activities designed to reduce the incidence of diarrheal disease.

Donors want to invest in development efforts and then have the benefits resulting from their investment carried on without the need for continued outside support. The developing countries themselves would prefer to avoid recipient country dependency on donor funding over the long term. This translates into donors trying to avoid paying recurrent costs, such as salaries, routine supervision, and transportation. When these costs are regularly paid by donors, the program is felt to be in jeopardy of being dropped or critically under-funded when the donor project runs out and the program reverts from donor support to the routine

government budget. If the government does not have sufficient funds to match the level of donor funding, the program's organization and activities may break down to the point where they are no longer effective. This describes what happens to an unsustainable program, one in which insufficient thought has been given to how the host country can support the program.

DEVELOPING UNICEF'S ORS PROGRAM

Within one week Allison had to develop a program for UNICEF to be presented to the UNICEF staff. Among the issues she considered were:

> How to increase the supply of ORS.
>> Increase imports?
>> Provide subsidies for local manufacturing?
>> Purchase from local manufacturers?
> How to make the distribution of ORS more effective.
> How to encourage private manufacturing and distribution.
> How to educate effectively health care providers and parents about when ORS is necessary and the correct use of ORS.
> How to package ORS.
>> Standardized at 250 ml., one-liter, or two sizes?
>> Any role for premixed ORS?

She realized that she could recommend a variety of activities, but not everything could be accomplished within the UNICEF budget of $87,000 in 1991. UNICEF was willing to spend as much $113,000 annually in the years 1992 through 1994 if they felt that their objectives were likely to be met. She suspected that there were some actions that would greatly improve the functioning of the system and had begun to think about the processes involved in the flow of ORS from supply by the manufacturer to demand and use by the consumer. She was also concerned about the flow of ORS information. Where were the leverage points? How could appropriate use be achieved on a sustainable basis?

NOTE

1. The kwacha, the Zambian currency. In 1991 K70 equaled US $1.

The First Four Letters Say It All: Lovelace Medical Center, Inc.

Lovelace Medical Center is contemplating the best posture it can take in providing a wide range of health care services to Southwestern communities during the 1990s. Over the past three decades, Lovelace has grown considerably in size and complexity and has progressively enlarged its scope of services. A committed board and dedicated management have been engaged in ongoing planning efforts to guide the substantial growth that has been occurring in recent years. A focal point of this planning effort is the Lovelace Health Plan (LHP), New Mexico's largest health maintenance organization.

The board and management of Lovelace have turned their attention to strategic planning and plotting the future course of the organization. As part of this process the following mission statement has been adopted: "To provide high quality, cost effective health care that is consumer oriented and physician directed." This statement is generally regarded as a satisfactory public expression of the overall purpose of Lovelace. The mission statement makes clear that the primary emphasis is on low-cost and high-quality health care delivery. Consumer emphasis and physician direction play important supporting roles.

It is acknowledged that, beyond the mission statement, a set of specific strategic objectives has not been developed for the organization. There is a need at this time for an explicit list of objectives that can guide further planning efforts and to which Lovelace staff can be consciously committed. At a time when competition among health care providers is likely to increase markedly, it is recognized that an ongoing planning process, including the development of departmental long- and short-range plans, is essential for competitive responses in Lovelace's market. Lovelace management is especially concerned with promoting organizational renewal and with the competitive viability of the LHP.

BACKGROUND

Since its inception in 1922, Lovelace has attempted to deliver high-quality health care services in New Mexico and the Southwestern region. Now, almost three-quarters of a century later, the Lovelace consortium of organizations continues to pursue strategies that advance health care delivery. The Lovelace approach recognizes the changing expectations, con-

This case was prepared by Derick P. Pasternak and Howard L. Smith. It is intended as a basis for classroom discussion rather than to illustrate effective or ineffective handling of an administrative situation. Used with permission from Derick Pasternak and Howard Smith.

straints, and opportunities of a new age in health care. Nonetheless, the original vision, mission, and standards characterizing Lovelace services have not been forgotten. The Lovelace organization seeks to maintain its leadership in health care delivery even though it has encountered numerous challenges. The spirit for meeting these problems has prevailed and a solid foundation has been created for service delivery. The past and present efforts of Lovelace represent a rich experiential basis that other health and medical providers can consider when establishing missions, goals, and strategies.

Dr. William Randolph Lovelace is credited with the formation of the Lovelace Clinic in 1922 along with his brother-in-law, Dr. Edgar Lassetter. Both physicians settled in Albuquerque, New Mexico, for health reasons at a time when the Southwest was expanding economically. Prior to the formation of the clinic, Dr. Lovelace had developed personal and professional ties with the Mayo Clinic. Using knowledge and contacts from his Mayo affiliation, Dr. Lovelace was instrumental in attracting specialists to an otherwise underserved rural area. The creation of a multispecialty group practice can be traced to this time. Thereafter, until 1946, the Lovelace clinic experienced steady growth consistent with regional trends and national events. At this point, Dr. William Randolph Lovelace II (Randy), the nephew of Dr. Lovelace, joined the partnership.

Due to Dr. Randy Lovelace's affiliation with the group practice, a number of strategic changes occurred that transformed the Lovelace Clinic into a diversified health care provider on the cutting edge of the field. Notable among the many advances were the following:

- The clinic moved to a new and expanded facility in 1950. This provided space for a medical staff that grew from approximately thirty physicians at the time of the move to about sixty in 1960.
- The Bataan Memorial Methodist Hospi-

tal, a 110-bed inpatient facility, was constructed next to the clinic.
- Organizationally, a group practice centered around the Mayo model was created. A supporting, nonprofit foundation guided by Dr. Clayton S. White was formed to stimulate education and research.
- The University of New Mexico, the clinic, and the Bataan Hospital were collaborating on medical education by 1965.
- Research programs expanded in scope to include many dimensions of biomedical and biophysical research.
- Research and medical services joined in serving aerospace interests, particularly in the area of manned spaceflights.

By 1968, the deaths of both Dr. William Lovelace and Dr. Randy Lovelace had altered the leadership and direction of the clinic and its affiliated units.

For the next ten years the Lovelace Clinic was led by Dr. Donald Kilgore, who had the vision necessary to respond to a radically changing health care environment. The foundation for Lovelace's involvement in alternative delivery systems was established at this time. Especially crucial were the merger of the clinic with the Bataan Hospital, the initiation of satellite clinics, and the founding of a health maintenance organization (subsequently known as the Lovelace Health Plan or LHP). These developments did not overshadow achievements in research, but they were complementary to the gradual broadening of research beyond aerospace medicine. In 1976, Dr. David J. Ottensmeyer assumed leadership, and over the next decade he refined the strategic thrust of Lovelace and the legacy of the approximately fifty-five years invested by many professionals, staff, volunteers, and philanthropists.

Throughout the Lovelace Clinic's history, the identity of the clinic as a physician-owned and operated organization oriented to patient care remained with exceptional clarity. This key underpinning has been instrumental in successfully negotiating turbulent periods in the health care environment. Although the Lovelace Clinic is affiliated with a hospital, acute care has never been the sole interest of Lovelace. Rather, the inpatient facility is one essential ingredient necessary to provide a comprehensive set of patient services. A more important determinant of Lovelace's success over the past seventy years is innovation in medical practice. Patient interests have been served through the quality of care and diverse skills available from a multispecialty group practice. Patients have had access to care that not only involves the finest facilities and equipment, but is also cost-effective and affordable. These are the historical precedents that have helped Lovelace serve the Southwest.

THE CURRENT STRUCTURE OF LOVELACE

Until 1984, the Lovelace Medical Foundation (LMF) was a 501(c)(3) private, not-for-profit medical foundation. It engaged in four broad areas of activity: operation of the Lovelace Medical Center (a 235-bed acute-care/tertiary hospital); operation of the Lovelace Medical Clinic (a 135-physician multispecialty medical group delivery service at seven clinical sites in Albuquerque, New Mexico); a basic and applied research program involving 300 full-time research personnel; and the Lovelace Health Plan (a 110,000-member health maintenance organization).

During the strategic planning process, Lovelace determined that its capital needs over the next five years would approximate $75 million. The organization had been growing rapidly in the health plan area, which improved its market share position. Furthermore, the highly competitive health care market in Albuquerque demanded sophisticated management

and marketing systems to ensure financial solvency. Lovelace planners noted that by the end of 1984, it was the only major health care organization in the Albuquerque area that did not have governmental sponsorship or was not a member of a multiinstitutional hospital chain. Together, these factors suggested that Lovelace should review its strategic plans for meeting capitalization and market share management.

Premerger Planning

Lovelace engaged in discussions with a broad variety of health care and financial organizations from 1982 to 1984. These discussions had three major objectives:

1. to improve access to capital;
2. to examine the benefits of a multi-institutional health care system; and
3. to strengthen the financial position of Lovelace for accomplishing its mission in research and medical education.

These strategic planning issues are not unique among health providers who perceive the need to grow beyond their current capacities, who may lack sufficient resources to attain this growth, and who are amenable to innovative methods of resolving these problems.

Lovelace developed a number of optional proposals on the basis of discussions with other health care organizations. As part of this process, top management and the board of trustees established a set of criteria to be used in evaluating the alternatives:

1. Lovelace must have sufficient resources and annual revenue to carry on activities central to its mission and goals.
2. Lovelace should retain management control in any resulting health care system that depended on the medical staff of the Lovelace Clinic for medical care delivery.

3. Lovelace must have an equity position in any health care facilities that develop from the proposals.
4. Medical education and research must be reinforced and integrated with health care delivery.
5. Lovelace should have 50 percent representation on any board of directors and should have authority to appoint the management team responsible for health care delivery activities.
6. The job security of the medical staff and the employees of Lovelace must be assured in any organizational arrangements.

Discussions were held with nine different organizations, and extensive negotiations were pursued with four. Two of the proposals were from investor-owned hospital corporations and two were from not-for-profit, multiinstitutional hospital organizations. After serious contemplation, discussion, assessment, and projection, it was decided that negotiations with the Hospital Corporation of America presented the most promising avenue of effort.

The Decision to Merge

In August 1984, the Lovelace Medical Foundation and the Hospital Corporation of America (HCA) announced a contractual agreement for a joint venture to restructure, rebuild, and operate the Lovelace Medical Center as a for-profit health care organization. This merger is remarkable, though not unique, because it brings a for-profit chain together with a not-for-profit medical foundation. This change represents a significant transformation because a formerly not-for-profit organization must reorient its service delivery philosophy to be consistent with proprietary status. Despite this metamorphosis, the affiliation with HCA was viewed as consistent with the innovation in health care delivery that has characterized Lovelace over its past seventy years.

A central consideration for LMF was the history of HCA as a physician-oriented health care corporation. Historically, HCA was established by a physician and has been managed by physicians. Looking at the HCA organization provides evidence of physicians at the corporate board level, throughout the corporate management levels, and at the individual institutional board level as well.

The decision to develop the LMF joint venture with HCA was derived from many complex factors that can best be summarized as a harmonious chemistry between the two organizations. LMF discovered that attaining the terms of the predetermined planning criteria was not overly difficult. In contrast, several of the other organizations under consideration were unable to commit the needed total and long-term financial resources. However, the ultimate selection of a partner went far beyond the partner's ability to simply provide the needed financial resources. The total package available from HCA was in distinct contrast to other options. It offered the best means of achieving each criterion.

The Present Lovelace Configuration

Beginning in 1985, Lovelace shifted its structural configuration to that shown in Exhibit 4.1. Most obvious is the retention of the major operating entities that have come to characterize the Lovelace image, notably the:

1. *Lovelace Medical Foundation (LMF).* A completely independent organization responsible for education and research. Consisting of the Lovelace Biomedical and Environmental Institute as well as Lovelace Scientific Resources, Inc., it conducts research on a wide variety of topics including toxicology, clinical applications, blood flow and ultrasound, pulmonary physiology, immunology, and health services research. It is staffed by over 300 personnel, almost 40 percent of whom hold doctorates.

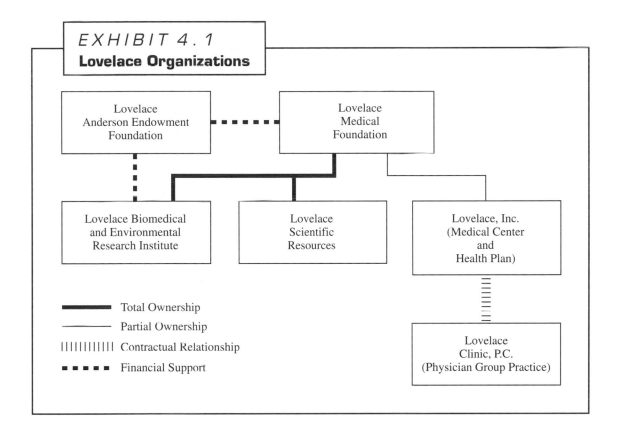

EXHIBIT 4.1
Lovelace Organizations

Lovelace Anderson Endowment Foundation

Lovelace Medical Foundation

Lovelace Biomedical and Environmental Research Institute

Lovelace Scientific Resources

Lovelace, Inc. (Medical Center and Health Plan)

Lovelace Clinic, P.C. (Physician Group Practice)

Total Ownership
Partial Ownership
Contractual Relationship
Financial Support

2. *Lovelace Medical Center, Incorporated (LCMI).* A for-profit hospital, clinical facilities, and equipment, including all personnel support. LMCI occupied its 238-bed inpatient facility in July 1987. Central to the consistently high occupancy rate (normally greater than 85 percent) is a referral system incorporating satellite clinics in Albuquerque and Santa Fe.

3. *Lovelace Health Plan (LHP).* A 110,000-member health maintenance organization based on the group model. The LHP has been a critical factor in maintaining efficient utilization of facilities and equipment. It has been a competitive tool that has allowed Lovelace to expand market share in an otherwise very competitive market.

4. *Lovelace Clinic Professional Corporation (LCPC).* A 135-physician member medical staff that serves LMCI and LHP.

Each entity has a separate board that, in addition to HCA, provides representation and guidance to the entire organizational configuration shown in Exhibit 4.1.

Currently, Dr. Derick Pasternak is the chief executive officer responsible for the operations of LMCI, LHP, and LCPC (see Exhibit 4.2). His present challenge is to stabilize the organization after the past three years of restructuring, ownership changes, and merger affiliations. Following in the tradition of physician executives who have managed the Lovelace family of organizations, Dr. Pasternak must achieve this stabilization during a

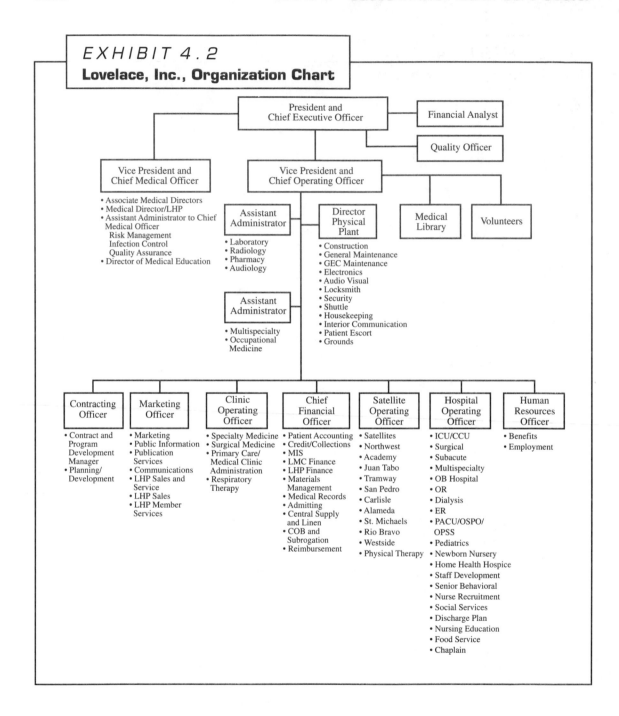

EXHIBIT 4.2
Lovelace, Inc., Organization Chart

President and Chief Executive Officer

Financial Analyst

Quality Officer

Vice President and Chief Medical Officer

- Associate Medical Directors
- Medical Director/LHP
- Assistant Administrator to Chief Medical Officer
  Risk Management
  Infection Control
  Quality Assurance
- Director of Medical Education

Vice President and Chief Operating Officer

Assistant Administrator

- Laboratory
- Radiology
- Pharmacy
- Audiology

Director Physical Plant

- Construction
- General Maintenance
- GEC Maintenance
- Electronics
- Audio Visual
- Locksmith
- Security
- Shuttle
- Housekeeping
- Interior Communication
- Patient Escort
- Grounds

Medical Library

Volunteers

Assistant Administrator

- Multispecialty
- Occupational Medicine

Contracting Officer

- Contract and Program Development Manager
- Planning/ Development

Marketing Officer

- Marketing
- Public Information
- Publication Services
- Communications
- LHP Sales and Service
- LHP Sales
- LHP Member Services

Clinic Operating Officer

- Specialty Medicine
- Surgical Medicine
- Primary Care/ Medical Clinic Administration
- Respiratory Therapy

Chief Financial Officer

- Patient Accounting
- Credit/Collections
- MIS
- LMC Finance
- LHP Finance
- Materials Management
- Medical Records
- Admitting
- Central Supply and Linen
- COB and Subrogation
- Reimbursement

Satellite Operating Officer

- Satellites
- Northwest
- Academy
- Juan Tabo
- Tramway
- San Pedro
- Carlisle
- Alameda
- St. Michaels
- Rio Bravo
- Westside
- Physical Therapy

Hospital Operating Officer

- ICU/CCU
- Surgical
- Subacute
- Multispecialty
- OB Hospital
- OR
- Dialysis
- ER
- PACU/OSPO/ OPSS
- Pediatrics
- Newborn Nursery
- Home Health Hospice
- Staff Development
- Senior Behavioral
- Nurse Recruitment
- Social Services
- Discharge Plan
- Nursing Education
- Food Service
- Chaplain

Human Resources Officer

- Benefits
- Employment

tumultuous period in the health care field. Furthermore, it must be attained while simultaneously creating a foundation for future growth in the LHP through innovative strategies. At a point where cost control is an everpresent consideration and quality of care is an imperative in view of the history of Lovelace, Dr. Pasternak and the Lovelace organizations face a difficult challenge.

HEALTH PLAN AND COMPETITORS

Lovelace Health Plan faces competition from acute-care providers (described in Exhibit 4.3), from managed-care plans (defined in Exhibit 4.4), and from physicians (specialists and generalists) practicing in Lovelace's markets. As the descriptive statistics of Bernalillo County (i.e., Albuquerque) suggest, many hospitals are competing for inpatients. Fluctuations in occupancy and census have created very intense competition. Strategic reactions to this competition include marketing, health plan affiliation, price and service differentials, multiinstitutional affiliations, and similar strategic responses prevalent in the health field today.

As Exhibit 4.4 indicates, Lovelace Health Plan confronts a number of competitors who have been gaining strength over the four years prior to the merger. At the end of 1986, Lovelace possessed approximately 65.4 percent of the HMO market. At the beginning of 1990, LHP's market share was approximately 55.7 percent. The market had effectively doubled between 1986 and 1990. It should be noted that this decrease in market share was to a great extent intentional on LHP's part. LHP has been concerned with maintaining economic viability, not simply enrolling the largest number of members. Some potential corporate, public, and third-sector consumers have an excessively high risk level that could threaten LHP's long-run viability. Consequently, such organizations may choose one of LHP's competitors who might offer a lower price for a

similar set of services despite the experience rating.

LHP has developed a number of options that vary services and prices as a means to remain competitive. These options include:

1. *Standard 500.* A basic plan wherein hospital admissions include a copayment of $500 and a series of other copayments and cost-sharing elements that allow a lower premium (see Exhibit 4.5).
2. *Standard 200.* A basic plan with lower cost sharing and copayment than the "Standard 500" plan. Hospital admissions include a copayment of $200. Outpatient charges (copayment) parallel the "Standard 500" option (see Exhibit 4.6).
3. *Standard Plus.* A plan with minimal cost sharing and copayment. Hospital admissions require a copayment of $100 per admission. Outpatient charges are greatly reduced relative to the "Standard 500" and "Standard 200" plans (see Exhibit 4.7).
4. *Custom.* A plan with virtually no copayment or cost sharing for hospital admissions or clinic visits (see Exhibit 4.8).

The LHP options provide the mechanism to compete on the premium side while maintaining services essential in managed care.

To gain an appreciation of which New Mexico organizations are attracted to the LHP options, Exhibit 4.9 lists the major LHP accounts. Some of the very largest organizations and corporations in New Mexico are affiliated with LHP, notably, Public Service Company of New Mexico (PNM), Honeywell, U.S. West Communications, the City of Albuquerque, the University of New Mexico, New Mexico Public Schools, Los Alamos National Laboratories, Albuquerque Public Schools, and the State of New Mexico. Exhibit 4.9 lists the number of eligible members and the percent-

EXHIBIT 4.3
Bernalillo County Health Facilities

Institution	Ownership	Beds	Admissions	Census	Occupancy	Births	Expenses (in thousands)		
							Total	Payroll	Personnel
Carrie Tingley	NG NFP	24	455	7	29.2%	0	$5,324	$2,069	102
Charter Hospital (P)	FP	80	*	*	*	*	*	*	*
HCA Heights Psychiatric (P)	FP	80	1,203	59	73.8	0	7,587	3,521	139
Kaseman Presbyterian	NG NFP	148	5,306	91	57.2	0	*	*	332
Lovelace	FP	197	11,520	124	63.3	1,889	149,066	34,082	1,851
Memorial (P)	FP	58	479	22	37.9	0	5,998	2,236	120
Northside Presbyterian	NG NFP	198	2,885	158	79.8	0	*	*	*
Presbyterian	NG NFP	413	21,211	279	67.6	3,467	*	*	1,420
St. Joseph	NG NFP	265	8,907	133	50.2	0	*	*	870
St. Joseph Rehab	NG NFP	50	438	36	72.0	0	8,225	4,009	162
St. Joseph West Mesa	NG NFP	128	2,912	46	35.9	618	16,079	5,834	221
St. Joseph Northeast Heights	NG NFP	120	3,406	35	29.2	921	15,261	5,581	218
USPHS Indian Hospital	PHS	28	904	14	50.0	0	6,632	5,309	152
University of New Mexico (UNM)	Gov	298	11,702	236	79.2	3,612	93,529	44,362	1,784
UNM Child Psychiatric (P)	State	53	103	50	94.3	0	5,480	3,172	166
UNM Mental Health (P)	County	74	1,343	60	81.1	0	13,428	8,748	392
Veterans Administration	VA	429	9,689	312	72.7	0	79,671	42,120	1,494

*Nonreporting.   P = psychiatric   NFP = not-for-profit   FP = for-profit   PHS = public health service   NG = nongovernment
Source: AHA Guide to the Health Care Field (Chicago: American Hospital Association, 1989).

EXHIBIT 4.4
Number of Members in New Mexico Managed-Care Plans

Plan	12/31/86	3/31/88	1/1/89	7/1/89	1/1/90
FHP	12,174	19,627	21,000	21,401	24,800
Firstsource	10,167	13,055	7,982	7,794	11,600
Healthplus	14,640	26,000	35,000	34,858*	27,008*
Lovelace	70,000	79,076	101,544	104,226	107,968
Qual-Med	—	—	24,269	22,228	22,424

*Includes PPO Indemnity
Source: Personal communication from Blue Cross/Blue Shield.

age of penetration for 1988, 1989, and 1990 (i.e., the percentage of eligibles who subscribe to LHP).

Exhibit 4.10 provides insight on the age of LHP enrollees. The 20–44-year-old age group represents the largest number of enrollees. More females than males are enrolled in LHP's options.

Lovelace has emphasized the importance of alternative delivery systems and attempted to incorporate them within its master strategy via satellite clinics and urgent-care centers to extend services in the community and LHP as a cost-effective delivery mechanism. The satellite clinics, currently housed in facilities that double as urgent-care centers, were a primary ingredient in Lovelace's efforts to expand its outreach. Development of the centers in the 1970s provided a logical convenience to patients and a reasonable method for avoiding a hospital orientation. Intensive care is still delivered at the central clinic location adjacent to the hospital, but the majority of care is outpatient oriented. The satellite clinics reinforce this philosophy and help Lovelace to expand the geographical areas served by the group practice. In turn, the clinics provide a mechanism for patient referral. Exhibit 4.11 diagrams the location of Lovelace facilities.

The satellite clinics are an integral aspect of service to a prepaid population of subscribers. Within the ten years prior to the merger, the number of LHP enrollees has grown to 110,000 members. Despite this growth, Lovelace continues to serve a large number of private patients (i.e., with other third-party insurance) in addition to its HMO population. LHP has encountered numerous competitors in the past three years as would be expected with the general trends in health insurance and the efforts of hospitals to capture a patient population through medical staff affiliations. Nonetheless, LHP has remained a vital component in an overall plan of care. The health plan benefits from its linkage to a physician group (offering a ready supply of physicians) with an orientation toward outpatient clinics where patients have access to clinical resources at a convenient neighborhood location.

RECENT PERFORMANCE TRENDS

LMCI's performance in terms of clinic visits, hospital utilization, and fiscal trends are shown in Exhibits 4.12 to 4.15 for the years 1987 to 1989. When considering these statistics, it is important to remember the multispecialty group-practice configuration that sustains

EXHIBIT 4.5
Standard 500

Lovelace
Lovelace Health Plan
Summary of Benefits

LHP Provides the Following Benefits when Medically Necessary and only when Provided or Arranged by your Primary Care Physician. Copayments are due at the time of service.

Services		Cost
Office Visits	Physician, Nurse Practitioner, and Physician Assistant Services—Diagnosis and treatment—Specialist's care and consultation when referred by your Primary Care Physician—Adult or Pediatric check-ups—Minor surgery—Radiation therapy—No limit on number of encounters	$10.00 per visit
Outpatient Surgery	Services not requiring hospital admission	$30.00 per visit
Other Outpatient Services	Laboratory and X-ray procedures	No charge
	Mammography	
	Casts and dressings	
	Administered drugs and medications	
	Injections—Specified immunizations—Allergy injections	$5.00 per visit
	Allergy Testing	$30.00 per visit
Hospital Admission	Physician's and surgeon's services, including operations and specialist's consultations	$500.00 per admission
	Room and board in semi-private accommodations—Private room (when medically necessary), intensive care, and coronary care—Use of the operating room, anesthesia, general nursing	
	Drugs and medications-injections—X-ray—Radiation therapy—Laboratory tests—Inhalation therapy	
	Casts and dressings—Administration of blood and blood derivatives	
Emergency Room For medical emergencies only*	All necessary services and supplies	$30.00 per visit in and out of the service area
Urgent Care	All necessary services and supplies at Lovelace Urgent Care facilities	$10.00 per visit
Surgical Sterilizations	Outpatient Procedures	$30.00 per visit
	Inpatient Procedures	$500.00 per admission

***SEE MEMBER HANDBOOK & CERTIFICATE FOR EXCLUSIONS, LIMITATIONS AND EMERGENCY CARE INFORMATION.**

LMCI's strategy. Unlike other health providers in Albuquerque or the state, LMCI has not restricted its strategy to inpatient services.

Like all health care providers, LMCI has had its share of good times and bad. However, the periods of low performance can generally be attributed to phenomenal growth in the LHP segment of LMCI services. Rapid expansion of the LHP has put stress on the system's ability to function. This is immediately apparent in 1987, when LHP enrollments expanded greatly (during 1986 and 1987).

EXHIBIT 4.5 *cont'd*

Services		Cost
Mental Health	Inpatient Services	Not covered
	Outpatient services—up to 80 units per contract year or a minimum of 20 visits 1 unit is equal to 15 minutes	50% of charges
Maternity Care	Pre-natal and post-natal care	$10.00 per visit
	All physician and hospital services for mother during confinement, including but not limited to, full term delivery, miscarriage, or termination of pregnancy	$500.00 per admission
Newborn Care	Child is covered from birth but must be enrolled within 31 days	No charge for hospital. $10.00 per outpatient visit
Extended Care	Skilled nursing care—Room and board—Laboratory and X-ray—Tests—Physician's services—Physical therapy—Drugs and medications	No charge up to 30 days
Home Health Services	Physician house calls	$10.00 per visit
	Prescribed home nursing care	No charge
Other Services	Ambulance service* *(unless transport is between medical facilities or results in hospital admission)*	$30 per transport
	Up to 6 months of short-term physical therapy, occupational therapy, chiropractic therapy, and speech therapy per condition which is reasonably expected to improve significantly within two months	Inpatient services are covered by the $500.00 hospital admission fee
	Outpatient: physical therapy, occupational therapy, speech therapy/audiology, respiratory therapy	$10.00 per visit
	Alcohol and drug abuse detoxification	$500.00 per admission
	Hemodialysis (member must make prompt application for Medicare benefits)	No charge
	Specified hospice care services which are reasonable and necessary for the palliation or management of terminal illness	No charge
	Eye and ear screening exams by Primary Care Physician to determine need for correction through age 17	$10.00 per visit
	Special Programs: —Infertility treatment —Weight reduction for morbid obesity	50% of charges
Health Education	Classes and specialty programs	Some require copayments

EXCLUSIONS

LHP will not provide or cover services for:

1. Rehabilitative treatment programs for alcoholism or drug addiction unless specifically listed as an additional benefit.

2. Outpatient prescription drugs unless specifically listed as an additional benefit.

3. Care for military service connected disabilities.

4. Unusual circumstances such as complete or partial destruction of facilities, war, riot, disability of a significant number of providers, or similar events, provided LHP shall make a good faith effort to provide or arrange covered benefits.

5. Organ transplants, except services to recipient for kidney and corneal transplants, and liver transplants for children with biliary atresia, where the recipient is a Member, and bone marrow transplants for specified blood conditions.

6. The medical and hospital services of a donor when the recipient of an organ transplant is not a Member.

7. Prayer or spiritual healing or religious counseling.

8. Eye refractions and eyeglasses (unless specifically included as a benefit), corrective lenses, the fitting of either eyeglasses or hearing aids, and hearing aid batteries.

9. Experimental services.

10. Custodial care.

11. Medical supplies not provided during hospital confinement or a doctor's office visit.

12. Whole blood and blood plasma. (Currently New Mexico providers do not charge for blood.)

13. Long-term physical therapy and rehabilitation.

14. Services not generally recognized as medically necessary, such as:
   a. Behavioral training   c. Reversal of voluntary sterilization.
   b. Sex change procedures.   d. Extra corporeal insemination and *in vitro* pregnancies.

15. Vocational rehabilitation.

EMERGENCY CARE

An emergency is a sudden, acute and unexpected medical condition which, if not immediately diagnosed and treated, could lead to disability or death.

1. Within a 40-mile radius of a Lovelace facility, LHP covers reasonable charges for emergency service received at a non-Lovelace medical facility only if delay caused by coming to a Lovelace facility would result in death or serious disability.

2. For members residing in Santa Fe, Los Alamos or Espanola, local emergency rooms may be used.

3. Elsewhere, LHP covers reasonable charges for emergency services.

4. Members need to notify LHP within 48 hours after care is provided at a non-Lovelace facility.

5. All follow-up or continuing care must be arranged through your LHP Primary Care Physician.

EXHIBIT 4.6
Standard 200

✚ LOVELACE
Lovelace Health Plan
Summary of Benefits

LHP Provides the Following Benefits when Medically Necessary and only when Provided or Arranged by your Primary Care Physician. Copayments are due at the time of service.

Services		Cost
Office Visits	Physician, Nurse Practitioner, and Physician Assistant Services—Diagnosis and treatment—Specialist's care and consultation when referred by your Primary Care Physician—Adult or Pediatric check-ups—Minor surgery—Radiation therapy—No limit on number of encounters	$10.00 per visit
Outpatient Surgery	Services not requiring hospital admission	$30.00 per visit
Other Outpatient Services	Laboratory and X-ray procedures Mammography Casts and dressings Administered drugs and medications Voluntary family planning services Injections—Specified immunizations—Allergy injections	No charge
Hospital Admission	Physician's and surgeon's services, including operations and specialist's consultations Room and board in semi-private accommodations—Private room (when medically necessary), intensive care, and coronary care—Use of the operating room, anesthesia, general nursing Drugs and medications-injections—X-ray—Radiation therapy—Laboratory tests—Inhalation therapy Casts and dressings—Administration of blood and blood derivatives	$200.00 per admission
Emergency Room For medical emergencies only*	All necessary services and supplies	$30.00 per visit in and out of the service area
Urgent Care	All necessary services and supplies at Lovelace Urgent Care facilities	$10.00 per visit

*SEE MEMBER HANDBOOK & CERTIFICATE FOR EXCLUSIONS, LIMITATIONS AND EMERGENCY CARE INFORMATION.

Clinic Visits

Exhibit 4.12 displays trends for clinic visits at the main Gibson site, at other Albuquerque satellite clinics, and in Santa Fe. Normally, two figures are reported: clinic visits and urgent-care visits, except for the main Gibson site, which offers true emergency care but has no separate urgent-care center. The data indicate that total visits increased 12.7 percent between 1987 and 1988, and an 8.2 percent increase was registered between 1988 and

EXHIBIT 4.6 cont'd

Services		Cost
Surgical Sterilizations	Outpatient Procedures	$30.00 per visit
	Inpatient Procedures	$200.00 per admission
Mental Health	Inpatient Services	Not covered
	Outpatient services up to 80 units per contract year or a minimum of 20 visits	50% of charges
	1 unit is equal to 15 minutes	
Maternity Care	Pre-natal and post-natal care	$10.00 per visit
	All physician and hospital services for mother during confinement, including but not limited to, full term delivery, miscarriage, or termination of pregnancy	$200.00 per admission
Newborn Care	Child is covered from birth but must be enrolled within 31 days	No charge for hospital $10.00 per outpatient visit
Extended Care	Skilled nursing care Room and board Laboratory and X-ray Tests Physician's services Physical therapy Drugs and medications	No charge up to 30 days
Home Health Services	Physician house calls	$10.00 per visit
	Prescribed home nursing care	No charge
Other Services	Ambulance service* *(unless transport is between medical facilities or results in hospital admission)*	$30 per transport
	Up to 6 months of short-term physical therapy, occupational therapy, chiropractic therapy, and speech therapy per condition which is reasonably expected to improve significantly within two months	No charge for outpatient visits. Inpatient services are covered by the $200.00 hospital admission fee
	Alcohol and drug abuse detoxification	$200.00 per admission
	Hemodialysis (member must make prompt application for Medicare benefits)	No charge
	Specified hospice care services which are reasonable and necessary for the palliation or management of terminal illness	No charge
	Eye and ear screening exams by Primary Care Physician to determine need for correction through age 17	$10.00 per visit
	Special Programs: -- Infertility treatment -- Weight reduction for morbid obesity	50% of charges
Health Education	Classes and specialty programs	Some require copayments

EXCLUSIONS

LHP will not provide or cover services for:

1. Rehabilitative treatment programs for alcoholism or drug addiction unless specifically listed as an additional benefit.

2. Outpatient prescription drugs unless specifically listed as an additional benefit.

3. Care for military service connected disabilities.

4. Unusual circumstances such as complete or partial destruction of facilities, war, riot, disability of a significant number of providers, or similar events, provided LHP shall make a good faith effort to provide or arrange covered benefits.

5. Organ transplants, except services to recipient for kidney and corneal transplants, and liver transplants for children with biliary atresia, where the recipient is a Member, and bone marrow transplants for specified blood conditions.

6. The medical and hospital services of a donor when the recipient of an organ transplant is not a Member.

7. Prayer or spiritual healing or religious counseling.

8. Eye refractions and eyeglasses (unless specifically included as a benefit), corrective lenses, the fitting of either eyeglasses or hearing aids, and hearing aid batteries.

9. Experimental services.

10. Custodial care.

11. Medical supplies not provided during hospital confinement or a doctor's office visit.

12. Whole blood and blood plasma. (Currently New Mexico providers do not charge for blood.)

13. Long-term physical therapy and rehabilitation.

14. Services not generally recognized as medically necessary, such as:
    a. Behavioral training
    b. Sex change procedures.
    c. Reversal of voluntary sterilization.
    d. Extra corporeal insemination and *in vitro* pregnancies.

15. Vocational rehabilitation.

EMERGENCY CARE

An emergency is a sudden, acute and unexpected medical condition which, if not immediately diagnosed and treated, could lead to disability or death.

1. Within a 40-mile radius of a Lovelace facility, LHP covers reasonable charges for emergency service received at a non-Lovelace medical facility only if delay caused by coming to a Lovelace facility would result in death or serious disability.

2. For members residing in Santa Fe, Los Alamos or Espanola, local emergency rooms may be used.

3. Elsewhere, LHP covers reasonable charges for emergency services.

4. Members need to notify LHP within 48 hours after care is provided at a non-Lovelace facility.

5. All follow-up or continuing care must be arranged through your LHP Primary Care Physician.

EXHIBIT 4.7
Standard Plus

✚ LOVELACE
Lovelace Health Plan
Summary of Benefits

LHP Provides the Following Benefits when Medically Necessary and only when Provided or Arranged by your Primary Care Physician. Copayments are due at the time of service.

Services		Cost
Office Visits	Physician, Nurse Practitioner, and Physician Assistant Services—Diagnosis and treatment—Specialist's care and consultation when referred by your Primary Care Physician—Adult or Pediatric check-ups—Minor surgery—Radiation therapy—No limit on number of encounters	$5.00 per visit
Outpatient Surgery	Services not requiring hospital admission	$5.00 per visit
Other Outpatient Services	Laboratory and X-ray procedures	No charge
	Mammography	
	Casts and dressings	
	Injections—Specified immunizations—Administered drugs and medications	
	Allergy injections	
	Voluntary family planning services	
Hospital Admission	Physician's and surgeon's services, including operations and specialist's consultations	$100.00 per admission
	Room and board in semi-private accommodations—Private room (when medically necessary), intensive care, and coronary care—Use of the operating room, anesthesia, general nursing	
	Drugs and medications-injections—X-ray—Radiation therapy—Laboratory tests—Inhalation therapy	
	Casts and dressings—Administration of blood and blood derivatives	
Emergency Room For medical emergencies only*	All necessary services and supplies	$20.00 per visit in and out of the service area
Urgent Care	All necessary services and supplies at Lovelace Urgent Care facilities	$5.00 per visit
Surgical Sterilizations	Outpatient Procedures	$5.00 per visit
	Inpatient Procedures	$100.00 per admission
Extended Care	Skilled nursing care—Room and board—Laboratory and X-Ray—Tests—Physician's services—Physical therapy—Drugs and medications	No charge

*SEE MEMBER HANDBOOK & CERTIFICATE FOR EXCLUSIONS, LIMITATIONS AND EMERGENCY CARE INFORMATION.

1989. Urgent-care visits increased 4 percent, from 158,648 in 1987 to 165,022 in 1989. A 4.8 percent increase was experienced between 1988 and 1989. The profile that emerges is one of more rapid growth in clinic visits than in urgent-care visits.

Sites with the highest level of visit growth include the Gibson, Northwest, San Pedro, and Santa Fe offices. Occupational medicine also expanded significantly, by 39.5 percent from 1988 to 1989. The Santa Fe operations increased 76.1 percent from 1988 to 1989, pri-

EXHIBIT 4.7 cont'd

Services		Cost
Mental Health	Inpatient services (hospital, physician, and other professional services) - up to 30 days per contract year. One day of inpatient care is equivalent to *two* days of partial hospitalization. (Partial hospitalization is a non-residential program which includes various daily and weekly therapies.) A member is therefore entitled to 30 inpatient days or 60 partial hospitalization days, or any combination thereof, per contract year. Using one inpatient day uses up two partial hospitalization days; using two partial hospitalization days uses one inpatient day. At no time will LHP allow a greater benefit than 30 inpatient days per contract year.	50% of charges
	Outpatient services—up to 80 units per contract year or a minimum of 20 visits. 1 unit is equal to 15 minutes	50% of charges
Maternity Care	Pre-natal and post-natal care	$5.00 per visit
	All physician and hospital services for mother during confinement, including but not limited to, full term delivery, miscarriage, or termination of pregnancy	$100.00 for first admission due to pregnancy. Subsequent admissions related to same pregnancy No charge
Newborn Care	Child is covered from birth but must be enrolled within 31 days	No charge for hospital $5.00 per outpatient visit
Home Health Services	Physician house calls	$5.00 per visit
	Prescribed home nursing care	No charge
Other Services	Ambulance service* *(unless transport is between medical facilities or results in hospital admission)*	$30 per transport
	Up to 6 months of short-term physical therapy, occupational therapy, chiropractic therapy, and speech therapy for condition which is reasonably expected to improve significantly within two months	No charge for outpatient visits. Inpatient services are covered by the $100.00 hospital admission fee
	Alcohol and drug abuse detoxification	$100.00 per admission
	Hemodialysis (member must make prompt application for Medicare benefits)	No charge
	Specified durable medical equipment and appliances when prescribed	20% of charges

Other Services (continued)	Specified hospice care services which are reasonable and necessary for the palliation or management of terminal illness	No charge
	Eye and ear screening exams by Primary Care Physician to determine need for correction through age 17	$5.00 per visit
	Special Programs: —Infertility treatment —Weight reduction for morbid obesity	50% of charges
Health Education	Classes and specialty programs	Some require copayments

EXCLUSIONS

LHP will not provide or cover services for:

1. Rehabilitative treatment programs for alcoholism or drug addiction unless specifically listed as an additional benefit.
2. Outpatient prescription drugs unless specifically listed as an additional benefit.
3. Care for military service connected disabilities.
4. Unusual circumstances such as complete or partial destruction of facilities, war, riot, disability of a significant number of providers, or similar events, provided LHP shall make a good faith effort to provide or arrange covered benefits.
5. Organ transplants, except services to recipient for kidney and corneal transplants, and liver transplants for children with biliary atresia, where the recipient is a Member, and bone marrow transplants for specified blood conditions.
6. The medical and hospital services of a donor when the recipient of an organ transplant is not a Member.
7. Prayer or spiritual healing or religious counseling.
8. Eye refractions and eyeglasses (unless specifically included as a benefit), corrective lenses, prosthetic eyes and other eye appliances, the fitting of either eyeglasses or hearing aids, and hearing aid batteries.
9. Experimental services.
10. Custodial care.
11. Medical supplies not provided during hospital confinement or a doctor's office visit.
12. Whole blood and blood plasma. (Currently New Mexico providers do not charge for blood.)
13. Long-term physical therapy and rehabilitation.
14. Services not generally recognized as medically necessary, such as:
    a. Behavioral training
    b. Sex change procedures.
    c. Reversal of voluntary sterilization.
    d. Extra corporeal insemination and *in vitro* pregnancies.
15. Vocational rehabilitation.

EMERGENCY CARE

An emergency is a sudden, acute and unexpected medical condition which, if not immediately diagnosed and treated, could lead to disability or death.

1. Within a 40-mile radius of a Lovelace facility, LHP covers reasonable charges for emergency service received at a non-Lovelace medical facility only if delay caused by coming to a Lovelace facility would result in death or serious disability.

EXHIBIT 4.8
Custom

✚ LOVELACE
Lovelace Health Plan
Summary of Benefits

LHP Provides the Following Benefits when Medically Necessary and only when Provided or Arranged by your Primary Care Physician. Copayments are due at the time of service.

Services		Cost
Office Visits	Physician, Nurse Practitioner, and Physician Assistant Services—Diagnosis and treatment—Specialist's care and consultation when referred by your Primary Care Physician—Adult or Pediatric check-ups—Minor surgery—Radiation therapy—No limit on number of encounters	No charge
Outpatient Surgery	Services not requiring hospital admission	No charge
Other Outpatient Services	Laboratory and X-ray procedures	No charge
	Mammography	
	Casts and dressings	
	Injections—Specified immunizations—Administered drugs and medications	
	Allergy injections	
	Voluntary family planning services	
Hospital Admission	Physician's and surgeon's services, including operations and specialist's consultations	No charge
	Room and board in semi-private accommodations—Private room (when medically necessary), intensive care, and coronary care—Use of the operating room, anesthesia, general nursing	
	Drugs and medications-injections—X-ray—Radiation therapy—Laboratory tests—Inhalation therapy	
	Casts and dressings—Administration of blood and blood derivatives	
Emergency Room For medical emergencies only*	All necessary services and supplies	$20.00 per visit in and out of the service area
Urgent Care	All necessary services and supplies at Lovelace Urgent Care facilities	No charge
Surgical Sterilizations	Outpatient Procedures	No charge
	Inpatient Procedures	No charge
Extended Care	Skilled nursing care—Room and board—Laboratory and X-Ray—Tests—Physician's services—Physical therapy—Drugs and medications	No charge

*SEE MEMBER HANDBOOK & CERTIFICATE FOR EXCLUSIONS, LIMITATIONS AND EMERGENCY CARE INFORMATION.

marily because of LHP expansion. In contrast, the modest growth trends among the Albuquerque clinics is attributed to the expansion of the entire clinic system in Albuquerque, the completion of new facilities at the Gibson site, and responses by competitors (i.e., competitive actions to capture market share).

Hospital Utilization

LMCI had recently completed construction on a new 238-bed general hospital. The old hospital was converted into clinic space. The new facility provided additional diagnostic and treatment ability. The LMCI philosophy of out-

EXHIBIT 4.8 cont'd

Services		Cost
Mental Health	Inpatient services (hospital, physician, and other professional services)—up to 30 days per contract year. One day of inpatient care is equivalent to *two* days of partial hospitalization. (Partial hospitalization is a non-residential program which includes various daily and weekly therapies.) A member is therefore entitled to 30 inpatient days or 60 partial hospitalization days, or any combination thereof, per contract year. Using one inpatient day uses up two partial hospitalization days; using two partial hospitalization days uses one inpatient day. **At no time will LHP allow a greater benefit than 30 inpatient days per contract year.**	No charge
	Outpatient services—up to 80 units per contract year or a minimum of 20 visits. 1 unit is equal to 15 minutes	$5.00 per unit not to exceed $20.00 per visit
Maternity Care	Pre-natal and post-natal care	No charge
	All physician and hospital services for mother during confinement, including but not limited to, full term delivery, miscarriage, or termination of pregnancy	No charge
Newborn Care	Child is covered from birth but must be enrolled within 31 days	No charge
Home Health Services	Physician house calls	$5.00 per visit
	Prescribed home nursing care	No charge
Other Services	Ambulance service* *(unless transport is between medical facilities or results in hospital admission)*	$30 per transport
	Up to 6 months of short-term physical therapy, occupational therapy, chiropractic therapy, and speech therapy per condition which is reasonably expected to improve significantly within two months	No charge for outpatient visits
	Alcohol and drug abuse detoxification	No charge
	Hemodialysis (member must make prompt application for Medicare benefits)	No charge
	Specified hospice care services which are reasonable and necessary for the palliation or management of terminal illness	No charge
	Eye and ear screening exams by Primary Care Physician to determine need for correction through age 17	No charge
	Specified durable medical equipment and appliances when prescribed	20% of charges
	Special Programs: —Infertility treatment —Weight reduction for morbid obesity	50% of charges
Health Education	Classes and specialty programs	Some require copayments

EXCLUSIONS

LHP will not provide or cover services for:

1. Rehabilitative treatment programs for alcoholism or drug addiction unless specifically listed as an additional benefit.
2. Outpatient prescription drugs unless specifically listed as an additional benefit.
3. Care for military service connected disabilities.
4. Unusual circumstances such as complete or partial destruction of facilities, war, riot, disability of a significant number of providers, or similar events, provided LHP shall make a good faith effort to provide or arrange covered benefits.
5. Organ transplants, except services to recipient for kidney and corneal transplants, and liver transplants for children with biliary atresia, where the recipient is a Member, and bone marrow transplants for specified blood conditions.
6. The medical and hospital services of a donor when the recipient of an organ transplant is not a Member.
7. Prayer or spiritual healing or religious counseling.
8. Eye refractions and eyeglasses (unless specifically included as a benefit), corrective lenses, prosthetic eyes and other eye appliances, the fitting of either eyeglasses or hearing aids, and hearing aid batteries.
9. Experimental services.
10. Custodial care.
11. Medical supplies not provided during hospital confinement or a doctor's office visit.
12. Whole blood and blood plasma. (Currently New Mexico providers do not charge for blood.)
13. Long-term physical therapy and rehabilitation.
14. Services not generally recognized as medically necessary, such as:
    a. Behavioral training
    b. Sex change procedures.
    c. Reversal of voluntary sterilization.
    d. Extra corporeal insemination and *in vitro* pregnancies.
15. Vocational rehabilitation.

EMERGENCY CARE

An emergency is a sudden, acute and unexpected medical condition which, if not immediately diagnosed and treated, could lead to disability or death.

1. Within a 40-mile radius of a Lovelace facility, LHP covers reasonable charges for emergency service received at a non-Lovelace medical facility only if delay caused by coming to a Lovelace facility would result in death or serious disability.
2. Elsewhere, LHP covers reasonable charges for emergency services.
3. Members need to notify LHP within 48 hours after care is provided at a non-Lovelace facility.
4. All follow-up or continuing care must be arranged through your LHP Primary Care Physician.
5. For members residing in Santa Fe, Los Alamos or Espanola, local emergency rooms may be used.

EXHIBIT 4.9

Major LHP Accounts

Organization	Number of Eligibles	Percent of Penetration		
		1988	1989	1990
Public Service Company of New Mexico (PNM)	2,700	16	18	25
Intel Corporation	1,650	38	48	42
General Electric	1,300	42	43	58
Sunwest Bank	2,300	25	30	25
Honeywell	3,500	44	49	48
U.S. West Communications	4,200	19	19	27
City of Albuquerque	3,000	59	67	69
University of New Mexico (UNM)	6,000	28	41	42
New Mexico Public Schools	7,000	11	10	15
Los Alamos National Laboratories	7,000	6	7	9
Albuquerque Public Schools	6,500	39	49	43
State of New Mexico	13,000	49	42	50
Signetics	800	53	72	42
Albuquerque Publishing	600	56	79	70

Note: Numbers are disguised.
Source: Company documents.

EXHIBIT 4.10

Lovelace Health Plan Enrollment by Age in September 1990

Age	Male	Female	Total
0–1	1,565	1,373	2,938
2–4	2,719	2,644	5,363
5–19	17,001	16,324	33,325
20–44	21,669	24,732	46,401
45–64	11,334	12,763	24,097
65–69	1,543	2,630	4,173
70–74	1,100	1,473	2,573
75–79	643	1,211	1,854
80–84	334	673	1,007
85+	213	379	592
Unknown	7	6	13
Total	58,128	64,208	122,336

Note: Numbers are disguised.
Source: Company documents.

EXHIBIT 4.11
Location of Lovelace Facilities

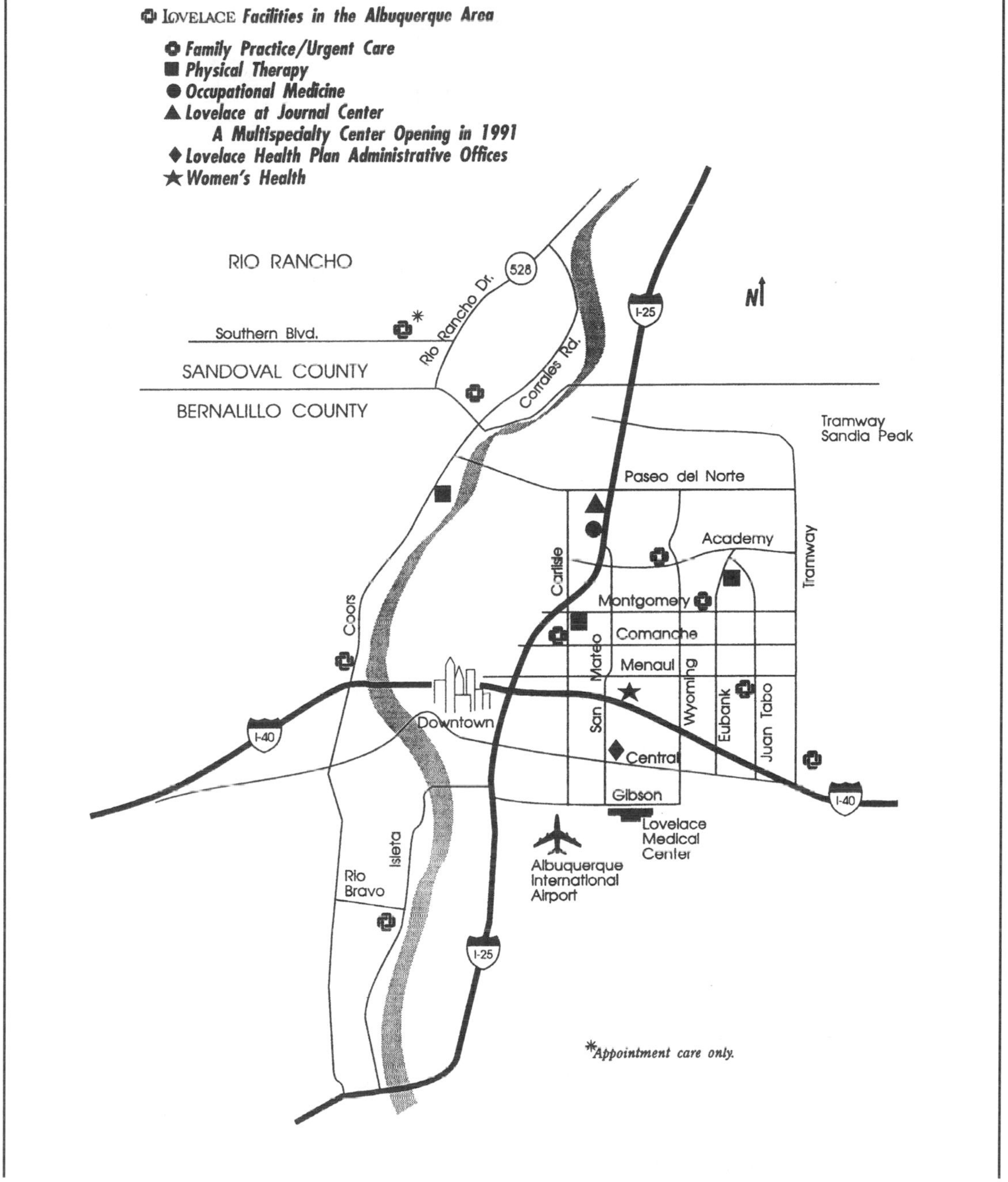

Lovelace *Facilities in the Albuquerque Area*

✚ *Family Practice/Urgent Care*
■ *Physical Therapy*
● *Occupational Medicine*
▲ *Lovelace at Journal Center*
    A Multispecialty Center Opening in 1991
◆ *Lovelace Health Plan Administrative Offices*
★ *Women's Health*

RIO RANCHO

Southern Blvd.

SANDOVAL COUNTY

BERNALILLO COUNTY

Rio Rancho Dr.

Corrales Rd.

528

I-25

N↑

Tramway
Sandia Peak

Paseo del Norte

Academy

Carlisle

Montgomery

Comanche

Menaul

San Mateo

Wyoming

Eubank

Juan Tabo

Tramway

Coors

I-40

Downtown

★

◆ Central

Gibson

Lovelace
Medical
Center

I-40

I-25

Isleta

Rio
Bravo

Albuquerque
International
Airport

Appointment care only.

EXHIBIT 4.11　*cont'd*

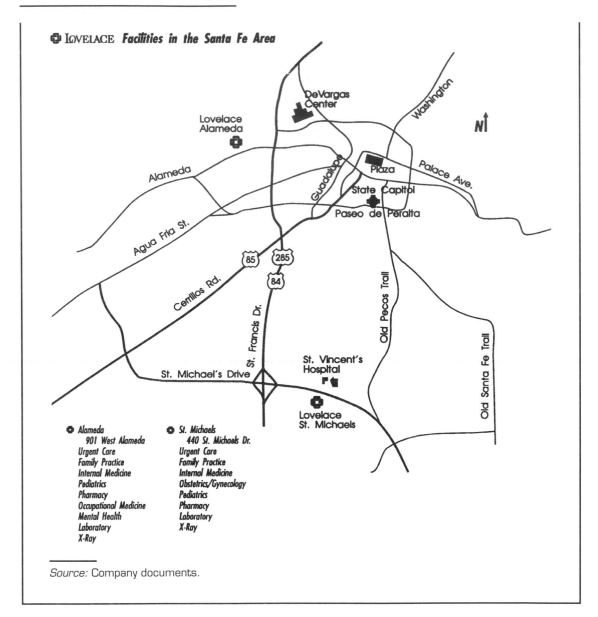

✚ LOVELACE *Facilities in the Santa Fe Area*

DeVargas Center

Washington

N↑

Lovelace Alameda

Alameda

Guadalupe

Plaza

Palace Ave.

State Capitol

Paseo de Peralta

Agua Fria St.

85　285

84

Cerrillos Rd.

St. Francis Dr.

Old Pecos Trail

Old Santa Fe Trail

St. Michael's Drive

St. Vincent's Hospital

Lovelace St. Michaels

✚ *Alameda*
　901 West Alameda
Urgent Care
Family Practice
Internal Medicine
Pediatrics
Pharmacy
Occupational Medicine
Mental Health
Laboratory
X-Ray

✚ *St. Michaels*
　440 St. Michaels Dr.
Urgent Care
Family Practice
Internal Medicine
Obstetrics/Gynecology
Pediatrics
Pharmacy
Laboratory
X-Ray

Source: Company documents.

patient care has been substantially aided by the new facility. As the 1987 through 1989 statistics in Exhibit 4.13 imply, LMCI continues to register a slight decrease in admissions. There were declines of 1.1 percent for 1987–1988 and .9 percent for 1988–1989.

Despite the gradual decrease in admissions, the average length of stay (ALOS) has been increasing. For any capitated health care provider (HMO), a longer ALOS is a potential danger signal, but this trend must be seen in relation to LMCI's attempts to lower admis-

EXHIBIT 4.12
Lovelace Clinic Visits, 1987–1989

	1987	1988	1989
TOTAL VISITS	**640,000**	**721,000**	**780,000**
Gibson Office			
Clinic visits	333,000	364,715	387,803
Northwest Office			
Clinic visits	18,930	24,070	26,256
Urgent care	20,620	21,297	23,510
Juan Tabo Office			
Clinic visits	30,423	33,055	32,518
Urgent care	25,916	26,289	25,487
Academy Office			
Clinic visits	33,803	36,937	36,034
Urgent care	14,648	15,196	15,600
Rio Bravo Office			
Clinic visits	13,859	19,855	19,116
Urgent care	27,831	26,288	24,938
San Pedro Office			
Clinic visits	0	2,995	6,152
Urgent care	20,056	18,746	15,820
Tramway Office			
Clinic visits	17,465	20,410	21,093
Urgent care	16,451	17,969	18,127
Carlisle Office			
Clinic visits	11,831	19,411	21,752
Urgent care	13,408	19,079	19,775
Occupational Medicine			
Clinic visits	9,915	13,865	19,335
Santa Fe Office			
Clinic visits	10,817	19,966	35,155
Urgent care	19,718	20,188	29,662

Note: Numbers are disguised; subject to rounding error.
Source: Company documents.

sions. It may be that more severe cases are being admitted, and it is also possible that physicians are altering their practice patterns to ensure high-quality care. Another explanation for the rise in ALOS could be that severe cases are entering from emergency care. Between 1988 and 1989, emergency cases increased 28.5 percent.

Services to mothers and children in the acute-care side of LMCI's business show some

---

EXHIBIT 4.13
Hospital Statistical Summary, 1987–1989

	1987	1988	1989
Admissions	10,930	10,806	10,706
Patient days			
Obstetrics	5,005	5,332	5,172
Pediatrics	3,036	3,111	2,872
Other	37,913	39,224	42,876
Newborn nursery	3,683	3,875	3,995
Deliveries	1,910	2,061	2,024
Average length of stay (in days)	4.58	4.76	4.92
Emergency Center visits	22,868	27,732	29,208

Note: Numbers are disguised; subject to rounding error.
Source: Company documents.

---

fluctuations. There is no consistent trend for hospital use by obstetrics or pediatrics or in the number of deliveries. The newborn nursery has shown slight increases from 1987 to 1989.

Fiscal Trends

LMCI's income statement and balance sheet are shown in Exhibits 4.14 and 4.15. It should be noted that the 1987 reported loss (before taxes) was $16,020,000. This was the only year in the past six years in which a loss was reported. Causal factors explaining the loss include high operating expenses and low revenue relative to the capitated population. LMCI had not raised its HMO rates for several years as a way to remain competitive (given its full range of services and interest in delivering high quality). This strategy may have been effective despite the poor showing in 1987 in view of the turmoil among capitation plans in Albuquerque over the preceding six years. Few competitors reported positive income figures, and there have been several consolidations and restructurings of plan benefits and options.

It is interesting to observe fluctuations between fee-for-service and capitation revenues. There has been considerable discussion among medical staff members regarding the proper balance of service goals. Some concern has been expressed that LMCI neglected fee-for-service patients to promote the growth of the LHP. Others think that fee-for-service has a limited future as a payment policy.

PERTINENT PLANNING DATA

Strategic planning for LMCI's future should consider data on population growth, morbidity and mortality, and economic potential at the local and state levels. With LMCI's expansion to Santa Fe it is appropriate to consider changes occurring not only in Bernalillo and Santa Fe counties, but across the state as well.

Demographic and Economic Trends

Exhibit 4.16 depicts New Mexico's 1988 population density by county in terms of persons per square mile. Of the thirty-three counties,

EXHIBIT 4.14
Lovelace, Inc., Income Statement, 1987–1989

	1987	1988	1989
Revenues			
Fee-for-service	$63,800,000	$94,800,000	$110,000,000
Discounts and allowances	14,900,000	22,800,000	33,000,000
Net fee-for-service	48,900,000	72,000,000	77,000,000
Prepaid revenue	62,200,000	77,400,000	103,500,000
Other operating revenue	780,000	1,000,000	961,000
Total operating revenue	111,880,000	150,400,000	181,461,000
Expenses			
Payroll	42,000,000	48,500,000	55,000,000
Physician services	23,700,000	25,400,000	32,800,000
Lovelace Health Plan outside services	17,700,000	21,100,000	25,200,000
Supplies	15,500,000	16,800,000	22,600,000
Occupancy expense and other contracted services	21,100,000	24,400,000	26,850,000
Gross receipts tax	5,600,000	6,800,000	4,800,000
Interest expense	1,700,000	3,400,000	4,000,000
Other expenses	800,000	1,200,000	2,400,000
Total operating expenses	128,100,000	147,600,000	173,650,000
Net operating gain (loss)	(16,220,000)	2,800,000	7,811,000
Nonoperating gain (loss)	200,000	170,000	270,000
Net gain (loss) before taxes	$(16,020,000)	$2,970,000	$8,081,000

Note: Numbers are disguised; subject to rounding error.
Source: Company documents.

nine (27 percent) have a population density greater than thirteen people per square mile. The highest-density counties of Los Alamos, Sandoval, Santa Fe, Bernalillo, and Valencia are contiguous and present feasible service-expansion opportunities. The low population densities for other counties suggest serious obstacles to expanding LHP services. Over 80 percent of the counties qualify as rural for the majority of their populations. The rural nature of New Mexico implies limited economic development and the lack of a necessary base for

EXHIBIT 4.15

Lovelace, Inc., Balance Sheet, 1987–1989

	1987	1988	1989
Assets			
Cash	$1,000,000	$40,000	$2,640,000
Receivables	19,690,000	27,750,000	29,000,000
Less: doubtful accounts	(10,420,000)	(6,100,000)	(3,900,000)
Other receivables	112,000	2,400,000	1,540,000
Net receivables	9,382,000	24,050,000	23,560,000
Inventories and prepaid expenses	2,130,000	3,350,000	6,930,000
Total current assets	12,512,000	27,440,000	33,130,000
Notes receivable (HCA)	23,700,000	23,400,000	23,100,000
Other long-term assets and bonds	9,520,000	4,660,000	4,460,000
Property, plant, and equipment	77,840,000	93,020,000	101,200,000
Less: depreciation	(11,540,000)	(16,980,000)	(22,400,000)
Net property, plant, and equipment	99,520,000	104,100,000	106,360,000
Total assets	$112,032,000	$131,540,000	$139,490,000
Liabilities and equity			
Current liabilities			
Accounts payable	$4,592,000	$7,880,000	$10,840,000
Deferred medical expenses	4,144,000	8,658,000	7,480,000
Other	10,078,000	10,484,000	10,818,000
Total current liabilities	18,814,000	27,022,000	29,829,000
Other liabilities			
Bonds payable	28,000,000	28,150,000	27,830,000
Note payable (HCA)	35,620,000	43,179,000	42,170,000
Total other liabilities	63,620,000	71,329,000	70,000,000
Equity			
Capital	33,266,000	32,967,000	32,670,000
Retained earnings (deficit)	(3,668,000)	222,000	6,991,000
Total equity	29,598,000	33,189,000	39,661,000
Total liabilities and equity	$112,032,000	$131,540,000	$139,490,000

Note: Numbers are disguised; subject to rounding error.
Source: Company documents.

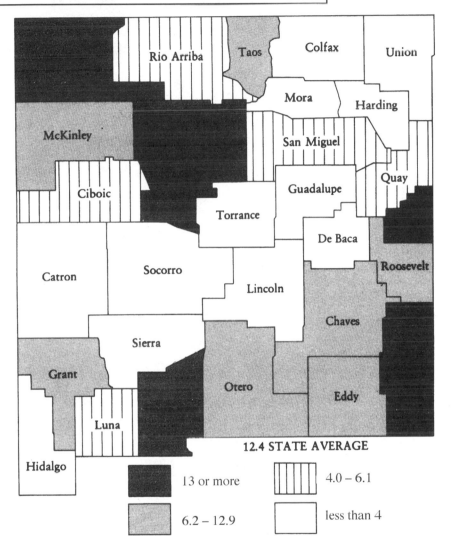

EXHIBIT 4.16

New Mexico Population Density by County, Persons per Square Mile, 1988

12.4 STATE AVERAGE

13 or more

4.0 – 6.1

6.2 – 12.9

less than 4

Source: *Selected Health Statistics New Mexico 1988* (Santa Fe: Health and Environment Department, Public Health Division, Vital Records and Statistics, May 1990), p. 10. Reprinted by permission.

EXHIBIT 4.17

**Per Capita Personal Income for
New Mexico and Selected Counties**

	1982	1983	1984	1985	1986	1987
New Mexico	$9,503	$9,837	$10,495	$11,188	$11,444	$11,861
Metropolitan areas						
Albuquerque	10,898	11,429	12,303	13,261	13,783	14,305
Las Cruces	7,758	8,315	8,524	9,051	9,331	9,578
Santa Fe	11,835	12,455	13,536	14,576	14,933	15,428
Counties						
New Mexico, Metropolitan	10,523	11,064	11,342	12,733	13,177	13,638
New Mexico, Nonmetropolitan	8,622	8,769	9,304	9,801	9,855	10,195
Bernalillo	10,898	11,429	12,303	13,261	13,783	14,305
Santa Fe	11,027	11,470	12,486	13,439	13,777	14,213

Source: Regional Economic Information System, Bureau of Economic Analysis, University of New Mexico, April 1989.

health insurance coverage via HMO models. Twenty-eight percent of all New Mexicans lack health insurance.

Greater insight of the economic considerations for HMO planning are gained from Exhibit 4.17, which presents the per capita income for New Mexico as a whole and selected counties from 1982 to 1987. The average per capita income for New Mexico in 1987 was $11,861. In contrast, Bernalillo and Santa Fe counties reported per capita incomes of $14,305 and $14,213, respectively, approximately 20 percent higher than the state average. Income in the metropolitan portion of Santa Fe county was even higher, at $15,428. Note that Las Cruces, which had the third-highest population density, had a per capita income of $9,578, or 67 percent of Albuquerque's figure.

Population projections for Bernalillo County and Santa Fe County are presented, respectively, in Exhibits 4.18 and 4.19. By 1990, Bernalillo was predicted to have over one-half million people, of whom 51.6 percent would be female. In contrast, Santa Fe County is projected at 94,600 people, of whom 51 percent would be female. The population of Bernalillo County grew by 10.2 percent from 1980 to 1985 and by 9.4 percent from 1985 to 1990.

The ethnic distribution in New Mexico is displayed in Exhibit 4.20. The data indicate that 36.3 percent of the state's population is Hispanic and 8.1 percent is Indian. By comparison, 55.0 percent of Santa Fe County's population is Hispanic and 2.8 percent is Indian. Bernalillo County is predominantly white non-Hispanic (56.9 percent). The county has 36.4 percent Hispanic residents.

EXHIBIT 4.18
Population Projections for Bernalillo County

Age Group	1980 Total	1980 Male	1980 Female	1985 Total	1985 Male	1985 Female	1990 Total	1990 Male	1990 Female
Total	421,500	205,800	215,700	464,500	225,600	238,900	508,300	246,100	262,200
<5 yrs	32,700	16,700	16,000	39,000	20,000	19,000	43,600	22,300	21,300
5–9	31,300	15,900	15,400	33,400	16,900	16,500	39,700	20,200	19,500
10–14	33,800	17,200	16,600	32,700	16,600	16,100	34,600	17,500	17,100
15–19	41,300	20,600	20,700	34,700	17,500	17,200	33,400	16,900	16,500
20–24	44,100	21,700	22,400	43,500	21,200	22,300	36,600	18,100	18,500
25–29	41,800	20,700	21,100	47,300	23,100	24,200	46,200	22,400	23,800
30–34	36,700	18,400	18,300	43,900	21,600	22,300	49,000	23,800	25,200
35–39	27,300	13,400	13,900	37,800	18,800	19,000	44,900	22,000	22,900
40–44	22,200	10,800	11,400	27,800	13,600	14,200	38,200	19,000	19,200
45–49	20,600	10,000	10,600	22,200	10,700	11,500	27,700	13,500	14,200
50–54	19,800	9,400	10,400	20,500	9,800	10,700	22,000	10,500	11,500
55–59	19,800	9,300	10,500	19,700	9,200	10,500	20,500	9,600	10,900
60–64	15,600	7,500	8,100	19,400	8,900	10,500	19,400	8,900	10,500
65–69	13,000	5,800	7,200	14,900	7,000	7,900	18,400	8,300	10,100
70–74	9,200	3,900	5,300	11,700	5,000	6,700	13,500	6,100	7,400
>75 yrs	12,000	4,400	7,600	15,800	5,500	10,300	20,500	7,100	13,400

Source: Bureau of Census, *Current Population Report,* Bureau of Economic Analysis, University of New Mexico, April 1989.

EXHIBIT 4.19
Population Projections for Santa Fe County

Age Group	1980 Total	1980 Male	1980 Female	1985 Total	1985 Male	1985 Female	1990 Total	1990 Male	1990 Female
Total	75,700	37,100	38,600	84,100	41,200	42,900	94,600	46,400	48,200
<5 yrs	5,900	3,000	2,900	7,100	3,600	3,500	8,700	4,400	4,300
5–9	5,900	3,000	2,900	6,300	3,200	3,100	7,500	3,800	3,700
10–14	6,400	3,300	3,100	6,200	3,100	3,100	6,500	3,300	3,200
15–19	7,000	3,500	3,500	6,600	3,400	3,200	6,400	3,200	3,200
20–24	6,200	3,100	3,100	7,200	3,600	3,600	6,700	3,400	3,300
25–29	7,100	3,500	3,600	6,700	3,300	3,400	7,600	3,800	3,800
30–34	7,300	3,700	3,600	7,800	3,800	4,000	7,500	3,700	3,800
35–39	5,400	2,700	2,700	7,800	3,900	3,900	8,300	4,100	4,200
40–44	4,300	2,100	2,200	5,600	2,800	2,800	8,100	4,100	4,000
45–49	3,600	1,800	1,800	4,400	2,200	2,200	5,800	2,900	2,900
50–54	3,400	1,600	1,800	3,600	1,800	1,800	4,500	2,200	2,300
55–59	3,200	1,500	1,700	3,400	1,600	1,800	3,700	1,800	1,900
60–64	2,800	1,300	1,500	3,200	1,500	1,700	3,500	1,600	1,900
65–69	2,400	1,100	1,300	2,700	1,200	1,500	3,100	1,400	1,700
70–74	1,900	800	1,100	2,300	1,000	1,300	2,500	1,100	1,400
>75 years	2,600	1,000	1,600	3,300	1,200	2,100	4,100	1,500	2,600

Source: Bureau of Census, *Current Population Report,* Bureau of Economic Analysis, University of New Mexico, April 1989.

EXHIBIT 4.20
New Mexico Racial Distribution by County, 1980

	White		Black	Indian	Other
	Non-Hispanic	Hispanic			
New Mexico	52.6%	36.3%	1.8%	8.1%	1.1%
Bernalillo	56.9	36.4	2.3	2.7	1.7
Santa Fe	40.8	55.0	.5	2.8	.8

Source: Selected Health Statistics New Mexico 1988 (Santa Fe: Health and Environment Department, Public Health Division, Vital Records and Statistics, May 1990), p. 11. Reprinted with permission.

Statewide Mortality and Morbidity

Exhibit 4.21 compares the leading causes of death in New Mexico with those in the United States. Most notable is the higher rate of heart disease for the United States as a whole compared to New Mexico. However, the proportions of deaths due to accident, suicide, or diabetes are twice the figures reported for the United States. The accident mortality rate may be explained by factors such as the rural, agrarian, and medically underserved nature of New Mexico. The higher diabetes rate may be attributed to the high prevalence of the disease among some Native American tribes, a mortality rate that is twice that of white non-Hispanics.

Further insight into mortality in New Mexico is gained from Exhibit 4.22, which lists the leading causes of death by ethnic group and race. Note among whites that although Hispanics are less likely than non-Hispanics to die due to diseases of the heart, malignant neoplasms, or chronic pulmonary disease, they are more likely to die due to accidents (especially automobile accidents), suicide, homicide, diabetes, or chronic liver disease/cirrhosis. Native Americans are especially susceptible to accidental death, suicide, diabetes, homicide, and chronic liver disease/cirrhosis relative to all races.

Finally, Exhibit 4.23 displays the communicable disease pattern for New Mexico from 1970 to 1988. Overall, the statistics imply mixed results for control of communicable disease. There are generally decreasing trends for shigellosis, tuberculosis, gonorrhea, and syphilis considering population growth. However, the rise in AIDS, hepatitis, and salmonella are alarming. By comparison, gains have been made in controlling rabies, plague, rubella, and typhoid.

Births and Deaths in Bernalillo County

Bernalillo county averaged 30 percent of all state births from 1986 to 1988, as suggested by the data in Exhibit 4.24. The three-year trends show mixed results among both Hispanic and non-Hispanic whites, but the Hispanic birth rate is the highest in Bernalillo County. Almost half (48 percent) of all births are to Hispanic mothers. Exhibit 4.24 indicates that roughly 60 percent of all births are to mothers ages 20 to 29 in both Bernalillo County and in the entire state.

Exhibit 4.25 examines births and deaths in Bernalillo County from the perspective of key residential areas. The data indicate that

EXHIBIT 4.21
Leading Causes of Death (percent of all deaths)

Causal Factor	New Mexico	United States
Diseases of the heart	27.0	35.3
Malignant neoplasms	21.2	22.5
Accidents	8.5	4.5
Stroke	6.0	6.9
Chronic obstructive pulmonary disease	4.4	3.8
Influenza and pneumonia	3.4	3.6
Suicide	3.3	1.4
Diabetes mellitus	2.7	1.8
Cirrhosis of the liver	1.9	1.2
Homicide	1.6	1.0
Conditions of perinatal period	1.1	0.9
Atherosclerosis	1.1	1.1
Nephritis, nephrotic syndrome, and nephrosis	1.0	1.0
Congenital anomalies	1.0	0.6
Alcoholism	0.7	0.2
Septicemia	0.7	1.0

Source: Selected Health Statistics New Mexico 1988 (Santa Fe: Health and Environment Department, Public Health Division, Vital Records and Statistics, May 1990), p. 39. Reprinted by permission.

2.7 births occur for each death. More births per death occur in rural Albuquerque, Tijeras, and at Sandia/Kirtland Air Force Base compared to other settings in Bernalillo County. These trends may have implications for planning HMO clinic locations.

The leading causes of death in Bernalillo County for the three-year period from 1986 to 1988 are portrayed in Exhibit 4.26. For the most part, Bernalillo County has death rates similar to New Mexico as a whole. These trends are fairly consistent with the data presented in Exhibit 4.21. Previous discussion already underscored the comparative differences with U.S. mortality rates.

Turning to mortality trends by age, Exhibit 4.27 depicts that 64.8 percent of all deaths in New Mexico occur among people 65 years of age or older. The age range of 75–84 years

has the highest mortality rate. The statistics for Bernalillo County are remarkably similar. Infant mortality is also shown in Exhibit 4.27. Again, there is consistency between Bernalillo County and New Mexico. Total infant and neonatal mortality rates have been declining slowly.

Births and Deaths in Santa Fe County

Santa Fe County has averaged 5.4 percent of all state births from 1986 to 1988, as displayed in Exhibit 4.28. The Hispanic birth rate is the highest of all ethnic groups in Santa Fe County. About 62 percent of all births are to Hispanic mothers. Exhibit 4.28 indicates that almost 60 percent of all births in New Mexico are to

---

EXHIBIT 4.22

Leading Causes of Death in New Mexico by Ethnic Group/Race, Percentage Distribution

Cause	All Races	White Non-Hispanic	Hispanic	Black	Indian
All causes	100.0%	100.0%	100.0%	100.0%	100.0%
Diseases of the heart	27.4	30.5	23.8	29.8	14.5
Malignant neoplasms	21.1	32.1	18.9	20.4	12.1
Accidents	8.7	6.0	10.9	6.4	23.0
(Motor vehicle)	(4.9)	(2.9)	(6.8)	(3.9)	(15.0)
(All other accidents)	(3.7)	(3.1)	(4.1)	(2.6)	(8.0)
Cerebrovascular disease	5.7	5.9	5.9	6.3	3.0
Chronic obstructive pulmonary disease	4.9	6.3	3.0	2.8	1.1
Influenza and pneumonia	3.4	3.4	3.3	1.8	3.7
Suicide	3.0	2.7	3.6	1.5	3.7
Diabetes mellitus	2.6	2.0	3.5	3.5	3.9
Chronic liver disease and cirrhosis	2.0	1.2	3.2	0.9	4.7
Homicide	1.7	0.9	2.9	4.6	3.7
Conditions of the perinatal period	1.1	0.7	1.5	3.7	1.9
Nephritis, nephrotic syndrome, and nephrosis	1.0	0.9	1.0	2.0	1.4
Atherosclerosis	1.0	1.1	0.8	0.9	0.2
Congenital anomalies	0.9	0.5	1.4	1.5	2.3
Alcoholism	0.7	0.3	0.9	0.0	3.0
Septicemia	0.6	0.6	0.6	0.4	1.1
All other	14.3	13.8	14.7	13.6	16.8

Source: Selected Health Statistics New Mexico 1988 (Santa Fe: Health and Environment Department, Public Health Division, Vital Records and Statistics, May 1990), p. 40. Reprinted with permission.

---

mothers ages 20 to 29 years. Santa Fe County only reports 51.2 percent of all births occurring in this age range. In contrast, Santa Fe County reports 33.7 percent of all births are to mothers ages 30 to 39; only 24.1 percent of all births in New Mexico are for mothers in this age range. Hence, a higher percentage of older mothers are giving birth in Santa Fe County relative to the rest of New Mexico.

Exhibit 4.29 examines births and deaths

EXHIBIT 4.23
Selected Communicable Diseases in New Mexico, 1970–1988

	1970	1971	1972	1973	1974	1975	1976	1977	1978	1979	1980	1981	1982	1983	1984	1985	1986	1987	1988
AIDS	*	*	*	*	*	*	*	*	*	*	*	1	0	0	4	16	31	51	56
Animal rabies	16	9	10	7	78	43	22	21	27	49	45	28	23	15	12	12	7	3	15
Dog	0	0	3	0	31	5	0	0	0	8	2	0	2	0	0	0	0	0	0
Cat	0	0	0	1	6	3	0	0	2	1	1	0	0	1	1	1	0	0	2
Bat	6	1	4	5	30	19	7	10	10	12	17	18	13	7	2	9	3	3	4
Skunk	8	7	2	1	11	13	10	9	14	27	25	10	8	7	8	2	4	0	6
Other	2	1	1	0	0	3	5	2	1	1	0	0	0	0	1	0	0	0	3
Diphtheria	1	8	12	42	17	9	3	5	0	0	0	0	0	0	0	0	0	0	0
Hepatitis	369	605	522	519	755	554	449	771	663	1,149	440	419	581	405	486	828	903	736	834
Measles	306	364	129	115	63	17	17	257	0	38	12	9	0	0	88	6	38	317	0
Pertussis	13	3	4	14	21	109	18	76	42	30	29	16	8	13	13	15	29	13	54
Plague	9	1	0	1	7	16	9	8	5	4	13	6	9	26	16	14	5	5	7
Rubella	237	251	128	174	130	19	4	11	4	12	5	5	6	0	1	2	0	0	0
Salmonella, nontyphoidal	102	88	94	154	104	96	83	116	265	184	212	327	259	409	327	406	410	461	329
Shigellosis	208	259	261	224	250	361	323	345	551	622	627	419	351	432	353	400	544	386	788
Tuberculosis	202	141	208	222	195	146	181	152	149	153	146	152	122	116	112	94	111	99	101
Typhoid	6	3	2	9	5	1	2	0	2	4	3	0	0	3	3	4	1	11	1
Gonorrhea	2,382	2,969	4,377	4,805	5,433	7,023	7,137	5,941	5,600	4,918	4,676	4,636	4,402	3,553	3,372	3,181	2,601	2,167	1,546
Syphilis																			
Infectious	128	162	223	183	184	284	285	180	145	159	218	248	321	350	189	237	162	122	134
Noninfectious	430	236	253	344	328	223	207	182	133	74	52	100	62	79	68	89	114	211	295

Source: Selected Health Statistics New Mexico 1988 (Santa Fe: Health and Environment Department, Public Health Division, Vital Records and Statistics, May 1990), p. 69. Reprinted by permission.

EXHIBIT 4.24

Birth Distribution by Age and Ethnicity of Mother in Bernalillo County

	1986	1987	1988
Live births	**8,074**	**8,468**	**8,157**
White			
Non-Hispanic	3,430	3,378	3,411
Hispanic	3,869	4,204	3,942
Black	249	275	255
Indian	371	421	394
Other	155	190	155
County percent of total state births	29.6%	31.1%	30.3%

Age of Mother	Bernalillo		New Mexico
	Number	**Percent**	**Percent**
All ages	**8,157**	**100.0%**	**100.0%**
<15	20	0.2	0.2
15–17	429	5.3	5.6
18–19	689	8.4	9.9
(15–19)	(1,118)	(13.7)	(15.5)
20–24	2,321	28.5	30.0
25–29	2,429	29.8	29.0
30–34	1,615	19.8	17.7
35–39	573	7.0	6.4
>40	81	1.0	1.1

Source: Selected Health Statistics New Mexico 1988 [Santa Fe: Health and Environment Department, Public Health Division, Vital Records and Statistics, May 1990], p. 11. Reprinted by permission.

in Santa Fe County in terms of key residential areas. The data indicate that 2.5 births occur in the same period for each death (this figure is slightly lower than that for Bernalillo County). The highest numbers of births per death are reported in rural Santa Fe and Pojoaque. Again, it is important to consider these trends when planning HMO services and site locations.

The leading causes of death in Santa Fe County for the three-year period from 1986 to 1988 are portrayed in Exhibit 4.30. For the most part, mortality rates in Santa Fe County by cause of death are strikingly parallel to New Mexico as a whole. However, it is important to remember that causes of death in the United States differ slightly from those in Santa Fe County.

Finally, 68 percent of all deaths in Santa Fe County occur among those 65 years of age or older, as shown in Exhibit 4.31. For the

EXHIBIT 4.25

Births and Deaths in Bernalillo County

Place of Residence, 1988	Births	Deaths	Births per 1 Death
Albuquerque, urban	7,268	2,899	2.5
Albuquerque, rural	472	128	3.7
Corrales*	0	9	0.0
Tijeras, all	102	19	5.4
Sandia/Kirtland AFB (military)	230	7	34.1
Other and unspecified	76	15	5.1
County total	8,157	3,077	2.7

Percent of County Resident Births

Born in county	98.93%
Born in other NM county	0.87%
Born out of state	0.20%

*Community in more than one county; includes births/deaths in county portion only.
Source: Selected Health Statistics New Mexico 1988 (Santa Fe: Health and Environment Department, Public Health Division, Vital Records and Statistics, May 1990), p. 72. Reprinted by permission

state, 64.8 percent of all deaths occur in this age range, indicating that people die at a later age in Santa Fe County. Turning to infant mortality in Exhibit 4.31, the infant and neonatal mortality rates for Santa Fe are considerably lower than for the rest of New Mexico.

CHALLENGE FOR THE FUTURE

Lovelace has been steadfastly willing to innovate and evolve. In contrast, many organizations become overly satisfied with their success and therefore are reluctant to take the next step forward. Lovelace has accepted the necessity of taking risks to develop and more effectively accomplish its mission. Not all of these efforts has been successful. For example, Lovelace attempted to establish a system of associated group practices throughout New Mexico during the late 1970s and early 1980s for the purpose of serving rural community health needs while offering a referral service. This experiment was only marginally successful and was ultimately dropped because it seemed unlikely that the initial objectives of the associated group practice system would be attained and other investment opportunities could be pursued.

The Lovelace Clinic and its subsequent configurations have remained a key source of effective health care in the Southwest. Like other providers, Lovelace has experienced its share of setbacks. However, by following several strategies centered around the multispecialty group practice model of organization, the adoption of an HMO model for financing and delivering services, the cultivation of patients and markets, and openness to innovation, Lovelace has remained resilient over the years. At this point, Lovelace must chart the future

EXHIBIT 4.26

Leading Causes of Death in Bernalillo County, 1986–1988

Cause	Deaths Observed	Deaths Expected	SMR[1]	Percent of Total Deaths		YPLL Rate[2]	
				County	NM	County	NM
Diseases of the heart	2,412	3,572	68	25.7%	27.4%	6.8	8.1
Malignant neoplasms	2,095	2,385	88	22.3	21.1	12.7	12.3
All accidents	692	543	127	7.4	8.7	15.7	20.6
Motor vehicle accidents	370	288	128	3.9	4.9	10.8	14.6
All other accidents	322	255	126	3.4	3.7	4.9	6.1
Cerebrovascular disease	562	687	82	6.0	5.7	1.3	1.3
Chronic obstructive pulmonary disease	486	374	130	5.2	4.9	1.2	1.1
Influenza and pneumonia	275	314	88	2.9	3.4	0.7	0.7
Suicide	322	179	180	3.4	3.0	8.2	7.6
Diabetes	234	188	124	2.5	2.6	1.1	1.2
Liver disease, cirrhosis	189	143	132	2.0	2.0	2.3	2.6
Homicide	211	127	166	2.2	1.7	6.4	5.1
Certain perinatal conditions	118	119	99	1.3	1.1	0.1	0.1
Nephritis, nephrotic syndrome	95	104	91	1.0	1.0	0.2	0.3
Congenital anomalies	96	77	125	1.0	0.9	1.1	0.9
Atherosclerosis	86	98	88	0.9	1.0	0.0	0.0
Alcoholism	51	24	213	0.5	0.7	0.8	1.1
Septicemia	49	93	53	0.5	0.6	0.1	0.2
All other causes	1,405	1,375	102	15.0	14.3	11.2	9.8
Total for all causes	9,378	10,402	90	100.0	100.0	69.9	73.0

[1]The SMR (standard mortality ratio) is the ratio of the observed deaths to the expected deaths times 100. The number of expected deaths is derived using national mortality as a standard and is age/sex adjusted.

[2]The YPLL (years of potential life lost) rate is per 1,000 population with deaths and population specific to ages 1–64.

Source: Selected Health Statistics New Mexico 1988 (Santa Fe: Health and Environment Department, Public Health Division, Vital Records and Statistics, May 1990), p. 72. Reprinted by permission.

EXHIBIT 4.27

Mortality Trends by Age in Bernalillo County

	Percent of Total Deaths	
Age	Bernalillo	New Mexico
All	100.0%	100.0%
<1	2.6	2.4
1–4	0.6	0.6
5–14	0.7	0.8
15–24	3.2	3.4
25–34	4.9	4.5
35–44	5.0	4.5
45–54	5.9	6.1
55–64	13.3	12.8
65–74	21.3	21.4
75–84	24.9	25.7
85+	17.6	17.7

EXHIBIT 4.27   cont'd

Infant Mortality

Bernalillo County	Total Infant		Neonatal		Postneonatal	
	Number	**Rate[1]**	**Number**	**Rate[1]**	**Number**	**Rate[1]**
1983	90	11.8%	52	6.8%	38	5.0%
1984	76	9.8	57	7.3	19	2.4
1985	99	12.5	60	7.6	39	4.9
1986	88	10.9	60	7.4	28	3.5
1987	71	8.4	42	5.0	29	3.4
1988	80	9.8	53	6.5	27	3.3
New Mexico, 1988	268	9.9	164	6.1	104	3.9

Infant = <1 year, Neonatal = <28 days, Postneonatal = 28 days to <1 year
[1]Rate per 1,000 live births
Source: Selected Health Statistics New Mexico 1988 (Santa Fe: Health and Environment Department, Public Health Division, Vital Records and Statistics, May 1990), p. 72. Reprinted by permission.

EXHIBIT 4.28

Birth Distribution by Age and Ethnicity of Mother in Santa Fe County

	1986	1987	1988
Live births	**1,486**	**1,451**	**1,484**
White			
Non-Hispanic	424	489	465
Hispanic	957	883	926
Black	16	12	11
Indian	76	56	68
Other	13	11	14
County percent of total state births	5.4%	5.3%	5.5%

Age of Mother	Santa Fe		New Mexico Percent
	Number	**Percent**	
All ages	**1,484**	**100.0%**	**100.0%**
<15	0	0.0	0.2
15–17	57	3.8	5.6
18–19	138	9.3	9.9
(15–19)	(195)	(13.1)	(15.5)
20–24	356	24.0	30.0
25–29	403	27.2	29.0
30–34	336	22.6	17.7
35–39	164	11.1	6.4
>40	30	2.0	1.1

Source: Selected Health Statistics New Mexico 1988 (Santa Fe: Health and Environment Department, Public Health Division, Vital Records and Statistics, May 1990), p. 123. Reprinted by permission.

EXHIBIT 4.29
Births and Deaths in Santa Fe County

Place of Residence, 1988	Births	Deaths	Births per 1 Death
Santa Fe, urban	966	482	2.0
Santa Fe, rural	282	33	8.5
Tesuque, all	16	6	2.7
Pojoaque, all	33	5	6.6
Espanola*	14	9	1.6
Chimayo*	8	5	1.6
Nambe, all	8	3	2.7
Other and unspecified	157	51	3.1
County total	1,484	594	2.5

Percent of County Resident Births
Born in county	86.93%
Born in other NM county	12.74%
Born out of state	0.34%

*Community in more than one county; includes births/deaths in county portion only.
Source: Selected Health Statistics New Mexico 1988 (Santa Fe: Health and Environment Department, Public Health Division, Vital Records and Statistics, May 1990), p. 124. Reprinted by permission.

EXHIBIT 4.30
Leading Causes of Death in Santa Fe County, 1986–1988

Cause	Deaths Observed	Deaths Expected	SMR[1]	Percent of Total Deaths County	NM	YPLL Rate[2] County	NM
Diseases of the heart	433	747	58	25.1%	27.4%	5.8	8.1
Malignant neoplasms	367	476	77	21.3	21.1	10.1	12.3
All accidents	141	104	136	8.2	8.7	15.9	20.6
Motor vehicle accidents	87	53	164	5.0	4.9	12.8	14.6
All other accidents	54	51	106	3.1	3.7	3.9	6.1
Cerebrovascular disease	102	147	69	5.9	5.7	1.0	1.3
Chronic obstructive pulmonary disease	87	74	118	5.0	4.9	0.4	1.1
Influenza and pneumonia	52	66	79	3.0	3.4	0.7	0.7
Suicide	73	35	209	4.2	3.0	9.9	7.6
Diabetes	46	39	118	2.7	2.6	1.0	1.2
Liver disease, cirrhosis	45	27	167	2.6	2.0	3.6	2.6
Homicide	24	21	114	1.4	1.7	3.3	5.1

EXHIBIT 4.30 cont'd

Cause	Deaths Observed	Deaths Expected	SMR[1]	Percent of Total Deaths		YPLL Rate[2]	
				County	NM	County	NM
Certain perinatal conditions	11	21	52	0.6	1.1	0.0	0.1
Nephritis, nephrotic syndrome	17	21	81	1.0	1.0	0.2	0.3
Congenital anomalies	15	11	136	0.9	0.9	1.5	0.9
Atherosclerosis	17	22	77	1.0	1.0	0.0	0.0
Alcoholism	15	4	375	0.9	0.7	1.3	1.1
Septicemia	8	18	44	0.5	0.6	0.0	0.2
All other causes	274	282	97	15.9	14.3	9.0	9.8
Total for all causes	1,727	2,115	82	100.0	100.0	63.6	73.0

[1]The SMR (standard mortality ratio) is the ratio of the observed deaths to the expected deaths times 100. The number of expected deaths is derived using national mortality as a standard and is age/sex adjusted.

[2]The YPLL (years of potential life lost) rate is per 1,000 population with deaths and population specific to ages 1–64.

Source: Selected Statistics New Mexico 1988 (Santa Fe: Health and Environment Department, Public Health Division, Vital Records and Statistics, May 1990), p. 124. Reprinted with permission.

EXHIBIT 4.31
Mortality Trends by Age in Santa Fe County

Age	Percent of Total Deaths, 1986–1988	
	Santa Fe	New Mexico
All	100.0%	100.0%
<1	1.5	2.4
1–4	0.3	0.6
5–14	0.4	0.8
15–24	3.5	3.4
25–34	4.7	4.5
35–44	5.3	4.5
45–54	5.9	6.1
55–64	10.4	12.8
65–74	19.9	21.4
75–84	27.0	25.7
85+	21.1	17.7

EXHIBIT 4.31   *cont'd*

	Infant Mortality					
	Total Infant		Neonatal		Postneonatal	
Santa Fe County	Number	Rate[1]	Number	Rate[1]	Number	Rate[1]
1983	5	3.7%	1	0.7%	4	2.9%
1984	13	9.2	9	6.3	4	2.8
1985	6	4.1	4	2.8	2	1.4
1986	11	7.4	7	4.7	4	2.7
1987	4	2.8	2	1.4	2	1.4
1988	11	7.4	5	3.4	6	4.0
New Mexico, 1988	268	9.9	164	6.1	104	3.9

Infant = <1 year, Neonatal = <28 days, Postneonatal = 28 days to <1 year
[1]Rate per 1,000 live births
Source: Selected Health Statistics New Mexico 1988 (Santa Fe: Health and Environment Department, Public Health Division, Vital Records and Statistics, May 1990), p. 124. Reprinted by permission.

course of its health plan and determine how the LHP fits relative to the rest of the organization.

NOTE

Sections of this case have been adapted from R. Gillock, H. L. Smith, and N. F. Piland, "For-Profit and Nonprofit Mergers: Concerns and Outcomes," *Hospital & Health Services Administration* 31, no. 6 (November/December 1986), pp. 74–84; and N. F. Piland and H. L. Smith, "The Lovelace Medical Center: Strategies for Advancing Health Care Services in the Southwest," *Journal of Medical Practice Management* 4, no. 3 (Winter 1989), pp. 190–196. Additional insight on Lovelace can be gained from J. W. Spidle, *The Lovelace Medical Center* (Albuquerque: University of New Mexico Press, 1987).

New England Health Plan

I'm really exasperated, Jim! I can't get my cases booked during my scheduled OR sessions because the hospital tells me there isn't enough time. I can get the emergency cases on the schedule, but the patients who need nonemergency surgery have to wait longer than they'd like. Then I have to wait around for over an hour between cases. I don't get it. The schedule isn't that tight, but we can't get cases booked!

To Dr. James Stevens, the planwide chief of Obstetrics and Gynecology (OB/GYN) at New England Health Plan (NEHP), Dr. Julia Hartman's complaint was familiar: the surgeons did not have enough operating room (OR) time to schedule their patients' surgery. Nonemergency surgical cases were placed on waiting lists because there was no available time. These patients were waiting two months for surgery, sometimes longer, and even though these waits did not affect their health, Dr. Stevens believed the delays lowered patient perception of service quality.

To top off his morning, no sooner had Dr.

This case was prepared by Janelle Heineke and Paul E. Morrison from Boston University. It is intended as a basis for classroom discussion rather than to illustrate effective or ineffective handling of an administrative situation. Copyright © 1993 by the *Case Research Journal* and the authors. Used with permission from Janelle Heineke.

Hartman left his office than Dr. Gordon called. Dr. Gordon, the Chairman of the Surgical Care Committee, told Dr. Stevens that he had been watching the OB/GYN OR utilization:

Jim, your OR utilization is way too low! You tell me your service needs OR time and then your doctors don't book it. There are other services that need the time more than OB/GYN apparently does. Use it or lose it! I'll see you at the surgical care committee meeting in three days. You can tell us your plan then, but at this point I can't think of any reason not to reallocate 20 percent of OB/GYN's operating time to specialties that will use it.

Dr. Stevens wondered how there could be low utilization and long waits at the same time. It just didn't make sense. He looked around his office. His desk was buried under stacks of papers, his in-box was full of work he needed to sort through, he had a full afternoon schedule of his own patients booked at the Health Center, and he was due in the OR in twenty minutes.

Dr. Stevens had been planwide chief nearly one year and was still struggling to find enough hours in the day to practice medicine half-time and to deal with his new administrative responsibilities. He spent hours each week in meetings with the three associate medical directors to whom he reported and with the health center chiefs who reported to him (see Exhibits 5.1 and 5.2). He was actively trying to recruit new doctors and trying to keep the ones already on his staff satisfied with their NEHP practices. Dr. Stevens had known that the OR was a problem—but there just hadn't been time to analyze the situation. Now he had to find the time. He leaned back in his chair and thought to himself, "Maybe Dr. Gordon's right. We aren't using the OR time and other doctors need it. Are the OB/GYN doctors just griping, or are their complaints legitimate?"

HEALTH MAINTENANCE ORGANIZATIONS

In March 1989 the Health Centers Division of NEHP was New England's largest staff model health maintenance organization (HMO). HMOs became popular in the late 1970s and early 1980s with increasing public and private concern over rapidly rising health care costs. In 1989, one-fourth of Massachusetts residents belonged to an HMO and NEHP's share of the Massachusetts HMO market was 27 percent.

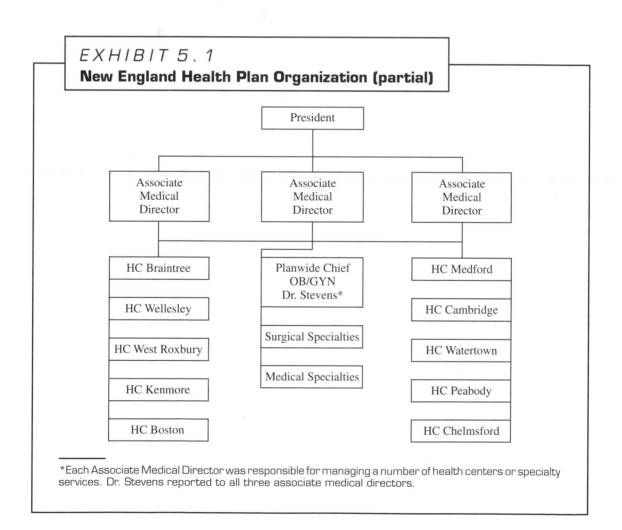

EXHIBIT 5.1
New England Health Plan Organization (partial)

*Each Associate Medical Director was responsible for managing a number of health centers or specialty services. Dr. Stevens reported to all three associate medical directors.

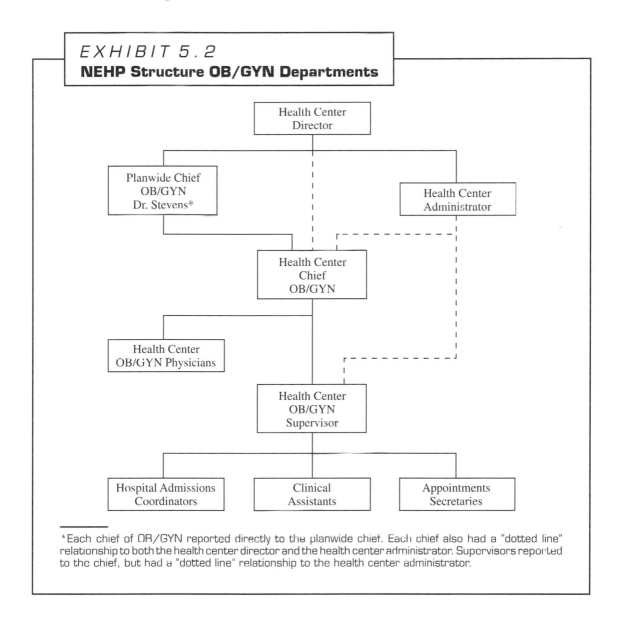

EXHIBIT 5.2
NEHP Structure OB/GYN Departments

```
                    Health Center
                      Director

  Planwide Chief
    OB/GYN                      Health Center
   Dr. Stevens*                 Administrator

                    Health Center
                       Chief
                      OB/GYN

  Health Center
  OB/GYN Physicians

                    Health Center
                      OB/GYN
                     Supervisor

Hospital Admissions      Clinical        Appointments
   Coordinators         Assistants        Secretaries
```

*Each chief of OB/GYN reported directly to the planwide chief. Each chief also had a "dotted line" relationship to both the health center director and the health center administrator. Supervisors reported to the chief, but had a "dotted line" relationship to the health center administrator.

As the name implies, HMOs focus not only on treatment of episodes of illness, but on maintaining the health of their patient members. Emphasis is placed on early diagnosis and treatment of medical problems, the philosophy being that such an approach is both better for the patient and less costly for the HMO.

HMO members and their employers choose HMOs for different reasons. Employers look for low premium rates for a given package of benefits. Members are concerned with their options for choice of physicians and facilities, services provided for the base premium fee, and out-of-pocket expense (which includes payments made at the time of visits and the employee's share of premium costs). HMO premiums are generally lower than traditional indemnity insurance plans.

HMO Cost Control Strategy

HMOs control costs in several ways. They take advantage of economies of scale when possible by negotiating reduced payment contracts with hospitals, specialty ambulatory services, supply and equipment vendors, pharmaceutical companies, and physician subspecialists. A primary care physician, usually a general practice or internal medicine physician, controls access to specialty services for individual patients. This physician "gatekeeper" refers patients for only those specialty services that are medically indicated, and to only those physicians employed by the HMO or community agencies under agreement to the HMO as preferred vendors.

Staff-Model and Group-Model HMOs

Staff-model physicians are typically salaried employees of the HMO. They usually provide services only to HMO members, although small numbers of fee-for-service patients may be accepted. Patients see physicians in their offices at health centers owned or leased by the HMO. For their medical care to be considered a covered part of their HMO benefit, staff-model HMO members must see HMO physicians.

Group-model HMOs differ from staff-model HMOs in that the physician groups also provide care to patients covered by traditional indemnity medical insurance; HMO members make up only part of their patient panel. In the group model, the physician group is paid on a per patient basis for each HMO member enrolled for care. The group is then responsible for providing care within the budget defined by the total payment. The group makes a profit if total costs of care for that panel are con-

tained, and may suffer a loss if costs exceed the total per patient amount.

IPAs

Individual practice associations (IPAs) are more loosely structured systems. Physicians practicing in their own offices in the community contract individually with a central insurer which contracts with and specifies the benefits available to member enrollees. IPA primary care physicians are usually paid on a capitated basis for their patient panel, and specialists are paid on a reduced fee-for-service basis for individual services provided. Both primary care and specialist physicians may share in profits achieved by the insurer if costs are contained, but the primary care physicians also carry some insurer risk if the care of the patient panel is not managed cost-effectively.

In IPAs, as in staff- and group-model systems, primary care gatekeepers are responsible for managing referrals to specialists, and agreements with hospitals and other vendors are negotiated centrally.

NEW ENGLAND HEALTH PLAN (NEHP): BACKGROUND AND HISTORY

NEHP opened its first staff-model health center in 1969 in Boston with 53,000 members and 35 full-time staff physicians. By February 1989, NEHP had ten health centers, with three more scheduled to open during the next year, a total membership of over 400,000, and a recently acquired group model division. Each health center housed physician offices, a clinical lab, a pharmacy, and administrative offices. In fiscal 1988 the Health Centers Division of NEHP received 1.3 million member visits, performed 1.4 million tests in its own health center labs, filled over 1 million prescriptions, and delivered nearly 5,000 babies.

Each health center was affiliated with one or more hospitals for inpatient care. Hospitals were chosen by location, facility standards, and reputation. Dr. Stevens was most concerned with the five health centers that used MassBay Hospital for inpatient care. These five centers were all located within five to thirty minutes from MassBay.

HEALTH CENTER STRUCTURE

Each health center provided office care in three primary care areas: internal medicine, pediatrics, and OB/GYN. Chiefs in each primary care area were responsible for managing that specialty's practice within the health center, including hiring staff physicians, reviewing clinical protocols, developing procedures for managing medical follow-up, and scheduling physician coverage for offices, on-call, and operating rooms. Each health center chief reported to the health center director (responsible for the financial control and operations of the health center), who in turn reported to one of the three associate medical directors, each of whom was responsible for managing a number of health centers or specialty services. Exhibit 5.2 shows the OB/GYN NEHP administrative structure.

OBSTETRICS AND GYNECOLOGY AT NEHP

Obstetrics (OB) is the branch of medicine that deals with pregnancy, whereas gynecology (GYN) is concerned with the reproductive system of women throughout their lives. OB/GYN physicians are also trained to perform surgery.

From the mid-1980s OB/GYN physicians had been in increasingly short supply. Fewer young physicians were choosing OB/GYN because it demands more nights on-call and awake than most other specialties, and because of the high risk of malpractice litigation and the associated costs of malpractice insurance.

OB/GYN staffing levels at NEHP were based on health center membership: one full-time OB/GYN physician was budgeted for each 2,750 adult female members. Each health center OB/GYN department had an OB/GYN hospital admissions coordinator (HAC) who scheduled major tests, procedures, and surgical operations. HACs reported to the supervisor for that health center's OB/GYN department, who in turn reported directly to the OB/GYN chief and indirectly on a "dotted line" relationship to the health center administrator. The chiefs of OB/GYN reported directly to the planwide chief, but also had a "dotted line" relationship to both the health center director and the health center administrator.

DR. STEVENS: THE PLANWIDE CHIEF

NEHP's decentralized structure had been designed with center-based specialties in mind. Pediatricians at one health center, for example, worked relatively independently of pediatricians at other health centers. In contrast, OB/GYN physicians spent half their time at the hospital, often working with physicians from other health centers. The unpredictability of patient arrivals in labor and in the emergency room meant OB/GYN health center groups needed to work together to cover busy times. Major practice issues were common to all NEHP OB/GYN health centers, including the need for a formalized back-up system for labor and delivery coverage, coordinated physician recruiting procedures to hire increasingly scarce doctors, and communication with hospital management and nursing staff.

To address those issues, the position of planwide chief of OB/GYN was created in 1988, and Dr. Stevens was appointed. Each health center OB/GYN chief continued to report to his or her health center director but also reported to Dr. Stevens. Dr. Stevens met every other week with the health center chiefs to discuss policies and procedures for OB/GYN practice at NEHP. He also joined several committees, such as the surgical care committee, which addressed issues that concerned several specialty services at NEHP.

THE SURGICAL CARE COMMITTEE

The surgical care committee was formed in 1988 to improve communication between MassBay Hospital OR leadership and NEHP surgeons and managers. The committee met each month to discuss problems that were encountered in the day-to-day use of the ORs, on-going systems issues, utilization statistics, and allocation of NEHP OR block time. Each month the committee reviewed statistics on the number of operations and hours for scheduled, add-on, and emergency surgery. Utilization rates were computed by dividing the total operating hours for each service, including required set-up times, by the total block time hours assigned to that specialty. The committee also reviewed canceled operations and no-shows so that downtime in NEHP operating rooms could be minimized.

The chairman of the surgical care committee was the Chief of General Surgery for NEHP, Dr. Gordon. General surgery's utilization rates were the highest of the specialties (105 percent), followed by orthopedics (95 percent), genitourinary surgery (74 percent), and OB/GYN (60 percent). General surgery's utilization rate of greater than 100 percent indicated that cases were booked outside that specialty's allocated block time, either as add-ons for urgent problems or as routine cases booked into nonallocated time through the "wait list" process. The general surgeons were pressuring Dr. Gordon for more OR time, so he was reviewing all specialty utilization, intending to reallocate if necessary. He said:

> The general surgeons and the orthopedic surgeons have made excellent use of their assigned block time. They

shouldn't have to backlog their operations because GYN time is poorly utilized. Now, I know that GYN is a different kind of practice than general surgery, but maybe the gynecologists are just going to have to be more flexible. This committee expects Dr. Stevens to either present a plan of action at April's surgical care committee meeting or to release 20 percent of his OB/GYN block time to other services to use. This reduction will clearly not cut into OB/GYN's active surgical hours—their utilization is only 60 percent.

SCHEDULING PHYSICIAN TIME

OB/GYN physician work schedules actually incorporated three schedules: operating room, on-call, and office service. The on-call schedule was constructed first. One health center of the five affiliated with MassBay Hospital covered its own on-call, while the other four worked in teams, two health centers on each team. Operating room time was then allocated to each physician, and finally the office schedule was developed.

About half of the work time of an OB/GYN physician was spent at the health center and the other half was spent at the hospital. Each week an OB/GYN physician at NEHP spent one 24-hour period on-call at the hospital covering the labor-delivery unit, the emergency room, and the high-risk prenatal service; 20 hours in the office; and 4 hours on continuing education. Each physician also expected to have one half-day session per month to perform GYN surgery. Exhibit 5.3 shows an OB/GYN physician's schedule for a typical month.

NEHP was committed to providing good service to its members. Access standards for OB/GYN had been established, stating that patients should be able to schedule a routine appointment within two weeks. Patients with

EXHIBIT 5.3

Typical Month's Schedule for an OB/GYN Physician

		Sunday	Monday	Tuesday	Wednesday	Thursday	Friday	Saturday
Week 1	A.M.	On-call	Off	Office	Education	Office	Off	Off
	P.M.	On-call	Off	Office	Office	Office	Off	Off
Week 2	A.M.	Off	Office	On-call	Education	Office	OR	Off
	P.M.	Off	Office	On-call	Off	Office	Office	Off
Week 3	A.M.	Off	On-call	Off	Education	Office	Office	Off
	P.M.	Off	On-call	Off	Office	Office	Office	Off
Week 4	A.M.	Off	Office	Office	Education	On-call	Off	Off
	P.M.	Off	Office	Office	Office	On-call	Off	Off

Note: On-call days involved twenty-four hours on-site at MassBay Hospital.
Office sessions were scheduled for four-hour blocks in either the morning or the afternoon.

urgent problems were seen within two days, usually by a physician designated "officer of the day" who was responsible for add-ons. Patients with emergency problems were seen in the MassBay Hospital emergency room by the on-call physician.

NEHP's policy stated that physicians should schedule their office times at least three months in advance so that patients could book appointments conveniently. Because NEHP patient members were "prepaid," patients could not be refused appointments when the schedule was full, as can happen in fee-for-service practices, which meant that appointments slots needed to be made available for last minute add-ons.

Despite the official policy, OB/GYN chiefs were reluctant to prepare schedules too far in advance for two reasons. First, a single change in an office, on-call, or OR schedule had a ripple effect: not only the physician in question but other physicians in the same office, physicians from other health centers on the same on-call team, and the MassBay OR schedule could be affected. Once the schedule had been finalized, usually four weeks or less

in advance, both supervisors and chiefs tried to keep changes to a minimum. As one chief said:

> I know we're supposed to have the schedules made out three months in advance, but who knows that far ahead what weekends they want off or what days their babysitters aren't available? I do my best to make out a schedule that won't need to be changed, and that usually means waiting until the middle of one month to finalize the schedule for the next month. Doctors get the schedules they want and the office staff are less likely to have to reschedule patients because their doctors decided to take a day off or leave on a last-minute vacation.

Another reason that the chiefs were reluctant to change the schedule was concern about member satisfaction. At NEHP patients expected scheduled appointments to be kept. This was considered part of their benefit, and was an important consideration for NEHP in a competitive environment. By contrast, most fee-for-service OB/GYN physicians spend time in the hospital only when they make rounds, have patients in labor, or perform surgery. If one patient requires care in the delivery room during office hours, other patients are rescheduled.

ALLOCATING AND SCHEDULING THE MASSBAY OPERATING ROOM

NEHP had negotiated the use of MassBay Hospital ORs in large blocks of time to permit efficient scheduling of NEHP surgeons. Block time allowed the physicians to schedule their surgical cases without affecting their office schedules.

Both NEHP and MassBay Hospital wanted OR utilization to be high. As a high-volume MassBay customer, NEHP negotiated an annual contract with the hospital. NEHP paid for full-time use of four operating rooms – one of them assigned to OB/GYN. If OR utilization was low, NEHP was essentially "overpaying." MassBay lost, too, because the rates paid by fee-for-service insurers were higher than the rates paid by NEHP. And Mass-Bay suffered an additional cost: when private physicians (non-NEHP) wanted OR time and couldn't get it, they considered taking their patients to other hospitals.

The OR was open for scheduled operations on weekdays; weekend and holiday surgery was performed on an urgent basis only. The first operation of the day could be booked to start at 7:30 A.M., and the last was scheduled for completion by 3:30 P.M. ORs functioned throughout the day, with no scheduled breaks. On Wednesday mornings surgery started later because the anesthesiologists and general surgeons held their department meetings from 7:30 to 9:30 A.M.

The OR schedules were usually distributed two months in advance of booking dates. Tuesdays were blocked off for the NEHP fertility and endocrinology service, a subspecialty OB/GYN department that also reported to Dr. Stevens. One of the health center supervisors to-

taled the number of remaining OR days available in the month and allocated time to the health centers in half-day blocks based on the number of members enrolled in each center. Exhibit 5.4 provides membership data for the second half of 1988, and Exhibit 5.5 shows NEHP OB/GYN allocations for a typical month.

After the hospital on-call schedule was completed, the OB/GYN chiefs assigned each of the half-day OR blocks to a single physician. If there were more blocks assigned than OB/GYN physicians working in a health center during a given month, the busiest physician at that center would be assigned additional blocks. Once the OR time had been assigned to physicians and the on-call schedule fixed, the chief could prepare the office schedule and the appointment secretaries could "open the books" for members to schedule office visits.

If an OB/GYN physician at one health center needed additional OR time during a given month, the responsible hospital admissions coordinator might try to "borrow" time from another health center's HAC. However, calling each of the other four HACs was a time-consuming process that was rarely fruitful. Other than these contacts, HACs had no regular opportunities to communicate with each other in person. In fact, although some had occasionally talked on the telephone, they had not all met.

Although some OB/GYN physicians performed more surgery than others (either because of personal practice style or because of differences in their mix of patients), even the less surgically inclined physicians were reluctant to give up their OR time. One HAC said:

> I don't dare give away my doctors' OR time. If an operation came up at the last minute and the time was gone there would be a real scene. And never mind asking the doctors. None of them will give their time away – they hold onto it "just in case." And besides, I

EXHIBIT 5.4
Membership in NEHP, June–December 1988

	June	July	Aug.	Sept.	Oct.	Nov.	Dec.
Center							
Kenmore	54,905	54,905	54,905	54,448	53,581	52,608	52,608
Wellesley	31,191	31,191	31,191	31,205	31,444	31,802	31,802
Braintree	29,909	29,909	29,909	30,479	32,000	32,213	32,213
Boston	24,923	24,923	24,923	26,527	27,170	28,391	28,391
West Roxbury	13,569	13,569	13,569	14,142	14,690	15,662	15,662
Total	154,497	154,497	154,497	156,801	158,885	160,676	160,676
Blocks assigned	Actual	Actual	Actual	Actual	Actual	Actual	Actual
Kenmore	13	11	11	9	9	10	10
Wellesley	7	6	7	7	7	6	6
Braintree	7	6	6	7	7	6	6
Boston	6	5	6	6	5	5	6
West Roxbury	3	3	3	3	4	3	4
Total	36	31	33	32	32	30	32
Total available half-day blocks	44	39	43	40	40	40	40
Blocks assigned to fertility	8	8	10	8	8	10	8
Blocks available for GYN	36	31	33	32	32	30	32

Note: NEHP membership data updating had been done every third month prior to September, 1988.
Source: NEHP.

EXHIBIT 5.5
Typical OB/GYN Monthly Block Assignment

		Monday	Tuesday	Wednesday	Thursday	Friday
Week 1	A.M.		Fertility	Braintree	Wellesley	Kenmore
	P.M.		Fertility	Boston	Kenmore	Boston
Week 2	A.M.	Kenmore	Fertility	Kenmore	Braintree	Kenmore
	P.M.	Braintree	Fertility	Braintree	Wellesley	Boston
Week 3	A.M.	Holiday	Fertility	Wellesley	Boston	Wellesley
	P.M.	Holiday	Fertility	Wellesley	Kenmore	West Roxbury
Week 4	A.M.	Kenmore	Fertility	Boston	West Roxbury	Kenmore
	P.M.	Braintree	Fertility	Kenmore	Kenmore	Braintree
Week 5	A.M.	West Roxbury	Fertility			
	P.M.	Wellesley	Fertility			

can never get time from anyone else when my doctors need it, so why should I give my time away?

BOOKING OPERATIONS FOR OPERATING ROOMS

Once blocks were assigned to individual physicians, the procedure for booking an operation was fairly simple. The HAC called the hospital scheduling office to provide the necessary information, including the time the surgeon anticipated the operation would require. More detailed patient information was then sent from NEHP to MassBay by mail.

The HACs often had trouble trying to book more than one operation in a block. One stated:

> The scheduling department at the hospital won't let me book an operation out of my time. If I have two major procedures to schedule for one doctor, I can never book them together because the two operations would run longer than a single block, and some other health center has the other half of the day. I have no way to move operations around to solve the problem.

Another commented:

> I do try to borrow time, and every once in a while I can find some time that no one is using, but I have to make so many phone calls. I have to call each health center, sometimes more than once, to be sure the doctor approves. Then I have to call the hospital to let them know that I'll be booking outside my usual times. It's such a hassle.

When NEHP block time for any service was still unscheduled five working days before the date, the time was given back to MassBay Hospital for use by any surgeon – NEHP or not – who could use it. Surgeons who wanted to schedule an operation but who had no block time remaining could put an operation on the hospital wait list. Two days before the requested date, the hospital would contact the surgeon to confirm whether the operation was scheduled. Although this procedure created uncertainty, it did help the surgeons schedule more operations than they could perform if they were limited to assigned blocks.

MANAGEMENT OF THE MASSBAY HOSPITAL OPERATING ROOM

Like Dr. Hartman, most of the OB/GYN physicians complained about the difficulty in scheduling surgery. They also complained about very long waits between operations.

"Major" operations take two to three hours to perform, whereas "minor" operations usually require fifteen to sixty minutes of actual operating time. Generally, OB/GYN physicians at NEHP performed one or more major operations and two or more minor operations per month, but this varied widely. These operations could be booked either at a particular start time (such as 7:30 A.M.) or, if a surgeon was performing two or more operations in succession, on a "to follow" basis. "To follow" means that the second operation would start as soon as the OR was ready after the first. Although the standard time scheduled for cleaning and set-up between operations was thirty minutes, the average was actually forty minutes. Surgeons often complained of waiting an hour or more between operations. This was especially frustrating because they believed that the cleaning and set-up could be accomplished in fifteen minutes or less. This belief was based on their experiences at other hospitals and at for-profit "surgi-centers," where patients are not admitted overnight and only minor surgical procedures are performed. One physician said:

> The waits drive me crazy, especially between minor operations! Even if I finish my first one early, there's no way I get to start the "to-follow" before the scheduled time. In fact, usually that operation starts late, too.

The cleaning and set-up tasks between operations were straightforward and were carried out by an OR support crew. First, nurses brought the patient from the OR to the recovery room. Next, the clean-up crew removed soiled instruments from the OR and the room was cleaned (see Exhibit 5.6). Staff members then brought in instruments and supplies for the next operation and set them up. Finally, the next patient was brought into the room and prepared for surgery. While the anesthetic was being administered, the surgeon and his or her assistant scrubbed their hands and donned masks, gowns, and gloves. At the same time, the circulating nurse made sure that all equipment and supplies were in order, and the scrub nurse or technician opened and arranged the appropriate instruments.

Anesthesiologists were employed by MassBay Hospital and paid a flat monthly sal-

---

EXHIBIT 5.6
Procedure for Cleaning the Operating Room

Equipment:
  Mop
  Floor bucket (change water as necessary)
  Spray disinfectant solution
  Rubber gloves

Step[1]	Time[2]
1. Note time on clean-up sheet	
2. Call anesthesia	1 minute
3. Put gloves on	
4. Pick up trash and soiled linen and place in dirty case cart (3)	3 minutes
5. Check wall suction bottle; if soiled, place in dirty case cart and replace with clean unit. (3)	4 minutes
6. Remove case cart	2 minutes
a. Push case cart out of room (4, 5)	
b. Send to Central Sterilizing Area on elevator (6a)	
7. Move operating table (6a)	.5 minute
8. Wash room (7)	4 minutes
a. Wipe furniture	
b. Wipe lights	
c. Wipe spots from walls as needed	
d. Mop floor (8a, b, c)	
9. Bring clean linen into room (8)	1 minute
10. Make bed (9)	2 minutes
11. Put new linen and trash bags in place (8)	1 minute
12. Note time room cleaning completed on clean up sheet (all)	

---

[1]Numbers in parentheses are steps which must be completed before task can be performed.
[2]Times are observed times for one worker to perform task.

ary. OR nurses and support staff, both union-ized groups employed by MassBay, were paid flat salaries as well, earning overtime pay when the standard forty-hour work week was ex-ceeded. OR staff was usually assigned by room, rather than by operation. The support staff felt that working on multiple short opera-tions was more stressful and hectic than work-ing on a single, long, complicated operation.

SOLVING THE OPERATING ROOM PROBLEM

Dr. Stevens had been very successful at recruit-ing new physicians and at standardizing poli-cies—but those issues did not affect individual health center practices. The OR problem was different. Dr. Stevens said:

It's not up to me to tell the chiefs or the HACs how to handle their surgical booking. It is up to me to do some-thing, or OB/GYN will lose some of its block time. I don't like to think of what that will do to waiting times for nonemergency surgical services. Not to mention the effect on the offices!

Dr. Stevens requested data on OB/GYN's utilization of OR time throughout the day and week and the number of operations performed and total OR hours by physician. Exhibits 5.7 and 5.8 present this information in tabular form. Exhibit 5.7 shows all blocks of ninety minutes or longer either unused or used by services other than NEHP OB/GYN during the month of January 1989. For example, there were two Mondays during January when, start-

---

EXHIBIT 5.7
Unused and Non-OB/GYN OR Time, January 1989

Time	Monday	Tuesday	Wednesday	Thursday	Friday	Total
07:30 AM	2	3		1	2	8
08:00 AM					1	1
08:30 AM						0
09:00 AM	1	1				2
09:30 AM		1				1
10:00 AM			1	1	1	3
10:30 AM	1	2	1	1		5
11:00 AM		1		1		2
11:30 AM			1		1	2
12:00 PM	1	1		2	1	5
12:30 PM		2		1		3
01:00 PM			2	1	1	4
01:30 PM		2	1			3
02:00 PM	1			1		2
02:30 PM			1			1
03:00 PM						0
03:30 PM						0
Total	6	13	7	9	7	42

EXHIBIT 5.8
Operating Room Registry – NEHP OB/GYN
Total Surgeon Time June–December, 1988

Surgeon	Health Center	Total Volume	Total Hours	Percent of Total Hours
NEHP				
Hartman	West Roxbury	33	61.08	6.91
Mayes	Kenmore	38	51.78	5.86
Fletcher	Boston	32	46.37	5.25
Lister	Wellesley	29	44.87	5.08
Andrews	Infertility	21	43.65	4.94
Rosen	Wellesley	28	39.73	4.50
Peters	Kenmore	32	36.72	4.16
Davidson	Boston	32	35.60	4.03
Meryl	West Roxbury	22	35.28	3.99
Long	Wellesley	22	31.45	3.56
Johns	Braintree	26	31.27	3.54
Patricks	Braintree	28	31.13	3.52
Moody	Infertility	16	30.87	3.49
DeBourgh	Boston	25	30.30	3.43
Arthur	Kenmore	25	29.37	3.32
Harris	Boston	19	24.38	2.76
Silvers	Boston	15	21.15	2.39
Jaknap	Kenmore	15	18.65	2.11
Gaylord	Boston	15	17.53	1.98
Bryan	Infertility	11	16.90	1.91
Rogers	Wellesley	18	15.03	1.70
Sandler	Braintree	14	12.72	1.44
Markewitz	Wellesley	8	11.93	1.35
Stevens	Kenmore	8	10.50	1.19
Vickers	Kenmore	12	9.98	1.13
Dorey	Braintree	3	1.48	0.17
Rivers	West Roxbury	1	1.25	0.14
Ackerson	Kenmore	2	0.87	0.10
Non-NEHP		91	141.74	16.04

ing at 7:30 A.M., NEHP assigned time was either unused until at least 9:00 A.M. or was used by another specialty. Exhibit 5.8 shows NEHP operating room time by surgeon and health center. Dr. Stevens hoped he would be able to use this information to understand the source of the problems and to design solutions.

HEALTHSOUTH Rehabilitation Corporation

When other people were recovering from Thanksgiving and preparing for Christmas, Richard Scrushy, chairman and CEO of HEALTHSOUTH Rehabilitation Corporation (HRC), was negotiating with the CEO of Santa Monica–based National Medical Enterprises, Inc., to purchase twenty-eight rehabilitation hospitals and forty-five outpatient rehabilitation centers. The negotiation involved the purchase of NME facilities for $300 million plus about $50 million for the net book value of certain inventory, receivables, and prepayments. It was expected that with these additional hospitals and outpatient centers HEALTHSOUTH annual revenues would increase to more than $1 billion. Papers were signed and the deal closed. Investors appeared to like the decision as HEALTHSOUTH common stock jumped more than $3.25 per share on the basis of the purchase.

The acquisition of the NME facilities increased the number of HEALTHSOUTH facilities to 265 located in thirty-two states, the District of Columbia, and Ontario, Canada. The company employed more than 13,000 people. Scrushy justified the purchase of NME by pointing out that it was less expensive to purchase existing hospital beds than to build new ones. Estimates showed that it cost between $150,000 and $180,000 for each newly constructed hospital bed. HEALTHSOUTH acquired the NME facilities for about $109,000 per bed. Moreover, many of the states where the NME facilities were located required certificates of need (CON) for new facilities.

Borrowing $300 million from NationsBank to finance the acquisition was frightening. The rate, however, was a good one – one point under prime. "It's always risky when you acquire a company as large as you are," said one industry expert. He continued, "But where there's risk there's opportunity. That's what HEALTHSOUTH is counting on as it prepares to manage the new properties."

HEALTHSOUTH Rehabilitation Corporation was one of the most successful business ventures in modern health care. Its growth was nothing less than phenomenal. Yet, growth involved its own challenge. As Richard M. Scrushy reviewed selected operating results at the beginning of the fourth quarter, 1993 (Exhibit 6.1), and reflected on the company's position as it neared the end of its first decade of growth, he wondered about HRC's future. The ultimate direction of health care reform remained uncertain. In addition, some observers expected significantly more competition in the rehabilitation market, and a few actually

This case was prepared by W. Jack Duncan and Peter M. Ginter of the University of Alabama at Birmingham and Michael D. Martin of HEALTHSOUTH Rehabilitation Corporation. It is intended as a basis for classroom discussion rather than to illustrate effective or ineffective handling of an administrative situation. Used with permission from Jack Duncan.

EXHIBIT 6.1
HEALTHSOUTH Rehabilitation Corporation, Selected Operating Indicators, September 1993

Indicator	Value
Stock price	$17⅛
52-week range of stock price	$26⅝–12⅛
Book value per share	$10.49
Shares outstanding	29.2 million
Return on equity	11.6%
Debt/capital ratio	53%
Estimated 3-year growth in earnings per share	15%

Source: Adapted from research reports published by CS First Boston (October 27, 1993) and Wessels, Arnold, and Henderson (October 18, 1993).

---

forecasted a decline in the demand for rehabilitation services.

By the end of 1992, HEALTHSOUTH had experienced twenty-seven consecutive profitable quarters. HEALTHSOUTH was the darling of Wall Street. The medical rehabilitation niche within the health care industry had been as successful as Scrushy originally believed. HRC had achieved or exceeded all of the objectives in its original business plan.

Scrushy realized that, to sustain growth, continued hard work was even more necessary than during the startup period. Additionally, he realized that some key strategic decisions would have to be made, including, Should HRC continue to focus on the rehabilitation business? Should HRC concentrate more on one business segment? Should HRC diversify even more into the acute care hospital business? What pitfalls lie ahead? Can success continue? Where should HRC go from here?

BEGINNING OF SUCCESS

HRC was organized in 1983 as AMCARE, Inc., but in 1985 changed its name to HEALTHSOUTH Rehabilitation Corporation. HEALTHSOUTH was founded by a group of health care professionals, led by Scrushy, who were formerly with LifeMark Corporation, a large publicly held, for-profit health care services chain that was acquired by American Medical International (AMI) in 1984.

In 1982, Richard Scrushy reflected on how he first recognized the potential for rehabilitation services, "I saw the TEFRA (Tax Equity and Fiscal Responsibility Act) guidelines and the upcoming implementation of Medicare's prospective payment system as creating a need for outpatient rehabilitation services. It was rather clear that lengths of stay in general hospitals would decrease and that patients would be discharged more quickly than in the past. It became obvious to me that these changes would create a need for a transition between the hospital and the patient's home." Medicare provided financial incentives for outpatient rehabilitation services by giving comprehensive outpatient rehabilitation facilities (CORFs) an exemption from prospective payment systems and allowed the services of these facilities to continue to be reimbursed on a retrospective, cost-based basis.

Scrushy anticipated the impact of the upcoming reimbursement changes.

I also saw that LifeMark, my current employer, would suffer significant reductions in profitability as the use of the then lucrative ancillary inpatient services was discouraged under the new reimbursement guidelines. I discussed my concerns about the upcoming changes in Medicare with LifeMark management and proposed that we develop a chain of outpatient rehabilitation centers.

I saw that the centers I proposed were LifeMark's chance to preserve its profitability under PPS, and when they rejected my proposal, I saw cutbacks and a low rate of advancement in the future.

Scrushy repeated his proposal for AMI's management when it acquired LifeMark, but AMI could not implement the program immediately after a major acquisition. Scrushy resigned his position and then founded HEALTHSOUTH Rehabilitation Corporation in conjunction with three colleagues from Life-Mark.

Early Development

HRC began operations in January 1984. Its initial focus was on the establishment of a national network of outpatient rehabilitation facilities and a rehabilitation equipment business. In September 1984, HRC opened its first outpatient rehabilitation facility at Little Rock, Arkansas, followed by another one at Birmingham, Alabama, in December 1984. Within five years, HRC was operating twenty-nine outpatient facilities located in seventeen states throughout the Southeastern United States. By the end of 1992, HRC operated in more than 145 locations – from California to New Hampshire, from Florida to Wisconsin – and business was booming, as illustrated in Exhibit 6.2. It was estimated that every day,

nearly 5,000 people depended on HEALTH-SOUTH outpatient centers for rehabilitative care.

In June 1985, HRC started providing inpatient rehabilitation services with the acquisition of an 88-bed facility in Florence, South Carolina. During the next five years, the company established eleven more inpatient facilities in nine states, with a twelfth under development. Although the rehabilitation equipment business portion of the corporation had grown rapidly, in August 1989 most of it was sold to National Orthopedic and Rehabilitation Services, Inc. (NORS) in order to concentrate resources on HRC's core business. However, in January 1992, HRC exchanged its note receivable from NORS for 3,743,000 shares of series a convertible preferred stock of the parent company of NORS, Caretenders Health Corporation, and became affiliated once again with the rehabilitation equipment business. The investment was initially valued at approximately $7.25 million and represented a 24 percent ownership interest in Caretenders Health Corporation. HRC stock was listed on the New York Stock Exchange.

South Highlands Hospital

A key development in HRC's growth strategy was the December 1989 acquisition of the 219-bed South Highlands Hospital in Birmingham, Alabama. Although South Highlands had been marginally profitable, its inability to obtain financing meant that it was unable to meet the needs of its physicians, particularly James Andrews and William Clancy, both world-renowned orthopedic surgeons. As Scrushy noted: "My immediate concern was to maintain the referral base that Drs. Andrews and Clancy provided. HRC had benefited from the rehabilitation referrals stemming from the extensive orthopedic surgery performed at South Highlands. The surgeons needed a major expansion at South Highlands to practice at maximum effectiveness and Drs. Andrews and Clancy would seek the facilities they needed

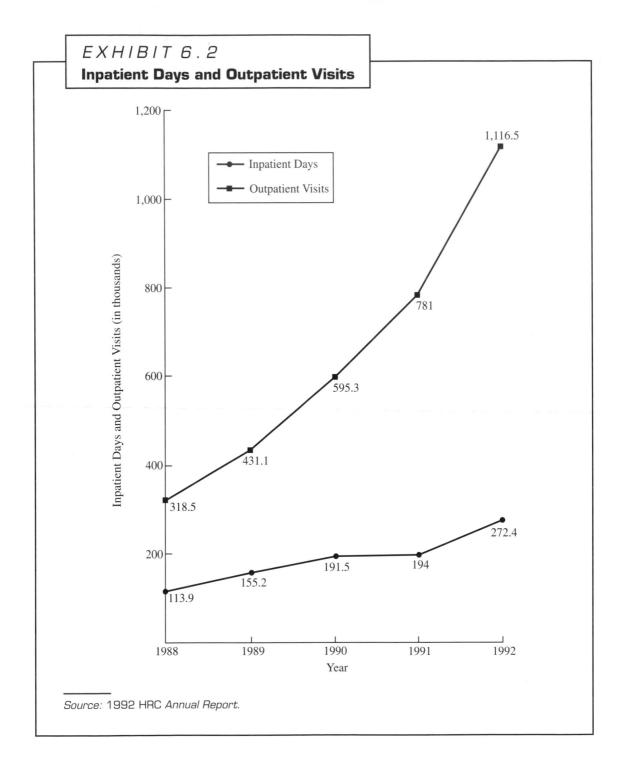

EXHIBIT 6 . 2
Inpatient Days and Outpatient Visits

Source: 1992 HRC *Annual Report.*

elsewhere if something wasn't done. On the surface our acquisition of South Highlands was defensive."

The purchase of South Highlands Hospital for approximately $27 million was far from a defensive move. Renamed HEALTHSOUTH Medical Center (HMC), this hospital was developed into a flagship facility. HRC immediately began construction of a $30 million addition to the hospital. Even during construction, referrals continued to flow from HMC to other HRC facilities. The construction created interest in the medical community, which in turn, created business. The emergency facility at HMC eliminated the necessity of delaying evaluation and treatment of athletic injuries that could be quickly transferred to the facility through HRC's extensive linkages with 396 high school and college athletic programs. A brief overview of selected events in HRC's history is shown in Exhibit 6.3.

INDUSTRY OVERVIEW

Every year more than 3 million people have need of rehabilitative health care services as the result of automobile and industrial accidents, sports and recreational injuries, crime and violence, or cardiac, stroke, and cancer episodes. It is estimated that at any particular time, 13 percent of the U.S. population and almost one-half of Americans over 75 years of age require some form of rehabilitative health services. With the population aging, this suggests even higher demand for rehabilitative health services in the future.

Medical rehabilitation involves the treatment of physical limitations through which therapists seek to improve their patients' functional independence, relieve pain, and ameliorate any permanent disabilities. Patients using medical rehabilitation services include the handicapped and those recovering from automobile, sports, and other accidents, strokes, neurological injuries; surgery, fractures and disabilities associated with diseases, and con-

ditions such as multiple sclerosis, cerebral palsy, arthritis, and heart disease.

In 1993, a great deal of uncertainty was created in view of promises by President Clinton to reform the health care system. Particular concern resulted from the possibility that cost containment efforts might result in the extension of Medicare reimbursement rates to *all* payers. Because Medicare payments were significantly below those of private payers, there would be a significant financial impact on rehabilitation service providers, and HEALTH-SOUTH was no exception.

Rehabilitation Services

Medical rehabilitation provider services include inpatient rehabilitation in dedicated freestanding hospitals and distinct units of acute-care hospitals; comprehensive outpatient rehabilitation facilities; specialty rehabilitation programs (such as traumatic brain injury and spinal cord injury); pediatric rehabilitation; occupational and industrial rehabilitation; and rehabilitation agencies. An illustration of the primary types of services provided by HRC are provided in Exhibit 6.4.

The availability of comprehensive rehabilitation services was limited in the United States. Provision of rehabilitation services by outpatient departments of acute-care hospitals was fragmented because services were provided through several departments, and private practice therapists rarely provided a full-range of comprehensive rehabilitation services. Often, patients requiring multidisciplinary services would be treated by different therapists in different locations, which could result in uncoordinated care.

Comprehensive inpatient rehabilitation services were provided by freestanding rehabilitation hospitals, distinct units in acute-care hospitals, and skilled nursing facilities. According to industry estimates, at the beginning of 1992, there were 152 dedicated rehabilitation hospitals and 692 distinct-part, inpatient

Year	Key Events
1984	Company started by Richard Scrushy and others Raised $1 million from CitiBank Venture Capital Opened two outpatient centers
1985	Acquired first inpatient facility Opened four new outpatient facilities
1986	Initial public offering raised $15 million Acquired two inpatient facilities Opened three outpatient centers
1987	Secondary stock offering raised $24 million Acquired two inpatient centers Opened four outpatient centers
1988	Developed and acquired three inpatient facilities Opened eight outpatient centers
1989	Issued $52 million of subordinated convertible debentures Listed on the New York Stock Exchange Developed two inpatient facilities Acquired South Highland Hospital (HEALTHSOUTH Medical Center) Opened eight outpatient facilities Divested rehabilitation equipment operations
1990	Developed one inpatient and opened ten outpatient facilities Listed as thirty-fifth largest percentage gainer on New York Stock Exchange by *Fortune Magazine* Secondary stock offering raised $49 million
1991	Acquired or opened fourteen outpatient facilities Consolidated the operations of four existing outpatient facilities into two entities Opened one new rehabilitation hospital Two new facilities under construction Acquired Humana Hospital—Richmond, renamed HEALTHSOUTH Medical Center/Richmond Expansion of HEALTHSOUTH Medical Center/Birmingham
1992	Acquired or opened twenty-three outpatient facilities Consolidated six existing facilities into three entities Added one new rehabilitation hospital Two new medical centers located in Miami, Florida Obtained interest in Caretenders Reorganized into three operating divisions—HEALTHSOUTH Inpatient Operations, HEALTHSOUTH Outpatient Operations, and HEALTHSOUTH International, Inc., and New Business Ventures

> ### EXHIBIT 6.4
> **Estimate of Services Provided**
>
> | Outpatient Services | Percent | Inpatient Services | Percent |
> |---|---|---|---|
> | General orthopedic and sports injuries | 64 | Strokes | 28 |
> | Back injuries | 17 | Fracture of femur | 23 |
> | General orthopedic hand injuries | 7 | Other | 21 |
> | Work hardening | 7 | Polyarthritis | 8 |
> | Other | 4 | Brain injury | 7 |
> | Neurological disorders | 1 | Spinal cord injuries | 5 |
> | | | Neurological disorders | 4 |
> | | | Amputation | 3 |
> | | | Major multiple trauma | 1 |

rehabilitation units in acute-care hospitals. This had grown from approximately 100 dedicated rehabilitation hospitals and 565 distinct-part units in 1988.

Analysts with Goldman Sachs estimated that the rehabilitation services segment of the health care industry in the United States would grow at a rate of 15 to 20 percent through 1993. A number of factors would influence this growth.

- *Increasing need for services.* The incidence of major disability increases with age. Improvements in medical care have enabled more people with severe disabilities to live longer. Data compiled by the National Center for Health Statistics showed that, in 1989, 35 million people in the United States (one out of every seven people) had some form of disability. The National Association of Insurance Commissioners pointed out that seven out of ten workers would suffer a long-term disability between the ages of 35 and 65. Increases in leisure time among the middle age population resulted in more physical activity and thus more sports injuries, a major portion of

HRC's business. At the same time, the greater proportion of the population in the elderly age group increased the demand for rehabilitation services associated with the elderly such as treatments for strokes and amputations.

- *Economic benefits of services.* Purchasers and providers of health care services, such as insurance companies, health maintenance organizations, businesses, and industry were seeking economical, high-quality alternatives to traditional health care services. Rehabilitation services, whether outpatient or inpatient, represented such an alternative. Often early participation in a disabled person's rehabilitation prevented a short-term problem from becoming a long-term disability. Moreover, by returning the individual to the work force, the number of disability benefit payments was reduced, thus decreasing long-term disability costs. Independent studies by companies such as Northwestern Life have shown that of every dollar spent on rehabilitation a savings of $30 occurred in disability payments. Insurance companies generally agreed that every rehabilitation dollar spent on patients with serious functional impairments saved from $10 to $30 in long-term health care costs such as nursing care.

- *Favorable payment policies for services.* As noted previously, inpatient rehabilitation services organized as either dedicated rehabilitation hospitals or distinct units, were eligible for exemptions from Medicare's prospective payment system. Outpatient rehabilitation services, organized as comprehensive outpatient rehabilitation facilities or rehabilitation agencies were eligible to participate in the Medicare program under cost-based reimbursement. Inpatient and outpatient rehabilitation services were typically covered for payment by the major medical portion of commercial health insurance policies. Moreover, Medicare reimbursement and the policies of private insurance companies encouraged early discharge from acute care hospitals thereby providing opportunities for outpatient rehabilitation, home health, and long-term-care facilities.
- *Technological advances in medical science.* Advances in medical science and trauma care made it possible to save the lives of numbers of victims of accidents, greater violence, and serious sports injuries. These victims were provided with therapeutic options that offered opportunities for inpatient and outpatient rehabilitation facilities.

Competition

At the close of the 1992 calendar year, HRC's operating units were located in twenty-seven states and consisted of four medical centers, twelve rehabilitation hospitals, and seventy-three outpatient clinics (see Exhibits 6.5 and 6.6). The competition faced in each of these markets was similar although unique aspects did exist, arising primarily from the number of

health care providers in specific metropolitan areas. The primary competitive factors in the rehabilitation services business were quality of services, projected patient outcomes, responsiveness to the needs of the patients, community and physicians, ability to tailor programs and services to meet specific needs, and the charges for services.

HEALTHSOUTH faced competition every time it initiated a certificate of need project or sought to acquire an existing facility or CON. The competition would arise from national or regional companies or from local hospitals that filed competing applications or that opposed the proposed CON project. Although the number of states requiring CON or similar approval was decreasing, HRC continued to face this requirement in several states. The necessity for these approvals, which was somewhat unique to the health care industry, demanded that organizations planning to open new facilities or purchase expensive and specialized equipment convince a regulatory or planning agency that such facilities or equipment were really needed and would not merely move patients from one provider to another. CONs, as noted previously, can provide a major incentive for acquiring facilities in CON states that already have approval to operate. They served as an important barrier to entry and potentially limited competition by creating a franchise to provide services to a given area.

The market for rehabilitation services represented a relatively small part of the overall health care system. The market was highly fragmented with HRC's primary competitors being rehabilitation units in acute-care hospitals, private practice therapists, and rehabilitation agencies. At the end of 1992, the inpatient rehabilitation market was estimated to be approximately $7 billion. Primary competitors were National Medical Enterprises, Inc.; Continental Medical Systems; ReLife; NovaCare; and AdvantageHEALTH. The degree of fragmentation is indicated by the fact that estimates illustrated that the top six competitors in the

EXHIBIT 6.5

Location of Facilities December 1992

State	Medical Centers	Rehabilitation Hospitals	Outpatient Facilities
Alabama	1		3
Arkansas			1
Arizona			3
California			8
Colorado			3
District of Columbia			1
Florida	2	2	14
Georgia			2
Iowa			1
Kentucky			1
Louisiana			1
Maryland			4
Minnesota			1
Mississippi			1
Missouri		1	6
Nebraska			1
New Jersey			3
New Hampshire		1	1
New Mexico		1	1
North Carolina			1
Ohio			1
Oklahoma		1	
Pennsylvania			1
South Carolina		2	
Tennessee		2	3
Texas		2	4
Wisconsin			1
Virginia	1	—	6
Total	4	12	73

inpatient rehabilitation market account for less than 20 percent of the market. The rehabilitation operations of the previous major player, National Medical Enterprises, Inc., were acquired by HRC.

Experts estimated the market for outpa-tient rehabilitation services to be about $5 bil-lion per year. The largest service provider in this market in 1992 was National Rehabilita-tion Centers with almost $100 million in reve-nues. HRC was a close second with about $80 million. Other primary competitors were Con-

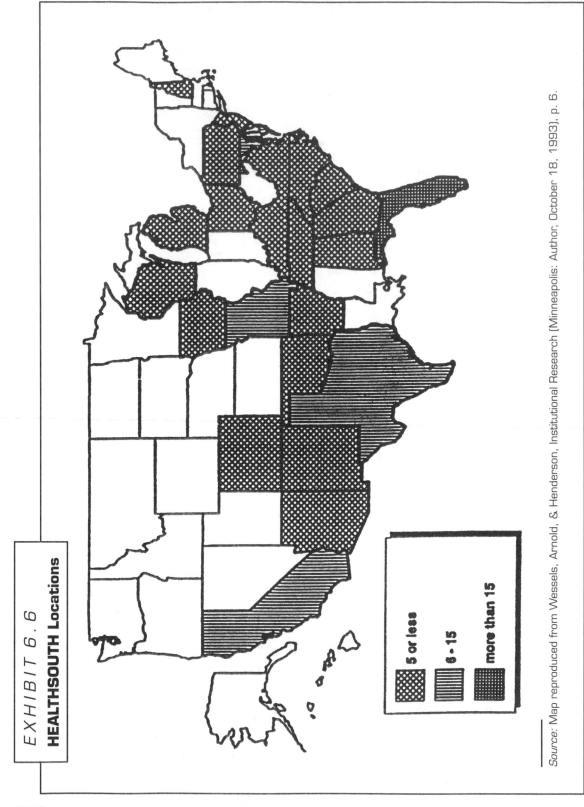

EXHIBIT 6.6
HEALTHSOUTH Locations

5 or less

6 - 15

more than 15

Source: Map reproduced from Wessels, Arnold, & Henderson, Institutional Research (Minneapolis: Author, October 18, 1993), p. 6.

tinental Medical Systems, RehabClinics, National Medical Enterprises, and Caremark. The top four competitors in the outpatient market accounted for less than 7 percent of the entire market. In the outpatient market, as in the inpatient market, competition was varied and highly fragmented.

Reimbursement

Reimbursement for services provided by HRC were divided into three distinct categories: commercial or private pay, workers' compen-

sation, and Medicare. The percentage of each varied by business segment and facility. As illustrated in Exhibit 6.7, private payment represented about 53 percent of total company receipts – about 53 percent in outpatient clinics, 35 percent in rehabilitation hospitals, and 60 percent in medical centers (Exhibit 6.8). Medicare accounted for 21 percent of overall HRC revenues, with 7 percent in outpatient clinics, 15 percent in rehabilitation hospitals, and about 10 percent in medical centers. Workers' compensation comprised 26 percent of overall revenues for HRC, 40 percent in out-

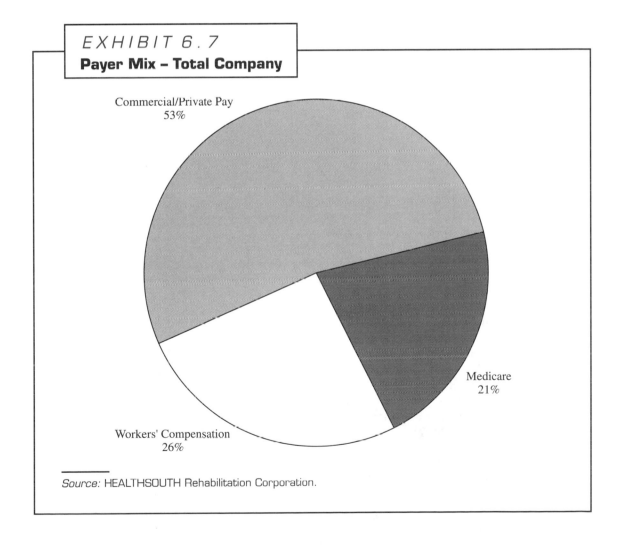

EXHIBIT 6.7
Payer Mix – Total Company

Commercial/Private Pay
53%

Medicare
21%

Workers' Compensation
26%

Source: HEALTHSOUTH Rehabilitation Corporation.

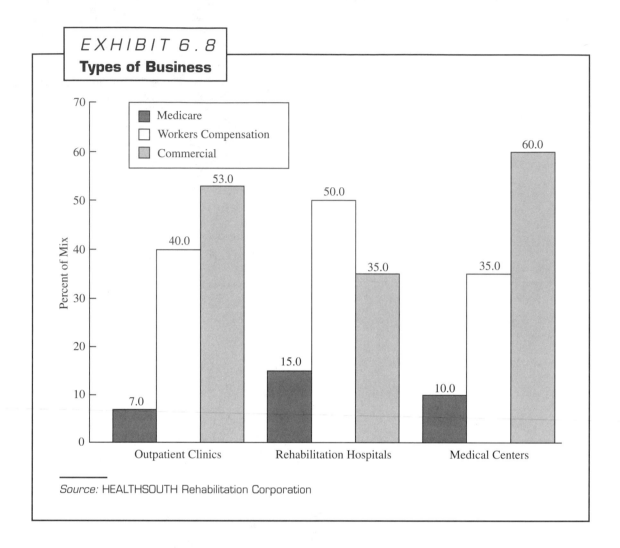

EXHIBIT 6.8
Types of Business

Percent of Mix

Legend:
- Medicare
- Workers Compensation
- Commercial

Outpatient Clinics: Medicare 7.0, Workers Compensation 40.0, Commercial 53.0
Rehabilitation Hospitals: Medicare 15.0, Workers Compensation 50.0, Commercial 35.0
Medical Centers: Medicare 10.0, Workers Compensation 35.0, Commercial 60.0

Source: HEALTHSOUTH Rehabilitation Corporation

patient clinics, 50 percent in rehabilitation hospitals, and 35 percent in the three medical centers.

Private Pay. Approximately 80 percent of the population under age 65 had medical insurance coverage. The extent of the coverage varied by location. Generally, charges for inpatient rehabilitation were completely (100 percent) reimbursed under general hospitalization benefits, and outpatient rehabilitation was reimbursed 100 percent similar to other outpatient

services. Studies conducted by the Life Insurance Marketing and Research Association found that more than 70 percent of the employers in their sample provided some financial assistance for employees who participated in company-approved rehabilitation programs. Northwestern National Life Insurance Company reported that complete rehabilitation was possible in 66 percent of the light-industry injuries and in 62 percent of heavy-industry injuries.

Insurers preferred established programs

with demonstrated functional outcomes. The private-pay segment included general medical insurance, workers' compensation, health maintenance organizations, preferred provider organizations, and other managed-care plans.

Medicare. Although rehabilitation had grown to an estimated $2 to $5 billion a year market, it continued to represent a relatively small portion of Medicare expenditures. Since 1983, the federal government had employed a prospective payment system as a means of controlling general acute-care hospital costs for the Medicare program. In the past, the Medicare program provided reimbursement for reasonable direct and indirect costs of the services furnished by hospitals to beneficiaries, plus an allowed return on equity for proprietary hospitals. As a result of the Social Security Act Amendments of 1983, Congress adopted a prospective payment system to cover the routine and ancillary operating costs of most Medicare inpatient hospital services.

Under PPS, the Secretary of Health and Human Services established fixed payment amounts per discharge based on diagnosis-related groups. With limited exceptions, a hospital's reimbursement for Medicare inpatients was limited to the DRG rate, regardless of the number of services provided to the patient or the length of the patient's hospital stay. Under PPS, a hospital could retain the difference, if any, between its DRG rate and the operating costs incurred in furnishing inpatient services, and was at risk for any operating costs that exceeded the DRG rate. HMC is generally subject to PPS with respect to Medicare inpatient services.

In 1993, Medicare paid certain defined units, freestanding rehabilitation facilities, and certified outpatient units on the basis of "reasonable costs" incurred during a base year (the year prior to being excluded from Medicare's prospective payment system or the first year of operation) adjusted by a market basket index. However, many rehabilitation providers faced

an increase in rates that was less than that of their actual costs. In addition, many Medicare intermediaries had an incomplete understanding of rehabilitation services and, therefore, might deny claims inappropriately; further education was necessary.

Workers' Compensation. The increasing cost of medical services for workers' compensation and the number of injured workers claiming disability was a primary driving force in the growth of HRC's outpatient and inpatient business. Unlike many types of health insurance, workers' compensation provided "first dollar" coverage (no deductible) and in most states required only that the worker missed three days of work to qualify. Benefits were usually equal to a percentage of the injured worker's salary, up to a specified maximum.

Since 1975, workers' compensation benefits increased by 17 percent annually. HRC viewed workers' compensation as a major opportunity for growth. Its ability to offer lower cost, high-quality services with better patient outcomes than most providers constituted a major competitive advantage for HRC.

Another way to look at the sources of HRC revenue was to distinguish between cost-based and non-cost-based revenue. The trend over the past three years is illustrated in Exhibit 6.9. Private pay and other non-cost-based revenue sources represented the majority of HRC revenue. Medicare was included in the cost-based revenue although Medicaid reimbursements were non-cost-based. Clearly, the trend was for an increasing share of revenue coming from non-cost-based revenue.

Regulation

The health care industry was subject to regulation by federal, state, and local governments. The various levels of regulatory activity affected organizations by controlling growth, requiring licensure or certification of facilities, regulating the use of properties, and control-

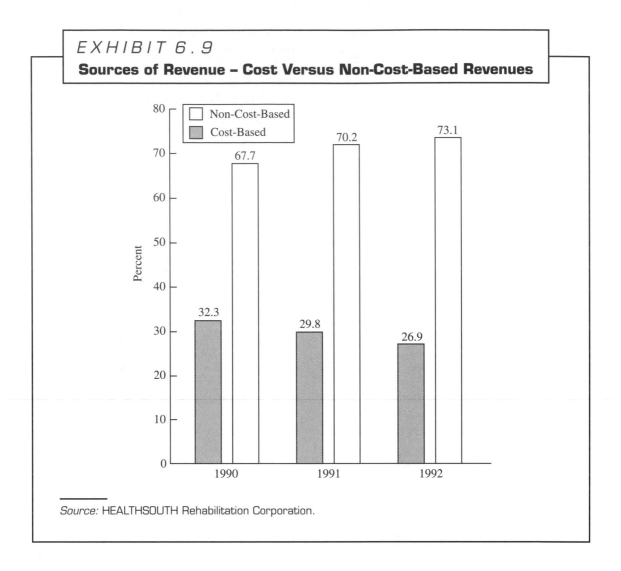

EXHIBIT 6.9
Sources of Revenue – Cost Versus Non-Cost-Based Revenues

Source: HEALTHSOUTH Rehabilitation Corporation.

ling the reimbursement for services provided. In some states, regulations controlled the growth of health care facilities.

Capital expenditures for the construction of new facilities, addition of beds, or acquisition of existing facilities could be reviewed by state regulators under a statutory scheme, usually referred to as a *CON program*. States with CON requirements placed limits on the construction and acquisition of health care facilities as well as the expansion of existing facilities and services.

Licensure and certification were separate but related regulatory activities. The former was usually a state or local requirement, and the latter was a federal requirement. In almost all instances, licensure and certification would follow specific standards and requirements set forth in readily available public documents. Compliance with the requirements was monitored by annual on-site inspections by representatives of various government agencies.

To receive Medicare reimbursement, each facility had to meet the applicable conditions of participation set forth by the U.S. Department of Health and Human Services relating to the type of facility, equipment, personnel, and standards of medical care, as well as compliance with all state and local laws and regulations. In addition, Medicare regulations generally required entry into such facilities through physician referral.

HEALTHSOUTH TODAY

When patients were referred to one of HEALTHSOUTH's rehabilitation facilities, they underwent an initial evaluation and assessment process that resulted in the development of a rehabilitation care plan designed specifically for each patient. Depending upon the patient's disability, this evaluation process could involve the services of a single discipline (such as physical therapy for a knee injury) or of several disciplines (such as physical and speech therapy in the case of a complicated stroke patient). HRC developed numerous rehabilitation programs, including ones for stroke, head injury, spinal cord injury, neuromuscular, sports, and work injury, that combined certain specific services to address the needs of patients with similar disabilities. When a patient entered one of these programs, the professional staff tailored the program to meet the needs of the patient. In this way, all of the facility's patients, regardless of the severity and complexity of their disabilities, could receive the level and intensity of those services necessary for them to be restored to as productive, active, and independent a lifestyle as possible.

The professional staff at each facility consisted of licensed or credentialed health care practitioners. The staff, together with the patient, his or her family, and the referring physician, formed the "team" that assisted the patient in attaining the rehabilitation goals. This approach permitted the delivery of coordinated, integrated patient care.

Outpatient Rehabilitation Services

HEALTHSOUTH operated the largest group of affiliated proprietary CORFs in the United States. Comprehensive outpatient rehabilitation facilities played an important role in the health care industry by offering quality care at a reasonable price. The continuing emphasis on reducing health care costs, as evidenced by PPS, reduced the length of stay for patients in acute-care facilities. Some critics even suggested patients did not receive the intensity of services that may be necessary for them to achieve a full recovery from their diseases, disorders, or traumatic conditions. CORFs satisfied the increasing need for outpatient services because of their ability to provide hospital-level services at the intensity and frequency needed.

HEALTHSOUTH had much to offer when compared to most small therapy centers. It possessed state-of-the-art equipment that could cost $100,000 for an individual item. HEALTHSOUTH's experience in operating its many outpatient centers offered:

- an efficient design, which aided in the delivery of rehabilitation services in terms of quality and cost;
- efficient management of the business office function – accounting, billing, managing, staffing, and so on;
- the ability to provide a full spectrum of comprehensive rehabilitation services;
- the ability to draw referrals from a large mass of sources due to its lack of affiliation with one specific group.

Inpatient Rehabilitation Services

HEALTHSOUTH was one of the largest independent providers of inpatient rehabilitation services in the United States. HRC's inpatient rehabilitation facilities provided high-quality comprehensive services to patients who required intensive institutional rehabilitation care. These patients were typically experiencing physical disabilities due to various conditions, such as head injury, spinal cord injury, stroke, certain orthopedic problems, and neuromuscular disease. Except for the St. Louis facility, which provided only head injury rehabilitation services, these inpatient facilities provided the same professional health care services as the company's outpatient facilities, but on a more intensive level. In addition, such facilities provided therapeutic recreation and twenty-four-hour nursing care. An interdisciplinary team approach, similar to that used in the outpatient facilities, was employed with each patient to address rehabilitation needs.

HEALTHSOUTH Specialty Medical Centers

HRC's specialty medical centers provided general acute-care services as well as services in orthopedics, sports medicine, and inpatient and outpatient rehabilitation. HRC owned four specialty medical centers located in Birmingham, Alabama; Richmond, Virginia; Coral Gables and Miami, Florida. In 1991, a major $25 million expansion plan was completed at the Birmingham facility that included an addition of a professional office building, four surgery suites, a magnetic resonance imaging unit, and renovation of the hospital. The facility was the home of the American Sports Medicine Institute, a private organization dedicated to educating physicians treating sports and orthopedic injuries.

HRC's Birmingham facility was a world class orthopedic surgery and sports medicine complex. It was an acute-care hospital reimbursed under the prospective payment system. The key to the hospital's success was the affiliation with a group of renowned orthopedic surgeons. These surgeons have treated famous patients such as Jane Fonda, Bo Jackson, the king and the prince of Saudi Arabia, golfers Jack Nicklaus and Greg Norman, Charles Barkley of the Philadelphia 76ers, and Troy Aikman of the Dallas Cowboys.

The prestige and publicity of these patients enhanced the demand for local services, HEALTHSOUTH's main business. One patient's father stated, "If HEALTHSOUTH was good enough for Charles Barkley then it's good enough for my son" (a high school football player who suffered a knee injury). The group of surgeons has eight to ten "fellows" or physicians who spent a year studying under the group before returning to their practices. This provided a network for future business and additional outpatient and inpatient development for HEALTHSOUTH. Since the development of the first specialty medical center in 1989, the prominence of the affiliation lead to several new acquisitions and many more opportunities.

Rehabilitation Management

HEALTHSOUTH Rehabilitation Corporation provided, as an extension of its outpatient and inpatient rehabilitation services, one or more of its clinical services to outside client facilities on a contractual basis. These contract opportunities represented a limited investment and capital risk and were only a small portion of the company's total revenues.

HRC effectively obtained economies of scale and filled some existing capacity by contract managing. In addition, it used contract management as a marketing strategy to enhance its presence through contractual management affiliations. For example, HRC managed a clinical services department in acute-care hospitals in San Antonio, Texas, and Menlo Park, California. It managed twenty-bed inpatient units in its Richmond and Birmingham specialty medical centers.

FUNCTIONAL CONSIDERATIONS

HRC's management was a group of young energetic professionals. In 1992, HEALTHSOUTH formally created three operating divisions, each with its own president and controller. All presidents reported to Scrushy, who remained as chairman of the board and chief executive officer. The three operating divisions were HEALTHSOUTH Inpatient Operations, HEALTHSOUTH Outpatient Operations, and HEALTHSOUTH International, Inc., and New Business Ventures. The goal of the reorganization was to ensure clarity of focus on operating goals and responsiveness to changing marketplaces. The management team was young, with an average age of about 40.

The corporate climate was characterized by a sense of urgency that was instilled in all of HEALTHSOUTH's employees directly by the chairman and CEO. Scrushy founded HEALTHSOUTH at the age of 32. As with many entrepreneurs, he was a visionary, but had the ability to make things happen. He worked virtually 365 days a year, 16 to 20 hours a day for the first five years, waiting until 1989 before taking his first vacation. His pace remained furious, working over 75 hours a week.

As a result of Scrushy's "hands-on" style, HRC was run; it did not drift. This was not likely to change with the three operating divisions reporting directly to the chairman and CEO. One of the company's most effective tools was a weekly statistical report, compiled every Thursday and distributed on Friday. The report included weekly statistics and trends such as payer mix, census, and revenue. It was reviewed over the weekend; and, if there was a negative trend, it was corrected. Thus, any problem was short lived. In this manner the management team was focused on real and developing problems.

Another tool was effective communications. Every Monday morning at 7:00 A.M. there was a meeting of the company's officers that included personnel from operations, development, finance, and administration. In this meeting each employee made a presentation, detailing what he or she accomplished in the previous week and what was planned for the current week. Questions were answered and problems were resolved. One additional benefit was that each employee was held accountable for his or her actions. Although this could be perceived to be overkill, it was believed to be necessary and helpful to the participants. At one time the meetings were stopped for about six weeks. After the company experienced a slight dip in performance and coordination, the meetings were immediately reinstated.

Staffing and Compensation

Unlike many other health care companies, HEALTHSOUTH had not experienced staffing shortages. Clinicians were in short supply, but HRC was able to recruit and maintain excellent personnel. The ability to offer a challenging environment was a key factor. A HEALTHSOUTH inpatient facility in a metropolitan location typically competed favorably against other hospitals and nursing homes for the skills of new therapists. HEALTHSOUTH's outpatient facilities offered an attractive alternative to the clinician by offering eight-hour workdays with weekends and holidays off.

All of the company's employees were competitively compensated. One compensation tool used was employee incentive stock options, which were granted to key corporate and clinical personnel. The options required a vesting period of four years with 25 percent of the amount being vested annually. If the employee left for another job, the options were lost. With the tremendous success of the company, the stock options had created "golden hand cuffs." Some employees had options that could be exercised at prices near $10 a share. Although HRC stock was trading for $38 per share in October 1991, throughout 1992 it traded in a range of $15.25 to $37.13 per share. Additionally, in 1991 the company created an employee stock ownership plan (ESOP) for the purpose of providing substantially all employees with the opportunity to save for retirement and acquire a proprietary interest in the company.

Development

A key element of HEALTHSOUTH growth was its ability to develop and acquire new facilities. The company had a development team led by three individuals who had been with the HRC from the beginning. Each was responsible for the development of facilities in a particular business segment. Before seeking to develop or acquire an inpatient or outpatient facility, a number of factors had to be considered including population, number of orthopedic surgeons and physical therapists, industry concentrations, reimbursement, competition, and availability of staff. Scrushy was quoted as saying his ten-year plan was "to take HRC to 500 centers and all 50 states." Management of the company believed that with revenues projected to exceed $2 billion over the next decade along with earnings of $4.00 per share, the goal could be realized without issuing additional stock.

Outpatient Development. HEALTHSOUTH believed that it operated the largest group of affiliated outpatient rehabilitation facilities in the United States. These units were usually acquired and, once purchased, were seeing fifty or more patients per day. Almost all new centers were set up as limited partnerships, typically with the former owners (physicians and therapists) maintaining a limited partnership interest. This provided an incentive to continue referring patients to the center, and the limited partners shared in the cash flow. HRC retained control of the facility by serving as general partner with at least 50 percent ownership and a management agreement. The cost of acquiring and opening a center ranged from $800,000 to $2.2 million.

Inpatient Development. Inpatient facilities were usually developed but were sometimes acquired. They were customarily located in regulated environments requiring a CON. The company has targeted a number of markets for rehabilitation hospitals; however, HEALTHSOUTH's competition was usually seeking the same markets.

To date, HRC was successful in securing each of the CONs or similar approvals it sought. The success was based primarily on (1) the quality of care provided by existing HEALTHSOUTH facilities and (2) the lower cost of the facility, which led to lower health care costs. There was, however, no guarantee that such success would always be the case.

HEALTHSOUTH's inpatient facilities were typically located on or near the campus of an acute-care hospital that served as a trauma center. This provided a steady stream of patients when trauma victims were discharged from the hospital. Additionally, physical therapy could be conducted by HEALTHSOUTH for the hospital on an inpatient and outpatient basis. Typically, HEALTHSOUTH's inpatient facilities cost around $10 million but, depending on the location and facilities provided, the costs could be considerably higher.

The development of additional acute-care medical centers stressing orthopedics, such as those in Birmingham, Richmond, Coral Gables, and Miami, remained a possibility in the future. A potential acute-care hospital acquisition had to possess an orthopedic concentration. The cost of an acute-care hospital meeting HEALTHSOUTH's criteria ranged from $20 to $50 million depending on its size and type of equipment.

Marketing

The company's marketing efforts were similar for each business segment. The demand was controlled by physicians, workers' compensation managers, insurance companies, and other intermediaries. Administrators and clinicians were involved in the marketing effort. The company hired a number of individuals who were formerly case managers with local intermediaries, such as insurance companies and HMOs. Every outpatient clinic had its own marketing director.

HRC entered into contracts to be the exclusive provider for rehabilitation services directly to industry. Firms such as General Motors were excellent targets because they had many employees in various markets that HEALTHSOUTH served. In such cases, significant new business could be generated and in return HEALTHSOUTH could afford to discount its charges. HRC expanded its marketing efforts to include a focus on national contracts with large payers and self-insured employers.

HEALTHSOUTH established a national marketing effort with training programs, national account managers, case managers, and a carefully developed marketing plan for each facility based on a number of factors, including population demographics, physician characteristics, and localized disability statistics. The objective was to put into place a consistent sales methodology throughout HEALTHSOUTH and take advantage of its national system of rehabilitation facilities. This national coverage enabled HEALTHSOUTH to provide services for national as well as regional companies.

Marketing programs were directed toward the development of long-term relationships with local schools, businesses and industries, physicians, health maintenance organizations, and preferred provider organizations. In addition, HRC attempted to develop and enhance its image with the public at large. One example was the company's joint promotional arrangement with the Ladies Professional Golf Association, whereby HRC provided and staffed a rehabilitation van for the players while they were on tour.

HEALTHSOUTH's pricing was usually lower than that of competition. However, this was not used as a major selling point, but rather a bonus. HEALTHSOUTH focused mainly on quality of services and outcomes as the best marketing tool.

Financial Structure

HEALTHSOUTH's growth was funded through a mix of equity and debt. The company raised $13 million in venture capital before going public in 1986. Because of the company's startup nature in its early years, commercial banks were reluctant to lend significant funds for development. After the company's initial public offering, commercial bankers were more responsive to financing growth plans. HRC continued to use a conservative mix of equity and debt and believed its cost of capital was the lowest in the health care industry. A decision to give up ownership was an easy one. The founders understood that a smaller percentage ownership of a larger company would be worth more and would not carry as much risk.

Earnings increases were significant, with compounded earnings growth of 416 percent from 1986 to 1990. During the 1990 to 1993 period growth rates declined, as expected, but remained impressive by industry standards. About 70 percent of HRC's revenues were generated primarily through inpatient services. Profit margins were expected to increase until at least 1995. Although some observers believed margin increases would be offset to a great extent by cost containment pressures, increasing wages for licensed therapists, and so on, profit margins of 20 percent were possible. Moreover, specialty medical centers tended to have lower overall profit margins. Considering all these factors, the most likely scenario would be that profit margins would gradually increase from the present 14 to 15 percent to 17 to 18 percent by 1995. HRC financial statements are included as Exhibits 6.10 to 6.13.

EXHIBIT 6.10

Condensed Consolidated Balance Sheet (in thousands)

	December 31, 1991	December 31, 1992
Current Assets		
Cash and marketable securities	$82,930	$70,842
Other marketable securities	24,170	15,074
Accounts receivable, net inventories	61,401	94,381
Prepaid expenses and other current assets	11,207	21,444
Total current assets	185,447	212,541
Other assets	10,973	12,203
Property, plant, and equipment, net	220,562	335,058
Intangible assets, net	44,640	81,997
Total assets	$461,622	$641,799
Liabilities and Stockholders Equity		
Current liabilities		
Accounts payable and other current liabilities	$18,389	$39,508
Current portion of long-term debt and leases	1,534	2,907
Total current liabilities	19,923	42,415
Long-term debt and leases	164,314	299,508
Deferred income taxes	7,808	12,050
Other long-term liabilities	329	49
Minority interests – limited partnerships	(93)	(2,355)
Total liabilities	192,281	351,667
Stockholders' Equity		
Common stock, $.01 par value – 50,000,000 shares authorized: 28,823,000 in 1992 and 28,044,000 in 1991, issued and outstanding	280	288
Additional paid-in capital	230,213	241,093
Retained earnings	48,848	68,393
	279,341	309,774
Receivable from employee stock ownership plan	(10,000)	(19,642)
Total stockholders' equity	269,341	290,132
Total liabilities and stockholders' equity	$461,622	$641,799

EXHIBIT 6.11

Condensed Consolidated Statement of Income (in thousands except per share amounts)

	Year Ending December 31, 1991	Year Ending December 31, 1992
Revenues	$225,485	$406,968
Operating expenses		
Operating units	157,654	303,604
Corporate general and administrative	7,947	10,245
Provisions for doubtful accounts	5,298	11,000
Depreciation and amortization	14,718	25,485
Interest expense	9,912	10,836
Interest income	(5,483)	(4,340)
Terminated merger expense		3,665
	190,046	360,495
Income before minority interest and income taxes	35,439	46,473
Minority interests	1,568	1,402
	33,871	45,071
Provision for income taxes	11,500	15,333
Net income	$22,371	$29,738
Weighted average common and common equivalent shares outstanding	25,905	29,887
Net income per common and common equivalent share	$.86	$1.00
Net income per common share – assuming full dilution	$.83	n/a

WHERE DOES HEALTHSOUTH GO FROM HERE?

Richard Scrushy was reviewing company projections for continued success of HEALTH-SOUTH Rehabilitation Corporation. He could not help but wonder if it were possible for HRC to continue such rapid growth. All the questions raised earlier were in his thoughts. What will I need to do to make it happen? Are there things we should be doing differently? How can I ensure that HEALTHSOUTH does not outgrow its resources (capital and management)? Does the market provide ample opportunity to grow at 20 to 30 percent per year?

What external factors do we face? What should we do to ensure that medical rehabilitation continues to be favorably reimbursed? What is the real number of facilities needed, and how many acquisition targets are there?

Scrushy focused on answering the questions. He knew that he could formulate a plan to ensure HEALTHSOUTH's success. In fact, in a probing interview in *Rehabilitation Today* (May 1991), Scrushy was careful to state that he would consider any acquisition where he believed "value could be added" and dismissed the possibility that the company's "regional name" implied that his aspirations were regional. Clearly, he was willing to go any-

EXHIBIT 6.12

Consolidated Statement of Stockholders' Equity (in thousands)

	Common Shares	Common Stock	Additional Paid In Capital	Retained Earnings	Receivables from ESOP	Total Stockholders' Equity
Balance December 31, 1991	28,044	$280.4	$230,212.7	$48,848.0	($10,000.0)	$269,341.1
Proceeds from exercise of options	762	$7.6	6,648.6	—	—	6,656.2
Income tax benefits of incentive stock options	—	—	3,827.7	—	—	3,827.7
Common shares exchanged in exercise of stock options	(4)	—	(95.6)	—	—	(95.6)
Loan to ESOP	—	—	—	—	(10,000.0)	(10,000.0)
Reduction in receivables from ESOP	—	—	—	—	358.0	358.0
Purchase of limited partnership units	21	.2	499.8	(10,193.4)	—	(9,693.4)
Net income	—	—	—	29,738.0	—	29,738.0
Balance December 31, 1992	28,823	$288.2	$241,093.2	$68,392.6	($19,642.0)	$290,132.0

EXHIBIT 6.13

Condensed Consolidated Statement of Cash Flows (in thousands)

	Year Ending December 31, 1991	Year Ending December 31, 1992
Operating Activities		
Net income	$22,371	$29,738
Adjustments to reconcile net income to net cash provided by operating activities:		
Depreciation and amortization	14,718	25,485
Provisions for doubtful accounts	5,298	11,000
Income applicable to minority interests of limited partnerships	1,568	1,402
Provision for deferred income taxes	3,168	4,695
Provision for deferred revenue from contractual agencies	(109)	(279)
Changes in operating assets and liabilities, net of effects of acquisitions	(21,305)	(4,000)
Net cash provided by operating activities	25,709	31,241
Investing activities:		
Purchase of property, plant, and equipment	(71,974)	(86,240)
Additions to intangible assets, net of effects of acquisitions	(8,270)	(24,976)
Assets obtained through acquisitions, net of liabilities assumed	(41,693)	(41,343)
Changes in other assets	(648)	1,834
Proceeds received on sale of long-term marketable securities	11,286	14,041
Investments in marketable securities	(26,339)	(4,945)
Net cash used in investing activities	(137,638)	(141,629)
Financing Activities		
Proceeds from borrowing	$102,158	$169,800
Principal payments on debt and leases	(35,524)	(58,890)
Proceeds from exercise of options	5,756	6,561
Commons stock issued on acquisition	*	*
Proceeds from issuance of common stock	69,604	*
Loans to employee ownership plan	(10,000)	(10,000)
Reductions in receivables from employee ownership plan	*	358
Tax benefits of incentive stock options	4,373	3,828
Transactions related to limited partners	(3,592)	(13,357)
Net cash provided by financing activities	132,775	98,300
(Decrease) Increase in cash and cash equivalents	20,846	(12,088)
Cash and cash equivalents at beginning of year	62,984	82,930
Cash and cash equivalents at end of year	82,930	70,842
Supplemental disclosures of cash flow information		
Cash paid during year for		
Interest	12,205	12,469
Income taxes	$6,701	$9,201

Noncash Financing Activities:

The holders of the company's $52 million in aggregate principal amount of $7^3/_4$ percent convertible subordinated debentures due 2014 surrendered the debentures for conversion into 3,081,446 shares (on a pre-split basis) of the company's common stock on various dates during 1991.

During 1991 the company had a three-for-two stock split on its common stock, which was effected in the form of a 50 percent stock dividend.

where, anytime he believed opportunities existed. To date, nothing had changed his mind.

REFERENCES

Sources used for quotes and information to supplement public documents of HEALTHSOUTH include the following.

Brown, Alex & Sons, Inc. Research Report, Health Care Group, October 23, 1991.

Hansen, Jeffrey. "HealthSouth Finishes Deal Doubling Size." *Birmingham News* (January 6, 1994), pp. 6D and 10D.

"Deal Will Double Size of HealthSouth." *Birmingham News* (December 4, 1993), pp. 1A and 12A.

Hicks, W. G., and K. M. Miner. "The Post-Acute Spectrum of Care." *Gowen Industry Strategies* (May 19, 1993).

Smith Barney. Research Report, August 14, 1992.

Wessel, Arnold, and Henerson. Institutional Report, October 18, 1993.

Wilder, Marvin. "The Powerhouse Behind HEALTHSOUTH." *Rehabilitation Today* (May 1991), pp. 22–31.

Supportive HomeCare: Operating Under Reform Uncertainties

The early 1980s was not the best time to start a new business. The economic climate was dismal, with the country going through a severe recession and interest rates hovering above 15 percent. Oshkosh, Wisconsin, was no different than the rest of the nation. Yet in 1983, two people decided that it was a good time to start a business in the home health care industry.

At the age of 28, Terri S. Hansen, RN-MSN, quit her full-time job because she saw a gap in home care services and knew she could provide what was needed. She began Supportive HomeCare in the upstairs of her home with a partner, John Westphal, and three part-time employees. The company was structured as a private, proprietary agency to target clients needing long-hour home health aide services any time of the day or night, any day of the week, including weekends and holidays. In the first four years of business, the company grew rapidly in sales and number of employees. During the next four years, however, critical financial challenges faced the agency. Things were beginning to turn around when a

This case was prepared by Jeffrey W. Totten and Linda E. Swayne. It is intended as a basis for classroom discussion rather than to illustrate effective or ineffective handling of an administrative situation. Used with permission from Jeff Totten.

nonlicensed, nonregulated competitor (Lakeshore Home Care) began offering services at half the cost, Appleton Visiting Nurses Association agreed to a merger with two of the area hospitals, and another shortage of nurses had its impact on all home care organizations in the area.

THE HOME HEALTH CARE INDUSTRY

Home health care provides health and social services in the patient's home rather than in a medical facility. The National Association for Home Care defines home care as a service to the recovering, disabled, or chronically ill person providing for treatment or effective functioning in the home environment.[1] Services include skilled nursing care; medical care; physical, speech, and occupational therapy; social work; nutrition; personal care and housekeeping; patient transportation; respite care; medical equipment; and meals on wheels. The National Association for Home Care identified 13,951 home-care agencies in the United States in 1993.[2] The major advantage for patients and third-party payers is that home health care is considered to be less expensive than institutionalization. Another advantage for patients is that home care is less disruptive, and many people "feel better" in familiar surroundings. Exhibit 7.1 contains a comparison of home health care costs with institutional costs. Exhibit 7.2 illustrates the changes in average expenses for a home-care visit between 1987 and 1993.

Expenditures for home health care exceeded $21.2 billion in 1993.[3] Although it was a small portion of the total $800 billion spent on personal health care that year, the amount and proportion for home care was expected to increase because of the growing number of people age 65 and over, innovation in services and technology, the increasing interest in coor-

dination of care, the generally lower cost of home care, support by insurers, and Medicare endorsement of home care as an alternative to institutionalization.

Home-care agencies of various types have been providing high-quality, in-home services to Americans since the 1880s.[4] However, Medicare's enactment in 1965 greatly accelerated the industry's growth. Medicare made home health services available to the elderly and, in certain cases, disabled younger Americans. Utilization of home health care agencies increased each year from 1980 until the mid-

---

EXHIBIT 7.1

Comparison of Various Home Health Care Costs with Institutional Costs

Average cost per day for relatively intensive treatment
    Home care $25–200 per day
    Hospital $300–500 per day

Average cost of care for a ventilator-dependent patient
    Home care $21,192 per year
    Hospital $270,830 per year

Average cost of care for an AIDS patient
    Home care $94 per day
    Hospital $773 per day

Average cost of care for a quadriplegic patient with spinal cord injury
    Home care $13,931 per month
    Hospital $23,862 per month

Average cost of care for infant born with breathing and feeding problems
    Home care $20,209 per month
    Hospital $60,970 per month

Average cost for routine skilled nursing
    Home care $750 per month
    Hospital $2,000 per month

Source: Robin Richman, "High-Tech Home Care: What's in It for Hospitals?" *Health Care Strategic Management* 8, no. 3 (March 1990), p. 21.

EXHIBIT 7.2
Average Expenses per Home Care Visit

	1987	1993[1]
Nurse	$62	$84
Therapist	57	77
Home health aide	34	46
Homemaker/companion	33	44
Other[2]	56	75
Average	49	66

[1]Updated based on an average annual increase of Medicare per-visit charges of 5.1 percent.
[2]Includes social workers and other professionals.
Source: National Association for Home Care, August 1993.

1980s. At that time, because of the increasing amount of paperwork and unreliable payment policies, the number of visits declined. Because home health care had been growing at a rate of 20 percent a year, the "dip" in 1987 was unusual, especially as there was an increasing proportion of people over age 65. In 1987, the over-65 population accounted for 30 percent of total medical expenditures.[5]

It appears that the lessening demand for home health care in 1987 may have been caused by a misunderstanding by the Health and Human Services Department concerning the number of days a week an eligible home-care patient could receive care under full-time and part-time services. The misunderstanding was resolved by litigation in favor of the beneficiary (see Duggan v. Bowen, USDC(DC), No. 87—0383, August 1, 1988).[6] Home care usage increased slightly in 1988 and expanded significantly thereafter (see Exhibit 7.3).

Currently, the home health care market is divided into three basic services: home health care services (sometimes referred to as custodial care), home medical equipment, and home infusion therapy. Home health services accounted for 68 percent, home medical equip-

ment 20 percent, and home infusion therapy 12 percent when this was a $16 billion industry.[7] Medical equipment, because of changes in Medicare reimbursement, has been a loss rather than a profit center for many in this competitive market. Cost-containment pressures and the changes in the composition of the patient population have caused home health care to shift from custodial to acute care. Therefore, the home infusion therapy segment is predicted to grow and be more profitable than home health services (custodial care) or home medical equipment. Home infusion therapies, such as intravenous (IV) antibiotic therapy and chemotherapy, allow patients the flexibility of being treated at home instead of in the hospital.

Senior citizens represent 73.1 percent of the patients receiving IV therapies. AIDS patients are another growing segment of the patient mix that can benefit from home infusion therapy. There were approximately 58,000 new AIDS patients in 1991 in the United States, and another 120,000 to 190,000 were newly diagnosed with HIV-related severe immunosuppression.[8] A growing number of providers are developing specialized home health ser-

EXHIBIT 7.3

Trends in Home Health Care Utilization, Medicare Certified Agencies

Year	Visits (in thousands)	Patients Served (in thousands)	Expenditures (in millions)	Average Cost per Visit
1975	10,800	500	$208	$19.30
1980	22,428	957	662	29.52
1985	39,742	1,589	1,773	44.61
1986	38,359	1,600	1,796	46.82
1987	35,591	1,565	1,879	52.79
1988	37,154	1,582	2,033	54.72
1989	46,270	1,685	2,525	54.57
1990	69,431	1,940	3,900	56.17
1991	99,938	2,370	5,706	57.10
1992	138,540	2,870	8,236	59.45
1993	184,397	3,450	11,707	63.49

Source: HCFA, Office of the Actuary, unpublished information prepared for FY1994 Trustees Report.

vices for AIDS patients. Although outpatient care is estimated to be 25 percent of the total costs for AIDS patients, home care is only about 2.5 percent of all home care spending.[9]

Another growing home service is in the area of rehabilitation care. Because of advances in medical technology, many patients are now surviving severe trauma. Their rehabilitative care is extended and expensive. Home care can be a viable option.[10] In addition, many hospitals are discharging patients to home care for rehabilitative care because of shortened hospital stays. The percentage of Medicare patients discharged to home health care nearly doubled between 1981 and 1985 according to a study by Abt Associates. Major joint procedures including hip/femur procedures, stroke, and heart failure were the DRGs most likely to result in home care rehabilitation after discharge from the hospital.[11]

Additional new services are being contemplated by many home-care agencies because of the availability of high-tech equipment in a size that can be used at home. Home monitoring for high-risk pregnancies and subacute care for neonates are two examples of new services that hold promise for expanding home-care companies.

Within the industry, the most important segment is the Medicare-certified home health agency, because the federal government is the single largest payer for home care services. In 1993, there were over 6,900 Medicare-certified home health agencies. Most were proprietary, although there is a growing number that are hospital based (Exhibit 7.4). In 1993 it was estimated that more than 60 percent of the nation's hospitals provided at least some level of home care (not necessarily Medicare certified).[12]

Medicare pays for only a limited array of medically related services to those patients needing skilled nursing care. Thus, the bulk of payments for unskilled services come from

EXHIBIT 7.4
Number of Medicare-Certified Home Health Agencies by Type

Type	1987		1993	
	Number	Percent	Number	Percent
Hospital based	1,439	24.9	1,934	28.0
Private, nonprofit	766	13.3	551	8.0
Proprietary	1,846	31.9	2,440	35.3
Public	1,073	18.5	1,176	17.0
Visiting Nurses Association	551	9.5	646	9.4
Other	110	1.9	155	2.3
Total	5,785	100.0	6,902	100.0

Source: National Association for Home Care, August 1993.

the clients or their families. Private insurance carriers sometimes provide coverage, although it often depends on the patient having been discharged from a hospital or nursing home. Exhibit 7.5 illustrates the sources of payment for home health care.

Since the implementation of the prospective payment system in 1983, hospital-based home-care agencies have more than doubled in number, from 700 in 1983 to over 2,000.[13] Hospitals are actively seeking additional revenues because third-party payer policies and practices are resulting in shorter hospital stays. Home care seems to offer an opportunity to add services, remain visible in the community, and obtain a competitive advantage. Because many hospitals provide referrals (98.4 percent of patients are referred by a hospital to a home health care agency), they have a decided advantage in developing home-care services. They are motivated to enter the market because it helps to reduce a patient's hospital stay but still provides care for the patient. However, according to a study by SMG Marketing Group reported in the Marion *Long Term Care Digest, Home Health Care Edition* for 1989, long-term

EXHIBIT 7.5
Sources of Payment for Home Care, 1992

Source	Percent
Medicare	37.8
Medicaid	24.7
Private insurance	5.5
Out-of-pocket	31.4
Other	.6
Total	100.0

Source: National Association for Home Care, August 1993.

patients tend to choose proprietary agencies over hospital-based home care (Exhibit 7.6).

Hospitals originally entered the home-care area because they predicted significant profits. "Hospitals are no longer looking at home health care as moneymaking, but rather as providing that continuum of care that is critical,"

EXHIBIT 7.6
Home Health Care Choice

Type of Patient	Government	Hospital	Proprietary	Nonprofits/ Visiting Nurses Association	Average
Male	35.9%	39.0%	36.9%	35.2%	36.8%
Female	64.1	61.0	63.1	64.8	63.2
Adult	24.0	23.3	25.9	24.0	24.5
Pediatric	4.7	3.6	5.1	5.0	4.6
Senior Citizen	71.3	73.1	69.0	70.9	70.9
Patient <30 Days	27.5	35.0	27.0	33.5	30.3
Patient >30 Days	72.5	65.0	73.0	66.5	69.7
1 Visit/Week	44.5	36.6	18.2	24.9	29.8
2–3 Visits/Week	39.3	51.3	47.3	50.7	47.1
3 + Visits/Week	16.2	12.1	34.5	24.4	23.1
24-Hour Care	7.0	7.9	15.8	10.4	12.3

Source: "Planning Indicators," *Health Care Strategic Management* 8, no. 4 (April 1990), p. 23.

according to Carol Schaffer, CEO of Health Care Ventures, a wholly owned subsidiary of the Cleveland Clinic Foundation.[14] David Baker, corporate director of home-care services for Saint Frances, Inc., in Peoria, Illinois, agrees. He predicted that home health care will play an important role in integrated delivery systems especially as the nation moves toward capitated care.[15] As third-party payers continue to control the timing and amount of reimbursements, hospitals are losing control to alternative-site providers. The most rapid growth area in home care is the high-tech therapy that directly competes with hospitals for more acutely ill patients.[16]

As home care has shifted from custodial to acute care, hospitals have increased their diversification efforts into home infusion therapy, Medicare-certified home health agencies, hospices, home medical equipment companies, and private-duty nursing/supplemental staffing agencies. Home infusion is gaining favor over

Medicare-certified home health agencies because agencies that rely on people as inventory are more difficult to operate.[17] Hospital-based home health care agencies experienced turnover rates of 18.7 percent for registered nurses and 47.8 percent for occupational therapists.

Hospitals are entering into the home infusion therapy business in various ways. In the past many hospitals developed arrangements with existing providers. They accomplished these arrangements through informal efforts, affiliations, contract services, fee-for-service, or joint ventures. For example, one hospital entered the home infusion therapy market through a joint venture with the local visiting nurses association (VNA). It was mutually beneficial for both parties because they expanded services without either having to invest full startup costs.

Some for-profit home health care agencies have started offering bonuses to hospital discharge planners as a method to increase business. Similar to the frequent flyer programs implemented by airlines, the agencies provide free service to hospitals that refer private paying patients. Olsten Health Care Services returns to each participating institution (350 are enrolled) 10 percent of reimbursed service hours generated from private referrals within that institution. The more hours referred, the more hours of free care accumulated. The institutions use the free hours for indigent patients. "What we're doing is giving something back to the community," according to Sal Morici, marketing manager in Olsten's health care division.[18] Not all hospitals are enthusiastic about the program. Public scrutiny of referrals (especially Medicare referrals) have made some hospitals reluctant to participate. Others have been pleased to be able to offer the free home care to patients so that they could be discharged earlier.

Reimbursement for home infusion therapy is generally at a satisfactory level. Most private insurance carriers and health maintenance organizations provide sufficient reimbursement. However, Medicare does not pay for most intravenously administered drugs outside of the hospital setting. Case managers are becoming common for in-home infusion therapy patients. Case managers are expected to scrutinize health care costs and bring more checks and balances to the home infusion industry.[19]

The largest home-care agencies have branches in multiple states and have continued to expand. In 1993, Caremark was the largest home care agency in terms of revenues. It was involved in a spinoff from its parent, Baxter International, causing Caremark to report a 58.7 percent decline in net income.[20] A combination that is agreed to but awaiting final stockholder approval will position Olsten (after its purchase of Lifetime Corporation) as the largest home-care agency in terms of revenues. Statistics for the ten largest agencies, based on number of branches, are included in Exhibit 7.7.

EXHIBIT 7.7

Top Ten Home Care Companies by Total Number of Branches in 1992

Company	No. Branches	No. States	No. Visits	Revenues*	Profit*
Kimberly Quality Care	364	40	9,095,900	n/a	n/a
Visiting Nurse Preferred Care	251	46	n/a	n/a	n/a
ABC Home Health Services	239	17	3,800,000	$213.1	$2.7
Homedco	235	40	n/a	303.3	17.6
Interim Healthcare	226	45	n/a	n/a	n/a
Olsten HealthCare	220	38	15,971,000	341.0	21.0
T² Medical	197	34	n/a	242.1	59.3
Option Care	196	41	n/a	40.7	3.5
Tokos Medical Corporation	120	40	n/a	159.9	6.5
Lincare	115	27	n/a	117.4	15.1

*In thousands
Source: Mary Wagner, "Home Infusion Growth Fosters Advances for Home-Care Firms," *Modern Healthcare* 23, no. 21 (May 24, 1993), pp. 82, 84.

Because of the substantial cost savings, home care is expected to benefit from health care reform. Currently there are two major reasons home care has not been used aggressively for cost containment: Medicare does not cover the cost of most IV-administered drugs and Medicare does not reimburse physicians for treating patients at home. In addition physicians do not want to take time to travel to patients' homes, and they are still legally liable for patients' care once they authorize home care. With the expected increase in use of managed care, home care is positioned to provide services for non-acute-care patients and their families.

HOME HEALTH CARE IN OSHKOSH

In 1983, before Terri Hansen started Supportive HomeCare, only Upjohn Health Care provided twenty-four-hour home health care for the Oshkosh area. The Visiting Nurses Association (VNA) and the Winnebago County nurses provided part-time, intermittent home care. Several hospitals in the Fox River Valley, including Mercy Medical Center (350 licensed beds, 256 used, in Oshkosh), Theda Clark Regional Hospital (350 licensed beds, 250 used, in Neenah), St. Elizabeth's Hospital (287 licensed and used beds in Appleton), Appleton Medical Center (220 licensed beds, 150 used, in Appleton), Kaukauna Community Hospital (52 beds in Kaukauna), and St. Agnes (191 staffed beds in Fond Du Lac) provided acute (inpatient) care.[21] Exhibit 7.8 is a map of the Oshkosh area including the locations of the Fox River Valley hospitals and Supportive HomeCare offices.

Oshkosh is a small urban community of approximately 55,000 people located on the western shore of Lake Winnebago in Winnebago County, Wisconsin. The city is located on a major state highway, about ninety minutes from Madison, the state capital. Oshkosh has a strong Polish, German, and Scandinavian heritage and is tied economically to the paper industry that is concentrated along the Fox

River Valley. The city is also the home for Oshkosh Truck (heavy-duty vehicles), Leach (garbage trucks), Oshkosh B'Gosh (well-known children's clothing), the Experimental Aircraft Association, the University of Wisconsin – Oshkosh, Miles Kimball (catalog merchandise), Georgia Pacific (paper), and Mercury Marine (boat motors).

GETTING STARTED

Hansen started very small. "I did not want a lot of overhead, so I started the business in my home. I wanted to make sufficient income for myself and for my workers." She did not expect to generate any cash for at least six months. In fact, she had to borrow money from the bank to pay her own salary. Because she could afford so little help, she handled the nursing management, typing, telephone answering, and marketing herself. In the beginning, the company was a two-person office operation, with three part-timers in the field.

Before she could actually get started, she had to apply for a license from the state. A lengthy proposal had to be written and submitted to the Wisconsin Department of Health and Social Services to show need for the service. Letters from physicians and social services agencies indicating support for the idea had to be included. Three-year projections of operations were required to show that the business could be maintained for at least that period of time. The certificate of need was granted in January 1983; Supportive HomeCare became a privately owned, independent, state-licensed home-care agency. It took the company until April to get certification for third-party billing by Medicare and Medicaid. During those four months, the company could accept only private-pay patients.

Hansen spent the first months talking about the company to agencies, churches, and doctors without generating any business. Finally, in March, the company cared for its first patient, followed quickly by five more. "For that first year, I was on call twenty-four hours a

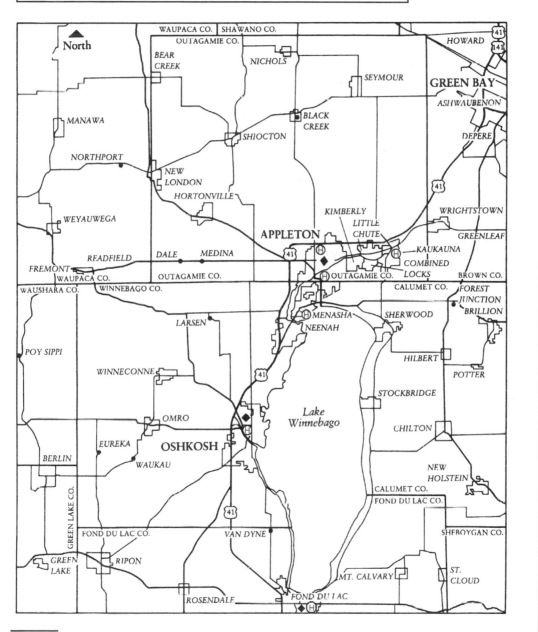

EXHIBIT 7.8

Map of Oshkosh and Surrounding Counties with Hospitals and Supportive Homecare Offices

Ⓗ Hospital ◆ Supportive HomeCare Office
Source: Company documents.

day, seven days a week," remembered Hansen. The company grew to two full-time and two part-time office personnel and thirty employees in the field by the end of its first year of operation.

Target Market

Hansen targeted her services toward hospital discharge planners, doctors, county nurses, county social service agencies, and the Visiting Nurses Association. According to Terri Hansen, "We wanted to find a niche in the market where the company could fit in without rocking the boat, yet still provide a needed service. My goal was to provide a service with a positive image, one that works with other competitors, to be collaborative rather than competing against them." The population target was Winnebago County, where Hansen had her strongest contacts and greatest credibility as a health care professional. Potential consumers of home care included individuals recuperating from accidents and outpatient surgery; handicapped and disabled individuals; the frail and elderly; those suffering from a chronic illness such as heart disease, diabetes, arthritis, and so on; single and working parents; and private-duty individualized care for loved ones who were gravely ill. Exhibit 7.9 lists the client base for 1989 and 1993.

EXHIBIT 7.9
Supportive HomeCare Client Base

	1989	1993
Primary Diagnosis of Clients Served		
AIDS	0	2
Cardiovascular	53	60
Cancer	17	18
Arthritis	25	42
Cerebral vascular incident	24	11
Diabetes	21	6
Respiratory	22	10
Cerebral palsy	5	4
Fractures	21	30
Paralysis	12	3
Mental illness	13	1
Senile dementia	19	10
Mental retardation	8	6
Other conditions	69	59
Total Clients	309	262
Referral Sources for Admissions		
Hospitals	36	22
Social services	28	30
SHC employees	12	11
Newspaper	10	2
Client/former client	26	15

EXHIBIT 7.9 *cont'd*

	1989	1993
Nursing homes	2	8
Yellow pages	4	19
Home health agency	19	10
Presentation	4	0
Other and continuing patients	168	145
Total referrals and continuing patients	309	262
Number of Clients Discharged		
To nursing homes	33	29
By death	26	7
To self-care	78	39
To family	6	19
Other	32	46
Hospitalized	57	34
Total	232	174
Number of Clients by Age		
17 and under	19	12
18–54	23	19
55–64	40	19
65–74	150	59
75–84	70	85
85–94	7	64
95 +	0	4
Total	309	262
Client Totals		
Number of clients carried over from previous year	140	136
Number of new admissions	169	126
Total clients served	309	262

Source: Supportive HomeCare Annual Reports.

Choosing Home Health Care

In general, if the person who would be utilizing the home health care service were currently in the hospital, he or she would rely on the advice of the discharge planner, then the family in choosing a home health care agency. The discharge planner is supposed to give hospitalized patients a choice of agencies. It is not clear if such a choice is given. The hospital's VNA may be the only "choice" given by the discharge planner. Outside the hospital, Hansen has found that prospective clients rely primarily on a female member of the family.

Supportive HomeCare has found that clients or referral sources who make service inquiries are at one of four possible stages in their decision making: gathering information, semi-interested, desiring home-care services, or deciding to use a different alternative. The personnel answering the telephones try to respond promptly to all inquiries, assessing the level of decision making and determining the client's needs.

Fees for home health care vary considerably based on the type of care required as well as the company providing the care. Supportive HomeCare was competitively priced for the services offered (see Exhibit 7.10).

Service Growth

Growth, measured in terms of hours of service provided, was quadrupling every quarter during 1983 and 1984. By June 1984, Supportive HomeCare employed forty people, including office personnel, nurses, and nurses' aides. Growth compelled the company to move out of Hansen's home. A vacant house on Mt. Vernon Street (two blocks east of Oshkosh's main street) became available and the company moved during the summer of 1985.

Although Hansen had no formal business training, she had developed and was managing a very successful company. Her concern was that the health care industry was changing rapidly. More competitors were entering the market, and the VNA was the acknowledged market leader in Winnebago County. In addition, she was concerned about the rumors warning that changes in private insurance and Medicaid would make home care less financially beneficial for patients.

To grow, Hansen opened an office in Appleton in January 1986. Outagamie is the largest of the three counties (Outagamie, Winnebago, and Calumet) that make up the Appleton/Fox cities metropolitan statistical area (see Exhibit 7.11 for population statistics). She found that the Oshkosh market had been much

easier to break into than the Appleton market. The two major reasons for this more-difficult entry appeared to be the fact that she did not live in Appleton (although some of her connections there have helped the company) and the strong visiting nurses programs in the area. The Appleton Visiting Nurses Association is well entrenched in that market, plus the Neenah-Menasha VNA is strong. Neenah and Menasha lie between Oshkosh and Appleton, and are relatively closed communities (supportive of home-grown, lived-here-all-our lives businesses).

The company continued strong growth through 1986, although not at the rapid pace of 1983 and 1984. By January 1987, Supportive HomeCare employed thirty full-time personnel in the office and forty-nine full-time and 150 part-time personnel in the field. It became evident that the company had to move again. Hansen investigated several options and chose a site on a corner of Main Street in Oshkosh. Supportive HomeCare wanted to stress being visible to potential customers. The new office had 5,500 square feet of space and included a computer department, billing and payroll, nursing department, marketing, personnel, financial services, and general administration. The location's high visibility did bring in additional growth in terms of walk-in business, which the company had never had before. Hansen anticipated that the new location would adequately serve the company for the next five years.

At the end of December 1989, the staff was somewhat smaller, reflecting the difficulty of recruiting employees. The office staff included twenty full-time and three part-time employees. In the field, there were 13 full-time and 121 part-time employees. The job market shifted in the early 1990s, making it easier to hire employees. However, by 1993, it had tightened up again, as in 1989, requiring Supportive HomeCare to have a strategic recruiting plan. The company expanded services to the Fond du Lac area (south of Oshkosh)

EXHIBIT 7.10
Home Health Care Rate Comparisons

Type of Helper	Supportive Homecare	Visiting Nurses of Mercy Medical Center	Preferred Health Care	Caregivers Homehealth	Neenah-Menasha VNA
Registered Nurse	$80/visit $35/add. hr.	$99/2-hr. visit $39/add. hr.	$80 ($70)/2-hr. visit[1] $30 ($26)/add. hr.	$32 ($27)/hr.[2]	$96/2-hr. visit $29/add. hr.
Licensed Practical Nurse	$55/2-hr. visit $27/add. hr.	n/a	$70/2-hr. visit $22/add. hr.	$25 ($22)/hr.[2]	$96/2-hr. visit $25/add. hr.
Home Health Aide	$36/2-hr. visit $16.45/add. hr.	$47/2-hr. visit $22/add. hr.	$41/2-hr. visit $16.44/add. hr.	$18/hr.	$52/2-hr. visit $16/add. hr.
Personal Care Worker/Homemaker/Companion	$28/2-hr. visit $14/add. hr.	n/a	$21/2-hr. visit $9/add. hr.	$11.50/hr.	$15.75/hr. (2-hr. minimum) $45/overnight (8–10 hrs.)
Live-in Companion	n/a	n/a	$100/day	$8.50/hr.	$12.25/hr.
Home-Care Attendant	$28/2-hr. visit $13/add. hr.	n/a	n/a	$8.50/hr.	$15.75/hr.
Medical Social Worker	n/a	$143/2-hr. visit	n/a	n/a	$134/visit
Speech Pathologist	n/a	$99/2-hr. visit	n/a	n/a	$96/visit
Occupational Therapy	n/a	$99/2-hr. visit	n/a	n/a	$96/visit
Physical Therapy	n/a	$99/2-hr. visit	n/a	n/a	$96/visit

[1]Higher fees for specialized RN (e.g., pediatrics)
[2]Higher for "hi-tech" RNs, LPNs
Sources: Telephone interviews, October 1993; N-M VNA Rate Sheet, October 1993; Supportive HomeCare Rate Sheet, October 1993.

> ### EXHIBIT 7.11
> **Population Statistics for the**
> **Appleton/Oshkosh MSA and Fond du Lac**

	1980	1990	2000
Calumet County	30,867	34,291	29,129
Appleton	5,484	9,075	n/a[1]
Fond du Lac County	n/a	n/a	93,701
Fond du Lac Area	35,863[2]	n/a	52,050
Outagamie County	128,730	140,510	150,823[3]
Appleton	53,424	56,177	73,154[2]
Winnebago County	131,772	140,320	147,918
Appleton	5	443	n/a[1]
Menasha	14,728	14,638	n/a[2]
Neenah	22,432	23,219	n/a[2]
Oshkosh	49,740[4]	55,006	66,290
Town of Menasha	12,307	13,975	n/a[2]

n/a = not available.
[1] Projections rolled into population for Appleton under Outagamie County.
[2] City of Fond du Lac only; city-only statistic not available for projections.
[3] Projections include Fox Cities (pulling Neenah and Menasha from Winnebago County).
[4] City of Oshkosh only; city-only statistic not available for projections.
Source: 1990 Census of Population and Housing, Population and Housing Unit Counts, Wisconsin (Washington, D.C.: Tables 8 and 9; Bureau of the Census, U.S. Department of Commerce, issued April 1993), and *Population Projections for Communities in East Central Wisconsin,* East Central Wisconsin Regional Planning Commission, January 1989, pp. 5, 6, 9, 13.

in 1991 and opened an office there in mid-1993.

Entrepreneurial Style

Terri Hansen is an entrepreneur who learned how to manage an "overnight success." She developed a team concept in managing the company. Currently, she is grooming her team, which is composed of the nurse manager, the personnel director, the financial director, and the marketing manager. Her partner, John Westphal, served as director of computer services until she bought his share of the partnership in late July 1987. Exhibit 7.12 is a copy

of Hansen's organization chart. "My team is very strong, especially because of the different backgrounds of the members. Decisions are made as a team and I seldom override them. But I will if I think something else is best for the company."

Marketing meetings are held once every six weeks. Team members are encouraged to refer both employees and clients to Supportive HomeCare. Customer service is a key focus of these meetings. The company added a customer service representative, who calls two weeks after a person becomes a SHC client. With the assistance of the marketing department, all clients receive phone calls once per

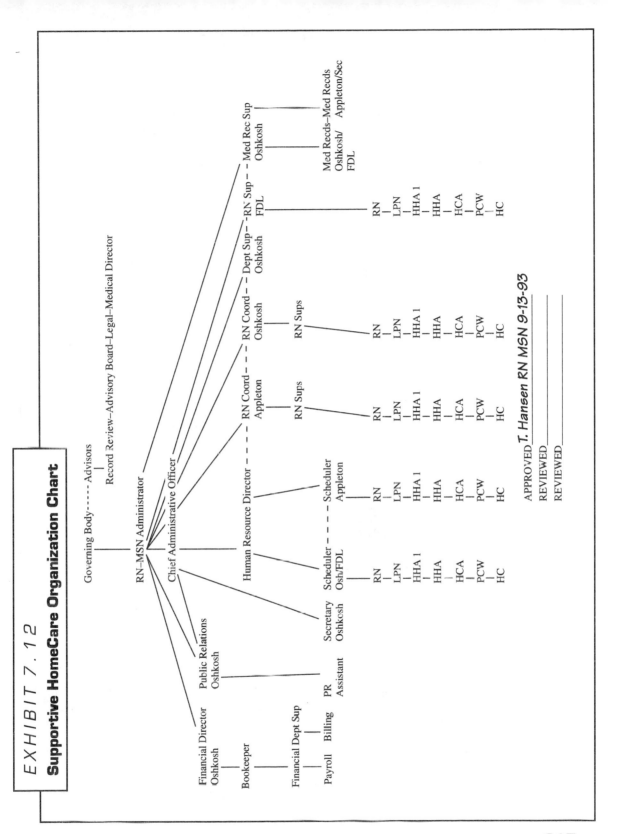

EXHIBIT 7.12
Supportive HomeCare Organization Chart

quarter. This helps the company identify problems and make corrections.

Her nurses and office staff are involved in marketing. Each office employee is given certain marketing assignments to complete. The team is working on a company wide plan to "keep Supportive HomeCare in the community's mind." Ms. Hansen acknowledges the market leadership of the local VNA in the area outside Oshkosh (see Exhibit 7.13 for its market position). "We are aiming at being number two in the market outside of Oshkosh – a strong number two at that." She does not see her company taking over the top spots occupied by the VNA in Appleton and Neenah-

Menasha, unless the VNAs were to increase their rates. Hansen summed up her style of management: "I believe in a strong management philosophy – I was never taught that; I just use common sense."

Hansen recognized the value of good community relations and is very active in the community. She has taken advantage of opportunities to speak to clubs in the area whenever possible and has held an open house at Supportive HomeCare's offices. Her company was Wisconsin's 1991 Blue Chip Enterprise Initiative contest winner (out of more than 800 applicants), and she is the first woman president of the Oshkosh Chamber of Commerce.

EXHIBIT 7.13
Market Positions for the Major Home Care Providers in the Oshkosh Area

Position	1987	1990	1993[1]
Oshkosh			
1	Supportive HomeCare	Supportive HomeCare	Supportive HomeCare
2	Mercy VNA	Mercy VNA	Mercy VNA
3	Upjohn	Upjohn	CareGivers HomeHealth
4	County Nurses	Lakeshore	County Nurses
5	Preferred Health	County Nurses	
Appleton			
1	Appleton VNA	Appleton VNA	Appleton VNA
2	Supportive HomeCare	Supportive HomeCare	Supportive HomeCare
3	Upjohn	Upjohn	CareGivers HomeHealth
4	Preferred Health	Preferred Health	Preferred Health
5	St. Elizabeth's	Lakeshore	
Neenah/Menasha			
1	Neenah-Menasha VNA	Neenah-Menasha VNA	Neenah-Menasha VNA
2	Supportive HomeCare	Supportive HomeCare	Supportive HomeCare[2]
3	Upjohn	Upjohn	Preferred Health[2]
4	Preferred Health	Preferred Health	CareGivers HomeHealth
5		Lakeshore	

[1]Lakeshore was no longer in business; Upjohn became CareGivers HomeHealth.
[2]Tied in market share.
Source: Observations of Terri Hansen, August 1990, November 1993.

A Different Industry

The changes in the environment made for a greater challenge in running a small business in health care. More competitors entered the market, and many private insurance companies decided to drop coverage of home health care programs. This really hurt the funding outlook for home care in general and Supportive HomeCare was not immune to the problem. As shown in Exhibit 7.14, the funding mix changed for Supportive HomeCare, reflecting the problems created by insurance companies' modifications in the coverage granted for home care.

In addition, Medicaid made changes that have had a major impact on Supportive HomeCare. Like many others, the company had come to depend on third-party funding, but it appears that third-party payments will continue to diminish. Hansen has been attempting to contract with other businesses, such as the city of Oshkosh, Georgia Pacific, or Mercury Marine, in order to move away from dependency on third-party payments. She has contracts with the Appleton and Neenah-Menasha VNAs to provide extended care for hospice patients and with nearly all nursing homes in the Fox River Valley to provide staffing when needed.

Supportive HomeCare Services

Supportive HomeCare provides a variety of services, including registered nurses, licensed practical nurses, home health aides/nurses' aides, homemaker-companions, night service, insurance counseling, private duty, institutional staffing, and home care attendant/personal care worker. Services were provided 24-hours a day and seven days a week.

Two new programs were introduced in 1987 when the use of home health care appeared to be declining. Personnel Resource Network (PRN) had two divisions, Home Management and Staffing. PRN Home Management was considered to be a burgeoning area primarily because of the increasing number of two-income families. Services offered included routine and extensive cleaning, laun-

---

EXHIBIT 7.14
Supportive HomeCare Funding Mix

Sources	September 1986	1989–1990	1992–1993
Private pay	17%	22.33%	25.19%
Medicaid	33	43.68	33.55
Private insurance	40	10.10	14.07
Medicare	3	3.71	10.08
County funds	7	13.80	10.14
PRN*	n/a	3.21	1.58
LSC*	n/a	.66	.17
Other	0	2.51	5.22

*New programs started in 1987.
Source: Supportive HomeCare company records.

dry and ironing, grocery shopping and errands, meal preparation, and help with entertaining. Hansen admitted that she had not invested the money necessary to market this service. "This program is just about dead," said Hansen in October 1993. "I plan to change the name to HomeMaids and market the program to professionals as a maid and home management service." She considered PRN Staffing to be successful because it provided temporary staff for hospitals, nursing homes, and other health care providers.

The other new service, LifeStyle Connections (LSC), provided custom services, including health assessment screenings, behavior-modification classes, fitness assessments, lifestyle assessments, and informational mini seminars. Only a few companies used the services of LSC. According to Hansen, "LSC is still a concept before its time. It may be revitalized now that President Clinton wants to pay for preventative health measures such as screening tests."

SHC Goals and Philosophy

Hansen outlined her goals for Supportive HomeCare:

- To provide quality nursing and supportive services;
- To provide a quality agency by providing superior services at a competitive cost; monitoring agency expansion to meet the needs of the community; functioning within local, state, and federal guidelines; and monitoring and evaluating agency operations continuously;
- To hire and retain qualified employees;
- To increase community and consumer awareness via marketing and community relations;
- To achieve maximum reimbursement from third-party payers.

Supportive HomeCare's unique selling proposition and philosophy are provided in Exhibit 7.15.

Staffing

In 1989 Hansen stated, "Staffing is our biggest problem. The nursing and other medical personnel shortage is real and it's everywhere. But we are not only competing with other health care organizations to get good people but with restaurants, factories, and so forth. Home health care has a problem with retaining people, too. It is difficult to predict or ensure working hours, the individual is isolated on the job because there are no other staff to talk to, the hours are often inconvenient, and travel – sometimes longer distances than I'd like – is often required."

The nursing shortage of the 1980s eased up in the early 1990s; however, the market has shifted and tightened once again in 1993. "The big need today is for Certified Nursing Assistants or CNAs," said Hansen. "The CNA is one of the highest demanded jobs right now." The state regulates who can work as a CNA and more training is being required for nurses. "This training is both extensive and costly," she commented. "As a result, the market for CNAs and nurses has tightened up."

The government also instituted tougher regulations for training home health care "aides." However, a new category of health care providers was added that fit the old job description for "home health aide." A "personal care worker" (PCW) could be reimbursed $11.50 an hour in 1993. Medicaid changed the amount of reimbursement for home health aide services, effective July 1992. A four-hour visit used to generate $63.30 in reimbursements from Medicaid; after July 1992 Medicaid would only pay $37.00. According to Ms. Hansen, "Medicaid makes us jump through hoops to get reimbursed for home health aides versus personal care workers. The company will submit hours for home health aides – HHAs – and Medicaid will cross out HHAs and write PCWs and only pay PCW rates for reimbursements. It's a real problem," said Hansen.

> ### *EXHIBIT 7.15*
> **Supportive HomeCare Positioning**
>
> #### Unique Selling Proposition
>
> Supportive HomeCare provides skilled nursing, personal care, and homemaker/
> companion services for up to twenty-four hours a day, seven days a week to clients in
> their homes. Initial contact, assessment of service needs, and exploration of payment
> options are at no charge to the client. Quality services are offered at a competitive price.
>
> Supportive HomeCare maintains a reputation for being the quality service that truly
> cares about people and considers meeting its clients' needs as the number one goal.
> The agency acts as a client advocate. The staff have professional expertise in dealing
> with third-party payment sources and continually remain abreast of issues dealing with
> home care.
>
> Supportive HomeCare maintains strict supervision policies, agency rules and regula-
> tions, service, and employment standards. Employees are thoroughly screened, trained,
> oriented, and provided inservice training on an ongoing basis.
>
> Supportive HomeCare prides itself on case management. It maintains close communi-
> cation with the client, family, physician, and significant others involved. The agency
> strives to develop a cooperative working relationship with other community agencies
> and facilities.
>
> #### Philosophy of the Agency
>
> It is the philosophy of the agency to provide quality and dependable nursing care,
> therapies, and homemaker/companion services, thus enabling individuals to remain as
> independent as possible in the least-restrictive environment. Services will be provided
> by employees who are qualified, experienced, and empathetic to the needs of home care
> clients. All aspects of the agency will be monitored to provide efficient and cost-effective
> quality care.
>
> Supportive HomeCare will promote cooperative working relationships with other
> home health providers and community resources, to attain a comprehensive level of
> care.

Supportive HomeCare attempted to market itself to potential employees to entice them to come to work, and developed retention strategies to keep the individuals once they were hired. On July 1, 1990, Supportive HomeCare instituted a number of changes for the field staff, including increased employee benefits, higher wages to be more in line with competition, increased personal contact by Hansen and the office staff, and development of a "retention budget." Employees were rewarded with small gifts for beyond-the-call-of-duty service, flowers were sent for special occasions, and gift certificates were given for a holiday remembrance.

Hansen met with the personnel department twice a month to actively work on problem solving for staffing. "We have the patients.

We just don't have the staff," she lamented. "We stress the flexible hours we offer for part-time and some full-time staff. We are a compassionate employer. We know and understand the needs of employees. And we are a company that anyone can be proud to work for because we provide quality care and we have the reputation for providing quality care."

In 1993, the key addition has been "benefit positions," designed for top-quality home health aides and homemakers. Personnel holding benefit positions get guaranteed hours with benefits prorated on the number of hours worked. Employees rely on working a certain number of hours for income. Normally, income loss results when a patient is moved to the hospital, a nursing home, or dies. Benefit position employees are guaranteed the hours and benefits without regard to the patient changes – an effective retention tool.

WHAT LIES AHEAD?

Some challenges lay ahead for Hansen and her company. Competition was more intense and would be a factor.

> Our competitors control discharges from the hospitals – Visiting Nurses of Mercy Medical Center for Mercy Hospital, Neenah-Menasha VNA for Theda Clark, St. Agnes VNA for St. Agnes Hospital in Fond du Lac, and the Appleton VNA for Appleton Medical Center and St. Elizabeth's Hospital. It's tough to compete.
>
> The whole economy in health care is changing. Aurora Health Care [in the Milwaukee area] is buying hospitals and other health care providers. Health care reform is both a threat and an opportunity for our business. Big guys are gobbling up little guys. . . . Where does fair competition play in this? Independent agencies will be ap-

proached to be bought by larger conglomerates.

> The environment continues to change. In the 1980s, there was a shortage of qualified nurses – not just in Oshkosh and Appleton, but all over the country. The situation eased a little during the early 1990s. However, in 1993 nurses are demanding hospital-based wages – $20 per hour – to change to home care and there is a shortage of CNAs. I'm worried that Fox Valley Technical College will discontinue CNA training. They're considering it right now.

Hansen had several other concerns for home health care. As noted before, the government instituted tougher regulations for training and certifying both home health aides and CNAs. There were reductions in reimbursements from Medicaid, Medicare, and county funds. In Wisconsin, insurance coverage for home care is mandated; however, insurance companies get around paying for it. Reform efforts should help with this problem. Private insurance paid very few claims. Hansen does foresee a turnaround. Although there was an increased need for home care as the population aged, there was insufficient staff that was affordable.

> People just can't afford personal home care. It is a real balancing act when the environment is hostile, there is a shortage of health care providers, and demand exceeds supply. People are having to pay more out of pocket for home care.
>
> Then there are new government laws and regulations to comply with, which add to overhead costs. One headache is the OSHA blood-borne pathogen law, where employees must get hepatitis injections, wear protective gloves and clothing, and receive

costly training. When you visit your dentist who wears a mask and gloves, he or she is complying with the law. We spend $150 per employee for three hepatitis injections.

Then there is the living will law. . . . The public and patients must be informed of their rights to living wills. Compliance with this law is expensive for us. Each patient has to receive a packet of information and the company must get a copy of the patient's living will. *Every* time a patient is admitted to the hospital, forms must be signed and the entire process is basically repeated for every admittance. Then there's the paperwork that goes with the new Americans with Disabilities Act (ADA).

A combination of all these new regulations added to the increase in costs.

Supportive HomeCare has made some internal changes in response to these external forces. According to Hansen, "Nurses are now dictating their notes, instead of writing them down on paper. We'll move to handheld computers when the prices come down." The company has added computerized scheduling, which has improved efficiency, cut mistakes, and yielded time savings. "We're doing electronic billing, where claims are sent in over modems ('paperless claims'), and we'll be doing electronic payroll in a month or two, for time and energy savings. Three facsimile machines let the three offices talk quickly to each other."

Hansen saw some possible new targets coming from health care reform. "People will be released from the hospital 'quicker and sicker.' This is better for home care but maybe not better for the patients. New mothers are being discharged from the hospital in 24 hours for a normal delivery and 48 hours for a C-section. Regardless of the length of labor, the clock's ticking. There will be a need for home care to check on new mothers and their babies, a greater need if there were complications."

Preparing for new targets, Supportive HomeCare is adding new services such as IV therapy, more skilled nursing, and "My Baby and Me" (a class for new mothers on well-baby care).

Hansen continued, "Our billing is higher than it's ever been. Reimbursement is poorer than it has ever been. The demand is here, but if Medicaid and Medicare are a big part, reimbursement is a big problem." Hansen added, "The specific objective for SHC in 1993 is to increase the case load for the year. I hope to do that by accomplishing four objectives: (1) increase the number of new cases, (2) increase the number of referrals from clients and former clients, (3) keep rates as low as possible, and (4) grow the Fond du Lac market."

Hansen concluded, "It's going to be another busy year for Supportive HomeCare. It will be interesting to see what reform will do to this industry. It should expand because of better reimbursement if the Clinton proposal is enacted, but it will probably become even more competitive . . ."

NOTES

1. National Association for Home Care, *How to Choose a Home Care Agency,* 1992 brochure, p. 1.
2. *Basic Statistics About Home Care* (Washington, D.C.: National Association for Home Care, 1993), p. 1.
3. Ibid.
4. Ibid.
5. Robin Richman, "High-Tech Home Care: What's in It for Hospitals?" *Health Care Strategic Management* 8, no. 3 (March 1990), p. 19.
6. "Health Services," *U.S. Industrial Outlook 1990* (Washington, D.C.: U.S. Department of Commerce, January 1990), p. 49-5.

7. Sandy Lutz, "Hospitals Reassess Home Care Ventures," *Modern Healthcare* 20, no. 37 (September 17, 1990), p. 26.

8. "Projections of the Number of Persons Diagnosed with AIDS and the Number of Immunosuppressed HIV-Invested Persons – United States, 1992–1994," *Journal of the American Medical Association* 269, no. 6 (February 10, 1993), p. 733.

9. Howard J. Anderson, "Providers Develop Specialized AIDS Home Care Programs," *Hospitals* (July 5, 1992), p. 144.

10. Mary Wagner, "Despite Gains in Home Infusion Therapy, Home-Care Revenue Growth Remains Flat," *Modern Healthcare* 20, no. 20 (May 21, 1990), p. 96.

11. *Basic Statistics About Home Care,* p. 6.

12. Kevin O'Donnell, "Home Care Shaping up as Competitive Necessity," *Modern Healthcare* 23, no. 23 (June 14, 1993), p. 34.

13. Lutz, "Hospitals Reassess Home Care Ventures," p. 23.

14. Frank Cerne, "Homeward Bound," *Hospitals* (February 20, 1993), p. 52.

15. David Baker, "Home Care's Role in Integrated Healthcare Delivery Systems," *The Remington Report* (March/April 1993), p. 12.

16. O'Donnell, "Home Care Shaping Up," p. 34.

17. Richman, "High-Tech Home Care," p. 1.

18. Sandy Lutz, "Home-Care Agencies Offer Bonuses for Business," *Modern Healthcare* 20, no. 33 (August 20, 1990), pp. 73–74.

19. "Providers Eye Entry of Case Managers in Home Infusion," *Modern Healthcare* 20, no. 37 (September 17, 1990), p. 30.

20. Mary Wagner, "Home Infusion Growth Fosters Advances for Home-Care Firms," *Modern Healthcare* 23, no. 21 (May 24, 1993), p. 82.

21. Telephone calls during November 1993.

Lamprey Health Care: A Model Health Center

Ann Peters, executive director of Lamprey Health Care, was lost in the moment, reflecting on the events of the past year. Lamprey Health Care (LHC) celebrated its twentieth year as a primary care community health center in 1991 and was heralded by health care leaders as a model center.

LHC had continued its phenomenal growth, surpassing even Peters's wildest imagination. Peters was busy putting the final touches on her executive director's report to be presented to the Executive Committee of the Board of Directors the next day. She could not help thinking about a 1989 article she had pinned to her wall regarding the rise and fall of Wang Computer. She was struck by a quote in the Wang article: "Success is nice. It can also be dangerous. It can destroy the very things that make a company click in the first place and in doing so, set the stage for decline."

The article identified three dangers Wang's senior management failed to consider:

1. Successful companies get big fast
2. Success breeds arrogance
3. Success breeds conservatism

This case was prepared by Michael J. Merenda, University of New Hampshire, and Timothy W. Edlund, Morgan State University. It is intended as a basis for classroom discussion rather than to illustrate effective or ineffective handling of an administrative situation. Copyright © 1994 by Michael Merenda and Timothy W. Edlund. Used with permission from Tim Edlund.

Peters wondered as she read through the historical summary of her director's report and contemplated the challenges facing LHC. "What are the lessons to be learned from Wang's decline, especially its failure to recognize the need to focus on service and control of growth? Does the Wang story parallel some of the challenges we are facing? Will 1992 be our watershed year, given the poor condition of New Hampshire's economy and the severe problems facing the health care industry in the United States?"

LHC BACKGROUND INFORMATION

In 1980 the Newmarket Center opened its doors in the basement of the Newmarket (New Hampshire) Town Hall as a walk-in clinic. The center was started by Volunteers in Service to America (VISTA), first as a referral and coordinating agency. It added a blood pressure screening service and ultimately became an agency providing lifelong preventive health care for individuals of all ages and incomes. Originally called Newmarket Regional Health Center, the name was changed to Lamprey Health Care in 1987 by a vote of the Board of Directors to better reflect the enlarged service area that extended far beyond the town of Newmarket.

In fiscal year 1991 (the year ending September 30, 1991), the Newmarket and Raymond Centers provided over 37,000 medical

EXHIBIT 8.1

Lamprey Health Care Performance Summary, Budget Year 1990–1991

Program	September 1991			Year-to-Date			
	Sept. Actual	Projected	Variance	Total Actual	Projected	Variance	Budget
Medical provider visits[1]							
Newmarket	1,552	1,855	(303)	19,133	22,260	(3,127)	22,255
Raymond	1,431	1,638	(207)	18,140	19,656	(1,516)	19,650
Total	2,983	3,493	(510)	37,273	41,916	(4,643)	41,905
Other health visits[2]							
Newmarket	219	218	1	3,531	2,616	915	2,616
Raymond	234	234	0	2,776	2,808	(32)	2,808
Total	453	452	1	6,307	5,424	883	5,424
Number new prenatal patients	27	25	2	253	300	(47)	300
Number prenatal deliveries	20	20	0	212	240	(28)	240
Patient fee collections							
Newmarket	$64,039	$75,591	($11,552)	$871,888	$956,852	($84,964)	$957,428
Raymond	67,571	63,363	4,208	798,009	802,067	(4,058)	801,492
Total—avg		138,954	(138,954)	1,669,897	1,758,919	(89,022)	1,758,920
Outstanding A/R							
Newmarket	$126,578	$239,979	$(113,401)				$239,979
Raymond	250,331	193,010	57,321				193,010
Total	376,909	432,989	(56,080)				432,989
Days A/R							
Newmarket	42	90	(48)				90
Raymond	82	90	(8)				90
Total	62	90	(28)				90
Information							
Number problems—I&R	372	314	58	3,421	3,768	(347)	3,768
Number referrals— I&R	411	389	22	4,231	4,668	(437)	4,668
Number Tel Med calls	9,104	5,500	3,604	64,631	66,000	(1,369)	66,000
Transportation Rides	1,956	2,109	(153)	26,907	25,308	1,599	25,308
Ratios							
Medical cost/all visits	40	55	(15)	56	55	1	55
Percent collections of total billable charges	0.93	0.95	−0.02	1.10	0.95	0.15	0.95

[1]Does not include nutritional and mental health
[2]Other health visits include nutrition, mental health and community health worker visits, and special clinics

provider visits, over 6,000 other visits (including hospital visits), and delivered 212 babies (see Exhibit 8.1). The center's combined revenues from all sources for FY 1991 were almost $2.8 million.

The rapid pace of change affecting the health care industry in the 1980s was expected to accelerate well into the 1990s. Managing change, especially as it affected the center's ability to meet its primary mission of providing quality community-based health and medical services was seen by Ann Peters as the center's major challenge. She identified several issues and trends in her executive report. How these issues affected the center's mission (Exhibit 8.2) and long-term position as a community health center would probably dominate her meeting with the board.

EXHIBIT 8.2
Lamprey Health Care Mission Statement

The primary mission of Lamprey Health Care is to provide quality community-based family and medical services. Our goal is "To Be the Best We Can Be" and to provide patient satisfaction in all aspects of our services. Lamprey Health Care is in the business of caring—caring for our patients, our communities, and our staff. We provide care for individuals of all ages and incomes who reside in Southeastern New Hampshire, centered on the Lamprey River basin. Services provided shall be carried out in a friendly, prompt, cost-effective, and caring manner.

Lamprey Health Care is an organization that values its communities, its employees, and its patients. Lamprey Health Care supports an environment for professional growth and development based on the shared values of its community board members and staff toward the delivery of community health care.

The center offers a range of primary health and medical care services, including health education, social services, transportation and information services that support the philosophy of keeping the person as independent and close to home as practical and clinically indicated. Practitioners will provide continuity of care from outpatient through inpatient hospital follow-up, social, and nutritional services.

Lamprey Health Care is committed to continuing its high standards of service delivered in a cost-effective manner. This requires the maintenance of financial integrity and appropriate utilization of resources. Lamprey Health Care places a high value on patients and employees, our communities, and others who support these goals.

Lamprey Health Care plays a leadership role in addressing and responding to state, regional, and local health and related needs. The foundation and orientation of Lamprey Health Care comes from its strong relationships with the communities it serves. This includes policy setting by community members of the Board of Directors, advisory committee input and support, and responsiveness to the needs of our patients and users of all programs.

EARLIER DEVELOPMENTS

This case continues an earlier case (Case 17) that describes the choices facing Newmarket Regional Health Center (NRHC) in early 1987. Among these were the choice between two hospitals for inpatient treatment of NRHC clients, completion of fund raising for a new facility in Raymond to replace an inadequate one (where the lease could not be renewed in any case), and efforts to obtain satisfactory reciprocal coverage for clients, particularly for Obstetrics (delivery of babies). However, the greatest challenge was meeting costs incurred in a newly instituted prenatal health care program, used primarily by poor women who previously could not obtain any such service. The program was attracting many clients from areas outside NRHC's normal service area because it was unique in all New Hampshire. Should that program be continued, and if so, how could it be kept from bankrupting NRHC?

The new facility (for LRC) was built at Raymond. By the time it opened, nearly all of its cost had been raised from a variety of contributors: individuals, foundations, and some businesses. It opened on schedule and had a growing client base and intensive use. Exhibit 8.1 may be used to compare utilization of both centers in FY 1991 with the 1984 figures in Exhibit 17.10 of the Newmarket Case.

Exeter Hospital was chosen to continue as NRHC's hospital. Ann Peters and her administration and the nonmedical board members favored Elliott Hospital at Manchester for reasons of cost, capabilities, and client convenience. The physicians strongly preferred Exeter for its location, despite its coverage and reciprocity restrictions. John Russell resigned as board chair, in part over this issue, although he continued as a board member.

The prenatal care program was continued, as an essential part of NRHC's mission. Deficits were expected to grow as the client list grew. Recognizing that inadequate prenatal care for rural areas existed throughout the state,

NRHC determined that the proper funding agency was the state government. NRHC took the lead in building a statewide coalition that placed the issue before the state legislature. Ann Peters was the lead witness in providing testimony. Despite New Hampshire's tradition of handling most program funding locally, an annual appropriation of $500,000 was passed to provide adequate prenatal care to those not able to afford it. That funding has been continued, although LHC and all other recipients suffered a 19 percent cut in funding for FY1991 and further cuts were expected.

Because NRHC was the lead group in the coalition and one of the few existing not-for-profit medical organizations giving prenatal care to the medically underserved, NRHC received a substantial portion of that funding.

Analysis of NRHC's increasing prenatal caseload showed heavy usage from clients outside its usual service area. Women were coming to NRHC because no similar capability existed where they lived. NRHC identified appropriate community agencies in those areas and assisted them in starting similar services and obtaining funding. Not only did such care become more convenient for clients in those areas, but losses for prenatal care at NRHC were kept within acceptable limits. Moreover, Ann Peters's expertise was increasingly sought by others planning facilities intended to serve similar clients.

Several years later, LHC was asked to manage a similar center that had been started in Seabrook, New Hampshire. The town of Seabrook, site of the long-delayed nuclear power plant that had driven New Hampshire Public Service Company into bankruptcy, was on the seacoast southeast of Exeter, about 15 miles from Newmarket. After an extensive exploration of this opportunity, LHC's board decided not to accept the offer, believing that it would unduly endanger continued accomplishment of LHC's mission in its existing centers. There was no shortage of new challenges and opportunities, however.

HEALTH CARE REFORM

Peters reviewed several national proposals for health care reform in her executive director's report. Among those proposed were (1) a Canadian-style system, (2) play or pay, (3) the Administration's (Bush) health plan, (4) consumer choice, and (5) managed care. These five proposals are summarized in Exhibit 8.3. More details on the Canadian system are contained in Exhibit 8.4.

The major impetus for change reflected both decreased coverage and rising health care costs, which were 11.5 percent of gross national product in 1991. Approximately 37 million people had no health care insurance; that number was expected to increase to 40 million in 1992. In a March 1992, *Fortune* article, Joseph A. Califano, former Secretary of Health and Human Services, stated, "The shifting of financial responsibility for health care costs from hospitals to government to taxpayers becomes a macabre dance of despair and an unconscionable cop-out." Compared to other industrialized nations, Americans had higher hospital and doctor costs despite lower average physician contacts per capita. Exhibit 8.5 highlights some comparisons.

Peters stated in her report, "The health care safety net has disappeared and the newest class of uninsured are white working adults. The patchwork quilt of the health care system is failing." She identified several areas for health reform: outcomes assessment, managed care, technology and information, Medicare, malpractice, and primary-care physicians.

Outcomes Assessment

One of the most controversial proposals coming from Washington was a statistical tool called *outcomes assessment*. Spurred by skyrocketing health care costs, it was described as an attempt to establish objective means of measuring success rates for treatment. Peters stated in her executive report,

The lack of standards in medical care will no longer be tolerated. A new body, the 'Agency for Health Care Policy Research Standards,' has been created nationally and funded for outcomes research and technology assessment. Currently, data on quality standards are missing and payers are demanding it. The push is to develop Standards of Practice. In the future, deviation from the standards will have to be justified in both clinical and cost terms; for example, currently Quaker Oats makes use of price and quality data in developing its Health Insurance Plan. It makes this data available to its employees. This type of activity will expand in the future. Both employers and insurers are demanding it. Corporate health benefits programs now total 45 percent of net earnings according to a New York based employee benefit consulting firm. If left unchecked, health care benefits will consume all potential raises. Thus, the pressure for accountability will be stronger than ever.

In a contemporary article, "Health Care by the Numbers," proponents of outcomes assessment argued that outcomes assessment gives physicians, hospitals, and regulators a system for determining the medical practices that work and those that do not. They foresaw a day when physicians would be able to access massive computerized data banks that would help them make better informed medical decisions.

Managed Care

Managed care is a mechanism to control costs. In 1991, its use increased nationwide, with one-half of all workers in companies having more than 200 employees enrolled in managed care. Although health care benefit costs in-

EXHIBIT 8.3
Major Health Care Reform Proposals

Plan	How It Works	Who's for It	How It Would Limit Costs
Canadian-Style System	A tax-supported, government-run system would pay all medical bills	Sixty-six Democratic Congressmen – and one Republican – led by Representative Russo (D-Illinois)	Government budgeting process
Play or Pay	Employers would have to provide minimum health coverage or pay new taxes to finance a government-run plan	Democratic Senate leadership (Mitchell bill); Representative Rostenkowski in the House	Payers and providers negotiate prices within national guidelines (Mitchell); government gradually limits rise in health spending to GNP growth rate
Administration's Health Plan	Tax credits up to $3,750 a year for low-income families and deductions for the middle class would help many of the uninsured buy basic health insurance	Bush Administration	Find offsetting efficiencies throughout the health care system
Consumer Choice	Individuals would be required to buy health insurance on their own or through employers, paying with a proposed tax credit	Heritage Foundation	Market forces: comparison shopping by individuals
Managed Competition	Employers would have to offer – and workers would have to join – one of several comprehensive, accountable health plans	Jackson Hole Group of health industry experts and executives	Market forces: comparison shopping by individuals from plans screened by employers or other intermediaries

Source: Fortune (March 23, 1992), p. 49.

to process information from various sources. Information technology was expected to change the structure of health care delivery. For example, bedside ICU computers were already directing care in some hospitals. Clinical information systems were connected directly to monitoring equipment and flow sheets, providing analysis of the patient's progress against a large data base. Patient progress was already being evaluated against that data, and information provided to the physician for decision making had been greatly expanded. It was believed that the next logical step for this type of development was application to labor and delivery.

Machines were expected to get smarter. NASA and the Department of Defense were working on a smart battlefield stretcher. Cited examples were cutting edge developments, but new technology was being rapidly assimilated, and Lamprey Health Care was expected to need to evaluate technology as it developed. However, in the near future their major investments in technology was planned to be focused on their strategic thrusts, that is on practice standards.

Medicaid

Nationwide, Medicaid grew by 3.1 million enrollees in 1991 because of increased poverty and expanded eligibility. However, there was a drive to cap Medicaid. There were proposals to put a 6 percent cap on Title XIX (for Medicaid). LHC had an increasing proportion of its patients covered by Medicaid. Therefore, any changes in Title XIX were very important for its financial viability.

Malpractice

All versions of health care reform had malpractice reform components, and it was the general consensus that the $7 billion spent on insurance and the $15 billion spent on defensive medi-

creased 11.5 percent in 1991, it was the lowest cost increase since 1987. The decrease was due in part to a shift to managed care that better controlled costs. Thus managed care was expected to be a growth component of LHC business. The potential existed for developing a public sector managed care option with capitation, such as Medicaid prepayment.

Technology and Information

Growth and development in information technology was expected to drive the health care system in the future. Clinicians would be able

EXHIBIT 8.5

U.S. Hospital Tabs Compared to Four Other Advanced Countries

	United States	Canada	France	Germany	Switzerland
Average cost per day in hospital, 1988	$780	$500	$350	$170	$220
Average annual expenditure per capita	$430	$250	$150	$190	$250
Average annual physician contacts per capita	5.2	6.4	7.0	11.3	5.9

Source: M. Moremont, G. Schares, S. Toy, and S. Garland, "Can Europe Help Cure America's Health Care Mess?" *Business Week* (March 9, 1992), pp. 52–54.

cine could not be tolerated any longer. Legislative efforts were expected to establish dispute resolution processes with limits on noneconomic damages (awards for pain and suffering) and to create mandatory binding arbitration systems.

In addition, legislative proposals were being developed to support coverage of CHC (community health center) providers under the Federal Tort Claims Act much in the same manner that NHSC physicians were covered in the 1980s. LHC was currently spending $100,000 on malpractice insurance. Potential savings were significant; however, possible threats existed with area obstetricians and their liability concerns when they provide care for LHC patients.

Primary-Care Physicians

The supply of primary care physicians was decreasing. In 1990, only 70.4 percent of family practice residency programs were filled and only 59.9 percent were filled with U.S. graduates. At the same time, HMOs and other managed-care options were growing and increasing the demand for these physicians. It

was estimated that HMOs alone could absorb all primary care graduates for the next ten years. In addition, fewer graduating primary-care physicians were selecting rural areas and those graduating had ever-increasing debt loads.

LHC was therefore in a highly competitive market for family physicians. Furthermore, family physicians who also provide obstetrics care were a truly scarce resource. It was therefore important that LHC retain its current physicians and be competitive in recruiting new physicians. These personnel issues would affect any expansion activities.

Exhibit 8.6 details trends in physician choice of primary-care versus specialization and specialization choices within primary care.

FINANCE

Financial information is included in Exhibits 8.7 through 8.12. Management budget reports are Exhibits 8.1, 8.7, 8.8, and 8.9; financial statements are Exhibits 8.10 through 8.12; and definitions of selected financial terms used by LRC are included in Exhibit 8.13.

Financial highlights included revenues

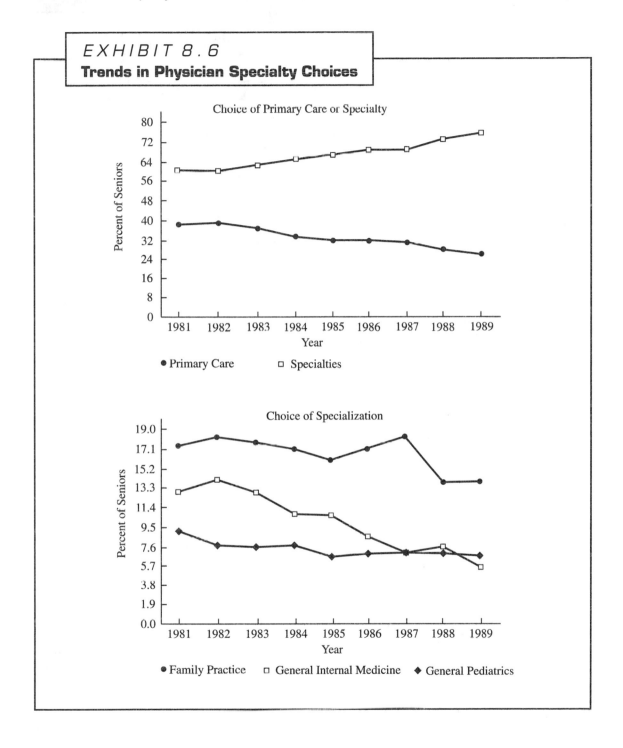

EXHIBIT 8.6
Trends in Physician Specialty Choices

Choice of Primary Care or Specialty

● Primary Care □ Specialties

Choice of Specialization

● Family Practice □ General Internal Medicine ◆ General Pediatrics

EXHIBIT 8.7

Operating Budget
(10/01/90–9/30/91, period ending September 1991)

	Month to Date			Year to Date			
	Actual	Projected	Favorable/ Unfavorable Variances	Actual	Projected	Favorable/ Unfavorable Variances	Total Budget
Patient fees	$131,600	$138,954	($7,354)	$1,697,485	$1,758,919	$61,434	$1,758,920
Total receipts	230,400	215,776	14,624	2,716,300	2,797,215	80,915	2,804,000
Expenses							
Personnel/ fringe	98,200	147,700	49,500	1,735,300	1,889,400	154,100	1,829,200
Malpractice insurance	10,400	11,100	700	124,600	133,000	8,400	132,700
Facility	10,700	16,300	5,600	197,500	225,300	27,800	195,400
Practice administration	11,000	15,900	4,900	181,300	190,900	9,600	189,200
Office administration	11,500	15,200	3,700	175,200	182,400	7,200	184,300
General insurance	3,600	4,100	500	46,000	49,400	3,400	49,700
Other	8,900	12,200	3,300	101,900	116,700	14,800	146,500
Total operating expenses	154,300	222,500	68,200	2,561,800	2,787,100	225,300	2,727,000
Other income/ expenses	–	–	–	–	–	–	–
Excess revenue/ expenses						*(163,866)	

*Estimated accruals not included: approximately $50,000.

EXHIBIT 8.8

Capital Budget—Expenses
(10/01/90–9/30/91, period ending August 1991)

	Month to Date			Year to Date			
	Actual	Projected	Favorable/ Unfavorable Variances	Actual	Projected	Favorable/ Unfavorable Variances	Total Budget
Office equipment	0	0	0	$10,900	0	$10,900	0
Medical equipment	0	0	0	8,000	$5,000	(3,000)	$5,000
Mortgage	$700	$700	0	8,400	8,400	0	8,400
Reserve fund	50,000	0	($50,000)	50,000	6,000	(44,000)	12,000
Total expenses	$50,700	$700	($50,000)	$77,300	$19,400	($57,900)	$25,400
Estimated total budget net							$55,966

EXHIBIT 8.9
Cash Flow Budget, September 1991

	Month to Date			Year to Date			
	Actual	Projected	Favorable/ Unfavorable Variance	Actual	Projected	Favorable/ Unfavorable Variance	Total
Collections							
Patient fees	$131,600	$138,900	($7,300)	$1,697,300	$1,758,900	($61,600)	$1,758,900
PHS grants	60,000	60,700	(700)	747,600	715,700	31,900	715,700
Other grants	18,700	12,600	6,100	214,900	193,000	21,900	193,000
Towns/ United Way	4,800	500	4,300	84,600	101,500	(16,900)	101,500
Interest	600	0	600	1,800	0	1,800	0
Building fund	100	0	100	3,200	0	3,200	0
Other income	14,600	3,100	11,500	68,800	28,100	40,700	28,100
Total collections	$230,400	$215,800	$14,600	$2,818,200	$2,797,200	$21,000	$2,797,200
Payments							
Personnel	$124,900	$140,700	$15,800	$1,584,200	$1,859,200	$275,000	$1,859,200
Malpractice insurance	22,100	25,500	3,400	139,400	129,900	(9,500)	129,900
Facility	14,700	16,300	1,600	180,500	195,600	15,100	195,600
Practice administration	20,700	17,100	(3,600)	195,800	191,200	(4,600)	191,200
Office administration	17,700	14,900	(2,800)	159,200	178,800	19,600	178,800
General insurance	20,200	2,100	(18,100)	49,000	46,700	(2,300)	46,700
Other	43,100	11,000	(32,100)	371,300	150,100	(221,200)	150,100
Capital	*50,800	3,400	(47,400)	80,200	24,800	(55,400)	24,800
Total payments	$314,200	$231,000	($83,200)	$2,759,600	$2,776,300	$16,700	$2,776,300
Net Cash (gain/ loss)	($83,800)						

*Includes $50,000 capital reserve.

and support from all programs increased 6 percent from $2,554,184 to $2,719,737; accounts receivable (A/R) were reduced to forty-one days in Newmarket and eighty-two days in Raymond. Medicaid eligibility expansion and in-house aggressive efforts resulted in a doubling of Medicaid users from 7 to 14 percent. The new cost-based FQHC (federally qualified health center) reimbursement program was finally negotiated and approved to cover 100 percent of reasonable costs in December 1991.

Previously, Lamprey Health Care was receiving approximately fifty cents on the dollar.

A time line plan to implement the resource based relative value scale (RBRVS), adopted by Medicare, Medicaid, and most payer sources had been developed in 1992. This represented training in coding, chart documentation, and billing for medical and office billing staff. The process was integrated with the new quality assurance requirements to minimize unnecessary paperwork.

EXHIBIT 8.10
Balance Sheets (years ended September 30)

	1990	1991
Assets		
Current assets		
Cash	$69,025	$154,505
Accounts receivable		
Services	210,987	206,752
Grants	581,110	636,685
Friends of Lamprey Health Care, Inc.	53,647	6,656
Prepaid operating expenses	91,703	82,266
Total current assets	1,006,472	1,086,864
Cash – board designated	—	67,544
Property assets	590,782	533,515
	$1,597,254	$1,687,923
Liabilities and Fund Balance		
Current liabilities		
Accounts payable and accrued expenses	$102,311	$99,325
Accrued salaries and wages	95,119	103,467
Deferred grant revenue	569,566	654,803
Deferred revenue	18,683	22,422
Total current liabilities	785,679	880,017
Mortgage payable	266,217	256,983
Contingencies		
Fund balance	545,358	550,923
	$1,597,254	$1,687,923

Internal controls to meet A133 regulations (federal program report requirements of health care centers) were revised. Initial testing in October 1991 indicated 90 percent compliance.

Full financial reports on a quarterly basis were provided to the finance committee of the LRC Board of Trustees to permit better planning and monitoring of fund balances. In addition, a system for tracking monthly accruals using LOTUS 1-2-3 was developed in 1991. The cost flow projections and budgeting models were further refined based on historical data to provide even greater accuracy in monitoring and tracking.

FACILITIES

LHC completed one expansion and several improvements to its existing facilities in 1991.

> ### *EXHIBIT 8.11*
> **Statements of Support, Revenue, and Expenses and Changes in Fund Balance (years ended September 30)**

	1990	1991
Support and Revenue		
Patient service charges	$1,905,925	$2,214,545
Less: contractual allowances and adjustments	382,902	542,511
Net patient charges	1,523,023	1,672,034
Grant funds used to defray operating expenses	877,454	929,307
Donated services	12,577	9,607
Contributions	120,920	100,719
Miscellaneous	20,210	8,070
Total support and revenue	2,554,184	2,719,737
Operating Expenses		
Personnel	1,601,954	1,741,895
Supplies	118,484	132,495
Contractual services	102,926	119,738
General	595,883	629,264
Fund raising	556	808
Depreciation	79,370	72,858
Total Expenses	2,499,173	2,697,058
Excess of support and revenue over operating expenses	55,011	22,679
Nonoperating revenue (expense)		
Interest income	2,025	2,294
Interest expense	(22,780)	(19,408)
	(20,755)	(17,114)
Excess of revenue over expenses	34,256	5,565
Fund balance at beginning of year	511,102	545,358
Fund balance at end of year	$545,358	$550,923

The parking lot in Raymond was expanded to include additional space for twenty cars. An agreement with Newmarket School was reached that provided for use of ten spaces on school property for LHC staff. The quality service management goals to provide clean, neat, attractive, well-equipped offices was achieved and provider space in Raymond was modified to improve privacy and confidentiality.

EXHIBIT 8.12

Detailed Statements of Operating Expenses, Operating Fund (years ended September 30)

				1991		Total Allocated to	
	1990 Total	Amount Expended	Donated Services	Total	Medical	Transportation	Information and Referral
General							
Legal and audit	$11,200	$8,950	$	$8,950	$7,924	$826	$200
Dues and publications	18,705	25,708		25,708	24,776	261	721
Insurance	151,575	176,465		176,465	149,298	27,167	–
Travel	26,179	35,327		35,327	32,192	2,792	343
Education	22,746	27,000		27,000	26,443	522	35
Recruitment and advertising	6,688	4,416		4,416	4,382	34	–
Telephone	72,951	77,647		77,647	54,869	3,961	18,817
Utilities	25,252	22,697		22,697	21,900	(98)	895
Housekeeping	50,474	55,985		55,985	53,162	1,085	1,708
Equipment repair	6,646	3,772		3,772	3,655	317	–
Vehicle expense	26,300	29,533		29,533	–	29,373	–
Rent	107,634	118,793		118,992	109,387	5,726	3,879
Printing and copying	19,595	25,852		25,852	24,038	577	1,237
Miscellaneous	18,712	(11,581)		(11,581)	(12,028)	390	57
Payroll service	3,152	3,542		3,542	3,724	147	71
Computer operations	19,420	24,919		24,919	19,499	–	5,420
	595,883	629,264	0	629,264	522,771	73,080	33,413

Supplies							
Medical	71,322	79,331		79,331	79,331		1,433
Office	47,102	53,164		53,164	50,745	986	
	115,486	132,495	0	132,495	130,076	986	$1,433
Contractual Service							
Laboratory	64,062	79,459	—	79,459	79,459	—	—
Dictation	15,033	19,377	—	19,377	19,377	—	—
Physician Service	20,000	16,975	—	16,975	16,975	—	—
Consultants	3,765	3,927	—	3,927	3,927	—	—
	102,926	119,308	0	119,738	119,738	—	—
Personnel							
Salaries and Wages	1,371,507	1,486,325	9,607	1,495,932	1,361,464	111,598	22,870
Payroll Taxes	97,648	103,872	—	193,872	94,978	7,268	1,626
Employee Benefits	121,749	138,791	—	138,791	124,527	11,027	3,237
Fund Raising	11,050	3,300	—	3,300	3,300	—	—
	$1,601,954	$1,732,288	$9,607	$1,741,895	$1,584,269	$129,893	$27,733

EXHIBIT 8.13
Glossary of Terms

Borrowing as a Percent of Fund Balance:	The amount of debt in relation to the net worth of LHC.
Borrowing for Period:	The amount of the line of credit that was drawn down during the period.
Capital Expenses:	Cost of equipment or mortgage during period. Equipment cost greater than $500 per item.
Costs:	Actual cash outflow for period.
Days A/R:	The number of days it takes, on average, to collect the adjusted charges for the previous year (360 days).
Days Cash on Hand:	The number of days of operating the undesignated cash will cover.
Designated Cash:	Cash reserved to cover future expenses: busses, deferred grant revenue.
Excess Revenue/Expenses:	Receipt less operating expenses for the period.
Operating Expenses:	Actual operating costs based on goods and services ordered during period.
Receipts:	Actual cash collected for period.

MARKETING

In 1990–1991 an updated comprehensive marketing plan was implemented that included a number of specific activities. LHC was to focus on retention of new patients. To implement this focus, visit trends by type and time of year were to be monitored; changes in demographics and the health care environment (health resources and the economy) were to be monitored; and other marketing research would be conducted for the area.

The focus on quality service management – "To Be the Best We Can Be" – would continue by revision of the new employee orientation program as well as front desk and nurse training. In addition, there would be a focus on marketing that targeted prevention services such as Pap and breast exams and sigmoidoscopy.

Public relations would provide an annual schedule of press releases and multimedia presentations of the accomplishments, staff training, and services offered by LHC. In August 1991, Lamprey Health Care co-sponsored with Fleet Bank, a 5K road race as part of Old

Home Weekend in Newmarket. Over 130 runners participated.

HUMAN RESOURCES MANAGEMENT

Staff retention and professional development was the continuing focus of the human resources management plan. LHC worked to strengthen its individual employee education plan in accordance with LHC needs. All employees were supported for continuing professional education.

A number of staff were highlighted for their achievements. The fiscal officer completed the MBA degree at Boston University, and the perinatal coordinator attended the nurse management development program at Harvard. One LHC physician was certified in family practice and two physicians were recertified. One of the nurse practitioners was enrolled in training for pediatrics and obstetrics to qualify as a family nurse practitioner.

Recruitment

Recruitment activities for 1990–1991 centered on the need for obstetrical services following the departure of Dr. Rasmussen in June 1991. An analysis of the problems inherent in the continued search for an OB physician to replace her, and a strong desire by the family physician staff to *not* bring on an obstetrician resulted in focused attention to develop a coverage contract with Exeter Hampton OB/GYN Professional Association. In August 1991, these negotiations fell apart. Because the contract could not be arranged, as well as the recognition on the part of LHC family physicians that the call coverage responsibilities and demand for care required additional staff, a recruitment strategy for an additional family physician was undertaken.

The provision of specialty coverage in obstetrics was a very time-consuming problem.

Contracts had been signed and notice to discontinue given. However, Exeter Hospital's enlightened commitment and leadership in providing access to the indigent were invaluable. The vagaries and mercurial whims of existing obstetricians had to be worked through to cover LHC family physicians. The plan was to secure coverage from March to July 1992 through Exeter obstetricians. After July, additional staff would be in place. Although recruiting was underway, finding a family physician qualified and interested in obstetrics to practice in New Hampshire was challenging.

The demand for family physicians was intense and the supply had been decreasing. Because it was likely to recruit a physician no sooner than the summer 1992, demand for in-office care in Raymond would have to be met by a family nurse practitioner. However, this option did not reduce the call/coverage load or obstetrical load per physician. LHC must evaluate the options to address this issue. Exeter Hospital was fully committed to assisting LHC in this process.

Employee Benefits and Personnel Relations

LHC improved benefits for employees by selecting a new vendor for health insurance, short-term disability and sick time were modified, and long-term disability was added at no cost to the employee. Auto, home, and life insurance were added to payroll deduction options.

An incentive program for physicians was developed by the practice management committee of the board and approved by the entire board. It was the product of medical staff issues on workload, financial feasibility, and ease of administration of the program. The plan provided flexible reimbursement for off-site care including after-hours delivery, hospital visits, surgical assists, after-hours office visits, and others. The plan was working as envisioned and on budget.

An employee handbook, to provide knowledge of Lamprey Health Care mission, policies, and benefits was undergoing final revisions. All personnel forms were revised to be more user-friendly and improve consistency.

MEDICAL SERVICES AND HEALTH CARE PLAN

Summary statistics and key administrative aspects of medical services were provided by reports from the medical staff. Lamprey Health Care continued to expand its clinical services to meet the needs within its service area. Users increased from 10,508 in 1990 to 11,717 in 1991; medical visits increased to 31,401. Despite the loss of one OB/GYN physician, the prenatal population increased. The obstetrical workload for family practice and the number of deliveries (235 deliveries by four family

physicians) became too high and consumed too large a percentage of their clinical time. Pull-outs for deliveries increased, patient waiting time increased, and staff burnout strongly underscored the need for an additional family physician.

Lamprey Health Care continued to increase team productivity (Exhibit 8.14). However, medical users per FTE (full-time equivalent) medical team (1,762) and medical users per FTE physicians (2,311) increased beyond levels appropriate for continuity of care. In 1990, the growth in users per physician was due to maternity leave, which was temporary. However, in 1991, users continued to increase 12 percent, further indicating the need for additional staff. The waiting time in both offices, but more so in Raymond, exceeded twelve weeks for a physical exam and further supported the need for additional staff.

Lamprey Health Care exceeded BHCDA

EXHIBIT 8.14
LHC Performance, 1988–1991

	1988	1989	1990	1991	Standards
Team Productivity[1]	4,247	4,212	4,744	5,085	4,200–6,000
Medical Users/ FTE Medical Team	1,443	1,476	1,622	1,762	900–1,200
Medical Users/ FTE Physician	1,968	1,751	2,044	2,311	1,500–2,000
Medical Encounter/ Medical User	3.52	3.93	3.54	3.41	2.5
Charges/ Reimbursable Costs	94%	106%	93%	94%	90%
Collections/Billings	98%	87%	106%	101%	80%

[1]On site visits only.

(Bureau of Health Care Delivery and Assistance) performance screen for charges as a percentage of reimbursable costs (94 percent) and collections as a percentage of billings (101 percent).

LHC developed a management tool and planning process to assess need, resources and cost, and priority of adding new services. The tool provided data for analysis and processes that involved administrative and medical staff input and board review and approval. With this process, the addition of sigmoidoscopy was accomplished in 1991. The addition of Norplant was under review. Pharmacy services for the sliding-fee scale population were to be expanded according to an agreed-on formula and a phased-in approach, and dental service needs were under review.

LHC refined its community-oriented primary-care model by integrating the new clinical measures with the existing outcomes/health care plan. This quality assurance process was completely revised and involved community input and evaluation of the health care problems in the service area.

COMMUNITY SERVICES

LHC was involved with some specific activities in the state, including continuation of championing the issue of access to care for the indigent statewide. LHC was a member of the Bi State Community Health Center Association, A Healthy Start Task Force on Prenatal Care, Congressman Zeliff's Health Care Committee, and the Governor's Health Care Data Committee.

In addition, LHC provided expertise and support to other health care agencies and groups in Berlin, Warren, and Manchester, New Hampshire. Assistance was provided for MUA (medically underserved area), HPSA (health professional shortage area), Rural Health Outreach, and CHC (community health center) funding. This was in concert with LHC's long-standing commitment to needs of

the indigent statewide and BHCDA's new policy of "Adopt a Health Center."

In addition to statewide activities, LHC was very active in its own service area. It provided service to teen and young parent support groups in Newmarket and Raymond to enhance parenting skills, decrease the incidence of substance abuse, and support teen parents to finish high school. It provided over 60,575 messages via the Tel Med Program.

LHC provided over 4,167 referrals via the Information and Referral (I&R) Program. Loss of county financial support for the I&R program became reality in 1991; however, the program has continued with a focus on the LHC service area rather than a total countywide effort. LHC pursued and received a Harmon Foundation Grant to automate the I&R data. The purchase of hardware, software, and the original entry of data was completed through the grant. The program was fully operational in March 1992, and reports using the data base were generated based on market potential. The goal was to generate funds to support I&R by the sale of these products.

Another grant was received from the New Hampshire Housing Authority to develop a support service for the elderly in Newmarket. This program consisted of outreach, education, information, referral, and support. One morning a week office hours were held at the housing units to assist the elderly with problems. Educational programs, including Medigap information, pharmaceutical review clinics, and advanced medical directives have been presented. Further expansion of the program needed to be reviewed as part of the strategic plan for community service. In addition, LHC provided 27,219 rides to seniors.

ISSUES FOR CONSIDERATION

Ann Peters pondered the uncertainties that faced LHC this year. Needed were additional exam rooms and provider space at the Raymond Center. In the longer range, major facili-

EXHIBIT 8.15
The Medically At-Risk and Underserved in New England

	Total Population	At-Risk Population	Medically Underserved Persons
Maine	1,227,928	231,433	105,231
New Hampshire	1,109,252	97,314	84,421
Vermont	562,758	84,448	29,570

Source: B. Heller, "Missing Data on Basic Health Care: Growing Disparity Showing in Rural New England," *Boston Globe* (March 20, 1992), pp. 1, 12–13.

ties expansion would be needed, either in Raymond, in Epping, or in another MUA (medically underserved area) town. Relocating other services, such as orthopedics, X ray, physical therapy, and OB/GYN were all possibilities for the future. Approaches had been made to LHC by medical groups in Exeter.

A competitive position was needed for recruitment and retention of staff. Ann was also concerned about risks, including those arising from medical practice, those arising from hazardous substances, and those involved in facility-related accidents and incidents.

A chart (see Exhibit 8.15) and quote from a *Boston Globe* article highlighted an issue fundamental to LHC: "Lives in balance: Basic health care for many in rural New England is hard to find according to a report by the National Association of Community Health Centers. 'The problem is severe. Isolated, rural populations are being ignored or poorly served, and, unfortunately, the trend is not promising,' Dr. Bruce Bates, associate dean, College of Osteopathic Medicine, University of New England."

The Veterans Administration Medical Care System

As he climbed the steps of the Veterans Administration (VA) building in Washington, D.C., on the way to his office, Chief Medical Director John Gronvall's glance came to rest on the immortal words of Abraham Lincoln etched across the entrance: "Care for him who shall have borne the battle and for his widow, and his orphan."

How ironic those words seem, Gronvall thought, given the current situation: a medical system $221 million short of needed cash with 13,000 beds out of service and 7,000 medical jobs vacant. With a budget proposal for the next fiscal year already $604 million short, they could not even begin to treat all the patients they had treated last year, much less fulfill Lincoln's lofty goal. Somehow, the VA Medical Care System had to provide quality medical treatment to this country's veterans amid budget constraints and demands to decrease public spending. What was the answer? Would the current strategy work? Should he seek a more radical alternative?

HISTORY AND BACKGROUND

The origin of the VA can be traced to the time immediately after the Civil War when

This case was prepared by Sharon Topping and Peter M. Ginter. It is intended as a basis for classroom discussion rather than to illustrate effective or ineffective handling of an administrative situation. Used with permission from Sharon Topping.

the National Asylum for Disabled Volunteer Soldiers was founded. Union veterans who had suffered economic distress from disabilities incurred during the war were eligible. Concurrently, a number of states established state homes for the domiciliation of disabled soldiers and sailors. Operated initially at state expense, in 1888 the homes started receiving federal aid for the care of certain disabled soldiers and sailors at the annual rate of $100 for each veteran domiciled in a state home. At that time, medical care was only ancillary to residency at the federal and state homes.

Growth in Programs and Facilities

Significant changes in benefits to veterans occurred after World War I, including medical and hospital care for those suffering from wounds or diseases incurred while in service. Due to the lack of facilities, medical care had to be provided by the Public Health Service or through contracts with civilian hospitals as well as Army and Navy hospitals. Eventually, a number of the Public Health Service hospitals were transferred to the Veterans Bureau. In 1930, the Veterans Bureau, Pension Bureau, and the National Home for Disabled Veterans were consolidated into a new agency, the Veterans Administration. At that time, it had a budget of $100 million for the operation of forty-seven hospitals (22,732 beds), ten branches of the National Home, and a sanitarium.

World War II caused further expansion in benefits and medical care for veterans. Seventy-two new hospitals were authorized. In 1946, the Department of Medicine and Surgery was established to be headed by a chief medical director who reported directly to the administrator of veteran affairs. Under this department, a three-point program – medical care, research, and education – was initiated to improve the quality of care to veterans.

At that time, affiliations with medical schools began. This program, in a little over three decades, grew to 107 medical school and 58 dental school affiliations. Today, the VA provides residency training for one-third of all U.S. physicians. Numerous affiliations also exist with schools of pharmacy, nursing, psychology, social work, and other allied health disciplines. The research program began with a budget of $1 million; today, its budget is well over $150 million. Moreover, two VA researchers, Rosalyn Yalow and Andrew Schally, were awarded the Nobel Prize.

Over the years, the VA has become one of the largest federal agencies, with approximately 250,000 employees and a budget of over $28 billion. Recently, Congress voted to make it the fourteenth Cabinet department, thereby giving veterans a voice in policy making at the White House. A major part of the VA budget is related to the provision of medical services. In 1988, the Department of Medicine and Surgery spent over $10 billion on VA medical programs. The medical system has over 350 facilities that include over 28,000 medical beds, 16,000 surgical beds, 23,000 psychiatric beds, and 10,000 nursing home beds. From a budget of $100 million and 60 facilities, the VA medical system has become the single-largest centrally directed health care system in the country.

The Eligibility Criteria

Initially established to provide medical care for the veteran with service-connected disabilities,

VA eligibility criteria have changed many times throughout the years. In 1920, the lack of community facilities encouraged Congress to permit the VA to provide care for needy veterans with non-service-related problems. Through the years, Congress gradually has returned to the idea of entitlements in terms of disabilities. A veteran with service-related disabilities was given care on an inpatient and outpatient basis; a veteran with a non-service-connected condition was treated on an inpatient basis only. This meant that the latter had to have a serious ailment that required hospital care but had no legal right to care before or after hospitalization.

In the 1960s, changes again were made in the criteria. Care was authorized before and after hospitalization, nursing home care was authorized within the VA (or by contract with community nursing homes), and comprehensive care for veterans totally disabled from service was granted. The requirement that veterans aged 65 or more had to certify their inability to defray the cost of hospital care for nonrelated conditions was removed. As would be expected, these changes led to a sharp drop in the average length of stay in the hospitals.

Currently, all veterans with an honorable discharge are technically eligible for VA services. Whether this request is granted is determined by a three-tiered system of priorities that was established in 1986 along with a "means test" where appropriate. This system is described in Exhibit 9.1. At the same time, Congress removed the automatic age eligibility of those 65 or over. Now, a copayment indexed to the Medicare deductible is required. The income levels are adjusted annually and based on the increment associated with increases in VA pensions. Taken as a whole, the new eligibility criteria changed the focus of VA medical services to place emphasis on veterans with disabilities related to military service and with low incomes. Veterans who do not have service-connected conditions and who have

---

EXHIBIT 9.1
Three-Tiered System of Eligibility Priorities

First Priority: Veterans requesting treatment for service-connected illness or injury

Second Priority: Veterans with service-connected injuries or illnesses, whose current injury or illness is not service-related

Space-Available Priority: Veterans without service-related injuries or illnesses who sign an affidavit stating that they are unable to pay for medical care elsewhere

"Means" Test Thresholds: Income that falls at or below $15,000 for single veterans and $18,000 for veterans who have one dependent with this increasing $1,000 for each dependent

Special Groups: Prisoners of war (POW), World War I veterans, and VA pension recipients receive medical care from the VA

Source: D. Kosloski, C. Austin, and E. Borgatta, "Determinants of VA Utilization," *Medical Care* 25 (1987), pp. 830–846.

---

higher incomes can use the health care system only on a space-available basis.

The overriding goal of the VA medical care program is to provide timely high-quality care within government laws and regulations to eligible veterans now and in the future (see Exhibit 9.2).

As ways to decrease the deficit have continued to be sought, the question of eligibility has received more and more attention. The question always comes back to whether the American taxpayer should pay for veterans' care regardless of income or the existence of a service-related disability. It has been estimated that without eligibility constraints the cost of VA medical care would exceed $30 billion by the year 2000. In addition, there have been problems with the definition of *service-related disability*, for it includes a wide range of conditions that may be incurred or aggravated during military service. For example, a knee problem for which an inductee was not exempted but that became worse before discharge was pre-

sumed to be service-related and treatable by the VA. There were also fifty-seven chronic illnesses and tropical diseases that, if discovered within one to seven years of discharge, qualified the veteran for VA medical benefits.

ENVIRONMENTAL DEMANDS: THE AGING POPULATION

The issue of eligibility involved not only budget reduction but also demographics. In 1900, individuals age 65 and over were 4 percent of the population; by 1987, they were 14.6 percent. By 2020, one in every five persons is expected to be over 65. However, the veteran population was aging at an even faster rate since the population served by the VA is about ten years older than the general population. The aging peak that will occur in the general population in 2020 will hit the VA in 2010. Furthermore, an increasing proportion of elderly men will be veterans. In 1987, over 30 percent of all American men over 65 were veterans. By

---

EXHIBIT 9.2
Veterans Administration Mission and Goals

The Veterans Administration will serve America's veterans and their families with dignity and compassion and will be their principal advocate in ensuring that they receive the care, support, and recognition earned in service to this nation.

Medical: To ensure quality medical care is provided on a timely basis to eligible veterans.

Benefits: To ensure benefits and services are provided to eligible veterans and their families in an efficient, timely, and compassionate manner.

Memorial Affairs: To ensure the memorial affairs of eligible veterans and dependents are conducted with dignity and compassion.

Leadership: To serve as the leader and advocate within the federal government on all matters directly affecting veterans and their families.

People: To ensure the people of the Veterans Administration receive quality leadership, adequate compensation, decent working conditions, necessary training and education, equal opportunity, and earned recognition.

Management: To integrate technological advances and innovative management techniques into an efficient system for providing quality care and benefits.

---

the year 2000, this proportion was expected to be 63 percent (two out of every three).

The Veteran Population

Veterans tend to cluster in age groups that relate to service in major conflicts or wars. Although there is a steady influx of veterans during peacetime, these numbers are small compared to the number of those who enter the military after a major mobilization. Therefore, there are large peaks in the veteran population that represent the last three conflicts: World War II, the Korean War, and the war in Vietnam. The veterans from the first two currently are entering into the age group that seeks the most medical care. Although woman veterans tend to cluster in similar age groups, it should be noted that they constitute less than 3 percent of the total veteran population.

The total veteran population increased steadily during the 1970s because of the Viet-

nam War (see Exhibit 9.3). It has been declining since 1980 and is estimated to fall by 13.5 percent by the year 2000. According to VA Chief Medical Director Gronvall, the only age group that will increase between 1986 and 2000 is the age 65 and older. In 1980, 10 percent of veterans were 65 or older. This should increase to 37 percent by 2000 and peak at approximately 47 percent by 2020. Currently, VA facilities serve 10 percent to 12 percent of all veterans each year. The larger elderly veteran population is expected to place new stresses on the VA, for this is the age when they are more likely to seek care. People who are 65 or older tend to have diseases that are generally chronic and require more long-term care.

Persons in that age group also tend to affect hospital utilization rates because they require more care. In 1980, the average hospital stay of patients age 65 or older was 28.9 days. No other group has an average stay of longer than

EXHIBIT 9.3

Veteran Population by Age, 1970–2000 (in thousands)

Age	1970	1980	1986	1990*	2000*
Total	27,976	28,640	27,682	26,914	23,951
Under 45	13,652	11,189	9,538	8,349	4,940
45–64	11,111	14,283	12,637	11,515	10,140
65–74	1,292	2,308	4,395	5,586	5,063
75 and over	921	860	1,112	1,464	3,808

*Projected
Source: J. A. Gronvall, "Medical Care of Low-Income Veterans in the VA Health Care System," *Health Affairs* (Spring 1987), pp. 167–175.

22.5 days. With a growing population of veterans in this age group, long-term-care beds should be in demand. It had been estimated by some that by 1990 the system would be providing nursing home care to 90 percent more veterans than received care in 1980. This is especially true in states such as Florida with growing elderly populations. In that state, new facilities will be added to the five already in existence and contracts with community hospitals will be used to meet the demands.

In addition, of the population of male veterans age 25 and older, the elderly are the poorest (see Exhibit 9.4). Over 50 percent of those veterans 65 years or older have annual incomes below $20,000. In a recent survey conducted by Louis Harris and Associates for the VA, which was restricted to veterans over

EXHIBIT 9.4

Veterans' Annual Total Family Income in 1986 by Age

Age	$1–$9,999	$10,000–$19,999	$20,000–$39,999	$40,000 or More	None or Not Available
Under 25	106,800	91,000	48,100	3,400	13,900
25–44	557,600	1,113,700	2,868,600	2,745,000	568,500
45–64	1,003,700	1,649,600	3,677,400	4,319,900	1,500,700
65 or over	1,204,300	1,794,100	1,376,700	776,900	741,500

Source: Veterans Administration, 1987 Survey of Veterans, U.S. Bureau of the Census, Washington, D.C., 1989, p. 103.

the age of 55, information was obtained on the sources of medical care that age group would select if they needed it. Of those below the $10,000 income level, 42 percent would use VA hospitals and 13 percent would use VA outpatient clinics. As income increased, the number who would use the VA facilities declined rapidly. Furthermore, for veterans with good insurance coverage, their choices of medical care providers were private physicians followed by non-VA hospitals. For those who lacked insurance, VA hospitals replaced all sources of care most likely to be used.

The Veteran Patient

A number of recent studies have found that those who use the VA system are somewhat different from the rest of the population. On the average, VA patients are more likely to have lower educational attainment, to have less annual income, to be retired due to health reasons, to be out of the labor force and live alone, to be unable to perform usual activity due to limitations of chronic conditions, and to rate health status as poor.

From these characteristics, certain outcomes have been inferred. For instance, research findings show that there are higher death rates in the lower-income classes. Persons of lower income, regardless of race, stay in the hospital an average of two days longer than other income levels. They have more trouble securing medical care, which in turn leads to more incidence of delayed care and more serious ailments when access to the system is finally obtained. The health problems of the poor tend to be more numerous and more complex than those in middle- and upper-income levels. Between the ages of 45 and 64, chronic conditions such as arthritis, diabetes, hearing and visual impairments, heart condition, and hypertension are two to three times higher for those with low incomes.

According to certain authorities, these characteristics affect the need for care in varying ways:

Patients with multiple diagnoses, chronic conditions, and lower health status require more intensive medical and nursing care and closer observation and assessment when they are hospitalized. They require additional services such as discharge planning, nutritional counselling, and other patient education programs on a more frequent basis. The lower health status and presence of complicating chronic conditions will extend the required length-of-stay per admission. In addition, more intensive resource utilization per admission will occur.[1]

Past VA hospital usage tends to support many of these conclusions. For instance, VA studies have shown that the hospital discharge rates in the system decrease when income levels increase. Those in the lowest income groups are hospitalized almost twice as much as those with incomes over $10,000. In addition to income, the availability of insurance plays a large role in determining the users of VA. According to a 1987 Bureau of the Census report, 46.8 percent of the veterans using a VA hospital were not covered by health insurance. Of those covered, there was a reliance on non-private types of insurance such as Medicare, Medicaid, and military programs.

OTHER PROBLEMS IN THE VA's FUTURE

The VA is not only struggling to keep pace with a growing number of elderly veterans but also is facing a growing AIDS problem, the threat of more debilitating diseases among the aging veterans, and significant staffing shortages.

AIDS Among Veterans

The VA estimates that it will spend $40 million annually to provide treatment to veterans with AIDS. In January 1987, the VA was treating

1,600 AIDS patients. Of the VA's 172 medical centers, 112 are actively treating AIDS, but 77 percent of the cases are concentrated in twenty-four facilities. Manhattan Veterans Medical Center treats more cases than any other in the country. Twenty-three of its 120 acute-care beds are occupied by AIDS patients. Presently, the VA is establishing separate, specialized treatment units for veterans with AIDS.

According to the eligibility requirements, veterans unable to pay for care are entitled to free care. AIDS patients usually fall in this category. According to VA statistics, the length of stay for an AIDS patient is twenty-four to twenty-five days at an estimated cost of $50,000 per admission; some AIDS patients are admitted four or five times a year. The Centers for Disease Control in Atlanta estimated that the average general hospital care for each AIDS patient can range as high as $147,000 annually.

Debilitating Diseases

The VA is becoming increasingly strained by the long-term-care needs of those with Alzheimer's disease and other forms of dementia. An increase in these types of diseases is expected. By the year 2000, the VA predicts the number of veterans with dementia to reach 550,000, up from 200,000 in 1983. To prepare for the influx of veterans with Alzheimer's disease, the VA has community-based test projects that provide respite care for family members who care for veterans with dementia at home. Currently, only one exists, in Bedford, Massachusetts.

Staff Retention and Recruitment

A 1986 survey found the average turnover rate at the VA to be 16.1 percent among registered nurses, 22.6 percent for pharmacists, 23.4 percent for occupational therapists, and 25.5 percent for physical therapists. The most severe shortages were in the major metropolitan areas, the northeast, and California. The VA was at-

tempting to enhance its image as an employer by increasing its tuition reimbursement and scholarship programs. It spent approximately $2.5 million on tuition reimbursement in 1990 with funds directed at areas with the largest shortages. The VA plans to broaden its scholarship program, which has traditionally been for nurses only. Under this plan, the program would be increased for nurses and would add physical therapists. This could lower turnover as 73 percent of the full-time nurses who received scholarships remained at the VA after completing their programs, while 100 percent of the part-time nurses who received scholarships stayed.

Another way that the VA is approaching the turnover problem is through supplemental pay. Because the pay scale in some areas is not competitive, the VA allocated about $36 million for special pay rates in fiscal 1987 with the expectation that the amount would increase to $50 million in 1988. About 9,700 employees are paid based on a special rate scale. For registered nurses, pharmacists, and physical therapists, salaries are provided that are 4 percent to 21 percent higher than the normal pay scale. In 1987, an entry-level registered nurse earned an average salary of $20,340. At the VA, the same nurse would earn $16,500 on regular pay with an additional 19 percent supplement for a total of $19,700. Nurses are offered the supplemental rate in ninety markets. A task force has been appointed to deal with recruitment and retention problems. Among the many options they will consider are provision of child care services, recruitment bonuses, and improved working conditions.

THE POLITICAL SITUATION

The VA is scrutinized by congressional committees, veterans' service organizations, and the President's Office of Management and Budget (OMB). The House and Senate Veterans Affairs Committees have legislative authority over the VA, and they are highly protective of this interest, as are the House and Senate Appropriations subcommittees that approve the VA annual budget. In addition, both the House and Senate Committees on Aging, although they have no authority to legislate, exert pressure on the VA through public hearings and published works. These groups become particularly active if the department is trying to close or relocate a facility. In addition, an individual legislator can become a factor in these situations, usually when the questionable facility is in his or her district.

Congress powerfully influences priorities in the VA medical construction program. For instance, the House and Senate Appropriations Committees have tried to mandate the location of outpatient ambulatory clinics, although the construction program is an area on which the legislators do not always agree. The House Veterans Affairs Committee tends to favor continued construction, whereas its Senate counterpart tends toward promoting alternatives to outpatient care. Congress has been known to become involved at times in some of the smallest details concerning the VA. On different occasions, for example, they have directed the VA to hire an assistant medical director for geriatrics and service chiefs for podiatry and optometry at its central office.

The "Iron Triangle"

Actually, the VA and its advocates represent an "iron triangle" of interests in Washington policy making. The triangle is made up of the department itself, congressional committees that oversee and promote its interests, and veterans' service organizations. Members of this triangle never miss an opportunity to support the cause of the VA. Never has the influence of this lobby been felt more than by the Reagan administration.

The Reagan administration experienced the power of the VA's vast lobby in its first assault on the budget deficit, the Omnibus Budget Reconciliation Act of 1981. Packaged in this act was a scheme to decrease VA spend-

ing by $863 million, nearly two-thirds of which was to come from reductions in medical care and construction programs. To get approval in a Democratic Congress, Reagan needed more than the Republican vote, so the administration tried to put together a block of votes from conservative Democrats. One of these was the chairman of the Veterans Affairs Committee. He, of course, objected to the reductions in VA medical care and would support other cuts only if VA medical care was maintained. Furthermore, for his vote, he elicited an informal agreement from the administration that they would not seek any sizable VA budget reductions in the future.

Commitment by Congress to the VA has been steadfast over the years, but will be tested in the future in light of the department's need to shift resources, convert hospital beds into long-term care, and prepare for the care of the elderly veteran. Republican leaders in the Senate have been more willing to trim VA spending in the early 1990s. One outgrowth has been the decision by Congress to focus the VA's limited dollars on veterans with service-connected injuries in an attempt to improve services and decrease the budget. Federal legislators are encouraging resource-sharing agreements between community hospitals and the VA as an alternative to building or replacing VA hospitals. For instance, one proposed bill would allow for contracting private health care whenever VA medical services are geographically inaccessible.

Political Opponents

A powerful lobby that has been opposed to the VA from its inception is the American Medical Association (AMA), which represents private medicine. At the end of World War II, the AMA mounted a major but unsuccessful offensive. Recently, a report by the National Academy of Sciences recommended the integration of VA health facilities with those of the community, with the ultimate goal of relegating the department's functions to the private sector. This was supported but not pursued by the Reagan administration.

Although the budget-reduction efforts failed, the Reagan administration did not give up its attack on the VA. For instance, the General Accounting Office (GAO) released a report in August 1985 that said:

> GAO performed two different reviews of patients at VA hospitals. In one review of seven hospitals, GAO's consultant team of physicians and nurses from the Washington State Professional Standards Review Organization reviewed 350 randomly selected medical files of patients who had been discharged from these hospitals during fiscal year 1982. Based on the consultants' review, GAO estimates that nearly 43 per cent of the total days spent by medical and surgical patients at these seven hospitals were medically avoidable. About 20 per cent of the total days were attributable to the absence of efficient management practices at the hospitals, while 23 percent were attributable to the unavailability of less costly levels of care. The VA service chiefs in the hospitals agreed with 86 per cent of the avoidable days identified by the consultant.[2]

The second review during fiscal 1984 found similar results; however, in both instances, the GAO pointed out that less-costly levels of care for patients were often not available.

THE VA BUDGET

Total spending for veterans (including income security, medical care, education, training, and rehabilitation) peaked in 1976 in inflation-adjusted terms. A decline in spending will continue if the projections for 1990 are sustained.

Spending for the medical care program in 1975 was $3.5 billion; this has grown marginally in inflation-adjusted terms from $5.7 billion in 1981 to $6.6 billion in 1982, $7.4 billion in 1983, $7.8 billion in 1984, and $8.9 billion in 1985. The 1989 fiscal year budget proposal was for approximately $11 billion.

In the past, VA medical centers received a finite amount of funding each year. Called a *target allowance,* it represented the historical share of what the VA received from Congress. Using this method, the reward for efficiency and cost containment for each center was survival, and it was effective to a degree in containing cost. In 1981, private hospital cost per patient rose 15.9 percent. According to VA sources, the system's cost rose 8 percent.

Currently, with the prospective payment system using diagnostic-related groups (DRGs), the budget is distributed differently. The distribution is determined by the efficiency of each hospital within the overall system. This has motivated many of the systems to attempt improvements. West Side Medical Center in Chicago, for instance, implemented a venture capital program in which a pool of capital within the budget was set aside for trial implementation of ideas that would decrease costs or increase revenues. They saved $40,000 a year by hiring a wheelchair mechanic instead of contracting out the repair.

THE ORGANIZATION OF THE VA

To decentralize the provision of medical care, the VA is organized into seven major geographic groupings within the United States: Northeastern, Mid-Atlantic, Southeastern, Great Lakes, Mid-Western, Western, and Southwestern (see Exhibit 9.5). The regions are divided into twenty-eight districts that contain several hospitals and medical centers.

Administratively, the VA is divided into three major divisions: Department of Medicine and Surgery, Department of Benefits, and Department of Memorial Affairs. The Depart-

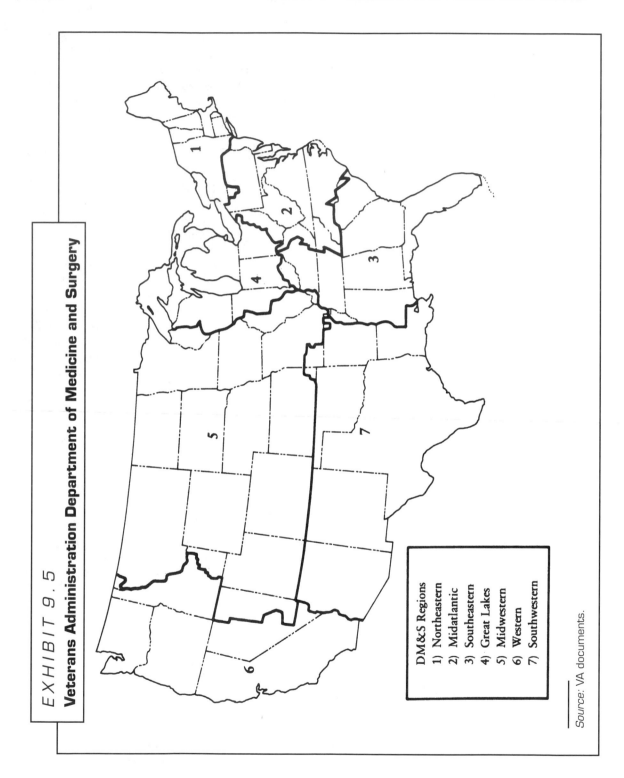

EXHIBIT 9.5
Veterans Administration Department of Medicine and Surgery

DM&S Regions
1) Northeastern
2) Midatlantic
3) Southeastern
4) Great Lakes
5) Midwestern
6) Western
7) Southwestern

Source: VA documents.

ment of Medicine and Surgery is headed by the chief medical director. The organization of the department is shown in Exhibit 9.6. The administrator of each hospital in a particular district reports directly to the regional director.

THE VA STRATEGY

The VA has been involved in a "grassroots" planning process involving the administrators of each medical center who studied the demographic changes in the VA's twenty-eight districts. Given the assumption that there will *not* be another war, all districts have identified the aging veteran's medical needs as a prime concern. Therefore, the critical issue is how to meet the needs of aging veterans between now and at least the year 2010. A new comprehensive plan will remove VA hospitals from the center of medical services and strengthen ambulatory care and alternative services such as adult day care and hospital-based home care. Exhibit 9.7 describes some of these services. If the aging plan is successful, the hospital will function only as the support system, the focal point will be outpatient and noninstitutional care.

The 1988 fiscal budget of $28 billion contained no allocation for construction of new nursing homes. Rather, the budget called for conversion of 282 hospital beds to long-term-care beds and a $26.9 million increase in expenditures for state and community nursing homes. Usually, VA is criticized for spending too much on capital expansion and not enough on alternatives to construction. The strategy, according to the Office of the VA Chief Medical Director, is to rely increasingly on state and community homes. Community hospitals and nursing homes will be called to help especially during peak years – 2000 for VA hospitals and 2010 for long-term-care services.

OTHER STRATEGIC ALTERNATIVES

The VA faces an uncertain future especially in light of so many opposing factors: the humani-

tarian instincts of society, the political emphasis on decreased public spending, a population of veterans that is rapidly aging, and a private health sector that may have more hospital beds and physicians than needed. As a result, various groups have developed their own proposals as to what the VA's future strategy should be.

Mainstreaming Services

This proposal calls for phasing out the VA's direct involvement in the provision of medical care. It is believed that the VA should finance rather than provide services through some form of insurance or voucher system that would allow veterans to purchase health care. Often, partial "mainstreaming" is advocated where either outpatient or hospital care for acute illness would be phased out. Proponents believe that full or partial mainstreaming would ensure quality control because quality of services is monitored directly by the customer. Proponents of this proposal often base their rationale on the assumption that a national health care system is inevitable.

On the other hand, opponents of this proposal often cite the Medicaid program as evidence against it. They believe that poor patients were shifted to the community unsuccessfully in Medicaid. Furthermore, many believe that if the VA does not meet the burden of the aging veteran, it will be shifted onto state and local governments. Regardless, the needs will have to be met by one social agency or another, and the VA at least knows the veteran population.

Integration into the Private Health Care System

In this proposal, VA health services would be integrated into the larger system of health and social services for older Americans. This would allow both systems to achieve economies of scale and it would eliminate the problem of the VA constructing facilities where

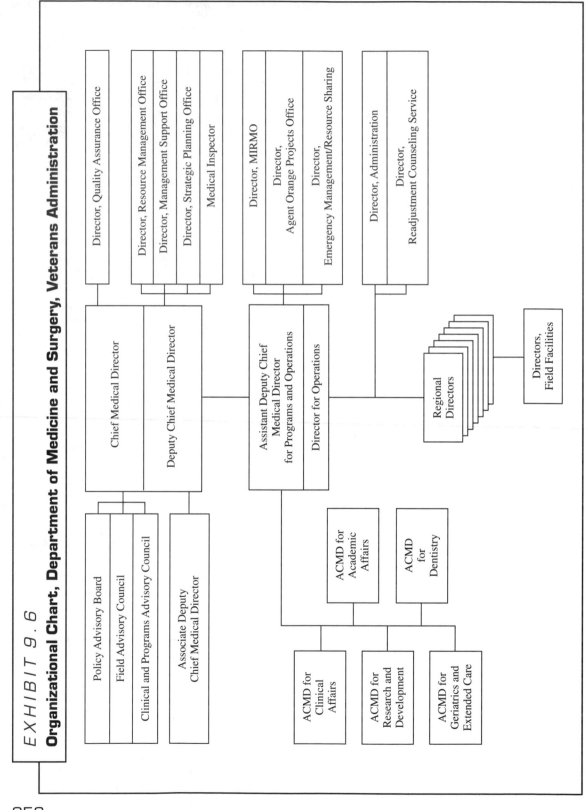

EXHIBIT 9.6

Organizational Chart, Department of Medicine and Surgery, Veterans Administration

Director, Quality Assurance Office

Director, Resource Management Office
Director, Management Support Office
Director, Strategic Planning Office
Medical Inspector

Director, MIRMO
Director, Agent Orange Projects Office
Director, Emergency Management/Resource Sharing

Director, Administration
Director, Readjustment Counseling Service

Chief Medical Director

Deputy Chief Medical Director

Assistant Deputy Chief Medical Director for Programs and Operations
Director for Operations

Policy Advisory Board
Field Advisory Council
Clinical and Programs Advisory Council

Associate Deputy Chief Medical Director

Regional Directors

Directors, Field Facilities

ACMD for Academic Affairs

ACMD for Dentistry

ACMD for Clinical Affairs

ACMD for Research and Development

ACMD for Geriatrics and Extended Care

EXHIBIT 9.7
Geriatric and Extended-Care Programs

VA Nursing Home Care: 115 nursing homes located in VA medical centers.

Community Nursing Home Care: Contract program for veterans who require skilled or intermediate nursing care to assist in transition from a hospital to the community.

VA Domiciliary Care: Located in fifteen medical centers and one independent facility for eligible ambulatory vets who are disabled by age, disease, or injury and are in need of care but not hospitalization or skilled services.

Hospital-Based Home Care: Forty-nine medical centers provide chronically ill veterans with services in their own homes. In 1985, there were 219,000 home visits to 11,353 patients.

Community Residential Care Programs: 125 medical centers provide residential care in privately operated facilities to veterans who do not require hospitalization or nursing home care, but who cannot resume independent living due to health conditions.

Adult Day Health Care: Provides health maintenance and therapeutic activities in eight VA centers for veterans who otherwise would require institutionalization.

Geriatric Evaluation Units (GEU): Fifty units provide assessment of older patients' medical, functional, psychologic, and social-economic status in order to improve diagnosis, treatment, and placement.

State Veterans Home Program: Per diem program to aid states in providing direct hospital, nursing home, and domiciliary care to eligible veterans.

Source: J. H. Mather and R. W. Abel, "Medical Care of Veterans," *Journal of the American Geriatrics Society* 34 (1986), pp. 757–760.

---

underutilized ones already exist in the community. Proponents believe that in attempting to solve the problem of the aging veteran, the political atmosphere must be considered. They think that this plan is the only politically realistic one that simultaneously provides a basis for good health care for the elderly.

Conversely, others believe that this plan, like the mainstreaming alternative, will shift the burden of aging veterans onto state and local governments or onto what they perceive as an already failing Medicaid program. As Representative G. V. (Sonny) Montgomery, a Mississippi Democrat and chairman of the House Veterans' Affairs Committee, asks, "Why dump all of those people on a system that does not work very well – Medicare and Medicaid?"[3]

Specialization in Long-Term Care

Many believe that the VA should narrow its focus and specialize in the provision of long-term care. The VA has developed a reputation for providing better long-term care than is available in the general health care system. By focusing on this area, it could take advantage of its distinctive competency. Others believe that this area is less well covered by public and private insurance; therefore, as veterans age, more will turn to the VA for nursing home care. The advantages from specialization should lower costs and increase the quality of care. On the other hand, opponents of this alternative regard the eligible VA population as an attractive market whose needs would be best served by the private sector. Amid problems of federal budget constraints, they assert that the VA cannot obtain the budgetary increases required to build and support the facilities necessary to meet this growing demand.

Construction of Long-Term-Care Facilities

The Veterans Affairs Committees in Congress are supporting the addition of major long-term-care construction projects. This alternative is also supported by the Paralyzed Veterans of America, who fear that there is not enough planning for the long-term needs of the elderly. They believe that most public facilities are running near or at full capacity and cannot accommodate the growing elderly population as called for by the VA plan. With this proposal, veterans' medical services would remain with the VA; there would be no change except for the emphasis on construction of long-term-care facilities. This alternative is opposed not only by those who maintain that the quality of care provided by the VA is suspect but also by those who believe that the VA will not be able to meet the future demands of the aging veterans.

Integration with the Military

This proposal calls for the gradual integration of the VA with the armed forces. Many believe that this solution will maintain the organizational integrity of the VA and help solve the military problem of physician shortages. However, the opposite view is that neither the VA nor the armed forces can provide adequate

care; therefore, the merging of the two would resolve no problems while creating worse obstacles to veteran care.

Operational Efficiency Focus

One alternative proposes to change the focus of the VA strategy to increasing operational efficiency. GAO reports that nearly 43 percent of the VA medical and surgical days reviewed were medically avoidable. Some were the result of poor management practices; others were attributable to the unavailability of less-costly levels of care. From this, the proponents believe that the reimbursement mechanism provides incentives to keep the beds filled; therefore, to focus on operational efficiency, incentives would be changed. The opponents do not believe that a new focus would change any of the existing problems such as the long-term needs of an aging veteran population or the perceived lack of quality care.

Expansion of the Array of Services

This proposal is based on the fact that 30 percent of VA nursing home care is provided by community facilities. It is believed that this should be eliminated so that the veteran can obtain all services from the VA. This would allow substitution of one more-costly service by another of lesser cost. It is believed that when acute care is delivered in one service system while long-term care is delivered elsewhere, providers have little incentive to substitute one for the other to reduce costs. Moreover, the movement of patients between the two disrupts the continuity and quality of care. Inherent in this proposal is the need to broaden the patient base to include all veterans regardless of eligibility. Others, such as spouses of veterans, could even be included. This alternative, however, is considered politically impracticable by many. Among other things, there is the concern of Congress to reduce costs coupled with the perceived reluctance of the taxpayer to support all veterans' medical expenses regardless of service-related disability.

THE FUTURE DIRECTION OF THE VA HEALTH CARE SYSTEM

With Lincoln's quote still in mind, Dr. Gronvall reflected on the many changes facing the VA medical care program in the future. Knowing that the agency was moving into a period fraught with more uncertainty than ever before in its history, he could not help but question the appropriateness of the current strategy. Would the conversion of existing VA beds and reliance on state and community facilities meet the long-term-care needs of the aging veterans both now and in the year 2010? Would the VA be able to successfully refocus from hospital-based care to outpatient and alternative means of care? Or, given the future environment, would a more radical strategy be feasible, such as mainstreaming services, specializing in long-term care, or even integrating with the armed forces medical organization?

NOTES

1. M. Randall, K. E. Kilpatrick, J. F. Pendergast, K. R. Jones, and W. B. Vogel, "Differences in Patient Characteristics Between Veterans Administration and Community Hospitals," *Medical Care* 25, no. 11 (1987), p. 1104.
2. J. K. Iglehart, "The Veterans Administration Medical Care System Faces an Uncertain Future," *The New England Journal of Medicine* 313, no. 18 (1985), p. 1172.
3. J. Davidson, "Veterans Are Angry over Proposals to Trim Health-System Budget," *The Wall Street Journal* (April 22, 1985), p. 19.

REFERENCES

Alexander, C. F. "Fifty Years of VA Health Care." *Urban Health* (July–August 1980), p. 10.

Andries, G. H., Jr. "Venture Capitalism at the Veterans Administration." *Hospital & Health Services Administration* 31, no. 4 (Winter 1986), pp. 25–31.

Davidson, J. "Veterans Are Angry over Proposals to Trim Health-system Budget." *The Wall Street Journal* (April 22, 1985), pp. 1, 19.

Farber, S. J. "The Future Role of the VA Hospital System: A National Health-policy Dilemma." *The New England Journal of Medicine* 298, no. 11 (1978), pp. 625–628.

Firshein, J. "AIDS Stretching VA's Ability to Treat Veterans." *Hospitals* (February 20, 1986), pp. 33–34.

Franklin, B. A. "Congress Approves Making VA a Cabinet Department." *The New York Times* (October 19, 1988), p. 8.

Gronvall, J. A. "Medical Care of Low-Income Veterans in the VA Health Care System." *Health Affairs* (Spring 1987), pp. 167–175.

Horgan, C., A. Taylor, and G. Wilensky. "Aging Veterans: Will They Overwhelm the VA Medical System?" *Health Affairs* 2, no. 3 (1983), pp. 77–86.

Iglehart, J. K. "The Veterans Administration Medical Care System Faces an Uncertain Future." *The New England Journal of Medicine* 313, no. 18 (1985), pp. 1168–1172.

Kosloski, D., C. Austin, and E. Borgatta. "Determinants of VA Utilization." *Medical Care* 25, no. 9 (1987), pp. 830–846.

Maino, J. H., T. I. Messer, and D. H. Messer. "Veterans Administration Residency Programs: An Overview." *Journal of the American Optometric Association* 58, no. 5 (1987), pp. 378–379.

Mather, J. H., and R. W. Abel. "Medical Care of Veterans." *Journal of the American Geriatrics Society* 34, no. 10 (1986), pp. 757–760.

Randall, M., K. E. Kilpatrick, J. F. Pendergast, K. R. Jones, and W. B. Vogel. "Differences in Patient Characteristics Between Veterans Administration and Community Hospitals." *Medical Care* 25, no. 11 (1987), pp. 1099–1104.

Romeis, J. C., K. N. Gillespie, and R. M. Coe.

"Older Veterans' Future Use of VA Health Care Services." *Medical Care* 26, no. 9 (1988), pp. 854–866.

Schlesinger, M., and T. Wetle. "Care of the Elder Veteran: New Directions for Change." *Health Affairs* (Summer 1986), pp. 59–71.

Special Medical Advisory Group of the Veterans Administration. "Helping to Meet the Health Care Needs of the Nation." *Journal of the American Medical Association* 220, no. 10 (1972), pp. 1334–1337.

Thomas, J. W., S. E. Berki, L. Wyszewianski, and M. L. E. Ashcraft. "Classification of Hospitals Based on Measured Output: The VA System." *Medical Care* 21, no. 7 (1983), pp. 715–723.

Veterans Administration. *1987 Survey of Veterans* (Washington, D.C.: U.S. Bureau of the Census, 1989).

Wagner, L. "VA Hospitals Struggling to Keep Pace with Patient Demands, Staff Shortages." *Modern Healthcare* (June 5, 1987), pp. 162–164.

Wallace, C. "VA's New Aging Plan Downplays Hospitals, Stresses Alternatives." *Modern Healthcare* (May 15, 1984), pp. 172–174.

Wolinsky, F. D., R. M. Coe, and R. R. Mosely. "Length of Stay in the VA." *Medical Care* 25, no. 3 (1987), pp. 250–253.

Wolinsky, F. D., R. M. Coe, R. R. Mosely, and S. M. Homan. "Some Clarification About Health Planning in the VA." *Medical Care* 25, no. 11, (1987), pp. 1105–1110.

Wolinsky, F. D., R. M. Coe, R. R. Mosely, and S. M. Homan. "Veterans' and Nonveterans' Use of Health Services." *Medical Care* 23, no. 12 (1985), pp. 1358–1371.

Orthopedic Services, Inc.

On Thursday, March 19, 1992, Jeffrey S. Levitt, President of Orthopedic Services, Inc. (OSI) was in his office at 7:30 A.M. as usual. The morning newspaper opened to the NASDAQ National Market Quotations showed OSI had closed the day before at 32⅞, selling at seventy-three times earnings. It was the last listing of OSI, for on the nineteenth of March the shareholders of NovaCare, Inc., listed on the New York Stock Exchange, had approved a merger with OSI and OSI had become a subsidiary of NovaCare at the close of business. NovaCare was a leading national provider of contract rehabilitation services to health care institutions, offering speech-language pathology, occupational therapy, and physical therapy, as well as operating seven comprehensive medical rehabilitation hospitals, one hospital-based rehabilitation unit, and six community-based transitional care programs.

OSI, in less than five years, had gone from a concept to become the nation's largest provider of orthotic and prosthetic patient care services. Its 104 branches in 20 states from the East to the West coasts generated $55 million in sales. The next five years had promised

to be different for OSI and for Jeff. As President, he had seen that he would have to manage what he called a "jump shift" in emphasis from the acquisition psychology that had excited and motivated OSI's managers to an internal growth psychology if they were to achieve the objective of 60 percent revenue growth in 1992. The jump shift was needed, he felt, because industry growth was projected at 6 to 7 percent and after OSI's forty-one acquisitions the remaining acquirable practices were few and small in size. Also, with an almost 200 percent increase in net income planned, productivity would have to improve. And, of course, OSI would have to continue seeking to influence as favorably as possible future changes in health care reimbursement. Now all would have to be done in the context of NovaCare as a parent.

THE O & P INDUSTRY

The orthotics and prosthetics (O & P) industry was part of the $19 billion medical rehabilitation market. Orthotics involves the design, fitting, and fabrication of custom-made braces and support devices for the treatment of musculoskeletal conditions resulting from illness, injury, or congenital anomalies. Prosthetics involves the design, fitting, and fabrication of custom-made artificial limbs typically required by people who have suffered the loss of a limb from vascular disease, diabetes, cancer,

This case was prepared by Robert J. Paven of Rutgers University. It is intended as a basis for classroom discussion rather than to illustrate effective or ineffective handling of an administrative situation. All rights reserved jointly to the author and the North American Case Research Association. Used with permission from Robert Paven.

or traumatic injuries. In 1992, the market for O & P patient care was estimated at $750 million with 6 to 7 percent annual growth.

Traditionally, O & P practices had been small, highly profitable, family-run businesses which capitalized on strong demand for their expertise and the limited supply of qualified professionals. The American Orthotic and Prosthetic Association (AOPA) estimated there were about 1,500 local practices averaging less than $500,000 per year in revenue, five regional firms, and two multiregional firms. OSI and AOPA estimated O & P market shares as follows: 76 percent for independents, 5 percent for the five regionals, 3 percent for Hanger Orthopedic Group, 9 percent for OSI, and 7 percent for other providers such as drugstores.

The supply of certified O & P practitioners at the end of 1990 was 2,780, with expansion at 3 to 4 percent per year. Certification in both orthotics and prosthetics could take up to seven years, including a four-year baccalaureate degree. Fewer than ten schools offered certification programs, and two of the largest (New York University and the University of California – Los Angeles) had closed their O & P programs recently because of a lack of federal funding.

The O & P industry generated high gross margins (see Exhibit 10.1) and was more profitable than most other health care businesses. This was seen as a result of the custom nature of the devices; the technical expertise of the practitioner; the three-stage service, which consisted of fitting, fabrication, and delivery; the limited supply of certified practitioners; and the more favorable payer mix. Nearly all O & P services were billed to third-party payers – payers other than the patients.

For 1990, the O & P payer mix was 70 percent from private and third-party insurance companies; 18 percent from Medicare, 9 percent from Medicaid, and 4 percent from the Veterans Administration. With the increase in the elderly portion of the patient population, the proportion of industry revenue coming from Medicare would increase from its current level of 19 percent. Until 1990, O & P services had been subject to Medicare reimbursement amounts defined by the rules for durable medical equipment (DME). DME rules, however, failed to recognize either the custom nature of the devices or the care component of O & P. In 1990, Medicare reimbursement for O & P was removed from the DME schedule, and the Health Care Financing Administration (HCFA) worked with the industry to devise a new reimbursement plan. The new plan developed maximum allowable charges for each of ten geographic regions (instead of limits set by each state), but in no case would the amount be less than 85 percent or more than 195 percent of the national average charge. The plan would be phased in starting January 1, 1992, using weighted averages of local and regional fees to determine the total allowable charge, and be fully in place by 1994. Barring any legislative action, the O & P industry knew what to expect in regard to Medicare reimbursement levels for the next few years.

Normal industry sales growth was estimated at 6 to 7 percent a year, with 2 percent from yearly price increases and 4 to 5 percent from normal volume expansion. The following factors were identified by OSI as driving the unit growth rate in the future:

Societal demand. Many handicapped individuals aggressively seek to regain independence through rehabilitation programs. Studies by major insurance carriers and the federal government have demonstrated that investment in rehabilitation dramatically reduces ongoing health care expenses.

Aging population. The 65 and over age group is expected to increase from approximately 32 million in 1990 to approximately 34 million in 1995. Vascular

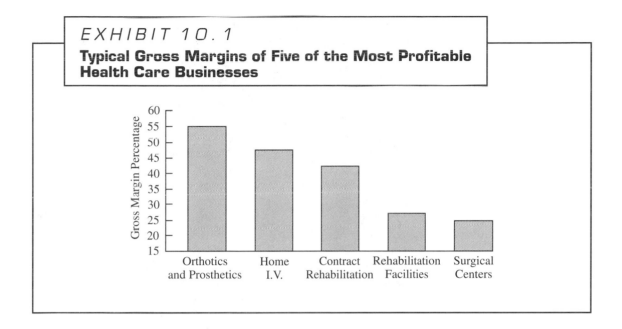

EXHIBIT 10.1

Typical Gross Margins of Five of the Most Profitable Health Care Businesses

disorders and musculoskeletal conditions in this age group often result in the need for an orthotic or prosthetic device.

High value-added. Patients generally value O & P products and services highly because (1) most are custom devices, (2) individualized services and technical expertise are important components of the price for products and services, and (3) ongoing patient care involving adjustments, refittings, and replacements is provided.

Technology and materials. Significant advances in both have resulted in lighter, more sophisticated, and more comfortable devices, which, while frequently more expensive, are applicable to a wider range of patients.

Underserved market. OSI's analysis of the businesses it has acquired shows that the O & P businesses have not actively marketed their services in various health set-tings, such as nursing homes, the home health care system, and rural environments, but have instead relied on relationships with hospital-based referral sources and with physicians. The unsophisticated sales and marketing programs and dearth of adequate consumer and referral source education, along with a shortage of O & P practitioners, suggested an unmet need of $250 million a year.

COMPANY HISTORY

The concept for OSI originated in 1986, when John H. Foster, of Foster Management Company, a venture capital firm he founded in 1972, followed the suggestion of an investor to "look into the O & P industry." Foster hired a consultant to research the industry economics, identify the leaders, and determine if there was an opportunity for consolidation. The report showed that the O & P industry had a high gross margin and was highly fragmented, with no one attempting consolidation. With a list of the ten largest companies in hand, the acquisition quest began.

Early Acquisitions

OSI had begun operations on August 1, 1987, upon completing the acquisition of Missouri Valley Orthotics and Prosthetic Center, Inc., the fourth largest regional company. Located in Omaha, Nebraska, Missouri Valley had three offices each in Nebraska and Kansas, plus two in South Dakota. On December 4, 1987, Foster acquired Orthopedic Service Center, Inc., adding its Kansas office. The third acquisition, on May 31, 1988, was Orthomedics, Inc. Orthomedics, based in Brea, California, was the second largest regional company, with nineteen offices in California and two in Washington. The initial goal of acquiring "platform companies" had been achieved.

As President Jeffrey S. Levitt explained:

> What John did then, basically, was draw a 500-mile radius around the Midwest and West platforms. With input from the former owners, John then identified which firms to acquire in order to "densify." It was very important to start with industry leaders. To acquire two of the ten largest, OSI paid well. There was a larger component of cash used to acquire these businesses than in later deals.

Exhibit 10.2 summarizes the acquisitions completed from 1987 through 1991.

Later Acquisitions

Jeff described the desirable acquisition candidate as: (1) a private practice with a reputation for quality care; (2) at least $1 million in revenue with the potential for quickly achieving a minimum 20 percent operating margin; (3) key practitioners who were willing to help sustain the practice and preserve referral sources and

work with OSI to implement its systems and vision; and (4) respected practitioners who would serve as magnets to attract other motivated sellers who like themselves sought an opportunity to expand their practices as part of OSI. He said, "Our experience is that these sellers typically fall into three broad categories: (1) professionals in business many years who are seeking an exit strategy without retiring; (2) those lacking management or capital resources to expand but who have the drive and talent to do so; and, (3) owners frustrated with the increasing administrative burden placed on them by third-party payers."

By mid-March of 1992, OSI had closed 41 deals, after looking at 275 potential acquisitions. "We have been able to close most of the deals we wanted," claimed Levitt. "Many of the practices are too small, and some are dying businesses. There are also the family businesses that don't want to sell because 'Grandpa started this business and we can't let him down.' The second, fourth, and fifth largest private practices are examples. There have only been three or four sellers who sold to someone else who was willing to pay more."

Typically, OSI paid a price about equal to "trailing annual sales," defined as sales for the twelve months prior to the acquisition agreement. For a business with the potential for quickly achieving a 20 percent pretax margin, that was five times potential pretax earnings. As Jeff noted, "Many family-owned firms report lower pretax margins because of higher owner salaries, related benefits, and discretionary expenses which often run through the business."

Usually, the price paid exceeded the value of the assets acquired. Payment was a combination of cash, five-year notes, and OSI stock. The agreements included three- to five-year employment contracts for the principals with financial incentives if the acquired practices met or exceeded performance targets.

For all of its eighteen acquisitions in 1991, OSI paid 87 percent of trailing revenues, ac-

EXHIBIT 10.2
OSI Acquisitions of O & P Businesses, 1987–1991

	1987	1988	1989	1990	1991	Total
West						
Arizona				2	3	5
California		21		6	14	41
Oregon					6	6
Washington	—	2	—	—	1	3
	0	23	0	8	24	55
Midwest						
Colorado				2	3	5
Iowa		2			1	3
Kansas	4			1		5
Missouri			4	2		6
Nebraska	3					3
Oklahoma			1	1		2
South Dakota	2					2
Texas	—	—	—	—	6	6
	9	2	5	6	10	32
East						
Connecticut					2	2
Georgia					1	1
Kentucky				1	2	3
Massachusetts				1	1	2
Maine					1	1
New Hampshire					5	5
Tennessee	—	—	—	4	2	6
	0	0	0	6	14	20
No. of locations	9	25	5	20	48	107
No. of companies	2	3	3	13	18	39

Source: OSI; excludes start-ups and branch consolidations.

cording to Jeff. "As to payment, OSI would prefer to pay 100 percent in stock, while the seller would like all in cash, so we negotiate."

The average 1991 deal provided 30 percent in cash at closing, 10 percent in OSI five-year 7 percent notes, and 60 percent earnout over five years, paid in a combination of cash and stock. (Earnout is that portion of the purchase price paid during the five years after acquisition, and is dependent upon the acquired business achieving an agreed upon sales threshold.)

Integration of the Acquisitions

OSI had developed a systematic approach to the integration of its acquisitions. Integration began before the transaction closed, with the regional president explaining employee responsibilities, benefits, and opportunities to the owners and key employees. Following the closing, OSI typically maintained a regional management presence on site for thirty to ninety days to enhance integration.

"We have found," said Jeff, "that having someone immediately available to answer questions before they become problems is critical. There are many issues which seem small to an outsider that can affect employee attitudes if left unanswered, such as 'Mr. Jones always gave us our birthdays off with pay, will OSI?' "

Most acquired practices carried roughly 52 percent gross margins as compared to OSI's existing locations which typically ran 57 percent. To improve the gross margin, OSI worked on reducing expenses, improving efficiency, and expanding revenues. All superfluous functions and expenses were eliminated. OSI's proprietary management information system, TOPS (Total Orthotic and Prosthetic System), was installed to connect the local offices with the regional headquarters for the management of cash, receivables, and other administrative tasks required of small businesses. Regional purchasing of components and supplies was installed where economies of scale were possible. A materials management system was introduced to reduce inventory and improve inventory turnover. Where feasible, fabrication of O & P devices was regionally centralized.

On the revenue side, billing procedures were reviewed and revised when necessary to ensure that all services rendered were properly classified. Professional marketing programs were instituted. In order to retain the goodwill of acquired businesses, OSI's policy was to initially operate sites under their existing names and to slowly shift name recognition to that of OSI. The ability of practitioners to provide services and generate revenues was enhanced not only by reducing the time formerly devoted to administrative tasks, but also by OSI instituting education and training programs for O & P assistants and technicians who could attend to more routine professional services for the practitioner.

OSI's experience was that within a few months after acquisition, they were able to add 2 to 3 percentage points to a typical branch's gross margin. In the subsequent six to twelve months, further margin improvement was derived from changes in practitioner productivity and billing efficiency. Simultaneously, OSI's marketing initiatives and recruiting efforts helped the branches pursue revenue growth more aggressively than previously possible.

A strategic plan for each acquired business was worked out by OSI with the former owners. The plan accommodated the particular nature of the specific practice, while adhering to OSI's overall corporate strategy of enhancing both patient care and productivity. It was Jeff's belief that "issues involving the consistent delivery of high-quality care and physician and patient satisfaction are given as much attention as those relating to financial and operational procedures."

COMPANY OPERATIONS

Management Personnel

OSI had sought to create a strong, seasoned management team (see Exhibit 10.3). Founder John Foster had been involved in the rehabilitation services industry for a decade. Jeffrey Levitt and Alan Vinick had extensive experience in identifying and integrating acquisitions in the health care delivery field. Barry Roth was experienced in monitoring the reimbursement environment. As a certified orthotist, Thomas Bart provided sensitivity at the top levels of management to practitioner needs.

The three regional presidents, Brian Mur-

EXHIBIT 10.3

Orthopedic Services, Inc., Management Team (March 1992)

John H. Foster, B.A., M.B.A. (49): Founder, Chairman, CEO (1987–present)

Williams College and Amos Tuck School of Business Administration; Morgan Guarantee Trust (1967–72), venture capital, left as Assistant Vice President; Founder, Chairman, CEO (1972–present), Foster Management Co., venture capital; Founder, Chairman (1979–83) The Aviation Group, Inc., all cargo carrier, Director (1979–86) until sold; Founder, Chairman, CEO (1980–84) Foster Medical Corp. until sold to Avon Products, Inc.

Jeffrey S. Levitt, B.S., J.D., C.P.A. (43): President, COO (1989–present)

University of Pennsylvania and Villanova University; Arthur Andersen & Co. (1974–77), Senior Tax Accountant; V.P. (1977–82) Johnson Rents, Inc., medical equipment; President (1982–84) Home Health Care Division, Foster Medical Corp; President (1984–86) Home Health Care Division, Avon Products, Inc.; President, COO (1986–89) Heritage Health Systems, Inc., owner and manager of health maintenance organizations.

Thomas R. Bart, Certified Orthotist (46): V.P. Development (1989–present)

Chairman, President (1978–87), Missouri Valley Orthotic & Prosthetic Center, Inc.; President, OSI Midwest Region (1987–89); former President, American Orthotics and Prosthetics Association.

Barry M. Roth, B.S., L.L.B. (48): V.P. Regulatory Affairs, General Counsel, Secretary (1990–present)

V.P., General Counsel (1984–87) Foster Medical Corp.; V.P. Government Affairs (1987–88), V.P. General Counsel (1988–90) Heritage Health Systems, Inc.

Alan N. Vinick, B.S., M.B.A. (48): V.P., CFO, Treasurer (1990–present)

V.P., CFO, Heritage Health Systems, Inc. (1988–90); V.P., CFO, John Hancock Health Plans (1984–88).

Marilyn J. Twombley, B.S., M.S., R.N. (45): Director – Marketing (1987–present)

Director – Marketing (1982–87), Foster Medical Corp.; prior position, Director, Stein Medical, home health care equipment and respiratory business.

Scott Kessler, B.S. in Business Administration (34): Director – Reimbursement (1991–present)

American Express, Director of Reimbursement Services (1986–91); Foster Medical Corp., Director of Claims Administration (1980–85); Accountant/Controller (1975–80).

John Gardner, B.S. in Business Administration (35): Director – Human Resources (1991–present)

Manager – Human Resources (1983–91), Decision Data, Inc.; Manager – Human Resources (1978–83), United Engineers & Contractors, Inc.

EXHIBIT 10.3   *cont'd*

Jeffrey Allgood, B.S. in Industrial Engineering, M.B.A. in Marketing (40): Director – Logistics (1991–present)

Manager-Purchasing, Managing Buyer, Customer Service and Distribution (1979–91), Johnson & Johnson.

William Torzolini, B.S. in Business Administration, C.P.A. (31): Director – Finance (1990–present)

Peat, Marwick, Main & Co. (1981–84); Senior Auditor (1984–87), Alco Standard Corp., Director – Finance (1987–90) Chilton Co./ Capital Cities ABC.

William McGinnis, B.S. in Business Administration, C.P.A. (32): Controller (1990–present)

Senior Manager (1984–90), Pannell Kerr Forster CPAs; Senior Auditor (1982–84), Peat, Marwick, Main & Co.

Brian G. Murphy, B.S. in Health Education (31): President, Midwest Region (1989–present)

Prior positions: President, AmeriPlan Health Services; President – Heritage Health Plans; Director – Development, Partners National Health Plans.

Floyd W. Pastor, B.S. (51): President, East Region (1991–present)

Group Vice President (1985–89) Foster Medical Corp.; District Manager (1965–85) United Parcel Service.

Richmond L. Taylor, B.S. in International Affairs (43): President, West Region (1989–present)

V.P. (1984–88), Home Health Care Division, Avon Products, Inc.; V.P. Sales (1988–89) Integrated Medical Systems, Inc., developer of medical information systems; currently Director, California Orthotics and Prosthetics Association.

William M. Clover, Jr., B.A., M.A. (46): President, Products Division (1990–present)

Director, Engineering (1984–88), V.P. Operations (1988–89), Products Division, Orthomedics, Inc.

phy, Bill Pastor, and Rick Taylor, all had considerable experience with national health care companies and had worked with Foster and Levitt in other businesses. Bill Clover, president of the Products Division, combined engineering and administrative experience. The additions, within the past year, of directors for marketing, reimbursement, human resources, and logistics were intended to provide greater depth to OSI's corporate management.

The headquarters executives, despite their professional experience, perhaps because of their relative youth (most were in their forties) and OSI's rapid growth, appeared to interact in an informal manner. A visitor on a Saturday morning found standard office decor, office doors open, and people popping in and out of each other's office. Half the offices were in use, with their occupants casually dressed, including Jeff Levitt in his warm-up suit. A shared story was that at OSI, there were three types of people: certified orthotists, certified prosthetists, and overhead – with Jeff Levitt as certified overhead! If you were overhead, the question was, "What have you done to help an orthotist or prosthetist today?"

MANAGEMENT STYLE AND SYSTEMS

"This is a people business, so the focus is on people in how we manage," Jeff stated. "I see my job as creating an atmosphere of winning. I keep a checklist of the top fifty people at OSI with the aim of spending, at a minimum, one to two quality hours per quarter talking to each one in person. I actually keep track of who I have talked to. The idea is to have a 'quality time' chat, not a broad discussion of 'how is your job going?' We focus on 'Where are you today in your career plan?' and 'How can I help you succeed?' Each regional president is encouraged to do the same with a checklist of the top thirty people in their region. This is really important considering how fast we are moving. Our voice mail also helps. We have ninety-five people on that system. It has eliminated interoffice memos for communications."

Jeff genuinely enjoyed talking to people at all levels in the organization. "I think I'm good at listening and people like to talk to me. I'll hear of a problem from an employee and ask, 'What should we do about it?' Often the initial look is, 'Do you really want to know?' but after reassuring them that I do, they respond. I listen and then get the views of others

on the suggestion. This probably comes from when I was a kid working at all the low-level jobs in the meat packing plant my father managed. At home I would hear the management responses to union demands, and then at work, hear the worker reactions. Workers were not dumb. They knew what would and would not work, and whether management was sincere or not."

OSI had a formal review and bonus system with quarterly reviews by the president. A quarterly bonus was determined for the regional presidents and corporate officers with financial goals and MBO goals (the agreed-upon set of "to dos") weighted equally, while for regional officers and corporate staff financial goals carried a 30 percent weight and MBO goals 70 percent. The bonus for branch managers was a function of specific branch key success variables including sales growth, cash collection, material cost percentage, and turnover rate. OSI believed that a quarterly bonus evened out performance and made sure that the business and strategic plans were used.

The overall business plan set up what Jeff called quarterly "to dos." Managers submitted their own list of "to dos," and an agreed-upon set of goals was negotiated. Each week Jeff received a status report on the "to dos." Jeff, in turn, reported weekly to John Foster. An end-of-the-quarter review was conducted with written comments. John Foster, at year end, received written reviews of Jeff from the regional presidents and corporate vice presidents.

As Jeff said:

We all get our report cards. The system provides discipline and detail. Tons of feedback, but on what is important, not just a "data dump." Each person gets a one-page form telling: here is where I am; here is where I am off; here is what I have to do. I have never had a person who was unclear on where they stood. The system is self-policing. Nonperformers replace themselves.

Organization

"Corporate executives have to learn not to run local health care businesses from their centralized corporate offices. Our decentralized philosophy enables management to be more responsive in providing prompt follow-up and decision making so that local practitioners can provide high-quality patient care services in their local branches. This approach also allows for the efficient and rapid integration of acquired businesses," explained Jeff Levitt.

OSI had no formal organization chart. It preferred to emphasize its "conceptual" organization chart (see Exhibit 10.4), which reflected the philosophy that it was the practitioner at the branch level who made money for OSI while everyone else was overhead. The purpose of all overhead was to assist the branch-level practitioners in providing patient care most efficiently while maintaining quality. The knowledge and resources available at what are traditionally viewed as "higher" organization levels were of value only to the extent that they supported the task of the practitioner.

When fully developed, the Eastern, Midwestern, and Western operating regions were intended to be stand-alone businesses with a complete staff providing all support functions, including accounting, information systems, professional services, operations, central fabrication, and sales. In early 1992, the regions varied in their staffing (see Exhibit 10.5). The Western region had a full-scale fabrication center to serve all branches, while the Midwest region fabrication center only served about 60 percent of its patient care centers. The Eastern region had not yet focused on the development of its fabrication capability, as it was the last region to be started by OSI in January 1990.

The regions varied in their use of principals from acquired companies to head up pa-

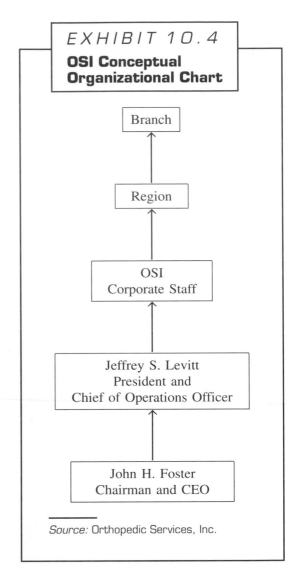

EXHIBIT 10.4
OSI Conceptual Organizational Chart

Branch

↑

Region

↑

OSI Corporate Staff

↑

Jeffrey S. Levitt
President and Chief of Operations Officer

↑

John H. Foster
Chairman and CEO

Source: Orthopedic Services, Inc.

tient care centers, as seen in Exhibit 10.6. Among the principals shown in the exhibit were two in the West who managed two branches, whereas both the East and Midwest had one who was doing double duty. The Midwest had one branch where two principals served as co-managers.

The Products Division was responsible for the design and manufacture of a line of noncus-

---

EXHIBIT 10.5
OSI Regional Staffing – As of March 1992

East	Midwest	West
President	President	President
V.P.—Professional Development	V.P.—Operations	V.P. and General Manager
V.P.—Operations	V.P.—Finance	V.P.—Professional Development
V.P.—Finance	Director—Reimbursement	V.P.—Field Operations
Director—Materials Management	Director—Human Resources	V.P.—Finance and Administration
Director—MIS	Director—Materials Management	Director—Customer Fabrication
Director—Human Resources	Director—Operations (3)	Director—Sales/Operations (2)
Director—Operations (2)	Director—Professional Education	Director—MIS
Director—Reimbursement	Director—MIS	
	Director—Fabrication	

EXHIBIT 10.6
Branch Management

Region	Managers		Assistant Managers Not Principal	Without Manager	Total Branches
	Not Principal	Principal			
East	14	6	0	1	21
Midwest	23	13	0	1	37
West	31	11	2	2	46
	68	30	2	4	104

---

tomized O & P devices for sale to OSI branches, non-OSI branches, orthopedic surgeons, and international markets. The Products Division manufactured both customized and noncustomized O & P devices, but its principal product line was a family of standard low-end orthotic braces. Current division sales were approximately $3.5 million and were 90 per-

cent to external customers. The gross margin ran 70 percent.

A critical success factor in the O & P industry, OSI had concluded, was branch location and not the number of facilities. This impacted on decisions concerning acquisitions and branch operations. Take, for example, a situation in which an acquiree had two branches, one of which duplicated an OSI branch. Since the earnout contract with an acquiree set a minimum sales threshold, OSI, when it changed the acquiree's business, adjusted the threshold. If it ended up closing the second branch, it reduced the threshold; if the decision was to close an existing OSI branch, OSI increased the threshold.

The TOPS system generated for each branch a monthly operating statistics report for the previous twelve months (Exhibit 10.7). The report helped identify areas of needed corrective action(s). If, from the TOPS system, a branch showed declining revenues for five to six months, closing the branch was considered.

Sales and Marketing

To increase its referral base, OSI had introduced sales and marketing, a largely unheard of activity in the O & P industry. The typical small practice depended upon walk-in trade. OSI employed a variety of mailed promotions directed at principal referral sources – physicians, hospitals, and managed care organizations. In addition it used a professionally trained sales force to actively call on the same referral sources. The marketing efforts aimed to project a reputation for quality, increase a referral source's comfort with Orthopedic Services, and lure referrals away from competing practitioners.

The company also conducted a patient-focused marketing program, including patient feedback and follow-up systems. The objectives were to retain patients and to inform them about applicable technological developments.

Orthotics services accounted for roughly half of OSI revenues. Of this, 50 percent was for injury victims and represented nonrecurring business; the balance was for congenital defects and age-related disorders, which tended to generate long-term patients. Prosthetic services provided 42 percent of OSI sales. The patient base was relatively small, but revenue contribution was disproportion-

ately large. O & P products and their services represented the balance of the company's revenue.

Finance

On July 17, 1990, Lehman Brothers and Paribas Corporation successfully comanaged OSI's initial public offering (IPO). Originally scheduled to sell 3 million shares at $19.00 per share, the underwriters sold 3.45 million shares. The net proceeds of $49,311,000 were used by OSI to repay about $5 million in bank debt, and to redeem Foster Management's more than $18 million in notes with accrued interest and almost $4 million in cumulative preferred stock and unpaid dividends.

At the time of the IPO, the company had issued 3,610,804 common shares for approximately $450,000 to the Foster Management partnerships, plus another 60,000 common shares for $7,200 to these investors for their guarantee to repay a $20 million bank line of credit extended to OSI. In addition, 217,111 common shares were issued for $25,000 in connection with the first seven acquisitions. The Foster Management partnerships also paid $3.6 million for 36,000 shares of 10 percent cumulation preferred stock.

Following the IPO, management believed it was amply funded to pursue its acquisition plans. Projections indicated that cash flow would just about cover operational needs and notes due in 1991 and 1992 of $1.9 million and $2.7 million, respectively. Consolidated statements of operations and balance sheets are shown in Exhibits 10.8 and 10.9.

OSI and NovaCare, Inc., jointly announced on November 19, 1991, an agreement to merge, with OSI to become a wholly owned subsidiary. Each outstanding share of OSI common was to be converted into 1.3 shares of NovaCare common stock which was listed on the New York Stock Exchange. The exchange was to be treated as a pooling of interests and a tax-free reorganization subject to the approvals of each company's board of directors and of two-thirds of NovaCare common stockholders and a majority of OSI common stockholders. Shares beneficially owned by John Foster in each company were excluded from voting. The merger was completed on March 19, 1992.

John Foster, Chairman and CEO of both Nova Care and OSI, stated, "Driven by a desire to improve patient care, enhance financial performance, and reduce reimbursement risk, the rehabilitation industry will continue to undergo dramatic consolidation. NovaCare will lead the industry in that consolidation. The merger with OSI is another important step in that process."

NOVACARE, INC.

Founded in 1985 as InSpeech, Inc., by John H. Foster, NovaCare's initial strategic plan was to consolidate the high-margin, highly fragmented market for the provision of speech-language pathology (SP) services to nursing homes on a contract basis. Nursing homes were a receptive market; SP was the least cost-effective therapy for a nursing home's own staff to provide, since the average 190-bed nursing home generated relatively low demand.

Having gained entry into nursing homes, Foster added physical and, later, occupational therapy to further serve his nursing home clients. Expansion into these therapy services was by acquisition (nineteen in nineteen months). By including these diverse services in one company and by introducing professional management techniques, economies of scale were sought and new treatment programs were developed.

In recognition of these modifications, the company name was changed to NovaCare in 1988. The financial management organization was strengthened to further improve economies of scale, cash management, and the timeliness and accuracy of financial reporting. In the following fiscal year a president and chief

operating officer was appointed. In 1991, the top management positions were chairman and CEO; president and chief operating officer; senior vice president – finance and administration and chief financial officer; vice president – MIS and customer accounting; vice president and controller; vice president – regulatory affairs; vice president – professional services; vice president – human resources; and vice president – operations.

As NovaCare grew, it learned that therapists are not motivated by money alone. They need to work for an organization that first and foremost is concerned with the quality of care delivered. In 1988–89, the company implemented many programs to improve hiring and retention of therapists. By the fall of 1989 the company had decentralized into four geographic operating divisions, empowering regional and district supervisors (most of whom were therapists) to solve problems and create programs to enhance productivity of the therapists and the well-being of their patients. In addition it had integrated physical, speech, and occupational therapists into multidisciplinary teams to provide a level of cooperative, comprehensive care, previously available only in acute care and rehabilitation hospitals.

In fiscal 1989 NovaCare revenues were $70 million; in fiscal 1990 revenue had grown to $102 million, with net income as a percent of sales increasing from 7.3 percent to 19.1 percent. (See Exhibits 10.10 and 10.11 for financial statements.) The annual average number of full-time equivalent therapists (FTEs) for fiscal 1990 had increased to almost 2,000 (1,975), but the average annual therapist turnover rate was at 32 percent. NovaCare had discovered an industry truth: nursing homes are very difficult places for which to recruit talented professionals such as therapists because geriatric patients rarely experience full recovery.

NovaCare was well on its way to dominating the contract rehabilitation market. Fiscal 1991 closed with over 1,900 rehabilitation

EXHIBIT 10.7
TOPS Monthly Operating Statistics Report

Orthopedic Services, Inc.
Branch Operational Statistics
Region: _____
Branch: _____

	1991									
	MAR	APR	MAY	JUN	JUL	AUG	SEP	OCT	NOV	DEC
Adjusted net revenues										
Orthotics	$49,806	$57,174	$59,966	$40,752	$47,909	$50,347	$32,922	$34,066	$47,322	$35,244
Prosthetics	3,532	4,854	23,849	6,777	25,373	8,651	15,473	28,140	13,407	15,221
Other	1,544	3,495	1,923	1,560	1,699	1,567	1,271	631	1,833	1,092
Total net revenues	$54,882	$65,523	$84,738	$49,089	$74,981	$60,565	$49,666	$62,837	$62,562	$51,557
Number of billed patients										
Orthotics	70	88	68	70	80	68	60	53	61	67
Prosthetics	4	9	14	5	5	6	10	10	6	9
Other	12	22	18	10	12	14	12	6	10	9
Total billed patients	86	119	100	85	97	88	82	69	77	85
Total patient visits	141	190	178	187	254	207	206	198	195	NA
Number of work days	21	22	22	20	22	22	20	23	19	21
FTEs										
Number of practitioners	2.0	3.0	3.0	2.0	3.0	3.0	3.0	1.0	1.0	1.0
Number of board eligibles	0.0	0.0	0.0	0.0	0.0	0.0	0.0	1.0	2.0	2.0
Number of practitioner assistants	0.0	0.0	0.0	0.0	0.0	0.0	0.0	0.0	0.0	0.0
Total practitioners	2.0	3.0	3.0	2.0	3.0	3.0	3.0	2.0	3.0	3.0
Number of technicians	0.0	0.0	0.0	0.0	0.0	0.0	0.0	0.0	0.0	0.0
Number of administrative	1.0	1.0	1.0	1.0	1.0	1.0	1.0	1.0	1.0	1.0
Total FTEs	3.0	4.0	4.0	3.0	4.0	4.0	4.0	3.0	4.0	4.0
Revenue per billed patient										
Orthotics	$712	$650	$867	$582	$599	$740	$549	$643	$776	$526
Prosthetics	883	539	1,704	1,355	5,075	1,442	1,547	2,814	2,235	1,691
Other	129	159	107	158	142	112	106	105	183	121
Total	$638	$551	$847	$578	$773	$688	$606	$911	$812	$607
Revenue per practitioner	$27,441	$21,841	$28,246	$24,545	$24,994	$20,188	$16,555	$31,419	$20,854	$17,186
Revenue per FTE	$18,294	$16,381	$21,185	$16,363	$18,745	$15,141	$12,417	$20,946	$15,641	$12,889
Patients seen per practitioner	71	63	59	94	85	69	69	99	65	0
Patients seen per practitioner per day	3.4	2.9	2.7	4.7	3.8	3.1	3.4	4.3	3.4	0.0
Patients billed per practitioner	43	40	33	43	32	29	27	35	26	28
Patients billed per practitioner per day	2.0	1.8	1.5	2.1	1.5	1.3	1.4	1.5	1.4	1.3
Patient conversion ratio	1.6	1.6	1.8	2.2	2.6	2.4	2.5	2.9	2.5	0.0

EXHIBIT 10.7 *cont'd*

Orthopedic Services, Inc.
Branch Operational Statistics
Region: _____
Branch: _____

	1992 JAN	1992 FEB	YTD	1991 Full Year	FEB 1992 Actual	FEB 1992 Budget	Variance +/(−)	YTD 1992 Actual	YTD 1992 Budget	Variance +/(−)
Adjusted net revenues										
Orthotics	$26,427	$27,781	$54,208	$532,481	$27,781	$21,446	$6,335	$54,208	$79,323	($25,115)
Prosthetics	4,102	18,942	23,044	174,726	18,942	5,130	13,812	23,044	18,974	(4,070)
Other	483	593	1,076	20,238	593	1,966	(1,373)	1,076	7,271	(6,195)
Total net revenues	$31,012	$47,316	$78,328	$727,445	$47,316	$28,542	$18,774	$78,328	$105,568	($27,240)
Number of billed patients										
Orthotics	51	52	103	832	52	33	19	103	123	(20)
Prosthetics	11	12	23	92	12	3	9	23	10	13
Other	5	7	12	165	7	16	(9)	12	59	(47)
Total billed patients	67	71	138	1,089	71	52	19	138	191	(53)
Total patient visits	213	205	418	NA	205	92	113	418	342	76
Number of work days	22	20	42	254	20	20	0	42	42	0
FTEs										
Number of practitioners	2.0	2.0	2.0	2.2	2.0	3.0	(1.0)	2.0	3.0	(1.0)
Number of board eligibles	1.0	1.0	1.0	0.4	1.0	0.0	1.0	1.0	0.0	1.0
Number of practitioner assistants	0.0	0.0	0.0	0.0	0.0	0.0	0.0	0.0	0.0	0.0
Total practitioners	3.0	3.0	3.0	2.6	3.0	3.0	0.0	3.0	3.0	0.0
Number of technicians	0.0	0.0	0.0	0.0	0.0	0.0	0.0	0.0	0.0	0.0
Number of administrative	1.0	1.0	1.0	1.0	1.0	1.5	(0.5)	1.0	1.5	(0.5)
Total FTEs	4.0	4.0	4.0	3.6	4.0	4.5	(0.5)	4.0	4.5	(0.5)
Revenue per billed patient										
Orthotics	$518	$534	$526	$640	$534	$646	($112)	$526	$646	($120)
Prosthetics	373	1,579	1,002	1,899	1,579	1,918	(340)	1,002	1,918	(916)
Other	97	85	90	123	85	124	(39)	90	124	(34)
Total	$463	$666	$568	$668	$666	$552	$115	$568	$552	$16
Revenue per practitioner	$10,337	$15,772	$156,656	$281,592	$15,772	$9,514	$6,258	$26,109	$35,189	($9,080)
Revenue per FTE	$7,753	$11,829	$117,492	$203,008	$11,829	$6,343	$5,486	$19,582	$23,460	($3,878)
Patients seen per practitioner	71	68	139	0	68	31	38	139	114	25
Patients seen per practitioner per day	3.2	3.4	3.3	0.0	3.4	1.5	1.9	3.3	2.7	0.6
Patients billed per practitioner	22	24	46	422	24	17	6	46	64	(18)
Patients billed per practitioner per day	1.0	1.2	1.1	1.7	1.2	0.9	0.3	1.1	1.5	(0.4)
Patient conversion ratio	3.2	2.9	3.0	0.0	2.9	1.8	1.1	3.0	1.8	1.2

EXHIBIT 10.8

**OSI Consolidated Statement of Operations –
Year Ended December 31 (dollars in thousands)[1]**

	1987[2]	1988	1989	1990	1991[3]	1992E
Net sales	$3,134	$16,158	$22,754	$35,049	$55,002	$87,969
Direct cost: products and services sold	1,475	7,086	9,778	15,860	25,003	38,737
Gross profit	1,659	9,072	12,976	19,189	29,999	49,232
Selling and indirect	310	2,067	2,930	4,285	7,223	10,867
General and administrative	965	4,386	7,212	10,803	15,812	24,188
Operations income	384	2,619	2,834	4,101	6,964	14,177
Interest expense	291	1,843	2,692	2,025	895	1,025
Interest income	(19)	(41)	(40)	(713)	(866)	(236)
Amortization: excess cost over net assets acquired[4]	69	356	514	723	1,050	1,604
Other expense (income)	0	(1)	130	14		
Income (loss) before minority interest and income taxes	43	462	(462)	2,052	5,885	11,784
Minority interest in income	0	221	237	299	143	164
Income (loss) before income taxes	43	241	(699)	1,753	5,742	11,620
Income tax (benefit)	7	193	(85)	648	1,797	3,835
Net income (loss)	$36	$48	($614)	$1,105	$3,945	$7,785
Shares outstanding at year end (in thousands)	3,866	3,979	4,037	7,654	7,654	n/a

[1]Includes results of businesses acquired from effective date of each acquisition.
[2]Includes results of Missouri Valley from August 1, 1987.
[3]1991 pro forma excludes merger related expenses with NovaCare.
[4]Excess of cost over the fair value of net assets acquired is amortized on a straight-line basis over a 40-year period.
Source: July 10, 1990, prospectus and 1990 *Annual Report* prepared by Price Waterhouse, and OSI 1991 pro forma and 1992 estimate.

EXHIBIT 10.9

OSI Consolidated Balance Sheet – Year Ended December 31 (dollars in thousands)

	1987	1988	1989	1990	1991[1]
Assets					
Cash	$495	$216	$1,821	$21,830	$9,363
Accounts receivable	810	3,110	3,325	7,020	12,406
Doubtful accounts receivable	(142)	(229)	(317)	(886)	(1,198)
Income tax recoverable	89	312	96	107	104
Inventories	501	1,570	1,803	3,423	5,752
Other	143	156	251	404	763
Total current assets	1,896	5,135	6,979	31,898	27,190
Net property, plant, and equipment	586	4,272	4,263	4,724	5,569
Excess cost over net assets acquired	7,403	19,659	20,061	30,600	53,250
Other assets	173	250	325	438	448
Total assets	$10,058	$29,316	$31,628	$67,660	$86,457
Liabilities and Stockholders' Equity					
Notes payable – bank	$2,931	$65	$0	$0	$0
Accounts payable	220	445	679	1,223	2,443
Accrued expenses and liabilities[2]	598	1,134	2,324	3,576	5,972
Long-term debt (current)	328	512	1,385	1,727	1,903
Income tax payable	27	0	0	363	1,814
Total current liabilities	4,104	2,156	4,388	6,889	12,132
Long-term debt	5,381	25,624	22,290	8,812	10,356
Deferred income tax	0	547	217	0	0
Other liabilities	0	64	806	1,625	4,812
Total Liabilities	9,485	28,391	27,701	17,326	27,300
Minority interest	0	290	299	351	146
Stockholders' equity	573	635	3,628	49,983	59,011
Total liabilities and equity	$10,058	$29,316	$31,628	$67,660	$86,457

[1]1991 pro forma excludes merger-related expenses with NovaCare.
[2]Lease expense for office space and vehicles and equipment charged to operations was $727,000, $1,085,000, and $1,571,000 in 1988, 1989, and 1990.
Source: July 10, 1990, prospectus and 1990 *Annual Report* prepared by Price Waterhouse, and OSI 1991 pro forma.

EXHIBIT 10.10

NovaCare, Inc., Consolidated Operations—Year Ended June 30 (dollars in thousands)[1]

	1987	1988	1989	1990	1991
Net revenues	$26,869	$56,612	$69,975	$102,110	$151,532
Cost of services	15,364	35,941	44,389	62,632	95,129
Gross profit	11,505	20,671	25,586	39,478	56,403
Selling, general, and administrative expenses	6,645	17,509	16,587	19,944	25,935
Merger expenses	–	–	–	–	593
Income from operations	4,860	3,162	8,999	19,534	29,875
Interest expense	(696)	(1,516)	(1,636)	(1,383)	(552)
Interest and dividend income	1,357	1,416	1,358	1,750	2,293
Amortization of excess cost of net assets acquired	(341)	(887)	(886)	(905)	(960)
Loss on marketable securities	(710)	(2,468)	–	–	–
Income (loss) before income taxes and extraordinary item	4,470	(293)	7,835	18,996	30,656
Income taxes	2,157	752	2,728	6,614	10,341
Income (loss) before extraordinary item	2,313	(1,045)	5,107	12,382	20,315
Extraordinary item: tax benefit from utilization of net operating loss carryforward	566	–	–	–	–
Net income (loss)	$2,879	($1,045)	$5,107	$12,382	$20,315
Shares outstanding[2] (at year end, in thousands)	13,215	13,376	26,764	26,945	32,060

[1]Includes results of acquisitions from effective date of acquisition.
[2]Stock splits of two for one in June 1987 and July 1991.
Source: Annual reports; prepared by Price Waterhouse.

EXHIBIT 10.11

NovaCare, Inc. Consolidated Balance Sheet—Year Ended June 30 (Dollars in thousands)

	1987	1988	1989	1990	1991
Assets					
Cash and cash equivalents	$1,053	$2,760	$19,668	$22,713	$25,799
Marketable securities	0	20,486	1,953	5,067	7,311
Accounts receivable, net	8,445	15,303	18,460	25,899	43,394
Income taxes receivable	–	–	–	–	1,793
Other current assets	1,416	1,011	951	975	1,245
Deferred income taxes	0	1,019	338	811	378
Total current assets	10,914	40,597	41,370	55,465	79,920
Marketable securities	25,197	–	–	–	14,205
Property and equipment, net	1,291	1,907	1,753	2,219	2,584
Excess cost of net assets acquired, net of accumulated amortization	20,451	29,900	30,152	29,295	28,291
Other assets	252	–	–	933	2,389
Total assets	$58,105	$72,386	$73,275	$87,912	$127,489
Liabilities and Stockholders' Equity					
Current portion long-term debt and credit agreement	$1,179	$1,456	$1,385	$3,159	$634
Accounts payable and accrued expenses	3,733	6,462	6,293	8,552	12,565
Income taxes payable	612	1,146	478	1,667	–
Deferred income taxes	1,110	0	0	407	–
Total current liabilities	6,634	9,064	8,156	13,785	13,199
Long-term debt and credit agreement, net of current portion	8,337	17,459	14,523	10,916	403
Deferred income tax	121	1,158	818	406	373
Total liabilities	15,092	27,781	23,497	25,107	13,975

EXHIBIT 10.11   *cont'd*

Commitments and contingencies					
Stockholders' equity					
Common stock, $0.01 par value;[1]	132	134	134	269	321
Additional paid in capital	41,317	43,914	43,955	44,605	74,947
Retained earnings	1,638	593	5,700	18,082	38,397
	43,087	44,641	49,789	62,956	113,665
Less: common stock in treasury (at cost)[2]	(74)	(36)	(11)	(151)	(151)
Total stockholders' equity	43,013	44,605	49,778	62,805	113,514
Total liabilities and stockholders' equity	$58,105	$72,386	$73,275	$87,912	$127,489

[1]Authorized 50,000,000 shares; issued 32,060,440 shares in 1991 and 26,945,402 shares in 1990.
[2]204,372 shares in 1991 and 1990.
Source: Annual reports; prepared by Price Waterhouse.

contracts in thirty-four states; $191 million in revenue; return on sales at 19.4 percent; and average FTE therapists at 1,929 with turnover rate down to 27 percent. Diversification of its patient base and reduction of dependence on Medicare appeared desirable. On August 9, 1991, NovaCare acquired Rehab Systems Company (RSC), which operated seven rehabilitation hospitals, an in-patient rehab unit in an acute care hospital, and six transitional living centers. In all, RSC had 463 licensed beds. Its revenue for the twelve months ended July 30, 1991, was $65 million. Its payer base included more private-pay patients and fewer Medicare-dependent patients than Nova-Care's. RSC's patient base was younger and more acutely ill than the nursing home patient base and thus more challenging and satisfying to therapists. "Additionally," as John Foster noted, "NovaCare generates cash and has vir-

tually no debt, while RSC requires capital to continue its expansion."

NovaCare saw itself as a national provider of comprehensive medical rehabilitation services. The rehabilitative therapy industry in the United States was estimated in 1989 to exceed $3.7 billion in annual revenues. With an aging population and advancing medical technology, experts projected annual growth exceeding 10 percent, with 1993 revenue of about $5.5 billion. It viewed the rehabilitation industry as consisting of seven primary settings on a spectrum from greater to lesser intensity of care:

Acute care hospital
Dedicated in-patient rehabilitation hospital
Long-term hospitals
Transitional care units
Nursing homes

Out patient clinics
Home care

Patients moved through the system according to their specific needs and progress.

Each of these primary settings was served by ancillary service segments, such as orthotics and prosthetics, clinical supplies, and psychological, social, and audiological services. Many of these segments were seen as economically attractive. Insurance sources varied from segment to segment, and most were characterized by a shortage of qualified clinical professionals.

NovaCare's strategy was to integrate the most profitable and logical rehabilitation segments which leverage local management and corporate infrastructure, thus providing broadened patient care, diversified revenue sources, and attractive, long-term career opportunities for care givers. The goal for 1993 was revenue of $275 million and a 5 percent market share. John Foster firmly believed:

> There is going to emerge over the next five or ten years a company which is the leader in rehabilitation, and that company will provide a full range of services. That is where I'm going. That is my vision. We're all betting that we will be part of the team that will be the Johnson & Johnson of rehabilitation services.

OSI: THE NEXT FIVE YEARS

In less than five years, OSI had established itself as the largest provider of orthotic and prosthetic patient care services in the United States, an attractive niche within the dynamic medical rehabilitation industry. Basic to its growth was a very aggressive and, management believed, well thought out acquisition program. It saw its management structure, operations systems, and policies as the most sophisticated in the industry. With OSI's reputation for quality care, size, access to capital, and management systems, the base was in place to achieve $190 million in sales in 1994. The next five years would be interesting and challenging.

OSI and the "Jump Shift"

"Our acquisition plans for 1992 through 1994 are to acquire some fifteen companies a year," explained Jeff Levitt. He went on to add, "Although we can enunciate an acquisition strategy, are there enough companies out there willing to be acquired at an economical price? Only six did more than $5 million a year and three of them joined OSI. The others are family-owned and somewhat resistant to selling. Periodically, we talk to them to remind them, in a friendly way, of our interest."

Beyond the largest firms were the 1,300 practices which shared 76 percent of O & P revenues, with an average annual revenue of less than $500,000.

The second five years also raised the question of what to do with the former owners of previously acquired companies who were coming to the end of their five-year employment contracts. OSI faced this issue for the first time in 1992, with thirteen cases. Did OSI want them to stay? Did they want to stay? Some had indicated yes, if they could get a premium to "re-up." This seemed more likely to be the case with minority owners who had spent the money they received when their business was first acquired. Jeff's initial reaction was, "They want us to buy them a second time, now that they see what we have accomplished!"

Employment agreements contained a covenant not to compete in the area for two years after leaving OSI. If anyone tried to ignore this constraint, OSI's legal counsel and the lawyer side of Jeff felt the company should legally enforce the covenant. The business manager side of Jeff wondered about the risk of adverse local publicity.

I can see the possibility of local news stories that focus on the small local guy vs. the distant big guy. Remember, competition among providers for referrals occurs at the local level. . .

Of course a person could move and open a small shop in a new market. If they do that, we think they will find they have lost touch with the management side of the practice, which was the weakness for many of them in the first place. Also, they now have the use of the TOPS computer system which is proprietary, and support of all of the professional programs we developed. Don't forget – they must also replicate a central fabrication capability as well. It's not an easy decision if OSI has done its job right.

Though acquisitions were fundamental to OSI's strategy in the first five years, OSI had from the beginning sought internal growth through the integration of its acquisitions. It saw integration as differentiating OSI from its only competition in consolidating the O & P industry nationally. The competition's strategy appeared to be to "only build a confederation." For OSI to achieve its growth goal, internal growth would have to play an increasingly greater role. The company's record on revenue gains by businesses acquired at least one year earlier is given in Exhibit 10.12.

Managing what Jeff called the "jump shift" from acquisitions psychology to internal growth psychology would be critical. As he reviewed the accomplishments of OSI, Jeff was pleased but concerned: "I think we are a great group of business builders. We have shown that we can acquire businesses successfully, but we need to marry that ability with the ability to operate a multisite franchise-like business." He had been looking for a vice president – operations and found, "When I interview applicants from companies like Sears or Pizza Hut and describe our regional and branch operations they seem very comfort-

EXHIBIT 10.12
Internal Growth

Region	1989	1990	1991
Midwest	+8%	+11%	+10%
West	–	+13%	+13%
East	–	–	+19%
	+8%	+12%	+12%

able with our needs. Do we have the ability to be business operators as well as business builders? Will our people find it is as exciting and fun to operate as it is to build a business?" As John Foster had observed, "The idea is to benefit from economies of scale. It sounds easy. Well we can all cook a hamburger, but there's only one McDonald's."

OSI and the Industry Dynamics

A new dimension of OSI's marketing was its commitment to become a major sponsor of two national disabled ski events hosted by National Handicapped Sports (NHS), the "Ski Spectacular" and the U.S. Disabled Ski Championships. NHS was the nation's largest sports and recreation program for the disabled. Its sixty-six community-based chapters served annually an estimated 55,000 people of all ages. The NHS press release hailed its partnership with Orthopedic Services, Inc., because ". . . they share our philosophy of excellence in service to disabled people. The quality of a prosthesis can mean the difference for a disabled person between a full and active life or one that is doomed to reclusiveness and inactivity." When "Good Morning America" on January 6, 1992, covered the U.S. Disabled Ski Championship, the OSI logo was prominently displayed. A segment of the program showing a high-tech leg prosthesis was conducted in front of a Orthopedic Services, Inc., banner.

The "Good Morning America" segment showed that computers could analyze how an amputee would walk if the person had real legs and then design "artificial legs that will work almost as well." The computer created a custom-designed tight-fitting plastic socket and a carbon-fiber knee mechanism that eliminated knee buckling when the user walked. The "foot," with its linked carbon-fiber components, simulated the movement of foot bones. The leg and foot were very lightweight, and the foot mechanism and materials were designed to store energy (in contrast to old-style solid models, which lost energy), allowing the amputee to push off.

OSI believed that developing a reputation for introducing and using leading-edge O & P devices would enhance its competitive position. In fact, because of OSI's marketing efforts, it had received calls from manufacturers and universities about possibly working together in this area. However, when it pushed for commitment, OSI found that the other parties were not ready to move.

Research and development on new O & P products was fragmented. Companies such as DuPont did research on materials which were or might be used in prosthesis, and colleges did some research on components. Most development was done by small practitioners who created what they thought was needed, without any

systematic way to determine the market's needs. OSI, with 66,000 orthotic and 19,000 prosthetic patients (annualized fourth-quarter 1991 rate), felt it was in a position to better identify market needs. OSI knew that it was capable of partnering in new product development, testing a device on a sample of patients, and publishing a joint paper, but OSI wanted to be in on the initial product specifications as well.

In the past few years as OSI had grown, it had met with its twenty-five largest vendors, seeking distributor status, with mixed results. It seemed to Jeff that manufacturers, distributors, and practitioners were all making money with the status quo and saw no reason to change. In addition to the strategic advantage of leadership in new product development, Jeff saw potential operational advantages: "It would be great if we could go from inventorying 8,000 different items to 1,000 items."

Promoting OSI nationally also intensified the "brand name" question. Regional policies in identifying branches varied. In the West, branches carried the Orthomedics name together with either a geographic location or the name of another acquired company – e.g. Orthomedics–San Diego and Orthomedics–Barnhart; Midwestern branches mostly carried the OSI name; and in the East all carried the name of the acquired company. Regional practices are shown in Exhibit 10.13.

EXHIBIT 10.13
Regional Branch Name Policy (March 2, 1992)

Region	OSI	Various Acquirees	Orthomedics – Geographic	Orthomedics – Acquiree's Name
East	0	21	0	0
Midwest	31	6	0	0
West	0	0	17	29
	31	27	17	29

With the shortage of O & P practitioners, firms expected that practitioner compensation would increase faster than inflation. Successful recruiting and retention of practitioners would be essential for competitors to remain viable and grow. Historically, the industrywide retention rate was high; i.e., once certified, few persons left the profession. OSI's turnover figures showed steady improvement, from 19.5 percent in 1989, to 7.5 percent in 1990, and 6.5 percent in 1991. The 1992 operating goal was 5.0 percent.

To improve its retention rate (and aid in recruiting), OSI had adopted a number of policies and practices. A clear career path had been established with defined levels of technician and assistant responsibilities, coupled with promotions from within and transfer of individuals to accommodate personal circumstances. OSI provided on-the-job training for practitioners who had yet to obtain certification and might then offer sponsorship to accredited schools. It ran mock testing clinics to better prepare individuals for their exams. To date, all who had participated in these clinics had passed their exams. The adoption in 1991 of the *OSI Vision* (see Exhibit 10.14) after fifteen months of companywide discussions was thought to contribute greatly to improving retention. The *Vision* was promoted throughout

---

EXHIBIT 10.14
Vision Statement

Vision

Patients are our most important priority.

We treat them professionally with compassion, respect, and dignity in a manner that makes a positive difference in their lives. To this end, we provide the highest levels of quality care that meet the patients' needs.

Employees are OSI's most valuable resource.

In our pursuit of excellence, we create a challenging and rewarding atmosphere that encourages personal and professional growth. By providing an environment of mutual respect and teamwork, we attract the best people in the industry.

Referral sources are the lifeblood of our company.

Mutual concern for our patients' well-being fosters a partnership between us. We enhance the value of that partnership by contributing our unique professional expertise.

We commit to providing the highest quality, most cost-effective services.

We distinguish ourselves through our leadership in the profession and the industry.

OSI is a community of people living this VISION.

OSI, using video tape, literature, and group meetings.

Recruiting was increasingly treated as a "professionalized" activity. The company offered a formal residency program and actively recruited recent graduates from accredited schools to complete their residency requirements at OSI. It supported its practitioners in meeting their continuing education requirements by reimbursing them for attendance at national and regional industry and supplier-sponsored training programs and by offering company-sponsored education programs.

An issue increasingly discussed by OSI management was whether OSI should become even more directly involved in the education business, to expand the number of practitioners that would be needed as demand grew, particularly as the "unmet need" was tapped. Should OSI set up a school? A joint venture with a school? Was it in OSI's interest to increase the total supply of practitioners? Perhaps OSI might gain a competitive advantage from a practitioner shortage by advancing its recruiting and retention capabilities relative to the competition. As the well-staffed competitor, OSI would be best positioned to provide high-quality services, continuity of care, and increased access, which might prove particularly attractive to contracting managed care organizations. OSI had over 200 exclusive provider agreements, including the Oregon Health Sciences University Hospital in Portland, Oregon, a premier teaching institution.

OSI had also pursued increased revenues by opening nineteen new branches. Start-up branches were in response to excess demand at an existing center or to an invitation from a referral source. Before opening a new branch, regional headquarters had to answer the "buy or build" question. The market had to clearly show sufficient demand from a strong referral base and availability of qualified personnel. Start-ups were viewed as a high return-on-investment activity.

A typical start-up required leased space and computer hardware, office furniture, and tools. With OSI's regional fabrication and warehousing, the space and tools needed were less than for an independent practice. A recent start-up had required an initial investment of $43,000. Working capital needs would be primarily for personnel, fifty-five days of accounts receivable, and leasing costs. The rent for the 1500-square-foot branch was $10 per square foot annually. Salaries were $50,000 for a practitioner, $25,000 for a practitioner assistant, and $20,000 for an office administrator (plus 20 percent for benefits and taxes). Staffing needs based on past experience were related as shown in Exhibit 10.15.

Revenue expectations were an annual rate

EXHIBIT 10.15
Typical Branch Start-up Staffing Needs

Revenue (in thousands)	Practitioner	Practitioner Assistant	Office Administrator
$0–100	1	0	1
100–300	1	0.5	1
300–500	1	1	1
500–700	1	2	2
700–900	2	3	2

of $200,000 by the end of nineteen months; $400,000 by twenty-four months; and $600,000 by thirty-six to forty-eight months, which was average for a mature branch.

OSI and Productivity

Besides working to expand the demand for its products and services, gain a larger share of the market, and increase the number of practitioners, management believed it needed to improve productivity. Materials were slightly less than 50 percent of the cost of sales; practitioner compensation was the balance.

OSI was unique in its focus on materials management. The two principal areas of focus were: (1) the development of efficient central fabrication (i.e., production or assembly) capability within each region, and (2) better material purchasing from third-party manufacturers and distributors.

The Western region operated the most comprehensive fabrication center, acquired as part of the 1988 Orthomedics acquisition, which in part accounted for its above-average profit margin. The Midwest region fabrication center served only some of the branches in its area.

Patients were treated in a multistep process involving consultation between the O & P practitioner, the physician, and the patient to assess the individual's needs and rehabilitative goals. The practitioner then made a cast of the patient's affected area, took measurements, and/or made drawings to assure an intimate fit of the device. A custom device was designed and fabricated by trained technicians using an increasing array of materials and technologies. Next, the patient was carefully fitted and trained in the use and care of the device by the practitioner. For prosthetic patients, the practitioner might use gait analysis, which involved videotaping the patient walking. Patient follow-up with the practitioner included adjustments, refittings, or replacement as needed, along with follow-up reporting to the physician

and assistance with insurance paperwork and billing.

The initial increase in practitioner productivity was achieved by freeing practitioners from certain nonclinical tasks by transferring those tasks to the regional or corporate headquarters, thereby maximizing the time available for branch practitioners to provide patient care. Further increase in productivity could be obtained through greater use of supervised practitioner assistants for less complex care. OSI continued to study other staffing models for health care provision, e.g., group practitioner dentistry. A current OSI model of staffing to improve productivity at the branch level is shown in Exhibit 10.16.

Practitioner productivity at OSI, measured as revenue per practitioner, had increased yearly: $195,000 in 1988; $225,000 in 1989; $285,000 in 1990; and $305,000 in 1991. "We have learned that beyond the structural changes to improve practitioner productivity, you can't say 'work harder' or set sales or output quotas. Practitioners are professionals who care about their patients," Jeff noted. "What you can say is 'Are there any other patients who could have benefited from our services today and need it?' The impact of the *OSI Vision* has been remarkable." Continuing education programs in the design and use of increasingly sophisticated O & P technology also contributed.

OSI and the Reimbursement Environment

Productivity gains were sought in part to offset future expected pressure from payers in all health care fields, to reduce payments. With perhaps some exaggeration, John Foster commented, "Health care is a strange business. It's the only business where you provide the service first, then see how much you can get paid for it later."

OSI, a major proponent of regional pricing for Medicare patients, employed experienced reimbursement professionals and expected to

---

EXHIBIT 10.16
Branch Staffing for $1 Million in Revenue

	OSI Model	Industry Model
Certified practitioners	2	3–4
Practitioner assistants	3–4	0
Technicians	0	3–4
Office administration	2–3	3–4
	7–9	9–12
Central fabrication	Yes	No

---

implement the new HCFA rules in a timely fashion. TOPS would allow OSI to update reimbursement data at both branch and state levels as each phase occurred, whereas less proficient providers might face delays in reimbursement while the new system was digested, adversely affecting cash flow.

In addition, OSI would continue its effort to improve reimbursement levels on a state-by-state basis by challenging the data upon which state reimbursement limits were set. In a few states, OSI had achieved a 20 percent increase in allowable charges. The company's activity in the reimbursement area promised to be vigorous.

OSI AND NOVACARE

Both OSI and NovaCare expected to benefit from the merger. OSI's expectations were access to management systems and expertise; capital availability; new market opportunities; and better administrative cost leverage. For its part, NovaCare looked forward to seeing corporate selling, general, and administrative (SG&A) expenses spread over a large sales base; Medicare dependence reduced and mitigated; expanded market opportunities; increased local scale/leverage economies; and diversification of customer base.

To reach OSI's goals of $150 million in 1994 revenue and 15 percent of an expanded market, Jeff Levitt believed he would have to go back to the public market for funds. NovaCare had committed to supplying capital. There were also opportunities for savings, e.g., the approximately $500,000 a year it cost OSI to satisfy the reporting requirements of a listing on the NASDAQ Market.

OSI and NovaCare operations overlapped in more than forty geographic markets, but until now OSI had only begun to serve the needs of NovaCare's in-patient clients in one of those markets. Nor had OSI yet tapped NovaCare's nursing home clients in those markets. Overlap selling was expected to increase. OSI expected to establish branches that would be advantageously positioned to obtain referrals from NovaCare's 1991 acquisition of Rehab Systems Company (RSC). The expectation was that branches adjacent to RSC facilities should be able to obtain referrals more economically than the strategy of capturing market share through acquisitions.

Access by OSI to NovaCare's management system and expertise was highly valued by Jeff: "NovaCare has highly skilled senior staff in place, which we can benefit from as we manage the jump shift from an acquisition emphasis to an integration emphasis. We would like advice from their consultants, much as we would like our regions to provide consulting help and services to our branches. An OSI branch manager is free to use the services of the regional staff or go outside." Exhibit 10.17 shows the services offered by one of OSI's regional service centers to its branches.

In contrast, spreading corporate SG&A over a larger sales base was seen by NovaCare as a means of achieving integrated operating control. As Jeff stated: "They have a well-run machine. They have a disciplined model set up for operations, and their staff feels we should adopt their systems. We agree that there should be technical integration of NovaCare and OSI systems, but as to content, OSI, for example, needs its own inventory and cost accounting systems. Tell us what the end game is – what output information does NovaCare need from the systems we use?"

Also to be decided was whether OSI would develop its own systems or NovaCare would do it. If NovaCare did it, would OSI run into conflict with other NovaCare subsidiaries for its highly valuable systems development resources?

Differences had arisen in regard to the legal function. Barry Roth, OSI's general counsel, had developed a relationship of trust, credibility, and responsiveness with the regional and branch managers, and they felt comfortable calling upon him. OSI had recently hired a staff attorney to assist Barry. NovaCare thought their corporate general counsel staff should be expanded to handle all legal matters of the subsidiaries. OSI's general counsel was proud of his accomplishments in serving growing OSI branches, handling acquisitions, and successfully dealing with the Securities and Exchange Commission for the initial public offering of OSI shares. The relationship with the NovaCare general counsel office remained to be determined.

NovaCare and OSI were also different in regard to human resources management and compensation. NovaCare used a consulting firm which specialized in job evaluation and prepared for each position a salary schedule with steps. The management at NovaCare, using their Performance Planning and Review System (PPR), met with a subordinate at the beginning of the year to review his or her job description and reach agreement on expected achievement that year. John Foster saw PPR as the company's way of making good on its commitment to the employee. He thought OSI should use PPR.

OSI did not have well-delineated or communicated job descriptions. Throughout the company, it was felt that before OSI could integrate into a PPR process, it would have to roll out standardized job descriptions and gain widespread acceptance and understanding of these job descriptions deeply within the company. Yet there were many other tasks with higher priority. When John Gardner, OSI's director of human resources, tried to discuss job descriptions with regional and branch managers, he found they wanted to talk about more immediate needs.

At NovaCare a human resources information system was in operation. OSI did not have such a system. John Gardner had agreed with the NovaCare staff on such a project, but then found no one was available from NovaCare to work with him. OSI wanted help in the form of actual staff assistance, but felt what it was getting was an attitude of "we know best" which showed disrespect for the OSI staff.

The NovaCare staff also believed its compensation plan should be used in OSI for senior managers. It saw OSI's regional presidents as comparable to NovaCare's regional vice presidents since they, in broad terms, managed similar amounts of sales revenue. OSI's view was that its regional presidents were general managers with control over their own profit-and-loss statements and capital budgets – with, in effect, accountability for their own decentralized business – whereas NovaCare's regional vice presidents did not have those financial responsibilities.

EXHIBIT 10.17
Service Listing: OSI Regional Center

Business Management and Reporting

Financial Reporting and Analysis

At the OSI Regional Service Center, we prepare monthly, quarterly and annual reports on your operations and provide business analysis of various plans and programs which drive your business.

Business Planning

We will support you in preparing your annual business plan, including goals, objectives, and financial statements. We also prepare special pro forma analysis including sales growth trends, "what if?" analysis, fabrication cost, alternative staffing levels, and other factors you may specify.

Accounts Payable Processing

The Regional Service Center handles all payments to your vendors, and responds to communications between vendors and your branch.

Daily Cash Management

- We will manage your daily bank deposits and pool your excess cash balances for investment.
- We will fund weekly payrolls, vendor payments, and petty cash needs through the Service Center.
- For newly acquired businesses and start ups, we advance funds to meet working capital needs.

Business Loans

The Regional Service Center provides funds needed for building improvements, equipment, and other asset additions.

Accounts Receivable Management and Training

We provide hands-on training in these areas:

- Working effectively with patients
- Accelerating collections
- Establishing goals and communicating results

We also establish and maintain national contracts with "pre-collect" and "collection" services.

Reimbursement Management

We provide training and guidance in insurance carrier relations. And, we monitor changes in government programs and communicate that information to you.

Physical Inventories and Pricing

We monitor and analyze the movement of your inventory, and we help you to establish the inventory levels best suited for your branch.

We also will assist with organizing and taking periodic physical inventories and compiling these results.

OSI East Region Services

We serve the needs of our people who serve the needs of our patients.

Dear Partner:

The OSI Regional Service Center has developed this service menu to show you the wide range of resources which we make available to you. We hope it will be helpful to you in becoming familiar with the services the Regional Center has to offer in furthering our continued success in the O & P profession!

EXHIBIT 10.17 cont'd

Management Information Systems

TOPS System Conversion

We offer initial training and assistance in converting existing billing systems to the OSI TOPS system for maximum efficiency.

User Training

Training programs are established for all system users. The Regional Center provides system overviews to branch managers, and, for each individual, sets up needed training programs.

TOPS System Upgrades and Modifications

• We coordinate system enhancement requests from user committees.

• We provide demonstrations and training in periodic new system release information.

24 Hour Telephone Support

We provide 24 hour system support to all users and resolve all errors in a timely manner. And, we acknowledge the receipt of an error within one hour of the time that it comes to our attention.

Human Resources

Benefits Administration

The Regional Service Center monitors and processes all employee enrollments and disenrollments for health, life, disability and 410K programs. We work with employees on resolving any outstanding employee insurance and workers' compensation claims. We handle all COBRA conversions.

Payroll Processing

We process bi-weekly payroll checks and update any employee changes such as their address, W-4 rate, etc. We also offer employees the choice of direct deposit.

Employee Recordkeeping

The Regional Service Center maintains and updates employee personnel files, employment applications, performance review information, and personnel action reports. We also track employee vacations and sick time.

Training and Employee Development

Through human resource programs, we offer employee training and development programs.

Professional Development

Practitioner Education Programs

We provide inservices, educational materials, and other continued education opportunities such as professional seminars and workshops.

Representation at Professional Societies

The Regional Service Center is actively involved with ABC, AOPA and AAOP on a national, regional, and local level.

Nationwide Professional Recruitment

Recruitment is provided on a nationwide basis in order to hire needed practitioners and technicians.

Practitioner Certification

We assist in certification preparation up to, and including a mock examination.

Quality Assurance Program Development and Implementation

The Regional Service Center assists with the implementation of local and national quality assurance initiatives.

Operations

Material Management System Development and Implementation

We assist in developing policies and procedures for purchasing, shipping, and receiving to ensure patients receive the highest level of service available.

National and Regional Materials Discount Negotiation

Assistance is provided in negotiating discounts with vendors. We offer OSI's national purchasing power and our discount arrangements to each branch that becomes part of the OSI system.

Facilities Management Assistance

The Regional Service Center can help with the review of facility layouts, appearance as it relates to our patients, equipment capabilities, and base renewals.

Operations

Patient Programs

We implement programs for our branches in which patients are routinely asked to rate the services we provide them. This is done through questionnaires sent to each patient and ranking results. This program helps to measure our patients' perceptions of our services and will help to resolve potential problems early on.

Sales and Marketing Program Development

The Regional Center can assist in implementing a patient recall program, patient follow-up program, and physician follow-up program. These are all done as part of our automated revenue system. And, patient service representatives may be hired to help further develop the market.

Legal Assistance

We provide access to corporate legal counsel both inside and outside. We also make arrangements for local counsel to represent the company in any legal actions or legal matters.

Business Growth

Acquisition Candidate Analysis

The Regional Service Center provides both financial and operational evaluations of potential acquisition candidates.

Acquisition Negotiations and Deal Closings

We facilitate all contract negotiations and closings of a potential acquisition.

Business Integration

The Center provides a detailed integration plan for each acquired company, which includes a business plan. We convert many of the financial functions to the Regional Service Center and enhance our branches' ability to service their patients and generate revenues.

"NovaCare looks at OSI as an $85 million company in 1992, whereas I see OSI as forty to fifty small companies. There is a great difference in cultures. For the most part, Nova-Care has evolved to be run by professional managers and operators, while we are still in the entrepreneurial phase. We don't want to lose our locker-room spirit too quickly," Jeff stated. OSI's corporate group felt it must be a buffer and translator between those regional companies and NovaCare. Moreover, it felt its decentralization model was necessary to further build OSI. With a smile, Jeff noted, "We, for the first time, are feeling what probably every other company we acquired has felt."

Jeff believed that John Foster shared his view. He had worked with John before, and was pleased that John had named him a senior vice president of NovaCare and had included him in his Office of the Chairman to help facilitate fitting OSI into NovaCare. Of course, the issues might be complicated by NovaCare's relationships with companies acquired in its other health care businesses. Frederick C. Powell, President and CEO of RSC, for example, would undoubtedly be watching to see if the NovaCare compensation system was applied only to RSC.

Northwest Hospital's Health Intervention and Wellness Program

In the early hours one evening in late April 1985, Susan Smith, controller of Northwest Hospital, settled back in the seat of her TWA flight to Seattle, Washington. Susan reviewed the events of the day, a day that had been spent with the division president and vice president and other divisional hospital administrators and controllers discussing an immediate plan of action for the $4 million, 15 percent shortfall in the 1985 earnings. She reviewed the several factors that had contributed to this shortfall. First, patient days for the division were 42,812 under budgeted year-to-date levels and 23,556 under prior year levels. Second, occupancy for the division was 60.8 percent but had been budgeted to be 66.6 percent. Northwest Hospital was maintaining a better-than-division average occupancy of 71.1 percent for the year-to-date. Although Northwest Hospital was exceeding its budgeted pretax, premanagement-fee profit by 14.5 percent, Susan had been instructed by the divisional president to reduce staffing and cut operational costs by $2 million during the remainder of 1985. Susan

was faced with the responsibility of formulating a proposal to achieve the $2 million reduction. An area that had been up for consideration was the recently launched Health Intervention and Wellness Program (HI&W). The HI&W Program had generated $10,028 in revenue and incurred $22,579 in operating expenses through April 1985. This equated to 125 percent negative gross margin. Startup capital-equipment cost for the program had exceeded $50,000 (see Exhibit 11.1). Advertising expenditures for the same period had been $36,336 (see Exhibit 11.2).

COMPANY HISTORY

Northwest Hospital is a large, seven-story, 470-bed comprehensive hospital located in Seattle, Washington. The hospital was founded in 1970 and was the first hospital in Southside Seattle. Also, in 1970 a three-phase construction project began to build twenty-five doctors' office units adjacent to the main hospital. In 1976, Jones Pavilion, a three-story, 113-bed psychiatric facility, which was formerly located in downtown Seattle, became part of Northwest Hospital. The Northwest complex is located on a 43-acre tract of land adjacent to a major metropolitan thoroughfare. Northwest Hospital was

This case was prepared by Thomas D. Giese and T. M. Weisenberger. It is intended as a basis for classroom discussion rather than to illustrate effective or ineffective handling of an administrative situation. Used with permission from Thomas D. Giese.

EXHIBIT 11.1

Startup Costs, Northwest Hospital Health Intervention and Wellness Program

Item Description	Amount
Weight machines	$13,714
Ergometer	6,368
Jog-O-Matic	2,866
Renovation of wellness center facility	15,632
Resurface jogging trail	10,000
Exercise bicycles	810
Lockers	744
Refrigerator	177
Skin fold calipers	150
Total	$50,461

---

built and is owned by National Hospital Corporation, one of the largest hospital ownership companies in the world, with current revenues exceeding $4 billion a year.

THE HOSPITAL INDUSTRY

For the past ten years the health care system has been like a cancer growing out of control. In the past four years, costs have increased by 118 percent and the total health care bill for the United States reached more than $20 billion in 1983. Each individual in the United States pays approximately $1,500 annually for health care, and the business sector contributes over $90 billion toward health care for its employees. Of our gross national product 11 percent is now directed toward health care, and the industry has grown to be the third-largest in the country. The causes of this growth are numerous and include the advancement and evolution of medical technology; escalation in construction and renovation costs; lack of competition; cost shifting; the increase in hospital

malpractice claims; and the abusive use of insurance by consumers. The primary cause, however, is poor health.

Hospitals around the country are redefining their missions largely because of recent changes in federal regulations. A prospective payment system for Medicare patients was implemented on October 1, 1983. Hospitals now receive a set payment for each Medicare patient according to his or her diagnosis. Since that time, the rate of increase in health care costs has subsided, the average length of stay has declined by an average of one full day, and the number of admissions has decreased dramatically. Many hospitals that were ill-prepared for these changes are paying the price. Massive layoffs are becoming commonplace and in some areas of the country hospitals are closing their doors.

Health care has become a consumer-driven market, but hospitals have traditionally built the foundation of their business on treatment of ill health. What the health care industry is discovering, however, is that simply providing

---

EXHIBIT 11.2

Advertising Expenditures, Northwest Hospital Health Intervention and Wellness Program

Brochures: Three brochures had been developed to market the Wellness Program. One brochure was aimed to the corporate sector, another to physicians, and the third to participants in the program.

Art direction, layout	$2,225
Typography, photos, and retouching	3,540
Printing	8,101
Total	$13,866

(The concept, photo selection, and writing had been performed by Northwest Hospital's public relations staff.)

Slide Show: A slide show had been prepared and shown to the physician staff and to corporations and individuals who had shown interest in the Wellness Program.

Photos, programming, technical work performed by Merlin Productions	$5,885
Convert slides to videocassettes	178
Total	$6,063

(The show had been conceptualized, written, and directed by Northwest Hospital's public relations staff.)

Logo: Northwest $95

TV Spot: A ten-second television spot had been developed to be used on local television.

Production	$ 600
Air time	1,400
Total	$2,000

(Written and produced by Northwest Hospital's public relations staff.)

Magazine Advertisement: Four advertisements had been run on a regional basis, one each in *Newsweek, Time Magazine, U.S. News and World Report,* and *Sports Illustrated.*

Newspaper Advertisement: Four newspaper ads had been placed in local newspapers, one targeted toward employers and three targeted toward employees.

Magazine and newspaper ads	$14,312
Total	$36,336

treatment for illness and emergencies without a commitment to disease prevention, health promotion, and medical self-help is not beneficial to either physical health or the financial health of the hospital. Modern marketing and management concepts are the key to survival in the current and future environment.

WHAT IS WELLNESS?

One of the fastest growing social trends in the past two decades has been the fitness movement, which has swept through the country carrying millions of Americans with it. Some have only dabbled in it, but others have adopted fitness as a permanent part of their lives. A new expansion of this fitness movement is the "wellness" concept. Wellness is not only the absence of disease but also the presence of vitality, energy, and well-being.

Although physical fitness, nutrition, and stress management are emphasized in most wellness endeavors, personal safety and environmental sensitivity are also components of wellness. Wellness programs can range from health education classes and aerobics to a full-scale fitness facility. Basically, any program that encourages a healthy lifestyle change by an individual can be considered part of the wellness movement.

Current research shows that 80 percent, or 1.6 million, of all U.S. deaths are due mainly to lifestyle or self-inflicted health hazards. Despite an enormous amount of data showing that smoking, alcohol abuse, overeating, and driving too fast can lead to an early grave, hundreds of thousands of Americans are dying annually from indulging in these hazards. Exhibit 11.3 shows the leading causes of preventable deaths. These twelve leading health problems account for as much as 90 percent of the total years of life lost by Americans and 84 percent of the cost of direct personal health care.

Wellness means fostering attitudes and actions that can lead to health. It is believed that half of the death, sickness, and health care costs that pile up each year could be avoided if people made reasonable efforts to avoid well-known hazards to health.

HISTORICAL PERSPECTIVE OF DEATH AND ILLNESS

In 1900, the top three killers were infections, caused either by bacteria or viruses. In the next thirty to forty years, these infections were eliminated or reduced greatly. Public health measures and improved hygiene decreased the exposure to the bacterial or viral cause and antibiotics or vaccines killed them.

Today, after more than eighty years, the picture has changed dramatically. Exhibit 11.4 shows the five current leading causes of death in the United States. The infectious problems have dropped to sixth place, or off the chart altogether, and cardiovascular disease, cancer, and accidents have replaced them. It is interesting to note that half of all deaths in 1900 were due to three different infectious diseases, but today close to half of all deaths are from a single cause, arteriosclerosis or "hardening and plugging" of the arteries.

In summary, a comparison of the leading causes of death from 1900 to 1980 reveals a marked shift away from contagious diseases toward what are generally referred to as hypokinetic diseases, or diseases caused by lifestyle.

THE WELLNESS PROGRAM AT NORTHWEST HOSPITAL

Wellness is a way of life, a lifestyle. Wellness involves self-directed behavioral change and is a lifelong learning process. Wellness programs are geared not merely toward avoiding illness, but rather toward enhancing health. Moreover, wellness is related not only to those who are without illness. Rather, it encourages each person to achieve his or her maximum potential

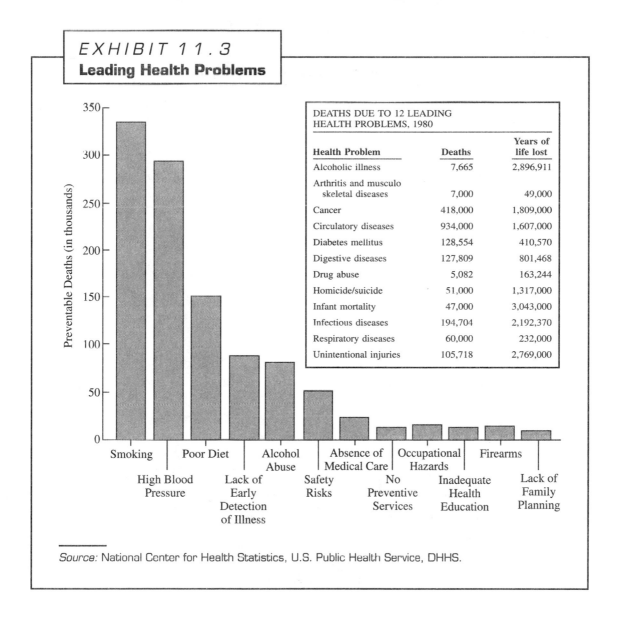

EXHIBIT 11.3
Leading Health Problems

DEATHS DUE TO 12 LEADING
HEALTH PROBLEMS, 1980

Health Problem	Deaths	Years of life lost
Alcoholic illness	7,665	2,896,911
Arthritis and musculo skeletal diseases	7,000	49,000
Cancer	418,000	1,809,000
Circulatory diseases	934,000	1,607,000
Diabetes mellitus	128,554	410,570
Digestive diseases	127,809	801,468
Drug abuse	5,082	163,244
Homicide/suicide	51,000	1,317,000
Infant mortality	47,000	3,043,000
Infectious diseases	194,704	2,192,370
Respiratory diseases	60,000	232,000
Unintentional injuries	105,718	2,769,000

Source: National Center for Health Statistics, U.S. Public Health Service, DHHS.

and is consequently achievable by the aged, the chronically ill, and the handicapped. Wellness success lies in effecting change in four major areas of life: nutrition, physical fitness, stress management, and the environment in which we live. A wellness program integrates a number of health education programs into a total approach rather than concentrating on a single dimension. From a marketing perspective, a wellness program can be considered a distinct product in a hospital service mix.

As part of the initial planning for the wellness program, several environmental forces were evaluated.

1. *Demography.* Statistics such as the number of males and females and their various age brackets in the Seattle area

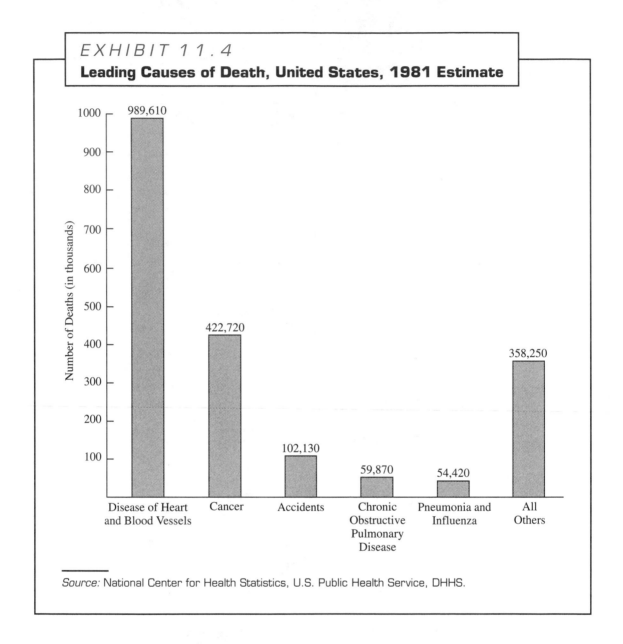

EXHIBIT 11.4

Leading Causes of Death, United States, 1981 Estimate

Number of Deaths (in thousands)

Disease of Heart and Blood Vessels	989,610
Cancer	422,720
Accidents	102,130
Chronic Obstructive Pulmonary Disease	59,870
Pneumonia and Influenza	54,420
All Others	358,250

Source: National Center for Health Statistics, U.S. Public Health Service, DHHS.

and specifically in the Southside of Seattle were researched.

2. *Economic Conditions.* Income levels of Seattle inhabitants, and specifically Southsiders, were researched to determine if the population had money to spend on a wellness program and if they would be willing to support the program.

3. *Social and Cultural Programs.* It is felt that the nation is becoming more health conscious. Commercial health clubs and celebrities such as Jane Fonda and Richard Simmons have done a tremen-

dous job of stimulating people's interest in exercise and fitness.

4. *Political and Legal Forces.* An investigation was made to see if insurance carriers would compensate for costs of the program. The results showed that some medical insurance plans would not cover the preventive aspects of the program but would pay for the rehabilitative measures. However, the industry is moving toward an acceptance of the concept of wellness and it is felt that there will be an increase in the number of carriers who will compensate for the wellness program in the near future.

5. *Technology and Competition.* Research showed that a number of hospital and health-care-related businesses in Seattle have wellness educational programs. In addition, it was found that Seattle had over fifty health and fitness centers, which are considered to be in direct competition. Management came to the following conclusion: The modern hospital is the one institution with the potential for providing or assuming responsibility for the provision of the full range of comprehensive health services – prevention, treatment, rehabilitation, and after care.

Because a substantial portion of acute illness is the accumulated result of an individual's personal living habits, the greatest potential for improving health is to be found in what people do and do not do for themselves. Consequently, the nation's health strategy has been moving toward, and is now emphasizing, the maintenance of health through preventive medicine, health education, and environmental management, in addition to the traditional medical aspects of diagnosis, treatment, and cure.

Consumer demand for wellness is high, as evidenced by the current multimillion-dollar fitness industry, which includes do-it-yourself health books, magazines, and articles; health food stores; Weight Watchers and other weight-loss programs; and health clubs. The popularity and success of the industry testifies to the widespread hunger for intelligent and educational health guidance.

It has been said that the traditional hospital that continues to focus exclusively on acute, disease-oriented care will become extinct. The future belongs to those hospitals that can identify consumer needs, and then organize and market a delivery system that effectively, efficiently, and economically meets those needs. Buyers and consumers of health care will increasingly seek such systems.

Based on these findings, the management of Northwest Hospital concluded that the market for hospital-based health promotion and disease prevention among businesses and community groups will continue to expand. Also, health-promotion programs can be an effective means to improve the image of the hospital. People feel positive about institutions that help them stay healthy. A program directed to high-risk groups can have an impact on the health care costs of the area, and a well-designed and well-marketed program will generate an alternative source of revenue.

Because of the competitive nature of the wellness market, management considered cutting prices to a level that would be competitive with area health spas and fitness clubs. However, the product would be differentiated from those of competitors because it would be a medically based wellness program with the quality and credibility lacking in most exercise and fitness centers in the Seattle area. In addition, the market appeal would be broader than existing commercial centers because hospitals have the flexibility to alter their programs to meet the needs of the individual.

TARGET MARKETS

Three target markets were identified for the wellness program: physician referrals, corporations, and employees of Northwest Hospital. A marketing program was designed for each of the target markets and a different version of the basic product was developed for each segment.

Physician Referrals

The first phase of the wellness program to be implemented was the physician referral program. This program is for individuals with potential or diagnosed health problems. The medically based program was designed to provide a highly structured and supervised environment for individuals with problems such as obesity, hypertension, diabetes, and arthritis. The program is marketed totally by physician referral and is performed on an outpatient basis. A medical advisory board, composed of a broad range of specialists, provides guidance and consultation to the program.

The participant is required to receive a physical exam prior to entering the program. The wellness staff contacts the client and schedules the introductory visit for lifestyle and physical analysis. After physical testing, nutritional assessment, and stress evaluation, the client is given a custom-tailored exercise prescription, nutritional guidelines, and a list of recommended educational classes, all of which is sent to the referring physician for approval. If approval is given, the client's first exercise and nutritional counseling session is then scheduled.

The components of the assessment are as follows:

1. *Blood Chemistry.* A complete blood analysis is performed, which includes cholesterol, HDL cholesterol, cholesterol/HDL ratio, LDL cholesterol, triglycerides, hematocrit, hemoglobin, and lipoprotein levels (fats in the blood). These are helpful in assessing the risk of developing heart disease.
2. *Pulmonary Functions.* Spirometry is performed in Respiratory Therapy and the results are interpreted by a physician. It includes forced vital capacity and forced expiratory volume, along with other pertinent respiratory data to identify any breathing abnormalities.
3. *Cardiovascular Function.* A cardiovascular bicycle ergometer test administered by an exercise physiologist is used to predict the client's maximum oxygen uptake. For high-risk clients, EKG interpretation by a cardiologist is provided. Physical measurements (height, weight, and percent of body fat) are taken and compared to normal values. Posture is examined to assess muscular balance. Endurance testing measures the ability of the body to process oxygen, proteins, and carbohydrates. Strength is tested, to measure the maximum tension generated in selected muscles and to identify areas of overdevelopment or underdevelopment. Flexibility tests measure the ability of muscles to stretch to appropriate lengths in order to identify areas of greater or lesser capacity, as well as to identify muscles that may be vulnerable to inner injury. Pulse and blood-pressure testing are done to determine the rate of the heart before and during exercise. The physician provides the hospital with the client's health history, which notes the presence of any physical condition that may affect the exercise plan.
4. *Nutritional Assessment.* A computerized nutritional analysis is done, and the results are interpreted by a registered dietitian. Dietary guidelines are designed to meet each individual's needs and dietary counseling is provided throughout the client's enrollment.

The individual then visits the wellness center three times a week for supervised exercise sessions, dietary counseling, and educational classes. Some of the educational classes provided include stress management, smoking cessation, health/fitness, nutrition, weight management, learning to relax, stretching, aerobics, wellness lecture series, yoga, cardiopulmonary resuscitation, Lamaze, alcoholism, and drug abuse. In addition, resources in the library are available. At the end of the three- or six-month program the individual is evaluated by a second physical assessment. If needed, a maintenance program is available for continued support.

In summary, the components of the wellness program include education, activity, counseling, and assessment.

A strong fitness program was identified as the area of greatest consumer need. It was felt that this program needed to be taught by an exercise physiologist and housed in a facility with space for aerobic exercises, running, weightlifting, and showers. Northwest built the following facilities to meet that consumer need: an exercise room with stationary bicycles, treadmill, stretching station, and Nautilus station; a one-mile walking/jogging fitness trail; locker rooms; a testing laboratory; classrooms; and shower facilities. Management felt that an attractive, well-equipped facility was required to meet the needs of the consumer.

Plans are currently under way to acquire roughly half-interest in the Rugby Racquet Club in Southside Seattle. Management felt that a distinct separation from the hospital, which is perceived as a place to go when one is sick, was needed. They also felt that the facilities were needed to be competitive with the local health and racquetball and tennis clubs, and that the program could benefit from the advantage of piggybacking onto an ongoing concern.

The program staff consists of an exercise physiologist, exercise specialist, and dietitian. The spokesman for the program was Ken Macho, an area sports and fitness personality. Ken was the latest inductee into the Washington Sports Hall of Fame and had retired from playing football with the Seattle Seahawks in 1978. It was felt that Mr. Macho would be an asset to the program because of his many corporate contacts as well as his service as an honorary chairman for the Governor's Counsel on Health and Physical Fitness. Management felt that a professional athlete would play a visible role in promoting the center and, at the same time, could assess overall community wellness needs and oversee total programming of the center, teach classes, and bring in guest speakers.

Corporations

The second segment of the wellness program was marketing the package to corporations. The key to successful corporate marketing is to convince the firm that if its employees are in good physical shape they contribute significantly to productivity. The lack of physical fitness causes employees to be ill more often and recover more slowly than workers who are fit, affects efficiency and productivity, and increases the risk of on-the-job accidents caused by chronic fatigue and lethargy. Many statistics back up these claims and Northwest used these statistics in its marketing efforts to corporations. The following are quotes from the hospital's corporate-oriented brochure that show how these statistics can be used to persuade the corporation to enroll in the wellness program.

> Studies show that stress-related illnesses now cost businesses from $50 to $75 billion per year, more than $750 per employee, through increased absenteeism, higher company medical expenses, and low productivity. Stress-related illnesses include hypertension, heart disease, and high blood pressure. These, of course, contribute to major medical problems. If a company can prevent just one heart attack, it is worth it.

The key to marketing the program was to emphasize the differential advantage that Northwest's Health Intervention and Wellness Program had in being the only health and fitness program that helps individuals with potential or diagnosed health problems. Another corporate marketing tool was to cite the results of a survey of more than 250 firms that had been conducted by William M. Mercer-Meidinger, Inc., a consulting firm that specializes in such fields as employee benefits. The survey showed that 90 percent of the respondents believe their employees' lifestyles had a moderate to significant impact on their firm's medical costs. One-third to more than half of the firms surveyed reported having health-promoting programs such as blood pressure screening, stress management, and physical fitness programs for their employees. Two-thirds of the firms in the survey said they believe they could positively affect their employees' lifestyles either moderately or significantly.

In summary, to effectively market to corporations, they must be convinced, first, that Northwest has a quality product to offer; second, that the product has a differential advantage over any other competitive product in the market; third, that the cost of the programs will be recaptured by decreased health care costs and increased employee productivity and morale; and fourth, that the program can be made available to the company on-site. (Exhibit 11.5 shows the on-site services that are offered to a corporation.)

Northwest Hospital Employees

The third marketing effort was to target the program to Northwest Hospital employees. The establishment of health programs at the work site may not only make good sense economically, but may also make good sense in the area of employee and community relations as well. The program was marketed to employees by offering a 50 percent discount from the retail price. The program was also offered to employees' families at a discount. This encourages similar wellness commitments by families, dependents, and thus, entire communities. Because Northwest Hospital currently employs over 1,600 people in the community, it was felt that the impact could be significant. Northwest felt that the wellness benefit could become an excellent recruiting tool as well as an aid in retaining employees. The program could also boost morale and enhance the employee's perception of the company, in addition to reinforcing the corporate philosophy of wellness. The headquarters for National Hospital Corporation, Northwest's parent company, contains a full-scale fitness center with an indoor track, racquetball courts, saunas, and weight rooms. Corporate employees are paid for each mile that they run, which encourages increased wellness.

PROMOTION

A number of hospitals and health-care-related businesses in Seattle have wellness educational programs, so when Northwest created its program, it had to be better and more comprehensive than the others, and fill a consumer need. The public relations challenge was to get publicity and wellness clients for its new program while competing with seventeen other hospitals and numerous insurance and fitness firms.

Objectives

The objectives of the hospital's promotional efforts were:

1. To make consumers, physicians, area corporations, and hospital employees aware of the Health Intervention and Wellness Program;
2. To enlist clients in the program through publicity efforts; and
3. To enroll employees in wellness classes created especially for them.

EXHIBIT 11.5

Health Intervention and Wellness Program, On-Site Services

Needs and Interest Survey This is a survey designed to assess the needs and interests of *your* employees, including the areas of nutrition, exercise, stress management, blood pressure, alcohol, smoking, and back problems. Statistics are then compiled that indicate the areas your company should emphasize.

Lifestyle Assessment This computerized assessment is an excellent health-awareness tool, which is based on one's lifestyle and health background. This confidential report is designed to help employees learn how their lifestyles influence their health and well being, and what they can do to improve their health. A group analysis is provided for the employer.

Nutritional Analysis This is a computerized analysis based on a three-day food diary, including an evaluation of nutrients, vitamins, and food choices and recommendations on how to improve eating habits. Results are interpreted and explained by a registered dietitian.

Physical Assessment This is an excellent method to raise an employee's awareness level about the condition of one's body. The assessment can range from simple blood pressure screening to a sophisticated analysis including a cardiovascular test, a blood analysis, a pulmonary function test, body composition, strength, and flexibility. Results are interpreted by physicians and lab technicians, and explained by an exercise physiologist. Exercise prescriptions are also available as an addition to the physical assessment.

Love Life This is a two-year health education and awareness program that emphasizes a different theme each month, including nutrition, smoking, alcohol, exercise, stress, self-image, and other areas affecting health problems. The program comes in the form of letters home to the employees, articles in the house organ, paycheck stuffers, posters, and audio-visual aids. We feel this program is popular because of its cost effectiveness and its professional and attractive approach; and is effective due to the concept of continuously and consistently reminding and educating employees about unhealthy lifestyle habits.

Educational Classes and Seminars Depending on the needs and interests of your employees, our qualified instructors can present virtually any topic. These can range from a two-hour seminar to a six-week class. Our most common requests are the topics of stress management, back care, health/fitness, and nutrition.

Aerobic Classes We can provide the service of coordinating aerobics classes for your employees at your company site at a convenient time.

The market was segmented into three target areas of physician referrals, corporate employees, and employees of Northwest Hospital after an analysis of buyers' motivations, better known as psychographic segmentation. For example, the physician referral market segment would choose to participate in the wellness program based on a physician's recommendation. Thus, the marketing strategy for this target market was to market the wellness program to the physicians. The objective when marketing to corporations was to convince them that any up-front outlay for the wellness program would be recovered through reductions in health insurance costs, increased employee productivity, and reductions in sick days. The wellness program was positioned so that a majority of the services could be performed on-site at the corporation's office. The objectives in marketing to employees was to use the reduced membership fees as an incentive for employees to participate. It was felt that employees would be the best public relations representatives for the program.

For many reasons, the hospital employees were considered the primary target group when it came to promoting wellness. Statistics verified the benefits in terms of decreased absenteeism, decreased morbidity and mortality, decreased turnover, increased productivity, and improved morale. In addition to all these benefits, however, having healthy, happy, and productive employees should help the hospital serve as an example for the community by establishing itself as a wellness role model. It was felt that employees would choose to participate in the program not only for the functional value of improving their health, but also because of the program's appeal to their feelings of self-worth.

Strategy

The components of the hospital's promotional strategy included:

1. Developing promotional materials, including brochures for physicians, wellness participants, and corporate managers, and a short slide show describing wellness and the various programs offered by the hospital.
2. Hiring a noted area sports and fitness personality to be the wellness spokesman.
3. Developing a ten-second spot television commercial using Mr. Macho as the talent to sell the program.
4. Initiating a media campaign consisting of television talk shows, newspaper and television features, and national magazine advertisements emphasizing the uniqueness and the differential advantage of the program.
5. Publicizing the wellness program for hospital employees using the monthly newsletter and weekly bulletins.
6. Encouraging the wellness staff to participate in community relations activities, including public speaking engagements.
7. Increasing the quantity and promotion of educational classes featuring the wellness topics.
8. Developing a wellness menu to be offered to hospital employees in the cafeteria. This also included expanding the menu board to include the caloric value of items offered.

ENROLLMENT

Because the program largely targeted "at-risk" people in the beginning, it was hoped that twenty-five clients would be enrolled within the first four months. At-risk clients are people with potential health or medical problems or those with diagnosed health problems such as obesity, hypertension, diabetes, or arthritis. The actual number of enrollees exceeded the target, and by the end of the four-month period, thirty-two people had been enrolled in the program. The interest shown by corporate managers to enroll their employees in portions of the wellness program was gaining momentum. One computer company sent several key people to the program and one local government with more than 2,000 employees signed up for a portion of the on-site services. Many other companies invited the wellness staff to make presentations to their executives, and one major employer asked Northwestern to sponsor a Wellness Health Fair for 8,000 employees and their families.

PUBLICITY

Stories on the Health Intervention and Wellness Program appeared in two newspapers, one of which was a front-section Sunday story reaching more than half a million readers.

Features were aired on "Good Morning Seattle," a local television talk show, and two other stations did news features on their evening and late-night news shows. In addition, one of the reporters did a follow-up interview on one of the clients, stating her accomplishments since signing up for the program. "Tonight Magazine," a syndicated show, aired a five-minute segment on the wellness program.

EMPLOYEES

Employee participation in the educational classes has been better than anticipated, but at this time, the number of employees who have signed up was still minimal. (See Exhibit 11.6 for the Health Intervention and Wellness packages and fee schedule.) It was felt that the employees were not willing to pay for even a portion of the program. To increase employee participation, the hospital would have to offer it free of charge or at a very reduced rate. However, employees were requesting the wellness entrees in the cafeteria.

COMMUNITY RELATIONS

The wellness staff participated in several health fairs, and the wellness coordinator became an active member of the hospital's speakers bureau. The publicity and exposure prompted a fitness expert, Mr. Don Myers, to ask the wellness coordinator to write a chapter on wellness to be used in his next book, *Fundamentals of Human Resource Management*.

OVERALL EFFECTIVENESS

In every case, each piece of publicity, whether it was a newspaper article or a television story, generated telephone calls and clients for Northwest's Health Intervention and Wellness Program. It was felt that the advertising had been successful because there was a growing primary demand for the wellness product. Also, the wellness program could easily be associated with the client's potential self-image. Another factor that contributed to the effectiveness of the advertising campaign was that the program was differentiated from others because it was the only health and fitness program in Seattle for individuals with potential or diagnosed health problems. It was felt that Northwest's other services would benefit from advertising that stimulated demand for health awareness and wellness. The advertising emphasis was on improving consumer awareness that the product existed and educating consumers about the program. The program was marketed using pull tactics to get consumers to seek the program.

CONCLUSION

As the plane taxied along the runway at the airport, Susan wondered whether the high capital startup costs, coupled with the large advertising expenditures, had been wisely spent on the Health Intervention and Wellness Program. Susan knew another major advertising cam-

EXHIBIT 11.6

**Health Intervention and Wellness Program
Program Packages/Fee Schedule**

1. TOTAL WELLNESS PACKAGE—6 months—$550
   • Physical, Nutritional, and Lifestyle Assessments
   • Exercise Prescription
   • Supervised Exercise Sessions
   • Nutritional Counseling
   • Educational Classes
   • Evaluation including second Physical Assessment
     Maintenance Program—$30/month
   • Supervised Exercise Sessions
   • Nutritional Counseling

2. BASIC WELLNESS PACKAGE—3 months—$350
   • Physical and Lifestyle Assessments
   • Exercise Prescription
   • Supervised Exercise Sessions
   • Educational Classes
   • Evaluation including second Physical Assessment
     Maintenance Program—$25/month
   • Supervised Exercise Sessions

3. EDUCATIONAL CLASSES
   • Health/Fitness • Nutrition • Stress Management
     1 topic for 6 weeks: $75   1 topic for 3 weeks: $50
     2 topics for 6 weeks: $85   3 topics for 9 weeks: $95
     3 week extension: $25

4. PHYSICAL ASSESSMENT—$200
   • Cardiovascular Bicycle Ergometer Test
   • Pulmonary Function
   • Blood Analysis
   • Flexibility
   • Strength
   • Body Composition
   • Consultation with exercise physiologist to interpret results

5. NUTRITIONAL ANALYSIS—$25
   • Computerized with Recommendations
   • Consultation with Dietitian to interpret results

paign was not planned in the near future. However, with the possible purchase of the Jones Fitness Center, Susan was afraid the hospital would throw more good money after bad. She remembered a saying she had once heard, "More business isn't good business if it's going to put you out of business."

Susan knew her recommendations would have to be made as quickly as possible to achieve the $2 million savings for the remainder of 1985.

REFERENCES

Bills, Sharon Sweeney. "Wellness and the Workplace." *Promoting Health 5*, no. 2 (March–April 1984).

Block, Carl E., and Kenneth J. Roering. *Essentials of Consumer Behavior.* Hinsdale, Illinois: The Dryden Press, 1979.

Boyd, Harper W., Jr., and Joseph W. Newman. *Advertising Management.* Homewood, Illinois: Richard D. Irwin, 1965.

Brook, Charles C. "Lifestyle Hazards Linked to U.S. Death Toll." *The Atlanta Constitution* (November 27, 1984).

"Northwest Hospital's Wellness Center." *Chesterfield Gazette* (October 10, 1984).

Cunningham, Robert M., Jr. "Wellness at Work: A Report on Health and Fitness Programs for Employees of Business and Industry." Blue Cross and Blue Shield, 1982.

Gelman, David. "Fitness Corporate Style." *Newsweek* (November 5, 1984).

Gillette, Paul. "Competition Heats up in Wellness Market." *Modern Health Care* (March 1, 1985).

Percy, Larry, and John R. Rossiter. *Advertising Strategy: A Communication Theory Approach* Greenwood, Illinois: Praeger Publishing, 1980.

"Hospital's Wellness Unit Tailored to Client Need." *Seattle Times* (October 7, 1984).

"Employer Efforts Shield Lower Medical Costs." *Seattle Times* (December 7, 1984).

Smith, Joseph P. "Is Bad Health Good Business?" *Optimal Health* (September/October 1984).

Stanton, William J. *Fundamentals of Marketing.* New York: McGraw-Hill, 1984.

Costs of Care: Two Vexing Cases in Health Care Ethics

"Hospitals are places where, in general, well-intentioned and capable health professionals do their best to fulfill the goal of delivering the best medical care they can. Responsibility for promoting and maintaining trust and appropriate clinical goals is the central feature of the ethical practice of medicine."
—*George Agich and Stuart Younger*

PROLOGUE

Mr. Blackwell decided to consult the Institutional Ethics Committee (IEC) of Regional Memorial Hospital. Blackwell is the CEO of this large, public health facility, which has over 900 beds and serves a countywide population of over 1 million persons. His concerns center around two clinical cases that have plagued his medical and administrative staffs for months. The questions just do not go away. The cases of Baby Boy-X and Annie O. are not typical, but they raise ethical issues that are troublesome, fairly common, and not easily

This case was prepared by John M. Lincourt, the University of North Carolina at Charlotte. The situations come from *Ethics Without a Net, a Case Workbook in Bioethics*, by John M. Lincourt, Dubuque, Iowa: Kendall/Hunt Publishing Company, 1991. Production of the cases is by permission of the publisher. The prologue and background sections were written especially for *Strategic Management of Healthcare Organizations, Second Edition*. Used with permission from John Lincourt.

managed. The major issue here is cost. Even with a combined expenditure of over half a million dollars, questions about the nature, duration, and efficacy of care provided remain. Blackwell sought the advice of the hospital's IEC on the appropriateness of the care given and special help on what would constitute a fair level of care in such cases.

BACKGROUND

Cranford and Doudera's description of hospital ethics committees is still useful. "Institutional Ethics Committees are interdisciplinary groups within health care institutions that advise about pressing ethical problems that arise in clinical care."[1] A primary assumption on which IECs are founded is that cooperative, reasoned reflection is likely to assist decision makers to reach better conclusions. These committees provide information and education to staff and surrounding communities about ethical questions, propose policies related to ethically difficult issues, and review patient care situations (prospectively and retrospectively) in which ethical questions are at stake. Contributions provided by IECs include the following: (1) they serve as a locus for discussion, clarification, dialogue, and advice (not decision); (2) they supply protection and support for health care providers making difficult decisions; and (3) they increase awareness of and sensitivity to ethical dimensions of clinical cases.

IECs are not without their critics. Some claim such advisory groups threaten to undermine the traditional doctor/patient relationship and impose new and untested regulatory burdens on patients, families, physicians, and hospitals. Labeling an issue as *ethical* removes it from the category of those that are strictly medical and declares that relevant considerations are not just technical in nature. Many health care providers are unaccustomed to working in this area of ethical values, and some insist their training and experience provide scant preparation for it. Conversely, others claim that ethics is woven into the very fabric of medicine thereby rendering them eminently capable, if not the most capable, to make such decisions. These individuals tend to view IECs as "God Squads," that is, generally lacking in moral authority and ill-equipped to handle the ethical challenges of life and death decisions. Such attitudes still persist in some quarters.[2]

The operation of IECs is similar to other hospital committees, but there are some important differences. These include the interdisciplinary composition, sliding orientation period, and varied utilization pattern. IECs tend to be large committees with between ten and twenty members. Membership includes nurses and physicians (frequently from Oncology and Pediatrics), administrators including an outside attorney, members of the clergy and Social Services, a citizen or two, plus an ethicist (if available). Orientation for a new committee or new members can range from a week or two up to a full year. Typically, this period is devoted to a careful review of institu-

tional and community standards of care, an introduction to the bioethical literature, which is becoming vast, and most important, practice sessions involving ethics cases. Such reviews are usually retrospective in nature and come from that institution, one of similar status, or the literature.

Committee utilization patterns vary. The IEC may be convened on a case requiring immediate action, the careful review of past cases that are known to include ethical misjudgments, and cases that upon review are not ethical at all but center on some other problem or issue, such as a legal or procedural one. Finally, The Patient Self-Determination Act (PSDA), passed by Congress as part of The Omnibus Reconciliation Act of 1990 became effective on December 1, 1991, and helped to legitimize IECs and socialize them more completely into hospital medical practice.

THE CASE OF BABY BOY-X

Baby Boy-X was born to a 37 year old woman at thirty-six weeks gestation. The birth was a spontaneous vaginal delivery and the patient's medical history gave no clue to the future difficulties associated with the birth of this child. The first indications of fetal risk were revealed when the Apgar scores were computed. This child had scores of 2 at one minute and 1 at five minutes. These scores are used to assess the general condition of the neonate, by rating the child's status using the following criteria: color, pulse, respiration, reflex response, and muscle tone. A total score of 10 denotes a newborn in the best condition. Neonatal mortality rises rapidly as the total Apgar Score approaches 0. For example, scores of 1 and 2 predict a 12–15 percent survival rate. Baby Boy-X's score was cause for serious concern for the medical staff at Regional Memorial.

The patient's clinical, physical, and social histories support the Apgar assessment. These included:

- Deformed right leg
- Hydrocephalus
- Nonfunctioning G.I. track
- Irregular cessation of breathing requiring a ventilator
- Chronic anemia requiring transfusions and nutritional supplements
- Repeated grand mal seizures during the first two months
- Probable blindness
- Lowered and malformed ears
- Severe contractions of the limbs including fingers and toes
- Cerebral shrinkage and degeneration due to lack of oxygen to the brain
- Little brain activity except during seizures
- Gastrostomy, colostomy, and iliostomy tubes inserted surgically for proper nutrition and excretion

Baby-X was kept in the neonatal intensive care unit (NICU) for four months. He was on a ventilator and given drugs for his seizure disorder. The concensus among the NICU personnel was the prognosis was poor, and they expected the patient to die from massive infection or following violent seizure activity. The cost at four months was $182,265. The mother and father were separated and the family was on welfare. The father had not visited the child.

On numerous occasions, members of the medical and administrative staffs initiated discussions with the mother about her son's grim prognosis and poor quality of life. These conversations were started in the hopes she would realize the futility of all the heroic measures being employed and allow her son to die naturally and soon. Staff members stated privately that scarce and costly medical resources were being wasted. This patient would never leave the hospital alive and his life in the hospital was severely compromised and painful. Some administrators asked pointed questions about rethinking the *"Medical Full-Court-Press"* for

this patient. Resources expended here could be redirected to clients whose chances for survival and normal lifestyles were markedly better.

In the face of all these remarks, the mother remained adamant. The following text was taken from the NICU nursing notes and reflects poignantly the mother's attitude at the time. "She [mother] does not identify her child as a person with serious health problems. She does not understand the nature and extent of his high-risk problems plus his levels of pain and discomfort. She feels the baby is alright and she seems quite unrealistic about treatment outcomes. Because of car problems, she visits only once each week and usually for about one hour. She holds the baby briefly and combs his hair. The child's father has yet to visit the patient. She continually insists that everything medically possible should be done for her child."

THE CASE OF ANNIE O.

This case ranged over three years, cost the taxpayers in excess of $310,000, and could be considered *"a classic worst-case scenario"* in allocation. The initial encounter with the patient occurred in the Emergency Room of Regional Memorial Hospital. What follows is a description of some of the medical and nonmedical facts that shaped the case and led to the ethical dilemma.

The patient is a 41-year-old white female who was hospitalized forty-one times over a period of three years. The hospitalizations ranged from four to twenty-one days, and on several occasions, the patient signed herself out of the hospital against medical advice. She is a wheelchair-bound paraplegic subsequent to a gunshot wound to the spine. Her former husband was tried and convicted of the assault and is in prison. The patient's only child was placed in a foster home, because the court deemed the patient *"an unfit mother."*

The patient presented to the Emergency Room with the following problems and history:

- Fever >103°F.
- Insulin dependent diabetic
- Chronic urinary track infection
- Recurrent depression
- Allergies to most antibiotics
- Recurrent vaginal infection and pelvic rash
- Intermittant alcohol and substance abuse
- Multiple fractures due to Osteoporosis (hollowing of bones)
- Poor nutrition and overweight—5'4" and 197 pounds
- Deep and pitting ulcers on both buttocks due to poor hygiene/sanitation

The social history is relevant. The patient lives in an abandoned garage owned by a local farmer. There is no electricity or running water, and the garage has a dirt floor. Water and electricity are supplied by way of a garden hose and extension cord from the farmer's house. There are no toilet facilities. The patient is well known to the local medical community for her consistent noncompliance. Over the years, many adjectives have been used by health care providers and others to describe her behavior. These include: *"rude," "hostile," "obstinate," "uncooperative," "cunning," "mean,"* and *"blatantly self-destructive."* One physician described Annie as *"a bitch on wheels."* Even though Annie has many serious medical problems, her uncooperative attitude and risky lifestyle make her case extremely difficult to manage. On her most recent admission, she spiked a fever of >103°F., had a raging urinary track infection, and one of her ulcers had become reinfected. This combination of medical problems, though serious, was fairly typical for this patient. However, a new problem surfaced on this visit to the hospital. Annie O. was also pregnant.

NOTES

1. R. E. Cranford, A. E. Doudera, "The Emergence of Institutional Ethics Committees," *Proceedings of the American Society of Law and Medicine* (April 1983), p. 13.
2. M. Siegler, "Ethics Committees: Decision by Bureaucracy," *Hastings Center Report* 16, no. 3 (June/July 1986), p. 22.

Helicopter Emergency Medical Services at the Medical College of Georgia Hospital and Clinics

INTRODUCTION

The Medical College of Georgia Hospital and Clinics is the health sciences campus of Georgia and is located on the Medical College of Georgia (MCG) campus in Augusta. The 590-bed hospital and associated clinics function as integral parts of MCG teaching and research programs. The hospital is clearly recognized as a high-quality tertiary-care provider. (A tertiary-care provider is a hospital that provides state-of-the-art subspecialty services, such as neonatal intensive care.)

The city of Augusta is the health care center not only for its metropolitan statistical area (MSA) of 450,000 people, but also for the surrounding, predominantly rural area within a 100-mile radius. The MCG Hospital and Clinics, as providers of tertiary care, serve an even larger rural area.

University Health, Inc. (UH), a recently reorganized, aggressive, state-of-the-art, 840-bed acute-care hospital with a full range of support services, satellite services, and alternative delivery systems, is the largest inpatient facility in the Augusta MSA. UH also provides some tertiary specialties including neonatal care and the area's only heart transplant program. Augusta's emergency care is coordinated by UH, which also operates the area's predominant ambulance service.

Other area hospitals have carved out market niches by serving specialized populations. Humana Hospital, Inc., concentrates on burn care and renal dialysis. St. Joseph's Hospital provides home health services and family-oriented inpatient care. Augusta is also the home of a major military installation that includes a regional military referral hospital. Three major Veterans Administration facilities are also located in Augusta.

Augusta is a city in which health care is a major industry. Health care providers are major employers and health care topics are covered extensively by the news media. The citizens of Augusta and the surrounding rural areas have come to expect exceptional health care services, and despite the apparent abundance of such facilities, most area hospitals operate at high occupancy rates (75 percent to 90 percent). These rates are attributed to population growth in the local area, as well as increasing referrals from the surrounding region.

This case was prepared by Harry R. Kuniansky and Phil Rutsohn. It is intended as a basis for classroom discussion rather than to illustrate effective or ineffective handling of an administrative situation. Used with permission from Harry R. Kuniansky.

In June 1985, after tiring of attempts to collaborate with other area hospitals, UH unilaterally started a helicopter emergency medical services (HEMS) program, dubbed *Carebird*. This move was in character with UH's aggressive posture and heavy involvement in emergency care. Unfortunately for UH, however, only a quarter of the patients transported by helicopter were delivered to its hospital. Most patients transported by helicopter were taken to either MCG Hospital, the area's Level I trauma center, or to Humana Hospital for burn care. Some unfortunate incidents, negative publicity, aircraft vendor problems, and sizable revenue losses prompted UH to discontinue Carebird in November 1987.

In January 1988, UH approached area hospitals (MCG Hospital in particular) with a proposal for a HEMS Consortium. Based on lessons learned with Carebird, a restructured HEMS program would apportion program costs based on a given hospital's use of the service. MCG Hospital, as the single largest potential user, is considering UH's proposal.

HELICOPTERS IN HEALTH CARE

Helicopter use in civilian health care grew out of the heavily publicized successful military experience, especially during the Vietnam era. Because of their effectiveness in reducing mortality, medical specialists began to view helicopters as logical extensions of trauma care programs, especially those serving rural areas where a disproportionately high percentage of trauma injuries occur.

The first civilian programs were started in the mid-1970s, and now an estimated 150 to 200 programs are in operation, most of which had been established outside certificate-of-need (CON) legislation. (CON legislation requires that institutional capital expenditures that exceed an established threshold be reviewed by a state agency that has the authority to approve or disapprove the expenditure.) Almost every metropolitan area has a helicopter transport program. Some metropolitan areas have competing programs, and some rural communities have overlapping coverage areas of competing helicopter services.

Safety

Unfortunately, the safety record of HEMS programs is poor. HEMS aircraft experience thirty times the normal helicopter accident rate and one hundred times the scheduled airline accident rate. In 1986, HEMS aircraft were involved in twenty-one accidents, resulting in eleven deaths. This was not an isolated bad year, but part of a continuing trend, which the industry has not been able to reverse.

Safety has become a major industry concern. Television programs such as *60 Minutes* and other media attention have made it a public concern as well. A few states, not including Georgia, have attempted HEMS regulation through legislation, but most HEMS programs operate in an environment that is minimally regulated by the health care industry and the Federal Aviation Administration (FAA). Indeed, pilot rest requirements are due to be relaxed in the near future.

Meetings of the American Society of Hospital Based Emergency Air Medical Systems (ASHBEAMS) have provided a forum for safety discussions. Data presented at those meetings include the following:

- About 70 percent of fatal accidents resulted from flights at night, in marginal weather, or in unfamiliar terrain, and these were attributed to pilot error.
- The remaining 30 percent of fatal accidents were due to helicopter mechanical problems.

The industry appears to have concluded that multiple engine helicopters with redundant flight systems are an appropriate safety response. "Pilot error," however, is more difficult to address. The industry suggests:

- setting ceiling and visibility minimums, regardless of the nature of the injury reported;
- placing strict limits on pilot duty time, and requiring at least three pilots per helicopter in seven-day, twenty-four hour programs;
- using only instrument-rated pilots; and
- establishing better criteria for the air versus ground transport decision.

HEMS Benefits

On the positive side, major studies have shown reduced mortality with helicopter-transported patients, especially severely injured or critically ill patients in rural service areas. One study of more than 900 helicopter-transported trauma victims indicated that helicopter transport was essential to the victims' well being in 14 percent of those cases, helpful in another 13 percent, and not a factor in 57 percent of cases. Despite treatment and transport, 16 percent of the victims died as a result of injuries. Another study found a 39 percent mortality in ground-transported trauma patients compared to a 36 percent mortality in helicopter-transported trauma victims.

Patient Profiles

Various other studies have yielded the following:

- Of those transported by helicopter, 60 percent to 75 percent were legitimate traumas or critical illnesses.
- Of those qualifying as legitimate, 75 percent were trauma victims and 25 percent were critically ill patients.
- Only 30 percent of helicopter transports came from accident scenes; the remainder were transports from other hospitals.
- Helicopters seem most effective within an area farther than twenty miles but

less than one hundred miles from the receiving hospital.
- A study of nearly 3,600 helicopter-transported patients indicated the following distribution by diagnostic category:

Diagnostic Category	Number of Patients
Trauma	916
Cardiac	723
Neurologic	407
Neonatal	361
General Surgery	226
Burns	156
Toxic Ingestion	107
OB/GYN	96
Other	600
Total	3,592

Costs

Nationwide, first-year costs for HEMS programs have been in the $900,000 to $2 million range. Thereafter, continuing annual costs have ranged from $700,000 to $1.6 million. Costs usually include operation and maintenance of one helicopter, pilots, flight nurses, dispatchers, administrative personnel, and some flight physician expenses.

Many options exist to configure a one-aircraft operation. The institution may (1) purchase or lease the aircraft, contract for aviation management services, and provide its own medical staff; (2) do the same, except hire the aviation management expertise from another operating system; (3) contract for the aircraft and aviation management services, and provide its own medical staff; or (4) contract for a complete turnkey operation, including flight and medical service.

Most not-for-profit institutions have opted for an agreement in which the contractor provides the aircraft, pilots, maintenance, and aviation management. Most vendors of this type of contract provide backup aircraft availability as a bonus. These vendors usually do not compete based on price but rather on services offered. Most are regional companies that also provide other commercial helicopter services. Exhibit 13.1 shows national average vendor prices for three basic helicopter types. Other costs for helicopter programs are shown in Exhibit 13.2.

Reimbursement

Medicare and Medicaid currently reimburse at the ground ambulance rate of $125 for critical-care transports plus a mileage rate of $1.50 per mile to the county line. No major carrier has established a rate for reimbursement for helicopter services. Most commercial third-party payers will reimburse part of the cost of

---

EXHIBIT 13.1
Typical Helicopter Costs

| | Helicopter Categories | | |
	Single-Engine Light	Twin-Engine Light	Twin-Engine Medium
Options			
Purchase	$350,000	$800,000	$1,500,000
Lease monthly	29,500	37,500	56,000
Lease hourly (per flight hour)	300	305	415
Fuel (per hour)	40	50	50

EXHIBIT 13.2
Other Associated Program Costs

Helipad	$10,000
Communications	1,000
Staff[1]	
5 EFT RN @ .70 time	93,000
5 EFT EMT @ .70 time	66,500
1 EFT Secretary	13,500
½ EFT Management	12,500
Fringe benefits	25% of staff costs
Indirect costs	25% of staff costs
Ground transport (per trip)	$25

[1]EFT = Equivalent Full Time; RN = Registered Nurse; EMT = Emergency Medical Technician.

helicopter transport under major medical, if the treating physician states that the helicopter was medically necessary. These claims are handled on a case-by-case basis and reimbursement is not consistent.

No program currently in operation is breaking even. Revenues generated by patient transport do not cover the fixed and variable operating costs. Programs generally cover only 30 percent to 50 percent of operating costs from individual and third-party payments. Most programs consider the marginal inpatient revenues from new inpatient stays in their cost/benefit assessments because these "new captures" are patients who probably would not have been inpatients at the current institution if not for the helicopter system.

CAREBIRD

In June 1985, UH made the unilateral decision to begin a trial program, which meant accepting all risks and potential rewards. Metro Air Ambulance from Atlanta (approximately 150 miles from Augusta) offered UH a ninety-day free trial. Metro provided the helicopter,

crew, and flight service, and UH provided medical flight personnel. Dispatching and medical ground control were provided through UH's emergency room.

The ninety-day trial was deemed a success and Carebird began operations. Through October 1986, 958 missions involving approximately 2,000 flight hours were completed. Pertinent information concerning Carebird missions is shown in Exhibit 13.3. Of those transported, 59 percent went to MCG Hospital, 25 percent to UH, 14 percent to Humana Hospital, and the remaining 2 percent to other area hospitals.

For comparison, experience from other region MSAs is shown in Exhibit 13.4. Although a single helicopter could approach 700 flights per year, the national average is 1.5 flights per day. One major provider of helicopter services estimates annual usage at thirty flights per 100,000 people within a 100-mile radius. The reimbursement history of the program is shown in Exhibit 13.5.

Carebird was staffed by one full-time pilot twenty-four hours a day. He was occasionally relieved by another pilot from the Metro base.

EXHIBIT 13.3
Carebird Trips

Year	No. Trips	Annualized
1985 (24 weeks)	166	360
1986 (52 weeks)	425	425
1987 (42 weeks)	367	454

Types of patients transported by Carebird were as follows:

Diagnostic Category	Percent of Total Patients
Trauma	40%
Cardiovascular	20
Burns	14
Neonates	8
Other	18

EXHIBIT 13.4
Air Ambulance Service Growth Rate

	Jacksonville	Atlanta	Memphis	Pensacola
First three months' flights	110	39	48	50
First six months' flights	256	107	140	128
First full year's flights	633	304	306	366
Second full year's flights	755	420	450	630
Population within 50 miles	750,000	2,000,000	1,000,000	400,000
Population within 100 miles	1,000,000	3,000,000	1,500,000	750,000

EXHIBIT 13.5
Carebird Financial Review

	1985	1986	1987
Charges			
Air ambulance charges	$143,143	$331,857	$514,870
Supply charges	7,006	15,454	25,272
Total	$150,149	$347,311	$540,142
Receipts			
Paid by third party	$75,027	$134,971	$84,205
Paid by guarantor	6,899	18,654	7,035
Payment expected from third party or guarantor	0	23,027	328,357
Public relations (nonbillable)	10,282	5,068	947
Total	$92,208	$181,720	$420,544
Bad debt	$57,941	$165,591	$119,598

The service utilized a Bell Jet-Ranger helicopter. Medical staffing was provided by the EMT at the scene of the accident or the first available EMT was picked up by the pilot from a ground ambulance.

Several articles were written in the local newspaper concerning the appropriate use of the helicopter for transportation of patients. Some articles were negative, emphasizing safety problems and the fact that ground ambulances were more efficient; and some were positive, pointing out that lives were saved by the rapid transportation provided by the helicopter.

In late 1987, plagued by operational problems, negative publicity, a deteriorating relationship with Metro, and sizable financial losses, the contract with Metro was terminated after proper notice. Since then, the Augusta MSA and surrounding rural areas have been without local medical helicopter services.

MEDICAL COLLEGE OF GEORGIA (MCG)

The MCG Hospital is exclusively controlled by MCG and the State University System of Georgia. The MCG Hospital and Clinics mission is to support the MCG mission, which includes teaching, research, patient care, and community (state) service.

MCG Clinics accommodate 225,000 visits per year. The MCG Hospital is a modern 590-bed tertiary-care facility with an overall occupancy rate of 84 percent. Of the 590-bed total, 50 beds are configured for intensive or trauma care. Those beds have an occupancy rate of 91 percent. The average length of stay for all MCG patients is 7.8 days. The average length of stay for trauma victims is nearly fourteen days. MCG is a relatively high-cost provider, with daily inpatient variable costs at $300. Charges per inpatient day are approximately $800. The collection rate for all patients is 66 percent of charges.

The MCG Emergency Services volume has increased steadily over the past few years. This is attributed to a combination of population growth, increased emphasis on emergency medicine teaching programs, and designation as the area Level I trauma center. Trauma cases now arrive at MCG via ground transport.

The MCG Hospital and Clinics strategic plan for the next three to five years calls for increased emphasis on ambulatory care, emergency care, intensive care, and the care of children. New facilities are now being designed to increase the number of trauma/intensive-care beds and to supplement corresponding ancillary and support services. Expanded teaching programs in emergency medicine are planned to coincide with facility improvements.

MCG is also becoming more concerned with its community image as competition for paying and tertiary-care patients increases. Planners at MCG have been examining the UH HEMS proposal. Assuming that dispatching continues from UH, planners estimate HEMS nonflight costs as shown in Exhibit 13.6.

EXHIBIT 13.6
HEMS Nonflight Cost Estimates

Helipad	$10,000
Communications	1,000
Staffing	
3.5 FTE RN (5 @ .70 time)	93,000
3.5 FTE EMT	66,500
1.0 FTE Secretary	13,500
0.5 FTE Management	12,500
	185,500
Fringe benefits	46,375
Indirect costs	46,375
Total annual hospital costs	$289,250

AREA OUTLOOK

Exhibits 13.7 and 13.8 provide population data and projections for the Augusta MSA. The Augusta health care service area includes another twenty-one counties outside the MSA with an additional 500,000 persons, based on 1985 estimates.

THE DECISION

Barbara Hoskens, vice president for hospital services for MCG, was contemplating a plan submitted by Darren Whitten of UH, which proposed a cost-sharing consortium of area hospitals to support restarting helicopter emergency medical services in Augusta. The anticipated service would be similar operationally to Carebird with ground medical control provided by UH's emergency room. Two notable differences from the previous Carebird situation would be the cost sharing among hospitals and the use of a twin-engine helicopter to improve safety and increase range and capacity.

Whitten believed time to be of the essence and requested that MCG Hospital along with the other area hospitals respond to the proposal within sixty days.

EXHIBIT 13.7
Population Data, December 31, 1987

	Population	Percent of U.S. Pop.	Pop./Sq. Mi. (Density)	Households Total	Percent of U.S. Households
Total	378,700	.1571	193	133,300	.1508
County A	190,700	.0791	585	65,100	.0736
County B	53,100	.0220	183	18,100	.0205
County C	115,000	.0477	105	43,100	.0488
County D	19,900	.0083	78	7,000	.0079

EXHIBIT 13.8
MSA Population Trends/Projections

Year	Augusta	County A	County B	County C	County D	MSA Total*
1980	47,532	181,629	40,118	105,625	18,546	345,918
1988	49,147	208,390	59,164	118,278	20,621	406,453
1990	–	207,884	62,116	130,000	21,511	421,511
2000	–	237,160	88,153	150,000	24,088	499,401

*1980 Census Data with estimates by Augusta Planning Commission.

CASE 14

Dr. Louis Mickael: The Physician as Strategic Manager

INDUSTRY BACKGROUND

In the early 1900s hospitals were perceived by the majority of the population in this country as places where very sick people went to die. However, in the past five decades, rapid progress in medical technology, knowledge base, and expertise have enhanced professional capability, and the public now demands high levels of health care services.

In fifty years, many demographic changes have occurred. The population, longevity, and standard of living have continued to increase. To address the needs of this changing population, government health care insurance programs for the older and needy segments of society have been instituted. Private insurance companies have proliferated, and although workers have begun to expect employers to share with them the financial responsibility for their health service needs, employers are searching for less expensive ways to provide such care. The government, also, has been attempting to reduce costs associated with the insurance programs it sponsors.

By the early 1980s, costs to provide these health care services had reached epic proportions, and the financial ability of employers to cover these costs was being stretched to the breaking point. In addition, new government health care regulations had been enacted that have had far-reaching effects on this U.S. industry.

The most dramatic change came with the inauguration of a prospective payment system. In 1984, reimbursement shifted to a prospective system under which health care providers were paid preset fees for services rendered to patients. The current procedural terminology (CPT) codes that were initiated at that time designated the maximum number of billed minutes allowable for the type of procedure (service) rendered for each diagnosis. A diagnosis is now identified by the *International Classification of Diseases, Ninth Revision, Clinical Modification*, otherwise known as *ICD-9-CM*. The two types of codes, procedural and diagnosis, must logically correlate, or reimbursement is rejected.

Put simply, regardless of which third-party payer insures a patient for health care, the bill for an office visit is determined by the number of minutes that the regulation allows for the visit. This is dictated by the diagnosis of the primary problem that has brought the patient into the office and the justifiable procedures used to treat it.

These cost-cutting measures initiated through the government-mandated prospective payment regulation have added to physicians' overhead costs because more paperwork was needed to submit claims and collect fees. In addition, the length of time increased between billing and actual reimbursement, causing cash flow problems for medical practices unable to make the procedural changes needed to adjust. This new system had the effect of reducing income for most physicians, because the fees set by the regulation were usually lower than those physicians had previously charged.

Almost all other operating costs of office practice have increased. These include utilities, maintenance, and insurance premiums for office liability coverage, workers' compensation, and malpractice coverage (for which costs have tripled in the past few years). This changed the method by which government insurance reimbursement was provided for health care disbursed to individuals covered under the Medicare and Medicaid programs. Private insurers quickly adopted the system, and health care as an industry moved into a more competitive mode of doing business.

The industry profile of today is markedly different from that of only a decade ago. Hospitals are now complex blends of for-profit and not-for-profit divisions, joint ventures, and partnerships. In addition health care provided by individual physician practitioners has undergone change. These professionals have been forced to take a new look at just who their patients are; and what is the most feasible, competitively justifiable, and ethical mode of providing and dispensing care to them.

For the first time in his life, Dr. Lou Mick-ael has been reading about physicians who were going bankrupt. In actuality, Dr. Charles was having an intense financial struggle and was close to declaring bankruptcy.

JANUARY 6, 1994

The last patient had just left and Dr. Lou Mickael ("Dr. Lou") sat in his office thinking about the day's events. He had been delayed getting into work because a patient telephoned him at home to talk about a problem with his son. When he arrived at the office, and before there was time to see any of the patients waiting for him, the hospital called to tell him that an elderly patient, Mr. Spence, admitted through the emergency room last night, had taken a turn for the worse.

"My days in the office usually start with some sort of crisis," he thought. "In addition to that, the national regulations for physician and hospital care reimbursement are forcing me to spend more and more time dealing with regulatory issues. The result of all this is that I'm not spending enough time *with* my patients. Although I could retire tomorrow and not have to worry financially, that's not an alternative for me right now. Is it possible to change the way this practice is organized, or should I change the type of practice I'm in?"

PRACTICE BACKGROUND

Location

When Dr. Lou began medical practice over thirty-five years ago, he chose a location less than one-half mile from the main thoroughfare of a northeastern city. At that time the population was approximately 130,000 people, most of whom were blue collar workers with diverse ethnic backgrounds. By 1994, suburban development surrounded the city, more than doubling the population base. A large representation of service industries were added, along with an extensive number of upper and middle managers and administrators typically employed by such industries.

Dr. Lou has kept the same office over the years. It is housed in a medical building constructed specifically for the purpose of providing space for physicians' offices, and located in a neighborhood of single-family dwellings. The building is situated across the street from City General, the hospital where Dr. Lou continues to maintain staff privileges. Three physicians (including Dr. Lou) formed a corporation to purchase the building, and each doctor pays that corporation a monthly rental fee, which is based primarily on square footage occupied, with an adjustment for shared facilities such as a waiting room and restrooms.

Office Layout

One of the physicians, Dr. Salis, is an orthopedic surgeon who occupies the entire top floor of the building. Dr. Mickael and the other physician, Dr. Charles, are housed on the first

floor. Total office space for each (a small reception area, two examining rooms, and private office) encompasses a 15' × 75' area (see Exhibit 14.1). The basement is reserved for storage and maintenance equipment.

The reception area and each of the other rooms that make up the office space open onto a hallway that Dr. Lou shares with Dr. Charles. The two physicians and their respective staff members have a good rapport, and because the reception desks open across from each other, each staff is able to provide support for the other by answering the phone or giving general information to patients when the need arises.

The large, common waiting room is used by both physicians. After reporting to their own doctor's reception area, patients are seated in this room, then paged for their appointment via loud speaker.

Dr. Charles is in his mid-forties and in general practice as well. His patients range in age from 18 to their mid-eighties, and his office is open from 10:00 A.M. until 7:30 P.M. on

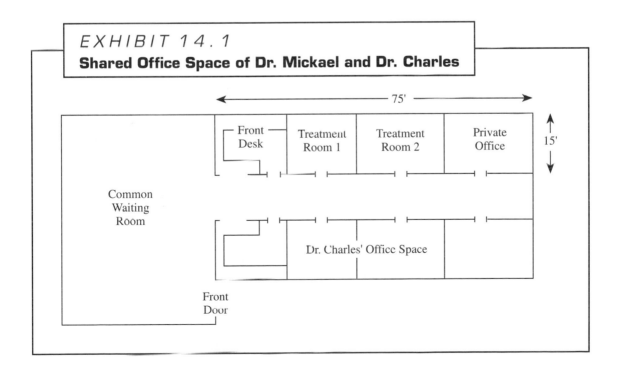

EXHIBIT 14.1
Shared Office Space of Dr. Mickael and Dr. Charles

Mondays and Thursdays, and from 9:30 A.M. until 4:30 P.M. on Tuesdays and Fridays; no office hours are scheduled on Wednesday. He and Dr. Lou are familiar with each other's patient base, and each covers the other's practice when necessary.

STAFF AND ORGANIZATIONAL STRUCTURE

Dr. Lou's staff includes one part-time bookkeeper (who doubles as office manager) and two part-time assistants. The assistants' and bookkeeper's time during office hours is organized in such a way that one individual is always at the reception desk and another is "floating," taking care of records, helping as needed in the examining rooms, and providing office support functions. There are never more than two staff people on duty at one time, and the assistants' job descriptions overlap considerably (see Exhibit 14.2 for job descriptions). Each staff member can handle phone calls, schedule appointments, and place patients in the examining rooms for their appointments.

Although Dr. Lou is "only a phone-call away" from patients on a twenty-four-hour basis, patient visits are scheduled only four days a week. On two of these days (Monday and Thursday) hours are from 9 A.M. to 5 P.M. The other two are "long days" (Tuesday and Friday), when office hours officially extend to 7 P.M. in the evening, but often run much later.

The fifth weekday (Wednesday) is reserved for meetings, which are an important part of Dr. Lou's professional responsibilities because he is a member of several hospital committees. He is one of two physicians residing on the ten-member board of the hospital,

---

EXHIBIT 14.2
Job Descriptions for Dr. Mickael's Office Staff

Job Description: Bookkeeper/Office Manager

In addition to responsibility for bookkeeping functions, ordering supplies, and reconciling the orders with supplies received, this person knows how to run the reception area, pull the file charts, and usher patients to treatment rooms. In addition, she can handle phone calls, schedule appointments, and enter office charges into patient accounts using the computer.

Job Description: Assistant 1

The main responsibility of this position is insurance billing. Additional duties include running the reception area, pulling and filing charts, ushering patients to treatment rooms, answering the phone, scheduling appointments, entering office charges into patient accounts, and placing supplies received into appropriate storage areas.

Job Description: Assistant 2

This is primarily a receptionist position. The duties include running the reception area, pulling and filing charts, ushering patients to treatment rooms, answering the phone, scheduling appointments, entering office charges into patient accounts, and placing supplies received into appropriate storage areas.

and this, along with other committee responsibilities, often demands attendance at a variety of scheduled sessions from 7 A.M. until late afternoon on "meetings" day. Wednesday is used by the staff to process patient insurance forms, enter patient data into their charts and accounts receivables, and prepare bills for processing.

When paperwork began to build after the PPS regulations came into effect in the 1980s, patients had many problems dealing with the forms that were required for reimbursement of services received in a physician's office. It is the option of physicians whether to "accept assignment" (the standard fee designated by an insurance payer for a particular health care service provided in a medical office). A physician who chooses to *not* accept assignment must bill patients for health care services according to a fee schedule ("a usual charge" industry profile) that is preset by Medicare for Medicare patients. Most other insurance follows the same profile. Dr. Lou agreed to accept the standard fee, but the patient had to pay 20 percent of that fee, so the billing process became quite complicated.

In 1988, Dr. Lou decided that he needed to computerize his patient information base to provide support for the billing function. He investigated the possibility of using an off-site billing service but it lacked the flexibility needed to deal with regulatory changes in patient insurance reporting that occurred with greater and greater frequency. Dr. Charles was asked if he wished to share expenses and develop a networked computer system. But the offer was declined; he preferred to take care of his own billing manually.

An information systems consultant was hired to investigate the computer hardware and software systems available at that time, make recommendations for programs specifically developed for a practice of this type, and oversee installation of the final choice. After initial setup and staff training, the consultant came to the office only on an "as needed" basis, mostly to update the diagnostic and procedure codes for insurance billing.

Computerization was an important addition to the record keeping process, and the system helped increase the account collection rate. However, at times problems would arise when the regulations changed and third-party payers (insurance companies) consequently adjusted procedure or diagnosis codes. For example, there was often some lag time between such decisions and receipt of the information needed to update the computer program. Fortunately, the software chosen remains technologically sound, codes have been easily adjusted, and vendor support has been very good.

Although the new system helped to adjust the account collection rate, fitting this equipment into the cramped quarters of current office space was a problem. To keep the computer paper and other supplies out of the way, Dr. Lou and his staff have had to constantly move the heavy boxes containing this stock to and from the basement storage area.

JANUARY 8, 1994 (MORNING)

On Dr. Lou's way in that day, the bookkeeper told him that something needed to be done about accounts receivable; lag time between billing and reimbursement was again getting out of hand, and cash flow was becoming a problem (see Exhibits 14.3 through 14.6 for financial information concerning the practice).

Cash flow had not been a problem prior to the PPS, when billing for the health care provided by Dr. Lou was simpler, and payment was usually retrospectively reimbursed through third-party payers. However, as the regulatory agencies continued to refine the codes for reporting procedures, more and more pressure was being placed on physicians to use additional or extended codes in reporting the condition of a patient. Speed of reimbursement was a function of the accuracy with which codes were recorded and subsequently reported to Medicare and other insurance

EXHIBIT 14.3
Trial Balance, December 31, 1993

	1991	1992	1993
Debits			
Cash	$15,994	$9,564	$8,666
Petty cash	50	100	100
Accounts receivable	19,081	25,054	28,509
Medical equipment	11,722	11,722	11,722
Furniture and fixtures	3,925	3,925	3,361
Salaries	117,455	124,608	132,325
Professional dues and licenses	1,925	1,873	1,816
Miscellaneous professional expenses	1,228	2,246	3,232
Drugs and medical supplies	2,550	1,631	2,176
Laboratory fees	2,629	524	1,801
Meetings and seminars	2,543	838	3,880
Legal and professional fees	5,525	2,057	5,400
Rent	16,026	16,151	18,932
Office supplies	4,475	3,262	4,989
Publications	1,390	406	401
Telephone	1,531	1,451	2,400
Insurance	8,876	9,629	11,760
Repairs and maintenance	3,547	4,240	5,352
Auto expense	1,009	1,487	3,932
Payroll taxes	3,107	2,998	3,780
Computer expenses	846	938	1,905
Bank charges	438	455	479
	$225,872	$225,159	$256,918
Credits			
Professional fees	$172,281	$172,472	$204,700
Interest income	992	456	210
Capital	46,122	43,137	40,117
Accumulated depreciation (furniture and fixtures)	1,692	2,151	2,796
Accumulated depreciation (medical equipment)	4,785	6,943	9,095
	$225,872	$225,159	$256,918

EXHIBIT 14.4
Gross Revenue and Accounts Receivable

	December 31	
	1979	**1986**
Gross revenue	$116,951	$137,126
Accounts receivable	15,684	32,137

EXHIBIT 14.5
Statements of Income for the Years Ended December 31

	1991	**1992**	**1993**
Operating Revenues			
Professional fees	$172,281	$172,472	$204,700
Interest income	992	456	210
Total revenues	173,273	172,928	204,910
Operating Expenses			
Salaries:	117,455	124,608	132,325
Dr. Mickael			
Staff			
Professional dues and licenses	1,925	1,873	1,816
Miscellaneous professional expense	1,228	2,246	3,232
Drugs and medical supplies	2,550	1,631	2,176
Laboratory fees	2,629	524	1,801
Meetings and seminars	2,543	838	3,880
Legal and professional fees	5,525	2,057	5,400
Rent	16,026	16,151	18,932
Office supplies	4,475	3,262	4,989
Publications	1,390	406	401
Telephone	1,531	1,451	2,400
Insurance	8,876	9,629	11,760
Repairs and maintenance	3,547	4,240	5,352
Auto expense	1,009	1,487	3,932
Payroll taxes	3,107	2,998	3,780
Computer expenses	846	938	1,905
Bank charges	438	455	479
Total operating expense	175,100	174,794	204,560
Net Income (Loss)	($1,827)	($1,866)	$350

EXHIBIT 14.6
Balance Sheets at December 31

	1991	1992	1993
Assets			
Capital equipment			
Medical equipment	$11,722	$11,722	$11,722
Furniture and fixtures	3,925	3,925	3,361
Less: accumulated depreciation	(6,477)	(9,094)	(11,891)
Total capital equipment	9,170	6,533	3,192
Current assets			
Cash	15,994	9,564	8,666
Petty cash	50	100	100
Accounts receivable	19,081	25,054	28,509
Total current assets	35,125	34,718	37,275
Total assets	$44,295	$41,271	$40,467
Liabilities			
Current liabilities			
Income taxes payable	($639)	($653)	$122
Dividends payable	1,158	1,154	1,154
Total current liabilities	519	501	1,276
New income	(1,188)	(1,213)	228
Less: dividends	1,158	1,154	1,154
Retained earnings	(2,346)	(2,367)	(926)
Capital	46,122	43,137	40,117
Total owner's equity	43,776	40,770	39,191
Total liabilities and owner's equity	$44,295	$41,271	$40,467

companies. In part, that was determined by a physician's ability to keep current with code changes required to report illness diagnoses and office procedures.

Cathy, the receptionist, had a list of patients who wanted Dr. Lou to call as soon as he came in. She also wanted to know if he could squeeze in time around lunch hour to look at her husband's arm; she believed he had a serious infection resulting from a work-related accident. The wound looked pretty nasty this morning, and Cathy thought maybe

it should not wait until the first available appointment at 7 P.M.

"I'm just starting to see my patients, and I've already done a half-day's work," Dr. Lou thought when he buzzed his assistant to bring in the first patient. He was forty-five minutes late.

PATIENT PROFILE

When Dr. Lou walked into Treatment Room 1 to see the first patient of the day, Doris

Cantell, he was thinking about how his practice had grown over the years. His practice maintained between 800 and 900 patients in active files. In comparison to other solo practitioners in the area, this would be considered a fairly large patient base.

"Well, how are you feeling today?" he asked the matronly woman. Doris and her husband, like many of his patients, were personal friends.

In the beginning years of practice, Dr. Lou's patients had been primarily younger people with an average age in the mid-thirties; their average income was approximately $15,000. Their families and careers were just beginning, and it was not unusual to spend all night with a new mother waiting to deliver a baby. Although often dead tired, he enjoyed the closeness of the professional relationships he had with his patients. He believed that much of his success as a physician came from "going that extra mile" with them.

Many things have changed. Today all pregnancies are referred to specialists in the obstetrics field. His patients range in age from 3 to 97, with an average of 58 years; their median income is $25,000. Most are blue collar workers or recently retired, and their health care needs are quite diverse.

Approximately 60 percent of Dr. Lou's patients are subsidized by Medicare insurance, and most of the retired patients carry supplemental insurance with other third-party payers. Three types of third-party payers are involved in Dr. Lou's practice:

1. private insurance companies, such as Blue Cross and Blue Shield,
2. government insurance (Medicare and Medicaid), and
3. preferred provider organizations.

Preferred provider organizations and health maintenance organizations are forms of group insurance that emerged in response to the need to cut the costs of providing health care to patients, which resulted in the prospective payment system. Both types develop a list of physicians who will accept their policies and fee schedules; using the list, subscribers choose the doctor from whom they prefer to obtain health care services.

Contrary to reimbursement policies of most other major medical third-party payers, PPOs and HMOs cover the cost of office visits, and the patient may not be responsible for any percentage of that cost. Although the physician must accept a fee schedule determined by the outside organization, there is an advantage to working with these agencies in that a physician may be on the list of more than one, and a practice can maintain or expand its patient base through the exposure gained from being listed as a health service provider for such organizations.

Those patients who are working usually have coverage through work benefits. Some are now members of a PPO; Dr. Lou is on the provider list of the Northeast Health Care PPO. Only a few of his patients are enrolled in the government welfare program.

"How's your daughter doing in college?" Dr. Lou asked. He had a strong rapport with the majority of his patients, many of whom continued to travel to his office for medical needs even after they moved out of the immediate area. "Are you heading south again this winter, and are you maintaining your 'snowbird' relationship with Dr. Jackson?"

It was not unusual for patients to call from as far away as Florida and Arizona during the winter months to request his opinion about a medical problem, and Doris had called last year to ask him to recommend a physician near their winter home in the South. Because of this personal attention, once patients initiate health care with him, they tended to continue. Dr. Lou lost very few patients to other physicians in the area since he began to practice medicine. The satisfaction experienced by his patients provides the only marketing function carried out for the practice. Any new patients (other than professional referrals) are drawn to the office through word-of-mouth advertising.

DR. LOU: PROFILE OF THE PHYSICIAN

Dr. Lou has grown older with many of his patients. His practice now spans more than three generations; a lot of families have been with him since he opened his doors in 1961. Caring for these people, many of whom have become personal friends, is very important to him. However, as the character of the health care industry is changing, Dr. Lou is beginning to feel that he now spends entirely too much time dealing with the "system" rather than taking care of patients.

Eighty-year-old Mr. Spence is a good example. Three weeks ago he was discharged from the hospital after having a pacemaker implanted. He had been living at home with his wife, and although she is wheelchair bound, they managed to maintain some semblance of independence with the assistance of part-time care. Lately, however, the man had become more and more confused. Last night he wandered into the yard, fell, and broke his hip. His reentry to the hospital so soon meant that a great deal of paperwork would be needed to justify this second hospital admission. In addition, Dr. Lou expected to receive calls from their children asking for information to help them determine the best alternatives for the care of both parents from now on. He has never charged a fee for such consultation, considering this to be an extension of the care he normally provides.

"Things are really different now," he thought. "Under this new system I don't have the flexibility I need to determine how much time I should spend with a patient. The regulations are forcing me to deal with business issues for which I have no background and these concerns for costs and time efficiency are very frustrating. Medical school trained me in the art and science of treating patients, and in that respect I really feel I do a good job, but no training was provided to prepare me to deal with the business part of a health care practice. I wonder if it's possible to maintain *my* standards for quality care and still keep on practicing medicine."

LOCAL ENVIRONMENT

The actual number of city residents had not changed appreciably since the early 1960s, although suburban areas have grown considerably. In the mid-1970s, a four-lane expressway, originally targeted for construction only one mile from the center of the downtown area, was put in place about eight miles farther away. Within five years, most of the stores followed the direction of that main highway artery and moved to a large mall situated about five miles from the original center of the city. Many of the former downtown shops then stood empty. Now, government offices, banking and investment firms, insurance and real estate offices, and a university occupy some of this vacated space; and it was used for quite different (primarily service-oriented) business activities.

A number of residential apartments devoted to housing for the elderly and low-income families have been built near the original, downtown shopping area. Several large office buildings (where much space is available for rent), and offices for a number of human services agencies have relocated nearby.

As he headed across the street to lunch in the hospital dining room, Dr. Lou was again thinking about how things had changed. At first, he had been one of a few physicians in this area. Within the past ten years, however, many new physicians have moved in.

COMPETITION

Two large (500-bed) hospitals within easy access of the downtown area have been in operation for over forty years. One is located immediately within the city limits on the north side of the city; the other is also just inside city limits on the opposite (south) side. They are approximately three miles apart and compete for a market share with City General, a 100-bed facility. This smaller hospital is only two blocks from the old business district; it is the only area hospital where Dr. Lou maintains staff privileges. Exhibit 14.7 contains a map showing the location of the hospitals and Dr. Lou's office.

The two large hospitals have begun to actively compete for staff physicians (physicians in private practice who pay fees to a hospital for the privilege of bringing their patients there for treatment). In addition, these two health care institutions now offer startup help for newly certified physicians by providing low-cost office space and ensuring financial support for a certain period of time while they work through the first months of practice.

City General recently began subsidizing physicians coming into the area by providing them with offices inside the hospital. Most of these physicians work in specialty fields that have a strong market demand, and the hospital gives them a salary and special considerations, such as low rent for the first months of practice, to entice them to stay in the area.

These doctors serve as consultants to hospital patients admitted by other staff physicians and can influence the length of time a patient remains in the hospital. This is an extremely important issue for the hospital, because under the new regulations a long length of stay can be costly to the facility. All third-party insurers reimburse only a fixed amount to the hospital for patient care; the payment received is based on the diagnosis under which a patient is admitted. Should a patient develop complications, a specialist can validate the extension of reimbursable time to be added to the length of stay for that patient.

In the past few years, many services to patients provided by all these hospitals have changed to care provided on an outpatient basis. Advancements in technology have now made it possible to complete in one day a number of services, including tests and some surgical procedures, that formerly required admission into the hospital and an overnight stay. Many such procedures can also be done by physicians in their offices, but insurance reimbursement is faster and easier if a patient has them done in a hospital. As an example of the degree of change involved, in the mid 1980s, outpatient gross revenue was only 18 percent of total gross revenue for City General. In 1992, this figure was projected to be approximately 30 percent.

January 8, 1994 (Lunchtime)

"May I join you?"

Dr. Lou looked up from his lunch to see Jane Duncan, City General's hospital administrator standing across the table. "I'd like to talk with you about something."

Dr. Lou thought he knew what this was about. The hospital had been recruiting additional staff physicians, doctors who own private practices in and around the city. A number of these individuals hold family practice certification, now a prerequisite for staff privileges in many hospitals. The recruitment program offers financial assistance to physicians who are family practice specialists wishing to move into the area, and also subsidizes placement of younger physicians who have recently completed their residencies. In contrast to physicians designated as general practitioners, who have not received training beyond that received through medical school and a residency, "family practitioners" have received additional training and have passed state board exams written to specifically certify a physician in that field.

Last week after a hospital staff meeting, Duncan had caught him in the hall and wanted to know if Dr. Lou had thought about his retirement plans. "It's really not too soon," she had said. Dr. Lou knew that one of the methods used to bring in "new blood" was to provide

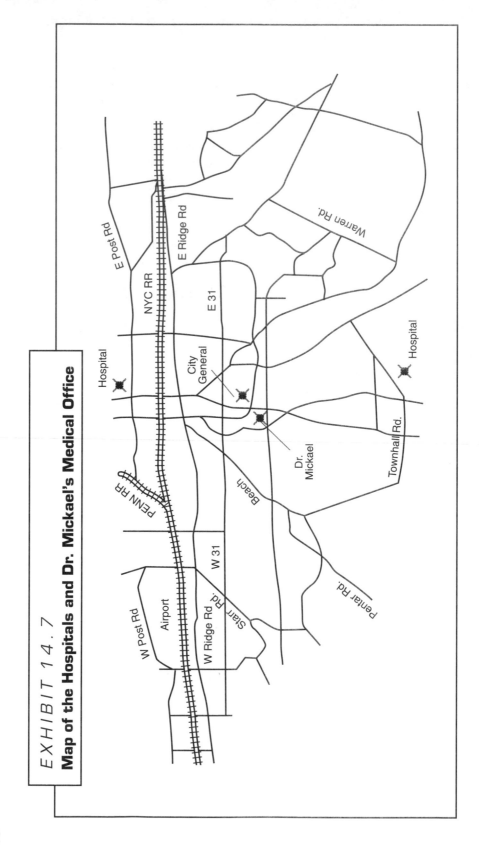

EXHIBIT 14.7
Map of the Hospitals and Dr. Mickael's Medical Office

financial backing to a physician wishing to ease out of practice, helping pay the salary of a partner (usually one with family practice certification) until the older physician retired.

"She wants to talk to me again about retirement and taking on a partner," he thought. "But I'm only in my late fifties. And I'm not ready to go to pasture yet! Besides, there is really no room to install a partner in my office."

January 8, 1994 (Afternoon)

After lunch Dr. Lou ran back to the office to take a look at Cathy's husband's arm before regular office hours started. This was a work-related case. As he treated the patient, he began thinking about industrial medicine as an alternative to full-time office practice. Right then the prospect seemed quite appealing. He had investigated the idea enough to know that there were only a few schools that provided this kind of training but one was within driving distance (Exhibit 14.8 contains information on industrial medicine).

As health costs rose over the past decade, manufacturing organizations began to feel the cost-pinch of providing health care insurance to employees. Some larger companies in the area began to recognize the cost-benefit of maintaining a private physician on staff who was trained in the treatment of health care needs for industrial workers. Dr. Lou had been considering going back for postgraduate train-

---

EXHIBIT 14.8
Industrial Medicine as a New Career for Dr. Mickael

"Industrial Medicine" is an emerging physician specialty. Training in this new field entails post-graduate work and board certification.

As yet, only a few schools provide such training. One is located in Cincinnati, Ohio, which is geographically close enough to be feasible for Dr. Mickael. The time spent in actual attendance amounts to one, two-week training period beginning in June of the year in which a physician is accepted for the training. Two additional training periods are each one week in duration; these take place in the following months of October and March. After this, the physician is expected to individually study for and take the board certification exams, which are given only once per year; the exams are comprehensive and extend over a two-day period.

TRAINING PROGRAM COSTS: INDUSTRIAL MEDICINE

University Residency:	
Three, on-site class sessions	$4,000.00
Per night cost for room	47.87
Books and Supplies (Total)	580.53
Transportation, Air:	
Three, round-trip fares	$1,650.00
Transportation, Ground:	
Car rental, per week with unlimited mileage	$125.45

ing in industrial medicine, and while wrapping the man's arm, he began to think about working for a large corporation.

"Work like that could have a lot of benefits; it would give me a chance to do something a little different, at least part time for now," he thought. "The income is almost comparable to what I net for the same time in the office, and some days I might even get home before nine P.M.!"

END OF THE DAY

As he was putting on his coat and getting ready to leave, Dr. Charles, the physician from across the hall, phoned to ask if Dr. Lou might be interested in buying him out. "I think you could use the space," he said, "and my practice is going down the tubes. I can't seem to get an upper hand with the finances. I've had to borrow every month to maintain the cash flow needed to pay *my* bills because patients can't keep up with theirs. City General has offered me a staff position and I'm seriously considering it. I thought I'd give you first chance." After some minutes of other "office talk," Dr. Charles said goodnight.

"If I wanted to take on a new partner, that could work out well," thought Dr. Lou. "It might be interesting to check into this; I wonder what his asking price would be? It could not be too much more than the value of my practice, although his patients are a bit younger and some of his equipment is a little newer. The initial hospital proposal to buy me out indicated that my practice was worth about $175,000. So that means I should be able to negotiate with Dr. Charles for a little less than $200,000."

It was 9:30 P.M. when Dr. Lou finally left the office, and he still had hospital rounds to make. "This is another situation caused by these insurance regulations," he thought. "I feel as though I'm continuously updating patients' hospital records throughout the day, and more of my patients require hospitalization more often than they did when they were younger. All things being equal, I'm earning considerably less for doing the same things I did a decade ago, and in addition the paperwork has increased exponentially. There has to be a better way for me to deal with this business of practicing medicine."

CASE 15

Calumet Community Hospital

INTRODUCTION

"When we hired a consulting firm to develop a long-range plan, we expected to receive a step-by-step plan for staged growth," commented Hospital Administrator Jon L. Smyth. "However, it seems we may be facing one or two giant steps instead."

Like most not-for-profit hospitals, Calumet Community Hospital operates at near the breakeven point. Extensive renovation of the hospital building or major new construction would require far greater financial reserves than Calumet has available at this time.

Other issues facing Smyth are increased competition from larger hospitals and other health providers, declining inpatient revenue due in part to a change in Medicare reimbursement, and a shortage of physicians. Smyth and the Calumet Board of Directors face tough decisions on future directions.

BACKGROUND

Calumet Community Hospital is a forty-five-bed general acute-care hospital located in a

small, rural community in the Southwest. As a hospital, it is one of the more complex organizational types in modern society.

The hospital originally was established in 1935 as the Jones Memorial Hospital. The present building was constructed on 12 acres leased from the nearby Central State University and opened for service on April 1, 1976.

The organization operated forty-five beds for general acute medical/surgical care until 1986. The number of days of care for medical/surgical patients has been slowly declining since 1983 (see Exhibit 15.1). In addition, the advancing age of the two physicians who accounted for over 75 percent of the hospital's revenue and increasing competition forced the hospital to look for new sources of revenue.

Like other hospitals, Calumet began searching for ways to reduce the hospital's dependence on inpatients. The Home Health Program was instituted in 1986 and now accounts for an average of seventy-five patients per week (see Exhibit 15.2).

In years past, the hospital did only one fourth of its own laboratory work and contracted for the remainder. Today, about 99 percent of lab work is done in-house. In addition the laboratory is contracting with physicians' offices and the veterinary clinic at the university. The lab procedures have increased dramatically since these actions were taken (see Exhibit 15.2).

In 1986, the hospital administrator decided to convert fourteen beds from medical/surgical care to treatment of substance abuse and alco-

This case was prepared by V. Aline Arnold. It is intended to be used as a basis for class discussion rather than to illustrate effective or ineffective handling of an administrative situation. The names of the organizations, individuals, and locations, as well as statistical information have been disguised to preserve the anonymity of the organization. Presented and accepted by the refereed Midwest Society for Case Research. All rights reserved to the author and the MSCR. Copyright © 1988 by Aline Arnold. Used with permission.

EXHIBIT 15.1

Inpatient Care Volume and Bed Utilization, Fiscal 1983–1987

	Fiscal Year Ending September 30,				
	1983	1984	1985	1986	1987
Patients					
Medicine/surgery	1,353	1,298	1,224	1,197	1,138
Obstetrics	239	187	207	279	328
Pediatrics	38	43	69	118	219
Subtotal, general acute	1,630	1,528	1,500	1,594	1,685
Substance abuse	0	0	0	146	299
Total	1,630	1,528	1,500	1,740	1,984
Newborn	192	149	150	194	217
Days of Care					
Medicine/surgery	5,465	5,132	4,824	4,487	4,118
Obstetrics	707	571	571	650	758
Pediatrics	99	102	184	277	525
Subtotal, general acute	6,271	5,805	5,579	5,414	5,401
Substance abuse	0	0	0	3,133	5,092
Total	6,271	5,805	5,579	8,547	10,493
Newborn	568	454	388	587	669
Average Length of Stay					
Medicine/surgery	4.0	4.0	3.9	3.7	3.6
Obstetrics	3.0	3.1	2.5	3.0	2.9
Pediatrics	2.6	2.4	2.7	2.3	2.4
Subtotal, general acute	3.2	3.2	3.0	3.0	3.0
Substance abuse	0	0	0	21.5	17.0
Total	3.2	3.2	3.0	24.5	20.0
Newborn	3.0	3.0	2.6	3.0	3.1
Average Daily Census					
Medicine/surgery	15.0	14.1	13.2	12.3	11.3
Obstetrics	1.9	1.6	1.4	1.8	2.1
Pediatrics	0.3	0.3	0.5	0.8	1.4
Subtotal, general acute	17.2	16.0	15.1	14.9	14.8
Substance abuse	0	0	0	8.6	14.0
Total	17.2	16.0	15.1	23.5	28.8
Newborn	1.6	1.2	1.1	1.6	1.8

EXHIBIT 15.1   cont'd

	Fiscal Year Ending September 30,				
	1983	**1984**	**1985**	**1986**	**1987**
Occupancy Percentage					
General acute	38.1	35.3	33.6	32.9	32.8
Substance abuse	0	0	0	61.3	99.6
Total	38.1	35.3	33.6	47.1	66.2
Newborn	20.0	15.0	13.8	20.0	22.5
Beds					
General acute	45	45	45	31	31
Substance abuse	0	0	0	14	14
Total	45	45	45	45	45
Newborn bassinets	8	8	8	8	8

holism in a unit called *CareUnit*. Calumet provides the beds and Care Corporation, in exchange for a share of the profits, provides the unit's professional counseling staff. This unit has been running at 100 percent occupancy most of the time.

The service mix for the forty-five beds is now six obstetric, two pediatric, fourteen alcohol/substance abuse, and twenty-three medical/surgical. Statistical information relating to utilization of these beds since 1983 is shown in Exhibit 15.1.

HOSPITAL MISSION

Calumet Community Hospital's mission statement is as follows:

Calumet Community Hospital's mission is to provide hospital services for Calumet, Randolph County, and the surrounding area by sustaining and strengthening its position in quality and scope of services:

- a general hospital where patients and their families receive personalized, efficient care under high technical standards in a setting that focuses on local needs;
- a center for the private solo or group practice of medicine, where physicians can concentrate their practices with maximum support from management and personnel staff, modern facilities, and a productive professional environment for themselves and their patients;
- an economically sound and responsible nonprofit entity that develops revenues and other resources effectively and achieves maximum volume from the use of these resources;
- a Calumet-centered institution and an active corporate citizen dedicated to serving residents of Calumet and its trade area and to enhancing the region's status through civic leadership and a wide range of contributions to the local economy; and
- an employer in a setting where talented personnel with a service attitude and ini-

EXHIBIT 15.2

Volume of Selected Diagnostic and Treatment Services, Fiscal 1983–1987

Services	Fiscal Year Ending September 30,				
	1983	**1984**	**1985**	**1986**	**1987**
Emergency room visits	2,789	2,370	3,417	3,342	3,155
Operating room					
Inpatient	533	487	490	492	474
Outpatient	20	28	18	35	116
Total	553	515	508	527	590
Diagnostic radiology Procedures					
Inpatient	1,947	2,180	2,097	2,436	2,136
Outpatient	2,744	2,816	3,205	2,436	2,262
Total	4,691	4,996	5,302	4,872	4,398
Laboratory tests					
Inpatient	9,513	9,734	11,112	61,054	63,592
Outpatient	8,794	8,912	8,797	23,024	23,828
Total	18,307	18,646	19,909	84,078[2]	87,420
Delivery room live births	189	160	150	192	217
Respiratory therapy treatments					
Inpatient	1,878	1,641	11,552	11,297	13,448
Outpatient	144	161	438	421	429
Total	2,022	1,802	11,990	11,718	13,877
Physical therapy treatments	0	0	0	0	1,925[1]
Speech therapy treatments	0	0	0	0	267
Electrocardiograms (ECG)					
Inpatient	609	440	644	909	1,159
Outpatient	184	219	188	175	226
Total	793	659	832	1,084	1,385
Home health visits	0	0	0	2,814	4,066

[1]Ten months of operation.
[2]Change in recording methodology.

tiative can practice and grow in their profession or vocation and receive job satisfaction and appropriate rewards for good performance.

BOARD OF DIRECTORS

Calumet Community Hospital has an eleven-member board of directors (see Exhibit 15.3). The board is appointed by the governing authority of Randolph County for a two-year term on a rotating basis.

The board of directors is legally responsible for the operation of the hospital. The board also establishes goals and objectives for evaluating the hospital's performance relative to those goals. The board recruits, selects, and evaluates the hospital's chief executive officer, called *hospital administrator,* who represents the board in implementing policies.

Smyth often calls on board members for their expertise but at the same time tries to keep them from being involved in day-to-day internal operations.

MANAGEMENT AND ORGANIZATION

Calumet's organizational structure is fairly typical of small hospitals (see Exhibit 15.4). All department heads report directly to Smyth. Smyth noted, "One of my strengths is my open-door policy and my accessibility when the department heads need me to make a quick decision. I also practice 'management by wandering around' to keep on top of things in the hospital."

Smyth has been with the hospital for the past nine years. Prior to joining Calumet, he was an assistant administrator at Union County

---

EXHIBIT 15.3
Calumet Community Hospital Board of Directors

Kenneth Owens (Board Chairperson)
President
First National Bank

Marjorie Crow
Housewife

Gene Barnett
Editor
Calumet Daily News

Joe Marchman
Retired School Teacher

Harold Borman
Office Manager
Calumet Paper Co.

Verna Shepperd
Principal
Armstrong Elementary School

James Stuckey
Owner
Stuckey's Feed & Seed

Andy Arthur
Private Investments

John Stuart
Owner
Stuart Insurance Agency

Eileen Fordham
Owner, Fordham Furniture

Bill Blake
Attorney
Blake, Jones & Associates

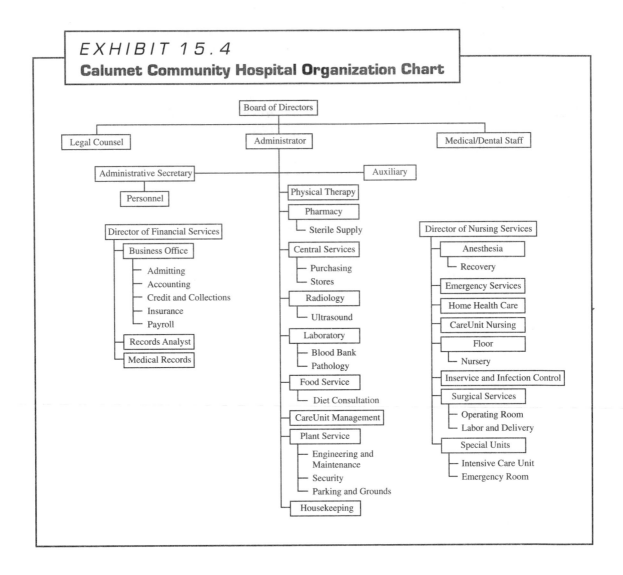

EXHIBIT 15.4
Calumet Community Hospital Organization Chart

- Board of Directors
  - Legal Counsel
  - Administrator
    - Administrative Secretary
      - Personnel
    - Auxiliary
    - Director of Financial Services
      - Business Office
        - Admitting
        - Accounting
        - Credit and Collections
        - Insurance
        - Payroll
      - Records Analyst
      - Medical Records
    - Physical Therapy
    - Pharmacy
      - Sterile Supply
    - Central Services
      - Purchasing
      - Stores
    - Radiology
      - Ultrasound
    - Laboratory
      - Blood Bank
      - Pathology
    - Food Service
      - Diet Consultation
    - CareUnit Management
    - Plant Service
      - Engineering and Maintenance
      - Security
      - Parking and Grounds
    - Housekeeping
    - Director of Nursing Services
      - Anesthesia
        - Recovery
      - Emergency Services
      - Home Health Care
      - CareUnit Nursing
      - Floor
        - Nursery
      - Inservice and Infection Control
      - Surgical Services
        - Operating Room
        - Labor and Delivery
      - Special Units
        - Intensive Care Unit
        - Emergency Room
  - Medical/Dental Staff

Hospital in Eureka. He holds a bachelor's degree in psychology from a small church-related university and is a member of the American College of Healthcare Executives. In addition he is an active and participating member of the State Hospital Association.

During Smyth's tenure at Calumet, the hospital has been financially successful and experienced steady growth until 1984. Smyth attributes much of the hospital's past success to his participatory style of management. Twice a month, department heads meet to develop ideas and discuss problems. A department head who brings a problem to the meeting is asked to bring at least one solution to the problem. This approach tends to keep the meeting from turning into a "gripe" session. New programs are discussed and old programs are examined to decide whether to retain or discontinue them.

Management by objectives is not practiced at Calumet because of time constraints. According to Smyth, "In facilities where MBO is used, the people spend all their time writing and hardly any time working. Too much time is spent deciding if goals are met, and assigning rewards and punishments instead of caring for patients." Smyth continued, "This is not to say Calumet is not goal oriented. I spend a great amount of my time helping personnel set goals and work toward those goals. Salary increases are based on employees reaching their goals."

Smyth is very popular with the hospital staff because of his friendly nature and willingness to roll up his sleeves and help out when necessary. It is not unusual to see him answering the telephone while the receptionist takes a coffee break or filling the soft drink machine when it is empty.

Smyth maintains control of billing and collections by working with the billing clerk on a regular basis. In addition to billing and collections, he "keeps on top" of purchasing. All purchase orders, except for food and pharmaceutical items, require his approval before issuance. Although he often works late into the evening on his paperwork, he feels this control is important if the hospital is to remain financially sound.

THE MEDICAL STAFF

As is the practice of most hospitals, physicians apply for admission to the medical staff and are appointed by the hospital's board of directors (see Exhibit 15.4).

Upon approval of the board of directors, a physician is granted the privilege of admitting patients to Calumet Community Hospital. The physician may be appointed to "active" medical staff, "courtesy" medical staff, or "consulting" medical staff. The difference between these categories is usually determined by how active a physician wishes to be in Calumet Community Hospital. Active status includes full rights and voting privileges along with an obligation to attend medical staff meetings and participate in medical staff committees. The active medical staff currently lists twenty-one physicians. However, only twelve physicians routinely admit patients to Calumet Community Hospital. Eight of the twelve physicians have offices in Calumet, and the other four practice in Eureka, ten miles away. Of the eight Calumet physicians, two family practitioners generate over 75 percent of the hospital's revenues; one is age 65 and the other is age 60.

The specialties of these twelve physicians are as follows: family/general practitioners (7); otolaryngologist (1); general surgeon (1); obstetrician/gynecologist (1); cardiologist (1); and urologist (1).

The active medical staff membership declined during the past five years. "To make my job even more difficult," noted Smyth, "the medical staff is fragmented and not pulling in the same direction. I end up spending a great deal of time solving problems created by the doctors."

The medical staff is governed by its own bylaws, rules, and regulations and is accountable to the board of directors. It conducts business through the executive committee, credentials committee, medical records committee, and medical audit committee. In addition, there is a joint conference committee consisting of three members each from the medical staff and board of directors. The administrator serves as an ex-officio member of that committee.

The hospital administrator is the liaison officer between the board of directors and the medical staff. The administrator facilitates the work of the medical staff by providing administrative assistance to the officers and committees on a routine basis. The administrator does not have direct line authority over the medical staff.

Smyth has employed a physician search

agency to recruit an orthopedic surgeon. An orthopedic surgeon is needed to overcome the community's perception that the hospital's emergency room is only a "first-aid" station. Currently, orthopedic cases that are too complicated for the attending physician are transferred to Eureka.

Physicians are particularly important to Calumet for two main reasons:

1. Only physicians admit patients and initiate treatment.
2. Physicians specify products and quantities purchased from the hospital (e.g., number of laboratory and X ray tests, days of care required, and so on).

Thus, physicians often are considered the hospital's most important marketing target. Hospitals must first market to their medical staff if they are to succeed in marketing their services and attracting patients.[1]

SERVICE AREA

The hospital's primary service area, Randolph County, has a population of 16,000. The population of the city of Calumet is approximately 11,000. In addition, 4,200 students attend Central State University; half of these students live in Calumet during the regular school session.

The university is a liberal arts institution and includes a School of Nursing. The hospital benefits from the nursing students who receive part of their clinical training at the hospital. In addition, the university conducts a "wellness program," and uses the hospital's classroom for lectures from time to time.

A small retirement village located a block from the hospital has approximately eighty-five residents. Residents of the service area, however, are younger than average; only 7 percent are over the age of 65 compared to the national average of 11 percent.

Although agriculture is the main industry in the local economy, the university is the largest employer. There are also several small industrial plants in the county, including a printing plant that employs 160 persons.

COMPETITION AND THE MARKET SITUATION

Calumet is a county-owned hospital, so it benefits from the tax support of Randolph County. Between 1986 and 1988, tax revenue totaled $1,119,000. These funds covered the cost of the care of indigent patients and the loss on bad debts. In addition, Calumet was just about able to break even from operations after absorbing the difference between Medicare reimbursement and actual cost of serving Medicare patients.

Even though there has been a decline in occupancy rate and Medicare reimbursement, direct charges to patients are generally 10 percent to 20 percent lower than in other area hospitals. According to Smyth, "This gives Calumet a competitive advantage over the other hospitals." In spite of lower rates, Calumet has felt the impact of competition from area hospitals and other health providers. Although there are no other hospitals in Randolph County, there are several hospitals in adjacent counties (see Exhibit 15.5).

Eureka, a city of approximately 162,000 population, is ten miles from Calumet. Eureka has three large hospitals: Main General, a 350-bed for-profit hospital; Union County, a 210-bed not-for-profit hospital; and St. Mary's, a 280-bed not-for-profit church-affiliated hospital.

Only two facilities within a fifty-mile radius treat alcohol or substance abuse patients. The CareUnit operated by Calumet has fourteen beds. The fifteen-bed Central Alcohol Recovery Center, located in Eureka, is operated by a private not-for-profit corporation.

All three large hospitals in Eureka plan to open adult or adolescent substance abuse units in the immediate future. Main General plans an adolescent chemical dependency unit, Union

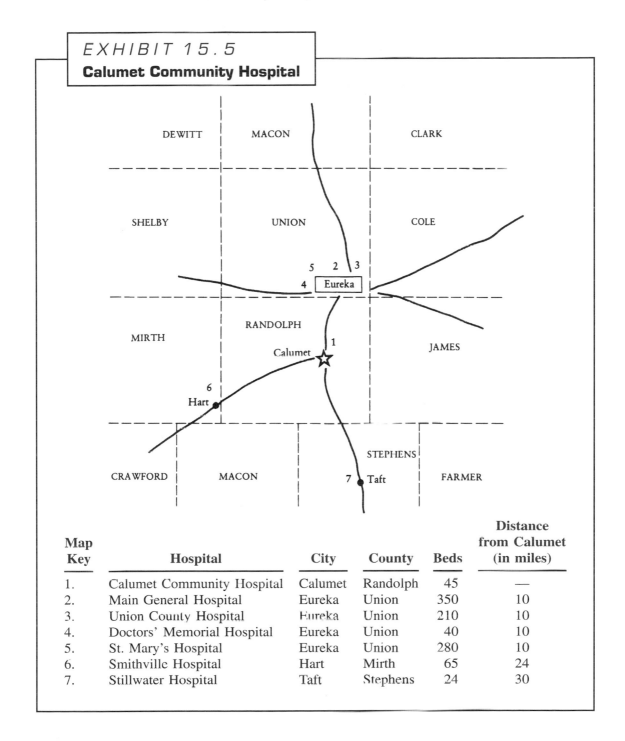

EXHIBIT 15.5
Calumet Community Hospital

Map Key	Hospital	City	County	Beds	Distance from Calumet (in miles)
1.	Calumet Community Hospital	Calumet	Randolph	45	—
2.	Main General Hospital	Eureka	Union	350	10
3.	Union County Hospital	Eureka	Union	210	10
4.	Doctors' Memorial Hospital	Eureka	Union	40	10
5.	St. Mary's Hospital	Eureka	Union	280	10
6.	Smithville Hospital	Hart	Mirth	65	24
7.	Stillwater Hospital	Taft	Stephens	24	30

County Hospital will open a twenty-one-bed adult substance unit, and St. Mary's will open a twenty-bed adolescent unit in six months.

Calumet must also compete with alternative health delivery systems including hospice organizations, home health agencies, and medical clinics.

THE CONSULTANTS' RECOMMENDATIONS

In late 1987, Mr. Smyth obtained approval from the board of directors to hire consultants to perform a marketing analysis of the service area and prepare a long-range plan that examined changes within the industry and competition from other health care providers. General Consultants, Inc., a national firm specializing in health facilities, was employed in October 1987. In March 1988, the consultants completed their study and presented Smyth with the hospital's new long-range plan, the first written plan for the hospital.

In the process of the study, the consultants did an analysis of strengths, weaknesses, opportunities, and threats (SWOT). The findings included the following:

Strengths

- Current services are of good quality
- Dedicated, qualified medical staff
- Well-equipped hospital for its size
- Dedicated department heads
- All rooms in hospital private
- Only hospital in Calumet
- Strong administrative leadership

Weaknesses and Problems

- Heavy dependence on two physicians
- Loss of active medical staff over past five years
- Factions within the medical staff
- Small size of hospital and absence of economies of scale
- Reputed to resist change

- Positive image lacking among some citizens
- Limited public relations and marketing activities
- Loss of 60 percent of all county patients in primary service area of other hospitals
- Inadequate plans and insufficient resources to meet increased competition

Opportunities

- Recruit physician specialists in selected fields
- Establish physicians' office building to assist in attracting new physicians
- Create a public relations/marketing program to enhance image and attract patients
- Expand home health services
- Improve student medical services
- Improve emergency and outpatient care

Threats

- Increased competition from larger hospitals nearby
- Consumer expectations for more specialized services than hospital can afford to offer
- Government reimbursement system for Medicare patients
- Competition from other substance abuse units
- Increasing technology in health field with limited resources to stay current
- Reduction in county's tax support

The consultants' final recommendations centered on five construction projects that would provide Calumet Community Hospital with additional space by 1995. The projects are as follows:

1. Construct a medical office building, estimated cost $900,000;
2. Expand CareUnit by fourteen beds, estimated cost $238,000;
3. Remodel and expand dietary area, estimated cost $150,000;

4. Construct a twenty-bed adolescent treatment unit, estimated cost $460,000;

5. Construct an addition to existing building to accommodate a new classroom and additional laboratory space, estimated cost $62,000.

WHERE DO WE GO FROM HERE?

The consultants' report has left the administrator and board with some hard decisions about what direction to take. A major problem is that almost no single part of the construction suggested can be undertaken without putting more pressure on available space – what one of the consultants called the *domino effect.*

How soon any of the projects can be undertaken, and how to pay for them, is still under consideration. The board has decided to investigate other alternatives before implementing the consultants' recommendations. These alternatives include:

1. Affiliate with one of the larger hospitals,
2. Convert hospital to outpatient and emergency center,
3. Convert hospital to a day-care facility for senior citizens and offer skilled nursing home services.

A referendum will be required to raise funds or "float bonds" to support any remodeling or major capital expenditures. However, what alternatives will the citizens of Randolph County have for primary health care if the mission of Calumet Community Hospital is drastically changed? The decisions will not be easy.

APPENDIX A: RURAL HEALTH CARE INDUSTRY NOTE

The health care industry has changed dramatically in recent years. Advanced technology, changing medical practices, increased special-ization, intense competition, government regulations, and alternative health delivery systems have forced hospitals to develop new and evolving goals. Systematic, strategic planning is more important now than ever before.

For the past few years, prophets of doom have predicted the closing of many small rural hospitals in this country. They question whether rural hospitals can remain economically viable in today's competitive environment, and predict the demise of many of them before the year 2000.[2] A 1987 study conducted by a large accounting firm predicted that 700 U.S. hospitals will close by 1995.[3]

DRG Reimbursement

In 1983, the federal government began reimbursing hospitals for services to Medicare and Medicaid patients on a preestablished fee based on treatment appropriate to the individual patient's admitting diagnosis rather than on the actual cost of service. This case-specific method is constructed around diagnostic related groups (DRGs). The concept behind DRGs is that certain categories or groups of medical diagnoses consume similar types and quantities of hospital resources. The DRG system subdivides inpatient hospital care into 383 separate diagnostic categories. Except for the fees of the attending physician, all other medical expenses are covered. The hospital is reimbursed one flat fee per illness rather than by patient day, service, or procedure rendered. In addition, some procedures and services are covered only on an outpatient basis.

The DRG system was phased in at hospitals over a four-year period. In 1983, 25 percent of total reimbursement to hospitals was under the new system, 50 percent in 1984, 75 percent in 1985, and 100 percent in 1986.

Problems of Rural Hospitals

An almost immediate impact of the DRG system was a dramatic decrease in hospital inpatient admissions. Although all hospitals have experienced lower occupancy rates and inadequate payments from the Medicare program, rural hospitals have been especially hard-hit. For example, DRG reimbursement for a pneumonia patient hospitalized for 4.5 days may be $950 less than reimbursement under the previous actual-cost-of-service method.

Between 1984 and 1986, 163 hospitals closed. Seventy-four were classified as small or rural.[4] When the DRG system was implemented, rural hospitals such as Calumet Community Hospital began receiving reimbursement for care of Medicare and Medicaid patients at a lower fee than that paid to larger city hospitals. For example, rural hospitals receive up to 30 percent less than urban hospitals for treating the same diagnosis, even though rural hospital costs are only 10 percent to 15 percent less. In addition, rural hospitals have difficulty attracting physicians and other health professionals and often have to pay premium salaries to attract qualified individuals.

Another concern for rural hospitals is the outmigration of patients to larger medical centers in nearby cities. More than four of ten consumers in rural areas indicate they do not believe specialized medical services are available in their area.[5] As many as 42 percent of rural residents travel to urban areas to receive medical treatment, usually to gain access to specialists and more sophisticated testing facilities than are available locally.[6]

Approximately 52 percent of rural hospitals are owned or leased by local governments. These organizations often face complex governmental structures that are unable to react quickly to changes in reimbursement, technology, and competition.

To increase revenues, and in some instances simply to survive, hospitals have established satellite emergency centers or outpatient clinics, eliminated unprofitable services, merged with other facilities, added services such as home health and hospice, and diversified into other businesses (medical office buildings, management consulting services, laundry services, food catering services, and so on).[7] Small rural hospitals have limited options for revenue enhancement, which complicates their planning for survival. However, many find a specific market niche to fill in their service area.

Historically, small rural hospitals did not feel a need to utilize marketing techniques or develop long-range strategic plans.[8] However, that attitude has changed significantly in recent years. A 1987 study of 476 small or rural hospitals, conducted by the American Hospital Association, noted that nearly 60 percent were active in marketing. Because of financial constraints, the administrator often is in charge of marketing and planning activities. Such activities are frequently restricted to public relations and advertising. So, the question remains, how effective are the marketing and planning functions when carried out on a part-time basis by the administrator?

NOTES

1. Julian G. Franks, "Zeroing in on the Targets," *L & H Perspective* (Fall/Winter 1980), p. 37.
2. Michael J. Rabinowitz and James J. O. Keefe III, "Rx for Rural Hospitals: Heal Thyself," *L & H Perspective* (Fall/Winter 1980), p. 28.
3. Arvin Rodrigues et al, "Strategic Planning for Rural Hospitals," Proceedings of the 1989 Conference of the Business and Health Administration Association, Midwest Business Administration 25th Annual Meeting, Chicago, March 1989, p. 32.
4. Ibid.
5. Joyce Jensen and Ned Miklovic, "Declining Censuses Plague Hospitals: Administrators Expect Further Drops," *Modern Healthcare* (August 16, 1985), pp. 86–87.
6. Ibid.
7. Sarah A. Grim, "Win/Win: Urban and Rural Hospitals Network for Survival," *Hospital & Health Services Administration* 31, no. 1 (Spring 1986), pp. 1–13.

8. Verna Aline Arnold, "The Application of Selected Marketing Concepts in the Hospital Planning Process," doctoral dissertation, North Texas State University, 1978, pp. 158–161.

REFERENCES

Jonas, Steven. *Health Care Delivery in the United States,* 2d ed. New York: Springer Publishing Company, 1981.

Rakich, Jonathon S., et al. *Managing Health Services Organizations,* 2d ed. Philadelphia: W. B. Saunders Co., 1985.

Roberts, Carolyn, and James G. Schuman. "Planning and Marketing in Small and Rural Hospitals." *Healthcare Planning and Marketing* (January/February 1988), pp. 4–9.

Sherman, James F., and Albert Zezulinski. "A New Procedure for Hospital Survival." *L & H Perspective* 11, no. 2 (1985), pp. 55–58.

Snook, I. Donald. *Hospitals: What They Are and How They Work.* Rockville, Maryland: Aspen Publishers, 1981.

Tye, Larry. "The Ins and Outs of Hospitals." *St. Louis Post-Dispatch* (September 9, 1989), p. 1D.

CASE 16

University of Texas Health Center at Tyler

The health care industry in the United States is in a state of crisis. Evidence of this crisis is apparent in spiraling health insurance premiums and health care costs, rural hospital closings, governmental reimbursement funding reductions, increasing liability litigation, and rising levels of indigent care loads. Compounding the problem are a nationwide nursing shortage, rapidly advancing and costly technology, and increasing competition among health care providers.

Against this backdrop, the University of Texas Health Center at Tyler attempts to fulfill its mission of providing patient care, conducting research, and providing education related to cardiopulmonary diseases. Because the Health Center receives a percentage of its operating resources from the state of Texas, it must provide indigent health care to the poor in its region. In addition, it must provide care to indigents with tuberculosis from anywhere in the state. However, the center has not refused services to any Texas indigent, regardless of the nature of the illness. As health insurance premiums have risen, more and more people have lost their coverage. As a result,

This case was prepared by Mark J. Kroll, the University of Texas at Tyler, and Vickie Noble, the University of Texas Health Center at Tyler. It is intended to be used as a basis for classroom discussion rather than to illustrate effective or ineffective handling of an administrative situation. Used with permission from Mark Kroll.

private hospitals frequently refuse treatment and refer patients to state-supported institutions. This trend, in conjunction with the closing of many of the region's rural hospitals, as well as federal reimbursement reductions, compel many individuals to seek care at the Health Center under indigency charity status.

Unfortunately, state funding levels for this type of care have not kept pace with demand, seriously undermining the financial base of the institution. However, the Health Center must provide competitive wages to attract nursing and other allied health personnel, who are in short supply. Additionally, the Health Center must operate in the competitive local hospital market for a paying patient base while providing costly technology and instrumentation. Most of the major strategic issues confronting the Health Center are ultimately related to the dilemmas faced by the health care industry. Compounding the Health Center's problems, however, have been reductions in state general revenue appropriations as a percentage of the total operating budget for research, operations, and maintenance.

The center is experiencing critical shortages of clinic treatment facilities that are needed to meet changing modes of care and reimbursement bases (more outpatient versus inpatient care). And local competition for specific patient groups has increased.

In addition to the issues just mentioned, there is the unique issue of the hospital's research mandate. Although the Health Center has successfully increased levels of grant-funded research, inadequate research laboratory facilities could potentially choke off further progress.

HISTORY

The Health Center was established in 1947 as a state tuberculosis sanatorium. It operated under the state Board of Control by act of the 50th Texas Legislature. Over the years, the institution has changed in a number of ways. Its role and scope were expanded to adapt to the new medical technology and changing health care needs of the state and region.

The institution was established at the site of a deactivated World War II army infantry training base, Camp Fannin, located eight miles northeast of Tyler, Texas. The state acquired 614 acres and the existing facilities of the base hospital from the federal government. Most of the base's 1,000 beds were in rows of wooden barracks, with each barrack accommodating 25 beds in an open ward. The first patients were accepted in 1949.

Supervision of the East Texas Tuberculosis Sanatorium was later transferred to a newly formed Board of Texas State Hospitals and Special Schools. In 1951, the Texas Legislature changed the hospital's name to the East Texas Tuberculosis Hospital. Its role and scope were changed from simple custodial care to treatment using newly developed drugs.

Although several legislative acts passed during the 1940s and 1950s changed the institution's governing authority, it was not until 1969 that its scope was expanded beyond the care and treatment of tuberculosis patients. In that year, the legislature authorized the institution to develop pilot programs aimed at treating other respiratory diseases, such as asthma, lung cancer, chronic bronchitis, emphysema, and occupational diseases related to asbestos. In 1971, the Texas Legislature gave the institution

a broader mission of education and research as well as patient care. The name was changed to the East Texas Chest Hospital, to be operated under the Texas Board of Health. This program expansion into education and research reflected the increasing stature of the facility and its scientific capabilities.

In 1977, Tyler senator Peyton McKnight introduced legislation transferring control of the hospital to the board of regents of the University of Texas system. This legislation authorized the regents to use the institution as a teaching hospital and to change its name to the University of Texas Health Center at Tyler. It also reaffirmed the institution's role and scope as a primary state referral center for patient care, education, and research in the diseases of the chest.

The physical face of the institution has also changed dramatically over the years. In 1957, the state completed a 320-bed, six-story brick and masonry structure, which allowed for removal of most of the wooden barracks. A few of these structures still remain and have been renovated for use as research laboratories. Other major building programs were initiated in the late 1960s and early 1970s. An outpatient clinic was added to the hospital in 1970. In 1976, the state appropriated $17 million for construction of a modern hospital facility. A six-story 320-bed hospital annex was built adjacent to the original structure, doubling the size of the complex. At the same time, the lower three floors of the old hospital building were renovated to house additional offices and allow for expansion of programs of cardiac and pulmonary rehabilitation and cancer treatment.

The Watson W. Wise Medical Research Library was dedicated in 1984, giving support to an expanded research faculty and the addition of new departments such as biochemistry, microbiology, and physiology. In 1987, the Health Center's Biomedical Research Building was completed. In 1991, construction began on an $11 million expansion of its ambulatory care facilities designed to house and expand the clinical laboratory, radiology, and surgical facilities. This change facilitated delivery and efficient handling of ambulatory patient services. The facility provided space for the Family Practice Residency Program and other clinics, as well as space for clinical research.

In carrying out its mission, the institution has evolved from a custodial-care facility only to an institution with the threefold purpose of patient care, education, and research. Open heart surgery became available in 1983, and the Health Center was designated as a national cystic fibrosis satellite center in 1985. The first postgraduate medical education program in east Texas, residency training in family practice, was launched in 1985 in cooperation with two Tyler hospitals. The residents are supervised and aided by specialists at the Health Center except in the areas of obstetrics and gynecology. They receive training in these areas at a local hospital. By the end of the 1992 fiscal year, the Health Center had twenty-four resident physicians in training.

Grant research funding increased dramatically in recent years. In 1983, funding was $78,347; by 1989, funding reached $2,387,658; but in 1992 funding dipped to $2,188,679. This research funding was, and continues to be, from external sources such as the National Institutes of Health, the Texas Affiliate of the American Heart Association, the American Lung Association of Texas, the Muscular Dystrophy Foundation, private medical-research foundations, and several industrial and pharmaceutical firms. Completion of the Biomedical Research Building in 1987, followed by the recruitment of research scientists, has helped the institution to aggressively pursue the research component of its mission.

In 1992 the following mission statement for the center was approved by the Board of Regents: "The mission of the University of Texas Health Center at Tyler is to provide the citizens of Texas with leadership and excellence in the diagnosis, prevention, and treatment of diseases related to cardiopulmonary, in primary patient care, in biochemical research, and in health education."

COMPETITION

Competition for paying customers between the two local general hospitals is intense. Each of the two major private hospitals averages between 12,000 and 16,000 inpatient admissions annually. Each has an operating budget of approximately $100 million and a medical staff of about 300 physicians. As a state agency that specializes in the treatment of cardiopulmonary diseases, the Health Center does not compete directly with these local hospitals. However, the institution competes indirectly for market share for specific patient groups, such as those with cardiopulmonary diseases.

It is important to recognize that the center's operating budget comes from general revenue appropriations from the state, research grant funding, and locally generated revenues from services rendered to patients who are able to pay. During the period 1981 to 1989, the percentage composition of the operating budget coming from appropriated versus generated funds has changed significantly. General revenue appropriations have decreased from 66 percent of the operating budget for fiscal year 1982 to 38 percent of the operating budget for fiscal year 1990. Consequently, the Health Center has been forced to generate local funds through the paying patient base (see Exhibit 16.1).

Complicating matters was the fact that the Health Center's operating budget must support educational programs as well as some of the research. State appropriations for indigent patient care, in actual dollars, have remained relatively constant over the 1983–1990 period (see item 12 of Exhibit 16.1, General Revenue Appropriations). However, the indigent and

EXHIBIT 16.1

University of Texas Health Center at Tyler, Financial Information

	FY 1988	FY 1989	FY 1990
1. Patient service revenue (gross)	$34,408,785	$33,642,732	$38,536,820
Annual percent increase	4.15%	(2.23%)	14.55%
2. Revenue adjustments (excluding			
bad debts, charity)	$4,525,220	$4,797,391	$6,932,712
Percent of patient revenue	13.15%	14.26%	17.99%
3. Charity	$12,947,936	$9,184,960	$9,172,281
As percent of gross revenue	37.6%	27.3%	23.8%
4. Bad debts	$1,984,674	$1,904,750	$2,795,851
As percent of gross revenue	5.8%	5.7%	7.3%
5. Subtotal, revenue reduction			
(adjustments, charity, and bad debts)	$19,457,830	$15,887,101	$18,900,844
As percent of gross revenue	57%	47%	49%
6. Net patient service revenue	$14,950,955	$17,755,631	$19,635,976
Annual percent increase	(8.84%)	18.76%	10.59%
7. Total patient cash collections	$15,694,463	$16,513,679	$19,546,082
8. Collection rate (#7 ÷ #6)	100.5%	93.0%	99.5%
9. Cost to charge ratio	86.1%	92.0%	97.4%
10. Collection by source			
Medicare	$9,529,772	$9,194,415	$11,071,994
Medicaid	860,152	1,347,954	1,645,293
Insurance	4,365,443	4,768,401	5,371,077
Private/self-pay	939,096	1,202,909	1,457,718
Total (same as #7)	$15,694,463	$16,513,679	$19,546,082
11. Budgeted operating revenue			
(as originally approved)	$36,331,730	$34,316,301	$36,892,387
12. Statement of revenue and expenses			
Net patient service revenue	$14,950,955	$17,755,631	$19,635,976
General revenue appropriations	12,209,063	12,209,063	13,296,372
Appropriations related to overhead	n/a	n/a	n/a
Other operating revenue	2,329,976	2,090,823	2,115,611
Total operating revenue	$29,489,994	$32,055,517	$35,047,959
Operating expenses			
Direct			
Salaries and wages	$16,332,959	$16,687,738	$17,381,939
Supplies and other	11,167,801	12,127,114	12,452,104
Depreciation	2,142,208	2,142,208	3,325,503
Total operating expenses	$29,642,968	$30,957,060	$33,159,546
Excess of revenues over expenses	($152,974)	$1,098,457	$1,888,413
Extraordinary items			
Interest	180,673	145,482	182,427
Medicare/Medicaid retroactive			
settlements	227,061	1,752,308	0
Total excess of revenues and extraordinary items over expenses	$254,760	$2,996,247	$2,070,840

charity care levels provided rose dramatically until 1988, at which point they leveled off (see item 5 of Exhibit 16.1, Subtotal, Revenue Reduction). Exhibit 16.2 illustrates the rapid growth in charity care during the 1980s.

The net result has been a large gap between funds received from the state to provide indigent care and the amount actually provided by the Health Center. In total dollars, indigent care services averaged $12 million per year from 1983 to 1985; however, indigent care services averaged approximately $18 million per year from 1986 to 1990. To help make up the difference the institution must compete for paying patients in service areas covered by other local hospitals. Currently, for each dollar of health care services the center provides, on average 50 percent is reimbursed through Medicare, approximately 6 percent is repaid through Medicaid, and 5 percent is paid by private insurers or patients. That leaves almost 40 percent to be borne by the center.

The two major competing hospitals offer similar health care programs in cardiology and cardiovascular surgery; therefore, competition for a market share exists. Both hospitals aggressively advertise and promote their image, services, and facilities. One of the two hospitals has recently completed a modernization and expansion project for cardiovascular surgery and intensive care units. In addition, it has been able to keep its profitability up and mortality rate down for cardiovascular services.

By law, however, the Health Center may not directly advertise in a manner competitive or comparative with that of the local hospitals.

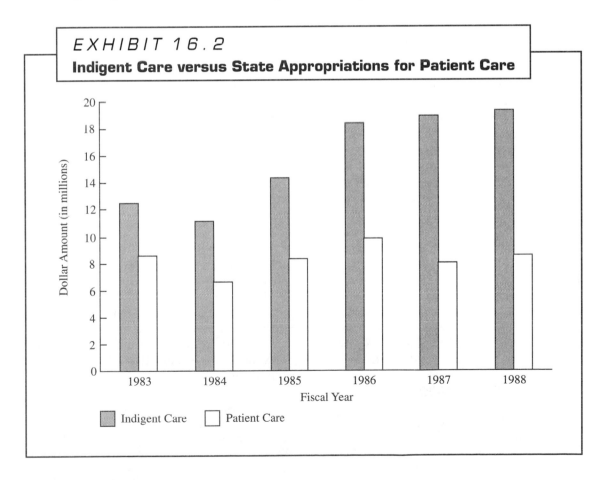

EXHIBIT 16.2

Indigent Care versus State Appropriations for Patient Care

Dollar Amount (in millions) — Fiscal Year

■ Indigent Care   □ Patient Care

The organization limits its promotional activities to presentations of programs and health care services as community service efforts. Ironically, the local hospitals could be in a position to claim unfair competition and disadvantage because the Health Center is partially funded by legislative appropriations. Further, the Health Center has a higher mortality rate because higher risk patients are treated. High-risk generally accompanies indigency status because patients have not received basic health care and wait longer before seeking medical attention. At this point, the disease process is advanced.

Given the Health Center's mission of patient care, education, and research, the focus of the institution is not one of direct competition with local hospitals. In effect, although the Health Center is a hospital in the traditional sense, it is also much more. To achieve all three dimensions of its mission, the hospital's resources must be divided, and these three elements combine to form the Health Center's "product." For example, in the treatment of asbestos-related disease, the patient benefits significantly through specialized treatment unavailable at the local hospitals. Grant-funded research provides the combined efforts of the clinical researcher, who works at the molecular level of the disease, with an experienced pulmonary disease physician specialist. The patient can participate in clinical trials, such as new drug therapy, which may lead to improvements in treatment of the disease. Further, the Health Center's advanced technology instrumentation base, which includes three electron microscopes, improves diagnostic capabilities. These microscopes provide ultra-high magnification for enhanced research studies and patient care. Therefore, the Health Center provides specialized products for research and patient care.

CUSTOMERS (MARKET)

The Health Center is located in the middle of Smith County, Texas, in an area known as east

Texas. The hospital's primary patient base is derived from the surrounding population of its twenty-four county service area. Only about 2.2 percent of the center's patients came from outside Texas for treatment. Exhibit 16.3 identifies the Health Center's service area in terms of admissions for 1990. It bases its forecasts for future patient loads and program implementation on the demographics of this region. East Texas, like the rest of the state, is increasing in population. The Health Center service area had a population of 1,155,317 in 1988. Analysts project a 1.4 percent to 2.1 percent annual population increase through the year 2000 (see Exhibit 16.4). Age is another important factor in the analysis of the Health Center service area demographics. Percentages of the state population by age group are provided in Exhibit 16.5.

For the years 1985–2025, the 0–17-year-old age group of the Texas population will decline 3.7 percent, whereas the 45–64 group will increase 6 percent. The 65 and older group of the Texas population will increase from 9.65 percent to 16.24 percent. Therefore, the population in Texas is both aging and growing. These trends are apparent in the average ages of the Health Center's patients (see Exhibit 16.6 for patient ages by county). Such a demographic profile will obviously have an impact on the direction of patient care for the elderly at the Health Center as well as on Texas and the nation.

Many hospitals and physicians statewide refer patients to the Health Center for diagnosis and treatment, especially when pulmonary problems are suspected. However, the bulk of patients come from the surrounding east Texas area. Patient admission data for the fiscal years 1988–1990 are provided in Exhibit 16.7 and Exhibit 16.8 lists admissions by county in the service area.

Patient referrals are from group practices, physicians, hospitals, governmental agencies, and self-referrals. Exhibit 16.9 illustrates a recent increase in referring physicians. Most pa-

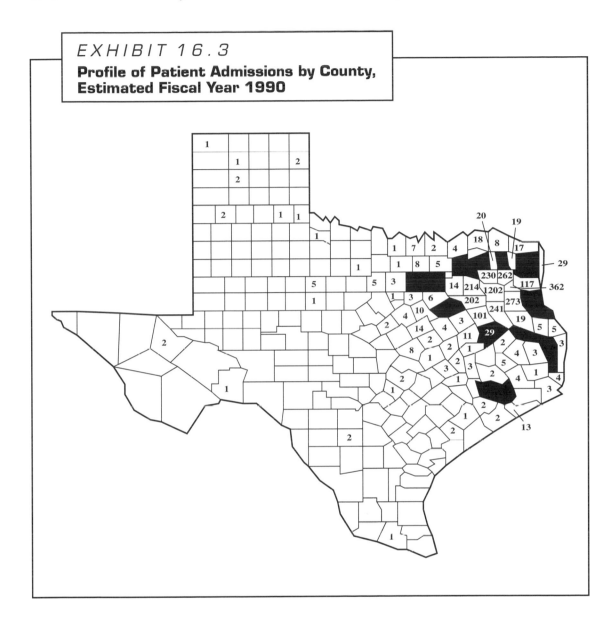

EXHIBIT 16.3

Profile of Patient Admissions by County, Estimated Fiscal Year 1990

tients admitted for diagnosis and treatment are referred because their clinical problems require specialized diagnosis and treatment provided by the Health Center. Exhibit 16.10 reports the percentages of outpatients admitted for treatment in each of the specialty areas. Many times, referrals are made for acutely ill pulmo-

nary patients requiring longer than average intensive care.

It is important to recognize that the Health Center has an unusual patient population because of its broader service area, commitment to indigent care, and aging population. These factors have resulted in increasing demands on

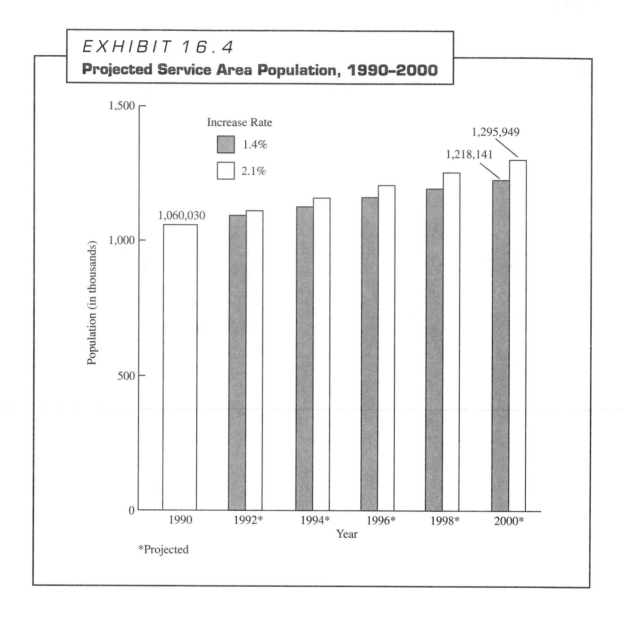

EXHIBIT 16.4

Projected Service Area Population, 1990–2000

Population (in thousands)

Increase Rate
- 1.4%
- 2.1%

1990: 1,060,030
2000* 1.4%: 1,218,141
2000* 2.1%: 1,295,949

Year

*Projected

the center for medical services. Indigent care provided by the hospital has increased from $10.9 million to $18.9 million in the 1982–1990 period. Beginning in 1988, a great deal of indigent care was provided not only to people in counties within the service area but also to a large number of Texans outside the east Texas service area. At present, approximately 28 percent of the indigent care the

Health Center provided was to patients residing outside the immediate east Texas service area. This accounted for $5,371,000 of the total $18,926,403 of indigent care services provided for 1990. In one attempt to rein in indigent care costs, the center has started limiting the prescription drugs it provided free of charge and placed limits on the amount of indigent care provided by the general Medicare clinic

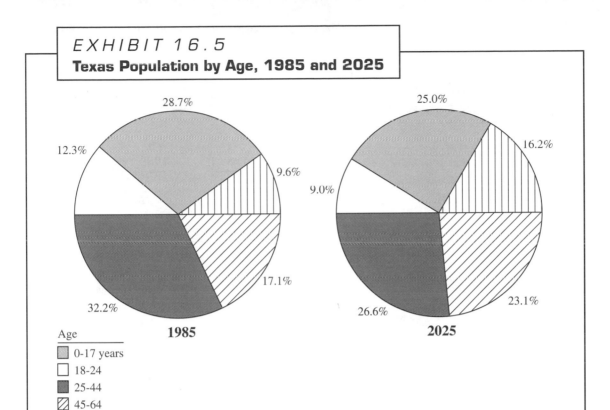

EXHIBIT 16.5
Texas Population by Age, 1985 and 2025

Age
- 0-17 years
- 18-24
- 25-44
- 45-64
- 65+

1985
- 28.7%
- 12.3%
- 9.6%
- 32.2%
- 17.1%

2025
- 25.0%
- 9.0%
- 16.2%
- 26.6%
- 23.1%

EXHIBIT 16.6
Average Age for Patients in East Texas Service Area (twenty-four counties)

County	Average Age	County	Average Age
Anderson	55	Morris	57
Angelina	52	Panola	53
Bowie	48	Rains	63
Camp	51	Rusk	57
Cass	51	Shelby	54
Cherokee	52	Smith	51
Gregg	48	Titus	51
Harrison	55	Upshur	55
Henderson	57	Van Zadt	58
Hopkins	54	Wood	57
Houston	62	Unknown	47
Hunt	57		
Kaufman	60		
Marion	53	Total average age	57

EXHIBIT 16.7
Statistical Information

	FY 1988	FY 1989	FY 1990
1. Average number of beds in operation			
Adult and pediatric	204	198	199
Infant	n/a	n/a	n/a
Special care bassinets	n/a	n/a	n/a
Total	204	198	199
2. Inpatients			
Total admitted	4,244	3,827	3,528
Adult and pediatric	4,244	3,827	3,528
Newborn	n/a	n/a	n/a
Total days	46,695	39,639	40,120
Adult and pediatric	46,695	39,639	40,120
Newborn	n/a	n/a	n/a
Average inpatients per day	127.6	109	110
Adult and pediatric	127.6	109	110
Newborn	n/a	n/a	n/a
Average stay (days) per patient	12.0	10.0	11.0
Adult and pediatric	12.0	10.0	11.0
Newborn	n/a	n/a	n/a
3. Outpatients			
Number of clinic visits	46,092	50,695	59,942
Average clinic visits per day	184	203	240
Number of emergency room visits	n/a	n/a	12,600
Average emergency room visits per day	n/a	n/a	35

and the family practice clinic. Exhibit 16.11 provides forecasts for Health Center financial operations data.

REGULATION AND ECONOMICS

In the health care field, regulations are an integral part of the economics that drive the industry. Regulations are promulgated by numerous government and industry agencies. These include the Healthcare Financing Administration (HCFA), the Department of Health and Human Services, the American Hospital Association, the Food and Drug Administration (FDA), the Texas Department of Health, and the Joint Commission on Accreditation of Healthcare Organizations (JCAHO).

Operational regulations for the Health

EXHIBIT 16.8

Admissions, Inpatient and Outpatient, East Texas Service Area, 1990

County	Inpatient Admissions	Outpatient Visits	Total
Anderson	78	1,061	1,139
Angelina	28	272	300
Bowie	21	175	196
Camp	19	325	344
Cass	23	473	496
Cherokee	119	2,295	2,414
Gregg	305	7,503	7,808
Harrison	66	899	965
Henderson	198	3,169	3,367
Hopkins	24	348	372
Houston	5	153	158
Hunt	14	175	189
Kaufman	24	199	223
Marion	14	186	200
Morris	13	485	498
Panola	23	306	329
Rains	14	187	201
Rusk	209	2,571	2,780
Shelby	24	322	346
Smith	1,051	25,779	26,830
Titus	22	487	509
Upshur	288	6,707	6,995
Van Zandt	143	2,264	2,407
Wood	244	3,927	4,171
Unknown	15	2,760	2,775
Total Admissions	2,984	63,028	66,012

Center are imposed by the state of Texas and the University of Texas system. Although these entities proscribe the operational parameters, the Prospective Payment System for Federal Medicare/Medicaid reimbursement had the most significant impact on the health care industry and the Health Center in recent years.

Enacted in October 1984, the system established diagnosis related groups whereby Medicare/Medicaid reimbursement payments to hospitals are based primarily on the diagnosis of the patient. This system does not reimburse for actual costs incurred for patient care if the required treatment varies from the average

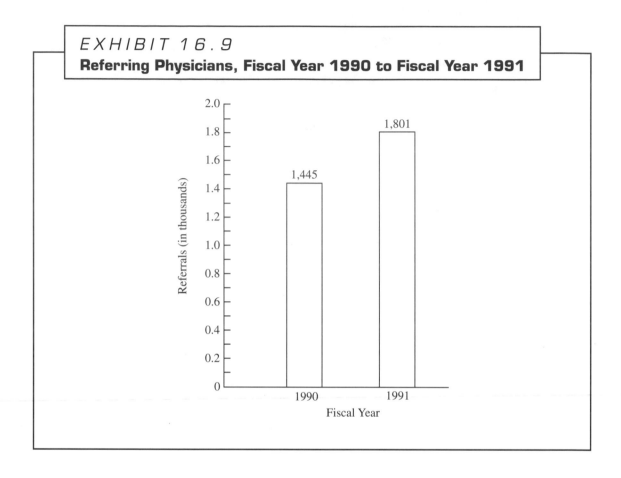

EXHIBIT 16.9
Referring Physicians, Fiscal Year 1990 to Fiscal Year 1991

costs related to the "normal" treatment routine. The system pays the hospital only the average costs associated with a particular course of treatment. In other words, a given rate and length of hospital stay is established for reimbursement payment, and any additional costs over the predetermined rate are borne by the hospital. In addition, many treatments are reimbursable only as an outpatient charge.

The initial intent of the system was to standardize rates, force efficiency, reduce utilization rates among Medicare patients, and shift some of the health care cost burden from the federal to state level. Cost control became a real objective for the health care industry. The

Health Center has monitored the progress of the new system and tried to anticipate its impact on the institution. As a result, inpatient hospital rooms were converted to outpatient clinics. The center's plans include the construction of additional ambulatory care clinic space.

In addition, the industry will be affected by another reduction in federal reimbursements. The Federal Budget Committee Agreement of 1990 targeted approximately $2 billion in Medicare spending reductions. These reductions specifically affect reimbursement adjustment factors for indirect medical education, such as the residency program at the Health Center. As a teaching facility that receives this benefit, the Health Center obviously would

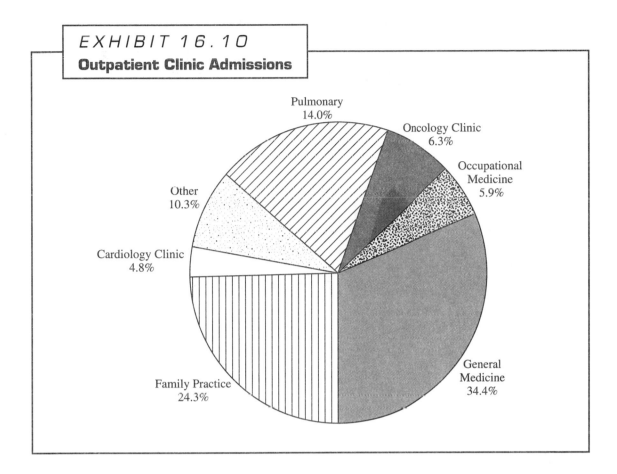

EXHIBIT 16.10
Outpatient Clinic Admissions

Pulmonary
14.0%

Oncology Clinic
6.3%

Occupational
Medicine
5.9%

Other
10.3%

Cardiology Clinic
4.8%

General
Medicine
34.4%

Family Practice
24.3%

face a negative impact, though the magnitude had not yet been assessed. The economic implications of all the factors mentioned are enormous for the Health Center. Currently, 50 percent of the institution's patients are covered by Medicare. This percentage is projected to increase significantly, based on an industry projection that the Medicare patient base will double by the year 2025.

GOVERNANCE

The Health Center's education mission has been affected by both federal and state funding reductions as well. It receives no funding from the University of Texas system for salaries of physician residents. Additionally, the federal government reduced special funding for physician residents.

The University of Texas system is presided over by a Board of Regents, made up of members from diverse professions and backgrounds, including business persons, educators, and physicians, each considered to be knowledgeable and successful in a given field. They are external to the University of Texas system and typically have significant positions of power and influence in their chosen career

EXHIBIT 16.11
Strategic Plan – Financial Analysis (current operation)

	1990–1991			Projected Increments (or decrements)			
		1993–1994	1994–1995	1995–1996	1996–1997	1997–1998	1998–1999
Projected income (1985–1986 constant dollars)							
General revenue	$17,266,989	$1,500,000	$2,000,000	$3,000,000	$3,500,000	$3,500,000	$3,500,000
Net student fees							
Income from patients	22,345,719	2,750,000	2,750,000	2,750,000	2,750,000	3,000,000	3,000,000
Available balances							
Other	3,310,123	300,000	300,000	300,000	300,000	350,000	350,000
Subtotal education and general funds	42,922,831	4,550,000	5,050,000	6,050,000	6,550,000	6,850,000	6,850,000
Contract and grant funds	3,449,012	275,000	275,000	275,000	275,000	275,000	300,000
PUF funds[1]							
Restricted funds	1,662,830	100,000	100,000	100,000	100,000	150,000	200,000
MSRDP (net)[2]	5,762,583	275,000	275,000	275,000	275,000	300,000	300,000
Auxiliary enterprises	152,817	10,000	10,000	10,000	10,000	12,500	15,000
Service department funds	2,311,614	15,000	15,500	16,000	16,500	17,000	17,500
Subtotal non– education and general funds	13,338,856	675,000	675,500	676,000	676,500	754,500	832,500
Total	$56,261,687	$5,225,000	$5,725,500	$6,726,000	$7,226,500	$7,604,500	$7,682,500
Projected expenditures (1990–1991 constant dollars)							
Planned changes		5,066,948	5,397,128	2,628,386	2,107,956	2,742,821	0
Projected increment available for general growth improvement		$158,052	$328,372	$4,097,614	$5,118,544	$4,861,679	$7,682,500

Note: All of these values (except 1990–1991) represent the anticipated annual "changes" in each of the items.
[1]PUF: Permanent university funds allocation – funds received from earnings on investments and assets.
[2]Medical Service Research and Development Plan.

fields. In addition, the members usually have political and persuasive powers with the Texas Legislature to secure funding and associated legislation for the system.

The Board of Regents sets the financial and operating guidelines of the University of Texas system through operating budgets, capital expenditure approvals, program implementation, and related activities confirmations. The board essentially supports or rejects recommendations from the administrators of the universities and medical centers in the system. The Board of Regents implements its decisions through the chancellor of the University of Texas system.

The Health Center's top management is organized along functional lines according to business, research, and medical classifications. The organization chart for the Health Center is illustrated in Exhibit 16.12. The medical and research divisions are directed by the executive associate director, who is a physician as well as a research scientist. He is highly regarded for his skills as an administrator, physician, and researcher, as evidenced by his membership on national and international committees in his fields. He is supported by assistant administrators along functional lines such as chief of staff and the associate director for patient services. The business decision is directed by the executive associate director for administration and business affairs who holds a master's degree in health care administration. He is supported by assistant administrators along functional lines. This group of directors, administrators, and assistant administrators makes up the administrative staff. They meet weekly to develop policy and to implement strategic plans and to perform various administrative functions.

The strategic plans developed by the directors are distributed to administrators and to the next management level, the department heads. Based on input from these groups, the plan is revised by a committee that includes represen-tation from the medical, research, and education divisions. The strategic plan that emerges forms part of the basis for budget requests for special programs, operating funds, equipment, and personnel.

Strategic decision-making authority is vested in the administrative staff. Both the department heads and administrative staff are responsible for making operational decisions. Most routine operations are managed by department heads who control departmental budgets. Accountability at each management level is maintained through a criteria-based job performance evaluation system.

Information at the Health Center is distributed through a communications channel. The organizational chart outlines the primary formal channels of communication. Memos and formal meetings are the primary means of formal communication. In addition to the weekly administrative staff meetings, task- or subject-specific meetings are held among the various administrators.

Standing committees form another formal communication channel. These committees utilize several techniques to communicate with employees at various levels of the organization. Formal meetings, hearings, interviews, questionnaires, and review of documentation enable the committees to perform their assigned functions. Most of the committees are required by health care accrediting and governmental agencies as well as the University of Texas system.

The communication network between management levels varies among the divisions. Medical management divisions generally communicate through formal meetings and memos. Weekly medical staff meetings are conducted by the chief of staff to discuss medical concerns, distribute policy changes, and solicit feedback from the staff.

Monthly department head meetings provide for communication among the medical, educational, business, and research groups.

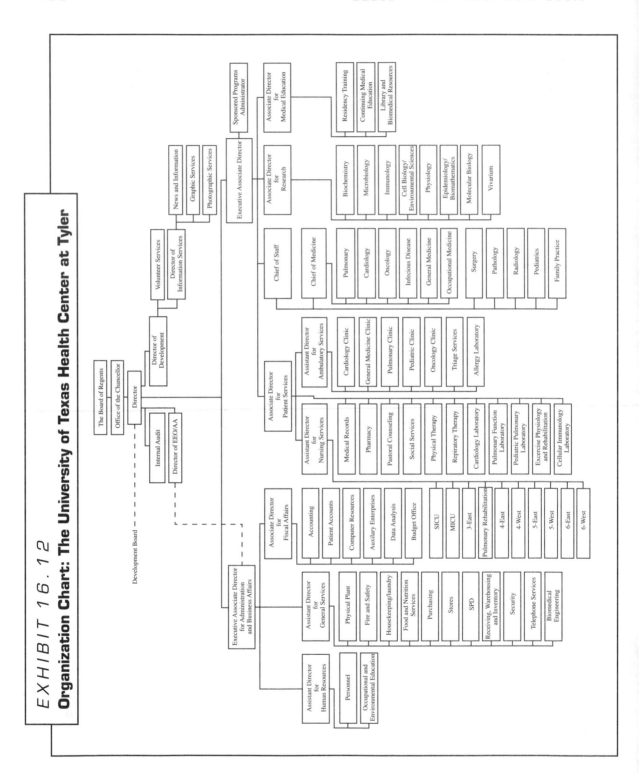

EXHIBIT 16.12
Organization Chart: The University of Texas Health Center at Tyler

This is a critical network communication link because of the complex and unique nature of a university health center. In addition, routine informal information exchange occurs at all levels in managing operations.

Given the Health Center's threefold mission, faculty members are appointed to positions in either research or clinical areas. All new faculty members initially receive one-year appointments, which are reviewed annually for renewal. Physician-faculty are in effect employed by the Health Center full time; therefore, they have no private medical practices. To fulfill the clinical practice dimension of their positions, physicians are provided with private offices; an outpatient clinic area; laboratory, radiology, and ancillary services; and nursing, clerical, and support staff personnel. In addition, the Health Center provides medical malpractice liability insurance and legal assistance, along with a retirement plan and other benefits. Although physicians are salaried, compensation for increases in patient visits and resultant income for the Health Center may lead to additions to a physician's base salary. To be appointed as a research faculty member, a candidate must have at least a Ph.D. or an equivalent doctoral degree in a medically related science.

CURRENT SITUATION

The Health Center at Tyler has made significant progress in the implementation of its threefold mission to provide patient care, conduct research, and provide education. Patient care services include inpatient and outpatient (ambulatory-care) services provided by nationally recruited, full-time clinical physicians and consulting staff. The Health Center has acquired additional medical and surgical intensive care suites, a heart catheterization laboratory, and an open-heart operating room. The Health Center provides a full range of services for cardiovascular diagnosis, treatment, and rehabilitation, including coronary angioplasty.

Coronary angioplasty, a new, advanced treatment for cardiovascular disease, eliminates the need for open-heart surgery in selected patients. Nationally known for its pulmonary disease capabilities, the Health Center has the most highly developed program for comprehensive evaluation and treatment of occupational lung diseases in Texas.

In fiscal year 1990, there were 3,528 hospital admissions and 40,120 patient days with an average length of stay of 11.0 days (refer to Exhibit 16.7). As a result of the decline in state funding, the Health Center has been forced to rely on its local income budget for capital expenditures. In addition, state funding reductions for research have resulted in recruitment delays for scientists.

However, changing economic conditions, reductions in both state and federal funding, and the increasing costs of providing health care programs present both opportunities and challenges. Being partially state funded requires the Health Center to provide indigent health care. In fact, the Health Center had to absorb large increases in indigent care because many private hospitals in the region refused to treat the indigent and instead referred them to state institutions. State and federal funding, however, has not kept pace with the increases in recent years nor does it appear that adequate funding for future indigent care will be forthcoming. Improving its services to paying patients and increasing the portion of the center's business became a key element of the Health Center's strategic plan to offset indigent care losses.

The Health Center has continued to work carrying out its threefold mission of patient care, research, and education despite the economic pressures felt by the health care industry. It has just graduated the first class of resident physicians completing the three-year Family Practice Residency Program. Four of its research investigators received awards, and the number of postdoctoral fellows coming on board to conduct research last year totaled twelve. In 1991, the Health Center was reaccredited for three years by the Joint Commission on Accreditation of Healthcare Organizations. Exhibit 16.11 provides an outline of anticipated changes in the sources of funds and expenditures for the Health Center in the coming years.

There has been an enormous increase in the number of ambulatory care patient visits. The Health Center is trying to address these needs through the construction of a new ambulatory care center, enabling the staff to take care of more patients with greater efficiency. Pursuit of additional research grants will also be a key component in the center's ability to build its status as a research institution. Given the decline in state support for research, attracting other funds will become more and more critical. Additionally, if the hospital is to keep its head above water financially, it will have to attract more paying customers, even though it does not promote itself in direct competition with regional private hospitals. As a result, the years ahead present both opportunities and threats to the center's ability to continue to build quality services in patient care, research, and education.

The Newmarket Regional Health Center

The Newmarket Regional Health Center (NRHC) and its satellite facility, the Lamprey River Clinic (LRC), recorded their thirteenth consecutive year of growth in both revenues and patients served. This growth was expected to continue through the 1980s, especially in those towns served by the center that were designated as medically underserved areas (MUA). See Exhibit 17.1 for the area served. For 1985, the NRHC expected to pass the million dollar mark in total revenues for the first time in its history. Since 1981, the center's revenues had risen an average of 25 percent per year. Visits by outpatients had grown as follows:

Year	Visits	Year	Projected Visits*
1980	8,490	1985	17,700
1981	9,872	1986	20,000
1982	12,309		
1983	14,700		
1984	16,000		

*Forecast totals by Strategic Long-Range Planning Committee

This case was prepared by Michael J. Merenda, the University of New Hampshire, and Timothy W. Edlund, Morgan State University. It is intended to be used as a basis for classroom discussion rather than to illustrate effective or ineffective handling of an administrative situation. Used with permission from Tim Edlund.

Several problems, however, were articulated during the center's long-range strategic planning process. The center utilized a three-year planning cycle, which was updated annually.

STRATEGIC CONCERNS

Ann Peters, executive director of NRHC, had just completed the first session of the annual strategic planning process with the strategic long-range planning committee of the center's board of directors. She was extremely pleased with the center's performance over the past several years (see financial statements, Exhibits 17.2 through 17.5), but she was concerned about several issues.

- Completing a capital fund drive to build a new 6,200 square foot medical facility for the Lamprey River Clinic (LRC) in Raymond, New Hampshire, and to renovate the existing headquarters facility in Newmarket, New Hampshire. The inadequate facility currently used for the LRC in Raymond was leased. That lease would expire December 31, 1985.
- Developing and implementing an inpatient hospital policy, choosing among two area hospitals for patients requiring inpatient service, and providing for prearranged obstetrician coverage at one or both of these hospitals whenever the

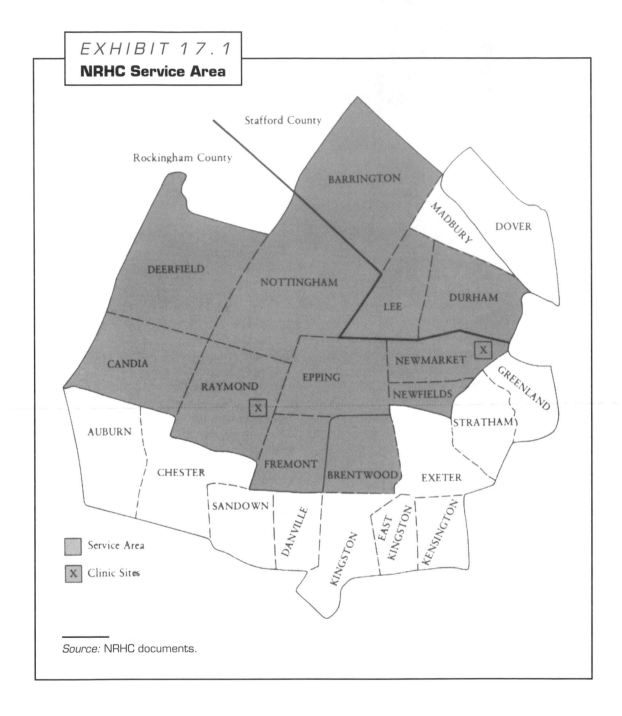

EXHIBIT 17.1
NRHC Service Area

Stafford County

Rockingham County

BARRINGTON

MADBURY

DOVER

DEERFIELD

NOTTINGHAM

LEE

DURHAM

CANDIA

RAYMOND

EPPING

NEWMARKET

GREENLAND

NEWFIELDS

AUBURN

STRATHAM

CHESTER

FREMONT

BRENTWOOD

EXETER

SANDOWN

DANVILLE

KINGSTON

EAST KINGSTON

KENSINGTON

Service Area

X   Clinic Sites

Source: NRHC documents.

EXHIBIT 17.2
Financial Highlights

	1982	1983	1984
Total assets at June 30	$184,304	$282,577	$328,608
Total revenues from services	149,002	226,657	320,668
Total grants received	257,515	275,974	296,904
Other revenues and services received	48,278	158,702	137,569
Total expenses	417,995	631,748	732,468

The percentage breakdown of revenues is as follows:

	1982	1983	1984
Patient services	32.8%	34.3%	42.5%
Operating grants	56.6	41.7	39.3
In-kind services	*	18.1	9.2
Other operating revenues	*	5.9	9.0
	100.0	100.0	100.0
Operating expenses (as percent of operating revenues)	91.9%	95.5%	97.0%

*Breakdown not available.

NRHC obstetrician might not be available.

- Retaining, recruiting, and developing key medical providers and staff in light of changes in the medical care needs of patients, the changing nature of the medical care industry, and potential cutbacks in government funding for health and welfare programs.
- Slowing and eventually eliminating the drains on financial resources and operating funds resulting from the recently created prenatal program.
- Assessing the impact of current and projected growth on the stated mission of the center, its programs, employees, systems, and patients.
- Developing a healthier payer mix to provide funds to meet the needs of those patients with limited ability to pay.

- Striving for financial independence; that is, less dependence on government grants and funds.

Board Chairman John Russell elaborated on these issues:

- The project budget is $550,000; $414,000 for LRC, including equipment; $16,000 fund-raising cost; $100,000 to renovate NRHC; and $20,000 contingency. We planned to cover that by a $220,000 mortgage and $330,000 from fund raising. To date we have spent $34,000 for the land, $10,000 for fund raising, and $10,000 toward the architect's fee, and we have raised $154,000. We expect a major grant of $75,000 and are continuing the general fund-raising effort.

EXHIBIT 17.3
Statements of Revenue and Expenses (years ended June 30)

| | | 1984 | | | | |
	1983 Total	Total	Self-Care for the Elderly	Information and Referral	Transportation	Medical
Support and revenue from:						
Patient service charges	273,797	401,093				401,093
(less contractual adjustments and increase in allowance for uncollectible accounts)	(47,140)	(80,425)				(80,425)
Net patient service charges	226,657	320,668				320,668
Grant funds used to defray operating expenses	275,974	296,904	14,016	13,225	89,480	180,183
In-kind services	119,780	69,614			7,611	62,003
Contributions	37,645	62,748			50,502	12,246
Miscellaneous	1,277	5,207		2,457	2,750	
Total support and revenue	661,333	755,141	14,016	15,682	150,343	575,100
Operating expenses (includes the in-kind service amount):						
Personnel	456,420	532,355	15,234	11,336	85,491	420,294
Supplies	34,948	37,855	185	463	2,548	34,659
Contractual services	14,225	19,008				19,008
General	126,155	143,250	147	6,376	53,718	83,009
Total operating expenses	631,748	732,468	15,566	18,175	141,757	556,970
Excess of support and revenue over (under) operating expenses	29,585	22,673	(1,550)	(2,493)	8,586	18,130
Non-operating revenue:						
Interest income	4,670	8,344				
Excess of revenue over (under) expenses	$34,255	$31,017				

- NRHC does not operate a hospital, nor do we expect to. Therefore, our patients have to go to an area hospital to deliver babies, for surgery, or for serious illness. Exeter Hospital is closest and is a fine hospital, but it is generally reluctant to give our physicians admitting privileges, particularly in the obstetrics (OB) specialty. Nor are their OBs willing to recip-rocally cover for our OBs should we have no one available due to overloads, schedules, resignations, and so forth. Care will be given, but it will cost us much more than at Elliott Hospital in Manchester.

- Of course, providing adequate medical staff is becoming especially critical. We will be getting less of our costs covered

EXHIBIT 17.4
Balance Sheets

| | June 30 | |
	1983	1984
Assets		
Current assets		
Cash and certificate of deposit	$69,982	$117,129
Accounts receivable, services	41,978	68,727
Accounts receivable, grants	75,658	15,949
Prepaid operating expenses	17,850	18,104
Total current assets	205,068	219,909
Property assets	77,509	108,699
Total assets	$282,577	$328,608
Liabilities and Fund Balance		
Current liabilities		
Accounts payable and accrued expenses	$27,615	$61,850
Accrued salaries and wages	28,320	38,571
Current portion of deferred grant revenue	56,258	15,605
Total current liabilities	112,193	116,026
Deferred grant revenue	19,564	30,745
Fund balance	150,820	181,837
Total liabilities and fund balance	$282,577	$328,608

by various governmental programs. We used to be able to get physicians relatively easily if the government had financed their education, but that program is almost finished. I'm not sure what we would do if two or three of our physicians left us. And we have started this prenatal program. It sure is a money loser, but that seems like something we must do because most of our clients come from the MUA around the LRC and have no health coverage and little family income.

• Somehow, we have to keep NRHC solvent. It is too important not to!

Russell and Peters turned to review their plans and the current environment.

THE HEALTH CARE INDUSTRY

The health care industry in the United States underwent major structural and competitive changes during the late 1970s and early 1980s. Once protected by government regulation, a strong national medical association, and tradition, the $360 billion industry faced stiff com-

EXHIBIT 17.5
Statements of Changes in Financial Position

	Years Ended June 30	
	1983	**1984**
Financial resources were provided by:		
Operating and nonoperating income:		
Excess of revenue over expenses	$34,255	$31,017
Depreciation, an item not affecting working capital	14,229	17,368
Working capital provided by operating and non-operating income	48,484	48,385
Addition to deferred grant revenue		26,986
	48,484	75,371
Financial resources were applied to:		
Acquisition of property assets	8,536	48,558
Current maturity of deferred grant revenue	9,872	15,805
Cumulative effect on prior year of accounting for compensated absences	12,242	
	30,650	64,363
Increase in working capital	$17,834	$11,008
Increase (decrease) in elements of working capital:		
Cash and certificate of deposit	$12,962	$47,547
Accounts receivable, services	22,952	26,749
Accounts receivable, grants	75,658	(59,709)
Prepaid operating expenses	(7,606)	254
Accounts payable and accrued expenses	(11,996)	(34,235)
Accrued salaries and wages	(28,320)	(10,251)
Current portion of deferred grant revenue	(45,816)	40,653
Increase in working capital	$17,834	$11,008

petition and rising public pressure to reform. Coddington, Palmquist, and Trollinger reported: "The health care industry has joined the list of major U.S. industries facing intensely competitive environments . . . revolutionary changes are sweeping the industry."[1]

Among the major forces affecting the health care industry were a glut of doctors and hospital beds; medical costs rising at an accelerating rate; governmental reform including changes in Medicare and Medicaid third-party payments; growth in alternative medical care and services (health maintenance organizations: walk-in centers, sometimes referred to as *Docs-in-a-Box;* preferred provider organizations); the entry of large, privately held, for-profit hospital chains, and the development of alliances and health care systems.

Industry Structural Changes

"We are going into an environment where so many changes are going to take place that you have to question (anyone's) long range forecasts of growth or profitability," predicted Robert Friedman, Jr., a health care security analyst.[2] Although they usually cater to a different patient than do private practices or hospitals, community health centers have not been immune to industry changes. Like school health services in the 1920s, health centers assumed a complementary relationship to private practices by diagnosing cases and sending patients to physicians, thus aiding doctors in their practice rather than competing with them. In the 1960s the aim of health center programs was to create a "one-stop" facility in low-income communities to provide virtually all necessary ambulatory services.[3]

Community health centers in the 1980s were undergoing a further transformation and, along with other private and for-profit organizations, were facing new and unexpected competition that changed not only what was provided, but how it was provided. The relative certainty and predictability associated with the medical industry in prior times was gone.

Many new products and services successfully gained entry into the medical industry and increased competition. For example, the advent of self-diagnosis kits and other medical equipment and supplies marketed directly to the patient, walk in clinics, self-help education programs, health maintenance organizations (HMOs), and increased emphasis on exercise and fitness have all contributed to changes in the way people use and receive medical care.

Growth in For-Profit Hospitals

Health care units "tend to compete on the basis of their availability and sophistication of their services and facilities."[4] However, the entry of new "competitors" into the medical arena is altering the way in which medical services are provided. A *U.S. News and World Report* article reported that there appeared to be shrinkage in the total number of hospitals since the 1970s, but that the number of institutions belonging to for-profit corporations had more than doubled.[5] Competition from for-profit providers increased the pressure on not-for-profit organizations to rethink past practices and strategies. Coddington et al. reported that hospital administrators were beginning to talk like *Fortune* 500 company executives. Some new strategies being considered were downsizing, specialization (coronary bypass surgery, high-risk maternity), low-cost providers, diversification into for-profit businesses, merging, and joint ventures.[6]

Rising Health Care Costs

Spiraling health care costs have forced many outside the health care industry to lobby for cost reduction and control. Between 1965 and 1978, health care costs rose at an annual rate of between 10 percent and 14 percent, and the future is not much brighter. A *Business Week* article noted: "The rising average age of Americans virtually guarantees that the U.S. will continue to demand more medical care. And the advent of modern, high cost medical techniques means that care is going to cost more."[7]

A *Business Week* survey of reasons for rising health care costs found 82 percent agreement that the major reason for spiraling health care costs was the purchase of expensive new equipment by hospitals and doctors.[8] This was followed by increased third-party medical coverage (government, insurance companies), increased patient testing, and long hospital stays. The survey asked, "Several reasons have been advanced for the big increase in health costs. Do you think each of these reasons is important or unimportant?" The question and responses follow in Exhibit 17.6.

EXHIBIT 17.6
Questions for Rising Health Care Costs

	Important	Not Sure	Unimportant
The purchase of expensive new equipment by hospitals and doctors	82%	5%	13%
The existence of such federal programs as Medicare and Medicaid	76%	8%	16%
Insurance companies paying claims without questioning if treatment really was necessary	74%	8%	18%
Doctors ordering more laboratory tests than are necessary	69%	7%	24%
Doctors permitting longer stays for minor ailments than are necessary	65%	7%	29%

Source: "The Upheaval in Health Care: Government Cost Controls Will Soon Have Hospitals Under the Knife, " *Business Week* (July 25, 1983), p. 56.

In another study, rising health care costs were attributed to five dimensions:

1. *Demand Pull.* Rising personal incomes and increased growth in medical insurance have created new and increased demand on a relatively inelastic supply of medical providers.
2. *Labor Cost Push.* Rising hospital staffing costs along with decreased provider productivity have driven expenses and overall medical costs up.
3. *Scientific Progress.* New technology and methods of care have been achieved at a higher cost.
4. *Capacity.* Prices have risen in response to increased capital investments and increased expenses in maintaining facilities that are underutilized.
5. *Cost Reimbursement.* Increases in medical supplies, equipment, staffs, and salaries have occurred with the increased growth in insurance coverage and other third-party reimbursement plans.[9]

Some users of medical services have begun to flex their muscles in light of rising medical costs. Susan Lee reported that business had every reason to be concerned with rising medical costs. On average, medical insurance was running about 10 percent of payroll, and health bills were rising 15 percent to 35 percent a year, outstripping inflation and payroll increases. According to Lee: "Business' newest weapon is the health care coalition. These are groups of employers dedicated to heavy-duty dealings with the medical establishment. The prevailing sentiment is that the private sector must do something."[10]

One option that was being touted by business executives was the growth and promotion of preferred provider organizations (PPOs). These were groups of physicians who agreed to provide medical services at negotiated rates in exchange for set contracted services.

Ethical Concerns

The appearance of for-profits in the medical arena, along with increased medical costs and an aging American population, raised several moral and ethical questions. Questions were raised about the health care industry's new concern for profitability. Is health care a service or business, or both? One argument that was advanced was that for-profit medical providers should not be expected to take on the responsibility of caring for the poor or medically disadvantaged. If profit is the objective, these critics argued, then to cater to the underprivileged would be a poor business decision and would drive the provider out of business. Furthermore, these critics claimed that the predominant and traditional not-for-profit structure in the medical care industry is antithetical to private for-profit competition and market constraints. *Business Week* reported that rising costs and an aging population "raise extremely difficult moral and ethical questions, including whether Americans want to pay $50,000 to $100,000 to care for an 85 year old patient whose quality of life is gone." Observes Harvey B. Karsh, a doctor of internal medicine in Denver, "People are unwilling to talk about such issues, but someone soon is going to have to make some decisions."[11]

NRHC's SERVICE AREA

NRHC was founded and its first clinic and headquarters was in Newmarket, New Hampshire, a small manufacturing town about ten miles west of Portsmouth and the Atlantic Ocean. Rockingham County includes the city of Portsmouth (population 26,254) and stretches thirty-five miles west to the outskirts of Manchester, New Hampshire's largest city (population 90,936).[12] Along the county's southern border are a string of boom towns, which became a tax haven for many seeking relief from high taxes in Massachusetts. But the upper central portion of the county contains a number of towns that are still rural and have high proportions of poor and indigent people. Six Rockingham towns (Candia, Deerfield, Epping, Fremont, Nottingham, and Raymond) are classified as medically underserved areas. NRHC's medical service area includes these towns as well as Brentwood, Newfields, and Newmarket in Rockingham County, and Lee, Durham, and Barrington in Strafford County immediately to the north. The University of New Hampshire, a medium-size land-grant institution, is in Durham, immediately north of Newmarket.

Travel in the service area is primarily by local roads and highways, except that State Highway 101 runs east – west through the service area, connecting Manchester to the coast, with a spur to Portsmouth. In the center of the county, it is a two-lane highway utilizing older roads, but both near Manchester and near the coast a new four-lane limited-access highway has replaced the old road. Reconstruction of the middle portion was underway and completion was estimated to take three or four years. Exhibit 17.7 is a map of Rockingham County and surrounding areas.

In 1985, New Hampshire had no general state sales taxes or income taxes, and retained the tradition of local control over most spending. Silber reported that New Hampshire schools derived 90 percent of their funding from local sources, the highest in the nation,[13] a pattern typical of all categories of spending.

New Hampshire towns retain the town meeting, in which spending for each year is determined by vote of all citizens in attendance. The state legislature has been reluctant to undertake new enterprises, generally leaving such initiatives to the towns and, in some cases, to the counties.

NRHC BACKGROUND

In 1969, a group of Volunteers in Service to America (VISTA) began a referral and coordinating agency in Newmarket, New Hampshire. From this beginning as an information and referral agency, the center expanded first into

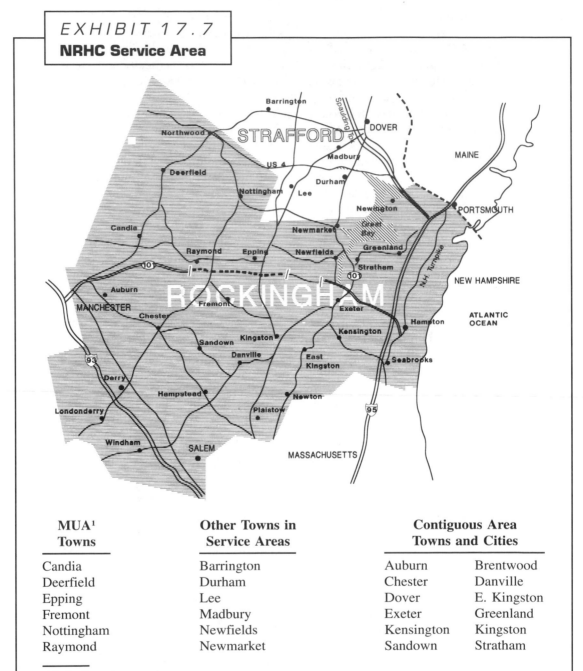

EXHIBIT 17.7
NRHC Service Area

MUA[1] Towns	Other Towns in Service Areas	Contiguous Area Towns and Cities	
Candia	Barrington	Auburn	Brentwood
Deerfield	Durham	Chester	Danville
Epping	Lee	Dover	E. Kingston
Fremont	Madbury	Exeter	Greenland
Nottingham	Newfields	Kensington	Kingston
Raymond	Newmarket	Sandown	Stratham

[1]Medically underserved areas
Note: Towns are legal municipalities and may contain several place names, generally having related names. Thus, the Town of Candia includes Candia Four Corners, Candia Station, and East Candia.
Source: NRHC documents.

blood pressure screening and eventually into providing lifelong preventive health care for individuals of all ages and incomes. Today, NRHC is the only not-for-profit, community-based health center in New Hampshire that provides primary health care and social services. "Since day one, we have had a tremendous amount of community support," noted Peters, "and we have found a great sense of community that you just don't see everywhere."

"We really make an effort to take care of the whole person," observed Dr. Sally Oxnard, NRHC's medical director. Care of the "whole person" was provided at the center through six interconnected and closely related programs (Exhibit 17.8). At the hub was the primary-care medical services program. The medical program was strongly supported, like the spokes in a wheel, by several social service and administrative programs including senior citizen transportation, health promotion and disease prevention, self-care for the elderly, social services (community health workers),

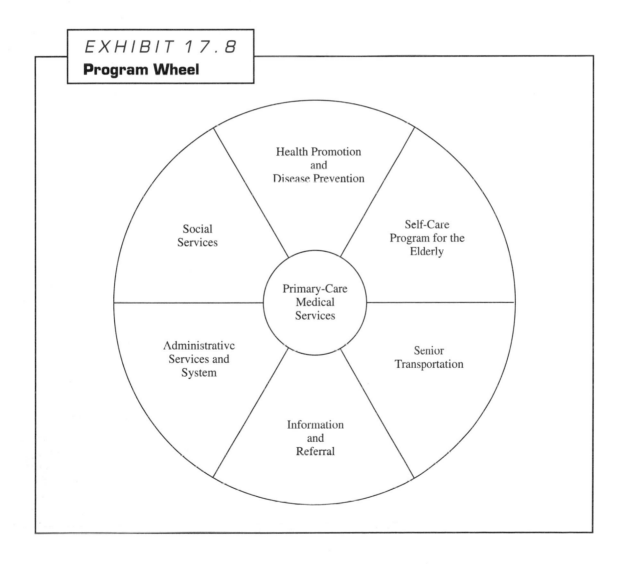

EXHIBIT 17.8
Program Wheel

and the original information and referral program. Oxnard continued, "Although not actually a program, the administrative services and system function is considered an integral part of the center's medical and social services programs."

Medical Program

The preceding three years were unprecedented years of growth and development for the Newmarket Regional Health Center and specifically for the medical program. The opening of a second facility and the addition of two new physicians and other support staff enlarged the size and scope of the medical program.

Newmarket Regional Health Care continued to focus on primary care for individuals of all ages. Care was provided by a medical and support staff of fifteen full- and part-time members, including four physicians, one nurse practitioner, one physician's assistant, four part-time medical receptionist/appointment clerks, two part-time registered nurses, one part-time nurse educator, and two medical assistants.

In 1982, the Newmarket Regional Health Center provided 7,542 encounters (patients seen) and LRC, the satellite facility in Raymond, provided 4,767. The strategic long-range planning committee examined growth pattern statistics from 1980 through 1984, and projected 17,700 patient visits for 1985 and 20,000 for 1986.

Revenues from patient fees were expected to increase from $320,668 in 1984 to $475,000 in 1985. Working with the medical staff, the strategic long-range planning committee identified several crucial issues for the medical program for the 1985–1988 strategic plan:

- Continued growth in patient utilization of services was expected to both strain the ability of the medical staff to provide needed services and place demands on the optimal size of the health center. Should limits be placed on utilization?

Should more staff members be recruited?
- There are questions concerning the ability of the medical staff to provide coverage for medical care in pediatrics, family practice, and obstetrics. How can the staff establish expanded admitting privileges at area hospitals?
- With regard to patient retention, should the medical program develop complete patient files in order to become each patient's primary physician? Should it refer patients to area physicians? Should it provide services on a first-come, first-served basis (similar to the "Doc-in-a-box" concept)?
- With regard to risk management or quality control, as new and expanded medical coverage is provided, does the center have the program quality assurance controls in place to adequately maintain quality care?
- Concerning long-term plans for the prenatal program, how can NRHC develop funding sources to support this program? Should it be continued? What contingency plans should be in place should the present obstetrician/gynecologist leave? Can coverage arrangements for the family practitioner in obstetrics be secured (to cover for vacations, several simultaneous births, and so on)?

Prenatal Care Program

The prenatal care program was the most recent addition to the Newmarket Regional Health Center and highlighted the crucial issues identified by the medical staff. Since its initiation in September 1983, the prenatal program was widely used by patients in the area, especially those patients from MUA towns. Moreover, this program was drawing patients from towns not normally served by NRHC. Ann Peters commented, "Some expectant mothers are coming from towns as far away as Derry.

There's almost no one else doing this, at least for the medically poor."

An MUA is a geographical area designated by the federal government as medically underserved and eligible for government-sponsored medical programs. It is defined by a weighted combination of four factors: (1) the number of area physicians per 1,000 population, (2) the percent of the area's population having family incomes below the poverty level ($5,000 in 1975), (3) the area's infant mortality rate, and (4) the percent of the area's population over 65 years of age.[14]

The obstetricians at the health center were delivering approximately 150 babies per year. These deliveries were done at the Elliott Hospital in Manchester, New Hampshire, which was adjacent to the western end of NRHC's service area.

Medically, the prenatal program was a success both in the number of patients served and in medical quality. However, the program faced serious financial problems that affected the center's finances. Dr. Oxnard commented: "The prenatal program is a real loser in terms of finances, but it's a service that needs to be provided. Many of these [prenatal] patients are indigent and cannot afford to pay the costs associated with prenatal care and the delivery of a child." The center was expecting to write off over $90,000 in bad debts in 1985–1986, almost all associated with the prenatal program.

Dr. Oxnard continued: "Although the costs of the prenatal program are high, it is one of the most needed services in the area, and it is vital that it remains within the Newmarket Regional Health Center structure."

Although the NRHC and LRC were still primarily outpatient facilities (all hospital coverage was by referral to non-health-center physicians), the prenatal program had drastically increased the center's need for inpatient care (hospital coverage), as well as for additional coverage by non-center physicians when the health center staff was overburdened. The cen-

ter was considering switching its existing coverage and inpatient care from Elliott Hospital in Manchester to Exeter Hospital. Ann Peters and the strategic long-range planning committee discussed the pros and cons of Elliott (Manchester) versus Exeter Hospital. A summary of that discussion follows.

Elliott provided excellent OB coverage for our physicians by Manchester physicians. Should we lose our OB, Elliott's staff will cover for us. The hospital is very supportive of us, and gives warm acceptance of our mid-level providers (nurse practitioners and other nonphysician care providers). They also can provide more extensive OB care for high-risk mothers, and have a Level 2 nursery, which provides needed care for higher risk newborns. But Elliott is farther away from Newmarket. It takes longer to get there for our physicians and other staff. Some live in or near Newmarket; others have chosen Durham, Dover, or the Portsmouth area. Route 101 still is slow in the two-lane portions, and its reconstruction (upgrading to a four-lane divided highway) only makes it worse right now. Moreover, should we choose Elliott, it would be hard to take advantage of and further build the close networks we have built with the Exeter pediatrics/family practice, surgical, and other medical staff.

At Exeter, we can get good coverage for our OB physicians, but it is not reciprocal (they will not permit our staff to cover for them), and they charge us much more to furnish coverage (compared to Elliott's charges). Exeter will not provide coverage reciprocity for our family practice physician. Their policy toward her is very restrictive, which may give her negative feedback. They are also restrictive toward our mid-level providers. However there is a supportive network of MDs in Exeter. Exeter is centrally located, which will cut down on staff travel time, thus increasing their productivity.

Social Services

Marge Clark, associate director of the health center, was responsible for several of the community and social service programs, including grants management, supervision and evaluation of the senior citizens' transportation program, information and referral, community health workers, self-care help for the elderly, nutrition, and the hypertension screening program. Marge reported, "The health center's team approach to patient care separates it from others. Our mission is to provide good health care, preventive education, and social services incorporated in a team approach – that's what makes us different. We coordinate the care of the patient – medical, administrative, transportation, or whatever. It's surprising, but when all the social services are added to the medical care, the patient's headaches go away a lot quicker." In commenting on the problems she faced as associate director, Marge noted: "My real problem is trying to coordinate all the programs. I have so many everyday programmatic problems that I feel that I never have enough time to devote to just one. I am always being split; I don't know how I do it, I just do it! I feel overwhelmed with the number of daily and weekly meetings."

Although it was not confirmed, the strategic long-range planning committee heard rumors that Clark was considering leaving the center after ten years of service.

Health Promotion and Disease Prevention

NRHC continued to develop its health promotion and disease prevention program via community clinics, work-site health promotion, and school health programs coordinated by the community health workers. In 1982–1983, the center received additional funds from the Rural Health Initiative Program and developed the nurse educator role for the prenatal program and classes. It was recruiting a health educator to continue expansion of health education activities with patients and area schools. A nutritionist was hired for a limited time to assist in prenatal classes, diet, and counseling patients when clinically recommended. "These public health endeavors continue to be a cornerstone of the health center's total philosophy toward medical care," according to Ann Peters.

Senior Citizen Transportation

The transportation program provided 24,226 rides to area senior citizens and handicapped in twenty-seven towns in Rockingham and Strafford counties. Twenty-four of these towns (shown in Exhibit 17.1) appropriated funds for the program in 1984. Over $150,000 in revenues were generated by the program; operating expenses were $141,757.

The transportation program staff included a director of transportation (Marge Clark), four full-time drivers, a substitute driver, volunteers in the community who took telephone reservations for the scheduled route, and volunteer drivers who carried individuals who did not fit into regularly scheduled bus runs or routes.

The capital assets of the program consisted of five vans and a station wagon: two passenger vans with more than 110,000 miles each (acquired in 1977); one thirteen-passenger van equipped with a hydraulic lift (acquired 1979); two sixteen-passenger vans equipped with hydraulic lifts for wheelchair passengers (acquired in 1981); and one station wagon, used for patient transportation, seniors, and general staff.

Clark estimated that the transportation program had excess capacity, because one of the vans had minimum scheduled route time and was available for new routes. The center was concerned about the age of two of the passenger vans and planned to apply for a grant to replace them.

Information and Referral

The information and referral program was NRHC's first program and had experienced many changes since its inception. In 1985, it operated as a telephone referral system for individuals with medical or other problems. In 1984, over 1,258 calls and 36 contacts were made in response to Rockingham County residents' medical and social services needs.

The staff consisted of two part-time information and referral specialists. Revenues were generated from funding by the Rockingham County budget (40 percent), pamphlet sales, garage sales, and Newmarket Regional Health Center general support.

Peters wanted to expand the focus and activities of the information and referral program. In 1982, the information and referral staff was combined with the transportation staff to maximize the benefits of each program. In 1984, the program experienced a small deficit of $2,493.

Community Health Workers

Two community health workers and a part-time mental health counselor provided the social services and counseling for center patients. The focus for community health workers was shifting from community development to direct patient services (i.e., prenatal social service needs assessment, pregnancy counseling, patient follow-up, and home visits). The community health workers direct patient contact and service was being further developed via the self-care program for the elderly.

The mental health counseling program was reduced in size in 1982 to one day of the counselor's time per clinic. "Due to lack of referrals and demand in Newmarket, mental health services will probably be deleted or curtailed at Newmarket's facility in 1985," Peters said.

The mental health counselor saw an average of five patients each week in Raymond. The focus of the mental health counseling program was on short-term counseling with referral to area mental health providers when appropriate.

Self-Care Program for the Elderly

In 1982, the Newmarket Regional Health Center initiated a self-care program for senior citizens. The purpose of the program was to promote maximum independence at home for the elderly by providing health screening, suggestions for home modification, and training in personal care and homemaking. The program was funded totally by the state of New Hampshire Division of Public Health Services, Bureau of Health Promotion ($29,526). This program was a cooperative effort with the Occupational Therapy Department at the University of New Hampshire.

The staff consists of the program coordinator, a registered nurse practitioner, a registered occupational therapist, and occupational therapy students. Community health workers provide social assessment and follow-up.

The program was started to meet the needs of the elderly and expand the capability of the Newmarket Regional Health Center staff in providing these services. It was the first program of the health center to focus on medical services for the elderly. At the end of 1985, when the contract would be completed, it was planned that the medical staff and program would continue as part of the health center. It would then be supported through the health center by patient fees and through an occupational therapy component provided by faculty and students of the University of New Hampshire.

Administrative Services and System

The size of the staff of the Newmarket Regional Health Center had grown to over forty-four full- and part-time members (Exhibit 17.9). As the health center grew, its administrative staff has remained approximately the same size. The administrative staff consisted of the executive director (Ann Peters), an administra-tive assistant, a part-time secretary, a fiscal officer, an accounts receivable bookkeeper, and an office manager.

The administration's efforts were focused on planning for the completion of the new building for the Lamprey River Clinic in Raymond, scheduled to open in January 1986. Ann noted, "The prenatal program is still in the process of being fully integrated into the over-

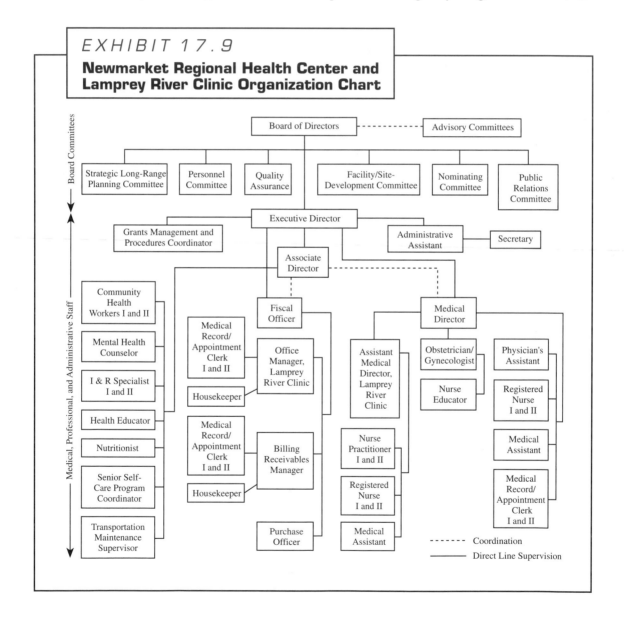

EXHIBIT 17.9
Newmarket Regional Health Center and Lamprey River Clinic Organization Chart

all agency operations. The new building in Raymond and the prenatal program problems have precipitated a need for change. We need to revise the center's management and supervisory functions, as well as its fiscal operating procedures."

"Just how the management and supervisory functions will be revised is not clear at this time, but it is considered a major concern that needs to be addressed in the 1985–1988 strategic plan," John Russell added.

CAPITAL FUND DRIVE

The center was in the midst of a major $550,000 capital fund-raising effort. The funds would be used for renovation of the Newmarket facility and construction of the Raymond

facility. This expansion would mark the fifth time in thirteen years that the center enlarged its facilities to meet the demand for its services. Exhibit 17.10 contains excerpts from the market study that helped support the expansion decision. It was estimated that there would be unmet demand for 2.32 (conservative estimate) to 5.22 FTE (full-time equivalent) medical providers in the center's service area by 1990, even with the proposed Raymond facility.

OPERATING STATISTICS

Ann Peters, along with the center's planning committee, viewed the capital fund drive as necessary and important to the future viability of the health center. Nevertheless, they were concerned with its timing. They were aware

---

EXHIBIT 17.10

Market Projections for Newmarket Regional Health Center, 1984–1990

Abstract

1. The service area population is 23,905.
2. There is a need for one to two more primary-care physicians on the staff of the Newmarket Regional Health Center based on conservative Method A.
3. The 1990 need for primary-care physicians would increase by approximately 0.5–1.0 FTE (full-time-equivalent medical providers).

These conclusions are very conservative based on the following assumptions that may prove to underestimate actual demand:

A. We estimated a total service area population increase of 20 percent from 1982 to 1990. From 1980 to 1982 there has been a 7.5 percent increase. If that rate continues to 1990, the increase would be 37 percent. The impact of the reconstruction of State Route 101 has not been estimated. Completion of this superhighway connecting Manchester and Portsmouth should lead to additional population increase.

B. We assumed that NRHC would capture only 50 percent of the unmet need for services. This may be too conservative considering that the center is located in the service area and current unmet need is being serviced in the contiguous market areas of Manchester and Exeter.

C. Our estimates do not consider the addition of other services and specialties to the staff of NRHC, which may provide a multiplying effect on demand.

EXHIBIT 17.10   cont'd

Demand for Primary Care

Method A (Conservative)

1984 Providers (FTE)
  NRHC 4.03–4.03
  Others 2.25–2.25

Total	6.28–6.28
Need	8.60–10.32[1]
Unsatisfied Need	2.32–4.04

Assume NRHC could capture 50 percent of need.
NRHC = 50 percent FTE level.
FTE needed by NRHC to satisfy needs of 1984 population = 1.16–2.02 FTE.

1990 Providers (FTE)
  NRHC 4.03–4.03
  Others 2.25–2.25

Total	6.28–6.28
Need	9.60–11.50[2]
Unsatisfied Need	3.32–5.22

Assume NRHC could capture 50 percent of increased service population.
Therefore, NRHC needs 50 percent FTE level.
FTE needed by NRHC to satisfy needs of 1990 population = 1.66–2.61.

Service Area Populations, Change per Annum

Service Area	1980	1982	Change 80–82	1990[3]
Candia	2,989	3,163	3%	3,796
Deerfield	1,979	2,181	5%	2,617
Epping	3,460	3,643	3%	4,372
Fremont	1,333	1,397	2%	1,676
Newfields	817	822	>1%	986
Newmarket	4,290	4,419	2%	5,303
Nottingham	1,952	2,200	6%	2,640
Raymond	5,427	6,080	6%	7,296
Total	22,247	23,905		28,686

[1]Based on standards of 1:2,500–3,000:
    25,800 divided by 3,000 = 8.60 FTE
    25,800 divided by 2,500 = 10.32 FTE
[2]Based on standards of 1:2,500–3,000:
    28,686 divided by 3,000 = 9.6
    28,686 divided by 2,500 = 11.5
[3]Projections: Change in population between 1970–1980 for service area was 13 percent. Change in population between 1980–1982 for service area was 1 percent–6 percent increase per annum. Therefore, we assume a change in population for 1982–1990 of 20 percent.

of the drastic changes occurring in the health care industry. Recent speeches by the Secretary of Health, Education, and Welfare and the President announcing an all-out effort to combat the massive federal budget deficit presented a major threat to the health care industry. Although the center had set fiscal autonomy and independence as an objective, only 42 percent of its revenues were provided by patient fees. Bad debt for the prenatal program was projected to be almost $100,000 for 1985–1986. Exhibits 17.11, 17.12, and 17.13 contain excerpts from the executive director's report on operating statistics. This report was presented monthly to the center's board of directors.

At the first board meeting of the new year, a new director inquired why the last three months' receivables and collection rates were not posted. Peters explained, "Those entries show how much of each month's adjusted charges are paid within ninety days. October's can't be posted until the end of January, and so forth." She went on, "You may spot what looks like another discrepancy, but it isn't. The medical visit data for each clinic in the management report (Exhibit 17.11) includes hospital stays. Such stays were eliminated from the data given to the strategic long-range planning committee." (That data is at the beginning of the case.)

Peters listed the following concerns of the administrative staff:

- Space needs in Newmarket and Raymond; both facilities were at capacity.
- Funding in general, especially given potential cutbacks in state and federal grant funding, which appeared almost inevitable.
- The impact of growth on all systems: medical records, accounts receivable and accounts payable areas, personnel, supervision, and program management functions. The center had no automated systems.
- The cost and utility of automated systems in receivables and payables areas. All bookkeeping was performed manually.
- The impact of growth and change on staff attitudes, staff retention, job functions, and general working relationships. Could the informal, caring, friendly, and supportive environment that existed at the center be maintained with continuing expansion in size, services, and geography?

CONCLUDING COMMENTS

In discussing recent changes in the health care industry and the possibility of NRHC sharing resources or joining forces with other social service agencies, Ann Peters commented:

> We serve a medically underserved area. We have a high percentage of medically indigent. We're not feeling direct competition in a classic industry sense; however, we have a very fragile economic base. Any creaming – and by that I mean capturing those services that are the cheapest to provide and the best in dollar reimbursement by the for-profit medical providers – even a small percent, can affect us negatively.
>
> Even though other providers are not directly competing for the majority of our patients, a little bite out of some of our paying patients by for-profits would affect us more than others.

She continued:

> The majority of our patients have no medical insurance whatsoever for outpatient medical service. Those who go to HMOs have greater coverage – ours do not. Our patients are coming from industries that do not have good

EXHIBIT 17.11

Summary Program Statistics for 1984 (total medical visits, including hospitalizations)

	Jan	Feb	Mar	Apr	May	Jun	Jul	Aug	Sep	Oct	Nov	Dec	1st Qtr	2nd Qtr	3rd Qtr	4th Qtr	Yearly Totals
NRHC																	
Actual 1984	850	719	797	756	816	881	711	880	1,098	1,012	929	724	2,366	2,453	2,689	2,665	10,173
Actual 1983	567	606	697	634	631	585	567	644	684	805	747	731	1,870	1,850	1,895	2,283	7,898
Actual 1982	497	473	651	516	625	626	551	677	597	843	612	874	1,621	1,767	1,825	2,329	7,542
LRC																	
Actual 1984	683	711	724	685	707	647	591	731	553	869	902	713	2,118	2,039	1,875	2,484	8,516
Actual 1983	528	484	524	537	498	519	543	659	579	645	659	578	1,536	1,554	1,781	1,882	6,753
Actual 1982	305	300	449	409	358	302	375	390	428	480	513	438	1,054	1,069	1,193	1,431	4,747

EXHIBIT 17.12
Newmarket Internal Management Report, 1984

	Jan	Feb	Mar	Apr	May	Jun	Jul	Aug	Sep	Oct	Nov	Dec
Charges												
General medical	$12,685	$13,593	$14,819	$14,589	$14,090	$14,368	$15,159	$16,374	$13,835	$16,663	$19,533	$15,662
Adj. charges	$10,604	11,380	11,476	12,490	12,739	11,336	13,071	15,962	9,638	14,961	16,294	12,448
Prenatal package	3,345	727	2,704	1,989	1,940	5,304	2,652	2,652	1,606	3,874	4,211	713
Adj. charges	1,395	727	2,141	1,696	1,104	2,079	2,262	1,052	1,606	3,150	4,176	713
In-hospital surgery	1,360	1,620	160	1,280	1,920	480	1,700	695	235	864	2,255	1,105
Adj. charges	1,360	1,442	160	1,280	1,470	480	1,700	695	184	686	2,255	904
Total charges	$17,390	$15,940	$17,683	$17,858	$17,950	$20,152	$19,511	$19,721	$15,676	$21,371	$25,999	$17,480
Total adjusted charges	$13,359	$13,549	$13,777	$15,466	$15,313	$13,895	$17,033	$17,709	$11,478	$18,797	$22,725	$14,065
Revenues												
Cash at door	$5,937	$7,301	$7,061	$7,479	$7,910	$8,227	$7,876	$9,033	$6,364	$8,637	$9,179	$7,089
Medicare	1,074	109	647	1,269	545	752	878	926	301	480	131	1,291
Medicaid	811	607	619	1,000	1,326	939	500	1,518	764	943	442	662
Other insurance	3,196	2,042	7,611	2,913	4,408	2,110	2,836	2,345	3,670	2,904	2,584	2,659
Direct billing	3,520	3,315	2,850	3,780	3,371	3,235	2,631	3,283	3,005	3,626	2,861	2,732
Percent at door	44%	54%	51%	48%	52%	59%	46%	51%	55%	46%	40%	50%
Total revenue:	$14,538	$13,374	$18,788	$16,441	$17,560	$15,263	$14,721	$17,105	$14,104	$16,590	$15,197	$14,443
Receivables to date	$32,376	$32,813	$28,718	$28,866	$27,771	$26,492	$29,197	$30,348	$27,966	$30,769	$38,500	$38,530
Receivables from charges, 90 days	$10,884	$12,278	$12,549	$12,779	$13,444	$14,723	$14,136	$15,411	$10,439			
Collection rate, 90 days (percent)	81%	91%	91%	83%	88%	106%	83%	87%	91%			

EXHIBIT 17.13
Lamprey River Clinic Internal Management Report, 1984

	Jan	Feb	Mar	Apr	May	Jun	Jul	Aug	Sep	Oct	Nov	Dec
Charges												
General medical	$10,613	$10,056	$10,742	$11,316	$10,101	$10,798	$10,542	$12,115	$7,682	$13,259	$15,968	$15,370
Adj. charges	9,117	8,339	8,625	9,602	7,619	10,491	8,457	8,977	4,674	10,998	13,769	12,005
Prenatal package	6,636	6,164	5,203	6,207	8,045	7,218	5,360	9,945	3,316	6,830	9,982	4,448
Adj. charges	3,923	4,111	3,983	4,604	4,136	4,972	4,026	6,204	1,015	4,910	7,790	3,899
In-hospital surgery	1,750	1,313	1,016	1,909	2,019	600	0	715	730	1,655	4,080	655
Adj. charges	1,255	810	858	1,579	1,643	390	0	0	361	1,237	3,483	655
Total charges	$18,999	$17,533	$16,961	$19,432	$20,165	$18,616	$15,902	$22,775	$11,728	$21,744	$30,030	$20,473
Total adjusted charges	$14,295	$13,260	$13,466	$15,785	$13,398	$15,853	$12,483	$15,181	$ 6,050	$17,145	$25,042	$16,559
Revenues												
Cash at door	$4,598	$4,546	$5,307	$5,527	$5,642	$6,297	$6,020	$6,192	$4,177	$6,255	$7,160	$5,793
Percent at door	32%	34%	39%	35%	42%	44%	48%	41%	69%	36%	29%	35%
Medicare	220	1,518	842	1,616	162	556	540	309	349	0	153	229
Medicaid	25	779	1,172	1,926	1,433	2,962	1,536	1,356	787	0	1,638	50
Other insurance	1,650	3,090	2,470	841	2,226	3,791	1,007	2,042	2,187	926	1,346	1,626
Direct billing	754	586	2,134	2,580	4,186	2,686	2,399	1,988	1,590	1,566	1,510	1,795
Total revenues	$7,247	$10,519	$11,925	$12,490	$13,649	$14,766	$11,502	$11,887	$9,090	$8,747	$11,807	$9,493
Receivables to date	$68,624	$71,365	$73,139	$78,342	$78,091	$79,178	$80,501	$85,050	$82,594	$91,440	$105,273	$112,930
Receivables from charges, 90 days	$7,123	$8,587	$9,264	$8,476	$9,356	$8,509	$7,184	$8,713	$5,494			
Collection rate, 90 days (percent)	50%	65%	69%	54%	70%	54%	58%	57%	91%			

medical plans or salaries. We are often talking about people that are technically below the federal poverty guidelines. We are dealing with people with limited resources. A segment of our patients come to us because of our location and because of the quality of service and the caring atmosphere in which it is provided. We need to maintain those paying patients, as well as adhere to our basic mission, which is to make medical care accessible to all, regardless of the ability to pay. We have to have a good patient mix to meet that objective.

NOTES

1. D. C. Coddington, L. E. Palmquist, and W. V. Trollinger, "Strategies for Survival in the Hospital Industry," *Harvard Business Review* 63, no. 3 (May–June 1985), pp. 129–138.
2. "The Upheaval in Health Care: Government Cost Controls Will Soon Have Hospitals Under the Knife," *Business Week* (July 25, 1983), p. 45.
3. Paul Starr, *The Social Transformation of American Medicine* (New York: Basic Books, 1982).
4. J. C. Goodman, *The Regulation of Medical Care: Is the Price Too High?* (Washington, D.C.: Cato Institute, 1980), p. 71.
5. *U.S. News and World Report* (December 10, 1984), pp. 61–62.
6. Coddington et al., "Strategies for Survival," p. 131.
7. "The Upheaval in Health Care," p. 52.
8. Ibid., p. 56.
9. Goodman, *Regulation of Medical Care,* p. 71.
10. Susan Lee, "Enough Is Enough," *Forbes* 139, no. 6 (September 10, 1984), pp. 109–112.
11. "The Upheaval in Health Care," p. 52.
12. 1980 data from *The World Almanac and Book of Facts, 1986* (New York: Newspaper Enterprise Association, 1985), pp. 283–284.
13. John Silber, *Straight Shooting* (New York: Harper and Row, 1989), p. 35.
14. G. P. Huber, *Managerial Decision Making* (Glenview, Illinois: Scott Foresman and Company, 1980), p. 57.

Riverview Regional Medical Center: Moving Beyond the Corporate Formula

In general, Health Management Associates (HMA), Inc., acquired and operated acute-care hospitals that were the dominant or only health care provider in the nonurban market areas they served. After each acquisition, HMA applied a proven formula to reduce costs and attract physicians and patients. By all accounts that formula was working well for Jon P. Vollmer, executive director of HMA's most recent acquisition and largest health care facility, Riverview Regional Medical Center (RRMC) in Gadsden, Alabama. For the first two years of his administration, Vollmer successfully pursued a turnaround strategy focused primarily on the internal operational problems of the hospital.

According to the corporate goals, he was right on target to "manage the acquired hospital to maximize operating margins and return on capital within the first thirty-six months of operations." At the end of that time, however, Vollmer knew he would need to focus more

closely on the external threats and opportunities for future growth, considering that (1) the health care industry was undergoing structural change, (2) the hospital's market service area was slowly declining in population, and (3) he was himself facing a challenge somewhat atypical for an HMA facility administrator, namely, strong competition from a larger local health care facility (Baptist Memorial Hospital in Gadsden) and the myriad of health care providers located in nearby Birmingham.

As he started his third year at the helm of RRMC in August 1993, Vollmer wondered whether the "proven corporate formula" for turnaround would be sufficient to stimulate growth in the coming years. Because of the autonomy accorded each hospital by the corporate office, Vollmer knew that HMA executives would look to him for specific strategies aimed at taking RRMC into the next century. He believed that simply improving operational inefficiencies was a necessary but not sufficient ingredient for future growth, and he supported Professor Elwood's perception that consumers would not freely choose physicians and hospitals who reacted to lost revenue and decreased market share by merely adopting a more intensive practice style or charging higher fees.[1] He recognized that the days of cost-shifting and price discrimination were coming to an end.

This case was prepared by Andrea Silvey, Donna J. Slovensky, and Woodrow D. Richardson from the University of Alabama at Birmingham. It is intended to be used as a basis for classroom discussion rather than to illustrate effective or ineffective handling of an administrative situation. Used with permission from Woody Richardson.

THE HEALTH CARE ENVIRONMENT

Current State of Affairs

Dissatisfaction with the current state of affairs was voiced by the popular vote in the 1992 presidential election. Health care costs had risen dramatically during the quarter century since implementation of Medicare and Medicaid in 1965. By 1992, health care costs accounted for as much as 14 percent of the GDP – more than $800 billion.[2]

Clinton was elected on a broad reform platform – promising economic recovery and health care system reform. The Clinton health care plan was intended to address two objectives: control of escalating costs and improved access for the more than 35 million underinsured and uninsured individuals in the United States.

Clinton's Health Care Reform Proposal

An interagency task force of more than 500 "experts," headed by Hillary Rodham Clinton, was chartered to formalize a proposal for system-wide health care reform. Despite media criticism, the task force operated under extreme secrecy in an effort to control the influence of special interests during the formulation phase. The information leaks employed to test public and political reaction to proposed funding mechanisms and coverage mandates engendered extreme opposition from legislators, providers, and payers. Public release of the proposal was delayed repeatedly, and health care reform at the national level was effectively gridlocked through the summer of 1993.

Clinton's health care reform proposal, The American Health Security Act, was introduced in Congress during October 1993. It included several main points. First, all Americans would be guaranteed coverage for a standard benefits package. Second, individuals would be permitted to choose from among plans offered through regional insurance purchasing pools. Third, premiums would be funded primarily by employers, who would pay 80 percent of the average plan cost. Individuals would be required to pay the remaining amount of the actual premium cost for the plan chosen.

Health Care Providers

Many of the more proactive players in the health care arena believed that bottom-up reform through state and local initiatives could be achieved more easily and would better protect individual provider interests than top-down reform. By 1993, several states (e.g., Oregon, Hawaii, Florida) had received waivers to implement alternative payment structures or purchasing coalitions. These "first movers" no doubt influenced the deliberations of the reform task force and served as models to stimulate others to attempt local market reform.

At the individual facility level, provider networks and managed care programs were initiated or expanded. Merrill Lynch (1993) predicted "In the larger urban areas, HMO's would . . . continue to be the coordinator and provider of health care services. However, in non-urban markets, . . . the hospital would be the cornerstone and coordinator of health care services for the health alliance purchasing cooperatives which would be formed under managed competition proposals."[3]

At the individual practitioner level, some experts insisted that the financial power base was moving away from solo practices and independent small groups toward integrated, cost competitive, comprehensive systems that produced a single patient bill including the charges of the physicians, the hospital, and the outpatient services. Integrated systems required a corporate structure to facilitate shared capitated risk. Over the past decade, mergers and other types of strategic alliances between physicians' practices, and hospitals and physicians' practices, had increased in an effort to reduce costs and become price competitive.

Small group practices often lacked the administrative and management expertise as well as the material resources necessary to improve efficiency. They were advised to look for such capabilities when they sought potential partners.

Many physicians remained skeptical of mergers, partnerships, and alliances offering any competitive advantage. That skepticism occurred most often in areas where managed care was absent or limited. Exhibit 18.1 shows the penetration of managed care throughout the regions of the country.

HEALTH MANAGEMENT ASSOCIATES

Health Management Associates was a professional hospital management company that operated acute care and psychiatric hospitals in nonurban areas in the southeastern and southwestern regions of the United States. The executive headquarters was located in Naples, Florida. Founded in 1977, the company went public in 1986. Unfortunately, the hospital management industry was out of favor with investors at that time, and despite solid growth earnings, the HMA shares did not perform well. A leveraged buyout in 1988 by the current management took the company private. However, in 1991 the company went public for the second time. In June 1992, the company's shares began trading on the New York Stock Exchange under the symbol *HMA*. Through all the corporate changes, HMA had maintained an efficient, tight-knit corporate structure, with only thirty-six employees, half of whom were in the clerical and support staff. Exhibit 18.2 contains information on corporate officers.

Corporate Philosophy and Mission

In 1992 HMA published "A Statement of Corporate Philosophy" that defined its goals and principles as a health care provider, employer, and publicly traded company. The corporate officers believed that success in the health care industry was determined by the ability of providers to deliver services in the most cost-effective and efficient manner possible. Their guiding objectives were stated as follows:

- Providing the highest quality service to our patients, physicians, and the communities we serve.
- Providing an attractive return on investment to those who are investors in our company.

EXHIBIT 18.1

Regional Penetration of Managed Care (market share of employer-sponsored insurance 1991)

	Northeast	North Central	South	West
Conventional	58%	55%	66%	16%
HMO	16	13	12	50
PPO	21	14	19	33
POS	5	18	3	1

Source: Merrill Lynch New Buy Recommendation, June 23, 1993.

EXHIBIT 18.2
HMA Corporate Officers' Background Information

Name	Age	Position	Year Elected
William J. Schoen	57	Chairman, Board of Directors, President and CEO	1983
Kent P. Dauten	37	Director	1981
Robert A. Knox	40	Director	1985
Charles R. Lees	73	Director	1988
Kenneth D. Lewis	45	Director	1991
Earl P. Holland	47	Executive Vice President, Operations and Development	1982
Kelly E. Curry	37	Executive Vice President and Chief Financial Officer	1985
Robb L. Smith	48	Senior Vice President and General Counsel, Corporate Secretary	1982
Stephen M. Ray	44	Senior Vice President, Administrative Services	1983

William J. Schoen joined the company's Board of Directors in February 1983, and in December 1983 became its president and chief operating officer. He became co-chief executive officer in December 1985, and chairman of the Board of Directors and chief executive officer in April 1986. From 1982 to 1987 Schoen was chairman of Commerce National Bank, Naples, Florida; and from 1973 to 1981 he was president, chief operating officer, and chief executive officer of the F & M Schafer Corporation, a consumer products company. From 1971 to 1983, Schoen was president of the Pierce Glass subsidiary of Indian Head, Inc., a diversified company. In addition to serving on the company's board, Schoen also serves on the Board of Directors of First Union National Bank of Florida.

Kent P. Dauten served as a director of the company from March 1981 through May 1983, and again from June 1985 through September 1988. He was again elected a director in November 1988. Dauten is a senior vice president of Madison Dearborn Partners, Inc. which is the management company both for Madison Dearborn Capital Partners, L.P., a private equity investment fund, and Madison Dearborn Advisors, L.P., that provides venture capital investment advisory services to First Chicago Corporation. Dauten was formerly a senior vice president of First Chicago Investment Corporation and First Capital Corporation of Chicago, the venture capital subsidiaries of First Chicago Corporation, where he had been employed in various investment management positions since 1979. He is a general partner of Madison Dearborn Partners, IV, a venture capital

EXHIBIT 18.2   cont'd

investment partnership. In addition, he serves on the Board of Directors of Genesis Health Ventures, Inc.

Robert A. Knox has been a director of the company since June 1985. Knox has been employed by The Prudential Insurance Company of America since 1975, and since 1984 he has been president of Prudential Equity Investors, Inc., a venture capital firm. He also serves on the Board of Directors of Lechters, Inc.

Charles R. Lees served as director of the company from April 1988 through September 1988. He was again elected a director in February 1989. Lees has been in the private practice of law, concentrating in tax matters, since May 1985. He was a project director for the Governor's Tax Reform Advisory Commission in California from August 1984 to September 1985. From 1979 to 1983 he was a visiting professor at the School of Accounting, University of Southern California. For more than twenty years prior to his retirement in 1979, Lees was a partner of the accounting firm of Peat, Marwick, Mitchell & Co. specializing in tax matters.

Kenneth D. Lewis was elected to the Company's Board of Directors in May 1991. He is president of NationsBank Corporation, a position that he has held since December 1991. Prior to that, Lewis was employed by NCNB Corporation in various capacities, including president of NCNB-Texas from 1988 to 1990, and president of NCNB National Bank of Florida from 1986 to 1988.

Earl P. Holland joined the company in 1981 as senior vice president—operations. He became senior vice president—marketing and development in 1984 and executive vice president—operations and development in 1989. For more than five years prior to 1981, he was employed by Humana, Inc., where he served as assistant regional vice president and executive director of two hospitals.

Kelly E. Curry, a certified public accountant, joined the company in 1982 and has served as director of internal audit and director of reimbursement. He became vice president—operations and finance in January 1985 and senior vice president and chief financial officer in 1987. In 1992, Curry was made executive vice president and chief financial officer. Prior to 1982, he was employed by Humana, Inc., and by Touche, Ross & Co.

Robb L. Smith joined the company as vice president and general counsel in 1981 after eleven years of private law practice in Louisville, Kentucky. His private practice included representing the company as outside counsel. Smith was appointed secretary in 1986, and senior vice president and general counsel in 1988.

Stephen M. Ray, a certified public accountant, joined the company in 1981 as controller and became a vice president in 1983. In 1992, Ray was promoted to senior vice president—administrative services. He served as treasurer from 1987 to 1988. He is currently responsible for the company's system-wide supply procurement and contract negotiations. From 1979 until 1981, Ray was employed by Hospital Affiliates International, Inc., a hospital management company, where he was responsible for reporting compliance and corporate technical accounting.

Source: Merrill Lynch et al. *Prospectus,* February 2, 1993.

- Providing employees with a satisfying and rewarding work environment.
- Functioning as a good corporate citizen in the communities we serve.
- Managing HMA in a manner that maintains uniform strength and identity while allowing individual hospitals the degree of independence necessary to maximize innovation and efficiency and meet the individual needs of the communities we serve.

Furthermore, they believed that the experience of contracting directly with employers to provide health care services would be very important in the future. For that reason, HMA had established its own PPO in some of the markets with low managed-care penetration.

Corporate Strategy

When originally established in 1977, HMA intended to compete as a national firm owning, leasing, and managing hospitals throughout the United States. In 1983 HMA redirected its focus to a niche of hospitals located in non-urban communities in the southeast and southwest with 20,000 to 150,000 in population. The officers believed the very nature and size of the facilities (generally 200 beds or fewer) located in nonurban communities precluded the individual, non-system-affiliated hospitals from attracting experienced and professional medical practitioners in each area of specialty. On the other hand, they believed that through system affiliation with HMA and its concomitant infusion of capital and management expertise, the same hospitals could be profitable.

In other words, to optimally penetrate the niche markets, HMA executives believed it was necessary to provide the management expertise and medical technology in specific areas to reduce costs, attract physicians, and increase the scope and quality of service within a profitable framework and to halt the outmigration of patients to larger metropolitan areas

for as many surgical procedures as possible. They believed that achieving these objectives allowed the communities they served to forge the viable and effective health care delivery facilities that their patients desperately needed.

Facilities

In 1992 HMA operated sixteen facilities. Thirteen were general acute-care hospitals (totaling 1,432 beds) that offered a broad range of inpatient and outpatient health services with an emphasis on primary care. Inpatient programs at all facilities included a broad range of medical and surgical services, diagnostic services, intensive and cardiac care, plus emergency services that were staffed by physicians at all times. At various facilities other specialty services such as full-service obstetrics, oncology, and industrial medicine were available. In addition, HMA also operated three freestanding psychiatric hospitals with a total of 226 beds. Exhibit 18.3 presents location, size, and other information concerning the corporation's facilities.

Selected Financial Data and Operating Statistics

As of June 1993, HMA's acute care hospitals accounted for 89 percent of the company's net operating revenue and 88 percent of the company's profit. The psychiatric hospitals accounted for the remaining 11 percent of revenue and 12 percent of profit. Exhibit 18.4 shows the very strong and stable financial performance of the corporation for fiscal years 1989 through 1992, along with selected operating statistics.

RIVERVIEW REGIONAL MEDICAL CENTER (RRMC)

The 281-bed acute-care facility at which Jon Vollmer was executive director, originally chartered as The Holy Name of Jesus Hospital,

EXHIBIT 18.3
HMA Facilities in 1992

Hospital	Location	Type	Licensed Beds	Owned/ Leased	Date Acquired
Paul B. Hall Regional Medical Center	Paintsville, KY	Acute Care	72	Owned	1/79
Williamson Memorial Hospital	Williamson, WV	Acute Care	76	Owned	6/79
Highlands Regional Medical Center	Sebring, FL	Acute Care	126	Leased	8/85
Lake Norman Regional Medical Center	Mooresville, NC	Acute Care Psychiatric	109 12	Owned	1/86
Palmview Hospital	Lakeland, FL	Psychiatric	66	Owned	5/86
Fishermen's Hospital	Marathon, FL	Acute Care	58	Leased	8/86
Franklin Regional Medical Center	Louisburg, NC	Acute Care Psychiatric	70 15	Owned	8/86
Biloxi Regional Medical Center	Biloxi, MS	Acute Care	153	Leased	9/86
Medical Center of Southeastern Oklahoma	Durant, OK	Acute Care	103	Owned	5/87
Crawford Memorial Hospital	Van Buren, AK	Acute Care	103	Leased	5/87
Hamlet Hospital	Hamlet, NC	Acute Care Psychiatric	54 10	Leased	8/87
Northeast Medical Center	Bonham, TX	Acute Care	65	Owned	10/87
Upstate Carolina Regional Medical Center	Gaffney, SC	Acute Care	125	Owned	3/88
University Behavioral Center	Orlando, FL	Psychiatric	100	Owned	1/89
Sandy Pines	Tequesta, FL	Psychiatric	60	Owned	1/90
Riverview Regional Medical Center	Gadsden, AL	Acute Care	281	Owned	7/91
Total Licensed Beds			1,658		

Source: Merrill Lynch et al., *Prospectus*, February 2, 1993.

was the first hospital built in Etowah County back in the 1940s. Owned and operated by an order of Catholic nuns, it remained under their ownership and control until financial considerations persuaded them to sell the hospital to HMA in August 1991. At that time the name was changed to Riverview Regional Medical Center.

EXHIBIT 18.4

HMA Summary of Financial and Other Information
(in thousands, except per share and other data)

| | Year Ended September 30 | | | |
	1989	1990	1991	1992
Income Statement				
Net operating revenue	$141,970	$191,661	$226,140	$277,961
Earnings before depreciation, interest, income tax	27,703	36,653	47,009	58,353
Income before income tax and extraordinary items	4,130	9,155	21,803	38,419
Extraordinary items	–	–	–	797
Net income	$1,980	$4,644	$11,991	$22,678
Earnings per share				
Before extraordinary items	.16	.37	.79	1.16
Extraordinary items	–	–	–	.04
Net income	$.16	$.37	$.79	$1.20
Weighted average number of shares outstanding	12,413	12,413	15,156	18,898

| | September 30, 1992 | |
	Actual	Adjusted
Balance Sheet[1]		
Working capital	$22,590	$47,195
Total assets	242,793	267,398
Total debt	67,644	67,644
Stockholders' equity	135,338	159,943

| | Year Ended September 30 | | | |
	1989	1990	1991	1992
Selected Operating Statistics				
Total hospitals owned or leased at end of period	13	15	16	16
Licensed beds at end of period	1,157	1,374	1,658	1,658
Admissions	30,251	36,412	40,217	46,756
Patient days	179,728	233,607	254,754	290,026
Acute-care average length of stay in days	5.4	5.6	5.5	5.6
Psychiatric average length of stay in days	20.7	21.9	22.5	17.7
Occupancy rate[2]	44%	49%	49%	48%
Outpatient utilization	22%	22%	25%	26%
Earnings before depreciation, interest, income tax	20%	19%	21%	21%

[1]Adjusted to reflect sale by the company of 1 million shares of Class A common stock.
[2]Hospital occupancy rates are affected by many factors, including the population size and general economic conditions within the service area, the degree of variation in medical and surgical services, outpatient use of hospital services, quality and treatment availability at competing hospitals, and seasonality. Generally, the company's hospitals experience a seasonal decline in occupancy in the first and fourth fiscal quarters.

Local Demographics

RRMC was located in the city of Gadsden, Etowah County, in northeastern Alabama. Etowah County was the ninth largest county in the state of Alabama. Exhibit 18.5 shows population growth in Alabama by county. Etowah County included twelve incorporated cities with a total population of 99,840 in 1993. Gadsden was the largest city in Etowah County. Exhibit 18.6 shows the relationship and proximity of the cities in Etowah County to one another.

Gadsden was a growing transportation hub connecting many of the major metropolitan areas in the southeastern region of the country. It was located at the southern foothills of the Appalachian Mountains in an area 60 miles northeast of Birmingham, 70 miles southeast of Huntsville, 110 miles west of Atlanta, and 95 miles southwest of Chattanooga. Situated astride Lookout Mountain and the Coosa River, the city had grown from sparsely populated Indian country in the early 1800s to a city with a population that peaked at more than 58,000 residents in the early 1960s. The population had since declined to slightly more than 42,500 residents. Exhibit 18.7 shows the population trends for Etowah County and Gadsden between 1940 and 1990.

Local Economy and Tax Base

As shown in Exhibit 18.8, Gadsden's employment market was based largely on industrial manufacturing. According to a 1992 Gallup Institute poll, the reasons given most frequently for young people leaving Etowah County in general and Gadsden in particular, had to do with lack of job opportunities in the area and better jobs elsewhere. More than 35 percent of the jobs in Etowah County were in manufacturing compared to only 16 percent of the jobs in Jefferson County (where the city of Birmingham was located). Exhibit 18.9 shows a comparison between the employment

opportunities in Etowah and Jefferson counties.

Only about 11 percent of the 476 Etowah County residents that participated in the survey rated the job market in their own county as very good or good. Exhibit 18.10 shows the largest employers in the area in 1993. Exhibit 18.11 shows the financial support of the community given by the county's top ten property taxpayers in 1991.

Health Care Competition

Both acute-care hospitals located in Gadsden were among the nine largest employers in the county. As mentioned earlier, unlike many of the other facilities operated by HMA, Riverview Regional Medical Center was neither the sole community provider nor even the dominant provider of health care in the market service area. Baptist Memorial Hospital (BMH) had approximately sixty more beds, and over twice as many employees as Riverview Regional Medical Center. Unlike the key BMH medical staff members, who were housed in a hospital-owned professional office building, RRMC's key medical staff members and group practices maintained separate offices throughout the city. For the most part, the two hospitals had a common medical staff membership, with the exception of the Emergency Department physicians. The composition of the medical staffs for RRMC and BMH is shown in Exhibit 18.12. Exhibit 18.13 shows a comparison of the services offered by Baptist Memorial Hospital and RRMC.

Primary Market Area. Baptist Memorial Hospital was a 346-bed nonprofit, nonaffiliated, acute-care community hospital. Although it was not owned by the Goodyear Tire and Rubber Company (Etowah county's largest employer and fourth largest taxpayer), it was located on the property adjacent to the Goodyear plant.

Recently, BMH had been approached by the director of the HEALTHSOUTH

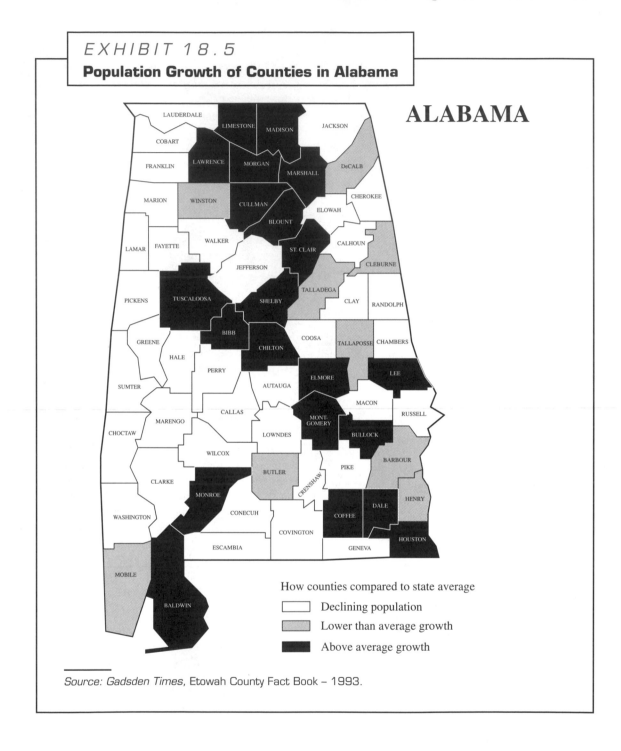

EXHIBIT 18.5

Population Growth of Counties in Alabama

ALABAMA

How counties compared to state average

☐ Declining population

▦ Lower than average growth

■ Above average growth

Source: Gadsden Times, Etowah County Fact Book – 1993.

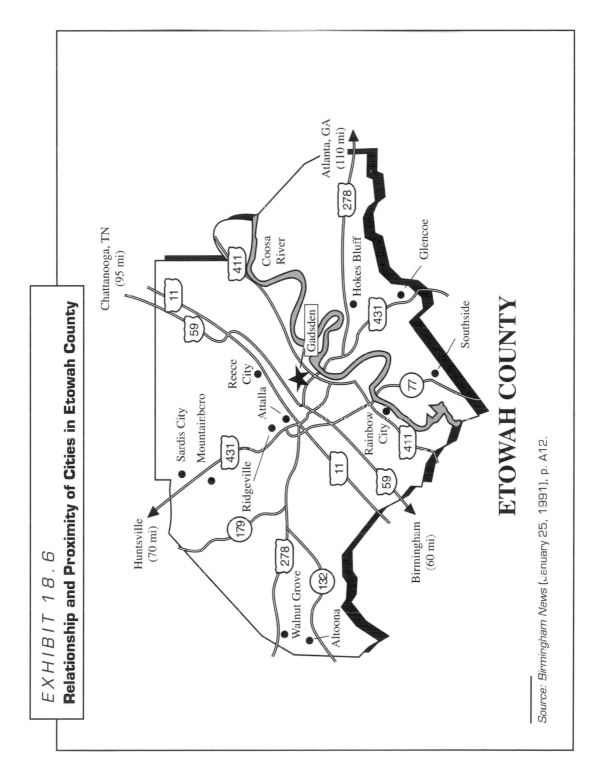

Source: *Birmingham News* (January 25, 1991), p. A12.

EXHIBIT 18.6
Relationship and Proximity of Cities in Etowah County

EXHIBIT 18.7
Population Trends, Etowah County/Gadsden 1960–1990

	1960	1970	1980	1990
Etowah County	**92,980**	**96,980**	**103,057**	**99,840**
Altoona	744	781	928	960
Attalla	8,257	7,510	7,737	6,859
Gadsden	58,088	53,928	47,565	42,523
Glencoe	2,592	2,901	4,648	4,670
Walnut Grove	237	224	510	717
Hokes Bluff	1,619	2,133	3,216	3,739
Rainbow City	1,626	3,107	6,792	7,673
Reece City	470	496	718	657
Southside	436	983	5,139	5,580
Mountainboro	—	311	266	261
Sardis City	—	368	883	1,301
Ridgeville	—	—	182	178

EXHIBIT 18.8
Selected Manufacturers of Etowah County

Name of Company	Number Employed	Year Est.	Location	Products
AAA Plumbing Pottery	151–200	1949	Gadsden	Vitreous china, plumbing fixtures
AMC Pattern and Tooling	1–5	1991	Rainbow City	Patterns
Accucare Health Technologies	6–10	1991	Gadsden	Pharmaceutical intravenous solutions
Airco Industrial Gas	1–5	1983	Gadsden	Oxygen, nitrogen, acetylene/welding supply distribution
Arkridge's Cabinet Shop, Inc.	1–5	1965	Gadsden	Custom cabinets
Alabama Contractors and Equipment	41–50	1957	Gadsden	Rent contract equipment and industrial supplies
Alabama Earth Products	1–5	1992	Gadsden	Sludge de-watering, animal feed ingredients, composting material
Alabama Easel Company	6–10	1970	Gadsden	Floral easels
Alabama Gas Corporation	51–75	1978	Gadsden	Public utility
Alabama Outdoor Advertising	11–15	1950	Gadsden	Advertising displays, outdoor advertising
Alabama Power Company	201–250	1907	Gadsden	Public utility

EXHIBIT 18.8   cont'd

Name of Company	Number Employed	Year Est.	Location	Products
Alabama Structural Beams	11–15	1949	Gadsden	Steel H-Beams for mobile homes
Associated Tool	21–30	1980	Gadsden	Dies, parts
Attalla Cabinet Works	1–5	1971	Attalla	Custom kitchen cabinets
AVCO Meat Company	41–50	1976	Gadsden	Pork processing
BACCA Sportswear	16–20	1992	Sardis	Cut and sew blue jeans
Barricks Manufacturing Company	21–30	1982	Gadsden	Institutional furniture
Bearings and Hydraulic Co.	1–5	1990	Gadsden	Hydraulic hose assembly, band saw blades, electric motors
Beaver Cleaning Systems	1–5	1983	Gadsden	Detergent chemicals
Betty Lane Bow Co.	76–100	1989	Gadsden	Hairbows and accessories
Bigelow Septic Tank Products Co.	6–10	1950	Attalla	Concrete septic tanks
Bin-Bak, Inc.	16–20	1984	Gadsden	Steel containers, container repairs
Birch Andersen and Company, Inc.	1–5	1915	Gadsden	Commercial printing
Boaz Lowbed International	31–40	1991	Gadsden	Semi trailers
Bolin Cabinet Shop	6–10	1949	Attalla	Kitchen cabinets for mobile homes
Bragg's Factory Outlet	6–10	1977	Glencoe	Storm windows, wood doors
Buffalo Rock Company, Inc.	101–150	1977	Gadsden	Bottling
Burns Fabricating Co.	1–5	1957	Gadsden	Step rails, fences, staircases, burglar bars
C & H Manufacturing	6–10	1992	Hokes Bluff	Truck parts, truck rebuilding
Calhoun Asphalt Company, Inc.	n/a	1948	Gadsden	Paving mix
Center Star Manufacturing	76–100	1991	Gadsden	T-shirts, sweat shirts, jogging pants
Choice Fabricators, Inc.	76–100	1979	Attalla	Sheet metal fabrication, stamping, precision machining
Cleaners Hangers Company, Inc.	41–50	1939	Gadsden	Wire garment hangers
Cloud Pulpwood Company	1–5	1940	Attalla	Logging, pulpwood
Cofield Quick Printing	1–5	1980	Rainbow City	Offset printing, quick signs, banners
Coil Clip, Inc.	11–15	1990	Gadsden	Metal cutting
Commercial Printing Co., Inc.	1–5	1945	Gadsden	Printing
Connie Signs	1–5	1940	Gadsden	Signs and advertising displays
Conservation Management, Inc.	6–10	1991	Gadsden	Non-hazardous waste water treatment plant

EXHIBIT 18.8   cont'd

Name of Company	Number Employed	Year Est.	Location	Products
Coosa Millwork and Components, Inc.	21–30	1971	Glencoe	Wood windows, door, custom cabinets
Coosa Valley Steel, Inc.	21–30	1977	Attalla	Steel fabrication
Craft Plating and Finishing Co., Inc.	11–15	1955	Attalla	Electroplating metals
Custom Creations	6–10	1988	Attalla	Athletic sportswear and uniforms
Data Preparation, Inc.	101–150	1971	Gadsden	Data processing
Dean Sausage Co., Inc.	51–75	1955	Attalla	Sausage processing and packing
Dixie-Pacific Mfg.Co., Inc.	151–200	1967	Gadsden	Colonial wood columns, turnposts
EMCO, Inc.	650–750	1978	Gadsden	Military ordnance
ESI Metals Corporation	51–75	1948	Gadsden	Sheet metal fabrication
East Gadsden Manufacturing	21–30	1991	Gadsden	Ladies' sportswear
Equity Group Alabama, Division of Keystone	301–350	1988	Gadsden	Further processed poultry
Etowah Asphalt Company, Inc.	6–10	1977	Attalla	Paving mix
Flowers Distributing Company	31–40	1989	Gadsden	Bakery product distribution
Gadsden Printing Company, Inc.	1–5	1930	Gadsden	Commercial printing
Gadsden Times	101–150	1861	Gadsden	Newspaper publishing, printing
Gadsden Tool Inc.	41–50	1985	Rainbow City	Tools
Goodyear Distribution Center	101–150	1952	Gadsden	Tire warehousing / distribution
Goodyear Tire and Rubber Co., Inc.	2,001–2,500	1929	Gadsden	Automobile, truck, tractor tires, tubes, tread rubber
Gulf States Steel, Inc.	2,001–2,500	1986	Gadsden	Carbon steel plates, hot/cold rolled steels
Haney Company	51–75	1952	Glencoe	Custom machines, machine parts
Hanna Steel Corporation	41–50	1953	Gadsden	Steel processing (service center)
Holiday Lamp and Lighting, Inc.	21–30	1982	Glencoe	Lamps, lighting fixtures
International Jets, Inc.	6–10	1989	Gadsden	Aircraft purchase and reassembly
Jeffrey's Steel Co., Inc.	21–30	1989	Attalla	Steel fabrication
Jones Sawmill Inc.	21–30	1925	Gadsden	Lumber, sawed and planed
KANS, Inc.	41–50	1985	Rainbow City	Refuse containers
Kentucky Farm Kitchens	21–30	1992	Attalla	Pre-cooked sausage products
L B Chemical Company, Inc.	6–10	1950	Gadsden	Commercial chemicals, soaps, detergents

EXHIBIT 18.8 cont'd

Name of Company	Number Employed	Year Est.	Location	Products
L & M Matkin Machine Shop	6–10	1991	Sardis	Screw machine products
Lemanco	51–75	1958	Gadsden	Storage bins, containers, silos
Liberty Trouser Company	76–100	1988	Altoona	Men's, boys', and children's trousers
Liberty Trouser Company	101–150	1991	Sardis	Men's, boys', and children's trousers
M & M Chemical Co., Inc.	41–50	1976	Attalla	Solvent distillation, fuel from ignitable liquid waste
Martin's Grill Meats	21–30	1939	Gadsden	Beef processing and packaging
Max Packaging Co.	51–75	1990	Attalla	Plastic tableware
Meadow Gold Dairies, Inc.	151–200	1956	Gadsden	Dairy products, juices
Mid-South Electrics, Inc.	451–550	1977	Gadsden	Appliances, computer assemblies, electric assemblies
Mindis Recycling Inc.	101–150	1947	Attalla	Metal processing
Miss Martha Originals, Inc.	76–100	1980	Glencoe	Doll figurines
Osborn Brothers, Inc.	76–100	1947	Gadsden	Commercial food distribution
Post Welding Supply Company	10–15	1943	Rainbow City	Welding supplies
Praxair (formerly Union Carbide)	41–50	1961	Gadsden	Oxygen, nitrogen, argon
Rainbow Mattress Co., Inc.	11–15	1920	Gadsden	Mattresses, boxsprings
Sherman Ready-Mix Co.	31–40	1921	Glencoe	Ready-mix concrete, concrete block
South Central Bell	151–200	1883	Gadsden	Telephone communications
Stamped Products	31–40	1983	Glencoe	Metal stamping
Stephenson Diversified Electronics, Inc.	75–100	1988	Gadsden	Electronic circuit boards
Trambeam Corp.	41–50	1983	Attalla	Overhead cranes, monorails, miscellaneous fabricated products
Tyson Feed Mill	31–40	1987	Attalla	Feed Grains
Tyson Foods, Inc.	1,001–1,500	1970	Gadsden	Poultry processing
Vulcan Materials Co., Inc.	11–15	1930	Glencoe	Crushed stone

EXHIBIT 18.9
Comparison of Etowah and Jefferson County Employment

Industry		Number of Employees Week of 3/12/93	Total Number of Establishments	Number of Establishments by Employment-Size Class								
				1–4	5–9	10–19	20–49	50–99	100–249	250–499	500–999	1000+
Total												
Jefferson	1988	304,181	17,271	8,655	3,602	2,325	1,658	579	318	74	37	23
Etowah	1988	30,266	1,949	1,012	419	264	171	48	25	3	5	2
Etowah	1990	31,319	1,948	964	474	251	170	55	36	3	3	3
Agriculture/ Forestry/Fishing												
Jefferson	1988	871	120	66	28	18	7	—	1	—	—	—
Etowah	1988	35	9	5	4	—	—	—	—	—	—	—
Etowah	1990	29	11	9	2	—	—	—	—	—	—	—
Construction												
Jefferson	1988	26,730	1,352	645	276	194	150	48	28	5	4	2
Etowah	1988	1,494	136	65	30	20	15	4	2	—	—	—
Etowah	1990	1,382	149	72	30	20	13	5	—	—	—	—
Manufacturing												
Jefferson	1988	47,755	839	232	148	138	141	87	59	252	4	5
Etowah	1988	11,223	120	29	17	21	33	7	6	2	3	2
Etowah	1990	11,129	138	41	25	18	28	10	10	—	1	3

Transportation and Public Utilities

	Year											
Jefferson	1988	31,018	525	211	77	74	89	36	25	3	3	7
Etowah	1988	1,356	65	22	18	9	8	4	4	—	—	—
Etowah	1990	1,285	72	28	14	14	10	3	3	—	—	—

Wholesale Trade

	Year											
Jefferson	1988	26,260	1,746	697	397	320	230	71	23	7	1	—
Etowah	1988	1,461	140	59	33	31	13	3	1	—	—	—
Etowah	1990	1,601	135	55	35	27	12	3	3	—	—	—

Retail Trade

	Year											
Jefferson	1988	58,237	4,150	1,789	1,059	620	449	148	76	7	2	—
Etowah	1988	6,800	585	284	143	81	51	18	8	—	—	—
Etowah	1990	6,785	568	247	187	71	53	19	11	—	—	—

Finances, Insurance, and Real Estate

	Year											
Jefferson	1988	29,343	1,761	1,027	519	199	135	35	27	9	7	3
Etowah	1988	1,250	136	79	18	19	17	3	—	—	—	—
Etowah	1990	1,268	145	86	22	16	16	5	—	—	—	—

Services

	Year											
Jefferson	1988	82,859	5,708	3,059	1,231	721	439	150	73	16	13	6
Etowah	1988	6,421	637	363	148	76	34	9	5	—	2	—
Etowah	1990	7,614	666	360	166	82	37	10	8	1	2	—

EXHIBIT 18.10

Gadsden/Etowah County Largest Employers, June 1993

Company	Number Employed
Goodyear Tire and Rubber Company	2,300
Gulf States Steel Corporation	1,950
Mid-South Industries	1,340
Dixie Tool and Die	155
EMCO, Inc.	600
Mid South Corporate	18
Mid South Electric	455
Mid South Product Engineering	21
Precision Automatics	22
Stamped Products, Inc.	31
Weaver Division Machining	38
Tyson Foods	1,300
Baptist Memorial Hospital	1,190
Etowah County Board of Education	860
Gadsden City Schools	791
Riverview Regional Medical Center	550
City of Gadsden	542
Gadsden State Community College[1]	470
Gregerson's Foods	350
Equity Group of Alabama	350
Wal-Mart[2]	335
Etowah County	250
Liberty Trouser Company[2]	220
Attalla City Schools	200
Center Star Manufacturing	193
K-Mart[2]	189
South Central Bell	189
Alabama Power Company	178
AAA Plumbing Pottery	175
Dixie Pacific Manufacturing	174
Meadow Gold Dairies	155
Mountain View Hospital	145
Sears	130
Buffalo Rock Company, Inc.	119
Mindis Metals, Inc.	115
Gadsden Times Publishing	114
McRae's	110
Department of Human Resources	103
Miss Martha Originals	100

[1]Three campus locations.
[2]All locations within the county.
Source: Gadsden Times, County Fact Book – 1993.

EXHIBIT 18.11
Etowah County Top Property Taxpayers, 1991

Taxpayer	Real Property	Personal Property
Gulf States Steel	$333,009.62	$1,031,588.46
Alabama Power	1,057,909.04	–
South Central Bell	552,987.15	–
Goodyear	181,806.66	299,042.03
Gadsden Mall	151,669.70	897.68
Tyson Foods	45,978.96	56,074.94
Alabama Gas	98,627.74	–
Riverview Regional Medical Center	93,985.92	59,326.26
Alabama Great Southern	45,589.90	–
Hopper Telephone	35,860.14	–

Source: Gadsden Times, Etowah County Fact Book – 1993.

EXHIBIT 18.12
Number of Medical Staff by Area of Specialization

Specialty Area	BMH	RRMC	Specialty Area	BMH	RRMC
Allergy, Asthma, and Immunology	0	3	Oncology	1	1
Anesthesiology	10	10	Ophthalmology	4	4
Cardiology	8	5	Oral Surgery/Dentistry	6	5
Dermatology	2	1	Orthopedic Surgery	6	3
Emergency Medicine	9	6	Otolaryngology	0	4
Facial/Cosmetic Surgery	1	1	Pathology	4	4
Family Practice	21	12	Pediatrics	10	7
Gastroenterology	4	3	Plastic/Reconstructive Surgery	1	1
General/Vascular Surgery	12	12	Psychiatry	4	1
Internal Medicine	15	17	Pulmonary Disease	2	1
Nephrology	2	1	Radiology	3	3
Nepurology	2	3	Thoracic/Cardiac/Vascular Surgery	2	2
Obstetrics/Gynecology	9	4	Urology	4	3

Source: Riverview Regional Medical Center and Baptist Memorial Hospital company documents.

EXHIBIT 18.13

Major Services Offered by BMH and RRMC

Services	BMH	RRMC
24-Hour Emergency Services	✓	✓
Angioplasty	✓	x
Arthrectomy	✓	✓
Birthing Room	✓	✓
Blood Bank	✓	✓
Cancer Center Chemotherapy	✓	✓
Cardiac Catheterization Laboratory	✓	✓
Care-A-Van	✓	x
COPD Services	✓	✓
Community Health Promotion	✓	x
CT Scanning	✓	✓
Education Department	✓	✓
Endoscopy/Gastroenterology	✓	✓
Heart Center	✓	x
Histopathology Laboratory	✓	✓
Home Health Services	✓	✓
Hospice Organization	✓	x
Hospital Auxiliary	✓	✓
Intensive Care unit—Cardiac	✓	✓
Intensive Care Unit—Medical	✓	✓
Intensive Care Unit—Surgical	✓	✓
Lifeline Personal Emergency Response	✓	✓
Lithotripsy	✓	x
Magnetic Resonance Imaging	✓	x
Neurodiagnostic Services/Electroencephalogram	✓	✓
Nuclear Medicine	x	✓
Obstetrical Services	✓	✓
Occupational Therapy	✓	x
Open Heart Surgery	✓	✓
Outpatient Surgery	✓	✓
Pastoral Care	✓	x
Pediatric Acute Inpatient Services	✓	✓
Physical Therapy	✓	✓
Psychiatric Services	✓	x
Radiation Oncology	✓	x
Respiratory Therapy Services	✓	✓
Social Work Services	✓	✓
Speech-Language Pathology	x	✓
Stroke Clinic	x	✓
Support Group—Arthritis	✓	✓
Support Group—Cancer	✓	✓
Support Group—Compassionate Friends	x	x
Support Group—Diabetes	✓	✓
Support Group—Head Trauma	✓	x
Support Group—Multiple Sclerosis	✓	✓
Support Group—Ostomy	✓	x
Support Group—Spinal Cord Injury	✓	x
Surgical Services—General	✓	✓
Surgical Services—Laparoscopic	✓	✓
Surgical Services—Neurological	✓	✓
Surgical Services—Oncological	✓	✓
Surgical Services—Ophthalmological	✓	✓
Surgical Services—Oral	✓	✓
Surgical Services—Orthopedic	✓	✓
Surgical Services—Plastic and Reconstructive	✓	x
Surgical Services—Vascular	✓	✓
Tel-Med Tape Library	✓	x
Ultrasound	✓	✓
Walking Club	✓	x
Women's HealthPLUS	✓	x

Source: Adapted from *Gadsden Times, Etowah County Fact Book—1993.*

✓ = service offered   X = service not offered

Corporation in Birmingham regarding the possibility of establishing some sort of joint-venture rehabilitation service in Gadsden. Baptist Memorial Hospital was an aggressive competitor that made extensive use of newspaper advertising, promoting an image of clinical superiority as shown in Exhibit 18.14. Also, since HMA's acquisition and secularization of Gadsden's formerly Catholic hospital, Baptist Memorial Hospital placed increasingly greater emphasis on its own status as "A Christian Medical Center."

The only other competitor for inpatient services in Gadsden was Mountain View Hospital, a psychiatric and chemical dependency hospital for children, adolescents, and adults. Although Mountain View Hospital was not a direct competitor of RRMC by virtue of its target population, it nonetheless influenced the local market forces with respect to certain health care services.

Mountain View Hospital implemented professional and educational programs that brought in national specialists in the field of mental health. Through a relationship with Northeast Alabama Psychiatric Services, neuropsychiatry (focusing on mental or behavioral disorders resulting from head injury and trauma) was available as well as extensive outpatient services. In addition, the hospital specialized in child and adolescent treatment of attention deficit hyperactivity disorders. In June 1991, an adult psychiatric unit was opened to treat depression, stress, anxiety, and panic attacks. An intensive care center for psychiatric care was opened in January 1993. Other services provided by Mountain View Hospital included substance abuse treatment, a year-round academic program, a state-licensed private school, partial hospitalization, community education, and a free twenty four-hour crisis evaluation. Physicians were being recruited from various nationally respected hospitals throughout the country with specialized areas of expertise in the field of mental health.

Outmigration to Birmingham. None of the hospitals in Gadsden could ignore the opportunity for residents to travel outside the local area for nonemergency care. As shown earlier in Exhibit 18.6, Gadsden's proximity to the interstate network facilitated outmigration to urban areas boasting larger medical facilities. Although exact figures were unknown, the volume was estimated to be in excess of 25 percent.

The Birmingham metropolitan area included approximately twenty hospitals, many of which offered specialty programs attractive to individuals who were predisposed to self-select health care services. Among those hospitals were HEALTHSOUTH, an internationally acclaimed sports medicine and rehabilitation facility, Baptist Medical Centers, Carraway Methodist Medical Center, Children's Hospital of Alabama, Brookwood Medical Center, the Eye Foundation Hospital, the Veterans' Administration Medical Center, and the University of Alabama at Birmingham (UAB) Medical Center.

The UAB Medical Center campus was located approximately one hour's drive from Gadsden via Interstate 59. It was an internationally acclaimed patient care, education, and research complex, comprising the Schools of Medicine, Dentistry, Nursing, Optometry, Health Related Professions, and Public Health, the University of Alabama Hospital, and several of the specialty hospitals mentioned previously.

The medical center was dominated by the University of Alabama Hospital, a 903-bed teaching facility with more than fifty clinical services. University Hospital encompassed the Alabama Heart Hospital, the Lurleen Wallace Complex for comprehensive cancer treatment, Spain Rehabilitation Center, and the Diabetes Hospital. More than twenty-five educational, instructional, and patient care "centers of excellence" and approximately twenty specialty units providing treatment, screening, and laboratory services were sponsored by the hospital.

Alabama's Reputation For Heart Surgery Is Worldwide.

Your Closest Point Of Access:

Gadsden

Now you and your family don't have to go any farther than Gadsden to take advantage of Alabama's world renowned treatment for heart problems. Open heart surgeries are being performed daily right here at the **Baptist Heart Center**, part of Baptist Memorial Hospital.

Dr. Terry Robinson and Dr. Alan Stansfield, both Board Certified cardiovascular surgeons, are members of the Heart Center's highly trained and experienced staff. They have at their disposal the most modern equipment, the latest techniques and the finest support staff available for this lifesaving operation.

Home is where the heart is. And right here at home is where you'll find the best care and treatment for your heart.

 Share The Vision

Baptist Memorial Hospital
A Christian Medical Center
Gadsden, Alabama

The University of Alabama Hospital was third in a listing of the top twenty-five hospitals in the United States in *The Best in Medicine.*[4]

The medical staff (faculty for the UAB School of Medicine) practiced privately in the Kirklin Clinic, an ultra-modern, high-technology facility that opened in 1992. The multispecialty Kirklin Clinic marketed aggressively throughout and beyond the Birmingham market area.

Operational Changes at RRMC

HMA named Jon Vollmer as executive director of RRMC in August 1991. Vollmer had more than ten years of experience in hospital administration and held an MBA from Cornell University. Early in his tenure at RRMC, Jon introduced substantial tangible and intangible changes into the organization. The members of the administrative team changed to some degree, as a new financial officer was brought on board in the reorganization and the data processing manager chose to make a lateral move within the hospital when HMA's proprietary cost management and information systems were implemented. Downsizing was initiated through consolidation of jobs, elimination of some positions, and attrition. In all, staffing decreased by about sixty full-time-equivalent positions. These changes occurred without reducing the services offered by RRMC.

Policies at RRMC were revised to decentralize decision making and give the department heads more operational control. The organizational culture began evolving from the previous one of strict conformity (under the administration of the nuns) that discouraged risk taking and participation in problem solving, to a culture in which the administrator was much more visible throughout the hospital and encouraged and reinforced employees' and management's input. Four new physicians were recruited and added to the staff in the areas of internal medicine, general surgery, pediatrics, and neurology. Recently, two additional physicians were added to the Emergency Department.

All of these changes were in keeping with the objectives of a well-orchestrated plan that included improving bottom-line accountability by spending the capital necessary to bring the facility up-to-date, increase efficiency, and improve accounts receivables and to expand and improve the services offered based on the geographic, demographic, and economic characteristics of the community.

Although the overall turnaround strategy was formulated at the corporate level, the details for implementation were developed and refined at the hospital level through the work of the administrative team and the managers, with particular support from the Board of Trustees and the marketing department.

Physical Plant Changes at RRMC

Physical changes in the plant were begun on a large scale. Facility renovations and relocation of clinical services left an older wing of the hospital vacant. The most notable physical improvements were in the Emergency Department (ED), which was completely remodeled to a level of medical sophistication usually observed only in larger urban hospitals. The ED was expanded to eighteen patient treatment rooms with monitoring capabilities that included hardwire and telemetry electrocardiograms, noninvasive blood pressure measurement, noninvasive arterial blood gases, respiratory rate, and temperature. The ED was supported by a full-service, fully equipped twenty-four hour lab, and state-of-the-art CT and ultrasound imaging units. Medical staffing was provided twenty-four hours a day, seven days a week, by six emergency physicians from Emergency Medical Services Associates, a specialty group practice based in Atlanta, Georgia. Although annual patient visits to the ED had increased from 23,000 to 26,000 since the renovation, excess capacity still existed.

New capital purchases increased the hospital's technological capabilities, and new services and programs were added in areas such as women's health, where the previous administration had not kept pace with the community's needs. In addition, Rehab Care (an independent service provider) had recently approached Vollmer about leasing a twenty-bed unit. Not only were clinical services changing, but innovative programs such as Nurse First and MedKey, aimed at marketing the hospital's new efficient and upscale image, were also implemented.

Innovative Programs

The Nurse First program, developed and instituted by the Emergency Department staff in conjunction with the physical plant renovations, was conceptualized as an advanced triage system. Patients were observed and immediately assessed upon entering the emergency room, prior to registration and nonmedical processing. No longer did paperwork take precedence over patient treatment.

The MedKey system employed computer technology to streamline patient registration and admission procedures through the use of a plastic "smart card" with a magnetic strip on which pertinent patient information was encoded and changed quickly and easily, as necessary. Initially, MedKey translated into increased operational efficiency and better service for patients by substantially decreasing the amount of time required to process an admission and verify insurance coverage. Both of these programs portrayed a patient-oriented rather than a profit-oriented image.

Marketing

Subsequently the MedKey system was exploited as a focused marketing strategy that used the patient data base to promote RRMC facility utilization through membership in-

centives and rewards via discounts and extra services for MedKey "members." Marketing efforts were directed at recruiting individual members and employer-group memberships. As a marketing vehicle, MedKey was viewed by Vollmer as more effective and cost efficient than mass advertising.

An in-house newsletter featuring new and existing programs and services as well as new benefits for MedKey members, was developed and mailed on a regular basis. Promotional flyers were developed and mailed to inform members of upcoming events and activities. A recent flyer promoted RRMC's cardiac services as shown in Exhibit 18.15.

By August 1993, there were 17,000 individual MedKey members. Exhibit 18.16 provides a listing of the companies that added momentum toward a WIN/WIN/WIN relationship between area businesses, RRMC, and MedKey members. The hospital would win by improving its membership incentives through the discounts provided by the cosponsoring enterprises. The companies would win by reaching a larger market through the hospital's direct-mailings to the ever-growing list of MedKey members to promote upcoming events, new services, and membership discounts. The members would win by receiving savings on services at RRMC as well as savings on the products and services of cosponsoring enterprises.

The Future of RRMC

As Jon Vollmer considered the progress of RRMC over the past two years, he was pleased with the results. Operational efficiencies and the quality of the physical plant had improved markedly. However, he knew that these improvements would not be sufficient to garner the growth expected by HMA management in the years to come. A guiding strategy must be adopted to provide a point of reference, an anchored perspective upon which to base all future administrative decisions in order to

EXHIBIT 18.15
RRMC Promotional Flyer

Dear MED-KEY Member,

You're invited to be our guest on Tuesday or Wednesday, August 10th and 11th, when Riverview Regional Medical Center hosts a healthful and hearty celebration to announce The Chest Pain Unit in our Emergency Center and the opening of our newly redesigned Third Floor Coronary Care facility. As a MED-KEY member, you will receive:

 **Free**
... cholesterol screenings
... heart disease profile testing
... blood pressure screenings

 Information about THE CHEST PAIN UNIT in Riverview's Emergency Center

 *The·Chest·Pain·Unit*

 25 percent discount on HEART HEALTHY lunch and dinner menu items in the Riverview Cafeteria

 PLUS educational material from the American Heart Association on the prevention and treatment of heart disease.

Tuesday, August 10th	**R.S.V.P**
Wednesday, August 11th	**Call 543-5440,**
12 noon until 6:00 p.m.	**543-5874**
Third Floor	**or 543-5785**

As you know, Riverview Regional Medical Center has long been a leader in the treatment of heart disease in Northeast Alabama. Riverview was the first hospital to offer cardiac catheterization services in this area and the region's first open heart surgery was performed at Riverview in 1982. We provide a full range of services for our coronary patients including balloon angioplasty and cardiac rehabilitation.

And now The Chest Pain Unit in Riverview Regional's Emergency Center stands ready to serve you and your family around the clock. Patients experiencing chest pain receive immediate medical evaluation by a team of doctors and nurses skilled in emergency cardiac care. The Chest Pain Unit features monitored beds, specialized equipment, supplies and medications -- including "CLOT BUSTERS", advanced forms of early heart attack treatment.

For more information, telephone 543-5440 or 543-5874

 **RIVERVIEW**
Regional Medical Center
600 South Third Street in Gadsden

EXHIBIT 18.16
Healthy Discounts Directory

Arby's in Gadsden and Boaz
15% on Price of Meal

Apple-A-Day Health World
Inside Gregerson's Midtown Plaza
10% on Natural Vitamin

Brice Thomas Radiator
5% on Stock Items

Cellular ONE
New Customers—10% on Equipment
Existing Customers—60 min. Free Airtime

Colours Paint & Decorating Center
Buy 1 Roll Wallpaper—Get 2nd ½ Price

Days Inn
10% for Visiting Family Members

Dominoes Pizza (four locations)
10% on Menu Price Items

Flowers By Rita's One Hour Photo
10% on Film—Discounts on Developing

Framing Plus
10% on Menu Priced Items

Fuller Medical
10% on Non-Medicare Covered Items

Gadsden Motor Inn
10% on Regular Room Rate

Gaines Florist in Boaz
10% on All Arrangements

George Gruver Optical
10% on All Services

Gingerbread House
Free Wrapping, Delivery and Mailing

Gregerson's Pharmacy
Wholesale Price Plus $1.00

Hick's Shoe Store
10% on All Merchandise

Herb Ford Photography
25% on Photograph Copies

Holiday Inn in Attalla
25% on Regular Room Rate

International Tours of Gadsden
$25.00 off Cruise Trip

Joy's Flowers
10% on Cash & Carry Order over $10.00

King's Pool World
Free Local SPA Delivery, Chemical Kit
Cleaner & Additional $50.00 on SPA Purchase

Klingbeck's Optical Dispensary
15% on Prescription Eyewear

Little Ceasar's Pizza (2 locations)
10% on Menu Priced Items

Little Rascal's Kids Clothing
10% on Regular Priced Items

Merry Maids
$10.00 off First Cleaning

Nelson's Variety
5% on All Merchandise

Noble Yocum Photography
10% on Minimum Wedding Coverage

Northeast Alabama Audiology Clinic
10% on All Services

Pasquale's Pizza in Boaz
$2.00 on 15″ Regular Priced Pizza

PC Land Computers, INC.
10% on Software—5% on Hardware

Piggly Wiggly Pharmacy in Boaz
Wholesale Plus $1.00

**Pizza Huts in Gadsden and Attalla
(3 locations)**
10% on Price of Meal (Buffet Excluded)

Physicians Home Health Care
10% on Cash Purchases

p.k. yates printing
10% on Business Cards

Rainbow City Western Store
10% on Non-Sale Items

Rials Plumbing
10% on Labor

Regis Hairstylist
10% on Regis Services & Regis Products

Shepherd's Heart Christian Bookstore
10% on Non-Sale Items

Southside Academy
No Registration Fee When You Pay for Initial
3 Weeks

Subway Sandwiches and Salads
in Gadsden, Rainbow City and Boaz
10% on Price of a Meal

**Taco Bell in Gadsden and Attalla
(4 locations)**
10% on Price of a Meal

Tee Shirt Limited
10% on Non-Sale Items

Villa Fiesta Mexican Restaurant
10% on Price of Meal

Willows Gift Shop
10% on All Merchandise

Western Sizzlin in Gadsden and Fort Payne
10% on Price of a Meal

Works of Art Restaurant
10% on Price of a Meal

achieve smooth implementation of the ultimate plan. Vollmer reflected on the potential of several approaches he was considering to achieve growth in a declining market area. How could he maximize utilization of the newly renovated emergency department? What could be done with unused space in older sections of the building? What about leasing portions of it to other providers? Should a lease proposal be evaluated on contribution to profits alone? What other criteria might be appropriate? What new services or products could be developed with existing facilities? What services should be strengthened and promoted to control out-migration from the primary market service area? How could the hospital best position itself to deal with impending health care reforms? Did the demographics of Etowah County suggest or provide an alternative course of action? Could RRMC establish relationships with the various smaller businesses that form the industrial base of the county?

Vollmer knew that modifications to HMA's efficiency-focused "success formula" would need to be made in the near future and he was contemplating what crucial information was necessary to support any proposals he would make. Although the trend toward managed care presented an opportunity for RRMC, the medical staff as a group opposed the PPO concept and the majority of large businesses in the area were insured by Blue Cross. For the plan to have optimum strategic value, Vollmer recognized that proposals for future activity and growth must seriously consider the increasing political movement toward simpler and more comprehensive service arrangements.

NOTES

1. P. M. Elwood, Jr., "Alternative Delivery Systems: Health Care on the Move," *Journal of Ambulatory Care Medicine* 8, no. 4 (1985), pp. 1–30.
2. T. W. Elwood, "A View from Washington—Health Care Reform: Part I," *Journal of Allied Health* 22, no. 2 (1993), pp. 195–204.
3. Merrill Lynch, *Health Management Associates, New Buy Recommendation,* June 23, 1993.
4. H. J. Dietrich and V. H. Biddle, *The Best in Medicine* (New York: Harmony Books, 1986).

Mercy Health Services

"Today in the United States, Catholic health care extends the mission of the Church in every State of the Union, in major cities, small towns, rural areas, on the campuses of academic institutions, in remote outposts, and in inner-city neighborhoods. By providing health care in all these places, especially to the poor, the neglected, the needy, the newcomer, your apostolate penetrates and transforms the very fabric of American society."

—Pope John Paul II
September 14, 1987
Address to the Catholic
Health Association
Phoenix, Arizona

Judith Pelham became president and CEO of Mercy Health Services (MHS) in February 1993. In doing so, she assumed a key leadership role in the nation's second-largest Catholic

This case was prepared by Monty L. Lynn of Abilene Christian University and is intended to be used as a basis for class discussion rather than to illustrate either effective or ineffective handling of the situation. Appreciation is expressed to Maxine Kollasch for providing information for the case. Presented and accepted by the Midwest Society for Case Research. All rights reserved to the author and the MSCR. Copyright © 1994 by Monty L. Lynn. Used with permission from Monty Lynn.

health care system. MHS is ranked in the top 500 employers in the United States and has a total of $1.8 billion in assets. But it is not size alone that distinguishes MHS from other providers; its mission sets it apart as well. MHS's mission is not only to accept indigent care but to *seek out* opportunities to provide medical care for the poor (see Exhibit 19.1).

In accepting the presidency, Pelham was faced with managing a continuing challenge – how to pursue a mission of maximizing medical care to the poor and yet remain financially sound. In today's health care marketplace, such a task requires perceptive strategy as well as divine guidance. For although MHS's mission may separate it from some, it operates in the same competitive environment as other voluntary and proprietary providers. In the face of health care reform, shifting alliances, and increasing competitiveness, Pelham and her MHS colleagues must answer the question, "What strategy and tactics should MHS pursue to ensure strategically and financially sound delivery of care to the poor?" She knew that a good understanding of MHS history was important to set the stage for the future.

INDIGENT CARE

Many voluntary hospitals in nineteenth century America were created to provide lodging for poor and traveling persons who became ill.[1] Catholic orders established hospitals in large

EXHIBIT 19.1

Mercy Health Services Vision Statement

Catherine McAuley, foundress of the Sisters of Mercy, heeded the call of Jesus to reach out with courage and love to the needy of her time. Inspired by her personal interaction with Dublin's poor and by the centuries-old tradition of the Roman Catholic Church, Catherine created new and more responsive structures to meet needs unmet by current social structures. She gathered about her dedicated persons, lay and religious, and she trained women to exercise specific skills and general leadership with both competency and compassion. Catherine chided those responsible for service to be more responsive to the need, "not next week, but today."

Today, Mercy Health Services, under the sponsorship of the Sisters of Mercy Regional Community of Detroit, continues these efforts to provide health care to people in need, giving priority to those who are economically poor. Our organization depends on the energies of many dedicated persons serving throughout the system whose values enhance the mission of Mercy Health Services. In our service and through our influence, Mercy Health Services is striving to promote a society that assures access to needed health services for all, provided with dignity, competency, and compassion.

Catherine McAuley's example and inspiration translate to present and future needs. In a rapidly shifting health care environment marked by complexity, competition, high technology and fragmented service, a compassionate, direct response to human need remains essential. What must be central in our service, regardless of future change, is that persons deserve quality care, that systems exist to serve human needs, and that respect for the dignity of every person constitutes a fundamental principle of our action. Mercy Health Services is growing in the understanding that individuals have primary responsibility for their health and that the earth is the primary health resource. A healthy environment will be necessary for healthy people. Working with others who hold common values and relying on God's care will be essential to the works of Mercy in the present and future.

Within this framework, Mercy Health Services will work toward creating the future envisioned in these statements:

I. Mercy Health Services will apply the values and spirit of the Sisters of Mercy throughout its health care ministry.

II. Mercy Health Services will demonstrate a preferential option for the economically poor.

III. Mercy Health Services will work with others in providing comprehensive health services to improve the health status of the communities we serve.

IV. Mercy Health Services will work with other health care providers to facilitate intercongregational and lay-sponsored health care in order to strengthen Catholic health care in the United States.

V. Mercy Health Services will participate in shaping public policy to improve health status at local, state, national and international levels, emphasizing in these efforts the needs of the economically poor.

VI. Mercy Health Services will assist people in taking responsibility for their own health by actively promoting wellness and facilitating healing.

and small communities across the United States beginning in about 1840. Due to increased need and efficacy of institutional care, hospitals became more attractive to middle and upper income groups after 1900. Hill-Burton legislation in 1946 and Medicaid and Medicare legislation in 1965 provided additional revenues for growth and services but also weakened the welfare role of hospitals. Although hospitals could not add indigent costs to Medicaid or Medicare reimbursements, the revenues granted were generous enough to help cover bad debts. Many hospitals paid for charity care by shifting costs to commercially insured patients.

Rapidly rising health care costs earned the attention of federal, state, and commercial insurers in the 1960s and 1970s. Hospital competition began heating up after the diagnosis related groups system of reimbursement for Medicare patients was implemented in 1983. Additional cost containment pressures increased from the commercial side as insurers refused to pay above-average charges for medical services. Health maintenance organizations and large purchasers of health care – such as corporations, public agencies, and commercial insurers – who negotiate for low cost, reduced hospital financial margins further. Faced with overbedding, declining revenues, and rapidly escalating costs, many hospitals over the past three decades have edged-down the percentage of charity care in their case mix.

Some U.S. hospitals closed in the 1970s and 1980s in part because they generated insufficient revenues from commercially covered patients to offset growing charity care expenses. Because insurance coverage is often supplied as an employment benefit and individual policies are relatively expensive, many of the unemployed go without health insurance. Companies rarely provide health coverage for part-time employees and as costs have risen, some of the self-employed remain uninsured as well.

Although the Catholic Health Association urged "additional, immediate commitments on behalf of the poor,"[2] authors of a major study published in the *New England Journal of Medicine* warned that "The probability . . . a hospital will incur deficits (or become financially distressed) rises significantly at institutions where service to the poor . . . is substantial and where area resources are limited."[3] Partially because of their commitment to indigent care, Catholic hospitals have been found to have "less financial resiliency than the median U.S. hospital."[4]

Studies of hospitals that closed due to financial reasons between 1970 and 1980 indicated that the strongest predictors of closings are a physician-to-population ratio smaller than 196; East North Central and West North Central census regions (which include Indiana, Iowa, and Michigan); diversification in fewer than eight medical services; occupancy rate of less than 50 percent; location in a metropolitan statistical area; for-profit status; capacity of fewer than 200 beds; and the presence of a state rate-setting agency.[5]

A study of Catholic hospitals found that financial distress was associated with similar characteristics, specifically the following: urban location; lack of membership in a multi-institutional system; affiliation with a medical school; lower than average occupancy rates; the offering of several complex medical services (e.g., organ transplants); large proportion of outpatient, Medicare, or Medicaid patients to total revenue; and long patient lengths of stay.[6] Some of these characteristics are directly or indirectly associated with charity care, such as urban location and a large percentage of Medicaid patients to total revenue.

To remain solvent, many community hospitals have attempted to reduce the amount of charity care provided resulting in an increase in the number of poor without medical care. Although prohibited by a 1985 federal law, some hospitals have been accused of "patient dumping," transferring uninsured patients to other hospitals. In other attempts to contain costs, hospitals have experimented with relocating facilities from inner-city to suburban areas; eliminating high-cost or low revenue-producing services (e.g., emergency medicine or OB/GYN units); merging with other institutions or creating an alliance to increase volume; and selling less profitable facilities to employees. No hospital has been completely immune from responding to the level of indigent care that it provides, not even public hospitals.[7]

MERCY HEALTH SERVICES

The Sisters of Mercy of the Union in the United States of America is a female Roman Catholic order. Catherine McAuley established the Sisters of Mercy in 1831 and dedicated herself to providing care for needy Dublin, Ireland, residents. Mother M. Francis Xavier Warde was the first sister to take the order's ministry to the United States. In 1843, she helped establish the first Mercy hospital in the western part of Pennsylvania. The year 1879 marked the completion of the first hospital now owned by the Sisters of Mercy Regional Community of Detroit. Several other hospitals followed, most of which were constructed within the next sixty years.[8]

Hospitals were operated autonomously by the Detroit province under the MHS umbrella until the early 1970s when the Sisters recognized the need for increased coordination among their hospitals. Following thirty-six months of in-depth study, the Sisters created the Sisters of Mercy Health Corporation (SMHC) in 1976. This corporation was charged with overseeing all hospitals owned by the Sisters of Mercy Regional Community of Detroit. Between 1976 and 1980, a number of acquisitions were made resulting in an expansion of SMHC-owned hospitals, skilled and intermediate nursing facilities, home health care agencies, and ambulatory-care clinics. Many of the acquisitions were in communities where MHS hospitals already existed.

Thus, they developed the basis needed for a strategy of horizontal integration and related service diversification.[9]

To diversify services more effectively, the corporation was reorganized again in 1983. Five other subsidiaries besides SMHC now existed. The six subsidiaries – SMHC, Accord Insurance, Mercy Services for Aging, Mercy Health Foundation, Mercy Alternative, and Mercy Information Systems – reported directly to then president, Edward J. Connors. In June 1988, MHS headquarters were moved to a campus in Farmington Hills, Michigan, so top management and all subsidiary operations could be further integrated. (Formerly they were spread out over Southeast Michigan.) After assuming president and CEO roles in 1993, Judith Pelham initiated another strategic reshuffling, inserting a chief operational officer over hospital operations and more fully integrating all MHS operations (see Exhibit 19.2). To further extend integration of services and operations, SMHC was scheduled to be consolidated into MHS in July 1994.

Less visible structurally were MHS's health care alliances. Fifteen community health care systems were operational, linking together services in a "seamless continuum of care" and yielding better coordinated care and stronger strategic positioning. Hospital care, long-term care, home care, hospice, ambulatory care, health maintenance, and preferred provider organizations as well as other community services formed parts of each network. Additionally, MHS created a joint venture with Henry Ford Health System to improve access to care throughout Southeast Michigan. Additionally, MHS participated in the Community Care Partnership (also with Henry Ford), contracting with Blue Cross/Blue Shield of Michigan to provide its members' health care at fixed rates.

MHS diversified across the health care delivery spectrum. In 1994, MHS owned twenty-three hospitals, managed twelve, and had one affiliate hospital (6,338 beds total). Located

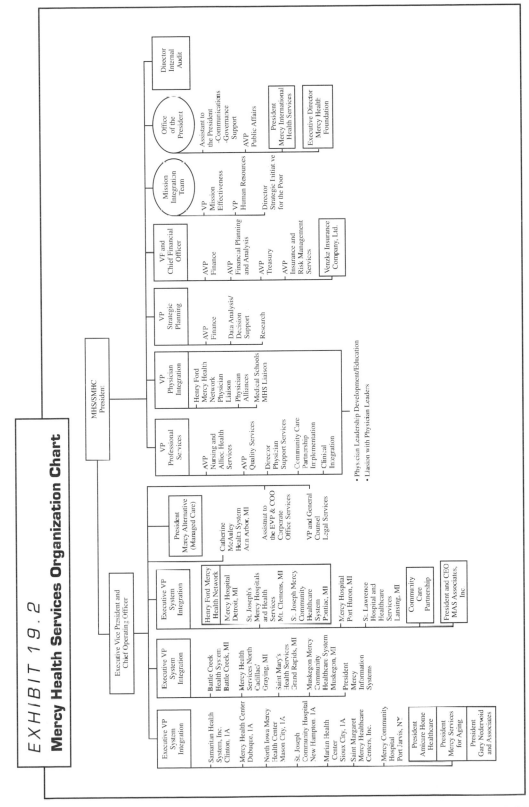

EXHIBIT 19.2
Mercy Health Services Organization Chart

1123

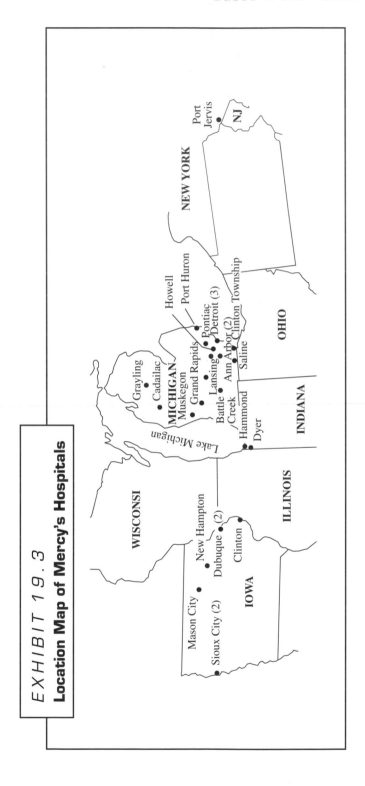

EXHIBIT 19.3
Location Map of Mercy's Hospitals

EXHIBIT 19.4
Hospitals Operated by MHS, 1993

Hospital/Location	Year Established (year acquired)	Number of Beds	Occupancy 1988 (percent)	Estimated Primary Market Size	Approximate Market Share 1986 (percent)	Population Growth (loss) 1980–1986 (percent)	Population over Age 65 1984 (percent)	Families Earning under $15,843 1989 (percent)	County Unemployment 1986 (percent)
St. Margaret Mercy Healthcare Centers, Inc. Hammond, IN	1942	264	63.3	522,900	5	(6)	10.3	9.2	12.2
St. Mary's Health Services Grand Rapids, MI¹	1893	370	55.7	485,000	–	7.4	10.6	6.7	7.7
Saline Community Hospital Saline, MI	–	–	–	–	–	.5	7.1	5.7	4.7
Samaritan Health System, Inc. Clinton, IA	1892	141	45.8	69,600	31	(6.2)	13.9	5.7	9.1
St. Joseph Mercy Hospital Ann Arbor, MI¹						.5	7.1	5.7	4.7
St. Joseph Mercy Hospital Mason City, IA	1915	318	46.5	57,000	81	.8	15.4	5.6	7.1
St. Joseph Mercy Hospital Pontiac, MI		–	–	–	–	1.4	10.1	4.1	6.5
St. Joseph's Mercy Hospitals and Health Services Clinton Township, MI		–	–	–	–	.4	9.8	3.9	8.1
St. Lawrence Hospital and Healthcare Services Lansing, MI¹	1920	451	69.1	410,000	15	.8	8.3	8.4	7.3
Battle Creek Health System Battle Creek, MI¹	1925	209	57.4	180,000	50	(3.3)	12.4	8.5	9.1
Catherine McAuley Health System Ann Arbor, MI¹	1911	614	80.3	402,000	35	.5	7.1	5.7	4.7
Marian Health Center Sioux City, IA¹	1890	484	54.8	119,013	47	(1.0)	13.0	7.5	4.7

EXHIBIT 19.4   cont'd

Hospital/Location	Year Established (year acquired)	Number of Beds	Occupancy 1988 (percent)	Estimated Primary Market Size	Approximate Market Share 1986 (percent)	Population Growth (loss) 1980–1986 (percent)	Population over Age 65 1984 (percent)	Families Earning under $15,843 1989 (percent)	County Unemployment 1986 (percent)
McPherson Hospital Howell, MI	–	–	–	–	–	4.3	7.9	4.3	6.2
Mercy Community Hospital Port Jervis, NY	–	–	–	–	–	8.5	10.8	7.9	5.1
Mercy Health Center Dubuque, IA[1]	1879	740	60.5	169,000	–	(2.9)	11.9	6.1	7.7
Mercy Health Services North – Mercy Hospital Cadillac, MI	1908	174	49.7	60,000	65	6.4	13.8	9.9	13.9
Mercy Health Services North – Mercy Hospital Grayling, MI	1911	104	77.9	40,000	44	6.9	n/a	11.7	9.6
Mercy Hospital Detroit, MI[1]	1939	347	80.0	820,000	10	(7.4)	11.5	11.8	8.9
Mercy Hospital Muskegon, MI[1]	1903	228	50.4	133,000	37	.6	12.0	10.0	11.0
Mercy Hospital Port Huron, MI	1954	119	53.8	160,000	23	1.2	11.7	8.0	10.9
St. Joseph Community Hospital New Hampton, IA	–	–	–	–	–	(4.0)	n/a	9.4	10.2

[1]Hospital located in a Metropolitan Statistical Area (MSA).
Sources: American Hospital Association Guide, 1993 (Chicago: AHA, 1993); City and County Data Book, Washington, D.C.: Government Printing Office, 1983.

throughout the Midwest (see Exhibits 19.3 and 19.4), these hospitals provided the bulk of MHS's revenues. MHS operates over 100 affiliated walk-in clinics in Iowa and Michigan; owns 17 and manages 2 residential facilities for the aged (2,367 beds) in Michigan, Iowa, and New York; owns 7 skilled nursing and intermediate care facilities (237 beds) in Iowa; owns 144 and manages 194 apartments for the aged in Michigan and Iowa; and owns 4 housing facilities for the aged (267 beds) in Michigan. MHS owns twenty-one branches of home health care in Michigan, Iowa, Illinois, and Nebraska and five hospices in Michigan and Iowa. The home-care and managed-care enterprises are growing as a percent of revenues generated.

Selected other MHS organizations are described as follows:

- Mercy Alternative provides managed care products, such as Care Choices HMO and Preferred Choices PPO, and performs third-party administration of claims for self-insured companies.
- Mercy Services for Aging provides clinical and outreach services, such as, adult day care, education, recreation, and wellness programs for the elderly.
- Mercy Health Foundation seeks funding from philanthropists and local and national donors.
- Mercy International Health Services provides management, training, development, and supplies to health care providers in other countries.
- Amicare is a provider of home health care services and medical equipment for in-home use.
- Venzke Insurance Company, Ltd., reinsures liability insurance policies issued by domestic insurance companies.

MHS's ongoing social welfare commitment is embodied in its Strategic Initiative to the Poor. This corporate division assists the fifteen community health care systems in developing needs analysis and creating strategies to improve the quality of community health and life.

MHS continues to operate directly under the auspices of the Sisters of Mercy Regional Community of Detroit. Seven of the eleven members of MHS's Board of Directors are sisters in the sponsoring community. The sisters on the board and in administrative posts exert substantial influence on the strategic direction of the organization. The 1976 guidelines, for example, state that lay chief executive officers may be appointed on the condition that they understand and support the history, spirit, and corporate personality of the Sisters of Mercy and that some formal means of ensuring the philosophy and mission of the Sisters of Mercy can be located within the governance/ management system.[10] Five top management members are nuns from several different orders.

The objective of Judith Pelham who became president in 1993, was to fully integrate MHS service lines in the communities it serves. A continuum of services would be created for patients' care to be coordinated among the various services and clinicians. Patients would receive the most appropriate care in the most appropriate setting – which may not be the hospital.

Another of her goals for MHS was to collaborate with other providers in the community. Duplicate and unnecessary services would be eliminated and resources devoted to more needed services enabling organizations such as MHS to provide more preventive care for people who need it but could not afford to pay. In FY93, MHS provided $16 million in community services in addition to the $46 million in charity hospital care.

To achieve the objective of integration, the structure and culture began to change. One of Pelham's first steps was to reaffirm that the local sites were "clients" of the Mercy system. She challenged her staff to determine "What can the system do – collectively – to help management, including clinicians, achieve integration in the local area?"

THE FUTURE

MHS appears to be well positioned and generally healthy financially (see Exhibits 19.5 and 19.6). Not surprisingly, however, it continued to incur losses due to charity care at some facilities. Mercy Hospital, Detroit, for example, lost $7.1 million in fiscal 1993.[11] MHS has experimented with financially forecasting various patient care and hospital operation designs to more carefully monitor costs and improve the quality of care offered.[12] However,

> ## EXHIBIT 19.6
> ### Consolidated Statement of Revenues and Expenses (dollars in thousands)
>
> | | 1991 | 1992 | 1993 |
> |---|---|---|---|
> | **Revenues** | | | |
> | Net patient service revenues | $1,389,186 | $1,517,385 | $1,575,694 |
> | Other revenues | 230,600 | 268,297 | 286,385 |
> | Total revenues | 1,619,786 | 1,785,682 | 1,862,079 |
> | **Expenses** | | | |
> | Salaries, wages and fringe benefits | 793,126 | 852,909 | 886,290 |
> | Bad debts | 54,692 | 70,487 | 56,793 |
> | Other | 627,176 | 684,566 | 739,503 |
> | Interest | 47,071 | 53,544 | 47,137 |
> | Depreciation and amortization | 81,228 | 86,396 | 85,538 |
> | Total expenses | 1,603,293 | 1,747,902 | 1,815,261 |
> | Income (loss) from operations | 16,493 | 37,780 | 46,818 |
> | **Nonoperating Gains (losses)** | | | |
> | Investment income | 12,625 | 14,698 | 10,102 |
> | Loss on hospital facility | – | (5,000) | – |
> | External financial interest | 659 | (2,846) | (3,263) |
> | Excess of revenues over expenses Before extraordinary loss and change in accounting principle | 29,777 | 44,632 | 53,657 |
> | Extraordinary loss | – | (2,608) | (14,401) |
> | Cumulative effect of accounting change | | – | (33,942) |
> | Excess (deficit) of revenues over expenses | $29,777 | $42,024 | $5,314 |
>
> *Source:* Mercy Health Services 1992 and 1993 annual reports.

such adjustments would not be potent enough to offset major losses due to charity care. The likelihood of national health care reform with its possible mandate for universal coverage may pose a unique dilemma for MHS – if charity care ceases to exist in the United States, must MHS alter its strategy so it can continue to provide health care for the poor? Should

MHS's mission be redefined? Should it increase its involvement in nations with greater inequities in health care? What strategies should it develop? For what future scenarios must it be prepared?

According to Mercy studies, there was 40 to 60 percent overbedding in each of the communities that Mercy serves. Pelham noted,

"We need to refocus our investments away from buildings and into physician practices and information systems while removing excess hospital capacity. We need to put our money where our mouth is to make the changes necessary. Our mission is the reason MHS exists and mission is the reason for good strategy and management practices."

NOTES

1. For a brief history of hospitals see J. Rogers Hollingsworth and Ellen Jane Hollingsworth, *Controversy about American Hospitals: Funding Ownership, and Performance* (Washington, D.C.: American Enterprise Institute for Public Policy Research, 1987), Chapter 2.
2. *No Room in the Marketplace, The Health Care of the Poor* (St. Louis: Catholic Health Association, 1986).
3. John Hadley, Ross Mullner, and Judith Feder, "The Financially Distressed Hospital," *New England Journal of Medicine* 307 (November 11, 1982), pp. 1285–1287.
4. William Cleverley, "Fiscal Fitness: Ten Principles for Evaluating Financial Health," *Health Progress* (January–February 1986), p. 27.
5. Daniel R. Longo and Gary A. Chase, "Structural Determinants of Hospital Closure," *Medical Care* 22 (May 1984), pp. 395–396; Jonathan D. Mayer, Elizabeth R. Kohlenberg, G. Eric Siefferman, and Roger A. Rosenblatt, "Patterns of Rural Hospital Closure in the United States," *Social Science and Medicine* 24 (1987), p. 331.
6. Ik-Whan Kwon, Scott R. Safranski, David Martin, and William R. Walker, "Causes of Financial Difficulty in Catholic Hospitals," *Health Care Management Review* 31, no. 1 (1988), pp. 29–37.
7. Judith Feder, Jack Hadley, and Ross M. Mullner, "Falling Through the Cracks: Poverty, Insurance Coverage, and Hospitals' Care of the Poor, 1980 and 1982," in *Hospitals and the Uninsured Poor* (New York: United Hospital Fund, 1985), pp. 21–22.
8. For further information, see Mary Kathryn Grant, *A History of the Establishment of the Sisters of Mercy Health Corporation,* (Farmington Hills, Michigan: Sisters of Mercy Regional Community of Detroit, and the Sisters of Mercy Health Corporation, 1979).
9. Sisters of Mercy Regional Community of Detroit, *Report of the Five-Year Evaluation of the Sisters of Mercy Health Corporation,* (Farmington Hills, Michigan: Sisters of Mercy Regional Community of Detroit, 1982), pp. 1–5.
10. Elizabeth Mary Burns, "Developing a Catholic Health Care System," *Health Progress* (December 1976), pp. 49–50.
11. "Sisters of Mercy Health Corp. Series O (IA) & Series P (Mich.) Bonds Rated 'A' by Fitch," *Fitch Financial Wire* (October 27, 1993), p. 1027.
12. Mary A. Grayson, "System Uses Financial Data and Grass-Roots Ideas to Restructure Care Delivery," *Hospitals* 65 (August 5, 1991), pp. 31–32.

CASE 20

Wills Eye Hospital

INTRODUCTION

D. McWilliams Kessler, chief executive officer and executive director of Wills Eye Hospital in Philadelphia, was deep in thought as he prepared to present his 1992 annual report to the Board of Directors of City Trusts. The past year had been a successful one for Wills by hospital industry standards, and Wills enjoyed an international reputation for quality in the care and treatment of the eye. Indeed, Wills had been listed consistently among the top hospitals in the nation by *U.S. News and World Report* in its "Annual Guide to America's Best Hospitals."[1]

Kessler knew better than most, however, that the health care industry was in the midst of a radical transformation, one that would become more turbulent as political reforms took shape under the Clinton administration. Not all hospitals would survive the shake-out. Research by the American Hospital Association revealed two ominous trends – hospital closings and mergers – were both on the rise.[2]

As Kessler reflected on the past year's

This case was prepared by Elizabeth B. Davis and Stephen J. Porth of St. Joseph's University. It is intended as a basis for classroom discussion rather than to illustrate effective or ineffective handling of an administrative situation. Copyright © 1994 by the *Case Research Journal* and Elizabeth B. Davis and Stephen J. Porth. Used with permission.

experience, he was both pleased and concerned. Wills's reputation and recent financial performance were sources of pride. At the same time, the momentum for health care reform and the costs of keeping pace with medical technologies threatened the very existence of small, highly specialized hospitals such as Wills. As the area's least efficient hospital (as measured by capacity utilization), Wills was beginning to feel the squeeze.

In consultation with his executive team, Kessler had formulated a set of options to be examined over the upcoming planning period. Although maintaining the independence of the institution seemed a primary goal in the past, industry pressures and uncertainty forced the team to consider all options, including strategic alliances, mergers, and acquisitions.

HOSPITAL INDUSTRY TRENDS

The health care industry from 1970 to the 1990s had continually demonstrated not only its complexity but its volatility as well. The industry comprised a myriad of products and services and a corresponding variety of organizational types. The health care industry was defined as those companies and institutions that directly interact with patients and those that supply medical products or services to the directly interacting companies.[3] Organizational types included hospitals, clinics, HMOs, nursing homes, medical and dental practices, manufacturers of medical products and technologies, and pharmaceutical companies. These organizations fell into the categories of both not-for-profit and for-profit institutions.

Slowing the growth rate of national health care expenditures had been the subject of great debate during the decade of the 1980s and continued into the 1990s. Exhibit 20.1 shows that health care spending exploded from $25.4 billion in 1960 to over $730 billion in 1991, a compound annual growth rate of 11.8 percent. By comparison, the GNP expanded at an annual rate of 8.5 percent over the same period. Medical expenditures grew faster than GNP in all but three years between 1960 and 1990. Health care costs in 1992 were approximately 13.4 percent of GNP or $850 billion; projections for the year 2000 were that health care costs would represent 16.4 percent of the GNP or over $1,600 billion.[4] A variety of issues contributed to the unbridled surging of health care costs in the United States.

Government Health Care Programs. In the 1960s the government enacted the Medicare and Medicaid programs. Medicaid is a program, jointly funded by state and federal governments, that provides medical aid for people who are unable to finance their own medical expenses. Medicare is a program under the Social Security Administration that provides medical care for the aged. These programs experienced tremendous growth over the years, with the Medicare program representing close to 40 percent of hospital revenues, on average.

In addition, in 1984, the government enacted a new Prospective Payment System (PPS), in which reimbursement moved from a cost-based approach to a fixed-fee reimbursement system. That is, health care providers were paid based not on the costs of services rendered but on a predetermined schedule established for various medical conditions known as diagnosis-related groups (DRGs).

The enactment of PPS along with the growth of the Medicare and Medicaid programs resulted in fundamental changes in the delivery of health care services. Changes included declining trends in hospital admissions, average lengths of stay, and other utilization measures and a corresponding increase in services provided in less expensive settings, such as outpatient clinics and home health care.[5]

The proliferation of government policy and regulation aimed at solving the rising health care cost problem produced uncertainty and instability, and contributed to the high-risk, high-cost environment of the hospital industry.

Demographic Shifts. The "graying of America" (i.e., the aging U.S. population) created an increase in demand for medical services and contributed to rising national health care expenditures. As the elderly segment of the population grew, there was a corresponding increase in medical services designed to serve this population's needs. This increased demand produced a deficit-ridden Medicare program, with the deficit reaching $100 billion in 1991.

Medical Technology. The rapid increase and development of new medical technologies created a fast-paced health care system in which organizations fought to maintain and provide the best quality services through capital equipment acquisitions. These expensive technologies contributed to higher operating costs and, in many cases, shifted medical procedures from inpatient to outpatient services or from hospital to off-site delivery.

Third-Party Payer Systems. Most consumers of health care services had been insulated from rising health care costs through the evolution of the third-party payer system. The majority of U.S. medical expenditures was made by third-party payers such as large corporate employers, the government, and insurance companies. Accordingly, corporate medical expenses increased 20.4 percent in 1990, with medical plan costs per employee amounting

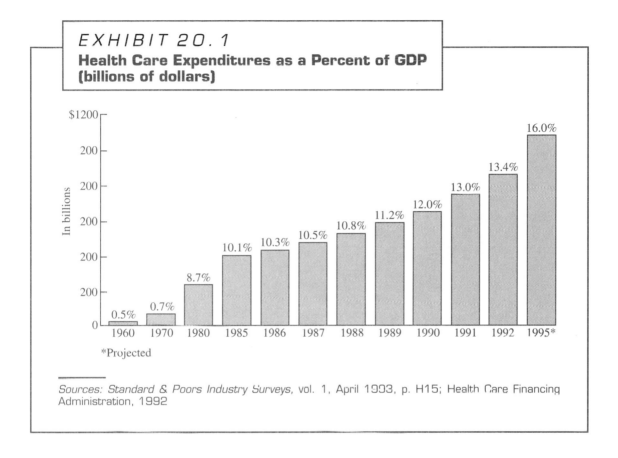

EXHIBIT 20.1

Health Care Expenditures as a Percent of GDP (billions of dollars)

Sources: *Standard & Poors Industry Surveys,* vol. 1, April 1993, p. H15; Health Care Financing Administration, 1992

to $3,616, compared to $2,600 in 1989 and $2,160 in 1988.[6]

Because of caps placed on reimbursement under the Medicare and Medicaid programs, hospitals increasingly incurred uncompensated costs. Hospitals shifted the burden of these uncompensated costs to the private insurers. The corporate response was the creation of private insurer's managed-care approach toward utilization of medical services. Both private insurers and corporations sought to minimize and scrutinize use of services, thereby controlling corporate expenses. Although individuals were relieved of a good portion of their health care costs, the fee-for-service system provided an incentive for hospitals to expand medical-related diagnostic testing and the provision of services.

DELAWARE VALLEY HEALTH CARE INDUSTRY

The Philadelphia metropolitan area was well known for its heavy concentration of health care institutions. Nationally, the Philadelphia area ranked second in the number of teaching hospitals and medical schools behind the New York/northern New Jersey area.[7] The region had six medical schools, twenty-four teaching hospitals, and in 1992 prepared over 4,000 students for medicine.[8] In addition, approximately 125 hospitals were considered part of the Philadelphia metropolitan region,[9] along with over 125 pharmaceutical, biotechnology and research institutions employing over 14,000 people.[10] Total health care employment in the area was about 75,000 people in 1992.[11]

EXHIBIT 20.2
Philadelphia Metropolitan Hospital Industry, 1987–1992

	1987	1992	Percent Change
Outpatient visits	4.4 million	6 million	+36.4%
Inpatient days	4.9 million	4.6 million	−6.1%
Beds	18,158	16,862	−7.1%
Average stay	7.9 days	7.5 days	−5.1%
Occupancy	73.3%	74.9%	+2.2%

Source: American Hospital Association Statistical Yearbook, 1992.

Exhibit 20.2 provides data on the Philadelphia metropolitan hospital industry, comparing the years 1987 and 1992.

The Delaware Valley Hospital Council reported that two out of every three hospitals in the city of Philadelphia and one out of every three in the surrounding suburbs ended fiscal year 1990 with operating losses.[12] Average operating margins were between 0 and 1 percent, far below the 4 percent margin that most health care experts say is needed to maintain the physical plant.[13] Operating margins in 1990 by hospital type fell into the categories shown in Exhibit 20.3.[14]

The overall weak financial performance of Delaware Valley hospitals in 1990 set the tone for a highly competitive hospital arena. Despite the statistics, Wills Eye Hospital consistently performed above the national average of 4 percent operating margins, posting margins in the 5 percent range. This alone made Wills an attractive candidate for strategic alliances in the Delaware Valley. Potential alliance partners for Wills were dictated in part by physical proximity of general acute-care hospitals (i.e., urban environment) and medical staff teaching, research, and practice affiliations.

Competitive strategies of nearby hospitals

EXHIBIT 20.3
Delaware Valley Hospitals—Operating Margins, 1990

Hospital Type	Operating Margin
Medical school	−1.0%
City teaching	−3.9%
City community	−5.0%
City specialty	+1.5%
Suburban teaching	+1.0%
Suburban community	+2.0%

in recent years ranged from the Graduate Hospital's ongoing practice of acquiring failing hospitals and executing turnarounds, to Pennsylvania Hospital's conservative search for alliances with premier revenue-generating programs and services. Both hospitals and their corporate offices were within a twelve block radius of Wills.

Thomas Jefferson Hospital on the other hand, had been affiliated with Wills Eye Hospital for many years. Occupying a side-by-side physical arrangement with Wills, it maintained a formal arrangement in which the opthalmologist-in-chief of Wills had an appointment in the Jefferson system as chair of the Ophthalmology Department. This dual appointment had facilitated the teaching and research partnership that Wills established with Jefferson and placed them in a position of close affiliation. Jefferson and its medical school complex continued to search for profitable arrangements that would contribute to their bottom line, and Wills Eye Hospital's past performance made it a highly desirable candidate for merger or acquisition in Jefferson's eyes.

The Presbyterian Hospital was located on the fringe of center city Philadelphia (in the area known as University City) but still relatively close to Wills, Pennsylvania, Jefferson, and Graduate Hospitals. Presbyterian had been repeatedly plagued by a high Medicare and Medicaid market population. Like others, this institution was searching for potential alliances to boost its profitability. Although hardly a profitable organization itself, Presbyterian offered its strong teaching and practice affiliation with the Hospital of the University of Pennsylvania and maintained a robust activity in ophthalmology through the Scheie Eye Institute. Linkage with Presbyterian meant a direct connection with the prestigious operations of the University of Pennsylvania Medical Complex. A Wills Eye/Presbyterian Hospital alliance might solidify eye care in the Delaware Valley.

The Main Line Health System, a multihospital system, represented another potential opportunity for Wills Eye. Specifically, the Lankenau Hospital located just beyond the Philadelphia border held the flagship position in the Main Line Health Corporation. Lankenau was home to a fair number of Wills Eye physicians, who had established additional medical offices in Lankenau's Ophthalmology Department as well as maintaining a major teaching affiliation with the Thomas Jefferson Hospital located in Center City. As a multi-institutional system, Mainline Health had suc-

ceeded in recent years in building a corporate suburban structure that included not just Lankenau but the Bryn Mawr Hospital, Paoli Memorial Hospital, Bryn Mawr Rehabilitation Hospital, and Community Health Affiliates. This made Main Line Health one of the more powerful players in the Delaware Valley region. The system tended to serve the more affluent communities of Philadelphia, and as a consequence, its financial performance was better than some of its center city Philadelphia counterparts. The Main Line Health System paid constant attention to the identification of potential candidates to increase its base and scope of operations and programs. This interest did not exclude examination of opportunities beyond the current suburban focus of the system. With the involvement of some of the Wills medical staff already at Lankenau, and with both hospitals being financially viable and having major teaching affiliations with Thomas Jefferson Hospital, a formalized arrangement involving program sharing, technology sharing, program introduction, patient referrals, or joint marketing might prove mutually beneficial.

The focus of Delaware Valley hospitals in the years to come would be survival. Both failing and profitable institutions were searching for strategies that would guarantee their viability in the 1990s. Wills Eye Hospital was hardly immune to the pressure being exerted by its external environment; in fact, Wills had arrived at a crossroads in determining its future place in the Philadelphia area.

HISTORY AND BACKGROUND OF WILLS EYE HOSPITAL

Wills Eye Hospital was founded in 1832 through a bequest of James Wills, Jr., a Quaker merchant. At the time of his death in 1825, James Wills left the city of Philadelphia $108,000 to build an institution for the relief of the indigent blind and lame. The first Wills

Hospital was a three-story, seventy-bed institution.

Before Wills's founding, general surgeons treated ophthalmic patients. Specialized training was rare. Wills played a vital role in establishing ophthalmology (the medical field encompassing treatment of the eye) as a separate branch of medicine in the United States. The first cataract operation was performed at Wills in 1834, by a Wills physician, Dr. Isaac Parish. In 1839, just seven years after the hospital's founding, Wills further helped the growth of ophthalmology by establishing the first ophthalmology residency with the enrollment of Dr. John Neill.

In the 1960s, Wills remained at the forefront of ophthalmic care and began to develop subspecialty services in addition to its General Ophthalmology Service (now the Cataract and Primary Eye Care Service). During the 1980s, Wills treated approximately 1 million patients, including over 107,000 operating room cases; 46,000 day surgery cases; 180,000 emergency room cases; 570,000 outpatient visits; and 78,000 inpatient admissions. In 1993 Wills employed over 500 people and occupied a new six-floor building with 115 inpatient beds in center city Philadelphia.

The mission of Wills was as follows:

> Wills Eye Hospital, through its dedication to the preservation of vision, serves as a comprehensive center for ophthalmology and other specialized services. Wills is committed to excellence in the provision of patient care, to the education of health care professionals and the community, and to participation in basic and clinical research. Wills Eye Hospital will carry out this mission by operating as an independent, not-for-profit, private practice-oriented center with a sound financial base.

Wills was structured in a unique way. Overseeing the institution was the Board of Directors of City Trusts. The board was a group of political appointees, made up primarily of local business people and politicians, that oversaw Wills as well as 120 other organizations. The primary function of the board was to review and decide the fate of new strategic initiatives developed by Wills's executive staff. The board had the authority to make policy and develop strategies for Wills, but it had not assumed this role. Since 1985, the executive staff of Wills had, without exception, obtained the approval of the board for each of its strategic initiatives. The board included a five-member subcommittee on hospital and research issues whose primary function was to advise the CEO of Wills on administrative issues.

Reporting directly to the board was not only the executive director/CEO (D. Mc-Williams Kessler), but also the ophthalmologist in chief (William Tasman, M.D.). Exhibit 20.4 details this arrangement. As executive director and CEO, Kessler was responsible for management and administration of the business side of Wills. This included, for example, strategic and financial planning, operations, purchasing, budgeting, human resources, accounting, and MIS. Exhibit 20.5 is an organizational chart of the business side of the hospital.

Also reporting directly to the board was the ophthalmologist in chief (OIC), Dr. Tasman. The OIC was responsible for the medical staff at Wills, which consisted of approximately 200 private practice physicians and 9 service chief physicians. The service chiefs were appointed by the OIC and acted as department heads, responsible for medical care within their respective departments. Wills physicians rented office space and equipment from the hospital, and practiced in the fee-for-service, private practice mode (and, therefore, were not salaried employees of the hospital). Exhibit 20.6 provides information on the background and expertise of the key decision makers at Wills.

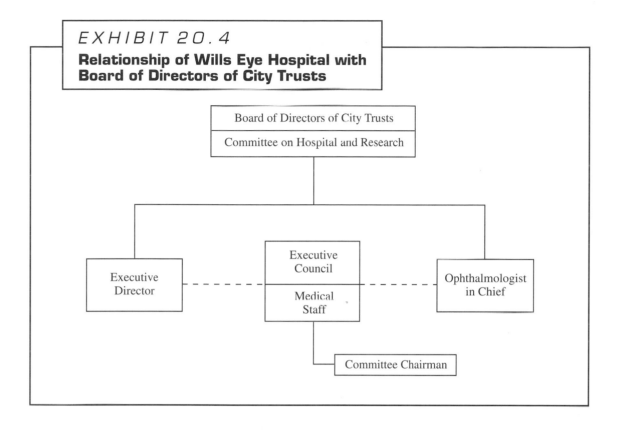

EXHIBIT 20.4

Relationship of Wills Eye Hospital with Board of Directors of City Trusts

The structural arrangement shown in Exhibit 20.4 created special challenges for strategic planning at Wills. Specifically, it meant that both the business side and the medical side of the institution needed to agree on strategy. Because the business executives and physicians often saw things from different points of view and had different sets of priorities for the institution, achieving this agreement was a formidable task.

The case of cataract operations illustrates the difference in perspectives of the medical and executive staffs. Cataract operations, one of the most common procedures performed at Wills, had shifted from inpatient to almost exclusively outpatient delivery. This shift had little impact on physicians: they continued to be paid the predetermined fee for the procedure. Not so for the hospital, however, which

was squeezed by a reimbursement system that was not cost-based (and typically did not cover all costs). The burden to cover overhead expenses (e.g., operating room, emergency room, educational programs) fell primarily on inpatient services at the same time that Wills was performing a steadily decreasing proportion of these services.

"Finding ways to subsidize underreimbursed outpatient services, educational programs and medical research is one key for the future of Wills," according to Kessler. "Another is to utilize our slack resources to produce new income." Dr. Peter Laibson, chair of the Medical Staff Planning Committee, concurred with Kessler on the need for teamwork. "Ophthalmologists have a huge challenge before them, what with HMO and provider networks redirecting patient flow, and the need to deliver

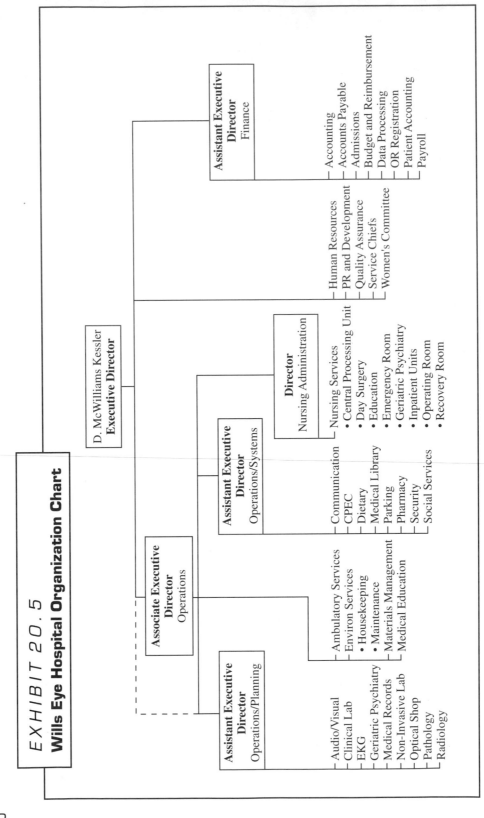

EXHIBIT 20.5
Wills Eye Hospital Organization Chart

D. McWilliams Kessler
Executive Director

Associate Executive Director
Operations

Assistant Executive Director
Operations/Planning

- Audio/Visual
- Clinical Lab
- EKG
- Geriatric Psychiatry
- Medical Records
- Non-Invasive Lab
- Optical Shop
- Pathology
- Radiology

- Ambulatory Services
- Environ Services
- Housekeeping
- Maintenance
- Materials Management
- Medical Education

Assistant Executive Director
Operations/Systems

- Communication
- CPEC
- Dietary
- Medical Library
- Parking
- Pharmacy
- Security
- Social Services

Director
Nursing Administration

- Nursing Services
  • Central Processing Unit
  • Day Surgery
  • Education
  • Emergency Room
  • Geriatric Psychiatry
  • Inpatient Units
  • Operating Room
  • Recovery Room

- Human Resources
- PR and Development
- Quality Assurance
- Service Chiefs
- Women's Committee

Assistant Executive Director
Finance

- Accounting
- Accounts Payable
- Admissions
- Budget and Reimbursement
- Data Processing
- OR Registration
- Patient Accounting
- Payroll

EXHIBIT 20.6
Wills Eye Hospital Executives

D. McWilliams Kessler, Executive Director and CEO

Sixteen years experience in management, finance, planning, education, research, marketing, and development in general and specialty acute-care teaching hospitals. Appointed CEO in 1985, after serving as the associate executive director and COO for the previous four years. Special expertise in financial turnarounds, strategic planning, product development, marketing, physician recruitment, and service diversification.

Kessler was regarded by his executive team as a creative, strategic thinker with vision. Although his relationships with the physicians on staff at the hospital had been stormy at times, he repeatedly demonstrated his finesse and skills at negotiation. This combined with his participatory approach toward his management team had fostered great loyalty and commitment on the part of his staff.

James Mulvihill, Associate Executive Director and COO

Twenty years experience in hospital management with special expertise in physician recruitment, purchasing, and operations management. Appointed COO in 1985, after serving as assistant executive director since 1979. Mulvihill had been asked to speak about current health care issues at various national meetings and was instrumental in organizing a national buying group to purchase hospital surgical supplies and pharmaceuticals at volume discount prices.

His career was in the operational aspects of the institution with a particular focus on cultivating physician relations.

William Tasman, M.D., Ophthalmologist in Chief (OIC)

Tasman, a retina specialist, came to Wills as a resident in 1959. After several hospital appointments as attending surgeon and consulting surgeon, in 1985 he was named the chairman of the Department of Ophthalmology for Thomas Jefferson University Hospital, located next to Wills. Later that same year he was appointed OIC of Wills Eye Hospital.

Tasman had long been a figure in the international medical ophthalmic arena and was a well-known lecturer in his field. His many years of experience in the medical care system made him decisive in his actions and unpredictable in his approach toward management. Senior to most of the young management team at Wills, he was an independent thinker.

---

care in lower cost settings. Joint planning [among the executive and medical staffs] needs to begin now."

Despite a distressed industry, Wills had succeeded in posting an operating margin that was consistent with national standards and un-

usually high by Pennsylvania state and local industry statistics. Wills had increased its charges in 1992 and the new Geriatric Psychology Service was increasing the overall length of stay for the hospital. Occupancy from 1991–1992 had increased from 31.9 to 39.1

percent, respectively. Kessler's predictions were that the introduction of these revenue-generating methods would not be enough to counter the sweeping changes in the industry. In fact, he forecast that in the near future Wills would begin to feel the pinch. This would first be felt by a financial downturn in net patient service revenues in 1993. Financial statements are provided in Exhibit 20.7, a four-year "Statement of Revenues and Expenses," and Exhibit 20.8, a four-year balance sheet. It is important to note that board-designated assets (i.e., funds held by Trustee and Board designated investments) are not restricted funds.

These monies are not donor-endowment assets with restrictions as to eventual use or generated yearly income suffering a restriction.

STRATEGIC OPTIONS

Wills Eye Hospital had gone through a decade of major strategic changes in the midst of the government regulations and demographic shifts described earlier. One change was in the hospital's mix of inpatient versus outpatient services. Before 1982 all of Wills's services were inpatient. By 1992 fully half of Wills's services were outpatient.

EXHIBIT 20.7
Statement of Revenues and Expenses

	June 30, 1989	June 30, 1990	June 30, 1991	June 30, 1992
Revenues				
Patient service revenue	$59,756,893	$69,168,762	$74,027,808	$95,446,416
Less uncollectable accounts, free care, and contractual allowances	26,021,387	31,635,434	34,275,982	44,859,815
Net patient service revenue	$33,735,506	$37,533,328	$39,751,826	$50,586,601
Other operating revenue	3,530,083	3,518,685	3,472,281	3,524,522
Unrestricted investment income	2,948,270	4,229,062	4,819,225	4,005,073
Unrestricted gifts	2,802,301	3,033,223	1,043,210	362,709
Total revenues	$43,016,160	$48,314,298	$49,086,542	$58,478,905
Expenses				
Salaries and wages	$15,014,080	$15,819,737	$16,609,843	$18,070,941
Supplies and expenses	17,048,048	17,815,890	19,677,629	21,098,548
Interest expense	1,122,480	1,101,018	1,076,948	1,051,327
Depreciation and amortization	2,025,170	2,092,752	2,196,088	2,387,888
Provision for bad debt[1]				3,562,232
Funds available for new services and equipment	7,806,382	11,484,901	9,526,034	12,307,969
Total expenses and fund balance	$43,016,160	$48,314,298	$49,086,542	$58,478,905

[1]The appearance of this new category was a direct response to the Medical Staff's request to offer more charity care to the surrounding community.

EXHIBIT 20.8
Operating Funds Balance Sheet

	June 30, 1989	June 30, 1990	June 30, 1991	June 30, 1992
Current Assets				
Cash and certificates of deposit	$16,701,121	$30,887,897	$36,932,413	$51,049,658
Accounts receivable, net of allowances	5,849,660	3,045,195	850,027	371,959
Inventories	419,463	533,659	595,937	566,797
Due from restricted funds	505,944	706,385	2,007,306	394,496
Other current assets	1,094,374	989,488	929,596	960,120
Total current assets	24,570,562	36,162,624	41,315,279	53,343,030
Other Assets				
Property, plant and equipment	34,825,355	36,142,979	39,777,160	41,952,668
Less: accumulated depreciation	16,904,136	18,683,830	20,825,656	23,065,523
	17,921,219	17,459,149	18,951,504	18,887,145
Funds held by trustee	12,728,615	14,586,435	16,060,477	18,033,179
Investments, board designated	6,569,299	8,843,347	12,292,477	12,868,794
Deferred financing costs, net	428,714	392,507	361,026	330,296
Total other assets	37,647,847	41,281,438	47,665,484	50,119,414
Total operating assets	$62,218,409	$77,444,062	$88,980,763	$103,462,444
Current Liabilities				
Current portion of long-term debt	$395,000	$420,000	$445,000	$470,000
Accounts payable	2,466,725	2,528,558	2,839,130	3,213,699
Accrued expenses	1,873,901	2,047,191	2,207,780	2,498,806
Due to restricted fund		38,493	138,056	128,120
Payable to third parties		3,423,782	4,290,238	5,686,600
Total current liabilities	4,735,626	8,458,024	9,920,204	11,997,225
Other Liabilities and Fund Balances				
Long-term debt	$16,250,000	$15,830,000	$15,385,000	$14,915,000
Fund balances				
Board designated	6,569,299	8,843,347	12,292,477	12,868,794
Other	34,663,484	44,312,691	51,383,082	63,681,425
Total fund balances	$41,232,783	$53,156,038	$63,675,559	$76,550,219
Total other liabilities and fund balances	$57,482,783	$68,986,038	$79,060,559	$91,465,219
Total operating liabilities and fund balances	$62,218,409	$77,444,062	$88,980,763	$103,462,444

One physician on staff at Wills described the magnitude of this change when he remarked, "When I was considering whether to join the staff at Wills in 1985, I was advised by more than one colleague to stay away. Wills had just finished building a new six-floor, 115-bed hospital. At the same time government regulations were making it increasingly difficult to fill the beds by putting pressure on hospitals to serve more patients in an outpatient mode. Some people at the hospital were afraid the new building was a white elephant that would intensify the financial burdens on Wills."

As feared, filling beds was a challenge at Wills where occupancy rates lagged behind other area hospitals (see Exhibit 20.9). Further, Wills served a disproportionately high percentage of Medicare patients and was forced to absorb costs not covered because of Medicare reimbursement caps.

In the early 1980s top management recog-nized the need to expand the hospital's range of services to fill more beds and attract a greater proportion of non-Medicare patients. As a result, new specialty programs and services, such as the hand center unit (performing hand operations like carpal tunnel surgery) and the geriatric psychiatry unit, were established. These changes produced a modest level of diversification for Wills but occupancy rates continued to lag behind other area hospitals. The changes created internal controversy at Wills as some of the medical staff, who were used to thinking of Wills as a renowned eye hospital, resisted any attempt by management to expand outside of eye care. Exhibit 20.10 provides some insight into Wills's changing mix of services and revenue sources from 1987 to 1992.

As CEO of Wills, Kessler was concerned. Few local competitors could compare to the preeminent medical expertise located at Wills or offer the full range of ophthalmologic services that were housed there. For the time

---

EXHIBIT 20.9
Philadelphia-Area Hospitals, Inpatient Data—1992

Hospital	Code	Service	Beds	Admissions	Occupancy
Graduate	UM	1	320	11,601	73.4%
Pennsylvania	U	1	489	22,179	76.9%
Presbyterian[1]	U	1	334	11,589	85.3%
Thomas Jefferson	U	1	707	26,312	80.6%
Lankenau	SM	1	408	16,630	83.9%
Wills Eye	U	2	115	5,481	39.1%

LEGEND:
U = Urban
S = Suburban
M = Multiinstitutional System
1 = General Medicine/Surgery
2 = Specialty Medicine

[1]Includes Scheie Eye Institute.
Source: AHA Guide to Health Care Field, 1993.

EXHIBIT 20.10

Wills Eye Hospital, Activity and Revenue, 1987/1992

Hospital Activity/Service	Activity 1987	Activity 1992	Revenue Percent 1987	Revenue Percent 1992
Ophthalmology/inpatient surgery cases	5,695	5,293	45.6	41.8
Ophthalmology/outpatient surgery cases	5,740	6,714	32.5	33.7
Other services/clinic visits, ER, ancillary	85,262	68,872	19.9	18.5
Hand surgery cases	336	296	2.0	1.5
Geriatric psychiatry cases	0	167	0	4.5

being, however, even these competitive advantages would not suffice. The strategic challenge was survival in the uncontrollable and unpredictable climate of health care reform and technology revolution.

With this in mind, Kessler considered his strategic options. Given the number of hospitals in the region, Kessler had ample opportunity to consider potential strategic alliances, joint ventures, or integration with a wide variety of partners. Exhibits 20.9, 20.11, and 20.12 provide data on potential strategic partners for Wills Eye Hospital. Specifically, Kessler felt that the following strategic options needed to be further explored:

1. *Strategic Alliances.* With many highly diverse hospitals in the metropolitan

EXHIBIT 20.11

Strategic Alliance Options, Hospital Inpatient Data, 1992

Hospital	Expense (thousands)	Payroll (thousands)	Personnel	Total Revenue (millions)
Graduate	$158,167	$55,039	1,621	n/a
Pennsylvania	238,218	102,992	2,980	$397.3
Presbyterian	127,122	57,810	1,597	n/a
Thomas Jefferson	357,283	161,162	4,121	639.8
Lankenau	148,782	65,837	2,188	153.4
Wills Eye	42,609	17,020	534	58.5

n/a = Data not available.
Sources: Annual reports of the respective organizations, 1992; AHA Guide to Health Care Field, 1993.

EXHIBIT 20.12
Hospital Statistics

Hospital	Admissions		Occupancy (percent)		Total Expenses (thousands)	
	1989	1992	1989	1992	1989	1992
Graduate	11,619	11,601	82.8	73.4	n/a	$158,167
Pennsylvania	17,569	22,179	77.6	76.9	$152,391	238,218
Presbyterian	9,888	11,589	73.9	85.3	92,216	127,122
Thomas Jefferson	24,629	26,312	86.0	80.6	273,476	357,283
Lankenau	15,519	16,630	87.3	83.9	n/a	148,782
Wills Eye	5,782	5,481	35.0	39.1	35,210	42,609

n/a = Data not available.
Sources: AHA Guides to the Health Care Field, 1990, 1993.

area, Wills could forge partnerships and strategic alliances to cut costs or to gain access to new services and programs.

2. *Merger.* It was clear that the area offered the option of merger partners in both the specialty and general acute-care arenas. One clear partner was the Scheie Eye Institute operated by the Presbyterian Hospital in Philadelphia.

3. *Acquisition.* The option of acquisition also existed. Thomas Jefferson Hospital, the massive acute care medical center located close to Wills, had often expressed their interest in acquiring the operational, technical, and clinical expertise and facilities of Wills.

4. *Internal Growth.* Wills had been frugal and prudent with its operating surpluses in the past three years. Investments and expansion of unrestricted funds had contributed to a base of capital in excess of $76 million. The idea of internal development of new programs and services seemed a viable option.

5. *Liquidation.* The Board of Directors of City Trusts currently controlled and administered the Wills Eye Hospital as only one of 120 trusts. Although the board heralded Wills as its flagship trust, the fact remained that the board's depth of experience and understanding of the constantly shifting circumstances in the industry was limited. The possibility seemed remote, but Kessler worried that liquidation might prove highly attractive to a board with backgrounds and interests as diverse as education, politics, insurance, and utilities.

Kessler's task as CEO of Wills was to work with his executive staff, the medical staff, and the board, to chart a course for the 1990s through the murky waters of the health care industry. The upcoming board meeting appeared to pose no immediate threat for Kessler, however, the future was anything but certain. His frustration was evident when Kessler remarked, "I wish I would only have to be as accountable for my predictions as are economists and meteorologists."

NOTES

1. "1992 Annual Guide, America's Best Hospitals," *US News & World Report* (June 15, 1992).
2. Jay Greene, "Hospitals Now Merge Rather Than Close," *Modern Health Care* (July 6, 1992), pp. 20–21.
3. L. Jauch and W. Glueck, "Humana Case," in *Business Policy and Strategic Management,* 5th ed. (New York: McGraw-Hill Book Company, 1988), p. 702.
4. "Bitter Pill," *Business Philadelphia* 3, no. 5 (May 1992), pp. 33–37, 60.
5. Standard & Poor's Industry Surveys, Health Care, Insurance and Investments (August 22, 1991), pp. 15–17, 30–34.
6. Ibid.
7. Delaware Valley Hospital Council Facts & Data Sheet on Hospitals, Directory of American Medical Education, 1992.
8. Center for Greater Philadelphia Economic Development Coalition, 1992.
9. American Hospital Association, *Hospital Statistics 1992–1993,* pp. 156, 160.
10. Philadelphia Economic Monitoring Project R & D Survey, 1990.
11. *American Hospital Association Statistical Yearbook, 1992.*
12. "Bitter Pill."
13. Ibid.
14. Ibid.

REFERENCES

American Hospital Association Guide to the Health Care Field, 1993, A374–A385.
Kessler, D. McWilliams, personal interviews, July 15, 1992, April 2, 1993, May 12, 1993.
Lankenau Hospital, Annual Report, 1992.
Mulvihill, James, personal interviews, July 15, 1992, May 5, 1993.
Pennsylvania Hospital, Annual Report, 1992.
Standard & Poor's Industry Reports, Volume 1, April 1993, p. H15.
Thomas Jefferson Medical Center, Annual Report, 1992.
U.S. Department of Labor, Bureau of Labor Statistics, CPI Detailed Report, November 1993.
Wills Eye Hospital, Annual Reports, 1988, 1989, 1990, 1991, 1992.
Wills Eye Hospital, Long Range Strategic Plan (internal corporate document), 1991–1992.

Index

Note: Italicized numbers refer to material located in the exhibits.

system (subsystem) providing a unique contribution. Many contemporary health care strategies are driven by systems approaches as evidenced by the growth of health care systems, networks, cooperatives, and alliances. Perspective 1–4 indicates the type of systems thinking required by health care managers.

WHAT IS STRATEGIC MANAGEMENT?

In developing a definition of strategic management, first it is useful to define *strategy* and *strategic planning*. Although these terms are often used interchangeably with strategic management, each has a unique meaning.

Strategy and Strategic Planning

The term *strategy* has three related meanings or usages common in health care management. A strategy may be viewed as a sequence of decisions, an organization's behavior, or a plan. Consistency is the central theme that ties together the three usages of *strategy*.

PERSPECTIVE 1–4
Conceiving the System: A South Florida Health Care Alliance

Six Broward County hospitals, two Dade County hospitals, and all the associated physicians, have joined together to create South Florida's most comprehensive health care alliance. The alliance, Affiliated Health Providers, Inc., includes Plantation General Hospital, Hollywood Medical Center, North Ridge Medical Center, Cleveland Clinic Hospital, Florida Medical Center, Northwest Regional Hospital, Parkway Regional Medical Center, and Palmetto General Hospital.

Because of the varied services provided by each member hospital, Affiliated Health Providers is expected to be very appealing to managed-care providers. Each part of the system provides a unique contribution toward making the alliance more than the mere sum of its parts. Cleveland Clinic Hospital has a national reputation; Hollywood Medical Center and Northwest Regional Hospital have a large base of primary care physicians; North Ridge Medical Center and Florida Medical Center are premier open-heart facilities; and Plantation General is a leader in women's and pediatric programs with its maternity and tertiary-level neonatal services. By adding the northern Dade hospitals, the alliance will provide a broader spectrum of services to the Dade and Broward communities. In addition, most of the member hospitals already have strong utilization management programs enabling the member hospitals to bid for at-risk or capitation contracts.

Source: "South Florida Alliance Allows New Comprehensive Area Partnerships," *Health Care Strategic Management* 11, no. 9 (1993), p. 8.

First, a strategy may be viewed as a pattern that emerges in a stream of decisions concerning the positioning of the organization within its environment. In other words, when a sequence of decisions relating the organization to its environment exhibits a logical consistency over time, a strategy will have been formed.[21]

In a broader context, as illustrated in Exhibit 1–4, strategy also may be

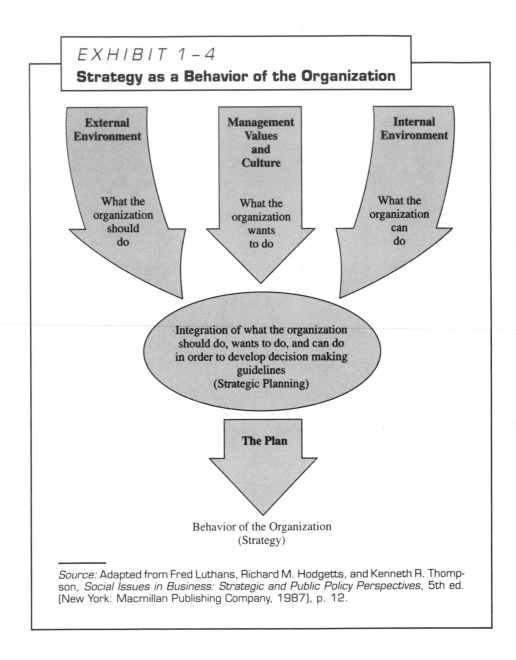

EXHIBIT 1–4
Strategy as a Behavior of the Organization

External Environment

What the organization should do

Management Values and Culture

What the organization wants to do

Internal Environment

What the organization can do

Integration of what the organization should do, wants to do, and can do in order to develop decision making guidelines (Strategic Planning)

The Plan

Behavior of the Organization (Strategy)

Source: Adapted from Fred Luthans, Richard M. Hodgetts, and Kenneth R. Thompson, *Social Issues in Business: Strategic and Public Policy Perspectives,* 5th ed. (New York: Macmillan Publishing Company, 1987), p. 12.

viewed as the "behavior" of the organization. The forces in the external environment influence the strategic behaviors of the organization and suggest "what the organization *should* do." Strategic behavior is additionally influenced by the internal capabilities of the organization and represents "what the organization *can* do." The consistency of the behavior is "driven" by a set of common organizational values and goals. These values and goals are often the result of considerable analysis by top management and indicate "what the organization *wants* to do."

When management considers all of these forces and develops a series of consistent top-level decisions, the organization has a strategy. Only when there is consistency is there a strategy. When there is a formal planning process, decision consistency is borne out of extensive situational analysis. For instance, in the late 1980s and early 1990s both Hospital Corporation of America (HCA) and Humana studied the situation and developed strategies that resulted in consistent, albeit different, streams of decisions that reflected the unique "behavior" of each organization. HCA's strategy was based on the ownership of state-of-the-art hospitals (horizontal integration) whereas Humana's strategy was based on the ownership of an HMO and other managed-care providers (vertical integration).

The requirements of decision consistency suggest that a strategy is the means an organization chooses to move from where it is today to a desired state some time in the future. Thus, strategy also may be viewed as a set of guidelines or a plan that will help assure consistency in decision making. Strategic plans indicate what types of decisions are appropriate or inappropriate for an organization. As illustrated in Exhibit 1–5, strategy links management's understanding of the organization today with where it wants, can, and should be at some well-defined point in the future (say, for example, five years from now).

The organizational process for identifying the desired future and developing decision guidelines is called *strategic planning*. Thus, the result of the strategic planning process is a plan or strategy.

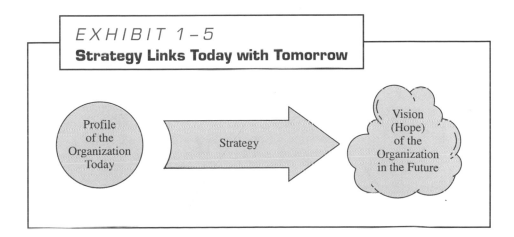

EXHIBIT 1–5
Strategy Links Today with Tomorrow

Strategic Management

Although sometimes used interchangeably with strategic planning, *strategic management* is the broadest of the three terms and should be viewed as encompassing the process of strategic planning. *Strategic management* is an externally-oriented philosophy of managing an organization that links strategic planning to operational decision making. Strategic management attempts to achieve a fit between the organization's external environment (political, regulatory, economic, technological, social, and competitive forces) and its internal situation (vision, values, culture, finance, organization, human resources, marketing, information systems, and so on).

Strategic management goes beyond the traditional focus of strategic planning. Strategically managed organizations have excelled at the execution of strategy because they:

- are adept at building new capabilities consistent with strategy,
- heed behavioral aspects of planning and change, and
- skillfully blend the roles of line managers and planning staff.[22]

Strategic management is based on the belief that organizations should continually monitor internal and external events and trends so that timely changes can be made as needed. Strategic managers constantly relate the organization to its external environment, not just to assure compatibility and survival, but also to understand the environmental trends sufficiently well to "create the future." Strategic managers successfully anticipate the future, positioning their organizations to be at the right place at the right time with the right products and services. As noted earlier in Perspective 1–3, strategic management uses systems concepts to structure *thinking* about the organization and its environment.

Definitions of strategic planning, strategy, and strategic management are summarized in Exhibit 1–6.

Strategic Management Abilities and Commitments

The strategic management process as a philosophy or way of managing may be summarized as a series of abilities and commitments. The basic elements of strategic management are these:

1. the ability to understand competitive behavior as a system in which competitors, customers, money, people, and resources continually interact;
2. the ability to use this understanding to predict how a given strategic move will restore competitive equilibrium;
3. the commitment of resources that can be permanently dedicated to new uses although the benefits will be deferred;
4. the ability to predict risk and return with enough accuracy and confidence to justify the commitment; and
5. the ability and commitment to act.[23]